S0-ABC-189

RON SHANDLER's
Baseball
Forecaster

2008

Point of Contact Edition

Shandler Enterprises, LLC
Roanoke, VA

Copyright © 2007, Shandler Enterprises LLC

Shandler Enterprises LLC
P.O. Box 20303
Roanoke, VA 24018

Offices	540-772-6315
Fax	540-772-1969
Customer service	800-422-7820

E-mail	http://help.baseballhq.com/contact.shtml
Internet	http://www.baseballhq.com

Ron Shandler's Baseball Forecaster is intended for entertainment purposes only. Neither the author nor publisher assume any liability beyond the purchase price for any reason.

Shandler Enterprises LLC ("Publisher") creates the content of this book through extensive work. Financially, the Publisher can publish this book only if all users purchase a copy. Accordingly, by purchasing this book, you agree that you may not reproduce, resell, distribute, transmit, or display this book or any part of it for any commercial purpose, such as selling any part of the materials in this book or incorporating them into a Web site. You may not create derivative works based upon this book. The limitations in this paragraph apply not only to the Publisher's Intellectual Property, but also to any non-copyrightable information provided by this book. If you disagree, please return this book to the point of purchase for a refund.

Also, this Service contains material that is the copyright, trademark, service mark and trade dress property of the Publisher or of third parties who have licensed material to the Publisher (collectively, "Publisher's Intellectual Property"). The Publisher's Intellectual Property includes the following: logos, trademarks, service marks, photographs and other images, articles and columns, other text, graphics and illustrations, other artwork, unique names for statistical categories, formulas used for creating unique statistical categories, opinions expressed as to the meaning of statistical performance levels (e.g. benchmark analytical levels), the selection of statistics and information included within the Service (and the structure and sequence of it), and software. You may use this book for your personal use only, and the limitations in the first paragraph apply to Publisher's Intellectual Property.

Rotisserie League Baseball is a registered trademark of the Rotisserie League Baseball Association, Inc.

Statistics provided by Baseball Info Solutions.

Cover design by Jon Resh@Go-Undaunted.com
Front cover photograph: Aflo Photography/Veer
Author photograph by Kevin Hurley

ISBN 978-1-891566-08-0
Printed in the United States of America

Acknowledgments

I have to share a comment that my friend, Steve Moyer, made in the acknowledgments in this year's *Bill James Handbook*. He wrote that the only people who read the acknowledgments are the folks mentioned. That may well be true, but I took it as a challenge. There is a hidden message within *my* acknowledgments that may make them worth the read, even for those not mentioned.

This book has my name on the cover but only because it apparently has become a "brand." In truth, I am just one of many noble warriors who have a hand in its existence.

First, the *Forecaster's* two editors, Ray Murphy and Rod Truesdell. As the number of contributors has grown, I've relied heavily on Ray and Rod to keep them all in line, even me on occasion. They are both heavily armed and you simply don't mess with them.

There are 5,345,902 pieces of data in this book (I counted). Paul Petera is in charge of the compiling and crunching operation, ably assisted by Baseball HQ's data analysts, Andy Andres, Matt Dodge, Phil Hertz, Mike Shears and Peter Sheridan.

Deric McKamey has been contributing his minor league expertise to this publication for about a dozen years, by last count. Over that time, he has become one of the leading analysts in the field and now writes his own book, *Minor League Baseball Analyst*. *On January 25*

Rick Wilton runs BaseballInjuryReport.com, and has been a friend and colleague for 14+ years. When it comes to injury analysis, he was the industry trailblazer and I am honored to be able to share his insights in this book.

Each September, I look back over all the great essays published on BaseballHQ.com® over the past year and select a few that merit inclusion in this book. Then there is always a bunch of original pieces I can't refuse. This year's "chosen" fanalytic contributors were Matt Beagle, John Burnson, Doug Dennis, Brandon Kruse, Craig Neuman, Stephen Nickrand and Joshua Randall. *February 22*

Thank you to "Old Tom" Mulhall for his contributions on the Japanese Baseball League. We're now international!

In addition to many of the names already mentioned above, the rest of the player commentaries were expertly written by Dave Adler, Harold Nichols, Jock Thompson and Tom Todaro. *and March 21*

The rest of the Baseball HQ staff... Matt Baic, Neil Bonner, Hal Cohen, Patrick Davitt (HQ Radio!), Jeremy Deloney, Rob Gordon, Brent Grooms, Dylan Hedges, Brent Hershey, Joe Hoffer, Gerald Holmes, Tom Kephart, Craig Kronzer, Troy Martell, Scott Monroe, Frank Noto, Josh Paley, Mike Roy, Brian Rudd, Michael Sanderson, Skip Snow and Jeffrey Tomich – these are the guys who make HQ the industry's #1 site for fantasy baseball analysis, er... fanalytics.

Matt Yonkovit, Mike Krebs and Rob Rosenfeld, our tech team, creators of the most leading edge tools in the fantasy baseball industry. *there will be a link on Baseball HQ*

Lynda Knezovich, the voice you'll likely hear on the other end of the 800 line, who does an amazing job keeping everything running, even when you want it yesterday and have a draft in Tokyo.

Greg Ambrosius, Jeff Barton, Pete Becker, Matthew Berry, Scott Burton, Jim Callis, Don Drooker, Jeff Erickson, Brian Feldman, Jason Grey, Eric Karabell, Peter Kreutzer, Gene McCaffrey, Lenny Melnick, John Menna, Lawr Michaels, Steve Moyer, Rob Neyer, Alex Patton, Peter Schoenke, Joe Sheehan, John Sickels, Perry Van Hook, Sam Walker, Brian Walton, Jeff Winick, Trace Wood, Todd Zola and Irwin Zwilling – an elite club of baseball's top analysts, writers, editors and toughest fantasy players, of which I am proud to be a member. *with the name of a player from page 75*

It is an interesting experience running a primarily male sports enterprise in a house full of women. But without them, there would be no reason to drive myself crazy like this. Since we checked in last, Darielle is now driving for real *(cringe),* has taken over my Hyundai (though I keep telling her it's not "her car," it's "the car that she drives"), and is charting her course to a college in some big city; as our resident theater geek, bet on New York. Justina entered high school having spent the summer in a recording studio, cutting a four-song CD of original compositions, and between marching band, her new guitar and today's social drama, there's never a minute of silence.

And finally there's Sue. In every cohesive unit, there is always one person who works tirelessly behind the scenes, without fanfare, but also without whom everything would come crashing to the ground. Sometimes it's a thankless role, so I'll use this space to publicly say, THANK YOU! Your support is more valuable to me than anything else I do in this life.

If you've read this far, you are close to seeing the entire hidden message (I know, it's not hidden all that well). But more important, I am eternally grateful to every one of you who've purchased this book over the past 22 years, and have supported my work, even if you're not reading this. *containing an important message about the future.*

Acknowledgments

CONTENTS

"First of all, it wasn't B.J. Ryan's back that was bothering him. It was his elbow that was bothering him. We said it was his back so he could have a little bit more time.

"There are a lot of things we do not tell the media, because the media does not need to know it and the fans do not need to know it. There are a lot of things that happen that if you let it play out it ends up solving itself. If you bring attention to it then a lot is made out of things that don't end up being a big deal."
— J.P. Ricciardi, May 3, 2007

"General managers do lie regularly, but usually it's either a small lie or a Big Lie, both of which are fairly easy to get away with. But this was sort of a medium Lie, and those are the ones that get you in trouble."
— Rob Neyer, May 5, 2007

NOISE

Coming into 2007, I projected that Aubrey Huff was going to have a terrific year.

It was one of those projections for which I sometimes break from the pack. After several uninspiring seasons, most touts were beginning to write him off. But, after a little bit of digging into the skills beneath the stats, I was seeing a different picture.

Huff had shown solid skills in the past, consistently hitting over 20 home runs and batting around .300 for three consecutive years. After his 2003 peak — 34 HRs and .311 — he started a slow downward spiral. Most folks saw the HR trend — 34, 29, 22, 21 — and started losing interest.

However, once a player displays a skill, he owns it. And Huff had several things going for him...

There was his consistent contact rate, which ran between 85% and 90%. His expected batting average levels were mostly above .290. Essentially, his underlying skills pointed to, at minimum, a .290 hitter, even during the seasons when he batted under .270.

There was also a smidge of batting average bad luck that had been working against him in 2005 and 2006. His hit rate — a gauge that tends to regress to a player's previous three-year average — had been running low. He was due for a correction.

On the home run side, his power index (PX) — which measures underlying power skill as compared to league average — had been consistently above league average.

Yet the numbers were still fading... until June 14, 2006.

Beginning on that day, Huff went on a streak in which he would not go two straight games without a hit for six weeks; he batted .351 during that span. During the rest of the season, Huff looked like his 2003 vintage self. He hit at a 32 HR pace with an expected batting average over .300. His PX was 148 (in 2003, it was 141). His .883 OPS was the highest it had been since 2003's .919. Once he was signed by the Orioles — and he would be playing half his games in hitter-friendly Camden Yards — the stage was set for a 2007 return to high level productivity.

In last year's *Forecaster*, we projected 25 HRs, 93 RBIs and a .292 batting average. After the trade to Baltimore, our batting average projection was bumped to .304 on BaseballHQ.com. Yes, it was a bold statement.

Oh, there was one more thing. It may have sounded trivial, but Huff was going to have an advantage that he never benefited from at any time in his career. He was going to get to face the Tampa Bay pitching staff.

And that is about the only thing that went right in 2007. Amidst his disappointing 15-72-.280 campaign was the performance against his former Devil Ray teammates: 7 HRs and a .365 average. It couldn't trump the fact that he struggled against nearly everyone else.

What happened? There are four reasons why a well-constructed projection could go wrong.

1. We used the wrong process. Our knowledge about what makes baseball tick keeps getting better every year, but to ever conclude that we've gone as far as we can is short-sighted. Ten years ago, all we had for projecting batting average was batting eye; since then, we've added gauges like contact rate, hit rate, even power and speed to the equation. Tomorrow's analyses will include even more variables, thereby improving the process.

So Huff's missed projection might only mean that the process has not come far enough. Despite all the indicators pointing us to conclude that he'd have a great 2007, maybe there was something else that would have tempered our enthusiasm. Perhaps opposing teams figured out that he struggles against certain types of pitches when thrown in certain locations. Perhaps the plane of his swing was not conducive to Camden Yards' wind currents. We are only beginning to measure variables like these. The next step would be to amass enough data to use these insights to project the future.

2. We analyzed the results incorrectly. Our focus on *results* often leads us to look at the wrong measures of performance. Huff's projection was off by 10 HRs, an outward drop in power that might have been made up in other areas that reflect power skill, like extra base hits. He did, in fact, have 54 total extra base hits, a total exceeded only by his performances in 2003 and 2004, including more doubles (34) than he's hit since 2003.

We often forget that a .290 hitter can bat anywhere from .255 to .325 and still be within a statistically valid range for his skill set. Huff's .280 average was clearly within a range of normal variability for a .292 projection, and on the fringes for even a .304 projection.

There were even signs of life from *within* his 2007 season stats. Huff batted over .300 in three out of the six months, and .346 from August 1 on. He displayed consistently rising walk and contact rates as the season progressed. If not for a poor July when he batted only .179, he would have batted .298 for the season. Finally, his August - September power numbers put him on a 27 HR full-season pace. Perhaps he's just a dog-days-of-summer hitter.

But we have to be careful here. While the above analyses may have some merit, any set of numbers can be made to look better than it is via the deft employment of selective analysis. Regarding this in-season treasure hunt, remember that we still judge performance based on a full season of stats. And Huff still only batted .280 with 15 home runs. The intra-season view might hold some clues to 2008, though. Of course, that same analysis didn't work for 2007.

3. We did not have complete information. Frankly, this is the bane of our fanalytic existence. Information is the life blood of everything we do in this game, but it is only as valuable as it is accurate and reliable. Lately, if I had to assign a Reliability Score to the information we've been getting, I'd probably give it something like a 45.

The problem is nothing new. We've always known that Major League teams only feed the media the specific information they are willing to let us know. Major League players micro-manage their personal information as a means of self-preservation. And no matter how adept investigators are at extracting the truth, there is a limit to how much truth will filter into the information.

Nothing new, but getting worse.

Where did Huff's power go in 2007? Was he hurt? Were his prior numbers inflated by artificial means? Does he have personal issues? We may never know the truth. These days, facts can be elusive. For example:

The Health Insurance Portability and Accountability Act (HIPAA) has limited how much health-related information will make its way into public knowledge. If you compared the depth of content provided by injury analysts today with what they were able to report even two years ago, you'd notice a huge difference.

To gauge market reaction, teams feed columnists informational trial balloons that are composed of 10% speculative fact and 90% filler and meat by-products. The ultimate in media manipulation occurred in July 2006 when the following note appeared in two respected sources:

"If I had to put a percentage on it now," said one AL executive, asked to predict the chances Alfonso Soriano will be traded, "I'd say 100 percent."
— *Washington Post*

"Multiple sources all over the sport now say it's 100 percent certain Alfonso Soriano will be traded."
— *Fox Sports*

And as we found out days later, Soriano was *not* traded.

A Major League general manager admitted that he lied about a player's injury. Toronto Blue Jays GM J.P. Ricciardi reported in the spring that B.J. Ryan's back was bothering him. The truth was, Ryan had an elbow injury that was serious enough to require surgery, forcing him to miss most of the 2007 season. The *Toronto Star* reported that "the club's original injury report was an intended fabrication" made in order to buy some time.

Why is this important?

First, this was not just an error of omission. Many baseball sources will obfuscate the truth by not revealing all information. In this case, we were deliberately fed *false information*. That is a huge difference.

The second reason why this is important, particularly to us fantasy leaguers... *Some of you would not have paid $25 for B.J. Ryan if you had known he had a bum elbow.*

Reliable sources are drying up but we still need accurate information. However, if we allow ourselves to get forced into a corner, we'll end up clinging onto whatever nuggets we can find, and believing nearly everything. .

Don't think that could happen? It already does. This March, I predict the following with near-100% certainty:

- Orioles' manager Dave Tremblay will announce his "closer du jour" and that pitcher's value will spike, even if he clearly does not have the skills for the job and a better candidate is just a few blown saves away from claiming the role.
- Travis Snider's (or pick a name) superb winter play will have over-eager minor league analysts hailing his potential to open the season in the bigs, even though he is barely 20 and untested above A-ball.
- Alex Rodriguez will be *over-valued* in auctions based on his incredible 2007 season and the New York hype

machine. In this post-steroid era, players are unlikely to hit 50-plus HRs in back-to-back seasons (Hello, Ryan Howard!) and A-Rod's own recent track record is one of year-to-year inconsistency.
- Some $20+ player will have a lousy spring and state publicly that he is not hurt. He will get drafted at near full value and be placed on the DL before May 1.

This is not working. There has to be a better way.

That better way is to take control of our own information management. Rather than accept what the media feeds us, we have to turn each piece of information into its own laboratory subject. We have to look under the hood, poke and prod, validate, test and re-test, analyze, deconstruct, reassemble, then often break it all down and start again.

The problem with this approach is, at the end of the day, you still cannot prove absolute fact. *But maybe that's okay. Maybe we don't need absolute fact.*

In the world of projective accuracy, I didn't necessary need for Aubrey Huff to hit 25 HRs to proclaim success. Twenty four would have been perfectly fine. Heck, 23 would have been acceptable. Even if he had posted a 22-85-.295 season off my 25-92-.304 projection, I don't think I would have received nearly as much hate mail.

Similarly, perhaps we don't need absolute accuracy when it comes to information. Let's create a scale:

0%   **No truth**
J.P. Ricciardi says that B.J. Ryan is perfectly healthy.

25%   **Minor truth**
Ricciardi says that Ryan is hurt (true) but lies about the type of injury.

50%   **Mixed truth**
Ricciardi says that Ryan is hurt (true) and says that it's an elbow injury (true) but lies about how serious it is.

75%   **Mostly truth**
Ricciardi says that Ryan has a serious elbow injury (true) but lies that team doctors say he could be back by June.

100%   **Perfect truth**
Ricciardi says that Ryan is a player on the Toronto Blue Jays. Beyond that, I'm not sure that there is such a thing as a perfect truth. But it's good to have a goal.

The Ricciardi fiasco was a 25% truth (or, 75% lie) so we have to give him at least some credit, right?

I think our goal has to be to try to reach 75% as much as we can. That means taking all the 0%, 25% and 50% information and working hard to poke and prod, validate, test and re-test, analyze, deconstruct and reassemble... until we've built it up closer to 75%. And since 100% is probably darned near impossible, this may sometimes mean stringing together nuggets of small facts and assembling them into educated speculations.

I've been doing this more and more often each year, and some readers find the process repugnant. But we are finding more and more instances where keeping an open mind has led to valid insights and realizations that would have been summarily dismissed otherwise.

Consider it again... Assembling factoids into educated speculations can provide 75% truth. And that is enough. It may be the best we can ever expect.

Okay, let's look at some educated speculations. Time to put on your protective gear...

Given that several of the accusations listed in Jose Canseco's book turned out to be true, isn't it possible that he might be at least a somewhat more reliable source?

Rafael Palmeiro denied using steroids before Congress but then failed a drug test. Jason Giambi admitted to steroid use before a grand jury. Mark McGwire all but admitted he used performance enhancing drugs (PEDs). Ivan Rodriguez avoided media attention but saw his body mass and productivity plummet after the accusations came out. Juan Gonzalez ceased all comeback attempts and was never heard from again.

There are a variety of nuggets here. Only the I-Rod one has questionable value since he might have just been on the downside of his career anyway. Taken individually, there's not much here. But stringing them together creates a more interesting picture to speculate on.

While there was not enough firm evidence in "Game of Shadows" to convict Barry Bonds beyond a reasonable doubt, wouldn't it have taken an amazing amount of effort for the authors to have created such an elaborate hoax?

Was the book a complete work of fiction? Were only parts of it false? We can read into Bonds' response to the book's publication... he sued the publisher for engaging in unfair business practices, citing that secret grand jury testimony was used. He never sued for libel (though, granted, that's a tough case to win because there has to be proof of malicious intent). Still, Bonds never even intimated that anything about the book was false. He never denied using steroids.

There are those who've been staunch Bonds supporters, insisting that he never failed a drug test. However, given that there is no test for human growth hormone (HGH) and that players may have been given a two-day heads-up on the arrival of "random" testers for other PEDs, the integrity of the entire program is questionable. Of course, now with Bonds' indictment, all this fuss could be moot.

Isn't it possible that the massive power outage in 2007 could have been due, at least in part, to players ceasing use of PEDs?

All right. I know that some of you are probably getting tired of this discussion. I understand that. The reason that I keep writing about it is that the use, and cessation of use, of PEDs impacts our ability to project performance. Baseball forecasting is why you are reading this book, so our ability to do a good job of it holds a good deal of importance to us. Even though we do not have definitive information about who, and when, and how much, we do have tons of nuggets of small facts from which we can draw educated speculations. If the exercise can shed even a little bit of light, that's better than being completely in the dark. So let's examine some nuggets…

The chart at the top right of this page lists the 33 batters who hit at least 31 HRs in 2006. Thirty of them (91%) experienced a power decline in 2007. Of those power declines, nearly two thirds were off by at least 30%. Now, we would typically expect some drop-off in power from among the league's leading power hitters. That's just regression to the mean, injuries and the "gravity principle" at work. However, this 27% power outage seems extreme.

	HOME RUNS		
PLAYER	2006	2007	VAR
Howard,R	58	47	-19%
Ortiz,D	54	35	-35%
Pujols,A	49	32	-35%
Soriano,A	46	33	-28%
Berkman,L	45	34	-24%
Dye,J	44	28	-36%
Thome,J	42	35	-17%
Hafner,T	42	22	-48%
Beltran,C	41	33	-20%
Jones,A	41	26	-37%
Dunn,A	40	40	0%
Thomas,F	39	26	-33%
Delgado,C	38	24	-37%
Ramirez,A	38	26	-32%
Glaus,T	38	20	-47%
Giambi,J	37	14	-62%
Lee,C	37	32	-14%
Hall,B	35	14	-60%
Bay,J	35	21	-40%
Swisher,N	35	22	-37%
Rodriguez,A	35	54	54%
Konerko,P	35	31	-11%
Ramirez,M	35	20	-43%
Morneau,J	34	31	-9%
Sexson,R	34	21	-38%
Holliday,M	34	36	6%
Teixeira,M	33	30	-9%
Ibanez,R	33	21	-36%
Guerrero,V	33	27	-18%
LaRoche,A	32	21	-34%
Utley,C	32	22	-31%
Wells,V	32	16	-50%
Hunter,T	31	28	-10%
MEAN	**38**	**28**	**-27%**

(Joshua Randall's essay on page 4 has more detail.)

I am not saying that PED discontinuance is the lone cause of these power outages. I am saying that you cannot dismiss the possibility that it *might* be a contributing factor just because we don't have 100% perfect information, or just because the topic is unsavory to think about.

And neither will I dismiss the possibility that these power outages are simply normal statistical fluctuations. Joshua's essay provides at least some support for that argument.

If PEDs did not have a positive effect on performance, why would players be using them and why would this even be a story?

To me, this is the core of the entire argument. We can argue all day about who did and who didn't. But the facts seem immutable that *somebody* must have used PEDs for it to have caused such a stir.

How much do baseball's power brokers control the course of events via their manipulation of the media?

This is a touchy area – probably a 50% truth at best – but I just wanted to make the point that anything is possible.

Since this past summer, the release of information into the media about PED use appears random. However, there seem to be too many coincidences to rule out that it might have been more orchestrated.

- News of Rick Ankiel's HGH purchases hit the media just as he was riding a huge hitting streak. As soon as the news hit, his bat went cold.
- News of Paul Byrd's HGH purchases hit the media

The Power Outage of 2007

by Joshua Randall

Anecdotally, it appears that Major League Baseball experienced a "power outage" in 2007. Only five players managed 40+ HR, compared to at least nine in each of the previous three seasons. But what if we include players who hit at least 30 HR and look at things systematically?

Year	N	30+	%	AB/HR
2002	425	25	6%	31.2
2003	426	30	7%	30.7
2004	419	37	9%	29.2
2005	417	27	6%	31.4
2006	405	34	8%	29.7
2007	427	26	6%	32.4

At the aggregate level, there's not much year-to-year fluctuation in either the percentage of batters hitting 30+ HR nor in the rate at which HRs are hit league-wide (AB/HR). So in that sense, 2007 was not a year of a power outage — at least not across the board.

However, if we restrict our scope to only those batters who have been consistent sluggers, a new picture emerges. We looked for batters who averaged at least 30 HR over a three year span, then examined their HR output in the following year. If that output was less than 80% of their three year average, we considered that batter to have noticeably underperformed.

	'01-'03	'02-'04	'03-'05	'04-'06
# Who avg'd 30+ HR	23	23	20	23
"4th yr" HR < 80%	8	9	3	12
Percentage	35%	39%	15%	52%

When we examine things in this fashion, we see that 2007 (the "4th yr" after 2004-06) did represent a power outage when compared to prior seasons. Over half of those batters who averaged 30 or more HR in 2004-06 failed to reach 80% of their three-year average in 2007. (It's also worth noting that only three consistent 30+ HR batters failed to live up to expectations in 2006, a remarkably low number that makes 2007 seem even worse in contrast.)

Who were the players who most disappointed us in '07?

Player	Avg HR 04-06	HR 2007
Ortiz, David	47.3	35
Pujols, Albert	45.3	32
Ramirez, Manny	41.7	20
Jones, Andruw	40.3	26
Teixeira, Mark	38.0	30
Ramirez, Aramis	35.0	26
Guerrero, Vlad	34.7	27
Delgado, Carlos	34.3	24
Hafner, Travis	34.3	24
Bay, Jason	31.0	21
Glaus, Troy	31.0	20
Edmonds, Jim	30.0	12

Year	40+ HR hitters	35+ HR hitters
2004	9	20
2005	9	14
2006	11	23
2007	5	8

In this light we can see that 2007 had fewer players at the top of the heap in terms of HR. But given that AB/HR was nearly the same in all years, this must mean there were more guys in 2007 hitting HR in, say, the 25-34 range.

just prior to Game 7 of the ALCS, a game the Indians needed to win. They didn't.

- News of 11 free agents being questioned by George Mitchell's investigation hit the media just days after they had all declared their free agency. At our press time, it is too early to see whether that might suppress their price tags.

Taken individually, all seem like unrelated random events, but the timing is suspicious. Why were these items leaked *when* they were leaked?

Note that Scott Boras' announcement that Alex Rodriguez had opted out of his Yankees contract, which broke during Game 4 of the World Series, proves how much the media can be controlled. Did they have to break the story during a game that should have been the focal point of our attention? No, but Boras knew they couldn't sit on it either.

The point here… We must remember that the media is the conduit through which we receive our information but there are others who are driving the process. Make sure you know the true source of the information and whether there may be ulterior motives for its release.

Since one GM has lied to us, isn't it possible that others have done it, or might do it, as well?

With J.P. Ricciardi's deception regarding B.J. Ryan's injury, we now have proof that people in power will lie to us. But for some of you, Ricciardi's lie was just an isolated event, unrelated to anything else. What if it's not? It could be symptomatic of a larger problem where information is perhaps routinely disseminated for self-serving purposes, not for disclosure of the truth.

(On the next two pages, Baseball HQ's Managing Editor, Ray Murphy, takes a hard look at the many ways in which Major League GMs might be lying to us.)

It is unfortunate, but the timing of the publication of this book precludes us from knowing what's in the Mitchell Report, due to be released before the end of 2007. The results of his study were described as "salacious." How Bud Selig responds, how the owners, the players union and players respond, will be Grand Theatre. I will peg the ensuing spin festival at about 45% truth, tops.

One last reason why a well-constructed projection could go wrong…

4. It just does. There is a limit to how much we can really project. All of our advanced metrics and models only provide us with percentage plays. Even if we were 90% confident that the variables were pointing in a certain direction, Aubrey Huff just might have fallen in the other 10%. It happens. There is nothing we can do about it.

During 2007, there were many players that even the most sophisticated projections model would have missed. Carlos Pena's playing time. Andruw Jones' power. Fausto Carmona's ERA. Jorge Posada's batting average. Travis Hafner and Jason Bay confounded us all season.

At this past November's First Pitch Arizona conference, we had a panel discussion on the realities of projective accuracy. One of these realities helps put things into perspective:

What Else are GMs Lying About?

by Ray Murphy

We have long talked about the "news vs. noise" filter that we need to employ in evaluating statements from sources within the game. J.P. Ricciardi's case expands the scope of that filter. Now we need to consider the possibility that, not only is there noise in the information we receive, but those generating that noise may be doing so intentionally.

Here are several broad categories of information that we think are ripe for this kind of deception, and some current examples that may require closer inspection as a result:

The true nature of injuries

The Ricciardi example directly relates to how MLB teams disclose injuries. Recent changes to federal law (in particular HIPAA) were making this a touchy subject long before Ricciardi crossed the "blatant misinformation" line.

One particular situation that looks suspicious in this light is in Washington, where Nick Johnson and John Patterson's careers have been derailed by injury. Both are key cogs in whatever future the Nationals have, at this critical time when they are trying to build a loyal fan base in advance of their new stadium.

Patterson missed the second half of 2006 with arm problems. The Nationals were adamant that they were being overly cautious with Patterson at that time, saying that he could have pitched late in 2006 if needed. Then in April 2007, Patterson struggled. His velocity was down, his results were terrible (7.47 ERA). While Patterson continued to get hit hard, the Nationals stated that his arm was sound, and that he simply needed to build arm strength. Finally in May, Patterson was DL'd again with forearm problems similar to what shut him down in 2006. Patterson later sought experimental treatment outside the US, and did not pitch again in 2006.

Johnson's case was similar. His broken leg, suffered in September 2006, was initially thought to have a minor impact on his 2007 outlook. But the timeline for his 2007 return was repeatedly pushed back, and in the end he missed the entire season.

Given both of these players' importance to the franchise, was the severity of their respective injuries under-reported intentionally? Full disclosure may have adversely impacted the Nationals' bottom line at this critical point in franchise history. That can be a powerful motivator.

Are teams always playing to win?

Astute fans know that there are considerations in roster decisions that go beyond "who is the best player for the job". While you are not likely to hear a GM admit that publicly, their actions often speak to their motivations quite clearly. For instance, when MIN signed Ramon Ortiz and Sidney Ponson entering 2007, the transactions were met with confusion and even ridicule.

With the benefit of hindsight, we now see that the motivation for those signings was to delay the service-time clocks of Kevin Slowey and Matt Garza. Sinking a few extra budget dollars into those fungible vets may have saved millions down the line by delaying Slowey and Garza's first arbitration and free agency dates for a year.

Similarly, can it be a coincidence that Homer Bailey's call-up was delayed despite some woeful options eating innings in CIN? Or that it took Yovani Gallardo until late July to "earn" a role in the thin Brewers rotation? Gallardo's example may exhibit the "penny wise, pound foolish" aspect of this approach. The delay in utilizing Gallardo at the MLB level, compounded with keeping Ryan Braun in the minor leagues until late May, likely cost MIL the NL Central title.

Regardless of the wisdom or folly of the approach, its use appears to be expanding. In assessing rookie contributions in future years, it may become standard to think of June 1 as a sort of "magic" date after which rookies are called up, especially for more budget-conscious teams.

Complicit in the steroid coverup

Initially, MLB management had at least been quietly supportive of MLB's "crackdown" on performance enhancing drugs (PEDs) in the game. For instance, witness the lack of opportunities offered to Rafael Palmeiro following his 2005 suspension for steroid use. The perception of "possible Hall of Famer busted for steroid use", then suddenly no team wanting to be associated with him, made for a powerful image. But did that image match reality?

There is a set of marginal or declining major leaguers who were also suspended, and seem to have been treated similarly to Palmeiro: Matt Lawton, Carlos Almanzar, and Felix Heredia to name a few. But for the few younger, better players who have been suspended, the experience has been different. Rafael Betancourt is still a key contributor in the CLE bullpen. Juan Rincon's high-leverage position in the MIN bullpen was unaffected by his suspension. Both have seen their salaries escalate normally through their arbitration years. For all intents and purposes, in terms of their career progression, the suspensions of Betancourt and Rincon have proven irrelevant.

Perhaps the most telling example is that of Guillermo Mota. After a terrible first half of 2006 with CLE, Mota was dealt to the Mets in August 2006, and promptly turned into a lights-out reliever late in the season. Mota was subsequently hit with a 50-game suspension for PED use after the end of the season. A month after the suspension, the Mets signed Mota to a two-year contract extension.

Not only did the Mets decide to retain Mota's services after his PED suspension, but they even structured his contract (2 years/$5M, but $1.8M in 2007 and $3.2M in 2008) in such a way that at least gives the appearance of doing Mota a favor: lowering the 2007 salary minimizes the financial impact of the unpaid suspension, and back-loading the deal essentially funnels that money back to him in the end. The accompanying message seems clear: "Job well done. Thanks for doing whatever you had to do for us in 2006. Now, here's a sack of money for your trouble."

In this light, the high-profile blackballing of Palmeiro appears to be more the exception than the norm. If even some organizations are implicitly or explicitly rewarding (or at least condoning) PED use, they are therefore complicit in the ongoing scandal.

Taking this line of thought a step further, those who are expecting more recent PED revelations (involving players like Troy Glaus, Rick Ankiel and Jay Gibbons) to adversely affect their future career options, may need to revisit those expectations.

Sunk costs

GMs are often unwilling to get away from a sunk cost, especially if it means admitting a mistake. For instance, the Mariners surprisingly hung in the AL West race for most of the 2007 season. While the big-league club was over-performing, top prospect Adam Jones was crushing the ball in Triple-A. Jones got a call-up to SEA in early August, while they were still very much alive in the pennant race. But he only received 65 AB over the season's final two months.

One way to get Jones' potent bat into the lineup would have been at the expense of Jose Vidro. An empty .314 BA was Vidro's only contribution from the DH slot, as his OPS (.779) was certainly sub-par for that position. It is difficult to predict how smoothly a rookie will handle the initial transition to MLB, but it's certainly possible that Jones would have outperformed Vidro over the stretch run.

Why did Jones not get the opportunity? Perhaps because of the Mariners' investment in Vidro ($6M/year for 2007 and 2008), they were unwilling to risk "losing" Vidro by benching him, even if Jones might have been productive in the spot.

We are already seeing more examples of this line of thought this off-season. Consider the MIN 2B situation entering 2008. "Incumbent" Nick Punto hit an anemic .210 over 472 AB in 2007. Rookie Alexi Casilla did not fare much better (.222) in his callup, but is only 23 years old and a reasonably well-regarded prospect.

When asked after the 2007 season about the 2B position in 2008, Twins manager Ron Gardenhire said that Punto has "got a lead going into spring training, as far as I'm concerned." Why? Perhaps because Casilla will make the rookie minimum salary in 2008, while Punto is under contract at $2.4M. Organizations hate to admit mistakes, and starting Casilla over Punto might constitute such an admission. (Of course, this could be another example of "not playing to win", with MIN looking to stall Casilla's service clock. Let's see if Casilla is called up in early June to replace Punto.)

Relevance of personal situations

We will stipulate up front that ballplayers' off-the-field situations are not our business. But an inherent conflict arises when we start to consider the possibility that those situations can impact player performance. In a hierarchy of information disclosure, these issues are the best-kept secrets in baseball.

Two thousand seven was the least-productive season of Nomar Garciaparra's career. As injury-plagued as his career has been, he has always produced when in the lineup, until now. In a possibly related or un-related story, Garciaparra has infant twins at home. Anyone who has had children, let alone twins, can likely appreciate the concept that Garciaparra may not be reporting to work in the sharpest frame of mind under those circumstances. Is there a cause-and-effect relationship here?

Even the media is complicit. During a 2007 ESPN Sunday Night Baseball game shortly after Alex Rodriguez's "extra-marital issues" hit the New York tabloids, the ESPN announcers spent innings discussing the fallout of the incident, *without ever identifying the nature of the incident.* The Rodriguez situation was the exception in that it became public. More often than not, we're left to chew on scraps of information and draw our own (possibly inaccurate) conclusions.

Also in the summer of 2007, the *Boston Globe* made a cryptic reference to "personal issues" in Coco Crisp's life, as a possible contributing factor to his underachieving season. This highlights the conflict in play here: while we don't have any right to know of such matters, wouldn't that have been another useful data point while trying to assess whether Crisp was (or is) a rebound candidate? Further muddying the waters, the *Globe's* parent company has an ownership stake in the Red Sox. Where can we turn in our search for objectivity?

All we can do is speculate.

Of all the players in the entire MLB population, about 65% are reasonably projectable by using any rudimentary tool such as "Marcel the Monkey." For those unfamiliar, Marcel is a forecasting model discussed in the works of Tom Tango. Marcel simply takes each player's last three years, computes a weighted average, and adjusts for age. This says, in essence, that it doesn't matter what forecasting model you use for that 65%.

About 20-25% of the remaining players are virtually unprojectable. No matter what history-based model you used, nobody would have seen the Carmonas, Posadas and Hafners. Unfortunately, these are often the players who can make or break a fantasy season. But when you are dealing with human beings, there will never be 100% accuracy.

Finally, the last 10-15%. These are the players for whom all our systems are essentially trying to "beat the Monkey." We are looking for any incremental gain we can find, and it is only for this group that we might actually succeed. Even though the variances between systems may not be statistically significant, any gain can make the difference in a fantasy setting. All you need is one service like ours to tell you that Kevin Gregg is the best saves option in the Marlins' pen, or that Barry Zito won't earn his salary.

For those, we managed to beat the Monkey. For Aubrey Huff, the Monkey beat us. Or so it seems. Until we find a way to cut through all the noise to find out what really happened in 2007, we can't legitimately pass judgment on any projection.

Welcome to the *Baseball Forecaster*, Edition #22.

This book was conceived as a well-timed collision of sabermetrics and fantasy. The unique, hybrid brand of analysis that we perpetrate here is what we call **fanalytics**, which is a measured, deliberate approach to evaluating and projecting player performance within the context of fantasy baseball. It takes from both schools and provides deeper insight than any other analytical process. Sabermetrics becomes more than just a bunch of incomprehensible formulas, and fantasy becomes more than just blindly picking a bunch of players and praying.

New Readers – Welcome!

The *Baseball Forecaster* was the first book to approach prognostication by breaking performance down into its component parts. Rather than predicting batting average, for instance, we look at the elements of skill that make up that stat — a batter's ability to distinguish between balls and strikes, his propensity to make contact with the ball, and what happens after he makes contact — and reverse-engineer those skills back into batting average. This process has proven itself as being a better predictor than any quantitative model using the actual gauges themselves.

In all, we call this "component skills analysis."

You should know that there is some rudimentary math involved and there is a bit of a learning curve. The nice thing about the math, though, is that most of it is logical and intuitive. For instance, when we talk about "contact rate," that's just the percentage of time a batter makes contact with the ball. It is calculated simply as $((AB - K) / AB)$. As you would expect, the more contact a batter makes, the higher his batting average tends to be. We have benchmarks at the upper and lower ends of the scale — 70% and 90% — and we can project a player's batting average off of that.

And the pieces all fit together very neatly in the end.

Naturally, I think this approach is the best way to evaluate and project performance, but I'll let you decide for yourself. I do ask, however, that you keep an open mind. These tools do work, but you may have to toss away some of your preconceptions in order to embrace the possibilities.

There's a ton of information here. At first glance, it will seem overwhelming. But you don't have to take it in all at once. Start slow; take as much time as you need.

And please heed the consumer advisory on this page.

CONSUMER ADVISORY

AN IMPORTANT MESSAGE FOR FANTASY LEAGUERS ABOUT THE RISKS OF INCORRECTLY USING THE BASEBALL FORECASTER

This document is provided in compliance with authorities to outline the prospective risks and hazards possible in the event that the Baseball Forecaster is used incorrectly. Please be aware of these potentially dangerous situations and avoid them. Shandler Enterprises LLC assumes no risk related to any financial loss or stress-induced illnesses caused by ignoring the items as described below.

1. The statistical projections in this book are intended as general guidelines, not as gospel. It is highly dangerous to use the projected statistics alone, and then live and die by them. That's like going to a ballgame, being given a choice of any seat in the park, and deliberately choosing the last row in the right field corner with an obstructed view. The projections are there, you can look at them, but there are so many better places to sit. We have to publish those numbers, but they are stagnant, inert pieces of data. Performance is highly variable. Use the player commentaries and your own analysis of the data to draw more robust, colorful pictures of the future.

2. This book is not intended to provide absorbency for spills of over 6.5 ounces.

3. The player commentaries in this book are written by humans, just like you. These commentaries provide an overall evaluation of performance and likely future direction, but 40-word capsules cannot capture everything. Your greatest value will be to use these as a springboard to your own analysis of the data. Odds are, if you take the time, you'll find hidden indicators that we might have missed. *Forecaster* veterans say that this self-guided excursion is the best part of owning the book.

4. This book is not intended to provide stabilizing weight for more than 15 sheets of 20 lb. paper in winds over 45 mph.

5. The dollar values in this book are intended solely for player-to-player comparisons. They are not driven by a finite pool of playing time – which is required for valuation systems to work properly – so they cannot be used for in-draft bid values. There are two reasons for this: 1. The finite pool of players that will generate the finite pool of playing time will not be determined until much closer to Opening Day. 2. Your particular league's construction will drive the values; a $10 player in a 10-team mixed league will not be the same as a $10 player in a 13-team NL-only league.

Note that book dollar values also cannot be compared to those published on BaseballHQ.com as the online values *are* generated by the finite player pool.

6. The pages of this book are not recommended for avian waste collection. In independent laboratory studies, most migratory water fowl refuse to excrete on interior pages, even when coaxed.

7. Do not pass judgment on the effectiveness of this book based on the performance of individual players. The test, rather, is on the collective predictive value of the book's methods. Are players with better underlying base skills more likely to produce good results that bad ones? Years of research suggest that the answer is "yes." Does that mean that every high skilled player will perform well? No. But many more of them will perform well than will the average low-skilled player. So you should always side with the better percentage plays, but recognize that there are factors we cannot predict. Good decisions that beget bad outcomes do not invalidate the methods used in this book.

8. A good benchmark for success… If your copy of this book is not marked up and dog-eared by Draft Day, you probably did not get as much out of it as you might have.

What's New?

1. Japanese League coverage: Thanks to Baseball HQ forum regular, Tom Mulhall, we now have an expanded discussion of the Japanese Leagues and scouting reports on the top players who might cross over during the next few years.

2. Expanded injury coverage: Thanks to Rick Wilton of Baseball-Injury-Report.com, we now have detailed injury histories for all players.

3. +/- Scores: Many of you have suggested that the player boxes include some type of indicator for breakout and breakdown candidates. The +/- scores encapsulate our general expectation for each player and how we project his performance to vary from 2007. We also include +/- ranking lists in the back of the book.

4. Home run to fly ball ratio has been added to the batter profiles. Unlike the pitcher version where HR/F regresses to about 10%, the batter ratios tend to regress to each batter's own mean level.

5. Pitching type snapshot: The Power/Finesse indicator has been changed and now denotes Power (Pwr) and Contact (Con) as well as Ground Ball (GB), Extreme Ground Ball (xGB), Fly Ball (FB) and Extreme Fly Ball (xFB) pitchers.

6. Rising and Bull Durham Prospects: In addition to an essay in the Prospects section on "Bull Durham" prospects, the Major League Equivalency charts also include indicators for (a) young players with superior BPIs and (b) players between 26 and 30 who also have superior BPIs.

Updates

Content Update page: If there are any corrections or clarifications on the information in this book, go to:
http://www.baseballhq.com/books/bfupdates.shtml

Free Projections Update: As a buyer of this book, you get one free 2008 projections update, available online at
http://www.baseballhq.com/books/freeupdate/index.shtml.
These are spreadsheet data files, to be posted on or about March 1, 2008.

Electronic book: The complete PDF version of the *Forecaster* – plus MS Excel versions of most key charts – is available free to those who bought the book directly through Shandler Enterprises. These files will be available in February 2008; contact us if you do not receive information via e-mail about accessing them. If you purchased the *Forecaster* through an online vendor or bookstore, you can purchase these files from us for $8.95. Call 1-800-422-7820 for more information.

Beyond the *Forecaster*

The *Forecaster* is just the beginning. The following companion products and services are described in more detail in the back of the book.

BaseballHQ.com is our home website. It provides regular updates to everything in this book, including daily updated projections, plus a ton more. In 2008, we'll be adding some robust new tools for managing your teams.

First Pitch Forums are a series of conferences we run all over the country, where you can meet some of the top industry analysts and network with fellow fantasy leaguers. In 2008, we'll have sessions in the San Francisco Bay area, Los Angeles, Chicago, Cleveland, Washington DC, New York and Boston. Check in the back for the schedule.

RotoHQ.com is a very, very large online library of fantasy strategy essays and tools.

Graphical Player, the fifth edition of John Burnson's book, provides Forecaster-style data and more, in a series of insightful graphs and charts. *Available now.*

Minor League Baseball Analyst, the third edition of Deric McKamey's book, is a minor league version of the Forecaster, with stat boxes for over 1000 prospects, and more. *Available in January.*

How to Value Players for Rotisserie Baseball is the second edition of Art McGee's ground-breaking book on valuation theory. *Available now.*

RotoLab is the best draft software on the market, and not just because it comes bundled with our player projections. It's a terrific tool for those who use laptops on Draft Day.

Enough talk. It's time to get started. I've often been told that once you turn this page, the baseball season officially begins. Good luck to your teams in 2008!

— *Ron Shandler*

II.
FANALYTICS

Foundation Principles

Forecasting is the systematic process of determining likely end results. Baseball, as in most disciplines, uses some type of quantitative analysis in this process.

Baseball performance forecasting is inherently a high-risk exercise with a very modest accuracy rate. This is because the process involves not only statistics, but also unscientific elements, from random chance to human volatility. And even from within the statistical aspect there are multiple elements that need to be evaluated, from skill to playing time to a host of external variables.

Every system is comprised of the same core elements:

- Players will perform within the framework of their past history and/or trends.
- Skills will develop and decline according to age.
- Statistics will be shaped by a player's health, expected role and home ballpark.

While all systems are built from these same elements, they also are constrained by the same limitations. We are all still trying to project:

- a bunch of human beings
- each with their own individual skill sets
- each with their own individual rates of growth and decline
- each with different abilities to resist and recover from injury
- each limited to opportunities determined by other people
- and each generating a group of statistics largely affected by tons of external noise. For instance, pitching wins requires the analysis of not only the pitcher's skill, but the skills of his team's offense, defense, bullpen and the tendencies of his manager. *All* these variables must be analyzed.

Based on the research of multiple sources, the best accuracy rate that can be attained by any system is about 70%. In fact, a simple system that uses three-year averages adjusted for age can attain a success rate of 65%. This means all the advanced systems are fighting for occupation of the remaining 5%.

Other Variables

Playing time: Beyond the small group of players who have guaranteed jobs each year, there are hundreds of others whose roles change frequently. Injuries, ill-timed slumps and managerial whim can all impact a player's chances to put up AB and IP. This book does not attempt to tackle playing time. Rather than making arbitrary decisions about how roles will shake out, we focus on performance. The playing time projections presented here are merely to help you better evaluate each player's talent. Our online pre-season projections update provides more current AB/IP expectations based on how roles are being assigned.

Perpetuity: Forecasting is not an isolated exercise that produces a single set of numbers. It is dynamic, cyclical and ongoing. Conditions are constantly changing and we must react to those changes by adjusting our expectations. A pre-season projection is just a snapshot in time. Once the first batter steps to the plate on Opening Day, that projection has become obsolete. Its value to fantasy leaguers is merely to provide a starting point, a baseline for what is about to occur.

During the season, if a projection appears to have been invalidated by current performance, the process continues. It is then that we need to ask... What went wrong? What conditions have changed? In fact, has *anything* changed? We need to analyze the situation and revise our expectation, if necessary. This process must be ongoing.

Process and outcomes: The outcomes of forecasted events should not be confused with the process itself. Outcomes may be the components that are the most closely scrutinized, but as long as the process is sound, the forecast has done the best job it can do. *In the end, forecasting is about analysis, not prophecy.*

Component Skills Analysis

Our brand of forecasting is more about finding logical journeys than blind destinations.

Familiar gauges like HR and ERA have long been used to measure skill. In fact, these gauges only measure the outcome of an individual event, or series of events. They represent statistical output. They are "surface stats."

Raw skill is the talent beneath the stats, the individual elements of a player's makeup. Players use these skills to create the individual events, or components, that we record using measures like HR and ERA. Our approach:

1. It's not about batting average, it's about seeing the ball and making contact. We target hitters based on elements such as their batting eye (walks to strikeouts ratio) and how often they make contact. We then combine these components into an "expected batting average." By comparing each hitter's actual BA to how he *should* be performing, we can draw conclusions about the future.

2. It's not about home runs, it's about power. From the perspective of a round bat meeting a round ball, it may be only a fraction of an inch at the point of contact that makes the difference between a HR or a long foul ball. When a ball is hit safely, often it is only a few inches that separate a HR from a double. Yet we tend to neglect these facts in our analyses, although the outcomes — the doubles, triples, long fly balls — may be no less a measure of that batter's raw power skill. We must incorporate all these components to paint a complete picture. Only then can we track trends and see who might be primed for a breakout or letdown.

3. It's not about ERA, it's about getting the ball over the plate and keeping it in the park. Forget ERA. You want to draft pitchers who walk few batters (control), strike out many (dominance) and succeed at both in tandem (command). You also want pitchers who keep the ball on the ground (because home runs are bad). All of this translates into an "expected ERA" that you can use to compare to a pitcher's actual performance.

4. It's never about wins. Winning ballgames is less about pitching skill and more about offensive support. As such, projecting wins is futile and valuing hurlers based on their win history is dangerous. Focus on skills and the wins will come.

5. It's not about saves, it's about skill and opportunity. While the highest skilled pitchers have the best potential to succeed as closers, they still have to be given the ball with the game on the line in the 9th inning, and that is a decision left to others. Over the past 10 years, about 40% of relievers drafted for saves failed to hold the role for the entire season. The lesson: Don't take chances on draft day. There will always be saves in the free agent pool.

Luck

Luck has been used as a catch-all term to describe random chance. When we use the term here, we're talking about unexplained variances that shape the statistics. Yes, these variances are often random, but they are also often measurable and projectable. In order to get a better read on "luck," we use formulas that capture the external variability of the data.

Through our research and the work of others, we have learned that when raw skill is separated from statistical output, what's remaining is often unexplained variance. The aggregate totals of many of these variances, for all players, is often a constant. For instance, while a pitcher's ERA might fluctuate, the rate at which his opposition's batted balls fall for hits will always be about 30%. Large variances in this rate can be expected to regress to 30%.

Why is all this important? Analysts complain about the lack of predictability of many traditional statistical gauges. The reason they find it difficult is that they are trying to project performance using gauges that are loaded with external noise. Raw skills gauges are more pure and follow better defined trends during a player's career. Then, as we get a better handle on the variances — explained and unexplained — we can construct a complete picture of what a player's statistics really mean.

The Process

The next step is to assemble these evaluators in such a way that they can be used to validate our observations, analyze their relevance and project a likely future direction.

In a perfect world, if a player's raw skills improve, then so should his surface stats. If his skills decline, then his stats should follow as well. But, sometimes a player's skill may increase while his surface stats may decline. These variances may be due to a variety of factors.

Component skills analysis is based on the expectation that events tend to move towards universal order. Surface stats will eventually approach their raw skill levels. Some unexplained variances will regress to the mean. And from this, we can identify players whose performance, as a whole, may change.

This process provides an important starting point for any forecasting analysis. For most of us, that analysis begins with the previous season's numbers. Last season provides us with a point of reference, so it's a natural way to begin the process of looking at the future.

Component skills analysis allows us to validate last year's numbers. A batter with few HRs but a high linear weighted power level has a good probability of improving his future HR output. A pitcher whose ERA was solid while his command ratio was poor is a good bet for an ERA spike.

Of course, these leading indicators do not always follow the rules. There are more shades of greys than blacks and whites. When indicators are in conflict – for instance, a pitcher who is displaying both a rising strikeout rate and a rising walk rate – then we have to find ways to sort out what these indicators might be saying.

It is often helpful to look at leading indicators in a hierarchy, of sorts. In fact, a hierarchy of the most important pitching base performance indicators might look like this: command (k/bb), control (bb/9), dominance (k/9) and GB/FB rate. For batters, contact rate might top the list, followed by power, walk rate and speed.

Assimilating Additional Research

Once we've painted the statistical picture of a player's potential, we then use additional criteria and research results to help us add some more color. These other criteria include the player's health, age, changes in role, ballpark, and a variety of other factors. We also use our *Forecaster's Toolbox* research results, which are described in the next section. These analyses look at things like traditional periods of peak performance and breakout profiles.

The final element of the process is assimilating the news into the forecast. This is the element that many fantasy leaguers tend to rely on most since it is the most accessible. However, it is also the element that provides the most noise.

Players, management and the media have absolute control over what we are allowed to know. Factors such as hidden injuries, messy divorces and clubhouse unrest are routinely kept from us, while we are fed red herrings and media spam. *We will never know the entire truth.*

And so... as long as we do not know all the facts, we cannot dismiss the possibility that any one fact is true, no matter how often the media assures it, deplores it, or ignores it. Don't believe everything you read; use your own judgment. If your observations conflict with what is being reported, that's powerful insight that should not be ignored.

Quite often, all you are reading is just other people's opinions... a manager who believes that a player has what it takes to be a regular, a team physician whose diagnosis is that a player is healthy enough to play. These words from experts have some element of truth, but cannot be wholly relied upon to provide an accurate expectation of future events. As such, it is often helpful to develop an appropriate cynicism for what you read.

For instance, if a player is struggling for no apparent reason, and there are denials about health issues, don't dismiss the possibility that an injury does exist. There are often motives for such news to be withheld from the public.

Also remember that nothing lasts forever in major league baseball. *Reality is fluid.* One decision begets a series of events that lead to other decisions. Any reported action can easily be reversed based on subsequent events. My favorite examples are announcements of a team's new bullpen closer. Those are about the shortest realities known to man.

We need the media to provide us with context for our analyses, and the *real* news they provide is valuable intelligence. But separating the news from the noise is difficult. In most cases, the only thing you can trust is how that player actually performs.

Embracing Imprecision

Precision and accuracy in baseball prognosticating is a fool's quest. There are far too many unexpected variables and noise that can render our projections useless. The truth is, the best we can ever hope for is to accurately forecast general tendencies and percentage plays.

However, even when you follow an 80% percentage play, for instance, you will still lose 20% of the time. Those 20% worth of outlying players are what skeptics like to use as proof that all prognosticators are frauds. The paradox, of course, is that fantasy league titles are often won or lost by those exceptions. Still, long-term success dictates that you always chase the 80% and accept the fact that you will be wrong 20% of the time. Or, whatever that percentage play happens to be.

For fantasy league purposes, playing the percentages can take on an even less precise spin. The best projections are often the ones that are just far enough away from the field of expectation to alter decision-making. In other words, it doesn't matter if I project Player X to bat .320 and he only bats .295; it matters that I projected .320 and everyone else projected .280.

Or, perhaps we should evaluate projections based upon their intrinsic value. For instance, coming into 2007, would it have been more important for me to tell you that Adam Dunn was going to hit 40 HRs or that Dan Uggla's batting average would drop 20 points from 2006? By season's end, the Dunn projection would have been more accurate, but the Uggla projection would have been more *valuable.*

And that should be enough. Actually, it *has* to be enough. Any tout who exactly projects any player's statistics dead-on will have just been lucky with his dart throws that day.

About Us Touts

As a group, there is a strong tendency for all pundits to provide numbers that are more palatable than realistic. That's because committing to either end of the range of expectation poses a high risk. Few touts possess the courage to put their credibility on the line like that, even though we all know that those outliers are inevitable. So they take the easy road and just split the difference. I am a member of that group and I can say that we are cowards, all of us.

In the world of prognosticating, this can be called the *comfort zone.* This represents the outer tolerances for the public acceptability of a set of numbers. In most circumstances, even if the evidence is outstanding, published prognosticators will not stray from within the comfort zone.

As for me, occasionally I do commit to outlying numbers when I feel the data supports it. But on the whole, most of my numbers can be nearly as cowardly as everyone else's. I get around this by providing "color" to the projections in the capsule commentaries. That is where you will find the players whose projection has the best potential to stray beyond the limits of the comfort zone.

As Baseball HQ writer John Burnson once wrote: "The issue is not the success rate for one player, but the success rate for all players. No system is 100% reliable, and in trying to capture the outliers, you weaken the middle and thereby lose more predictive pull than you gain. At some level, everyone is an exception!"

And Just So You Know

We began the conversation about component skills analysis right here in the 1993 edition of the *Baseball Forecaster.* The LIMA Plan in 1998 pioneered the application of these concepts for fantasy baseball. Since then, we continue to further the discussion, enhancing and refining the process of winning with such tools as Pure Quality Starts and strategies such as the Portfolio3 Plan.

Thanks to the internet, its community of sharing and the easy dissemination of information, other sources have picked up on the power of these tools. When you see things like contact rate and strand rate cited elsewhere, know that the research and application of these gauges originated *here,* whether these other services provide fair attribution or have adopted the concepts as their own. But the source of the original thought, and the place that continues to pioneer innovative new ideas, is the *Baseball Forecaster* and BaseballHQ.com. This is where you stay ahead of the curve.

For a deeper discussion about my take on baseball forecasting, read "The Great Myths of Projective Accuracy" online at
http://www.baseballhq.com/books/myths.shtml

Forecaster's Toolbox

The following tools, rules and research findings represent the work of many authors, from industry icons like Bill James to many of our own baseball analysts from Baseball HQ.

There are two types of information here. There are analytical tools, which are methods to put events and performances into context. And there are actual research results. Generally, we only include the results of each particular piece of research, rather than take up space with all the methodologies and minutia. The back-up data have appeared in our other publications and on Baseball HQ in the past. Our purpose here is to give you the tools you need to make evaluations, and quickly. So pardon the lack of support data. Rest assured we're not making this stuff up.

Be aware that these research findings represent tendencies, not absolutes. If we tell you that 96% of batters with eye ratios over 1.50 will hit over .250, don't send us hate mail if the former batting champion you drafted in the second round falls into the other 4%. It happens. It's not our fault. Consider this a universal disclaimer.

Beyond that, there is great value here. Consider this your own fanalytic arsenal.

Validating Overall Performance

Performance Validation Criteria

When a player puts up numbers that vary from expectation, we can assemble a set of support variables that can help us determine whether his statistical output is an accurate reflection of his skills, or if other variables have come into play that have skewed the stats. Essentially, we're asking, is this performance a "fact or fluke?"

1. The player's age... Is he at the stage of development when we might expect a change in performance?

2. Health status... Is he coming off an injury, reconditioned and healthy for the first time in years, or a habitual resident of the disabled list?

3. Minor league performance... Has he ever shown the potential for greater things at some level of the minors? Or does his minor league history show a poor skill set that might indicate a lower skills ceiling?

4. Historical trends... Have his skill levels over time been on an upswing or downswing?

5. Hidden indicators behind traditional stats... Looking beyond batting averages and ERAs, what do his support ratios look like?

6. Change in ballpark, team, league... Pitchers going to Texas will see their ERA spike. Pitchers going to Petco Field will see their ERA improve. Stuff like that.

7. Change in team performance... Has a player's performance been affected by overall team chemistry or the environment fostered by a winning or losing club?

8. Change in batting stance, pitching style... Has a change in performance been due to an adjustment made during the off-season?

9. Change in usage, lineup position, etc.... Has a change in RBI opportunities been a result of moving further up or down in the batting order? Has pitching effectiveness been impacted by moving from the bullpen to the rotation?

10. Change in managerial strategy, or opportunity... Does his sudden change in performance have less to do with ability than with playing time, or perhaps not having a well-defined role?

11. Coaching effects... Has the coaching staff changed the way a player approaches his conditioning, or how he approaches the game itself?

12. Off-season activity... Has a player spent the winter frequenting workout rooms or banquet tables?

13. Personal factors... Has the player undergone a family crisis? Experienced spiritual rebirth? Given up red meat? Taken up testosterone?

Skills Ownership

Once a player displays a skill, he owns it. That display could occur at any time – earlier in his career, back in the minors, or even in winter ball play. And while that skill may lie dormant after its initial display, the potential is always there for him to tap back into that skill at some point, barring injury or age. That dormant skill can reappear at any time given the right set of circumstances.

Caveat... The initial display of skill must have occurred over an extended period of time. An isolated 1-hit shut-out in Single-A ball amidst a 5.00 ERA season is not enough. The shorter the display of skill in the past, the more likely it can be attributed to random chance. The longer the display, the more likely that any re-emergence of that skill is for real. Typically, you'd want to see a consistent level of performance over at least a several month period.

Corollaries:

1. Once a player displays a vulnerability or skills deficiency, he owns that as well. That vulnerability could be an old injury problem, an inability to hit breaking pitches, or just a tendency to go into prolonged slumps.

2. The probability of a player addressing and correcting a skills deficiency declines with each year he allows that deficiency to continue to exist.

Categories of Surprises

When a player has an uncharacteristically good or bad season, it is helpful to characterize that performance to determine its likelihood of being repeated. By answering a question such as, "Was Hanley Ramirez's 2007 breakout a career year, maturation, or aberration?" we can start the process of projecting what he is likely to do in 2008.

Career year: These are players who have established a certain level of performance over several years, then suddenly put up exceptional numbers. Career years may be explained from the list of validation criteria, but are usually one-shot deals.

Maturation: These players have also established a certain level of performance over time, but the performance spike is truly indicative of their potential and will likely be maintained.

Off year: These are players who have established a certain level of performance over several years, then suddenly drop off. This could be a performance blip, an adjustment period or an injury-induced decline. These players have the potential to bounce back.

Comedown: These players have also established a certain level of performance over time, but their performance drop is indicative of a new level at which they will likely plateau. The typical 30-something syndrome.

Opportunity: Sometimes a surprise isn't a change in performance at all but the effect a change in playing time has on performance. Often, a role player gets thrust into a full-time job and suddenly puts up extraordinary numbers. This can work both ways — a player may rise to the occasion, or find that the regular day-to-day grind has an adverse effect on his numbers. Opportunity surprises are created by events like injuries or changes in managerial strategy and can last as long as the opportunity lasts.

No surprise: We sometimes form unrealistic expectations about players due to media hype or short-term performance levels. Rookies fall into this category, for instance, but the success or failure of unproven commodities should not be unexpected. In addition, frequently injured players who've lowered our expectations, then bounce back to previous productivity levels when healthy, should not be surprises either (except, perhaps, that they managed to stay healthy).

Aberration: These are the performances that simply cannot be adequately explained by the validation criteria. Chance occurrences do happen, and sometimes in bunches. There are stretches in a player's career when a spray hitter might see a few week's worth of fat, juicy homer balls, or a pitcher might face a string of wiffle bats. It just happens, then it stops. Most times, it will never happen again.

Risk Management and Reliability Scores

Forecasts are constructed with the best data available, but there are factors that can impact the variability around that projection. One way we manage this risk is to assign each player a Reliability Score (Rel). The more certainty we see in a data set, the higher the potential reliability of the forecast. The following variables are evaluated:

Experience: The greater the pool of major league history to draw from, the greater our ability to construct a viable forecast. Length of service is important, as is length of consistent service. So players who bounce up and down from the majors to the minors are higher risk players. And rookies are all high risk.

Consistency: Consistent performers are easier to project and garner higher reliability scores. Players that mix mediocrity, or worse, with occasional flashes of brilliance generate higher risk projections.

Health: Players with an injury history — whether or not they are healthy now — will generate lower Rel scores.

Age: Players' skills develop and erode as they age. During the rise of that skills curve, as well as during their late career descent, their performance will be more prone to fluctuation, and hence, higher risk.

Burnout potential: For a pitcher, workload levels need to be monitored, especially in the formative years of his career. Exceeding those levels elevates the risk of injury, burnout, or breakdown.

The reliability scores are expressed on a scale of 0-100. A perfect score of 100 would represent the following:

Batters
- Between 27 and 30 years of age
- Average min. 550 PA in MLB each of the past three years
- Spent no time on the DL over the past three years
- RC/G over the past three years was perfectly consistent

Starting Pitchers
- Between 28 and 31 years of age
- Averaged at least 200 MLB innings each of the past 3 years
- Spent no time on the DL over the past three years
- For pitchers currently 29 years or younger, did not pitch an excessive number of innings prior to age 25
- xERA over the past three years was perfectly consistent

Relief pitchers
Same criteria as starting pitchers with one exception:
- The total of IP plus (saves x 5) over the past three years averaged at least 200

The benchmark for acceptability is a score of 50. Any levels above this represent gradually increasing reliability (or gradually decreasing risk). Players with levels under 25 should generally be avoided, especially by the risk averse.

You'll note that relief pitchers have low scores. This is by design since playing time is one of the elements that drive these scores. Just one bad outing can completely skew a stat line. Those with the higher scores are typically closers who've been consistent in that role over time.

Remember that these levels have nothing to do with *quality* of performance; they strictly refer to consistency and confidence in our expectations. So a Rel of 81 for Josh Fogg, for instance, only means that there is a high probability he will perform as poorly as we've projected.

Reliability and Experience

Peak batting reliability occurs at ages 29 and 30, followed by a minor decline for four years. So, to draft the most reliable batters, and maximize the odds of returning at least par value on your investments, you should target the age range of 28-34.

The most reliable age range for pitchers is 29-34. While we are forever looking for "sleepers" and hot prospects, these charts indicate that, it is very risky to draft any pitcher under 27 or over 35.

RELIABILITY SCORE		
Age	Batters	Pitchers
22-	10	8
23	19	10
24	23	12
25	33	16
26	31	19
27	39	28
28	44	30
29	50	32
30	50	36
31	48	48
32	47	46
33	46	38
34	46	34
35	30	25
36	35	19
37	38	15
38	35	23
39	32	29
40+	28	40

April Performance as a Leading Indicator

We isolated all players who earned at least $10 more or $10 less than we had projected in March. Then we looked at the April stats of these players to see if we could have picked out the $10 outliers after just one month.

	Identifiable in April
Earned $10+ more than projected	
BATTERS	39%
PITCHERS	44%
Earned -$10 less than projected	
BATTERS	56%
PITCHERS	74%

Nearly three out of every four pitchers who earned at least $10 less than projected also struggled in April. For all the other surprises — batters or pitchers — April was not a strong leading indicator. Another look:

	Pct.
Batters who finished +$25	45%
Pitchers who finished +$20	44%
Batters who finished under $0	60%
Pitchers who finished under -$5	78%

April surgers are less than a 50/50 proposition to maintain that level all season. Those who finished April at the bottom of the roto rankings were more likely to continue struggling, especially pitchers. In fact, of those pitchers who finished April with a value *under -$10,* 91% finished the season in the red. Holes are tough to dig out of.

Courtship Period

Any time a player is put into a new situation, he enters into what we might call a *courtship period.* This period might occur when a player switches leagues, or switches teams. It could be the first few games when a minor leaguer is called up. It could occur when a reliever moves into the rotation, or when a lead-off hitter is moved to another spot in the lineup. There is a team-wide courtship period when a manager is replaced. Any external situation that could affect a player's performance sets off a new decision point in evaluating that performance.

During this period, it is difficult to get a true read on how a player is going to ultimately perform. He is adjusting to the new situation. Things could be volatile during this time. For instance, a role change that doesn't work could spur other moves. A rookie hurler might buy himself a few extra starts with a solid debut, even if he has questionable skills.

It is best not to make a decision on a player who is going through a courtship period. Wait until his stats stabilize. Don't cut a struggling pitcher in his first few starts after a managerial change. Don't pick up a hitter who smacks a pair of HRs in his first game after having been traded. Unless, of course, talent and track record say otherwise.

Half-Season Fallacies

A popular exercise at the midpoint of each season is to analyze those players who are *consistent* first half to second half surgers or faders. There are several fallacies with this analytical approach.

1. Half-season consistency is rare. There are very few players who show consistent changes in performance from one half of the season to the other.

Research results from a three-year study conducted in the late-1990s: The total of all batters who compiled a minimum of 300 full season ABs, and a minimum of 150 first half ABs in this study was 98. Of that group, 40% demonstrated a consistent first half to second half trend in at least one statistical category for all three years. Only 18% demonstrated any half-season tendency in more than one category. Only 3% demonstrated consistent tendencies in more than two categories over the three-year period.

The total of all pitchers who compiled a minimum of 100 full season IPs, and a minimum of 50 first half IPs in this study was only 42. Of that group, 57% demonstrated a consistent first half to second half trend in at least one stat category for all three years. Only 21% demonstrated any half-season tendency in more than one category. And only 5% had consistent tendencies in more than two categories.

When the analysis was stretched to a fourth year, only 1% of all players showed consistency in even one category.

2. Analysts often use false indicators. Situational statistics provide us with tools that are often misused. Several sources offer up three and 5-year statistics intended to paint a picture of a long-term performance. Some analysts look at a player's half-season batting average swing over that multi-year period and conclude that he is demonstrating consistent performance.

The fallacy is that those multi-year scans may not show any consistency at all. They are not individual season performances but *aggregate* performances. A player whose 5-year batting average shows a 15-point rise in the 2nd half, for instance, may actually have experienced a BA *decline* in several of those years, a fact that might have been offset by a huge BA rise in one of the years.

3. It's arbitrary. The season's midpoint is really an arbitrary delineator of performance swings. Some players are slow starters and might be more appropriately evaluated as pre-May 1 and post-May 1. Others bring their game up a notch with a pennant chase and might see a performance swing with August 15 as the cut-off. Each player has his own individual tendency, if, in fact, one exists at all. There's nothing magical about mid-season as the break point, and certainly not over a multi-year period.

Contract Year Performance

There is a contention that players step up their game when they are playing for a new contract. Research looked at contract year players, their performance during that year (as compared to career levels) and whether they reverted to form in the first year of their new contract. Of the batters and pitchers studied, 53% of the batters performed as if they were on a salary drive, while only 15% of the pitchers managed to exhibit some level of contract year behavior.

Batting Toolbox

Batting Eye as a Leading Indicator

There is a strong correlation between the ability to distinguish between balls and strikes — strike zone judgment — and batting average. However, research shows that this is more descriptive than predictive:

Batting Average

Batting Eye	2003	2004	2005	2006	2007
0.00 - 0.25	.247	.235	.244	.251	.250
0.26 - 0.50	.261	.262	.261	.267	.265
0.51 - 0.75	.270	.276	.274	.279	.276
0.76 - 1.00	.281	.279	.279	.286	.280
1.01 and over	.294	.300	.290	.287	.305

We can create percentage plays for the different levels:

For Eye Levels of	Pct who bat .300+	.250-
0.00 - 0.25	7%	39%
0.26 - 0.50	14%	26%
0.51 - 0.75	18%	17%
0.76 - 1.00	32%	14%
1.01 - 1.50	51%	9%
1.51 +	59%	4%

Any batter with an eye ratio over 1.50 has about a 4% chance of hitting under .250 over 500 at bats.

Of all .300 hitters, those with ratios of at least 1.00 have a 65% chance of repeating as .300 hitters. Those with ratios under 1.00 have less than a 50% chance of repeating.

Only 12% of sub-.250 hitters with ratios between 0.50 and 0.99, and only 4% with ratios under 0.50, will mature into .300 hitters the following year.

In a 1995-2000 study, only 37 batters hit .300-plus with a sub-0.50 eye ratio over at least 300 AB in a season. Of this group, 30% were able to accomplish this feat on a consistent basis. For the other 70%, this phenomenon was a short-term aberration.

Contact Rate as a Leading Indicator

It follows intuitively that the more often a batter makes contact with the ball, the higher the likelihood that he will hit safely. Not rocket science here, but good to see that the numbers do bear this out.

Batting Average

Contact Rate	2003	2004	2005	2006	2007
0% - 60%	.161	.187	.207	.181	.204
61% - 65%	.201	.186	.221	.220	.228
66% - 70%	.240	.242	.244	.251	.237
71% - 75%	.247	.249	.252	.256	.250
76% - 80%	.264	.265	.266	.270	.269
81% - 85%	.271	.273	.270	.274	.277
86% - 90%	.280	.283	.279	.287	.284
Over 90%	.284	.298	.282	.295	.289

Contact Rate & Walk Rate as Leading Indicators

A matrix of contact rates and walk rates can provide expectation benchmarks for a player's batting average:

		bb% 0-5	6-10	11-15	16+
ct%	65-	.179	.195	.229	.237
	66-75	.190	.248	.254	.272
	76-85	.265	.267	.276	.283
	86+	.269	.279	.301	.309

A contact rate of 65% or lower offers virtually no chance for a player to hit even .250, no matter how high a walk rate he has. The .300 hitters most often come from the group with a minimum 86% contact and 11% walk rate.

Hit Rate (BABIP) as a Leading Indicator *(Patrick Davitt)*

Every hitter establishes his own individual hit rate (batting average on balls-in-play) that stabilizes over time. A batter whose seasonal hit rate (H%) varies significantly from the H% he has established over the preceding three seasons is likely to improve or regress to his individual H% mean (with over-performer declines both more likely and sharper than under-performer recoveries). H% levels for a three-year period strongly predict a player's H% in the succeeding year.

Batting Eye and Power

We often ignore the batting eye ratio when evaluating power because so many batters achieve their lofty HR numbers by opening up their swing, thereby increasing their strikeout totals and depressing their eye ratio. However, this path to power success is a riskier one.

During a four-year study period, any batter who slammed 30 HRs in a season had less than a 3 in 10 chance of improving his power skills the following year. But eye ratios better define the power decline.

	YEAR 2	
Batting eye	PX increased	PX declined
Less than 0.50	13%	87%
0.50 - 0.99	24%	76%
1.00 and over	31%	69%

Batters with lower ratios were more likely to experience a power drop-off in the year following a 30-HR campaign.

Power Breakouts

It is not easy to predict which batters will experience a power spike. We can categorize power breakouts to determine the likelihood of a player taking a step up or of a surprise performer repeating his feat.

1. Increase in playing time. A HR spike might not be skills-related but just the result of a playing time increase.

2. History of power skills. A player may have displayed power skills sometime in the past, be it in his early major league career or prior.

3. Distribution of extra base hits. There is not much difference in skill between a double and a HR. A HR breakout may merely be a random redistribution of already demonstrated extra base hit power.

4. Normal skills growth. The power spike may be a normal occurrence along a batter's growth curve. A batter's breakout year may have been easily predicted from a review of his power index (PX) trend.

5. Situational breakouts. No matter how impressive the HR-hitting feats of Vinny Castilla were in the past, the fact that he played half his games in Coors Field discounted any true spike in skills. Similar for any player moving into a more power-conducive venue.

6. Fly ball tendency. See Olkin research below.

7. Steroids. A power spike might be the result of a player using illegal performance-enhancing substances.

8. The unexplained. Sometimes, a power spike makes no logical sense and cannot be explained by any of the previous criteria. These power surges hold the lowest probability for a comparable follow-up performance.

Fly Ball Tendency and Power *(Mat Olkin)*

There is a proven connection between a hitter's ground ball-fly ball tendencies and his power production.

1. Extreme ground ball hitters generally do not hit for much power. It's almost impossible for a hitter with a ground/fly ratio over 1.80 to hit enough fly balls to produce even 25 HRs in a season. However, this does not mean that a low G/F ratio necessarily guarantees power production. Some players have no problem getting the ball into the air, but lack the strength to reach the fences consistently.

2. Most batters' ground/fly ratios stay pretty steady over time. Most year-to-year changes are small and random, as they are in any other statistical category. A large, sudden change in G/F, on the other hand, can signal a conscious change in plate approach. And so...

3. If a player posts high G/F ratios in his first few years, he probably isn't ever going to hit for all that much power.

4. When a batter's power suddenly jumps, his G/F ratio often drops at the same time.

5. Every so often, a hitter's ratio will drop significantly even as his power production remains level. In these rare cases, impending power development is likely, since the two factors almost always follow each other.

Handedness Notes

1. While pure southpaws account for about 27% of total ABs (RHers about 55% and switch-hitters about 18%), they hit 31% of the triples and take 30% of the walks.

2. The average lefty posts a batting average about 10 points higher than the average RHer. The on base averages of pure LHers are nearly 20 points higher than RHers, but only 10 points higher than switch-hitters.

3. LHers tend to have a better batting eye ratio than RHers, but about the same as switch-hitters.

4. Pure righties and lefties have virtually identical power skills. Switch-hitters tend to have less power, on average.

5. Switch-hitters tend to have the best speed, followed by LHers, and then RHers.

6. On an overall production basis, LHers have an 8% advantage over RHers and a 14% edge over switch-hitters.

Batting Average Perception

Early season batting average strugglers who surge later in the year get no respect because they have to live with the weight of their early numbers all season long. Conversely, quick starters who fade late get far more accolades than they deserve.

For instance, take Kevin Kouzmanoff's 2007 month-by-month batting averages. Perception, which is typically based solely on a player's cumulative season stat line, was that he struggled in batting average pretty much all season. Reality is different. He had one truly off-month, and it happened to occur in April. How many people knew he batted .303 from May 1 on and .320 in the second half?

Month	BA	Cum BA
April	.113	.198
May	.303	.204
June	.247	.219
July	.275	.234
August	.292	.248
September	.380	.275

Optimal Ages

Players develop at different paces, but in general terms, age can be helpful to determine where they should be along the developmental curve. Bill James' original research showed that batters tended to peak at about age 27. More recent research suggests that a variety of factors have pushed that average up closer to 30. More tendencies:

"26 With Experience" *(John Benson):* While batters may peak at about age 27, the players most likely to exhibit the most dramatic spike in performance are those aged 26 who have several years of major league experience.

Power: Batting power skills tend to grow consistently between ages 24 and 29. Many batters experience a power peak at about age 30-31. Catchers often experience a power spike in the mid-30's.

Speed: Base-running and speed are skills of the young. When given the choice of two speedsters of fairly equivalent abilities and opportunity, always go after the younger one. A sharp drop-off in speed skills typically occurs at age 34.

Batting eye: For batters who continue to play into their 30's, this is a skill that can develop and grow throughout their career. A decline in this level, which can occur at any age, often indicates a decline in overall skills.

Thirtysomethings *(Ed Spaulding):* Batters tend to lose points on their BA but draw more walks. While players on the outside of the defensive spectrum (1B, 3B, LF, RF, DH) often have their best seasons in their 30's, players in the middle (2B, SS, CF) tend to fade. Many former stars move to new positions (Ripken, Molitor, Banks, etc.).

Catchers *(Ed Spaulding):* Many catchers — particularly second line catchers — have their best seasons late in their careers. Some possible reasons why:

1. Catchers, like shortstops, often get to the big leagues for defensive reasons and not their offensive skills. These skills take longer to develop.

2. The heavy emphasis on learning the catching/defense/pitching side of the game detracts from their time to learn about, and practice, hitting.

3. Injuries often curtail their ability to show offensive skills, though these injuries (typically jammed fingers, bruises on the arms, rib injuries from collisions) often don't lead to time on the disabled list.

4. The time spent behind the plate has to impact the ability to recognize, and eventually hit, all kinds of pitches.

Spring Training Leading Indicator *(John Dewan)*

A hitter with a positive difference between his spring training slugging percentage and his lifetime slugging percentage of .200 or more correlates to a better than normal season.

Projecting In-Season RBI *(Patrick Davitt)*

Evaluating players in-season for RBI potential is a function of the interplay among four factors:

- Teammates' ability to reach base ahead of him and to run the bases efficiently;
- His own ability to drive them around by hitting, especially for extra bases
- Number of Games Played
- Place in the batting order

3-4-5 Hitters:
$(0.69 \times GP \times TOB) + (0.30 \times ITB) + (0.275 \times HR) - (.191 \times GP)$

6-7-8 Hitters:
$(0.63 \times GP \times TOB) + (0.27 \times ITB) + (0.250 \times HR) - (.191 \times GP)$

9-1-2 Hitters:
$(0.57 \times GP \times TOB) + (0.24 \times ITB) + (0.225 \times HR) - (.191 \times GP)$

...where GP = games played, TOB = team on-base pct. and ITB = individual total bases (ITB).

Apply this pRBI formula after 70 games played or so (to reduce the variation from small sample size) to find players more than 9 RBI's over or under their projected RBI. There could be a correction coming.

You should also consider other factors, like injury or trade (involving the player or a top-of-the-order speedster) or team SB philosophy and success rate.

As well, remember that the player himself has an impact on his TOB. When we first did this study, we excluded the player from his TOB and got slightly better results. The formula overestimates projected RBI for players like Barry Bonds, whose high OBP skews his teams' OBP upwards but who can't benefit in RBI from that effect.

Pitching Toolbox

Fundamental Skills

"There's no way to project pitchers accurately from year to year." — Bill James.

"Starting pitchers are the most unreliable, unpredictable, unpleasant group of people in the world, statistically speaking that is." — John Benson

"Not the most astute major league scout nor the world's top number cruncher, can correctly project the statistical output of more than a couple a dozen of the game's 400 hurlers." — Steve Mann

It is difficult to argue with these top baseball writers, but their perception is tainted. Unreliable pitching performance is a fallacy driven by the practice of attempting to project pitching stats using gauges that are poor evaluators of skill.

How can we better evaluate pitching skill? We can start with the three statistical categories that are generally unaffected by external factors. These three stats capture the outcome of an individual pitcher versus batter match-up without regard to supporting offense, defense or bullpen:

Walks Allowed, Strikeouts and Ground Balls

Even with only these stats to observe, there is a wealth of insight that these measures can provide.

Command Ratio as a Leading Indicator

The ability to get the ball over the plate — command of the strike zone — is one of the best leading indicators for future performance. Command ratio (K/BB) can be used to project potential in ERA as well as other skills gauges.

1. Research indicates that there is a high correlation between a pitcher's Cmd ratio and his ERA.

	Earned Run Average				
Command	**2003**	**2004**	**2005**	**2006**	**2007**
0.0 - 1.0	5.85	6.24	6.22	6.42	6.48
1.1 - 1.5	5.05	5.16	4.93	5.06	5.12
1.6 - 2.0	4.51	4.63	4.41	4.65	4.58
2.1 - 2.5	4.22	4.30	4.28	4.48	4.28
2.6 - 3.0	3.80	3.80	3.60	4.15	3.89
3.1 and over	3.30	3.30	3.45	3.49	3.49

We can create percentage plays for the different levels:

For Cmd	Pct who post	
Levels of	**3.50-**	**4.50+**
0.0 - 1.0	0%	87%
1.1 - 1.5	7%	67%
1.6 - 2.0	7%	57%
2.1 - 2.5	19%	35%
2.6 - 3.0	26%	25%
3.1 +	53%	5%

In general, pitchers who maintain a command ratio of over 2.5 have a high probability of long-term success. Pitchers with a ratio over 3.0 have only a 5% chance of posting a 4.50-plus ERA. For fantasy drafting purposes, it is best to avoid pitchers with sub-2.0 ratios. Bullpen closers should be avoided if they have a ratio under 2.5.

2. A pitcher's command in tandem with dominance (strikeout rate) provides even greater predictive abilities.

	Earned Run Average	
Command	**-5.6 Dom**	**5.6+ Dom**
0.0-0.9	5.36	5.99
1.0-1.4	4.94	5.03
1.5-1.9	4.67	4.47
2.0-2.4	4.32	4.08
2.5-2.9	4.21	3.88
3.0-3.9	4.04	3.46
4.0+	4.12	2.96

This helps to highlight the limited upside potential of soft-tossers with pinpoint control. The extra dominance makes a huge difference.

3. Research also suggests that there is a strong correlation between a pitcher's command ratio and his propensity to win ballgames. Over three quarters of those with ratios over 3.0 post winning records, and the collective W/L record of those command artists is nearly .600.

The command/winning correlation holds up in both leagues, although the effect was much more pronounced in the NL. Over four times more NL hurlers than AL hurlers have command ratios over 3.0, and it appears that higher command ratios are required in the NL to maintain good winning percentages. While a ratio between 2.0 and 2.9 might be good enough for a winning record for over 70% of AL pitchers, that level in the NL will generate an above-.500 mark only slightly more than half the time.

In short, in order to have at least a 70% chance of drafting a pitcher with a winning record, you must target NL pitchers with at least a 3.0 command ratio. To achieve the same odds in the AL, a 2.0 command ratio will suffice.

Strand Rate as a Leading Indicator

Strand Rate finds great utility in explaining variances between a pitcher's ERA and his performance indicators.

Pitchers with rates over 80% always have exemplary ERAs. Starters and middle relievers with 80%-plus rates in a given season have an 80% likelihood of seeing their ERA rise the following year. The percentage drops to 50% for short relievers.

Pitchers with strand rates under 65% always have inflated ERAs, but have an 89% likelihood of seeing their ERA improve the following year. In addition, 83% will improve their ERA by more than one run.

Important! These 65% and 80% benchmarks are firm. Other analysts may project ERA regression off of rates closer to the mean of 71%. These analyses are wrong.

Hit Rate as a Leading Indicator *(Voros McCracken)*

In 2000, Voros McCracken published a study that concluded that "there is little if any difference among major league pitchers in their ability to prevent hits on balls hit in the field of play."

His assertion was that, while a Johan Santana would have a better ability to prevent a batter from getting wood on a ball, or perhaps keeping the ball in the park, once that ball was hit in the field of play, the probability of it falling for a hit was virtually no different than for any other pitcher.

Among the findings in his study were:

- There is little correlation between what a pitcher does one year in the stat and what he will do the next. This is not true with other significant stats (BB, K, HR).
- You can better predict a pitcher's hits per balls in play from the rate of the rest of the pitcher's team than from the pitcher's own rate.

This last point brings a team's defense into the picture. It begs the question, when a batter gets a hit, is it because the pitcher made a bad pitch, the batter took a good swing, or the defense was not positioned correctly to field it? McCracken's findings take the onus away from the pitcher and puts it on the shoulders of the batter and defense.

Pitchers will often post hit rates per balls-in-play that are far off from the league average, but then revert to the mean the following year. As such, we can use that mean – approximately 30% – in much the same way we use strand rate to project the direction of a pitcher's ERA.

Subsequent research has shown that ground ball or fly ball propensity may have a small impact on hit rate.

HR/FB Rate as a Leading Indicator *(John Burnson)*

McCracken's work focused on "balls in play," omitting home runs from the study. However, pitchers also do not have much control over the percentage of fly balls that turn into HR. Research shows that there is an underlying rate of HR as a percentage of fly balls of 10%. A pitcher's HR/FB rate will vary each year but always tends to regress to that 10%. The element that pitchers *do* have control over is the number of fly balls they allow. That is the underlying skill or deficiency that controls their HR rate.

Pitchers who keep the ball out of the air more often correlate well with Roto value. The formula *(K + 0.3GB) / Batters Faced* provides a strong gauge for "air superiority."

Line Drive Pct. as a Leading Indicator *(Seth Samuels)*

Also beyond a pitcher's control is the percentage of balls-in-play that are line drives. Line drives do the most damage; from 1994-2003, here are the expected hit rates and number of total bases per type of BIP.

	|—— Type of BIP ——|	
	GB	FB	LD
H%	26%	23%	56%
Total bases	0.29	0.57	0.80

Despite the damage done by LDs, pitchers do not have any innate skill to avoid them. There is little relationship between a pitcher's LD% one year and his rate the next year. All rates tend to regress towards a mean of 22.6%.

However, ground ball pitchers do have a slight ability to prevent line drives (21.7%) and extreme ground ball hurlers even moreso (18.5%). Extreme fly ball pitchers have a slight ability to prevent LDs (21.1%) as well.

Ground Ball Tendency as a Leading Indicator
(John Burnson)

Ground ball pitchers tend to give up fewer HRs than do fly ball pitchers. There is also evidence that GB pitchers have higher hit rates. In other words, a ground ball has a higher chance of being a hit than does a fly ball that is not out of the park.

GB pitchers have lower strikeout rates. We should be more forgiving of a low strikeout rate (under 5.5 K/9) if it belongs to an extreme ground ball pitcher.

GB pitchers have a lower ERA than do fly ball pitchers but a higher WHIP. On balance, GB pitchers come out ahead, even when considering strikeouts, because a lower ERA also leads to more wins.

Ground Ball and Strikeout Tendencies as Indicators
(Mike Dranchak)

Pitchers were assembled into 9 groups based on the following profiles (minimum 23 starts in 2005):

Profile	Ground Ball Rate
Ground Ball	higher than 47%
Neutral	42% to 47%
Fly Ball	less than 42%

Profile	Strikeout Rate (k/9)
Strikeout	higher than 6.6 k/9
Average	5.4 to 6.6 k/9
Soft-Tosser	less than 5.4 k/9

Findings: Pitchers with higher strikeout rates had better ERA's and WHIPs than pitchers with lower strikeout rates, regardless of ground ball profile. However, for pitchers with similar strikeout rates, those with higher ground ball rates had better ERA's and WHIPs than those with lower ground ball rates.

Pitchers with higher strikeout rates tended to strand more baserunners than those with lower K rates. Fly ball pitchers tended to strand fewer runners than their GB or neutral counterparts within their strikeout profile.

Ground ball pitchers (especially those who lacked high-dominance) yielded more home runs per fly ball than did fly ball pitchers. However, the ERA risk was mitigated by the fact that ground ball pitchers (by definition) gave up fewer fly balls to begin with.

Projecting Wins

Using regression analyses, we can rank the importance of the variables that impact pitching win totals. In order:

1. Team offense (run support)
2. Pitching Effectiveness (base performance value)
3. Run Prevention (strand rate)
4. Bullpen support (inherited runners stranded %)
5. Managerial Tendencies (quick hooks/slow hooks)
6. Team Defense (fielding percentage)

When a fantasy leaguer needs to draft or beef up the Wins category, the most prudent approach is to target pitchers on teams with good offensive support.

Projecting Breakout Performances

Research has provided us with a set of criteria that can be used to identify candidates with the potential to experience large-scale ERA improvement. For pitchers that have consistently posted ERAs at or above the league average, target those that...

- will be between 24 and 28 years of age (and eliminate anyone over 29)
- have a minimum of two full years of major league experience
- have a history of command ratios over 2.0 (although the most recent year may be below 2.0)
- have had consistent strikeout rates of 6.0 or above
- have had consistent opposition OBA under .350
- have had strand rates of 70% or less and the promise of improved bullpen support in the next season.
- have had BPVs that showed potential for 50-plus levels, either via rising trends or in the minors.

Very few pitchers will meet all seven criteria; target those who meet the most, with a minimum of five. *(See the new breakout research in the Research Abstracts section.)*

Skill versus Consistency

Two pitchers have identical 4.50 ERAs and identical 3.0 PQS averages. Their PQS logs look like this:

PITCHER A:	3	3	3	3	3
PITCHER B:	5	0	5	0	5

Which pitcher would you rather have on your team? The risk-averse manager would choose Pitcher A as he represents the perfectly known commodity. Many fantasy leaguers might opt for Pitcher B because his occasional dominating starts show that there is an upside. His Achilles Heel is inconsistency. Is there any hope for Pitcher B?

- If a pitcher's inconsistency is characterized by more poor starts than good starts, his upside is limited.
- Pitchers with extreme inconsistency rarely get a full season of starts.
- However, inconsistency is neither chronic nor fatal.

The outlook for Pitcher A is actually worse. Disaster avoidance might buy these pitchers more starts, but history shows that the lack of dominating outings is more telling of future potential. In short, consistent mediocrity is bad.

Pitching Streaks

It is possible to find predictive value in strings of DOMinating or DISaster starts:

Once a pitcher enters into a DOM streak of any length, the probability for his subsequent start is going to be a better-than-average outing. The further a player is into a DOM streak, the higher the likelihood that the subsequent performance will be of high quality. In fact, once a pitcher has posted six DOM starts in a row, there is greater than a 70% probability that the streak will continue. When it does end, there is less than a 10% probability that the streak-breaker is going to be a DISaster.

Once a pitcher enters into a DIS streak of any length, the probability is that his next start is going to be a below average outing, even if that outing breaks the streak. However, DIS streaks erode quickly. Once a pitcher hits the skids, there is little potential for him to start posting productive numbers in the short term, even though the duration of the plummet itself should be brief.

Projecting Saves: Origin of Closers

History has long maintained that ace closers are not easily recognizable early on in their careers, so that every season does see its share of the unexpected. Al Reyes, C.J. Wilson, Brad Hennessy, Manny Corpas... who would have thought it a year ago?

Some accepted facts...

- You cannot find major league closers from pitchers who were closers in the minors.
- Closers begin their careers as starters.
- Closers are converted set-up men.
- Closers are pitchers who were unable to develop a third effective pitch.

All four statements are true. But the reality is a lot more simple... closers are a product of circumstance.

Are the minor leagues a place to look at all?

From 1990-2004, there were 280 twenty-save seasons in Double-A and Triple-A, accomplished by 254 different pitchers.

Of those 254, only 46 ever made it to the majors.

Of those 46, only 13 ever saved 20 games in a season.

Of those 13, only 5 ever posted more than one 20-save season in the majors: John Wetteland, Mark Wohlers, Ricky Bottalico, Braden Looper and Francisco Cordero.

Five out of 254 pitchers over 15 years, a rate of 2%.

One of the reasons that minor league closers rarely become major league closers is because, in general, they do not get enough innings in the minors to sufficiently develop their arms into big-league caliber.

In fact, organizations do not look at minor league closing performance seriously, assigning that role to pitchers who they do not see as legitimate prospects. In 2007, the average age of all Double-A and Triple-A pitchers who posted 20-plus saves was 28. In 2006, it was 27. In 2005, it was 28.

Projecting Saves

The task of finding future closing potential comes down to looking at two elements:

Talent: The raw skills to mow down hitters for short periods of time. Optimal BPVs over 100, but not under 75.

Opportunity: The more important element, yet the one that pitchers have no control over.

There are pitchers that have *Talent, but not Opportunity.* These pitchers are not given a chance to close for a variety of reasons (e.g. being blocked by a solid front-liner in the pen, being left-handed, etc.), but are good to own because they will not likely hurt your pitching staff. You just can't count on them for saves, at least not in the near term.

There are pitchers that have *Opportunity, but not Talent.* MLB managers decide who to give the ball to in the 9th inning based on their own perceptions about what skills are required to succeed, even if those perceived "skills" don't translate into acceptable BPI levels. Those pitchers without the BPIs may have some initial short-term success, but their long-term prognosis is poor and they are high risks to your roster. Classic examples of the short life span of these types of pitchers include Matt Karchner, Heath Slocumb, Ryan Kohlmeier, Dan Miceli and Danny Kolb.

Projecting Holds *(Doug Dennis)*

Here are some general rules of thumb for identifying pitchers who might be in line to accumulate Holds. The percentages represent the portion of 2003's top Holds leaders who fell into the category noted.

1. Left-handed set-up men with excellent BPIs. (43%)

2. A "go-to" right-handed set-up man with excellent BPIs. This is the one set-up RHer that a manager turns to with a small lead in the 7th or 8th innings. These pitchers also tend to vulture wins. (43%, but 6 of the top 9)

3. Excellent BPIs, but not a firm role as the main LHed or RHed set-up man. Roles change during the season; cream rises to the top. Relievers projected to post great BPIs often overtake lesser set-up men during the season. (14%)

Optimal Ages

As with batters, pitchers develop at different rates, but a look at their age can help determine where they should be along the developmental curve. Here are some tendencies...

While peaks vary, most all pitchers (who are still around) tend to experience a sharp drop-off in their skills at age 38.

Starting pitchers *(Rick Wilton):* Their first productive season in the majors (10 wins, 150 IP, sub-4.00 ERA) is at age 25 or 26. Starters who experience a career year after age 31 are far less likely to repeat that performance than those who achieve their career year at a younger age.

Relief aces *(Rick Wilton):* Their first 20-save season arrives at about age 26. About three of every four relievers who begin a run of 20-save seasons in their 20's will likely sustain that level for about four years, with their value beginning to decline at the beginning of the third year.

Many aces achieve a certain level of maturity in their 30's and can experience a run of 20-save seasons between ages 33 and 36. For some, this may be their first time in the role of bullpen closer. However, those who achieve their first 20-save season after age 34 are unlikely to repeat.

Thirtysomethings *(Ed Spaulding):* Older pitchers, as they lose velocity and movement on the ball, must rely on more variety and better location. Thus, if strikeouts are a priority, you don't want many pitchers over 30. The over-30 set that tends to be surprising includes finesse types, career minor leaguers who break through for 2-3 seasons often in relief, and knuckleballers (a young knuckleballer is 31).

Career Year Drop-off *(Rick Wilton)*

Research shows that a pitcher's post-career year drop-off, on average, looks like this...

- ERA increases by 1.00
- WHIP increases by 0.14.
- Nearly 6 fewer wins

Usage Warning Flags

Research suggests that there is a finite number of innings in a pitcher's arm. This number varies by pitcher, by development cycle, and by pitching style and repertoire. We can measure a pitcher's potential for future arm problems and/or reduced effectiveness:

- *Sharp increases in usage from one year to the next...* Any pitcher who increases his workload by 50 IP or more from year #1 to year #2 is a candidate to experience symptoms of burnout in year #3.

- *Starters' overuse...* Consistent "batters faced per game" (BF/G) levels of 28.0 or higher, combined with consistent seasonal IP totals of 200 or more may indicate burnout potential. Within a season, a BF/G of over 30.0 with a projected IP total of 200 may indicate a late season fade.

- *Relievers' overuse...* Warning flags should be up for relievers who post in excess of 100 IP in a season, while averaging fewer than 2 IP per outing.

When focusing solely on minor league pitchers, research results are striking:

Stamina: Virtually every minor league pitcher who has had a BF/G of 28.5 or more in one season will experience a drop-off in BF/G the following year. Many will be unable to ever duplicate that previous level of durability.

Performance: Most pitchers experience an associated drop-off in their BPVs in the years following the 28.5 BF/G season. Some are able to salvage their effectiveness later on by moving to the bullpen.

Protecting Young Pitchers *(Craig Wright)*

There is a link between some degree of eventual arm trouble and a history of heavy workloads in a pitcher's formative years. Some recommendations from this research:

Teenagers (A-ball): No 200 IP seasons and no BF/G over 28.5 in any 150 IP span. No starts on three days rest.

Ages 20-22: Average no more than 105 pitches per start with a single game ceiling of 130 pitches.

Ages 23-24: Average no more than 110 pitches per start with a single game ceiling of 140 pitches.

When possible, a young rookie starter should be introduced to the major leagues in a long relief role before he goes into the rotation.

Catchers' Effect on Pitching *(Thomas Hanrahan)*

A typical catcher handles a pitching staff better after having been with a club for a few years. Research has shown that there is an improvement in team ERA of approximately 0.37 runs from a catcher's rookie season to his prime years with a club. For fanalytic purposes, you should expect a pitcher's ERA to be higher than expected if he is throwing to a rookie backstop.

Handedness Notes

1. LHers tend to peak about a year after RHers.
2. LH post only 15% of the total saves. Typically, LHers are reserved for specialist roles so few are frontline closers.
3. RHers have slightly better command and HR rate.
4. There is no significant variance in ERA.
5. On an overall basis, RHers have about a 6% advantage.

Minor League Toolbox

Minor League Information Management
(Terry Linhart)

The increased attention that the minor leagues are getting has created some dangerous analytical by-products.

Hype: With the minor leagues still largely uncovered by the media, one reporter's short-term observations can make their way into the mainstream as fact. This growing subjective information base is often not rooted in fact at all, yet drives perception about prospects.

Rush: There is a rush to scour the lower minors statistically for the next phenom before anyone else does. But statistics alone do not tell the whole story. Often, there is an exaggerated emphasis on short-term performance in an environment (major league player development) that is supposed to focus on the long-term. Two poor outings don't mean a 21-year-old pitcher is washed up.

Other common factors that affect statistics:

League variances: Some leagues favor hitters or pitchers.

Ballpark variances: Dimensions and altitude create hitters parks and pitchers parks, but a factor rarely mentioned is that many ballparks in the lower minors are inconsistent in their field quality. Minor league clubs have limited resources to maintain their field conditions, and this can artificially depress defensive statistics while inflating gauges like batting average.

Widely variant skills: Some players' skills are so superior to the competition at their level that you can't get a true picture of what they're going to do from their stats alone.

Player development assignments: Many pitchers are told to work on secondary pitches while moving through the minors, throwing curveballs and change-ups on 3-2 or 2-2 counts to gain confidence in the pitch. The result is an increased number of walks. The bigger picture is the long-term development for a major league club. They may be able to get hitters out with a sharp, moving fastball, but are trying to work on keeping hitters off-stride.

Pitching rotations: The #3, #4, and #5 pitchers in the lower minors are truly longshots to make the majors. They often possess only two pitches and can barely go five innings. The most obvious weakness is the inability to disguise the off-speed pitches with their delivery and arm speed. Hitters can see inflated statistics in these leagues.

Minor League Level versus Age

When evaluating minor leaguers, look at the age of the prospect in relation to the median age of the league he is in:

Low level A	Between 19-20
Upper level A	Around 20
Double-A	21
Triple-A	22

These are the ideal ages for prospects at the particular level. If a prospect is younger than most and he holds his own against older and more experienced players, elevate his status. If a prospect is older than the median, reduce his status. These adjustments are taken into account in the Major League Equivalents section.

Call-up Success Rates I

The probability that a minor leaguer will immediately succeed in the Majors can vary depending upon the level of Triple-A experience that player has amassed at the time of call-up. Research conclusions:

	BATTERS		PITCHERS	
	≤ 1 Yr	Full	≤1 Yr	Full
Performed well	57%	56%	16%	56%
Performed poorly	21%	38%	77%	33%
2nd half drop-off	21%	7%	6%	10%

The odds of a batter achieving immediate major league success, no matter what his minor league experience, remains slightly more than 50-50. However, over 80% of all minor league pitchers promoted with less than a full year at Triple-A will struggle in their first year in the majors. Those pitchers who do have a full year in Triple-A increase their success rate to a level equal to that of batters.

Call-up Success Rates II

Historical BPIs have some value in determining which minor league pitching call-ups fare well. The percentage of hurlers that were good investments in the year that they were called up varied by the level of their historical BPIs *prior* to that year.

Pitchers who had:	Fared well	Fared poorly
Good indicators	79%	21%
Marginal or poor indicators	18%	82%

The minor league data used to classify these pitchers were MLE levels from the previous two years, not the season in which they were called up. What is the significance of this? Typically, it is solid current year performance that merits the call-up in the first place, but those numbers had little bearing on who fared well. Early season performance in the minors is not a good indicator of short-term major league success, for two reasons:

1. The performance data set is too small, typically just a few month's worth of statistics. For pitchers, this is not nearly enough data to draw any reasonable conclusions.

2. For those pitchers putting up those stats at a new minor league level, there has not been enough time for the scouting reports to make their rounds, so we do not know if they have truly mastered that level yet.

Minor League BPV as a Leading Indicator *(Al Melchior)*

There is a link between minor league skill and how a pitching prospect will fare in his first 5 starts upon call-up.

PQS Avg	MLE BPV < 50	50-99	100+
0.0-1.9	60%	28%	19%
2.0-2.9	32%	40%	29%
3.0-5.0	8%	33%	52%
TOTAL	100%	100%	100%

Pitchers who demonstrate sub-par skills in the minors, as indicated by a sub-50 BPV, tend to fare poorly in their first big league starts. Three-fifths of these pitchers register a PQS average below 2.0, while only 8% average over 3.0.

At the other end of the spectrum, fewer than one out of five minor leaguers with a 100+ MLE BPV go on to post a sub-2.0 PQS average in their initial major league starts, but more than half average 3.0 or better.

Projecting Second Year Success

One of the most accurate indicators of a rookie's future potential is his performance during the second half of his debut season in the majors. First year players often get off to particularly fast or slow starts. During their second tour of the league is when we get to see whether the slow starters have adjusted to the level of play or whether the rest of the league has figured out the fast starters. That second half "adjustment" performance level is the baseline for projecting the sophomore campaign and beyond.

Late Season Performance of Rookie SP *(Ray Murphy)*

Given that a rookie's second tour of the league provides insight as to future success, do rookie pitchers typically run out of gas? To find out, we studied 2002-2005 and identified 56 rookie SP who threw at least 75 IP in their rookie season. We assembled their PQS logs and sliced them a few different ways.

The performance of the entire set of pitchers:

All rookies	#	#GS/P	DOM%	DIS%	qERA
before 7/31	56	13.3	42%	21%	4.56
after 7/31	56	9.3	37%	29%	4.82

Rookie pitchers on the whole do tend to fade later in the season. However, a quarter-run degradation in qERA is hardly cause for panic. What if we start shrinking our study class? The qERA variance increased to 4.44-5.08 for the busiest rookies, those who made at least 16 starts before July 31. The variance also was larger (3.97-4.56) for the best rookies, those who had a PQS-3 average prior to July 31. The pitchers who intersected these two sub-groups:

PQS>3+GS>15	#	#GS/P	DOM%	DIS%	qERA
before 7/31	8	19.1	51%	12%	4.23
after 7/31	8	9.6	34%	30%	5.08

While the sample size here is small, the degree of flameout by these guys is significant: the group's qERA rose by over three quarters of a run after July.

Adjusting to the Competition

All players must "adjust to the competition" at every level of professional play. When a player gets promoted to, say, Triple-A, he is, in fact, a "rookie" during his first year at that level. An analysis of his second half Triple-A performance gives us a better indication of his true ability there. And... premature major league call-ups often negate the ability for us to evaluate a player's true potential.

E.g. A hotshot Double-A player opens the new season in Triple-A. After putting up solid numbers for a month, he gets a call to the bigs, and struggles. We wonder why. The fact is, at the point of call-up, we do not have enough evidence that the player has mastered the Triple-A level. We don't know whether the rest of the league would have caught up to him during his second tour of the league. But now he's labeled as an underperformer in the bigs when in fact he has never truly proven his skills at the lower levels.

Bull Durham Prospects

There is some potential talent in older players — age 26, 27 or higher — who, for many reasons (untimely injury, circumstance, bad luck, etc.), don't reach the majors until they have already been downgraded from prospect to suspect. Equating potential with age is an economic reality for Major League clubs, but not necessarily a skills reality.

Skills growth and decline is universal, whether it occurs at the major league level or in the minors. So a high skills journeyman in Triple-A is just as likely to peak at age 27 as a major leaguer of the same age. The question becomes one of opportunity — will the parent club see fit to reap the benefits of that peak performance?

Prospecting these players for your fantasy team is, admittedly, a high risk endeavor, though there are some criteria you can use. Look for a player who is/has:

- Optimally, age 27-28 for overall peak skills, age 30-31 for power skills, or age 28-31 for pitchers.
- At least two seasons of experience at Triple-A. Career Double-A players are generally not good picks.
- Solid base skills levels.
- Shallow organizational depth at their position.
- Notable winter league or spring training performance.

Players who meet these conditions are not typically draftable players, but worthwhile reserve or FAAB picks. *(A more detailed discussion is in the Prospects section.)*

Team Toolbox

Johnson Effect *(Bryan Johnson)*: Teams whose actual won/loss record exceeds or falls short of their statistically projected record in one season will tend to revert to the level of their projection in the following season.

Law of Competitive Balance *(Bill James)*: The level at which a team (or player) will address its problems is inversely related to its current level of success. Low performers will tend to make changes to improve; high performers will not. This law explains the existence of the Plexiglass and Whirlpool Principles.

Plexiglass Principle *(Bill James)*: If a player or team improves markedly in one season, it will likely decline in the next. The opposite is true but not as often (because a poor performer gets fewer opportunities to rebound).

Whirlpool Principle *(Bill James)*: All team and player performances are forcefully drawn to the center. For teams, that center is a .500 record. For players, it represents their career average level of performance.

Japanese Baseball Toolbox
by Tom Mulhall

Background on Japanese Baseball

Japanese professional baseball presently has 12 teams, divided equally between the Central and Pacific Leagues. The Central League is generally considered the more prestigious and traditional league, and contains the country's most popular team, the Yomiuri Giants. The Pacific League has faster-paced games and uses the DH.

Baseball in Japan is currently experiencing turbulent times. Some teams are struggling financially since there is no revenue sharing system and the league has no integrated broadcast or merchandising rights. An unhealthy competition exists between the owners.

Once a point of pride, there is a growing backlash against the talent drain of players to America. Not only are they losing top players to MLB, American managers and players are infiltrating their league in growing numbers. Four of the 12 managers in the 2007 season were American: Marty Brown, Terry Collins, Trey Hillman (now with Kansas City) and Bobby Valentine. Originally limited to two foreign players, and later three, teams are now allowed to carry four foreign players. These players are referred to as *gaijin* — meaning "outside person" – a term which usually carries a derogatory connotation.

In addition to these problems, a payola scandal broke in late 2006. Several professional teams reportedly paid college and high school teams large sums of money to steer top players their way. This violated the Japan Student Baseball Association's charter, which strictly forbids the giving and receiving of cash gifts.

These types of inducements appear to be endemic in Japanese baseball, where professional managers will openly give envelopes of money to players after good performances. The payments are commonly referred to as "fight money."

Comparing ML Baseball and Japanese *Besuboru*

The Japanese major leagues are generally considered to be equivalent to very good Triple-A ball and the pitching may be even better. However, statistics are difficult to convert to a major league equivalent due to a variety of differences in the way the game is played in Japan.

1. While strong on fundamentals, Japanese baseball's guiding philosophy is risk avoidance. Mistakes are not tolerated. Since fewer risks are taken, runners rarely take extra bases, batters focus on making contact rather than driving the ball, and managers play for one run at a time rather than the big inning. As a result, offenses score fewer runs than they should given the number of hits. Pitching stats tend to look better than the talent behind them.

2. Stadiums in Japan usually have shorter fences. Normally this would mean more HRs, but given #1 above, it is the American players who make up the majority of Japan's power elite. This skews offensive statistics. Power hitters do not make an equivalent transition to the MLB. In his last four years in Japan, Hideki Matsui hit 170 HR.

In his first four years with the Yankees, he hit just 78 HR despite having 82 more at-bats.

3. There are more artificial turf fields, which increases the number of ground ball singles. Only a few stadiums have infield grass and some still use dirt infields.

4. The quality of umpiring is questionable; there are no sanctioned umpiring schools in Japan. Fewer errors are called, reflecting the cultural philosophy of low tolerance for mistakes and the desire to avoid publicly embarrassing a player. Moreover, umpires are routinely intimidated. (In one game, unable to decide if a ball was a HR or a ground-rule double, and after being struck by one of the managers, the umpire ruled it a "ground-rule triple." He was again assaulted by the manager after the game.)

5. Teams have smaller pitching staffs, sometimes no more than about seven deep. Three-man pitching rotations are not uncommon and the best starters often work out of the pen between starts. Despite superior conditioning, Japanese pitchers tend to burn out early due to overuse. (After winning 38 games in 1959, Tadashi Sugiura pitched *all four games* of their World Series – his career was over before he reached 30.)

6. Japanese leagues use a slightly smaller baseball, making it easier for pitchers to grip and control.

7. Tie games are allowed. If the score remains even after 12 innings, the game goes into the books as a tie. On two recent occasions, the Pacific League pennant winner did not have the most wins but had a higher winning percentage due to tie games.

The Posting System

In 1995, Hideo Nomo, who was ineligible for free agency, announced his retirement. He subsequently signed with the Los Angeles Dodgers. As a result, in 1998 a new agreement between the leagues went into effect known as the posting system, established to compensate Japanese teams facing the loss of players to the U.S. It is impossible to predict which players may come to the Majors without understanding the posting system and each team's attitude about the system.

Japanese players cannot become free agents until they have completed nine full seasons with the parent club. In most cases, that amounts to 10 seasons, or more, since few rookies will begin the new year with their major league team. Moreover, time spent on the disabled list does *not* count towards free agency, with some exceptions during the final year of a contract. If a player wishes to leave Japan early for the Majors, he must have permission from his club, which can then auction the right to negotiate with that player to the highest bidding MLB team. This usually occurs in the penultimate year of their contract. If the player does not sign with the MLB team winning bidding rights, the Japanese team must return the posting money.

Some Japanese teams are more likely to post a player than other teams, mostly due to economic considerations. Other organizations are on stronger financial ground and those teams have a strong policy against posting players. The Fukuoka Softbank Hawks lost both Kenji Johjima and Tadahito Iguchi to free agency without compensation rather than post them early. The Yomiuri Giants also oppose posting players.

Japan is a less litigious society than the U.S. and the concept of *wa* is still very important. Wa essentially means harmony and balance, and is applied to society in general and to your social grouping in particular. It emphasizes loyalty to the group and frowns on individualism. According to one Japanese proverb, "the nail that sticks up gets hammered down." To go against his own team and disturb group unity by filing a lawsuit would take a very progressive player.

The feeling of loyalty and duty towards the team can cause some Japanese players to delay or forgo their dream of playing in the Majors. For example, Ichiro Suzuki delayed his departure for a year at the request of his manager. Nevertheless, the concept of wa is less binding than in the past and we may expect increasing defections.

Sooner or later, the posting system will be overturned or modified. Until then, not only would a player face societal pressures, he would not have the backing of a strong players union. The first player strike in the history of Japanese baseball took place in 2004. It lasted just one weekend, at which point the players and their union felt compelled to apologize for the stoppage and then provide free autograph sessions and baseball clinics for the fans.

This may be slowly changing. In 2007, the players union voted unanimously to seek greater rights with regard to free agency, hinting at a lawsuit. Unfortunately for the players, most teams exist in large part as advertising for their corporate owners and are not maintained for profit. Since few of the teams are expected to make money, it is difficult to pressure them economically through a strike. A strike may be embarrassing for the owners, but not financially damaging.

Japanese Players as Fantasy Reserve/Farm Selections

Many fantasy leagues have large reserve or farm teams with rules allowing them to draft foreign players before they sign with a MLB team. Previously, you could use your final reserve selection to draft a Hideki Matsui the year before he joined the ML. Those days are coming to an end. With increased coverage by fantasy experts, the internet, and exposure from the World Baseball Classic, anyone willing to do a minimum of research can compile an adequate list of good players.

However, the key is not to identify the *best* Japanese players – the key is to identify impact players who have the desire and opportunity to sign with a MLB team. Players who might make the move this coming season and beyond are covered in the Prospects section.

It is easy to overestimate the value of drafting these players. Since 1995, only 31 Japanese players have made a big league roster, and 14 were middle relievers. But for owners who are allowed to carry a large reserve or farm team at reduced salaries, these players could be a real windfall, especially if your competitors do not do their homework.

A list of Japanese League players who could jump to the Majors appears in the Prospects section.

Other Diamonds
The Fanalytic Fundamentals
1. This is not a game of accuracy or precision. It is a game of human beings and tendencies.
2. This is not a game of projections. It is a game of market value versus real value.
3. Draft skills, not stats.
4. A player's ability to post acceptable stats despite lousy BPIs will eventually run out.
5. Once you display a skill, you own it.
6. Virtually every player is vulnerable to a month of aberrant performance. Or a year.
7. Exercise excruciating patience.

Aging Axioms
1. Age is the only variable for which we can project a rising trend with 100% accuracy. (Or, age never regresses.)
2. The aging process slows down for those players who maintain a firm grasp on the strike zone. Plate patience and pitching command can help preserve whatever waning skill they have left.
3. Negatives tend to snowball as you age.

Age 26 Paradox: 26 is when a player begins to reach his peak skill, no matter what his address is. If circumstances have him celebrating that birthday in the majors, he is a breakout candidate. If circumstances have him celebrating that birthday in the minors, he is washed up.

A-Rod 10-Step Path to Stardom: Not all well-hyped prospects hit the ground running. More often they follow an alternative path...
1. Prospect puts up phenomenal minor league numbers.
2. The media machine gets oiled up.
3. Prospect gets called up, but struggles, Year 1.
4. Prospect gets demoted.
5. Prospect tears it up in Triple-A, Year 2.
6. Prospect gets called up, but struggles, Year 2.
7. Prospect gets demoted.
8. The media turns their backs and fantasy leaguers reduce their expectations.
9. Prospect tears it up in Triple-A, Year 3. The public shrugs its collective shoulders.
10. Prospect is promoted in Year 3 and explodes. Some lucky fantasy leaguer lands a franchise player for under $5.

Some players that are currently stuck at one of the interim steps, and may or may not ever reach Step 10, include Edwin Jackson, Andy Marte, Dan Johnson and Chris Iannetta.

Ashley-Perry Statistical Axioms:
1. Numbers are tools, not rules.
2. Numbers are symbols for things; the number and the thing are not the same.
3. Skill in manipulating numbers is a talent, not evidence of divine guidance.
4. Like other occult techniques of divination, the statistical method has a private jargon deliberately contrived to obscure its methods from non-practitioners.
5. The product of an arithmetical computation is the answer to an equation; it is not the solution to a problem.
6. Arithmetical proofs of theorems that do not have arithmetical bases prove nothing.

Steve Avery List: Players who hang onto major league rosters for six years searching for a skill level they only had for three.

Bylaws of Badness

1. Some players are better than an open roster spot, but not by much.

2. Some players have bad years because they are unlucky. Others have *many* bad years because they are bad... and lucky.

Rickey Bones List: Pitchers with BPIs so incredibly horrible that you have to wonder how they can possibly draw a major league paycheck year after year.

George Brett Path to Retirement: Get out while you're still putting up good numbers and the public perception of you is favorable. *(See Steve Carlton Path to Retirement.)*

Steve Carlton Path to Retirement: Hang around the major leagues long enough for your numbers to become so wretched that people begin to forget your past successes. *(See George Brett Path to Retirement.)*

Among the many players who have taken this path include Roberto Alomar, Kevin Brown, Eric Davis, Doc Gooden, Hideo Nomo, Tim Raines and of course, Steve Carlton. Current players who look to be on the same course include Byung Hyun Kim, David Wells, perhaps Mike Mussina and most certainly Jose Mesa (who so epitomizes this list that we might be forced to rename it in his honor).

Chaconian: Having the ability to post many saves despite sub-Mendoza BPIs and an ERA in the stratosphere. In 2007, Joe Borowski was darned near Chaconian.

Christie Brinkley Law of Statistical Analysis: Never get married to the model.

Chicken and Egg Problem: Did irregular playing time take its toll on the player's performance or did poor performance force a reduction in his playing time?

Chronology of the Classic Free-Swinger with Pop

1. Gets off to a good start.

2. Thinks he's in a groove.

3. Gets lax, careless.

4. Pitchers begin to catch on.

5. Fades down the stretch.

Crickets: The sound heard when someone's opening draft bid on a player is also the only bid.

Developmental Dogmata

1. Defense is what gets a minor league prospect to the majors; offense is what keeps him there. *(Deric McKamey)*

2. The reason why rapidly promoted minor leaguers often fail is that they are never given the opportunity to master the skill of "adjusting to the competition."

3. Rookies who are promoted in-season often perform better than those that make the club out of spring training. Inferior March competition can inflate the latter group's perceived talent level.

4. Young players rarely lose their inherent skills. Pitchers may uncover weaknesses and the players may have difficulty adjusting. These are bumps along the growth curve, but they do not reflect a loss off skill.

5. Late bloomers have smaller windows of opportunity and much less chance for forgiveness.

6. The greatest risk in this game is to pay for performance that a player has never achieved.

7. Some outwardly talented prospects simply have a ceiling that's spelled AAA.

Bull Durham List: Older minor leaguers who sneak onto major league rosters and shine for brief periods, showing what a mistake it is to pigeon-hole talented players just because they are not 24 and beautiful.

Edwhitsonitis: A dreaded malady marked by the sudden and unexplained loss of pitching ability upon a trade to the New York Yankees.

Scott Elarton List: Players you drop out on when the bidding reaches $1.

Employment Standards

1. If you are right-brain dominant, own a catcher's mitt and are under 40, you will always be gainfully employed.

2. Some teams believe that it is better to gainfully employ a pitcher with *any* experience because it has to be better than the devil they don't know.

3. It's not so good to go pffft in a contract year.

FAAB Forewarnings

1. Spend early and often.

2. Emptying your budget for one prime league-crosser is a tactic that should be reserved for the desperate.

3. If you chase two rabbits, you will lose them both.

Fantasy Economics 101: The market value for a player is generally based on the aura of past performance, not the promise of future potential. Your greatest advantage is to leverage the variance between market value and real value.

Fantasy Economics 102: The variance between market value and real value is far more important than the absolute accuracy of any individual player projection.

Brad Fullmer List: Players whose leading indicators indicate upside potential, year after year, but consistently fail to reach that potential. Current members of that list include Michael Barrett, David Bush and Aubrey Huff.

The Gravity Principles

1. It is easier to be crappy than it is to be good.

2. All performance starts at zero, ends at zero and can drop to zero at any time.

3. The odds of a good performer slumping are far greater than the odds of a poor performer surging.

4. Once a player is in a slump, it takes several 3 for 5 days to get out of it. Once he is on a streak, it takes a single 0 for 4 day to begin the downward spiral.

Corollary: Once a player is in a slump, not only does it take several 3 for 5 days to get out of it, but he also has to get his name back on the lineup card.

5. Eventually all performance comes down to earth. It may take a week, or a month, or may not happen until he's 45, but eventually it's going to happen.

Health Homilies

1. Staying healthy is a skill.

2. A $40 player can get hurt just as easily as a $5 player but is eight times tougher to replace.

3. Chronically injured players never suddenly get healthy.

4. There are two kinds of pitchers: those that are hurt and those that are not hurt... yet.

5. Players with back problems are always worth $10 less.

6. "Opting out of surgery" usually means it's coming anyway, just later.

Bill James 2007

1. "One thing that changed when I started working for the Red Sox is that I'd talk to Theo and John Henry, but couldn't run out and talk to other people as I always had. Science is conversation. Knowledge is community property. When you cut yourself off from that, you lose something. If you respect (confidentiality) too much, it's like your thumbs have been cut off. There is a real limit to how much good work you can do in a closet."

2. "Long-term decision-making is antithetical to human nature. If you go out on a date with a girl and she has bad breath, you don't look at it as a small sample size. You move along. If you go to a restaurant and your food is bad, you don't go back four or five times to get more data. If a player comes up from the minors and struggles, people want to move on. That's just natural. I always see it as being my role to argue for the longer-term view, maybe suggest some mouthwash."

Jason Jennings Rationalization: Occasional nightmares (2/3 inning, 11 ER) are just a part of the game.

Kamin's Sixth Law (fantasy baseball variation): When attempting to forecast player performance, never be misled by what a player says; instead watch what he does.

The Knuckleballers Rule: Knuckleballers don't follow any of the rules.

Monocarp: A player whose career consists of only one productive season.

Lance Painter Lesson: Six months of solid performance can be screwed up by one bad outing. (In 2000, Painter finished with an ERA of 4.76. However, prior to his final appearance of the year — in which he pitched 1 inning and gave up 8 earned runs — his ERA was 3.70.)

The Pitching Postulates

1. Never sign a soft-tosser to a long-term contract.
2. Right-brain dominance has a very long shelf life.
3. A fly ball pitcher who gives up a lot of HRs is expected. A ground ball pitcher who gives up a lot of HRs is making mistakes.
4. Never draft a contact fly ball pitcher who plays in a hitter's park.
5. Only bad teams ever have a need for an inning-eater.
6. Never chase wins.

Quack!: An exclamation in response to the educated speculation that a player has used performance enhancing drugs. While it is rare to have absolute proof, there is often enough information to suggest that, "if it looks like a duck and quacks like a duck, then odds are it's a duck."

Reclamation Conundrum: The problem with stockpiling bench players in the hope that one pans out is that you end up evaluating performance using data sets that are far too small to be reliable.

Rule 5 Reminder: Don't ignore the Rule 5 draft lest you ignore the 1% possibility of a Johan Santana.

The Five Saves Certainties:

1. On every team, there *will* be save opportunities and *someone* will get them. In fact, at a bare minimum, there will be at least 30 saves to go around, and not unlikely that there could be over 45.
2. *Any* pitcher could end up being the chief beneficiary. Bullpen management is a fickle endeavor.

3. Relief pitchers are often the ones that require the most time at the start of the season to find a groove. The weather is cold, the schedule is sparse and their usage is erratic.
4. Despite the talk about "bullpens by committee," managers prefer a go-to guy. It makes their job easier.
5. As many as 50% of the available saves in any given year will come from pitchers who are in the free agent pool at the end of Draft Day.

Small Sample Certitude: If players' careers were judged based what they did in a single game performance, then Tuffy Rhodes and Mark Whiten would be in the Hall of Fame.

Esix Snead List: Players with excellent speed and sub-.300 on base averages who get a lot of practice running down the line to first base, and then back to the dugout. Also used as an adjective, as in "Esix-Sneadian."

Standings Vantage Points

First Place: It's lonely at the top, but it's comforting to look down upon everyone else.

Sixth Place: The toughest position to be in is mid-pack at dump time.

Last Place in April: The sooner you fall behind, the more time you will have to catch up.

Last Place, Yet Again: If you can't learn to do something well, learn to enjoy doing it badly.

Tenets of Optimal Timing

1. If a second half fader had put up his second half stats in the first half and his first half stats in the second half, then he probably wouldn't even have had a second half.
2. Fast starters can often buy six months of playing time out of one month of productivity.
3. Poor 2nd halves don't get recognized until it's too late.
4. "Baseball is like this. Have one good year and you can fool them for five more, because for five more years they expect you to have another good one." — Frankie Frisch

The Three True Outcomes

1. Strikeouts
2. Walks
3. Homeruns

The Three True Handicaps

1. Has power but can't make contact.
2. Has speed but can't hit safely.
3. Has potential but is too old.

Mike Timlin List: Players who you are unable to resist drafting even though they have burned you multiple times in the past.

Walbeckian: Possessing below replacement level stats, as in "Guzman's season was downright Walbeckian." *Alternate usage:* "Guzman's stats were so bad that I might as well have had Walbeck in there."

Mark Wohlers Lament: When a closer posts a 65% strand rate, he has nobody to blame but himself.

Seasonal Assessment Standard: If you still have reason to be reading the boxscores during the last weekend of the season, then your year has to be considered a success.

The Three Cardinal Rules for Winners: If you cherish this hobby, you will live by them or die by them...

1. Revel in your success; fame is fleeting.
2. Exercise excruciating humility.
3. 100% of winnings must be spent on significant others.

Research Abstracts

BATTING

Home run to flyball ratios

by Joshua Randall

Prior research has shown that for pitchers, the expected rate of home runs can be stated as 1/10 of fly balls, or HR/F = 10%. Do batters also have predictable HR/flyball rates? We looked at 231 batters who had 900+ AB from 2004-2006. The distribution of three-year HR/F averages formed a bell curve with a peak around 11%-12%, median and mean at 11%, and outliers ranging from 1% to 37%.

Ranges and Rebounds

To offset the effect that a single fluky year may have had on our three-year results, we examined HR/F using rolling three-year averages. For batters active since 2001, 76% had HR/F ranges within four percentage points, and more than half of those were within two points. A minority of players show large ranges, but most batters establish relatively narrow HR/F ranges over rolling three-year periods.

Once batters establish their HR/F ranges, do they *stay* in those ranges in subsequent seasons? We looked at the "fourth years" following the three-year averages.

% Pt Diff	# in 2004 vs. 01-03	# in 2005 vs. 02-04	# in 2006 vs. 03-05	Total
+7 +	13	14	15	42 (5%)
+6	11	3	5	19 (2%)
+5	15	8	8	31 (4%)
+4	13	11	12	36 (5%)
+3	16	14	12	42 (5%)
+2	16	16	17	49 (6%)
+1	32	11	23	66 (9%)
0	35	29	14	78 (10%)
-1	24	34	26	84 (11%)
-2	31	21	23	75 (10%)
-3	12	22	28	62 (8%)
-4	9	20	15	44 (6%)
-5	7	14	15	36 (5%)
-6	9	16	11	36 (5%)
-7 -	13	23	32	68 (9%)

Batters' HR/F was within two percentage points of their three-year average 46% of the time, within three points 59% of the time, and within four points 70% of the time. Combined with what we learned earlier, this shows that *batters establish reliable 3-year HR/F levels, and these levels strongly predict the HR/F in the subsequent year.*

Regression to the Mean

What happens to outliers whose "fourth year" HR/F varies by unusual margins from their 3-year levels? We compared players' 2004 HR/F with their 2001-2003 three-year averages and examined how they did the following year (2005). As expected, the "correction" was stronger as the variance from the norm grew.

2005 Movement after 2004 Variance

2004 Diff	N	min	max	avg	median
+7 + pts	13	-21	+ 6	-8.0	-6.4 pts
+6	11	-12	+ 8	-4.3	-3.9
+5	15	-16	+ 3	-4.8	-4.7
+4	13	-11	+ 2	-4.0	-4.4
+3	16	-20	+10	-5.5	-5.3
+2	16	-14	+ 7	-3.3	-2.4
+1	32	- 7	+ 7	-1.0	-1.3

2004 Diff	N	min	max	avg	median
0	35	-10	+ 7	-0.9	-1.1
-1	24	- 7	+ 8	-0.3	-1.3
-2	31	- 7	+13	+0.6	+0.5
-3	12	- 7	+ 6	-1.5	-1.4
-4	9	- 5	+17	-3.9	+1.6
-5	7	- 2	+ 3	+0.6	+0.4
-6	9	- 5	+ 7	+1.8	+0.0
-7 - pts	13	-13	+19	+4.5	+4.4 pts

Batters do move towards their three-year HR/F averages, particularly those whose "fourth year" HR/F was higher than their three-year levels. In other words, *over-performers decline more than underperformers improve.*

Players close to their preceding three-year level also experienced small declines. By including only batters active over a long period, we necessarily chose an aging sample with the attendant inevitable decline in ability.

Testing Predictive Value

Can we use a batter's HR/F variance to predict the subsequent year's level? To test this, we looked at batters with at least 200 AB each season from 2001-2005 whose 2005 HR/F was more than six percentage points different than their 2002-2004 three-year HR/Fs. We expected to see a regression (i.e., the "bounce" in 2006 offsetting the "+/-" of 2005 vs. 02-04) which is generally what happened.

Player	01-03	02-04	05	+/-	06	bounce
Pena,C	14%	15%	27%	+12%	11%	-16%
Wilson,P	18%	18%	29%	+11%	12%	-17%
Cruz Jr.,J	14%	11%	21%	+10%	6%	-15%
Mientkiewicz	7%	6%	13%	+ 7%	4%	- 9%
Lopez,F	10%	10%	17%	+ 7%	10%	- 7%
Roberts,B	3%	3%	10%	+ 7%	6%	- 4%
Pierzynski,AJ	7%	7%	14%	+ 7%	11%	- 3%
Beltran,C	17%	17%	8%	- 9%	22%	+14%
Wilkerson,B	13%	15%	6%	- 9%	15%	+ 9%
Ordonez,M	17%	17%	8%	- 9%	13%	+ 5%
Lowell,M	11%	12%	4%	- 8%	9%	+ 5%
Podsednik,S	6%	7%	0%	- 7%	3%	+ 3%
Bellhorn,M	16%	16%	9%	- 7%	10%	+ 1%
Finley,S	12%	15%	8%	- 7%	4%	- 4%
Clayton,R	10%	9%	2%	- 7%	0%	- 2%
Green,S	23%	21%	14%	- 7%	12%	- 2%

All seven of the over-performers regressed; only two were able to maintain any of their gains. Six of the nine underperformers rebounded, with only one exceeding his previous HR/F levels. These results fit expectations: gains in HR/F followed by sharp declines, losses in HR/F followed by more modest recoveries or continued losses.

Conclusions

HR/F should not be used in isolation, particularly as it is a ratio that by itself tells us nothing about a player's HR or fly ball proclivity. However, we can state with confidence:

Each batter establishes an individual HR/F that stabilizes over rolling three-year periods; those levels strongly predict the HR/F in the subsequent year.

A batter who varies significantly from his HR/F is likely to regress toward his individual HR/F mean, with over-performance decline more likely and more severe than under-performance recovery.

Wasted talent

What do Julio Lugo and Chris B. Young have in common?

Not a lot, actually. One is 31, the other is 24. They each play different positions. One is a rookie. One has power. What make these players similar is that they are the only two players in Major League Baseball this year with at least 20 SBs and an on base average under .300.

I refer to this phenomenon as having "wasted talent." Defined in the glossary as "a player with a high level skill that is negated by a deficiency in another skill," the duo above possesses all that great speed but can't get on base consistently. In the "Other Diamonds" section of the Forecaster's Toolbox, I used to define the "Doug Glanville List" as players with excellent speed and sub-.300 on base averages who get a lot of practice running down the line to first base, and then back to the dugout.

The fact that this duo has managed 60 SBs between them is a tribute to their respective "green lights." Young has attempted a stolen base in 29% of his available opportunities; for Lugo, 28%. The MLB average in 2007 was under 9%. If this duo had a collective on base average of even .325 — which is still not great — and maintained their SBO, their current stolen base output might be as much as 80, a full 33% higher.

However, if they had a more sedate 15% SBO, that SB output of 60 would drop to 30. That's the real danger here. Those bags are tied so tightly to the green light that any change in managerial strategy could completely derail the value of these players. A higher OBA mitigates that downside.

Plate patience is not an innate skill like speed; it can be taught. That alone should tell us that there is hope for these players with "wasted talent." But how often does this really happen?

Over the past 10 years, the following Major League players had a season where they posted at least 20 SBs but with an on base average under .300:

PLAYER	TM	YEAR	AB	SB	OBA	SBO
Cameron,Mike	CHW	1999	396	27	277	42%
Encarnacion,Juan	DET	1999	509	33	275	51%
Everett,Adam	HOU	2005	549	21	282	23%
Glanville,Doug	PHI	2001	634	28	283	24%
Gonzalez,Alex S.	TOR	1998	568	21	275	22%
Goodwin,Tom	LA	2001	286	22	288	42%
Grissom,Marquis	MIL	2000	595	20	290	20%
Grudzielanek,Mark	MON	1997	649	25	298	24%
Guzman,Cristian	MIN	2000	631	28	298	26%
Hairston Jr.,Jerry	BAL	2001	532	29	292	31%
Hunter,Brian L.	DET	1998	595	42	296	36%
Hunter,Brian L.	SEA	1999	539	44	281	37%
Kennedy,Adam	ANA	2000	598	22	299	22%
Martin,Al	PIT	1998	440	20	290	21%
Reese,Pokey	CIN	1997	397	25	284	27%
Reese,Pokey	CIN	2001	428	25	281	29%
Williams,Gerald	MIL	1997	566	23	277	27%

Only 15 players (and 17 instances) since 1997, and only one in the past five years, which makes this season's duo all that more interesting. More important is that there are very few players on this list who've had careers worth

investing in. We might conclude that Mike Cameron successfully developed into a solid on base player. For Marquis Grissom, 2000 (and also 2001) was the point at which his otherwise fine career started heading south. Al Martin's 1998 campaign was a blip on the radar of a solid career. All the others constitute a wasteland of mediocrity, with SB success wholly driven by inflated SBO rates.

At the minor league level, the situation is equally stark. There have been plenty of low-OBA speedsters over the past 10 years, but few have seen much more than a cup of coffee in the bigs:

YEAR	Avg Age	No.	No. with even 100 MLB At Bats	No. with minimum one full MLB season
1997	26	15	11	2
1998	26	3	2	0
1999	26	5	3	0
2000	24	13	1	1
2001	25	16	4	3
2002	25	18	3	1
2003	25	8	3	1
2004	25	5	2	0
2005	26	22	4	0
2006	27	6	0	0
TOT	25	111	33 (30%)	8 (7%)

The lucky eight who've managed at least one full season of play in the bigs are Marlon Anderson, Miguel Cairo, Cesar Izturis, Willie Bloomquist, Adam Everett, Chone Figgins, Ryan Freel and Omar Infante. These players show a wide range of fantasy value. Figgins was a first-rounder in most leagues in 2006, but he, and perhaps Freel, are the lone stars in this group. However, neither have been able to maintain their value. The other six players are all end-game roster filler.

The 33 players who've managed at least 100 major league ABs include lots of familiar names. The large 1997 class had failed fantasy commodities like Kim Bartee, Lou Frazier, Charles Gipson and Dante Powell. Other familiar failures include Reggie Taylor, Gene Kingsale, Elvis Pena and Kerry Robinson.

Of the 111 players, 17 appear more than once. Most of these are names that never came close to the majors, such as Dwaine Bacon, Pat Hallmark, Belvani Martinez and Demond Smith. A few that had a fleeting glimpse of the bigs include Justin Baughman, Trent Durrington and Tim Raines, Jr.

But there is one player who exemplifies this phenomenon more than any other...

ESIX SNEAD

YEAR	AB	SB	OBA	SBO
1999	249	35	281	73%
2001	520	64	307	64%
2003	472	61	287	84%

You will be hard pressed to find SBOs that high anywhere else (except maybe Herb Washington in 1974-75). It is in honor of this accomplishment that I have renamed the Toolbox entry as the "Esix Snead List."

All of this only goes to confirm what we already know: Stay away from these types of players.

29

Batter breakout profile

by Brandon Kruse

Breakouts players — particularly those you draft late, buy cheap, or just grab out of the free agent pool — are fantasy baseball's jewels. Unfortunately, owning them is often a matter of good luck or good timing rather than managerial skill. Still, a historical view of past breakouts might help us better identify those players in the future.

For the purposes of this study, we classified a breakout season as one where a player posts a Rotisserie value of $20 or higher. And to isolate "unexpected" breakouts, we looked for players who had never posted a Rotisserie value higher than $10 at the major league level prior to their $20 season. We also required at least one season of minimum Double-A skill stats prior to the breakout season (which eliminated players like Rafael Furcal and Albert Pujols who jumped from A-ball to the majors). We looked at seven season of data, from 2000-2006, and found 38 qualifying players; somewhat borderline for sample size, so any findings here should be kept in proper perspective.

It was an interesting group. With the exception of a couple of players, this was not about simply gaining more playing time; the breakouts came from improved performance and increased skill. We tracked some of the changes in skill, in the season before their breakout and then during their breakout season, by getting the average of their combined skill stats in six core offensive skill categories:

	bb%	ct%	h%	Eye	PX	SX
Pre-Breakout*	7	84	30	0.53	97	85
Breakout	8	82	33	0.55	116	103

*Contains full or partial-season MLEs from 34 of the 38 players

As the pre-breakout skills show, this was not a particularly distinguished group. Most didn't have the skill or the job security to make anyone think they would suddenly become $20 players, and as we established earlier, they definitely didn't have the track record.

Let's look at what percentage of the 38 players saw increases, decreases or no change in those six categories:

	bb%	ct%	h%	Eye	PX	SX
Increased	53%	32%	76%	55%	74%	82%
No Change	24%	5%	3%	0%	3%	3%
Decreased	24%	63%	21%	45%	24%	16%

In this table and the one above, the most significant changes were improvements in hit rate, PX and SX; but that's not all that surprising, as those metrics are very closely tied to production. In fact, 95% of the players saw an increase in one of those three categories, 82% saw an increase in two categories, and 55% saw an increase in all three categories.

The most interesting change was that 24 of the 38 hitters, or 63%, saw a *decrease* in their contact rate. That goes against what we'd expect, as we tend to view skill growth as a key part of improved performance. Did the decrease in contact reflect a more aggressive approach at the plate, one that led to increased power? Not necessarily.

Among the 24 hitters who saw a drop in their contact rate, 17 (71%) saw their PX go up. Among the steady/rising contact hitters, 11 of 14 (78%) saw their PX go up. The falling contact hitters averaged a PX gain of 18.9 points; the steady/rising contact hitters averaged a PX gain of 20.2 points. One last slice of the data: among the 28 hitters who saw their PX go up, 17 (61%) saw their contact rate go down.

Some other general observations from the sample pool:

- The average age of these players during their breakout season was 24.6 years. 90% of them were 27 or younger.
- Elite-level plate discipline was not common. Only two batters (5%) had a batting eye of 1.00 or higher during their breakout season. Only seven (18%) had a batting eye of 0.75 or higher.
- Thirty-six (95%) hitters had a contact rate of 75% or higher.
- As you might expect, an above-average batting average was important: 34 hitters (90%) had a BA of .275 or higher during their breakout season.
- Good overall skill was important. Thirty-four (90%) hitters had an xBA of .270 or higher during their breakout season.
- Above-average power and speed skills were common. Twenty-eight (74%) hitters had a PX higher than 100 during their breakout season. Twenty-two (58%) hitters had an SX higher than 100. Every player had a 100+ in one of those two categories.

So perhaps we can use some of these observations to create a profile of these unexpected breakouts. We could look for the following when it appears that a player might be making a surprise jump to a $20 season:

1. They should be 27 years old or younger.

2. They should see an increase in at least two of the following categories: H%, PX or SX.

3. They should have a 100+ level in either PX or SX.

4. They should have a contact rate of 75% or higher.

5. They should have an xBA of .270 or higher.

Obviously there were exceptions to all of these, but for the most part, this is the meat of what we've seen in the last seven years. So how did this profile work for 2007's breakout players? There were six first-time $20+ players this past season, and four of them (Ryan Braun, Corey Hart, Hunter Pence, Troy Tulowitzki) were a perfect match for the profile. B.J. Upton and Delmon Young were not.

Still, if there's one lesson to take here, it's this: surprise earners shouldn't be easily dismissed. We've averaged 5.5 of them per season over the last eight seasons. Odds are we'll see at least a couple more reach that $20 pinnacle in 2008; applying this skill profile can help you identify the best ones to own.

In the pitching section: Breakout pitchers

Survival of the fittest

by John Burnson

For some time now, we at Baseball HQ have been interested in forecasting reliability – ensuring that you get what you pay for. Our Reliability Score (REL) metric looks *backward* – it tells whether we could have relied on a player in the recent past. Thinking that it would be helpful to complement REL with a *forward*-looking indicator, we examined the "predictive reliability" of individual BPI's.

Our method is to track survivorship rates of players within a season based on their exhibited skills in the first three weeks. According to the players' rate of one of four skills, we divided the pool of players into five groups. We then followed each group and tracked the change in their usage over the season. We desire skills that hint that a player will have a long season, if not a productive one.

Naturally, the five groups eat 100% of the available playing time in the first three weeks, but their use slips as the season progresses. Every group slides with time – no player is immune to injury, and hot call-ups have to steal *someone's* job. However, good skills *are* good insurance.

Hitters

Contact rate: In general, contact rate is not an acute predictor of survivability. The exceptions are "slap hitters" – those batters with a contact rate of at least 90%. These guys consistently maintain more than 90% of their original playing time. Why are high-Ct hitters so durable? With so many hit balls, these hitters' stats might be more apt to converge to the performance that is expected by their managers. Making consistent contact might also be a proxy for good health.

Walk rate: There is little difference in usage by skill here – the strongest and poorest quintiles finish at the same level. The weak predictive power of walk rate might stem from the fact that taking a walk does not reflect physical well-being. Sure, it takes discipline to not swing at bad pitches; at the end of the day, though, most hitters are paid to hit, and walks don't pay the bills.

Power (HR/AB): The groups that fare the best in power are the ones at the extremes – those with a homer rate under 1% or above 5%. The batters with a homer rate below 1% are generally contact hitters, and as we saw above, they tend to keep their jobs. On the other hand, batters with a homer rate above 5% are the sluggers who provide the pop that most teams can't do without. Between these extremes are batters who bring enough power to attract attention but not enough to keep it.

Speed (SB/(1B+BB)): Moreso even than walk rate, an early display of speed confers no benefit. Base-stealing might be too sensitive to even slight deterioration in health, or perhaps speedsters don't have enough other talents to ensure playing time, so that when their speed goes, so do they. Whatever the cause, the hitters with the wildest swings in fortunes are the ones with the greatest speed. This is another reason for fantasy GM's to forgo steals.

Pitchers

Dominance (K/9): Dominance is well correlated with survivorship – pitchers with a strikeout rate over 7.0 K/9 in April are still logging 80% of their playing time into August, versus a figure of 65% for pitchers who start the year under 5.0 K/9. To keep one's job, keep the ball out of play. However, by September, the differences among the groups compressed; maybe the stress of five months of pitching falls particularly hard on the flame-throwers.

Control (BB/9): If you want to wreck a roster spot, keep a starter who is walking three batters or more a game in April – these pitchers plunge to 60% of their original usage by the All-Star Break. A steady arm – in the form of a walk rate below 3.0 BB/9 – wins out, with usage through August around 80%.

Command (K/BB): Pitchers with below 1.5 K/BB in April are ridden out of town on a rail, falling to 65% of their playing time after only one month. Meanwhile, the top pitchers – those with 4.0 K/BB in the first three weeks – retain their original playing time virtually into September. The lesson: There's nothing fluky about masterful K/BB.

Homerun rate (HR/9): There are essentially three groups of pitchers: those with a homer rate in April below 0.5 HR/9, those with a homer rate above 2.0 HR/9, and everyone else. The relative usage of the low-homer group never dips below 90%. Meanwhile, the high-homer hurlers fall to 75% after only one month and are logging only 50% of their original playing time by the Break.

Of all our indicators for pitchers, nothing is a better predictor of survivability than HR/9. This is somewhat surprising – in the congress of BPI's, homer rate has been relegated to a less vital seat following the discovery of a strong tendency of HR% toward FB/10. However, our research says that the responsibility of pitchers in preventing homers should not be understated. Maybe HR/9 is instructive because it is the product of two separate skills: strikeout rate (which prevents hit balls) and G/F (which keeps hit balls in play). A high HR/9 might also be a sign of injury or immaturity.

In conclusion, we can state that higher-quality pitchers – those with a strikeout rate over 7 K/9, walk rate below 3 BB/9, and homer rate near 0.5 HR/9 – are safer bets on Draft Day not simply because they should post *better* stats than their less-skilled brethren but also because they should post *more* stats. Their talent simultaneously promises a healthy arm and provides protection against infringement by newcomers. LIMA-caliber pitchers aren't just better, they're also hardier.

Overall, the prospects for hitters to survive into September are less tied to visible skills than they are for pitchers. Unlike with pitchers, there are no BPI's for hitters where the relative usage of a group falls below 60%; in fact, usage for hitters rarely falls below 80% for any skill.

The fact that there are so many things that pitchers can't control (such as hit rate on balls in play and HR rate on fly balls) magnifies the few things they *can* control (such as strikeout rate and walk rate). And most all the skill they do possess resides in one fragile area of the body, the arm. Hitters, on the other hand, are more robust: They can contribute either by becoming baserunners or by scoring baserunners, they can travel via either power or speed, and they can excel in either offense or defense. This is not news to fantasy GM's, but it is nice to see our intuition reinforced.

PITCHING
Pitch counts and PQS

One hundred and twenty pitches. Some groundbreaking sabermetric work anointed 120 as the magic number for when a pitcher had reached the point of no return. Warning flags went up every time a pitch count hit 120, heralding the coming of Abuse, Burnout and Injury.

Driving the argument was a wasteland littered with failed careers. Bill Pulsipher, Paul Wilson and Jason Isringhausen were the New York Mets' 1990s wunderkind, a rotation core that was supposed to take them into the next century. Only Izzy survived, and only because he cut down his workload in the bullpen. More recently, Mark Prior, Kerry Wood and Carlos Zambrano fit the mold, and while Zambrano seems to have risen above the workload, his periodic struggles might presage a coming downfall.

Further research, improved conditioning and a greater awareness of workloads have tempered the alarmists. However, we still shudder when we see a young arm like Matt Cain post consecutive high-pitch games. We still see a string of pitch counts — 119, 118, 112, 124, 101, 66 — and wonder if injury-prone Ben Sheets is being pushed too hard. Or A.J. Burnett, who averaged 124 pitches over a three game span, iced with a 130 pitch outing on June 7, then failed to get out of the 5th inning in his subsequent two starts prior to hitting the disabled list.

Long-term analysis of workload is an ongoing science. However, there have also been questions whether we can draw any conclusions from short-term trends. Certainly, we can look at Sheets and Burnett above, and speculate. But are there more conclusions to be drawn? Can we look at a 125-pitch complete game outing and safely say that the pitcher's next start is more likely to be worse? Simple regression to the mean would say, "yes," but is there more?

For this analysis, all pitching starts from 2005-2006 were isolated — looking at pitch counts and PQS scores — and compared side-by-side with each pitcher's subsequent outing. So we were examining two-start trends, essentially the immediate impact that one type of pitching performance would have on the very next start.

We start with a simple look at pitch count trends:

Pitch cts	Pct	< 80	80 -89	90 -99	100 -109	110 -119	120+
Under 80	13%	23%	20%	28%	20%	8%	1%
80-89	14%	18%	18%	31%	23%	7%	2%
90-99	28%	14%	15%	30%	28%	11%	2%
100-109	30%	12%	11%	25%	34%	16%	3%
110-119	13%	8%	7%	24%	37%	20%	5%
120+	3%	10%	8%	21%	29%	27%	5%
MEAN		14%	14%	27%	29%	13%	3%

Pitch counts are divided into six tiers, from "under 80" to "120 and over." The "Pct." column shows the distribution of starts by tier; in other words, pitchers threw under 80 pitches in 13% of all starts in this study. In the very next start, 23% of those pitchers again threw fewer than 80 pitches, 20% tossed between 80 and 89 pitches, and so on.

These days, only about 3% of all starts clock in with 120+ pitches so it is difficult to draw conclusions from that small sample. Still, we'll see what we can unearth.

The effect on subsequent pitch counts is one small slice.

More important is *how* each pitcher fares in the subsequent start. And for that, we'll look at PQS...

Under 80 Pitches

PQS	Pct.	Next start PQS	DOM	DIS	qERA
0	72%	2.47	31%	29%	4.90
1	4%	2.30	26%	35%	5.13
2	7%	2.68	32%	20%	4.60
3	10%	2.80	42%	27%	4.74
4	5%	2.79	38%	28%	4.82
5	2%	3.50	57%	14%	3.97
MEAN		2.55	33%	28%	4.90

This first chart looks at all starts of under 80 pitches. You'll note that 72% of these starts resulted in a PQS score of zero. This is not surprising; you would expect most sub-80-pitch outings to be caused by a pitcher getting blown out. Perhaps more surprising is the fact that even 2% of these starts generated a PQS-5 score.

The subsequent starts were all over the board. If an initial outing resulted in a PQS-2, for instance, 32% of the next starts were DOMinating (PQS-4 or 5); 20% were DISasters (PQS-0 or 1). That equates to a qERA of 4.60. The average PQS score for all the subsequent starts was 2.68.

Overall, the result of the subsequent start was nearly the same no matter if a pitcher scored a PQS-0 or a PQS-4 in that initial start. The only notable difference was for the 2% that managed a PQS-5 in the initial start; here, the subsequent start showed a bit more life.

80-89 Pitches

PQS	Pct.	Next start PQS	DOM	DIS	qERA
0	27%	2.46	35%	34%	5.00
1	10%	2.57	33%	27%	4.90
2	15%	2.57	41%	32%	4.92
3	22%	2.60	33%	27%	4.90
4	18%	2.53	30%	26%	4.90
5	8%	2.78	40%	27%	4.74
MEAN		2.56	35%	29%	4.82

For those who hurled between 80 and 89 pitches in the initial start, the subsequent start was not much better. In fact, in some ways it was worse. Fewer of these initial outings were outright disasters. This leads one to speculate that this group was composed of more bad pitchers whereas the Under 80 group was composed more of better pitchers having bad outings.

90-99 Pitches

PQS	Pct.	Next start PQS	DOM	DIS	qERA
0	9%	2.49	36%	31%	5.00
1	9%	2.39	32%	32%	5.08
2	15%	2.41	27%	31%	5.13
3	29%	2.57	34%	26%	4.90
4	21%	2.89	41%	25%	4.56
5	17%	3.08	50%	20%	4.53
MEAN		2.68	37%	26%	4.82

For those initial starts between 90 and 99 pitches, we see the continuing shift away from disaster. Whereas the Under 80 group generated 76% disasters in the initial start, and 37% of the 80-89 group were disasters, only 18% of these initial starts generated a PQS score of 0 or 1.

On the DOM side, now 38% of the initial starts were PQS-4s and 5s, and the subsequent outings generated qERA levels at least close to league average.

100-109 Pitches

PQS	Pct.	PQS	DOM	DIS	gERA
0	5%	2.68	36%	25%	4.64
1	6%	2.47	30%	29%	4.90
2	13%	2.68	39%	28%	4.82
3	28%	2.82	39%	22%	4.64
4	25%	2.90	42%	22%	4.56
5	23%	3.10	49%	21%	4.53
MEAN		2.86	41%	23%	4.56

Next start columns: PQS, DOM, DIS, gERA

The 100-pitch mark is where we first see some significant improvement in subsequent outings. We can assume that most hurlers who made it to pitch #100 had a certain minimum skill level.

110-119 Pitches

PQS	Pct.	PQS	DOM	DIS	gERA
0	1%	2.57	29%	29%	4.93
1	3%	2.59	29%	24%	4.73
2	12%	2.89	41%	20%	4.44
3	24%	2.99	41%	18%	4.44
4	32%	3.07	48%	21%	4.53
5	29%	3.30	52%	13%	4.23
MEAN		3.07	46%	18%	4.40

The improvement continues at the 110-119 pitch level. Over 60% of these initial starts are DOMinating and the subsequent outings for that group all generated an average PQS score of over 3. In essence, good pitching begets good pitching at this workload level.

Now is where it gets interesting. What would we expect to happen with the "Over 120 pitch" group? If we go with the straight trend, we'd expect these numbers to continue to improve. If we believe that #120 is the demarcation point for Abuse, Burnout and Injury, then we might expect to see a drop-off. We already saw a minor drop-off on the pitch count side, but what about performance?

120+ Pitches

PQS	Pct.	PQS	DOM	DIS	gERA
0	0%				
1	2%	2.50	0%	0%	4.50
2	6%	2.57	29%	29%	4.93
3	25%	2.64	29%	29%	4.93
4	32%	3.19	57%	22%	4.23
5	35%	3.18	45%	13%	4.28
MEAN		3.00	43%	20%	4.56

And we do see a small drop-off in performance. Fully two thirds of these initial starts are DOMinating, and for those, the subsequent starts are all solid. In fact, beginning at the 110 pitch mark, any PQS-4 or 5 outing has a 50% chance of yielding another PQS-4 or 5, and only a 17% chance of seeing a PQS-0 or 1 follow-up.

However, for every initial outing of PQS-3 or below, the potential for the subsequent start was just bad. Does this mean that good pitchers can be stretched out to over 120 pitches but less-skilled pitchers should not be? Of the group that survived, there were rubber arms like Aaron Harang, Jason Schmidt, John Smoltz and Carlos Zambrano. Among the group that failed to follow up, there were Livan Hernandez, Mark Redman and Dontrelle Willis.

There does appear to be merit to the concern about 120 pitches. However, the impact does not appear to be all that great and the fallout might just affect those pitchers who have no business pitching that deep into games anyway.

Days of rest and PQS

Workload is only part of the equation. The other part is how often a pitcher is sent out to the mound. For instance, it's possible that a hurler might see no erosion in skill after a 120+ pitch outing if he pitched only once every other week. So we took another slice out of our data set and looked at the number of days rest in between starts.

Three days rest

Pitch ct	Pct.	PQS	DOM	DIS	gERA
Under 100	72%	2.8	35%	17%	4.60
100-119	28%	2.3	44%	44%	5.21
120+	0%				

These days, managers are reluctant to put a starter on the mound with any fewer than four days rest. In fact, that practice has become so rare, that this first group constitutes only 1% of the total population. That makes this sample size a bit small, and more suspect.

However, we can note a few interesting data points. First, the hurlers who tossed fewer than 100 pitches on three days rest were not able to maintain much dominance (35% DOM) but *were* able to avoid disaster to a great degree (17% DIS). This is evidence of a more deliberate, careful approach to pitching, and to protecting the pitcher. More research is needed, but it's possible that finesse pitchers might fare better than power pitchers on shorter rest.

For those who tossed 100-119 pitches on three days rest, the results were over two and a half times more disastrous. Thankfully, nobody in the study group was left on the mound for 120 or more pitches on three days rest.

Four days rest

Pitch ct	Pct.	PQS	DOM	DIS	gERA
Under 100	52%	2.7	36%	27%	4.82
100-119	45%	2.9	42%	22%	4.56
120+	3%	3.0	42%	20%	4.44

About 55% of all pitchers fell into this category. Note that there is no performance drop-off in the 120+ pitch group as we had seen earlier. The conclusion? Perhaps it's okay to let a starter go over 120 pitches if he goes every fifth day.

Five days rest

Pitch ct	Pct.	PQS	DOM	DIS	gERA
Under 100	54%	2.7	38%	25%	4.79
100-119	43%	3.0	44%	19%	4.44
120+	3%	3.2	48%	14%	4.28

We typically think in terms of a standard of four days rest with three days being the outlier. However, this "five days" group constitutes a full 31% of the population and the results are notable. That extra day of rest improves performance across the board and squeezes even more productivity out of the 120+ pitch outings.

Five days rest means that a pitcher is probably in a regular rotation but might get held back a day due to the game schedule (off days) or rainouts. For the daily fantasy leaguer, those blank Mondays and Thursdays could be beneficial to our Tuesday and Friday starters.

Six days rest

Pitch ct	Pct.	PQS	DOM	DIS	qERA
Under 100	58%	2.7	39%	30%	5.00
100-119	40%	2.8	40%	26%	4.82
120+	3%	1.8	20%	60%	7.98

If six days rest is better than five, then seven should be better than six, right? Wrong. Only 4% of the pitchers studied pitched once per week and the results were not good. Six days between outings is usually due to spot starting or a pitcher being held back due to an injury. In any case, these are not situations where you want a pitcher active on your roster.

7-8 days rest

Pitch ct	Pct.	PQS	DOM	DIS	qERA
Under 100	72%	2.4	32%	32%	5.08
100-119	28%	2.7	40%	26%	4.74
120+	1%	1.0	0%	100%	15.00

9-19 days rest

Pitch ct	Pct.	PQS	DOM	DIS	qERA
Under 100	76%	2.4	26%	28%	4.93
100-119	24%	2.7	38%	22%	4.64
120+	0%				

These two groups each constitute about 3% of the total. For the most part, you do not want to start a pitcher when he's had that long of a layoff.

20+ days rest

Pitch ct	Pct.	PQS	DOM	DIS	qERA
Under 100	85%	1.8	20%	46%	6.12
100-119	15%	2.3	33%	33%	5.08
120+	0%				

Despite being only 3% of the total population, this is an intriguing group. The pitchers here were almost entirely injury rehabs and failed call-ups, and the length of the "days rest" was occasionally well over 100 days. A pitcher would get hurt, or pitch poorly enough to get sent down, and a long time lapse would follow. This chart shows the result of their performance in their first start back.

The good news is that the workload was monitored for 85% of these returnees. The bad news is that these are not pitchers you want active. So for those who obsess over getting your DL returnees activated in time to catch every start, the better percentage play is to avoid that first outing (Aaron Cook notwithstanding.). Odds are it won't help you.

DAVITT   BEAGLE   KRUSE   McKAMEY

Uncover the inner workings of what it takes to win with Baseball HQ's weekly radio podcast. Join host Patrick Davitt, our top analysts and special guests, each week from February through August, for interviews and insights. All shows are FREE 30+ minute mp3 files available for download or subscription through iTunes.

SAMPLE 2007 PROGRAMS (Still available at the URL below)

February 16: Rob Gordon on four prospects to watch in Spring Training ... Harold Nichols and Matt Beagle look at the NL and AL in their regular Market Watch segments... Brandon Kruse's "Metric Minute" looks at "Eye Ratio"... Ron Shandler talks about the shifting nature of the "Top Five" players in his regular Master Notes segment.

March 3: Ray Murphy discusses his 2007 Straight Draft Guide... Deric McKamey on Giants pitching prospect Tim Lincecum ... Brandon Kruse's "Metric Minute" on "Contact Rate"... Ron Shandler talks about the dangers of believing too strongly in last year's outcomes.

March 17: Ron Shandler talks about his new Portfolio3 draft strategy and his yearly pre-season "Draft Radar Alerts"... Deric McKamey reports on Red Sox 2B Dustin Pedroia ... Brandon Kruse looks at Walk Rate.

March 31: Draft time! Ron Shandler and Ray Murphy conduct a roundtable discussion of trends, players, and memorable draft experiences... Deric McKamey looks at Cincinnati comeback kid Josh Hamilton... Brandon Kruse looks at "Power Index".

April 21: Special guest, Jeff Erickson, talks about his fantasy baseball history, how he manages his 12 to 15 fantasy teams in multiple formats, and his gigs with RotoWire and XM Radio... Deric McKamey looks at Astros OF Hunter Pence... Brandon Kruse looks at "Strand Rate".

May 5: "Dr. HQ" columnist Rick Wilton talks about injuries to pitchers and hitters, and teams that do well keeping their players off the DL... Brandon Kruse looks at Ground Ball Percentage... Ron Shandler talks about not acting too quickly as the season enters May.

May 26: We ask the critical question: Should you go for the title? Or start to rebuild? And how do you do it? Ron Shandler and Ray Murphy discuss... Brandon Kruse looks at Hit Rate... Deric McKamey looks at Reds' prospect Joey Votto.

July 7: Doug Dennis talks about how he analyzes bullpen pitching, which closers are solid in their roles, and where to look for saves in the second half... Brandon Kruse on Pure Quality Starts... Ron Shandler continues his discussion about the trading process.

July 28: Matt Beagle on Strat-O-Matic... Brandon Kruse talks about Base Performance Value for pitchers... Rob Gordon on Brewers' call-up pitcher Manny Parra... Ron Shandler talks about how to manage risk in the critical pre-deadline period.

August 18: Special guest Todd Zola of fantasybaseball.com talks about his choice of games and his observations on the 2007 season... Brandon Kruse on Expected Batting Average (xBA)... Deric McKamey looks at Dodgers reliever John Malone... Ron Shandler on making big moves even with six weeks to go.

LISTEN NOW — it's FREE!
http://www.baseballhq.com/radio/

Short-term predictive value of xERA

by Brandon Kruse

Last year, we took a look at the short-term predictive value of Expected Batting Average — specifically, whether hitters with large gaps between their BA and their xBA tend to experience a surge or fade in their batting average over a short period of time. We also examined the value of targeting high BA "stud" hitters with a strong supporting xBA. The results were positive; for the most part, the studs kept on raking, the surgers surged and the faders faded.

So we decided to perform a similar short-term test with Expected ERA. To do this, we collected pitching data from the first four weeks of the season, then gathered pitchers into groups, using only starters for a better innings sample size. Once again, there were Surgers and Faders — those pitchers with at least a half-run difference between their ERA and xERA. We again collected a group of Studs — 10 starters with the best xERAs in the league (but varied ERA/xERA differentials). And we added a group whose xERA closely matched their actual ERA (we'll call them the Stables), just to see how well xERA predicts short-term stability. Then we tracked their results over the next four weeks, from April 29 through May 26.

There were 34 Surgers, 56 Faders and 19 Stables, for a total of 109 pitchers (the 10 Studs pulled double duty in one of those three groups). For all pitchers, there was a minimum requirement of 18 IP on April 28, and 10 IP over the study period.

Here's a look at the composite skills of the four groups:

Group	ERA	xERA	Diff	Cmd	H%	S%
Faders	2.87	4.27	1.40	1.9	27	78
Studs	3.20	3.11	-0.09	3.8	30	73
Stables	4.16	4.20	0.04	2.4	30	71
Surgers	5.69	4.15	-1.55	2.3	33	64

The Studs are clearly superior, skill-wise. According to xERA, the other three groups are nearly identical; the main difference has been varying degrees of luck. An observer going by actual ERA would say there's no way the Surgers should outperform the Faders; going by skill, we beg to differ. Here's what really happened:

Group	ERA	IP	Cmd	H%	S%
Studs	3.32	339	3.1	29	74
Surgers	4.10	1009	1.9	30	73
Faders	4.23	1665	1.9	30	71
Stables	4.24	603	2.8	30	72

The Surgers did produce a slightly better ERA than the Faders, as both groups saw their hit and strand rates normalize. The difference between the two wasn't dramatic, but then again, the difference in their xERAs wasn't that dramatic either — just a 12-point differential. In fact, the most amazing result is how close the Surgers, Faders and Stables came to their April 28 xERA targets — all within 0.05 of their respective marks. The Studs posted an ERA 21 points higher than their earlier xERA, but still had the best ERA and maintained elite-level command.

Now let's look from another angle — did any group do a better job of producing hot hands? As a benchmark, let's go with a 4.00 ERA, which is half a run below what is generally a league-average ERA. Overall, 48 of the 109

pitchers, or 44%, posted an ERA of 4.00 or lower during the study period. How many did each group produce?

Group	Sub-4.00	Pct
Studs	6/10	60%
Surgers	18/34	53%
Faders	23/56	41%
Stables	7/19	37%

Again, as we would expect, targeting elite pitchers with strong xERAs was the best method for netting a strong short-term ERA. Targeting Surgers wasn't a bad strategy either, producing an above-average number of sub-4.00 pitchers in the short-term; it's a nice alternative, since just going out and grabbing an elite pitcher is not generally an option. The Faders produced a below-average number of sub-4.00 ERAs, and the Stables did the worst job of it, though that's not necessarily a surprise, as their composite xERA was 4.20 (above our ERA target), and the whole point of their group was consistency.

What about downside risk? How did each group fare in terms of pitchers to avoid? As a benchmark, we'll go with a 5.00 ERA, a half-run above the league average. Overall, 33 of the 109 pitchers, or 30%, posted an ERA of 5.00 or higher during the four-week period. Here's how many each group produced:

Group	5.00+	Pct
Studs	0/10	0%
Surgers	9/34	27%
Faders	18/56	32%
Stables	6/19	32%

The Studs didn't disappoint; theirs was the clear path to avoiding disaster. The other three groups all hovered right around that 30% average, suggesting that perhaps among non-elite pitchers, a certain amount of short-term bad luck is going to find you no matter what.

Finally, one last angle. With the Surgers, Faders and Stables, did pitchers' overall ERA move in the direction predicted by their April 28 xERA? We'll again use half-run benchmarks: *ERA Down* means their ERA moved half a run or more lower, *ERA Up* means it moved half a run or more higher, and *ERA Same* means their ERA stayed within half a run of their April 28 mark. The results were definitive:

Group	ERA Down	Pct	ERA Up	Pct	ERA Same	Pct
Surgers	23/34	68%	4/34	12%	7/34	21%
Stables	5/19	26%	3/19	16%	11/19	58%
Faders	4/56	7%	32/56	57%	20/56	36%

Even over four weeks, xERA successfully predicted the performance direction of a significant number of individual pitchers.

Overall, the results of this study proved quite similar to the results of last year's short-term xBA study. Again we confirmed the value of targeting elite-level skills. And as with xBA, it seems that xERA can provide useful input when it comes to making roster decisions... If you're choosing between two pitchers and one is a Surger and one is a Fader, going with the Surger looks like the better strategy. That makes xERA a tool worth adding to your regular mix of decision-making resources.

The power of ground ball pitchers

by Stephen Nickrand

The search for the next Fausto Carmona has begun.

The reason is clear. Many owners earned a greater profit from Carmona than from any other starter. He seemed to develop overnight from a failed closer to a superstar SP.

Carmona's emergence defied many of our analytical tools. His base skills didn't indicate that he was a prime breakout target. He posted a mediocre 5.6 Dom and 4.1 Ctl with CLE in 2006. As a result, he was M.I.A. from most pre-season breakout lists.

He also never had a stud prospect pedigree. He was known as a good prospect who needed a good defense behind him to succeed. He gave up a lot of hits and didn't pile up strikeouts in the minors. Not exactly a guy worthy of breakout speculation.

So how can a guy with middling skills transform from a struggling starter into a Cy Young candidate? Well, there were signs. He did post a 9.0+ Dom in three separate months with CLE, even though much of that came in relief. But his emergence was really fueled by a unique combination: dominant raw stuff and an extremely high ground ball rate.

Our previous research has shown that high Dom, groundball pitchers are worth a premium. So perhaps it also is true that a high GB% can help a starter with good raw stuff emerge quicker.

Sometimes a plus fastball or slider can manifest itself in a high dominance rate for pitchers who are otherwise struggling. Other times, a starter may post pedestrian 6.0 or 6.5 Dom rates despite having the potential for much more.

As it turns out, there were just nine starters in 2007 aged 26 or under who met both of the following criteria: 5.6+ Dom and 50%+ GB%

Here they are, sorted in descending order of Dom…

PItcher	Dom	GB%
Hernandez, Felix	7.8	61%
McGowan, Dustin	7.6	53%
Cabrera, Daniel	7.3	50%
Gaudin, Chad	7.0	51%
Loewen, Adam	6.5	52%
Gabbard, Kason	6.1	54%
Hill, Shawn	6.0	55%
Morales, Franklin	5.9	54%
Carmona, Fausto	5.7	64%

Let's take a closer look at some guys who have a good shot to follow a Carmona-like path to stardom in 2008.

Felix Hernandez has all the goods you want from a breakout target: good skills, elite raw stuff, and a forgiving home park. He just needs to align his ability with some better fortune. He posted a 9.6 Dom and 2.8 Ctl in the first half of 2007, but a 39% H% kept his ERA above 4.00. In the second half, his H% normalized, but his skills faded a bit. With some better luck, he has a great shot to have a Carmona-like season in 2008.

Dustin McGowan doesn't have the King Felix fanfare, but he finished the season stronger. He posted a 100+ BPV in both August and September, including an 8.0+ Dom and 56% GB%. Among starters who finished with a 4.00+ ERA, McGowan may be the best bet to emerge among the game's elite.

Daniel Cabrera is one of those guys on whom many risk-averse owners never bid. After all, for every PQS-5 he throws, there seem to be an equal number of PQS-0/1 scores. Yet this is a guy who has both the goods and groundball ability to emerge quickly.

Adam Loewen is coming off a stress fracture in his throwing elbow, so his status in 2008 is up in the air. But he was all over our 2007 pre-season breakout lists because of his high Dom plus GB% approach. He is ahead of where teammate Erik Bedard was at the same age.

Shawn Hill enjoyed a breakout of sorts in 2007, but injuries got in the way again. If healthy, he could become a top 10 National League hurler, even after RFK Stadium goes away.

Franklin Morales looked really good in September: 7.2 Dom, 2.2 Ctl, 104 BPV. He is a top prospect with elite raw stuff who keeps the ball on the ground.

The problem with this approach is knowing which pitchers have the raw stuff to become top hurlers. Few pitchers can throw a moving sinker in the upper 90s like Carmona can. Nevertheless, identifying this qualitative aspect and linking it to our groundball metrics can provide a competitive edge.

While Carmona's 60% GB% clearly is a unique skill, perhaps our 50% GB% cutoff is setting the bar too high. In fact, lowering our criteria to a 45%+ GB% gives us some more interesting names of guys with top-shelf raw stuff:

PItcher	Dom	GB%
Lincecum, Tim	9.2	47%
Miller, Andrew	7.9	49%
Snell, Ian	7.7	46%
Jimenez, Ubaldo	7.5	46%
Garza, Matt	7.3	48%
Jackson, Edwin	7.2	45%
Pelfrey, Mike	5.6	48%
Bailey, Homer	5.6	47%

Tim Lincecum is a known commodity in most leagues. As a result, you'll be unlikely to earn a big profit from him. But expect his growth to continue.

Andrew Miller had a terrible MLB debut on the surface: 5.63 ERA, 1.75 WHIP but still had the Dom/GB% combo.

Ubaldo Jimenez isn't as good of a breakout target as teammate Franklin Morales is. Yet he did post a 7.5 Dom, along with an 94 BPV in 33 IP in August. And he offers upper-90s, moving stuff that hasn't been consistently evident in his strikeout totals.

Matt Garza finished with a 1.54 WHIP, due in large part to a 35% H%. But he has some of the best raw stuff in the game, and he knows how to use it to generate groundballs.

Edwin Jackson could be the most intriguing longshot bet to emerge in 2008. He showed flashes of his ability in the second half; consistency was the issue. Most scouts will tell you that he has all the tools to be a top-of-the-rotation starter.

Mike Pelfrey had a horrible MLB debut with NYM. But behind his 5.57 ERA and 1.71 WHIP lies a 47% GB%. And we know his raw stuff is good.

Homer Bailey just needs to translate his Triple-A success into MLB results. At age 21 and after flopping with CIN, now's the perfect time to buy him low.

Pitcher breakout profile

by Brandon Kruse

Previously we looked at breakout seasons among batters, specifically those hitters who took a big jump in value with little to no track record of value prior to that season. We found that many showed improvement in their core skills, and we were able to set up a profile that could guide us in analyzing in-season breakouts.

For pitchers, the guidelines are the same: pitchers who had never posted a Rotisserie value higher than $10 at the major league level prior to posting a $20 season, and a requirement of at least one season of MLE or MLB skill stats prior to the breakout season. We removed Japanese free agents from consideration, since almost all had solid track records from their time in Japan. We covered the 2000-2006 seasons, giving us seven years of data, and found 31 qualifying pitchers; again, these are somewhat borderline in terms of sample size, so any findings should be kept in proper perspective.

As with hitters, most of these breakouts were about improved performance rather than increased playing time (with the exception of some closers, where a role change makes a huge difference). We'll start by analyzing their combined pre-breakout and breakout skill stats in a mixture of core pitching skill and luck categories (since we have both starters and relievers, these are weighted averages):

	ERA	WHIP	Ctl	Dom	Cmd	H%	S%	BPV
Pre-Bkout*	4.15	1.36	3.2	7.4	2.5	31	72	70
Breakout	3.27	1.18	2.7	7.2	2.9	28	75	86

*Contains full or partial-season MLEs from 24 of 31 pitchers

Unlike the batters, who had sub-par skills in their pre-breakout season, the pitchers were average to above-average in surface stats and skills prior to their breakout. Of course, average pitchers don't often post $20 seasons, so improvement was required and they delivered, in the form of better control and command, slightly fewer home runs, and good luck with hit and strand rates. Looking at those changes, it appears that luck had as much to do with the breakout as skill.

Now let's check what percentage of the 31 pitchers saw improvement, a decline or no change in their skills:

	Ctl	Dom	Cmd	hr/9	H%	S%	BPV
Improved	71%	52%	71%	61%	77%	58%	68%
No Change	7%	0%	3%	7%	7%	10%	3%
Declined	23%	48%	26%	32%	16%	32%	29%

Improvement was the majority in every category, with strikeout rate barely making the cut. A lower hit rate was the biggest common denominator, and if we add in the pitchers whose hit rate held steady, we have 84% of the field that had a hit rate equal to or lower than their pre-breakout hit rate.

Broken down into starters and closers, we found that while both groups improved their command (65% of the starters, 88% of the closers), they took different routes; both cut down on walks, but the closers also struck out more batters. Hit rate took on even greater significance for the starters, as 92% of them had a rate equal to or lower than they had the previous season.

Some further observations from the sample pool:
- The average age of these players during their breakout season was 24.2 years. 94% of them were 27 or younger.
- During their breakout season, 24 (77%) had a walk rate equal to or lower than 3.3, which is right around the typical league average.
- Twenty-seven (87%) had a strikeout rate of 5.6 or higher (a mark that previous Baseball HQ research has shown to be a tipping point for a sub-4.00 ERA).
- Twenty-six (84%) pitchers had a command ratio of 2.0 or higher (and three others were very close at 1.9). No pitcher had a K/BB ratio lower than 1.5.
- Twenty-eight (90%) had a hr/9 rate of 1.1 or lower.
- Reinforcing the importance of good luck, 28 pitchers (90%) had a hit rate of 30% or lower, and 29 of them (94%) had a strand rate of 71% or higher.
- Twenty-eight pitchers (90%) had a BPV over 50.
- And finally, good overall skill was important. Twenty-nine (94%) pitchers had an xERA below 4.00 during their breakout season.

So as we did with the hitters, we'll use these observations to create an in-season profile for unexpected breakouts. We could look for the following when it appears that a player might be making a surprise jump to a $20 season:

1. They should be 27 years old or younger.

2. They should meet or exceed our standard skill benchmarks: 5.6 Dom, 2.0 Cmd, 1.1 hr/9 and 50 BPV.

3. They should have a hit rate of 30% or lower and a strand rate of 71% or higher.

4. If they're a starter, they should have a hit rate equal to or lower than the hit rate in their previous season; if they're a closer, they should show improved command.

5. They should have an xERA of 4.00 or lower.

Obviously there were exceptions to all of these, but mostly, this is what we've seen in the last seven years. So how did this profile match up with breakout players in 2007?

There were three first-time $20+ pitchers this past season, but only one, Fausto Carmona, matched the profile. Jeremy Accardo and Manny Corpas matched everything except the command improvement we highlighted for closers. As an additional note, this profile, when applied at the end of June, did successfully predict that five pitchers who were performing at a $20 pace (Kevin Gregg, Jeremy Guthrie, Rich Hill, John Maine and James Shields) would not finish the season at that level.

Overall, the lesson from the batters applies once again here: surprise earners shouldn't be easily dismissed. We've averaged just over four per season over the last eight years. We'll likely see at least a few more reach the $20 mark in 2008; applying this skill profile can help you target the right ones to pursue.

BPV and saves success

by Doug Dennis

From 1999 to 2007, there have been 221 20-save seasons. The number each season has been steady, with about five teams failing to have even one 20-save closer each year:

1999	26	2002	25	2005	25
2000	24	2003	25	2006	25
2001	25	2004	23	2007	23

The glossary in this book defines Base Performance Value (BPV) and explains that "the elite of the bullpen aces will have BPVs in excess of 100 and it is rare for these stoppers to enjoy long term success with consistent levels under 75." I often hear from others that this is wrong, and then get an earful of Jose Mesa. Let's examine the successes, or lack thereof, of poor skilled relievers.

Here are those nine years broken down by BPV:

		Base Performance Values		
Year	No.	Over 100	Over 75	Under 75
1999	26	7	14	12
2000	24	6	13	11
2001	25	14	20	5
2002	25	15	18	7
2003	25	9	16	9
2004	23	14	14	9
2005	25	9	16	9
2006	25	13	18	7
2007	23	12	17	6

Out of 221 20-save seasons, 99 (45%) are by elite relievers with 100+ BPVs, 146 (66%) are by solid 75+ BPV relievers and a full-third are by relievers who did not manage a 75 BPV. That is a significant number of crappy relievers getting save chances. But of course, the Glossary does not claim that relievers cannot get 20-saves with a BPV under 75 — it claims that it is rare for these sub-75 BPV relievers to "enjoy long-term success."

How many of these sub-75 BPV relievers with 20-saves repeated that 20-save season the following year?

Year	BPV < 75	Repeaters
1999	12	6
2000	11	7
2001	5	3
2002	7	2
2003	9	4
2004	9	2
2005	9	2
2006	7	5
2007	6	?

Forty-five percent of closers with a sub-75 BPV retain their job and get 20+ saves the following year. That's something of a surprise (and we will come back to why this happens in a minute). But here is another interesting question: How many of those with 20 or more saves and a BPV under 75 that repeat have a BPV under 75 *both years*?

Year	BPV < 75	Both years <75
1999	12	2
2000	11	2
2001	5	1
2002	7	2
2003	9	3
2004	9	2
2005	9	1
2006	7	3
2007	6	?

Only 16. The other 15 times that the closer managed another 20-save season, he also managed to hike his BPV above 75. Two consecutive 20-save seasons with a BPV under 75 for both is rare indeed; only 8% of all 20-save seasons buck the need for BPV to exceed 75 for that closer to repeat that 20-save season. Here are those 16 times:

Alfonseca (1999-2000)	Mesa (2002-2003)
Alfonseca (2000-2001)	Mesa (2003-2004)
D.Baez (2004-2005)	Mesa (2004-2005)
C.Cordero (2006-2007)	Percival (2003-2004)
Dempster (2006-2007)	T.Jones (2006-2007)
Graves (1999-2000)	M.Williams (2000-2001)
Isringhausen (2005-2006)	M.Williams (2001-2002)
Julio (2003-2004)	M.Williams (2002-2003)

If we cut this by pitchers, that makes 11 closers who managed the trick out of 90, and only three of those 90 managed it for more than two seasons — Antonio Alfonseca, Mike Williams and Jose Mesa.

How does it happen that teams actually let these sub-par relievers repeat the feat — and some multiple times?

There are a number of possibilities, and each pen situation is a bit different. First, 20 saves is not a very high threshold. Twenty saves represents a little more than half a season's saves for the average team in an average year. So it can easily represent partial seasons — either in gaining the job, or in losing it, or even in some job-share arrangement. Graves, Julio and Baez are examples of that.

Second, some of these closers have other seasons with a 75+ BPV, either before or after the two-year aberration. Isringhausen and Percival are examples of that. Even Jose Mesa managed a 102 BPV just before his 2002-2005 run.

Sometimes it is because these teams simply lacked talented relievers and had to stick *someone* in at the end of games. It fell to the reliever who had the best skills, even with a sub-75 BPV. Alfonseca, perhaps, is an example.

So just as one might expect, the odds are long for Todd Jones to repeat with a 20-save season in 2008. But Alfonseca, Williams and Mesa show that it is not completely unprecedented.

Besides Jones, five other 20-save closers — Ryan Dempster, Chad Cordero, Trevor Hoffman, David Weathers and Bob Wickman — posted a sub-75 BPV in 2007. It should not be a surprise to see some of these six repeat, but history tells us that only one or two of them is likely to manage it.

Chad Cordero seems the safest at the moment. It would seem possible that Ryan Dempster gives way to Carlos Marmol or Angel Guzman, and David Weathers gives way to Jared Burton or some free agent. Wickman has already given way in Atlanta, going from closer to cut overnight. And Joel Zumaya's freak injury may save Todd Jones for another season.

These data have particular importance to Trevor Hoffman owners, given his BPV trend (188, 131, 98, 65) over the past four years, with BPV-studs Cla Meredith (97) and Heath Bell (134) in set-up and out-pitching him. It may seem difficult from here to see the Padres pry Hoffman out of the job, but Bell is ready and able to close immediately, and Hoffman's BPV trend is so stark — it is more likely than not that it will happen in 2008.

III.
GAMING

Gaming Research

The changing face of fantasy

According to latest estimates, we are among over 17 million people who participate in fantasy sports. Fantasy football continues to be the overwhelming industry leader, but baseball has been experiencing its own consistent, albeit smaller, growth rate.

At BaseballHQ.com, we've been keeping tabs on ongoing industry trends by means of our weekly HQ Poll, which we've been running since December 1998. In each edition of the *Forecaster*, we look back at some of these questions and share the results. There are dozens of trends that we track so we rotate the topics each year in this space.

Since these questions are asked at Baseball HQ, they only represent the opinions of folks who a) visit Baseball HQ, and b) respond to online polls. So these are clearly not 100% scientific representations of the industry as a whole. However, even from among our smaller group, we can glean some interesting tidbits about where our hobby may be headed.

(Note that all poll results had at least 500 responses.)

Be honest... What is your core motivation for playing fantasy sports?

	2003	2005	2007
The sense of control in owning a team	8%	11%	15%
The challenge of proving your knowledge	44%	44%	43%
The thrill of competition	32%	29%	26%
The social and camaraderie aspect	11%	12%	12%
The chance to win money	4%	4%	4%

I've cited this poll's results many times in talking about the importance of information in playing these games. Yet, as this industry has evolved into big business, the focus has been on high stakes and formats where luck plays a bigger role. Proving your knowledge becomes quite a challenge if the results of your efforts are largely random.

But respondents want more control, which supports the growth of daily games, which increases the element of luck, which diminishes the amount of control. In last year's *Baseball Forecaster*, John Burnson wrote an article that proved how streaming players (notably pitchers) yielded poorer results by the end of the season than just sticking with them.

But I guess it's all in the thrill of the chase.

Rotisserie players: What is your preferred category format?

	2003	2005	2007
Eight standard categories (4x4)	23%	22%	20%
5x5, adding Runs and Innings Pitched	6%	4%	4%
5x5, adding Runs and Strikeouts	58%	52%	56%
6x6, or more categories	5%	10%	10%
Some other Rotisserie variation	8%	12%	10%

The decline of *Rotisserie League Baseball's* 4x4 standard continues. In tandem, more folks are venturing out beyond 5x5. From an analytical standpoint, the only danger I see in these multi-mega-category formats is potential skill redundancies. For instance, what's the point of having Home Runs *and* Slugging Pct? More appropriate might be Doubles plus Triples. I am seeing many leagues that add categories just for the sake of piling on categories, without regard to the analytical implications. The Founding Fathers created a delicate balance with 4x4; 5x5 was a natural enhancement. 10x10 seems like overkill, frankly.

The spring annuals start hitting the newsstands each February. Admit it — you always buy at least one. What's your primary reason?

	2005	2006	2007
Despite the dated information, they are still a fun read	15%	16%	14%
I rely on them from their frequent insights	2%	3%	3%
I need to know what the other owners In my league are reading.	23%	23%	25%
Good bathroom entertainment	12%	12%	14%
It's like a drug at that time of year. I can't help myself.	45%	42%	40%
Some other reason	3%	4%	4%

I've been asking this question for the past few years because, frankly, I was curious. Every year, there seemed to be a thread on BaseballHQ.com's reader forum where one or more of the spring magazines was trashed. On the baseball side, there are about a dozen mags (triple that for football). Some are better than others, many employ a cookie-cutter approach to information, but all are anxiously awaited around Super Bowl time. Like the arrival of Strat-O-Matic cards, first pitch on Opening Day and perhaps, for some, this book.

Yes, definitely a drug.

Does your Rotisserie league use the category of holds?

	2004	2006	2007
Yes, and we think it works fine.	10%	13%	19%
Yes, but we don't like it	2%	3%	2%
No, but we are considering it.	9%	9%	7%
No, we have no interest in it.	78%	76%	72%

Getting back to the analytical integrity of this game, I am never against change so long as it makes sense. The rise in adoption of Holds is in response to a perceived need to reward the role of the middle reliever. Unfortunately, the "hold" statistic is so flawed as to render it almost useless. The official definition:

A relief pitcher is credited with a hold any time he enters a game in a save situation, records at least one out and leaves the game never having relinquished the lead. A pitcher cannot finish the game and receive credit for a hold, nor can he earn a hold and a save in the same game.

Lots of grey area here, including the fact that, perhaps the most critical game situation — when the score is tied — still offers no reward for talented pitchers. More to the point, however, is that Holds can be even more difficult to project than saves.

Despite that fact, the category's growth continues. I've resisted adding it to our arsenal for several years. Although it does not appear in this book, mostly due to space constraints, Holds will now appear on BaseballHQ.com in our 2008 projections. But it's little more than a shot in the dark.

For weekly transaction leagues, which of the following is the closest to your transaction deadline?

	2003	2005	2007
Friday noon	3%	2%	2%
Friday 5 or later	3%	2%	2%
Saturday noon	0%	1%	1%
Saturday 5 or later	1%	2%	2%
Sunday noon	3%	2%	3%
Sunday 5 or later	19%	24%	22%
Monday noon	38%	38%	38%
Monday 5 or later	15%	17%	16%
Tues., Wed., or Thurs.	17%	12%	14%

I wish I started asking this question about 10-15 years ago because I think we would have seen a large scale shift over that time.

The Founding Fathers set their deadline for noon Friday because that was when their source of stats — *The Sporting News* — came out. When *USA Today* became the primary source of stats, many leagues moved their deadlines to Tuesday (AL) and Wednesday (NL). Once commissioner services started becoming popular, deadlines began moving to the weekend.

What is your preferred mode of player acquisition on draft day?

	2005	2006	2007
Auction	62%	63%	65%
Pick-a-player/salary cap	3%	3%	2%
Straight/serpentine/snake	33%	32%	30%
Some other method	2%	2%	2%

Industry research conducted by the Fantasy Sports Trade Association keeps showing that snake drafts are far more popular than auctions. The people they survey obviously are not the same people who visit Baseball HQ. The preference for auctions makes more sense to me as that has been the Rotisserie standard for over two decades. Snake drafting has only become popular since the internet era; early game providers did not have the technical capability to offer online auctions. I suppose all those ESPN and Yahoo players flooded the FSTA ballot box.

What are your baseball viewing habits?

	2005	2006	2007
I don't watch much baseball on TV at all	9%	13%	12%
I watch about one game each week.	13%	12%	13%
I watch about 2-3 games per week.	28%	26%	27%
I watch about 4-6 games per week.	29%	24%	24%
I watch a game every day, on average.	21%	25%	24%

What I'd really like to do is run a correlation between these results and fantasy league success. I have a sneaking, and somewhat horrifying suspicion that success and viewership might have an inverse relationship.

Consider... the more games you watch, the less objectivity you tend to bring to the decision-making process. Even if you watch a lot of games, your opinions are shaped by small sample sizes of performance. We would never pass judgment on a player based on 30 or 40 games of stats; it would be equally dangerous to pass judgment based on 30 or 40 games of observation.

However, how can we not watch games? My approach is to watch games as a fan and run my fantasy teams from a more objective, analytical perspective. At least I try.

When do you start taking the standings seriously in order to start working your roster?

	2005	2006	2007
Immediately after draft day	11%	9%	9%
Mid-April	9%	6%	7%
May 1	27%	30%	33%
May 15	27%	28%	27%
June 1	26%	21%	18%
After June 1	0%	6%	5%

We have always advised that it takes at least six weeks for the early season dust to clear and player stats to begin to stabilize. So my vote here would go to May 15. Many respondents share that opinion.

But there is a growing faction that gets itchy about two weeks earlier. That's not horrible, but those two weeks can make a difference. Last year, I proffered that you could trade away April's top performers with soft BPIs for April's bottom-feeders with strong BPIs and experience a net gain by season's end. I did orchestrate a mock 10 for 10 deal in my May 1 Baseball HQ column and, in fact, did profit. But had I waited until May 15, the tide would have already started to turn. Two weeks is two weeks.

What is your opinion on player dumping at this point in the season?

	MAY	
	2004	2006
All's fair in fantasy baseball	38%	34%
Dumping is okay but not this early	20%	20%
Dumping is never acceptable under any conditions	18%	18%
My league has rules to prohibit/discourage dumping	24%	28%

	JUNE	
	2002	2007
All's fair in fantasy baseball	50%	44%
Dumping is okay but not this early	16%	15%
Dumping is never acceptable under any conditions	12%	17%
My league has rules to prohibit/discourage dumping	22%	24%

	JULY	
	1999	2000
All's fair in fantasy baseball	48%	57%
Dumping is okay but not this early	10%	12%
Dumping is never acceptable under any conditions	16%	16%
My league has rules to prohibit/discourage dumping	26%	15%

Forgetting the timing of these polls for a moment, the entire issue of player dumping remains as controversial as ever. I would have thought by now, with the industry maturing, that participants would have begun to figure out how to navigate the sometimes treacherous waters of fantasy's free market economy. Instead, many online competitions and high stakes games have just opted to outlaw trading completely. So much for fantasy baseball being a social activity.

The eight-year span when these polls were run provides some interesting food for thought. For starters, the deeper into the season that the question is asked, the more likely that respondents are content with "all's fair." Similarly, those who feel that "dumping is okay" will qualify that opinion depending upon how early it is in the season.

Finally, there has been no real increase in the adoption of anti-dumping rules... which I suppose makes sense if more leagues are completely eliminating trading as a part of the experience.

Changing standards

Last May, in one of my ESPN chats, I received the following question:

"I could use some help at SP. I have Jake Peavy, Randy Johnson, Erik Bedard, Anthony Reyes, Nate Robertson and Jason Schmidt. I have plenty of closers. I was offered Barry Zito for Trevor Hoffman and Curtis Granderson. Should I do it or is he asking too much? Right now I lead in saves and am in second in WHIP but my wins and ERA are horrendous! I am in a 10 team league and start 15 position players and 10 pitchers with 5 bench spots."

There was a time when I lived in his world. My first foray into Rotisserie baseball was 1985 when I helped form a 6-team league that drafted from baseball's two East divisions. The player pool penetration was about 40%, a level we were perfectly comfortable with. Several years later, I graduated to the "standard" 12-team single league format. It was a step up to the big boys; that was where the "real" players played.

And that was fine too. For many years.

My approach to this game comes from the perspective of having to know all the second string catchers and every middle reliever in line for possible saves. But the game has been changing over the past decade. Since the internet opened up fantasy sports to the masses, and the market has been flooded with more casual — but no less obsessive — participants, leagues more akin to my 1985 experience have risen from the ashes.

In our annual reader survey, one of the questions we ask is about participation in shallow and mixed leagues. As of last year, 48% of our readers participate in at least one mixed league, up from 27% in 1999. Shallow league participation is currently at 37%, up from 22% in 1999.

This is not necessarily good or bad. There are plusses and minuses to each format. But they do require different mindsets. To wit, here was my response to the chat question:

"I think you hold tight on this one. Zito is not a clear upgrade for any of your pitchers and certainly not enough to give up Hoffman and Granderson. If your ERA is hurting, just wait -- Bedard is poised to surge, Reyes has upside and if Schmidt is healthy, he should contribute in the 2nd half."

In trying to race through about 40 questions in 60 minutes, I do as best a job I can of addressing each issue. In this case, however, I missed an important point that being second in WHIP is a terrific indicator that his staff is probably better than it is showing. However, it was on another point that a subsequent poster took me to task.

He contended that Robertson and Reyes have no business being on a roster in a 10-team league. This is a point that I had not even considered.

At ESPN, *their* standard is a 10-team mixed league, with 9 batters, 6 pitchers, 5 bench spots and 1 DL. That means a total of 200 players are drafted, a penetration rate of 27%. What does a 27% league look like? It has teams with rosters like this: Michael Barrett, Carlos Delgado, Jeff

Kent, David Wright, Michael Young, Vlad Guerrero, Carlos Lee, Juan Pierre, Dave Roberts, Jeremy Bonderman, Erik Bedard, Ted Lilly, James Shields, Huston Street and Takashi Saito. On the bench, including injury replacements, are Shane Victorino (for Roberts), Kevin Gregg (for Street), Dan Johnson, David Bush, Tom Gorzelanny and Roger Clemens.

Any guesses where this team finished in 2007?

Ninth.

In this league, Reyes is on a roster (though benched) but Robertson is not. The chatter's league is a little bit deeper. His is a 40% league, so it is likely that both pitchers *would* be rostered. The poster who challenged me was wrong.

Still, given that the "old standard" is an 80% league (not including reserves), a 40% league is quite a different animal. Here are some of the players that would have been *in the free agent pool* at the end of draft day 2007 in a 40% league:

Casey Blake, Kevin Youkilis, Curtis Granderson, Chris Duncan, Shane Victorino, Mark DeRosa, Shawn Green, Ted Lilly, Mark Buerhle, Daniel Cabrera, Tim Hudson, Joel Zumaya, Tom Gorzellany, Salomon Torres, Bartolo Colon...

For a more interesting perspective, a typical 40% league might have had the following caliber of players in its free agent pool after draft day:

- 59 batters projected to get at least 400 AB.
- 6 of those players projected to hit at least .290.
- 10 batters projected to hit at least 20 HRs. Another 18 projected to hit at least 15 HRs.
- 12 players projected to steal at least 10 bases.
- 27 pitchers projected for at least 190 IP.
- 11 of those projected for an ERA under 4.50.
- 20 pitchers projected to get at least 130 strikeouts.
- 37 pitchers projected to win at least 10 games.
- 7 pitchers projected to get at least 10 saves.

Imagine what these numbers would look like in the 27% ESPN standard league!

By now, deep leaguers are shaking their heads in disbelief. This is not what fantasy baseball was supposed to be! Perhaps, not by the original design, but this is what it has become.

When I first started writing over 20 years ago, I kept making arguments for playing the game whatever way was best for your league. Admittedly, once I got involved with deep leagues, I became a bit of a deep-league snob. After all, "The Book" — *Rotisserie League Baseball* — said shallow leagues were bad because:

"In such mutant organizations, a GM inevitably puts together a team made exclusively of first-rank players... That's too easy.

"If you stick to (drafting at least 75% deep), you have to find a decent second-string catcher, decide which utility infielder has the most speed, figure which fourth and fifth outfielders will get more playing time, and pick a middle-inning reliever who won't slaughter your ERA and Ratio." Essentially, there's no challenge otherwise.

"There's too much talent in the free agent pool. A lucky owner could greatly benefit by having injured players so that he could grab the most desirable free agents.

"With considerably less disparity between the top and bottom players chosen, luck may be more of a factor than in other leagues.

"There may be less trading activity since no one has a glaring need."

These are all legitimate issues. However, most shallow leagues online exacerbate these problems by having few rules that provide a more realistic structure to the game. In the league above, when Dave Roberts hit the DL, players like Shane Victorino and Kenny Lofton were available. ("The Book" also said that "injuries should hurt at least a little bit.") When David Wright got off to a slow start, there was an abundance of better-performing replacements to choose from. The question is often not so much "should I do this?" as "which one should I pick?"

At the far end of the spectrum are daily games where roster churn is promoted because that means more online traffic for the hosting website. These games focus on highly volatile and unpredictable individual match-ups as opposed to a level of longer-term analysis that can evaluate talent more accurately. I know many of you hate me repeating this tired analogy but it still fits — it's the difference between playing chess and pinball.

However... nearly all of the arguments above are easily resolvable with a single rule tweak... **Restrict access to the free agent pool.**

If you limit most of the active roster movement to a team's own roster, you essentially change the overall composition of the player population. That levels the playing field. Yes, your 40% league might not draft Daniel Cabrera or Curtis Granderson, but for all intents and purposes, those commodities simply do not exist. For now.

To provide further structure, you might also consider the following:

1. Draft deep reserve squads to reduce the size of the free agent pool. This also serves to promote more trading, as each team has more depth to deal from.

2. Limit access to the free agent pool to one player per team per week. There can be unlimited daily movement between a team's active and reserve rosters.

3. Institute a rule that injury replacements must come from your reserves before the free agent pool can be accessed.

I'll talk more about these types of rules later on in the article, "Quest for the Perfect Format."

A shallow league may be a different animal, but it does not require much tweaking to make it just as challenging as a deep league. It's all a matter of creating an environment where the same type of decision-making can take place. Right now, that's not being done because... well, playing pinball is fun too.

Pigskin to Cowhide:
The optimal way to ease football fantasy leaguers into fantasy baseball
by Matt Beagle

That great group of guys in your football league would be even more fun in your baseball league. Every time you ask, they bring their "A" game of excuses.

"The season's too long."

"I don't have time for all the lineups and transactions."

"An auction takes too much effort. You'll take my money."

Here's a plan to start a baseball league with your football buddies that you'll all enjoy.

For starters, limit the smack talking and high-level statistical analysis. Your league must be easy to understand and friendly to get them involved.

1. Avoid the word Rotisserie. The word intimidates. Better yet, avoid the Roto format initially. Head-to-Head is the fastest growing format for several reasons. It mirrors the "Win or Lose" instant gratification you get each week from fantasy football. It's simple. Add up the category wins and losses. Head-to-head requires less time to analyze and is easier to track. It also keeps everyone interested all season long. Even two last place teams going at it in August feel the thrill of the competition against each other for bragging rights.

2. Use a few, basic categories. With too many categories, luck replaces skill. Pick a few good categories everyone understands. A basic points league also works well. Give one point for each total base, run scored, stolen base, and RBI. A Win earns fifteen points, five for a save, and one point for pitcher strikeouts. This makes it easy to calculate points as you watch a game. A solo homer yields the same six point instant gratification as a touchdown.

3. Keep the stakes low. The more money involved, the less likely your friends will enjoy themselves. They're more likely to try it for $20 than $200.

4. Shallow penetration of the talent pool. Make sure first-timers know, or have heard of, most of their selections. Fifty percent penetration represents the maximum for this kind of league. Later you can increase the penetration through additional teams or larger rosters.

5. Draft, don't auction. For beginners, a snake draft works best. Especially in the initial season, you want parity to keep as many managers energized as possible. An auction invites dissatisfaction with the extra preparation time, budgeting, and inflation issues. Few auction football leagues exist for a reason.

6. Limit transactions. Beginners won't or can't commit the time to daily transactions. They don't know what "streaming" is, but they do know they're at a disadvantage if they spend one day a week on lineups and others are playing match-ups every day. Have weekly lineups or make all players active every day, limiting the need for lineup adjustments. Limit the number of waiver wire pickups and trades.

7. No keepers. Start out each year with a fresh talent pool and values. Different managers have the thrill of owning Albert Pujols or Alex Rodriguez each year. Parity exists from day one.

Why are we fighting?

by John Burnson

If you have spent any time at BaseballHQ.com, you're familiar with the idea of Standings Gain Points (SGP). SGP denominators describe a league by the average gaps in the standings for a category. An SGP denominator of 30 means that adjacent ranks in the category tend to be 30 units apart, and thus the addition of 30 units of the stat should lead to a gain of one point in the standings.

Every year at HQ, we post SGP denominators derived from a pool of actual fantasy leagues. Here are the projected SGP denominators for the counting stats for a standard 5x5 NL league for 2007:

HR	11.3	Wins	3.4
RBI	32.1	Strikeouts	35.6
SB	8.9		
Runs	31.4		

On a lark, we decided to simulate SGP denominators for this same league. From final NL stats, we took all hitters with at least 200 AB and all pitchers with at least 40 IP. We then randomly created a thousand 13-team leagues and calculated the average SGP denominators for each category. Here are the simulated SGP denominators:

HR	10.3	Wins	3.3
RBI	28.0	Strikeouts	34.5
SB	9.9		
Runs	27.5		

The SGP denominators in real fantasy leagues are rather close to those in our simulated leagues. If anything, the denominators in real leagues are *bigger* than those in our simulated leagues – in other words, real teams are further apart in each category. That finding suggests that real fantasy leagues are characterized by weaker, not stronger, competition than randomly generated leagues. This conclusion runs counter to our expectations: We would have expected real standings to be much tighter, as owners jostle and scrape for the title. Apparently, all that fighting is for naught.

There are several explanations for the similarity in SGP denominators. First, it might be that some fantasy categories are, at bottom, random, and thus any effort to master them will ultimately be thwarted by chance. The category of Wins comes to mind as a good candidate – we may be able to broadly target pitchers by Win-generating potential, but questing for greater precision is folly.

Another explanation is human nature. We at HQ are constantly pointing out chances to sell high and buy low; however, hearing those recommendations and heeding them are different things. It is the rare person who, when considering an overachieving player, is not too greedy to sell him, nor, when considering an underachieving player, is not too fearful to buy him. The upshot is that both sorts of players are given enough time on their original rosters to regress toward a typical performance, so the standings are not as compressed as they would be if everyone was fighting for an advantage. (Alternatively, fantasy leaguers

might now be so experienced that they know not to sell low or buy high, in which case the end is the same: settled rosters and stale leagues.)

We don't stand much of a shot at conquering either randomness or psychology. However, there is a third culprit that is more amenable to remedy: the difficulty of trading. After all, the easiest way to tighten the gap with the team ahead of you is to trade away what you have a lot of for what you need more of.

In a typical league, an owner has only 11 or 12 potential trading partners. This is limit enough on vigorous trading, but the constraint goes further than that. We sometimes view a roster as a single portfolio of 23 players, but in truth it contains a number of "mini-portfolios" of players at similar positions, and trades must satisfy balance among all of the mini-portfolios. This balancing can be hard to orchestrate. How many trade talks are opened only to get dragged down in discussions of how to balance the final rosters?

Fortunately, this is a structural problem, and there is a fix: *Expand active rosters.* Expanding rosters would have two complementary and salubrious effects. First, expanded rosters would grant each owner more slots to play with. Second, expanded active rosters would yield a flatter value curve. We're not proposing to also raise budgets, so owners would have to spread the same number of dollars among more stats. The result would be flatter prices: the price of each player falls, and prices of better players fall more. This facilitates trading because a flatter value curve scrunches differences between players, which in turn makes it easier to find a workable bargain.

At the most radical end, we could eliminate all positional-eligibility requirements and have a roster of utility men. But such a change saps Roto of its charm. Here is a less radical proposal:

1. Add spots at Middle infield and Corner infield. In theory, we have mini-portfolios of three players at these positions, but in practice, many owners have one position filled by only one player. For example, you may have two SS but one 2B. As a result, your 2B is often untradeable unless you get a 2B in return. Adding a spot gives you another place to hold a back-up second baseman.

2. Eliminate the second CA spot. Yes, this change reduces the size of the roster. However, catchers have so little variation among them, and so few worthy stats, that the second CA spot is typically deadweight for trading purposes. It would be better to drop the slot entirely so that your payroll is dedicated to players who could make a difference, either for you or for a fellow owner.

3. Add one UT spot. This is a catch-all to grease the wheels.

On balance, we are adding only two spots, but the new roster is markedly better for deal-making. And easier deal-making is our best shot to shake the whims of chance and the structural flaws of Roto. There is the paradox: To make our leagues more competitive, we'll have to work together.

A new look at player valuation

by John Burnson

Tenets of player valuation say that the number of ballplayers with positive value – either (before the season) positive *projected* value or (after the season) positive *actual* value – must equal the total number of roster spots, and that, before the season, the value of a player must match our expected production from that player. These are appealing propositions. They are also wrong.

What's the unit of production in Rotisserie? You might answer "the player" or "the statistic," but those aren't quite right. The unit of production is the *player-week*. If you own a player, you must own him for at least one week, and if you own him for more than one week, you must own him for multiples of one week. Moreover, you cannot break down his production – everything that a player does in a given week, you earn. (In leagues that allow daily transactions, the unit is the *player-day*. The point stays.)

When you draft a player, what have you bought? "You have bought the stats generated by this player." No: You have bought the stats generated by his *slot*. Initially, the drafted player fills the slot, but he need not fill the slot for the season, and he need not contribute from Day One. If you trade the player during the season, then your bid on Draft Day paid for the stats of the original player *plus* the stats of the new player. If the player misses time due to injury or demotion, then you bought the stats of whomever fills the weeks while the drafted player is missing.

The point is that you're not drafting 23 players; rather, you are drafting 23 *player-seasons*, each of which consists of 26 player-weeks. Why is this important? Because focusing on players rather than player-seasons creates gaps in our universe. Suppose that you draft a player who is coming back from an injury and won't see play until July. You will almost certainly pick up a free agent in the first week of the season. Let's say that you drop this guy when the original player returns (and the fill-in is sent down). After the season, both your original player and his fill-in could have contributed positive value – that is, each of them may outplay a replacement-level player over the stretch of the season. But the two players did not fill two slots on your roster, they filled only one. They combined for one player-season. Thus, our final player values are short by a player-season.

Of course, it's not required for a free agent to contribute positive value; however, there's certainly value to be found. From Opening Day to October 1, the pool of draftable hitters loses about 1/5 of its value, and pitchers lose about 2/5. Not all of this value will be collected by owners, but a good chunk will be. Even if a given free agent does not have an *overall* value above replacement level, you may still see a benefit from owning him. Why? Because most owners do not battle in every category. If you need RBI, you may be happy with a batter who hits .240 if he also clubs 20 HR.

Note, too, that the relationship between a player-season and playing time is loose. We're not demanding that each slot provide a full 600 PA or 200 IP – we just want to see *some* weekly production so that, in most leagues, you would not have cause to drop the player.

How many player-weeks comprise a season? If **R** is the total number of roster slots, and **W** is the number of weeks, then **RW** is the total number of player-weeks. For a typical AL league, **R** = 276 (12 teams x 23 players) and **W** = 26, so **RW** = 7,176 (4,368 for hitters, 2,808 for pitchers). For a 13-team NL league, the totals are 4,732 **RW** for hitters and 3,042 for pitchers. So the targets over both leagues are 9,100 player-weeks for hitters, and 5,850 player-weeks for pitchers.

To get a handle on our undercount of player-seasons, we looked at the final values for 2006. For each player with positive value, we tabulated the number of calendar weeks in which the player played. In 2006, the hitters who were noted as having positive value combined for 7,825 player-weeks – only 86% of the needed total. That shortfall is as if every team in the league owned no hitters for September. The loss is even greater for pitchers – only 79% of the total. Some 1,200 pitcher-weeks are unaccounted for.

In other words, from the pool of players who were denoted as providing positive final values for 2006, you couldn't build a league! This discrepancy strikes us as critical. In valuation theory, the final draftable player is supposed to have a value of $1. However, if we're overlooking 15-20% of the production needed to flesh out a fantasy season, then our stated replacement level is too high.

Where does this analysis leave us? Before the season, the number of players projected for positive value should equal **R** – after all, we can't order owners to draft more players than can fit on their rosters. However, the projected productivity should be adjusted by the potential to capture extra value in the slot. This is especially important for injury-rehab cases and late-season call-ups. For example, if we think that a player will miss half the season, then we would augment his projected stats with a half-year of stats from a replacement-level player at his position. Only then would we calculate prices. Essentially, we want to apportion $260 per team among the *slots*, not the players.

After the season, the story is different. We could (and almost certainly should) assign positive value to *more* than **R** players, because many players will have provided fewer than **W** weeks of production. Ideally, we would determine the most productive pool of **N** players who filled **RW** player-weeks. As an approximation, we could step down the list of players in order of final worth and accumulate player-weeks until the players contribute **RW** weeks. This method is not perfect, because what we truly want is the pool of **N** players who contribute **R** slots of production at *each* of the **W** weeks of the season, but it will do. This challenge marks the frontier of player valuation.

Fanalytic Gaming Strategies

The LIMA Plan

The LIMA Plan is a strategy for Rotisserie leagues (though the underlying concept can be used in other fantasy formats) that allows you to target high skills pitchers at very low cost, thereby freeing up dollars for offense. LIMA is an acronym for Low Investment Mound Aces, and also pays tribute to Jose Lima, a $1 pitcher in 1998 who exemplified the power of the strategy. In a $260 league:

1. *Budget a maximum of $60 for your pitching staff.*
2. *Allot no more than $30 of that budget for acquiring saves.* In 5x5 leagues, it is reasonable to forego saves at the draft table (and acquire them during the season) and re-allocate this $30 to starters ($20) and offense ($10).
3. *Draft only pitchers with:*
... Command ratio (K/BB) of 2.0 or better.
... Strikeout rate of 5.6 or better.
... Expected home run rate of 1.0 or less.
4. *Draft as few innings as your league rules will allow.* This is intended to manage risk. For some game formats, this should be a secondary consideration.
5. *Maximize your batting slots.* Target batters with:
... Contact rate of at least 80%
... Walk rate of at least 10%
... PX or SX level of at least 100

Spend no more than $29 for any player and try to keep the $1 picks to a minimum.

The goal is to ace the batting categories and carefully pick your pitching staff so that it will finish in the upper third in ERA, WHIP and saves (and IP or K's in 5x5), and an upside of perhaps 9th in wins. In a competitive league, that should be enough to win, and definitely enough to finish in the money. Worst case, you should have an excess of offense available that you can deal for pitching.

The strategy works because it better allocates resources. Fantasy leaguers who spend a lot for pitching are not only paying for expected performance, they are also paying for better defined roles – #1 and #2 rotation starters, ace closers, etc. – which are expected to translate into more IP, wins and saves. But roles are highly variable. A pitcher's role will usually come down to his skill and performance; if he doesn't perform, he'll lose the role.

The LIMA Plan says, let's invest in skill and let the roles fall where they may. In the long run, better skills should translate into more innings, wins and saves. And as it turns out, pitching skill costs less than pitching roles do.

In *straight draft leagues*, don't start drafting starting pitchers until Round 10. In *shallow mixed leagues*, the LIMA Plan may not be necessary; just focus on the BPI benchmarks. In *simulation leagues*, also build your staff around BPI benchmarks.

Variations on the LIMA Plan

LIMA Extrema: Limit your total pitching budget to only $30, or less. This can be particularly effective in shallow leagues where LIMA-caliber starting pitcher free agents are plentiful during the season.

SANTANA Plan: Instead of spending $30 on saves, you spend it on a starting pitcher anchor. In 5x5 leagues where you can reasonably punt saves at the draft table, allocating those dollars to a high-end LIMA-caliber starting pitcher can work well as long as you pick the right anchor.

One way to approach that selection is...

The RIMA Plan

LIMA is based on optimal resource allocation. These days, however, no matter how good of a team you draft, player inconsistency, injuries and unexpected *risk factors* can wreak havoc with your season. The RIMA Plan adds the element of **RI**sk **MA**nagement.

Players are not risks by virtue of their price tags alone. A $30 Johan Santana, for example, might be a very good buy since he is a healthy, stable commodity. But most LIMA drafters would not consider him because of the price.

The RIMA Plan involves setting up two pools of players. The first pool consists of those who meet the LIMA criteria. The second pool includes players with high Reliability scores. The set of players who appear in both pools are our prime draft targets. We then evaluate the two pools further, integrating different levels of skill and risk, and creating six hierarchical tiers of players to draft from:

TIER A: LIMA-caliber with high Reliability scores
TIER B: LIMA-caliber with moderate Reliability scores
TIER C: Non-LIMA with high Reliability scores
TIER D: LIMA-caliber with low Reliability scores
TIER E: Non—LIMA with moderate Reliability scores.
TIER F: Non-LIMA with low Reliability scores.

Tier C is where RIMA opens up more opportunities. While we'd typically stay away from low-skilled players, carefully-chosen "C" bodies can provide valuable support if you are careful. In this group you might find inning-eater hurlers who could help boost your strikeout totals, though might have elevated ERAs. If the rest of your staff has a solid skills foundation, you can often weather the mediocre numbers that come along with these arms. The fact that they are low risk means that you know exactly what you will be getting and so you can better plan for it.

The goal for your roster is to assemble a balanced portfolio of solid performers and steady AB and IP-eaters that provide good return on your investment.

The RIMA concept is also applicable in non-Rotisserie formats. The process of integrating skill and risk management is universal for all types of league formats.

Hybrid strategies

by Craig Neuman

Most veteran readers are familiar with strategies such as LIMA, LIMA Extrema, Portfolio3, SANTANA, Labadini, etc. Each of these has benefits and drawbacks so, in an effort to take the best from each, we offer a few hybrid plans for your consideration...

Double LIMA Extrema

A cross between LIMA and LIMA Extrema. In Double LIMA Extrema, the pitching budget remains $60. However, instead of acquiring one saves source, the majority of the pitching budget will be spent on saves while the rest will be $1 pitchers. This should allow you to maximize three pitching categories and all offensive categories. The typical LIMA Extrema caveats apply (shallower league with low innings requirement) but it can be quite successful. Yet, while LIMA and LIMA Extrema have been more difficult to implement in a 5x5 league due to the extra counting category (strikeouts), Double LIMA Extrema gives you more of a fighting chance as it allows you to finish at the top of the saves category instead of the middle of the pack.

Sanlimadini

A cross between SANTANA, LIMA and Labadini. In this plan, draft a frontline starter (from SANTANA), a closer (from LIMA) and seven $1 pitchers (from Labadini) into a pitching budget around $60 (another LIMA principle). The benefit of this plan is in leagues with a "significant" innings requirement. By including a staff workhorse from the beginning, it won't be as difficult to reach the innings goal through in-season trading. And, having a Santana-type on your staff will ensure that the addition of those starters won't kill your ERA and WHIP.

The Great Santini

A cross between SANTANA and Labadini. Add Santana or another ace to a staff of $1 middle relievers and a $220 offense, and you've got the recipe for success. A $220 offense should allow you to maximize all of the offensive categories while your pitching should finish at or near the top of ERA and WHIP. That's likely good enough to finish in the money but potentially not enough to win. The reason to add a pitcher like Santana into the mix is twofold. First, if you're in a league with a "significant" IP requirement, it gives you the same head start on achieving that total as Sanlimadini. But, if you're not, then you've got another chip to bargain with when trading to strengthen your team.

Conclusion

These Hybrid Plans are not for everyone. Admittedly, they are best implemented in shallow, 4x4 leagues with low innings requirements. That said, they can be excellent options for players in keeper leagues looking for the start of a two-year plan. If your keeper list is weak and your chances of competing this year are slim, you might want to give one of these plans a shot. If things break right, great — you've managed to parlay a poor keeper list into a money team. And, if it doesn't work, at least you've got Santana and/or a closer(s) and/or a big budget offense from which to trade for the future.

Art McGee's
HOW TO VALUE PLAYERS FOR ROTISSERIE® BASEBALL
Second Edition

Learn how to calculate the best player values for your draft or auction! Art McGee applies concepts from economics, finance, and statistics to develop a pricing method that far surpasses any other published. His method is highly sophisticated, yet McGee explains it in terms that any fantasy baseball owner can understand and apply. Includes...

- Discover the power of Standings Gain Points (SGP)
- Learn how to adjust values for position scarcity, injury risk and future potential
- Set up your own pricing spreadsheet, as simple or sophisticated as you want
- Make better decisions on trades, free agents, and long-term contracts
- Apply these methods even if your league uses non-standard categories or has a non-standard number of teams
- PLUS... 10 new essays to expand your knowledge base.

How to Value Players for Rotisserie Baseball
.... **$17.95**
plus $5.00 Priority Mail shipping and handling

orders.baseballhq.com
1-800-422-7820

Total Control Drafting

Part of the reason we play this game is the aura of "control," our ability to create a team of players we want and manage them to a championship. We make every effort to control as many elements as possible. But in reality, the players that end up on our teams are largely controlled by the other owners. *Their* bidding affects your ability to roster the players you want. In a snake draft, the other owners control your roster to an even greater extent. We are really only able to get the players we want within the limitations set by others.

However, an optimal roster can be constructed from a fanalytic assessment of skill and risk. We can create our teams from that "perfect player pool" and not be forced to roster players that don't fit our criteria. It's now possible. It's just a matter of taking *Total Control*.

Why this makes sense

1. Our obsession with projected player values is holding us back. Fact: Only about 65% of players drafted provide a return within +/-$5 of projection. To get that percentage up to about 85%, you'd have to open the range to +/- $9. This is not indicative of poor forecasting; it's the nature of the beast. So, if a player on your draft list is valued at $20 and you agonize when the bidding hits $23, odds are about two chances in three that he could really earn anywhere from $15 to $25. What this means is, in some cases, and within reason, you should just pay what it takes to get the players you want.

2. There are no such things as bargains. Most of us *don't* just pay what it takes because we are always on the lookout for players who go under value. But we really don't know which players will cost less than they will earn because prices are still driven by the draft table. The concept of "bargain" assumes that we even know what a player's true value is. To wit:

If we target Hideki Matsui at $23 and land him for $20, we might *think* we got a bargain. In reality, Matsui might earn anywhere from $19 to $26 (which is, incidentally, his career range for full season performances), making that $3 perceived savings virtually irrelevant.

The point is, a "bargain" is defined by your particular marketplace at the time of your particular draft, not by any list of canned values, or an "expectation" of what the market value of any player might be. So any contention that TCD forces you to overpay for your players is false.

3. "Control" is there for the taking. Most owners are so focused on their own team that they really don't pay much attention to what you're doing. There are some exceptions, and bidding wars do happen, but in general, other owners will not provide that much resistance.

How it's done

1. Create your optimal draft pool.
2. Get those players.

Start by identifying which players will be draftable based on the RIMA criteria. Then, at the draft:

Early Game: Your focus has to be on your roster only. When it's your bid opener, toss a player you need at about 50%-75% of your projected value. Bid aggressively. Forget about bargain-hunting; just pay what you need to pay. Of course, don't spend $40 for a $25 player, but it's okay to exceed your projected value within reason.

Mix up the caliber of openers. Instead of tossing out an Albert Pujols at $35 in the first round, toss out a Randy Winn at $11. *Wise Guy Baseball's* Gene McCaffrey suggests tossing all lower-end players in the early-going, which does make a lot of sense. It helps you bottom-fill your roster with players most others won't chase early, and you can always build the top end of your roster with players others toss out.

Another good early tactic is to gauge the market value of scarce commodities with a $19 opener for Joe Nathan or a $29 opener for Jose Reyes.

Other owners may pick up on the fact that you are only throwing out names of players you want, so mix in a few non-targets to throw them off. Also, bid aggressively on *every player*; it will obscure which ones you really want.

Mid-Game: If you've successfully rostered 10-12 players with high skills and Reliability scores, you will have likely built a solid foundation for your team. At that point, you can relax some of the reliability constraints and take a few chances on players with high upside, but higher risk, like upwardly mobile rookies.

End game: You will need to relax the reliability targets for your last picks, so it might be a good idea to make sure those last buys are all pitchers (who are inherently more risky). You'll note that most high-skilled end-game LIMA pitchers have low reliability scores by nature.

At the end of the draft, you may have rostered 23 players who could have been purchased at somewhat lower cost. It's tough to say. Those extra dollars likely won't mean much anyway; in fact, you might have just left them on the table. TCD almost ensures that you spend all your money.

In the end, it's okay to pay a slight premium to make sure you get the players with the highest potential to provide a good return on your investment. It's no different than the premium you'd pay to get the last valuable shortstop, or for the position flexibility a player like Willie Bloomquist provides. With TCD, you're just spending those extra dollars up front on players with high skill and low risk.

The best part is that you take more control of your destiny. You build your roster with what you consider are the best assemblage of players. You keep the focus on your team. And you don't just roster whatever bargains the rest of the table leaves for you, because a bargain is just a fleeting perception of value we have in March.

The Portfolio3 Plan

Optimal draft strategy involves integrating the elements of expected player performance, risk and market conditions. For well over a decade now, I have been writing about different elements of this process, trying to get a handle on the best way to win our leagues.

The first true breakthrough was the **LIMA Plan**. This has been the foundation for our approach to player performance since 1998. LIMA teaches us to focus on skills, not stats, often to the exclusion of roles. By now, nobody who has been a regular reader of my work should feel skittish about drafting a pitcher with a 5.00 ERA if his peripherals are solid. Neither should you be targeting .300 hitters if their contact rates are under 75%.

But it's not all about skill. If it was only about skill, Ben Sheets would be a first round pick and $35 player every year. He's not because the probability of him returning fair value on your investment is highly suspect due to injury risk. The **RIMA Plan** took the foundation of LIMA and incorporated risk. RIMA says, let's separate players into groups based on varying levels of skill and risk, and then draft from a hierarchical sorting of those groups.

And that should have been enough to provide the framework for a successful draft plan. However, there was one little problem... Despite a wealth of excellent analytical tools, we are not all that good at projecting skill and risk. Projective accuracy, no matter what system you use, caps out at about 70%.

So last year, I showed how a reliance on prognosticating precision was destined to lead us astray. A player projected to return $20 had a 65% chance of returning anywhere from $15 to $25. "Go the extra buck, if warranted" became the impetus for the **Total Control Drafting** plan. TCD taught us to toss off the shackles of player values and better respond to market conditions.

Looking back, these three strategies have had important roles in furthering our potential for success. The problem is that they all take a broad-stroke approach to the draft. The $35 first round player is evaluated and integrated into the plan in the same way that the end-gamer is. But each player has a different role on your team by virtue of his skill set, dollar value, position and risk profile. When it comes to a strategy for how to approach a specific player, one size does not fit all...

We need some players to return fair value more than others. When you spend $40 on a player, you are buying the promise of putting over 15% of your budget in the hands of 4% of your roster. By contrast, the $1 players are easily replaceable. If you're in a snake draft league, you know that a first-rounder going belly-up is going to hurt you far more than a 23rd round bust.

We rely on some players for profit more than others. Those first-rounders are not where we are likely going to see the most profit potential. The $10-$20 players are likely to return more pure dollar profit; the end-gamers are most likely to return the highest profit percentage.

We can afford to weather more risk with some players than with others. Since those high-priced early-rounders need to return at least fair value, we cannot afford to take on excessive risk. Since we need more profit potential from the lower priced, later-round picks, that might mean opening up our tolerance for risk more with those players.

Players have different risk profiles based solely on what roster spot they are going to fill. Catchers are more injury prone. A closer's value is highly dependent on fickle managerial whim. These types of players are high risk even if they have the best skills on the planet. That needs to affect their draft price or draft round.

For some players, the promise of providing a scarce skill, or productivity at a scarce position, may trump risk. Not always, but sometimes. At minimum, we need to be open to the possibility. The determining factor is usually price. A $7, 15th round Joakim Soria is not something you pass up, even with a Reliability Score of only 13.

In the end, we need a way to integrate all these different types of players, roles and needs. We need to put some form to the concept of a diversified draft approach. Thus:

The **Portfolio3 Plan** takes all the work we've done to date and provides a three-tiered approach to the draft. Just like most folks prefer to diversify their stock portfolio, P3 advises to diversify your roster with three different types of players. Depending upon the stage of the draft (and budget constraints in auction leagues), P3 uses a different set of rules for each tier that you'll draft from. The three tiers are:

1. Core Players
2. Mid-Game Players
3. End-Game Players

Nothing fancy here.

TIER 1: CORE PLAYERS

Roster		BATTERS				PITCHERS	
Slots	Budget	Rel	Ct%	PX or SX		Rel	BPV
5-8	Up to $160	70	80%	100	100	70	75

These are the players who will provide the foundation to your roster. These are your prime stat contributors and where you will invest the largest percentage of your budget. In snake drafts, these are the names you pick in the early rounds. There is no room for risk here. Given their price tags, there is usually little potential for profit. The majority of your core players should be batters.

The above chart shows general roster goals. In a snake draft, you need to select core-caliber players in the first 5-8 rounds. In an auction, any player purchased for $20 or more should meet the Tier 1 filters.

The filters are not terribly strict, but they are important, so you should stick to them as best as possible. An 80% contact rate ensures that your batting average category is covered. PX and SX ensure that you draft players with a minimum league average power or speed. On the pitching side, a BPV of 75 ensures that, if you must draft a pitcher in your core, it will be one with high-level skill. For both batters and pitchers, a minimum reliability score of 70 should cover your risk.

Since these are going to be the most important players on your roster, the above guidelines help provide a report card, of sorts, for your draft. For instance, if you leave the table with only three Tier 1 players, then you know you have likely rostered too much risk or not enough skill. If you manage to draft nine Tier 1 players, that doesn't necessarily mean you've got a better roster, just a better core. There still may be more work to do in the other tiers.

TIER 2: MID-GAME PLAYERS

Roster		BATTERS				PITCHERS	
Slots	Budget	Rel	Ct%	PX or SX		Rel	BPV
7-13	$75-$125	40	80%	100	100	40	50
	All players must be under $20						

In Tier 2, we start relaxing the filters a bit. On the batting side, we hold tight to the skills requirements but are now starting to take on a bit more risk. It is important to stockpile as much playing time as you can.

On the pitching side, both skill and risk filters are relaxed so that we can open up more opportunities for starting pitchers (who tend to have somewhat lower BPVs). For those who opted to pass on pitchers in Tier 1, Tier 2 will provide many solid-skilled arms. Closers who drop to this level may be rostered carefully.

Tier 2 is often where the biggest auction bargains tend to be found as the blue-chippers are already gone and owners are reassessing their finances. It is in that mid-draft lull where you can scoop up tons of profit.

In a snake draft, these players should take you down to about round 18.

TIER 3: END-GAME PLAYERS

Roster		BATTERS				PITCHERS	
Slots	Budget	Rel	Ct%	PX or SX		Rel	BPV
5-8	Up to $25	n/a	80%	100	100	n/a	75
	All players must be under $10						

For some fantasy leaguers, the end game is when the beer is gone and you have to finish your roster with any warm body whose name pops out of a magazine. In the Portfolio3 Plan, these are your gambling chips, but every end-gamer must provide the promise of upside. For that reason, the focus must remain fixed on high skills and conditional opportunity. P3 drafters should fill the majority of their pitching slots from this group.

By definition, end-gamers are typically high risk players, but risk is something you'll want to embrace here. You probably don't want a Pedro Feliz-type player at the end of the draft. His 99 reliability score would provide stability, but there is no upside in his skill set, so there is little profit potential. This is where you need to look for profit opportunity so it is better here to ignore reliability; instead, take a few chances in your quest for those pockets of possible profit. If the player does not pan out, he can be easily replaced.

As such, a Tier 3 end-gamer should possess the BPI skill levels noted above, and...

... playing time upside as a back-up to a risky front-liner

... an injury history that has depressed his value

... solid skills demonstrated at some point in the past

... minor league potential even if he has been more recently a major league bust

Notes on draft implementation...

Auction leagues: As you might expect, auction leaguers would acquire these players via the Total Control Drafting method — simply, pay whatever it takes, within reason, particularly with Tier 1 names. Be willing to pay a small premium for the low risk and high skills combination.

Snake drafters will have choices in the first six rounds or so. There are no guarantees — a swing-pick seed might negate any chance you have for rostering some players — but at least there are some options. If you miss out on the cream, you can either drop down and select a lower round player early, or relax the filters a bit to grab someone who might have higher value but perhaps greater risk. You have to decide which way to go.

Position scarcity: While we still promote the use of position scarcity in snake drafts, it may be more important to have solid foundation players in the early rounds. However, as it turns out this year, there are some nice middle infield options in the early rounds.

Drafting pitchers early is still something we advise against. However, if you are going to grab a pitcher in the first six rounds, at least make sure it's a Tier 1 name. It is still a viable strategy to hold off on starting pitchers until as late as Round 10 or 11; however, if it's Round 7 and John Lackey is still sitting out there, by all means jump.

LIMA Plan: Although LIMA says no starting pitchers over $20, Tier 1 typically provides a few options for which it would be okay to break the rules. You can adjust your $60 pitching budget up to accommodate, or downgrade your saves targets.

Punting saves: Still viable, unless a Tier 1 closer falls into your lap. These are extremely rare commodities anyway. (There were only two Tier 1 closers last year; only one this year.)

Keeper leagues: When you decide upon your freeze list, you should be looking for two types of keepers — the best values *and* the most valuable players. Freezing a $6 Tim Lincecum is a no-brainer; where some drafters struggle is with the $30 Paul Konerko. Given that TCD says that we should be willing to pay a premium for the Tier 1-type players above, any name on the Tier 1 list should be a freeze consideration.

Adding in the variable of potential draft inflation, you should be more flexible with the prices you'd be willing to freeze players at. For instance, if you currently own a $48 Alex Rodriguez, you might be tempted to throw him back. After all, his projected value is likely to be a bit lower than that. However, between draft inflation and the premium you should be willing to pay for a Tier 1 commodity, his real value is probably well over $50.

The 2008 lists of Tier 1, 2 and 3 players appear in the Ratings & Rankings section.

Fanalytic Gaming Formats

Rotisserie7

Rules

1. Mixed league. Any number of teams.

2. 25-man roster, stocked any way you like so long as all your positions are covered. Each week, 16 of those players will be designated as "active:" 9 position players (1B, 2B, 3B, SS, CA, OF, OF, OF, DH), 5 man starting rotation and 2 relief pitchers. Nine reserves at any position.

3. 4x4 game with the following categories:

> **BATTERS: HR, (Runs scored + RBIs - HR), SB, BatAvg**
> **PITCHERS: Wins, Saves, Strikeouts, ERA**

4. Snake draft or auction is fine. For auctions, budget for the 16 active players only, followed by a snake draft for the remaining 9 players.

5. Rotisserie's category ranking system is converted into a weekly won-loss record. Depending upon where your team finishes for that week's isolated statistics determines how many games you win for that week. Each week, your team will play seven games, hence Rotisserie7.

*Place	Record	*Place	Record
1st	7-0	7th	3-4
2nd	6-1	8th	2-5
3rd	6-1	9th	2-5
4th	5-2	10th	1-6
5th	5-2	11th	1-6
6th	4-3	12th	0-7

* Based on overall Rotisserie category ranking for the week.

At the end of each week, all the roto stats revert to zero and you start over. You never dig a hole in any category that you can't climb out of, because all categories themselves are incidental to the standings.

6. There is unlimited once-weekly movement allowed between the active and reserve rosters during the season. Access to the free agent pool is limited to one player per week per team. Free agents are acquired via a straight draft in reverse order of the standings.

7. The regular season lasts for 23 weeks, which is 161 games. Weeks 24, 25 and 26 are for play-offs. The top six teams make the play-offs. In larger leagues (minimum 15 teams), the top eight teams can make the play-offs. Here it becomes a head-to-head game, but Rotisserie standings again determine the victors.

> **Week 24**: Teams 1 and 2 get byes. Team 3 meets Team 6, Team 4 meets Team 5. In larger leagues, Teams 1 and 2 would meet teams 8 and 7, respectively.
> **Week 25**: Team 1 versus Team 4 or Team 5; Team 2 versus Team 3 or Team 6
> **Week 26**: Two winners meet for the championship

The pot is divided 70% for regular season standing and 30% for play-off results.

Stratified Rotisserie

Rules

1. Start with the same basic rules as a standard Rotisserie competition, but this is a pick-a-player contest.

2. A league may include any number of owners. You will be drafting from both American and National leagues.

3. Each team will have a 25-man roster and a 15-man reserve squad. Each active roster will have 15 batters and 10 pitchers. Standard roto positional structure applies, with two DH/utility slots on the offense side. Reserve rosters have no positional restrictions.

4. *The only players available are those who posted a dollar value of $5 or less in the previous season.*

5. Each team stocks its roster individually. There is no draft or auction. While players may end up on more than one team, the narrow spread of talent will likely ensure that no two teams look exactly alike.

6. There is unlimited once-weekly movement allowed between the active and reserve rosters during the season. There is no trading in this league.

7. On June 1 and August 1, you may select up to five new players to add to your team. For each player who is added, an active or reserve player must be dropped. New players cannot come from the original list of ineligibles (over $5).

Strategic considerations

The players with the best upside value are last year's injury rehabs and minor leaguers looking at significant playing time.

In drafting for your active roster, your key goal is to accumulate quality playing time.

Since you will be playing most of the season from the roster you draft, your reserve squad becomes very important. Naturally, you'll want to grab as many positional backups as possible to protect against injury and excessive bench-sitting of your active players. Your reserve also is a good place to stash upwardly mobile minor leaguers who could get promoted mid-season and have an impact.

Rule modification options for the truly masochistic

1. Draft from only one league, rather than both.

2. Reduce the strata threshold to $3 instead of $5.

3. Make all injury rehabs ineligible if they posted a roto value over $5 in their last healthy season.

4. Limit the number of players with less than 20 games of major league experience to 5 per roster.

5. No more than 3 players with less than 20 games of major league experience can be active at any time.

Quint-Inning

Object: To assemble a group of players that will amass the most points during a single baseball game.

Auction draft: A player auction is conducted among five "owners" before the ballgame and must be completed prior to the start of the game. Each owner must acquire 5 players from the current 25-man rosters of the two major league teams playing in that game, at a cost not to exceed $55. There are no positional requirements for the 5 players other than one must be a pitcher. All 5 roster spots must be filled.

An owner need not spend his entire auction dollar allotment. Any unspent dollars may be added to an owner's Free Agent Acquisition Budget (FAAB).

The "salaries" paid for the five players have no further relevance once the draft is over. They are essentially acquisition costs only.

Points and standings: Team standings are calculated based on a ranking of points accumulated by players at the time they are on an owner's roster.

BATTERS accumulate points for bases gained or lost:

Single = +1	Double = +2
BB = +1	Triple = +3
HBP = +1	Home run = +4
SB = +1	Error = -2
CS = -1	

Batting stats accumulated by pitchers in the National League do count, however, the pitcher must be drafted or acquired separately as a batter. A pitcher may appear as both a batter and a pitcher in a given game, accumulate points separately, and appear on different rosters.

PITCHERS accumulate points for IP minus ER:

IP = +1	Earned Run allowed = -1

The IP point is awarded to the pitcher who is on the mound when the third out of the inning is registered.

Win = +5	Save = +3

These points are awarded to the owner who has the pitcher of record on his team at the end of the game, even if the owner did not draft that pitcher. If an unrostered pitcher gets a win or save, these points are not awarded.

"The Quint:" At the beginning of the 5th inning, any owner has the option of doubling the points (positive and negative) for one player on his roster for the remainder of the game. Should that player be traded, or dropped and then re-acquired, his "Quint" status remains for the game.

Ninth Inning: Beginning in the 9th inning, all batting points (positive and negative) are doubled.

FAAB points: Unused FAAB units can be converted to scoring points at the end of the game. The conversion rate is 10 FAAB = 1 point.

In-game roster management: The five drafted players must remain on each owner's roster for at least the first inning. Then, players may be dropped, added or traded, and all roster size restrictions are then lifted, except:

- Rosters must contain at least one player at all times.
- Rosters must contain at least one pitcher at all times.

All player moves take effect at the beginning of each half inning. All player moves must be announced prior to the first pitch of that half inning; otherwise, the move will not take effect until the following half inning.

Dropping players: Any player can be cut from an owner's roster at any time after the first inning. Players who are cut may not be re-acquired by the original owner.

Adding players: Each owner is allotted a free agent acquisition budget (FAAB) of $50 per game for the purpose of acquiring players. Available for FAABing are...

- undrafted players on one of the 25-man rosters
- players that had been cut by other owners
- players of those owners who drop out of the game

An owner can announce that he is placing a bid on a free agent at any time after the first inning. Other owners can then bid until a winner is determined. No other player needs to be dropped. All players accumulate points from the half inning after which they were acquired. Owners are limited to one player per half inning acquired via FAAB.

Trading: A trade can be consummated at any time after the first inning, between any two or more owners. The only commodities that may be traded are rostered players and FAAB dollars. Uneven trades are allowed and roster sizes do not have to be squared up at any time. However, should a team's only pitcher be traded to another owner, a pitcher must be received in return or a free agent pitcher acquired immediately. If a pitcher is not added to a roster before the first pitch of the next half-inning, the trade is nullified.

Stakes: Quint-Inning can be played as a no-stakes, low stakes, moderate or higher stakes competition.

- It costs ($1/$5/$55) to get in the game.
- It costs (25 cents/$1/$5) per inning to stay in the game for the first four innings.
- Beginning with the 5th inning, the stakes go up to (50 cents/$2/$10) per inning to stay in the game.
- Should the game go into extra innings, the stakes rise to ($1/$5/$25) to stay in the game until its conclusion.

Each owner has to decide whether he is still in the game at the end of each full inning. Owners can drop out at the end of any inning, thus forfeiting any monies they've already contributed to the pot. When an owner drops, his players go back into the pool and can be FAABed by the other owners.

Determining the winner: The winner is the owner who finishes the game with the most points. Tie-breakers:

- Team with the most number of players contributing positive scoring points.
- Team with the most pitching points.
- Team with the most FAAB remaining.

Scorekeeping: A Quint-Inning scoresheet, along with more detailed rules and strategies, can be downloaded from http://www.baseballhq.com/free/free050819.shtml

---

The anti-Internet gambling bill that was signed into law in October 2006 has carve-out language that clearly defines the legality of fantasy sports. This language states that fantasy games are exempt as long as they follow several stipulations. The second stipulation states:

2. Winning outcomes are determined by skill for contests that use results from multiple real-life games.

Quint-Inning fails at this stipulation, which only means we won't be setting up QI games on the internet. But you can feel free to continue playing at home.

The quest for the perfect format

Our Founding Fathers invented Rotisserie as an elegant confluence of baseball and economics. Whether by design or accident, the result has lasted for over two decades.

But I wonder what Rotisserie would have been like if the Founding Fathers knew then what we know now about statistical analysis and game design. What if we tried to emulate real baseball a little bit more? What if we just turned everything upside down and started over? You can be sure things would be different.

Most folks know that I am fascinated by the rules of this crazy game. I have developed hybrids of my own as a means to tinker and test. I truly believe we have yet to tap the ultimate competitive format.

So last spring, I set out with nine other hardy souls to do some experimentation with the standard Rotisserie constitution. I updated some archaic rules, closed off some Roto loopholes, and structured the format to better approximate the types of decisions a real general manager might make. And then we took it all out for a test run.

The results were interesting, but since this was undertaken in a laboratory setting, we continued to tinker. What follows is a description of the rules we played with in 2007, but also incorporating some changes we deemed necessary for 2008. A hybrid of the hybrid, I suppose.

I expect that most of you are already familiar with standard Rotisserie rules. The following are the changes we'd make for this Laboratory League...

Teams

As noted last year in these pages, we determined that an optimal league depth would have 75% player pool penetration. So for this experiment, we used a 10-team AL-only league. The smaller player population would also be easier to manage and observe.

Rosters

The Founding Fathers used a 23-man roster. MLB uses a 25-man roster; so this Lab League did too. Rotisserie's roster structure is somewhat artificial. For this league, the only fixed slots are the eight defensive positions (nine with a DH), a four-man rotation and two short relievers. These constitute the 15-man "active roster" and are the only players that accumulate stats.

The remaining 10 roster spots – the bench – are up for grabs. If an owner wants to draft 8 outfielders, that would be his prerogative. If an owner ended up drafting lousy starting pitchers and wanted to stock his bullpen with 10 relievers, he could go nuts.

There are real-world consequences, however. In this league, access to additional talent is far more restrictive than in than typical fantasy leagues. (This is discussed shortly.) So, if your starting 3Bman hits the DL, you'll want to have someone else on your roster to move into that slot. As such, it's probably best to play it like a real GM and make sure you draft depth and have backups at each position. How you structure that bench is up to you.

The Draft

Snake draft? Auction? Each has its positives and negatives. To add a small dose of reality, this league has a financial component, so an auction is used for just the active roster slots. Those are the guys who everyone should have an equal opportunity to buy. If you absolutely need to have Alex Rodriguez, a low snake seeding shouldn't prevent you from having a fair shot at him.

So, you *have to buy* one player each at DH, CA, 1B, 2B, 3B, SS, LF, CF, RF (or just three outfielders), four starting pitchers and two relievers. A total of 150 active players are auctioned off in this 10-team league. In a typical 10-team AL league, the top 150 players should go for about $2375, so to maintain comparable values, each team's budget for this auction is $235.

The 10 bench spots are snake drafted. At this depth of the talent pool, there is little advantage to seeding, so it can be random, at least in the league's first year. The first five players are assigned an arbitrary salary of $4 and the last five a salary of $1. Each team's total roster budget would then be $260. Check.

However, to ensure that active players are priced appropriately, the opening bid in the auction is $5.

Stats/Standings

If our goal is to emulate some level of realism, then the Rotisserie format would probably lose out to some type of head-to-head style of play. Rotisserie7 is a possible compromise, but for this particular experiment, we stuck with Rotisserie. This format offers some interesting strategic and tactical options that provide for a more interesting experience. I know, I'm biased.

The original roto categories were selected by our Founding Fathers because they were easily accessible in the pre-internet days. Accessibility, or perhaps, familiarity, is still important. This league goes with a blend of simplicity and accuracy. 5x5 may be the present norm, but I've always found that you can better value players and manage your roster when there are fewer, but more meaningful, categories. This league is 4x4, using the following categories:

Extra Bases: The allure of HRs is that we can watch our players on SportsCenter and know immediately that we're cashing in some big numbers. Extra bases takes nothing away from that excitement, and in fact, enhances it. Now we can cheer the doubles and triples too. The formula for this category is $(2B + (3B \times 2) + (HR \times 3))$.

Runs Produced: I'm not a fan of using situation-dependent stats to measure individual performance. However, combining Runs and RBIs (actually, R+RBI-HR) gives at least a little credit to those who put themselves in position to help their teams (Runs) and those who take advantage of the opportunities presented them (RBI). One thing I don't like about traditional 5x5 is that we devote two categories to situational stats; using Runs Produced at least lessens the impact.

Net steals: One of the biggest complaints about roto is that it values HR and SB equally. I do think that speed is a component of the game that should be incorporated somehow (and defense too, but that's another story), but giving credit for SB without the penalty for CS is not equitable. This is not perfect, but it's better. If I want to pay for Willie Harris' 17 SBs, I'm going to have to cringe 11 times for each CS.

On base average: Walks are far too valuable to ignore.

Innings pitched: You have to be good to get the chance to run up innings, and so IP seems like the purest way to measure both that and stamina. I suppose that begs the question, "Why not at-bats on the batting side?" I don't know; it didn't seem right.

Net saves: Similar to stolen bases, you can't get credit for the good stuff without also being responsible for the bad. In a 4x4 league, saves tend to hold too much value; netting out the blown saves helps a bit.

(Strikeouts - (HR x 4)): I was tempted to just use strikeouts, or perhaps (strikeouts - walks), but this somewhat convoluted statistic is probably a lot more valuable than it seems. It captures the opposite ends of the spectrum of pitching outcomes – strikeouts and home runs.

How does it look in practice? The top five strikeout artists in 2007 were Jake Peavy (240), Scott Kazmir (239), Johan Santana (235), Erik Bedard (221) and Aaron Harang (218). The top five in this stat were Jake Peavy (188), Scott Kazmir (167), Brandon Webb (146), Erik Bedard (145) and C.C. Sabathia (129). Santana and Harang drop to 13th and 12th respectively. Chris Young jumps from 24th to 6th!

WHIP: Oddly enough, the only category I've chosen to salvage from the original roto rules. This is essentially the pitching side of on base average, so it complements that batting category well.

This unique set of categories wreaked havoc with our valuation systems. HQ analyst Mike Roy – also one of the league participants – noted some interesting findings:

1. Catchers are worth even less in this Lab League than in traditional Roto.

2. Though speed is arguably more valuable in this league (net SB are 25% of hitting), the base stealers consistently are worth less. Lab rewards true run-producers (runs *and* RBI) who hit in the middle of the lineup and get on base. I view this "deflation" of base stealers as more realistic.

3. The "scarce" middle infielders are worth less in Lab than in Roto. As stated above, Lab rewards the all-around hitter, and the middle infielders just don't do enough. The guys who hit for BA, but don't walk or hit for power – they're worthless.

4. There are not too many significant differences in starting pitcher valuation, though the anchor starters who eat innings and strike out batters come out high. Interestingly, the solid relievers are worth more in Lab than in Roto, though this may be expected due to Net Saves being 25% of pitching categories.

Trades

Trades may be made at any time between October 1 and July 31. Between August 1 and September 30, a player must pass through waivers before he can be traded.

MLB trades that send players to the other league have no effect in the current season so long as that player remains on the Lab League team that drafted him. At the conclusion of the season, however, that player must be cut.

Reserve List

In real baseball, there is no such thing. Given that this league uses a small active roster, the bench serves the same purpose as a reserve list.

Free Agents

There is a free agent pool comprised solely of
- players who were not drafted
- players who were cut by other teams
- players called up from the minors who are not already on a farm roster.

MLB players traded into the league, or signed into the league after draft day, are not be available as free agents.

Owners have limited access to this pool. Each owner can claim one player per week, conducted in a draft, in reverse order of the standings. Additional picks in a given week are available only to teams in need of multiple DL replacements. To clarify, in a given week:

If you have no players go on the DL, you can claim one free agent to replace any player.

If you have one player go on the DL, you can claim one free agent to replace him.

If you have two players go on the DL, you can claim two free agents to replace them.

If you have five players go on the DL, you can claim five free agents to replace them.

If you have one player go on the DL and one healthy player you want to replace, you still can only claim one free agent.

Disabled List

There is a disabled list of unlimited size. When an active player goes on the DL, you must replace him by activating someone from your farm or bench, or claiming a free agent. When a bench player goes on the DL, you have the option of replacing him from your farm or claiming a free agent. When the DLed player returns, he must be activated, benched, cut or demoted to farm. If activated or benched, another player must be benched, cut, or demoted to farm.

Farm System

Each team has a 5-man farm system which is snake-drafted after the 25-man roster draft. The only players eligible to be drafted are those in the minors (whether their rookie eligibility is exhausted or not). Farm players can be activated at any time once they are called up by their major league club. In order to fit a farm player on your roster, another player would have to be DLed or cut outright. The only time an activated farm player can be returned to your farm system is if he is demoted by his major league club, or any time prior to him accumulating 50 at bats or 10 innings pitched in the majors.

Continuity

Beyond trying to win each year, teams need to be constructed to create continuity and longevity. So this is a keeper league. There is no limit to how many players you can keep from one year to the next, however, every protected player must be given a $5 salary raise. This is a self-regulating method of ensuring roster turnover each year as it is impossible for any team to keep their entire team intact from one season to the next.

The $4 and $1 bench players may be protected at the same $5 raise and remain as part of the bench, though you must work them in under the $260 cap. The advantage to doing this is to free up active roster spots for other higher-priced players you want to keep, but decreases the amount you can spend on the remaining open active slots.

IV.
MAJOR
LEAGUES

The Teams

The following four pages contain stat boxes for all 30 major league teams plus summary boxes for both leagues. The stats themselves will be mostly familiar to you from the player boxes, however, we have included both batter and pitcher BPIs on each line.

Each team box is divided into three sections.

At Home represents all batting and pitching statistics accumulated by that team in its home ballpark.

Away represents all batting and pitching statistics accumulated by that team in its games on the road.

Opp@ represents all batting and pitching statistics accumulated by all visiting teams when they played at the home ballpark.

Within each section are BPIs from the past three years, 2005-2007. Teams that have changed ballparks during that time may cause some inconsistent data.

To get a sense of ballpark effects, look at both the At Home and Opp@ sections in tandem. If the levels are similar, then it may indicate a particular ballpark tendency. If the levels are not similar, then it may be team dependent. You can compare this data from one team's box to another for additional insight.

As an example, the Cubs's batters have a contact rate at home in the low-to-mid 80%'s but the opposition at Wrigley Field has levels consistently about 5%-7% lower. This could indicate the success of the Chicago pitching staff as opposed to any park effects.

In contrast, Milwaukee's At Home and Opp@ contact rates are both in the high 70%'s, which might be more telling of Miller Park park effects.

In the pitching section of each chart, we also show the number of wins (W) each team had, the Pythagorean projected wins (Py) they should have had based on their runs scored and runs allowed, and the percentage of save opportunities successfully converted. For those who had been following Arizona's negative run differential in support of their divisional title, you can see how many

games they *should* have won. This 90-win team's Pythagorean win total was a meager 79.

The save opportunities data are interesting. We don't typically consider that a closer's success might hinge on the friendliness of his environment. However, look at teams like Boston and the White Sox. In 2005-2006, Opposing relief pitchers visiting Fenway and U.S. Cellular converted barely 50% of their opportunities while the home-team arms were as much as 20% more successful. That phenomenon corrected itself a bit in 2007. The reverse was true in Baltimore where visiting bullpens have been out-pitching the Orioles' relievers over the past two years. And look at the K.C. Royals... At home in 2007, opposing bullpens shut down the Royals late-inning offense 93% of the time!

Other things to look at include a team's SX and SBO rates, which provide insight into which teams are easier or more difficult to run on. Note that opposing teams visiting MIN ran under 10% of the time with SX rates far below league average. Compare that to the opposition coming into Coors Field, which ran just as frequently but with much greater success.

Some other interesting tidbits...

There are wider home/road splits for pitchers than for batters. You find much larger variances between Home and Away BPVs than you do for RC/G.

Opposing pitchers have a horrible time in Fenway Park, posting a 5.61 ERA there the past three years. In 2007, even opposing xERA broke through the 5.00 barrier, making the Sox one of only two teams whose offense so brutalizes opposing pitchers at home. The other team? The Yankees.

Home runs per fly ball tend to regress to 10%, but there are a few ballparks where the base rate has been consistently higher over the past three years, including Atlanta, Cincinnati, Colorado, Houston, Philadelphia and Toronto. As you'd expect, consistent sub-10% rates can be found in places like Anaheim, Pittsburgh, San Diego, Seattle, San Francisco and Washington.

BATTING / PITCHING

ARI	Yr	Avg	OB	Slg	OPS	bb%	ct%	h%	Eye	G	L	F	PX	SX	SBO	xBA	RC/G	W	Py	Sv%	ERA	WHIP	H%	S%	xERA	Ctl	Dom	Cmd	hr/f	hr/9	BPV
At Home	05	258	330	427	758	10	81	29	0.57	45	20	35	108	96	5%	277	4.90	36	28	66%	5.27	1.51	32%	67%	4.45	3.5	6.3	1.8	13%	1.2	38
	06	283	342	461	803	8	84	31	0.57	46	20	35	114	105	7%	293	5.42	39	38	64%	4.81	1.45	31%	70%	4.06	3.5	6.9	2.0	13%	1.2	46
	07	260	331	445	776	10	81	29	0.56	41	18	41	119	124	10%	276	5.15	50	42	70%	4.11	1.39	30%	73%	3.80	3.4	6.5	1.9	10%	1.1	50
Away	05	254	328	415	743	10	80	29	0.54	45	20	34	109	83	7%	275	4.73	41	38	80%	4.45	1.40	31%	71%	3.83	3.1	6.5	2.1	13%	1.2	48
	06	251	312	388	701	8	82	28	0.48	43	19	38	92	101	8%	260	4.15	37	42	62%	4.16	1.34	31%	70%	3.88	3.1	6.9	2.2	9%	0.8	65
	07	241	305	382	687	8	78	28	0.41	41	17	42	98	111	9%	245	3.95	40	37	88%	4.17	1.38	30%	72%	3.79	3.4	7.1	2.1	10%	1.0	57
Opp @ ARI	05	284	349	470	819	9	82	32	0.56	46	22	32	122	110	7%	302	5.65	45	53	58%	3.96	1.40	29%	76%	3.47	3.7	6.6	1.8	13%	1.2	43
	06	273	340	453	793	9	80	31	0.51	47	20	33	117	110	8%	287	5.33	42	43	60%	4.55	1.46	31%	71%	4.08	3.2	5.6	1.8	10%	1.1	36
	07	265	332	427	759	9	81	30	0.52	43	19	38	106	94	8%	268	4.90	31	39	67%	4.75	1.38	29%	68%	4.46	3.6	6.4	1.8	10%	1.2	44

ATL	Yr	Avg	OB	Slg	OPS	bb%	ct%	h%	Eye	G	L	F	PX	SX	SBO	xBA	RC/G	W	Py	Sv%	ERA	WHIP	H%	S%	xERA	Ctl	Dom	Cmd	hr/f	hr/9	BPV
At Home	05	284	352	462	814	10	81	32	0.55	43	23	34	118	121	9%	294	5.62	53	49	69%	3.82	1.33	29%	73%	3.61	3.0	5.7	1.9	9%	0.8	54
	06	280	342	457	800	9	80	32	0.46	42	22	36	118	84	5%	280	5.37	40	43	59%	4.33	1.41	31%	73%	3.70	3.2	7.1	2.2	13%	1.2	54
	07	266	335	416	751	9	79	31	0.50	45	19	36	100	97	6%	263	4.80	44	42	75%	3.96	1.34	29%	74%	3.66	3.4	7.0	2.0	11%	1.1	57
Away	05	247	309	409	718	8	80	28	0.44	46	19	35	107	97	8%	270	4.32	37	41	55%	4.16	1.45	30%	74%	3.68	3.5	5.8	1.7	12%	1.0	39
	06	261	324	453	777	9	79	29	0.44	45	19	36	126	94	6%	279	5.06	39	42	54%	4.87	1.51	31%	70%	4.37	3.9	6.0	1.5	11%	1.1	35
	07	282	339	452	790	8	80	33	0.43	43	19	38	116	93	6%	272	5.24	40	46	67%	4.27	1.38	30%	72%	3.83	3.2	6.7	2.1	11%	1.1	53
Opp @ ATL	05	262	321	390	711	8	83	30	0.52	48	22	31	85	92	8%	275	4.30	28	32	50%	5.21	1.52	32%	68%	4.47	3.7	6.7	1.8	12%	1.2	42
	06	271	333	433	765	8	80	31	0.46	44	22	33	107	106	9%	280	4.93	41	38	71%	4.79	1.47	32%	71%	4.04	3.3	7.2	2.2	13%	1.3	49
	07	254	323	407	730	9	79	29	0.49	44	19	37	100	113	9%	262	4.54	37	39	61%	4.41	1.43	31%	72%	3.95	3.6	7.1	2.0	11%	1.1	55

BAL	Yr	Avg	OB	Slg	OPS	bb%	ct%	h%	Eye	G	L	F	PX	SX	SBO	xBA	RC/G	W	Py	Sv%	ERA	WHIP	H%	S%	xERA	Ctl	Dom	Cmd	hr/f	hr/9	BPV
At Home	05	263	328	427	755	9	85	28	0.64	42	19	38	96	83	7%	272	4.85	36	35	73%	4.22	1.39	29%	72%	3.87	3.7	6.6	1.8	11%	1.1	48
	06	290	344	454	798	8	86	31	0.57	43	20	36	96	109	10%	283	5.27	40	41	55%	4.73	1.47	30%	71%	4.09	3.6	6.2	1.7	13%	1.3	35
	07	280	338	430	768	8	84	31	0.57	44	17	38	90	107	12%	264	4.97	35	33	48%	5.38	1.54	31%	66%	4.91	4.2	6.5	1.5	9%	1.0	40
Away	05	274	318	441	759	6	83	30	0.38	43	21	36	104	101	10%	281	4.73	38	39	61%	4.93	1.47	31%	69%	4.19	3.6	6.7	1.9	13%	1.2	43
	06	265	323	393	717	8	83	30	0.51	46	19	35	82	97	10%	263	4.37	30	29	72%	6.02	1.63	32%	65%	5.11	4.2	6.7	1.6	13%	1.4	26
	07	264	324	395	719	8	82	30	0.50	44	18	38	87	108	12%	257	4.42	34	38	61%	4.99	1.50	30%	68%	4.57	4.5	7.2	1.6	10%	1.0	49
Opp @ BAL	05	256	328	395	724	10	81	29	0.56	46	19	35	86	91	8%	256	4.47	45	46	73%	4.03	1.39	28%	75%	3.79	3.4	5.2	1.6	11%	1.2	30
	06	277	345	442	787	9	82	31	0.57	44	20	36	99	81	9%	273	5.22	41	40	71%	4.91	1.49	31%	70%	4.29	2.9	5.2	1.8	12%	1.3	26
	07	276	354	423	777	11	82	31	0.65	45	17	38	93	98	7%	258	5.22	46	48	72%	4.64	1.44	31%	70%	4.34	3.1	5.5	1.8	9%	1.0	38

BOS	Yr	Avg	OB	Slg	OPS	bb%	ct%	h%	Eye	G	L	F	PX	SX	SBO	xBA	RC/G	W	Py	Sv%	ERA	WHIP	H%	S%	xERA	Ctl	Dom	Cmd	hr/f	hr/9	BPV
At Home	05	280	360	459	819	11	81	32	0.67	42	23	35	116	100	3%	289	5.77	54	48	70%	4.46	1.37	31%	69%	4.12	2.8	6.2	2.2	9%	1.0	54
	06	285	360	448	808	10	82	32	0.65	41	20	39	106	72	3%	271	5.61	48	42	65%	4.70	1.41	32%	68%	4.27	3.0	6.8	2.2	9%	0.9	60
	07	297	376	465	841	11	82	34	0.71	41	18	40	108	116	7%	271	6.08	51	51	79%	4.13	1.30	31%	70%	4.00	2.7	7.0	2.6	8%	0.9	73
Away	05	281	351	450	801	10	82	31	0.59	41	23	36	104	86	3%	279	5.43	41	42	63%	5.04	1.41	31%	66%	4.55	2.7	5.9	2.2	10%	1.1	47
	06	253	335	422	757	11	80	28	0.62	39	20	41	105	82	6%	262	4.93	38	39	69%	4.97	1.48	31%	70%	4.24	3.3	6.6	2.0	13%	1.4	39
	07	262	341	424	764	11	81	30	0.62	42	18	40	103	102	7%	260	5.07	45	50	81%	3.60	1.24	28%	75%	3.50	3.3	7.4	2.2	10%	1.0	67
Opp @ BOS	05	269	324	436	759	7	83	30	0.46	43	21	36	108	109	8%	284	4.86	27	33	57%	5.68	1.62	32%	67%	4.89	4.5	6.7	1.5	12%	1.2	33
	06	274	332	432	764	8	81	32	0.45	44	20	35	106	111	8%	276	4.94	33	39	45%	5.28	1.60	32%	68%	4.78	4.2	6.4	1.5	9%	1.1	36
	07	261	315	407	721	7	80	31	0.39	43	17	40	99	97	8%	254	4.38	30	30	63%	5.86	1.72	34%	67%	5.23	4.6	6.5	1.4	9%	1.0	32

CHW	Yr	Avg	OB	Slg	OPS	bb%	ct%	h%	Eye	G	L	F	PX	SX	SBO	xBA	RC/G	W	Py	Sv%	ERA	WHIP	H%	S%	xERA	Ctl	Dom	Cmd	hr/f	hr/9	BPV
At Home	05	257	315	442	756	8	82	28	0.46	43	20	37	110	98	16%	279	4.73	47	43	73%	3.82	1.28	28%	74%	3.43	2.9	6.4	2.2	13%	1.2	53
	06	281	342	480	822	8	82	30	0.51	42	20	38	118	91	9%	284	5.55	49	46	70%	4.43	1.36	30%	72%	3.92	2.8	6.3	2.2	12%	1.3	45
	07	247	316	419	735	9	80	27	0.51	43	18	40	104	80	10%	257	4.55	38	32	70%	4.94	1.43	32%	67%	4.39	2.9	6.4	2.2	10%	1.1	51
Away	05	267	317	409	727	7	82	30	0.41	45	21	35	87	96	13%	267	4.37	52	48	75%	3.39	1.23	28%	75%	3.39	2.7	6.3	2.3	8%	0.9	67
	06	280	336	448	785	8	81	32	0.44	42	20	38	105	94	10%	269	5.13	41	41	76%	4.82	1.36	31%	67%	4.36	2.5	6.3	2.5	10%	1.1	55
	07	246	311	390	701	9	78	29	0.42	45	17	37	95	87	7%	245	4.14	34	35	60%	4.60	1.42	30%	70%	4.30	3.3	6.2	1.9	9%	1.1	45
Opp @ CHW	05	254	313	412	725	8	81	28	0.45	44	22	34	96	101	11%	275	4.38	34	38	50%	4.47	1.29	27%	70%	3.91	2.9	6.2	2.2	15%	1.5	43
	06	268	322	440	763	7	82	29	0.45	43	18	39	104	108	10%	269	4.82	32	35	50%	5.47	1.47	30%	68%	4.46	3.3	6.4	2.0	16%	1.7	26
	07	282	337	437	774	8	82	32	0.45	44	19	37	97	102	8%	266	4.99	43	49	60%	4.26	1.32	27%	73%	3.83	3.5	6.8	2.0	13%	1.4	45

CHC	Yr	Avg	OB	Slg	OPS	bb%	ct%	h%	Eye	G	L	F	PX	SX	SBO	xBA	RC/G	W	Py	Sv%	ERA	WHIP	H%	S%	xERA	Ctl	Dom	Cmd	hr/f	hr/9	BPV
At Home	05	271	321	447	768	7	84	29	0.45	44	21	35	112	92	8%	293	4.87	38	40	55%	4.04	1.32	29%	73%	3.48	3.5	7.9	2.3	14%	1.2	66
	06	279	327	440	767	7	84	31	0.44	47	20	33	102	116	12%	286	4.88	36	35	60%	4.68	1.35	29%	70%	3.94	3.8	8.5	2.2	15%	1.5	57
	07	278	340	439	779	9	81	32	0.49	45	19	36	110	109	8%	275	5.15	44	44	75%	4.19	1.35	30%	72%	3.98	3.6	7.7	2.1	9%	1.0	65
Away	05	268	320	433	754	7	83	29	0.46	45	21	34	107	79	7%	286	4.73	41	40	74%	4.36	1.37	30%	71%	3.77	3.7	7.8	2.1	13%	1.2	60
	06	256	305	405	710	7	83	28	0.41	47	19	34	92	111	13%	271	4.17	30	34	67%	4.81	1.55	31%	71%	4.38	4.8	7.1	1.5	10%	1.1	44
	07	265	321	404	725	8	82	30	0.46	45	19	36	95	93	8%	267	4.45	41	43	72%	3.89	1.29	28%	73%	3.73	3.5	7.4	2.1	10%	1.0	64
Opp @ CHC	05	247	316	405	722	9	77	29	0.44	46	21	33	109	89	10%	268	4.42	43	41	55%	4.30	1.33	29%	72%	3.80	2.6	5.7	2.2	13%	1.3	43
	06	244	321	441	762	10	75	28	0.46	43	18	39	132	121	10%	267	4.96	45	46	63%	4.36	1.37	31%	71%	3.88	2.5	5.7	2.3	11%	1.0	50
	07	251	322	408	730	10	77	30	0.47	41	18	42	110	113	11%	254	4.57	37	37	61%	4.61	1.47	32%	71%	4.06	3.4	6.9	2.0	10%	1.1	51

CIN	Yr	Avg	OB	Slg	OPS	bb%	ct%	h%	Eye	G	L	F	PX	SX	SBO	xBA	RC/G	W	Py	Sv%	ERA	WHIP	H%	S%	xERA	Ctl	Dom	Cmd	hr/f	hr/9	BPV
At Home	05	268	340	472	812	10	78	30	0.49	42	22	36	138	94	6%	290	5.56	42	40	71%	5.16	1.50	32%	69%	4.29	2.9	6.2	2.1	13%	1.4	34
	06	271	350	459	809	11	78	30	0.56	43	19	38	122	94	10%	274	5.54	42	38	58%	4.78	1.38	31%	70%	4.10	2.8	6.9	2.5	13%	1.4	50
	07	265	333	456	789	9	80	29	0.51	40	19	41	124	105	7%	275	5.24	39	39	48%	4.94	1.37	30%	67%	4.39	2.8	6.7	2.4	12%	1.4	49
Away	05	254	329	422	750	10	75	31	0.45	45	22	33	119	94	7%	272	4.85	31	35	61%	5.19	1.50	31%	68%	4.57	3.2	5.8	1.8	11%	1.3	31
	06	244	314	407	721	9	78	28	0.47	44	19	37	112	100	11%	267	4.43	38	38	62%	4.28	1.44	31%	74%	3.73	3.0	6.2	2.1	11%	1.2	43
	07	269	328	418	746	8	80	31	0.45	44	19	37	99	96	10%	262	4.68	33	36	61%	4.98	1.51	33%	69%	4.41	3.2	6.6	2.1	10%	1.1	47
Opp @ CIN	05	294	347	495	842	8	83	32	0.48	42	21	37	131	103	7%	300	5.81	39	42	62%	5.28	1.47	31%	68%	4.25	3.8	7.8	2.0	16%	1.6	42
	06	273	327	460	788	7	80	31	0.41	41	20	39	123	73	5%	277	5.12	39	43	60%	4.84	1.51	30%	73%	3.95	4.2	7.5	1.8	16%	1.6	35
	07	272	326	455	781	7	81	30	0.42	40	18	42	120	97	8%	272	5.05	42	42	67%	4.90	1.42	30%	70%	4.26	3.6	7.0	2.0	13%	1.5	41

CLE	Yr	Avg	OB	Slg	OPS	bb%	ct%	h%	Eye	G	L	F	PX	SX	SBO	xBA	RC/G	W	Py	Sv%	ERA	WHIP	H%	S%	xERA	Ctl	Dom	Cmd	hr/f	hr/9	BPV
At Home	05	267	333	437	770	9	81	30	0.52	45	20	34	110	79	6%	278	5.04	43	48	82%	3.32	1.16	27%	75%	3.16	2.3	6.5	2.8	11%	1.0	77
	06	280	349	458	807	10	78	33	0.49	41	21	38	118	91	4%	273	5.55	44	47	58%	4.05	1.36	31%	72%	3.72	2.7	6.1	2.2	9%	0.9	57
	07	277	348	444	792	10	79	32	0.53	42	19	40	106	93	7%	259	5.33	49	44	74%	4.25	1.35	33%	70%	3.83	2.5	7.3	2.8	9%	0.9	77
Away	05	276	329	467	797	7	80	31	0.41	44	20	36	118	94	8%	282	5.25	50	48	74%	3.91	1.29	29%	73%	3.65	2.8	6.5	2.3	10%	1.0	61
	06	281	342	456	798	8	79	33	0.43	43	20	37	114	98	6%	271	5.36	34	42	46%	4.84	1.47	32%	70%	4.22	2.7	5.9	2.2	11%	1.2	42
	07	260	327	411	737	9	78	31	0.45	40	19	41	102	86	7%	249	4.66	44	45	79%	3.92	1.29	29%	72%	3.83	2.5	5.6	2.3	9%	0.9	55
Opp @ CLE	05	240	289	378	667	6	81	27	0.35	45	21	33	89	88	10%	265	3.61	38	33	81%	4.33	1.42	30%	73%	3.78	3.5	6.8	1.9	12%	1.2	47
	06	273	325	408	733	7	83	31	0.45	46	21	34	85	105	12%	268	4.49	37	34	71%	5.21	1.52	33%	68%	4.45	3.8	7.6	2.0	12%	1.2	50
	07	274	323	409	731	7	79	32	0.35	46	19	35	90	83	9%	252	4.44	28	33	60%	5.08	1.52	32%	69%	4.39	3.9	7.4	1.9	12%	1.3	45

BATTING | PITCHING

COL	Yr	Avg	OB	Slg	OPS	bb%	ct%	h%	Eye	G	L	F	PX	SX	SBO	xBA	RC/G	W	Py	Sv%	ERA	WHIP	H%	S%	xERA	Ctl	Dom	Cmd	hr/f	hr/9	BPV
At Home	05	300	362	460	822	9	82	34	0.55	43	25	32	104	109	6%	294	5.67	40	41	58%	5.19	1.57	33%	68%	4.41	3.6	6.2	1.7	11%	1.0	39
	06	294	362	459	821	10	82	34	0.60	45	23	32	107	117	9%	292	5.74	44	44	55%	4.72	1.47	31%	70%	4.09	3.4	5.9	1.8	12%	1.1	38
	07	298	369	480	849	10	82	34	0.61	43	22	35	118	109	7%	292	6.06	51	48	64%	4.34	1.36	30%	70%	4.02	2.8	5.6	2.0	10%	1.0	48
Away	05	232	293	359	652	8	78	28	0.39	45	20	35	88	81	6%	248	3.50	27	28	59%	5.08	1.54	31%	69%	4.51	4.1	6.3	1.5	11%	1.2	33
	06	247	312	408	720	9	78	29	0.43	42	19	38	111	96	9%	263	4.41	32	36	60%	4.60	1.43	31%	69%	4.47	3.5	5.9	1.7	7%	0.8	48
	07	261	332	395	727	10	78	31	0.48	44	20	37	94	110	8%	254	4.55	39	42	53%	4.29	1.36	29%	71%	4.04	3.4	6.2	1.8	10%	1.0	48
Opp @ COL	05	295	359	457	816	9	83	33	0.58	46	23	31	108	103	7%	297	5.63	41	40	67%	5.36	1.61	34%	68%	4.44	3.5	6.4	1.8	12%	1.1	38
	06	282	345	454	800	9	83	31	0.57	48	20	32	110	115	8%	292	5.40	37	37	71%	5.41	1.57	33%	66%	4.72	3.8	6.3	1.7	10%	1.0	41
	07	274	327	438	765	7	84	30	0.49	46	19	35	106	116	7%	287	4.92	31	34	52%	5.68	1.65	34%	68%	4.70	4.1	6.6	1.6	13%	1.3	30

DET	Yr	Avg	OB	Slg	OPS	bb%	ct%	h%	Eye	G	L	F	PX	SX	SBO	xBA	RC/G	W	Py	Sv%	ERA	WHIP	H%	S%	xERA	Ctl	Dom	Cmd	hr/f	hr/9	BPV
At Home	05	277	324	442	766	6	82	31	0.40	44	20	36	97	106	4%	274	4.84	39	39	67%	4.07	1.36	30%	73%	3.76	2.9	5.8	2.0	10%	1.0	47
	06	273	325	424	749	7	81	31	0.41	43	19	37	94	97	6%	261	4.68	46	45	72%	3.92	1.33	29%	73%	3.70	3.0	6.1	2.0	10%	1.0	52
	07	287	345	475	819	8	82	32	0.50	40	21	39	113	127	9%	283	5.59	45	43	64%	4.65	1.43	30%	70%	4.29	3.5	6.4	1.8	10%	1.1	46
Away	05	266	313	415	727	6	81	31	0.35	45	20	35	96	98	9%	265	4.37	32	36	63%	5.01	1.38	29%	67%	4.34	2.9	5.5	1.9	14%	1.4	32
	06	276	327	472	799	7	79	31	0.35	41	19	40	123	93	8%	270	5.25	49	51	76%	3.78	1.31	29%	74%	3.52	3.1	6.4	2.1	10%	1.0	56
	07	286	338	442	779	7	81	33	0.41	43	19	38	102	109	8%	267	5.08	43	46	72%	4.51	1.43	30%	71%	4.08	3.6	6.6	1.9	11%	1.1	47
Opp @ DET	05	270	327	419	746	8	83	30	0.50	45	19	35	89	80	6%	265	4.67	42	42	71%	4.09	1.35	31%	73%	3.64	2.4	6.2	2.5	11%	1.1	56
	06	259	318	404	722	8	82	29	0.50	46	19	35	89	85	6%	262	4.41	35	36	59%	4.53	1.37	31%	69%	4.12	2.7	6.6	2.4	10%	1.0	60
	07	268	334	431	765	9	82	30	0.54	44	18	38	100	103	7%	266	4.99	36	38	74%	5.36	1.50	32%	66%	4.69	3.1	6.3	2.0	11%	1.3	39

FLA	Yr	Avg	OB	Slg	OPS	bb%	ct%	h%	Eye	G	L	F	PX	SX	SBO	xBA	RC/G	W	Py	Sv%	ERA	WHIP	H%	S%	xERA	Ctl	Dom	Cmd	hr/f	hr/9	BPV
At Home	05	269	340	398	737	10	82	31	0.60	43	22	34	86	94	7%	270	4.72	45	41	78%	3.83	1.34	31%	72%	3.68	3.4	7.6	2.2	7%	0.6	77
	06	258	326	427	754	9	77	31	0.44	44	19	37	116	105	11%	264	4.87	42	39	63%	4.07	1.43	31%	74%	3.81	3.9	7.3	1.9	9%	1.0	57
	07	271	333	466	800	9	76	32	0.40	40	20	40	134	115	9%	271	5.41	36	36	58%	4.80	1.58	34%	71%	4.30	4.4	7.9	1.8	9%	0.9	56
Away	05	276	329	420	750	7	85	31	0.51	45	23	32	95	105	11%	291	4.74	38	38	61%	4.56	1.47	32%	70%	4.18	3.6	6.4	1.8	9%	0.8	51
	06	270	324	442	766	7	78	32	0.36	44	20	37	118	112	12%	271	4.91	36	41	58%	4.69	1.48	30%	71%	4.25	3.9	6.4	1.6	11%	1.1	39
	07	263	326	431	756	8	76	32	0.39	40	19	41	118	109	10%	257	4.86	35	36	67%	5.13	1.58	32%	70%	4.45	3.8	6.3	1.7	11%	1.3	31
Opp @ FLA	05	257	325	383	708	9	77	32	0.45	46	22	33	90	116	11%	259	4.33	36	40	58%	4.12	1.43	31%	72%	3.99	3.7	6.2	1.7	8%	0.7	52
	06	262	337	415	752	10	79	31	0.54	41	20	39	102	90	7%	259	4.90	39	42	74%	4.15	1.37	31%	73%	3.70	3.5	7.9	2.3	11%	1.1	66
	07	280	361	431	792	11	78	34	0.56	41	21	38	107	112	9%	262	5.48	45	45	71%	4.70	1.41	32%	71%	3.97	3.2	8.2	2.5	13%	1.4	62

HOU	Yr	Avg	OB	Slg	OPS	bb%	ct%	h%	Eye	G	L	F	PX	SX	SBO	xBA	RC/G	W	Py	Sv%	ERA	WHIP	H%	S%	xERA	Ctl	Dom	Cmd	hr/f	hr/9	BPV
At Home	05	271	334	436	771	9	82	30	0.52	43	20	37	104	116	12%	275	5.00	53	51	87%	3.08	1.13	27%	77%	2.82	2.4	7.3	3.0	12%	1.0	87
	06	254	328	430	758	10	81	28	0.57	42	19	40	114	89	5%	270	4.91	44	41	72%	4.03	1.27	29%	72%	3.58	2.7	7.2	2.6	12%	1.1	69
	07	266	333	422	755	9	82	30	0.56	43	18	39	100	101	6%	265	4.86	42	40	48%	4.05	1.33	31%	74%	3.53	2.9	7.7	2.6	12%	1.3	65
Away	05	242	299	381	681	8	80	28	0.41	44	19	37	96	98	11%	260	3.88	36	40	68%	3.98	1.33	30%	73%	3.56	3.1	7.2	2.3	11%	1.0	66
	06	256	325	390	714	9	80	29	0.52	45	19	36	89	94	10%	256	4.36	38	42	68%	4.16	1.33	29%	72%	3.78	3.2	7.0	2.2	11%	1.1	59
	07	254	319	403	722	9	81	29	0.49	44	17	39	100	77	7%	255	4.42	31	33	72%	5.42	1.51	31%	66%	4.77	3.4	5.9	1.8	11%	1.3	32
Opp @ HOU	05	233	285	369	654	7	78	27	0.33	48	20	31	91	78	8%	258	3.43	28	30	78%	4.34	1.41	30%	73%	3.87	3.3	6.3	1.9	12%	1.2	43
	06	255	310	419	729	7	79	29	0.38	46	20	35	110	96	7%	272	4.43	37	40	59%	4.43	1.36	28%	71%	4.13	3.7	6.5	1.8	12%	1.2	43
	07	262	319	439	758	8	78	30	0.38	44	16	40	120	98	8%	261	4.81	39	41	63%	4.26	1.40	30%	72%	4.07	3.4	6.1	1.8	9%	1.0	45

KC	Yr	Avg	OB	Slg	OPS	bb%	ct%	h%	Eye	G	L	F	PX	SX	SBO	xBA	RC/G	W	Py	Sv%	ERA	WHIP	H%	S%	xERA	Ctl	Dom	Cmd	hr/f	hr/9	BPV
At Home	05	269	324	395	719	8	84	31	0.49	46	20	34	82	93	6%	264	4.41	34	32	74%	5.21	1.51	32%	66%	4.74	3.4	5.8	1.7	9%	1.0	39
	06	289	348	437	785	8	81	34	0.49	47	20	32	97	104	6%	276	5.23	34	35	59%	5.68	1.62	31%	67%	4.97	4.1	5.4	1.3	12%	1.3	20
	07	267	321	403	724	7	82	31	0.44	46	20	34	89	105	7%	267	4.46	35	36	76%	4.61	1.47	32%	70%	4.29	3.3	6.1	1.9	9%	1.0	46
Away	05	256	307	397	704	7	80	30	0.36	44	20	37	90	85	6%	256	4.10	22	28	40%	5.95	1.64	33%	66%	4.98	4.0	6.0	1.5	12%	1.3	23
	06	254	308	385	693	7	81	29	0.42	48	19	33	86	92	7%	262	4.05	28	28	49%	5.66	1.59	32%	67%	4.87	3.9	6.0	1.5	12%	1.4	22
	07	256	309	373	682	7	79	31	0.37	48	18	33	78	103	10%	246	3.87	34	38	59%	4.39	1.41	30%	72%	4.05	3.3	6.3	1.9	10%	1.1	45
Opp @ KC	05	285	348	445	793	9	84	32	0.59	44	20	36	101	87	6%	278	5.34	47	49	62%	4.07	1.34	30%	70%	4.04	2.8	5.7	2.0	7%	0.6	59
	06	294	367	477	844	10	85	32	0.76	44	21	36	112	87	5%	293	6.02	47	46	72%	4.80	1.50	33%	69%	4.22	3.2	6.6	2.0	9%	0.8	55
	07	283	343	450	794	8	83	32	0.53	41	20	39	111	92	6%	278	5.34	46	45	93%	4.29	1.32	31%	68%	4.20	2.7	6.2	2.3	7%	0.6	68

LA	Yr	Avg	OB	Slg	OPS	bb%	ct%	h%	Eye	G	L	F	PX	SX	SBO	xBA	RC/G	W	Py	Sv%	ERA	WHIP	H%	S%	xERA	Ctl	Dom	Cmd	hr/f	hr/9	BPV
At Home	05	248	325	399	724	10	80	28	0.58	46	21	34	102	82	7%	272	4.52	40	41	75%	3.94	1.24	28%	72%	3.58	2.7	6.8	2.5	12%	1.1	66
	06	293	369	463	831	11	84	32	0.74	42	21	37	108	116	12%	286	5.90	49	47	71%	4.11	1.37	31%	72%	3.73	3.2	7.1	2.2	10%	0.9	63
	07	277	344	407	750	9	84	31	0.65	48	18	34	82	109	13%	266	4.83	43	41	72%	4.24	1.34	32%	70%	3.89	3.0	7.8	2.5	9%	0.9	77
Away	05	258	317	392	708	8	80	30	0.42	42	22	36	92	87	6%	261	4.23	31	34	63%	4.86	1.44	30%	69%	4.28	3.3	5.8	1.8	12%	1.2	36
	06	260	324	404	727	9	82	30	0.53	46	19	36	93	124	9%	269	4.55	39	40	61%	4.35	1.39	31%	70%	3.96	2.9	6.1	2.1	10%	0.9	53
	07	273	328	405	732	8	85	30	0.54	44	19	37	86	102	10%	269	4.57	39	41	71%	4.16	1.37	30%	72%	3.82	3.4	6.9	2.0	10%	0.9	59
Opp @ LA	05	250	305	406	710	7	80	28	0.39	47	18	34	105	100	11%	269	4.19	41	40	71%	4.07	1.36	28%	73%	3.75	3.8	6.7	1.7	11%	1.0	51
	06	265	326	408	734	8	80	31	0.45	48	17	35	99	106	12%	261	4.56	32	34	74%	5.36	1.63	32%	69%	4.78	4.3	5.8	1.4	10%	1.1	26
	07	263	323	394	717	8	77	32	0.39	45	19	36	93	93	10%	250	4.33	38	40	71%	4.50	1.48	31%	71%	4.20	3.5	5.5	1.5	9%	0.9	38

LAA	Yr	Avg	OB	Slg	OPS	bb%	ct%	h%	Eye	G	L	F	PX	SX	SBO	xBA	RC/G	W	Py	Sv%	ERA	WHIP	H%	S%	xERA	Ctl	Dom	Cmd	hr/f	hr/9	BPV
At Home	05	268	324	406	730	8	85	29	0.55	44	19	37	83	112	15%	267	4.51	49	46	80%	3.46	1.23	29%	75%	3.44	2.6	6.9	2.7	8%	0.9	76
	06	279	339	418	757	8	84	31	0.55	44	18	38	87	103	13%	266	4.86	45	43	81%	3.76	1.27	30%	73%	3.64	2.7	7.2	2.7	8%	0.9	78
	07	305	368	445	813	9	85	34	0.66	47	17	36	89	109	12%	268	5.61	54	51	68%	3.85	1.32	31%	73%	3.80	2.9	7.1	2.5	7%	0.8	72
Away	05	273	324	412	736	7	85	30	0.50	42	22	36	85	110	14%	275	4.55	46	47	72%	3.90	1.32	30%	74%	3.61	2.9	7.0	2.4	10%	1.1	64
	06	270	326	432	757	8	84	30	0.51	45	20	36	99	110	14%	279	4.82	44	42	77%	4.33	1.32	29%	70%	4.03	3.2	7.2	2.3	10%	1.1	62
	07	263	319	393	712	8	83	30	0.50	47	18	35	83	97	13%	260	4.29	39	37	88%	4.64	1.41	32%	69%	4.11	3.0	7.5	2.5	10%	1.0	65
Opp @ LAA	05	247	300	387	686	7	80	29	0.37	41	19	40	91	81	8%	250	3.90	32	35	66%	4.38	1.37	30%	70%	4.25	2.9	5.3	1.8	8%	0.9	43
	06	257	310	392	702	7	79	30	0.37	42	19	39	90	91	9%	247	4.10	36	38	71%	4.38	1.45	31%	71%	4.18	3.2	5.8	1.8	8%	0.9	45
	07	260	316	397	713	8	80	31	0.41	42	17	41	92	101	10%	246	4.28	27	30	64%	5.43	1.62	34%	66%	4.96	3.6	5.4	1.5	7%	0.8	35

MIL	Yr	Avg	OB	Slg	OPS	bb%	ct%	h%	Eye	G	L	F	PX	SX	SBO	xBA	RC/G	W	Py	Sv%	ERA	WHIP	H%	S%	xERA	Ctl	Dom	Cmd	hr/f	hr/9	BPV
At Home	05	259	329	433	762	9	79	30	0.49	42	22	36	118	98	7%	279	4.95	46	45	66%	3.76	1.27	28%	74%	3.49	3.5	7.7	2.2	11%	1.1	67
	06	260	329	438	767	9	77	30	0.46	41	19	40	123	101	7%	267	5.02	48	39	71%	4.46	1.31	30%	68%	4.12	3.2	7.7	2.5	10%	1.0	72
	07	268	333	476	809	9	80	30	0.48	41	17	41	137	113	10%	280	5.48	51	47	81%	4.06	1.32	30%	72%	3.78	3.2	7.6	2.3	10%	1.0	67
Away	05	260	321	414	735	8	79	30	0.43	44	22	34	109	86	9%	275	4.57	35	39	72%	4.21	1.44	31%	73%	3.85	3.6	7.0	1.9	10%	1.0	53
	06	256	312	403	715	8	77	30	0.36	44	20	36	103	78	8%	259	4.26	27	32	55%	5.22	1.46	31%	66%	4.59	3.3	6.7	2.0	11%	1.2	45
	07	256	314	437	750	8	79	29	0.41	41	19	40	116	106	8%	268	4.69	32	37	61%	4.85	1.48	34%	69%	4.36	3.1	7.0	2.3	9%	1.0	59
Opp @ MIL	05	235	308	390	697	10	77	27	0.46	42	21	37	107	84	9%	261	4.13	35	36	76%	4.57	1.38	30%	70%	4.05	3.6	7.3	2.1	12%	1.2	55
	06	251	314	412	725	8	77	30	0.41	43	19	38	113	113	9%	264	4.47	33	42	52%	4.54	1.39	30%	71%	4.02	3.6	7.8	2.2	12%	1.3	58
	07	252	316	401	717	9	78	30	0.43	42	18	40	104	95	8%	253	4.33	30	34	74%	5.23	1.43	30%	68%	4.46	3.4	7.2	2.1	14%	1.6	41

		BATTING																PITCHING													
MIN	Yr	Avg	OB	Slg	OPS	bb%	ct%	h%	Eye	G	L	F	PX	SX	SBO	xBA	RC/G	W	Py	Sv%	ERA	WHIP	H%	S%	xERA	Ctl	Dom	Cmd	hr/f	hr/9	BPV
At Home	05	264	324	399	723	8	82	30	0.48	50	20	31	85	100	10%	266	4.43	45	42	73%	3.62	1.16	28%	72%	3.46	1.8	6.1	3.3	10%	1.0	82
	06	298	351	439	790	8	84	33	0.52	45	23	32	84	106	8%	281	5.21	54	52	95%	3.40	1.16	30%	74%	3.17	1.8	7.5	4.1	10%	1.0	106
	07	263	326	376	702	9	85	29	0.64	50	18	33	70	110	10%	259	4.29	41	39	70%	3.84	1.27	30%	73%	3.66	2.6	7.1	2.8	9%	1.0	75
Away	05	254	313	384	697	8	83	29	0.51	50	18	31	81	96	9%	263	4.12	38	42	73%	3.83	1.31	30%	75%	3.51	2.5	5.7	2.3	11%	1.1	51
	06	276	338	412	750	9	84	31	0.60	49	20	31	83	95	9%	273	4.79	42	41	71%	4.54	1.41	32%	72%	3.76	2.6	7.1	2.7	13%	1.3	57
	07	266	328	405	733	8	84	29	0.58	50	17	33	86	109	9%	266	4.60	38	41	76%	4.54	1.42	32%	72%	3.85	2.7	6.5	2.4	12%	1.3	48
Opp @ MIN	05	252	291	390	681	5	82	28	0.30	45	20	35	85	82	6%	260	3.72	36	39	56%	4.07	1.35	30%	72%	3.71	3.1	6.4	2.1	10%	0.9	59
	06	251	289	392	681	5	78	30	0.24	44	19	37	92	84	8%	250	3.71	27	29	59%	4.91	1.51	33%	68%	4.34	2.9	5.5	1.9	9%	0.9	42
	07	255	307	403	711	7	79	30	0.36	42	18	40	96	85	7%	250	4.18	40	42	76%	3.82	1.36	29%	72%	3.88	3.2	5.0	1.6	6%	0.6	47

NYM	Yr	Avg	OB	Slg	OPS	bb%	ct%	h%	Eye	G	L	F	PX	SX	SBO	xBA	RC/G	W	Py	Sv%	ERA	WHIP	H%	S%	xERA	Ctl	Dom	Cmd	hr/f	hr/9	BPV
At Home	05	261	324	411	735	9	81	29	0.50	45	20	35	98	121	14%	273	4.57	48	46	66%	3.48	1.27	29%	75%	3.45	2.9	6.3	2.2	8%	0.8	66
	06	256	325	434	759	9	81	28	0.54	44	17	38	117	128	13%	278	4.92	50	45	70%	3.77	1.27	29%	73%	3.62	3.1	7.2	2.3	10%	1.0	68
	07	270	335	425	760	9	83	30	0.58	44	19	37	99	117	16%	274	4.92	41	40	65%	4.20	1.33	29%	70%	4.10	3.5	7.1	2.0	9%	1.0	62
Away	05	256	313	421	733	8	80	29	0.41	44	21	35	109	114	13%	277	4.50	35	43	63%	4.10	1.35	29%	72%	3.87	3.3	6.4	1.9	9%	0.9	54
	06	272	335	455	790	9	81	31	0.48	42	20	38	120	121	12%	282	5.26	47	45	79%	4.58	1.38	30%	70%	4.01	3.4	7.1	2.1	12%	1.3	52
	07	280	344	439	783	9	82	31	0.55	45	20	35	103	119	15%	279	5.18	47	46	73%	4.34	1.41	30%	72%	4.04	3.6	6.9	1.9	10%	1.1	52
Opp @ NYM	05	253	312	377	689	8	81	29	0.45	44	21	35	85	104	10%	264	4.00	33	35	66%	4.27	1.37	30%	72%	3.87	3.3	6.6	2.0	11%	1.1	52
	06	245	309	388	697	9	79	29	0.44	43	19	38	98	94	12%	255	4.08	31	36	54%	4.56	1.37	29%	70%	4.18	3.5	6.5	1.9	11%	1.2	45
	07	247	316	393	709	9	79	29	0.49	41	18	41	99	109	9%	254	4.29	40	41	63%	4.40	1.42	30%	71%	4.08	3.4	5.9	1.7	10%	1.1	41

NYY	Yr	Avg	OB	Slg	OPS	bb%	ct%	h%	Eye	G	L	F	PX	SX	SBO	xBA	RC/G	W	Py	Sv%	ERA	WHIP	H%	S%	xERA	Ctl	Dom	Cmd	hr/f	hr/9	BPV
At Home	05	290	362	478	839	10	82	31	0.64	46	18	36	110	99	7%	279	5.87	53	49	68%	4.22	1.34	31%	71%	3.83	2.5	6.4	2.6	10%	1.0	63
	06	284	358	470	829	10	82	31	0.66	44	18	37	113	108	10%	280	5.79	50	49	74%	3.97	1.29	29%	72%	3.81	2.9	6.2	2.1	10%	1.0	54
	07	300	374	474	848	11	84	33	0.72	45	19	36	105	114	10%	282	6.05	52	52	65%	4.32	1.37	30%	71%	4.10	3.3	6.7	2.1	9%	1.0	56
Away	05	263	338	423	761	10	82	29	0.65	47	17	36	97	83	6%	263	4.96	42	41	69%	4.87	1.40	30%	67%	4.47	3.3	6.0	1.8	11%	1.1	42
	06	285	358	453	811	10	80	33	0.58	46	20	34	107	104	10%	278	5.61	47	46	69%	4.90	1.42	31%	67%	4.49	3.3	6.5	2.0	10%	1.1	49
	07	280	348	453	801	9	82	31	0.58	46	19	35	108	106	9%	280	5.45	42	45	59%	4.69	1.50	31%	70%	4.50	3.9	5.8	1.5	8%	0.9	40
Opp @ NYY	05	272	320	414	734	7	82	31	0.39	47	18	35	88	106	12%	260	4.46	28	32	52%	5.69	1.62	32%	69%	4.55	4.1	6.4	1.6	15%	1.7	18
	06	253	311	400	711	8	82	28	0.47	44	18	38	93	90	10%	258	4.25	31	32	67%	5.47	1.58	31%	69%	4.63	4.1	6.3	1.5	13%	1.5	24
	07	263	326	412	738	9	81	30	0.49	42	18	39	97	97	10%	257	4.63	29	29	60%	6.32	1.70	33%	65%	5.26	4.3	6.0	1.4	13%	1.4	18

OAK	Yr	Avg	OB	Slg	OPS	bb%	ct%	h%	Eye	G	L	F	PX	SX	SBO	xBA	RC/G	W	Py	Sv%	ERA	WHIP	H%	S%	xERA	Ctl	Dom	Cmd	hr/f	hr/9	BPV
At Home	05	268	331	415	746	9	87	29	0.71	42	22	36	90	57	3%	285	4.80	45	45	73%	3.82	1.25	27%	72%	3.73	3.2	6.5	2.0	10%	0.9	61
	06	259	334	409	743	10	83	28	0.67	42	18	41	91	90	4%	257	4.77	49	43	75%	3.97	1.38	30%	73%	3.90	3.1	5.9	1.9	8%	0.9	51
	07	240	325	385	709	11	82	27	0.71	41	19	40	89	90	4%	256	4.42	40	38	55%	3.79	1.31	29%	72%	3.85	3.4	6.2	1.8	7%	0.7	60
Away	05	257	323	399	722	9	84	28	0.62	44	20	36	87	80	4%	266	4.47	43	48	65%	3.57	1.26	28%	75%	3.33	3.1	6.9	2.2	11%	1.0	64
	06	261	342	414	756	11	82	29	0.67	43	21	36	95	90	6%	270	4.96	44	42	71%	4.47	1.46	31%	72%	3.99	3.5	6.6	1.9	11%	1.2	45
	07	271	346	427	773	10	78	32	0.51	40	19	41	105	67	4%	252	5.13	36	41	63%	4.85	1.45	32%	68%	4.37	3.2	6.7	2.1	9%	1.0	53
Opp @ OAK	05	239	304	372	676	9	81	27	0.49	44	22	35	85	97	9%	263	3.85	36	36	69%	4.68	1.42	29%	68%	4.57	3.3	4.7	1.4	8%	0.9	31
	06	268	328	410	738	8	83	30	0.53	43	19	38	89	96	8%	261	4.64	32	38	64%	4.33	1.43	29%	72%	4.20	3.9	5.9	1.5	9%	1.1	37
	07	249	317	372	689	9	82	29	0.54	46	18	36	77	114	10%	251	4.08	41	43	69%	3.85	1.37	27%	75%	3.91	4.2	6.0	1.4	9%	1.0	43

PHI	Yr	Avg	OB	Slg	OPS	bb%	ct%	h%	Eye	G	L	F	PX	SX	SBO	xBA	RC/G	W	Py	Sv%	ERA	WHIP	H%	S%	xERA	Ctl	Dom	Cmd	hr/f	hr/9	BPV
At Home	05	281	357	453	810	11	83	31	0.69	41	24	34	109	120	8%	293	5.62	46	43	60%	4.48	1.32	30%	70%	3.69	2.7	7.3	2.8	15%	1.3	64
	06	274	346	462	808	10	80	31	0.54	46	20	34	123	109	6%	287	5.52	41	43	61%	4.70	1.42	31%	71%	3.74	3.1	7.5	2.4	16%	1.5	51
	07	280	350	475	825	10	79	32	0.52	43	19	38	126	132	10%	282	5.73	47	43	60%	4.79	1.43	30%	71%	3.92	3.4	6.8	2.0	16%	1.5	39
Away	05	259	333	395	728	10	78	31	0.51	43	23	34	94	108	9%	266	4.58	42	46	68%	3.93	1.28	28%	73%	3.63	3.5	7.2	2.1	12%	1.1	62
	06	260	334	433	767	10	78	30	0.51	42	20	38	114	118	8%	269	5.04	44	43	68%	4.52	1.42	31%	71%	4.08	3.2	6.5	2.0	10%	1.1	48
	07	268	345	442	787	10	78	31	0.54	40	19	41	120	123	10%	266	5.35	42	44	73%	4.74	1.47	31%	69%	4.44	3.5	6.1	1.7	8%	0.9	45
Opp @ PHI	05	265	317	450	767	7	79	30	0.36	45	24	32	124	101	8%	295	4.88	35	38	77%	5.22	1.57	31%	69%	4.54	4.2	6.1	1.4	12%	1.2	29
	06	275	334	471	805	8	79	31	0.42	45	21	34	130	109	9%	292	5.40	40	38	68%	5.10	1.50	31%	70%	4.17	3.9	7.2	1.9	15%	1.4	39
	07	273	338	474	811	9	80	30	0.49	44	21	35	131	84	7%	294	5.49	34	38	63%	5.34	1.54	32%	69%	4.40	3.9	7.4	1.9	14%	1.5	38

PIT	Yr	Avg	OB	Slg	OPS	bb%	ct%	h%	Eye	G	L	F	PX	SX	SBO	xBA	RC/G	W	Py	Sv%	ERA	WHIP	H%	S%	xERA	Ctl	Dom	Cmd	hr/f	hr/9	BPV
At Home	05	265	327	407	734	8	81	31	0.47	44	22	34	97	108	5%	275	4.61	34	36	64%	4.26	1.43	30%	72%	3.91	3.6	6.3	1.8	10%	1.0	47
	06	283	339	423	762	8	80	33	0.42	43	22	35	98	99	7%	268	4.90	43	42	68%	4.09	1.44	32%	73%	3.83	3.5	6.5	1.8	8%	0.8	55
	07	272	327	415	742	8	80	32	0.41	42	20	38	101	89	6%	264	4.65	37	39	54%	4.55	1.39	31%	69%	4.22	2.9	6.0	2.1	9%	0.9	52
Away	05	254	308	394	701	7	80	29	0.39	47	19	34	93	96	9%	262	4.08	33	36	84%	4.62	1.46	29%	70%	4.34	4.1	5.7	1.4	10%	1.1	35
	06	243	299	370	669	7	77	29	0.35	46	19	36	90	80	5%	244	3.66	24	29	62%	5.06	1.58	32%	71%	4.31	4.3	6.8	1.6	13%	1.2	37
	07	254	312	408	720	8	79	29	0.41	42	17	41	104	105	7%	254	4.35	31	31	74%	5.36	1.58	33%	68%	4.64	3.6	6.4	1.8	11%	1.3	34
Opp @ PIT	05	269	337	420	758	9	82	30	0.57	44	22	34	101	86	7%	279	4.92	47	45	68%	3.94	1.37	31%	73%	3.73	3.2	6.7	2.1	8%	0.7	64
	06	275	342	408	750	9	81	32	0.54	46	20	34	92	92	10%	267	4.85	38	39	68%	4.40	1.44	33%	71%	3.94	3.0	7.1	2.4	9%	0.9	65
	07	280	335	425	760	8	83	32	0.48	45	20	36	98	89	8%	272	4.86	44	42	79%	4.42	1.36	32%	68%	4.20	2.8	6.8	2.4	8%	0.8	68

SD	Yr	Avg	OB	Slg	OPS	bb%	ct%	h%	Eye	G	L	F	PX	SX	SBO	xBA	RC/G	W	Py	Sv%	ERA	WHIP	H%	S%	xERA	Ctl	Dom	Cmd	hr/f	hr/9	BPV
At Home	05	255	327	377	704	10	82	30	0.58	41	22	37	80	101	10%	260	4.30	46	39	79%	3.52	1.24	29%	74%	3.47	3.0	7.3	2.4	8%	0.8	78
	06	245	316	388	705	9	80	28	0.51	41	18	41	94	114	10%	251	4.25	43	38	73%	3.77	1.23	28%	73%	3.59	2.8	7.1	2.5	10%	1.1	68
	07	235	305	378	684	9	76	28	0.42	41	18	41	100	105	6%	242	3.96	47	46	86%	3.02	1.16	29%	75%	3.27	2.6	7.1	2.7	6%	0.5	92
Away	05	259	334	404	738	10	83	29	0.65	43	22	35	95	103	9%	279	4.74	36	37	59%	4.79	1.45	32%	69%	4.24	3.2	6.6	2.1	10%	1.0	51
	06	279	344	443	786	9	81	32	0.51	43	21	36	111	115	10%	280	5.25	45	48	68%	4.00	1.31	29%	73%	3.81	2.9	6.4	2.2	10%	1.1	55
	07	265	330	440	770	9	80	30	0.49	40	19	42	120	82	5%	268	5.04	42	44	53%	4.46	1.37	31%	69%	4.12	3.2	6.7	2.1	9%	0.9	58
Opp @ SD	05	241	303	378	682	8	78	29	0.41	43	22	36	96	110	8%	262	3.92	35	42	73%	3.64	1.35	29%	74%	3.74	3.6	6.2	1.7	7%	0.7	57
	06	244	302	396	698	8	79	28	0.40	41	20	40	100	116	12%	258	4.04	38	43	65%	3.74	1.32	29%	74%	3.72	3.5	6.9	1.9	9%	0.9	59
	07	235	290	336	626	7	79	28	0.37	45	18	37	71	119	14%	237	3.17	34	35	72%	3.87	1.25	29%	71%	3.82	3.4	8.0	2.4	9%	0.9	78

SEA	Yr	Avg	OB	Slg	OPS	bb%	ct%	h%	Eye	G	L	F	PX	SX	SBO	xBA	RC/G	W	Py	Sv%	ERA	WHIP	H%	S%	xERA	Ctl	Dom	Cmd	hr/f	hr/9	BPV
At Home	05	260	317	390	708	8	81	30	0.44	45	20	34	85	103	11%	260	4.22	39	40	61%	4.15	1.35	29%	71%	4.09	3.1	5.8	1.9	8%	0.9	48
	06	265	315	416	731	7	82	30	0.41	45	18	37	91	108	10%	263	4.43	44	39	71%	4.26	1.38	29%	72%	4.01	3.7	6.9	1.9	10%	1.0	54
	07	283	334	417	752	7	84	32	0.47	47	18	35	82	95	9%	258	4.70	49	39	74%	4.50	1.43	32%	70%	4.24	3.3	6.8	2.0	8%	0.9	57
Away	05	252	310	393	703	8	83	28	0.51	46	21	33	88	101	10%	273	4.20	30	36	73%	4.86	1.42	29%	69%	4.38	3.1	5.4	1.7	12%	1.3	28
	06	277	325	432	757	7	83	31	0.42	44	19	37	93	111	9%	271	4.73	34	39	69%	4.96	1.47	31%	69%	4.30	3.3	6.3	1.9	12%	1.2	40
	07	290	331	432	763	6	86	32	0.43	47	19	34	87	97	5%	276	4.80	39	40	75%	4.98	1.52	32%	68%	4.55	3.5	6.0	1.7	9%	0.9	41
Opp @ SEA	05	261	322	394	717	8	83	29	0.54	41	20	40	82	82	9%	256	4.36	42	41	76%	4.09	1.33	30%	70%	3.88	2.9	6.6	2.3	8%	0.8	66
	06	255	327	410	737	10	80	29	0.53	42	19	39	101	83	8%	260	4.67	37	42	73%	4.35	1.30	30%	69%	4.05	2.5	6.2	2.5	10%	1.0	59
	07	272	335	416	751	9	81	32	0.49	44	17	39	96	83	8%	252	4.81	32	42	55%	4.34	1.42	32%	72%	3.95	2.7	5.8	2.1	9%	1.0	48

BATTING / PITCHING

SF

SF	Yr	Avg	OB	Slg	OPS	bb%	ct%	h%	Eye	G	L	F	PX	SX	SBO	xBA	RC/G	W	Py	Sv%	ERA	WHIP	H%	S%	xERA	Ctl	Dom	Cmd	hr/f	hr/9	BPV
At Home	05	260	316	396	711	8	85	29	0.54	47	19	33	88	92	9%	274	4.30	37	34	62%	4.26	1.37	29%	70%	4.20	3.5	6.0	1.7	8%	0.8	51
	06	264	329	415	744	9	85	29	0.63	44	19	37	98	117	6%	278	4.81	43	40	67%	4.38	1.33	29%	68%	4.35	3.4	6.4	1.9	8%	0.8	57
	07	259	325	382	706	9	84	29	0.62	47	17	35	79	109	10%	260	4.33	39	38	62%	4.02	1.41	31%	73%	3.89	3.3	6.4	2.0	7%	0.8	58
Away	05	262	315	396	711	7	82	30	0.43	41	22	37	91	87	6%	269	4.24	38	37	62%	4.45	1.47	30%	72%	4.12	3.9	6.1	1.6	10%	1.0	39
	06	254	312	428	740	8	83	28	0.49	43	18	39	108	97	6%	271	4.59	33	36	60%	4.92	1.48	30%	69%	4.59	3.9	6.1	1.6	10%	1.1	37
	07	249	314	391	706	9	83	28	0.56	44	17	39	92	112	11%	260	4.26	32	39	61%	4.39	1.39	29%	70%	4.37	4.1	6.7	1.6	8%	0.9	53
Opp @ SF	05	259	328	397	725	9	82	29	0.58	42	21	37	90	92	8%	265	4.54	44	47	74%	3.76	1.28	28%	73%	3.73	2.7	5.1	1.8	9%	0.8	48
	06	253	321	392	713	9	81	29	0.54	42	19	38	93	107	9%	262	4.38	38	41	61%	4.49	1.38	29%	68%	4.49	3.3	5.3	1.6	7%	0.8	44
	07	270	333	412	745	9	82	31	0.51	44	19	37	96	115	8%	267	4.76	42	43	68%	3.74	1.36	29%	73%	3.83	3.3	5.3	1.6	7%	0.7	49

STL

STL	Yr	Avg	OB	Slg	OPS	bb%	ct%	h%	Eye	G	L	F	PX	SX	SBO	xBA	RC/G	W	Py	Sv%	ERA	WHIP	H%	S%	xERA	Ctl	Dom	Cmd	hr/f	hr/9	BPV
At Home	05	271	336	437	773	9	84	29	0.62	46	20	34	105	94	8%	287	5.08	50	49	67%	3.44	1.28	29%	77%	3.02	2.7	6.3	2.4	12%	1.0	61
	06	273	339	429	768	9	84	30	0.62	44	20	36	99	92	5%	279	5.03	49	45	70%	3.93	1.30	28%	73%	3.60	3.1	6.0	2.0	12%	1.1	49
	07	283	343	405	749	8	85	31	0.62	43	19	38	80	81	6%	261	4.79	43	39	78%	4.17	1.37	30%	71%	4.11	3.0	5.6	1.9	7%	0.8	50
Away	05	269	332	410	741	9	82	31	0.51	46	23	31	92	103	8%	278	4.67	50	49	80%	3.54	1.27	28%	75%	3.28	2.9	5.8	2.0	11%	0.9	55
	06	265	327	434	761	8	83	29	0.53	45	19	36	108	91	7%	280	4.87	34	38	63%	5.20	1.48	31%	68%	4.41	3.3	6.2	1.9	13%	1.3	35
	07	265	326	405	731	8	82	30	0.51	44	18	37	93	72	6%	260	4.52	35	33	72%	5.21	1.45	30%	67%	4.59	3.4	6.2	1.8	12%	1.3	37
Opp @ STL	05	258	312	398	710	7	81	29	0.42	51	19	30	92	54	4%	265	4.20	31	32	72%	4.65	1.44	30%	71%	4.15	3.5	5.5	1.6	12%	1.2	32
	06	253	315	410	725	8	82	28	0.51	47	19	34	101	85	7%	273	4.44	31	35	56%	4.78	1.46	30%	69%	4.36	3.5	5.7	1.6	10%	1.1	35
	07	269	326	409	735	8	84	30	0.53	43	20	38	92	101	7%	269	4.60	38	42	65%	4.29	1.45	31%	72%	4.22	3.2	5.2	1.6	7%	0.8	40

TAM

TAM	Yr	Avg	OB	Slg	OPS	bb%	ct%	h%	Eye	G	L	F	PX	SX	SBO	xBA	RC/G	W	Py	Sv%	ERA	WHIP	H%	S%	xERA	Ctl	Dom	Cmd	hr/f	hr/9	BPV
At Home	05	279	333	429	761	7	82	32	0.46	45	21	34	92	124	14%	274	4.87	40	36	72%	4.94	1.46	31%	68%	4.50	3.6	6.4	1.8	10%	1.1	42
	06	259	321	437	758	8	80	29	0.45	44	18	38	109	114	14%	267	4.83	41	37	66%	4.70	1.49	31%	71%	4.17	3.8	6.4	1.7	11%	1.2	37
	07	256	320	421	741	9	77	30	0.42	42	18	40	104	107	11%	253	4.63	34	32	55%	5.06	1.49	34%	68%	4.42	3.4	7.7	2.3	10%	1.1	59
Away	05	268	315	421	736	6	82	30	0.38	44	20	36	95	109	14%	270	4.47	27	29	55%	5.90	1.62	31%	65%	5.27	4.3	5.6	1.3	11%	1.3	19
	06	250	300	403	703	7	80	29	0.35	44	20	36	97	99	13%	262	4.06	20	29	53%	5.26	1.62	33%	69%	4.69	3.9	6.0	1.5	9%	1.1	32
	07	276	341	442	782	9	75	34	0.40	43	20	38	114	112	12%	258	5.25	29	33	58%	6.09	1.62	34%	64%	5.06	3.8	7.3	2.0	12%	1.4	38
Opp @ TAM	05	272	339	433	772	9	82	30	0.56	41	21	39	98	98	7%	269	5.06	41	45	68%	4.76	1.40	32%	67%	4.33	2.8	6.2	2.2	9%	0.9	55
	06	275	345	446	791	10	82	31	0.59	43	19	37	106	99	10%	274	5.33	40	44	67%	4.34	1.34	29%	72%	3.83	3.1	7.0	2.2	12%	1.3	53
	07	284	347	452	799	9	78	34	0.44	42	18	40	111	105	7%	260	5.41	44	46	62%	4.25	1.33	30%	72%	3.80	3.2	7.7	2.4	12%	1.2	63

TEX

TEX	Yr	Avg	OB	Slg	OPS	bb%	ct%	h%	Eye	G	L	F	PX	SX	SBO	xBA	RC/G	W	Py	Sv%	ERA	WHIP	H%	S%	xERA	Ctl	Dom	Cmd	hr/f	hr/9	BPV
At Home	05	278	338	509	847	8	81	29	0.49	38	20	41	136	113	6%	289	5.85	44	44	70%	4.80	1.44	31%	68%	4.34	3.0	5.7	1.9	10%	1.0	43
	06	283	343	458	801	8	81	32	0.47	42	20	38	114	84	5%	277	5.38	39	42	61%	4.68	1.42	31%	69%	4.16	3.2	5.9	1.9	11%	1.0	44
	07	277	338	451	789	8	78	33	0.42	42	20	38	111	119	8%	265	5.25	47	42	76%	4.30	1.45	30%	72%	3.99	3.9	6.4	1.7	9%	0.9	49
Away	05	258	314	430	743	8	80	29	0.40	41	21	38	109	99	6%	271	4.60	35	37	66%	5.15	1.50	32%	67%	4.57	3.5	6.0	1.7	10%	1.0	40
	06	272	331	434	765	8	82	31	0.48	44	20	37	102	92	5%	271	4.92	41	44	68%	4.54	1.45	32%	71%	4.05	3.1	6.3	2.0	10%	1.0	49
	07	249	311	402	712	8	78	29	0.40	42	18	40	101	103	8%	251	4.27	28	36	74%	5.25	1.63	31%	69%	4.71	4.6	5.9	1.3	10%	1.1	28
Opp @ TEX	05	277	334	430	764	8	84	31	0.53	46	20	34	95	100	5%	279	4.93	37	37	72%	5.66	1.48	30%	68%	4.54	3.3	6.7	2.0	16%	2.0	22
	06	273	333	420	753	8	83	30	0.53	47	21	33	91	85	7%	275	4.78	42	39	83%	5.12	1.49	33%	68%	4.42	3.2	6.9	2.1	11%	1.2	48
	07	263	336	402	738	10	82	30	0.60	47	19	34	89	88	8%	263	4.72	34	39	67%	5.00	1.45	33%	68%	4.27	3.3	7.8	2.4	12%	1.2	60

TOR

TOR	Yr	Avg	OB	Slg	OPS	bb%	ct%	h%	Eye	G	L	F	PX	SX	SBO	xBA	RC/G	W	Py	Sv%	ERA	WHIP	H%	S%	xERA	Ctl	Dom	Cmd	hr/f	hr/9	BPV
At Home	05	275	331	434	766	8	83	31	0.51	44	21	34	99	101	8%	283	4.96	43	45	59%	3.84	1.28	29%	75%	3.31	2.4	6.3	2.6	13%	1.2	57
	06	295	352	505	858	8	84	31	0.57	41	20	39	126	95	6%	295	6.01	50	49	65%	4.04	1.31	29%	73%	3.55	3.0	7.0	2.3	13%	1.1	60
	07	260	328	433	761	9	80	30	0.50	40	20	40	113	95	5%	268	4.94	49	46	71%	3.67	1.18	27%	72%	3.36	2.7	7.1	2.6	12%	1.0	75
Away	05	256	317	381	698	8	82	29	0.51	45	20	34	80	98	7%	261	4.15	37	43	66%	4.30	1.38	29%	71%	3.98	3.1	5.6	1.8	10%	1.1	42
	06	274	337	421	758	9	83	31	0.57	44	19	37	93	82	7%	266	4.89	37	37	71%	4.74	1.43	31%	70%	4.13	3.3	6.6	2.0	12%	1.2	45
	07	258	321	406	727	8	82	29	0.52	40	20	40	95	89	6%	263	4.51	34	40	58%	4.35	1.39	30%	71%	4.03	3.2	6.1	1.9	9%	0.9	50
Opp @ TOR	05	264	312	422	734	7	82	29	0.39	46	20	34	96	93	11%	272	4.41	38	36	71%	4.81	1.41	31%	67%	4.39	3.0	5.9	2.0	10%	1.0	47
	06	252	313	409	722	8	80	29	0.44	47	20	33	98	110	11%	269	4.36	31	32	81%	5.60	1.53	31%	67%	4.73	3.2	5.6	1.8	13%	1.6	20
	07	235	292	385	677	7	79	27	0.38	49	19	32	96	111	12%	266	3.78	32	35	73%	4.61	1.39	30%	70%	4.22	3.5	7.0	2.0	11%	1.2	52

WAS

WAS	Yr	Avg	OB	Slg	OPS	bb%	ct%	h%	Eye	G	L	F	PX	SX	SBO	xBA	RC/G	W	Py	Sv%	ERA	WHIP	H%	S%	xERA	Ctl	Dom	Cmd	hr/f	hr/9	BPV
At Home	05	236	304	362	665	9	80	28	0.48	44	21	35	89	83	7%	259	3.79	41	37	77%	3.56	1.28	29%	74%	3.64	3.1	6.6	2.1	8%	0.8	66
	06	262	334	409	743	10	80	30	0.55	41	19	40	100	103	10%	259	4.76	41	37	59%	4.66	1.36	29%	68%	4.51	3.1	6.1	2.0	9%	1.1	48
	07	259	323	383	706	9	81	31	0.49	47	18	35	89	96	5%	257	4.29	40	37	65%	4.08	1.36	29%	72%	4.16	3.3	6.0	1.8	8%	0.9	49
Away	05	266	323	407	731	8	80	31	0.42	47	22	31	98	68	6%	273	4.51	40	40	70%	4.19	1.46	31%	73%	3.96	3.6	5.7	1.6	9%	0.9	40
	06	261	334	425	759	10	78	31	0.49	46	20	34	116	88	14%	274	4.95	30	33	58%	5.43	1.60	31%	69%	4.80	4.3	5.9	1.4	11%	1.3	22
	07	254	319	397	716	9	79	30	0.44	45	20	35	99	100	7%	261	4.36	33	33	62%	5.11	1.53	30%	70%	4.56	3.9	5.6	1.4	12%	1.4	20
Opp @ WAS	05	247	310	371	680	8	81	29	0.47	39	22	39	85	85	8%	257	3.90	40	44	69%	3.49	1.22	28%	72%	3.68	3.2	6.7	2.1	6%	0.6	74
	06	263	323	423	746	8	82	29	0.50	39	18	43	103	113	9%	263	4.70	40	44	57%	4.37	1.40	30%	71%	4.21	3.7	6.7	1.8	9%	0.9	54
	07	259	325	402	726	9	83	29	0.56	39	17	43	95	102	8%	254	4.52	41	44	74%	3.81	1.34	31%	72%	3.80	3.2	6.6	2.0	6%	0.6	68

AL

AL	Yr	Avg	OB	Slg	OPS	bb%	ct%	h%	Eye	G	L	F	PX	SX	SBO	xBA	RC/G	W	Py	Sv%	ERA	WHIP	H%	S%	xERA	Ctl	Dom	Cmd	hr/f	hr/9	BPV
At Home	05	271	332	433	765	8	83	30	0.53	44	20	36	100	100	8%	277	4.94	44	42	71%	4.14	1.33	30%	71%	3.85	2.9	6.2	2.2	10%	1.0	55
	06	280	342	447	789	9	82	31	0.53	43	20	37	100	100	8%	271	5.23	45	43	69%	4.30	1.37	30%	71%	3.94	3.1	6.4	2.1	10%	1.1	52
	07	274	340	432	772	9	82	31	0.55	44	19	38	100	100	9%	267	5.07	44	42	68%	4.38	1.38	31%	70%	4.09	3.2	6.8	2.1	9%	0.9	58
Away	05	264	321	416	737	8	82	30	0.46	44	20	35	100	100	8%	275	4.56	38	40	66%	4.60	1.40	30%	70%	4.16	3.2	6.1	1.9	11%	1.1	44
	06	270	331	427	758	8	82	30	0.49	44	20	36	100	100	8%	271	4.85	38	39	67%	4.84	1.46	31%	69%	4.27	3.3	6.5	2.0	11%	1.2	43
	07	266	328	414	742	8	81	31	0.47	44	18	37	100	100	8%	263	4.68	37	40	68%	4.67	1.44	31%	70%	4.26	3.5	6.5	1.9	10%	1.1	47

NL

NL	Yr	Avg	OB	Slg	OPS	bb%	ct%	h%	Eye	G	L	F	PX	SX	SBO	xBA	RC/G	W	Py	Sv%	ERA	WHIP	H%	S%	xERA	Ctl	Dom	Cmd	hr/f	hr/9	BPV
At Home	05	266	333	424	757	9	81	30	0.54	44	22	35	100	100	8%	277	4.89	50	47	69%	4.07	1.34	30%	72%	3.71	3.1	6.7	2.2	11%	1.0	59
	06	271	338	437	775	9	81	31	0.53	43	20	37	100	100	9%	268	5.11	50	47	65%	4.33	1.36	30%	71%	3.90	3.2	7.0	2.1	11%	1.1	56
	07	269	335	430	765	9	81	31	0.52	43	19	38	100	100	8%	264	4.97	50	47	66%	4.22	1.36	30%	71%	3.94	3.2	6.8	2.1	10%	1.0	58
Away	05	257	319	405	724	8	80	30	0.46	45	21	34	100	100	8%	272	4.43	42	44	67%	4.40	1.42	30%	71%	3.98	3.5	6.4	1.8	11%	1.1	47
	06	259	321	418	739	8	80	30	0.46	44	19	37	100	100	9%	264	4.62	41	44	63%	4.67	1.45	31%	70%	4.21	3.6	6.5	1.8	11%	1.1	44
	07	263	325	416	741	9	80	30	0.47	43	19	38	100	100	9%	260	4.66	42	44	66%	4.67	1.44	31%	70%	4.25	3.5	6.5	1.9	10%	1.1	47

The Batters

QUALIFICATION: All batters who accumulated at least 100 at bats in the majors in 2007 have been included. Nearly all who accumulated 50-99 AB are also included. A handful of players with fewer than 50 AB are included if we believe that they will have an impact in 2008. Players who may have a role in 2008 but have spent several years battling injuries are often not included, though an injury status update appears on page 178. All of these players will appear on BaseballHQ.com over the winter as their roles and projected impacts become clearer.

POSITIONS: Up to three positions are listed for each batter and represent those for which he appeared a minimum of 20 games in 2007. Positions are shown with their numeric designation (2=CA, 3=1B, 7=LF, 0=DH, etc.)

AGE: Each batter's current age is shown, along with a description of the associated stage in his career.

BATS: Shows which side of the plate he bats from — right (R), left (L) or switch-hitter (S).

RELIABILITY SCORE: An analysis of each player's forecast risk, on a 0-100 scale. High scores go those batters who receive regular playing time, are healthy, are in a stable age range and have displayed consistent performance over the past three years (using RC/G).

BATTING AVERAGE POTENTIAL (BAvg Potl): The probability that a batter will improve his batting average in 2008 over 2007, based on an evaluation of contact rate, xBA variance and walk rate. These percentages are in 5% increments, ranging from 10% to 90%, though most will be centered closer to the mean. If a batter's BAvg Potl says 60%, for instance, it means that he has a 60% chance of improving his batting average in 2008. This is a strict, computer-generated calculation; often, the projection will not reflect the percentage play cited here.

LIMA PLAN GRADE: Rating that evaluates how well a batter would fit into a team using the LIMA Plan. Best grades go to batters who have excellent base skills, are expected to see a good amount of playing time, and are in the $10-$30 Rotisserie value range. Lowest grades will go to poor skills, few at bats and values under $5 or over $30.

+/- SCORE: A score that measures the probability that a batter's 2008 performance will exceed or fall short 2007's numbers. Two types of variables are tracked: 1) Multi-year trends in bb%, ct%, PX and SX, and 2) Outlying 2007 levels for h%, hr/f, xBA and LH/RH variance. Positive scores indicate both rebounds and potential breakouts. Negative scores indicate both corrections and breakdowns.

PLAYER STAT LINES: The past five year's statistics represent the total accumulated in the majors as well as in Triple-A, Double-A ball and various foreign leagues during each year. All non-major league stats used have been converted to their equivalent major league performance level. Minor league levels below AA are not included.

Nearly all baseball publications separate a player's statistical experiences in the major leagues from the minor leagues and outside leagues. While this may be appropriate for the sake of official record-keeping, it is not an accurate snapshot of a player's complete performance for the year.

Bill James has proven that minor league statistics, at Double-A level or above, are accurate indicators of future potential. Other researchers have also devised conversion factors for foreign leagues. Since these are accurate barometers of potential performance, then we should be including them in the pool of historical data.

TEAM DESIGNATIONS: An asterisk (*) appearing with a team name means that major league equivalent Triple-A and/or Double-A numbers are included in that year's stat line. A designation of "a/a" means the stats were accumulated at both levels that year. "JPN" means Japan, "MEX" means Mexico, "KOR" means Korea, "TWN" means Taiwan, "CUB" means Cuba and "ind" means independent league. All stats that appear with these designations are converted to major league equivalents.

The designation "2TM" appears whenever a player was on more than one major league team, crossing leagues, in a season. "2AL" and "2NL" represent more than one team in the same league. Complete season stats are presented for players who crossed leagues during the season.

SABERMETRIC CATEGORIES: Descriptions of all the sabermetric categories appear in the glossary. The decimal point has been suppressed on several categories to conserve space. *Notes:*

- Platoon data (vL, vR) and Ball-in-play data (G/L/F) are for major league performance only.
- xBA only appears for years in which G/L/F data is available.

2008 FORECASTS: It is far too early to be making definitive projections for 2008, especially on playing time. Focus on the skill levels and trends, then consult Baseball HQ for playing time revisions as players change teams and roles become finalized. A free projections update will also be available online in March.

Forecasts are computed from a player's trends over the past five years. Adjustments were made for leading indicators and variances between skill and statistical output. After reviewing the leading indicators, you might opt to make further adjustments.

Although each year's numbers include all playing time at the Double-A level or above, the 2008 forecast only represents potential playing time at the major league level, and again is highly preliminary.

CAPSULE COMMENTARIES: For each player, a brief analysis of their BPIs and the potential impact on performance in 2008 is provided. For those who played only a portion of 2007 at the major league level, and whose isolated MLB stats are significantly different from their full-season total, their MLB stats are listed here. Note that these commentaries generally look at performance related issues only. Playing time expectations may impact these analyses, so you will have to adjust accordingly, especially as we get closer to Opening Day. Upside (UP) and downside (DN) statistical potential appears for some players. These are less grounded in hard data and more speculative of skills potential.

Abreu,Bobby			AB	R	H	HR	RBI	SB	Avg	vL	vR	OB	Slg	OPS	bb%	ct%	h%	Eye	xBA	G	L	F	PX	hr/f	SX	SBO	RC/G	RAR	R$
Pos	9	03 PHI	577	99	173	20	101	22	300	272	312	411	468	879	16	78	35	0.87	292	50	23	27	114	16%	91	14%	6.82	19.6	$29
Age	34	04 PHI	574	118	173	30	105	40	301	267	318	428	544	972	18	80	33	1.09	309	42	21	37	154	18%	115	20%	8.05	44.0	$37
Past Peak		05 PHI	588	104	168	24	102	31	286	275	292	404	474	879	17	77	33	0.87	297	47	24	29	129	18%	101	18%	6.84	26.7	$32
Bats	Left	06 2TM	548	98	163	15	107	30	297	293	299	427	462	889	18	75	37	0.90	283	45	26	29	117	13%	105	16%	7.23	30.8	$27
Reliability	72	07 NYY	605	123	171	16	101	25	283	262	289	370	445	815	12	81	33	0.73	284	46	20	34	109	9%	129	17%	5.83	19.5	$26
BAvg Potl	55%	1st Half	288	54	73	4	35	12	253			345	358	702	12	80	31	0.68	260	47	21	32	74	6%	123	16%	4.43	-2.3	$9
LIMA Plan	B+	2nd Half	317	69	98	12	66	13	309			393	524	917	12	82	35	0.79	308	44	19	37	140	13%	122	18%	7.06	20.7	$18
+/- Score	17	08 Proj	536	103	156	17	96	23	291			397	466	862	15	79	34	0.83	289	45	22	32	119	12%	110	15%	6.58	24.5	$25

Low hr/f and nice 2nd half might make you think the power is back. But overall PX trend means the days of 25+ HR are over. 2nd half will salvage some value and consistent speed keeps him a solid contributor.

Abreu,Tony			AB	R	H	HR	RBI	SB	Avg	vL	vR	OB	Slg	OPS	bb%	ct%	h%	Eye	xBA	G	L	F	PX	hr/f	SX	SBO	RC/G	RAR	R$
Pos	54	03	0	0	0	0	0	0	0							0									0				
Age	23	04	0	0	0	0	0	0	0							0									0				
Growth		05	0	0	0	0	0	0	0							0									0				
Bats	Right	06 aa	457	64	123	6	53	8	269			316	365	681	6	85	31	0.45					62		91	10%	3.90	-17.8	$11
Reliability	0	07 LA	* 400	60	120	4	32	4	300	214	290	332	435	767	5	88	34	0.38	290	52	15	32	91	4%	104	4%	4.89	1.2	$11
BAvg Potl	45%	1st Half	270	43	81	3	19	4	300			335	433	768	5	86	34	0.38	293	56	15	29	89	5%	113	6%	4.91	0.9	$8
LIMA Plan	F	2nd Half	130	17	39	1	13	0	300			326	438	764	4	90	33	0.38	286	48	15	38	96	2%	60	0%	4.86	0.3	$3
+/- Score	4	08 Proj	233	33	67	2	23	2	288			324	410	733	5	87	32	0.41	274	50	15	35	82	4%	91	6%	4.52	-2.8	$6

2-17-.271 in 166 AB at LA. Not seeing much time against LHP; if he can do well against them, will garner more ABs. Lack of power and speed limits short-term value, but defensive flexibility is a plus.

Adams,Russ			AB	R	H	HR	RBI	SB	Avg	vL	vR	OB	Slg	OPS	bb%	ct%	h%	Eye	xBA	G	L	F	PX	hr/f	SX	SBO	RC/G	RAR	R$
Pos	5	03 aa	271	34	67	3	20	7	247			309	336	645	8	89	27	0.78					53		113	10%	3.72	-5.3	$5
Age	27	04 aaa	483	49	132	5	46	5	273			326	391	718	7	89	30	0.73					79		71	6%	4.53	-6.2	$9
Peak		05 TOR	481	68	123	8	63	11	256	195	264	326	383	708	9	88	28	0.88	288	46	20	33	80	6%	116	10%	4.51	0.1	$12
Bats	Left	06 TOR	* 412	49	103	3	42	4	249	135	234	310	340	650	8	85	29	0.58	242	36	20	44	62	2%	80	7%	3.70	-16.1	$5
Reliability	54	07 TOR	* 491	64	114	12	56	5	232		259	289	362	651	7	87	25	0.59	294	33	30	37	81	8%	76	8%	3.62	-13.1	$8
BAvg Potl	70%	1st Half	281	36	68	7	32	2	242			311	370	681	9	90	25	1.04					76		65	4%	4.17	-2.8	$5
LIMA Plan	F	2nd Half	210	28	46	5	24	3	219			258	351	609	5	81	25	0.28	280	33	30	37	88	8%	89	15%	2.88	-10.6	$3
+/- Score	31	08 Proj	291	37	70	5	32	4	241			298	358	656	8	86	27	0.57	270	40	22	38	75	5%	89	9%	3.71	-8.2	$5

2-12-.233 in 60 AB at TOR. 2005 offered promise, but he hasn't progressed. Sure, he makes decent contact, but what else? No power, no speed, no wonder he can't stick in the majors.

Alou,Moises			AB	R	H	HR	RBI	SB	Avg	vL	vR	OB	Slg	OPS	bb%	ct%	h%	Eye	xBA	G	L	F	PX	hr/f	SX	SBO	RC/G	RAR	R$
Pos	7	03 CHC	565	83	158	22	91	3	280	346	260	352	462	814	10	88	29	0.94	306	38	24	39	108	11%	59	2%	5.64	0.8	$20
Age	41	04 CHC	601	106	176	39	106	3	293	298	292	365	557	922	10	87	28	0.85	316	39	19	43	144	18%	79	2%	6.78	22.4	$28
Decline		05 SF	427	67	137	19	63	5	321	372	303	400	518	917	12	90	32	1.30	309	42	20	38	109	13%	85	4%	6.90	17.8	$21
Bats	Right	06 SF	345	52	104	22	74	2	301	349	286	354	571	925	8	91	28	0.90	335	40	20	40	142	18%	52	4%	6.65	13.3	$17
Reliability	17	07 NYM	328	51	112	13	49	3	341	360	335	392	524	916	8	91	35	0.90	305	42	20	38	102	11%	65	3%	6.61	10.8	$16
BAvg Potl	50%	1st Half	110	15	35	2	13	1	318			380	445	826	9	90	34	1.00	293	41	23	37	83	6%	45	3%	5.82	1.4	$4
LIMA Plan	C	2nd Half	218	36	77	11	36	2	353			397	564	962	7	91	35	0.84	311	42	19	39	112	14%	66	3%	7.00	9.2	$12
+/- Score	-56	08 Proj	302	47	94	14	50	1	311			370	521	890	8	90	31	0.96	313	41	20	39	116	13%	46	1%	6.38	8.6	$13

Maintains good skills even with 40 in the rear-view mirror. The problem is the lure of the DL, but injury-prone 40somethings never suddenly get healthy. Should remain productive - but the days of 500 AB are gone.

Amezaga,Alfredo			AB	R	H	HR	RBI	SB	Avg	vL	vR	OB	Slg	OPS	bb%	ct%	h%	Eye	xBA	G	L	F	PX	hr/f	SX	SBO	RC/G	RAR	R$
Pos	8	03 aaa	317	44	98	2	36	11	309			342	403	745	5	90	34	0.52					61		105	23%	4.67	-1.7	$11
Age	30	04 aaa	135	11	29	1	10	5	216			263	280	543	6	90	23	0.65					38		101	15%	2.51	-9.0	$1
Peak		05 aaa	185	20	54	1	9	10	293			337	375	712	6	89	33	0.59					58		99	35%	4.37	-0.3	$6
Bats	Both	06 FLA	334	42	87	3	19	20	260	91	294	327	332	659	9	86	29	0.72	248	51	17	33	41	3%	111	30%	3.85	-6.0	$9
Reliability	46	07 FLA	400	46	105	2	30	13	263	224	269	322	358	679	8	87	30	0.67	267	47	21	33	54	2%	122	17%	4.11	-5.3	$8
BAvg Potl	60%	1st Half	222	24	57	1	19	8	257			318	338	656	8	88	29	0.77	270	47	22	31	46	2%	116	17%	3.88	-4.5	$4
LIMA Plan	D	2nd Half	178	22	48	1	11	5	270			326	382	708	8	85	31	0.58	262	46	19	35	64	2%	116	18%	4.42	-0.8	$4
+/- Score	3	08 Proj	323	38	86	2	21	14	266			323	353	676	8	87	30	0.65	262	48	19	33	52	2%	118	24%	4.03	-5.1	$8

He plays everywhere, and the speed is real. SB drop due to FLA's teamwide drop in SBO%. WIth more of a green light, he'll return to the 20+ SB level. But beyond the speed, these AB are as empty as they come.

Anderson,Garret			AB	R	H	HR	RBI	SB	Avg	vL	vR	OB	Slg	OPS	bb%	ct%	h%	Eye	xBA	G	L	F	PX	hr/f	SX	SBO	RC/G	RAR	R$
Pos	70	03 ANA	638	80	201	29	116	6	315	310	318	347	541	888	5	87	33	0.37	319	44	20	36	134	14%	73	6%	6.11	13.4	$28
Age	35	04 ANA	442	57	133	14	75	2	301	262	321	344	446	790	6	83	34	0.39	278	42	23	35	87	11%	56	2%	5.07	1.5	$15
Decline		05 ANA	575	68	163	17	96	1	283	330	259	311	435	746	4	85	31	0.27	282	42	21	38	97	9%	43	1%	4.45	-4.4	$17
Bats	Left	06 LAA	543	63	152	17	85	1	280	248	294	327	433	760	7	83	31	0.40	275	41	22	37	94	10%	51	1%	4.75	-6.5	$14
Reliability	64	07 LAA	417	67	124	16	80	1	297	288	300	340	492	832	6	87	31	0.50	301	40	19	41	121	11%	60	1%	5.59	10.0	$16
BAvg Potl	50%	1st Half	129	20	34	3	15	0	264			269	411	680	1	87	28	0.06	278	39	18	43	100	6%	55	0%	3.58	-4.3	$3
LIMA Plan	D+	2nd Half	288	47	90	13	65	1	312			369	528	897	8	87	32	0.70	311	41	19	40	131	13%	60	1%	6.46	13.5	$13
+/- Score	6	08 Proj	426	59	123	15	74	1	289			327	462	789	5	85	31	0.39	289	41	20	39	108	10%	55	1%	5.05	2.0	$14

Once he put hip problems behind him, he produced. Two thirds of his HR/RBI came in August/Sept. Regular DH duty is his future, but even that isn't a magic elixir. Plan for 400 AB; any more is profit.

Anderson,Joshua			AB	R	H	HR	RBI	SB	Avg	vL	vR	OB	Slg	OPS	bb%	ct%	h%	Eye	xBA	G	L	F	PX	hr/f	SX	SBO	RC/G	RAR	R$
Pos	8	03	0	0	0	0	0	0	0							0									0				
Age	25	04	0	0	0	0	0	0	0							0									0				
Pre-Peak		05 aa	524	61	140	1	23	46	267			300	335	635	5	86	31	0.34					42		157	47%	3.33	-17.2	$17
Bats	Left	06 aa	561	67	152	3	41	35	271			298	339	637	4	88	30	0.33					43		123	34%	3.34	-20.1	$16
Reliability	33	07 HOU	* 580	58	138	2	43	31	238	389	347	274	292	566	5	87	27	0.37	281	64	19	17	34	2%	120	28%	2.55	-35.5	$10
BAvg Potl	55%	1st Half	292	31	74	1	25	18	253			292	308	600	5	89	28	0.48					35		114	29%	3.03	-13.4	$7
LIMA Plan	D	2nd Half	288	27	64	1	18	13	223			255	275	530	4	85	26	0.29	274	64	19	17	33	2%	113	25%	2.05	-22.4	$3
+/- Score	28	08 Proj	369	40	93	1	25	22	252			284	312	596	4	87	29	0.34	286	64	19	17	38	2%	124	33%	2.87	-18.8	$9

0-11-.358 in 67 AB at HOU. The high GB% is a good thing - but must improve plate patience to capitalize on big-time speed. If he earns regular playing time: UP: 30 SB

Ankiel,Rick			AB	R	H	HR	RBI	SB	Avg	vL	vR	OB	Slg	OPS	bb%	ct%	h%	Eye	xBA	G	L	F	PX	hr/f	SX	SBO	RC/G	RAR	R$
Pos	98	03 aa	25	2	6	1	5	0	228			256	380	636	4	92	22	0.45					82		0	0%	3.31	-1.6	$0
Age	28	04 aa	5	0	0	0	0	0	0			167	0	167	17	80	0	1.00							0	0%	-2.27	-1.4	($0)
Peak		05 aa	136	11	24	6	19	0	179			214	352	566	4	81	17	0.24					105		17	0%	2.22	-12.1	$1
Bats	Left	06	0	0	0	0	0	0	0							0									0				
Reliability	21	07 STL	* 559	72	132	31	97	3	236	391	246	275	445	720	5	77	25	0.23	262	44	15	41	125	18%	68	6%	4.06	-20.0	$16
BAvg Potl	50%	1st Half	259	35	62	17	47	2	239			273	483	756	4	81	23	0.24					139		64	13%	4.44	-6.4	$8
LIMA Plan	D+	2nd Half	300	37	70	14	50	1	233			276	412	688	6	73	27	0.22	240	44	15	41	112	16%	68	1%	3.74	-13.6	$7
+/- Score	-35	08 Proj	433	48	112	22	69	2	259			294	450	744	5	78	28	0.23	256	44	15	41	114	16%	44	3%	4.36	-10.0	$13

11-39-.285 in 172 AB in STL. Feel-good story of the year felt less good after HGH report. PRO: Power is real. CON: Low bb%, ct%, and LD% mean BA will drop. Still... UP: 30 HR, .260 BA

Antonelli,Matt			AB	R	H	HR	RBI	SB	Avg	vL	vR	OB	Slg	OPS	bb%	ct%	h%	Eye	xBA	G	L	F	PX	hr/f	SX	SBO	RC/G	RAR	R$
Pos	4	03	0	0	0	0	0	0	0							0									0				
Age	23	04	0	0	0	0	0	0	0							0									0				
Growth		05	0	0	0	0	0	0	0							0									0				
Bats	Right	06	0	0	0	0	0	0	0							0									0				
Reliability	0	07 aa	187	31	50	6	22	9	267			360	422	782	13	82	30	0.79					97		103	20%	5.38	5.7	$7
BAvg Potl	45%	1st Half	0	0	0	0	0	0	0							0							0						
LIMA Plan	D	2nd Half	187	31	50	6	22	9	267			360	422	782	13	82	30	0.79					97		103	20%	5.39	5.7	$7
+/- Score	14	08 Proj	245	45	67	7	32	10	273			374	416	791	14	80	32	0.81					93		99	17%	5.58	8.9	$9

Speed and plate discipline make him an ideal leadoff candidate; unexpected power was a nice surprise. Expect growing pains, but this is one to track on draft day.

DAVE ADLER

Atkins,Garrett

			AB	R	H	HR	RBI	SB	Avg	vL	vR	OB	Slg	OPS	bb%	ct%	h%	Eye	xBA	G	L	F	PX	hr/f	SX	SBO	RC/G	RAR	R$
Pos	5	03 aaa	439	60	134	12	50	1	305			355	458	813	7	92	31	0.94					91		43	5%	5.53	14.0	$14
Age	28	04 COL *	473	63	157	13	72	0	332	333	385	386	510	896	8	93	34	1.31	315	58	15	27	105	11%	40	0%	6.55	18.4	$19
Peak		05 COL	519	62	149	13	89	0	287	291	285	344	426	770	8	86	31	0.63	295	46	24	30	90	10%	34	1%	5.02	3.5	$17
Bats	Right	06 COL	602	117	198	29	120	4	329	341	327	407	556	963	12	87	34	1.04	314	37	22	41	131	13%	67	2%	7.44	30.9	$32
Reliability	32	07 COL	605	83	182	25	111	3	301	286	307	371	486	856	10	84	32	0.70	289	31	24	44	111	11%	48	2%	6.09	21.8	$24
BAvg Potl	50%	1st Half	279	34	69	9	40	3	247			327	409	736	11	82	27	0.67	262	31	20	49	104	8%	53	4%	4.71	-0.6	$6
LIMA Plan	C	2nd Half	326	49	113	16	71	0	347			408	552	960	9	86	37	0.72	315	32	28	40	117	14%	32	1%	7.23	20.6	$17
+/- Score	-6	08 Proj	604	90	188	24	110	2	311			379	498	877	10	86	33	0.79	300	36	24	41	112	11%	48	2%	6.34	22.8	$26

Looked like he recovered 2006 power and BA after a slow start, but it may not sustain into 2008. 2nd half BA surge was due to a h% spike; 2nd half PX not up to '06 level and not supported by the FB% dip.

Aurilia,Rich

			AB	R	H	HR	RBI	SB	Avg	vL	vR	OB	Slg	OPS	bb%	ct%	h%	Eye	xBA	G	L	F	PX	hr/f	SX	SBO	RC/G	RAR	R$
Pos	35	03 SF	505	65	140	13	58	2	277	277	277	325	410	735	7	84	31	0.44	276	37	25	39	85	8%	57	3%	4.49	-14.7	$13
Age	36	04 2TM	399	49	98	6	44	1	246	257	240	310	353	663	8	82	29	0.52	242	40	18	42	72	4%	67	1%	3.77	-20.0	$6
Decline		05 CIN	426	61	120	14	68	2	282	272	286	339	444	783	8	84	31	0.55	283	41	21	38	101	10%	70	2%	5.13	-5.7	$15
Bats	Right	06 CIN	440	61	132	23	70	3	300	347	276	350	518	868	7	88	30	0.67	303	38	20	42	117	14%	59	3%	6.00	0.0	$18
Reliability	16	07 SF	329	40	83	5	33	0	252	240	260	299	368	667	6	86	28	0.49	271	39	22	38	74	5%	52	0%	3.79	-17.5	$5
BAvg Potl	55%	1st Half	191	22	45	2	19	0	236			274	346	619	5	86	26	0.38	265	40	21	39	71	3%	65	0%	3.20	-13.8	$2
LIMA Plan	D	2nd Half	138	18	38	3	14	0	275			333	399	732	8	86	30	0.63	280	38	24	38	79	7%	29	0%	4.59	-4.0	$3
+/- Score	-7	08 Proj	367	48	97	11	46	1	264			317	413	730	7	86	28	0.56	281	39	22	39	90	8%	55	1%	4.50	-12.9	$9

Move from CIN to SF was not kind to his power. But the bigger problem... turned back into a pumpkin vs LHP. Consistent skills otherwise, so his true level is probably somewhere between '06 and '07. At 35, closer to '07.

Ausmus,Brad

			AB	R	H	HR	RBI	SB	Avg	vL	vR	OB	Slg	OPS	bb%	ct%	h%	Eye	xBA	G	L	F	PX	hr/f	SX	SBO	RC/G	RAR	R$
Pos	2	03 HOU	450	43	103	4	47	5	229	237	227	300	291	592	9	85	26	0.70	251	49	21	31	40	3%	70	6%	3.03	-17.3	$5
Age	39	04 HOU	403	38	100	5	31	2	248	308	234	305	325	630	8	86	28	0.59	251	52	18	30	48	5%	49	4%	3.40	-4.9	$5
Decline		05 HOU	387	35	100	3	47	5	258	293	251	345	331	675	12	88	29	1.06	274	54	21	25	52	3%	47	6%	4.25	5.2	$7
Bats	Right	06 HOU	439	37	101	2	39	3	230	266	220	302	285	586	9	84	27	0.63	243	53	19	28	38	2%	52	3%	2.95	-18.5	$2
Reliability	35	07 HOU	349	38	82	3	25	6	235	239	234	308	324	632	10	79	29	0.50	244	51	17	31	63	3%	95	7%	3.42	-3.9	$4
BAvg Potl	50%	1st Half	192	23	50	2	17	3	260			317	365	682	8	82	31	0.47	263	46	20	34	74	4%	80	8%	3.99	1.1	$3
LIMA Plan	F	2nd Half	157	15	32	1	8	3	204			298	274	572	12	75	27	0.53	220	58	14	28	47	3%	96	7%	2.64	-5.6	$0
+/- Score	-1	08 Proj	221	21	52	2	18	3	235			312	307	619	10	81	28	0.60	245	53	18	29	51	3%	67	6%	3.31	-4.3	$2

Catchers sometimes have late-career surges. Then again, sometimes they don't. Though 2005 might have been his. You can see why it was easy to miss. Occasional SBs, otherwise nothing left here.

Aybar,Erick

			AB	R	H	HR	RBI	SB	Avg	vL	vR	OB	Slg	OPS	bb%	ct%	h%	Eye	xBA	G	L	F	PX	hr/f	SX	SBO	RC/G	RAR	R$
Pos	46	03	0	0	0	0	0	0	0							0									0				
Age	24	04	0	0	0	0	0	0	0							0									0				
Growth		05 aa	535	78	142	7	42	38	265			294	376	670	4	93	28	0.55					65		144	53%	3.84	-8.3	$19
Bats	Both	06 LAA *	379	56	98	5	39	27	259	250	250	291	370	660	4	91	27	0.48	280	70	3	27	66	6%	137	58%	3.70	-5.0	$13
Reliability	14	07 LAA	194	18	46	1	19	4	237	304	216	275	289	563	5	84	28	0.31	217	52	12	36	35	2%	79	16%	2.40	-10.3	$2
BAvg Potl	40%	1st Half	156	15	37	0	15	2	237			274	269	544	5	85	28	0.33	219	54	14	32	28	0%	54	15%	2.22	-9.2	$1
LIMA Plan	F	2nd Half	38	3	9	1	4	2	237			275	368	643	5	79	28	0.25	193	45	3	52	67	6%	108	22%	3.23	-1.0	$1
+/- Score	-42	08 Proj	258	33	66	2	23	13	256			288	340	628	4	89	28	0.43	264	55	13	32	53	3%	118	40%	3.31	-6.5	$7

What happened to the speed? Well, there was no way LAA was going to give him a 50+% SBO in the majors. Add in his sub-.300 OBAs and two DL stints. He should improve, but temper expectations for now.

Baker,Jeff

			AB	R	H	HR	RBI	SB	Avg	vL	vR	OB	Slg	OPS	bb%	ct%	h%	Eye	xBA	G	L	F	PX	hr/f	SX	SBO	RC/G	RAR	R$
Pos	3	03	0	0	0	0	0	0	0							0									0				
Age	26	04	0	0	0	0	0	0	0							0									0				
Pre-Peak		05 aaa	228	25	60	8	26	2	263			294	439	733	4	89	27	0.38					105		66	6%	4.37	-6.5	$6
Bats	Right	06 COL *	539	65	158	22	101	7	292	438	341	335	497	832	6	83	32	0.38	319	44	28	28	120	17%	89	6%	5.59	-6.1	$21
Reliability	6	07 COL	144	17	32	4	12	0	222	246	205	287	347	634	8	72	28	0.33	223	40	20	39	75	10%	72	0%	3.20	-10.5	$1
BAvg Potl	40%	1st Half	92	8	22	2	7	0	239			300	370	670	8	76	29	0.36	236	44	19	37	76	8%	65	0%	3.74	-5.1	$1
LIMA Plan	F	2nd Half	52	9	10	2	5	0	192			263	308	571	9	65	25	0.28	200	32	24	44	73	13%	56	0%	2.19	-5.6	$1
+/- Score	-17	08 Proj	260	33	64	9	33	2	246			299	402	701	7	77	29	0.33	254	38	22	40	96	11%	75	3%	4.01	-13.1	$6

June virus and July concussion laid waste to his 2nd half. Frankly, 1st half wasn't so hot either, especially given his numbers in 2006. At 26, there won't be too many more chances.

Bako,Paul

			AB	R	H	HR	RBI	SB	Avg	vL	vR	OB	Slg	OPS	bb%	ct%	h%	Eye	xBA	G	L	F	PX	hr/f	SX	SBO	RC/G	RAR	R$
Pos	2	03 CHC	188	19	43	0	17	0	229	200	233	310	330	639	10	75	30	0.47	250	46	22	32	82	0%	80	2%	3.62	-3.9	$1
Age	35	04 CHC	138	13	28	1	10	1	203	95	222	281	283	564	10	79	25	0.52	239	49	19	33	63	3%	46	3%	2.57	-5.4	($0)
Decline		05 LA	40	1	10	0	4	0	250	250	250	362	300	662	15	70	36	0.58	118	67	19	15	52	0%	0	0%	4.02	0.3	$0
Bats	Left	06 KC	153	7	32	0	10	0	209	200	210	262	229	491	7	70	30	0.24	179	56	19	24	20	0%	11	0%	1.21	-15.2	($1)
Reliability	0	07 BAL	156	13	32	1	8	0	205	192	208	275	256	531	9	68	30	0.30	215	56	23	21	40	5%	52	2%	1.83	-10.7	($1)
BAvg Potl	40%	1st Half	102	5	23	1	6	0	225			275	284	560	6	74	30	0.26	225	53	23	24	37	5%	41	0%	2.17	-5.7	($0)
LIMA Plan	F	2nd Half	54	8	9	0	2	0	167			274	204	478	13	57	29	0.35	195	65	23	13	47	0%	60	7%	1.07	-5.3	($1)
+/- Score	-14	08 Proj	127	11	25	0	8	0	197			272	237	509	9	69	28	0.33	206	55	21	24	39	2%	35	3%	1.55	-10.4	($1)

Back in the day, you could count on him for a strong BA, but that day was in 1998. Doubled his PX - and was still 60% below league average. But check out that SX trend -- I want a piece of that. Could net me 1 SB.

Baldelli,Rocco

			AB	R	H	HR	RBI	SB	Avg	vL	vR	OB	Slg	OPS	bb%	ct%	h%	Eye	xBA	G	L	F	PX	hr/f	SX	SBO	RC/G	RAR	R$
Pos	8	03 TAM	637	89	185	11	78	27	290	298	285	322	418	740	4	80	35	0.23	271	50	20	30	84	7%	137	23%	4.47	-5.0	$23
Age	26	04 TAM	518	79	145	16	74	17	280	331	264	319	436	756	5	83	31	0.34	273	52	13	35	94	11%	119	16%	4.65	-0.9	$19
Pre-Peak		05 TAM	0	0	0	0	0	0	0							0									0				
Bats	Right	06 TAM *	411	66	128	16	61	10	311	297	303	340	527	867	4	81	36	0.22	299	51	16	34	134	14%	134	13%	5.96	14.6	$18
Reliability	0	07 TAM	137	16	28	5	12	4	204	156	219	253	358	611	6	74	24	0.26	241	38	18	44	106	11%	78	19%	2.78	-6.5	$2
BAvg Potl	55%	1st Half	137	16	28	5	12	4	204			253	358	611	6	74	24	0.26	241	38	18	44	106	11%	78	19%	2.78	-6.5	$2
LIMA Plan	D	2nd Half	0	0	0	0	0	0	0							0													
+/- Score	11	08 Proj	298	42	79	10	37	9	265			304	429	733	5	79	31	0.27	269	48	16	36	106	11%	113	17%	4.36	-0.5	$9

Hot April, stone-cold May, DL rest of the year. '03/'04 shows the potential, but '05/'06 shows the danger. Owns speed and power, but the hamstrings might break your heart.
UP: 20 HR/25 SB. DN: 5/5.

Barajas,Rod

			AB	R	H	HR	RBI	SB	Avg	vL	vR	OB	Slg	OPS	bb%	ct%	h%	Eye	xBA	G	L	F	PX	hr/f	SX	SBO	RC/G	RAR	R$
Pos	2	03 ARI	220	19	48	3	28	0	218	244	212	265	327	592	6	80	26	0.33	245	32	21	47	83	4%	25	0%	2.76	-10.3	$2
Age	32	04 TEX	362	51	91	15	58	0	251	248	249	277	453	730	3	82	27	0.20	255	29	13	57	125	9%	55	2%	4.22	-1.2	$9
Past Peak		05 TEX	410	53	104	21	60	0	254	272	251	298	466	764	6	83	26	0.37	284	29	20	51	131	12%	27	0%	4.70	8.2	$12
Bats	Right	06 TEX	344	49	88	11	41	0	256	156	279	291	410	701	5	85	27	0.33	255	32	17	51	94	7%	41	0%	3.97	-4.4	$7
Reliability	32	07 PHI	122	16	28	4	10	0	230	226	231	343	393	736	15	80	26	0.88	244	31	15	54	109	8%	29	3%	4.91	4.2	$2
BAvg Potl	65%	1st Half	96	12	21	4	9	0	219			342	406	748	16	80	23	0.95	248	31	14	55	120	10%	26	3%	5.07	3.8	$1
LIMA Plan	D	2nd Half	26	4	7	0	1	0	269			345	346	691	10	81	33	0.60	229	30	20	50	68	0%	39	0%	4.29	0.4	$0
+/- Score	8	08 Proj	335	43	85	13	42	0	254			316	434	750	8	82	27	0.51	258	30	17	53	113	9%	29	1%	4.72	7.5	$8

Battled injuries most of the year, but couldn't win the starting job even when healthy. The seeds for success are still there, and '07's BPIs even took a step up. In the right situation, could return to 2006 levels.

Bard,Josh

			AB	R	H	HR	RBI	SB	Avg	vL	vR	OB	Slg	OPS	bb%	ct%	h%	Eye	xBA	G	L	F	PX	hr/f	SX	SBO	RC/G	RAR	R$
Pos	2	03 aaa	115	13	36	5	19	1	310			379	499	879	10	86	33	0.80					114		31	8%	6.35	6.9	$5
Age	30	04 a/a	186	22	36	3	16	0	194			245	285	530	6	86	21	0.47					60		42	0%	2.17	-11.2	$0
Peak		05 CLE	83	6	16	1	9	0	193	148	214	272	277	549	10	87	21	0.82	238	43	18	39	59	4%	16	0%	2.63	-3.6	($0)
Bats	Both	06 2TM	249	30	83	9	40	1	333	333	333	405	522	927	11	83	37	0.71	301	52	21	27	120	16%	30	1%	7.05	17.4	$10
Reliability	8	07 SD	389	42	111	5	51	0	285	376	250	367	404	770	11	85	33	0.86	272	52	18	30	81	5%	39	1%	5.31	16.7	$9
BAvg Potl	55%	1st Half	180	17	46	3	22	0	256			333	367	700	10	84	29	0.75	255	46	19	35	76	6%	17	0%	4.37	3.0	$3
LIMA Plan	D	2nd Half	209	25	65	2	29	0	311			395	435	830	12	86	36	0.97	285	56	18	26	85	4%	53	1%	6.12	13.2	$6
+/- Score	-16	08 Proj	372	42	107	7	50	1	288			362	420	782	10	85	32	0.76	280	52	19	29	88	8%	38	2%	5.35	14.5	$10

Solid plate patience means he can be counted on for a good batting average. A #2 catcher who won't hurt your BA is a rare find because everything else he contributes is gravy.

DAVE ADLER

Barfield,Josh			AB	R	H	HR	RBI	SB	Avg	vL	vR	OB	Slg	OPS	bb%	ct%	h%	Eye	xBA	G	L	F	PX	hr/f	SX	SBO	RC/G	RAR	R$
Pos	4	03	0	0	0	0	0	0	0							0									0				
Age	25	04 aa	521	71	117	15	81	4	225			282	367	649	7	80	26	0.40					90		82	5%	3.44	-14.4	$10
Pre-Peak		05 aaa	512	61	142	11	60	17	277			335	386	721	8	84	31	0.55					71		88	15%	4.42	1.2	$16
Bats	Right	06 SD	539	72	151	13	58	21	280	331	266	318	423	741	5	85	31	0.37	266	39	19	42	87	7%	110	20%	4.52	-1.3	$18
Reliability	17	07 CLE	420	53	102	3	50	14	243	211	255	267	324	591	3	79	30	0.16	221	40	17	43	61	2%	122	21%	2.56	-19.8	$8
BAvg Potl	35%	1st Half	274	30	72	2	36	6	263			284	350	634	3	81	32	0.15	232	42	17	41	61	2%	107	14%	3.10	-8.2	$6
LIMA Plan	D	2nd Half	146	23	30	1	14	8	205			237	274	511	4	75	27	0.16	199	35	17	48	59	2%	129	36%	1.49	-12.2	$3
+/- Score	-14	08 Proj	366	49	93	6	42	13	254			292	361	652	5	80	30	0.27	236	39	18	44	74	4%	115	20%	3.41	-7.8	$9

Started slowly and never recovered. Already-borderline bb% and ct% dipped, and 2H uppercut swing didn't help. Young enough to rebound, and consistent speed skills set a nice floor on his value.

Barmes,Clint			AB	R	H	HR	RBI	SB	Avg	vL	vR	OB	Slg	OPS	bb%	ct%	h%	Eye	xBA	G	L	F	PX	hr/f	SX	SBO	RC/G	RAR	R$
Pos	6	03 aaa	493	47	129	7	40	9	262			286	375	662	3	91	28	0.39					74		69	16%	3.66	-8.8	$9
Age	29	04 aaa	533	70	155	13	35	14	292			316	442	758	3	93	30	0.48					88		95	20%	4.71	6.3	$16
Peak		05 COL	350	55	101	10	46	6	289	289	283	320	434	754	4	90	30	0.44	288	36	23	41	87	8%	90	11%	4.63	6.7	$13
Bats	Right	06 COL	478	57	105	7	56	5	220	267	209	254	335	589	4	85	25	0.31	241	34	18	48	72	4%	92	10%	2.75	-23.8	$5
Reliability	34	07 COL	* 465	50	106	8	30	6	229	444	143	255	337	592	3	86	25	0.26	210	21	17	63	64	3%	87	12%	2.73	-17.6	$4
BAvg Potl	55%	1st Half	271	33	82	3	22	3	303			337	413	750	5	89	33	0.48		21	14	64	68	2%	78	11%	4.71	5.7	$7
LIMA Plan	F	2nd Half	194	17	24	5	8	3	126			136	230	365	1	82	13	0.06		20	20	60	58	5%	117	18%	-0.22	-27.9	($3)
+/- Score	-3	08 Proj	237	27	53	5	20	3	224			250	346	596	3	86	24	0.26	255	35	20	45	73	5%	96	13%	2.79	-9.4	$3

0-1-.216 in 37 AB at COL. 1st half performance in AAA resembled 2005 debut, but once again proved unsustainable. At 29, a utility role is looking less likely. Yet another player whose ceiling is spelled "AAA."

Barrett,Michael			AB	R	H	HR	RBI	SB	Avg	vL	vR	OB	Slg	OPS	bb%	ct%	h%	Eye	xBA	G	L	F	PX	hr/f	SX	SBO	RC/G	RAR	R$
Pos	2	03 MON	226	33	47	10	30	0	208	205	209	275	398	674	9	84	21	0.57	286	48	17	35	109	15%	73	0%	3.81	-3.4	$4
Age	31	04 CHC	456	55	131	16	65	1	287	248	299	335	489	824	7	86	31	0.52	310	48	20	32	118	13%	70	5%	5.59	22.9	$14
Past Peak		05 CHC	424	48	117	16	61	0	276	320	254	338	479	817	9	86	29	0.66	319	43	24	33	127	13%	44	3%	5.60	22.1	$13
Bats	Right	06 CHC	375	54	115	16	53	0	307	313	305	363	517	880	8	89	31	0.80	311	45	20	36	116	13%	50	1%	6.27	19.7	$14
Reliability	24	07 2NL	344	29	84	9	41	2	244	222	249	284	372	656	5	83	27	0.33	255	40	19	41	81	8%	35	5%	3.46	-3.4	$5
BAvg Potl	50%	1st Half	233	23	59	9	30	2	253			304	412	716	7	82	27	0.40	261	40	19	41	96	11%	37	7%	4.19	2.7	$5
LIMA Plan	D+	2nd Half	111	6	25	0	11	0	225			239	288	527	2	86	26	0.13	239	39	20	41	52	0%	17	0%	1.97	-6.1	($0)
+/- Score	-0	08 Proj	409	42	112	14	52	1	274			317	451	768	6	86	29	0.45	289	42	20	38	105	11%	46	2%	4.84	10.4	$10

BPIs were off in 1H, then injury and move to Petco ruined 2H. Skills history says he should rebound; how much will depend on new team and health. He still owns intriguing skills upside.
UP: 20 HR, .300

Bartlett,Jason			AB	R	H	HR	RBI	SB	Avg	vL	vR	OB	Slg	OPS	bb%	ct%	h%	Eye	xBA	G	L	F	PX	hr/f	SX	SBO	RC/G	RAR	R$
Pos	6	03	0	0	0	0	0	0	0							0									0				
Age	28	04 aaa	269	46	83	2	25	6	309			376	439	815	10	88	35	0.88					76		129	10%	5.81	11.2	$9
Peak		05 MIN	* 453	68	123	7	44	6	272	290	226	339	375	714	9	85	31	0.68	262	47	18	35	67	5%	92	6%	4.47	-1.2	$11
Bats	Right	06 MIN	* 568	85	172	3	51	16	303	314	307	339	407	746	5	87	35	0.42	279	44	22	34	72	2%	112	15%	4.69	4.4	$16
Reliability	63	07 MIN	510	75	135	5	43	23	265	319	245	330	361	691	9	86	30	0.68	260	44	20	36	60	3%	140	17%	4.23	-4.9	$14
BAvg Potl	55%	1st Half	218	24	55	1	19	13	252			324	303	626	10	87	29	0.79	263	42	26	32	38	2%	93	19%	3.52	-6.7	$5
LIMA Plan	B	2nd Half	292	51	80	4	24	10	274			335	404	740	8	85	31	0.61	260	46	16	39	77	4%	143	15%	4.77	1.8	$8
+/- Score	15	08 Proj	547	83	148	7	48	25	271			330	385	714	8	86	30	0.63	270	44	20	36	71	4%	138	19%	4.46	-0.9	$16

BA normalized as h% reverted. Still showed some skill growth in 2nd full season, until August hamstring injury slowed him. BA vRHP is a concern, but SX trend says...
UP: 30 SB

Barton,Daric			AB	R	H	HR	RBI	SB	Avg	vL	vR	OB	Slg	OPS	bb%	ct%	h%	Eye	xBA	G	L	F	PX	hr/f	SX	SBO	RC/G	RAR	R$
Pos	3	03	0	0	0	0	0	0	0							0									0				
Age	22	04	0	0	0	0	0	0	0							0									0				
Growth		05 aa	212	32	62	4	30	1	292			376	451	826	12	89	31	1.24					106		60	3%	6.04	4.1	$7
Bats	Left	06 aaa	147	22	36	2	19	1	247			366	367	732	16	88	27	1.51					68		88	2%	5.16	-2.4	$3
Reliability	8	07 OAK	* 588	87	164	11	67	4	279	296	378	360	423	784	11	89	30	1.12	291	32	24	44	96	5%	67	5%	5.50	7.0	$15
BAvg Potl	65%	1st Half	293	41	88	5	41	1	300			375	444	819	11	90	32	1.25					96		45	4%	5.89	6.5	$9
LIMA Plan	A	2nd Half	295	46	76	6	26	3	258			346	403	750	12	87	28	1.03	284	32	24	44	96	5%	77	6%	5.11	0.1	$6
+/- Score	13	08 Proj	518	77	139	14	62	4	268			363	437	801	13	88	28	1.26	294	32	24	44	103	7%	80	4%	5.76	8.6	$13

4-8-.347 in 72 AB at OAK. Lots of positives in this skill set: patient, makes contact, fly ball tendency. Power will need more time to develop, but he is well worth tucking away.

Bautista,Jose			AB	R	H	HR	RBI	SB	Avg	vL	vR	OB	Slg	OPS	bb%	ct%	h%	Eye	xBA	G	L	F	PX	hr/f	SX	SBO	RC/G	RAR	R$
Pos	59	03	0	0	0	0	0	0	0							0									0				
Age	27	04 2TM	88	6	18	0	2	0	205			263	239	502	7	55	38	0.18					44		31	5%	1.54	-9.6	($1)
Peak		05 PIT	* 515	53	122	16	69	7	238			294	390	684	7	82	26	0.45					98		66	10%	3.89	-13.9	$12
Bats	Right	06 PIT	* 501	70	122	18	60	4	243	283	216	323	420	743	11	74	29	0.46	238	40	13	47	117	10%	71	7%	4.79	-10.6	$11
Reliability	53	07 PIT	532	75	135	15	63	6	254	256	253	338	414	752	11	81	29	0.67	261	40	16	43	106	8%	73	6%	4.97	3.1	$13
BAvg Potl	55%	1st Half	272	42	74	7	26	4	272			357	434	791	12	82	31	0.75	272	44	16	40	109	8%	78	6%	5.51	5.7	$7
LIMA Plan	C+	2nd Half	260	33	61	8	37	2	235			318	392	711	11	80	27	0.60	248	37	16	47	103	8%	60	6%	4.40	-3.0	$5
+/- Score	17	08 Proj	511	68	126	16	63	5	247			325	410	735	10	79	28	0.55	250	40	15	45	108	9%	69	7%	4.68	-4.1	$12

Skills are unremarkable, but in PIT that is good enough for 500+AB. Second half BPI fade tempers optimism for further growth. 500 AB should be worth $10-12 again, but little upside beyond that level.

Bay,Jason			AB	R	H	HR	RBI	SB	Avg	vL	vR	OB	Slg	OPS	bb%	ct%	h%	Eye	xBA	G	L	F	PX	hr/f	SX	SBO	RC/G	RAR	R$
Pos	7	03 aaa	307	52	80	15	49	19	261			353	443	796	13	80	28	0.72					106		113	24%	5.44	-0.2	$15
Age	29	04 PIT	411	61	116	26	82	4	282	265	287	347	550	897	9	69	35	0.32	274	40	17	43	183	22%	81	10%	6.97	18.1	$19
Peak		05 PIT	599	110	183	32	101	21	306	342	292	401	559	960	14	76	36	0.67	301	38	22	40	170	17%	133	11%	7.76	39.6	$34
Bats	Right	06 PIT	570	101	163	35	109	11	286	304	280	394	532	926	15	73	34	0.65	268	41	15	44	155	19%	87	7%	7.43	35.0	$27
Reliability	44	07 PIT	538	78	133	21	84	4	247	227	254	322	418	740	10	74	30	0.42	241	38	17	45	114	12%	73	3%	4.68	-10.5	$14
BAvg Potl	45%	1st Half	293	41	79	12	49	1	270			346	461	806	10	75	32	0.46	262	40	19	41	127	13%	62	2%	5.60	2.2	$9
LIMA Plan	C+	2nd Half	245	37	54	9	35	3	220			293	367	660	9	73	27	0.37	214	36	13	51	99	10%	71	5%	3.55	-13.4	$5
+/- Score	-4	08 Proj	560	90	158	27	94	10	282			367	487	854	12	74	34	0.51	257	38	17	45	134	15%	92	7%	6.29	15.2	$23

BA decline was a h% fluke, and should revert. PX and SX plunges are more difficult to explain, and make a rebound tougher to project. But he owns the skills, and age is on his side.
UP: see 2005.

Belliard,Ronnie			AB	R	H	HR	RBI	SB	Avg	vL	vR	OB	Slg	OPS	bb%	ct%	h%	Eye	xBA	G	L	F	PX	hr/f	SX	SBO	RC/G	RAR	R$
Pos	4	03 COL	447	73	124	8	50	7	277	345	254	349	409	758	10	84	32	0.69	298	50	23	27	90	8%	97	7%	5.04	8.1	$13
Age	33	04 CLE	599	78	169	12	70	3	282	319	263	347	426	773	9	84	32	0.61	276	44	19	37	98	6%	54	3%	5.17	18.4	$14
Past Peak		05 CLE	536	71	152	17	78	2	284	287	285	327	450	777	6	87	30	0.49	290	45	18	37	105	10%	50	3%	4.98	12.8	$17
Bats	Right	06 2TM	544	63	148	13	67	2	272	220	295	317	403	720	6	85	30	0.44	267	46	19	35	81	8%	44	4%	4.31	-0.7	$13
Reliability	81	07 WAS	511	57	148	11	58	3	290	329	275	334	427	761	6	86	32	0.47	270	44	17	39	89	6%	59	2%	4.83	3.8	$13
BAvg Potl	50%	1st Half	197	15	59	2	17	1	299			327	381	708	4	86	34	0.29	244	49	17	34	57	3%	31	2%	4.06	-2.7	$4
LIMA Plan	C	2nd Half	314	42	89	9	41	2	283			338	455	794	8	86	31	0.59	282	42	16	42	110	8%	61	3%	5.30	6.5	$9
+/- Score	-17	08 Proj	519	62	147	15	63	3	283			330	440	770	6	86	31	0.48	280	45	18	37	98	9%	57	3%	4.91	5.1	$14

Skill set was stable and not all that exciting, until he started uppercutting in 2nd half and lifting balls over the fence. Maintained rest of his skills while doing so, which means...
UP: 2005, maybe even 20 HR

Bellorin,Edwin			AB	R	H	HR	RBI	SB	Avg	vL	vR	OB	Slg	OPS	bb%	ct%	h%	Eye	xBA	G	L	F	PX	hr/f	SX	SBO	RC/G	RAR	R$
Pos	2	03 aa	57	2	10	0	3	0	175			203	246	449	3	77	23	0.15					49		62	0%	0.82	-6.2	($1)
Age	26	04 aa	285	25	72	1	27	1	253			292	316	608	5	83	30	0.33					47		56	1%	2.98	-9.1	$3
Pre-Peak		05	0	0	0	0	0	0	0							0									0				
Bats	Right	06 aaa	321	24	63	6	37	1	196			221	287	507	3	86	21	0.22					54		37	5%	1.68	-27.4	$0
Reliability	0	07 aaa	223	29	62	7	33	1	278			317	444	761	5	90	29	0.54					101		46	2%	4.78	5.5	$7
BAvg Potl	40%	1st Half	135	22	47	5	25	1	348			393	541	934	7	91	36	0.83					116		48	2%	6.79	10.0	$7
LIMA Plan	F	2nd Half	88	7	15	2	8	0	172			195	295	491	3	87	17	0.23					77		26	0%	1.57	-6.7	($0)
+/- Score	-21	08 Proj	168	16	38	4	20	1	226			258	340	598	4	87	24	0.32					71		40	3%	2.82	-6.3	$2

0-0-.000 in 2 AB at COL. Fared better in second tour of AAA. Has never topped 321 AB in a season, so durability is a concern. If he sustains 2007's gains and stays healthy, he could earn a part-time role.

RAY MURPHY

Beltran,Carlos			AB	R	H	HR	RBI	SB	Avg	vL	vR	OB	Slg	OPS	bb%	ct%	h%	Eye	xBA	G	L	F	PX	hr/f	SX	SBO	RC/G	RAR	R$
Pos	8	03 KC	521	102	160	26	100	41	307	325	300	391	522	913	12	84	32	0.89	303	47	20	33	113	18%	164	25%	6.88	30.6	$34
Age	31	04 2TM	599	121	160	38	104	42	267	276	264	365	548	912	13	83	27	0.91	304	39	15	46	157	17%	167	27%	6.92	38.9	$35
Past Peak		05 NYM	582	83	155	16	78	17	266	308	254	331	414	745	9	84	30	0.58	277	44	19	37	96	9%	102	14%	4.75	3.2	$20
Bats	Both	06 NYM	510	127	140	41	116	18	275	247	288	388	594	983	16	81	27	0.96	318	37	17	47	186	21%	108	14%	7.87	50.2	$31
Reliability	19	07 NYM	554	93	153	33	112	23	276	304	265	356	525	882	11	80	29	0.62	296	38	19	43	150	17%	113	16%	6.44	29.7	$28
BAvg Potl	55%	1st Half	282	40	76	10	44	12	270			350	447	797	11	83	29	0.73	276	39	19	42	108	10%	106	17%	5.48	7.5	$11
LIMA Plan	B+	2nd Half	272	53	77	23	68	11	283			363	607	969	11	77	29	0.54	317	38	19	44	198	25%	107	16%	7.53	22.7	$17
+/- Score	-4	08 Proj	**523**	**100**	**147**	**33**	**105**	**17**	**281**			**368**	**541**	**909**	**12**	**81**	**29**	**0.71**	**302**	**39**	**18**	**43**	**155**	**18%**	**111**	**13%**	**6.81**	**33.5**	**$28**

Bothered by leg issues in 1st half. Opened up swing in 2nd half but 25% hr/f won't hold up. Skills fluctuate but remain excellent though dogged by injuries. Rel score / price point combo is dangerous.

Beltre,Adrian			AB	R	H	HR	RBI	SB	Avg	vL	vR	OB	Slg	OPS	bb%	ct%	h%	Eye	xBA	G	L	F	PX	hr/f	SX	SBO	RC/G	RAR	R$
Pos	5	03 LA	559	50	134	23	80	2	240	232	242	287	424	711	6	82	26	0.36	283	43	20	37	114	14%	46	3%	4.11	-2.3	$12
Age	29	04 LA	598	104	200	48	121	7	334	291	347	389	629	1017	8	85	33	0.61	326	41	18	40	159	23%	61	5%	7.67	41.0	$38
Peak		05 SEA	603	69	154	19	87	3	255	281	249	300	413	712	6	82	28	0.35	277	46	19	35	104	11%	56	3%	4.16	-6.0	$15
Bats	Right	06 SEA	620	88	166	25	89	11	268	280	264	319	465	784	7	81	30	0.40	282	37	21	42	121	12%	98	11%	5.07	1.1	$19
Reliability	88	07 SEA	595	87	164	26	99	14	276	280	274	319	482	801	6	83	30	0.37	295	44	17	39	132	13%	101	12%	5.21	12.0	$23
BAvg Potl	50%	1st Half	248	37	64	10	31	5	258			303	452	755	6	85	27	0.42	279	40	13	46	124	10%	77	13%	4.67	1.3	$7
LIMA Plan	C+	2nd Half	347	50	100	16	68	9	288			331	504	835	6	81	32	0.33	304	46	19	35	138	17%	103	11%	5.61	10.8	$15
+/- Score	31	08 Proj	**623**	**87**	**169**	**30**	**104**	**11**	**271**			**318**	**485**	**802**	**6**	**82**	**29**	**0.38**	**295**	**42**	**18**	**39**	**133**	**15%**	**90**	**10%**	**5.22**	**10.2**	**$23**

Fifth straight 2H HR increase of 50+% over 1H. Stable skill set with value derived from power and durability. PX is trending up toward 2004 and 2 year SB success rate is near 80%. Bid full value.

Bennett,Gary			AB	R	H	HR	RBI	SB	Avg	vL	vR	OB	Slg	OPS	bb%	ct%	h%	Eye	xBA	G	L	F	PX	hr/f	SX	SBO	RC/G	RAR	R$
Pos	2	03 SD	307	26	73	2	42	3	238	218	248	293	306	599	7	84	28	0.50	266	47	24	29	52	3%	55	4%	3.01	-11.8	$4
Age	36	04 MIL	219	18	49	3	20	1	224	256	217	295	329	623	9	85	25	0.69	247	50	14	36	72	5%	35	2%	3.43	-2.6	$1
Decline		05 WAS	199	11	44	1	21	0	221	200	241	295	271	567	10	81	27	0.57	243	43	25	32	40	2%	14	2%	2.63	-7.1	$0
Bats	Right	06 STL	157	13	35	4	22	0	223	400	172	274	331	605	7	81	25	0.37	244	48	20	31	65	10%	16	0%	2.84	-7.2	$2
Reliability	20	07 STL	155	12	39	2	17	1	252	227	261	288	335	624	5	90	27	0.50	245	43	17	40	54	4%	35	5%	3.28	-2.4	$2
BAvg Potl	50%	1st Half	96	6	22	1	10	1	229			260	302	562	4	91	24	0.44	225	42	13	44	47	3%	37	5%	2.59	-3.5	$1
LIMA Plan	F	2nd Half	59	6	17	1	7	0	288			333	390	723	6	88	31	0.57	278	45	23	32	65	6%	32	6%	4.42	1.1	$1
+/- Score	-6	08 Proj	**163**	**13**	**40**	**2**	**19**	**0**	**245**			**295**	**334**	**630**	**7**	**85**	**27**	**0.49**	**252**	**45**	**20**	**35**	**58**	**5%**	**28**	**3%**	**3.31**	**-3.1**	**$2**

When discussing #2 catcher possibilities, mention both his 2nd half BA and career-high ct%. Then hope that other owners ignore the five-year declining AB trend and career-long skill set emptiness.

Berkman,Lance			AB	R	H	HR	RBI	SB	Avg	vL	vR	OB	Slg	OPS	bb%	ct%	h%	Eye	xBA	G	L	F	PX	hr/f	SX	SBO	RC/G	RAR	R$
Pos	39	03 HOU	538	110	155	25	93	5	288	282	290	406	515	921	17	80	32	0.99	298	41	20	38	142	15%	99	4%	7.34	27.7	$24
Age	32	04 HOU	544	104	172	30	106	9	316	272	329	446	566	1012	19	81	34	1.26	310	40	21	39	151	17%	74	7%	8.57	38.9	$30
Past Peak		05 HOU	468	76	137	24	82	4	293	296	295	408	524	931	16	85	30	1.26	327	46	23	32	142	19%	62	3%	7.37	23.0	$21
Bats	Both	06 HOU	536	95	169	45	136	3	315	266	335	421	621	1042	15	80	32	0.92	313	39	19	42	173	25%	55	3%	8.58	37.4	$32
Reliability	38	07 HOU	561	95	156	34	102	7	278	265	282	382	510	891	14	78	30	0.75	285	44	18	38	139	21%	70	5%	6.75	18.4	$24
BAvg Potl	50%	1st Half	261	40	68	11	45	4	261			381	410	791	16	77	30	0.86	247	47	18	35	89	16%	48	7%	5.59	-0.1	$9
LIMA Plan	B	2nd Half	300	55	88	23	57	3	293			382	597	979	13	78	31	0.65	316	42	18	40	183	25%	80	3%	7.73	17.7	$16
+/- Score	-2	08 Proj	**535**	**93**	**157**	**35**	**107**	**5**	**293**			**400**	**551**	**951**	**15**	**80**	**31**	**0.88**	**303**	**43**	**19**	**38**	**153**	**22%**	**66**	**4%**	**7.51**	**26.9**	**$26**

Premier hitter traded some patience for big 2nd half. Eye and xBA trends may be first hints of decline. A .300 BA may be more difficult to attain going forward, but 2H PX says elite power is intact.

Betancourt,Yuniesk			AB	R	H	HR	RBI	SB	Avg	vL	vR	OB	Slg	OPS	bb%	ct%	h%	Eye	xBA	G	L	F	PX	hr/f	SX	SBO	RC/G	RAR	R$
Pos	6	03	0	0	0	0	0	0	0							0									0				
Age	26	04	0	0	0	0	0	0	0							0									0				
Pre-Peak		05 SEA *	621	57	157	7	58	17	253	283	248	282	367	649	4	91	27	0.47	257	38	17	45	66	3%	113	25%	3.60	-18.0	$12
Bats	Right	06 SEA	558	68	161	8	47	11	289	240	303	310	403	713	3	90	31	0.31	276	46	18	36	67	4%	101	14%	4.16	-3.9	$13
Reliability	81	07 SEA	536	72	155	9	67	5	289	333	277	309	418	726	3	91	30	0.31	290	43	19	38	84	5%	78	7%	4.31	-3.7	$14
BAvg Potl	50%	1st Half	262	35	74	4	28	4	282			306	389	696	3	92	30	0.41	279	40	20	39	70	4%	68	11%	4.01	-4.1	$7
LIMA Plan	C	2nd Half	274	37	81	5	39	1	296			311	445	756	2	91	31	0.23	300	46	18	36	97	6%	76	3%	4.60	0.3	$8
+/- Score	-9	08 Proj	**612**	**76**	**174**	**13**	**66**	**7**	**284**			**305**	**426**	**732**	**3**	**91**	**30**	**0.33**	**290**	**44**	**19**	**37**	**85**	**6%**	**85**	**11%**	**4.36**	**-2.6**	**$16**

Hacking ways still limit upside of excellent ct%. 2H PX spike and six Safeco HRs from a RH hitter are intriguing. High CS rate is reducing SBO, but youth should give him more chances. Pay for a repeat.

Betemit,Wilson			AB	R	H	HR	RBI	SB	Avg	vL	vR	OB	Slg	OPS	bb%	ct%	h%	Eye	xBA	G	L	F	PX	hr/f	SX	SBO	RC/G	RAR	R$
Pos	5	03 aaa	478	57	132	9	68	9	276			330	428	758	7	80	33	0.40					95		117	11%	4.91	7.2	$14
Age	27	04 aaa	356	42	91	11	52	3	256			310	421	731	7	76	31	0.33					111		70	7%	4.48	-5.3	$9
Peak		05 ATL	246	36	75	4	20	1	305	260	323	362	435	797	8	78	38	0.40	276	48	25	27	88	8%	91	5%	5.44	4.5	$7
Bats	Both	06 2NL	373	49	98	18	53	3	263	189	281	328	469	797	9	73	32	0.35	270	42	21	37	139	18%	48	4%	5.40	-1.0	$11
Reliability	56	07 2TM	240	33	55	14	50	0	229	239	227	335	454	789	14	66	28	0.46	250	42	18	40	167	22%	20	0%	5.64	7.3	$7
BAvg Potl	45%	1st Half	122	17	24	8	20	0	197			333	434	768	17	68	21	0.64	241	47	12	41	165	23%	17	0%	5.28	2.4	$2
LIMA Plan	D	2nd Half	118	16	31	6	30	0	263			336	475	810	10	64	36	0.30	257	36	25	39	168	21%	22	0%	6.06	4.8	$4
+/- Score	1	08 Proj	**264**	**36**	**68**	**17**	**45**	**1**	**258**			**336**	**511**	**847**	**11**	**70**	**30**	**0.40**	**283**	**43**	**21**	**36**	**172**	**25%**	**53**	**3%**	**6.18**	**10.7**	**$9**

BA vs. RHPs plunged due to poor 1H h% and a ct% in the danger zone. But FB% and bb% growth, plus PX trend and ideal age point to power breakout.
UP: 400 AB, 25 HR

Biggio,Craig			AB	R	H	HR	RBI	SB	Avg	vL	vR	OB	Slg	OPS	bb%	ct%	h%	Eye	xBA	G	L	F	PX	hr/f	SX	SBO	RC/G	RAR	R$
Pos	4	03 HOU	628	102	166	15	62	8	264	267	264	326	412	738	8	82	30	0.49	288	46	23	32	102	9%	96	7%	4.65	4.5	$17
Age	42	04 HOU	633	100	178	24	63	7	281	303	276	324	469	793	6	85	30	0.43	300	39	23	38	116	12%	78	6%	5.12	9.2	$21
Decline		05 HOU	590	94	156	26	69	11	264	243	269	308	468	776	6	85	27	0.41	296	43	17	41	127	13%	102	10%	4.89	5.6	$21
Bats	Right	06 HOU	548	79	135	21	62	3	246	297	233	298	422	719	7	85	26	0.48	278	39	19	41	104	11%	56	4%	4.29	-5.0	$13
Reliability		07 HOU	517	68	130	10	50	4	251	323	227	283	381	664	4	78	30	0.21	250	45	17	38	90	6%	83	6%	3.51	-16.0	$4
BAvg Potl		1st Half	282	44	67	5	26	3	238			276	387	663	5	79	28	0.25	261	44	16	40	104	6%	113	9%	3.59	-8.2	$5
LIMA Plan		2nd Half	235	24	63	5	24	1	268			292	374	667	3	77	33	0.15	232	46	17	37	73	7%	40	4%	3.41	-7.8	$4
+/- Score		08 Proj																											

Ends 20-year, 3000-hit HOF run as an OPS-challenged hacker after years of lead-off excellence. Eight years with a .380+ OBA, eight with 20+ HR, nine with 20+ SB. "BEE-GEE-OH!" indeed!

Blake,Casey			AB	R	H	HR	RBI	SB	Avg	vL	vR	OB	Slg	OPS	bb%	ct%	h%	Eye	xBA	G	L	F	PX	hr/f	SX	SBO	RC/G	RAR	R$
Pos	5	03 CLE	557	80	143	17	67	7	257	245	261	304	411	715	6	80	29	0.35	274	42	21	37	104	10%	64	12%	4.21	-5.0	$14
Age	34	04 CLE	587	93	159	28	88	5	271	243	284	347	486	832	10	76	31	0.49	274	43	17	40	137	16%	70	8%	5.88	16.7	$20
Past Peak		05 CLE	523	72	126	23	58	4	241	241	241	299	438	736	8	78	27	0.37	277	37	20	42	132	13%	63	8%	4.49	-0.1	$13
Bats	Right	06 CLE	401	63	113	19	68	6	282	272	286	354	479	833	10	77	33	0.48	279	40	23	37	124	17%	82	5%	5.84	9.4	$15
Reliability	22	07 CLE	588	81	159	18	78	4	270	256	276	332	437	769	8	79	32	0.44	262	39	18	43	113	9%	71	6%	5.01	8.7	$16
BAvg Potl	45%	1st Half	286	45	78	11	39	2	273			350	465	815	11	78	32	0.53	270	38	18	43	130	11%	72	6%	5.70	10.0	$9
LIMA Plan	D+	2nd Half	302	36	81	7	39	2	268			314	411	724	6	80	31	0.34	255	40	17	43	97	7%	71	5%	4.36	-1.3	$7
+/- Score	-7	08 Proj	**485**	**69**	**130**	**16**	**67**	**5**	**268**			**330**	**433**	**763**	**8**	**78**	**31**	**0.43**	**264**	**40**	**20**	**41**	**110**	**10%**	**71**	**6%**	**4.92**	**3.8**	**$14**

Power is his only real skill at at this point, working with high AB totals to drive his value. PX trend and age suggest that the ABs might decline sooner than later.
DN: 325 ABs, 10 HR

Blalock,Hank			AB	R	H	HR	RBI	SB	Avg	vL	vR	OB	Slg	OPS	bb%	ct%	h%	Eye	xBA	G	L	F	PX	hr/f	SX	SBO	RC/G	RAR	R$
Pos	5	03 TEX	567	89	170	29	90	2	300	209	329	350	522	872	7	83	32	0.45	292	33	21	45	132	14%	63	3%	6.08	24.6	$23
Age	27	04 TEX	627	108	173	33	114	2	276	282	273	354	504	858	11	76	31	0.51	271	34	18	48	144	15%	68	2%	6.23	23.5	$24
Peak		05 TEX	647	80	170	25	92	1	263	196	290	317	431	748	7	80	30	0.39	283	39	24	36	111	13%	38	1%	4.61	2.1	$18
Bats	Left	06 TEX	591	76	157	16	89	1	266	216	284	324	401	725	8	83	30	0.52	267	42	21	37	81	9%	62	1%	4.44	-9.7	$14
Reliability	19	07 TEX	208	32	61	10	33	4	293	298	292	358	543	901	9	82	32	0.55	304	33	21	46	157	13%	103	9%	6.65	12.5	$9
BAvg Potl	50%	1st Half	144	20	41	5	16	3	285			340	493	833	8	81	32	0.44	289	37	19	43	136	10%	102	11%	5.78	5.2	$5
LIMA Plan	C+	2nd Half	64	12	20	5	17	1	312			397	656	1053	12	83	31	0.82	339	25	25	51	204	19%	93	6%	8.55	7.0	$4
+/- Score	44	08 Proj	**495**	**75**	**141**	**24**	**88**	**3**	**285**			**351**	**512**	**863**	**9**	**82**	**31**	**0.56**	**296**	**35**	**22**	**43**	**139**	**14%**	**86**	**3%**	**6.14**	**20.8**	**$19**

PX and FB% slide began in June 2005, followed closely by two years of shoulder. problems. Encouraging post-surgery Sept suggests that a rebound could be imminent.
UP: 2004. DN: 2006.

JOCK THOMPSON

Blanco,Henry		AB	R	H	HR	RBI	SB	Avg	vL	vR	OB	Slg	OPS	bb%	ct%	h%	Eye	xBA	G	L	F	PX	hr/f	SX	SBO	RC/G	RAR	R$
Pos 2	03 ATL	151	11	30	1	13	0	199	281	176	248	272	520	6	86	22	0.48	240	30	22	48	54	2%	23	0%	2.10	-10.4	($0)
Age 36	04 MIN	315	36	65	10	37	0	206	204	207	256	368	624	6	82	22	0.38	247	36	14	50	101	8%	52	5%	3.13	-11.9	$3
Decline	05 CHC	161	16	39	6	25	0	242	194	254	291	391	682	6	85	25	0.46	256	42	17	41	88	11%	19	0%	3.81	0.1	$4
Bats Right	06 CHC	241	23	64	6	37	0	266	325	236	306	419	725	5	84	29	0.37	284	38	24	38	93	8%	42	0%	4.35	0.1	$5
Reliability 0	07 CHC	54	3	9	0	4	0	167	50	235	196	222	419	4	78	21	0.17	193	29	17	55	51	0%	24	0%	0.44	-5.9	($1)
BAvg Potl 55%	1st Half	36	3	7	0	3	0	194			237	250	487	5	81	24	0.29	218	31	21	48	49	0%	31	0%	1.47	-2.6	($0)
LIMA Plan F	2nd Half	18	0	2	0	1	0	111			111	167	278	0	72	15	0.00		23	8	69	55	0%	-9	0%	-1.75	-3.5	($1)
+/- Score -6	08 Proj	**164**	**16**	**38**	**4**	**22**	**0**	**232**			**278**	**380**	**658**	**6**	**84**	**25**	**0.40**	**263**	**36**	**20**	**45**	**91**	**7%**	**49**	**2%**	**3.58**	**-1.9**	**$2**

Battled neck and shoulder injuries for most of season. Strictly backup material, but makes contact and pops the occasional homer. A $1, last gasp, beer-is-all-gone-and-you-have-to-catch-a-bus catcher.

Bloomquist,Willie		AB	R	H	HR	RBI	SB	Avg	vL	vR	OB	Slg	OPS	bb%	ct%	h%	Eye	xBA	G	L	F	PX	hr/f	SX	SBO	RC/G	RAR	R$
Pos 4567	03 SEA	196	30	49	1	14	4	250	242	257	316	321	638	9	80	31	0.49	248	49	21	30	49	2%	111	9%	3.47	-3.9	$3
Age 30	04 SEA	188	27	46	2	18	13	245	281	212	283	330	613	5	74	32	0.21	227	42	20	38	67	4%	121	34%	2.87	-6.8	$6
Peak	05 SEA	249	27	64	0	22	14	257	247	262	288	333	622	4	85	30	0.29	269	45	24	32	59	0%	131	26%	3.16	-7.0	$6
Bats Right	06 SEA	251	36	62	1	15	16	247	253	243	313	299	612	9	84	29	0.60	227	46	17	37	32	1%	132	25%	3.22	-6.8	$6
Reliability 36	07 SEA	173	28	48	2	13	7	277	238	290	317	329	646	5	80	34	0.29	248	61	19	20	35	7%	89	23%	3.28	-4.3	$5
BAvg Potl 35%	1st Half	85	14	24	2	10	3	282			315	376	691	4	74	36	0.18	244	56	19	24	64	13%	84	25%	3.75	-0.9	$3
LIMA Plan F	2nd Half	88	14	24	0	3	4	273			319	284	603	6	85	32	0.46	252	64	19	17	10	0%	89	21%	2.98	-3.0	$2
+/- Score -63	08 Proj	**197**	**24**	**52**	**1**	**14**	**7**	**264**			**310**	**319**	**629**	**6**	**82**	**32**	**0.37**	**245**	**53**	**19**	**27**	**37**	**3%**	**97**	**18%**	**3.22**	**-5.3**	**$4**

Spent three years contributing double-digit steals for an end-game buck. SBO says he got just as many chances in '07 but SX says the skill has faded. That's dangerous for a uni-skill player like him.

Blum,Geoff		AB	R	H	HR	RBI	SB	Avg	vL	vR	OB	Slg	OPS	bb%	ct%	h%	Eye	xBA	G	L	F	PX	hr/f	SX	SBO	RC/G	RAR	R$
Pos 4	03 HOU	420	51	110	10	52	0	262	135	274	295	379	674	5	88	28	0.40	279	42	23	35	71	8%	34	0%	3.72	-8.3	$9
Age 35	04 TAM	339	38	73	8	35	2	215	288	193	267	348	615	7	83	24	0.41	250	46	14	40	87	7%	51	7%	3.08	-10.5	$3
Decline	05 2TM	319	32	73	6	25	3	229	213	236	291	345	636	8	87	25	0.65	268	40	21	39	73	6%	69	8%	3.52	-8.1	$4
Bats Both	06 SD	276	27	70	4	34	0	254	167	267	297	366	663	6	82	30	0.33	257	36	23	41	77	4%	41	2%	3.62	-8.0	$4
Reliability 43	07 SD	330	34	83	5	33	0	252	238	256	318	367	684	9	84	29	0.62	255	36	20	44	79	4%	32	0%	4.10	-4.5	$4
BAvg Potl 55%	1st Half	95	8	18	1	9	0	189			260	295	554	9	77	24	0.41	209	38	13	50	85	3%	23	0%	2.35	-6.7	($0)
LIMA Plan F	2nd Half	235	26	65	4	24	0	277			341	396	737	9	87	30	0.77	272	36	23	42	76	5%	37	0%	4.76	1.3	$5
+/- Score -19	08 Proj	**194**	**20**	**47**	**3**	**20**	**0**	**242**			**300**	**363**	**663**	**8**	**83**	**28**	**0.50**	**258**	**38**	**20**	**42**	**81**	**5%**	**53**	**2%**	**3.76**	**-4.7**	**$2**

WHY WE HATE HIM: Every year without fail, he manages to get hot for a week (9 for 20, week of 7/29), then proceeds to burn anyone who plucked him from the pool (BA next 5 weeks = .222).

Bonds,Barry		AB	R	H	HR	RBI	SB	Avg	vL	vR	OB	Slg	OPS	bb%	ct%	h%	Eye	xBA	G	L	F	PX	hr/f	SX	SBO	RC/G	RAR	R$
Pos 7	03 SF	390	111	133	45	90	7	341	363	331	522	749	1271	28	85	31	2.55	370	30	24	46	221	30%	80	3%	11.90	63.6	$34
Age 43	04 SF	373	129	135	45	101	6	362	307	395	607	812	1419	38	89	31	5.66	391	35	19	46	230	29%	82	2%	14.33	83.3	$37
Decline	05 SF	42	8	12	5	10	0	286	600	243	412	667	1078	18	86	23	1.50	338	32	16	51	198	27%	14	0%	8.80	4.1	$3
Bats Left	06 SF	367	74	99	26	77	3	270	255	276	444	545	989	24	86	25	2.25	311	30	20	50	149	17%	46	2%	8.39	33.0	$17
Reliability 0	07 SF	340	75	94	28	66	5	276	265	283	479	565	1044	28	84	26	2.44	313	40	17	43	157	23%	54	3%	9.23	37.5	$18
BAvg Potl 75%	1st Half	187	38	55	15	35	5	294			502	578	1079	29	83	29	2.44	311	43	17	40	157	24%	52	5%	9.82	23.2	$11
LIMA Plan B+	2nd Half	153	37	39	13	31	0	255			449	549	998	26	86	22	2.45	314	36	18	45	156	22%	27	0%	8.52	14.2	$7
+/- Score 2	08 Proj	**302**	**74**	**79**	**22**	**60**	**1**	**262**			**470**	**532**	**1001**	**28**	**86**	**24**	**2.73**	**311**	**35**	**19**	**46**	**148**	**18%**	**34**	**0%**	**8.77**	**30.0**	**$14**

Walked 132 times in 126 games, so pitchers are still wary - as they should be. Can still bomb HRs, so it's just a question of health.
DN: Pulls a hammy on June 1 and retires.

Boone,Aaron		AB	R	H	HR	RBI	SB	Avg	vL	vR	OB	Slg	OPS	bb%	ct%	h%	Eye	xBA	G	L	F	PX	hr/f	SX	SBO	RC/G	RAR	R$
Pos 3	03 2TM	592	92	158	24	96	23	267	216	285	320	453	772	7	82	29	0.44	285	38	22	40	114	12%	126	18%	4.92	-9.0	$25
Age 35	04 2AL	0	0	0	0	0	0	0							0									0				
Decline	05 CLE	511	61	124	16	60	9	243	229	246	291	378	669	6	82	27	0.38	269	43	21	35	84	11%	82	10%	3.62	-22.4	$12
Bats Right	06 CLE	354	50	89	7	46	5	251	280	239	304	370	675	7	82	29	0.44	264	36	25	40	78	6%	79	10%	3.81	-17.0	$7
Reliability 26	07 FLA	189	27	54	5	28	2	286	213	310	357	423	780	10	78	34	0.51	255	26	26	48	95	7%	53	3%	5.24	-1.9	$6
BAvg Potl 35%	1st Half	189	27	54	5	28	2	286			357	423	780	10	78	34	0.51	255	26	26	48	95	7%	53	3%	5.24	-1.9	$6
LIMA Plan F	2nd Half	0	0	0	0	0	0	0							0													
+/- Score -51	08 Proj	**129**	**18**	**34**	**4**	**18**	**2**	**264**			**321**	**397**	**718**	**8**	**81**	**30**	**0.44**	**262**	**36**	**24**	**40**	**85**	**9%**	**63**	**8%**	**4.30**	**-5.3**	**$4**

Performed well in platoon role before injuring his left knee. The power/speed combo is long gone, though some health might yield one final swan song. More likely, he'll hobble through a few more token ABs.

Botts,Jason		AB	R	H	HR	RBI	SB	Avg	vL	vR	OB	Slg	OPS	bb%	ct%	h%	Eye	xBA	G	L	F	PX	hr/f	SX	SBO	RC/G	RAR	R$
Pos 7	03 aa	194	22	47	4	22	5	240			303	365	668	8	80	28	0.45					86		94	12%	3.77	-9.8	$4
Age 27	04 aa	476	68	130	23	74	6	273			356	475	831	11	77	31	0.54					126		69	7%	5.89	9.5	$17
Peak	05 TEX *	533	67	136	20	73	1	255		308	318	437	755	9	78	29	0.43		50	36	14	118	33%	59	4%	4.81	1.4	$13
Bats Both	06 TEX *	286	45	72	13	38	5	252	100	250	334	466	800	11	72	31	0.44	277	38	24	38	151	16%	88	6%	5.61	3.6	$8
Reliability 35	07 TEX *	536	68	133	12	69	1	248	333	208	341	397	738	12	70	33	0.47	250	40	22	38	120	8%	59	1%	4.96	3.8	$10
BAvg Potl 40%	1st Half	293	43	86	7	49	0	294			397	474	871	15	77	36	0.76					136		50	1%	6.78	16.8	$9
LIMA Plan D	2nd Half	243	25	47	5	20	1	193			270	304	574	9	61	29	0.27	204	40	22	38	95	9%	67	1%	2.52	-16.9	$0
+/- Score 14	08 Proj	**344**	**45**	**84**	**11**	**43**	**1**	**244**			**325**	**410**	**735**	**11**	**71**	**31**	**0.42**	**257**	**40**	**23**	**37**	**122**	**12%**	**60**	**1%**	**4.76**	**-1.2**	**$7**

2-14-.240 in 167 AB at TEX. Impressive PX, but has had problems making contact in the bigs. Could hit 20 HR with enough ABs, but may forever look up at a .250 BA.

Bourn,Michael		AB	R	H	HR	RBI	SB	Avg	vL	vR	OB	Slg	OPS	bb%	ct%	h%	Eye	xBA	G	L	F	PX	hr/f	SX	SBO	RC/G	RAR	R$
Pos 7	03	0	0	0	0	0	0	0							0									0				
Age 25	04	0	0	0	0	0	0	0							0									0				
Pre-Peak	05 aa	539	68	134	6	37	32	249			315	334	649	9	81	30	0.50					55		132	29%	3.59	-23.7	$15
Bats Left	06 a/a	470	91	129	5	39	42	274			345	379	724	10	81	33	0.56					56		181	31%	4.61	-8.2	$20
Reliability 10	07 PHI	119	29	33	1	6	18	277	154	312	348	378	727	10	82	33	0.62	272	58	18	24	56	4%	198	49%	4.67	-2.3	$7
BAvg Potl 50%	1st Half	51	12	15	0	4	11	294			390	373	762	14	84	35	1.00	254	51	21	28	33	0%	185	52%	5.40	0.1	$4
LIMA Plan C	2nd Half	68	17	18	1	2	7	265			315	382	697	7	81	31	0.38	284	63	16	22	74	8%	186	44%	4.10	-2.5	$3
+/- Score 7	08 Proj	**222**	**46**	**60**	**2**	**14**	**25**	**270**			**340**	**372**	**711**	**10**	**81**	**32**	**0.57**	**270**	**58**	**18**	**24**	**58**	**5%**	**189**	**40%**	**4.45**	**-5.7**	**$11**

Speed to burn, but injuries and crowded Philly outfield limited his playing time. Makes contact and slaps those grounders, so even a part-time role can net you 25 steals. Full-time? 50 bags.

Bowen,Rob		AB	R	H	HR	RBI	SB	Avg	vL	vR	OB	Slg	OPS	bb%	ct%	h%	Eye	xBA	G	L	F	PX	hr/f	SX	SBO	RC/G	RAR	R$
Pos 2	03 a/a	239	27	64	6	29	0	268			327	435	762	8	82	31	0.48					116		39	0%	4.96	5.3	$5
Age 27	04 aa	276	26	48	9	23	3	173			259	303	562	10	69	21	0.38					91		54	5%	2.22	-16.6	$0
Peak	05 aaa	258	32	63	5	20	0	244			328	368	696	11	78	30	0.55					87		56	3%	4.25	2.7	$4
Bats Both	06 SD	94	22	23	3	13	0	245			336	394	730	12	72	31	0.50	264	48	25	28	104	16%	67	4%	4.70	1.0	$3
Reliability 20	07 2TM	156	21	36	4	18	1	231	250	222	344	372	716	15	61	35	0.44	223	38	24	39	129	11%	40	6%	4.98	5.1	$2
BAvg Potl 30%	1st Half	95	13	23	2	12	1	242			357	389	747	15	64	36	0.50	231	38	20	42	136	8%	45	10%	5.39	4.3	$2
LIMA Plan F	2nd Half	61	8	13	2	6	0	213			324	344	668	14	56	34	0.37	213	36	30	33	117	18%	25	0%	4.32	0.8	$1
+/- Score -24	08 Proj	**123**	**15**	**28**	**3**	**12**	**0**	**228**			**323**	**363**	**686**	**12**	**68**	**31**	**0.43**	**241**	**37**	**26**	**37**	**109**	**10%**	**38**	**3%**	**4.19**	**0.5**	**$2**

Intriguing #2 catcher option. Good power, hits line drives... when he manages to make contact, which isn't often. But sees the ball well (15% bb rate) so there may be some hidden upside here.

Bradley,Milton		AB	R	H	HR	RBI	SB	Avg	vL	vR	OB	Slg	OPS	bb%	ct%	h%	Eye	xBA	G	L	F	PX	hr/f	SX	SBO	RC/G	RAR	R$
Pos 7	03 CLE	377	61	121	10	56	17	321	402	287	420	501	921	15	81	38	0.88	303	42	25	33	126	10%	98	17%	7.33	20.6	$19
Age 30	04 LA	516	72	138	19	67	15	267	295	257	356	424	780	12	76	32	0.58	259	47	19	34	102	14%	66	16%	5.30	-2.1	$18
Peak	05 LA	283	49	82	13	38	6	290	278	294	347	484	832	8	83	31	0.53	305	45	23	32	117	17%	99	9%	5.65	2.4	$13
Bats Both	06 OAK	351	53	97	14	52	10	276	293	270	368	447	815	13	81	31	0.78	275	52	15	33	99	15%	94	10%	5.75	5.7	$13
Reliability 3	07 2TM	209	37	64	13	37	5	306	304	307	396	545	941	13	80	33	0.76	290	39	19	43	141	18%	81	10%	7.25	12.8	$11
BAvg Potl 50%	1st Half	65	6	19	2	7	2	292			370	446	816	11	78	35	0.57	261	29	24	47	106	8%	43	14%	5.73	1.3	$2
LIMA Plan D	2nd Half	144	31	45	11	30	3	312			407	590	997	14	81	32	0.85	306	43	16	41	156	23%	88	8%	7.91	11.3	$9
+/- Score -14	08 Proj	**233**	**38**	**64**	**11**	**36**	**2**	**275**			**362**	**478**	**840**	**12**	**81**	**30**	**0.71**	**284**	**43**	**19**	**38**	**122**	**16%**	**63**	**6%**	**5.98**	**5.9**	**$9**

Plenty of talent, but injuries and temper make him a huge risk. 2004, 2003 and 2006 represent his top three season AB totals. Stash him away until 2H when knee rehab is complete, then cross your fingers.

TOM TODARO

Branyan,Russell

			AB	R	H	HR	RBI	SB	Avg	vL	vR	OB	Slg	OPS	bb%	ct%	h%	Eye	xBA	G	L	F	PX	hr/f	SX	SBO	RC/G	RAR	R$
Pos	5	03 CIN	176	22	38	9	26	0	216	250	205	320	438	758	13	61	30	0.39	243	31	20	49	187	17%	20	0%	5.49	6.7	$4
Age	32	04 2TM	* 499	76	120	32	97	7	240	167	250	330	493	823	12	62	32	0.35	242	29	19	53	190	20%	86	7%	6.37	20.7	$18
Past Peak		05 MIL	202	23	52	12	31	1	257	50	280	378	490	868	16	60	36	0.49	251	29	24	47	192	21%	24	1%	7.36	15.2	$7
Bats	Left	06 2TM	241	37	55	18	36	2	228	220	230	324	498	822	12	63	28	0.38	252	29	19	52	194	23%	49	3%	6.18	6.8	$7
Reliability	8	07 2NL	163	22	32	10	26	1	196	158	201	314	423	737	15	58	26	0.41	218	29	18	53	178	20%	66	2%	5.25	2.4	$3
BAvg Potl	45%	1st Half	94	14	20	6	17	1	213			351	457	808	18	63	26	0.57	238	33	13	53	187	19%	39	3%	6.17	4.0	$3
LIMA Plan	D	2nd Half	69	8	12	4	9	0	174			260	377	637	10	51	26	0.24	191	23	26	51	162	22%	69	0%	3.96	-1.8	$1
+/- Score	22	08 Proj	182	24	39	12	28	1	214			320	454	774	13	59	29	0.37	231	28	21	51	187	21%	61	2%	5.80	4.8	$4

A sub-60% ct% usually spells "unemployed." And his stats are propped up by April's 79% ct% and .292 BA. For rest of year, he had a 54% ct% and .180 BA. 2008 may be last gasp.

Braun,Ryan

			AB	R	H	HR	RBI	SB	Avg	vL	vR	OB	Slg	OPS	bb%	ct%	h%	Eye	xBA	G	L	F	PX	hr/f	SX	SBO	RC/G	RAR	R$
Pos	5	03	0	0	0	0	0	0	0							0									0				
Age	24	04	0	0	0	0	0	0	0							0									0				
Growth		05	0	0	0	0	0	0	0							0									0				
Bats	Right	06 aa	231	40	68	15	38	11	294			353	580	933	8	81	31	0.47					173		119	20%	6.92	10.7	$13
Reliability	0	07 MIL	* 568	116	183	43	116	19	322	450	282	370	637	1007	7	79	35	0.35	315	39	16	45	190	21%	124	19%	7.78	46.2	$37
BAvg Potl	35%	1st Half	236	51	76	15	40	10	322			382	627	1009	9	84	33	0.61	343	39	21	39	184	19%	125	22%	7.84	19.5	$15
LIMA Plan	D+	2nd Half	332	65	107	28	76	9	322			361	645	1005	6	75	36	0.24	300	39	14	47	195	24%	117	18%	7.80	27.2	$22
+/- Score	-3	08 Proj	582	112	176	39	100	18	302			355	592	947	8	79	32	0.39	309	39	16	45	177	19%	124	17%	7.07	34.3	$32

34-97-.324 in 451 AB at MIL. Strong, steady debut -- never had under .285 BA or .900 OPS for full month. Greater patience would be a boon but pitchers never did find a hole -- he hit .308 with .998 OPS in Sept.

Broussard,Ben

			AB	R	H	HR	RBI	SB	Avg	vL	vR	OB	Slg	OPS	bb%	ct%	h%	Eye	xBA	G	L	F	PX	hr/f	SX	SBO	RC/G	RAR	R$
Pos	39	03 CLE	* 506	67	123	19	68	8	243	175	276	299	417	716	7	80	27	0.39	274	39	22	38	107	12%	100	9%	4.23	-17.3	$13
Age	31	04 CLE	418	57	115	17	82	4	275	362	258	355	488	843	11	77	32	0.55	275	40	18	42	136	12%	92	5%	6.12	13.5	$14
Past Peak		05 CLE	466	59	119	19	68	2	255	225	264	303	464	767	6	79	29	0.33	294	41	22	37	136	14%	80	4%	4.86	-3.2	$13
Bats	Left	06 2AL	432	61	125	21	63	2	289	177	308	330	484	813	6	76	34	0.25	265	40	19	41	123	16%	47	3%	5.34	-1.0	$15
Reliability	56	07 SEA	240	27	66	7	29	2	275	250	277	323	404	727	7	79	32	0.34	252	42	20	38	86	10%	47	3%	4.33	-5.2	$6
BAvg Potl	35%	1st Half	91	12	25	4	13	1	275			320	440	759	6	79	31	0.32	254	40	18	42	102	13%	48	4%	4.63	-1.2	$3
LIMA Plan	D	2nd Half	149	15	41	3	16	1	275			325	383	708	7	79	33	0.35	250	44	21	35	76	7%	38	2%	4.14	-4.0	$3
+/- Score	-29	08 Proj	318	40	86	12	43	2	270			319	435	753	7	78	31	0.33	264	41	20	39	106	12%	65	4%	4.65	-4.8	$9

Terrifically reliable hitter until this year -- he might not have taken to unaccustomed reserve role. 2008 rides on whether he gets chance to re-establish himself. Ignore numbers vLHP -- he had only 19 PA against LH.

Brown,Emil

			AB	R	H	HR	RBI	SB	Avg	vL	vR	OB	Slg	OPS	bb%	ct%	h%	Eye	xBA	G	L	F	PX	hr/f	SX	SBO	RC/G	RAR	R$
Pos	79	03 aaa	369	44	96	10	47	14	260			298	406	704	5	83	29	0.32					93		112	20%	4.04	-15.4	$12
Age	33	04 aaa	149	14	38	2	15	4	257			287	373	660	4	84	30	0.26					79		84	23%	3.54	-7.4	$3
Past Peak		05 KC	545	75	156	17	86	10	286	315	273	344	455	799	8	80	33	0.44	288	42	24	34	110	12%	108	7%	5.36	9.8	$20
Bats	Right	06 KC	527	77	151	15	81	6	287	236	308	358	457	816	10	82	33	0.62	281	44	18	38	113	9%	75	6%	5.70	7.8	$17
Reliability	44	07 KC	366	44	94	6	62	12	257	317	217	303	347	650	6	81	30	0.34	233	44	17	39	61	5%	95	14%	3.41	-14.1	$10
BAvg Potl	40%	1st Half	190	20	44	2	29	7	232			295	311	605	8	79	28	0.43	221	39	18	43	56	3%	100	14%	2.98	-10.0	$4
LIMA Plan	D+	2nd Half	176	24	50	4	33	5	284			311	386	698	4	82	33	0.23	245	49	15	36	66	8%	77	15%	3.83	-4.5	$6
+/- Score	-29	08 Proj	391	51	106	9	63	10	271			322	401	723	7	81	31	0.40	260	44	18	37	85	7%	97	12%	4.36	-5.8	$12

xBA says that numbers should have been even drearier. Nothing on the surface to explain massive PX and hr/f collapse, which makes us suspicious. PT now in jeopardy, so double-digit SB also at risk.

Bruce,Jay

			AB	R	H	HR	RBI	SB	Avg	vL	vR	OB	Slg	OPS	bb%	ct%	h%	Eye	xBA	G	L	F	PX	hr/f	SX	SBO	RC/G	RAR	R$
Pos	8	03	0	0	0	0	0	0	0							0									0				
Age	21	04	0	0	0	0	0	0	0							0									0				
Growth		05	0	0	0	0	0	0	0							0									0				
Bats	Left	06	0	0	0	0	0	0	0							0									0				
Reliability	0	07 a/a	253	36	81	15	39	3	322			376	600	976	8	79	36	0.41					177		73	10%	7.51	21.2	$12
BAvg Potl	30%	1st Half	41	4	11	3	8	1	268			302	561	863	5	73	30	0.18					198		41	29%	6.00	1.9	$2
LIMA Plan		2nd Half	212	32	70	12	31	2	332			390	608	997	9	80	37	0.47					173		77	8%	7.79	19.0	$11
+/- Score	18	08 Proj	163	22	45	5	23	2	276			345	487	832	9	78	33	0.47					144		91	10%	5.94	6.8	$5

Jumped two levels in 2007 to reach AAA and eventually win Baseball America's Minor League Player of the Year. But temper expectations -- 187 AB in Triple-A is not full test, and low ct% could be picked apart.

Bruntlett,Eric

			AB	R	H	HR	RBI	SB	Avg	vL	vR	OB	Slg	OPS	bb%	ct%	h%	Eye	xBA	G	L	F	PX	hr/f	SX	SBO	RC/G	RAR	R$
Pos	6	03 aaa	324	43	80	2	24	8	248			313	296	609	9	86	28	0.66					35		78	12%	3.21	-10.3	$6
Age	30	04 aaa	332	38	73	5	28	11	219			276	313	589	7	83	25	0.45					56		115	19%	2.81	-15.4	$5
Peak		05 HOU	109	19	24	4	14	7	220	295	125	286	413	699	8	77	25	0.40	270	31	28	41	122	12%	172	39%	4.11	0.5	$4
Bats	Right	06 HOU	* 192	21	47	1	16	5	245	350	241	341	313	653	13	81	30	0.78	235	41	20	38	52	2%	57	13%	3.90	-2.7	$3
Reliability	17	07 HOU	* 365	36	77	1	28	14	210	237	253	286	265	551	10	82	26	0.58	231	46	19	35	38	1%	101	21%	2.48	-17.1	$3
BAvg Potl	60%	1st Half	247	31	63	1	19	11	255			331	332	663	10	85	30	0.76		64	29	7	47	7%	121	22%	3.98	0.2	$5
LIMA Plan	F	2nd Half	118	5	14	0	9	3	117			190	125	315	8	75	16	0.36		43	18	39	16	0%		18%	-0.97	-20.3	($3)
+/- Score	6	08 Proj	95	10	19	1	8	3	200			278	268	546	10	80	24	0.53	231	40	21	39	51	3%	72	20%	2.33	-5.3	$1

0-14-.246 in 138 AB at HOU. Each year, there seems to be one thing that sends him to positive earnings; this year, it was 6 SB. Keep perspective: This is a guy for whom 35 hits would be new ML career-high.

Buck,John

			AB	R	H	HR	RBI	SB	Avg	vL	vR	OB	Slg	OPS	bb%	ct%	h%	Eye	xBA	G	L	F	PX	hr/f	SX	SBO	RC/G	RAR	R$
Pos	2	03 aaa	274	29	68	2	35	1	248			280	350	630	4	82	29	0.25					75		77	2%	3.20	-8.0	$4
Age	27	04 2TM	* 465	61	118	22	58	1	254	222	241	300	437	737	6	77	29	0.28	254	45	16	39	113	16%	38	3%	4.37	4.2	$12
Peak		05 KC	401	40	97	12	47	2	242	310	214	283	389	672	5	77	29	0.24	247	44	17	40	103	10%	51	5%	3.60	-5.1	$7
Bats	Right	06 KC	371	37	91	11	50	0	245	246	245	295	396	691	7	77	29	0.31	258	45	20	35	101	11%	32	2%	3.91	-5.5	$6
Reliability	64	07 KC	347	41	77	18	48	0	222	189	231	295	429	724	9	73	25	0.39	249	43	13	44	142	16%	23	1%	4.39	3.9	$7
BAvg Potl	50%	1st Half	170	26	43	14	27	0	253			339	559	897	11	75	25	0.52	287	39	11	50	198	22%	19	0%	6.64	13.1	$6
LIMA Plan	D	2nd Half	177	15	34	4	21	0	192			251	305	556	7	72	24	0.28	215	47	16	38	87	8%	27	3%	2.13	-10.7	$0
+/- Score	25	08 Proj	375	40	94	19	54	0	251			307	463	770	7	75	28	0.33	265	44	16	40	140	17%	31	2%	4.89	8.4	$9

Uncharacteristic 28-HR pace in 1H could not be maintained. But he is still at prime age for power spike, and any chance to get 20 HR from CA is tempting. Bitter taste of his second half could create draft-day bargain.

Buck,Travis

			AB	R	H	HR	RBI	SB	Avg	vL	vR	OB	Slg	OPS	bb%	ct%	h%	Eye	xBA	G	L	F	PX	hr/f	SX	SBO	RC/G	RAR	R$
Pos	9	03	0	0	0	0	0	0	0							0									0				
Age	24	04	0	0	0	0	0	0	0							0									0				
Growth		05	0	0	0	0	0	0	0							0									0				
Bats	Left	06 aa	212	27	58	3	19	8	274			330	425	755	8	85	31	0.56					105		102	18%	4.95	-1.6	$6
Reliability	0	07 OAK	285	41	82	7	34	4	288	323	277	373	474	847	12	77	35	0.59	280	44	19	37	131	9%	107	6%	6.34	13.1	$9
BAvg Potl	40%	1st Half	180	29	51	6	20	1	283			383	489	872	14	77	34	0.69	282	43	20	37	135	12%	91	3%	6.71	10.2	$5
LIMA Plan	B	2nd Half	105	12	31	1	14	3	295			357	448	804	9	77	37	0.42	274	46	17	37	124	3%	92	11%	5.67	2.8	$3
+/- Score	5	08 Proj	411	54	117	12	45	11	285			354	485	839	10	80	33	0.54	297	45	18	37	139	10%	107	11%	6.02	12.2	$13

Pressed into play with injuries to OAK OF, he responded with solid skills across board. The former 1st-round pick was dinged-up at every turn; maybe elbow surgery will add durability. Don't tag with "fragile" just yet.

Burke,Chris

			AB	R	H	HR	RBI	SB	Avg	vL	vR	OB	Slg	OPS	bb%	ct%	h%	Eye	xBA	G	L	F	PX	hr/f	SX	SBO	RC/G	RAR	R$
Pos	48	03 aa	549	69	147	3	32	26	269			322	345	667	7	91	29	0.92					46		124	23%	4.02	-4.2	$14
Age	28	04 aaa	483	74	138	13	41	29	286			343	447	790	8	88	30	0.71					94		128	35%	5.30	13.5	$20
Peak		05 HOU	* 408	60	104	7	34	18	254	265	239	304	384	688	7	82	29	0.40	256	38	19	42	87	5%	137	24%	3.98	-7.0	$12
Bats	Right	06 HOU	366	58	101	9	40	11	276	327	257	326	418	744	7	79	33	0.35	258	36	23	41	95	8%	102	13%	4.62	0.2	$12
Reliability	32	07 HOU	* 385	49	85	8	33	12	222	292	197	279	344	622	7	85	24	0.51	247	38	17	45	77	5%	107	20%	3.26	-15.5	$6
BAvg Potl	65%	1st Half	181	24	42	3	13	9	232			291	348	639	8	85	26	0.56	260	39	19	42	80	5%	94	29%	3.51	-5.9	$4
LIMA Plan	C	2nd Half	204	25	43	5	20	3	213			268	340	607	7	84	23	0.48	239	38	15	47	74	6%	97	11%	3.04	-9.7	$2
+/- Score	21	08 Proj	441	61	108	9	40	15	245			299	374	673	7	83	28	0.46	253	37	19	44	83	6%	118	19%	3.82	-9.8	$10

6-28-.229 in 319 AB at HOU. H% abandoned him in '07. He might welcome return to 2B, where he put up .735 OPS vs. .604 OPS at RF. Still owns potentially lucrative combo of high-ct/high-speed. UP: 25 SB

Burke,Jamie			AB	R	H	HR	RBI	SB	Avg	vL	vR	OB	Slg	OPS	bb%	ct%	h%	Eye	xBA	G	L	F	PX	hr/f	SX	SBO	RC/G	RAR	R$
Pos	2	03 aaa	323	37	87	5	40	1	270			305	354	659	5	88	29	0.43					51		43	2%	3.58	-5.7	$7
Age	36	04 CHW *	254	31	66	2	24	0	260			307	335	642	6	89	29	0.63					51		36	0%	3.59	-5.5	$3
Decline		05 aaa	351	37	77	8	38	1	218			270	344	614	7	87	23	0.54					80		49	5%	3.17	-8.0	$4
Bats	Right	06 aaa	370	39	93	9	41	0	251			287	379	666	5	89	26	0.45					75		36	0%	3.69	-7.4	$6
Reliability	9	07 SEA	113	19	34	1	12	0	301	280	307	342	398	740	6	85	35	0.41	286	38	28	34	74	3%	52	3%	4.59	1.8	$3
BAvg Potl	40%	1st Half	49	10	19	0	6	0	388			434	510	944	8	86	45	0.57	303	43	24	33	105	0%	55	6%	7.19	3.9	$2
LIMA Plan	F	2nd Half	64	9	15	1	6	0	234			269	312	581	4	84	26	0.30	276	33	31	35	51	5%	48	0%	2.57	-2.8	$1
+/- Score	-42	08 Proj	99	12	24	2	10	0	242			284	337	621	5	87	26	0.44	284	37	28	34	60	6%	42	1%	3.16	-2.9	$1

Statistical oddity: despite paltry MLEs, he's a career .312 hitter in the majors. Of course, it's in only 247 AB. And he rarely plays. And he's 36. So don't get in a lather over him or anything.

Burrell,Pat			AB	R	H	HR	RBI	SB	Avg	vL	vR	OB	Slg	OPS	bb%	ct%	h%	Eye	xBA	G	L	F	PX	hr/f	SX	SBO	RC/G	RAR	R$
Pos	7	03 PHI	522	57	109	21	64	0	209	198	212	305	404	709	12	73	25	0.51	262	35	21	44	136	13%	51	0%	4.39	-19.4	$7
Age	31	04 PHI	448	66	115	24	84	2	257	271	253	367	455	822	15	71	31	0.60	247	35	20	45	130	17%	43	1%	6.00	7.3	$16
Past Peak		05 PHI	562	78	158	32	117	0	281	318	269	389	504	892	15	72	34	0.62	273	31	24	45	153	18%	27	0%	7.00	26.3	$24
Bats	Right	06 PHI	462	80	119	29	95	0	258	290	244	388	502	890	18	72	30	0.75	268	31	21	48	158	18%	32	0%	7.03	24.0	$18
Reliability	99	07 PHI	472	77	121	30	97	0	256	255	257	401	502	903	19	75	28	0.95	270	31	18	51	158	17%	18	0%	7.21	25.8	$18
BAvg Potl	55%	1st Half	206	25	42	8	31	0	204			369	374	743	21	75	23	1.06	239	29	18	53	115	10%	14	0%	5.17	-1.1	$3
LIMA Plan	C+	2nd Half	266	52	79	22	66	0	297			426	602	1028	18	74	33	0.87	295	32	18	50	193	22%	22	0%	8.82	25.5	$15
+/- Score	15	08 Proj	490	78	130	30	100	0	265			395	507	902	18	73	30	0.80	270	31	20	49	158	17%	32	0%	7.18	26.0	$19

Poster boy for the value of patience, and of looking past in-season volatility. His skills are improving, and he's a sim format stud. Instead of griping about what he isn't, maybe it's time to appreciate what he is.

Buscher,Brian			AB	R	H	HR	RBI	SB	Avg	vL	vR	OB	Slg	OPS	bb%	ct%	h%	Eye	xBA	G	L	F	PX	hr/f	SX	SBO	RC/G	RAR	R$
Pos	5	03	0	0	0	0	0	0	0							0									0				
Age	27	04	0	0	0	0	0	0	0							0									0				
Peak		05 aa	215	15	43	1	18	4	199			255	252	507	7	85	23	0.51					37		70	13%	1.94	-18.5	$0
Bats	Left	06 aa	467	40	109	6	45	5	233			288	330	618	7	82	27	0.43					62		66	7%	3.15	-29.8	$4
Reliability	13	07 MIN *	461	55	118	13	58	4	256	200	250	319	397	716	9	87	27	0.74	270	43	16	40	87	8%	61	5%	4.45	-0.7	$10
BAvg Potl	60%	1st Half	284	40	81	9	40	2	285			354	454	808	10	89	29	1.00					103		60	5%	5.59	8.8	$9
LIMA Plan	D	2nd Half	177	15	37	4	18	2	209			263	305	568	7	84	23	0.46	235	43	16	40	59	7%	47	5%	2.52	-10.9	$1
+/- Score	18	08 Proj	379	36	93	7	40	4	245			302	348	651	8	85	27	0.53	244	43	16	40	66	5%	58	6%	3.58	-12.0	$5

2-10-.244 in 82 AB at MIN.
Why big 1st half could be real:
- High pick finally "arriving"?
- Fully healthy for a change
Why it probably wasn't:
- Abysmal track record
- Likely to get unhealthy again

Butler,Billy			AB	R	H	HR	RBI	SB	Avg	vL	vR	OB	Slg	OPS	bb%	ct%	h%	Eye	xBA	G	L	F	PX	hr/f	SX	SBO	RC/G	RAR	R$
Pos	0	03	0	0	0	0	0	0	0							0									0				
Age	22	04	0	0	0	0	0	0	0							0									0				
Growth		05 aa	112	12	33	3	15	0	295			328	462	789	5	89	31	0.47					107		22	0%	5.07	-3.0	$3
Bats	Right	06 aa	477	67	147	11	79	1	308			354	447	801	7	90	33	0.71					84		55	1%	5.34	-14.0	$16
Reliability	13	07 KC *	532	72	150	18	92	1	282	340	272	360	457	817	11	85	31	0.79	298	47	21	33	110	12%	56	1%	5.73	-4.4	$17
BAvg Potl	55%	1st Half	256	36	67	11	45	1	262			359	449	809	13	85	27	1.03	297	37	23	40	112	13%	52	1%	5.71	-2.3	$8
LIMA Plan	C+	2nd Half	276	36	83	7	47	0	301			361	464	825	9	84	34	0.59	294	48	20	31	108	10%	49	0%	5.73	-2.2	$9
+/- Score	32	08 Proj	504	67	148	14	83	1	294			364	454	818	10	87	31	0.87	299	47	21	32	100	10%	50	1%	5.73	-3.9	$16

8-52-.292 in 329 AB at KC. Perspective: Most kids his age are at A-ball, and he's hitting a legit near-.300 in the majors. The power may take a while, but with his ct% and rising Eye, a batting title might not.

Bynum,Freddie			AB	R	H	HR	RBI	SB	Avg	vL	vR	OB	Slg	OPS	bb%	ct%	h%	Eye	xBA	G	L	F	PX	hr/f	SX	SBO	RC/G	RAR	R$
Pos	7	03 aa	510	66	113	4	46	17	223			284	299	582	8	77	28	0.37					51		129	20%	2.66	-44.5	$8
Age	28	04 a/a	523	62	124	2	37	30	237			283	304	587	6	81	29	0.33					47		130	33%	2.71	-39.9	$11
Peak		05 aaa	378	44	90	2	31	18	238			292	320	612	7	83	28	0.44					55		133	28%	3.13	-22.1	$8
Bats	Left	06 CHC	136	20	35	4	12	8	257	130	283	303	456	759	6	68	35	0.20	259	45	25	30	127	15%	143	40%	5.13	-0.5	$5
Reliability	1	07 BAL	96	21	25	2	11	8	260	263	260	276	448	723	2	69	36	0.07	250	42	15	44	150	7%	210	60%	4.46	-0.7	$4
BAvg Potl	25%	1st Half	37	12	9	2	7	3	243			243	486	730	0	73	28	0.00	278	43	9	48	176	15%	244	100%	4.09	-0.7	$2
LIMA Plan	D	2nd Half	59	9	16	0	4	5	271			295	424	719	3	66	41	0.10	234	41	18	41	132	0%	169	45%	4.72	0.0	$2
+/- Score	18	08 Proj	132	18	33	2	10	8	250			293	397	689	6	74	32	0.23	251	43	21	36	102	6%	152	36%	3.99	-3.5	$4

That 2/30 BB to K ratio in 100 AB isn't going to cut it. The handful of SB is only worth the baggage in a dire category crisis. These Esix-Sneadian fast guys will break your heart every time.

Byrd,Marlon			AB	R	H	HR	RBI	SB	Avg	vL	vR	OB	Slg	OPS	bb%	ct%	h%	Eye	xBA	G	L	F	PX	hr/f	SX	SBO	RC/G	RAR	R$
Pos	89	03 PHI	495	86	150	7	45	11	303	315	299	360	418	778	8	81	36	0.47	286	50	25	25	80	7%	124	8%	5.16	2.5	$18
Age	30	04 PHI *	498	58	112	7	46	4	225	213	232	269	325	594	6	83	26	0.35	258	58	14	28	65	6%	79	9%	2.81	-28.3	$5
Peak		05 2NL *	329	38	94	8	38	8	287	326	228	338	434	772	7	82	33	0.44	274	38	22	40	100	7%	92	11%	5.01	4.2	$11
Bats	Right	06 WAS *	352	44	79	10	42	6	223	188	242	293	361	654	9	78	26	0.44	256	45	21	34	87	11%	71	11%	3.54	-9.8	$6
Reliability	17	07 TEX *	590	78	169	14	89	7	286	327	300	328	432	761	6	79	34	0.30	268	47	20	33	94	9%	105	7%	4.79	8.6	$18
BAvg Potl	35%	1st Half	284	42	101	8	48	3	356			394	528	922	6	84	40	0.40	300	53	18	28	107	12%	86	8%	6.68	17.6	$14
LIMA Plan	D	2nd Half	306	36	68	6	41	4	222			267	343	610	6	74	28	0.24	241	45	20	35	80	7%	120	7%	2.88	-13.1	$4
+/- Score	-22	08 Proj	396	51	104	9	51	6	263			314	401	714	7	79	31	0.36	265	46	20	34	90	9%	100	9%	4.26	-1.8	$10

10-70-.307 in 414 AB at TEX. Rode insane 1st half to a full time gig, but that obscures both the 2nd half crash and the lack of any true skills gains. A 2008 Most Likely to be Overvalued on Draft Day" nominee.

Byrnes,Eric			AB	R	H	HR	RBI	SB	Avg	vL	vR	OB	Slg	OPS	bb%	ct%	h%	Eye	xBA	G	L	F	PX	hr/f	SX	SBO	RC/G	RAR	R$
Pos	798	03 OAK	414	64	109	12	51	10	263	286	251	331	459	790	9	83	29	0.59	280	38	19	44	119	8%	137	12%	5.38	0.6	$13
Age	32	04 OAK	569	91	161	20	73	17	283	344	260	337	467	804	7	80	32	0.41	264	34	18	47	117	9%	122	12%	5.37	7.0	$21
Past Peak		05 2TM	412	49	93	10	40	7	226	263	205	282	371	653	7	83	25	0.45	256	32	20	48	96	6%	102	10%	3.58	-18.3	$7
Bats	Right	06 ARI	562	82	150	26	79	25	267	323	244	309	482	791	6	84	28	0.39	287	38	18	44	124	12%	120	24%	5.06	-3.1	$22
Reliability	67	07 ARI	626	103	179	21	83	50	286	248	297	346	460	806	8	84	31	0.58	266	35	19	46	101	9%	148	32%	5.43	1.7	$32
BAvg Potl	45%	1st Half	318	48	99	13	44	14	311			360	513	872	7	84	34	0.46	275	34	20	46	114	11%	126	21%	6.11	6.8	$16
LIMA Plan	B	2nd Half	308	55	80	8	39	36	260			331	406	737	10	85	28	0.72	257	37	18	45	87	7%	161	44%	4.74	-5.4	$16
+/- Score	-15	08 Proj	582	90	157	20	74	35	270			326	450	776	8	84	29	0.51	270	36	19	46	107	9%	142	27%	5.04	-4.9	$25

Take more PT, add a bit of BA luck, and stir in an always-green light, and you get the recipe for this SB explosion. Hard to imagine SBO will stay this high... but it was hard to imagine after last season, too.

Cabrera,Asdrubal			AB	R	H	HR	RBI	SB	Avg	vL	vR	OB	Slg	OPS	bb%	ct%	h%	Eye	xBA	G	L	F	PX	hr/f	SX	SBO	RC/G	RAR	R$
Pos	4	03	0	0	0	0	0	0	0							0									0				
Age	22	04	0	0	0	0	0	0	0							0									0				
Growth		05	0	0	0	0	0	0	0							0									0				
Bats	Both	06 aaa	393	58	106	5	39	13	269			332	375	706	9	80	33	0.47					76		88	22%	4.31	-0.6	$10
Reliability	0	07 CLE *	565	108	167	9	75	23	295	340	259	365	423	788	10	87	33	0.86	282	44	20	36	84	5%	122	18%	5.44	20.8	$23
BAvg Potl	55%	1st Half	265	55	81	5	35	19	306			383	442	824	11	89	33	1.18					86		132	28%	5.94	13.5	$14
LIMA Plan	B	2nd Half	300	53	86	4	40	4	286			349	407	757	9	85	32	0.66	275	44	20	36	83	5%	96	7%	4.98	7.2	$9
+/- Score	4	08 Proj	508	87	141	7	60	18	278			345	398	742	9	84	32	0.65	271	44	20	36	82	5%	110	19%	4.83	10.4	$17

3-22-.283 in 159 AB at CLE. Took big step up, but is this level sustainable? Age and BPIs say yes. Now watch what CLE does to sort out 2B logjam. But remember: draft skills. He has them, and talent will win out.

Cabrera,Melky			AB	R	H	HR	RBI	SB	Avg	vL	vR	OB	Slg	OPS	bb%	ct%	h%	Eye	xBA	G	L	F	PX	hr/f	SX	SBO	RC/G	RAR	R$
Pos	8	03	0	0	0	0	0	0	0							0									0				
Age	23	04	0	0	0	0	0	0	0							0									0				
Growth		05 a/a	523	63	133	12	68	12	255			297	371	669	6	86	28	0.44					72		100	11%	3.71	-11.0	$14
Bats	Both	06 NYY *	582	93	175	11	73	15	301	286	278	372	423	795	10	89	33	0.98	279	49	17	33	73	7%	99	11%	5.50	13.7	$20
Reliability	24	07 NYY	545	66	149	8	73	13	273	250	282	327	391	717	7	88	30	0.63	287	51	20	29	71	6%	112	12%	4.46	2.8	$14
BAvg Potl	60%	1st Half	219	24	56	3	22	5	256			315	365	680	8	89	28	0.76	291	54	20	26	61	6%	109	10%	4.11	-1.1	$4
LIMA Plan	C+	2nd Half	326	42	93	5	51	8	285			334	408	742	7	87	32	0.56	283	49	19	32	77	6%	104	13%	4.70	3.9	$10
+/- Score	21	08 Proj	579	78	162	10	76	14	280			338	399	737	8	88	31	0.71	284	51	19	31	72	6%	107	11%	4.71	4.8	$17

PRO:
- Age, opportunity on his side
- Solid ct% suggests BA upside
CON:
- Mediocre skills overall
- BA is only thing with upside
- Overhyped means overvalued

ROD TRUESDELL

Cabrera,Miguel

		AB	R	H	HR	RBI	SB	Avg	vL	vR	OB	Slg	OPS	bb%	ct%	h%	Eye	xBA	G	L	F	PX	hr/f	SX	SBO	RC/G	RAR	R$
Pos 5	03 FLA	* 580	82	179	20	117	8	309	364	247	368	519	886	9	78	37	0.43	303	48	20	32	145	14%	95	10%	6.56	36.9	$26
Age 25	04 FLA	603	101	177	33	112	5	294	262	302	365	512	878	10	75	34	0.46	281	45	19	35	138	20%	70	4%	6.43	23.0	$27
Pre-Peak	05 FLA	613	106	198	33	116	1	323	304	329	387	561	948	9	80	36	0.51	311	38	24	37	154	18%	59	1%	7.22	39.7	$32
Bats Right	06 FLA	576	112	195	26	114	9	339	321	344	424	568	992	13	81	38	0.80	312	40	24	35	144	16%	74	7%	8.02	38.3	$32
Reliability 83	07 FLA	588	91	188	34	119	2	320	364	309	400	565	965	12	78	36	0.62	298	40	21	39	153	19%	50	2%	7.59	44.2	$29
BAvg Potl 40%	1st Half	284	46	92	17	55	0	324			389	592	980	10	76	38	0.44	304	36	23	42	174	19%	50	1%	7.76	22.6	$14
LIMA Plan D+	2nd Half	304	45	96	17	64	2	316			411	539	950	14	81	35	0.83	291	44	19	37	136	19%	39	2%	7.45	21.8	$15
+/- Score -12	08 Proj	**596**	**99**	**197**	**38**	**129**	**4**	**331**			**409**	**601**	**1009**	**12**	**79**	**37**	**0.64**	**315**	**41**	**22**	**37**	**166**	**22%**	**60**	**3%**	**8.09**	**49.6**	**$34**

At 24, he still hasn't come close to reaching his ceiling. Why 2008 could be the year...
- 2nd half bb%, ct% surges
- Rising FB trend
If he reports to camp in shape:
UP: 45-140-.340

Cabrera,Orlando

		AB	R	H	HR	RBI	SB	Avg	vL	vR	OB	Slg	OPS	bb%	ct%	h%	Eye	xBA	G	L	F	PX	hr/f	SX	SBO	RC/G	RAR	R$
Pos 6	03 MON	626	95	186	17	80	24	297	311	293	351	460	811	8	90	31	0.81	301	40	21	39	101	8%	116	15%	5.53	24.7	$27
Age 33	04 2TM	621	75	163	10	62	17	262	295	249	307	382	689	6	91	27	0.74	279	44	18	38	72	5%	104	14%	4.14	-2.8	$15
Past Peak	05 ANA	540	70	139	8	57	21	257	242	266	306	365	671	7	91	27	0.76	273	41	19	39	67	4%	123	17%	3.96	-9.5	$15
Bats Right	06 LAA	607	95	171	9	72	27	282	243	297	337	404	741	8	90	30	0.88	270	39	17	43	79	4%	114	18%	4.82	7.0	$20
Reliability 92	07 LAA	638	101	192	8	86	20	301	308	299	346	397	743	6	90	33	0.69	266	43	18	39	64	4%	100	13%	4.71	2.6	$23
BAvg Potl 50%	1st Half	314	50	105	4	44	9	334			378	446	824	7	92	35	0.88	281	39	20	41	76	3%	88	9%	5.65	9.0	$13
LIMA Plan C+	2nd Half	324	51	87	4	42	11	269			315	349	664	6	88	30	0.56	252	48	16	36	51	4%	103	16%	3.76	-7.6	$10
+/- Score -46	08 Proj	**606**	**92**	**169**	**9**	**75**	**17**	**279**			**328**	**388**	**716**	**7**	**90**	**30**	**0.74**	**270**	**42**	**18**	**40**	**70**	**4%**	**104**	**12%**	**4.45**	**-1.0**	**$18**

A model of consistency on the surface. But there are warning signs...
- 2nd half slide
- SX trend
- Outhit xBA by 35 points
Don't bet on a repeat.

Cairo,Miguel

		AB	R	H	HR	RBI	SB	Avg	vL	vR	OB	Slg	OPS	bb%	ct%	h%	Eye	xBA	G	L	F	PX	hr/f	SX	SBO	RC/G	RAR	R$
Pos 35	03 STL	261	41	64	5	32	4	245	244	246	281	375	657	5	89	26	0.43	271	40	18	42	81	5%	120	9%	3.62	-14.7	$6
Age 33	04 NYY	360	48	105	6	42	11	292	336	267	325	417	742	5	86	32	0.37	272	44	20	36	73	5%	128	15%	4.54	-4.5	$11
Past Peak	05 NYM	327	31	82	2	19	13	251	191	273	292	324	616	5	91	27	0.61	275	44	22	34	53	2%	88	20%	3.30	-22.4	$6
Bats Right	06 NYY	222	28	53	0	30	13	239	279	221	281	320	601	6	86	28	0.42	263	53	16	31	55	0%	148	27%	3.05	-15.8	$5
Reliability 28	07 2TM	174	20	44	0	15	10	253	254	252	297	328	625	6	86	29	0.46	232	43	14	43	53	0%	129	27%	3.34	-10.4	$4
BAvg Potl 50%	1st Half	81	8	20	0	5	5	247			299	296	595	7	86	29	0.55	206	43	10	47	41	0%	82	27%	3.03	-5.6	$2
LIMA Plan F	2nd Half	93	12	24	0	10	5	258			296	355	651	5	86	30	0.38	251	43	18	40	63	0%	143	27%	3.62	-4.7	$2
+/- Score -12	08 Proj	**160**	**19**	**40**	**0**	**16**	**8**	**250**			**292**	**333**	**625**	**6**	**87**	**29**	**0.45**	**250**	**45**	**17**	**38**	**55**	**1%**	**131**	**25%**	**3.34**	**-10.0**	**$4**

SX hints at SB potential, but a sub-.300 OBA won't cut it. xBA tanked while h% held steady, so don't fish for any BA value either. MLB clubs are catching on too... note the AB trend.

Callaspo,Alberto

		AB	R	H	HR	RBI	SB	Avg	vL	vR	OB	Slg	OPS	bb%	ct%	h%	Eye	xBA	G	L	F	PX	hr/f	SX	SBO	RC/G	RAR	R$
Pos 5	03	0	0	0	0	0	0	0							0									0				
Age 25	04 aa	550	62	139	4	39	12	253			301	325	626	6	96	26	1.81					45		70	19%	3.69	-21.7	$9
Pre-Peak	05 a/a	557	60	147	8	59	8	264			299	357	656	5	96	26	1.27					56		57	17%	3.85	-13.2	$12
Bats Both	06 ARI	* 532	74	162	6	59	6	305	278	208	362	427	789	8	95	31	1.78	247	46	8	46	63	3%	94	8%	5.50	0.2	$16
Reliability 16	07 ARI	* 370	48	100	5	31	2	271	219	214	329	380	709	8	92	28	1.11	291	47	21	32	68	4%	60	5%	4.53	-2.7	$7
BAvg Potl 70%	1st Half	176	18	48	2	13	0	273			330	386	716	8	92	29	1.07	286	50	18	32	72	4%	46	4%	4.61	-0.8	$3
LIMA Plan D	2nd Half	194	30	52	3	18	2	270			328	374	703	8	92	28	1.14	328	27	40	33	63	5%	77	5%	4.45	-1.9	$4
+/- Score 11	08 Proj	**111**	**14**	**31**	**1**	**10**	**1**	**279**			**333**	**388**	**721**	**7**	**94**	**29**	**1.31**	**291**	**46**	**20**	**34**	**64**	**4%**	**77**	**9%**	**4.67**	**-0.9**	**$3**

0-7-.215 in 144 AB at ARI. Completely overmatched in MLB debut. While high ct% gives hope of a .300 BA, PX/SX history suggests his upside is limited. Lots of contact, lots of ground outs and soft liners.

Cameron,Mike

		AB	R	H	HR	RBI	SB	Avg	vL	vR	OB	Slg	OPS	bb%	ct%	h%	Eye	xBA	G	L	F	PX	hr/f	SX	SBO	RC/G	RAR	R$
Pos 8	03 SEA	534	74	135	18	76	17	253	286	240	339	431	770	12	74	31	0.51	266	32	28	40	122	11%	113	16%	5.23	7.8	$17
Age 35	04 NYM	493	76	114	30	76	22	231	216	235	311	479	790	10	71	26	0.40	259	31	16	53	167	16%	108	25%	5.36	10.8	$20
Decline	05 NYM	308	47	84	12	39	13	273	311	261	335	477	813	9	72	34	0.34	277	42	21	38	151	14%	126	18%	5.71	10.1	$13
Bats Right	06 SD	552	88	148	22	83	25	268	252	273	352	482	833	11	74	32	0.50	260	38	17	45	137	12%	134	22%	6.08	26.5	$23
Reliability 51	07 SD	571	88	138	21	78	18	242	294	222	321	431	752	11	72	30	0.42	251	37	19	44	131	12%	122	16%	4.96	6.9	$17
BAvg Potl 45%	1st Half	295	41	78	10	38	8	264			320	444	764	8	75	32	0.32	254	39	18	43	121	10%	108	17%	4.94	3.3	$9
LIMA Plan B+	2nd Half	276	47	60	11	40	10	217			323	417	740	13	69	27	0.50	247	35	20	45	143	13%	131	15%	4.95	3.3	$8
+/- Score -10	08 Proj	**531**	**83**	**133**	**18**	**75**	**15**	**250**			**331**	**436**	**767**	**11**	**72**	**31**	**0.44**	**252**	**37**	**19**	**44**	**130**	**11%**	**125**	**14%**	**5.21**	**10.3**	**$17**

Poor guy has spent the last 7 years hitting in pitcher-friendly parks. Now he's past peak and in the midst of a PX decline. Big BA drop vs. RH and 2nd half fade are worrisome. Expect the descent to continue.

Cano,Robinson

		AB	R	H	HR	RBI	SB	Avg	vL	vR	OB	Slg	OPS	bb%	ct%	h%	Eye	xBA	G	L	F	PX	hr/f	SX	SBO	RC/G	RAR	R$
Pos 4	03 aa	164	18	43	1	12	0	263			294	346	640	4	92	28	0.59					54		54	0%	3.55	-3.4	$2
Age 25	04 a/a	508	58	135	12	66	2	267			316	413	729	7	89	28	0.67					83		71	7%	4.57	3.3	$11
Pre-Peak	05 NYY	* 630	95	189	17	83	1	299	270	305	322	466	788	3	88	32	0.27	310	50	21	29	103	11%	76	3%	4.95	14.3	$21
Bats Left	06 NYY	482	62	165	15	78	5	342	287	363	366	525	891	4	89	36	0.33	321	52	20	28	112	12%	66	6%	6.10	24.8	$20
Reliability 49	07 NYY	617	93	189	19	97	4	306	328	296	348	488	835	6	86	33	0.46	305	52	17	31	112	12%	85	6%	5.66	26.0	$23
BAvg Potl 50%	1st Half	287	32	77	3	32	1	268			302	404	707	5	83	31	0.29	278	54	15	31	96	4%	80	8%	4.17	0.3	$5
LIMA Plan C	2nd Half	330	61	112	16	65	3	339			386	561	947	7	89	35	0.68	328	51	19	31	125	18%	90	4%	6.90	23.8	$18
+/- Score 9	08 Proj	**608**	**87**	**185**	**20**	**92**	**4**	**304**			**339**	**490**	**828**	**5**	**88**	**32**	**0.43**	**313**	**52**	**18**	**30**	**112**	**13%**	**77**	**5%**	**5.50**	**23.1**	**$22**

Monster 2nd half, but how can he sustain that 30 HR pace with a 50%+ GB%? If his 2nd half hr/f regresses to previous norms, the answer will be "he can't." But 20 HRs is realistic and a .300 BA is here to stay.

Cantu,Jorge

		AB	R	H	HR	RBI	SB	Avg	vL	vR	OB	Slg	OPS	bb%	ct%	h%	Eye	xBA	G	L	F	PX	hr/f	SX	SBO	RC/G	RAR	R$
Pos 3	03 a/a	358	39	93	6	45	2	260			291	391	683	4	88	28	0.37					88		57	8%	3.88	-16.5	$7
Age 26	04 TAM	* 541	76	157	20	89	3	290	373	270	320	505	825	4	82	32	0.25	310	46	20	34	140	13%	79	3%	5.45	7.0	$18
Pre-Peak	05 TAM	598	73	171	28	117	1	286	256	296	308	497	805	3	86	29	0.23	312	42	21	37	128	15%	44	1%	5.03	-1.0	$22
Bats Right	06 TAM	413	40	103	14	62	1	249	233	256	294	404	698	6	78	29	0.29	255	42	20	38	97	11%	50	2%	3.93	-18.1	$8
Reliability 50	07 2TM	* 300	33	77	4	33	0	257	232	283	310	377	686	7	81	31	0.40	269	45	22	34	89	5%	42	0%	4.00	-11.8	$4
BAvg Potl 45%	1st Half	123	12	31	0	12	0	252			308	317	625	8	78	32	0.37	237	47	21	32	53	0%	50	0%	3.25	-7.5	$1
LIMA Plan F	2nd Half	177	21	46	4	21	0	260			311	418	729	7	82	30	0.42	290	43	22	35	114	8%	28	0%	4.49	-4.4	$3
+/- Score 21	08 Proj	**254**	**28**	**68**	**8**	**35**	**0**	**268**			**311**	**441**	**752**	**6**	**81**	**30**	**0.34**	**282**	**43**	**21**	**36**	**113**	**11%**	**46**	**1%**	**4.65**	**-5.8**	**$6**

1-13-.252 in 115 AB at TAM and CIN. A lost season on the surface. Yet hidden in his MLB 2nd half were a .303 xBA and 143 PX. A little hr/f correction could do the trick. At age 26, a good speculative end-gamer.

Carroll,Jamey

		AB	R	H	HR	RBI	SB	Avg	vL	vR	OB	Slg	OPS	bb%	ct%	h%	Eye	xBA	G	L	F	PX	hr/f	SX	SBO	RC/G	RAR	R$
Pos 45	03 MON	227	31	59	1	10	5	260	268	255	317	326	643	8	83	31	0.49	254	47	22	31	49	2%	95	11%	3.53	-5.9	$4
Age 34	04 MON	219	36	63	0	16	5	288	250	310	378	370	748	13	90	32	1.52	291	48	23	29	57	0%	103	8%	5.31	4.3	$6
Past Peak	05 WAS	303	44	76	0	22	3	251	293	235	326	284	610	10	82	31	0.62	261	53	26	21	27	0%	76	7%	3.23	-12.1	$4
Bats Right	06 COL	463	84	139	5	36	10	300	359	283	376	404	780	11	86	34	0.85	281	49	23	29	64	4%	95	14%	5.39	10.3	$15
Reliability 8	07 COL	227	45	51	2	22	6	225	262	194	310	300	609	11	85	26	0.82	266	44	25	32	50	3%	113	12%	3.35	-8.4	$4
BAvg Potl 75%	1st Half	120	22	24	1	7	3	200			304	267	571	13	80	24	0.75	249	46	23	31	50	3%	85	14%	2.81	-6.7	$1
LIMA Plan F	2nd Half	107	23	27	1	15	3	252			316	336	653	9	91	27	1.00	283	41	26	32	49	3%	126	10%	3.90	-2.1	$3
+/- Score 32	08 Proj	**188**	**34**	**48**	**1**	**17**	**4**	**255**			**333**	**331**	**664**	**10**	**86**	**29**	**0.81**	**272**	**46**	**24**	**29**	**50**	**3%**	**103**	**11%**	**3.99**	**-3.2**	**$4**

2006 will go down as his career year, and that was hit rate-fueled. If '07 h% had corrected a little less, he still drew enough BB to reach 10+ SB again. But at age 34, the grease will keep coming off his wheels.

Casey,Sean

		AB	R	H	HR	RBI	SB	Avg	vL	vR	OB	Slg	OPS	bb%	ct%	h%	Eye	xBA	G	L	F	PX	hr/f	SX	SBO	RC/G	RAR	R$
Pos 3	03 CIN	573	71	167	14	80	4	291	320	278	349	408	758	8	90	31	0.88	306	45	27	27	65	10%	80	2%	4.93	-9.3	$18
Age 33	04 CIN	571	101	185	24	99	2	324	306	332	374	534	909	7	94	32	1.28	337	43	23	34	115	13%	74	1%	6.57	9.3	$27
Past Peak	05 CIN	529	75	165	9	58	2	312	335	298	369	423	793	8	91	33	1.00	290	52	19	29	73	6%	53	1%	5.40	-2.9	$18
Bats Left	06 2TM	397	47	108	8	59	0	272	287	266	328	388	716	8	89	29	0.77	284	44	23	33	71	7%	28	1%	4.45	-14.3	$9
Reliability 63	07 DET	453	40	134	4	54	2	296	365	285	352	393	745	8	91	32	0.93	282	46	21	33	68	3%	40	3%	4.88	-2.6	$10
BAvg Potl 60%	1st Half	232	20	69	1	30	1	297			361	388	749	9	91	32	1.10	282	45	21	34	69	1%	31	1%	5.04	-0.3	$5
LIMA Plan D	2nd Half	221	20	65	3	24	1	294			342	398	740	7	90	31	0.76	280	47	20	33	67	5%	44	5%	4.72	-2.3	$5
+/- Score -7	08 Proj	**424**	**47**	**121**	**7**	**54**	**1**	**285**			**341**	**399**	**740**	**8**	**90**	**30**	**0.88**	**289**	**46**	**21**	**32**	**73**	**5%**	**46**	**2%**	**4.79**	**-4.7**	**$10**

How does a player with 20+ HR power dive to single-digits overnight? And in a hitters park. If he's clean, his back injury could be a reason, but that happened in '06, not '05. As a cornerman, he's nearly worthless now.

STEPHEN NICKRAND

Casilla,Alexi			AB	R	H	HR	RBI	SB	Avg	vL	vR	OB	Slg	OPS	bb%	ct%	h%	Eye	xBA	G	L	F	PX	hr/f	SX	SBO	RC/G	RAR	R$
Pos	4	03	0	0	0	0	0	0	0							0									0				
Age	23	04	0	0	0	0	0	0	0							0									0				
Growth		05	0	0	0	0	0	0	0							0									0				
Bats	Both	06 aa	170	26	48	1	12	18	282			348	371	718	9	88	32	0.85					59		134	42%	4.63	1.3	$7
Reliability	0	07 MIN	* 509	67	126	3	29	35	248	274	181	302	308	611	7	84	29	0.50	266	62	16	22	43	3%	118	34%	3.13	-15.5	$13
BAvg Potl	55%	1st Half	267	40	72	1	17	23	270			341	341	682	10	84	32	0.66	288	65	19	16	55	3%	118	38%	4.14	0.1	$9
LIMA Plan	C	2nd Half	242	27	54	2	12	12	223			257	273	530	4	85	25	0.31	253	62	15	23	30	4%	111	28%	2.00	-16.0	$3
+/- Score	17	08 Proj	402	55	104	2	25	28	259			315	329	645	8	86	30	0.59	275	62	16	22	49	3%	124	32%	3.60	-6.3	$11

0-9-.222 in 189 AB at MIN. A disappointing debut. Walks will determine if he's the next Luis Castillo, or just another Doug Glanville. He's still raw, so exercise patience, and hope that he does too.

Castillo,Jose			AB	R	H	HR	RBI	SB	Avg	vL	vR	OB	Slg	OPS	bb%	ct%	h%	Eye	xBA	G	L	F	PX	hr/f	SX	SBO	RC/G	RAR	R$
Pos	54	03 aa	498	62	137	4	60	17	275			324	363	687	7	86	31	0.52					59		107	20%	4.06	-4.7	$14
Age	27	04 PIT	383	44	98	8	39	3	256	267	253	298	368	666	6	76	32	0.25	251	59	16	24	75	11%	75	5%	3.55	-17.0	$7
Peak		05 PIT	370	49	99	11	53	2	268	258	271	310	416	727	6	84	29	0.39	288	46	23	31	90	11%	76	5%	4.34	-4.7	$11
Bats	Right	06 PIT	518	54	131	14	65	6	253	259	251	296	382	679	6	81	29	0.33	259	46	19	34	81	10%	51	8%	3.72	-27.1	$11
Reliability	39	07 PIT	221	18	54	0	24	0	244	246	244	264	335	599	3	78	31	0.13	256	57	18	25	78	0%	41	0%	2.72	-13.5	$1
BAvg Potl	40%	1st Half	94	7	23	0	9	0	245			283	319	602	5	81	30	0.28	254	56	21	23	65	0%	21	0%	2.89	-5.3	$0
LIMA Plan	F	2nd Half	127	11	31	0	15	0	244			250	346	596	1	76	32	0.03	255	58	16	26	88	0%	56	0%	2.60	-8.2	$1
+/- Score	20	08 Proj	196	19	49	2	23	1	250			282	365	646	4	80	30	0.22	267	53	19	28	83	6%	67	5%	3.33	-9.4	$3

Power looks to be in a freefall but a scan of his PX trend says that it's more gradual... and that he really never had much power anyway. Increase in GB% nails that baby shut, and now there's nothing worth chasing at all.

Castillo,Luis			AB	R	H	HR	RBI	SB	Avg	vL	vR	OB	Slg	OPS	bb%	ct%	h%	Eye	xBA	G	L	F	PX	hr/f	SX	SBO	RC/G	RAR	R$
Pos	4	03 FLA	595	99	187	6	39	21	314	320	312	380	397	777	10	90	34	1.05	309	56	25	18	48	6%	111	18%	5.30	15.0	$22
Age	32	04 FLA	564	91	164	2	47	21	291	308	285	374	348	722	12	88	33	1.10	278	65	17	19	32	2%	131	11%	4.81	3.1	$18
Past Peak		05 FLA	439	72	132	4	30	10	301	423	259	391	374	764	13	93	32	2.03	312	63	22	15	41	6%	96	10%	5.47	11.2	$14
Bats	Both	06 MIN	584	84	173	3	49	25	296	256	316	358	370	728	9	90	33	0.97	289	61	18	21	44	3%	117	18%	4.74	10.2	$18
Reliability	90	07 2TM	548	91	165	1	38	19	301	296	303	363	359	722	9	92	33	1.18	289	67	15	18	37	1%	115	13%	4.73	5.9	$17
BAvg Potl	60%	1st Half	260	41	79	0	12	7	304			351	335	686	7	92	33	0.90	273	70	14	17	21	0%	94	11%	4.17	-1.3	$7
LIMA Plan	B+	2nd Half	288	50	86	1	26	12	299			373	382	755	11	92	32	1.42	300	64	16	20	51	2%	125	15%	5.23	7.1	$10
+/- Score	-7	08 Proj	564	91	169	2	42	20	300			368	368	735	10	91	33	1.22	294	64	17	19	41	3%	116	14%	4.92	9.0	$18

Has settled into a zone of quiet reliability despite ongoing knee issues. Sliding LD% is worth keeping an eye on; otherwise, with strong, stable BPIs, there's little here to worry about.

Castro,Ramon			AB	R	H	HR	RBI	SB	Avg	vL	vR	OB	Slg	OPS	bb%	ct%	h%	Eye	xBA	G	L	F	PX	hr/f	SX	SBO	RC/G	RAR	R$
Pos	2	03 FLA	53	6	15	5	8	0	283	409	194	333	604	937	7	79	27	0.36	346	24	24	53	185	23%	0	0%	6.71	3.6	$2
Age	28	04 FLA	* 312	31	56	4	28	4	179	143	134	254	279	532	9	81	21	0.52	192	32	11	58	61	3%	100	13%	2.18	-16.7	($0)
Peak		05 NYM	* 339	43	76	13	59	2	223	290	236	293	412	705	9	76	26	0.41	265	36	19	45	133	11%	61	3%	4.19	4.2	$8
Bats	Both	06 NYM	126	13	30	4	12	0	238	269	230	319	389	708	11	68	32	0.38	232	36	22	42	112	11%	17	0%	4.40	0.2	$2
Reliability	2	07 NYM	144	24	41	11	31	0	285	276	287	331	556	887	6	73	32	0.26	277	36	18	46	171	23%	30	0%	6.34	10.3	$7
BAvg Potl	35%	1st Half	63	9	16	4	13	0	254			329	476	805	10	71	29	0.39	262	26	24	50	142	18%	22	0%	5.47	3.1	$2
LIMA Plan	F	2nd Half	81	15	25	7	18	0	309			333	617	951	4	74	34	0.14	293	44	13	43	192	27%	37	0%	6.95	6.9	$5
+/- Score	-38	08 Proj	193	27	50	12	32	0	259			318	498	816	8	73	29	0.32	268	37	18	45	154	20%	33	2%	5.51	8.8	$7

Turned into a solid backup CA with career year, but most of it is likely not repeatable. Low ct% makes him a BA risk. hr/f was inflated and will regress. Even still, a reasonable #2 catcher option.

Catalanotto,Frank			AB	R	H	HR	RBI	SB	Avg	vL	vR	OB	Slg	OPS	bb%	ct%	h%	Eye	xBA	G	L	F	PX	hr/f	SX	SBO	RC/G	RAR	R$
Pos	7	03 TOR	489	83	146	13	59	2	299	176	318	345	472	818	7	87	32	0.56	309	42	24	34	105	9%	93	3%	5.54	2.8	$16
Age	34	04 TOR	249	27	73	1	26	1	293	227	307	338	390	728	6	87	33	0.52	295	44	27	29	70	2%	58	1%	4.56	-2.7	$5
Past Peak		05 TOR	419	56	126	8	59	0	301	290	302	357	451	809	8	87	33	0.70	295	45	21	35	96	6%	64	2%	5.56	9.7	$13
Bats	Left	06 TOR	437	56	131	7	56	1	300	237	306	374	439	814	11	92	32	1.41	296	48	19	34	88	5%	46	3%	5.86	8.2	$11
Reliability	54	07 TEX	331	52	86	11	44	2	260	231	261	318	444	762	8	89	27	0.76	316	51	19	30	108	12%	93	4%	4.97	2.4	$9
BAvg Potl	70%	1st Half	135	20	27	6	21	2	200			270	400	670	9	87	19	0.72	300	52	15	33	110	15%	110	7%	3.88	-3.6	$3
LIMA Plan	C+	2nd Half	196	32	59	5	23	0	301			351	474	825	7	90	31	0.79	326	51	21	28	107	10%	71	2%	5.69	5.2	$6
+/- Score	29	08 Proj	403	58	117	10	53	2	290			350	454	805	8	89	31	0.84	307	49	20	32	100	9%	75	3%	5.53	7.3	$12

Unfortunate 1st half hit rate ended his string of .290+ seasons, but xBA streak remains intact. And since he only had 13 AB vs. LH, drop in BA vs. RH can also be traced to h%. Expect a rebound.

Cedeno,Ronny			AB	R	H	HR	RBI	SB	Avg	vL	vR	OB	Slg	OPS	bb%	ct%	h%	Eye	xBA	G	L	F	PX	hr/f	SX	SBO	RC/G	RAR	R$
Pos	6	03	0	0	0	0	0	0	0							0									0				
Age	25	04 aa	384	34	96	5	42	9	250			291	349	640	5	82	29	0.32					64		83	22%	3.32	-11.4	$7
Pre-Peak		05 CHC	* 325	48	105	8	35	10	323	256	341	365	454	819	6	89	34	0.63	297	61	14	25	79	12%	91	14%	5.48	13.3	$15
Bats	Right	06 CHC	534	51	131	6	41	8	245	230	251	269	339	608	3	80	30	0.16	232	47	16	37	58	4%	96	14%	2.76	-25.8	$7
Reliability	7	07 CHC	* 361	48	106	13	42	7	294	176	225	343	451	794	7	84	32	0.45	268	33	23	44	92	9%	76	12%	5.16	12.3	$13
BAvg Potl	45%	1st Half	190	30	61	10	25	4	321			386	558	944	10	86	33	0.77	270	33	8	58	137	10%	73	14%	7.05	16.1	$9
LIMA Plan	F	2nd Half	171	18	45	3	17	3	264			292	333	625	4	81	31	0.20	259	33	33	33	39	6%	75	10%	2.94	-5.1	$3
+/- Score	-10	08 Proj	133	16	37	4	14	3	278			316	422	739	5	83	31	0.33	265	45	19	37	84	10%	82	14%	4.42	1.3	$4

4-13-.203 in 74 AB at CHC.
1st half success was nice, but:
- Big outliers in bb%, PX, FB%
- Was unable to repeat in 2H
- Has 0.18 Eye in 688 MLB AB

Too unskilled to take seriously, too young to dismiss just yet.

Chavez,Endy			AB	R	H	HR	RBI	SB	Avg	vL	vR	OB	Slg	OPS	bb%	ct%	h%	Eye	xBA	G	L	F	PX	hr/f	SX	SBO	RC/G	RAR	R$
Pos	79	03 MON	483	66	121	5	47	18	251	304	238	296	354	650	6	88	28	0.53	302	55	22	23	66	5%	133	21%	3.64	-28.3	$12
Age	30	04 MON	* 567	72	157	5	39	36	277	241	290	319	369	688	6	92	29	0.78	285	57	15	28	52	3%	143	29%	4.15	-21.2	$19
Peak		05 2NL	* 203	27	42	1	14	6	207	381	179	257	285	542	6	91	23	0.71	294	57	21	23	46	2%	137	19%	2.57	-17.8	$2
Bats	Left	06 NYM	353	48	108	4	42	12	306	333	298	350	431	781	6	88	34	0.55	301	55	20	25	76	5%	120	15%	5.15	-1.0	$13
Reliability	8	07 NYM	150	20	43	1	17	5	287	276	289	327	380	707	6	89	32	0.56	290	60	17	23	57	3%	111	17%	4.29	-4.5	$4
BAvg Potl	50%	1st Half	113	15	33	1	13	3	292			339	407	746	7	88	32	0.62	303	62	18	21	69	5%	110	16%	4.79	-1.8	$3
LIMA Plan	D	2nd Half	37	5	10	0	4	2	270			289	297	587	3	92	29	0.33	246	55	15	30	21	0%	88	20%	2.81	-2.7	$1
+/- Score	-14	08 Proj	220	29	61	2	21	7	277			323	380	703	6	89	30	0.63	297	58	19	23	62	4%	114	17%	4.29	-6.6	$6

Treads a fine line between modest value and irrelevance, as 1H/2H splits showed. SX trend is worrisome, but he has the skill potential for one more .300 BA, 10+ SB season, so long as playing time obliges.

Chavez,Eric			AB	R	H	HR	RBI	SB	Avg	vL	vR	OB	Slg	OPS	bb%	ct%	h%	Eye	xBA	G	L	F	PX	hr/f	SX	SBO	RC/G	RAR	R$
Pos	5	03 OAK	588	94	166	29	101	8	282	220	312	351	514	864	10	85	29	0.70	321	40	25	35	136	16%	98	7%	6.16	27.4	$24
Age	30	04 OAK	475	87	131	29	77	6	276	306	257	396	501	898	17	79	29	0.96	278	41	18	42	131	19%	57	5%	6.91	27.3	$20
Peak		05 OAK	625	92	168	27	101	6	269	260	271	331	466	796	8	79	30	0.45	277	39	18	43	130	13%	77	4%	5.29	14.2	$22
Bats	Left	06 OAK	485	74	117	22	72	3	241	197	257	353	435	788	15	79	26	0.84	266	39	18	44	118	13%	68	2%	5.50	7.1	$12
Reliability	73	07 OAK	341	43	82	15	46	4	240	234	244	309	446	755	9	78	27	0.45	270	36	17	46	136	12%	78	8%	4.82	3.3	$8
BAvg Potl	55%	1st Half	284	32	69	12	37	4	243			309	444	752	9	76	28	0.39	262	37	16	47	136	12%	75	9%	4.79	2.5	$7
LIMA Plan	C+	2nd Half	57	11	13	3	9	0	228			312	456	769	11	88	21	1.00	313	32	22	46	136	13%	48	0%	5.13	1.1	$2
+/- Score	26	08 Proj	404	64	103	19	61	3	255			339	462	801	11	79	28	0.60	277	36	19	44	133	14%	66	3%	5.48	9.9	$12

Injuries have cut his production, though xBA and PX say little has changed. But he's hitting more FB with diminishing HR returns; could be the injuries, or maybe his power has peaked. Either way, buy only at a discount.

Church,Ryan			AB	R	H	HR	RBI	SB	Avg	vL	vR	OB	Slg	OPS	bb%	ct%	h%	Eye	xBA	G	L	F	PX	hr/f	SX	SBO	RC/G	RAR	R$
Pos	78	03 aa	371	41	87	11	45	4	236			288	382	670	7	83	26	0.44					89		74	8%	3.71	-19.6	$7
Age	29	04 aaa	347	54	107	14	58	0	307			374	537	911	10	86	33	0.78					135		73	1%	6.78	15.1	$14
Peak		05 WAS	268	41	77	9	42	3	287	367	277	346	466	812	8	74	36	0.34	280	46	24	30	125	15%	102	7%	5.64	2.3	$10
Bats	Left	06 WAS	* 390	47	91	17	60	10	232	265	279	316	425	741	11	72	28	0.44	251	39	18	43	130	13%	79	12%	4.76	-5.8	$11
Reliability	38	07 WAS	470	57	128	15	70	3	272	229	287	341	464	805	9	77	32	0.46	291	43	22	35	138	12%	53	4%	5.58	3.2	$13
BAvg Potl	50%	1st Half	258	30	68	7	35	3	264			340	438	778	10	80	31	0.59	296	46	22	32	124	11%	49	6%	5.28	-0.4	$6
LIMA Plan	C	2nd Half	212	27	60	8	35	0	283			342	495	837	8	74	35	0.34	284	38	23	39	155	13%	47	2%	6.01	4.0	$7
+/- Score	7	08 Proj	471	60	130	18	77	3	276			344	474	817	9	76	33	0.42	283	42	22	36	136	14%	64	5%	5.71	5.1	$15

Drops in FB% and hr/f led to doubles explosion (43, to be exact). Posted career-best PX, and topped it in 2H. BA vs LH limits his value, but in friendlier confines (maybe new WAS park?), could crack 20-HR mark.

BRANDON KRUSE

Cintron,Alex

			AB	R	H	HR	RBI	SB	Avg	vL	vR	OB	Slg	OPS	bb%	ct%	h%	Eye	xBA	G	L	F	PX	hr/f	SX	SBO	RC/G	RAR	R$
Pos	5	03 ARI	* 555	86	181	15	67	3	326	365	296	366	501	867	6	93	33	0.92	338	45	27	29	98	10%	96	4%	6.07	26.8	$22
Age	29	04 ARI	564	56	148	4	49	3	262	295	250	301	363	664	5	90	29	0.53	267	45	18	37	63	2%	82	4%	3.81	-20.5	$8
Peak		05 ARI	330	36	90	8	48	1	273	301	267	298	415	713	4	90	28	0.36	299	43	22	34	86	8%	61	4%	4.17	-5.8	$9
Bats	Both	06 CHW	288	35	82	5	41	10	285	274	288	309	392	701	3	88	31	0.29	280	46	23	31	60	6%	115	18%	3.97	-8.5	$9
Reliability	40	07 CHW	185	23	45	2	19	2	243	238	244	278	324	603	5	81	29	0.26	235	43	19	39	56	3%	84	7%	2.79	-9.4	$3
BAvg Potl	45%	1st Half	98	12	21	0	7	0	214			267	265	532	7	81	27	0.37	217	46	15	38	46	0%	52	4%	2.08	-7.4	$0
LIMA Plan	F	2nd Half	87	11	24	2	12	2	276			292	391	683	2	82	32	0.13	250	39	22	39	67	7%	104	10%	3.57	-2.3	$3
+/- Score	-10	08 Proj	264	32	71	4	33	4	269			298	375	673	4	85	30	0.28	265	43	21	36	66	5%	94	9%	3.65	-7.6	$6

Three stints on bereavement, elbow and hand injuries derailed 2007, so we should discount that a bit. Still, it's tough to ignore 5 year declining trend in ct%, Eye and PX. Should top '07 stats, but still eroding.

Cirillo,Jeff

			AB	R	H	HR	RBI	SB	Avg	vL	vR	OB	Slg	OPS	bb%	ct%	h%	Eye	xBA	G	L	F	PX	hr/f	SX	SBO	RC/G	RAR	R$
Pos	50	03 SEA	258	24	53	2	23	1	205	227	194	273	271	544	9	88	23	0.75	257	40	23	37	46	2%	41	3%	2.55	-15.8	$0
Age	38	04 SD	75	12	16	1	7	0	213	207	217	263	293	556	6	81	25	0.36	224	49	14	37	55	4%	60	0%	2.30	-6.4	$1
Decline		05 MIL	185	29	52	4	23	4	281	400	231	361	427	788	11	88	30	1.05	293	50	16	34	99	7%	71	11%	5.50	3.8	$6
Bats	Right	06 MIL	263	33	84	3	23	1	319	413	282	370	414	784	7	87	36	0.64	267	46	20	34	64	4%	38	2%	5.20	-2.0	$8
Reliability	2	07 2TM	193	24	48	2	27	2	249	271	236	316	368	684	9	90	27	1.00	292	49	19	32	77	4%	87	4%	4.30	-1.9	$3
BAvg Potl	75%	1st Half	111	10	30	1	16	1	270			336	369	705	9	92	29	1.22	288	50	20	30	62	3%	61	3%	4.57	-0.2	$2
LIMA Plan	F	2nd Half	82	14	18	1	11	1	220			289	366	655	9	88	24	0.80	297	48	18	34	98	4%	111	6%	3.93	-1.8	$1
+/- Score	25	08 Proj	141	19	38	1	17	1	270			334	370	704	9	89	30	0.85	278	48	19	34	70	2%	81	5%	4.49	-1.2	$3

Finally made the playoffs after 1,617 games. Still has skills -- 1.00 Eye, 90% contact rate, .292 xBA. But BA vs RH puts him on wrong side of platoon at best.

Clark,Brady

			AB	R	H	HR	RBI	SB	Avg	vL	vR	OB	Slg	OPS	bb%	ct%	h%	Eye	xBA	G	L	F	PX	hr/f	SX	SBO	RC/G	RAR	R$
Pos	7	03 MIL	* 349	37	93	6	43	14	266	263	279	312	393	704	6	87	29	0.50	275	44	18	38	85	5%	102	19%	4.22	-13.9	$11
Age	35	04 MIL	354	41	99	7	46	15	280	250	291	373	395	769	13	86	31	1.08	262	42	19	39	72	6%	79	18%	5.35	-0.9	$12
Decline		05 MIL	599	94	183	13	53	10	306	302	305	356	426	782	7	91	32	0.85	294	37	26	37	74	6%	70	12%	5.18	-2.8	$21
Bats	Right	06 MIL	415	51	109	4	29	3	263	273	258	332	335	667	9	86	30	0.72	252	40	23	37	45	3%	58	5%	3.93	-16.0	$6
Reliability	46	07 2NL	* 185	23	46	1	18	2	246	308	235	319	338	657	10	83	29	0.62	251	46	18	36	65	1%	83	11%	3.85	-8.4	$2
BAvg Potl	55%	1st Half	58	7	13	0	5	1	224			297	293	590	9	81	28	0.55	234	43	17	39	60	0%	63	20%	2.98	-4.4	$0
LIMA Plan	F	2nd Half	127	16	33	1	13	1	257			329	359	688	10	84	30	0.66	265	49	20	32	67	2%	88	7%	4.24	-4.2	$2
+/- Score	7	08 Proj	195	25	49	2	18	3	251			320	341	661	9	85	29	0.67	258	42	21	37	61	3%	76	11%	3.87	-8.6	$3

Let's see, 35 with no power, plummeting ct% and OBA despite increase in bb%. Caught stealing in 20 of last 34 steal attempts. Never known for glove work. Any questions?

Clark,Tony

			AB	R	H	HR	RBI	SB	Avg	vL	vR	OB	Slg	OPS	bb%	ct%	h%	Eye	xBA	G	L	F	PX	hr/f	SX	SBO	RC/G	RAR	R$
Pos	3	03 NYM	254	29	59	16	43	0	232	279	215	299	472	771	9	71	26	0.33	272	49	19	33	164	27%	15	0%	4.99	-4.0	$7
Age	35	04 NYY	253	37	56	16	49	0	221	196	236	294	458	752	9	64	28	0.28	240	52	12	36	173	27%	31	0%	5.04	0.4	$7
Decline		05 ARI	349	47	106	30	87	0	304	313	299	370	636	1007	10	75	33	0.42	331	43	22	34	215	33%	35	0%	8.04	23.2	$20
Bats	Both	06 ARI	132	13	26	6	16	0	197	125	213	269	364	633	9	70	23	0.33	235	38	22	40	109	16%	16	0%	3.11	-12.0	$1
Reliability	0	07 ARI	221	31	55	17	51	0	249	219	254	314	511	825	9	73	26	0.36	279	49	17	34	157	31%	39	0%	5.58	-0.1	$9
BAvg Potl	50%	1st Half	100	12	23	8	24	0	230			287	490	777	7	79	21	0.38	262	53	12	35	144	29%	12	0%	4.76	-2.5	$3
LIMA Plan	F	2nd Half	121	19	32	9	27	0	264			336	529	865	10	69	31	0.34	278	45	21	33	169	33%	58	0%	6.40	2.8	$5
+/- Score	-2	08 Proj	228	29	60	16	46	0	263			329	514	843	9	72	30	0.35	275	45	19	36	158	27%	36	0%	5.94	1.5	$9

Here's how regression works... (2005 HR/RBI) + (2006 HR/RBI) divided by 2 = (2007 HR/RBI) It's like the children's story... 2005 was too hot. 2006 was too cold. 2007 was just right, and his true production level.

Clayton,Royce

			AB	R	H	HR	RBI	SB	Avg	vL	vR	OB	Slg	OPS	bb%	ct%	h%	Eye	xBA	G	L	F	PX	hr/f	SX	SBO	RC/G	RAR	R$
Pos	6	03 MIL	483	49	110	11	39	5	228	240	225	299	333	632	9	81	26	0.53	251	54	16	29	67	10%	66	5%	3.34	-11.4	$6
Age	38	04 COL	574	95	160	8	54	10	279	288	276	334	397	732	8	78	34	0.38	267	57	17	26	84	7%	110	9%	4.58	7.3	$16
Decline		05 ARI	522	59	141	2	44	13	270	296	259	320	351	670	7	80	33	0.36	270	58	20	22	62	2%	109	11%	3.79	-2.6	$12
Bats	Right	06 2NL	454	49	117	2	40	14	258	303	239	304	341	645	6	81	31	0.35	263	53	20	27	64	2%	86	18%	3.46	-12.0	$8
Reliability	53	07 2AL	195	24	48	1	12	2	246	246	246	297	333	630	7	73	33	0.26	244	51	21	28	81	2%	61	6%	3.24	-7.7	$2
BAvg Potl	35%	1st Half	148	18	35	1	9	2	236			294	331	625	8	70	33	0.27	233	53	17	30	90	3%	64	6%	3.21	-6.0	$1
LIMA Plan	F	2nd Half	47	6	13	0	3	0	277			306	340	647	4	81	34	0.22	285	45	32	24	58	0%	54	8%	3.35	-1.7	$1
+/- Score	-28	08 Proj	158	19	38	1	13	1	241			296	341	637	7	77	30	0.34	257	55	18	27	79	4%	79	5%	3.36	-5.4	$2

Lost speed, lost eye, lost contact ability. Lost job to John McDonald! 4-28 in AAA, 0-6 in September for Red Sox. Turn out the lights.

Clevlen,Brent

			AB	R	H	HR	RBI	SB	Avg	vL	vR	OB	Slg	OPS	bb%	ct%	h%	Eye	xBA	G	L	F	PX	hr/f	SX	SBO	RC/G	RAR	R$
Pos	7	03	0	0	0	0	0	0	0							0									0				
Age	24	04	0	0	0	0	0	0	0							0									0				
Growth		05	0	0	0	0	0	0	0							0									0				
Bats	Right	06 aa	434	53	97	13	49	6	224	333	200	298	359	657	10	67	30	0.32	236	58	17	25	97	18%	85	7%	3.64	-21.0	$7
Reliability	0	07 aaa	332	32	68	6	33	4	205	167		283	328	611	10	68	28	0.34		33	33	33	91	8%	96	10%	3.05	-20.8	$2
BAvg Potl	25%	1st Half	135	11	27	0	9	3	200			285	281	566	11	67	30	0.36					64		104	11%	2.54	-10.7	($0)
LIMA Plan	F	2nd Half	197	21	41	6	24	1	208			281	360	642	9	69	27	0.32		33	33	33	109	13%	72	9%	3.40	-10.2	$2
+/- Score	8	08 Proj	126	13	27	3	13	2	214			291	338	629	10	67	29	0.33	236	53	20	27	92	13%	80	9%	3.26	-7.2	$1

0-0-.100 in 10 AB at DET Prospect displayed small signs of potential, but low ct% shows a lot of work remains. Solid bb% means he knows strike zone, just needs to translate knowledge to contact.

Conine,Jeff

			AB	R	H	HR	RBI	SB	Avg	vL	vR	OB	Slg	OPS	bb%	ct%	h%	Eye	xBA	G	L	F	PX	hr/f	SX	SBO	RC/G	RAR	R$
Pos	3	03 2TM	577	88	163	20	95	5	282	288	281	340	459	799	8	88	29	0.71	300	38	23	39	105	10%	93	3%	5.36	-1.5	$21
Age	41	04 FLA	521	55	146	14	83	5	280	275	282	341	432	773	8	85	31	0.62	274	35	21	43	96	7%	53	7%	5.08	-12.9	$16
Decline		05 FLA	335	42	102	3	33	2	304	288	311	375	403	778	10	83	36	0.66	275	40	27	33	72	3%	70	2%	5.32	-2.6	$9
Bats	Right	06 2TM	489	54	131	10	66	3	268	260	271	323	399	722	8	87	29	0.62	274	46	19	35	78	7%	70	4%	4.48	-17.3	$11
Reliability		07 2NL	256	25	65	6	37	4	254	252	257	325	383	708	10	86	28	0.75	258	38	19	44	79	6%	68	6%	4.40	-9.0	$6
BAvg Potl		1st Half	141	16	40	4	23	3	284			344	433	777	8	86	31	0.65	262	36	19	46	88	7%	79	7%	5.12	-1.9	$5
LIMA Plan		2nd Half	115	9	25	2	14	1	217			302	322	624	11	86	24	0.88	250	40	18	42	68	5%	33	3%	3.52	-7.3	$1
+/- Score		08 Proj																											

Mr. Consistency posted lowest xBA since injury-plagued 1998 but was able to retire with a ring. Of course, had the Mets not imploded, he might have had another shot at some more heavy jewelry.

Cora,Alex

			AB	R	H	HR	RBI	SB	Avg	vL	vR	OB	Slg	OPS	bb%	ct%	h%	Eye	xBA	G	L	F	PX	hr/f	SX	SBO	RC/G	RAR	R$
Pos	46	03 LA	477	39	119	4	34	4	249	308	240	274	338	611	3	88	28	0.27	270	46	21	33	59	3%	75	6%	3.01	-19.7	$5
Age	32	04 LA	405	47	107	10	47	3	264	239	267	341	380	721	10	90	27	1.15	261	46	17	37	59	7%	70	5%	4.67	0.7	$9
Past Peak		05 2AL	250	25	58	3	24	7	232	281	227	264	332	596	4	88	25	0.37	272	52	17	30	57	4%	121	17%	2.91	-9.3	$4
Bats	Left	06 BOS	235	31	56	1	18	6	238	333	219	295	298	593	7	88	27	0.66	248	51	16	32	37	2%	108	12%	3.06	-7.5	$3
Reliability	36	07 BOS	207	30	51	3	18	1	246	179	257	271	386	658	3	89	27	0.30	284	43	20	37	81	4%	115	5%	3.60	-3.2	$3
BAvg Potl	55%	1st Half	106	13	30	2	14	0	283			309	443	752	4	88	31	0.31	290	41	24	35	83	6%	89	4%	4.65	1.6	$3
LIMA Plan	F	2nd Half	101	17	21	1	4	1	208			231	327	557	3	90	22	0.30	278	46	16	38	79	3%	129	7%	2.54	-5.0	$0
+/- Score	18	08 Proj	190	25	47	2	15	3	247			283	355	638	5	89	27	0.44	270	47	18	35	63	4%	113	9%	3.45	-3.8	$3

PRO: High ct%, solid 1st half

CON: Low bb%, BA constantly under-performs xBA, falling SBO

PRO: Unlikely to get enough AB to matter anyway.

Costa,Shane

			AB	R	H	HR	RBI	SB	Avg	vL	vR	OB	Slg	OPS	bb%	ct%	h%	Eye	xBA	G	L	F	PX	hr/f	SX	SBO	RC/G	RAR	R$
Pos	7	03	0	0	0	0	0	0	0							0									0				
Age	26	04	0	0	0	0	0	0	0							0									0				
Pre-Peak		05 KC	* 370	41	88	7	41	4	238		268	282	357	639	6	92	24	0.79	321	63	19	18	71	12%	84	6%	3.60	-12.4	$6
Bats	Left	06 KC	* 444	51	128	10	47	5	288	244	281	314	443	758	4	89	31	0.33	306	43	24	33	94	7%	92	5%	4.67	-6.3	$11
Reliability	24	07 KC	* 336	48	87	4	23	6	259	125	232	312	384	696	7	88	29	0.62	293	49	20	31	85	4%	100	11%	4.25	-4.7	$6
BAvg Potl	65%	1st Half	145	25	42	1	10	3	290			344	400	744	8	83	34	0.50	272	51	19	30	71	3%	126	9%	4.79	0.3	$4
LIMA Plan	F	2nd Half	191	23	45	3	13	3	236			288	372	660	7	91	25	0.78	308	47	21	33	94	5%	66	13%	3.89	-4.8	$2
+/- Score	31	08 Proj	146	19	39	2	13	2	267			309	399	708	6	89	29	0.54	300	47	22	31	85	6%	83	8%	4.28	-2.5	$3

0-12-.223 in 103 AB in KC Has mastered AAA, posting .326/.402/.502 in Omaha. Needs to transfer 10% bb rate to majors. That, and struggles vs LHP keeping him from taking next step. Time is running out.

MATT BEAGLE

Coste,Chris			AB	R	H	HR	RBI	SB	Avg	vL	vR	OB	Slg	OPS	bb%	ct%	h%	Eye	xBA	G	L	F	PX	hr/f	SX	SBO	RC/G	RAR	R$
Pos	2	03 aaa	96	4	15	1	6	0	159			182	234	417	3	81	19	0.15					56		10	0%	0.50	-11.7	($1)
Age	35	04 aaa	262	25	63	2	20	2	240			280	337	617	5	87	27	0.42					68		64	8%	3.20	-6.9	$2
Decline		05 aaa	499	50	116	15	59	2	233			273	368	641	5	86	24	0.39					81		40	6%	3.31	-9.0	$8
Bats	Right	06 PHI	* 345	36	88	9	45	1	256	288	345	293	394	688	5	82	29	0.30	294	40	29	31	89	10%	35	2%	3.82	-5.2	$7
Reliability	12	07 PHI	* 327	29	74	9	49	0	228	405	228	258	341	600	4	85	24	0.28	238	43	17	40	66	8%	22	0%	2.74	-10.4	$4
BAvg Potl	60%	1st Half	204	19	50	5	34	0	245			290	363	653	6	88	26	0.52		25	25	50	70	6%	20	0%	3.57	-1.3	$4
LIMA Plan	F	2nd Half	123	10	24	4	15	0	198			202	306	508	0	81	21	0.03	221	44	16	40	59	10%	27	0%	1.28	-9.7	$1
+/- Score	-25	08 Proj	202	19	47	5	26	0	233			263	351	614	4	84	25	0.25	255	43	20	38	72	8%	35	2%	2.88	-6.6	$3

5-22-.279 in 129 AB at PHI. Drop in LD% dragged down his BA, but taking only 4 BB in 129 AB didn't help. 30something catchers often see late career power surges but he probably already had his at AAA in 2005.

Counsell,Craig			AB	R	H	HR	RBI	SB	Avg	vL	vR	OB	Slg	OPS	bb%	ct%	h%	Eye	xBA	G	L	F	PX	hr/f	SX	SBO	RC/G	RAR	R$
Pos	564	03 ARI	303	40	71	3	21	11	234	219	239	326	304	629	12	89	25	1.28	275	51	22	27	38	4%	116	15%	3.78	-4.4	$6
Age	37	04 MIL	476	60	116	2	24	17	244	184	254	327	317	644	11	82	30	0.67	255	47	23	30	50	2%	120	14%	3.72	-19.2	$8
Decline		05 ARI	578	85	148	9	42	26	256	269	253	345	375	720	12	88	28	1.13	292	49	20	31	77	6%	123	18%	4.79	0.2	$17
Bats	Left	06 ARI	372	56	95	4	30	15	255	256	255	313	347	659	8	87	28	0.66	269	48	20	31	53	4%	118	22%	3.81	-18.7	$9
Reliability	45	07 MIL	282	31	62	3	24	4	220	157	234	319	309	627	13	83	25	0.87	237	46	15	38	58	3%	77	7%	3.61	-10.2	$2
BAvg Potl	65%	1st Half	163	19	39	1	14	4	239			340	319	659	13	83	28	0.93	239	49	15	36	56	2%	78	11%	4.07	-3.5	$2
LIMA Plan	F	2nd Half	119	12	23	2	10	0	193			289	294	583	12	83	22	0.80	230	42	16	42	61	5%	47	0%	2.99	-6.7	($0)
+/- Score	-20	08 Proj	187	24	43	2	15	5	230			315	330	645	11	85	26	0.84	258	47	18	35	62	4%	99	12%	3.80	-6.6	$3

Nothing much unusual for a 37-year-old. Declining speed skill, declining SB opportunities, and declining playing time. Negatives snowball as you age.

Crawford,Carl			AB	R	H	HR	RBI	SB	Avg	vL	vR	OB	Slg	OPS	bb%	ct%	h%	Eye	xBA	G	L	F	PX	hr/f	SX	SBO	RC/G	RAR	R$
Pos	7	03 TAM	630	80	177	5	54	55	281	263	288	309	362	671	4	84	33	0.25	276	54	23	23	49	4%	159	38%	3.64	-30.8	$25
Age	26	04 TAM	626	104	185	11	55	59	296	296	296	333	450	783	5	87	33	0.43	289	48	20	33	82	6%	180	45%	5.10	2.8	$31
Pre-Peak		05 TAM	644	101	194	15	81	46	301	244	326	329	469	798	4	87	33	0.32	295	45	20	35	97	8%	172	34%	5.15	7.7	$32
Bats	Left	06 TAM	600	89	183	18	77	58	305	288	311	345	482	827	6	86	33	0.44	298	52	18	30	92	12%	168	40%	5.55	6.2	$33
Reliability	99	07 TAM	584	93	184	11	80	50	315	318	314	351	466	816	5	81	38	0.29	283	48	20	32	101	7%	160	38%	5.46	12.0	$31
BAvg Potl	30%	1st Half	307	41	89	6	49	20	290			337	463	800	7	80	35	0.36	281	49	16	34	112	7%	145	33%	5.40	6.0	$13
LIMA Plan	D+	2nd Half	277	52	95	5	31	30	343			366	469	835	3	82	41	0.20	286	46	24	30	90	7%	143	42%	5.52	5.8	$18
+/- Score	-22	08 Proj	609	96	179	18	76	54	294			329	470	799	5	84	33	0.31	297	49	20	31	105	11%	173	43%	5.17	5.0	$32

Possible cause for concern... Drop in skills-based ct% was covered up by rise in luck-based H%. His H% will regress and his BA is going to drop. Power BPIs on upswing, so... UP: 20+ HR DN: .280 BA

Crede,Joe			AB	R	H	HR	RBI	SB	Avg	vL	vR	OB	Slg	OPS	bb%	ct%	h%	Eye	xBA	G	L	F	PX	hr/f	SX	SBO	RC/G	RAR	R$
Pos	5	03 CHW	536	68	140	19	75	1	261	300	246	303	433	736	6	86	27	0.43	283	35	21	44	103	9%	56	2%	4.45	-1.0	$14
Age	30	04 CHW	490	67	117	21	69	1	239	256	230	288	418	707	6	83	25	0.42	259	34	16	49	105	10%	44	3%	4.07	-12.3	$11
Peak		05 CHW	432	54	109	22	62	1	252	277	246	293	454	747	5	85	25	0.38	283	36	18	45	119	13%	38	2%	4.47	-0.4	$12
Bats	Right	06 CHW	544	76	154	30	94	0	283	273	288	318	506	824	5	89	27	0.48	292	31	18	51	121	12%	28	2%	5.34	5.1	$19
Reliability	13	07 CHW	167	13	36	4	22	0	216	206	218	260	317	577	6	86	23	0.42	216	32	15	53	61	5%	23	3%	2.60	-9.8	$1
BAvg Potl	60%	1st Half	167	13	36	4	22	0	216			260	317	577	6	86	23	0.42	216	32	15	53	61	5%	23	3%	2.60	-9.8	$1
LIMA Plan	D+	2nd Half	0	0	0	0	0	0	0							0													
+/- Score	-2	08 Proj	482	56	124	20	70	1	257			299	426	724	6	86	26	0.42	261	34	17	49	99	10%	29	2%	4.26	-5.5	$12

Back problems impacted his numbers before surgery ended his season. Before injury, PX and FB% were trending in right direction. If he returns healthy, he should regain his 20+ HR form.

Crisp,Coco			AB	R	H	HR	RBI	SB	Avg	vL	vR	OB	Slg	OPS	bb%	ct%	h%	Eye	xBA	G	L	F	PX	hr/f	SX	SBO	RC/G	RAR	R$
Pos	8	03 CLE	* 639	94	187	4	49	33	293	321	245	341	396	737	7	89	33	0.64	295	44	26	29	65	2%	136	27%	4.71	-0.5	$22
Age	28	04 CLE	491	78	146	15	71	20	297	311	290	345	446	791	7	86	32	0.52	289	50	19	31	86	11%	103	23%	5.16	6.3	$21
Peak		05 CLE	594	86	178	16	69	15	300	252	325	348	465	813	7	86	33	0.54	300	46	20	34	106	9%	105	13%	5.47	19.7	$22
Bats	Both	06 BOS	413	58	109	8	36	22	264	277	259	315	385	700	7	84	30	0.46	263	48	16	36	77	6%	125	24%	4.14	-6.3	$12
Reliability	61	07 BOS	526	85	141	6	60	28	268	270	267	332	382	714	9	84	31	0.60	264	47	17	36	75	4%	146	23%	4.47	2.8	$17
BAvg Potl	45%	1st Half	263	41	69	4	22	15	262			314	365	680	7	86	29	0.56	257	49	15	36	65	5%	127	28%	3.96	-2.5	$8
LIMA Plan	B	2nd Half	263	44	72	2	38	13	274			348	399	747	10	82	33	0.63	269	44	20	35	87	3%	151	18%	5.00	5.4	$9
+/- Score	22	08 Proj	502	77	138	7	55	24	275			333	395	727	8	84	31	0.55	270	47	18	35	79	5%	132	21%	4.57	2.2	$17

PRO: SX rising, consistent SBO means SBs will remain high. CON: His power has never recovered since his finger injuries. With PX and hr/f stuck, double-digit HRs may be a thing of the past.

Crosby,Bobby			AB	R	H	HR	RBI	SB	Avg	vL	vR	OB	Slg	OPS	bb%	ct%	h%	Eye	xBA	G	L	F	PX	hr/f	SX	SBO	RC/G	RAR	R$
Pos	6	03 aaa	465	69	125	18	72	19	269			340	462	802	10	80	30	0.55					122		123	19%	5.47	16.2	$19
Age	28	04 OAK	545	70	130	22	64	7	239	194	254	312	426	737	10	74	28	0.41	263	45	17	38	127	14%	73	8%	4.65	3.1	$12
Peak		05 OAK	333	66	92	9	38	0	276	314	260	345	456	802	10	84	31	0.65	308	54	18	28	118	12%	86	0%	5.53	9.1	$10
Bats	Right	06 OAK	358	42	82	9	40	8	229	185	242	299	338	637	9	79	27	0.47	241	47	18	35	69	9%	75	9%	3.34	-11.6	$6
Reliability	14	07 OAK	349	40	79	8	31	10	226	222	228	274	341	615	6	82	25	0.37	267	48	20	32	77	9%	84	15%	3.01	-16.5	$6
BAvg Potl	60%	1st Half	273	31	64	6	28	7	234			282	352	633	6	82	27	0.36	273	49	21	30	81	9%	76	15%	3.23	-11.0	$5
LIMA Plan	D	2nd Half	76	9	15	2	3	3	197			247	303	550	6	84	21	0.42	242	44	16	40	63	8%	84	19%	2.25	-5.5	$1
+/- Score	33	08 Proj	355	47	87	9	32	9	245			304	376	679	8	82	28	0.46	263	48	18	35	84	9%	93	11%	3.85	-6.9	$8

Another year, another injury; this time, a broken hand. Even when healthy, his high GB% and low SX/PX spell trouble for BA. He's only 28, but it may be time to lower expectations.

Cruz,Jose			AB	R	H	HR	RBI	SB	Avg	vL	vR	OB	Slg	OPS	bb%	ct%	h%	Eye	xBA	G	L	F	PX	hr/f	SX	SBO	RC/G	RAR	R$
Pos	79	03 SF	539	90	135	20	68	5	250	304	233	370	414	783	16	78	29	0.84	264	41	21	38	107	13%	59	7%	5.53	-0.9	$16
Age	34	04 TAM	545	76	132	21	78	11	242	264	233	335	433	768	12	79	27	0.65	254	37	16	47	114	10%	113	11%	5.17	3.8	$15
Past Peak		05 2TM	370	46	93	18	50	0	251	325	232	365	473	838	15	73	30	0.65	279	43	20	37	157	18%	36	2%	6.27	13.6	$10
Bats	Both	06 LA	223	34	52	5	17	5	233	313	199	357	381	738	16	76	29	0.80	231	36	14	50	105	6%	85	8%	5.06	-1.3	$4
Reliability	9	07 SD	* 318	47	74	7	26	9	234	221	241	316	367	683	11	76	29	0.49	227	38	16	47	91	6%	114	11%	4.06	-12.3	$6
BAvg Potl	45%	1st Half	212	34	56	5	18	6	264			347	401	748	11	74	34	0.49	222	34	17	49	94	6%	112	11%	4.95	-2.4	$6
LIMA Plan	F	2nd Half	106	13	18	2	8	3	174			253	299	552	10	79	20	0.50	246	56	9	34	84	7%	107	13%	2.38	-10.2	$0
+/- Score	-1	08 Proj	131	18	30	3	12	3	229			328	363	691	13	76	28	0.62	236	40	16	44	95	6%	90	9%	4.28	-4.2	$2

6-21-.234 in 256 AB at SD. Hit .355 in April (39% h%), .196 the rest of the way (25% h%). Stopped battering lefties, which won't help him find playing time in 2008.

Cruz,Nelson			AB	R	H	HR	RBI	SB	Avg	vL	vR	OB	Slg	OPS	bb%	ct%	h%	Eye	xBA	G	L	F	PX	hr/f	SX	SBO	RC/G	RAR	R$
Pos	9	03 aaa	3	1	1	0	0	0	300			300	300	600	0	63	48	0.00							0	0%	2.54	-0.2	$0
Age	27	04 a/a	275	43	74	12	36	6	268			319	451	770	7	77	31	0.32					116		91	14%	4.88	-0.9	$9
Peak		05 a/a	455	57	111	20	60	14	244			313	438	752	9	76	28	0.42					134		73	21%	4.77	-2.8	$15
Bats	Right	06 2TM	* 501	75	133	25	87	16	265	217	226	327	465	792	8	75	31	0.36	255	46	12	42	126	16%	91	18%	5.23	0.3	$20
Reliability	33	07 TEX	* 469	57	117	21	66	3	249	212	245	303	441	743	7	74	29	0.30	251	38	16	46	129	13%	63	8%	4.58	-1.7	$12
BAvg Potl	40%	1st Half	215	28	51	10	28	1	237			293	428	721	7	73	28	0.29	240	41	12	47	133	14%	43	6%	4.28	-2.7	$5
LIMA Plan	C	2nd Half	254	29	66	11	38	2	259			311	452	763	7	75	31	0.30	259	34	20	46	126	12%	72	9%	4.83	1.0	$7
+/- Score	-3	08 Proj	429	57	109	19	63	8	254			311	447	759	8	75	30	0.33	254	39	16	45	128	13%	81	13%	4.80	-2.1	$13

9-34-.235 in 307 AB at TEX. The power's not in question, but low and declining ct% means he will always be BA-challenged. Until he starts hitting LHP, a regular role will be elusive.

Cuddyer,Michael			AB	R	H	HR	RBI	SB	Avg	vL	vR	OB	Slg	OPS	bb%	ct%	h%	Eye	xBA	G	L	F	PX	hr/f	SX	SBO	RC/G	RAR	R$
Pos	9	03 MIN	* 288	36	80	6	39	5	278	245	262	354	424	778	11	78	34	0.53	277	49	22	29	101	9%	88	11%	5.31	1.3	$8
Age	29	04 MIN	339	49	89	12	45	5	263	293	245	335	440	775	10	78	30	0.50	265	39	19	42	116	11%	75	11%	5.14	4.4	$10
Peak		05 MIN	422	55	111	12	42	3	263	280	260	328	422	750	9	78	31	0.44	277	53	18	29	109	13%	72	6%	4.81	1.4	$10
Bats	Right	06 MIN	557	102	158	24	109	6	284	297	276	355	504	860	10	77	33	0.48	292	44	21	35	145	16%	110	4%	6.28	9.7	$22
Reliability	28	07 MIN	547	87	151	16	81	5	276	308	263	352	433	785	10	80	32	0.60	272	45	19	36	102	10%	98	3%	5.32	9.7	$17
BAvg Potl	45%	1st Half	273	50	79	8	45	3	289			372	447	819	12	80	34	0.67	272	45	18	36	104	10%	92	3%	5.82	8.5	$10
LIMA Plan	B	2nd Half	274	37	72	8	36	2	263			331	420	751	9	81	30	0.53	270	45	19	36	99	10%	86	3%	4.83	1.0	$7
+/- Score	-2	08 Proj	536	84	147	17	80	5	274			347	450	797	10	79	32	0.52	279	46	19	35	115	12%	94	5%	5.45	7.4	$17

If you took his 2006 season and removed it from this chart, his BPIs would look consistent and stable for the other 4 years. If 2006 is then a random outlier, we probably should not expect much of a rebound.

DAVE ADLER

Cust,Jack			AB	R	H	HR	RBI	SB	Avg	vL	vR	OB	Slg	OPS	bb%	ct%	h%	Eye	xBA	G	L	F	PX	hr/f	SX	SBO	RC/G	RAR	R$
Pos	90	03 BAL	* 406	58	107	13	65	5	264			391	419	810	17	73	33	0.77					111		61	4%	6.04	10.5	$12
Age	29	04 aaa	344	48	73	16	48	4	213			327	394	721	15	68	26	0.53					124		75	4%	4.63	-3.8	$7
Peak		05 aaa	476	71	105	15	56	2	220			353	367	720	17	74	27	0.80					105		46	4%	4.76	-3.2	$8
Bats	Left	06 aaa	441	71	103	19	57	0	233			384	405	789	20	76	26	1.02					109		20	2%	5.73	6.9	$9
Reliability	17	07 OAK	* 475	73	119	32	96	0	250	218	273	400	507	906	20	58	35	0.60	257	42	23	35	214	34%	27	1%	8.25	49.9	$17
BAvg Potl	30%	1st Half	219	41	60	21	52	0	274			404	626	1030	18	62	34	0.57	301	44	20	36	275	44%	21	3%	9.77	32.0	$12
LIMA Plan	C+	2nd Half	256	32	59	11	44	0	229			396	405	800	22	55	36	0.61	218	41	25	34	155	24%	31	0%	6.79	16.2	$6
+/- Score	5	08 Proj	**453**	**69**	**108**	**23**	**75**	**1**	**238**			**384**	**445**	**829**	**19**	**66**	**31**	**0.70**	**258**	**42**	**23**	**35**	**152**	**23%**	**33**	**2%**	**6.46**	**20.5**	**$12**

26-82-.256 in 395 AB at OAK. The new poster child for "three true outcomes." If the PX isn't impressive enough - 1/3 of his FB cleared the fence. 2nd half gives a better idea of what to expect going forward.

Damon,Johnny			AB	R	H	HR	RBI	SB	Avg	vL	vR	OB	Slg	OPS	bb%	ct%	h%	Eye	xBA	G	L	F	PX	hr/f	SX	SBO	RC/G	RAR	R$
Pos	807	03 BOS	609	103	166	12	67	30	273	275	272	346	404	750	10	88	29	0.92	296	46	23	31	79	7%	137	20%	4.99	4.4	$22
Age	34	04 BOS	627	126	192	20	94	20	306	278	319	381	477	858	11	89	32	1.07	299	49	17	34	95	11%	125	14%	6.24	26.6	$29
Past Peak		05 BOS	624	117	197	10	75	18	316	327	310	369	439	808	8	89	34	0.77	295	45	23	32	77	6%	136	10%	5.53	21.0	$26
Bats	Left	06 NYY	593	115	169	24	80	25	285	297	280	358	482	840	10	86	30	0.79	293	41	19	40	113	12%	124	20%	5.93	21.7	$26
Reliability	83	07 NYY	533	93	144	12	63	27	270	281	266	351	396	746	11	85	30	0.84	277	48	18	33	81	8%	121	18%	4.93	10.0	$20
BAvg Potl	60%	1st Half	235	36	58	5	25	12	247			332	357	690	11	83	28	0.77	266	50	18	32	70	8%	113	16%	4.23	-0.4	$7
LIMA Plan	B+	2nd Half	298	57	86	7	38	15	289			365	426	791	11	87	31	0.90	285	47	18	35	89	8%	116	19%	5.47	10.1	$13
+/- Score	-6	08 Proj	**547**	**100**	**150**	**13**	**68**	**21**	**274**			**349**	**414**	**762**	**10**	**86**	**30**	**0.83**	**284**	**46**	**19**	**35**	**87**	**8%**	**122**	**16%**	**5.09**	**10.6**	**$20**

FB% returned to normal after the 2006 aberration, and the power numbers followed suit. Speed remains intact - that and a consistent plate approach secure his value. A gracefully-aging "idiot," apparently.

DaVanon,Jeff			AB	R	H	HR	RBI	SB	Avg	vL	vR	OB	Slg	OPS	bb%	ct%	h%	Eye	xBA	G	L	F	PX	hr/f	SX	SBO	RC/G	RAR	R$
Pos	8	03 ANA	* 390	64	108	14	53	20	277	342	274	356	446	802	11	83	30	0.72	291	41	25	35	103	12%	114	22%	5.52	8.9	$17
Age	34	04 ANA	285	41	79	7	34	18	277	136	289	378	418	795	14	81	32	0.85	229	40	12	48	82	6%	132	20%	5.66	7.8	$11
Past Peak		05 ANA	225	42	52	2	15	11	231	393	206	345	311	656	15	80	28	0.89	241	44	19	37	59	3%	111	22%	4.00	-2.0	$5
Bats	Both	06 ARI	221	38	64	5	35	10	290	205	308	377	448	825	12	81	34	0.74	285	51	20	29	95	10%	129	19%	5.99	9.8	$9
Reliability	0	07 2TM	* 147	22	32	1	7	2	218	429	173	303	271	574	11	73	29	0.46	208	56	14	30	40	2%	87	11%	2.60	-8.4	$1
BAvg Potl	45%	1st Half	0	0	0	0	0	0	0							0							0						
LIMA Plan	D	2nd Half	147	22	32	1	7	2	218			303	271	574	11	73	29	0.46	208	56	14	30	40	2%	87	11%	2.60	-8.4	$1
+/- Score	-33	08 Proj	**214**	**35**	**54**	**3**	**20**	**8**	**252**			**347**	**359**	**706**	**13**	**79**	**31**	**0.68**	**245**	**47**	**18**	**35**	**71**	**6%**	**113**	**18%**	**4.48**	**-0.0**	**$6**

0-6-.213 in 89 AB at ARI and OAK. Lost most of 2007 to shoulder woes, so let's give him a do-over. With a good OBA and above-average speed, should once again find a job on someone's bench.

Davis,Rajai			AB	R	H	HR	RBI	SB	Avg	vL	vR	OB	Slg	OPS	bb%	ct%	h%	Eye	xBA	G	L	F	PX	hr/f	SX	SBO	RC/G	RAR	R$
Pos	8	03	0	0	0	0	0	0	0							0									0				
Age	27	04	0	0	0	0	0	0	0							0									0				
Peak		05 aa	499	62	121	3	26	34	242			287	310	597	6	88	27	0.52					46		133	35%	3.02	-21.3	$13
Bats	Right	06 aaa	385	50	107	2	20	44	278			323	345	668	6	85	32	0.46					47		127	50%	3.77	-8.9	$16
Reliability	25	07 2NL	* 401	55	108	4	32	43	269	299	258	329	372	701	8	87	30	0.69	257	43	17	40	66	3%	144	51%	4.35	-2.6	$17
BAvg Potl	50%	1st Half	234	29	67	3	28	27	286			343	410	753	8	91	30	0.95	254	54	4	42	71	3%	146	54%	4.99	3.0	$12
LIMA Plan	C	2nd Half	167	26	41	1	4	16	244			310	319	629	9	81	30	0.51	238	41	20	39	58	1%	130	45%	3.40	-6.0	$5
+/- Score	9	08 Proj	**380**	**51**	**100**	**2**	**21**	**39**	**263**			**334**	**343**	**677**	**10**	**86**	**30**	**0.74**	**246**	**42**	**18**	**40**	**55**	**2%**	**129**	**43%**	**4.11**	**-5.1**	**$14**

1-9-.272-22 SB in 190 AB at PIT and SF.
PRO: Blazing speed; SBO!!
CON: ct%, GB%, OBA all dove when promoted to majors in 2nd half. If he raises OBA, he'd be an absolute monster.

De Aza,Alejandro			AB	R	H	HR	RBI	SB	Avg	vL	vR	OB	Slg	OPS	bb%	ct%	h%	Eye	xBA	G	L	F	PX	hr/f	SX	SBO	RC/G	RAR	R$
Pos	8	03	0	0	0	0	0	0	0							0									0				
Age	24	04	0	0	0	0	0	0	0							0									0				
Growth		05	0	0	0	0	0	0	0							0									0				
Bats	Left	06 aa	230	40	61	2	16	27	265			329	357	686	9	79	33	0.45					63		156	54%	4.06	-3.5	$10
Reliability	0	07 FLA	144	14	33	0	8	2	229	313	205	260	313	573	4	74	31	0.16	240	39	26	34	66	0%	103	7%	2.40	-9.4	$1
BAvg Potl	40%	1st Half	33	4	10	0	3	1	303			324	455	778	3	88	34	0.25	278	37	19	44	98	0%	116	14%	5.03	0.4	$1
LIMA Plan	F	2nd Half	111	10	23	0	5	1	207			241	270	512	4	70	29	0.15	231	40	29	31	55	0%	84	5%	1.51	-10.5	($0)
+/- Score	10	08 Proj	**164**	**20**	**38**	**1**	**9**	**9**	**232**			**279**	**303**	**582**	**6**	**74**	**31**	**0.25**	**243**	**40**	**29**	**31**	**59**	**2%**	**123**	**29%**	**2.55**	**-10.2**	**$3**

Surprise starter in the spring, but a broken ankle scuttled his season. Another Esix-Sneadian speedster who can't find his way to first base. With little time above AA, he's a work in progress.

DeJesus,David			AB	R	H	HR	RBI	SB	Avg	vL	vR	OB	Slg	OPS	bb%	ct%	h%	Eye	xBA	G	L	F	PX	hr/f	SX	SBO	RC/G	RAR	R$
Pos	8	03 a/a	286	52	84	6	27	7	294			369	437	806	11	90	31	1.13					89		100	16%	5.70	6.9	$10
Age	28	04 KC	* 560	89	163	12	52	14	291	224	309	349	429	778	8	87	32	0.67	281	50	17	33	81	8%	102	19%	5.16	7.4	$18
Peak		05 KC	461	69	135	9	56	5	293	270	303	352	445	797	8	84	34	0.55	292	45	22	32	100	7%	99	8%	5.41	14.7	$14
Bats	Left	06 KC	491	83	145	8	56	6	295	307	291	352	446	798	8	86	33	0.61	303	49	22	29	95	7%	113	7%	5.45	10.8	$14
Reliability	73	07 KC	605	101	157	7	58	10	260	240	267	330	372	702	10	86	29	0.77	268	46	19	36	71	4%	120	8%	4.42	2.5	$13
BAvg Potl	60%	1st Half	318	57	89	4	27	3	280			348	409	756	9	86	32	0.72	279	42	23	36	81	4%	116	5%	5.05	6.9	$8
LIMA Plan	B	2nd Half	287	44	68	3	31	7	237			311	331	642	10	87	26	0.84	256	50	15	36	59	3%	113	11%	3.75	-4.6	$5
+/- Score	21	08 Proj	**591**	**97**	**172**	**9**	**62**	**10**	**291**			**355**	**420**	**775**	**9**	**86**	**33**	**0.71**	**282**	**47**	**20**	**33**	**81**	**5%**	**113**	**9%**	**5.22**	**13.4**	**$17**

Took a step back, mostly due to low 2nd half h%. Expect a BA rebound. Struggled vs LHP and PX dropped despite FB% rise. Minimal progress over the years; the window for a breakout is closing.

Delgado,Carlos			AB	R	H	HR	RBI	SB	Avg	vL	vR	OB	Slg	OPS	bb%	ct%	h%	Eye	xBA	G	L	F	PX	hr/f	SX	SBO	RC/G	RAR	R$
Pos	3	03 TOR	570	117	172	42	145	0	302	284	310	414	593	1007	16	76	33	0.80	320	36	26	39	187	25%	40	0%	8.39	47.0	$32
Age	35	04 TOR	458	74	123	32	99	0	269	271	267	364	535	899	13	75	29	0.60	290	36	21	43	167	22%	24	1%	6.82	24.1	$19
Decline		05 FLA	521	81	157	33	115	0	301	229	327	386	582	968	12	77	34	0.60	320	40	23	37	186	22%	47	0%	7.71	30.1	$27
Bats	Left	06 NYM	524	89	139	38	114	0	265	226	282	356	548	904	12	77	28	0.62	297	42	18	40	168	23%	40	0%	6.78	11.8	$22
Reliability	45	07 NYM	538	71	139	24	87	4	258	267	254	324	448	772	9	78	29	0.44	265	39	18	43	122	13%	56	3%	4.98	-9.7	$16
BAvg Potl	50%	1st Half	287	35	64	11	42	2	223			278	394	672	7	78	25	0.34	256	36	19	45	112	11%	54	3%	3.65	-17.0	$5
LIMA Plan	C+	2nd Half	251	36	75	13	45	2	299			374	510	884	11	78	34	0.56	273	42	17	42	133	16%	44	3%	6.48	6.1	$11
+/- Score	1	08 Proj	**530**	**80**	**140**	**29**	**93**	**2**	**264**			**345**	**491**	**836**	**11**	**77**	**29**	**0.55**	**283**	**40**	**19**	**41**	**144**	**17%**	**57**	**1%**	**5.90**	**2.9**	**$19**

1st half h% and bb% depressed his BA. But the main problem was big drop in hr/f, which crunched his HRs. With a stronger 2nd half and rising FB%, expect some of the lost power to return.

Dellucci,David			AB	R	H	HR	RBI	SB	Avg	vL	vR	OB	Slg	OPS	bb%	ct%	h%	Eye	xBA	G	L	F	PX	hr/f	SX	SBO	RC/G	RAR	R$
Pos	7	03 2TM	216	26	49	3	23	12	227	132	247	301	352	653	10	73	30	0.40	250	47	21	32	92	6%	150	22%	3.67	-11.8	$5
Age	34	04 TEX	335	59	80	17	61	9	239	107	254	332	436	768	12	73	28	0.53	252	40	17	43	124	16%	98	14%	5.11	1.7	$12
Past Peak		05 TEX	435	97	109	29	65	5	251	242	254	362	513	875	15	72	28	0.63	279	41	16	43	170	22%	113	6%	6.68	25.3	$18
Bats	Left	06 PHI	264	41	77	13	39	1	292	200	299	360	530	890	10	77	34	0.45	276	37	19	44	142	15%	84	5%	6.62	10.2	$10
Reliability	17	07 CLE	178	25	41	4	20	2	230	167	240	297	382	679	9	78	28	0.43	265	43	20	37	106	8%	97	7%	3.95	-4.2	$3
BAvg Potl	55%	1st Half	175	25	41	4	20	2	234			302	389	691	9	78	28	0.45	268	43	20	37	107	8%	97	7%	4.10	-3.3	$3
LIMA Plan	D+	2nd Half	3	0	0	0	0	0	0			0	0	0	0	33	0	0.00			0	0	0					-1.7	($0)
+/- Score	14	08 Proj	**307**	**52**	**82**	**13**	**43**	**2**	**267**			**348**	**472**	**821**	**11**	**75**	**32**	**0.50**	**270**	**41**	**18**	**40**	**134**	**14%**	**92**	**5%**	**5.83**	**8.5**	**$10**

Missed most of 2nd half with hammy issues. As usual, he'll see little time vs LHP. xBA says he'll see a BA rebound, while hr/f normalization will help power. 2005 level is unlikely, but he's better than 2007.

DeRosa,Mark			AB	R	H	HR	RBI	SB	Avg	vL	vR	OB	Slg	OPS	bb%	ct%	h%	Eye	xBA	G	L	F	PX	hr/f	SX	SBO	RC/G	RAR	R$
Pos	459	03 ATL	266	40	70	6	22	1	263	277	257	305	383	688	6	82	30	0.33	264	45	20	35	82	8%	62	2%	3.86	-4.2	$6
Age	33	04 ATL	309	33	74	3	31	1	239	233	242	292	320	613	7	83	28	0.43	250	48	20	32	58	4%	41	5%	3.10	-14.1	$3
Past Peak		05 TEX	148	26	36	8	20	1	243	322	188	317	439	756	10	76	27	0.46	273	47	19	35	123	21%	60	3%	4.76	2.8	$5
Bats	Right	06 TEX	520	78	154	13	74	4	296	342	278	351	456	807	8	80	35	0.43	292	49	23	29	109	11%	70	6%	5.48	19.7	$16
Reliability	68	07 CHC	502	64	147	10	72	1	293	283	297	366	420	786	10	81	34	0.62	266	42	22	36	84	7%	50	2%	5.37	11.3	$14
BAvg Potl	45%	1st Half	226	28	63	7	40	0	279			353	451	805	10	81	32	0.60	272	43	18	39	110	10%	54	2%	5.56	6.5	$7
LIMA Plan	C	2nd Half	276	36	84	3	32	1	304			377	395	772	10	82	36	0.64	263	40	25	34	64	4%	52	2%	5.21	4.9	$8
+/- Score	-34	08 Proj	**508**	**71**	**144**	**11**	**69**	**1**	**283**			**350**	**413**	**762**	**9**	**81**	**33**	**0.52**	**267**	**45**	**22**	**34**	**87**	**8%**	**54**	**2%**	**4.99**	**6.2**	**$14**

Consistent numbers with regular playing time the past couple of years. Is there more power to come? Potential hr/f regression says yes. PX trend, age and 2nd half say no. EDGE: No.

DAVE ADLER

Diaz,Matt

Diaz,Matt		AB	R	H	HR	RBI	SB	Avg	vL	vR	OB	Slg	OPS	bb%	ct%	h%	Eye	xBA	G	L	F	PX	hr/f	SX	SBO	RC/G	RAR	R$
Pos 7	03 a/a	480	58	155	10	75	13	323			363	477	840	6	86	36	0.45					102		90	15%	5.74	3.7	$20
Age 30	04 aaa	503	68	147	16	78	13	293			323	484	807	4	83	33	0.25					123		109	16%	5.25	0.8	$19
Peak	05 KC	*374	44	103	10	51	8	276	370	143	303	436	739	4	83	31	0.23	295	51	20	29	101	11%	106	15%	4.40	-3.5	$11
Bats Right	06 ATL	297	37	97	7	32	5	327	295	358	351	475	825	4	84	37	0.22	294	50	24	27	87	11%	92	12%	5.39	1.1	$11
Reliability 35	07 ATL	358	44	121	12	45	4	338	356	318	366	497	864	4	82	39	0.25	283	46	21	34	101	12%	55	4%	5.82	4.5	$15
BAvg Potl 20%	1st Half	167	16	57	4	15	2	341			360	461	822	3	83	39	0.18	277	42	25	33	77	9%	42	4%	5.23	-0.5	$6
LIMA Plan D+	2nd Half	191	28	64	8	30	2	335			371	529	900	5	82	38	0.31	288	49	17	34	123	15%	52	4%	6.34	5.0	$9
+/- Score -60	08 Proj	436	54	129	13	56	5	296			325	459	784	4	83	33	0.26	292	48	22	31	101	12%	81	7%	4.92	-5.1	$14

xBA and h% say don't expect a repeat of the lofty BA. But bump in power numbers, partly due to 2nd half boost in hr/f, make a statement for increased playing time. Could fly under the radar on draft day.

Diaz,Victor

Diaz,Victor		AB	R	H	HR	RBI	SB	Avg	vL	vR	OB	Slg	OPS	bb%	ct%	h%	Eye	xBA	G	L	F	PX	hr/f	SX	SBO	RC/G	RAR	R$
Pos 9	03 aa	491	67	144	15	73	14	293			337	448	785	6	82	33	0.36					101		80	23%	5.03	-4.9	$19
Age 26	04 NYM	*579	85	166	26	96	5	287			321	484	805	5	78	33	0.23					125		64	10%	5.20	-1.5	$23
Pre-Peak	05 NYM	*450	66	119	21	67	11	264			326	478	804	8	73	32	0.33	286	47	22	32	149	20%	106	14%	5.50	3.3	$18
Bats Right	06 aaa	392	31	92	9	40	5	235			282	344	627	6	74	30	0.25					76		43	11%	3.03	-26.1	$5
Reliability 5	07 TEX	*375	43	99	21	75	3	263	212	269	296	483	779	4	71	32	0.16	259	61	6	33	150	23%	66	4%	4.94	2.6	$13
BAvg Potl 35%	1st Half	183	21	55	12	49	1	301			326	574	900	4	73	35	0.14	290	59	6	34	186	26%	55	3%	6.47	8.9	$9
LIMA Plan F	2nd Half	192	22	44	9	26	2	228			267	396	663	5	70	28	0.17		75	0	25	113	26%	70	4%	3.41	-7.5	$4
+/- Score -21	08 Proj	175	20	45	8	27	2	257			299	444	743	6	73	31	0.22	263	52	16	32	126	19%	74	9%	4.52	-2.3	$5

9-25-.240 in 104 AB at TEX. A mirror image of 2005, but beware the warning signs: Drop in bb% points to BA struggles. High GB% limits power upside. Still has time, but a breakout doesn't seem near.

Dobbs,Greg

Dobbs,Greg		AB	R	H	HR	RBI	SB	Avg	vL	vR	OB	Slg	OPS	bb%	ct%	h%	Eye	xBA	G	L	F	PX	hr/f	SX	SBO	RC/G	RAR	R$
Pos 5	03	0	0	0	0	0	0	0							0									0				
Age 29	04 SEA	*511	45	120	11	59	7	235			256	354	610	3	86	26	0.20					68		88	14%	2.86	-32.1	$7
Peak	05 SEA	*332	29	86	3	37	5	260			303	336	639	6	86	29	0.45	253	35	24	42	53	2%	66	8%	3.42	-10.4	$6
Bats Left	06 SEA	*406	51	110	7	47	11	270			321	385	706	7	85	30	0.51	287	52	22	26	70	8%	99	16%	4.23	-9.2	$10
Reliability 31	07 PHI	324	45	88	10	55	3	272	214	277	331	451	782	8	79	32	0.43	260	38	16	46	115	9%	98	4%	5.18	3.7	$10
BAvg Potl 40%	1st Half	142	24	42	7	31	1	296			333	556	890	5	82	32	0.31	302	38	18	44	155	14%	106	3%	6.28	5.9	$7
LIMA Plan F	2nd Half	182	21	46	3	24	2	253			330	368	698	10	77	31	0.51	225	39	15	46	82	5%	69	4%	4.26	-2.8	$3
+/- Score -5	08 Proj	288	35	75	7	40	4	260			313	402	715	7	82	30	0.43	251	38	17	45	88	6%	92	9%	4.30	-5.4	$7

Early numbers enticed, but he couldn't keep it going over the whole year. He is what he is - a replacement-level player in a platoon role with occasional pop in his bat.

Doumit,Ryan

Doumit,Ryan		AB	R	H	HR	RBI	SB	Avg	vL	vR	OB	Slg	OPS	bb%	ct%	h%	Eye	xBA	G	L	F	PX	hr/f	SX	SBO	RC/G	RAR	R$
Pos 92	03	0	0	0	0	0	0	0							0									0				
Age 27	04 aa	221	24	51	8	26	0	233			286	421	707	7	83	25	0.43					123		31	2%	4.19	-5.4	$3
Peak	05 PIT	*396	56	110	15	62	3	278	296	243	317	455	772	5	81	31	0.31	281	51	16	33	114	14%	64	9%	4.82	-4.9	$14
Bats Both	06 PIT	*171	18	38	6	24	0	222	208	208	292	397	689	9	73	27	0.37	248	46	17	38	118	13%	44	0%	4.01	-4.0	$2
Reliability 0	07 PIT	*305	44	87	12	47	4	285	246	282	345	489	834	8	77	34	0.40	284	42	21	38	136	14%	78	10%	5.85	5.2	$11
BAvg Potl 40%	1st Half	200	29	65	7	33	4	325			386	520	906	9	77	39	0.43	289	42	22	36	140	13%	57	10%	6.85	8.6	$9
LIMA Plan D+	2nd Half	105	15	22	5	14	0	210			265	429	694	7	77	22	0.33	275	41	19	40	129	16%	100	11%	3.94	-4.4	$2
+/- Score 4	08 Proj	341	44	93	13	49	2	273			329	470	799	8	77	32	0.37	276	44	19	38	127	13%	69	6%	5.34	1.9	$10

9-32-.274 in 252 AB at PIT. Yet again, had trouble avoiding the DL. Low h% hindered 2nd half, but nice power boost gets our attention. Main reason to have him on your list... He qualifies at catcher again.

Drew,J.D.

Drew,J.D.		AB	R	H	HR	RBI	SB	Avg	vL	vR	OB	Slg	OPS	bb%	ct%	h%	Eye	xBA	G	L	F	PX	hr/f	SX	SBO	RC/G	RAR	R$
Pos 9	03 STL	287	60	83	15	42	2	289	218	306	368	512	881	11	83	30	0.75	312	44	23	33	128	19%	101	5%	6.42	6.6	$13
Age 32	04 ATL	518	118	158	31	93	12	305	287	313	434	569	1003	19	78	34	1.02	300	43	19	38	158	20%	126	7%	8.52	46.0	$30
Past Peak	05 LA	252	48	72	15	36	1	286	235	304	406	520	926	17	80	30	1.02	290	46	15	39	142	19%	57	2%	7.30	14.6	$11
Bats Left	06 LA	494	84	140	20	100	2	283	244	296	393	498	891	15	79	33	0.84	287	45	19	36	133	14%	76	3%	6.94	30.4	$19
Reliability 46	07 BOS	466	84	126	11	64	4	270	224	286	376	423	799	14	79	32	0.79	267	46	18	37	107	8%	89	4%	5.77	14.4	$13
BAvg Potl 50%	1st Half	227	43	57	6	32	1	251			354	383	737	14	80	29	0.78	266	51	19	30	87	11%	68	4%	4.88	1.2	$6
LIMA Plan B	2nd Half	239	41	69	5	32	3	289			397	460	857	15	77	36	0.80	266	40	17	43	126	6%	100	4%	6.65	13.0	$8
+/- Score 8	08 Proj	471	86	132	17	74	4	280			389	474	863	15	79	32	0.84	281	45	18	37	126	12%	90	4%	6.58	21.6	$17

$70 million buys this? Output shouldn't be surprising: xBA, BA, and PX have dropped three straight years. Boosted FB% in 2nd half, but hr/f drop negated gains. Sept. surge (1.087 OPS) offers some hope of a rebound.

Drew,Stephen

Drew,Stephen		AB	R	H	HR	RBI	SB	Avg	vL	vR	OB	Slg	OPS	bb%	ct%	h%	Eye	xBA	G	L	F	PX	hr/f	SX	SBO	RC/G	RAR	R$
Pos 6	03	0	0	0	0	0	0	0							0									0				
Age 25	04	0	0	0	0	0	0	0							0									0				
Pre-Peak	05 aa	101	10	20	3	10	2	198			277	327	604	10	74	24	0.42					90		54	21%	2.85	-4.6	$1
Bats Left	06 ARI	*551	69	154	16	62	4	279	350	308	328	452	780	7	84	31	0.45	281	36	24	40	98	9%	89	6%	5.07	11.2	$15
Reliability 18	07 ARI	543	60	129	12	60	9	238	246	235	313	370	684	10	82	27	0.60	243	38	16	46	85	6%	96	6%	4.01	1.9	$9
BAvg Potl 55%	1st Half	268	29	63	4	27	2	235			303	351	653	9	82	27	0.55	241	40	17	43	74	4%	84	3%	3.70	-2.1	$3
LIMA Plan C+	2nd Half	275	31	66	8	33	7	240			324	389	713	11	81	27	0.64	246	36	16	48	96	8%	84	9%	4.44	3.9	$6
+/- Score 18	08 Proj	560	64	148	16	67	8	264			330	416	746	9	81	30	0.52	253	37	18	45	94	8%	87	8%	4.76	11.1	$14

Hello, sophomore slump. Took a step back in power and average; drop in LD% hurt. Some small signs of progress: bb%, 2nd half SBO. He owns better skills, so don't dismiss him yet.

Duffy,Chris

Duffy,Chris		AB	R	H	HR	RBI	SB	Avg	vL	vR	OB	Slg	OPS	bb%	ct%	h%	Eye	xBA	G	L	F	PX	hr/f	SX	SBO	RC/G	RAR	R$
Pos 8	03 aa	494	74	125	1	37	30	253			308	320	628	7	86	29	0.56					47		138	31%	3.42	-21.5	$14
Age 28	04 aa	453	65	122	6	31	23	268			306	369	675	5	86	30	0.40					62		131	27%	3.80	-11.7	$13
Peak	05 PIT	*434	64	126	6	33	15	291	355	337	320	396	716	4	85	33	0.30	292	62	18	20	64	8%	129	24%	4.18	-4.7	$15
Bats Left	06 PIT	*420	63	116	4	35	39	276	229	264	322	377	699	6	80	34	0.34	274	58	19	23	67	5%	154	37%	4.11	-4.0	$17
Reliability 17	07 PIT	241	31	60	3	22	13	249	211	261	309	357	666	8	82	29	0.49	270	56	17	27	69	6%	126	27%	3.81	-5.5	$6
BAvg Potl 55%	1st Half	241	31	60	3	22	13	249			309	357	666	8	82	29	0.49	270	56	17	27	69	6%	126	27%	3.81	-5.5	$6
LIMA Plan C	2nd Half	0	0	0	0	0	0	0							0													
+/- Score 17	08 Proj	403	57	110	4	33	23	273			318	376	694	6	84	32	0.40	277	57	18	25	65	5%	137	28%	4.06	-5.9	$13

Battled injuries all year. Still: PRO: Combination of high GB%, SX; increased bb%, ct%. CON: OBA still too low. Health, improved OBA and one more opportunity could lead to... UP: 40 SB.

Dukes,Elijah

Dukes,Elijah		AB	R	H	HR	RBI	SB	Avg	vL	vR	OB	Slg	OPS	bb%	ct%	h%	Eye	xBA	G	L	F	PX	hr/f	SX	SBO	RC/G	RAR	R$
Pos 8	03	0	0	0	0	0	0	0							0									0				
Age 23	04	0	0	0	0	0	0	0							0									0				
Growth	05 aa	443	61	114	14	61	16	257			315	413	728	8	84	28	0.54					93		113	24%	4.47	0.6	$15
Bats Right	06 aaa	283	57	82	9	49	8	289			383	471	854	13	85	31	1.00					103		122	13%	6.34	14.4	$13
Reliability 0	07 TAM	184	27	35	10	21	2	190	260	164	313	391	705	15	76	19	0.75	241	42	11	48	118	15%	79	11%	4.32	0.3	$3
BAvg Potl 70%	1st Half	184	27	35	10	21	2	190			313	391	705	15	76	19	0.75	241	42	11	48	118	15%	79	11%	4.32	0.3	$3
LIMA Plan D	2nd Half	0	0	0	0	0	0	0							0													
+/- Score 49	08 Proj	132	21	32	5	18	3	242			331	415	747	12	82	26	0.72	246	42	11	48	102	10%	91	16%	4.85	1.7	$4

A million dollar swing combined with a ten-cent head. Low h% and bb% trend means better BA lies ahead; PX trend promises power. He can even grab some SBs. Of course, off-field issues might preclude regular PT.

Duncan,Chris

Duncan,Chris		AB	R	H	HR	RBI	SB	Avg	vL	vR	OB	Slg	OPS	bb%	ct%	h%	Eye	xBA	G	L	F	PX	hr/f	SX	SBO	RC/G	RAR	R$
Pos 7	03 aa	25	1	5	1	3	0	200			200	360	560	0	76	22	0.00					104		0	0%	1.84	-2.8	$0
Age 26	04 aa	387	47	98	13	52	7	253			342	406	748	12	79	29	0.65					99		54	10%	4.90	-3.3	$10
Pre-Peak	05 aa	430	45	100	16	58	1	233			314	395	709	11	80	25	0.61					104		33	4%	4.32	-9.3	$8
Bats Left	06 STL	*461	81	128	28	71	1	277	170	318	351	519	870	10	75	31	0.45	286	44	21	35	148	23%	63	2%	6.34	14.4	$18
Reliability 13	07 STL	375	51	97	21	70	2	259	213	271	353	480	833	13	67	33	0.45	253	40	18	42	160	20%	36	3%	6.25	10.0	$13
BAvg Potl 40%	1st Half	209	34	57	14	37	2	273			350	531	882	11	71	32	0.41	275	42	16	42	175	23%	49	5%	6.64	7.8	$9
LIMA Plan C	2nd Half	166	17	40	7	33	0	241			357	416	773	15	63	34	0.48	225	37	21	42	138	16%	10	0%	5.69	1.8	$4
+/- Score -13	08 Proj	431	58	110	27	72	2	255			345	496	841	12	72	30	0.48	273	40	19	40	159	21%	43	3%	6.12	9.9	$15

Gangbuster 1st half, but drop in ct% and a hernia scuttled 2H. PRO: Gains in bb%, PX. CON: Continued struggles vs LHP, prodigious K totals. The power is for real, but BA won't return to 2006 level.

DAVE ADLER

Duncan,Shelley

Duncan,Shelley			AB	R	H	HR	RBI	SB	Avg	vL	vR	OB	Slg	OPS	bb%	ct%	h%	Eye	xBA	G	L	F	PX	hr/f	SX	SBO	RC/G	RAR	R$
Pos	0	03	0	0	0	0	0	0	0							0									0				
Age	28	04	0	0	0	0	0	0	0							0									0				
Peak		05 aa	533	64	101	26	69	3	189			247	379	626	7	73	21	0.29					126		65	5%	2.96	-52.0	$8
Bats	Right	06 a/a	394	39	81	17	53	3	205			262	382	644	7	75	23	0.32					114		46	5%	3.26	-39.0	$5
Reliability	17	07 NYY	* 410	65	106	29	84	2	259	303	220	332	517	849	10	75	28	0.44	296	35	24	41	164	23%	52	4%	5.96	-0.7	$17
BAvg Potl	55%	1st Half	270	42	76	18	53	1	281			360	541	900	11	76	31	0.51					166		48	4%	6.71	5.3	$12
LIMA Plan	F	2nd Half	140	23	30	11	31	1	214			276	471	748	8	74	21	0.32	286	35	24	41	158	26%	57	4%	4.46	-6.7	$5
+/- Score	19	08 Proj	**253**	**34**	**66**	**15**	**44**	**2**	**261**			**321**	**477**	**798**	**8**	**75**	**29**	**0.35**	**278**	**35**	**24**	**41**	**138**	**19%**	**41**	**3%**	**5.24**	**-5.7**	**$9**

7-17-.257 in 74 AB at NYY. Definitely a masher, as the PX and hr/f indicate, but ct% limits any BA upside, and the output vs RHP mean his future likely lies on the short end of a platoon role.

Dunn,Adam

Dunn,Adam			AB	R	H	HR	RBI	SB	Avg	vL	vR	OB	Slg	OPS	bb%	ct%	h%	Eye	xBA	G	L	F	PX	hr/f	SX	SBO	RC/G	RAR	R$
Pos	7	03 CIN	381	70	82	27	57	8	215	202	221	343	465	807	16	67	24	0.59	249	31	18	51	171	21%	94	9%	5.86	3.2	$14
Age	28	04 CIN	568	105	151	46	102	6	266	256	271	383	569	952	16	66	32	0.55	278	33	19	48	215	26%	62	4%	8.14	44.3	$27
Peak		05 CIN	543	107	134	40	101	4	247	199	273	377	540	917	17	69	28	0.68	288	36	17	47	209	23%	77	4%	7.50	34.8	$24
Bats	Left	06 CIN	561	99	131	40	92	7	234	270	215	361	490	851	17	65	28	0.58	256	28	24	49	176	22%	66	4%	6.63	23.3	$20
Reliability	33	07 CIN	522	101	138	40	106	9	264	239	278	384	554	937	16	68	31	0.61	279	35	19	47	197	24%	87	6%	7.76	36.7	$26
BAvg Potl	45%	1st Half	273	52	74	22	52	7	271			360	575	935	12	64	34	0.39	274	33	21	46	217	27%	107	12%	7.90	20.1	$14
LIMA Plan	B+	2nd Half	249	49	64	18	54	2	257			407	530	937	20	73	28	0.94	281	36	16	47	178	21%	47	2%	7.72	17.2	$11
+/- Score	10	08 Proj	**553**	**105**	**139**	**41**	**104**	**7**	**251**			**378**	**528**	**906**	**17**	**68**	**29**	**0.64**	**272**	**33**	**19**	**47**	**190**	**23%**	**76**	**5%**	**7.34**	**32.6**	**$24**

No secrets here; you know what you're going to get - HR, BB, K. Sure, a higher ct% would be nice, but it ain't gonna happen. If you draft the power, you'll need an Ichiro-esque bat to balance the BA hit.

Durham,Ray

Durham,Ray			AB	R	H	HR	RBI	SB	Avg	vL	vR	OB	Slg	OPS	bb%	ct%	h%	Eye	xBA	G	L	F	PX	hr/f	SX	SBO	RC/G	RAR	R$
Pos	4	03 SF	410	61	117	8	33	7	285	370	258	363	441	805	11	80	34	0.61	283	41	24	35	108	7%	100	11%	5.68	15.0	$12
Age	36	04 SF	471	95	133	17	65	10	282	333	263	360	484	844	11	87	29	0.95	294	44	16	40	112	10%	136	10%	6.08	19.7	$19
Decline		05 SF	497	67	144	12	62	6	290	290	292	352	429	781	9	88	31	0.81	298	47	21	32	90	9%	61	6%	5.24	9.5	$16
Bats	Both	06 SF	498	79	146	26	93	7	293	341	277	359	538	897	9	88	29	0.84	316	46	17	37	130	16%	102	7%	6.51	26.6	$22
Reliability	9	07 SF	464	56	101	11	71	10	218	200	224	298	343	641	10	84	24	0.71	247	45	13	41	77	7%	89	10%	3.59	-13.9	$8
BAvg Potl	65%	1st Half	245	38	62	7	42	3	253			325	408	733	10	83	28	0.63	255	47	11	43	98	8%	77	8%	4.65	0.7	$7
LIMA Plan	C+	2nd Half	219	18	39	4	29	7	178			268	269	538	11	84	19	0.79	237	44	17	40	54	5%	84	13%	2.42	-15.1	$1
+/- Score	13	08 Proj	**423**	**56**	**105**	**12**	**64**	**8**	**248**			**323**	**399**	**722**	**10**	**86**	**27**	**0.76**	**273**	**45**	**16**	**38**	**90**	**9%**	**97**	**9%**	**4.58**	**0.2**	**$11**

He's not THIS bad. H% hurt his 2nd half BA. Gave back 2006 power surge; PX, hr/f now show that was a fluke. Career is winding down, so don't be surprised by more regression: DN: 300 AB, 6 HR.

Dye,Jermaine

Dye,Jermaine			AB	R	H	HR	RBI	SB	Avg	vL	vR	OB	Slg	OPS	bb%	ct%	h%	Eye	xBA	G	L	F	PX	hr/f	SX	SBO	RC/G	RAR	R$
Pos	9	03 OAK	* 270	34	49	6	26	1	181	260	146	271	278	548	11	81	20	0.63	208	41	12	47	61	6%	52	1%	2.37	-24.1	$1
Age	34	04 OAK	532	87	141	23	80	4	265	280	259	327	464	791	8	76	31	0.38	263	39	18	43	127	13%	91	4%	5.27	8.8	$17
Past Peak		05 CHW	529	74	145	31	86	11	274	252	278	324	512	836	7	81	29	0.39	301	38	21	41	145	18%	86	12%	5.60	13.8	$22
Bats	Right	06 CHW	539	103	170	44	120	7	315	337	305	383	622	1004	10	78	33	0.50	314	39	20	40	179	26%	84	6%	7.86	32.1	$31
Reliability	17	07 CHW	508	68	129	28	78	2	254	292	241	315	486	801	8	79	27	0.42	288	35	19	46	152	15%	42	3%	5.29	8.7	$15
BAvg Potl	55%	1st Half	244	29	56	11	35	2	230			285	422	707	7	80	25	0.38	265	38	16	46	126	12%	49	6%	4.09	-4.5	$5
LIMA Plan	C+	2nd Half	264	39	73	17	43	0	277			341	545	887	9	78	29	0.46	311	31	22	46	176	18%	23	0%	6.40	12.8	$10
+/- Score	4	08 Proj	**512**	**92**	**144**	**36**	**102**	**4**	**281**			**343**	**555**	**898**	**9**	**79**	**29**	**0.45**	**305**	**37**	**20**	**44**	**168**	**20%**	**73**	**5%**	**6.47**	**21.8**	**$24**

An off year? Nah, just an off 1st half. 2nd half BPIs were right back to 2006 levels. PX says you can put the power in the bank, and xBA says the BA will come back as well.

Easley,Damion

Easley,Damion			AB	R	H	HR	RBI	SB	Avg	vL	vR	OB	Slg	OPS	bb%	ct%	h%	Eye	xBA	G	L	F	PX	hr/f	SX	SBO	RC/G	RAR	R$
Pos	4	03 TAM	107	8	20	1	7	0	187	184	188	202	262	464	2	83	22	0.11	242	45	20	35	46	3%	62	0%	1.07	-10.5	($1)
Age	38	04 FLA	223	26	53	9	43	4	238	149	294	312	457	769	10	84	25	0.67	302	41	18	41	138	12%	77	11%	5.10	3.3	$6
Decline		05 FLA	267	37	64	9	30	4	240	333	218	307	419	727	9	82	26	0.55	295	40	23	37	119	11%	87	8%	4.52	-0.3	$7
Bats	Right	06 ARI	189	24	44	9	28	1	233	245	217	310	418	728	10	84	23	0.70	266	45	15	40	99	14%	57	4%	4.50	-0.6	$4
Reliability	22	07 NYM	193	24	54	10	26	0	280	371	202	344	466	811	9	82	30	0.54	255	40	16	44	106	14%	21	2%	5.39	4.5	$6
BAvg Potl	45%	1st Half	136	16	34	7	18	0	250			315	441	757	9	82	26	0.52	254	38	15	46	110	14%	24	3%	4.73	0.7	$3
LIMA Plan	F	2nd Half	57	8	20	3	8	0	351			413	526	939	10	82	39	0.60	229	44	18	38	95	17%	1	0%	6.94	3.5	$3
+/- Score	-78	08 Proj	**168**	**21**	**40**	**8**	**23**	**0**	**238**			**307**	**410**	**717**	**9**	**83**	**25**	**0.58**	**263**	**43**	**17**	**40**	**99**	**14%**	**34**	**2%**	**4.30**	**-1.3**	**$4**

No real improvement here - just small sample size volatility. xBA trend shows the writing on the wall. 2nd half BA propped up by h%. BA vs RHP limits his role, further devaluing him. He's just about done.

Eckstein,David

Eckstein,David			AB	R	H	HR	RBI	SB	Avg	vL	vR	OB	Slg	OPS	bb%	ct%	h%	Eye	xBA	G	L	F	PX	hr/f	SX	SBO	RC/G	RAR	R$
Pos	6	03 ANA	452	59	114	3	31	16	252	256	251	307	325	633	7	90	27	0.80	276	50	20	30	50	2%	102	17%	3.58	-11.3	$9
Age	33	04 ANA	566	92	156	2	35	16	276	279	274	326	332	658	7	91	30	0.86	273	50	21	30	38	1%	104	12%	3.87	-9.7	$13
Past Peak		05 STL	630	90	185	8	61	11	294	262	306	353	395	748	8	93	31	1.32	296	46	23	31	59	4%	100	9%	5.00	18.4	$19
Bats	Right	06 STL	500	68	146	2	23	7	292	280	298	333	344	677	6	92	32	0.76	271	49	22	29	34	1%	67	8%	4.00	-5.0	$10
Reliability	56	07 STL	434	58	134	3	31	10	309	298	314	345	382	727	5	95	32	1.09	280	41	22	37	49	2%	82	8%	4.59	7.5	$13
BAvg Potl	60%	1st Half	192	25	60	2	12	2	313			340	385	725	4	96	32	1.14	266	41	19	40	44	3%	58	3%	4.49	2.7	$5
LIMA Plan	C+	2nd Half	242	33	74	1	19	8	306			349	380	729	6	94	32	1.07	289	40	25	35	52	1%	83	12%	4.67	4.7	$7
+/- Score	-22	08 Proj	**512**	**70**	**149**	**3**	**35**	**11**	**291**			**334**	**362**	**696**	**6**	**93**	**31**	**0.98**	**280**	**44**	**22**	**33**	**46**	**2%**	**84**	**9%**	**4.28**	**3.0**	**$13**

Consistent BPIs. Only cause for concern is the steep rise in FB%. He's got no power, so those fly balls are dying in the OF. SB total is unlikely to rise: SX is below average, and he doesn't run as much anymore.

Edmonds,Jim

Edmonds,Jim			AB	R	H	HR	RBI	SB	Avg	vL	vR	OB	Slg	OPS	bb%	ct%	h%	Eye	xBA	G	L	F	PX	hr/f	SX	SBO	RC/G	RAR	R$
Pos	8	03 STL	447	89	123	39	89	1	275	225	292	382	617	999	15	72	30	0.61	316	34	20	47	231	26%	58	3%	8.38	43.6	$23
Age	37	04 STL	498	102	150	42	111	8	301	330	293	419	643	1062	17	70	35	0.67	309	34	21	45	231	27%	89	7%	9.54	67.3	$31
Decline		05 STL	467	88	123	29	89	5	263	296	251	384	533	917	16	70	31	0.65	287	35	19	47	198	19%	65	7%	7.49	40.1	$21
Bats	Left	06 STL	350	52	90	19	70	4	257	156	295	355	471	826	13	71	31	0.52	257	35	20	44	142	17%	55	4%	6.00	15.9	$13
Reliability	28	07 STL	365	39	92	12	53	0	252	198	268	328	403	730	10	79	29	0.55	249	36	19	44	93	9%	37	2%	4.57	0.1	$8
BAvg Potl	45%	1st Half	193	20	46	7	24	0	238			310	394	704	9	79	27	0.50	250	40	19	41	89	11%	55	4%	4.17	-2.3	$3
LIMA Plan	D	2nd Half	172	19	46	5	29	0	267			347	413	760	11	80	31	0.60	250	32	20	48	97	8%	18	0%	5.01	2.2	$4
+/- Score	-16	08 Proj	**341**	**48**	**84**	**11**	**50**	**0**	**246**			**340**	**406**	**747**	**12**	**75**	**30**	**0.57**	**247**	**35**	**20**	**45**	**109**	**10%**	**47**	**2%**	**4.92**	**3.7**	**$8**

xBA, PX, hr/f are all in a free-fall. Sure, he battled the usual injuries, but this is now serious. With struggles vs LHP, he's become a replacement-level platoon player. Tough to come to terms with that reality, right?

Ellis,Mark

Ellis,Mark			AB	R	H	HR	RBI	SB	Avg	vL	vR	OB	Slg	OPS	bb%	ct%	h%	Eye	xBA	G	L	F	PX	hr/f	SX	SBO	RC/G	RAR	R$
Pos	4	03 OAK	553	78	137	9	52	6	248	217	259	308	371	679	8	83	28	0.51	266	40	22	38	81	5%	104	6%	3.96	-2.9	$10
Age	30	04 OAK	0	0	0	0	0	0	0							0									0				
Peak		05 OAK	434	76	137	13	52	1	316	313	318	379	477	856	9	88	34	0.86	292	47	18	35	93	10%	78	3%	6.10	23.1	$17
Bats	Right	06 OAK	441	64	110	11	52	4	249	278	242	312	385	697	8	83	28	0.53	260	39	19	42	87	7%	82	4%	4.15	0.3	$9
Reliability	43	07 OAK	583	84	161	19	76	9	276	313	263	327	441	768	7	84	30	0.47	259	32	18	50	104	8%	89	9%	4.90	12.8	$18
BAvg Potl	45%	1st Half	255	33	70	8	40	6	275			332	431	764	8	84	30	0.54	252	25	20	55	99	7%	81	12%	4.90	5.7	$8
LIMA Plan	C+	2nd Half	328	51	91	11	36	3	277			323	448	771	6	84	30	0.42	266	37	16	47	107	9%	82	6%	4.89	7.1	$10
+/- Score	-4	08 Proj	**535**	**80**	**141**	**20**	**75**	**6**	**264**			**321**	**445**	**765**	**8**	**84**	**28**	**0.53**	**277**	**37**	**19**	**44**	**110**	**10%**	**87**	**6%**	**4.90**	**12.0**	**$16**

DL-free since 2007! Steady BPIs, a rising FB%, and good health contributed to his best season to date. xBA says not to expect more BA growth, but there might be a few more ticks in the HR column.

Ellsbury,Jacoby

Ellsbury,Jacoby			AB	R	H	HR	RBI	SB	Avg	vL	vR	OB	Slg	OPS	bb%	ct%	h%	Eye	xBA	G	L	F	PX	hr/f	SX	SBO	RC/G	RAR	R$
Pos	7	03	0	0	0	0	0	0	0							0									0				
Age	24	04	0	0	0	0	0	0	0							0									0				
Growth		05	0	0	0	0	0	0	0							0									0				
Bats	Left	06 aa	198	25	57	3	16	14	289			358	407	765	10	89	32	0.94					70		113	35%	5.17	-0.2	$7
Reliability	0	07 BOS	* 552	89	172	5	53	44	312	346	356	358	418	776	7	89	35	0.63	291	52	19	29	70	4%	143	31%	5.12	6.1	$25
BAvg Potl	45%	1st Half	279	45	86	0	21	25	308			363	409	772	8	90	34	0.83					70		149	37%	5.24	4.1	$12
LIMA Plan	B	2nd Half	273	44	86	5	32	19	315			353	427	780	6	87	35	0.46	286	52	19	29	70	7%	130	24%	5.00	2.1	$13
+/- Score	1	08 Proj	**461**	**78**	**135**	**6**	**43**	**34**	**293**			**348**	**405**	**753**	**8**	**88**	**32**	**0.73**	**291**	**52**	**19**	**29**	**71**	**5%**	**140**	**33%**	**4.93**	**0.6**	**$20**

3-18-.353 with 9 SB in 116 AB at BOS. Speed, defense, and a solid plate approach - the real deal. Lack of time at AA and AAA may cause some short-term struggles, but he'll be SB gold for years to come.

DAVE ADLER

Encarnacion,Edwin

			AB	R	H	HR	RBI	SB	Avg	vL	vR	OB	Slg	OPS	bb%	ct%	h%	Eye	xBA	G	L	F	PX	hr/f	SX	SBO	RC/G	RAR	R$
Pos	5	03 aa	254	34	68	5	30	6	269			317	393	709	7	87	29	0.55					78		92	14%	4.27	-0.8	$7
Age	25	04 aa	469	65	123	13	67	15	262			328	418	746	9	85	28	0.66					100		90	15%	4.80	-2.5	$15
Pre-Peak		05 CIN	* 501	63	134	23	77	9	268	246	234	331	479	810	9	80	30	0.47	306	41	24	35	142	16%	70	9%	5.47	10.0	$18
Bats	Right	06 CIN	406	60	112	15	72	6	276	248	287	342	473	815	9	81	31	0.53	292	41	21	37	127	12%	72	9%	5.62	1.5	$14
Reliability	45	07 CIN	* 548	77	163	19	82	9	297	284	291	345	456	801	7	84	33	0.44	266	38	19	43	97	10%	78	6%	5.25	7.1	$21
BAvg Potl	40%	1st Half	269	37	78	7	35	4	290			344	420	764	8	83	33	0.47	255	37	21	42	81	7%	79	5%	4.87	0.7	$9
LIMA Plan	C+	2nd Half	279	40	85	12	47	5	305			347	491	838	6	85	33	0.42	277	38	17	44	111	11%	65	8%	5.60	6.2	$12
+/- Score	-14	08 Proj	517	72	147	20	81	9	284			339	467	807	8	83	31	0.48	282	40	20	41	114	11%	81	8%	5.38	6.3	$19

16-76-.289 in 502 AB at CIN. CON: Drop in PX; xBA 30 points below BA. PRO: Strong finish (9 HR, .337 in Aug/Sept), growth vs LHP. If he can build on the late surge, may take a real step forward.

Encarnacion,Juan

			AB	R	H	HR	RBI	SB	Avg	vL	vR	OB	Slg	OPS	bb%	ct%	h%	Eye	xBA	G	L	F	PX	hr/f	SX	SBO	RC/G	RAR	R$
Pos	9	03 FLA	601	80	162	19	94	19	270	267	270	312	446	758	6	86	29	0.45	298	42	21	37	106	10%	121	20%	4.75	-15.0	$22
Age	32	04 2NL	484	63	114	16	62	5	236	217	241	291	405	696	7	82	26	0.44	267	43	16	41	106	10%	78	9%	4.05	-18.2	$10
Past Peak		05 FLA	506	59	145	16	76	6	287	309	282	340	447	787	7	79	33	0.39	275	39	24	38	106	11%	71	8%	5.16	-1.4	$18
Bats	Right	06 STL	557	74	155	19	79	6	278	316	261	315	443	759	5	85	30	0.35	283	45	20	35	93	12%	85	8%	4.66	-1.8	$17
Reliability	44	07 STL	* 341	46	86	9	49	3	251	290	278	295	392	688	6	84	28	0.38	266	44	18	38	89	8%	68	6%	3.90	-13.7	$8
BAvg Potl	50%	1st Half	202	29	46	5	23	1	228			271	371	642	6	86	24	0.43	267	45	15	40	89	7%	82	3%	3.43	-11.1	$3
LIMA Plan	F	2nd Half	139	17	40	4	26	2	285			331	422	753	6	80	33	0.34	262	43	21	36	90	10%	47	10%	4.65	-2.4	$5
+/- Score	6	08 Proj	94	12	25	3	14	1	266			311	409	720	6	83	30	0.37	269	43	20	37	91	10%	54	8%	4.25	-2.5	$3

9-47-.283 in 283 AB at STL. Fractured eye socket ended his season and puts 2008, and his career, in question. xBA and power were down when he did play, but that's the least of his worries at this point.

Ensberg,Morgan

			AB	R	H	HR	RBI	SB	Avg	vL	vR	OB	Slg	OPS	bb%	ct%	h%	Eye	xBA	G	L	F	PX	hr/f	SX	SBO	RC/G	RAR	R$
Pos	5	03 HOU	385	69	112	25	60	7	291	316	282	370	530	899	11	84	29	0.80	304	38	21	41	133	19%	84	8%	6.54	24.7	$19
Age	32	04 HOU	411	51	113	10	66	6	275	282	273	333	411	745	8	89	29	0.78	285	45	20	35	78	8%	85	9%	4.79	-3.2	$13
Past Peak		05 HOU	526	86	149	36	101	6	283	293	278	383	557	940	14	77	30	0.71	297	37	17	45	173	19%	71	8%	7.36	38.8	$26
Bats	Right	06 HOU	387	67	91	23	58	1	235	245	232	393	463	856	21	75	25	1.05	255	38	15	48	138	17%	34	3%	6.61	13.2	$11
Reliability	37	07 2NL	282	47	65	12	39	0	230	257	215	322	404	726	12	76	26	0.57	254	35	20	45	112	12%	40	1%	4.54	-2.0	$6
BAvg Potl	55%	1st Half	173	32	37	7	21	0	214			317	376	692	13	78	23	0.68	256	39	20	41	101	13%	49	2%	4.17	-3.3	$3
LIMA Plan	D	2nd Half	109	15	28	5	18	0	257			331	450	780	10	73	31	0.41	254	28	21	51	131	12%	25	0%	5.20	1.3	$3
+/- Score	-6	08 Proj	319	51	80	16	50	0	251			354	458	813	14	77	28	0.69	264	35	19	46	129	15%	46	2%	5.74	7.6	$10

Injury-plagued 2006, slow start to 2007, then poof! - DFA. FB% rise helped power return in 2nd half, but he sacrificed plate patience to do so. Trouble with RHP could relegate him to a platoon role going forward.

Erstad,Darin

			AB	R	H	HR	RBI	SB	Avg	vL	vR	OB	Slg	OPS	bb%	ct%	h%	Eye	xBA	G	L	F	PX	hr/f	SX	SBO	RC/G	RAR	R$
Pos	83	03 ANA	258	35	65	4	17	9	252	302	227	301	333	634	7	84	29	0.45	271	50	23	27	49	7%	109	14%	3.31	-10.9	$6
Age	33	04 ANA	495	79	146	7	69	16	295	253	316	344	400	744	7	85	34	0.50	278	57	16	27	70	6%	114	12%	4.68	-0.4	$18
Past Peak		05 ANA	609	86	166	7	66	10	273	232	291	325	371	696	7	82	32	0.43	270	48	22	30	71	5%	100	8%	4.10	-3.1	$15
Bats	Left	06 LAA	95	8	21	0	5	1	221	192	232	267	326	594	6	81	27	0.33	245	51	12	37	82	0%	82	11%	2.91	-5.2	($0)
Reliability	12	07 CHW	* 357	36	82	4	34	7	231	157	282	295	306	601	8	83	27	0.55	250	53	17	30	52	4%	75	9%	3.03	-13.5	$4
BAvg Potl	55%	1st Half	182	21	48	2	21	7	264			313	341	653	7	87	29	0.57	263	49	19	32	53	4%	78	18%	3.65	-3.3	$5
LIMA Plan	F	2nd Half	175	15	34	2	13	0	197			277	271	548	10	79	24	0.53	225	59	14	27	50	5%	40	0%	2.33	-10.7	($1)
+/- Score	-10	08 Proj	253	31	63	3	25	5	249			308	337	645	8	83	29	0.50	261	52	19	29	60	5%	86	9%	3.52	-6.7	$4

4-32-.248 in 310 AB at CHW. Still waiting for another 20/20 season? That was 8 years ago - forget it. Even Ozzie Guillen predicted 500 AB - ha! Speed and power are gone, and he can't hit LHP any more. Pass.

Escobar,Yunel

			AB	R	H	HR	RBI	SB	Avg	vL	vR	OB	Slg	OPS	bb%	ct%	h%	Eye	xBA	G	L	F	PX	hr/f	SX	SBO	RC/G	RAR	R$
Pos	654	03	0	0	0	0	0	0	0							0									0				
Age	25	04	0	0	0	0	0	0	0							0									0				
Pre-Peak		05	0	0	0	0	0	0	0							0									0				
Bats	Right	06 aa	428	51	107	2	43	7	249			337	322	658	12	82	30	0.73					51		78	11%	3.93	-5.9	$6
Reliability	0	07 ATL	* 499	72	161	7	54	11	323	355	303	373	443	816	7	86	36	0.58	301	56	21	23	81	7%	83	11%	5.58	21.8	$18
BAvg Potl	40%	1st Half	262	30	82	3	32	8	313			355	424	779	6	87	35	0.50	298	64	17	19	72	7%	90	15%	5.07	8.0	$9
LIMA Plan	D	2nd Half	237	42	79	4	22	3	333			392	464	856	9	85	38	0.66	303	53	23	24	91	8%	62	6%	6.14	13.7	$9
+/- Score	-4	08 Proj	349	48	98	4	36	6	281			348	384	732	9	84	32	0.65	288	55	22	23	71	5%	83	11%	4.71	6.4	$9

5-28-.326 in 319 AB at ATL. Great BA in debut, but xBA and h% say it won't repeat. Other than that, there's not much here: little power, and AAA speed didn't show in ATL. Decent backup MI, but that's all for now.

Estrada,Johnny

			AB	R	H	HR	RBI	SB	Avg	vL	vR	OB	Slg	OPS	bb%	ct%	h%	Eye	xBA	G	L	F	PX	hr/f	SX	SBO	RC/G	RAR	R$
Pos	2	03 ATL	* 390	38	117	10	62	0	300	167	333	345	446	791	6	92	31	0.84	296	42	21	36	90	8%	17	0%	5.25	10.3	$12
Age	31	04 ATL	462	56	145	9	76	0	314	272	329	367	450	817	8	86	35	0.59	283	43	22	36	92	6%	24	0%	5.60	22.2	$16
Past Peak		05 ATL	357	31	93	4	39	0	261	214	277	300	367	667	5	89	28	0.53	294	36	26	38	76	3%	22	0%	3.82	0.3	$5
Bats	Both	06 ARI	414	43	125	11	71	0	302	296	304	323	444	768	3	90	31	0.33	279	39	20	41	83	7%	21	0%	4.70	4.1	$13
Reliability	49	07 MIL	442	40	123	10	54	0	278	313	263	297	403	700	3	90	29	0.28	273	40	20	40	76	6%	20	0%	3.95	2.0	$9
BAvg Potl	50%	1st Half	245	29	70	7	30	0	286			303	437	740	2	91	29	0.26	290	39	21	40	90	8%	29	0%	4.36	3.9	$6
LIMA Plan	D	2nd Half	197	11	53	3	24	0	269			291	360	651	3	90	29	0.30	249	40	20	40	57	4%	8	0%	3.44	-2.0	$3
+/- Score	-6	08 Proj	438	40	122	9	60	0	279			305	403	708	4	90	29	0.38	277	39	21	40	77	6%	19	0%	4.11	1.9	$10

xBA predicted drop in BA; low bb% means .300 is probably a longshot now. Still, high ct% will protect your BA downside, so he's a reasonable option at catcher. But BPIs are otherwise dull - not much power, no speed.

Ethier,Andre

			AB	R	H	HR	RBI	SB	Avg	vL	vR	OB	Slg	OPS	bb%	ct%	h%	Eye	xBA	G	L	F	PX	hr/f	SX	SBO	RC/G	RAR	R$
Pos	97	03	0	0	0	0	0	0	0							0									0				
Age	26	04	0	0	0	0	0	0	0							0									0				
Pre-Peak		05 a/a	516	81	145	14	64	1	281			332	424	756	7	85	31	0.52					91		58	4%	4.78	-2.8	$16
Bats	Left	06 LA	* 482	62	148	12	64	7	307	351	298	366	469	835	9	81	36	0.50	273	41	22	37	95	8%	98	9%	5.87	14.6	$17
Reliability	44	07 LA	447	50	127	13	64	0	284	279	286	351	452	803	9	85	31	0.68	281	46	18	36	106	10%	30	3%	5.50	3.1	$12
BAvg Potl	50%	1st Half	226	25	63	6	30	0	279			343	429	772	9	88	30	0.79	280	45	18	37	92	8%	37	5%	5.13	-0.8	$6
LIMA Plan	C	2nd Half	221	25	64	7	34	0	290			359	475	834	10	82	33	0.60	286	48	18	35	123	11%	35	2%	5.91	4.1	$7
+/- Score	-1	08 Proj	488	61	143	18	67	1	293			355	489	843	9	83	32	0.58	292	45	19	36	117	13%	51	4%	5.91	10.4	$16

PX improved a little, as did ct%. Otherwise, not much growth from rookie season. Spent much of the season in a platoon, despite even splits. Time to show something more if he wants regular playing time.

Everett,Adam

			AB	R	H	HR	RBI	SB	Avg	vL	vR	OB	Slg	OPS	bb%	ct%	h%	Eye	xBA	G	L	F	PX	hr/f	SX	SBO	RC/G	RAR	R$
Pos	6	03 HOU	* 487	71	122	9	59	11	251	324	240	299	372	671	7	84	28	0.43	266	38	24	38	78	6%	124	11%	3.77	-4.9	$12
Age	31	04 HOU	384	66	105	8	31	13	273	235	282	304	385	690	4	85	30	0.30	239	41	15	45	66	5%	134	15%	3.84	-3.2	$12
Past Peak		05 HOU	549	58	136	11	54	21	248	227	255	282	364	646	5	81	29	0.25	249	39	19	42	79	6%	107	23%	3.30	-10.9	$14
Bats	Right	06 HOU	514	52	123	6	59	9	239	250	237	286	352	639	6	86	27	0.48	255	37	20	43	69	3%	95	13%	3.48	-13.7	$8
Reliability	56	07 HOU	220	18	51	2	15	4	232	214	238	278	318	596	6	86	26	0.45	248	45	17	38	58	3%	70	12%	2.95	-6.8	$2
BAvg Potl	60%	1st Half	215	17	49	2	15	4	228			272	316	588	6	86	26	0.42	248	44	18	39	60	3%	70	13%	2.84	-7.4	$1
LIMA Plan	D	2nd Half	5	1	2	0	0	0	400			500	400	900	17	100	40			80	0	20	0	0%	31	0%	7.40	0.4	$0
+/- Score	1	08 Proj	473	52	116	5	44	7	245			286	339	625	5	84	28	0.36	245	40	19	41	62	3%	87	11%	3.20	-12.4	$7

Sure, a broken leg can hinder your speed. (What a wimp - get over it!) Since SX was down before the injury, double-digit SBs could be gone for good. No power, low xBA, but only 31. You can't take away his youth.

Feliz,Pedro

			AB	R	H	HR	RBI	SB	Avg	vL	vR	OB	Slg	OPS	bb%	ct%	h%	Eye	xBA	G	L	F	PX	hr/f	SX	SBO	RC/G	RAR	R$
Pos	5	03 SF	235	31	58	16	48	2	247	231	251	278	515	792	4	77	25	0.19	302	46	18	36	159	24%	95	10%	4.93	4.7	$9
Age	33	04 SF	503	72	139	22	84	5	276	291	269	308	485	793	4	83	30	0.27	292	47	15	37	125	14%	89	7%	5.01	-0.8	$18
Past Peak		05 SF	569	69	142	20	81	0	250	271	245	297	422	718	6	82	27	0.37	272	44	17	39	108	11%	55	2%	4.24	-9.0	$14
Bats	Right	06 SF	603	75	147	22	98	1	244	212	253	283	428	711	5	81	27	0.29	266	40	16	43	110	10%	69	2%	4.10	-25.0	$14
Reliability	99	07 SF	557	61	141	20	72	2	253	257	252	290	418	708	5	87	26	0.41	271	43	15	42	95	10%	53	3%	4.10	-11.1	$12
BAvg Potl	60%	1st Half	272	28	67	12	36	0	246			278	434	712	4	88	24	0.35	278	44	15	40	105	13%	34	0%	4.07	-5.7	$6
LIMA Plan	C	2nd Half	285	33	74	8	36	2	260			301	404	705	6	87	27	0.47	261	41	15	43	86	7%	61	6%	4.13	-5.4	$6
+/- Score	6	08 Proj	526	62	132	18	66	1	251			290	416	706	5	84	27	0.35	267	43	16	41	99	10%	56	2%	4.06	-13.8	$11

While he cut down on his K's, that did not really help his power or BA. Consistency and reliability are great, but not when you see all those little minus signs in the RAR column. An offensive drain.

DAVE ADLER

Fick,Robert

			AB	R	H	HR	RBI	SB	Avg	vL	vR	OB	Slg	OPS	bb%	ct%	h%	Eye	xBA	G	L	F	PX	hr/f	SX	SBO	RC/G	RAR	R$
Pos	3	03 ATL	409	52	110	11	80	1	269	135	289	337	418	755	9	89	28	0.89	294	35	24	41	92	7%	53	1%	4.98	-6.2	$12
Age	34	04 2TM	226	14	45	6	26	0	199	111	207	270	319	589	9	84	21	0.61	232	35	18	47	64	7%	37	0%	2.87	-18.4	$1
Past Peak		05 SD	* 262	29	70	5	38	1	267	297	259	352	379	731	12	87	29	0.97	258	42	19	39	69	5%	57	3%	4.82	-5.9	$6
Bats	Left	06 WAS	* 177	20	43	3	10	3	242	273	262	300	316	617	8	81	28	0.45	213	34	18	48	46	4%	53	9%	3.09	-15.5	$2
Reliability	4	07 WAS	197	24	46	2	16	0	234	143	258	301	305	605	9	79	29	0.45	249	35	29	36	48	4%	56	2%	2.99	-15.5	$1
BAvg Potl	50%	1st Half	85	11	19	0	4	0	224			290	259	549	9	75	30	0.38	227	29	31	40	33	0%	49	4%	2.22	-8.9	$0
LIMA Plan	F	2nd Half	112	13	27	2	12	0	241			309	339	648	9	81	28	0.52	266	39	28	33	59	7%	56	0%	3.56	-6.8	$1
+/- Score	-17	08 Proj	164	19	40	2	15	0	244			312	331	642	9	81	29	0.53	245	36	25	40	54	5%	55	3%	3.50	-10.8	$2

At the turn of the century, he was a power hitter with decent BA. But back then, McKinley was president and the Cardinals led the majors with 39 HRs. Things change.

Fielder,Prince

			AB	R	H	HR	RBI	SB	Avg	vL	vR	OB	Slg	OPS	bb%	ct%	h%	Eye	xBA	G	L	F	PX	hr/f	SX	SBO	RC/G	RAR	R$
Pos	3	03	0	0	0	0	0	0	0							0									0				
Age	23	04 aa	497	72	139	25	81	12	279			364	496	860	12	83	29	0.76					129		73	13%	6.22	10.7	$20
Growth		05 MIL	* 437	58	123	25	80	7	281	500	281	351	510	860	10	81	30	0.58	339	37	35	28	142	25%	49	11%	6.06	5.8	$19
Bats	Left	06 MIL	569	82	154	28	81	7	271	247	280	339	483	822	9	78	30	0.47	279	42	18	39	132	16%	70	6%	5.66	-5.6	$19
Reliability	34	07 MIL	573	109	165	50	119	2	288	261	301	385	618	1002	14	79	29	0.74	322	35	19	46	196	24%	53	2%	8.01	38.7	$31
BAvg Potl	60%	1st Half	291	54	82	27	63	0	282			363	622	985	11	78	28	0.57	324	37	19	44	205	27%	28	3%	7.66	17.0	$15
LIMA Plan	C+	2nd Half	282	55	83	23	56	2	294			406	613	1019	16	80	30	0.95	318	33	19	48	186	21%	71	2%	8.35	21.5	$15
+/- Score	42	08 Proj	585	97	171	45	107	1	292			377	592	969	12	80	30	0.67	313	38	19	43	177	23%	38	3%	7.51	29.5	$28

A fully supported breakout. bb% spike fueled BA gain; xBA shows it can go even higher. FB% climb was behind power boost. Scary thing? He's still in his growth years.
UP: .300 BA, 50+ HR.

Fields,Josh

			AB	R	H	HR	RBI	SB	Avg	vL	vR	OB	Slg	OPS	bb%	ct%	h%	Eye	xBA	G	L	F	PX	hr/f	SX	SBO	RC/G	RAR	R$
Pos	57	03	0	0	0	0	0	0	0							0									0				
Age	25	04	0	0	0	0	0	0	0							0									0				
Pre-Peak		05 aa	474	55	98	14	57	5	207			267	338	605	8	73	25	0.31					95		60	12%	2.79	-27.8	$7
Bats	Right	06 aaa	482	82	140	21	66	26	290	167	143	362	500	862	10	72	36	0.41		58	8	33	143	18%	126	22%	6.42	15.9	$23
Reliability	3	07 CHW	* 578	79	145	34	100	8	251	321	213	333	481	814	11	69	31	0.39	261	41	17	43	166	20%	60	9%	5.82	22.7	$20
BAvg Potl	35%	1st Half	272	31	72	13	44	7	265			359	467	826	13	70	33	0.49	277	39	26	34	149	20%	48	14%	6.06	12.6	$9
LIMA Plan	B	2nd Half	306	48	73	21	56	1	240			309	493	803	9	67	29	0.31	262	41	15	44	181	23%	57	2%	5.60	10.1	$10
+/- Score	7	08 Proj	504	74	130	25	77	8	258			332	469	801	10	71	32	0.38	258	42	16	43	149	16%	83	10%	5.58	13.9	$17

23-67-.244 in 373 AB at CHW. Seized opportunity when injuries pressed him into service.
PRO: 2H FB% and PX gains
CON: Low ct%, struggles vs RH.
If he runs like in AAA, his value goes even higher.

Figgins,Chone

			AB	R	H	HR	RBI	SB	Avg	vL	vR	OB	Slg	OPS	bb%	ct%	h%	Eye	xBA	G	L	F	PX	hr/f	SX	SBO	RC/G	RAR	R$
Pos	5	03 ANA	* 525	78	149	3	51	26	284	284	303	338	392	730	8	87	32	0.65	296	43	29	28	63	2%	145	26%	4.68	2.6	$17
Age	30	04 ANA	577	83	171	5	60	34	296	314	289	351	419	771	8	84	35	0.52	259	37	25	39	69	3%	150	27%	5.12	3.5	$22
Peak		05 ANA	642	113	186	8	57	62	290	244	313	354	397	751	9	84	33	0.63	260	41	22	37	66	4%	162	38%	4.92	7.7	$32
Bats	Both	06 LAA	604	93	161	9	62	52	267	233	280	338	376	714	10	83	31	0.65	258	44	21	36	65	5%	151	37%	4.48	-9.6	$24
Reliability	67	07 LAA	442	81	146	3	58	41	330	326	331	400	432	832	10	82	40	0.63	283	47	26	26	72	3%	147	32%	6.00	18.1	$25
BAvg Potl	35%	1st Half	200	31	62	1	21	18	310			364	395	759	8	87	35	0.63	292	49	26	25	58	2%	135	33%	4.98	2.7	$10
LIMA Plan	B	2nd Half	242	50	84	2	37	23	347			428	463	890	12	78	44	0.63	275	46	27	27	84	4%	148	32%	6.94	15.9	$16
+/- Score	-43	08 Proj	564	97	162	6	65	50	287			357	395	752	10	83	34	0.63	272	45	24	31	69	4%	158	35%	4.98	5.4	$26

He took off in June after broken fingers led to a slow start. SX and SBO remain elite, and increasing GB% helps, so you can continue to bank the SBs. xBA and h% say BA won't repeat.

Finley,Steve

			AB	R	H	HR	RBI	SB	Avg	vL	vR	OB	Slg	OPS	bb%	ct%	h%	Eye	xBA	G	L	F	PX	hr/f	SX	SBO	RC/G	RAR	R$
Pos	8	03 ARI	516	82	148	22	70	15	287	245	306	358	500	858	10	82	32	0.61	296	43	21	36	124	14%	132	15%	6.15	17.3	$22
Age	43	04 2NL	628	92	170	36	94	9	271	245	282	335	490	826	9	87	26	0.74	301	40	20	40	118	16%	64	10%	5.58	17.0	$24
Decline		05 ANA	406	41	90	12	54	8	222	271	201	269	374	643	6	83	24	0.37	262	40	18	43	96	8%	93	15%	3.35	-11.7	$7
Bats	Left	06 SF	426	66	105	6	40	7	246	255	244	320	394	714	10	87	27	0.84	270	46	15	38	81	4%	131	6%	4.63	2.3	$8
Reliability		07 COL	94	9	17	1	2	0	181	267	165	245	245	490	8	96	18	2.00	226	49	11	39	38	3%	31	0%	2.32	-6.8	($1)
BAvg Potl		1st Half	94	9	17	1	2	0	181			245	245	490	8	96	18	2.00	226	49	11	39	38	3%	31	0%	2.32	-6.8	($1)
LIMA Plan		2nd Half	0	0	0	0	0	0	0																				
+/- Score		08 Proj																											

The decline was slow and painful but the end was swift. Designated for assignment in June. A look at the LD% trend tells the story. Another former star who chose the Steve Carlton path to retirement.

Flores,Jesus

			AB	R	H	HR	RBI	SB	Avg	vL	vR	OB	Slg	OPS	bb%	ct%	h%	Eye	xBA	G	L	F	PX	hr/f	SX	SBO	RC/G	RAR	R$
Pos	2	03	0	0	0	0	0	0	0							0									0				
Age	23	04	0	0	0	0	0	0	0							0									0				
Growth		05	0	0	0	0	0	0	0							0									0				
Bats	Right	06	0	0	0	0	0	0	0							0									0				
Reliability	2	07 WAS	180	21	44	4	25	0	244	270	220	299	361	660	7	73	31	0.29	229	50	17	34	86	9%	34	2%	3.55	-1.3	$3
BAvg Potl	35%	1st Half	59	8	12	0	7	0	203			309	271	580	13	78	26	0.69	222	47	16	38	62	0%	48	6%	2.95	-1.6	$0
LIMA Plan	F	2nd Half	121	13	32	4	18	0	264			294	405	699	4	71	34	0.14	231	51	17	31	99	15%	24	0%	3.89	0.3	$3
+/- Score	3	08 Proj	134	16	32	3	18	0	239			297	351	648	8	74	30	0.32	229	49	17	34	83	8%	38	3%	3.42	-2.2	$2

Rule 5 pick who didn't play above Single-A until 2007; did OK considering the big jump. xBA and ct% say he needs more seasoning. Power will come when he reduces GB%. Still a few years away.

Floyd,Cliff

			AB	R	H	HR	RBI	SB	Avg	vL	vR	OB	Slg	OPS	bb%	ct%	h%	Eye	xBA	G	L	F	PX	hr/f	SX	SBO	RC/G	RAR	R$
Pos	9	03 NYM	365	57	106	18	68	3	290	262	305	377	518	895	12	82	31	0.77	294	38	18	44	141	14%	77	3%	6.71	11.2	$16
Age	35	04 NYM	396	55	103	18	63	11	260	239	269	339	462	801	11	74	31	0.46	268	43	18	40	138	16%	74	14%	5.53	2.8	$15
Decline		05 NYM	550	85	150	34	98	12	273	224	290	347	505	853	10	82	28	0.64	293	41	18	42	135	18%	94	9%	5.97	11.3	$26
Bats	Left	06 NYM	332	45	81	11	44	6	244	179	266	305	407	711	8	83	27	0.50	268	42	18	40	99	10%	85	8%	4.27	-5.0	$8
Reliability	26	07 CHC	282	40	80	9	45	0	284	303	281	363	422	785	11	83	31	0.74	256	46	17	37	81	10%	40	0%	5.31	0.4	$9
BAvg Potl	45%	1st Half	144	19	44	4	27	0	306			375	424	799	10	83	34	0.67	251	46	19	35	71	11%	23	0%	5.41	0.6	$5
LIMA Plan	F	2nd Half	138	21	36	5	18	0	261			350	420	771	12	83	28	0.83	259	47	15	38	91	11%	53	0%	5.19	-0.2	$4
+/- Score	-52	08 Proj	220	32	59	8	34	0	268			344	425	769	10	82	30	0.65	262	44	17	39	94	11%	49	1%	5.07	-0.5	$6

The GOOD: Rise in BA, bb%.
The BAD: xBA, FB%, PX trends.
The UGLY: Battled maladies all year long, as usual. Best-case is a platoon option at this point. He may not be that old, but the end is coming fast and furious.

Fontenot,Mike

			AB	R	H	HR	RBI	SB	Avg	vL	vR	OB	Slg	OPS	bb%	ct%	h%	Eye	xBA	G	L	F	PX	hr/f	SX	SBO	RC/G	RAR	R$
Pos	4	03 aa	449	59	134	13	62	15	298			365	441	806	10	81	35	0.55					90		102	13%	5.51	15.6	$18
Age	27	04 aaa	524	65	132	8	44	12	252			310	372	682	8	81	30	0.45					77		110	15%	3.97	-5.9	$10
Peak		05 aaa	375	45	87	5	30	2	232			315	348	664	11	84	27	0.74					76		87	4%	3.98	-4.2	$4
Bats	Left	06 aaa	362	49	98	8	32	5	271			348	418	766	11	83	31	0.70					96		76	8%	5.15	8.3	$8
Reliability	21	07 CHC	* 445	64	120	9	53	7	270	212	297	320	413	734	7	83	31	0.43	277	47	19	34	90	7%	107	11%	4.55	-0.1	$12
BAvg Potl	50%	1st Half	280	54	95	9	42	4	339			375	557	932	5	88	36	0.46	318	48	16	35	130	10%	117	8%	6.76	16.1	$14
LIMA Plan	F	2nd Half	165	10	25	0	11	3	152			231	170	400	9	75	20	0.41	201	47	21	33	11	0%	73	15%	0.25	-24.2	($2)
+/- Score	6	08 Proj	264	32	68	4	25	4	258			324	377	702	9	81	30	0.53	264	47	20	33	77	6%	92	10%	4.28	-2.2	$5

3-29-.278 in 234 AB at CHC. June was what dreams are made of (.397 BA, 156 PX). July the devil came to call ("about that contract, Mike...") led to 2nd half struggles. Serviceable BPIs, some SB upside.

Ford,Lew

			AB	R	H	HR	RBI	SB	Avg	vL	vR	OB	Slg	OPS	bb%	ct%	h%	Eye	xBA	G	L	F	PX	hr/f	SX	SBO	RC/G	RAR	R$
Pos	7	03 MIN	* 284	45	82	5	42	6	289	329	361	329	447	776	6	87	32	0.47	304	44	22	34	103	6%	110	16%	5.05	-2.3	$10
Age	31	04 MIN	569	89	170	15	72	20	299	293	301	373	446	819	11	87	32	0.89	290	52	17	31	87	10%	120	12%	5.77	13.0	$22
Past Peak		05 MIN	522	70	138	7	53	13	264	224	278	323	377	700	8	84	30	0.53	273	54	16	30	78	5%	105	13%	4.23	-7.4	$13
Bats	Right	06 MIN	234	40	53	4	18	9	226	206	242	276	312	588	6	82	26	0.37	245	52	16	32	51	7%	131	17%	2.68	-17.8	$4
Reliability	20	07 MIN	* 238	26	55	5	29	5	231	256	219	305	362	667	10	75	29	0.43	248	47	16	37	103	7%	61	11%	3.80	-6.7	$4
BAvg Potl	50%	1st Half	123	11	30	3	17	2	244			306	374	680	8	85	27	0.58	250	46	13	41	86	7%	46	6%	3.96	-2.8	$2
LIMA Plan	F	2nd Half	115	15	25	2	12	3	217			304	349	652	11	66	31	0.37	255	50	25	25	126	10%	67	17%	3.79	-3.3	$2
+/- Score	-4	08 Proj	110	15	26	2	12	3	236			302	345	647	9	78	29	0.43	250	51	17	32	79	7%	74	14%	3.49	-4.6	$2

3-14-.233 in 116 AB at MIN. His game used to be about speed, but not anymore. In the 2nd half, he couldn't hit a slow-moving bovine with a 2x4. (I've been living in the south too long.)

DAVE ADLER

Francisco,Ben

		AB	R	H	HR	RBI	SB	Avg	vL	vR	OB	Slg	OPS	bb%	ct%	h%	Eye	xBA	G	L	F	PX	hr/f	SX	SBO	RC/G	RAR	R$
Pos 7	03	0	0	0	0	0	0	0							0									0				
Age 26	04 aa	497	60	113	12	60	18	227			288	362	650	8	85	25	0.55					83		107	21%	3.59	-24.4	$11
Pre-Peak	05 a/a	330	39	91	5	39	12	276			319	400	719	6	85	31	0.41					81		119	20%	4.35	-6.5	$10
Bats Right	06 aaa	515	76	134	14	56	24	260			318	416	734	8	86	28	0.63					93		123	22%	4.62	-9.0	$17
Reliability 28	07 CLE	* 439	61	126	13	56	19	287	286	273	340	452	792	8	82	33	0.45	287	47	19	35	112	10%	91	26%	5.24	6.6	$17
BAvg Potl 50%	1st Half	242	35	73	5	30	13	302			357	438	795	8	85	34	0.58					95		90	23%	5.34	4.2	$10
LIMA Plan D+	2nd Half	197	26	53	8	26	6	269			319	469	788	7	78	31	0.34	290	47	19	35	135	15%	86	31%	5.14	2.5	$7
+/- Score -8	08 Proj	315	43	85	9	38	13	270			323	429	752	7	83	30	0.47	284	47	19	35	103	10%	103	24%	4.76	-1.1	$10

3-12-.274 in 62 AB at CLE. Three HR in four games after callup got people's attention, but didn't do much else after that. A touch of pop and a willingness to run have value. If he gets AB, worth keeping an eye on.

Francoeur,Jeff

		AB	R	H	HR	RBI	SB	Avg	vL	vR	OB	Slg	OPS	bb%	ct%	h%	Eye	xBA	G	L	F	PX	hr/f	SX	SBO	RC/G	RAR	R$
Pos 9	03	0	0	0	0	0	0	0							0									0				
Age 24	04 aa	76	7	13	2	8	1	171			171	263	434	0	79	19	0.00					53		10	10%	0.34	-11.5	$0
Growth	05 ATL	* 592	76	161	25	99	14	272	403	268	306	483	789	5	79	31	0.23	290	40	19	41	144	13%	96	17%	5.02	-3.9	$23
Bats Right	06 ATL	651	83	169	29	103	1	260	292	248	285	449	733	3	80	29	0.17	270	45	18	37	107	15%	60	5%	4.20	-11.0	$18
Reliability 57	07 ATL	642	84	188	19	105	5	293	317	281	336	444	780	6	80	34	0.33	267	43	19	37	101	10%	55	4%	4.99	-4.6	$22
BAvg Potl 30%	1st Half	307	32	86	8	49	1	280			322	417	739	6	80	33	0.32	262	45	20	35	92	9%	31	4%	4.47	-6.8	$8
LIMA Plan D+	2nd Half	335	52	102	11	56	4	304			349	469	818	6	79	36	0.33	268	41	19	40	110	10%	68	4%	5.47	2.0	$13
+/- Score -28	08 Proj	632	83	176	23	103	5	278			314	451	766	5	80	32	0.26	272	44	19	38	110	12%	71	6%	4.72	-7.8	$21

A 10-HR decline from '06 but PX and FB% were virtually identical. The difference was a 5% drop in hr/f. But he hasn't been playing long enough to establish a hr/f baseline so we don't know which level is real. UP: 30 HR, DN: 20

Frandsen,Kevin

		AB	R	H	HR	RBI	SB	Avg	vL	vR	OB	Slg	OPS	bb%	ct%	h%	Eye	xBA	G	L	F	PX	hr/f	SX	SBO	RC/G	RAR	R$
Pos 46	03	0	0	0	0	0	0	0							0									0				
Age 25	04	0	0	0	0	0	0	0							0									0				
Pre-Peak	05 a/a	218	31	61	3	26	6	280			296	394	690	2	93	29	0.33					77		89	23%	3.95	-2.5	$7
Bats Right	06 SF	* 386	47	99	4	30	5	256	200	217	279	368	647	3	90	28	0.32	264	48	13	39	71	3%	80	14%	3.49	-12.7	$6
Reliability 12	07 SF	* 331	36	94	6	36	7	282	262	274	337	392	729	8	91	30	0.92	296	53	21	26	66	7%	65	12%	4.65	0.8	$9
BAvg Potl 65%	1st Half	166	19	49	2	17	3	295			354	404	757	8	89	32	0.83	289	56	18	26	70	5%	70	12%	5.01	2.1	$4
LIMA Plan D	2nd Half	165	17	45	4	19	4	270			320	380	700	7	93	27	1.06	301	51	22	27	62	10%	54	12%	4.30	-1.2	$4
+/- Score 6	08 Proj	356	42	98	5	36	7	275			312	385	698	5	91	29	0.62	296	52	20	28	69	6%	74	14%	4.17	-4.1	$9

5-31-.269 in 264 AB at SF. PRO: Nice growth in patience fed BA rise, which xBA supports. CON: Not much else here. Way below average in power and speed. Minimal value, even if ABs increase.

Freel,Ryan

		AB	R	H	HR	RBI	SB	Avg	vL	vR	OB	Slg	OPS	bb%	ct%	h%	Eye	xBA	G	L	F	PX	hr/f	SX	SBO	RC/G	RAR	R$
Pos 8	03 CIN	* 352	52	92	7	22	28	261	326	266	310	378	688	7	89	28	0.64	310	44	30	27	70	8%	138	42%	4.07	-9.6	$14
Age 32	04 CIN	505	74	140	3	28	37	277	235	290	362	368	730	12	83	33	0.76	263	50	20	29	58	2%	150	27%	4.84	2.8	$18
Past Peak	05 CIN	369	69	100	4	21	36	271	302	263	360	371	731	12	84	31	0.86	291	53	24	24	68	5%	149	37%	4.86	3.3	$17
Bats Right	06 CIN	454	67	123	8	27	37	271	303	261	352	399	751	11	78	33	0.58	261	44	21	35	89	6%	114	34%	4.99	7.4	$17
Reliability 28	07 CIN	277	44	68	3	16	15	245	143	315	292	347	638	6	83	29	0.38	260	49	18	33	66	4%	141	34%	3.38	-10.0	$7
BAvg Potl 50%	1st Half	179	29	45	2	12	8	251			309	363	672	8	84	29	0.54	272	49	20	31	68	4%	137	30%	3.93	-3.5	$4
LIMA Plan C	2nd Half	98	15	23	1	4	7	235			257	316	574	3	81	28	0.16	237	49	14	36	61	3%	123	45%	2.35	-6.7	$2
+/- Score -2	08 Proj	395	62	105	5	22	29	266			349	372	721	11	82	31	0.70	263	48	19	32	72	5%	127	31%	4.66	1.2	$14

Concussion and knee injury cost him 3 months. Problems with LHP and drop in bb% hampered BA. SX returned and SBO remained high, so SB will return if he gets healthy - a big IF, given recent history.

Fukudome,Kosuke

		AB	R	H	HR	RBI	SB	Avg	vL	vR	OB	Slg	OPS	bb%	ct%	h%	Eye	xBA	G	L	F	PX	hr/f	SX	SBO	RC/G	RAR	R$
Pos 9	03 JPN	617	104	154	21	94	9	249			319	453	772	9	82	27	0.56					118		132	10%	5.13	-4.6	$19
Age 31	04 JPN	404	59	90	14	79	7	224			292	428	719	9	78	25	0.44					120		132	12%	4.44	-6.9	$11
Past Peak	05 JPN	612	99	158	17	100	12	257			338	434	772	11	80	30	0.62					115		126	10%	5.23	4.6	$20
Bats Left	06 JPN	578	114	162	19	101	10	281			349	485	834	10	85	30	0.69					123		133	8%	5.91	11.4	$22
Reliability 62	07 JPN	269	62	74	8	47	5	274			398	441	839	17	77	33	0.89					123		74	7%	6.43	11.3	$11
BAvg Potl 40%	1st Half	269	62	74	8	47	5	274			398	441	839	17	77	33	0.89					123		74	7%	6.43	11.3	$11
LIMA Plan B+	2nd Half	0	0	0	0	0	0	0							0													
+/- Score -31	08 Proj	515	97	134	16	89	9	260			349	447	796	12	80	30	0.68					121		121	9%	5.59	8.0	$18

Missed 2nd half after having bone fragments removed from elbow. Many will see power; also has good speed, but temper expectations for first season. His skills are being compared to those of Bobby Abreu.

Furcal,Rafael

		AB	R	H	HR	RBI	SB	Avg	vL	vR	OB	Slg	OPS	bb%	ct%	h%	Eye	xBA	G	L	F	PX	hr/f	SX	SBO	RC/G	RAR	R$
Pos 6	03 ATL	664	130	194	15	61	25	292	247	306	351	443	794	8	89	31	0.79	309	48	23	29	88	9%	163	14%	5.38	23.6	$27
Age 30	04 ATL	563	103	157	14	59	29	279	276	280	346	414	760	9	87	30	0.82	278	50	16	34	76	8%	139	20%	5.01	14.3	$23
Peak	05 ATL	616	100	175	12	58	46	284	288	280	350	429	778	9	87	31	0.79	302	47	24	30	86	8%	163	31%	5.27	23.1	$29
Bats Both	06 LA	654	113	196	15	63	37	300	324	293	370	445	815	10	85	33	0.74	290	50	21	29	83	9%	133	23%	5.70	24.8	$28
Reliability 73	07 LA	581	87	157	6	47	25	270	313	254	333	355	688	9	88	30	0.81	268	50	19	32	52	4%	116	17%	4.21	4.3	$16
BAvg Potl 60%	1st Half	282	34	76	1	27	7	270			335	348	683	9	89	30	0.88	271	49	20	31	50	1%	97	11%	4.24	2.3	$6
LIMA Plan B	2nd Half	299	53	81	5	20	18	271			331	361	692	8	88	29	0.75	265	50	17	32	53	6%	120	23%	4.19	2.0	$10
+/- Score -11	08 Proj	600	108	169	15	52	32	282			347	420	767	9	87	30	0.78	291	49	20	31	79	9%	138	22%	5.08	17.2	$24

Ankle slowed him down big time in 1st half, affecting all aspects of his game. 2nd half shows the good news: BPIs bounced back to 2006 levels. Expect a full recovery, and if he's REALLY back on track... UP: 20 HR too.

Garciaparra,Nomar

		AB	R	H	HR	RBI	SB	Avg	vL	vR	OB	Slg	OPS	bb%	ct%	h%	Eye	xBA	G	L	F	PX	hr/f	SX	SBO	RC/G	RAR	R$
Pos 35	03 BOS	658	120	198	28	105	19	301	357	281	340	524	864	6	91	30	0.64	300	33	20	47	119	10%	151	15%	5.95	10.4	$31
Age 34	04 2TM	326	55	103	10	44	4	316	240	329	365	494	859	7	91	33	0.83	303	34	24	42	101	8%	97	5%	6.02	4.6	$13
Past Peak	05 CHC	230	28	65	9	30	0	283	281	285	318	452	770	5	90	28	0.50	311	40	25	35	99	13%	26	0%	4.80	-5.1	$7
Bats Right	06 LA	469	82	142	20	93	3	303	341	294	360	505	865	8	94	29	1.40	312	38	20	42	107	11%	76	2%	6.15	1.9	$21
Reliability 11	07 LA	431	39	122	7	59	3	283	213	303	331	371	702	7	90	30	0.76	260	43	19	37	53	5%	40	3%	4.26	-16.3	$10
BAvg Potl 55%	1st Half	274	22	73	1	38	2	266			309	321	630	6	89	30	0.59	246	46	19	35	40	1%	40	4%	3.43	-17.2	$4
LIMA Plan D	2nd Half	157	17	49	6	21	1	312			368	459	827	8	92	31	1.17	283	39	21	40	76	10%	30	2%	5.67	0.3	$6
+/- Score -37	08 Proj	307	39	86	8	47	2	280			331	413	744	7	92	29	0.89	284	40	21	39	75	7%	62	3%	4.75	-8.3	$9

PRO: Only one DL stint. CON: Almost everything else. Still makes consistent contact, so batting eye is intact. It just seems like all his strength is suddenly gone. Where did it go? Where did it go?

Garko,Ryan

		AB	R	H	HR	RBI	SB	Avg	vL	vR	OB	Slg	OPS	bb%	ct%	h%	Eye	xBA	G	L	F	PX	hr/f	SX	SBO	RC/G	RAR	R$
Pos 3	03	0	0	0	0	0	0	0							0									0				
Age 27	04 a/a	192	25	57	4	34	1	297			341	438	779	6	86	33	0.48					93		48	2%	5.06	-2.2	$6
Peak	05 aaa	452	58	119	13	59	1	263			315	409	724	7	84	29	0.46					93		52	4%	4.38	-12.8	$11
Bats Right	06 CLE	* 549	69	137	20	100	4	250	333	281	321	413	734	9	81	28	0.56	259	42	17	41	102	11%	43	6%	4.58	-13.7	$14
Reliability 47	07 CLE	484	62	140	21	61	0	289	310	281	336	483	819	7	81	32	0.36	276	38	19	44	125	12%	34	1%	5.45	4.8	$15
BAvg Potl 40%	1st Half	216	30	63	9	29	0	292			335	463	798	6	80	33	0.32	266	39	20	40	105	13%	51	2%	5.13	0.3	$7
LIMA Plan C	2nd Half	268	32	77	12	32	0	287			337	500	837	7	81	32	0.40	282	36	17	46	141	12%	19	0%	5.70	4.5	$8
+/- Score -8	08 Proj	519	71	148	24	91	1	285			338	489	827	7	82	31	0.44	281	38	18	44	127	13%	45	3%	5.56	5.6	$18

BPIs held up well in first full season. xBA, PX, FB% all jumped in 2H, signalling more power is yet to come. Already established as a lefty-killer (.913 OPS), but has potential to be a complete hitter.

Gathright,Joey

		AB	R	H	HR	RBI	SB	Avg	vL	vR	OB	Slg	OPS	bb%	ct%	h%	Eye	xBA	G	L	F	PX	hr/f	SX	SBO	RC/G	RAR	R$
Pos 7	03 aa	85	11	31	0	5	11	365			400	376	776	6	84	44	0.36					10		100	40%	4.90	-1.3	$6
Age 27	04 a/a	362	51	112	0	14	39	309			357	356	714	7	81	38	0.39					36		128	48%	4.30	-9.4	$17
Peak	05 TAM	* 429	62	114	1	26	42	266	353	269	315	336	651	7	83	32	0.42	289	72	15	13	47	2%	160	46%	3.59	-14.6	$16
Bats Left	06 2AL	383	59	91	1	41	22	238	232	239	313	292	605	10	80	29	0.56	261	67	16	17	38	2%	129	26%	3.13	-24.2	$9
Reliability 37	07 KC	* 451	61	132	0	37	27	292	282	312	367	341	707	11	87	34	0.90	298	65	23	12	36	0%	102	26%	4.56	-2.1	$15
BAvg Potl 55%	1st Half	233	39	73	0	24	23	313			414	378	792	15	89	35	1.54	318	70	21	9	46	0%	121	30%	5.87	7.5	$12
LIMA Plan D+	2nd Half	218	22	59	0	13	4	270			311	301	612	6	85	32	0.40	276	64	23	12	25	0%	62	20%	3.06	-10.9	$3
+/- Score 0	08 Proj	351	48	96	0	28	23	274			337	328	665	9	84	33	0.60	281	67	19	14	38	1%	118	31%	3.89	-10.4	$11

0-19-.307 with 9 SB in 228 AB at KC. Starting to look like a AAAA talent. After callup, xBA only.232, bb% cut by half. SX also plummeted, with 8 CS. Running out of chances to show he can do it on the big stage.

DAVE ADLER

German,Esteban			AB	R	H	HR	RBI	SB	Avg	vL	vR	OB	Slg	OPS	bb%	ct%	h%	Eye	xBA	G	L	F	PX	hr/f	SX	SBO	RC/G	RAR	R$
Pos	45	03 aaa	467	68	124	2	41	26	266			329	338	667	9	88	30	0.81					46		133	25%	4.01	-3.6	$14
Age	30	04 OAK	* 291	34	80	2	28	14	275	167	271	317	344	661	6	88	31	0.50	274	67	13	20	40	4%	124	20%	3.71	-3.1	$8
Peak		05 aaa	489	68	128	4	46	29	262			323	348	671	8	89	29	0.81					56		132	26%	4.03	-4.5	$16
Bats	Right	06 KC	279	44	91	3	34	7	326	347	311	411	459	869	13	82	39	0.82	290	58	18	24	86	6%	113	10%	6.62	18.7	$10
Reliability	10	07 KC	348	49	92	4	37	11	264	277	255	345	376	722	11	83	31	0.72	276	52	20	27	71	5%	116	16%	4.68	5.7	$9
BAvg Potl	55%	1st Half	189	23	47	2	23	5	249			336	349	686	12	82	29	0.74	266	54	18	28	69	5%	96	14%	4.26	0.7	$4
LIMA Plan	C	2nd Half	159	26	45	2	14	6	283			356	409	765	10	84	33	0.69	285	51	22	27	74	6%	127	20%	5.17	4.8	$5
+/- Score	-1	08 Proj	**372**	**55**	**105**	**4**	**39**	**14**	**282**			**357**	**394**	**751**	**10**	**84**	**33**	**0.74**	**284**	**55**	**19**	**26**	**71**	**5%**	**125**	**17%**	**5.03**	**9.7**	**$11**

Let's assemble a great player - combine ct% and SX/SBO from 2003-05 with bb% from 2006/07. BA drop was no surprise due to inflated 2006 h%. Stable BPIs, and keeps the ball on ground. If old SBO returns... UP: 20 SB

Giambi,Jason			AB	R	H	HR	RBI	SB	Avg	vL	vR	OB	Slg	OPS	bb%	ct%	h%	Eye	xBA	G	L	F	PX	hr/f	SX	SBO	RC/G	RAR	R$
Pos	0	03 NYY	535	97	134	41	107	2	250	192	272	396	527	923	19	74	26	0.92	283	27	20	53	176	20%	38	2%	7.42	44.2	$23
Age	37	04 NYY	264	33	55	12	40	0	208	263	185	328	379	707	15	77	23	0.76	212	41	9	50	104	12%	22	1%	4.39	-7.5	$4
Decline		05 NYY	417	74	113	32	87	0	271	261	276	421	535	956	21	74	29	0.99	278	33	19	48	167	22%	18	0%	7.92	22.6	$19
Bats	Left	06 NYY	446	92	113	37	113	2	253	213	270	401	558	959	20	76	25	1.04	293	30	16	53	185	20%	48	1%	7.84	18.4	$21
Reliability	23	07 NYY	254	31	60	14	39	1	236	239	235	340	433	773	14	74	26	0.61	240	30	16	53	127	14%	29	1%	5.18	-6.4	$6
BAvg Potl	50%	1st Half	149	19	39	7	23	1	262			368	436	804	14	77	30	0.71	244	29	19	52	111	12%	33	2%	5.65	-1.6	$4
LIMA Plan	D	2nd Half	105	12	21	7	16	0	200			300	429	729	12	70	21	0.48	231	32	12	55	151	17%	12	0%	4.49	-5.0	$2
+/- Score	-31	08 Proj	**293**	**45**	**70**	**18**	**55**	**1**	**239**			**363**	**459**	**823**	**16**	**74**	**26**	**0.76**	**251**	**31**	**16**	**53**	**141**	**16%**	**33**	**1%**	**5.96**	**-0.5**	**$9**

Foot injury split his year in half. Power returned in 2H, while h% hurt his BA. At 37, he's still good enough for the occasional HR, but he's running out of juice.

Gibbons,Jay			AB	R	H	HR	RBI	SB	Avg	vL	vR	OB	Slg	OPS	bb%	ct%	h%	Eye	xBA	G	L	F	PX	hr/f	SX	SBO	RC/G	RAR	R$
Pos	70	03 BAL	625	80	173	23	100	0	277	273	279	329	456	785	7	86	29	0.55	301	40	24	36	109	12%	36	1%	5.12	-3.8	$19
Age	31	04 BAL	346	36	85	10	47	1	246	257	241	304	379	683	8	82	28	0.45	237	46	13	40	80	9%	44	2%	3.87	-10.9	$6
Past Peak		05 BAL	488	72	135	26	79	0	277	250	286	316	516	832	5	89	27	0.50	307	37	17	47	138	13%	52	0%	5.51	11.0	$18
Bats	Left	06 BAL	343	34	95	13	46	0	277	258	281	339	458	796	9	86	29	0.67	265	38	16	46	109	10%	13	0%	5.32	1.4	$8
Reliability	27	07 BAL	270	28	62	6	28	0	230	283	219	270	348	618	5	81	26	0.29	248	40	19	41	82	7%	28	0%	2.98	-14.2	$3
BAvg Potl	50%	1st Half	182	19	38	3	15	0	209			265	324	589	7	80	24	0.39	247	39	19	42	87	5%	30	0%	2.77	-11.0	$0
LIMA Plan	D	2nd Half	88	9	24	3	13	0	273			281	398	679	1	82	30	0.06	249	42	20	38	74	11%	24	0%	3.37	-3.4	$2
+/- Score	-5	08 Proj	**331**	**36**	**86**	**11**	**44**	**0**	**260**			**300**	**414**	**714**	**5**	**84**	**28**	**0.36**	**262**	**40**	**18**	**42**	**96**	**10%**	**26**	**0%**	**4.14**	**-7.1**	**$7**

Depressed hit rate hurt him in 1st half; patience went out the window in 2nd half (one walk). Net result: BPIs were down across the board. Torn labrum and HGH allegations may impact whether he gets more chances.

Giles,Brian			AB	R	H	HR	RBI	SB	Avg	vL	vR	OB	Slg	OPS	bb%	ct%	h%	Eye	xBA	G	L	F	PX	hr/f	SX	SBO	RC/G	RAR	R$
Pos	9	03 2NL	492	93	147	20	88	4	299	286	305	422	514	936	18	88	31	1.81	309	34	23	43	125	11%	89	4%	7.58	26.9	$22
Age	37	04 SD	609	97	173	23	94	10	284	237	309	375	475	850	13	87	30	1.11	285	37	20	44	106	10%	106	7%	6.24	16.3	$24
Decline		05 SD	545	92	164	15	83	13	301	289	306	426	483	909	18	88	32	1.86	306	37	24	39	110	8%	111	8%	7.35	31.8	$24
Bats	Left	06 SD	604	87	159	14	83	9	263	217	282	371	397	769	15	90	27	1.73	270	40	18	43	79	6%	63	6%	5.53	13.4	$16
Reliability	17	07 SD	483	72	131	13	51	4	271	241	286	356	416	773	12	87	29	1.05	275	40	19	40	87	8%	60	7%	5.31	0.8	$12
BAvg Potl	65%	1st Half	170	23	47	1	12	1	276			339	347	686	9	91	30	1.00	259	45	19	36	50	2%	50	2%	4.27	-4.7	$3
LIMA Plan	B	2nd Half	313	49	84	12	39	3	268			366	454	819	13	86	28	1.07	284	38	19	43	109	10%	63	9%	5.89	5.9	$9
+/- Score	-29	08 Proj	**441**	**67**	**119**	**12**	**55**	**3**	**270**			**369**	**422**	**791**	**14**	**88**	**28**	**1.34**	**281**	**39**	**20**	**41**	**90**	**7%**	**62**	**5%**	**5.67**	**6.7**	**$12**

Follow the agonizing decline of some solid BPIs. 1st half was brutal but then he looked like a different (younger) player after the break. Still, age never regresses and knee injury puts the start of 2008 in question.

Giles,Marcus			AB	R	H	HR	RBI	SB	Avg	vL	vR	OB	Slg	OPS	bb%	ct%	h%	Eye	xBA	G	L	F	PX	hr/f	SX	SBO	RC/G	RAR	R$
Pos	4	03 ATL	551	101	174	21	69	14	316	283	325	382	526	908	10	85	34	0.74	315	41	21	38	135	12%	106	11%	6.74	34.9	$27
Age	29	04 ATL	379	61	118	8	48	17	311	402	282	371	443	814	9	82	37	0.51	270	42	22	35	86	7%	116	17%	5.60	10.3	$17
Peak		05 ATL	577	104	168	15	63	16	291	304	289	362	461	823	10	81	34	0.59	281	41	19	40	117	8%	124	11%	5.81	20.2	$23
Bats	Right	06 ATL	550	87	144	11	60	10	262	229	273	337	387	724	10	81	31	0.59	264	42	22	36	82	7%	87	10%	4.58	-0.3	$14
Reliability	49	07 SD	420	52	96	4	39	10	229	237	225	302	317	618	9	80	28	0.54	244	44	20	36	61	3%	102	11%	3.27	-16.6	$6
BAvg Potl	55%	1st Half	288	44	74	4	29	7	257			329	358	687	10	81	31	0.56	256	43	21	36	73	5%	77	12%	4.11	-3.8	$7
LIMA Plan	D+	2nd Half	132	8	22	0	10	3	167			241	227	469	9	80	21	0.48	217	45	18	37	34	0%	105	10%	1.39	-13.7	($1)
+/- Score	19	08 Proj	**411**	**54**	**99**	**8**	**41**	**10**	**241**			**314**	**370**	**684**	**10**	**81**	**28**	**0.55**	**260**	**43**	**20**	**37**	**83**	**7%**	**109**	**11%**	**4.06**	**-6.2**	**$8**

Not an ideal performance for a contract push. Power, low all year, completely disappeared in 2nd half (5 XBH). Some rebound is conceivable, but three-year PX and xBA trends paint a very gloomy picture.

Glaus,Troy			AB	R	H	HR	RBI	SB	Avg	vL	vR	OB	Slg	OPS	bb%	ct%	h%	Eye	xBA	G	L	F	PX	hr/f	SX	SBO	RC/G	RAR	R$
Pos	5	03 ANA	319	53	79	16	50	7	248	303	226	342	464	806	13	77	27	0.63	278	35	22	43	137	15%	100	10%	5.63	10.6	$11
Age	31	04 ANA	207	47	52	18	42	2	251	242	255	349	575	924	13	75	25	0.60	305	39	16	45	196	26%	88	9%	7.07	13.4	$10
Past Peak		05 ARI	538	78	139	37	97	4	258	244	263	359	522	881	14	73	29	0.58	282	37	17	46	177	20%	54	4%	6.66	29.5	$22
Bats	Right	06 TOR	540	105	136	38	104	3	252	292	238	355	513	868	14	75	27	0.64	275	34	17	49	162	19%	55	3%	6.40	22.1	$21
Reliability	75	07 TOR	385	60	101	20	62	0	262	361	235	363	473	836	14	74	31	0.60	267	34	21	45	142	16%	35	1%	6.11	18.0	$12
BAvg Potl	45%	1st Half	189	34	53	11	35	0	280			382	524	906	14	77	31	0.70	291	38	19	43	163	18%	33	2%	6.98	13.3	$8
LIMA Plan	C	2nd Half	196	26	48	9	27	0	245			345	423	769	13	70	30	0.52	244	29	24	47	121	14%	40	0%	5.23	4.2	$5
+/- Score	-22	08 Proj	**480**	**80**	**123**	**27**	**82**	**0**	**256**			**357**	**476**	**833**	**14**	**74**	**29**	**0.60**	**265**	**34**	**19**	**46**	**145**	**16%**	**42**	**1%**	**6.04**	**19.5**	**$16**

Value continues to be power-driven; low ct% ensures low BA. While he only spent a month on the DL, his foot bothered him all year. These nagging injuries and 3-year slide in xBA and PX increase the risk going forward.

Gload,Ross			AB	R	H	HR	RBI	SB	Avg	vL	vR	OB	Slg	OPS	bb%	ct%	h%	Eye	xBA	G	L	F	PX	hr/f	SX	SBO	RC/G	RAR	R$
Pos	3	03 aaa	508	60	143	17	58	5	281			316	467	783	5	89	29	0.47					109		82	7%	5.01	-6.3	$15
Age	32	04 CHW	234	28	75	7	44	0	321	425	299	374	479	853	8	84	36	0.54	294	39	25	35	100	10%	22	4%	5.96	6.2	$9
Past Peak		05 aaa	236	34	73	13	34	0	308			353	555	909	6	86	32	0.50					149		44	2%	6.45	7.1	$10
Bats	Left	06 CHW	156	22	51	3	18	6	327	308	333	352	462	813	4	90	35	0.40	306	51	21	27	76	8%	121	14%	5.29	-0.5	$6
Reliability	15	07 KC	320	37	92	7	51	2	288	388	269	321	441	762	5	88	31	0.41	301	50	19	31	97	8%	74	5%	4.79	-2.7	$9
BAvg Potl	55%	1st Half	95	12	27	2	17	2	284			320	442	762	5	87	31	0.42	304	58	15	26	93	9%	111	13%	4.82	-0.7	$3
LIMA Plan	D	2nd Half	225	25	65	5	34	0	289			322	440	762	5	88	31	0.41	298	46	20	33	99	8%	44	2%	4.78	-2.0	$6
+/- Score	-13	08 Proj	**304**	**39**	**92**	**6**	**45**	**3**	**303**			**337**	**449**	**786**	**5**	**88**	**33**	**0.43**	**302**	**50**	**20**	**30**	**91**	**8%**	**87**	**6%**	**5.08**	**-0.9**	**$10**

Set career high in ABs and RBI which, given his skill set, is not a good thing. You can see how his BPIs tailed with the extra exposure. Has done fine vs LHP the past 2 years but only 88 AB vs them. Okay for a few bucks.

Gomes,Jonny			AB	R	H	HR	RBI	SB	Avg	vL	vR	OB	Slg	OPS	bb%	ct%	h%	Eye	xBA	G	L	F	PX	hr/f	SX	SBO	RC/G	RAR	R$
Pos	097	03 a/a	461	64	110	15	52	21	239			313	419	732	10	69	31	0.35					136		140	21%	4.74	-8.8	$14
Age	27	04 aaa	390	63	89	20	67	7	228			306	451	758	10	69	27	0.37					158		89	15%	5.00	0.1	$12
Peak		05 TAM	* 510	86	141	30	87	14	276	287	280	354	524	877	11	71	33	0.42	268	29	23	48	166	17%	118	14%	6.62	28.2	$24
Bats	Right	06 TAM	385	53	83	20	59	1	216	297	187	323	431	754	14	70	25	0.53	243	29	17	54	149	14%	44	6%	5.04	-7.4	$8
Reliability	14	07 TAM	* 391	54	97	18	56	16	247	313	218	326	451	777	10	64	34	0.32	232	26	21	53	163	14%	105	21%	5.58	10.3	$14
BAvg Potl	25%	1st Half	141	19	39	7	23	5	277			366	489	856	12	70	35	0.47	250	17	24	59	159	12%	62	14%	6.51	7.3	$6
LIMA Plan	C+	2nd Half	250	35	58	11	33	11	231			302	430	732	9	61	33	0.26	224	30	20	50	165	15%	120	26%	5.05	2.7	$8
+/- Score	-14	08 Proj	**404**	**58**	**98**	**20**	**61**	**11**	**243**			**328**	**454**	**782**	**11**	**67**	**31**	**0.39**	**241**	**27**	**20**	**53**	**156**	**14%**	**92**	**15%**	**5.49**	**6.4**	**$13**

17-49-.244-12 SB in 348 AB at TAM. Free-swinging ways lead to plenty of Ks; high FB gets the ball over the wall. Big jump in SX and SBO helps, but must hit RHP to break out. And there is little evidence he can do that.

Gomez,Carlos			AB	R	H	HR	RBI	SB	Avg	vL	vR	OB	Slg	OPS	bb%	ct%	h%	Eye	xBA	G	L	F	PX	hr/f	SX	SBO	RC/G	RAR	R$
Pos	79	03	0	0	0	0	0	0	0							0									0				
Age	22	04	0	0	0	0	0	0	0							0									0				
Growth		05	0	0	0	0	0	0	0							0									0				
Bats	Right	06 aa	430	54	122	6	48	42	283			326	410	736	6	80	34	0.31					84		148	46%	4.54	-8.4	$19
Reliability	0	07 NYM	* 265	34	65	4	23	26	245	254	212	301	336	637	7	83	28	0.46	238	45	16	39	58	5%	124	48%	3.37	-16.1	$9
BAvg Potl	50%	1st Half	229	31	60	4	22	22	262			316	367	683	7	82	30	0.44	243	43	17	40	68	5%	122	44%	3.91	-9.8	$9
LIMA Plan	D	2nd Half	36	3	5	0	1	4	139			205	139	344	8	86	16	0.60	202	50	14	36	0	0%	106	75%	0.10	-6.8	$0
+/- Score	10	08 Proj	**228**	**30**	**62**	**4**	**23**	**22**	**272**			**321**	**387**	**708**	**7**	**81**	**32**	**0.38**	**245**	**43**	**17**	**40**	**75**	**5%**	**139**	**45%**	**4.20**	**-7.6**	**$10**

2-12-.232-12 SB in 125 AB at NYM. Not impressed? What were YOU doing at 21? Solid speed skills, but no MLB team is going to give him the green light as often as he's gotten it. So temper the SB expectations.

DAVE ADLER

Gomez,Chris			AB	R	H	HR	RBI	SB	Avg	vL	vR	OB	Slg	OPS	bb%	ct%	h%	Eye	xBA	G	L	F	PX	hr/f	SX	SBO	RC/G	RAR	R$
Pos	35	03 MIN	175	14	44	1	15	2	251	251	252	280	354	635	4	93	27	0.54	296	48	22	30	61	2%	90	8%	3.51	-9.7	$2
Age	36	04 TOR	341	41	96	3	37	3	282	300	274	336	346	682	8	88	31	0.68	270	45	25	30	40	3%	63	5%	4.05	-9.1	$7
Decline		05 BAL	219	27	61	1	18	2	279	317	243	358	342	700	11	92	30	1.59	278	52	20	28	46	2%	49	4%	4.64	-2.8	$4
Bats	Right	06 BAL	132	14	45	2	17	1	341	333	345	374	439	813	5	92	36	0.64	286	51	21	28	61	6%	36	7%	5.38	-0.1	$5
Reliability	0	07 2AL	222	21	66	1	21	1	297	292	301	328	374	701	4	88	33	0.38	285	51	23	25	55	2%	50	5%	4.10	-6.1	$4
BAvg Potl	40%	1st Half	74	9	22	1	11	1	297			342	351	693	6	95	30	1.25	278	52	22	26	29	5%	49	8%	4.22	-1.8	$2
LIMA Plan	F	2nd Half	148	12	44	0	10	0	297			320	385	705	3	85	35	0.23	287	51	24	25	70	0%	46	3%	4.08	-4.1	$2
+/- Score	-19	08 Proj	**198**	**21**	**57**	**2**	**21**	**1**	**288**			**329**	**372**	**701**	**6**	**90**	**31**	**0.62**	**287**	**51**	**22**	**27**	**56**	**3%**	**56**	**6%**	**4.23**	**-5.4**	**$4**

BPIs support some BA value but AB history is instructive. At 36, versatility, experience and contact game keep him on MLB rosters. Lack of pop, speed and upside should keep him off of yours.

Gonzalez,Adrian			AB	R	H	HR	RBI	SB	Avg	vL	vR	OB	Slg	OPS	bb%	ct%	h%	Eye	xBA	G	L	F	PX	hr/f	SX	SBO	RC/G	RAR	R$
Pos	3	03 a/a	449	42	119	5	45	2	265			318	356	675	7	87	30	0.58					59		61	2%	3.93	-19.6	$7
Age	25	04 TEX *	499	55	144	13	77	1	289		286	334	435	769	6	88	31	0.58	271	34	20	46	87	6%	48	2%	4.93	-0.8	$14
Pre-Peak		05 TEX *	478	60	133	20	63	0	278	71	243	325	458	783	6	86	29	0.49	285	39	20	41	105	12%	40	0%	5.00	-1.3	$14
Bats	Left	06 SD	570	83	173	24	82	0	304	312	301	362	500	862	8	80	34	0.46	292	44	23	33	122	16%	35	1%	6.10	1.5	$21
Reliability	66	07 SD	646	101	182	30	100	0	282	263	290	347	502	849	9	78	32	0.46	283	37	19	44	143	14%	49	0%	6.02	7.6	$23
BAvg Potl	45%	1st Half	308	44	87	14	51	0	282			352	506	858	10	78	32	0.48	285	38	20	43	147	14%	49	0%	6.20	5.2	$11
LIMA Plan	D+	2nd Half	338	57	95	16	49	0	281			343	497	840	9	79	31	0.45	281	36	19	45	138	13%	50	0%	5.85	2.4	$12
+/- Score	13	08 Proj	**610**	**88**	**173**	**31**	**108**	**0**	**284**			**343**	**505**	**847**	**8**	**81**	**31**	**0.47**	**293**	**39**	**21**	**40**	**136**	**15%**	**45**	**0%**	**5.88**	**2.8**	**$23**

Hit our 30/100 upside target right on the screws. FB% rebound and rising PX trend validate power spike. Ct% trend suggests that another .300 BA may be unreachable. Pay for a 2007 repeat.

Gonzalez,Alex			AB	R	H	HR	RBI	SB	Avg	vL	vR	OB	Slg	OPS	bb%	ct%	h%	Eye	xBA	G	L	F	PX	hr/f	SX	SBO	RC/G	RAR	R$
Pos	6	03 FLA	528	52	135	18	77	0	256	274	251	299	443	743	6	80	29	0.31	271	35	20	45	121	9%	54	4%	4.55	6.8	$12
Age	31	04 FLA	561	67	130	23	79	3	232	278	220	267	419	686	5	78	26	0.21	247	33	16	51	118	10%	79	4%	3.71	-7.1	$12
Past Peak		05 FLA	435	45	115	5	45	5	264	216	277	313	368	681	7	81	32	0.38	241	37	18	45	80	3%	57	7%	3.90	-0.8	$9
Bats	Right	06 BOS	388	48	99	9	50	1	255	278	244	295	397	692	5	83	29	0.33	261	37	20	43	91	6%	68	1%	3.93	-5.4	$7
Reliability	58	07 CIN	393	55	107	16	55	0	272	234	287	314	468	782	6	81	30	0.32	284	34	22	44	125	12%	43	1%	4.97	11.4	$11
BAvg Potl	45%	1st Half	272	37	70	12	37	0	257			286	460	746	4	82	27	0.23	284	35	21	44	124	12%	53	2%	4.40	3.5	$7
LIMA Plan	D	2nd Half	121	18	37	4	18	0	306			373	488	861	10	78	37	0.48	284	33	25	42	129	10%	27	0%	6.27	7.6	$4
+/- Score	-11	08 Proj	**304**	**39**	**82**	**9**	**41**	**0**	**270**			**318**	**435**	**753**	**7**	**81**	**31**	**0.36**	**269**	**35**	**21**	**44**	**110**	**8%**	**51**	**1%**	**4.71**	**5.5**	**$8**

Showed good pop, marginal BA profile again in healthy 1st half. Injuries and bereavement time (sick child) sank 2nd half. His last issue-free year was '04.
UP: 20 HR from SS
DN: Extended DL time

Gonzalez,Andy			AB	R	H	HR	RBI	SB	Avg	vL	vR	OB	Slg	OPS	bb%	ct%	h%	Eye	xBA	G	L	F	PX	hr/f	SX	SBO	RC/G	RAR	R$
Pos	75	03	0	0	0	0	0	0	0							0									0				
Age	26	04 aa	112	18	19	3	8	1	170			238	277	514	8	86	17	0.63					60		86	4%	2.01	-11.6	$0
Pre-Peak		05 aa	430	39	103	4	49	5	239			315	309	624	10	82	28	0.63					50		53	8%	3.38	-21.5	$6
Bats	Right	06 aaa	402	44	105	6	47	15	261			331	368	699	9	82	30	0.59					75		71	21%	4.27	-11.3	$10
Reliability	7	07 CHW *	313	31	64	5	26	6	204	185	185	305	299	604	13	69	28	0.48	208	48	15	37	77	6%	64	13%	3.01	-17.1	$2
BAvg Potl	40%	1st Half	172	22	41	4	22	5	238			335	378	713	13	73	30	0.54					105		89	14%	4.55	-0.9	$4
LIMA Plan	F	2nd Half	141	9	23	1	4	1	161			269	202	471	13	64	24	0.41		48	15	37	37	3%		12%	0.94	-18.1	($2)
+/- Score	2	08 Proj	**142**	**14**	**30**	**2**	**12**	**3**	**211**			**299**	**297**	**596**	**11**	**75**	**27**	**0.51**	**216**	**48**	**15**	**37**	**65**	**5%**	**53**	**14%**	**2.90**	**-8.9**	**$1**

2-11-.185 in 189 AB at CHW. Budding journeyman without power, speed, or contact skills. He plays everywhere and could qualify at middle infield shortly after the season begins. But he still won't hit.

Gonzalez,Luis			AB	R	H	HR	RBI	SB	Avg	vL	vR	OB	Slg	OPS	bb%	ct%	h%	Eye	xBA	G	L	F	PX	hr/f	SX	SBO	RC/G	RAR	R$
Pos	7	03 ARI	579	92	176	26	104	5	304	223	354	401	532	933	14	88	31	1.40	321	40	21	40	135	13%	77	4%	7.28	27.0	$26
Age	40	04 ARI	379	69	98	17	48	2	259	244	266	371	493	865	15	85	27	1.17	291	36	16	48	137	11%	91	3%	6.55	12.4	$12
Decline		05 ARI	579	90	157	24	79	4	271	269	272	358	459	817	12	84	29	0.87	290	38	20	42	118	12%	59	3%	5.74	6.7	$20
Bats	Left	06 ARI	586	93	159	15	73	0	271	259	277	348	444	792	11	90	28	1.19	298	40	19	41	105	7%	44	1%	5.55	5.1	$15
Reliability	78	07 LA	464	70	129	15	68	6	278	317	267	356	433	789	11	88	29	1.00	280	42	19	39	89	9%	77	6%	5.41	1.0	$15
BAvg Potl	65%	1st Half	253	43	77	10	39	4	304			391	506	897	12	91	30	1.57	314	38	22	40	113	11%	88	5%	6.79	10.0	$11
LIMA Plan	D	2nd Half	211	27	52	5	29	2	246			312	346	658	9	84	27	0.61	233	48	14	38	59	7%	50	7%	3.67	-10.5	$4
+/- Score	-23	08 Proj	**361**	**55**	**93**	**10**	**50**	**1**	**258**			**339**	**404**	**743**	**11**	**87**	**27**	**0.97**	**275**	**41**	**18**	**40**	**89**	**8%**	**53**	**2%**	**4.92**	**-4.4**	**$9**

Ct% and Eye held up, but end is nearer than surface stats indicate. PX is in a free-fall. .413 Slg vs. RHP suggests regular AB might be elusive. At his age, across-the-board 2nd half plunge is scary.

Gordon,Alex			AB	R	H	HR	RBI	SB	Avg	vL	vR	OB	Slg	OPS	bb%	ct%	h%	Eye	xBA	G	L	F	PX	hr/f	SX	SBO	RC/G	RAR	R$
Pos	53	03	0	0	0	0	0	0	0							0									0				
Age	24	04	0	0	0	0	0	0	0							0									0				
Growth		05	0	0	0	0	0	0	0							0									0				
Bats	Left	06 aa	486	87	139	20	79	17	286			361	490	851	10	83	31	0.67					127		104	15%	6.09	11.6	$21
Reliability	3	07 KC	543	60	134	15	60	14	247	217	258	300	411	710	7	75	30	0.30	254	37	19	44	120	8%	100	15%	4.24	-4.2	$12
BAvg Potl	40%	1st Half	260	29	61	6	22	9	235			299	373	672	8	75	29	0.37	245	36	22	43	100	7%	107	17%	3.80	-5.5	$5
LIMA Plan	B	2nd Half	283	31	73	9	38	5	258			300	445	745	6	75	32	0.24	263	38	18	45	138	10%	86	12%	4.64	1.2	$7
+/- Score	13	08 Proj	**559**	**77**	**147**	**20**	**74**	**16**	**263**			**324**	**451**	**775**	**8**	**78**	**31**	**0.41**	**271**	**37**	**19**	**44**	**128**	**10%**	**103**	**15%**	**5.08**	**7.1**	**$18**

Rookie struggled with ct% and pitch selection. Aggressive 2nd half approach improved on wretched 1st half, but BA still lags power. SB success rate, 8 HR and 150 PX in Aug-Sept point to better days ahead.

Gotay,Ruben			AB	R	H	HR	RBI	SB	Avg	vL	vR	OB	Slg	OPS	bb%	ct%	h%	Eye	xBA	G	L	F	PX	hr/f	SX	SBO	RC/G	RAR	R$
Pos	4	03	0	0	0	0	0	0	0							0									0				
Age	25	04 KC *	556	78	154	10	74	8	277			340	408	748	9	85	31	0.65					79		93	12%	4.86	12.6	$15
Pre-Peak		05 KC *	392	48	87	7	40	2	222			279	339	618	7	85	25	0.52	244	38	16	46	78	5%	71	7%	3.23	-10.9	$4
Bats	Both	06 aaa	491	55	119	10	55	9	242			287	367	654	6	84	27	0.38					79		81	14%	3.53	-12.4	$9
Reliability	18	07 NYM *	272	35	74	6	34	4	272	194	318	338	412	750	9	80	32	0.49	284	46	24	29	97	9%	68	11%	4.84	2.2	$7
BAvg Potl	50%	1st Half	136	18	35	5	22	2	257			340	441	781	11	83	28	0.74	306	48	24	29	112	15%	74	8%	5.29	2.9	$4
LIMA Plan	F	2nd Half	136	17	39	1	12	2	287			336	382	718	7	76	37	0.31	261	46	25	30	80	3%	55	13%	4.38	-0.7	$3
+/- Score	-20	08 Proj	**161**	**20**	**42**	**3**	**19**	**2**	**261**			**318**	**393**	**711**	**8**	**82**	**30**	**0.46**	**275**	**44**	**22**	**33**	**88**	**7%**	**76**	**11%**	**4.31**	**-1.2**	**$4**

4-24-.295 in 190 AB at NYM. Decent BPIs for growth-year MI.
PRO: LD pop; .318/.367/.467 vs. RHP.
CON: GB% limits power; defensive issues cap upside. Watch list material.

Graffanino,Tony			AB	R	H	HR	RBI	SB	Avg	vL	vR	OB	Slg	OPS	bb%	ct%	h%	Eye	xBA	G	L	F	PX	hr/f	SX	SBO	RC/G	RAR	R$
Pos	45	03 CHW	250	51	65	7	23	8	260	303	176	325	428	753	9	85	28	0.65	303	41	26	32	102	10%	148	13%	4.89	5.4	$8
Age	35	04 KC	278	37	73	3	26	10	263	265	262	328	335	662	9	86	30	0.71	251	46	19	35	47	4%	88	14%	3.86	-1.8	$7
Decline		05 2AL	379	68	117	7	38	7	309	297	317	361	425	786	8	87	34	0.61	290	50	22	28	72	8%	109	7%	5.20	11.1	$14
Bats	Right	06 2TM	456	68	125	7	59	5	274	275	274	339	406	745	9	85	31	0.66	268	41	19	40	86	4%	83	7%	4.86	6.6	$11
Reliability	39	07 MIL	231	34	55	9	30	0	238	231	243	310	390	699	9	81	26	0.55	243	43	15	42	90	11%	37	2%	4.11	-3.2	$5
BAvg Potl	55%	1st Half	159	19	40	6	19	0	252			312	396	708	8	80	28	0.44	235	47	14	40	87	12%	29	2%	4.13	-2.0	$3
LIMA Plan	F	2nd Half	72	15	15	3	11	0	208			305	375	680	12	83	21	0.83	256	36	17	47	98	11%	56	0%	4.06	-1.1	$2
+/- Score	-28	08 Proj	**63**	**11**	**16**	**2**	**8**	**1**	**254**			**325**	**387**	**713**	**10**	**84**	**28**	**0.65**	**260**	**42**	**18**	**40**	**83**	**9%**	**60**	**5%**	**4.38**	**-0.3**	**$2**

Utility player with a little pop. Underwent two surgeries in September and December, the latter for a torn ACL in right knee. MLB return in late July at best. 2008 could be a lost year. Avoid.

Granderson,Curtis			AB	R	H	HR	RBI	SB	Avg	vL	vR	OB	Slg	OPS	bb%	ct%	h%	Eye	xBA	G	L	F	PX	hr/f	SX	SBO	RC/G	RAR	R$
Pos	8	03	0	0	0	0	0	0	0							0									0				
Age	27	04 aa	462	75	122	16	79	12	265			354	433	787	12	82	29	0.78					93		118	14%	5.42	10.1	$17
Peak		05 DET *	607	87	167	20	77	20	275	364	257	332	488	820	8	75	34	0.34	279	48	17	35	137	12%	137	19%	5.77	26.2	$22
Bats	Left	06 DET	596	90	155	19	68	8	260	218	274	334	438	772	10	71	34	0.38	251	39	22	39	122	12%	116	8%	5.28	10.8	$15
Reliability	27	07 DET	612	122	185	23	74	26	302	160	337	357	552	909	8	77	36	0.37	285	34	21	45	158	11%	165	18%	6.89	43.8	$29
BAvg Potl	30%	1st Half	296	56	87	10	40	9	294			347	564	911	8	76	36	0.33	292	35	19	46	175	10%	151	14%	7.03	22.5	$12
LIMA Plan	B+	2nd Half	316	66	98	13	34	17	310			366	541	907	8	78	36	0.41	280	33	23	44	142	12%	163	20%	6.78	21.4	$17
+/- Score	3	08 Proj	**615**	**108**	**173**	**22**	**76**	**20**	**281**			**345**	**496**	**841**	**9**	**76**	**34**	**0.40**	**271**	**36**	**21**	**42**	**137**	**11%**	**148**	**15%**	**6.06**	**28.7**	**$24**

PRO: Year-long consistency of PX and SX spikes; three-year FB trend; only 1 CS.
CON: BA unsustainable without further ct% gains and significant turnaround vs. LHP. Pay for 20-20 repeat but not much more.

JOCK THOMPSON

Greene,Khalil

		Year	AB	R	H	HR	RBI	SB	Avg	vL	vR	OB	Slg	OPS	bb%	ct%	h%	Eye	xBA	G	L	F	PX	hr/f	SX	SBO	RC/G	RAR	R$
Pos	6	03 a/a	548	54	137	10	58	6	250			289	365	654	5	83	29	0.32					79		55	11%	3.47	-13.2	$9
Age	28	04 SD	484	67	132	15	65	4	273	291	266	345	446	791	10	81	31	0.56	263	36	18	45	110	8%	86	4%	5.37	17.2	$14
Peak		05 SD	436	51	109	15	70	5	250	200	267	291	431	722	5	79	29	0.27	273	33	22	44	124	10%	92	6%	4.25	3.7	$12
Bats	Right	06 SD	412	56	101	15	55	5	245	271	237	310	427	738	9	79	28	0.45	261	35	19	46	115	10%	83	6%	4.60	3.0	$10
Reliability	75	07 SD	611	89	155	27	97	4	254	268	249	291	468	759	5	79	28	0.25	276	35	18	47	139	12%	90	4%	4.66	12.5	$18
BAvg Potl	45%	1st Half	281	43	68	13	45	1	242			278	477	755	5	81	26	0.26	288	36	17	47	146	12%	94	2%	4.61	5.4	$8
LIMA Plan	C+	2nd Half	330	46	87	14	52	3	264			302	461	762	5	78	30	0.24	266	34	18	48	132	11%	64	4%	4.70	7.1	$10
+/- Score	16	08 Proj	600	81	156	23	89	4	260			306	454	761	6	79	29	0.32	269	35	19	46	126	11%	83	4%	4.76	11.9	$17

Durability and aggressiveness at prime age fueled career year. Eye and bb% suffered, hinting that BA upside is uphill from here; see 2005. But PX peak and FB level / stability point to another 20/90 season.

Green,Shawn

		Year	AB	R	H	HR	RBI	SB	Avg	vL	vR	OB	Slg	OPS	bb%	ct%	h%	Eye	xBA	G	L	F	PX	hr/f	SX	SBO	RC/G	RAR	R$
Pos	9	03 LA	611	84	171	19	85	6	280	252	295	352	460	812	10	82	32	0.61	299	48	20	32	122	12%	78	5%	5.65	0.7	$20
Age	35	04 LA	590	92	157	28	86	5	266	232	281	345	459	804	11	81	29	0.62	284	54	15	30	115	19%	65	4%	5.47	3.0	$20
Decline		05 ARI	581	87	166	22	73	8	286	226	309	355	477	831	10	84	31	0.65	304	51	18	31	120	15%	92	7%	5.81	9.2	$22
Bats	Left	06 2NL	530	73	147	15	66	4	277	267	282	334	432	766	8	85	30	0.55	288	54	18	28	93	12%	68	6%	4.95	2.7	$15
Reliability	71	07 NYM	446	62	130	10	46	11	291	195	326	346	430	776	8	86	32	0.60	295	54	18	28	90	9%	91	10%	5.10	-1.9	$14
BAvg Potl	50%	1st Half	223	34	63	7	27	5	283			336	453	789	7	86	30	0.58	297	53	16	31	105	12%	89	10%	5.21	-0.3	$8
LIMA Plan	D+	2nd Half	223	28	67	3	19	6	300			355	408	763	8	86	34	0.61	292	54	21	25	75	6%	73	9%	4.99	-1.6	$7
+/- Score	-7	08 Proj	321	45	92	9	37	6	287			346	439	785	8	85	32	0.60	294	53	18	28	97	11%	78	8%	5.21	0.6	$10

Power decline found BPI floor. But loss of regular AB further erodes counting stats and value. Sub-par power and a .195/.264/.288 line vs LHP likely seal his part-time status, wherever he ends up.

Griffey Jr.,Ken

		Year	AB	R	H	HR	RBI	SB	Avg	vL	vR	OB	Slg	OPS	bb%	ct%	h%	Eye	xBA	G	L	F	PX	hr/f	SX	SBO	RC/G	RAR	R$
Pos	9	03 CIN	166	34	41	13	26	1	247	250	245	352	566	919	14	73	26	0.61	322	37	25	39	212	28%	85	2%	7.18	7.7	$7
Age	38	04 CIN	300	49	76	20	60	1	253	198	286	349	513	862	13	78	26	0.66	284	37	16	47	160	18%	42	1%	6.27	8.6	$12
Decline		05 CIN	491	85	148	35	92	0	301	278	314	371	576	947	10	81	31	0.58	315	34	22	44	168	20%	29	1%	7.09	24.9	$26
Bats	Left	06 CIN	428	62	108	27	72	0	252	204	278	315	486	801	8	82	25	0.50	273	42	15	43	130	18%	25	0%	5.21	5.5	$14
Reliability	18	07 CIN	528	78	146	30	93	6	277	236	300	377	496	873	14	81	29	0.86	271	35	16	49	128	14%	63	4%	6.46	18.1	$21
BAvg Potl	55%	1st Half	256	43	75	21	49	2	293			386	578	965	13	82	29	0.83	295	35	16	50	159	20%	42	2%	7.42	15.4	$13
LIMA Plan	C+	2nd Half	272	35	71	9	44	4	261			368	419	787	14	81	29	0.88	248	36	16	48	99	8%	65	5%	5.54	2.3	$8
+/- Score	-9	08 Proj	432	66	117	24	76	3	271			358	493	850	12	81	29	0.70	277	37	17	46	132	15%	59	3%	6.08	11.5	$16

FB and bb% spikes, along with h% reversal drove strong follow-up to 2005-2006. All held up as PX crashed in 2nd half, citing fatigue and injury as the culprits. If you take on the risk, sell into mid-season strength.

Gross,Gabe

		Year	AB	R	H	HR	RBI	SB	Avg	vL	vR	OB	Slg	OPS	bb%	ct%	h%	Eye	xBA	G	L	F	PX	hr/f	SX	SBO	RC/G	RAR	R$
Pos	9	03 a/a	492	63	139	10	63	3	283			373	437	810	13	81	33	0.77					109		62	4%	5.84	6.4	$13
Age	28	04 aaa	377	44	106	8	46	3	281			358	430	788	11	82	33	0.66					102		47	8%	5.43	4.7	$10
Peak		05 TOR	* 482	62	130	6	44	12	270	91	272	341	391	732	10	82	32	0.59	245	30	21	49	88	3%	104	11%	4.74	0.5	$12
Bats	Left	06 MIL	208	42	57	9	38	1	274	95	294	381	476	857	15	71	35	0.60	264	34	23	42	143	14%	52	1%	6.61	10.9	$8
Reliability	20	07 MIL	* 259	39	67	11	33	5	258	91	244	351	470	822	13	80	28	0.74	285	39	20	41	128	13%	108	8%	5.87	4.7	$8
BAvg Potl	60%	1st Half	71	10	14	3	7	2	197			337	380	717	17	75	22	0.83	245	37	19	44	111	13%	99	9%	4.67	-1.3	$1
LIMA Plan	D	2nd Half	188	29	53	8	26	3	281			357	504	861	11	83	30	0.68	302	41	20	39	135	13%	102	8%	6.26	5.4	$7
+/- Score	21	08 Proj	213	33	56	8	28	3	263			359	450	808	13	78	31	0.68	270	37	21	42	121	11%	92	6%	5.76	3.8	$7

7-24-.235 in 183 AB at MIL. PX and bb% ticked down from 2007 surge, but remain solid. Unlucky 1H h% depressed BA as ct% actually improved. Still time for a power breakout. With 400 ABs... UP: 20 HR.

Grudzielanek,Mark

		Year	AB	R	H	HR	RBI	SB	Avg	vL	vR	OB	Slg	OPS	bb%	ct%	h%	Eye	xBA	G	L	F	PX	hr/f	SX	SBO	RC/G	RAR	R$
Pos	4	03 CHC	481	73	151	3	38	6	314	360	302	354	416	770	6	87	36	0.47	305	48	27	26	77	3%	87	6%	4.98	7.5	$15
Age	37	04 CHC	257	32	79	6	23	1	307	220	349	346	432	777	6	88	33	0.47	286	41	24	34	73	8%	56	3%	4.95	2.4	$8
Decline		05 STL	528	64	155	8	59	8	294	296	288	327	407	734	5	85	33	0.32	289	48	24	28	77	6%	85	10%	4.42	-2.1	$16
Bats	Right	06 KC	548	85	163	7	52	3	297	277	305	332	409	740	5	87	33	0.41	299	52	23	25	71	6%	88	3%	4.55	6.5	$14
Reliability	84	07 KC	453	70	137	6	51	1	302	321	294	336	426	762	5	87	34	0.38	287	49	19	31	85	5%	69	3%	4.80	8.4	$13
BAvg Potl	40%	1st Half	206	28	55	4	26	0	267			301	417	718	5	88	29	0.42	295	49	18	34	101	7%	53	0%	4.32	1.2	$4
LIMA Plan	D+	2nd Half	247	42	82	2	25	1	332			365	433	799	5	85	38	0.36	279	50	21	29	71	3%	78	4%	5.22	7.1	$8
+/- Score	-23	08 Proj	437	65	127	5	46	1	291			326	401	727	5	87	33	0.38	288	50	22	29	75	4%	78	3%	4.41	3.4	$10

Skills showed no ill-effects after returning from an early season knee injury. A perfect, draftable end-game infielder... no power, no speed, but a BA that won't hurt you and under-the-radar counting stats.

Guerrero,Vladimir

		Year	AB	R	H	HR	RBI	SB	Avg	vL	vR	OB	Slg	OPS	bb%	ct%	h%	Eye	xBA	G	L	F	PX	hr/f	SX	SBO	RC/G	RAR	R$
Pos	90	03 MON	394	71	130	25	79	9	330	393	313	422	586	1009	14	87	33	1.19	329	45	21	34	141	21%	90	10%	8.04	25.6	$25
Age	32	04 ANA	612	124	206	39	126	15	337	342	335	389	598	987	8	88	33	0.70	328	42	20	38	142	19%	107	10%	7.35	42.5	$37
Past Peak		05 ANA	520	95	165	32	108	13	317	313	319	389	565	954	10	91	30	1.27	329	44	17	39	135	18%	100	9%	7.17	34.5	$31
Bats	Right	06 LAA	607	92	200	33	116	15	329	401	307	381	552	932	8	89	33	0.74	313	44	19	37	121	16%	76	11%	6.73	17.4	$32
Reliability	92	07 LAA	574	89	186	27	125	2	324	321	325	398	547	945	11	89	33	1.15	315	48	16	36	133	15%	38	3%	7.19	38.2	$28
BAvg Potl	60%	1st Half	276	44	91	14	69	1	330			424	565	989	14	89	33	1.50	323	47	18	36	141	16%	30	3%	7.89	23.4	$15
LIMA Plan	B	2nd Half	298	45	95	13	56	1	319			373	530	904	8	89	32	0.81	309	50	14	36	126	14%	53	2%	6.52	14.5	$13
+/- Score	-19	08 Proj	577	93	182	29	109	3	315			382	539	921	10	89	31	1.00	314	46	17	37	128	16%	48	4%	6.80	28.6	$26

Strength, aggressiveness and an uncanny ct% for a power hitter drive his output. GB% creeping upward, a likely first sign of decay in Slg and HR. But for now, bet on a replay in 2008.

Guillen,Carlos

		Year	AB	R	H	HR	RBI	SB	Avg	vL	vR	OB	Slg	OPS	bb%	ct%	h%	Eye	xBA	G	L	F	PX	hr/f	SX	SBO	RC/G	RAR	R$
Pos	63	03 SEA	388	63	107	7	52	4	276	265	280	361	394	756	12	84	32	0.81	275	43	24	33	76	7%	83	6%	5.10	7.5	$11
Age	32	04 DET	522	97	166	20	97	12	318	269	348	380	542	922	9	83	35	0.60	306	41	22	37	132	12%	134	11%	6.91	34.7	$25
Past Peak		05 DET	334	48	107	5	23	2	320	368	306	366	434	800	7	87	36	0.53	280	44	23	33	70	5%	82	5%	5.33	6.9	$10
Bats	Both	06 DET	543	100	174	19	85	20	320	291	332	399	519	918	12	84	35	0.82	297	42	20	38	122	11%	114	16%	7.01	38.6	$26
Reliability	38	07 DET	564	86	167	21	102	13	296	302	295	359	502	860	9	84	32	0.59	293	39	20	41	126	11%	112	13%	6.14	25.1	$24
BAvg Potl	45%	1st Half	246	45	80	12	56	5	325			394	577	971	10	86	34	0.82	331	42	21	36	149	16%	105	14%	7.48	19.6	$14
LIMA Plan	B	2nd Half	318	41	87	9	46	8	274			330	443	774	8	81	31	0.46	263	37	18	45	107	8%	114	13%	5.06	4.6	$10
+/- Score	9	08 Proj	553	94	169	23	95	13	306			370	516	886	9	84	33	0.64	300	41	20	39	126	13%	113	13%	6.44	29.7	$25

Played through late season injuries, stunting career year and 2nd half power. Health and BPIs should rebound and thrive now that he'll be manning 1B. Could produce CI numbers in final season of SS eligibility.

Guillen,Jose

		Year	AB	R	H	HR	RBI	SB	Avg	vL	vR	OB	Slg	OPS	bb%	ct%	h%	Eye	xBA	G	L	F	PX	hr/f	SX	SBO	RC/G	RAR	R$
Pos	9	03 2TM	485	77	151	31	86	1	311	315	310	344	569	913	5	80	33	0.25	320	45	23	32	156	25%	53	4%	6.40	13.5	$24
Age	31	04 ANA	565	88	166	27	104	5	294	299	292	337	497	835	6	84	31	0.40	295	47	18	34	116	17%	80	6%	5.56	13.5	$23
Past Peak		05 WAS	551	81	156	24	76	1	283	215	303	321	479	800	5	81	31	0.30	297	44	22	34	124	16%	61	2%	5.14	-1.8	$20
Bats	Right	06 WAS	241	28	52	9	40	1	216	200	221	262	398	660	6	80	23	0.31	257	41	14	45	113	10%	61	2%	3.50	-9.4	$4
Reliability	26	07 SEA	593	84	172	23	99	5	290	362	268	336	460	796	6	80	33	0.35	271	48	16	36	108	14%	75	4%	5.16	7.6	$21
BAvg Potl	40%	1st Half	257	35	66	9	41	1	257			310	412	723	7	79	29	0.37	258	40	19	41	104	11%	47	2%	4.31	-2.9	$7
LIMA Plan	C	2nd Half	336	49	106	14	58	4	315			356	497	853	6	81	36	0.33	281	54	14	32	112	16%	78	5%	5.79	9.9	$15
+/- Score	-26	08 Proj	592	82	161	24	97	4	272			316	454	770	6	81	30	0.33	276	46	17	37	114	14%	72	3%	4.81	-2.6	$19

Comeback season driven by good health, inflated 2nd half h%, and .362/.433/.616 vs LHP. GB spike troubling but in line with best HR years. Pedestrian BPIs say 2007 is his upside, pay for a little less in 2008.

Gutierrez,Franklin

		Year	AB	R	H	HR	RBI	SB	Avg	vL	vR	OB	Slg	OPS	bb%	ct%	h%	Eye	xBA	G	L	F	PX	hr/f	SX	SBO	RC/G	RAR	R$
Pos	9	03 aa	67	12	20	4	12	3	298			367	564	931	10	72	36	0.39					173		127	33%	7.32	3.8	$4
Age	25	04 a/a	289	36	77	4	33	5	265			313	400	712	6	75	34	0.28					105		83	14%	4.30	-5.9	$7
Pre-Peak		05 a/a	450	65	104	8	40	13	231			278	358	635	6	83	26	0.38					88		114	21%	3.33	-22.7	$9
Bats	Right	06 CLE	* 485	81	129	9	44	12	266	262	277	336	396	732	10	77	33	0.46	268	43	23	34	97	7%	83	15%	4.66	-14.3	$12
Reliability	20	07 CLE	* 400	66	113	16	50	14	283	330	232	329	463	792	7	76	34	0.29	259	43	15	42	120	13%	108	19%	5.17	5.3	$16
BAvg Potl	35%	1st Half	184	35	56	7	23	8	304			340	457	797	5	81	35	0.29	258	43	16	41	95	12%	98	21%	5.05	1.8	$9
LIMA Plan	D+	2nd Half	216	31	57	9	27	6	264			321	468	788	8	72	33	0.30	261	43	15	42	144	14%	107	18%	5.30	3.8	$7
+/- Score	-5	08 Proj	376	59	96	11	41	11	255			309	408	718	7	77	30	0.34	255	43	16	40	107	9%	98	19%	4.30	-7.4	$11

13-36-.266 in 271 AB at CLE. Toolsy OF with lots to prove. PRO: FB spike supports PX CON: Stagnant ct% and bb%; .232/.292/.429 vs. RHP. 1st half BA to xBA disconnect shows downside. Expect growing pains.

JOCK THOMPSON

Guzman,Cristian			AB	R	H	HR	RBI	SB	Avg	vL	vR	OB	Slg	OPS	bb%	ct%	h%	Eye	xBA	G	L	F	PX	hr/f	SX	SBO	RC/G	RAR	R$
Pos	6	03 MIN	534	78	142	3	53	18	266	268	276	305	363	668	5	85	31	0.38	270	50	21	29	54	2%	146	19%	3.77	-10.4	$14
Age	30	04 MIN	576	84	158	8	46	10	274	326	250	310	384	694	5	89	30	0.47	286	57	16	27	67	6%	104	10%	4.06	-6.6	$13
Peak		05 WAS	456	39	100	4	31	7	219	161	242	260	314	573	5	83	26	0.33	276	56	20	24	62	4%	106	11%	2.58	-19.4	$3
Bats	Both	06 WAS	0	0	0	0	0	0	0							0									0				
Reliability	0	07 WAS	174	31	57	2	14	2	328	357	318	381	466	846	8	88	36	0.71	299	60	17	23	72	6%	114	3%	6.02	9.5	$6
BAvg Potl	45%	1st Half	173	31	57	2	14	2	329			383	468	851	8	88	37	0.71	299	60	17	23	72	6%	114	3%	6.08	9.6	$6
LIMA Plan	F	2nd Half	1	0	0	0	0	0	0			0	0	0	0	100	0											-0.3	($0)
+/- Score	-68	08 Proj	197	28	55	2	16	3	279			322	393	715	6	87	31	0.49	287	57	18	25	65	5%	122	9%	4.36	1.6	$5

Good contact hitter with wild swings in hit rate his last two seasons. Has spent 304 days on the DL the past two years, but has enough speed to steal a few bags if given the oppty. Otherwise, at best an empty BA.

Guzman,Joel			AB	R	H	HR	RBI	SB	Avg	vL	vR	OB	Slg	OPS	bb%	ct%	h%	Eye	xBA	G	L	F	PX	hr/f	SX	SBO	RC/G	RAR	R$
Pos	5	03	0	0	0	0	0	0	0							0									0				
Age	23	04 aa	182	25	51	9	35	1	278			327	508	835	7	80	31	0.35					138		86	8%	5.68	3.6	$7
Growth		05 aa	439	54	112	14	63	6	256			309	414	723	7	77	30	0.34					110		72	10%	4.34	-3.9	$12
Bats	Right	06 aaa	424	46	111	12	59	8	261	143	250	309	404	713	6	83	29	0.41	257	41	18	41	85	8%	77	13%	4.20	-13.1	$11
Reliability	20	07 TAM	* 451	49	109	16	68	9	241	125	276	281	404	685	5	74	29	0.21	242	56	7	37	109	13%	101	12%	3.75	-10.1	$11
BAvg Potl	40%	1st Half	271	29	67	11	38	6	247			277	413	690	4	73	30	0.15					116		69	13%	3.72	-6.3	$7
LIMA Plan	F	2nd Half	180	20	42	5	30	3	232			288	389	677	7	76	28	0.32	241	56	7	37	98	9%	111	11%	3.81	-3.8	$4
+/- Score	10	08 Proj	197	23	49	6	30	3	249			296	413	709	6	78	29	0.30	250	56	7	37	105	11%	94	12%	4.12	-3.1	$5

0-4-.243 in 37 AB at TAM. Former LA prospect hit just .242 at AAA with a ton of strikeouts. At 23, there's still time, but there are better prospects further along the growth curve to invest in.

Gwynn,Tony			AB	R	H	HR	RBI	SB	Avg	vL	vR	OB	Slg	OPS	bb%	ct%	h%	Eye	xBA	G	L	F	PX	hr/f	SX	SBO	RC/G	RAR	R$
Pos	8	03	0	0	0	0	0	0	0							0									0				
Age	25	04 aa	534	73	126	2	36	33	236			303	300	602	9	83	28	0.55					44		130	32%	3.09	-26.4	$12
Pre-Peak		05 aa	505	65	117	1	32	24	232			313	286	599	10	88	26	0.94					38		108	27%	3.32	-17.4	$9
Bats	Left	06 MIL	* 524	71	145	4	42	30	277	167	268	329	361	690	7	82	33	0.44	268	50	23	27	54	3%	120	28%	4.05	-6.0	$16
Reliability	24	07 MIL	* 249	30	65	0	21	12	261	316	250	316	317	633	7	85	31	0.54	249	53	18	29	34	0%	125	21%	3.47	-8.0	$6
BAvg Potl	50%	1st Half	128	15	36	0	11	6	281			343	328	671	9	84	34	0.57	249	56	19	25	27	0%	109	23%	3.93	-2.4	$3
LIMA Plan	F	2nd Half	121	15	29	0	10	6	240			287	306	593	6	87	28	0.50	238	47	16	38	41	0%	139	19%	3.00	-5.6	$2
+/- Score	-9	08 Proj	194	25	51	0	15	10	263			321	322	643	8	85	31	0.55	249	52	18	30	38	1%	118	24%	3.57	-5.7	$5

0-10-.260 in 123 AB at MIL. Groundball hitter with good speed who could give you a few cheap steals. Just think, his best batting average is 117 points lower than Dad's.

Hafner,Travis			AB	R	H	HR	RBI	SB	Avg	vL	vR	OB	Slg	OPS	bb%	ct%	h%	Eye	xBA	G	L	F	PX	hr/f	SX	SBO	RC/G	RAR	R$
Pos	0	03 CLE	* 391	49	99	16	49	4	253	190	280	327	450	777	10	73	31	0.41	273	43	22	35	136	16%	82	6%	5.24	7.2	$10
Age	30	04 CLE	482	96	150	28	109	3	311	244	344	396	583	979	12	77	36	0.61	301	38	19	44	175	17%	82	3%	7.90	34.1	$25
Peak		05 CLE	486	94	148	33	108	0	305	269	319	402	595	996	14	75	35	0.64	316	43	20	37	201	25%	30	0%	8.26	29.6	$26
Bats	Left	06 CLE	454	100	140	42	117	0	308	321	300	433	659	1092	18	76	33	0.90	330	39	21	40	216	30%	37	0%	9.57	38.7	$28
Reliability	20	07 CLE	545	80	145	24	100	1	266	274	261	382	451	833	16	79	30	0.89	273	48	17	35	118	16%	44	1%	6.14	1.8	$18
BAvg Potl	55%	1st Half	259	46	67	12	51	1	259			398	448	846	19	78	29	1.07	275	48	18	34	116	17%	64	1%	6.45	3.2	$9
LIMA Plan	C+	2nd Half	286	34	78	12	49	0	273			366	455	820	13	79	31	0.71	263	48	17	35	119	15%	17	1%	5.82	-1.6	$9
+/- Score	7	08 Proj	504	86	147	30	104	1	292			400	537	938	15	77	33	0.79	295	44	19	37	158	21%	42	1%	7.45	20.1	$22

Power suffered with big jump in GB%. That, and deflated h% were BA killers for a low-contact hitter with no speed. Was his old self in September. (.306 xBA, 156 PX), but that's not enough to predict a full rebound.

Hairston,Jerry			AB	R	H	HR	RBI	SB	Avg	vL	vR	OB	Slg	OPS	bb%	ct%	h%	Eye	xBA	G	L	F	PX	hr/f	SX	SBO	RC/G	RAR	R$
Pos	87	03 BAL	218	25	59	2	21	14	271	255	276	340	372	712	10	89	30	0.92	273	37	24	39	65	3%	112	29%	4.58	-1.0	$7
Age	31	04 BAL	287	43	87	2	24	13	303	316	296	367	397	764	9	90	33	1.00	271	37	23	40	64	2%	100	22%	5.18	3.9	$10
Past Peak		05 CHC	380	51	99	4	30	8	261	255	263	316	368	685	8	88	29	0.67	285	43	22	34	75	4%	92	17%	4.13	-4.9	$8
Bats	Right	06 2TM	170	25	35	0	10	5	206	153	245	262	253	515	7	80	26	0.38	212	42	17	41	36	0%	119	17%	1.87	-14.4	$1
Reliability	16	07 TEX	159	22	30	3	16	5	189	228	150	241	289	530	6	85	20	0.46	222	35	14	52	66	4%	100	19%	2.13	-11.0	$2
BAvg Potl	65%	1st Half	86	16	21	3	9	2	244			293	395	689	7	85	26	0.46	266	38	18	44	93	9%	90	15%	3.91	-1.0	$2
LIMA Plan	F	2nd Half	73	6	9	0	7	3	123			179	164	344	6	85	15	0.45	166	31	8	61	35	0%	95	27%	0.03	-10.7	($1)
+/- Score	25	08 Proj	112	15	23	1	10	4	205			261	278	539	7	85	23	0.49	223	37	16	46	52	2%	90	20%	2.29	-7.6	$1

Those G/L/F splits are bad news for someone with no power and decent speed. Too many fly outs. Used to have a good line-drive bat, but without it, value is nil.

Hairston,Scott			AB	R	H	HR	RBI	SB	Avg	vL	vR	OB	Slg	OPS	bb%	ct%	h%	Eye	xBA	G	L	F	PX	hr/f	SX	SBO	RC/G	RAR	R$
Pos	7	03 a/a	337	40	85	8	36	5	252			300	415	715	6	83	28	0.40					101		114	9%	4.31	-11.5	$7
Age	27	04 ARI	* 454	59	116	17	43	3	256	307	223	300	458	758	6	78	30	0.28	265	38	19	44	123	11%	99	10%	4.76	-9.2	$11
Peak		05 ARI	* 229	31	59	12	28	2	259	182		305	471	776	6	85	26	0.43		29	7	64	119	9%	87	4%	4.85	-3.2	$7
Bats	Right	06 aaa	396	64	116	20	63	2	292	375	429	358	510	868	9	83	31	0.62		50	30	20	126	31%	62	2%	6.15	10.3	$16
Reliability	3	07 2NL	263	37	64	11	36	2	243	235	247	311	452	764	9	79	27	0.47	265	34	15	50	134	10%	79	3%	4.95	-3.0	$7
BAvg Potl	55%	1st Half	133	19	31	3	12	1	233			315	383	699	11	79	27	0.57	257	36	20	44	103	7%	77	3%	4.30	-4.2	$2
LIMA Plan	C	2nd Half	130	18	33	8	24	1	254			307	523	830	7	79	26	0.37	277	32	11	57	166	14%	75	4%	5.60	1.0	$5
+/- Score	39	08 Proj	390	56	102	18	55	3	262			322	476	798	8	81	28	0.47	267	34	15	51	129	11%	82	4%	5.28	-0.6	$12

Power in search of an opportunity. High PX and FB are bullish for his HR potential, but batting eye will keep his average down.
UP: 30 HR, .275 BA

Hall,Bill			AB	R	H	HR	RBI	SB	Avg	vL	vR	OB	Slg	OPS	bb%	ct%	h%	Eye	xBA	G	L	F	PX	hr/f	SX	SBO	RC/G	RAR	R$
Pos	8	03 MIL	* 496	75	131	10	49	10	264	185	278	307	403	711	6	80	31	0.31	281	48	22	30	98	8%	99	21%	4.19	-11.7	$13
Age	28	04 MIL	394	44	95	10	55	13	241	190	256	278	383	661	5	70	32	0.17	237	43	20	37	104	10%	116	23%	3.53	-13.5	$10
Peak		05 MIL	501	69	146	17	62	18	291	328	277	343	495	838	7	79	34	0.38	301	43	23	34	138	12%	124	20%	5.83	18.0	$21
Bats	Right	06 MIL	537	101	145	35	85	8	270	300	261	347	553	900	11	70	32	0.39	279	33	19	48	192	19%	92	13%	7.01	40.4	$23
Reliability	38	07 MIL	452	59	115	14	63	4	254	270	247	315	425	740	8	72	33	0.31	259	36	23	41	131	10%	50	8%	4.72	2.1	$11
BAvg Potl	40%	1st Half	266	38	72	9	35	2	271			340	455	795	10	74	33	0.41	276	39	23	39	135	12%	45	9%	5.47	7.1	$8
LIMA Plan	C	2nd Half	186	21	43	5	28	2	231			278	382	659	6	68	31	0.20	236	31	23	46	123	9%	56	8%	3.60	-5.4	$3
+/- Score	-22	08 Proj	451	65	117	17	64	7	259			318	457	775	8	72	32	0.31	265	36	22	42	143	13%	86	13%	5.17	8.2	$14

2006 was an outlier, but there are two other big changes since 2005: Dwindling ct% and SX/SBO. Without a decent batting average and double-digit steals, he won't retutn to the $20 level.

Hall,Toby			AB	R	H	HR	RBI	SB	Avg	vL	vR	OB	Slg	OPS	bb%	ct%	h%	Eye	xBA	G	L	F	PX	hr/f	SX	SBO	RC/G	RAR	R$
Pos	2	03 TAM	463	50	117	12	47	0	253	253	252	288	380	668	5	91	26	0.58	281	33	23	44	75	6%	29	1%	3.77	-4.4	$8
Age	32	04 TAM	404	35	103	8	60	0	255	294	242	297	366	663	6	90	27	0.59	243	40	15	44	67	5%	20	2%	3.75	-6.9	$7
Past Peak		05 TAM	432	28	124	5	48	0	287	302	281	313	368	681	4	91	31	0.41	256	41	21	39	54	3%	12	0%	3.84	-2.2	$8
Bats	Right	06 2TM	278	17	72	8	31	0	259	292	248	285	406	691	3	92	26	0.45	220	37	16	47	84	7%	0	4%	3.96	-3.4	$4
Reliability	17	07 CHW	116	8	24	0	3	0	207	288	141	227	241	468	3	90	23	0.25	221	41	17	41	28	0%	27	0%	1.46	-9.2	($1)
BAvg Potl	60%	1st Half	32	2	6	0	0	0	188			188	219	406	0	97	19	0.00	221	33	17	50	24	0%	31	0%	1.06	-3.0	($0)
LIMA Plan	F	2nd Half	84	6	18	0	3	0	214			241	250	491	3	87	25	0.27	221	45	18	38	30	0%	25	0%	1.64	-6.2	($1)
+/- Score	-1	08 Proj	134	10	34	2	12	0	254			283	341	624	4	90	27	0.40	247	40	18	42	56	4%	22	1%	3.22	-3.6	$1

Rehabbed torn labrum prior to season, but it clearly affected what little power he has. Whether 2008 brings improvement is the $1 question, but if he's stuck in backup duty, it won't matter. Bid limit: $0

Hamilton,Josh			AB	R	H	HR	RBI	SB	Avg	vL	vR	OB	Slg	OPS	bb%	ct%	h%	Eye	xBA	G	L	F	PX	hr/f	SX	SBO	RC/G	RAR	R$
Pos	8	03	0	0	0	0	0	0	0							0									0				
Age	26	04	0	0	0	0	0	0	0							0									0				
Pre-Peak		05	0	0	0	0	0	0	0							0									0				
Bats	Left	06	0	0	0	0	0	0	0							0									0				
Reliability	0	07 CIN	* 338	60	100	23	54	6	295	222	314	364	563	927	10	78	32	0.50	314	45	22	33	161	26%	88	10%	6.93	22.4	$17
BAvg Potl	50%	1st Half	207	35	57	16	30	5	275			364	560	925	12	77	28	0.62	314	45	21	34	169	30%	80	12%	7.00	14.6	$10
LIMA Plan	C+	2nd Half	131	25	43	7	24	1	325			364	567	930	6	80	37	0.30	314	45	23	33	149	20%	82	6%	6.76	7.7	$7
+/- Score	11	08 Proj	399	72	120	25	67	6	301			359	561	920	8	79	33	0.43	314	45	22	33	157	24%	91	8%	6.77	24.5	$20

19-47-.292 in 298 AB at CIN. Succession of ailments held him back all season. Excellent power, good line-drive bat, but can he stay healthy enough to get 500 AB? History says to bet against.

TOM TODARO

Hannahan,Jack

			AB	R	H	HR	RBI	SB	Avg	vL	vR	OB	Slg	OPS	bb%	ct%	h%	Eye	xBA	G	L	F	PX	hr/f	SX	SBO	RC/G	RAR	R$
Pos	5	03 aa	471	56	107	7	40	2	227			291	303	594	8	86	25	0.63					49		56	2%	2.98	-20.0	$5
Age	28	04 aa	374	40	86	6	32	6	229			306	325	631	10	86	25	0.79					61		70	8%	3.56	-16.3	$4
Peak		05 a/a	257	25	56	3	24	5	218			282	296	578	8	78	27	0.40					60		62	12%	2.59	-16.4	$2
Bats	Left	06 aaa	415	53	107	8	56	8	257			344	369	714	12	74	33	0.51					84		59	10%	4.51	-9.1	$10
Reliability	13	07 OAK	* 480	65	128	13	79	6	267	400	239	380	416	796	15	74	34	0.69	257	37	23	39	111	10%	55	6%	5.79	18.0	$14
BAvg Potl	40%	1st Half	219	37	65	8	43	4	297			414	457	871	17	78	35	0.90					108		50	9%	6.74	13.9	$9
LIMA Plan	F	2nd Half	261	28	63	5	36	2	243			351	382	733	14	70	32	0.56	247	37	23	39	114	8%	52	3%	4.96	3.5	$4
+/- Score	-12	08 Proj	153	19	39	3	21	2	255			349	371	721	13	75	32	0.59	246	37	23	39	86	7%	48	7%	4.63	-0.1	$3

3-24-.278 in 144 AB at OAK. Added some power in his third year at AAA, because, heck, players can peak at 27 no matter what their address is. But low contact rates don't translate to big-league success.

Hardy,J.J.

			AB	R	H	HR	RBI	SB	Avg	vL	vR	OB	Slg	OPS	bb%	ct%	h%	Eye	xBA	G	L	F	PX	hr/f	SX	SBO	RC/G	RAR	R$
Pos	6	03 aa	416	61	109	11	57	5	262			343	401	744	11	88	28	1.04					87		60	7%	4.94	8.2	$12
Age	25	04 aaa	101	15	27	4	18	0	270			320	489	808	7	93	26	1.10					125		34	0%	5.48	3.4	$3
Pre-Peak		05 MIL	372	46	92	9	50	0	247	245	240	327	384	711	11	87	26	0.92	282	44	20	35	88	8%	38	0%	4.54	6.3	$8
Bats	Right	06 MIL	128	13	31	5	14	1	242	294	223	297	398	696	7	82	26	0.43	265	47	19	34	90	14%	36	6%	3.96	-1.5	$2
Reliability	25	07 MIL	592	89	164	26	80	2	277	316	264	323	463	786	6	88	28	0.55	284	41	17	42	105	12%	50	3%	5.03	18.1	$19
BAvg Potl	55%	1st Half	292	44	82	18	50	0	281			340	510	850	8	84	28	0.57	282	37	17	47	129	16%	27	4%	5.79	15.3	$11
LIMA Plan	C	2nd Half	300	45	82	8	30	2	273			306	417	722	4	91	28	0.52	287	45	18	37	83	8%	75	3%	4.34	3.2	$8
+/- Score	11	08 Proj	584	78	163	17	74	2	279			331	420	751	7	87	30	0.59	271	44	18	38	84	9%	45	3%	4.74	11.1	$16

Discovered an uppercut swing in the 1st half and experienced a HR explosion. Discovered a higher contact rate in the 2nd half and returned to his ground ball hitting ways. Now the 1st half just looks like an aberration.

Harris,Brendan

			AB	R	H	HR	RBI	SB	Avg	vL	vR	OB	Slg	OPS	bb%	ct%	h%	Eye	xBA	G	L	F	PX	hr/f	SX	SBO	RC/G	RAR	R$
Pos	64	03 aa	435	51	110	5	48	6	252			326	377	703	10	83	29	0.65					86		91	11%	4.41	1.9	$8
Age	27	04 MON	* 436	55	114	14	47	0	261			297	431	728	5	87	27	0.39					103		42	4%	4.35	2.8	$10
Peak		05 aaa	470	49	106	9	58	7	225			270	331	601	6	88	24	0.51					64		78	12%	3.01	-18.2	$7
Bats	Right	06 CIN	* 409	55	110	11	54	4	269			329	421	750	8	80	31	0.44	224	37	9	54	101	6%	65	5%	4.79	5.0	$11
Reliability	17	07 TAM	521	72	149	12	59	4	286	345	264	339	434	773	7	82	33	0.44	280	43	21	35	102	8%	79	4%	5.04	7.0	$14
BAvg Potl	45%	1st Half	242	38	77	8	33	2	318			375	492	867	8	81	37	0.48	302	44	26	30	116	14%	69	3%	6.19	10.5	$10
LIMA Plan	D	2nd Half	279	34	72	4	26	2	258			308	384	691	7	82	30	0.40	259	43	17	40	90	4%	78	4%	4.05	-4.2	$5
+/- Score	-9	08 Proj	422	55	113	9	50	4	268			321	409	730	7	82	31	0.45	273	43	20	37	95	7%	76	6%	4.51	-0.0	$10

A perfect demonstration of how a player can turn a short-term hot start into a full-time job. By the time anyone realized he was batting .229 in August, the season was already over. His 2nd half is your new baseline.

Harris,Willie

			AB	R	H	HR	RBI	SB	Avg	vL	vR	OB	Slg	OPS	bb%	ct%	h%	Eye	xBA	G	L	F	PX	hr/f	SX	SBO	RC/G	RAR	R$
Pos	78	03 CHW	* 237	38	64	6	16	20	270	105	220	342	401	743	10	81	31	0.58	297	46	31	23	80	14%	139	34%	4.76	-4.0	$10
Age	29	04 CHW	409	68	107	2	27	19	262	181	279	343	323	666	11	81	32	0.65	247	51	20	29	43	2%	119	19%	3.95	-12.0	$11
Peak		05 CHW	* 230	33	56	2	16	18	242	286	252	317	335	652	10	79	30	0.53	256	52	19	30	68	4%	139	34%	3.70	-7.2	$7
Bats	Left	06 BOS	* 263	45	51	7	16	15	193			273	307	580	10	75	23	0.44	249	68	9	24	74	14%	133	33%	2.58	-22.3	$5
Reliability	9	07 ATL	* 402	70	111	3	37	22	277	191	283	351	408	760	10	81	34	0.60	264	42	21	37	88	2%	144	30%	5.16	-2.1	$14
BAvg Potl	45%	1st Half	187	36	69	2	18	16	369			430	513	943	10	86	42	0.74	322	44	31	25	100	5%	126	34%	7.28	9.5	$12
LIMA Plan	D	2nd Half	215	34	42	1	19	6	196			284	317	601	11	76	25	0.52	223	41	14	44	77	1%	136	26%	3.14	-15.5	$2
+/- Score	-2	08 Proj	188	31	46	2	15	11	245			322	367	689	10	79	30	0.54	256	46	20	35	82	5%	146	31%	4.20	-6.6	$5

2-32-.270, 17 SB in 344 AB at ATL. Bounced around pro ball for 9 years, and then a 42% hit rate in the 1st half got everyone's attention. Great speed but he's a career minor leaguer for a reason.

Hart,Corey

			AB	R	H	HR	RBI	SB	Avg	vL	vR	OB	Slg	OPS	bb%	ct%	h%	Eye	xBA	G	L	F	PX	hr/f	SX	SBO	RC/G	RAR	R$
Pos	98	03 aa	334	34	88	4	40	10	263			342	326	669	11	84	31	0.73					41		66	12%	3.95	-14.0	$8
Age	26	04 aaa	441	59	119	14	59	15	269			322	450	772	7	84	30	0.48					109		117	22%	5.01	0.2	$15
Pre-Peak		05 MIL	* 486	73	126	15	59	25	259	211	184	318	440	759	8	84	28	0.54	319	54	22	24	112	15%	146	29%	4.89	-5.2	$19
Bats	Right	06 MIL	* 337	47	94	13	50	14	279	304	272	332	474	806	7	75	34	0.32	263	42	17	41	128	12%	105	29%	5.47	6.9	$14
Reliability	45	07 MIL	505	86	149	24	81	23	295	331	278	342	539	881	7	80	33	0.36	288	37	17	46	147	13%	146	25%	6.26	14.3	$25
BAvg Potl	40%	1st Half	203	35	64	10	31	16	315			382	527	909	10	82	35	0.59	280	39	17	44	126	14%	118	28%	6.71	8.1	$13
LIMA Plan	B	2nd Half	302	51	85	14	50	7	281			313	546	860	4	79	31	0.23	294	36	17	47	161	12%	133	22%	5.94	6.0	$13
+/- Score	14	08 Proj	524	81	148	26	93	21	282			334	520	855	7	80	31	0.39	288	39	17	44	144	14%	127	25%	5.95	12.2	$25

Finally got a chance to play. His PX and FB trends tell the story of his power breakout. If he can regain and sustain the 1st half's bb% and ct% levels, there is even more upside.
UP: 30-30-.300

Hatteberg,Scott

			AB	R	H	HR	RBI	SB	Avg	vL	vR	OB	Slg	OPS	bb%	ct%	h%	Eye	xBA	G	L	F	PX	hr/f	SX	SBO	RC/G	RAR	R$
Pos	3	03 OAK	541	63	137	12	61	0	253	255	253	334	383	717	11	90	26	1.25	284	45	20	35	81	7%	24	1%	4.71	-10.7	$9
Age	38	04 OAK	550	87	156	15	82	0	284	285	283	367	420	787	12	91	29	1.50	273	42	18	40	78	7%	33	0%	5.52	8.2	$16
Decline		05 OAK	464	52	119	7	59	0	256	214	271	330	343	673	10	88	28	0.94	258	47	20	33	56	5%	26	1%	4.09	-13.6	$8
Bats	Left	06 CIN	456	62	132	13	51	2	289	231	302	389	436	825	14	91	30	1.80	295	46	21	33	84	9%	34	2%	6.11	1.4	$13
Reliability	9	07 CIN	361	50	112	10	47	0	310	205	323	393	474	866	12	90	32	1.40	311	43	23	34	99	9%	32	0%	6.45	8.3	$12
BAvg Potl	70%	1st Half	194	26	55	7	23	0	284			368	448	817	12	90	29	1.37	304	43	23	34	94	12%	22	0%	5.82	1.2	$6
LIMA Plan	D	2nd Half	167	24	57	3	24	0	341			421	503	924	12	90	36	1.44	317	42	24	34	105	6%	43	0%	7.19	6.9	$7
+/- Score	-29	08 Proj	215	29	64	5	27	0	298			383	441	824	12	90	31	1.41	297	44	22	34	88	8%	30	1%	5.98	1.6	$7

"Moneyball" hero continues to display one of the best eye/ contact combos around, but without much run production. Still, it's all about getting on base and his near-.400 OBAs make him a sim league staple.

Hawpe,Brad

			AB	R	H	HR	RBI	SB	Avg	vL	vR	OB	Slg	OPS	bb%	ct%	h%	Eye	xBA	G	L	F	PX	hr/f	SX	SBO	RC/G	RAR	R$
Pos	9	03 aa	346	39	90	16	51	1	260			308	471	779	6	81	28	0.37					136		31	5%	4.96	-4.3	$10
Age	28	04 COL	* 450	54	126	28	66	3	280	154	261	332	524	856	7	79	30	0.38	310	53	21	26	142	30%	59	6%	5.88	7.5	$17
Peak		05 COL	305	38	80	9	47	2	262	250	264	353	403	757	12	77	31	0.61	255	52	17	32	90	12%	76	4%	5.04	-1.9	$9
Bats	Left	06 COL	499	67	146	22	84	5	293	232	302	384	515	899	13	75	35	0.60	285	42	22	36	142	16%	77	6%	6.98	31.0	$19
Reliability	25	07 COL	516	80	150	29	116	0	291	214	315	387	539	926	14	73	35	0.59	284	36	21	43	165	18%	48	1%	7.37	30.6	$23
BAvg Potl	35%	1st Half	245	38	72	13	54	0	294			387	527	913	13	79	33	0.73	293	40	20	40	146	17%	37	0%	7.00	11.9	$11
LIMA Plan	C+	2nd Half	271	42	78	16	62	0	288			387	550	937	14	68	37	0.51	274	33	22	45	184	19%	60	2%	7.83	19.7	$12
+/- Score	-6	08 Proj	542	77	154	31	104	1	284			374	531	906	13	75	33	0.57	288	40	21	39	159	19%	58	3%	6.99	28.2	$22

Concurrent rise in FB, PX and hr/f is exciting, even moreso in COL. However, struggles vs. LHP put a ceiling on further growth. He needs to figure that out to get to the next level. But for now, ride him.

Headley,Chase

			AB	R	H	HR	RBI	SB	Avg	vL	vR	OB	Slg	OPS	bb%	ct%	h%	Eye	xBA	G	L	F	PX	hr/f	SX	SBO	RC/G	RAR	R$
Pos	5	03	0	0	0	0	0	0	0							0									0				
Age	23	04	0	0	0	0	0	0	0							0									0				
Growth		05	0	0	0	0	0	0	0							0									0				
Bats	Both	06	0	0	0	0	0	0	0							0									0				
Reliability	1	07 aa	451	73	130	17	69	1	288	167	250	382	492	874	13	74	36	0.59		36	21	43	144	12%	70	1%	6.72	26.2	$16
BAvg Potl	25%	1st Half	254	47	79	13	40	1	311			390	559	949	11	77	36	0.56		38	15	46	165	14%	76	1%	7.49	19.6	$12
LIMA Plan	D	2nd Half	197	26	51	4	29	0	259			371	406	777	15	71	35	0.61					113		57	0%	5.63	5.7	$4
+/- Score	8	08 Proj	121	19	33	4	18	0	273			372	462	834	14	73	34	0.59	274	33	26	40	136	11%	64	0%	6.25	5.0	$4

0-0-.222 in 18 AB at SD. Good walk rate, good power, but must make better contact. Has no AAA experience, so more seasoning is likely in order.

Helms,Wes

			AB	R	H	HR	RBI	SB	Avg	vL	vR	OB	Slg	OPS	bb%	ct%	h%	Eye	xBA	G	L	F	PX	hr/f	SX	SBO	RC/G	RAR	R$
Pos	5	03 MIL	476	56	124	23	67	0	261	314	249	322	450	771	8	72	31	0.33	259	39	22	39	128	17%	21	1%	5.00	10.3	$14
Age	31	04 MIL	278	25	74	4	29	0	266	306	248	325	367	691	8	78	33	0.39	231	43	18	39	71	5%	37	1%	4.04	-8.2	$4
Past Peak		05 MIL	168	18	50	4	24	0	298	305	294	352	458	810	8	82	34	0.47	276	44	18	38	111	8%	46	2%	5.51	3.4	$5
Bats	Right	06 FLA	240	30	79	10	47	0	329	336	323	383	575	958	8	77	39	0.38	306	38	26	36	155	15%	66	6%	7.48	12.9	$11
Reliability	7	07 PHI	280	21	69	5	39	0	246	282	221	294	368	662	6	78	30	0.31	244	39	20	41	90	6%	14	0%	3.59	-9.8	$4
BAvg Potl	40%	1st Half	168	11	41	1	17	0	244			302	315	618	8	77	31	0.37	225	40	21	39	59	2%	13	0%	3.11	-8.3	$1
LIMA Plan	F	2nd Half	112	10	28	4	22	0	250			282	446	728	4	79	29	0.21	275	37	19	44	137	10%	16	0%	4.29	-1.6	$3
+/- Score	-18	08 Proj	242	24	67	7	39	0	277			326	455	781	7	78	33	0.33	275	39	21	40	121	9%	50	2%	5.12	1.2	$6

The curse of the bad 1st half... Yes, his power went MIA. Yes, his BA vs. RHP plunged. But he started rebounding in the 2H. Problem: Not enough AB for anyone to notice, and at 31, he won't get many more chances.

TOM TODARO

Helton,Todd			AB	R	H	HR	RBI	SB	Avg	vL	vR	OB	Slg	OPS	bb%	ct%	h%	Eye	xBA	G	L	F	PX	hr/f	SX	SBO	RC/G	RAR	R$
Pos	3	03 COL	583	135	209	33	117	0	358	387	344	461	630	1091	16	88	37	1.54	349	33	28	39	158	16%	56	2%	9.22	55.0	$37
Age	34	04 COL	547	115	190	32	96	3	347	320	360	470	620	1090	19	87	36	1.76	329	35	21	44	158	15%	68	1%	9.42	48.5	$33
Past Peak		05 COL	509	92	163	20	79	3	320	245	351	437	534	972	17	84	35	1.33	312	33	24	42	140	11%	69	1%	8.01	32.7	$24
Bats	Left	06 COL	546	94	165	15	81	3	302	326	295	402	476	878	14	88	32	1.42	297	35	24	41	102	8%	76	3%	6.74	11.2	$20
Reliability	26	07 COL	557	86	178	17	91	0	320	285	334	437	494	931	17	87	35	1.57	305	40	24	36	109	10%	34	0%	7.53	28.7	$22
BAvg Potl	60%	1st Half	267	35	85	6	39	0	318			445	468	913	19	87	35	1.79	294	41	23	36	93	7%	41	1%	7.46	13.3	$9
LIMA Plan	B+	2nd Half	290	51	93	11	52	0	321			429	517	946	16	86	34	1.38	316	38	25	37	123	12%	26	0%	7.59	15.4	$13
+/- Score	-32	08 Proj	522	89	166	16	85	0	318			430	500	930	16	87	34	1.48	305	37	24	39	112	9%	49	1%	7.47	24.6	$21

Still owns one of the best batting eyes in the business, but PX was barely above average two years' running. He's still a line-drive machine, though, and that will keep him over .300.

Hermida,Jeremy			AB	R	H	HR	RBI	SB	Avg	vL	vR	OB	Slg	OPS	bb%	ct%	h%	Eye	xBA	G	L	F	PX	hr/f	SX	SBO	RC/G	RAR	R$
Pos	9	03	0	0	0	0	0	0	0							0									0				
Age	24	04	0	0	0	0	0	0	0							0									0				
Growth		05 FLA	* 427	77	115	19	67	22	269	200	306	415	480	895	20	78	31	1.12	281	31	24	45	142	13%	114	14%	7.20	24.0	$21
Bats	Left	06 FLA	307	37	77	5	28	4	251	219	261	324	368	692	10	77	31	0.47	251	45	20	35	84	6%	72	6%	4.15	-5.6	$5
Reliability	2	07 FLA	429	54	127	18	63	3	296	292	297	366	501	867	10	76	36	0.45	283	44	21	35	141	16%	45	6%	6.37	13.5	$15
BAvg Potl	35%	1st Half	141	14	32	6	22	1	227			314	411	726	11	71	28	0.44	247	47	16	36	131	17%	30	6%	4.58	-2.9	$3
LIMA Plan	C+	2nd Half	288	40	95	12	41	2	330			391	545	936	9	78	39	0.45	299	42	23	35	146	15%	51	6%	7.18	14.9	$13
+/- Score	-32	08 Proj	541	71	157	23	85	4	290			371	494	865	11	76	34	0.54	282	44	20	35	136	16%	53	4%	6.40	19.0	$20

2nd half BA and xBA show the .300 potential, backed by strong PX and LD. Improvement in ct% would help. Once had 20/20 potential, but he doesn't get the green light very often anymore. Still... UP: 25-100-.300

Hernandez,Luis			AB	R	H	HR	RBI	SB	Avg	vL	vR	OB	Slg	OPS	bb%	ct%	h%	Eye	xBA	G	L	F	PX	hr/f	SX	SBO	RC/G	RAR	R$
Pos	6	03	0	0	0	0	0	0	0							0									0				
Age	23	04	0	0	0	0	0	0	0							0									0				
Growth		05 aa	415	41	92	2	28	4	222			284	282	566	8	88	25	0.73					37		80	9%	2.80	-18.8	$2
Bats	Both	06 a/a	453	40	112	2	33	4	247			279	307	586	4	89	28	0.38					37		68	8%	2.80	-21.4	$4
Reliability	24	07 BAL	* 466	47	110	1	43	7	236	300	286	263	294	557	4	88	27	0.29	269	51	22	27	39	1%	89	13%	2.42	-30.4	$4
BAvg Potl	55%	1st Half	280	27	62	0	31	5	221			256	279	535	4	88	25	0.39					39		96	15%	2.28	-19.9	$2
LIMA Plan	F	2nd Half	186	20	48	1	12	2	258			274	317	591	2	87	29	0.16	266	51	22	27	40	2%	77	11%	2.65	-10.6	$2
+/- Score	32	08 Proj	134	13	34	1	10	3	254			285	310	595	4	88	29	0.36	267	51	22	27	36	2%	85	13%	2.88	-6.5	$2

1-7-.290 in 69 AB at BAL.
A fun game to play this March... In mid-draft, bring him up for $1 and watch others either panic or sit dumbfounded. At best, someone might say $2 for fear of losing out. At worst, it's $1.

Hernandez,Ramon			AB	R	H	HR	RBI	SB	Avg	vL	vR	OB	Slg	OPS	bb%	ct%	h%	Eye	xBA	G	L	F	PX	hr/f	SX	SBO	RC/G	RAR	R$
Pos	2	03 OAK	483	70	132	21	78	0	273	208	302	320	458	777	6	84	29	0.42	289	41	22	37	110	14%	43	0%	4.90	11.2	$16
Age	31	04 SD	384	45	106	18	63	1	276	310	264	337	477	813	8	84	27	0.78	303	47	19	34	113	16%	33	1%	5.48	18.2	$13
Past Peak		05 SD	369	36	107	12	58	1	290	238	304	323	450	773	5	89	30	0.45	302	46	21	33	93	11%	53	1%	4.84	10.8	$12
Bats	Right	06 BAL	501	66	138	23	91	1	275	291	270	333	479	812	8	84	29	0.54	293	44	19	38	119	14%	53	1%	5.42	14.4	$16
Reliability	41	07 BAL	364	40	94	9	62	1	258	250	261	325	382	707	9	84	29	0.61	253	49	16	35	81	8%	29	4%	4.30	3.0	$8
BAvg Potl	55%	1st Half	134	17	32	3	29	1	239			346	358	704	14	84	27	1.00	262	48	18	34	80	8%	41	2%	4.57	2.2	$3
LIMA Plan	D+	2nd Half	230	23	62	6	33	0	270			311	396	707	6	84	30	0.38	247	49	15	36	82	9%	23	5%	4.09	0.5	$5
+/- Score	-10	08 Proj	437	51	119	14	75	1	272			330	429	759	8	85	29	0.57	277	47	18	35	96	11%	41	2%	4.84	8.9	$12

Looks like his spring training oblique injury and June groin contusion slowed him down for the whole year. Just the sound of that makes me come to a complete halt as well.
If healthy. should rebound.

Hillenbrand,Shea			AB	R	H	HR	RBI	SB	Avg	vL	vR	OB	Slg	OPS	bb%	ct%	h%	Eye	xBA	G	L	F	PX	hr/f	SX	SBO	RC/G	RAR	R$
Pos	0	03 2TM	515	60	144	20	97	1	280	298	271	312	468	780	4	86	29	0.34	318	44	25	31	115	14%	49	1%	4.87	3.7	$17
Age	32	04 ARI	562	68	174	15	80	2	310	323	304	338	464	802	4	91	32	0.49	304	47	20	33	89	9%	69	1%	5.19	-1.7	$19
Past Peak		05 TOR	594	91	173	18	82	5	291	325	279	321	449	770	4	87	31	0.33	292	43	20	37	99	10%	89	4%	4.77	-20.7	$20
Bats	Right	06 2TM	530	73	147	21	68	1	277	338	256	305	451	756	4	85	29	0.26	287	46	20	34	100	14%	53	3%	4.51	-29.0	$15
Reliability	22	07 2TM	* 314	28	75	5	34	0	238	260	247	256	316	572	2	88	26	0.20	231	45	15	40	44	4%	48	4%	2.45	-33.9	$3
BAvg Potl	50%	1st Half	197	19	50	3	22	0	254			272	325	597	2	91	27	0.28	226	47	13	40	41	4%	33	4%	2.82	-18.7	$3
LIMA Plan	F	2nd Half	117	9	25	2	12	0	211			229	301	530	2	82	24	0.13	238	40	22	38	48	5%	77	4%	1.82	-15.4	$0
+/- Score	-9	08 Proj	271	30	70	7	33	0	258			282	385	667	3	86	28	0.23	266	44	19	37	73	8%	59	3%	3.52	-19.8	$5

Power vanished from first day of spring training, the start of a 3-team odyssey. Might revive in the right situation, but even at his best, he was barely replacement level. He's been far worse for three years..

Hill,Aaron			AB	R	H	HR	RBI	SB	Avg	vL	vR	OB	Slg	OPS	bb%	ct%	h%	Eye	xBA	G	L	F	PX	hr/f	SX	SBO	RC/G	RAR	R$
Pos	4	03	0	0	0	0	0	0	0							0									0				
Age	26	04 aa	480	75	134	11	77	3	279			360	417	777	11	88	30	1.03					84		70	3%	5.36	13.9	$15
Pre-Peak		05 TOR	* 517	67	143	7	45	4	277	298	269	325	398	723	7	89	30	0.67	291	43	22	36	81	4%	83	4%	4.54	6.0	$12
Bats	Right	06 TOR	546	70	159	6	50	5	291	298	288	342	386	728	7	88	32	0.64	267	46	19	35	61	4%	80	4%	4.57	6.9	$12
Reliability	79	07 TOR	608	87	177	17	78	4	291	317	283	336	459	795	6	83	33	0.40	288	40	21	39	114	9%	69	5%	5.21	18.4	$18
BAvg Potl	45%	1st Half	283	42	78	9	44	3	276			339	456	795	9	84	30	0.60	293	44	18	38	119	10%	74	5%	5.35	9.9	$9
LIMA Plan	C+	2nd Half	325	45	99	8	34	1	305			333	462	795	4	82	35	0.25	285	37	23	40	109	8%	54	4%	5.08	8.5	$10
+/- Score	-6	08 Proj	601	83	179	20	81	4	298			346	473	820	7	86	32	0.52	296	42	21	37	110	10%	73	4%	5.52	23.2	$20

PX, FB and hr/f trends show that he's developed an effective power stroke. Strong LD rate helps too. It all means there's room for even more growth.
UP: 25 HR, .300+ BA

Hinske,Eric			AB	R	H	HR	RBI	SB	Avg	vL	vR	OB	Slg	OPS	bb%	ct%	h%	Eye	xBA	G	L	F	PX	hr/f	SX	SBO	RC/G	RAR	R$
Pos	37	03 TOR	449	74	109	12	63	12	243	256	237	331	437	767	12	77	29	0.57	290	36	26	39	144	9%	119	13%	5.26	-1.6	$13
Age	30	04 TOR	570	66	140	15	69	12	246	268	236	311	375	686	9	81	28	0.50	250	43	18	39	79	8%	86	13%	3.98	-17.3	$12
Peak		05 TOR	477	79	125	15	68	8	262	172	281	327	430	757	9	75	32	0.38	263	41	20	39	122	11%	99	10%	4.91	-2.5	$15
Bats	Left	06 2AL	277	43	75	13	34	2	271	167	293	353	487	840	11	71	34	0.44	259	40	16	43	148	15%	77	5%	6.18	6.1	$8
Reliability	30	07 BOS	186	25	38	6	21	3	204	200	205	308	398	706	13	71	25	0.52	250	45	11	44	142	10%	112	7%	4.49	-3.5	$3
BAvg Potl	55%	1st Half	70	13	15	3	8	0	214			321	443	764	14	73	25	0.58	270	44	12	44	162	13%	87	0%	5.24	0.3	$1
LIMA Plan	D+	2nd Half	116	12	23	3	13	3	198			301	371	671	13	70	26	0.49	236	46	10	44	129	8%	108	11%	4.02	-3.9	$1
+/- Score	47	08 Proj	314	46	80	11	38	5	255			342	444	786	12	72	32	0.48	254	43	15	42	135	12%	97	7%	5.48	2.8	$8

Playing time, not skill, is the problem. Solid PX and SX. Low ct%, but h% points to BA gains. Likely relegated to a platoon role. Still, will be overlooked on draft day, but all he needs are some ABs to turn a profit.

Holliday,Matt			AB	R	H	HR	RBI	SB	Avg	vL	vR	OB	Slg	OPS	bb%	ct%	h%	Eye	xBA	G	L	F	PX	hr/f	SX	SBO	RC/G	RAR	R$
Pos	7	03 aa	522	49	126	12	55	12	241			286	375	662	6	89	25	0.59					79		89	19%	3.75	-27.2	$10
Age	28	04 COL	400	65	116	14	57	3	290	237	307	341	488	829	7	79	34	0.36	290	50	17	32	131	14%	86	6%	5.71	3.1	$15
Peak		05 COL	479	68	147	19	87	14	307	324	302	355	505	861	7	84	34	0.46	306	48	21	31	118	15%	125	13%	5.98	8.4	$24
Bats	Right	06 COL	602	119	196	34	114	10	326	327	325	374	586	961	7	82	35	0.43	320	45	21	34	153	20%	104	9%	7.19	31.2	$33
Reliability	67	07 COL	636	120	216	36	137	11	340	301	351	399	607	1006	9	80	38	0.50	319	44	20	36	166	20%	101	8%	7.92	42.9	$38
BAvg Potl	35%	1st Half	315	48	110	13	60	3	349			393	584	978	7	80	40	0.37	308	43	20	37	151	14%	90	4%	7.50	17.4	$17
LIMA Plan	D+	2nd Half	321	72	106	23	77	8	330			404	629	1034	11	80	35	0.63	331	45	20	35	180	25%	103	11%	8.31	25.4	$22
+/- Score	-22	08 Proj	620	112	200	38	122	12	323			378	595	973	8	81	35	0.48	325	45	20	35	163	22%	105	10%	7.39	34.3	$35

Coors monster. He slugs under .500 on the road, but who's complaining? That's the only thing keeping him from hitting 40 homers... but he might do it anyway. Pay up.

Hopper,Norris			AB	R	H	HR	RBI	SB	Avg	vL	vR	OB	Slg	OPS	bb%	ct%	h%	Eye	xBA	G	L	F	PX	hr/f	SX	SBO	RC/G	RAR	R$
Pos	87	03 aa	424	46	116	0	32	20	273			307	314	621	5	88	31	0.42					29		103	25%	3.22	-20.5	$11
Age	29	04 aa	363	37	87	0	31	14	240			290	263	553	6	90	27	0.67					14		96	19%	2.60	-23.1	$6
Peak		05 aa	447	47	104	1	24	17	234			262	269	531	4	92	25	0.49					24		99	23%	2.30	-29.1	$6
Bats	Right	06 CIN	* 468	51	136	1	35	25	290			329	330	659	5	93	31	0.77	272	52	21	27	25	1%	100	23%	3.80	-8.6	$14
Reliability	20	07 CIN	307	51	101	0	14	14	329	351	316	370	388	758	6	89	37	0.61	283	58	20	22	41	0%	110	19%	4.87	2.6	$12
BAvg Potl	40%	1st Half	107	13	28	0	1	5	262			301	336	637	5	89	29	0.50	272	51	19	31	52	0%	113	30%	3.52	-3.4	$2
LIMA Plan	F	2nd Half	200	38	73	0	13	9	365			407	415	822	7	90	41	0.67	290	62	20	18	36	0%	104	15%	5.60	5.3	$10
+/- Score	-38	08 Proj	246	33	68	0	14	11	276			316	324	640	5	90	31	0.61	278	57	20	23	33	0%	107	22%	3.55	-7.2	$6

High 2nd half BA driven by crazy 41% hit rate. SX is good, and the SB opps are decent, but none of this is "break the bank" awesome. If he reverts to 1st half levels, which are closer to his history, it all goes bust.

TOM TODARO

House,J.R.

House,J.R.			AB	R	H	HR	RBI	SB	Avg	vL	vR	OB	Slg	OPS	bb%	ct%	h%	Eye	xBA	G	L	F	PX	hr/f	SX	SBO	RC/G	RAR	R$
Pos	2	03 aa	63	11	19	2	10	0	308			357	493	850	7	85	34	0.52					124		40	0%	5.92	3.0	$2
Age	28	04 aaa	309	30	80	11	38	1	259			300	437	737	6	83	28	0.34					110		47	3%	4.43	3.2	$7
Peak		05	0	0	0	0	0	0	0							0									0				
Bats	Right	06 a/a	493	64	140	12	81	2	285			327	425	752	6	89	30	0.55					84		60	3%	4.73	4.9	$14
Reliability	5	07 BAL	* 457	53	123	13	65	1	269	77	280	331	427	757	8	85	29	0.61	227	33	7	59	103	6%	36	5%	4.90	11.6	$11
BAvg Potl	45%	1st Half	306	37	88	7	47	1	288			349	428	777	9	88	31	0.76					91		41	6%	5.19	10.2	$9
LIMA Plan	F	2nd Half	151	16	35	6	18	0	232			293	424	717	8	79	25	0.42	234	33	7	59	131	8%	27	3%	4.29	1.2	$2
+/- Score	-42	08 Proj	**130**	**15**	**35**	**4**	**19**	**0**	**269**			**320**	**429**	**749**	**7**	**85**	**29**	**0.50**	**227**	**33**	**7**	**59**	**104**	**6%**	**35**	**4%**	**4.70**	**2.1**	**$3**

3-3-.211 in 38 AB at BAL. Hit .298 at AAA. Gets his bat on the ball, with decent power. Not everyday-catcher material, but could be useful in a part-time role.

Howard,Ryan

Howard,Ryan			AB	R	H	HR	RBI	SB	Avg	vL	vR	OB	Slg	OPS	bb%	ct%	h%	Eye	xBA	G	L	F	PX	hr/f	SX	SBO	RC/G	RAR	R$
Pos	3	03	0	0	0	0	0	0	0							0									0				
Age	28	04 a/a	485	75	119	35	105	1	246			315	516	831	9	68	28	0.32					182		47	3%	5.93	6.7	$19
Peak		05 PHI	* 522	82	160	36	106	0	307	148	320	381	584	965	11	71	37	0.41	311	44	27	29	193	33%	43	1%	7.84	31.9	$27
Bats	Left	06 PHI	581	104	182	58	149	0	313	279	331	421	659	1080	16	69	36	0.60	305	42	22	36	220	40%	24	0%	9.69	57.7	$36
Reliability	44	07 PHI	529	94	142	47	136	1	268	225	297	392	584	976	17	62	34	0.54	283	31	24	44	233	32%	31	1%	8.78	48.2	$27
BAvg Potl	35%	1st Half	211	33	54	18	56	0	256			387	564	951	18	63	32	0.57	276	33	21	46	229	30%	13	0%	8.39	17.2	$10
LIMA Plan	B	2nd Half	318	61	88	29	80	1	277			395	597	992	16	62	35	0.52	287	30	27	43	236	34%	36	1%	9.03	30.9	$18
+/- Score	22	08 Proj	**566**	**98**	**155**	**49**	**138**	**1**	**274**			**382**	**587**	**969**	**15**	**66**	**33**	**0.51**	**292**	**37**	**24**	**40**	**219**	**33%**	**37**	**1%**	**8.31**	**41.9**	**$29**

Recipe for 45-point BA drop: 62 ct%, more fly balls, lower HR rate. Needs better contact to get even back to .280... but does it matter? Highest PX in the majors. Expect another run at 50 homers.

Hudson,Orlando

Hudson,Orlando			AB	R	H	HR	RBI	SB	Avg	vL	vR	OB	Slg	OPS	bb%	ct%	h%	Eye	xBA	G	L	F	PX	hr/f	SX	SBO	RC/G	RAR	R$
Pos	4	03 TOR	474	54	127	9	57	5	268	160	297	324	395	718	8	82	31	0.45	284	47	26	28	79	8%	92	7%	4.38	3.3	$11
Age	30	04 TOR	489	73	132	12	58	7	270	262	272	339	438	777	9	80	32	0.52	282	48	20	32	107	9%	112	8%	5.22	16.1	$13
Peak		05 TOR	461	62	125	10	63	7	271	227	288	316	412	728	6	86	30	0.46	297	52	20	28	88	9%	108	7%	4.45	4.2	$13
Bats	Both	06 ARI	579	87	166	15	67	9	287	338	270	355	454	809	10	87	31	0.78	295	49	19	32	95	9%	100	9%	5.62	16.8	$18
Reliability	81	07 ARI	517	69	152	10	63	10	294	281	298	378	441	819	12	83	34	0.80	289	52	20	28	90	8%	110	7%	5.90	19.4	$16
BAvg Potl	50%	1st Half	287	37	85	7	43	3	296			386	467	853	13	83	34	0.84	295	51	20	29	106	10%	87	5%	6.36	14.4	$9
LIMA Plan	B	2nd Half	230	32	67	3	20	7	291			368	409	777	11	84	34	0.76	281	53	20	27	71	6%	120	9%	5.34	5.0	$7
+/- Score	-8	08 Proj	**567**	**78**	**162**	**12**	**67**	**11**	**286**			**357**	**434**	**791**	**10**	**84**	**32**	**0.70**	**291**	**51**	**20**	**29**	**90**	**8%**	**116**	**8%**	**5.44**	**14.0**	**$17**

Validated 2006 results, holding on to improvement in batting eye. Since coming to ARI, his OPS is over 100 points higher at home; was the opposite in TOR. Prefers the arid desert to the cold northern wilderness.

Huff,Aubrey

Huff,Aubrey			AB	R	H	HR	RBI	SB	Avg	vL	vR	OB	Slg	OPS	bb%	ct%	h%	Eye	xBA	G	L	F	PX	hr/f	SX	SBO	RC/G	RAR	R$
Pos	03	03 TAM	636	91	198	34	107	2	311	318	308	364	555	919	8	87	31	0.66	333	47	21	32	141	19%	49	3%	6.64	21.9	$28
Age	31	04 TAM	600	92	178	29	104	5	297	304	293	357	493	850	9	88	30	0.76	297	46	18	36	106	15%	77	3%	5.88	14.8	$24
Past Peak		05 TAM	575	70	150	22	92	8	261	254	262	319	428	747	8	85	28	0.56	275	48	15	37	100	12%	69	10%	4.66	-7.2	$18
Bats	Left	06 2TM	454	57	121	21	66	0	267	233	278	339	469	808	10	86	27	0.78	294	45	19	36	114	15%	35	0%	5.51	-2.6	$13
Reliability	77	07 BAL	550	68	154	15	72	1	280	305	272	338	442	780	8	84	31	0.55	276	46	16	38	103	9%	64	1%	5.14	0.8	$14
BAvg Potl	45%	1st Half	275	24	73	5	35	0	265			303	389	693	5	81	31	0.29	245	47	15	38	88	6%	33	0%	3.93	-9.2	$5
LIMA Plan	C+	2nd Half	275	44	81	10	37	1	295			370	495	865	11	87	31	0.92	301	45	17	38	118	11%	81	2%	6.30	9.3	$9
+/- Score	1	08 Proj	**543**	**71**	**156**	**18**	**78**	**1**	**287**			**349**	**459**	**808**	**9**	**85**	**31**	**0.65**	**283**	**46**	**17**	**37**	**104**	**11%**	**57**	**2%**	**5.49**	**4.7**	**$16**

One advantage coming into '07 was that he'd finally get to face TAM pitching... and he did hit 7 of his 15 HRs and batted .365 vs them. But stunk it up against everyone else. It's time to set new baselines. Sigh.

Hunter,Torii

Hunter,Torii			AB	R	H	HR	RBI	SB	Avg	vL	vR	OB	Slg	OPS	bb%	ct%	h%	Eye	xBA	G	L	F	PX	hr/f	SX	SBO	RC/G	RAR	R$
Pos	8	03 MIN	581	83	145	26	102	6	250	250	249	309	451	760	8	82	27	0.47	293	48	18	34	122	16%	82	10%	4.80	1.1	$18
Age	32	04 MIN	520	79	141	23	81	21	271	255	278	323	475	798	7	81	30	0.40	287	48	15	37	129	15%	96	23%	5.23	7.9	$21
Past Peak		05 MIN	372	63	100	14	56	23	269	283	263	330	452	782	8	83	29	0.52	288	49	14	36	118	13%	119	32%	5.13	9.2	$17
Bats	Right	06 MIN	557	86	155	31	98	12	278	319	262	332	490	822	7	81	30	0.42	283	45	18	37	121	18%	88	12%	5.46	12.7	$23
Reliability	79	07 MIN	600	94	172	28	107	18	287	314	276	331	505	836	6	83	31	0.40	303	49	14	37	140	15%	88	20%	5.62	23.0	$27
BAvg Potl	45%	1st Half	280	45	85	15	59	11	304			343	546	890	6	82	33	0.34	308	43	16	40	154	16%	99	25%	6.22	15.2	$15
LIMA Plan	C	2nd Half	320	49	87	13	48	7	272			321	469	789	7	84	29	0.45	296	53	12	34	127	14%	75	15%	5.12	7.8	$11
+/- Score	0	08 Proj	**572**	**90**	**159**	**25**	**97**	**18**	**278**			**329**	**475**	**803**	**7**	**82**	**30**	**0.43**	**289**	**48**	**15**	**37**	**123**	**14%**	**91**	**19%**	**5.28**	**14.1**	**$24**

Followed up strong 2006 finish with a great 1st half, but battled through hamstring and shoulder woes in the 2nd half. This is still a flat skill set. Expect some regression.

Iannetta,Chris

Iannetta,Chris			AB	R	H	HR	RBI	SB	Avg	vL	vR	OB	Slg	OPS	bb%	ct%	h%	Eye	xBA	G	L	F	PX	hr/f	SX	SBO	RC/G	RAR	R$
Pos	2	03	0	0	0	0	0	0	0							0									0				
Age	25	04	0	0	0	0	0	0	0							0									0				
Pre-Peak		05 aa	60	6	12	1	9	0	200			284	283	567	10	72	26	0.41					64		25	0%	2.39	-2.9	$0
Bats	Right	06 COL	* 384	59	118	14	47	1	307	231	266	386	495	880	11	85	33	0.88	316	52	23	25	108	17%	59	2%	6.51	22.7	$14
Reliability	0	07 COL	* 251	29	57	5	33	0	228	204	223	322	354	676	12	75	29	0.55	231	41	18	41	85	6%	62	0%	4.03	1.8	$3
BAvg Potl	45%	1st Half	113	12	23	1	13	0	204			302	319	621	12	68	29	0.44	213	43	16	41	90	3%	74	0%	3.36	-1.5	$0
LIMA Plan	F	2nd Half	138	17	34	4	20	0	248			338	384	722	12	80	28	0.69	246	38	20	43	82	8%	46	0%	4.58	3.2	$3
+/- Score	14	08 Proj	**243**	**32**	**63**	**7**	**31**	**0**	**259**			**347**	**406**	**752**	**12**	**79**	**30**	**0.64**	**256**	**42**	**19**	**39**	**93**	**9%**	**61**	**1%**	**4.99**	**7.3**	**$5**

4-27-.218 in 197 AB at COL. Swung for the fences with poor results: ct% plummeted, and so did his BA. Skills for success are there, but he needs to prove he's not just a AAAA hitter.

Ibanez,Raul

Ibanez,Raul			AB	R	H	HR	RBI	SB	Avg	vL	vR	OB	Slg	OPS	bb%	ct%	h%	Eye	xBA	G	L	F	PX	hr/f	SX	SBO	RC/G	RAR	R$
Pos	7	03 KC	608	95	179	18	90	8	294	245	319	347	454	801	7	87	32	0.60	294	42	23	35	95	10%	95	7%	5.35	0.2	$22
Age	35	04 SEA	481	67	146	16	62	1	304	295	307	352	472	824	7	85	33	0.50	289	44	21	35	102	11%	47	2%	5.55	8.1	$16
Decline		05 SEA	614	92	172	20	89	9	280	274	283	355	436	791	10	84	31	0.72	287	46	21	34	98	12%	82	7%	5.37	11.3	$21
Bats	Left	06 SEA	626	103	181	33	123	2	289	243	308	356	516	872	9	82	31	0.57	294	42	19	39	132	17%	65	3%	6.22	18.4	$25
Reliability	80	07 SEA	573	80	167	21	105	0	291	256	305	351	480	831	8	83	32	0.55	283	42	18	40	118	11%	56	0%	5.74	16.3	$20
BAvg Potl	45%	1st Half	257	39	72	6	49	0	280			337	440	777	8	86	31	0.61	281	42	18	40	101	7%	70	0%	5.14	3.1	$8
LIMA Plan	C	2nd Half	316	41	95	15	56	0	301			363	513	876	9	81	33	0.51	285	43	17	40	133	15%	43	0%	6.28	13.5	$12
+/- Score	-22	08 Proj	**542**	**80**	**153**	**19**	**85**	**0**	**282**			**346**	**458**	**804**	**9**	**83**	**31**	**0.57**	**280**	**43**	**19**	**38**	**109**	**11%**	**55**	**1%**	**5.44**	**8.6**	**$17**

Saved his season with a strong 2nd half, but BPIs are flat. Possible cracks in the armor...
- 1st half power slump
- 2nd half drop in contact rate
- Declining LD rate
- 2nd season of mediocrity vs LH

Iguchi,Tadahito

Iguchi,Tadahito			AB	R	H	HR	RBI	SB	Avg	vL	vR	OB	Slg	OPS	bb%	ct%	h%	Eye	xBA	G	L	F	PX	hr/f	SX	SBO	RC/G	RAR	R$
Pos	4	03 JPN	515	109	163	16	106	38	317			393	488	882	11	85	35	0.85					109		129	26%	6.53	31.9	$34
Age	33	04 JPN	510	94	158	14	87	16	311			358	474	832	7	83	35	0.44					102		117	15%	5.68	18.7	$24
Past Peak		05 CHW	511	74	142	15	71	15	278	274	279	339	438	777	8	78	33	0.41	280	48	22	30	106	13%	118	14%	5.13	14.6	$18
Bats	Right	06 CHW	555	97	156	18	67	11	281	252	298	350	422	772	10	80	32	0.54	259	51	16	34	88	12%	80	9%	5.05	14.7	$18
Reliability	99	07 2TM	465	67	124	9	43	14	267	266	267	347	400	747	11	81	31	0.65	265	43	20	37	89	6%	114	11%	4.93	7.8	$12
BAvg Potl	50%	1st Half	235	29	59	3	17	7	251			328	349	677	10	82	30	0.63	259	43	22	35	69	5%	89	11%	4.04	-2.1	$4
LIMA Plan	C+	2nd Half	230	38	65	6	26	7	283			365	452	818	12	80	33	0.67	273	43	18	39	111	8%	119	11%	5.84	9.7	$8
+/- Score	19	08 Proj	**459**	**73**	**121**	**11**	**54**	**13**	**264**			**338**	**402**	**740**	**10**	**81**	**31**	**0.58**	**267**	**46**	**19**	**35**	**91**	**8%**	**112**	**12%**	**4.76**	**5.6**	**$14**

xBA saw this one coming. Lower PX plus higher FB rate just means more fly outs. Can still produce as a regular, but we've already seen his best.

Infante,Omar

Infante,Omar			AB	R	H	HR	RBI	SB	Avg	vL	vR	OB	Slg	OPS	bb%	ct%	h%	Eye	xBA	G	L	F	PX	hr/f	SX	SBO	RC/G	RAR	R$
Pos	4	03 DET	* 445	54	100	2	27	29	225	155	253	290	279	569	8	86	26	0.65	240	46	18	36	39	1%	117	30%	2.76	-19.0	$9
Age	26	04 DET	503	69	133	16	55	13	264	277	257	319	449	768	7	78	31	0.36	254	35	18	46	114	9%	130	17%	4.97	13.2	$14
Pre-Peak		05 DET	406	36	90	9	43	8	222	178	236	251	367	618	4	82	25	0.22	247	33	16	51	101	5%	101	12%	2.98	-14.3	$6
Bats	Right	06 DET	224	35	62	4	25	3	277	286	273	319	415	735	6	80	33	0.31	247	38	19	43	86	5%	122	9%	4.50	2.5	$6
Reliability	12	07 DET	* 204	27	58	2	21	5	284	281	265	326	362	688	6	85	33	0.42	232	33	21	47	53	2%	94	10%	3.96	-1.0	$5
BAvg Potl	35%	1st Half	98	15	31	0	11	3	316			343	367	710	4	80	40	0.20	219	42	19	38	38	0%	110	10%	4.08	-0.1	$3
LIMA Plan	F	2nd Half	106	12	27	2	10	2	253			312	357	669	8	90	27	0.81	246	21	22	57	65	4%	55	10%	3.94	-0.6	$2
+/- Score	-34	08 Proj	**165**	**21**	**44**	**3**	**17**	**4**	**267**			**310**	**373**	**683**	**6**	**83**	**31**	**0.38**	**239**	**34**	**19**	**47**	**71**	**4%**	**92**	**11%**	**3.88**	**-1.2**	**$4**

2-17-.271 in 166 AB at DET. His only productive season, and apparently his peak, was at age 22. That makes his career monocarpic, which is a neat vocabulary word that sounds like it's about fish, but isn't.

TOM TODARO

Inge,Brandon			AB	R	H	HR	RBI	SB	Avg	vL	vR	OB	Slg	OPS	bb%	ct%	h%	Eye	xBA	G	L	F	PX	hr/f	SX	SBO	RC/G	RAR	R$
Pos	5	03 DET *	472	46	102	12	44	7	216	245	182	270	354	624	7	79	25	0.35	256	42	20	38	91	9%	84	12%	3.11	-20.6	$6
Age	30	04 DET	408	43	117	13	64	5	287	327	258	339	453	792	7	82	32	0.44	265	44	17	39	93	10%	91	8%	5.21	3.4	$13
Peak		05 DET	616	75	161	16	72	7	261	288	257	330	419	749	9	77	32	0.45	253	40	18	42	105	8%	98	8%	4.84	6.2	$15
Bats	Right	06 DET	542	83	137	27	83	7	253	243	256	308	463	771	7	76	28	0.34	261	40	14	46	133	14%	85	9%	4.90	-1.8	$17
Reliability	87	07 DET	508	64	120	14	71	9	236	333	209	301	376	677	8	70	31	0.31	237	37	22	41	105	10%	93	9%	3.85	-9.9	$11
BAvg Potl	40%	1st Half	236	40	61	11	38	4	258			345	449	794	12	72	31	0.48	267	39	23	38	134	17%	68	7%	5.48	6.8	$8
LIMA Plan	C	2nd Half	272	24	59	3	33	5	217			260	312	573	6	69	30	0.19	211	35	22	44	79	4%	95	11%	2.37	-17.9	$2
+/- Score	-15	08 Proj	470	60	115	15	64	7	245			305	402	706	8	74	30	0.33	245	39	19	42	109	10%	91	9%	4.18	-6.5	$11

2006 PX now looks like an outlier, leaving an established track record of marginal-to-low BA without sufficient power to counterbalance. Lousy 2H gives another reason to stay clear, especially in sim games.

Iwamura,Akinori			AB	R	H	HR	RBI	SB	Avg	vL	vR	OB	Slg	OPS	bb%	ct%	h%	Eye	xBA	G	L	F	PX	hr/f	SX	SBO	RC/G	RAR	R$
Pos	5	03 JPN	232	42	57	7	34	5	245			299	391	690	7	78	29	0.34					87		136	10%	3.90	-3.3	$7
Age	29	04 JPN	533	97	149	27	100	7	280			349	464	813	10	69	36	0.34					123		74	7%	5.72	11.1	$23
Peak		05 JPN	548	81	163	18	95	5	298			357	475	832	8	75	37	0.37					122		99	5%	5.90	19.2	$22
Bats	Left	06 JPN	546	82	158	19	75	7	290			357	456	813	9	78	34	0.47					104		94	4%	5.59	5.1	$19
Reliability	90	07 TAM	491	82	140	7	34	12	285	323	268	361	411	772	11	77	36	0.51	254	46	20	34	84	6%	123	13%	5.27	10.9	$14
BAvg Potl	30%	1st Half	147	33	44	3	12	6	299			401	456	857	15	80	36	0.83	285	53	19	28	102	9%	135	16%	6.56	8.5	$6
LIMA Plan	C	2nd Half	344	49	96	4	22	6	279			342	392	735	9	76	36	0.39	241	43	21	36	76	4%	112	10%	4.70	2.0	$8
+/- Score	-17	08 Proj	441	73	122	9	50	11	277			349	412	761	10	77	34	0.47	258	47	20	33	90	8%	121	11%	5.05	5.1	$13

This may look like a decent MLB debut, but heed warning signs:
- 2nd half BPI fade (perhaps his lingering oblique injury)
- Large BA to xBA gap.
- Poor SB success rate

Don't expect JPN levels just yet.

Izturis,Cesar			AB	R	H	HR	RBI	SB	Avg	vL	vR	OB	Slg	OPS	bb%	ct%	h%	Eye	xBA	G	L	F	PX	hr/f	SX	SBO	RC/G	RAR	R$
Pos	6	03 LA	558	47	140	1	40	10	251	263	246	283	315	598	4	87	29	0.36	282	49	25	25	43	1%	99	11%	2.94	-19.4	$7
Age	28	04 LA	670	90	193	4	62	25	288	269	295	331	381	712	6	90	32	0.61	281	49	21	31	56	2%	129	18%	4.38	4.8	$21
Peak		05 LA	444	48	114	2	31	8	257	303	242	296	322	618	5	89	29	0.49	279	52	22	26	46	2%	81	14%	3.24	-9.5	$7
Bats	Both	06 2NL	252	21	61	1	20	1	240	206	253	296	308	603	7	94	25	1.23	261	52	16	31	43	1%	44	8%	3.41	-7.3	$1
Reliability	33	07 2NL	314	31	81	0	16	3	258	186	285	300	315	616	6	94	27	1.00	285	49	23	28	39	0%	69	7%	3.46	-4.6	$3
BAvg Potl	70%	1st Half	178	13	45	0	8	3	253			300	315	615	6	92	27	0.86	289	53	22	25	48	0%	52	7%	3.43	-2.8	$1
LIMA Plan	F	2nd Half	136	18	36	0	8	0	265			301	316	617	5	96	27	1.40	277	44	24	33	27	0%	82	8%	3.51	-1.8	$2
+/- Score	19	08 Proj	231	24	59	0	15	2	255			299	322	621	6	93	27	0.87	281	49	22	29	42	1%	75	9%	3.49	-4.0	$2

This high-contact, ground ball hitting skill set would have value if it was still accompanied by 2004's SX. Unfortunately the SX and SBO trends leave little hope of the running game returning. End-game filler.

Izturis,Maicer			AB	R	H	HR	RBI	SB	Avg	vL	vR	OB	Slg	OPS	bb%	ct%	h%	Eye	xBA	G	L	F	PX	hr/f	SX	SBO	RC/G	RAR	R$
Pos	54	03 a/a	519	67	132	3	45	26	254			311	347	658	8	91	28	0.91					58		128	28%	3.95	-6.8	$13
Age	27	04 aaa	376	50	116	2	28	11	309			378	383	761	10	94	32	1.91					48		71	19%	5.30	3.4	$12
Peak		05 ANA *	222	25	59	1	16	12	265	191	268	331	369	700	9	89	29	0.91	277	45	20	35	66	1%	128	28%	4.48	-0.2	$6
Bats	Both	06 LAA	352	64	103	5	44	14	293	247	307	362	412	773	10	90	31	1.09	291	49	19	32	73	5%	119	18%	5.31	3.0	$13
Reliability	16	07 LAA	336	47	97	6	51	7	289	280	291	352	405	757	9	88	31	0.85	270	45	17	38	73	5%	92	8%	5.00	4.7	$11
BAvg Potl	55%	1st Half	94	10	23	1	14	2	245			304	319	623	8	90	26	0.89	259	45	19	36	50	3%	58	8%	3.49	-2.8	$2
LIMA Plan	C+	2nd Half	242	37	74	5	37	5	306			371	438	809	9	88	33	0.83	273	46	16	38	82	6%	93	8%	5.60	7.3	$9
+/- Score	-23	08 Proj	477	68	134	8	60	15	281			346	402	748	9	90	30	0.95	280	46	18	35	74	5%	106	15%	4.94	4.0	$15

SX and SBO trends will hurt his roto value, but he continues to show some hints of becoming a more complete hitter. If he ever combines the power growth with the speed he still owns:
UP: 290-10-70-25

Jackson,Conor			AB	R	H	HR	RBI	SB	Avg	vL	vR	OB	Slg	OPS	bb%	ct%	h%	Eye	xBA	G	L	F	PX	hr/f	SX	SBO	RC/G	RAR	R$
Pos	3	03	0	0	0	0	0	0	0							0									0				
Age	25	04 aa	226	24	62	5	27	2	274			331	416	747	8	88	29	0.73					83		66	10%	4.81	-4.3	$5
Pre-Peak		05 ARI *	418	54	123	8	59	2	294	258	157	387	455	841	13	92	31	1.91	283	44	12	44	105	5%	52	4%	6.35	8.7	$13
Bats	Right	06 ARI	485	75	141	15	79	1	291	296	288	362	441	803	10	85	32	0.74	271	38	21	41	89	9%	52	1%	5.50	-6.8	$16
Reliability	55	07 ARI	415	56	118	15	60	2	284	320	270	365	467	833	11	88	29	1.06	293	38	20	43	110	10%	47	3%	5.96	4.2	$13
BAvg Potl	65%	1st Half	210	29	58	5	25	1	276			369	424	793	13	89	29	1.29	279	40	19	41	91	7%	53	3%	5.67	0.4	$5
LIMA Plan	B	2nd Half	205	27	60	10	35	1	293			361	512	873	10	87	30	0.85	307	34	21	44	129	13%	34	4%	6.26	3.8	$8
+/- Score	9	08 Proj	531	72	153	17	79	2	288			365	460	825	11	88	30	0.99	288	38	20	42	103	9%	53	3%	5.84	1.9	$17

Eye-catching season of across-the-board growth. Became a LHP killer, hit more FB in 2H and they started clearing the fence. If this is a stepping stone to further growth, then...
UP: .300, 20 HR.

Jacobs,Mike			AB	R	H	HR	RBI	SB	Avg	vL	vR	OB	Slg	OPS	bb%	ct%	h%	Eye	xBA	G	L	F	PX	hr/f	SX	SBO	RC/G	RAR	R$
Pos	3	03 aa	407	46	118	14	67	0	290			326	477	803	5	82	33	0.30					124		32	4%	5.22	-2.6	$13
Age	27	04 aaa	96	7	16	1	5	0	167			231	219	450	8	67	24	0.25					41		23	0%	0.54	-15.5	($1)
Peak		05 NYM *	533	67	148	30	91	1	277	400	305	322	522	843	6	81	29	0.34	316	41	23	37	156	19%	41	3%	5.68	1.2	$21
Bats	Left	06 FLA	469	54	123	20	77	3	262	182	281	327	473	800	9	78	30	0.43	282	40	20	40	138	14%	55	3%	5.41	-8.1	$14
Reliability	60	07 FLA	426	57	113	17	54	1	265	290	257	315	458	773	7	76	31	0.31	260	36	18	46	128	11%	57	3%	4.96	-7.9	$11
BAvg Potl	40%	1st Half	111	16	30	4	15	0	270			336	450	787	9	75	33	0.39	256	37	18	45	128	11%	30	0%	5.30	-1.0	$3
LIMA Plan	C	2nd Half	315	41	83	13	39	1	263			307	460	768	7	77	31	0.27	262	36	18	46	128	12%	64	4%	4.84	-7.0	$8
+/- Score	-4	08 Proj	557	71	150	23	82	2	269			322	473	795	7	78	31	0.35	274	38	19	44	134	12%	52	3%	5.24	-7.5	$17

On the surface, 2007 looks like a carbon copy of 2006. But two reasons for optimism:
- Made strides vs LHPs
- Rising FB%

Go the extra buck in anticipation of the 30-HR upside here.

Jenkins,Geoff			AB	R	H	HR	RBI	SB	Avg	vL	vR	OB	Slg	OPS	bb%	ct%	h%	Eye	xBA	G	L	F	PX	hr/f	SX	SBO	RC/G	RAR	R$
Pos	7	03 MIL	487	81	144	28	95	0	296	270	308	371	538	909	11	75	34	0.48	303	42	25	33	159	23%	50	0%	6.89	17.5	$22
Age	33	04 MIL	621	89	164	27	93	3	264	215	281	315	472	787	7	75	31	0.30	275	44	19	37	134	16%	93	3%	5.16	-5.0	$20
Past Peak		05 MIL	538	87	157	25	86	0	292	261	307	359	513	872	9	74	35	0.41	301	40	27	33	159	19%	43	0%	6.44	16.4	$22
Bats	Left	06 MIL	484	62	131	17	70	4	271	133	306	346	434	780	10	73	34	0.43	259	44	22	34	110	14%	59	3%	5.28	0.5	$14
Reliability	73	07 MIL	420	45	107	21	64	2	255	215	262	308	471	779	7	72	30	0.28	274	41	21	37	147	18%	51	4%	5.09	-3.1	$11
BAvg Potl	40%	1st Half	202	25	56	12	35	0	277			336	505	841	8	72	33	0.32	263	45	18	38	152	22%	20	4%	5.94	3.5	$7
LIMA Plan	C	2nd Half	218	20	51	9	29	2	234			280	440	721	6	73	28	0.24	278	38	25	37	142	15%	76	5%	4.31	-6.8	$4
+/- Score	-1	08 Proj	417	52	111	19	63	2	266			327	471	798	8	73	32	0.34	276	42	23	36	139	17%	61	3%	5.41	0.9	$13

Recovered some of the skills he lost last year. If h% follows suit, he could even get a little closer to 2003-05 levels. But at age 33 with a declining AB trend, odds are against him.

Jeter,Derek			AB	R	H	HR	RBI	SB	Avg	vL	vR	OB	Slg	OPS	bb%	ct%	h%	Eye	xBA	G	L	F	PX	hr/f	SX	SBO	RC/G	RAR	R$
Pos	6	03 NYY	482	87	156	10	52	11	324	370	312	379	450	829	8	82	38	0.49	298	54	25	21	83	12%	102	10%	5.74	17.1	$20
Age	33	04 NYY	643	111	188	23	78	23	292	314	285	340	471	811	7	85	32	0.46	300	49	19	32	109	13%	111	16%	5.38	16.5	$26
Past Peak		05 NYY	654	122	202	19	70	14	309	317	305	382	450	831	11	82	35	0.66	295	60	19	21	86	17%	108	8%	5.87	23.4	$27
Bats	Right	06 NYY	623	118	214	14	97	34	343	390	328	409	483	892	10	84	39	0.68	313	59	22	18	90	15%	125	17%	6.61	35.7	$34
Reliability	73	07 NYY	639	102	206	12	73	15	322	317	324	377	452	829	8	84	37	0.56	297	56	20	24	87	9%	93	11%	5.75	20.5	$25
BAvg Potl	35%	1st Half	300	52	103	5	36	7	343			408	483	892	10	89	38	0.97	314	55	20	25	90	8%	93	13%	6.64	16.6	$13
LIMA Plan	C	2nd Half	339	50	103	7	37	8	304			348	425	773	6	81	36	0.35	281	57	20	24	84	11%	90	9%	4.94	3.5	$12
+/- Score	-20	08 Proj	593	97	183	12	68	13	309			369	438	807	9	83	35	0.58	297	57	21	22	85	11%	96	10%	5.51	16.3	$21

PX has been below average for several years, now SX has crossed the same threshold. His hr/f says some power may return, but speed is a skill of the young.
DN: Under 10 SB

Jimenez,D'Angelo			AB	R	H	HR	RBI	SB	Avg	vL	vR	OB	Slg	OPS	bb%	ct%	h%	Eye	xBA	G	L	F	PX	hr/f	SX	SBO	RC/G	RAR	R$
Pos	6	03 2TM	561	69	153	14	57	11	273	273	273	349	415	765	11	84	30	0.74	292	42	27	31	85	10%	97	10%	5.11	13.7	$15
Age	30	04 CIN	563	76	152	12	67	13	270	240	281	363	394	757	13	82	31	0.83	264	42	22	37	79	7%	87	10%	5.14	16.5	$16
Peak		05 CIN *	427	50	90	7	33	13	210	355	176	304	308	612	12	87	23	1.07	284	41	26	33	66	5%	79	15%	3.50	-6.2	$6
Bats	Both	06 2AL *	196	30	45	4	25	2	228	188	182	341	344	685	15	87	24	1.36	255	45	16	40	70	6%	65	10%	4.49	0.5	$3
Reliability	15	07 WAS *	273	38	78	7	31	4	286	200	264	389	443	832	14	85	32	1.10	276	41	19	40	99	8%	72	7%	6.18	17.2	$8
BAvg Potl	55%	1st Half	188	26	59	6	23	2	314			408	495	903	14	87	34	1.25		36	0	64	106	6%	68	6%	6.96	15.4	$7
LIMA Plan	D	2nd Half	85	12	19	1	8	2	224			347	329	676	16	79	27	0.89	255	42	22	36	82	4%	59	11%	4.29	0.9	$1
+/- Score	-18	08 Proj	150	21	40	3	16	3	267			370	398	769	14	84	30	1.25	273	42	21	37	84	6%	78	10%	5.41	5.9	$4

2-10-.245 in 102 AB at WAS. Has one of the best batting eyes in MLB but still can't translate it into production, due to lack of power or speed. Now on the wrong side of 30, his upside is a decent BA in a utility role.

RAY MURPHY

Johjima,Kenji		AB	R	H	HR	RBI	SB	Avg	vL	vR	OB	Slg	OPS	bb%	ct%	h%	Eye	xBA	G	L	F	PX	hr/f	SX	SBO	RC/G	RAR	R$
Pos 2	03 JPN	628	98	170	21	116	8	270			317	439	756	6	92	27	0.90					96		94	8%	4.86	12.1	$22
Age 31	04 JPN	498	89	134	22	89	5	269			323	456	779	7	91	26	0.93					99		83	8%	5.09	14.8	$19
Past Peak	05 JPN	411	68	118	14	56	3	288			331	477	808	6	93	28	0.88					102		100	7%	5.41	17.5	$15
Bats Right	06 SEA	506	61	147	18	76	3	291	263	298	317	451	768	4	91	29	0.43	293	45	19	36	88	11%	56	3%	4.73	4.6	$15
Reliability 77	07 SEA	485	52	139	14	61	0	287	327	276	308	433	741	3	92	29	0.37	294	46	20	34	88	9%	24	2%	4.43	5.6	$12
BAvg Potl 55%	1st Half	228	27	70	8	32	0	307			325	482	807	3	92	31	0.32	321	40	24	36	105	11%	29	2%	5.10	6.7	$8
LIMA Plan C	2nd Half	257	25	69	6	29	0	268			293	389	682	3	91	28	0.41	271	51	16	33	73	8%	26	2%	3.83	-1.4	$5
+/- Score -27	08 Proj	504	63	141	16	70	2	280			309	439	748	4	92	28	0.50	301	46	19	35	91	10%	58	4%	4.59	6.4	$14

If not for some typical catcher dings in July and Sept, this could have been a carbon copy of 2006. Strong ct% limits BA downside, GB tendency does same for power upside. Safe, reliable choice behind the plate.

Johnson,Dan		AB	R	H	HR	RBI	SB	Avg	vL	vR	OB	Slg	OPS	bb%	ct%	h%	Eye	xBA	G	L	F	PX	hr/f	SX	SBO	RC/G	RAR	R$
Pos 3	03 a/a	542	71	134	21	89	6	247			313	419	732	9	87	25	0.75					97		76	8%	4.59	-13.9	$15
Age 28	04 aaa	536	72	140	23	84	0	260			342	449	791	11	86	27	0.89					106		45	1%	5.39	-1.3	$15
Peak	05 OAK *	557	81	153	21	89	0	275	276	275	361	453	814	12	87	29	1.04	306	38	24	38	110	11%	25	1%	5.74	10.4	$18
Bats Left	06 OAK *	458	56	113	14	70	0	246	217	238	338	398	736	12	85	26	0.95	265	49	15	36	91	10%	38	1%	4.86	-7.7	$9
Reliability 47	07 OAK	416	53	98	18	62	0	236	234	237	348	418	767	15	81	25	0.94	272	43	18	39	113	14%	28	0%	5.24	1.9	$9
BAvg Potl 70%	1st Half	197	25	50	6	27	0	254			369	416	785	15	83	28	1.06	271	49	16	35	106	10%	39	0%	5.62	3.0	$4
LIMA Plan C	2nd Half	219	28	48	12	35	0	219			329	420	749	14	80	22	0.84	275	38	20	42	121	16%	18	0%	4.90	-1.3	$5
+/- Score 22	08 Proj	426	55	109	17	66	0	256			354	431	785	13	84	27	0.93	277	44	18	38	107	12%	34	1%	5.42	3.0	$11

Low BA will scare others away, but xBA and good plate patience tell you to expect a BA rebound. 2nd half PX and FB levels hint at still-emerging power.
UP: 25 HR, .270 BA

Johnson,Kelly		AB	R	H	HR	RBI	SB	Avg	vL	vR	OB	Slg	OPS	bb%	ct%	h%	Eye	xBA	G	L	F	PX	hr/f	SX	SBO	RC/G	RAR	R$
Pos 4	03 aa	334	43	88	6	42	9	263			328	404	732	9	78	32	0.44					98		115	13%	4.64	3.6	$9
Age 26	04 aa	479	62	125	14	45	8	261			323	424	747	8	82	29	0.50					105		74	15%	4.75	5.7	$12
Pre-Peak	05 ATL *	445	77	114	16	59	8	256	257	236	357	438	795	14	79	29	0.74	294	44	26	30	117	15%	115	7%	5.61	13.7	$15
Bats Left	06 aaa *	39	3	12	1	7	1	308			400	487	887	13	85	34	1.00					121		32	8%	6.81	2.6	$2
Reliability 10	07 ATL	521	91	144	16	68	9	276	272	278	372	457	828	13	78	33	0.68	266	43	19	39	113	10%	116	8%	6.07	22.7	$18
BAvg Potl 45%	1st Half	273	46	74	8	37	5	271			372	451	823	14	78	32	0.73	271	46	19	35	110	11%	109	10%	6.04	11.8	$9
LIMA Plan B+	2nd Half	248	45	70	8	31	4	282			371	464	835	12	77	34	0.61	261	40	19	42	115	10%	112	6%	6.11	10.9	$9
+/- Score 2	08 Proj	528	86	142	18	66	10	269			357	454	811	12	78	31	0.63	276	43	20	37	116	12%	110	9%	5.74	18.0	$17

Strong, consistent debut, esp. given lost 2006. Only real wart in skill set is borderline ct%, but that is balanced by room for growth in power and speed. A rare five-category contributor at scarce MI position.

Johnson,Nick		AB	R	H	HR	RBI	SB	Avg	vL	vR	OB	Slg	OPS	bb%	ct%	h%	Eye	xBA	G	L	F	PX	hr/f	SX	SBO	RC/G	RAR	R$
Pos 3	03 NYY	324	60	92	14	47	5	284	282	285	411	472	883	18	82	31	1.23	314	45	27	28	117	19%	60	5%	6.89	13.9	$13
Age 29	04 MON	251	35	63	7	33	6	251	323	228	354	398	752	14	77	30	0.69	264	47	20	33	103	11%	65	11%	5.08	-6.5	$7
Peak	05 WAS	453	66	131	15	74	3	289	328	277	396	479	875	15	81	33	0.92	296	44	21	35	129	12%	59	7%	6.73	14.6	$17
Bats Left	06 WAS	500	100	145	23	77	10	290	303	285	418	520	938	18	80	32	1.11	309	42	22	36	148	16%	69	7%	7.65	23.1	$22
Reliability 5	07 WAS	0	0	0	0	0	0	0																				
BAvg Potl	1st Half	0	0	0	0	0	0	0																				
LIMA Plan C	2nd Half	0	0	0	0	0	0	0																				
+/- Score	08 Proj	324	54	89	15	48	1	275			390	487	876	16	79	31	0.92	298	45	22	33	138	17%	31	4%	6.72	9.4	$11

Missed season recovering from Sept. 2006 leg injury. Young enough to come back and contribute, but "injury prone" label seems well-earned at this point. Pay for 300 AB, hope for profit.

Johnson,Reed		AB	R	H	HR	RBI	SB	Avg	vL	vR	OB	Slg	OPS	bb%	ct%	h%	Eye	xBA	G	L	F	PX	hr/f	SX	SBO	RC/G	RAR	R$
Pos 7	03 TOR *	513	91	151	12	66	8	294	328	279	325	425	750	4	85	33	0.29	298	42	29	29	81	10%	108	9%	4.53	-11.5	$18
Age 31	04 TOR	537	68	145	10	61	6	270	301	255	306	380	686	5	82	31	0.29	270	55	19	26	71	9%	83	7%	3.81	-17.6	$12
Past Peak	05 TOR	398	55	107	8	58	5	269	279	262	307	412	719	5	79	32	0.27	284	51	22	27	95	9%	110	12%	4.27	-5.3	$11
Bats Right	06 TOR	461	86	147	12	49	8	319	323	316	364	479	844	7	82	37	0.41	288	47	20	33	105	10%	101	8%	5.83	8.0	$18
Reliability 9	07 TOR	275	31	65	2	14	4	236	325	202	278	320	598	5	80	29	0.29	244	47	19	34	62	3%	91	9%	2.80	-16.0	$2
BAvg Potl 45%	1st Half	34	6	9	1	7	2	265			286	412	697	3	76	32	0.13	220	44	4	52	106	7%	107	29%	3.79	-0.9	$2
LIMA Plan F	2nd Half	241	25	56	1	7	2	232			277	307	584	6	80	29	0.31	247	47	21	32	56	2%	77	7%	2.67	-15.0	$1
+/- Score 0	08 Proj	264	37	71	7	25	3	269			310	421	731	6	81	31	0.31	285	49	21	30	98	12%	88	9%	4.37	-3.9	$7

Missed three months with disc problems, clearly still had issues after his return. 2006's power levels probably represent a best-case for 2008. Only a bionic disc transplant could bring back the .300 BA, though.

Jones,Adam		AB	R	H	HR	RBI	SB	Avg	vL	vR	OB	Slg	OPS	bb%	ct%	h%	Eye	xBA	G	L	F	PX	hr/f	SX	SBO	RC/G	RAR	R$
Pos 7	03	0	0	0	0	0	0	0							0									0				
Age 22	04	0	0	0	0	0	0	0							0									0				
Growth	05 aa	228	32	65	6	19	8	286			349	428	777	9	81	33	0.51					89		107	18%	5.11	0.5	$8
Bats Right	06 SEA *	454	71	124	16	66	15	273	235	211	317	441	758	6	81	31	0.34	297	44	27	29	102	15%	111	19%	4.69	-6.5	$16
Reliability 13	07 SEA *	485	81	136	23	77	9	280	310	194	330	499	829	7	75	33	0.30	288	34	27	39	145	16%	104	15%	5.69	13.6	$19
BAvg Potl 40%	1st Half	306	48	87	15	54	4	284			336	507	843	7	77	33	0.34					147		80	13%	5.84	9.9	$12
LIMA Plan D	2nd Half	179	33	49	8	23	5	274			319	486	805	6	73	34	0.24	272	34	27	39	141	16%	136	19%	5.44	3.8	$7
+/- Score 18	08 Proj	326	53	85	10	45	6	261			311	421	732	7	78	31	0.33	275	38	27	35	104	11%	106	15%	4.44	-4.2	$10

2-4-.246 in 65 AB at SEA. Big numbers at Triple-A earned a callup, but couldn't get off the bench in SEA. Ct% is a concern, and may lead to a bumpy MLB adjustment. But the power is real, and will emerge in time.

Jones,Andruw		AB	R	H	HR	RBI	SB	Avg	vL	vR	OB	Slg	OPS	bb%	ct%	h%	Eye	xBA	G	L	F	PX	hr/f	SX	SBO	RC/G	RAR	R$
Pos 8	03 ATL	595	101	165	36	116	4	277	260	282	336	513	849	8	79	30	0.42	291	40	20	40	143	19%	76	5%	5.84	14.7	$27
Age 31	04 ATL	570	85	149	29	91	6	261	265	260	343	488	831	11	74	30	0.48	278	48	16	36	147	19%	78	8%	5.94	21.6	$20
Past Peak	05 ATL	586	95	154	51	128	5	263	254	265	335	575	910	10	81	24	0.57	320	42	16	42	180	26%	73	6%	6.56	34.1	$30
Bats Right	06 ATL	565	107	148	41	129	4	262	260	263	355	531	886	13	78	27	0.65	294	39	19	42	158	22%	59	3%	6.54	34.4	$26
Reliability 31	07 ATL	572	83	127	26	94	5	222	225	221	307	413	719	11	76	25	0.51	257	39	17	44	122	14%	74	5%	4.41	-2.6	$14
BAvg Potl 60%	1st Half	282	33	56	12	46	3	199			294	383	677	12	73	23	0.49	248	38	17	45	128	13%	53	5%	3.89	-5.9	$5
LIMA Plan C+	2nd Half	290	50	71	14	48	2	245			320	441	761	10	79	27	0.52	265	40	17	43	116	14%	82	5%	4.88	2.8	$9
+/- Score 28	08 Proj	548	89	139	28	99	4	254			335	460	796	11	77	28	0.54	269	40	18	42	128	15%	74	4%	5.38	13.3	$19

Lots went wrong in 2007 but the focal point was his power. Most of his BPIs rebounded in the 2nd half, EXCEPT his power. Perhaps most remarkable was that he still had nearly 100 RBIs with his .222 BA. Lotsa oddness.

Jones,Brandon		AB	R	H	HR	RBI	SB	Avg	vL	vR	OB	Slg	OPS	bb%	ct%	h%	Eye	xBA	G	L	F	PX	hr/f	SX	SBO	RC/G	RAR	R$
Pos 7	03	0	0	0	0	0	0	0							0									0				
Age 24	04	0	0	0	0	0	0	0							0									0				
Growth	05	0	0	0	0	0	0	0							0									0				
Bats Left	06 aa	176	17	46	7	24	4	261			319	466	785	8	79	30	0.41					121		101	14%	5.17	-0.2	$5
Reliability 0	07 a/a	554	75	152	17	93	15	274			339	444	783	9	79	32	0.46		58	17	25	112	16%	100	15%	5.22	3.0	$19
BAvg Potl 35%	1st Half	309	44	79	10	47	9	256			331	417	749	10	79	30	0.53					102		98	18%	4.83	-1.8	$10
LIMA Plan D	2nd Half	245	31	73	7	46	6	298			348	478	826	7	79	35	0.37		58	17	25	124	14%	97	11%	5.70	4.5	$10
+/- Score 12	08 Proj	248	29	68	7	39	6	274			334	449	782	8	79	32	0.42	292	58	17	25	113	15%	103	14%	5.19	0.6	$8

Oft-injured prospect finally showed what he can do over a full season. With athleticism and power/speed blend, could be in the running to replace Andruw as early as Opening Day.

Jones,Chipper		AB	R	H	HR	RBI	SB	Avg	vL	vR	OB	Slg	OPS	bb%	ct%	h%	Eye	xBA	G	L	F	PX	hr/f	SX	SBO	RC/G	RAR	R$
Pos 5	03 ATL	555	103	169	27	106	2	305	306	304	405	517	922	14	85	32	1.13	304	38	22	40	126	14%	61	2%	7.14	43.9	$27
Age 36	04 ATL	472	69	117	30	96	2	248	268	238	362	485	847	15	80	25	0.88	283	46	15	39	137	21%	51	1%	6.16	15.3	$17
Decline	05 ATL	358	66	106	21	72	5	296	254	303	414	556	970	17	84	30	1.29	336	42	23	35	162	20%	62	5%	7.84	30.3	$19
Bats Both	06 ATL	411	87	133	26	86	6	324	293	332	411	596	1007	13	82	34	0.84	314	41	19	40	156	19%	93	5%	8.07	28.2	$24
Reliability 52	07 ATL	513	108	173	29	102	5	337	274	378	429	604	1033	14	85	35	1.09	330	44	19	37	157	18%	87	3%	8.42	48.7	$30
BAvg Potl 55%	1st Half	208	39	68	13	32	1	327			412	601	1013	13	84	34	0.91	324	42	19	39	161	19%	62	1%	8.08	18.1	$11
LIMA Plan B+	2nd Half	305	69	105	16	70	4	344			418	607	1046	15	86	36	1.24	334	45	19	36	154	17%	94	4%	8.65	30.5	$19
+/- Score -29	08 Proj	400	81	129	23	81	4	323			418	583	1001	14	84	34	1.04	322	43	20	38	153	18%	83	4%	8.06	33.2	$23

The surprise in 2007 was not the skills he displayed, but the AB total. At his age and with his injury history, odds are steep that he'll be able to repeat that feat. Don't pay for more than 400 AB. '06 is a nice over/under.

RAY MURPHY

Jones,Jacque

Jones,Jacque			AB	R	H	HR	RBI	SB	Avg	vL	vR	OB	Slg	OPS	bb%	ct%	h%	Eye	xBA	G	L	F	PX	hr/f	SX	SBO	RC/G	RAR	R$
Pos	89	03 MIN	517	76	157	16	69	12	304	304	317	331	462	793	4	80	36	0.20	300	59	20	21	106	18%	101	10%	5.01	3.9	$20
Age	33	04 MIN	555	69	141	24	80	13	254	245	258	304	427	731	7	79	28	0.34	268	57	13	30	104	18%	77	17%	4.34	-6.2	$17
Past Peak		05 MIN	523	74	130	23	73	13	249	201	268	315	438	753	9	77	28	0.43	287	59	15	26	120	22%	110	13%	4.76	7.5	$17
Bats	Left	06 CHC	533	73	152	27	81	9	285	234	303	329	499	828	6	78	32	0.30	300	56	19	26	131	25%	80	8%	5.53	16.4	$21
Reliability	68	07 CHC	453	52	129	5	66	6	285	295	283	335	400	734	7	85	33	0.49	290	58	19	23	81	6%	72	7%	4.61	0.6	$12
BAvg Potl	50%	1st Half	202	23	47	2	20	2	233			289	327	616	7	85	27	0.52	280	58	19	23	64	5%	75	6%	3.23	-8.2	$2
LIMA Plan	D+	2nd Half	251	29	82	3	46	4	327			372	458	830	7	84	38	0.46	298	58	19	24	95	6%	68	8%	5.72	7.8	$10
+/- Score	7	08 Proj	**326**	**41**	**92**	**9**	**48**	**6**	**282**			**332**	**438**	**770**	**7**	**81**	**32**	**0.40**	**292**	**58**	**18**	**24**	**102**	**14%**	**79**	**9%**	**4.93**	**3.4**	**$11**

Made a nice gain in ct%, but it was overshadowed by complete loss of power. Should rebound a bit from hr/f regression alone, but high GB limited his power even at peak. At his age, it only gets tougher from here.

Kata,Matt

Kata,Matt			AB	R	H	HR	RBI	SB	Avg	vL	vR	OB	Slg	OPS	bb%	ct%	h%	Eye	xBA	G	L	F	PX	hr/f	SX	SBO	RC/G	RAR	R$
Pos	5	03 ARI	* 489	66	127	9	48	5	261			306	409	715	6	85	29	0.42					92		111	10%	4.33	1.2	$11
Age	30	04 ARI	162	17	40	2	13	4	247			303	364	667	7	82	29	0.45					77		105	13%	3.80	-6.1	$3
Peak		05 2NL	* 333	31	81	2	22	5	244			269	324	593	3	90	27	0.34	243	29	23	48	50	1%	94	12%	2.90	-18.9	$4
Bats	Both	06 aaa	331	40	78	8	31	4	236			271	379	650	5	85	26	0.32					87		84	11%	3.42	-18.4	$5
Reliability	19	07 2NL	* 230	29	49	5	19	3	213	113	276	246	352	598	4	82	24	0.24	253	47	13	40	90	7%	106	10%	2.74	-14.5	$2
BAvg Potl	60%	1st Half	119	18	25	4	9	3	210			271	353	624	8	81	23	0.43	246	40	18	42	81	10%	112	15%	3.12	-6.2	$2
LIMA Plan	F	2nd Half	111	11	24	1	10	0	216			216	351	568	0	83	25	0.00	257	51	10	39	98	3%	72	0%	2.29	-8.5	$0
+/- Score	11	08 Proj	**115**	**13**	**26**	**2**	**10**	**1**	**226**			**256**	**359**	**615**	**4**	**84**	**25**	**0.25**	**255**	**48**	**12**	**40**	**85**	**5%**	**96**	**11%**	**3.00**	**-6.9**	**$1**

3-16-.222 in 158 AB at TEX/PIT. Arrived in PIT mid-season, and went 88 AB without drawing a BB. Apparently whatever the problem is in PIT, it's highly contagious.

Kearns,Austin

Kearns,Austin			AB	R	H	HR	RBI	SB	Avg	vL	vR	OB	Slg	OPS	bb%	ct%	h%	Eye	xBA	G	L	F	PX	hr/f	SX	SBO	RC/G	RAR	R$
Pos	9	03 CIN	292	39	77	15	58	5	264	266	263	354	455	810	12	77	30	0.60	280	51	20	29	120	23%	56	8%	5.61	0.0	$12
Age	27	04 CIN	* 300	43	72	11	44	4	240	213	235	335	423	759	13	70	31	0.48	244	49	12	39	128	13%	95	7%	5.17	-1.0	$8
Peak		05 CIN	* 498	81	127	24	84	0	254	233	240	331	483	813	10	73	30	0.43	300	49	22	29	166	23%	46	0%	5.72	6.8	$17
Bats	Right	06 2NL	537	86	142	24	86	9	264	336	236	356	467	823	12	75	31	0.56	270	42	19	39	132	15%	78	8%	5.91	17.8	$19
Reliability	71	07 WAS	587	84	156	16	74	2	266	292	258	345	411	756	11	82	30	0.67	273	45	20	35	95	10%	47	2%	4.98	-4.6	$14
BAvg Potl	55%	1st Half	289	34	74	5	26	0	256			320	384	704	9	82	30	0.53	263	45	18	36	89	6%	44	1%	4.29	-8.2	$4
LIMA Plan	C+	2nd Half	298	50	82	11	48	2	275			368	436	805	13	82	31	0.80	282	45	22	33	100	14%	50	3%	5.64	3.3	$10
+/- Score	5	08 Proj	**584**	**89**	**159**	**22**	**87**	**5**	**272**			**356**	**449**	**805**	**11**	**78**	**32**	**0.59**	**277**	**45**	**20**	**35**	**117**	**14%**	**64**	**4%**	**5.60**	**7.5**	**$19**

RFK sapped his power again (SLG: .365 Hm/.454 Rd). New park could be very good news for him, especially in light of ct% gains. GB% uptick is a concern, but there is still a power bat lurking here.

Kemp,Matt

Kemp,Matt			AB	R	H	HR	RBI	SB	Avg	vL	vR	OB	Slg	OPS	bb%	ct%	h%	Eye	xBA	G	L	F	PX	hr/f	SX	SBO	RC/G	RAR	R$
Pos	9	03	0	0	0	0	0	0	0							0									0				
Age	23	04	0	0	0	0	0	0	0							0									0				
Growth		05	0	0	0	0	0	0	0							0									0				
Bats	Right	06 LA	* 535	93	157	16	84	28	293	229	264	343	464	806	7	79	34	0.36	278	40	24	36	107	10%	134	24%	5.40	9.5	$25
Reliability	0	07 LA	* 453	73	147	14	58	18	324	390	318	359	505	863	5	80	38	0.28	278	45	17	37	113	10%	132	20%	5.99	9.0	$22
BAvg Potl	30%	1st Half	213	36	70	5	24	10	329			367	498	865	6	84	38	0.37	291	48	18	35	111	8%	121	22%	6.04	4.5	$10
LIMA Plan	C+	2nd Half	240	37	77	9	34	8	319			351	511	862	5	78	38	0.22	269	45	17	38	115	13%	125	18%	5.96	4.7	$11
+/- Score	-15	08 Proj	**452**	**75**	**131**	**14**	**64**	**20**	**290**			**331**	**466**	**798**	**6**	**80**	**34**	**0.31**	**276**	**44**	**19**	**37**	**111**	**10%**	**142**	**23%**	**5.23**	**1.0**	**$20**

10-42-.342 in 292 AB at LA. xBA says he's not yet a .320 hitter. Will need to control the strike zone better at big-league level, but power/speed blend is legit. Invest in the speed while you wait on the power.

Kendall,Jason

Kendall,Jason			AB	R	H	HR	RBI	SB	Avg	vL	vR	OB	Slg	OPS	bb%	ct%	h%	Eye	xBA	G	L	F	PX	hr/f	SX	SBO	RC/G	RAR	R$
Pos	2	03 PIT	587	84	191	6	58	8	325	310	331	377	416	793	8	93	34	1.23	304	47	25	28	56	4%	77	7%	5.42	17.8	$21
Age	33	04 PIT	574	86	183	3	51	11	319	291	325	383	390	774	9	93	34	1.46	282	51	20	29	49	2%	67	9%	5.35	24.1	$19
Past Peak		05 OAK	601	70	163	0	53	8	271	293	264	327	321	648	8	94	29	1.28	283	53	21	26	38	0%	72	6%	3.92	-1.8	$11
Bats	Right	06 OAK	552	76	163	1	50	11	295	331	285	357	342	699	9	90	33	0.98	279	50	24	26	35	1%	72	8%	4.41	0.1	$13
Reliability	68	07 2TM	466	45	113	3	41	3	242	198	259	290	309	599	6	91	26	0.74	253	44	19	38	45	2%	53	6%	3.17	-10.4	$4
BAvg Potl	65%	1st Half	247	20	53	1	20	3	215			248	259	507	4	90	24	0.44	235	43	18	39	32	1%	57	7%	1.98	-14.7	$0
LIMA Plan	D	2nd Half	219	25	60	2	21	0	274			335	365	700	8	92	29	1.18	272	45	19	36	59	3%	43	5%	4.46	3.5	$4
+/- Score	-0	08 Proj	**402**	**47**	**108**	**2**	**36**	**4**	**269**			**324**	**333**	**657**	**8**	**92**	**29**	**0.97**	**271**	**47**	**21**	**32**	**43**	**2%**	**65**	**7%**	**3.91**	**-1.6**	**$7**

Even his days as "end-game catcher who can give you 10 SB" are gone. High ct% remains, but little other reason for hope here. Even in 2nd half resurgence, OBA spiked but he didn't run. Stay clear.

Kendrick,Howie

Kendrick,Howie			AB	R	H	HR	RBI	SB	Avg	vL	vR	OB	Slg	OPS	bb%	ct%	h%	Eye	xBA	G	L	F	PX	hr/f	SX	SBO	RC/G	RAR	R$
Pos	4	03	0	0	0	0	0	0	0							0									0				
Age	24	04	0	0	0	0	0	0	0							0									0				
Growth		05 aa	190	27	57	5	33	9	300			318	484	802	3	92	31	0.31					117		118	37%	5.14	4.3	$9
Bats	Right	06 LAA	* 557	70	171	14	79	15	307	264	295	329	476	804	3	85	34	0.22	296	52	15	33	107	9%	109	15%	5.14	15.6	$20
Reliability	12	07 LAA	* 388	63	122	8	49	6	315	325	322	332	451	783	3	82	37	0.14	279	54	16	30	94	8%	95	10%	4.83	7.4	$14
BAvg Potl	30%	1st Half	197	34	59	6	23	4	299			324	462	785	3	80	35	0.18	277	54	14	32	110	12%	102	13%	4.90	4.3	$7
LIMA Plan	D+	2nd Half	191	29	63	2	26	2	331			342	439	780	2	85	38	0.10	281	55	18	27	78	4%	82	8%	4.76	3.2	$7
+/- Score	-35	08 Proj	**477**	**69**	**139**	**10**	**66**	**11**	**291**			**310**	**443**	**753**	**3**	**85**	**33**	**0.18**	**294**	**54**	**16**	**30**	**100**	**9%**	**106**	**16%**	**4.51**	**5.2**	**$16**

5-39-.322 in 338 AB at LAA. In between two separate finger injuries, hacked his way to a lofty BA. That BA will make others think that he's arrived, but you'll see lack of supporting skills. Ceiling is high, but not here yet.

Kennedy,Adam

Kennedy,Adam			AB	R	H	HR	RBI	SB	Avg	vL	vR	OB	Slg	OPS	bb%	ct%	h%	Eye	xBA	G	L	F	PX	hr/f	SX	SBO	RC/G	RAR	R$
Pos	4	03 ANA	449	71	121	13	49	22	269	235	281	336	399	735	9	84	30	0.62	266	31	27	42	78	8%	105	23%	4.60	6.1	$17
Age	32	04 ANA	468	70	130	10	48	15	278	250	286	336	406	742	8	80	33	0.45	251	40	21	39	79	7%	125	15%	4.67	7.9	$14
Past Peak		05 ANA	416	49	125	2	37	19	300	296	302	346	370	716	7	85	35	0.45	261	41	24	35	55	2%	90	18%	4.34	2.5	$14
Bats	Left	06 LAA	451	50	123	4	55	16	273	193	291	331	384	714	8	84	32	0.54	280	41	27	32	72	3%	113	21%	4.44	4.3	$11
Reliability	37	07 STL	279	27	61	3	18	6	219	122	235	276	290	566	7	88	24	0.67	241	43	17	40	44	3%	81	11%	2.73	-15.3	$2
BAvg Potl	70%	1st Half	190	16	40	0	12	4	211			272	258	530	8	91	23	0.89	235	41	17	41	33	0%	81	10%	2.52	-12.1	$0
LIMA Plan	D	2nd Half	89	11	21	3	6	2	236			284	360	644	6	83	25	0.40	251	46	18	36	70	11%	63	14%	3.30	-3.4	$2
+/- Score	9	08 Proj	**376**	**43**	**100**	**6**	**33**	**9**	**266**			**319**	**363**	**682**	**7**	**85**	**30**	**0.52**	**258**	**42**	**21**	**37**	**60**	**5%**	**86**	**13%**	**3.96**	**-6.7**	**$8**

Knee surgery ended his season in August. Struggled mightily to that point, but BPIs were mostly intact while h% dip tortured him. Still, 30something speedsters with bad legs make for poor risks. End-game MI if healthy.

Kent,Jeff

Kent,Jeff			AB	R	H	HR	RBI	SB	Avg	vL	vR	OB	Slg	OPS	bb%	ct%	h%	Eye	xBA	G	L	F	PX	hr/f	SX	SBO	RC/G	RAR	R$
Pos	4	03 HOU	505	77	150	22	93	6	297	361	282	347	509	856	7	83	32	0.46	298	36	21	43	135	12%	80	6%	5.94	21.4	$22
Age	40	04 HOU	540	96	156	27	107	7	289	286	290	348	531	880	8	82	31	0.51	296	36	20	44	141	14%	121	7%	6.29	25.6	$25
Decline		05 LA	553	100	160	29	105	6	289	306	285	371	512	883	12	85	30	0.85	297	31	21	48	136	13%	69	5%	6.46	29.5	$27
Bats	Right	06 LA	407	61	119	14	68	1	292	347	275	377	477	853	12	83	32	0.80	282	34	23	43	111	10%	57	2%	6.24	18.6	$14
Reliability	71	07 LA	494	78	149	20	79	1	302	299	302	374	500	874	10	88	31	0.93	291	38	18	45	118	10%	43	3%	6.35	24.4	$19
BAvg Potl	55%	1st Half	259	41	67	10	36	1	259			338	448	786	11	86	27	0.84	278	35	17	47	114	10%	59	4%	5.34	5.9	$7
LIMA Plan	C+	2nd Half	235	37	82	10	43	0	349			414	557	971	10	90	36	1.08	303	40	18	42	123	11%	26	1%	7.42	17.2	$12
+/- Score	-30	08 Proj	**411**	**66**	**118**	**15**	**71**	**2**	**287**			**363**	**473**	**836**	**11**	**86**	**30**	**0.84**	**286**	**36**	**20**	**44**	**113**	**10%**	**55**	**3%**	**5.93**	**15.8**	**$15**

Enters his 40s with a lot to like:
- Extremely stable skill set.
- Late-career spike in ct%.
- Got stronger in 2nd half.
SX trend and rising GB% are the first signs of fade, but he's not done yet.

Keppinger,Jeff

Keppinger,Jeff			AB	R	H	HR	RBI	SB	Avg	vL	vR	OB	Slg	OPS	bb%	ct%	h%	Eye	xBA	G	L	F	PX	hr/f	SX	SBO	RC/G	RAR	R$
Pos	6	03	0	0	0	0	0	0	0							0									0				
Age	28	04 a/a	389	47	113	1	31	10	292			340	357	696	7	95	30	1.61					42		83	15%	4.42	1.4	$10
Peak		05 aaa	255	34	78	3	25	4	307			340	412	752	5	96	31	1.16					63		94	7%	4.84	4.1	$8
Bats	Right	06 KC	* 510	67	152	6	50	0	298	222	303	354	378	732	8	93	31	1.25	279	58	19	23	48	5%	31	2%	4.77	5.1	$11
Reliability	27	07 CIN	* 469	66	155	7	47	3	331	362	320	387	450	837	8	95	34	1.67	303	47	21	32	71	5%	66	3%	5.97	24.9	$16
BAvg Potl	60%	1st Half	212	27	72	2	11	1	340			394	439	833	8	95	35	1.73		50	13	38	62	3%	52	3%	5.93	10.9	$6
LIMA Plan	C+	2nd Half	257	39	83	5	36	2	323			381	459	840	9	94	33	1.63	311	46	22	32	79	6%	74	3%	6.00	14.0	$10
+/- Score	-13	08 Proj	**356**	**48**	**107**	**8**	**35**	**3**	**301**			**354**	**436**	**790**	**8**	**94**	**30**	**1.47**	**308**	**48**	**21**	**31**	**75**	**8%**	**69**	**5%**	**5.38**	**12.8**	**$11**

5-32-.332 in 241 AB at CIN. Journeyman finally found a gig, and delivered. BA was inflated by h%, but otherwise he's been doing this for years. High ct% sets BA floor, making him an excellent end game choice.

RAY MURPHY

Kinsler,Ian

		AB	R	H	HR	RBI	SB	Avg	vL	vR	OB	Slg	OPS	bb%	ct%	h%	Eye	xBA	G	L	F	PX	hr/f	SX	SBO	RC/G	RAR	R$
Pos 4	03	0	0	0	0	0	0	0							0									0				
Age 25	04 aa	271	42	78	8	37	6	288			352	454	806	9	85	31	0.68					106		71	13%	5.51	9.0	$10
Pre-Peak	05 aaa	526	71	127	18	64	13	241			291	395	687	7	88	24	0.61					91		89	16%	3.98	-5.7	$14
Bats Right	06 TEX	423	65	121	14	55	11	286	271	292	348	454	802	8	85	31	0.63	276	35	21	44	103	9%	89	13%	5.40	15.4	$15
Reliability 41	07 TEX	483	96	127	20	61	23	263	339	239	347	441	788	11	83	28	0.75	268	35	20	46	108	11%	125	17%	5.34	16.9	$20
BAvg Potl 55%	1st Half	258	50	62	14	35	11	240			331	450	781	12	83	24	0.80	278	31	20	49	125	13%	104	15%	5.21	8.3	$10
LIMA Plan B+	2nd Half	225	46	65	6	26	12	289			365	431	796	11	83	33	0.69	259	38	19	42	89	8%	134	19%	5.47	8.5	$10
+/- Score 23	08 Proj	**510**	**89**	**138**	**18**	**64**	**20**	**271**			**341**	**437**	**778**	**10**	**84**	**29**	**0.69**	**271**	**35**	**20**	**45**	**101**	**9%**	**114**	**17%**	**5.17**	**15.3**	**$19**

Started hot (9 HR, 1.046 OPS in April), but couldn't sustain.
PRO: 20/20 in under 500 AB, bb% growth, SX spike.
CON: Gave back PX gains in 2nd half, troubles vs RHP.
Best path to growth is more AB.

Klesko,Ryan

		AB	R	H	HR	RBI	SB	Avg	vL	vR	OB	Slg	OPS	bb%	ct%	h%	Eye	xBA	G	L	F	PX	hr/f	SX	SBO	RC/G	RAR	R$
Pos 3	03 SD	397	47	100	21	67	2	252	194	272	357	456	813	14	79	27	0.78	264	40	17	44	126	15%	24	6%	5.73	2.5	$12
Age 36	04 SD	402	58	117	9	66	3	291	325	278	400	448	848	15	83	33	1.09	289	44	22	35	104	8%	66	3%	6.45	5.7	$14
Decline	05 SD	443	61	110	18	58	3	248	200	263	357	418	775	14	82	27	0.94	265	42	17	41	104	12%	50	5%	5.34	-3.5	$12
Bats Left	06 SD	4	0	3	0	2	0	750	1000	667	833	1000	1833	33	100	75			25	50	25	172	0%	0	0%	19.36	0.5	$1
Reliability 0	07 SF	362	51	94	6	44	5	260	262	259	343	401	744	11	81	31	0.68	260	47	14	39	98	5%	90	6%	4.95	-6.9	$8
BAvg Potl 55%	1st Half	167	25	48	3	22	1	287			377	449	826	13	82	34	0.80	262	50	10	40	105	5%	92	4%	6.06	2.2	$5
LIMA Plan D	2nd Half	195	26	46	3	22	4	236			313	359	672	10	81	28	0.58	257	46	16	38	92	5%	73	8%	3.98	-9.5	$3
+/- Score -6	08 Proj	**213**	**29**	**55**	**4**	**29**	**2**	**258**			**354**	**386**	**740**	**13**	**81**	**30**	**0.80**	**255**	**45**	**16**	**39**	**88**	**6%**	**72**	**5%**	**4.97**	**-4.6**	**$5**

Skills decline was mostly complete even before he missed 2006. Soon pitchers will realize there's no risk in throwing him strikes, which would drop his bb% and OBA, thus negating his last shred of sim league value.

Konerko,Paul

		AB	R	H	HR	RBI	SB	Avg	vL	vR	OB	Slg	OPS	bb%	ct%	h%	Eye	xBA	G	L	F	PX	hr/f	SX	SBO	RC/G	RAR	R$
Pos 3	03 CHW	444	49	104	18	65	0	234	327	187	302	399	700	9	89	23	0.86	291	40	22	38	92	12%	20	0%	4.25	-15.0	$9
Age 32	04 CHW	563	84	156	41	117	1	277	288	273	356	535	891	11	81	28	0.64	290	42	17	41	144	22%	33	1%	6.42	22.8	$24
Past Peak	05 CHW	575	98	163	40	100	0	283	261	289	372	534	906	12	81	29	0.74	309	33	25	42	148	20%	26	0%	6.71	26.1	$26
Bats Right	06 CHW	566	97	177	35	113	1	313	318	310	379	551	930	10	82	33	0.58	303	33	25	42	139	18%	41	1%	6.88	22.2	$27
Reliability 85	07 CHW	549	71	142	31	90	0	259	296	244	351	490	841	12	81	27	0.76	286	38	17	45	145	16%	17	1%	5.99	14.4	$17
BAvg Potl 60%	1st Half	260	33	65	12	39	0	250			343	438	782	12	80	27	0.71	260	39	16	44	120	13%	19	0%	5.29	1.5	$7
LIMA Plan C	2nd Half	289	38	77	19	51	0	266			358	536	894	12	83	26	0.82	310	37	18	45	166	18%	17	1%	6.61	12.7	$10
+/- Score 21	08 Proj	**558**	**82**	**154**	**34**	**99**	**0**	**276**			**359**	**513**	**872**	**11**	**82**	**28**	**0.71**	**298**	**36**	**21**	**43**	**142**	**17%**	**25**	**1%**	**6.29**	**17.6**	**$21**

A mixed bag here...
CON: More GBs, clear trend in hr/f, sudden issues vs RHP.
PRO: xBA says BA crash wasn't real, PX is rock solid.
Bottom line: Pay for 30 HR, you might get a bonus 5 or 10 more.

Kotchman,Casey

		AB	R	H	HR	RBI	SB	Avg	vL	vR	OB	Slg	OPS	bb%	ct%	h%	Eye	xBA	G	L	F	PX	hr/f	SX	SBO	RC/G	RAR	R$
Pos 3	03	0	0	0	0	0	0	0							0									0				
Age 25	04 a/a	313	42	108	6	46	0	346			383	507	889	6	92	36	0.79					103		28	0%	6.31	6.8	$13
Pre-Peak	05 ANA	* 489	63	128	14	66	1	263	250	277	327	408	735	9	91	27	1.02	312	55	21	24	86	13%	43	4%	4.74	-5.0	$12
Bats Left	06 LAA	79	6	12	1	6	0	152	214	138	221	215	436	8	84	17	0.54	222	67	11	23	40	7%	37	6%	1.04	-11.7	($1)
Reliability 0	07 LAA	443	64	131	11	68	2	296	315	292	371	467	838	11	90	31	1.23	307	51	16	33	109	8%	58	5%	6.09	12.3	$14
BAvg Potl 70%	1st Half	216	29	69	8	36	2	319			388	532	920	10	92	32	1.41	326	55	14	32	122	13%	79	3%	6.91	10.5	$9
LIMA Plan C+	2nd Half	227	35	62	3	32	0	273			355	405	761	11	89	30	1.12	289	47	19	35	96	4%	36	6%	5.27	1.2	$5
+/- Score 33	08 Proj	**494**	**68**	**148**	**15**	**72**	**1**	**300**			**365**	**477**	**842**	**9**	**91**	**31**	**1.09**	**308**	**51**	**17**	**32**	**107**	**11%**	**46**	**4%**	**5.99**	**11.1**	**$16**

PRO: Stayed fairly healthy, hit LHPs well, spiked his ct%, cut high GB% in 2nd half.
CON: PX wore down in 2H, GB% still too high for a power hitter.
Young enough to show more. If so... UP: 20 HR, .310 BA

Kotsay,Mark

		AB	R	H	HR	RBI	SB	Avg	vL	vR	OB	Slg	OPS	bb%	ct%	h%	Eye	xBA	G	L	F	PX	hr/f	SX	SBO	RC/G	RAR	R$
Pos 8	03 SD	482	64	128	7	38	6	266	236	278	342	384	726	10	83	31	0.68	286	46	26	29	80	6%	90	6%	4.68	-4.2	$10
Age 32	04 OAK	606	78	190	15	63	8	314	336	239	371	459	829	8	88	34	0.79	282	38	21	41	86	7%	71	7%	5.76	17.3	$20
Past Peak	05 OAK	582	75	163	15	82	5	280	324	261	326	421	747	6	91	29	0.78	307	40	25	35	86	8%	58	7%	4.75	7.9	$17
Bats Left	06 OAK	502	57	138	7	59	6	275	265	278	333	386	720	8	89	30	0.80	275	46	19	35	70	4%	77	6%	4.56	-1.4	$10
Reliability 36	07 OAK	* 243	21	50	1	21	2	207	130	238	276	280	556	9	91	22	1.08	246	45	15	41	54	1%	50	6%	2.90	-10.5	$0
BAvg Potl 80%	1st Half	127	12	30	1	10	2	236			307	323	630	9	92	25	1.30	270	56	14	30	61	3%	51	6%	3.77	-1.9	$1
LIMA Plan F	2nd Half	116	9	20	0	11	0	175			242	233	474	8	90	19	0.89	225	36	15	49	47	0%	42	6%	1.93	-8.9	($1)
+/- Score 29	08 Proj	**294**	**31**	**75**	**3**	**31**	**3**	**255**			**316**	**352**	**669**	**8**	**90**	**27**	**0.89**	**265**	**43**	**18**	**39**	**64**	**3%**	**59**	**6%**	**4.03**	**-3.3**	**$4**

1-20-.214 in 206 AB at OAK. Long-time back problems finally escalated from "annoying" to "debilitating". Even early-season disc surgery doesn't seem to have helped. Ct% remains elite, but there's no authority there.

Kouzmanoff,Kevin

		AB	R	H	HR	RBI	SB	Avg	vL	vR	OB	Slg	OPS	bb%	ct%	h%	Eye	xBA	G	L	F	PX	hr/f	SX	SBO	RC/G	RAR	R$
Pos 5	03	0	0	0	0	0	0	0							0									0				
Age 26	04 aa	24	3	4	1	5	0	167			231	333	564	8	75	18	0.33					107		41	0%	2.21	-2.2	$0
Pre-Peak	05	0	0	0	0	0	0	0							0									0				
Bats Right	06 CLE	* 402	65	129	20	78	4	321	167	227	376	546	922	8	85	34	0.61	301	59	9	32	132	18%	61	7%	6.71	18.5	$19
Reliability 7	07 SD	484	57	133	18	74	1	275	356	240	320	457	776	6	81	31	0.34	273	41	18	41	116	11%	50	1%	4.93	2.1	$14
BAvg Potl 40%	1st Half	203	19	44	6	30	0	217			274	374	648	7	75	26	0.32	252	38	20	42	109	9%	39	0%	3.41	-8.6	$2
LIMA Plan D+	2nd Half	281	38	89	12	44	1	317			354	516	870	5	84	34	0.36	288	44	17	39	120	13%	54	1%	5.95	8.8	$12
+/- Score -38	08 Proj	**489**	**66**	**138**	**21**	**83**	**2**	**282**			**332**	**483**	**815**	**7**	**83**	**31**	**0.43**	**286**	**43**	**17**	**40**	**123**	**13%**	**60**	**4%**	**5.42**	**6.6**	**$17**

Terrible 1st half followed by a very nice 2nd half recovery (including .285 BA vs RHP). Petco will continue to put a drag on his pop (13 road HR), but with a few more AB...
UP: 25 HR

Kubel,Jason

		AB	R	H	HR	RBI	SB	Avg	vL	vR	OB	Slg	OPS	bb%	ct%	h%	Eye	xBA	G	L	F	PX	hr/f	SX	SBO	RC/G	RAR	R$
Pos 70	03	0	0	0	0	0	0	0							0									0				
Age 25	04 a/a	488	85	162	18	89	14	332			393	547	940	9	89	35	0.91					127		107	14%	7.07	24.4	$26
Pre-Peak	05 MIN	0	0	0	0	0	0	0							0									0				
Bats Left	06 MIN	* 340	41	86	12	48	4	253	243	240	302	415	717	7	80	29	0.35	277	49	21	31	99	14%	83	5%	4.21	-9.7	$8
Reliability 0	07 MIN	418	49	114	13	65	5	273	236	280	338	450	787	9	81	31	0.52	293	43	22	35	121	11%	79	5%	5.28	6.7	$12
BAvg Potl 55%	1st Half	206	21	52	5	26	2	252			303	398	701	7	81	29	0.38	292	43	26	32	104	9%	48	4%	4.11	-3.7	$4
LIMA Plan B	2nd Half	212	28	62	8	39	3	292			370	500	870	11	81	33	0.65	296	43	19	39	136	12%	82	5%	6.40	9.9	$8
+/- Score 42	08 Proj	**500**	**64**	**143**	**20**	**89**	**7**	**286**			**345**	**484**	**829**	**8**	**82**	**32**	**0.50**	**300**	**44**	**21**	**34**	**126**	**14%**	**84**	**6%**	**5.70**	**11.6**	**$18**

Another positive step in what has become a long, slow road back from lost 2005. 2nd half PX, FB%, bb% all point at imminent power surge. Not too late to get in on the ground floor.
UP: 30 HR, .300 BA

Laird,Gerald

		AB	R	H	HR	RBI	SB	Avg	vL	vR	OB	Slg	OPS	bb%	ct%	h%	Eye	xBA	G	L	F	PX	hr/f	SX	SBO	RC/G	RAR	R$
Pos 2	03 TEX	* 382	53	96	10	41	8	251	294	259	319	411	730	9	84	28	0.60	298	36	30	33	98	9%	116	11%	4.62	6.0	$9
Age 28	04 TEX	147	20	33	1	16	0	224	317	189	283	286	569	8	76	29	0.34	218	44	19	36	48	2%	51	3%	2.43	-8.6	$1
Peak	05 TEX	* 321	43	86	14	42	8	269			315	457	772	6	85	28	0.44	270	39	15	45	108	11%	104	14%	4.86	7.8	$11
Bats Right	06 TEX	243	46	72	7	22	3	296	400	241	329	473	803	5	78	36	0.22	263	34	19	46	124	8%	99	7%	5.27	5.8	$8
Reliability 26	07 TEX	407	48	91	9	47	6	224	239	218	277	349	626	7	75	28	0.29	205	33	12	55	89	5%	94	9%	3.10	-11.5	$6
BAvg Potl 35%	1st Half	222	24	53	5	25	3	239			299	360	659	8	78	28	0.40	205	30	13	57	79	5%	81	9%	3.59	-2.9	$4
LIMA Plan F	2nd Half	185	24	38	4	22	3	205			250	335	585	6	70	27	0.20	205	37	11	52	101	6%	101	9%	2.50	-8.8	$2
+/- Score -15	08 Proj	**272**	**38**	**67**	**7**	**30**	**4**	**246**			**293**	**395**	**688**	**6**	**77**	**30**	**0.29**	**233**	**35**	**15**	**50**	**102**	**7%**	**100**	**9%**	**3.89**	**-2.0**	**$6**

CON: H% reverted as expected, combo of PX dip and FB% spike led to a lot of harmless flies, ct% trend is worrisome.
PRO: PX bounced back in 2H, LD% should climb.
Just another low avg C with pop.

Lamb,Mike

		AB	R	H	HR	RBI	SB	Avg	vL	vR	OB	Slg	OPS	bb%	ct%	h%	Eye	xBA	G	L	F	PX	hr/f	SX	SBO	RC/G	RAR	R$
Pos 53	03 aaa	274	36	71	8	37	1	259			341	431	772	11	85	28	0.83					105		76	3%	5.24	6.9	$7
Age 32	04 HOU	278	38	80	14	58	1	288	349	277	359	511	870	10	77	33	0.49	290	44	22	34	135	19%	70	3%	6.33	9.9	$12
Past Peak	05 HOU	322	41	76	12	53	1	236	182	243	285	419	704	6	80	26	0.34	280	42	22	36	111	13%	94	3%	4.06	-6.9	$8
Bats Left	06 HOU	381	70	117	12	45	2	307	211	324	365	475	840	8	86	33	0.64	282	40	20	39	97	9%	75	5%	5.86	3.8	$14
Reliability 43	07 HOU	311	45	90	11	40	0	289	362	277	363	453	816	10	86	31	0.80	273	43	18	39	94	11%	46	0%	5.67	7.7	$10
BAvg Potl 55%	1st Half	154	25	46	6	20	0	299			365	461	826	9	83	33	0.62	278	47	20	33	97	14%	32	0%	5.67	3.8	$5
LIMA Plan F	2nd Half	157	20	44	5	20	0	280			362	446	807	11	88	29	1.05	267	40	16	45	91	8%	55	0%	5.68	4.0	$4
+/- Score -27	08 Proj	**258**	**38**	**72**	**8**	**35**	**0**	**279**			**347**	**438**	**785**	**9**	**84**	**30**	**0.67**	**274**	**42**	**19**	**39**	**94**	**9%**	**60**	**1%**	**5.25**	**2.2**	**$8**

History of part-time AB plus declining PX trend makes it difficult to commit a roster spot to him. Can still help in short bursts when he's getting more regular AB as a DL replacement, but that's about it.

RAY MURPHY

Lane,Jason

			AB	R	H	HR	RBI	SB	Avg	vL	vR	OB	Slg	OPS	bb%	ct%	h%	Eye	xBA	G	L	F	PX	hr/f	SX	SBO	RC/G	RAR	R$
Pos	8	03 aaa	248	32	70	7	34	2	282			350	431	782	9	90	29	1.04					91		48	4%	5.31	3.1	$8
Age	31	04 HOU	136	21	37	4	19	1	272	280	267	349	463	812	11	76	33	0.48	259	34	19	47	129	8%	99	3%	5.78	4.4	$4
Past Peak		05 HOU	517	65	138	26	78	6	267	237	277	310	499	809	6	80	29	0.30	281	30	19	51	148	12%	88	8%	5.29	10.9	$19
Bats	Right	06 HOU	288	44	58	15	45	1	201	198	203	318	392	710	15	74	22	0.65	225	28	14	58	117	12%	38	4%	4.36	-0.7	$6
Reliability	17	07 2NL	* 356	40	68	14	51	2	190	151	194	252	345	597	8	82	19	0.47	221	35	9	56	92	8%	51	6%	2.81	-19.9	$4
BAvg Potl	65%	1st Half	164	20	34	8	22	0	207			249	409	657	5	89	19	0.50	240	28	7	65	112	8%	40	4%	3.55	-5.2	$2
LIMA Plan	F	2nd Half	192	20	34	6	29	2	176			255	290	545	10	77	20	0.46	206	42	11	47	72	8%	54	7%	2.10	-15.3	$1
+/- Score	24	08 Proj	159	20	35	7	23	1	220			293	390	683	9	80	24	0.51	236	32	14	54	105	10%	47	5%	3.89	-3.2	$3

8-27-.175 in 171 at HOU/SD. Punished by low h% for 2nd straight year, but his skills are hurting him too. PX is in freefall, no longer hits LHPs. Without those two calling cards, there is not much left to hold our interest.

Langerhans,Ryan

			AB	R	H	HR	RBI	SB	Avg	vL	vR	OB	Slg	OPS	bb%	ct%	h%	Eye	xBA	G	L	F	PX	hr/f	SX	SBO	RC/G	RAR	R$
Pos	78	03 a/a	468	52	117	9	46	11	250			325	389	714	10	78	30	0.50					100		85	18%	4.46	-14.2	$10
Age	28	04 aaa	456	91	126	18	63	4	276			363	471	834	12	79	32	0.65					125		79	10%	6.01	10.9	$17
Peak		05 ATL	326	48	87	8	42	0	267	298	261	342	426	768	10	77	33	0.49	282	40	26	33	114	10%	66	2%	5.16	-1.7	$9
Bats	Left	06 ATL	315	46	76	7	28	1	241	308	232	345	378	723	14	71	32	0.55	237	41	21	38	96	8%	72	3%	4.76	-4.6	$5
Reliability	16	07 2TM	* 261	37	47	7	25	4	181	219	157	275	314	590	11	63	26	0.35	201	44	13	43	105	10%	102	8%	2.74	-19.3	$2
BAvg Potl	40%	1st Half	137	19	23	3	14	1	168			288	277	565	14	60	25	0.42	189	40	17	43	99	8%	53	5%	2.43	-11.7	$0
LIMA Plan	F	2nd Half	124	18	24	4	11	3	196			260	355	616	8	67	26	0.26	213	52	5	43	110	11%	131	12%	3.00	-7.9	$2
+/- Score	25	08 Proj	164	24	38	4	16	2	232			319	371	690	11	69	31	0.42	230	43	18	39	104	10%	82	6%	4.18	-4.6	$3

6-23-.167 in 210 AB w/ATL,OAK WAS. How to hit under .200:
- Forget how to hit LHPs.
- Strike out 3/8 of the time.
- Post lowest h% in 5 years.

Even if he reverses all of the above, he's still just mediocre.

LaRoche,Adam

			AB	R	H	HR	RBI	SB	Avg	vL	vR	OB	Slg	OPS	bb%	ct%	h%	Eye	xBA	G	L	F	PX	hr/f	SX	SBO	RC/G	RAR	R$
Pos	3	03 a/a	483	70	134	19	67	2	277			353	466	818	10	79	32	0.55					125		49	4%	5.70	3.5	$16
Age	28	04 ATL	324	45	90	13	45	0	278	250	280	333	488	821	8	76	33	0.35	284	46	19	35	145	15%	45	0%	5.67	-2.6	$10
Peak		05 ATL	451	53	117	20	78	0	259	191	269	318	455	773	8	81	28	0.45	289	44	21	34	127	16%	21	2%	4.95	-8.5	$14
Bats	Left	06 ATL	492	89	140	32	90	0	285	241	297	356	561	917	10	74	33	0.43	298	38	21	41	180	21%	41	2%	7.02	14.1	$21
Reliability	30	07 PIT	563	71	153	21	88	1	272	299	262	344	458	802	10	77	32	0.47	269	36	21	43	130	11%	31	1%	5.51	-1.4	$16
BAvg Potl	45%	1st Half	270	29	57	8	40	0	211			302	363	665	11	73	26	0.47	237	39	18	43	112	9%	24	1%	3.79	-15.2	$3
LIMA Plan	C	2nd Half	293	42	96	13	48	1	328			384	546	930	8	81	37	0.47	298	33	23	44	144	12%	37	1%	6.96	10.5	$13
+/- Score	3	08 Proj	534	76	149	28	93	1	279			347	509	856	9	77	32	0.45	290	38	21	41	152	16%	30	2%	6.12	6.2	$20

2006 PX looks like an outlier, but there's still hope for a power surge. hr/f should climb a bit, 2H ct% and PX growth are promising. Improvement vs LHP should keep him in lineup more. Return to 30+ HR is a good bet.

LaRoche,Andy

			AB	R	H	HR	RBI	SB	Avg	vL	vR	OB	Slg	OPS	bb%	ct%	h%	Eye	xBA	G	L	F	PX	hr/f	SX	SBO	RC/G	RAR	R$
Pos	5	03	0	0	0	0	0	0	0							0									0				
Age	24	04	0	0	0	0	0	0	0							0									0				
Growth		05 aa	223	33	53	7	34	2	238			312	377	688	10	80	27	0.55					91		59	7%	4.03	-4.1	$6
Bats	Right	06 a/a	432	66	122	17	69	8	282			363	461	824	11	87	29	0.96					102		71	10%	5.81	7.0	$16
Reliability	1	07 LA	* 358	60	92	16	48	4	257	200	235	350	453	802	12	83	27	0.82	284	41	19	40	118	14%	67	7%	5.57	8.3	$11
BAvg Potl	60%	1st Half	172	26	38	3	14	2	221			340	331	671	15	89	23	1.63	255	32	21	47	66	4%	73	7%	4.43	-1.8	$2
LIMA Plan	C+	2nd Half	186	34	54	13	34	2	290			359	565	924	10	77	32	0.47	308	50	17	33	173	27%	56	6%	6.92	11.1	$9
+/- Score	33	08 Proj	403	65	112	17	60	5	278			360	466	826	11	83	30	0.77	283	43	18	39	112	13%	68	8%	5.81	10.0	$15

1-10-.226 in 91 AB at LA. Showed neither power (70 PX) nor ct% (74%) in MLB debut, but he'll have more chances. Combo of high bb%/ct% and still-emerging power says that this is one to tuck away.

LaRue,Jason

			AB	R	H	HR	RBI	SB	Avg	vL	vR	OB	Slg	OPS	bb%	ct%	h%	Eye	xBA	G	L	F	PX	hr/f	SX	SBO	RC/G	RAR	R$
Pos	2	03 CIN	379	52	87	16	50	3	230	210	237	291	422	713	8	71	28	0.30	256	41	18	41	140	15%	74	8%	4.30	0.1	$9
Age	34	04 CIN	390	46	98	14	55	0	251	274	244	298	431	729	6	72	31	0.24	256	43	19	38	126	13%	49	2%	4.44	7.2	$9
Past Peak		05 CIN	361	38	94	14	60	0	260	257	262	336	452	787	10	72	33	0.41	271	42	23	36	145	15%	16	0%	5.42	17.1	$10
Bats	Right	06 CIN	191	22	37	8	21	1	194	235	179	294	346	639	12	73	22	0.53	239	44	20	36	94	16%	37	2%	3.34	-6.0	$2
Reliability	3	07 KC	169	14	25	4	13	1	148	160	143	226	272	498	9	61	21	0.26	207	48	17	35	114	11%	42	3%	1.27	-15.5	($2)
BAvg Potl	50%	1st Half	92	8	16	2	8	1	174			224	304	529	6	62	25	0.17	220	50	17	33	122	11%	52	7%	1.76	-6.7	($0)
LIMA Plan	F	2nd Half	77	6	9	2	5	0	117			227	234	461	12	60	16	0.35	167	45	17	38	104	11%	1	0%	0.62	-9.1	($1)
+/- Score	41	08 Proj	188	18	42	6	19	1	223			304	368	672	10	67	30	0.34	226	45	19	36	113	13%	31	2%	3.88	-1.5	$2

xBA shows that he was clearly not a .148 hitter. He was a far more valuable .207 hitter! Trends have headed south so fast that we haven't even had time to pack a bathing suit.

Lee,Carlos

			AB	R	H	HR	RBI	SB	Avg	vL	vR	OB	Slg	OPS	bb%	ct%	h%	Eye	xBA	G	L	F	PX	hr/f	SX	SBO	RC/G	RAR	R$
Pos	7	03 CHW	623	100	181	31	113	18	291	218	317	330	499	830	6	85	30	0.41	300	39	21	40	122	15%	98	15%	5.45	2.1	$29
Age	31	04 CHW	591	103	180	31	99	11	305	308	303	363	525	887	8	85	31	0.63	290	33	20	47	126	13%	76	10%	6.30	22.2	$27
Past Peak		05 MIL	618	85	164	32	114	13	265	261	267	327	487	814	8	86	26	0.66	300	34	20	46	134	13%	76	11%	5.47	2.4	$26
Bats	Right	06 2TM	624	102	187	37	116	19	300	313	296	359	540	899	9	90	29	0.89	318	40	20	40	128	16%	95	12%	6.42	20.8	$31
Reliability	86	07 HOU	627	93	190	32	119	10	303	338	292	357	528	885	8	90	30	0.84	303	38	16	46	126	13%	67	9%	6.26	16.0	$29
BAvg Potl	60%	1st Half	300	42	88	14	62	4	293			348	513	861	8	90	29	0.81	308	39	18	43	125	12%	65	11%	6.01	5.7	$13
LIMA Plan	D+	2nd Half	327	51	102	18	57	6	312			366	541	907	8	90	30	0.88	299	37	15	48	126	13%	66	8%	6.49	10.2	$16
+/- Score	-11	08 Proj	644	100	193	34	120	14	300			356	529	884	8	89	29	0.78	306	38	18	44	128	14%	80	10%	6.25	16.3	$31

In terms of both skill set and durability, he is as consistent as they come: you can practically bank a .300-30-110-10 line at the draft table. HOU may eventually regret this 6-yr deal, but right now it looks just fine.

Lee,Derrek

			AB	R	H	HR	RBI	SB	Avg	vL	vR	OB	Slg	OPS	bb%	ct%	h%	Eye	xBA	G	L	F	PX	hr/f	SX	SBO	RC/G	RAR	R$
Pos	3	03 FLA	539	91	146	31	92	21	271	333	256	373	508	882	14	76	31	0.67	296	42	22	36	154	21%	100	17%	6.68	18.4	$27
Age	32	04 CHC	605	90	168	32	98	12	278	306	271	351	504	855	10	79	31	0.53	288	41	19	40	141	17%	75	10%	6.09	2.4	$25
Past Peak		05 CHC	594	120	199	46	107	15	335	333	339	418	662	1080	13	82	35	0.78	347	39	22	39	202	24%	104	10%	8.91	51.7	$41
Bats	Right	06 CHC	175	30	50	8	30	8	286	292	283	375	474	849	13	77	33	0.61	268	41	20	38	118	16%	75	21%	6.19	1.0	$8
Reliability	23	07 CHC	567	91	180	22	82	6	317	339	312	393	513	907	11	80	37	0.62	288	41	21	38	129	13%	60	6%	6.86	19.4	$24
BAvg Potl	40%	1st Half	280	39	97	6	39	3	346			415	511	926	11	79	43	0.55	280	42	21	37	121	7%	56	7%	7.22	11.9	$12
LIMA Plan	C+	2nd Half	287	52	83	16	43	3	289			372	516	888	12	81	31	0.70	296	41	20	39	137	18%	58	5%	6.54	7.5	$12
+/- Score	-33	08 Proj	578	99	171	30	97	4	296			379	521	900	12	79	33	0.64	294	41	21	38	142	17%	51	6%	6.76	17.0	$25

It took another half-season for power to return; luckily high 1H h% propped up his value while we waited. 2H surge (and 7 HR/ 164 PX Sept.) gives hope for still more power recovery. Return to 40 HR level not out of question.

Lewis,Fred

			AB	R	H	HR	RBI	SB	Avg	vL	vR	OB	Slg	OPS	bb%	ct%	h%	Eye	xBA	G	L	F	PX	hr/f	SX	SBO	RC/G	RAR	R$
Pos	97	03	0	0	0	0	0	0	0							0									0				
Age	27	04	0	0	0	0	0	0	0							0									0				
Peak		05 aa	508	62	121	5	38	24	238			311	340	651	10	78	29	0.49					73		128	27%	3.68	-20.4	$11
Bats	Left	06 aaa	439	64	106	9	43	14	241			320	379	698	10	82	28	0.64					80		130	20%	4.31	-12.2	$10
Reliability	22	07 SF	* 328	57	85	8	42	11	259	276	289	327	413	739	9	80	30	0.50	272	55	15	30	92	10%	145	14%	4.71	-5.2	$11
BAvg Potl	50%	1st Half	238	41	61	7	34	10	256			322	441	763	9	82	29	0.55	294	59	13	29	106	13%	150	18%	5.01	-1.7	$8
LIMA Plan	D	2nd Half	90	16	24	1	8	1	267			340	337	677	10	73	35	0.41	212	51	17	32	48	6%	78	6%	3.90	-3.5	$2
+/- Score	16	08 Proj	293	46	74	5	30	14	253			326	373	699	10	79	30	0.51	255	53	16	31	75	8%	135	22%	4.23	-8.0	$9

3-19-.287-5 SB in 157 AB at SF. This speedster has the right approach: Hit ground balls, take walks. 1st half xBA and SBO% hint at his upside. If he can repeat those over an expanded opportunity... UP: 25 SB.

Lieberthal,Mike

			AB	R	H	HR	RBI	SB	Avg	vL	vR	OB	Slg	OPS	bb%	ct%	h%	Eye	xBA	G	L	F	PX	hr/f	SX	SBO	RC/G	RAR	R$
Pos	2	03 PHI	508	68	159	13	81	0	313	319	311	361	453	814	7	88	33	0.64	300	37	27	37	86	8%	34	0%	5.47	16.1	$19
Age	36	04 PHI	476	58	129	17	61	1	271	284	267	324	447	771	7	86	29	0.54	282	33	21	46	106	9%	46	2%	4.95	15.6	$13
Decline		05 PHI	392	48	103	12	47	0	263	276	259	323	418	742	8	91	26	1.00	296	38	21	40	94	8%	27	0%	4.79	11.4	$10
Bats	Right	06 PHI	209	22	57	9	36	0	273	286	269	300	469	768	4	91	27	0.42	285	38	17	45	108	11%	18	0%	4.73	2.3	$6
Reliability	6	07 LA	77	6	18	0	1	0	234	167	254	272	260	531	5	86	27	0.36	214	45	18	36	22	0%	24	0%	2.11	-3.9	($0)
BAvg Potl	45%	1st Half	38	2	7	0	1	0	184			225	211	436	5	87	21	0.40	214	45	18	36	22	0%	17	0%	1.09	-3.3	($1)
LIMA Plan	F	2nd Half	39	4	11	0	0	0	282			317	308	625	5	85	33	0.33	213	45	18	36	22	0%	28	0%	3.14	-0.7	$0
+/- Score	-37	08 Proj	131	16	36	5	19	0	275			321	442	763	6	89	28	0.60	287	36	21	43	98	9%	30	1%	4.83	3.3	$4

World's Greatest Job: Russell Martin's backup. Earned $16K per AB in this gig. It's not Roger Clemens' comp rate but it's still not a bad living.

Linden,Todd

		AB	R	H	HR	RBI	SB	Avg	vL	vR	OB	Slg	OPS	bb%	ct%	h%	Eye	xBA	G	L	F	PX	hr/f	SX	SBO	RC/G	RAR	R$
Pos 7	03 aaa	471	61	114	7	45	11	242			290	346	636	6	82	28	0.38					69		106	14%	3.33	-30.3	$9
Age 27	04 aaa	489	70	107	14	56	6	219			286	362	648	9	77	26	0.41					94		82	12%	3.46	-26.5	$8
Peak	05 SF	* 511	77	128	23	69	7	251	300	199	321	454	775	9	76	29	0.43	293	46	23	31	137	19%	97	8%	5.10	-3.7	$17
Bats Both	06 SF	* 264	38	66	6	22	5	249	208	302	326	397	723	10	80	29	0.56	283	42	28	30	92	9%	116	7%	4.59	-5.1	$5
Reliability 26	07 2NL	* 232	28	59	2	18	4	255	262	235	327	339	666	10	69	36	0.34	213	48	18	35	69	3%	92	7%	3.87	-10.0	$4
BAvg Potl 20%	1st Half	117	16	29	1	12	0	248			333	325	658	11	66	37	0.38	204	48	20	33	62	4%	72	3%	3.86	-5.2	$2
LIMA Plan F	2nd Half	115	12	30	1	6	4	262			320	354	674	8	72	36	0.30	224	48	17	36	75	3%	95	12%	3.89	-4.8	$2
+/- Score -40	08 Proj	**127**	**17**	**30**	**2**	**11**	**2**	**236**			**308**	**354**	**662**	**9**	**74**	**30**	**0.40**	**243**	**46**	**20**	**34**	**83**	**7%**	**96**	**8%**	**3.71**	**-6.2**	**$2**

1-11-.245 in 184 AB at SF/FLA. Will be hard pressed to maintain even that BA as h% masked freefall in ct%, xBA, and PX. Needs to find a ML team with a park more like Albuquerque or Fresno for success.

Lind,Adam

		AB	R	H	HR	RBI	SB	Avg	vL	vR	OB	Slg	OPS	bb%	ct%	h%	Eye	xBA	G	L	F	PX	hr/f	SX	SBO	RC/G	RAR	R$
Pos 7	03	0	0	0	0	0	0	0							0									0				
Age 24	04	0	0	0	0	0	0	0							0									0				
Growth	05	0	0	0	0	0	0	0							0									0				
Bats Left	06 TOR	* 517	66	171	26	91	3	331	444	353	389	559	948	9	79	38	0.44	284	35	19	46	148	14%	39	3%	7.21	27.6	$23
Reliability 0	07 TOR	* 464	51	118	17	70	1	254	194	251	297	420	717	6	78	29	0.28	264	45	19	37	109	13%	46	3%	4.15	-7.7	$11
BAvg Potl 45%	1st Half	249	26	59	10	35	1	237			272	406	678	5	77	27	0.21	260	46	18	36	113	14%	37	6%	3.57	-8.6	$5
LIMA Plan D	2nd Half	215	25	59	7	35	0	274			325	437	762	7	80	32	0.37	268	43	20	38	103	11%	52	0%	4.81	0.5	$6
+/- Score 10	08 Proj	**353**	**42**	**92**	**13**	**57**	**1**	**261**			**313**	**433**	**746**	**7**	**79**	**30**	**0.35**	**269**	**43**	**19**	**38**	**115**	**12%**	**48**	**3%**	**4.61**	**-2.7**	**$9**

11-46-.248 in 290 AB at TOR. Won't hit .300 in bigs until he regains past contact and walk rates. Solving LH would help, too. Has displayed solid BPIs in minors, so should develop. Breakout at least a year away.

Lo Duca,Paul

		AB	R	H	HR	RBI	SB	Avg	vL	vR	OB	Slg	OPS	bb%	ct%	h%	Eye	xBA	G	L	F	PX	hr/f	SX	SBO	RC/G	RAR	R$
Pos 2	03 LA	568	64	155	7	52	0	273	281	270	325	377	702	7	90	29	0.81	305	45	27	29	68	5%	43	1%	4.35	0.9	$10
Age 36	04 2NL	535	68	153	13	80	4	286	314	276	331	421	752	6	91	30	0.73	288	44	20	36	78	7%	64	6%	4.78	14.8	$16
Decline	05 FLA	445	45	126	6	57	4	283	314	277	334	380	714	7	93	29	1.10	300	45	24	30	61	5%	57	5%	4.52	9.2	$11
Bats Right	06 NYM	512	80	163	5	49	3	318	336	311	349	428	777	4	93	34	0.63	295	45	21	34	71	3%	70	2%	5.02	9.4	$16
Reliability 59	07 NYM	445	46	121	9	54	2	272	341	245	309	378	687	5	93	28	0.73	297	48	23	29	60	8%	54	2%	4.04	3.1	$9
BAvg Potl 65%	1st Half	249	28	70	4	21	2	281			317	361	678	5	92	29	0.65	290	48	24	27	47	6%	51	3%	3.90	0.8	$5
LIMA Plan D+	2nd Half	196	18	51	5	33	0	260			300	398	697	5	93	26	0.85	303	47	22	31	77	9%	33	0%	4.20	2.3	$4
+/- Score -12	08 Proj	**430**	**50**	**127**	**6**	**53**	**2**	**295**			**334**	**398**	**732**	**5**	**93**	**31**	**0.78**	**295**	**46**	**23**	**31**	**63**	**5%**	**57**	**2%**	**4.57**	**7.4**	**$11**

Raw stats show increased power at expense of BA. BPIs reveal opposite: Rise in xBA and declining PX. At 36, we've just witnessed his late career power spike. Now it's time to get back to a .290 BA.

Lofton,Kenny

		AB	R	H	HR	RBI	SB	Avg	vL	vR	OB	Slg	OPS	bb%	ct%	h%	Eye	xBA	G	L	F	PX	hr/f	SX	SBO	RC/G	RAR	R$
Pos 87	03 2NL	547	97	162	12	46	30	296	244	313	351	450	800	8	91	31	0.90	300	44	21	36	89	7%	155	25%	5.47	7.5	$24
Age 40	04 NYY	276	51	76	3	18	7	275	308	272	349	395	743	10	90	30	1.15	276	51	16	33	62	4%	140	11%	5.03	2.6	$7
Decline	05 PHI	367	67	123	2	36	22	335	348	333	388	420	808	8	89	37	0.78	298	49	26	25	53	3%	149	19%	5.57	9.7	$19
Bats Left	06 LA	469	79	141	3	41	32	301	214	319	362	403	765	9	91	33	1.07	277	45	22	33	52	2%	155	24%	5.20	9.9	$19
Reliability 50	07 2AL	490	86	145	7	38	23	296	223	313	368	414	782	10	90	32	1.10	269	39	19	41	72	4%	130	18%	5.43	15.9	$18
BAvg Potl 55%	1st Half	238	50	69	5	18	16	290			372	416	788	12	91	30	1.48	268	38	18	44	73	5%	133	24%	5.57	8.7	$11
LIMA Plan B+	2nd Half	252	36	76	2	20	7	302			365	413	777	9	88	34	0.83	270	41	21	39	71	2%	111	12%	5.31	7.2	$7
+/- Score -43	08 Proj	**408**	**70**	**113**	**4**	**34**	**16**	**277**			**344**	**387**	**732**	**9**	**90**	**30**	**1.00**	**277**	**43**	**21**	**36**	**64**	**3%**	**142**	**17%**	**4.82**	**4.7**	**$12**

Impressive skill maintenance for 40, but erosion has begun:
- High h% hid 2H BPI decline
- Inability to hit LH in '06, '07
- 3 year decline in xBA
- Falling GB rate for speedster
- Solid but declining SX

Logan,Nook

		AB	R	H	HR	RBI	SB	Avg	vL	vR	OB	Slg	OPS	bb%	ct%	h%	Eye	xBA	G	L	F	PX	hr/f	SX	SBO	RC/G	RAR	R$
Pos 8	03 aa	514	62	116	3	33	32	226			288	302	590	8	82	27	0.50					46		150	34%	2.90	-31.6	$11
Age 28	04 DET	* 560	71	140	2	34	41	250	395	222	291	330	621	5	81	30	0.30	244	51	17	32	48	1%	166	39%	3.13	-26.9	$15
Peak	05 DET	322	47	83	1	17	23	258	284	246	303	335	639	6	84	30	0.40	260	54	17	29	51	1%	157	34%	3.43	-8.2	$10
Bats Both	06 WAS	* 232	32	54	1	13	12	233	350	286	302	298	601	9	74	31	0.38	213	47	18	35	45	2%	129	26%	2.91	-11.0	$4
Reliability 34	07 WAS	325	39	86	0	21	23	265	305	237	305	345	650	6	74	36	0.22	244	56	19	26	65	0%	144	34%	3.48	-10.3	$9
BAvg Potl 25%	1st Half	86	9	19	0	5	6	221			256	302	558	4	73	30	0.17	247	55	20	25	68	0%	141	41%	2.21	-6.3	$1
LIMA Plan F	2nd Half	239	30	67	0	16	17	280			323	360	683	6	74	38	0.24	242	56	18	26	65	0%	140	32%	3.93	-4.3	$8
+/- Score -20	08 Proj	**262**	**33**	**65**	**1**	**16**	**17**	**248**			**297**	**319**	**616**	**7**	**76**	**32**	**0.29**	**239**	**54**	**18**	**28**	**53**	**1%**	**140**	**32%**	**3.05**	**-11.9**	**$6**

New league, bad team, green light, high h% = Peak at 28. Poor OBA, low ct%, no power, ineffective vs RHP = Valley at 29. Banjo hitters need high bb% or ct%. Contact gap too wide, so must regain patience.

Loney,James

		AB	R	H	HR	RBI	SB	Avg	vL	vR	OB	Slg	OPS	bb%	ct%	h%	Eye	xBA	G	L	F	PX	hr/f	SX	SBO	RC/G	RAR	R$
Pos 3	03	0	0	0	0	0	0	0							0									0				
Age 23	04 aa	395	37	88	4	34	5	223			295	303	598	9	83	26	0.60					54		59	11%	3.04	-29.8	$3
Growth	05 aa	500	59	121	9	51	0	242			306	350	656	8	86	27	0.65					71		37	4%	3.74	-24.2	$7
Bats Left	06 LA	* 468	73	156	10	74	8	333	350	268	379	503	882	7	92	35	0.96	292	49	12	39	96	6%	96	11%	6.32	4.0	$21
Reliability 4	07 LA	* 577	63	170	16	93	2	295	319	336	349	454	803	8	84	33	0.53	285	42	22	36	98	9%	61	2%	5.39	-3.4	$18
BAvg Potl 45%	1st Half	271	30	77	4	39	2	284			338	428	766	8	83	33	0.49	291	32	29	38	97	5%	78	4%	5.03	-4.4	$7
LIMA Plan C	2nd Half	306	33	93	12	54	0	304			358	477	836	8	85	33	0.58	284	43	20	36	98	13%	40	1%	5.70	0.8	$11
+/- Score -6	08 Proj	**554**	**67**	**161**	**15**	**80**	**4**	**291**			**345**	**447**	**793**	**8**	**87**	**31**	**0.62**	**286**	**43**	**20**	**37**	**94**	**9%**	**67**	**6%**	**5.28**	**-6.7**	**$17**

15-67-.344 in 334 AB at LA. Monster 2H means he'll be overhyped at the draft table. Will hit for solid Avg, but PX says the power is not there yet. Mind your wallet during any bidding wars.

Longoria,Evan

		AB	R	H	HR	RBI	SB	Avg	vL	vR	OB	Slg	OPS	bb%	ct%	h%	Eye	xBA	G	L	F	PX	hr/f	SX	SBO	RC/G	RAR	R$
Pos 5	03	0	0	0	0	0	0	0							0									0				
Age 22	04	0	0	0	0	0	0	0							0									0				
Growth	05	0	0	0	0	0	0	0							0									0				
Bats Right	06 aa	105	15	27	6	20	2	257			264	476	740	1	80	27	0.05					128		78	18%	4.08	-3.6	$4
Reliability 0	07 a/a	485	91	142	25	90	4	292			382	507	889	13	80	32	0.73					134		65	3%	6.63	26.8	$22
BAvg Potl 40%	1st Half	290	51	79	15	50	3	272			353	476	829	11	82	29	0.71					121		64	3%	5.76	9.3	$11
LIMA Plan D+	2nd Half	195	40	63	10	40	1	322			423	552	976	15	77	38	0.76					155		49	2%	8.00	17.4	$10
+/- Score 16	08 Proj	**321**	**56**	**91**	**17**	**62**	**4**	**283**			**343**	**502**	**845**	**8**	**79**	**31**	**0.45**					**136**		**68**	**6%**	**5.83**	**9.4**	**$14**

Power is real. Plate patience is real. Strike zone knowledge at 23 with high PX yields long term success. Grab him now.

Lopez,Felipe

		AB	R	H	HR	RBI	SB	Avg	vL	vR	OB	Slg	OPS	bb%	ct%	h%	Eye	xBA	G	L	F	PX	hr/f	SX	SBO	RC/G	RAR	R$
Pos 64	03 CIN	* 340	46	80	4	28	10	235	196	219	312	335	647	10	74	31	0.43	255	49	24	27	78	6%	103	22%	3.58	-5.6	$6
Age 27	04 CIN	* 557	75	135	15	66	3	242	292	226	299	384	683	7	75	30	0.33	245	44	18	38	96	9%	72	6%	3.87	-4.4	$11
Peak	05 CIN	580	97	169	23	85	15	291	244	312	355	486	841	9	81	33	0.51	308	54	20	27	124	18%	115	13%	5.89	31.6	$26
Bats Both	06 2NL	617	98	169	11	52	44	274	246	285	358	381	739	12	80	33	0.64	258	50	19	30	69	7%	118	27%	4.83	8.5	$24
Reliability 32	07 WAS	603	70	148	9	50	24	245	269	235	306	352	658	8	82	29	0.49	265	50	20	30	67	6%	113	20%	3.68	-5.0	$13
BAvg Potl 55%	1st Half	307	29	73	3	29	9	238			284	339	623	6	80	29	0.32	254	48	20	32	67	4%	107	21%	3.15	-7.6	$4
LIMA Plan C+	2nd Half	296	41	75	6	21	15	253			328	365	693	10	84	28	0.70	276	52	20	28	67	9%	115	20%	4.22	2.3	$8
+/- Score 24	08 Proj	**589**	**82**	**155**	**10**	**55**	**26**	**263**			**332**	**377**	**709**	**9**	**81**	**31**	**0.53**	**267**	**51**	**20**	**29**	**74**	**7%**	**120**	**20%**	**4.36**	**4.9**	**$17**

Past two seasons more similar than different, taking him from overpriced to potential bargain. 2H BPIs reveal skill progression and possible upside. If h% normalizes in his new friendlier park, then: UP: See 2006

Lopez,Jose

		AB	R	H	HR	RBI	SB	Avg	vL	vR	OB	Slg	OPS	bb%	ct%	h%	Eye	xBA	G	L	F	PX	hr/f	SX	SBO	RC/G	RAR	R$
Pos 4	03 aa	538	84	140	12	70	19	260			298	396	694	5	91	27	0.60					84		108	24%	4.10	-2.7	$18
Age 24	04 SEA	* 482	66	130	17	60	5	270	214	238	304	440	744	5	89	27	0.44	297	42	21	38	99	11%	66	8%	4.52	6.2	$13
Growth	05 SEA	* 372	44	103	6	54	6	277	273	235	303	430	733	4	88	30	0.30	295	41	19	40	110	5%	67	17%	4.43	3.2	$10
Bats Right	06 SEA	603	78	170	10	79	5	282	331	265	312	405	716	4	87	31	0.33	274	49	18	33	72	6%	100	5%	4.21	1.5	$15
Reliability 58	07 SEA	524	58	132	11	62	2	252	244	254	279	355	634	4	88	27	0.31	255	46	17	37	61	6%	58	4%	3.22	-14.1	$9
BAvg Potl 50%	1st Half	260	36	74	7	44	2	285			324	419	743	5	88	30	0.50	278	45	18	36	80	8%	69	4%	4.56	3.1	$8
LIMA Plan C	2nd Half	264	22	58	4	18	0	220			234	292	526	2	87	24	0.15	230	46	16	38	41	5%	46	4%	1.87	-18.4	$1
+/- Score 0	08 Proj	**607**	**71**	**169**	**12**	**74**	**5**	**278**			**305**	**395**	**700**	**4**	**88**	**30**	**0.31**	**267**	**46**	**17**	**37**	**72**	**6%**	**69**	**7%**	**3.98**	**-2.6**	**$14**

Never the same after death of brother in June. Discounting 2H swoon, BPIs still nothing special. You have to wonder when team puts weight clause in your contract at age 24. A PT risk despite youth.

MATT BEAGLE

Loretta,Mark

			AB	R	H	HR	RBI	SB	Avg	vL	vR	OB	Slg	OPS	bb%	ct%	h%	Eye	xBA	G	L	F	PX	hr/f	SX	SBO	RC/G	RAR	R$
Pos	6435	03 SD	589	74	186	13	72	5	316	307	318	373	445	818	8	89	34	0.87	311	36	31	33	76	8%	69	5%	5.64	24.5	$21
Age	36	04 SD	620	108	208	16	76	5	335	352	329	392	495	887	9	93	34	1.29	307	40	22	38	94	7%	72	4%	6.47	38.1	$27
Decline		05 SD	404	54	113	3	38	8	280	309	269	352	347	698	10	92	30	1.32	287	40	28	32	44	3%	80	9%	4.52	6.4	$11
Bats	Right	06 BOS	635	75	181	5	59	4	285	274	290	336	361	697	7	90	31	0.78	278	35	27	38	51	2%	56	3%	4.27	-2.6	$12
Reliability	64	07 HOU	460	52	132	4	41	1	287	317	278	349	372	721	9	91	31	1.07	272	41	22	36	54	3%	46	2%	4.67	9.2	$9
BAvg Potl	60%	1st Half	199	24	64	1	25	1	322			397	417	814	11	90	35	1.25	279	40	23	37	67	1%	50	3%	5.90	10.4	$6
LIMA Plan	D	2nd Half	261	28	68	3	16	0	261			311	337	648	7	92	27	0.90	267	43	22	36	45	3%	44	1%	3.74	-1.7	$3
+/- Score	-21	08 Proj	**444**	**54**	**125**	**4**	**41**	**0**	**282**			**342**	**365**	**707**	**8**	**91**	**30**	**1.01**	**279**	**39**	**25**	**36**	**54**	**3%**	**40**	**2%**	**4.49**	**5.2**	**$9**

BPIs are in a slow decline, displayed most clearly in xBA. Still, ct% and Eye show he can still help BA. Worth an extra few bucks on his positional flexiblity alone.

Lowell,Mike

			AB	R	H	HR	RBI	SB	Avg	vL	vR	OB	Slg	OPS	bb%	ct%	h%	Eye	xBA	G	L	F	PX	hr/f	SX	SBO	RC/G	RAR	R$
Pos	5	03 FLA	492	76	136	32	105	3	276	295	271	350	530	881	10	84	27	0.72	310	33	22	45	147	17%	61	3%	6.29	28.6	$23
Age	34	04 FLA	598	87	175	27	85	5	293	344	279	361	505	866	10	87	30	0.83	292	32	19	49	124	11%	64	4%	6.19	18.8	$23
Past Peak		05 FLA	500	56	118	8	58	4	236	308	222	300	360	660	8	88	25	0.79	268	32	21	47	84	4%	75	3%	3.91	-13.0	$8
Bats	Right	06 BOS	573	79	163	20	80	2	284	241	302	339	475	813	8	89	29	0.77	308	38	22	41	114	10%	48	3%	5.53	8.4	$17
Reliability	27	07 BOS	589	79	191	21	120	3	324	323	325	380	501	881	8	88	34	0.75	282	36	18	46	107	9%	55	3%	6.29	28.1	$25
BAvg Potl	40%	1st Half	266	33	78	12	54	2	293			352	515	867	8	89	29	0.80	299	35	16	49	134	10%	58	3%	6.13	12.0	$10
LIMA Plan	C+	2nd Half	323	46	113	9	66	1	350			403	489	893	8	87	38	0.71	270	36	20	44	85	7%	42	3%	6.42	16.0	$15
+/- Score	-48	08 Proj	**578**	**77**	**165**	**20**	**99**	**3**	**285**			**345**	**464**	**808**	**8**	**88**	**30**	**0.76**	**289**	**35**	**20**	**45**	**108**	**9%**	**62**	**3%**	**5.49**	**13.7**	**$19**

Second half hit rate was otherworldly compared to anything he's ever done, and will regress. So that .350 2nd half BA will not last, nor likely a .300+ season level. Production still hanging on but that might tail a bit too.

Lubanski,Chris

			AB	R	H	HR	RBI	SB	Avg	vL	vR	OB	Slg	OPS	bb%	ct%	h%	Eye	xBA	G	L	F	PX	hr/f	SX	SBO	RC/G	RAR	R$
Pos	8	03	0	0	0	0	0	0	0							0									0				
Age	23	04	0	0	0	0	0	0	0							0									0				
Growth		05	0	0	0	0	0	0	0							0									0				
Bats	Left	06 aa	524	72	131	10	54	9	250			322	399	721	10	84	28	0.67					91		106	12%	4.60	0.8	$10
Reliability	0	07 aa	409	45	98	12	48	3	240			304	391	695	9	82	27	0.51					95		60	11%	4.11	-3.9	$7
BAvg Potl	40%	1st Half	247	28	67	7	29	3	271			336	429	765	9	85	30	0.63					97		66	12%	5.01	4.3	$6
LIMA Plan	F	2nd Half	162	17	31	5	19	0	191			256	333	589	8	77	22	0.38					91		59	9%	2.65	-9.3	$1
+/- Score	14	08 Proj	**182**	**22**	**43**	**5**	**20**	**2**	**236**			**304**	**384**	**688**	**9**	**82**	**27**	**0.53**					**92**		**83**	**11%**	**4.07**	**-2.3**	**$3**

While still young, he lacks a single outstanding skill. BB% is solid, but mediocre ct% at Omaha limits BA upside. He still has plenty of work to do.

Ludwick,Ryan

			AB	R	H	HR	RBI	SB	Avg	vL	vR	OB	Slg	OPS	bb%	ct%	h%	Eye	xBA	G	L	F	PX	hr/f	SX	SBO	RC/G	RAR	R$
Pos	79	03 CLE	* 479	61	131	23	80	3	274			331	493	824	8	77	31	0.37					143		72	3%	5.63	4.1	$16
Age	29	04 CLE	* 242	24	52	8	29	0	217			259	387	646	5	72	27	0.20					124		24	0%	3.27	-12.4	$3
Peak		05 CLE	* 229	27	38	7	16	0	168			233	303	536	8	77	19	0.37	195	32	7	61	89	6%	61	5%	1.95	-20.9	($0)
Bats	Right	06 aaa	508	71	118	23	70	2	233			291	434	725	8	68	30	0.25					145		63	7%	4.51	-10.9	$11
Reliability	16	07 STL	* 409	59	105	19	75	5	257	221	298	311	459	770	7	77	29	0.34	265	37	16	47	134	13%	57	10%	4.90	-5.3	$14
BAvg Potl	45%	1st Half	202	32	54	10	44	4	267			302	475	777	5	80	29	0.24	272	39	15	45	130	14%	78	12%	4.80	-3.2	$8
LIMA Plan	F	2nd Half	207	27	51	9	31	1	246			319	443	762	10	75	29	0.42	258	36	17	48	138	12%	35	9%	4.98	-2.3	$5
+/- Score	-26	08 Proj	**240**	**32**	**56**	**10**	**35**	**2**	**233**			**291**	**418**	**710**	**8**	**74**	**27**	**0.32**	**247**	**36**	**16**	**48**	**126**	**12%**	**50**	**8%**	**4.16**	**-8.6**	**$6**

14-52-.267 in 303 AB at STL. Always had the power, just needed to make enough of a splash to earn AB's before poor ct% brought him down. 2nd half decline likely to continue as others exploit him.

Lugo,Julio

			AB	R	H	HR	RBI	SB	Avg	vL	vR	OB	Slg	OPS	bb%	ct%	h%	Eye	xBA	G	L	F	PX	hr/f	SX	SBO	RC/G	RAR	R$
Pos	6	03 2TM	498	64	135	15	55	12	271	240	284	330	410	740	8	80	31	0.44	274	47	23	30	84	13%	101	11%	4.58	4.5	$15
Age	32	04 TAM	581	83	160	7	75	21	275	300	267	337	396	733	9	82	33	0.51	269	49	18	33	84	5%	121	16%	4.67	3.4	$18
Past Peak		05 TAM	616	89	182	6	57	39	295	306	291	359	403	762	9	88	33	0.85	288	49	20	31	71	4%	131	26%	5.11	9.6	$24
Bats	Right	06 2TM	435	69	121	12	37	24	278	263	284	338	421	758	8	83	31	0.51	274	47	20	34	87	10%	114	27%	4.86	6.0	$16
Reliability	73	07 BOS	570	71	135	8	73	33	237	226	241	296	349	645	8	86	26	0.59	268	46	17	37	78	4%	120	28%	3.62	-16.3	$15
BAvg Potl	60%	1st Half	279	33	53	4	34	20	190			259	283	542	9	85	21	0.63	259	54	14	32	62	5%	132	32%	2.42	-19.0	$5
LIMA Plan	B	2nd Half	291	38	82	4	39	13	282			332	412	745	7	86	32	0.54	276	39	20	41	94	4%	99	25%	4.75	1.6	$10
+/- Score	27	08 Proj	**515**	**71**	**141**	**9**	**58**	**28**	**274**			**332**	**398**	**730**	**8**	**85**	**31**	**0.58**	**274**	**46**	**19**	**35**	**82**	**6%**	**117**	**25%**	**4.59**	**1.3**	**$18**

Poor start simply result of low h%. 2H is his normal baseline. 3-year decline in xBA and GB may cause concern, but he should be okay. At minimum, he will again be undervalued on draft day, and that's your edge.

Mackowiak,Rob

			AB	R	H	HR	RBI	SB	Avg	vL	vR	OB	Slg	OPS	bb%	ct%	h%	Eye	xBA	G	L	F	PX	hr/f	SX	SBO	RC/G	RAR	R$
Pos	79	03 PIT	* 391	37	92	8	38	12	235	257	273	288	358	646	7	75	29	0.30	263	48	25	27	81	10%	121	16%	3.38	-26.2	$7
Age	31	04 PIT	491	65	121	17	75	13	246	164	258	316	420	736	9	77	29	0.44	270	46	20	33	108	14%	121	13%	4.62	-12.1	$15
Past Peak		05 PIT	463	57	126	9	58	8	272	275	272	334	389	723	8	78	33	0.43	261	51	20	30	80	8%	92	9%	4.45	-11.9	$13
Bats	Left	06 CHW	255	31	74	5	23	5	290	222	308	360	404	764	10	77	36	0.47	249	54	17	29	78	9%	73	8%	5.06	-0.9	$7
Reliability	51	07 2TM	293	40	77	6	38	4	263	283	259	323	386	709	8	76	33	0.37	259	55	18	27	86	10%	89	6%	4.26	-6.6	$7
BAvg Potl	40%	1st Half	170	23	39	3	19	3	229			296	312	607	9	79	27	0.44	222	57	11	32	50	7%	88	8%	2.96	-10.7	$3
LIMA Plan	F	2nd Half	123	17	38	3	19	1	309			361	488	849	8	72	41	0.29	300	51	30	19	141	18%	76	3%	6.28	4.2	$4
+/- Score	-5	08 Proj	**192**	**25**	**51**	**4**	**24**	**3**	**266**			**328**	**392**	**721**	**9**	**76**	**33**	**0.39**	**262**	**53**	**20**	**27**	**89**	**10%**	**81**	**8%**	**4.43**	**-3.7**	**$5**

Lightning in a bottle in 2nd half thanks to 41% hit rate and 18% hr/f. Ct%, Eye and history tell us not to expect a repeat. Part-timers can juice you, but they can yield as much pain as pleasure.

Markakis,Nick

			AB	R	H	HR	RBI	SB	Avg	vL	vR	OB	Slg	OPS	bb%	ct%	h%	Eye	xBA	G	L	F	PX	hr/f	SX	SBO	RC/G	RAR	R$
Pos	9	03	0	0	0	0	0	0	0							0									0				
Age	24	04	0	0	0	0	0	0	0							0									0				
Growth		05 aa	120	19	39	3	28	0	325			413	533	946	13	78	40	0.69					158		65	3%	7.68	8.7	$6
Bats	Left	06 BAL	491	72	143	16	62	2	291	286	293	348	448	796	8	85	32	0.60	292	51	20	29	92	13%	67	1%	5.29	-5.0	$15
Reliability	22	07 BAL	637	97	191	23	112	18	300	274	311	361	485	846	9	82	33	0.54	290	45	18	37	120	12%	98	13%	5.94	22.0	$28
BAvg Potl	45%	1st Half	309	42	86	9	43	7	278			336	440	776	8	83	31	0.52	274	46	15	40	108	9%	88	10%	5.08	3.4	$10
LIMA Plan	B	2nd Half	328	55	105	14	69	11	320			384	527	911	9	82	36	0.57	303	44	21	35	133	15%	95	16%	6.76	18.4	$18
+/- Score	20	08 Proj	**604**	**92**	**178**	**25**	**103**	**15**	**295**			**360**	**500**	**860**	**9**	**83**	**32**	**0.59**	**305**	**47**	**19**	**34**	**129**	**15%**	**98**	**11%**	**6.12**	**19.4**	**$26**

The Magic of August 11...

	Home Ru	
	2006	20
20 weeks before	5	11
6 weeks after	11	12

If he can ever manage to warm up sooner... UP: 30 HR

Marte,Andy

			AB	R	H	HR	RBI	SB	Avg	vL	vR	OB	Slg	OPS	bb%	ct%	h%	Eye	xBA	G	L	F	PX	hr/f	SX	SBO	RC/G	RAR	R$
Pos	5	03	0	0	0	0	0	0	0							0									0				
Age	24	04 aa	387	48	101	21	64	1	260			352	499	851	12	78	29	0.63					152		38	2%	6.19	13.6	$12
Growth		05 ATL	* 446	53	117	20	76	0	262	174	118	362	468	830	14	82	28	0.88	263	35	13	52	130	10%	32	3%	5.99	15.9	$14
Bats	Right	06 CLE	* 521	69	128	19	69	1	246	227	225	310	433	742	8	78	28	0.42	261	34	17	48	125	9%	54	1%	4.66	-5.3	$11
Reliability	5	07 CLE	* 409	44	97	14	60	0	237	278	154	274	396	671	5	84	25	0.32	257	29	19	52	99	8%	35	0%	3.60	-11.0	$7
BAvg Potl	55%	1st Half	184	15	38	7	30	0	207			240	370	609	4	85	21	0.30	264	33	19	49	99	9%	15	0%	2.87	-9.4	$2
LIMA Plan	D	2nd Half	225	29	59	7	30	0	262			303	418	720	5	83	29	0.33					99		46	0%	4.23	-1.8	$5
+/- Score	12	08 Proj	**341**	**40**	**86**	**13**	**50**	**0**	**252**			**311**	**434**	**744**	**8**	**82**	**28**	**0.46**	**262**	**32**	**17**	**51**	**116**	**9%**	**39**	**1%**	**4.63**	**-0.2**	**$8**

1-8-.193 in 57 AB at CLE. Looks like another well-hyped Atlanta prospect who became a failed prospect after being dealt away. There are skills that he still owns but he has to stop swinging for the fences. (52% FB

Martinez,Ramon

			AB	R	H	HR	RBI	SB	Avg	vL	vR	OB	Slg	OPS	bb%	ct%	h%	Eye	xBA	G	L	F	PX	hr/f	SX	SBO	RC/G	RAR	R$
Pos	4	03 CHC	293	30	83	3	34	0	283	346	259	338	375	713	8	83	33	0.48	264	43	23	33	66	4%	42	1%	4.34	-0.5	$6
Age	35	04 CHC	260	22	64	3	30	1	246	243	247	315	346	661	9	85	28	0.65	248	39	19	42	68	3%	49	1%	3.85	-5.8	$3
Decline		05 2TM	112	11	31	1	14	0	277	255	292	314	330	644	5	90	30	0.55	261	47	23	30	34	3%	25	0%	3.50	-2.7	$2
Bats	Right	06 LA	176	20	49	2	24	0	278	289	275	335	364	699	8	89	31	0.75	253	44	19	37	51	3%	44	0%	4.28	-1.6	$4
Reliability	0	07 LA	129	10	25	0	27	1	194	200	189	257	225	482	8	88	22	0.73	238	43	21	36	25	0%	43	3%	1.86	-11.0	$0
BAvg Potl	75%	1st Half	59	2	9	0	7	1	153			231	186	417	9	92	17	1.20	253	38	24	38	26	0%	33	8%	1.41	-6.2	($1)
LIMA Plan	F	2nd Half	70	8	16	0	20	0	229			280	257	537	7	86	27	0.50	224	47	19	34	24	0%	37	0%	2.29	-4.8	$1
+/- Score	34	08 Proj	**120**	**11**	**28**	**1**	**21**	**0**	**233**			**290**	**282**	**573**	**7**	**88**	**26**	**0.67**	**244**	**44**	**21**	**36**	**34**	**2%**	**37**	**1%**	**2.82**	**-6.3**	**$1**

Falling xBA means the end is near, but h% makes him look worse than reality, if that's possible. Back, ankle & elbow injuries may hasten his exit. You can't play every position if you can't play. Utility futility.

MATT BEAGLE

Martinez,Victor

Martinez,Victor		AB	R	H	HR	RBI	SB	Avg	vL	vR	OB	Slg	OPS	bb%	ct%	h%	Eye	xBA	G	L	F	PX	hr/f	SX	SBO	RC/G	RAR	R$
Pos 23	03 CLE *	445	53	133	8	58	4	299	271	300	350	407	757	7	88	33	0.66	293	47	25	28	70	7%	43	7%	4.86	9.6	$13
Age 29	04 CLE	520	77	147	23	108	0	283	282	283	357	492	849	10	87	29	0.87	290	40	16	44	123	12%	38	1%	6.05	25.2	$19
Peak	05 CLE	547	73	167	20	80	0	305	274	320	377	475	852	10	86	33	0.81	293	48	21	32	106	13%	22	1%	6.08	30.8	$20
Bats Both	06 CLE	572	82	181	16	93	0	316	290	332	392	465	857	11	86	35	0.91	286	44	22	34	92	9%	25	0%	6.23	27.9	$20
Reliability 99	07 CLE	562	78	169	25	114	0	301	289	307	370	505	876	10	86	31	0.82	304	42	20	38	126	13%	22	0%	6.31	35.3	$22
BAvg Potl 60%	1st Half	270	40	85	14	62	0	315			373	530	903	8	87	32	0.71	316	41	23	36	126	16%	23	0%	6.47	17.8	$13
LIMA Plan C	2nd Half	292	38	84	11	52	0	288			368	483	851	11	86	30	0.90	292	42	18	40	126	11%	20	0%	6.15	17.4	$10
+/- Score 7	08 Proj	**565**	**78**	**171**	**21**	**101**	**0**	**303**			**374**	**482**	**856**	**10**	**86**	**32**	**0.84**	**294**	**43**	**20**	**37**	**111**	**12%**	**27**	**0%**	**6.13**	**30.8**	**$21**

Reversed decline in PX with a vengeance. But he is relying on rising FB%, which may hurt BA -- 2nd half shows downside. Increasing playing time at first base should help prolong effectiveness.

Martin,Russell

Martin,Russell		AB	R	H	HR	RBI	SB	Avg	vL	vR	OB	Slg	OPS	bb%	ct%	h%	Eye	xBA	G	L	F	PX	hr/f	SX	SBO	RC/G	RAR	R$
Pos 2	03	0	0	0	0	0	0	0							0									0				
Age 25	04	0	0	0	0	0	0	0							0									0				
Pre-Peak	05 aa	405	67	108	7	48	12	267			361	358	719	13	86	30	1.05					57		87	14%	4.74	10.0	$13
Bats Right	06 LA *	489	76	136	10	72	10	278	366	265	351	425	776	10	87	31	0.83	297	50	20	30	90	8%	92	12%	5.30	13.5	$16
Reliability 45	07 LA	540	87	158	19	87	21	293	357	273	371	469	839	11	84	32	0.75	289	48	18	34	108	12%	100	18%	5.99	33.8	$24
BAvg Potl 50%	1st Half	265	42	78	8	49	13	294			364	464	828	10	85	32	0.73	296	49	19	33	104	11%	115	19%	5.82	15.1	$13
LIMA Plan B	2nd Half	275	45	80	11	38	8	291			377	473	850	12	82	32	0.78	281	48	16	36	111	14%	78	16%	6.16	18.8	$11
+/- Score 6	08 Proj	**542**	**87**	**157**	**21**	**80**	**16**	**290**			**368**	**476**	**845**	**11**	**85**	**31**	**0.82**	**299**	**49**	**18**	**33**	**111**	**14%**	**94**	**15%**	**6.05**	**32.4**	**$23**

Bidders clamor for the speed he brings to the catcher position, but pay attention to his power: In last four halves of baseball, PX has risen from 85 to 96 to 104 to 111. At that rate, he could have a 15-HR second half in '08.

Mathis,Jeff

Mathis,Jeff		AB	R	H	HR	RBI	SB	Avg	vL	vR	OB	Slg	OPS	bb%	ct%	h%	Eye	xBA	G	L	F	PX	hr/f	SX	SBO	RC/G	RAR	R$
Pos 2	03 aa	95	17	26	2	13	1	276			348	453	801	10	86	30	0.79					125		68	13%	5.61	3.9	$3
Age 25	04 aa	432	46	87	10	45	2	201			268	331	599	8	81	23	0.47					83		70	3%	2.91	-15.7	$0
Pre-Peak	05 aaa	427	59	105	16	56	3	246			296	420	717	7	86	25	0.52					105		76	8%	4.29	4.9	$11
Bats Right	06 LAA *	439	57	106	6	41	2	241	133	150	285	364	650	6	83	28	0.37	221	29	12	59	85	3%	75	3%	3.52	-11.6	$5
Reliability 21	07 LAA *	421	57	90	8	45	3	214	242	203	264	333	597	6	78	26	0.32	230	42	13	45	87	5%	77	6%	2.76	-16.4	$4
BAvg Potl 50%	1st Half	250	35	57	4	23	3	228			272	336	608	6	84	26	0.37					74		90	7%	2.98	-7.9	$3
LIMA Plan F	2nd Half	171	22	33	4	22	0	193			254	327	582	8	70	25	0.27	220	42	13	45	110	7%	48	3%	2.51	-8.2	$1
+/- Score 8	08 Proj	**219**	**29**	**51**	**5**	**24**	**1**	**233**			**284**	**366**	**650**	**7**	**80**	**27**	**0.35**	**236**	**41**	**13**	**46**	**92**	**6%**	**74**	**5%**	**3.46**	**-4.5**	**$3**

4-23-.211 in 171 AB at LAA. Doing nothing to lock down a big-league job. Double-digit HR lurks but he will never get a shot by hitting .200. And it takes more power than he has to offset a 70% ct%.

Matsui,Hideki

Matsui,Hideki		AB	R	H	HR	RBI	SB	Avg	vL	vR	OB	Slg	OPS	bb%	ct%	h%	Eye	xBA	G	L	F	PX	hr/f	SX	SBO	RC/G	RAR	R$
Pos 70	03 NYY	623	82	179	16	106	2	287	287	287	353	435	788	9	86	31	0.73	302	55	21	24	95	12%	45	2%	5.32	-0.2	$19
Age 33	04 NYY	584	109	174	31	108	3	298	265	314	390	522	912	13	82	32	0.85	295	41	19	39	131	16%	75	2%	6.93	31.9	$26
Past Peak	05 NYY	629	108	192	23	116	2	305	354	278	368	496	865	9	88	32	0.81	303	47	16	36	117	12%	64	2%	6.18	25.1	$26
Bats Left	06 NYY	172	32	52	8	29	1	302	226	336	397	494	891	14	87	31	1.17	281	39	17	44	108	12%	49	2%	6.70	7.2	$7
Reliability 42	07 NYY	547	100	156	25	103	4	285	274	290	369	488	857	12	87	29	1.00	295	43	17	40	117	13%	83	3%	6.21	23.0	$22
BAvg Potl 65%	1st Half	234	35	65	8	46	1	278			355	449	804	11	86	30	0.85	285	49	16	36	109	11%	42	3%	5.56	5.6	$8
LIMA Plan B	2nd Half	313	65	91	17	57	3	291			380	518	897	13	87	29	1.13	298	38	18	44	123	14%	98	4%	6.69	17.2	$14
+/- Score 13	08 Proj	**525**	**95**	**153**	**23**	**95**	**3**	**291**			**375**	**491**	**866**	**12**	**87**	**30**	**0.99**	**294**	**43**	**17**	**40**	**115**	**13%**	**76**	**3%**	**6.31**	**21.0**	**$21**

Looks like replay of 2004-05 before last year's wrist injury, but stats hide unrest. He hit 13 of his HR in one month (July). In June/Aug/Sept he had only 18 extra-base hits total. Don't think he can't age. DN: 15 HR

Matsui,Kaz

Matsui,Kaz		AB	R	H	HR	RBI	SB	Avg	vL	vR	OB	Slg	OPS	bb%	ct%	h%	Eye	xBA	G	L	F	PX	hr/f	SX	SBO	RC/G	RAR	R$
Pos 4	03 JPN	587	101	167	20	82	12	284			334	468	802	7	80	33	0.38					117		126	10%	5.33	17.7	$23
Age 32	04 NYM	460	65	125	7	44	14	272	306	262	330	396	726	8	79	33	0.41	276	48	23	29	89	7%	107	14%	4.51	-1.3	$13
Past Peak	05 NYM	267	31	68	3	24	6	255	279	246	292	352	644	5	84	29	0.33	276	51	22	27	60	5%	123	11%	3.39	-9.2	$5
Bats Both	06 2NL *	370	56	98	6	40	13	266	119	299	309	375	684	6	82	31	0.35	264	48	20	31	69	6%	121	15%	3.87	-7.8	$11
Reliability 23	07 COL	410	84	118	4	37	32	288	271	291	342	405	747	8	83	34	0.49	270	45	21	34	77	3%	169	31%	4.81	2.9	$18
BAvg Potl 45%	1st Half	151	33	46	2	18	15	305			344	457	801	6	84	35	0.38	281	41	24	36	92	4%	187	40%	5.34	3.2	$9
LIMA Plan B	2nd Half	259	51	72	2	19	17	278			342	375	716	9	83	33	0.56	262	48	20	33	68	3%	142	26%	4.49	-0.6	$10
+/- Score 3	08 Proj	**504**	**88**	**139**	**7**	**50**	**27**	**276**			**325**	**392**	**717**	**7**	**83**	**32**	**0.42**	**272**	**47**	**21**	**32**	**76**	**5%**	**154**	**23%**	**4.35**	**-3.1**	**$18**

Blew out the speakers with 31% SBO and 32 SB. But he still has no power, even in COL, and xBA doesn't see cause for celebrating. Don't bid as if he can better these numbers. He runs at his manager's whim.

Matthews Jr.,Gary

Matthews Jr.,Gary		AB	R	H	HR	RBI	SB	Avg	vL	vR	OB	Slg	OPS	bb%	ct%	h%	Eye	xBA	G	L	F	PX	hr/f	SX	SBO	RC/G	RAR	R$
Pos 8	03 2TM	468	71	116	6	42	12	248	287	233	311	359	670	8	80	30	0.45	268	50	20	30	82	5%	102	17%	3.85	-14.3	$10
Age 33	04 TEX *	428	60	117	18	60	8	273	244	289	348	474	822	10	79	31	0.55	296	45	24	31	123	17%	100	8%	5.74	12.6	$14
Past Peak	05 TEX	475	72	121	17	55	9	255	241	260	322	436	758	9	81	28	0.52	290	51	17	32	114	14%	116	9%	4.88	8.4	$14
Bats Both	06 TEX	620	102	194	19	79	10	313	314	313	372	495	867	9	84	35	0.59	303	51	19	30	112	12%	97	9%	6.21	26.3	$23
Reliability 46	07 LAA	516	79	130	18	72	18	252	175	275	324	419	743	10	80	28	0.54	269	51	13	36	107	12%	110	16%	4.71	6.6	$17
BAvg Potl 55%	1st Half	281	47	80	10	42	11	285			343	452	795	8	80	32	0.45	266	47	14	39	105	11%	114	18%	5.27	7.9	$12
LIMA Plan C+	2nd Half	235	32	50	8	30	7	213			302	379	681	11	80	23	0.64	271	56	11	33	109	13%	94	14%	4.03	-1.8	$5
+/- Score 8	08 Proj	**462**	**71**	**122**	**15**	**60**	**12**	**264**			**334**	**435**	**768**	**9**	**81**	**30**	**0.56**	**282**	**51**	**15**	**33**	**109**	**12%**	**107**	**13%**	**5.05**	**8.4**	**$15**

We warned against a repeat, but even we weren't this down. Move out of Texas exposed average Eye and power, and retreat to 80% ct% didn't help. Still, xBA says 2nd-half tumble was false. Expect the ordinary.

Mauer,Joe

Mauer,Joe		AB	R	H	HR	RBI	SB	Avg	vL	vR	OB	Slg	OPS	bb%	ct%	h%	Eye	xBA	G	L	F	PX	hr/f	SX	SBO	RC/G	RAR	R$
Pos 2	03 aa	276	43	92	3	37	0	333			383	438	821	7	92	35	1.05					68		51	0%	5.70	10.9	$10
Age 25	04 MIN	107	18	33	6	17	1	308	182	365	373	570	943	9	87	31	0.79	328	46	18	36	146	18%	81	3%	7.04	7.9	$5
Pre-Peak	05 MIN	489	61	144	9	55	13	294	232	323	373	411	784	11	87	32	0.95	303	52	24	24	75	9%	93	8%	5.42	19.0	$16
Bats Left	06 MIN	521	86	181	13	84	8	347	331	356	433	507	940	13	90	37	1.46	325	49	25	26	94	11%	86	5%	7.38	40.0	$24
Reliability 22	07 MIN	406	62	119	7	60	7	293	283	299	380	426	806	12	87	32	1.12	298	55	18	28	87	7%	94	6%	5.80	20.2	$13
BAvg Potl 60%	1st Half	174	31	54	3	25	5	310			391	466	856	12	86	35	0.92	303	49	20	31	105	6%	114	9%	6.37	11.0	$7
LIMA Plan B	2nd Half	232	31	65	4	35	2	280			372	397	769	13	89	30	1.31	287	59	16	25	75	8%	60	4%	5.40	9.1	$6
+/- Score 29	08 Proj	**467**	**71**	**144**	**10**	**68**	**8**	**308**			**391**	**448**	**839**	**12**	**88**	**33**	**1.15**	**306**	**52**	**21**	**27**	**88**	**9%**	**88**	**6%**	**6.15**	**25.6**	**$17**

Bedeviled by quad, hamstring, and hernia, the latter of which may need surgery. Given these woes, a .298 xBA is testament to his natural talent. Any bid on Draft Day is a bet on his health, especially if he stays at catcher.

Maybin,Cameron

Maybin,Cameron		AB	R	H	HR	RBI	SB	Avg	vL	vR	OB	Slg	OPS	bb%	ct%	h%	Eye	xBA	G	L	F	PX	hr/f	SX	SBO	RC/G	RAR	R$
Pos 7	03	0	0	0	0	0	0	0							0									0				
Age 21	04	0	0	0	0	0	0	0							0									0				
Growth	05	0	0	0	0	0	0	0							0									0				
Bats Right	06	0	0	0	0	0	0	0							0									0				
Reliability 0	07 DET *	69	17	14	4	10	5	203		200	298	436	733	12	61	26	0.35	249	54	4	43	191	22%	138	33%	4.97	0.5	$3
BAvg Potl 45%	1st Half	0	0	0	0	0	0	0																				
LIMA Plan D+	2nd Half	69	17	14	4	10	5	203			298	436	733	12	61	26	0.35	249	54	4	43	192	22%	138	33%	4.97	0.5	$3
+/- Score 27	08 Proj	**61**	**17**	**14**	**3**	**10**	**6**	**230**			**330**	**437**	**767**	**13**	**57**	**35**	**0.35**	**231**	**54**	**4**	**43**	**187**	**19%**	**144**	**36%**	**5.93**	**1.9**	**$3**

1-2-.143 in 49 AB at DET. Signal accomplishment was batting .304/.393/.486 at High-A. Those numbers are flashy but he has to survive a very poor ct% for two more levels before he settles in the majors.

McCann,Brian

McCann,Brian		AB	R	H	HR	RBI	SB	Avg	vL	vR	OB	Slg	OPS	bb%	ct%	h%	Eye	xBA	G	L	F	PX	hr/f	SX	SBO	RC/G	RAR	R$
Pos 2	03	0	0	0	0	0	0	0							0									0				
Age 24	04	0	0	0	0	0	0	0							0									0				
Growth	05 ATL *	346	43	90	10	46	3	260	344	259	337	408	744	10	86	28	0.82	290	42	23	35	92	10%	55	7%	4.86	10.9	$9
Bats Left	06 ATL	442	61	147	24	93	2	333	266	351	389	572	962	8	88	34	0.76	317	35	22	43	135	14%	38	2%	7.16	32.6	$23
Reliability 7	07 ATL	504	51	136	18	92	0	270	264	273	317	452	770	6	85	29	0.47	282	39	19	43	115	10%	18	1%	4.90	16.1	$14
BAvg Potl 55%	1st Half	231	23	62	7	41	0	268			321	437	759	7	86	29	0.55	295	44	22	34	109	10%	17	0%	4.85	7.0	$6
LIMA Plan C	2nd Half	273	28	74	11	51	0	271			314	465	779	6	85	29	0.41	272	34	16	50	120	10%	20	2%	4.94	9.1	$8
+/- Score 12	08 Proj	**517**	**61**	**147**	**21**	**96**	**1**	**284**			**340**	**482**	**822**	**8**	**86**	**30**	**0.61**	**295**	**37**	**20**	**43**	**120**	**11%**	**32**	**2%**	**5.56**	**23.4**	**$18**

Decent sophomore numbers, but he was a shadow of his 2006 form: In 2007, he never hit *over* .300 in a month, while in '06, he never hit *under* .300. 2nd half power adjustment bodes well for 2008 growth.

JOHN BURNSON

McDonald,John			AB	R	H	HR	RBI	SB	Avg	vL	vR	OB	Slg	OPS	bb%	ct%	h%	Eye	xBA	G	L	F	PX	hr/f	SX	SBO	RC/G	RAR	R$
Pos	6	03 CLE	214	21	46	1	14	3	215	215	215	253	280	534	5	86	25	0.35	247	40	22	38	46	1%	79	13%	2.16	-15.2	$1
Age	33	04 CLE	93	17	19	2	7	0	204	200	220	237	344	581	4	88	21	0.36	259	43	13	44	81	6%	111	0%	2.74	-5.0	$1
Past Peak		05 2AL	166	18	46	0	16	6	277	298	253	322	325	647	6	86	32	0.46	264	55	21	24	36	0%	98	14%	3.55	-4.8	$4
Bats	Right	06 TOR	260	35	58	3	23	7	223	230	220	268	308	576	6	84	25	0.39	249	48	18	34	49	4%	128	15%	2.63	-14.3	$3
Reliability	32	07 TOR	327	32	82	1	31	7	251	329	223	275	333	608	3	85	29	0.23	263	40	23	37	62	1%	95	13%	2.95	-15.6	$5
BAvg Potl	50%	1st Half	134	19	39	1	9	3	291			307	381	687	2	86	33	0.16	273	44	22	34	68	3%	78	16%	3.75	-3.1	$3
LIMA Plan	F	2nd Half	193	13	43	0	22	4	223			254	301	554	4	85	26	0.28	255	38	23	39	58	0%	93	11%	2.39	-12.8	$1
+/- Score	-11	08 Proj	**282**	**31**	**70**	**1**	**26**	**5**	**248**			**282**	**323**	**605**	**4**	**85**	**29**	**0.32**	**255**	**45**	**21**	**35**	**52**	**2%**	**95**	**10%**	**2.95**	**-13.1**	**$4**

Runs fairly often once he gets on base -- and there's the rub. Contact rate is solid but he rarely walks. When a player's personal baseline hit rate is under 30%, the ceiling is going to be low.

McLouth,Nate			AB	R	H	HR	RBI	SB	Avg	vL	vR	OB	Slg	OPS	bb%	ct%	h%	Eye	xBA	G	L	F	PX	hr/f	SX	SBO	RC/G	RAR	R$
Pos	87	03	0	0	0	0	0	0	0							0									0				
Age	26	04 aa	515	76	153	6	59	25	297			345	414	759	7	91	32	0.81					76		116	23%	4.98	4.3	$20
Pre-Peak		05 PIT	* 506	68	133	9	42	28	263	100	292	307	374	680	6	88	29	0.52	279	52	16	31	70	6%	121	29%	3.92	-9.7	$17
Bats	Left	06 PIT	270	50	63	7	16	10	233	260	227	281	385	666	6	78	27	0.31	269	39	25	35	99	9%	141	20%	3.63	-6.6	$6
Reliability	12	07 PIT	329	62	85	13	38	22	258	269	256	337	459	796	11	77	30	0.51	250	31	16	53	132	10%	147	26%	5.47	8.8	$14
BAvg Potl	45%	1st Half	86	10	19	1	6	4	221			264	302	566	5	77	28	0.25	205	30	18	52	62	3%	89	21%	2.30	-5.9	$1
LIMA Plan	B	2nd Half	243	52	66	12	32	18	272			361	514	875	12	77	31	0.60	267	31	16	53	157	12%	157	28%	6.58	14.1	$13
+/- Score	15	08 Proj	**479**	**81**	**126**	**18**	**44**	**21**	**263**			**321**	**450**	**771**	**8**	**78**	**30**	**0.39**	**264**	**35**	**20**	**45**	**121**	**11%**	**132**	**21%**	**4.99**	**6.0**	**$17**

His 53% FB% was 18% above league average. This is good news for power growth. But fly balls have the lowest likelihood of falling for a hit, which is bad news for his BA and SB. And speed is (was?) his true value.

Mench,Kevin			AB	R	H	HR	RBI	SB	Avg	vL	vR	OB	Slg	OPS	bb%	ct%	h%	Eye	xBA	G	L	F	PX	hr/f	SX	SBO	RC/G	RAR	R$
Pos	79	03 TEX	* 241	29	67	6	28	3	278	346	301	351	436	786	10	87	30	0.84	302	37	25	38	105	8%	52	6%	5.39	0.4	$6
Age	30	04 TEX	438	69	122	26	71	0	279	319	259	329	539	868	7	86	28	0.52	306	36	17	46	146	15%	58	0%	6.00	13.1	$16
Peak		05 TEX	557	71	147	25	73	4	264	296	257	325	469	793	8	88	26	0.74	294	38	17	45	120	11%	67	5%	5.27	8.8	$17
Bats	Right	06 2TM	446	45	120	13	68	1	269	303	257	311	419	730	6	87	29	0.46	273	42	18	39	88	9%	49	1%	4.41	-10.2	$10
Reliability	66	07 MIL	288	39	77	8	37	3	267	314	212	306	441	747	5	93	27	0.76	297	42	17	41	98	7%	92	6%	4.74	-5.0	$8
BAvg Potl	70%	1st Half	158	18	43	2	17	2	272			277	405	682	1	91	29	0.07	283	43	16	40	86	3%	86	7%	3.74	-7.2	$3
LIMA Plan	D	2nd Half	130	21	34	6	20	1	262			338	485	823	10	95	24	2.14	314	40	17	43	113	11%	89	6%	5.87	2.0	$4
+/- Score	34	08 Proj	**294**	**38**	**81**	**10**	**41**	**2**	**276**			**324**	**454**	**779**	**7**	**90**	**28**	**0.73**	**291**	**41**	**17**	**42**	**101**	**9%**	**70**	**4%**	**5.08**	**-2.1**	**$9**

On the plus side, his PX didn't slip again. On the minus side, it didn't do much of anything. He has morphed to a guy who plays for contact. That's not a productive move for a guy who already lacks a line-drive swing.

Metcalf,Travis			AB	R	H	HR	RBI	SB	Avg	vL	vR	OB	Slg	OPS	bb%	ct%	h%	Eye	xBA	G	L	F	PX	hr/f	SX	SBO	RC/G	RAR	R$
Pos	5	03	0	0	0	0	0	0	0							0									0				
Age	25	04	0	0	0	0	0	0	0							0									0				
Pre-Peak		05	0	0	0	0	0	0	0							0									0				
Bats	Right	06 aa	425	41	85	7	29	8	199			262	288	550	8	77	24	0.37					59		80	16%	2.19	-41.8	$1
Reliability	1	07 TEX	* 422	56	96	10	52	2	227	237	265	285	374	659	7	77	27	0.35	257	39	19	42	109	7%	64	4%	3.60	-11.5	$6
BAvg Potl	45%	1st Half	231	37	59	7	33	2	255			317	429	746	8	82	28	0.51	264	50	8	42	121	9%	64	6%	4.74	1.7	$6
LIMA Plan	F	2nd Half	191	19	37	3	19	0	194			245	309	554	6	71	26	0.23	231	36	22	41	94	5%	58	3%	2.13	-14.4	$0
+/- Score	23	08 Proj	**143**	**16**	**35**	**3**	**14**	**1**	**245**			**301**	**373**	**674**	**7**	**76**	**30**	**0.34**	**244**	**38**	**20**	**42**	**92**	**6%**	**74**	**8%**	**3.79**	**-3.7**	**$2**

5-21-.255 in 161 AB at TEX. Hints of power, little else. He did hit .295 with 4 HR in Aug/Sept but the sample of 61 AB is not convincing, since he hit .146 with 0 HR in the same number of AB at AAA.

Michaels,Jason			AB	R	H	HR	RBI	SB	Avg	vL	vR	OB	Slg	OPS	bb%	ct%	h%	Eye	xBA	G	L	F	PX	hr/f	SX	SBO	RC/G	RAR	R$
Pos	79	03 PHI	109	20	36	5	17	0	330	382	278	411	569	980	12	80	38	0.68	321	41	24	34	164	17%	32	0%	7.86	6.5	$5
Age	31	04 PHI	299	44	82	10	40	2	274	286	270	364	415	778	12	73	34	0.53	237	40	20	40	95	12%	45	4%	5.33	-0.9	$9
Past Peak		05 PHI	289	54	88	4	31	3	304	323	289	396	415	812	13	84	35	0.98	276	41	25	35	75	5%	87	5%	5.89	4.4	$10
Bats	Right	06 CLE	494	77	132	9	55	9	267	291	252	326	391	717	8	80	32	0.43	261	40	23	38	87	6%	88	11%	4.37	-11.6	$12
Reliability	44	07 CLE	267	43	72	7	39	3	270	287	252	321	397	718	7	81	31	0.40	241	37	17	46	82	7%	78	10%	4.27	-3.5	$8
BAvg Potl	45%	1st Half	145	21	44	5	22	1	303			353	469	822	7	83	34	0.46	260	37	16	47	101	9%	69	10%	5.51	3.2	$5
LIMA Plan	F	2nd Half	122	22	28	2	17	2	230			282	311	594	7	79	28	0.35	218	37	18	45	57	5%	88	10%	2.71	-7.5	$2
+/- Score	-18	08 Proj	**219**	**36**	**57**	**5**	**29**	**3**	**260**			**324**	**387**	**711**	**9**	**81**	**30**	**0.49**	**253**	**39**	**20**	**41**	**84**	**7%**	**88**	**9%**	**4.32**	**-3.6**	**$6**

We said last year that his skills weren't worthy of full-time play. And they didn't improve. Woes vs. RHP spelled loss of 200 PA vs. RHers from '06 to '07. OPS against lefties unchanged at .800, so don't write totally off.

Mientkiewicz,Doug			AB	R	H	HR	RBI	SB	Avg	vL	vR	OB	Slg	OPS	bb%	ct%	h%	Eye	xBA	G	L	F	PX	hr/f	SX	SBO	RC/G	RAR	R$
Pos	3	03 MIN	487	67	146	11	65	4	300	300	310	392	450	842	13	89	32	1.35	308	38	26	36	97	7%	62	3%	6.27	11.9	$16
Age	33	04 2AL	391	47	93	6	35	2	238	220	246	321	350	672	11	86	26	0.86	258	43	18	39	74	5%	53	5%	4.10	-10.5	$4
Past Peak		05 NYM	275	36	66	11	29	0	240	214	245	319	407	726	10	86	24	0.82	273	49	16	35	100	13%	30	1%	4.59	-8.4	$6
Bats	Left	06 KC	314	37	89	4	43	3	283	274	286	355	411	766	10	84	33	0.70	276	41	22	37	88	4%	74	3%	5.18	-2.1	$7
Reliability	5	07 NYY	166	26	46	5	24	0	277	231	286	341	440	780	9	86	30	0.70	299	36	24	39	106	9%	35	0%	5.19	0.5	$5
BAvg Potl	60%	1st Half	124	17	28	4	16	0	226			284	379	663	7	87	23	0.63	292	37	24	39	95	9%	37	0%	3.75	-5.0	$2
LIMA Plan	D	2nd Half	42	9	18	1	8	0	429			500	619	1119	12	83	50	0.86	321	35	26	38	141	7%	33	0%	9.61	4.3	$3
+/- Score	-10	08 Proj	**320**	**41**	**90**	**12**	**43**	**0**	**281**			**352**	**458**	**810**	**10**	**86**	**30**	**0.78**	**293**	**42**	**21**	**38**	**108**	**11%**	**36**	**1%**	**5.58**	**3.6**	**$9**

The concurrent rise in LD, FB, PX and hr/f all point to a coming power surge. These would be exciting indicators if not for the fact that his role is defense, he'll only see 300 AB and he's 33.

Miles,Aaron			AB	R	H	HR	RBI	SB	Avg	vL	vR	OB	Slg	OPS	bb%	ct%	h%	Eye	xBA	G	L	F	PX	hr/f	SX	SBO	RC/G	RAR	R$
Pos	46	03 aaa	546	68	150	11	43	7	275			320	401	721	6	92	28	0.78					75		76	12%	4.48	3.3	$13
Age	31	04 COL	* 576	80	168	6	52	13	292	267	301	327	365	691	5	90	32	0.54	269	55	17	28	43	4%	97	13%	4.03	-9.5	$17
Past Peak		05 COL	* 356	41	97	2	29	5	271	234	292	287	344	631	2	89	30	0.20	288	54	23	23	45	3%	105	8%	3.18	-14.1	$7
Bats	Both	06 STL	426	48	112	2	30	2	263	291	256	323	347	671	8	90	29	0.90	286	55	20	25	51	2%	78	2%	4.09	-6.3	$5
Reliability	45	07 STL	414	55	120	2	32	2	290	286	292	330	348	678	6	90	32	0.63	263	54	18	28	39	2%	62	2%	3.96	-6.9	$8
BAvg Potl	55%	1st Half	179	20	55	0	13	0	307			340	352	692	5	91	34	0.56	251	52	18	30	35	0%	32	2%	4.08	-2.3	$4
LIMA Plan	D	2nd Half	235	35	65	2	19	2	277			323	345	667	6	90	30	0.67	269	55	18	27	42	4%	79	3%	3.86	-4.7	$5
+/- Score	-30	08 Proj	**325**	**41**	**86**	**2**	**25**	**2**	**265**			**307**	**335**	**643**	**6**	**90**	**29**	**0.62**	**275**	**54**	**19**	**26**	**45**	**3%**	**78**	**4%**	**3.59**	**-9.2**	**$5**

High contact, no power, no speed, ground ball hitter, which means about all he can do is try to leg out hits. He did a little better in '07, he'll do a little worse in '08.

Millar,Kevin			AB	R	H	HR	RBI	SB	Avg	vL	vR	OB	Slg	OPS	bb%	ct%	h%	Eye	xBA	G	L	F	PX	hr/f	SX	SBO	RC/G	RAR	R$
Pos	30	03 BOS	544	83	150	25	96	3	276	289	271	348	472	820	10	80	30	0.56	283	34	23	42	123	14%	60	3%	5.64	4.0	$20
Age	36	04 BOS	513	75	152	18	74	1	296	299	297	367	472	838	10	82	33	0.62	264	36	17	47	112	9%	38	1%	5.92	13.2	$17
Decline		05 BOS	449	57	122	9	50	0	272	246	283	350	399	749	11	84	31	0.73	255	34	20	46	87	5%	37	1%	4.94	-1.9	$10
Bats	Right	06 BAL	430	64	117	15	64	1	272	244	283	360	437	797	12	83	30	0.80	276	35	22	42	103	10%	38	1%	5.53	1.4	$12
Reliability	77	07 BAL	476	63	121	17	63	1	254	250	256	357	420	777	14	80	28	0.81	256	29	20	51	109	9%	41	1%	5.36	3.7	$11
BAvg Potl	60%	1st Half	189	22	49	6	23	0	259			369	407	777	15	80	29	0.89	253	27	21	53	99	8%	16	0%	5.43	1.8	$4
LIMA Plan	C	2nd Half	287	41	72	11	40	1	251			348	429	777	13	80	28	0.75	260	31	19	50	115	9%	52	2%	5.31	1.9	$7
+/- Score	-2	08 Proj	**429**	**59**	**113**	**14**	**58**	**1**	**263**			**355**	**427**	**783**	**12**	**81**	**29**	**0.77**	**263**	**32**	**20**	**48**	**106**	**9%**	**44**	**1%**	**5.38**	**2.5**	**$11**

Climbing Eye says that he is getting more selective at the plate, which should help his numbers at the margins. But this is still a 36-year-old with ordinary pop and no speed. But consistently ordinary.

Milledge,Lastings			AB	R	H	HR	RBI	SB	Avg	vL	vR	OB	Slg	OPS	bb%	ct%	h%	Eye	xBA	G	L	F	PX	hr/f	SX	SBO	RC/G	RAR	R$
Pos	9	03	0	0	0	0	0	0	0							0									0				
Age	23	04	0	0	0	0	0	0	0							0									0				
Growth		05 aa	193	27	61	3	20	9	316			354	446	800	6	81	38	0.32					99		86	29%	5.28	1.6	$9
Bats	Right	06 NYM	* 473	70	130	11	61	15	275	241	241	355	429	783	11	79	33	0.60	274	44	22	34	99	8%	102	20%	5.39	8.6	$15
Reliability	18	07 NYM	* 246	41	71	10	40	8	289	317	250	330	472	801	6	78	34	0.27	288	47	24	29	113	18%	117	16%	5.21	-0.3	$11
BAvg Potl	35%	1st Half	42	8	12	1	4	4	286			318	381	699	5	76	35	0.20					61		115	33%	3.85	-1.7	$2
LIMA Plan	D+	2nd Half	204	33	59	9	36	4	289			332	490	822	6	78	33	0.29	299	48	24	27	124	21%	104	12%	5.49	1.4	$9
+/- Score	22	08 Proj	**390**	**59**	**112**	**12**	**53**	**13**	**287**			**338**	**455**	**792**	**7**	**80**	**34**	**0.38**	**294**	**47**	**24**	**29**	**111**	**13%**	**100**	**22%**	**5.23**	**0.9**	**$15**

7-29-.272 in 184 AB at NYM. Above avg power and speed point to growth, but there's a ways to go. He ended '06 with improving Eye but went back to overeager ways. Patience would help, or just more power.

JOHN BURNSON

Miller,Damian			AB	R	H	HR	RBI	SB	Avg	vL	vR	OB	Slg	OPS	bb%	ct%	h%	Eye	xBA	G	L	F	PX	hr/f	SX	SBO	RC/G	RAR	R$
Pos	2	03 CHC	352	34	82	9	36	1	233	248	226	309	369	679	10	74	29	0.43	261	48	23	29	99	12%	50	1%	3.93	-3.8	$5
Age	38	04 OAK	397	39	108	9	58	0	272	290	264	337	403	740	9	78	33	0.45	265	43	24	33	92	9%	19	1%	4.69	4.1	$8
Decline		05 MIL	385	50	105	9	43	0	273	231	286	336	413	749	9	76	34	0.39	279	50	25	24	105	13%	42	1%	4.83	11.5	$10
Bats	Right	06 MIL	331	34	83	6	38	0	251	280	241	319	390	708	9	74	32	0.38	253	44	21	35	108	7%	21	0%	4.37	0.3	$5
Reliability	24	07 MIL	186	19	44	4	24	1	237	235	237	290	349	639	7	79	28	0.36	236	48	15	37	77	7%	41	2%	3.30	-2.7	$3
BAvg Potl	40%	1st Half	82	9	21	1	10	1	256			299	354	653	6	82	30	0.33	243	47	16	37	72	4%	51	5%	3.49	-0.7	$1
LIMA Plan	F	2nd Half	104	10	23	3	14	0	221			283	346	629	8	77	26	0.38	223	49	15	37	82	10%	20	0%	3.15	-2.0	$1
+/- Score	-4	08 Proj	**161**	**17**	**40**	**3**	**20**	**0**	**248**			**309**	**375**	**684**	**8**	**77**	**30**	**0.38**	**250**	**47**	**19**	**34**	**92**	**8%**	**34**	**1%**	**3.93**	**-0.1**	**$3**

A six-point drop in LD% fueled a sub-30 H% and tailspins vs. both RH and LH. It is difficult to find a silver lining in these BPIs. His LD% may rebound somewhat, but steadily sliding Eye points to vanishing skills.

Mirabelli,Doug			AB	R	H	HR	RBI	SB	Avg	vL	vR	OB	Slg	OPS	bb%	ct%	h%	Eye	xBA	G	L	F	PX	hr/f	SX	SBO	RC/G	RAR	R$
Pos	2	03 BOS	163	23	42	6	18	0	258	250	261	305	448	752	6	78	30	0.31	289	44	22	34	133	14%	36	0%	4.68	2.8	$4
Age	37	04 BOS	160	27	45	9	32	0	281	311	270	358	525	883	11	71	34	0.41	274	39	18	43	170	18%	32	0%	6.72	10.8	$6
Decline		05 BOS	136	16	31	6	18	2	228	245	212	300	412	712	9	65	30	0.29	233	36	18	45	146	15%	53	6%	4.46	1.8	$3
Bats	Right	06 2TM	183	13	35	6	25	0	191	200	188	253	328	580	8	68	25	0.25	189	39	13	48	98	10%	10	0%	2.40	-11.5	$1
Reliability	0	07 BOS	114	9	23	5	16	0	202	250	194	272	360	632	9	64	26	0.27	177	37	16	47	118	15%	0	0%	3.18	-3.0	$1
BAvg Potl	30%	1st Half	66	2	12	2	5	0	182			229	288	516	6	65	24	0.17	159	35	16	49	77	10%	-9	0%	1.37	-5.6	($0)
LIMA Plan	F	2nd Half	48	7	11	3	11	0	229			327	458	786	13	63	30	0.39	240	40	17	43	177	23%	23	0%	5.71	2.4	$2
+/- Score	-34	08 Proj	**97**	**9**	**20**	**4**	**12**	**0**	**206**			**268**	**364**	**632**	**8**	**68**	**26**	**0.26**	**219**	**38**	**16**	**45**	**116**	**13%**	**29**	**2%**	**3.13**	**-3.0**	**$1**

Playing time is rapidly drying up, and deservedly so. A little pop at catcher is always nice, but a 64% ct% is a deep hole in one's prospective productivity. We've never seen a .177 xBA before. Probably won't again.

Molina,Bengie			AB	R	H	HR	RBI	SB	Avg	vL	vR	OB	Slg	OPS	bb%	ct%	h%	Eye	xBA	G	L	F	PX	hr/f	SX	SBO	RC/G	RAR	R$
Pos	2	03 ANA	409	37	115	14	71	1	281	289	278	303	443	746	3	92	28	0.42	307	37	24	39	92	9%	28	2%	4.49	4.6	$12
Age	33	04 ANA	337	36	93	10	54	0	276	252	286	313	404	716	5	90	28	0.51	257	48	16	36	71	9%	25	1%	4.23	-1.0	$8
Past Peak		05 ANA	410	45	121	15	69	0	295	393	253	339	446	785	6	90	30	0.66	283	41	21	38	86	11%	18	2%	5.05	11.7	$14
Bats	Right	06 TOR	433	44	123	19	57	1	284	358	246	314	467	781	4	89	28	0.40	303	39	23	38	99	13%	37	2%	4.84	5.3	$12
Reliability	67	07 SF	497	38	137	19	81	0	276	271	277	297	433	729	3	89	28	0.28	270	37	19	44	85	10%	18	0%	4.20	5.8	$13
BAvg Potl	45%	1st Half	251	17	71	7	39	0	283			305	422	727	3	90	29	0.31	271	33	21	46	80	7%	22	0%	4.25	3.2	$6
LIMA Plan	D+	2nd Half	246	21	66	12	42	0	268			289	443	732	3	89	26	0.26	263	41	17	42	91	13%	8	0%	4.15	2.5	$7
+/- Score	-15	08 Proj	**481**	**44**	**135**	**18**	**76**	**0**	**281**			**308**	**440**	**748**	**4**	**90**	**28**	**0.38**	**281**	**39**	**20**	**41**	**87**	**10%**	**29**	**1%**	**4.47**	**7.1**	**$14**

Repeated 19 HR but had to crank up the FB% to do so. Note the 30-point drop in xBA from last year -- that's the cost of high FB%. Still, contact rate stays strong, so even typical power can generate earnings.

Molina,Jose			AB	R	H	HR	RBI	SB	Avg	vL	vR	OB	Slg	OPS	bb%	ct%	h%	Eye	xBA	G	L	F	PX	hr/f	SX	SBO	RC/G	RAR	R$
Pos	2	03 ANA	114	12	21	0	6	0	184	240	141	191	219	411	1	77	24	0.04	260	43	33	24	33	0%	59	0%	0.15	-14.4	($1)
Age	32	04 ANA	203	26	53	3	25	4	261	339	229	296	374	670	5	74	34	0.19	231	48	15	37	80	5%	113	10%	3.62	-4.2	$5
Past Peak		05 ANA	184	14	42	6	25	2	228	306	186	279	348	627	7	78	26	0.32	248	50	20	30	74	14%	39	4%	3.01	-5.6	$3
Bats	Right	06 LAA	225	18	54	4	22	1	240	218	254	269	369	638	4	78	29	0.18	250	42	18	39	96	6%	38	2%	3.18	-8.3	$2
Reliability	35	07 2AL	191	18	49	1	19	2	257	360	220	276	340	616	3	77	33	0.12	256	48	23	29	73	2%	55	8%	2.84	-6.6	$2
BAvg Potl	40%	1st Half	95	8	23	0	5	2	242			258	295	552	2	76	32	0.09	212	45	17	38	51	0%	63	15%	1.99	-5.8	$1
LIMA Plan	F	2nd Half	96	10	26	1	14	0	271			293	385	678	3	79	33	0.15	294	51	28	21	94	6%	30	0%	3.67	-1.0	$2
+/- Score	-8	08 Proj	**193**	**18**	**49**	**3**	**21**	**2**	**254**			**280**	**356**	**636**	**4**	**78**	**32**	**0.17**	**256**	**47**	**22**	**31**	**79**	**5%**	**48**	**5%**	**3.12**	**-5.8**	**$3**

Has much of his older brother's PX but none of supporting BPIs: Not a high ct% nor a fair Eye nor a reasonable FB%. The result is an amazingly lifeless BA that hints at greater value than he actually possesses.

Molina,Yadier			AB	R	H	HR	RBI	SB	Avg	vL	vR	OB	Slg	OPS	bb%	ct%	h%	Eye	xBA	G	L	F	PX	hr/f	SX	SBO	RC/G	RAR	R$
Pos	2	03 aa	364	30	94	2	47	0	258			306	313	619	6	88	29	0.58					37		33	1%	3.29	-9.6	$5
Age	25	04 STL	* 264	28	72	3	27	0	273	250	272	340	352	692	9	89	30	0.90	255	46	20	34	52	4%	26	1%	4.30	3.7	$5
Pre-Peak		05 STL	385	36	97	8	49	2	252	299	231	294	358	653	6	92	26	0.77	280	51	18	31	62	7%	48	5%	3.70	-1.1	$7
Bats	Right	06 STL	417	29	90	6	49	1	216	213	217	262	321	583	6	90	23	0.63	262	42	18	39	67	4%	26	4%	2.94	-18.0	$2
Reliability	13	07 STL	353	30	97	6	40	1	275	288	269	339	368	707	9	88	30	0.79	254	46	19	35	58	6%	25	2%	4.38	6.0	$7
BAvg Potl	50%	1st Half	128	12	35	1	12	0	273			340	344	684	9	85	31	0.68	249	44	22	34	51	3%	19	0%	4.13	1.2	$2
LIMA Plan	D	2nd Half	225	18	62	5	28	1	276			337	382	720	9	89	29	0.88	255	47	17	36	63	7%	24	3%	4.52	4.7	$5
+/- Score	-19	08 Proj	**407**	**34**	**106**	**8**	**47**	**1**	**260**			**316**	**369**	**685**	**8**	**89**	**28**	**0.74**	**263**	**46**	**19**	**35**	**66**	**7%**	**25**	**2%**	**4.08**	**1.5**	**$7**

Has his oldest brother's contact rate but less power and higher GB%. The result is a .250-level xBA, though his high ct% leads to better movement of men around bases to home.

Monroe,Craig			AB	R	H	HR	RBI	SB	Avg	vL	vR	OB	Slg	OPS	bb%	ct%	h%	Eye	xBA	G	L	F	PX	hr/f	SX	SBO	RC/G	RAR	R$
Pos	7	03 DET	* 472	64	119	25	76	5	252	293	209	298	466	764	6	79	27	0.32	283	47	16	37	130	18%	77	7%	4.70	-8.7	$15
Age	31	04 DET	447	65	131	18	72	3	293	256	314	336	488	824	6	82	32	0.37	283	46	16	38	117	13%	76	6%	5.49	6.8	$16
Past Peak		05 DET	567	69	157	20	89	8	277	303	270	325	446	771	7	83	30	0.42	292	49	19	32	106	13%	83	8%	4.88	2.7	$19
Bats	Right	06 DET	541	89	138	28	92	2	255	271	249	303	482	785	6	77	28	0.29	277	38	18	44	146	15%	73	4%	5.04	-2.1	$17
Reliability	28	07 2TM	392	53	86	12	59	0	219	271	194	268	370	638	6	73	27	0.24	231	36	16	48	111	9%	41	5%	3.19	-22.3	$6
BAvg Potl	40%	1st Half	241	40	56	9	41	0	232			286	415	701	7	72	29	0.26	254	35	20	45	136	12%	53	4%	4.09	-6.9	$6
LIMA Plan	D+	2nd Half	151	13	30	3	18	0	199			239	298	537	5	74	25	0.21	190	37	11	52	72	5%	34	7%	1.81	-15.5	$0
+/- Score	-5	08 Proj	**385**	**51**	**100**	**17**	**59**	**0**	**260**			**305**	**452**	**757**	**6**	**76**	**30**	**0.27**	**257**	**40**	**16**	**44**	**126**	**13%**	**40**	**4%**	**4.67**	**-4.9**	**$11**

From March on, he was hobbled by tendinitis in his left knee, and it showed. We don't know if he'll recover; that said, you could do worse than take a flyer on a guy who averaged $17 in four prior seasons. Bid.

Montero,Miguel			AB	R	H	HR	RBI	SB	Avg	vL	vR	OB	Slg	OPS	bb%	ct%	h%	Eye	xBA	G	L	F	PX	hr/f	SX	SBO	RC/G	RAR	R$
Pos	2	03	0	0	0	0	0	0	0							0									0				
Age	24	04	0	0	0	0	0	0	0							0									0				
Growth		05 aa	108	10	24	2	10	1	225			264	323	588	5	81	26	0.28					53		97	4%	2.60	-4.3	$1
Bats	Left	06 a/a	439	38	118	15	66	1	269	333	231	338	426	764	9	87	28	0.81		38	15	46	91	9%	13	5%	5.02	8.2	$10
Reliability	1	07 ARI	214	30	48	10	37	0	224	286	218	291	397	688	9	84	22	0.57	248	39	14	47	97	12%	32	0%	3.93	0.9	$5
BAvg Potl	65%	1st Half	110	16	24	4	19	0	218			289	355	644	9	85	22	0.69	244	44	15	42	76	10%	37	0%	3.52	-0.9	$2
LIMA Plan	D	2nd Half	104	14	24	6	18	0	231			292	442	734	8	82	23	0.47	254	33	14	53	121	13%	26	0%	4.39	1.9	$3
+/- Score	30	08 Proj	**353**	**40**	**85**	**14**	**54**	**0**	**241**			**304**	**401**	**705**	**8**	**84**	**25**	**0.57**	**244**	**38**	**14**	**48**	**91**	**10%**	**36**	**2%**	**4.17**	**2.3**	**$8**

Good stuff: 2nd half PX surge, H% regression will help BA
Bad stuff: FB tendency will limit BA upside.
We were expecting more in '07 but we'll just have to be patient.
UP: 20 HR

Moore,Scott			AB	R	H	HR	RBI	SB	Avg	vL	vR	OB	Slg	OPS	bb%	ct%	h%	Eye	xBA	G	L	F	PX	hr/f	SX	SBO	RC/G	RAR	R$
Pos	5	03	0	0	0	0	0	0	0							0									0				
Age	24	04	0	0	0	0	0	0	0							0									0				
Growth		05	0	0	0	0	0	0	0							0									0				
Bats	Left	06 a/a	505	58	137	25	79	12	271			346	479	826	10	73	33	0.42	284	61	18	21	139	32%	55	14%	5.85	8.8	$18
Reliability	0	07 BAL	* 373	51	89	17	67	3	239		250	311	442	753	9	72	29	0.37	263	46	16	38	141	17%	76	8%	4.87	4.2	$10
BAvg Potl	45%	1st Half	234	33	57	9	37	3	244			327	436	763	11	75	29	0.49					133		82	10%	5.08	4.1	$6
LIMA Plan	D	2nd Half	139	18	32	8	30	0	230			282	453	735	7	67	28	0.22	254	46	16	38	158	23%	63	4%	4.57	0.3	$4
+/- Score	24	08 Proj	**254**	**32**	**64**	**13**	**45**	**3**	**252**			**321**	**460**	**781**	**9**	**71**	**31**	**0.35**	**266**	**49**	**17**	**35**	**144**	**20%**	**68**	**10%**	**5.23**	**4.4**	**$8**

1-11-.231 in 52 AB at CHC/BAL. Free-swinging power hitter, but strong GB tendency is a flaw that will keep his HR ceiling low. Key indicator is grossly inflated hr/f. That won't hold up, and as it comes down, so will HRs.

Morales,Kendry			AB	R	H	HR	RBI	SB	Avg	vL	vR	OB	Slg	OPS	bb%	ct%	h%	Eye	xBA	G	L	F	PX	hr/f	SX	SBO	RC/G	RAR	R$
Pos	3	03	0	0	0	0	0	0	0							0									0				
Age	24	04	0	0	0	0	0	0	0							0									0				
Growth		05 aa	281	36	75	13	42	2	267			299	445	744	4	88	26	0.38					100		55	3%	4.41	-7.6	$9
Bats	Both	06 LAA	* 453	53	119	14	63	1	263	229	235	306	413	718	6	87	28	0.47	271	52	15	34	86	11%	46	6%	4.28	-15.2	$10
Reliability	22	07 LAA	* 374	48	113	8	47	0	302	241	311	335	445	779	5	87	33	0.37	257	47	11	42	96	6%	40	3%	4.95	-1.4	$11
BAvg Potl	35%	1st Half	190	23	53	3	24	0	279			305	389	694	4	88	30	0.30	258	61	11	29	76	6%	38	4%	3.93	-6.3	$4
LIMA Plan	F	2nd Half	184	25	60	5	23	0	326			365	501	866	6	86	36	0.43	270	41	11	47	118	6%	52	2%	6.03	4.6	$6
+/- Score	-34	08 Proj	**166**	**21**	**47**	**5**	**22**	**0**	**283**			**320**	**442**	**762**	**5**	**87**	**30**	**0.41**	**272**	**48**	**13**	**39**	**97**	**9%**	**58**	**4%**	**4.75**	**-2.0**	**$4**

4-15-.294 in 119 AB at LAA. His BPIs were largely static but he took a giant step up in FB. 2nd half numbers show a slugger who figured out where ball should travel. BA is puffy but you're not buying BA.

JOHN BURNSON

Mora,Melvin		AB	R	H	HR	RBI	SB	Avg	vL	vR	OB	Slg	OPS	bb%	ct%	h%	Eye	xBA	G	L	F	PX	hr/f	SX	SBO	RC/G	RAR	R$
Pos 5	03 BAL	344	68	109	15	48	6	317	324	315	402	503	905	12	79	36	0.69	291	40	26	34	116	16%	79	7%	6.87	22.1	$16
Age 36	04 BAL	550	111	187	27	104	11	340	303	352	411	562	973	11	83	37	0.69	303	40	21	39	135	15%	75	9%	7.54	38.0	$31
Decline	05 BAL	593	86	168	27	88	7	283	234	304	339	474	813	8	81	31	0.45	272	37	18	45	119	13%	66	7%	5.41	15.3	$22
Bats Right	06 BAL	624	96	171	16	83	11	274	253	282	332	391	723	8	84	30	0.55	254	39	20	41	71	7%	87	7%	4.41	-10.7	$18
Reliability 70	07 BAL	467	67	128	14	58	9	274	254	280	340	418	758	9	82	31	0.57	261	40	19	42	93	9%	80	9%	4.89	5.2	$14
BAvg Potl 45%	1st Half	282	44	70	11	37	7	248			321	426	746	10	83	26	0.63	272	40	17	43	110	11%	93	12%	4.75	2.1	$8
LIMA Plan C	2nd Half	185	23	58	3	21	2	314			371	405	777	8	81	37	0.49	244	41	21	39	65	5%	46	5%	5.10	3.0	$6
+/- Score -7	08 Proj	515	77	134	13	68	7	260			325	385	710	9	82	30	0.54	255	39	20	41	81	7%	82	7%	4.30	-5.3	$13

Raw numbers weren't helped by month lost to a foot sprain, but mediocre rates are the real problem. And don't go buying a 2nd-half BA of .314 -- PX was half of '04 peak, xBA says fluke. .275 could be a gift.

Morgan,Nyjer		AB	R	H	HR	RBI	SB	Avg	vL	vR	OB	Slg	OPS	bb%	ct%	h%	Eye	xBA	G	L	F	PX	hr/f	SX	SBO	RC/G	RAR	R$
Pos 8	03	0	0	0	0	0	0	0							0									0				
Age 27	04	0	0	0	0	0	0	0							0									0				
Peak	05	0	0	0	0	0	0	0							0									0				
Bats Left	06 aa	219	31	56	1	8	17	254			294	322	615	5	87	29	0.42					37		149	46%	3.16	-9.4	$6
Reliability 4	07 PIT *	271	37	71	1	14	25	262	259	313	310	332	642	7	83	31	0.41	252	57	16	27	41	2%	152	45%	3.46	-9.1	$9
BAvg Potl 45%	1st Half	130	20	37	0	8	19	285			340	315	656	8	86	33	0.61					19		142	53%	3.74	-3.2	$7
LIMA Plan F	2nd Half	141	17	34	1	6	6	241			282	347	629	5	80	30	0.28	256	57	16	27	63	3%	133	33%	3.22	-5.9	$2
+/- Score -3	08 Proj	230	31	62	1	11	12	270			313	343	656	6	84	32	0.40	256	57	16	27	43	2%	135	32%	3.61	-6.6	$6

1-7-.299 in 107 AB at PIT. .300 minor lg BAs don't convert well, but this GB-hitting SB machine may be more than his Esix-Sneadian BPIs appear. High SBO won't carry over to the bigs so there is a SB ceiling.

Morneau,Justin		AB	R	H	HR	RBI	SB	Avg	vL	vR	OB	Slg	OPS	bb%	ct%	h%	Eye	xBA	G	L	F	PX	hr/f	SX	SBO	RC/G	RAR	R$
Pos 3	03 a/a	344	47	90	18	48	0	262			321	471	792	8	82	27	0.48					122		48	2%	5.14	-3.1	$11
Age 26	04 MIN *	568	83	157	36	112	1	276	240	283	341	537	878	9	83	28	0.58	297	38	16	46	152	17%	34	1%	6.22	19.9	$22
Pre-Peak	05 MIN	490	62	117	22	79	0	239	205	254	301	437	738	8	81	25	0.47	277	42	18	41	121	14%	56	2%	4.54	-8.0	$12
Bats Left	06 MIN	592	97	190	34	130	3	321	315	325	377	559	936	8	84	34	0.57	312	36	24	41	137	17%	49	4%	6.85	22.8	$29
Reliability 39	07 MIN	590	84	160	31	111	1	271	228	294	343	492	834	10	85	28	0.70	295	45	16	39	130	16%	53	1%	5.77	11.5	$21
BAvg Potl 60%	1st Half	273	50	76	20	57	0	278			354	560	915	10	85	26	0.80	324	47	16	37	157	23%	56	0%	6.68	12.2	$13
LIMA Plan C	2nd Half	317	34	84	11	54	1	265			332	432	765	9	84	29	0.63	269	43	16	41	105	10%	44	2%	4.98	-1.0	$8
+/- Score 20	08 Proj	582	83	167	30	110	1	287			351	508	859	9	84	30	0.61	295	42	18	40	130	15%	53	2%	6.02	13.8	$22

20 HR and .324 xBA in 1st half set hearts racing, but then he hit 3 HR in his last 63 games. A .222 BA for Aug/Sept says that woes were genuine and deep. An injury? Nobody is saying. Tread carefully.

Munson,Eric		AB	R	H	HR	RBI	SB	Avg	vL	vR	OB	Slg	OPS	bb%	ct%	h%	Eye	xBA	G	L	F	PX	hr/f	SX	SBO	RC/G	RAR	R$
Pos 2	03 DET	313	28	75	18	50	3	240	208	250	316	441	757	10	81	24	0.57	265	43	16	41	115	17%	35	4%	4.76	6.2	$8
Age 30	04 DET	321	36	68	19	49	1	212	227	208	277	445	723	8	72	23	0.32	255	37	16	47	149	17%	58	3%	4.32	-0.1	$6
Peak	05 aaa	378	44	84	16	47	1	221			268	391	659	6	83	23	0.38					103		42	2%	3.48	-4.9	$7
Bats Left	06 HOU	141	10	28	5	19	0	199	318	176	257	348	604	7	77	22	0.34	198	39	17	44	93	11%	0	0%	2.78	-6.9	$1
Reliability 21	07 HOU *	305	31	64	9	32	1	210	216	242	283	351	634	9	83	23	0.57	231	37	13	50	90	7%	35	3%	3.39	-3.8	$3
BAvg Potl 65%	1st Half	209	28	52	7	25	1	249			329	435	764	11	84	27	0.74	279	41	16	44	123	9%	42	4%	5.11	8.2	$4
LIMA Plan F	2nd Half	96	3	12	2	7	0	125			176	167	343	6	79	14	0.30	109	36	11	53	14	5%	-2	0%	-0.55	-14.3	($2)
+/- Score 10	08 Proj	97	8	19	3	11	0	196			256	329	585	8	80	21	0.41	221	38	14	48	80	9%	24	2%	2.59	-4.2	$0

4-15-.235 in 132 AB at HOU. Four years of treading the Mendoza Line makes sense when you see a baseline hit rate of under 24%. This is about the weakest hitter we've come across in a long time.

Murphy,David		AB	R	H	HR	RBI	SB	Avg	vL	vR	OB	Slg	OPS	bb%	ct%	h%	Eye	xBA	G	L	F	PX	hr/f	SX	SBO	RC/G	RAR	R$
Pos 7	03	0	0	0	0	0	0	0							0									0				
Age 26	04	0	0	0	0	0	0	0							0									0				
Pre-Peak	05 aa	480	59	123	12	63	11	257			311	394	705	7	85	28	0.52					87		92	14%	4.22	-11.6	$13
Bats Left	06 a/a	490	59	127	10	61	6	259			327	422	749	9	85	29	0.67					106		80	9%	4.93	-4.1	$10
Reliability 29	07 2AL *	512	56	137	10	51	7	267	409	325	318	405	723	7	85	30	0.49	294	42	26	32	89	7%	95	7%	4.45	-4.0	$10
BAvg Potl 55%	1st Half	290	33	81	4	31	5	279			347	407	754	9	82	33	0.59					86		102	6%	4.97	2.1	$7
LIMA Plan D	2nd Half	222	23	56	6	20	2	251			278	402	680	4	87	27	0.30	309	43	26	31	93	9%	72	8%	3.76	-6.3	$4
+/- Score 11	08 Proj	325	37	85	7	36	4	262			315	410	726	7	85	29	0.53	302	43	26	31	96	8%	86	9%	4.51	-3.5	$7

2-14-.343 in 105 AB at BOS/TEX. Murphy has good gap power and strike zone. Hit a total of 20 HR and 60 doubles in his last two minor-league seasons. In the right lineup, he could drive in some runs.

Murphy,Donnie		AB	R	H	HR	RBI	SB	Avg	vL	vR	OB	Slg	OPS	bb%	ct%	h%	Eye	xBA	G	L	F	PX	hr/f	SX	SBO	RC/G	RAR	R$
Pos 6	03	0	0	0	0	0	0	0							0									0				
Age 25	04	0	0	0	0	0	0	0							0									0				
Pre-Peak	05 aa	214	25	58	7	24	1	271			304	430	733	4	89	28	0.42					93		59	4%	4.39	0.8	$6
Bats Right	06 aa	366	43	77	9	34	5	209			240	347	587	4	86	22	0.29					85		86	15%	2.70	-19.3	$3
Reliability 1	07 OAK *	293	46	76	8	39	4	259	279	187	313	433	747	7	75	32	0.32	262	35	19	46	133	8%	87	9%	4.75	1.7	$8
BAvg Potl 40%	1st Half	163	25	48	2	16	3	294			350	442	792	8	79	37	0.40		100	0	0	117		87	12%	5.42	3.9	$5
LIMA Plan F	2nd Half	130	21	28	6	23	1	215			266	423	689	6	71	26	0.24	261	33	20	47	155	14%	71	5%	3.89	-2.7	$3
+/- Score 1	08 Proj	269	37	70	9	33	3	260			301	438	739	6	81	29	0.30	270	34	19	46	119	9%	79	9%	4.47	-0.3	$7

6-21-.220 in 118 AB at OAK. Developed some pop but probably not enough to offset a 75% ct% in the majors. Still, with a high FB%, he could bring power to SS in a full-time job. UP: 15 HR

Murton,Matt		AB	R	H	HR	RBI	SB	Avg	vL	vR	OB	Slg	OPS	bb%	ct%	h%	Eye	xBA	G	L	F	PX	hr/f	SX	SBO	RC/G	RAR	R$
Pos 97	03	0	0	0	0	0	0	0							0									0				
Age 26	04	0	0	0	0	0	0	0							0									0				
Pre-Peak	05 CHC *	487	60	150	15	54	17	308	380	246	364	459	823	8	86	33	0.65	297	62	14	24	87	15%	104	15%	5.61	4.9	$20
Bats Right	06 CHC	455	70	135	13	62	5	297	301	295	360	444	804	9	86	32	0.73	296	58	18	24	84	14%	79	5%	5.47	8.8	$16
Reliability 57	07 CHC *	386	58	107	13	43	2	277	319	257	345	453	798	9	85	30	0.71	286	47	16	37	109	11%	62	2%	5.43	1.9	$11
BAvg Potl 60%	1st Half	175	28	47	2	14	2	269			337	383	730	11	86	30	0.88	275	50	17	33	82	4%	64	4%	4.82	-2.2	$4
LIMA Plan C	2nd Half	211	30	60	11	29	0	284			343	512	855	8	85	29	0.59	292	45	15	41	132	15%	44	0%	5.94	4.1	$7
+/- Score 23	08 Proj	428	63	124	18	52	3	290			354	483	836	9	86	30	0.70	303	53	17	30	112	16%	64	4%	5.80	7.8	$15

8-22-.281 in 235 AB at CHC. Almost a carbon-copy to 2006 except for a fall in BA, which xBA says was exaggerated. 2nd-half PX points to power, and rising FB says that he could take advantage. UP: 20/.300

Nady,Xavier		AB	R	H	HR	RBI	SB	Avg	vL	vR	OB	Slg	OPS	bb%	ct%	h%	Eye	xBA	G	L	F	PX	hr/f	SX	SBO	RC/G	RAR	R$
Pos 9	03 SD *	507	66	130	14	58	6	256	311	249	302	389	690	6	81	29	0.34	272	47	22	32	85	11%	83	6%	3.88	-25.7	$13
Age 29	04 SD *	368	50	102	19	66	2	277	344	178	320	492	812	6	87	27	0.49	320	58	17	25	119	24%	62	2%	5.27	-0.2	$14
Peak	05 SD	326	40	85	13	43	2	261	323	220	307	439	746	6	79	29	0.33	277	44	20	36	112	14%	75	4%	4.54	-6.7	$9
Bats Right	06 2NL	468	57	131	17	63	3	280	336	263	323	453	776	6	82	31	0.35	272	46	17	37	106	12%	52	5%	4.91	1.9	$14
Reliability 74	07 PIT	431	55	120	20	72	3	278	295	274	315	476	791	5	77	32	0.23	273	39	21	40	127	15%	60	4%	5.03	-2.7	$15
BAvg Potl 40%	1st Half	235	34	66	13	45	2	281			324	494	818	6	77	31	0.28	292	39	25	35	132	20%	51	5%	5.36	0.7	$10
LIMA Plan D+	2nd Half	196	21	54	7	27	1	276			304	454	758	4	76	33	0.17	250	38	16	46	121	10%	58	2%	4.64	-3.4	$5
+/- Score -6	08 Proj	449	60	123	22	76	3	274			313	483	797	5	79	30	0.27	282	42	19	39	130	16%	62	4%	5.09	-0.8	$16

Despite suffering from a strained hamstring for most of the year, still showed some growth. BPIs aren't overly strong but the seeds are here for at least one or two more growth seasons.

Napoli,Mike		AB	R	H	HR	RBI	SB	Avg	vL	vR	OB	Slg	OPS	bb%	ct%	h%	Eye	xBA	G	L	F	PX	hr/f	SX	SBO	RC/G	RAR	R$
Pos 2	03	0	0	0	0	0	0	0							0									0				
Age 26	04	0	0	0	0	0	0	0							0									0				
Pre-Peak	05 aa	439	71	87	22	74	9	199			299	398	697	13	75	21	0.57					131		89	13%	4.14	3.3	$12
Bats Right	06 LAA *	346	57	78	18	51	3	225	185	241	337	434	770	14	65	29	0.48	227	34	14	52	155	15%	50	7%	5.47	11.3	$9
Reliability 20	07 LAA	219	40	54	10	34	5	247	291	232	345	443	788	13	71	30	0.52	252	36	19	46	139	14%	94	11%	5.52	9.8	$7
BAvg Potl 45%	1st Half	171	33	42	7	28	4	246			338	439	777	12	72	30	0.50	256	36	20	44	139	13%	103	13%	5.35	6.8	$6
LIMA Plan C	2nd Half	48	7	12	3	6	1	250			368	458	827	16	69	30	0.60	232	35	15	50	139	18%	41	6%	6.10	2.9	$2
+/- Score 1	08 Proj	396	69	99	19	64	7	250			347	449	795	13	71	30	0.52	249	35	18	47	138	14%	78	10%	5.60	17.3	$14

Struggled with injuries (ankle, hamstring) but maintained solid walk rate and power. A 25-point jump in xBA points to improving contact. If healthy, could post continued PX gains. Soft BA, but not bad for a catcher.

JOHN BURNSON

Navarro,Dioner			AB	R	H	HR	RBI	SB	Avg	vL	vR	OB	Slg	OPS	bb%	ct%	h%	Eye	xBA	G	L	F	PX	hr/f	SX	SBO	RC/G	RAR	R$
Pos	2	03 aa	208	25	70	4	34	2	338			387	476	863	7	90	36	0.83					88		41	10%	6.09	10.6	$9
Age	24	04 a/a	391	46	101	3	42	2	259			332	349	681	10	88	29	0.89					59		73	2%	4.22	1.8	$6
Growth		05 LA	* 417	43	103	7	35	1	247	435	248	322	346	668	10	91	26	1.31	281	45	22	33	61	6%	29	4%	4.14	4.4	$6
Bats	Both	06 2TM	* 308	30	74	6	29	3	241	286	245	315	336	651	10	82	28	0.59	245	35	24	41	60	6%	47	4%	3.62	-6.9	$4
Reliability	30	07 TAM	388	46	88	9	44	3	227	226	227	287	356	643	8	83	25	0.49	254	42	17	41	84	7%	76	4%	3.47	-6.5	$5
BAvg Potl	60%	1st Half	186	15	35	1	11	1	188			249	274	523	7	84	22	0.52	231	40	15	44	60	1%	72	3%	2.17	-11.0	($1)
LIMA Plan	D	2nd Half	202	31	53	8	33	2	262			323	431	753	8	81	29	0.47	273	43	19	38	107	13%	58	6%	4.72	4.1	$6
+/- Score	44	08 Proj	415	47	106	12	46	3	255			321	394	714	9	84	28	0.61	265	40	20	40	85	9%	56	4%	4.36	2.7	$8

Might have cracked the secret of ML success with line of .294/.344/.492 for Aug/Sept. Two months of good play doesn't ensure gain, but with a ct% in the 80's, ANY uptick in power will pay dividends.

Nixon,Trot			AB	R	H	HR	RBI	SB	Avg	vL	vR	OB	Slg	OPS	bb%	ct%	h%	Eye	xBA	G	L	F	PX	hr/f	SX	SBO	RC/G	RAR	R$
Pos	9	03 BOS	441	81	135	28	87	4	306	219	330	395	578	973	13	78	34	0.68	296	29	24	48	164	17%	99	4%	7.75	31.5	$23
Age	34	04 BOS	149	24	47	6	23	0	315	133	336	378	510	888	9	84	34	0.63	272	37	17	46	115	10%	56	0%	6.44	6.9	$6
Past Peak		05 BOS	408	64	112	13	67	2	275	229	289	358	446	804	11	86	29	0.90	290	39	20	40	111	9%	61	2%	5.63	10.9	$13
Bats	Left	06 BOS	381	59	102	8	52	0	268	204	288	367	394	761	14	85	30	1.07	253	39	17	44	82	6%	31	2%	5.28	-4.2	$9
Reliability	45	07 CLE	307	30	77	3	31	0	251	224	256	345	336	680	13	81	30	0.75	224	39	18	44	66	3%	18	0%	4.20	-4.5	$3
BAvg Potl	45%	1st Half	205	24	49	2	25	0	239			336	327	663	13	80	29	0.71	222	40	16	43	70	3%	25	0%	3.97	-4.4	$2
LIMA Plan	F	2nd Half	102	6	28	1	6	0	275			362	353	715	12	83	32	0.82	230	35	20	45	58	3%	5	0%	4.63	-0.2	$1
+/- Score	-32	08 Proj	285	34	72	6	34	0	253			345	373	718	12	83	29	0.84	250	38	19	44	82	6%	30	1%	4.65	-2.6	$5

xBA and PX are plummeting, and his playing time is following suit -- from 95 AB in May to 14 AB in September. It figures... he finally stays off the DL for an entire season and there's no gas left in the tank.

Norton,Greg			AB	R	H	HR	RBI	SB	Avg	vL	vR	OB	Slg	OPS	bb%	ct%	h%	Eye	xBA	G	L	F	PX	hr/f	SX	SBO	RC/G	RAR	R$
Pos	0	03 COL	179	19	47	6	31	2	263	273	261	323	447	770	8	74	33	0.34	284	43	24	33	140	14%	47	7%	5.09	2.4	$5
Age	35	04 DET	* 270	30	46	5	15	1	170	182	167	253	256	509	10	75	21	0.45	201	40	15	45	54	6%	64	3%	1.65	-32.2	($1)
Decline		05 aaa	323	41	77	14	41	0	240			309	426	735	9	82	25	0.55					115		38	2%	4.55	-14.3	$8
Bats	Both	06 TAM	294	47	87	17	45	1	296	283	299	371	520	891	11	77	34	0.51	275	38	19	42	140	18%	32	7%	6.59	1.3	$12
Reliability	0	07 TAM	202	25	49	4	23	1	243	174	251	360	347	706	15	73	31	0.67	230	33	24	43	80	6%	35	3%	4.55	-8.9	$3
BAvg Potl	45%	1st Half	60	9	13	2	6	0	217			365	333	698	19	73	26	0.88	239	30	27	43	75	11%	25	0%	4.45	-2.9	$1
LIMA Plan	F	2nd Half	142	16	36	2	17	1	254			358	352	710	14	73	34	0.59	227	35	22	43	82	4%	36	4%	4.59	-6.0	$2
+/- Score	-48	08 Proj	244	33	59	8	30	1	242			340	391	730	13	75	29	0.60	251	35	23	42	101	11%	35	4%	4.69	-9.8	$5

Some aging players maintain their value by learning more plate patience. He's done just that, but at the cost of his contact rate when he does swing. Net effect is a decent OBA but zero productivity.

Nunez,Abraham			AB	R	H	HR	RBI	SB	Avg	vL	vR	OB	Slg	OPS	bb%	ct%	h%	Eye	xBA	G	L	F	PX	hr/f	SX	SBO	RC/G	RAR	R$
Pos	5	03 PIT	311	37	77	4	35	9	248	163	261	306	357	663	8	83	29	0.49	285	55	23	22	62	7%	135	14%	3.76	-4.6	$7
Age	31	04 PIT	182	17	43	2	13	1	236	158	245	276	319	595	5	80	28	0.28	233	63	12	25	60	5%	43	10%	2.71	-13.1	$1
Past Peak		05 STL	421	64	120	5	44	0	285	310	277	343	361	704	8	85	33	0.59	280	54	25	21	49	7%	56	1%	4.26	-6.2	$11
Bats	Both	06 PHI	322	42	68	2	32	1	211	171	225	300	273	574	11	82	25	0.71	241	62	15	23	40	3%	68	1%	2.84	-26.4	$2
Reliability	44	07 PHI	252	24	59	0	16	2	234	284	213	316	282	597	11	81	29	0.63	255	61	20	18	38	0%	61	3%	3.10	-12.7	$1
BAvg Potl	60%	1st Half	153	17	40	0	13	1	261			319	327	646	8	80	33	0.43	263	61	20	19	52	0%	71	2%	3.56	-5.4	$2
LIMA Plan	F	2nd Half	99	7	19	0	3	1	192			310	212	522	15	82	23	0.94	238	61	21	18	18	0%	33	3%	2.36	-7.6	($1)
+/- Score	11	08 Proj	206	23	47	1	16	1	228			310	285	596	11	82	27	0.66	256	60	19	20	40	3%	67	3%	3.08	-11.7	$1

For his career, he has a .313 OB and .314 SLG. Or is it other way around? I can never remember. Regardless, he has almost no power to repel a thrown ball. Even a wet noodle has a 20 PX.

Ojeda,Augie			AB	R	H	HR	RBI	SB	Avg	vL	vR	OB	Slg	OPS	bb%	ct%	h%	Eye	xBA	G	L	F	PX	hr/f	SX	SBO	RC/G	RAR	R$
Pos	4	03 aaa	283	33	59	2	18	3	207			276	269	545	9	92	22	1.14					37		88	4%	2.77	-13.2	$1
Age	33	04 MIN	* 386	54	87	4	23	6	226			300	303	604	10	91	24	1.17					50		71	12%	3.43	-7.8	$4
Past Peak		05 aaa	310	32	58	2	25	3	186			247	247	494	8	90	20	0.78					44		62	7%	2.04	-23.0	($0)
Bats	Both	06 aaa	306	33	65	3	21	4	212			300	274	574	11	87	23	1.00					38		68	5%	3.02	-12.7	$1
Reliability	13	07 ARI	* 210	27	51	1	22	2	243	250	292	312	310	621	9	88	27	0.81	253	43	21	36	42	2%	88	3%	3.49	-6.7	$3
BAvg Potl	65%	1st Half	114	20	35	1	17	2	307			373	395	768	10	90	33	1.09	306	33	33	33	60	3%	68	5%	5.23	2.1	$4
LIMA Plan	F	2nd Half	96	7	16	0	5	0	167			238	208	446	9	84	20	0.60	220	45	19	36	18	0%	73	0%	1.30	-10.2	($2)
+/- Score	-8	08 Proj	95	11	22	1	8	1	232			303	301	605	9	88	26	0.84	252	44	21	36	42	2%	79	4%	3.32	-3.6	$1

1-12-.274 in 113 AB at ARI. Don't be seduced by that 1 HR and 2 SB -- they are not leading indicators of better days ahead. I'm not even quite sure of what peak he is supposed to have passed.

Olivo,Miguel			AB	R	H	HR	RBI	SB	Avg	vL	vR	OB	Slg	OPS	bb%	ct%	h%	Eye	xBA	G	L	F	PX	hr/f	SX	SBO	RC/G	RAR	R$
Pos	2	03 CHW	317	37	75	6	27	6	237	302	212	280	360	639	6	75	30	0.24	261	41	26	33	92	8%	87	15%	3.25	-8.2	$5
Age	29	04 2AL	301	46	70	13	40	7	233	322	196	280	439	719	6	72	28	0.24	260	47	14	39	134	16%	132	22%	4.29	-0.4	$8
Peak		05 2TM	* 300	36	68	11	43	7	225	284	188	247	381	628	3	72	28	0.11	249	47	18	35	109	15%	103	17%	2.87	-9.5	$7
Bats	Right	06 FLA	430	52	113	16	58	2	263	273	258	278	440	717	2	76	31	0.09	260	42	19	39	112	13%	70	6%	3.99	-4.4	$11
Reliability	44	07 FLA	452	43	107	16	60	3	237	295	221	260	405	665	3	73	29	0.11	244	43	17	40	112	12%	75	6%	3.39	-5.4	$8
BAvg Potl	40%	1st Half	259	18	64	5	33	2	247			264	386	650	2	76	31	0.10	248	43	19	38	93	7%	80	8%	3.24	-4.2	$4
LIMA Plan	D	2nd Half	193	25	43	11	27	1	223			254	430	684	4	68	26	0.13	239	43	14	44	141	19%	52	3%	3.65	-0.8	$4
+/- Score	2	08 Proj	402	46	96	17	54	4	239			263	417	681	3	73	29	0.12	251	43	18	39	119	15%	79	9%	3.58	-4.6	$9

When he hits the ball into the air, there is a 1-in-8 chance that it will turn into a home run. That is his ONLY skill. That may suffice for fantasy, but eventually his *real* owners will stop smiling. DN: 200 AB

Ordonez,Magglio			AB	R	H	HR	RBI	SB	Avg	vL	vR	OB	Slg	OPS	bb%	ct%	h%	Eye	xBA	G	L	F	PX	hr/f	SX	SBO	RC/G	RAR	R$
Pos	9	03 CHW	606	95	192	29	99	9	317	317	317	376	546	922	9	88	32	0.78	327	42	22	36	134	15%	83	8%	6.76	26.4	$28
Age	34	04 CHW	202	32	59	9	37	0	292	339	273	344	485	829	7	89	29	0.73	290	49	15	36	100	14%	69	4%	5.61	5.1	$8
Past Peak		05 DET	305	38	92	8	46	0	302	308	300	364	436	800	9	89	32	0.86	291	44	23	34	84	9%	23	0%	5.45	6.2	$10
Bats	Right	06 DET	593	82	177	24	104	1	298	294	300	348	477	825	7	85	32	0.52	279	45	18	38	104	13%	35	3%	5.53	-2.2	$21
Reliability	34	07 DET	595	117	216	28	139	4	363	410	351	435	595	1030	11	87	39	0.96	323	42	19	39	146	14%	57	2%	8.22	52.4	$36
BAvg Potl	40%	1st Half	281	65	106	13	68	2	377			455	637	1092	12	88	40	1.21	347	41	20	39	168	13%	60	2%	9.03	29.7	$19
LIMA Plan	C+	2nd Half	314	52	110	15	71	2	350			417	557	974	10	85	38	0.78	300	43	19	39	126	15%	43	3%	7.47	22.3	$18
+/- Score	-27	08 Proj	539	89	163	23	108	2	302			369	503	872	9	87	32	0.79	305	43	19	37	122	13%	53	3%	6.25	19.1	$23

Decided to party like it's 2003. Were his BPI's strong? Yes. Did he maintain his numbers over both halves? Yes. Still, the percentage play has to be that he will slip back a bit, if only from his age.

Ortiz,David			AB	R	H	HR	RBI	SB	Avg	vL	vR	OB	Slg	OPS	bb%	ct%	h%	Eye	xBA	G	L	F	PX	hr/f	SX	SBO	RC/G	RAR	R$
Pos	0	03 BOS	448	79	129	31	101	0	288	216	313	370	592	961	11	81	29	0.70	344	34	27	39	187	22%	49	0%	7.42	35.1	$22
Age	32	04 BOS	582	94	175	41	139	0	301	250	326	381	603	984	11	77	33	0.56	311	35	20	46	189	20%	43	0%	7.83	40.3	$29
Past Peak		05 BOS	601	119	180	47	148	1	300	302	297	401	604	1005	15	79	31	0.82	323	31	23	46	189	21%	51	1%	8.13	34.8	$34
Bats	Left	06 BOS	558	115	160	54	137	1	287	278	292	412	636	1048	18	79	27	1.02	322	36	17	47	200	26%	51	1%	8.76	36.3	$31
Reliability	96	07 BOS	549	116	182	35	117	3	332	308	343	444	621	1065	17	81	36	1.08	324	38	17	45	188	17%	59	2%	9.09	44.3	$32
BAvg Potl	50%	1st Half	260	49	83	13	48	1	319			431	573	1004	16	81	35	1.04	317	39	19	42	173	15%	41	1%	8.37	16.3	$13
LIMA Plan	A	2nd Half	289	67	99	22	69	2	343			456	664	1120	17	81	36	1.11	329	36	16	49	201	19%	63	3%	9.74	27.9	$19
+/- Score	-9	08 Proj	549	113	167	40	126	2	304			417	602	1019	16	80	32	0.97	319	36	18	46	186	20%	56	1%	8.43	36.2	$30

Despite sharp HR decline, his 188 PX was identical to 2004-2005 when he hit 41 and 47. Part of that was due to fewer AB but most of it was due to lower overall league power. And RC/G says that this was his best year.

Ortmeier,Dan			AB	R	H	HR	RBI	SB	Avg	vL	vR	OB	Slg	OPS	bb%	ct%	h%	Eye	xBA	G	L	F	PX	hr/f	SX	SBO	RC/G	RAR	R$
Pos	37	03	0	0	0	0	0	0	0							0									0				
Age	26	04	0	0	0	0	0	0	0							0									0				
Pre-Peak		05 aa	503	68	120	14	64	29	238			291	385	677	7	80	27	0.37					92		139	35%	3.78	-24.4	$17
Bats	Both	06 a/a	429	45	94	7	36	12	219			265	328	593	6	84	25	0.38					69		101	25%	2.82	-39.2	$5
Reliability	23	07 SF	* 462	48	108	13	55	13	233	257	310	274	387	661	5	78	27	0.26	265	53	14	32	99	11%	115	17%	3.50	-29.4	$9
BAvg Potl	50%	1st Half	219	29	56	7	33	7	256			300	425	725	6	82	28	0.36	296	58	16	26	108	15%	98	17%	4.33	-8.2	$7
LIMA Plan	F	2nd Half	243	19	52	6	22	6	213			250	354	604	5	75	26	0.20	241	51	14	35	90	9%	108	18%	2.72	-21.8	$2
+/- Score	20	08 Proj	203	22	51	5	22	7	251			294	386	680	6	80	29	0.30	258	53	14	33	84	9%	102	21%	3.76	-11.9	$5

6-16-.287 in 157 AB at SF. Despite his dire MLEs, there may be more here, especially given the speed potential. But his nightmarish RARs are just begging for SF to say, "Welcome to Fresno."

JOHN BURNSON

Overbay,Lyle

		Year	AB	R	H	HR	RBI	SB	Avg	vL	vR	OB	Slg	OPS	bb%	ct%	h%	Eye	xBA	G	L	F	PX	hr/f	SX	SBO	RC/G	RAR	R$
Pos	3	03 ARI	* 373	41	100	7	40	1	268	291	268	364	405	768	13	78	33	0.69	291	43	28	29	105	8%	34	1%	5.33	-2.0	$8
Age	31	04 MIL	583	84	175	16	88	2	300	298	301	386	479	864	12	78	36	0.63	292	45	23	31	128	11%	48	2%	6.51	8.9	$20
Past Peak		05 MIL	537	80	148	19	72	1	276	270	278	367	449	816	13	82	31	0.80	298	51	21	27	114	16%	51	1%	5.81	3.2	$17
Bats	Left	06 TOR	581	82	181	22	92	5	312	284	322	371	508	879	9	83	34	0.57	308	46	22	32	124	14%	56	5%	6.32	14.2	$22
Reliability	26	07 TOR	425	49	102	10	44	2	240	287	224	316	391	706	10	82	27	0.60	288	49	21	31	105	9%	66	2%	4.37	-9.1	$6
BAvg Potl	65%	1st Half	207	25	53	8	27	0	256			330	464	794	10	81	28	0.59	308	53	20	27	135	17%	50	0%	5.41	1.9	$5
LIMA Plan	C+	2nd Half	218	24	49	2	17	2	225			302	321	623	10	82	27	0.62	265	44	22	34	76	3%	53	4%	3.40	-11.2	$1
+/- Score	41	08 Proj	**516**	**66**	**147**	**15**	**63**	**3**	**285**			**359**	**451**	**809**	**10**	**82**	**32**	**0.63**	**294**	**48**	**22**	**31**	**112**	**12%**	**56**	**2%**	**5.62**	**6.4**	**$14**

His season essentially ended on June 3 when he was struck by a pitch and broke his right hand. He was on his way to a career-high PX and xBA. A healthy upside projection would be 25-90-.300 but hand injuries linger.

Owens,Jerry

		Year	AB	R	H	HR	RBI	SB	Avg	vL	vR	OB	Slg	OPS	bb%	ct%	h%	Eye	xBA	G	L	F	PX	hr/f	SX	SBO	RC/G	RAR	R$
Pos	8	03	0	0	0	0	0	0	0							0									0				
Age	27	04	0	0	0	0	0	0	0							0									0				
Peak		05 aa	518	75	148	2	40	29	286			336	347	683	7	88	32	0.64					40		118	31%	4.06	-5.6	$18
Bats	Left	06 aaa	439	68	109	4	44	37	248			312	325	636	8	87	28	0.72					45		141	39%	3.58	-13.0	$15
Reliability	40	07 CHW	* 588	79	156	4	35	52	265	235	274	326	322	649	8	83	31	0.54	271	62	19	19	40	4%	120	37%	3.60	-11.9	$20
BAvg Potl	50%	1st Half	281	43	71	2	15	24	253			320	313	634	9	85	29	0.67	297	71	19	10	44	9%	108	38%	3.52	-6.6	$9
LIMA Plan	D+	2nd Half	307	36	85	2	20	28	277			332	331	663	8	82	33	0.45	260	60	19	21	35	4%	123	36%	3.69	-5.3	$11
+/- Score	-5	08 Proj	**317**	**45**	**84**	**2**	**24**	**26**	**265**			**325**	**330**	**655**	**8**	**85**	**31**	**0.60**	**279**	**62**	**19**	**19**	**42**	**4%**	**125**	**37%**	**3.72**	**-6.7**	**$11**

1-17-.267 and 32 SB in 356 AB at CHW. He has no power, but his career BA in minors is .295, and he won't refuse a walk. A name to remember for your draft's end game.

Ozuna,Pablo

		Year	AB	R	H	HR	RBI	SB	Avg	vL	vR	OB	Slg	OPS	bb%	ct%	h%	Eye	xBA	G	L	F	PX	hr/f	SX	SBO	RC/G	RAR	R$
Pos	5	03 a/a	278	21	58	1	13	10	209			230	298	528	3	91	23	0.30					53		131	36%	2.25	-19.0	$1
Age	33	04 aaa	472	58	114	5	57	23	242			269	324	593	3	91	26	0.39					51		120	35%	2.91	-30.1	$12
Past Peak		05 CHW	203	27	56	0	11	14	276	306	248	300	330	630	3	87	32	0.27	293	73	15	12	37	0%	137	39%	3.22	-7.7	$6
Bats	Right	06 CHW	189	25	62	2	17	6	328	322	348	352	444	796	4	92	35	0.44	293	49	19	32	71	4%	101	23%	5.15	0.7	$7
Reliability	0	07 CHW	78	9	19	0	3	3	244	256	231	272	282	554	4	88	28	0.33	228	51	13	37	32	0%	84	16%	2.41	-4.8	$1
BAvg Potl	45%	1st Half	78	9	19	0	3	3	244			272	282	554	4	88	28	0.33	228	51	13	37	32	0%	84	16%	2.41	-4.8	$1
LIMA Plan	F	2nd Half	0	0	0	0	0	0	0							0													
+/- Score	-29	08 Proj	**169**	**20**	**47**	**1**	**11**	**8**	**278**			**303**	**343**	**646**	**3**	**89**	**31**	**0.34**	**267**	**57**	**15**	**27**	**44**	**2%**	**107**	**26%**	**3.45**	**-5.9**	**$4**

Broke ankle on May 27. On the positive side, he wasn't rushed back, so he should be healthy. He's no racehorse, but he has just enough speed and contact to put up 6-12 SB and a .290 BA if you are lucky.

Pagan,Angel

		Year	AB	R	H	HR	RBI	SB	Avg	vL	vR	OB	Slg	OPS	bb%	ct%	h%	Eye	xBA	G	L	F	PX	hr/f	SX	SBO	RC/G	RAR	R$
Pos	89	03	0	0	0	0	0	0	0							0									0				
Age	26	04 a/a	494	72	129	3	55	28	261			315	360	676	7	82	31	0.43					66		153	27%	3.92	-11.1	$15
Pre-Peak		05 aaa	509	57	124	6	32	23	244			297	338	635	7	81	29	0.41					61		121	29%	3.35	-16.8	$11
Bats	Both	06 CHC	170	28	42	5	18	4	247	196	272	308	394	702	8	84	27	0.54	266	51	15	34	81	10%	112	14%	4.18	-1.3	$4
Reliability	2	07 CHC	* 264	34	62	7	28	8	237	236	289	283	391	674	6	80	27	0.33	249	36	18	46	96	7%	126	18%	3.74	-6.5	$6
BAvg Potl	50%	1st Half	196	29	49	6	20	8	250			303	418	722	7	82	28	0.42	242	30	18	53	100	7%	137	20%	4.36	-1.1	$6
LIMA Plan	F	2nd Half	68	5	13	1	8	0	198			221	313	534	3	77	25	0.13	242	43	18	39	85	3%	83	13%	1.87	-5.9	($0)
+/- Score	23	08 Proj	**146**	**18**	**37**	**3**	**15**	**4**	**253**			**299**	**384**	**683**	**6**	**81**	**30**	**0.33**	**252**	**45**	**17**	**39**	**83**	**6%**	**114**	**18%**	**3.87**	**-3.0**	**$3**

4-21-.264 in 148 AB at CHC. With a BPI line that screams mediocrity, he is not technically *awful*. But he doesn't do any one thing well, and a repeat of a .306 OBA shows limits. Better than an empty slot, but barely.

Patterson,Corey

		Year	AB	R	H	HR	RBI	SB	Avg	vL	vR	OB	Slg	OPS	bb%	ct%	h%	Eye	xBA	G	L	F	PX	hr/f	SX	SBO	RC/G	RAR	R$
Pos	8	03 CHC	329	49	98	13	55	16	298	289	301	328	511	839	4	77	36	0.19	290	40	26	34	134	15%	154	28%	5.71	6.8	$17
Age	28	04 CHC	631	91	168	24	72	32	266	289	258	315	452	767	7	73	33	0.27	255	40	19	41	123	13%	139	27%	4.93	5.2	$25
Peak		05 CHC	* 542	60	121	17	44	20	223	169	231	264	362	626	5	74	27	0.22	244	46	18	36	92	12%	115	23%	2.95	-26.9	$12
Bats	Left	06 BAL	463	75	128	16	53	45	276	207	301	308	443	751	4	80	32	0.22	262	39	21	40	99	11%	166	50%	4.51	-2.1	$23
Reliability	23	07 BAL	461	65	124	8	45	37	269	310	251	301	386	687	4	86	30	0.32	258	44	15	41	78	5%	132	42%	3.86	-5.6	$18
BAvg Potl	45%	1st Half	222	27	50	1	19	14	225			268	302	570	6	85	26	0.38	240	44	15	41	61	1%	108	38%	2.61	-11.5	$4
LIMA Plan	C	2nd Half	239	38	74	7	26	23	310			332	464	796	3	87	33	0.26	275	44	15	41	92	8%	142	46%	5.00	4.8	$13
+/- Score	5	08 Proj	**477**	**69**	**124**	**10**	**50**	**36**	**260**			**293**	**387**	**680**	**5**	**82**	**30**	**0.26**	**254**	**43**	**18**	**40**	**82**	**6%**	**150**	**41%**	**3.72**	**-9.9**	**$18**

Rising ct% is a good sign since he's been camped at a .300 OBA. But power continues its descent and it's tough to see that recovering. Truth is, If he came into the bigs with these BPIs, he might already be out.

Paulino,Ronny

		Year	AB	R	H	HR	RBI	SB	Avg	vL	vR	OB	Slg	OPS	bb%	ct%	h%	Eye	xBA	G	L	F	PX	hr/f	SX	SBO	RC/G	RAR	R$
Pos	2	03 aa	159	17	34	5	17	0	214			265	358	623	6	81	23	0.37					88		62	6%	3.08	-5.5	$2
Age	27	04 aa	369	43	93	12	48	2	252			298	410	709	6	87	26	0.50					93		56	5%	4.20	1.4	$8
Peak		05 a/a	436	54	115	14	46	5	265			312	412	724	6	87	28	0.51					89		79	4%	4.36	5.8	$11
Bats	Right	06 PIT	* 471	39	144	6	59	1	306	339	300	356	390	747	7	82	36	0.42	252	47	23	31	58	5%	25	1%	4.68	4.4	$12
Reliability	48	07 PIT	457	56	120	11	55	2	263	407	218	312	389	702	7	83	30	0.42	257	47	17	36	83	8%	44	3%	4.09	4.1	$10
BAvg Potl	50%	1st Half	216	23	49	5	22	1	227			271	347	618	6	81	26	0.31	243	54	13	33	81	9%	45	4%	2.99	-5.3	$2
LIMA Plan	D	2nd Half	241	33	71	6	33	1	295			349	427	776	8	85	33	0.54	270	41	21	39	85	8%	42	3%	5.05	8.4	$7
+/- Score	-8	08 Proj	**424**	**48**	**113**	**10**	**51**	**2**	**267**			**317**	**388**	**704**	**7**	**83**	**30**	**0.44**	**262**	**46**	**19**	**35**	**79**	**8%**	**43**	**3%**	**4.14**	**2.3**	**$9**

He didn't deserve a .300 BA in 2006, and he didn't get one in 2007, though 2nd-half xBA offers hope that he might someday get back to .280. He'll need to goose his ct% further and pray for musculature.

Paul,Josh

		Year	AB	R	H	HR	RBI	SB	Avg	vL	vR	OB	Slg	OPS	bb%	ct%	h%	Eye	xBA	G	L	F	PX	hr/f	SX	SBO	RC/G	RAR	R$
Pos	2	03 aaa	210	14	40	3	16	1	190			227	257	484	5	80	22	0.24					39		56	9%	1.29	-19.7	($1)
Age	32	04 ANA	70	11	17	2	10	2	243	316	216	312	371	683	9	76	29	0.41	235	46	15	38	86	10%	78	16%	3.90	-0.9	$2
Past Peak		05 ANA	* 70	9	15	2	9	0	214			286	357	643	9	76	25	0.41	240	44	15	41	104	9%	47	6%	3.40	-1.4	$1
Bats	Right	06 TAM	146	15	38	1	8	1	260	333	234	325	342	667	9	73	35	0.36	237	48	22	30	71	3%	41	7%	3.81	-2.6	$1
Reliability	0	07 TAM	105	8	20	1	9	1	190	242	167	234	248	482	5	71	26	0.20	181	39	15	46	46	3%	46	5%	1.05	-9.9	($0)
BAvg Potl	40%	1st Half	49	4	12	0	5	1	245			302	245	547	8	71	34	0.29	150	43	14	43	0	0%	45	6%	2.00	-2.9	$1
LIMA Plan	F	2nd Half	56	4	8	1	4	0	143			172	250	422	3	71	18	0.13	206	36	15	49	87	5%	31	0%	0.20	-7.2	($1)
+/- Score	-12	08 Proj	**142**	**11**	**29**	**2**	**10**	**1**	**204**			**246**	**288**	**533**	**5**	**76**	**26**	**0.22**	**217**	**41**	**18**	**40**	**63**	**4%**	**37**	**6%**	**1.82**	**-10.4**	**($0)**

Highlights for 2007:
April 5: Goes 2-for-3
April 18: Steals his only base
July 28: Hits his only home run
A good pick-up if you like to anticipate your pleasure. Rest should anticipate not owning.

Payton,Jay

		Year	AB	R	H	HR	RBI	SB	Avg	vL	vR	OB	Slg	OPS	bb%	ct%	h%	Eye	xBA	G	L	F	PX	hr/f	SX	SBO	RC/G	RAR	R$
Pos	7	03 COL	600	93	181	28	89	6	302	288	307	348	512	860	7	87	31	0.56	320	45	23	32	119	17%	88	6%	5.90	5.2	$26
Age	35	04 SD	458	57	119	8	55	2	260	283	248	323	367	690	9	88	28	0.77	250	43	16	41	61	5%	78	2%	4.20	-16.5	$9
Decline		05 2AL	408	62	109	18	63	0	267	283	258	308	444	751	6	88	27	0.51	291	42	19	38	98	13%	50	1%	4.59	-1.5	$13
Bats	Right	06 OAK	557	78	165	10	59	8	296	296	296	323	418	741	4	91	31	0.42	292	45	22	34	73	6%	94	8%	4.52	-10.3	$15
Reliability	69	07 BAL	434	48	111	7	58	5	256	285	244	292	376	667	5	90	27	0.52	282	50	17	33	72	5%	91	7%	3.80	-11.7	$8
BAvg Potl	60%	1st Half	198	24	55	1	26	2	278			313	374	686	5	92	30	0.67	303	51	22	27	63	2%	85	8%	4.11	-3.5	$4
LIMA Plan	D	2nd Half	236	24	56	6	32	3	237			274	377	651	5	89	25	0.44	266	49	13	39	79	7%	93	6%	3.53	-8.4	$4
+/- Score	13	08 Proj	**385**	**49**	**104**	**9**	**50**	**4**	**270**			**306**	**404**	**710**	**5**	**90**	**28**	**0.51**	**286**	**47**	**19**	**35**	**78**	**7%**	**86**	**6%**	**4.23**	**-7.2**	**$9**

With 90% ct%, he should have fared better than a .256 BA. At 35, he won't get much of a look from ML or fantasy GM's, so he may be undervalued. But nail in coffin might be putting half of hit balls on the ground.

Pearce,Steven

		Year	AB	R	H	HR	RBI	SB	Avg	vL	vR	OB	Slg	OPS	bb%	ct%	h%	Eye	xBA	G	L	F	PX	hr/f	SX	SBO	RC/G	RAR	R$
Pos	9	03	0	0	0	0	0	0	0							0									0				
Age	25	04	0	0	0	0	0	0	0							0									0				
Pre-Peak		05	0	0	0	0	0	0	0							0									0				
Bats	Right	06	0	0	0	0	0	0	0							0									0				
Reliability	10	07 PIT	* 480	74	141	15	78	12	293	429	259	342	482	823	7	87	31	0.57	315	48	20	32	117	11%	102	12%	5.59	4.6	$19
BAvg Potl	55%	1st Half	199	31	61	9	41	0	307			364	548	912	8	85	32	0.62					149		52	2%	6.68	7.8	$9
LIMA Plan	C	2nd Half	281	43	80	6	37	12	283			325	435	760	6	88	30	0.52	302	48	20	32	95	8%	116	19%	4.84	-3.2	$10
+/- Score	9	08 Proj	**326**	**50**	**95**	**10**	**53**	**8**	**291**			**340**	**480**	**820**	**7**	**87**	**31**	**0.56**	**315**	**48**	**20**	**32**	**117**	**11%**	**102**	**13%**	**5.56**	**3.7**	**$13**

0-6-.294 in 68 AB at PIT. Snuck onto lineup when Bay and Nady were hurt and did not embarrass himself. Do not mistake 0 HR for no power -- he has produced at a 30-HR pace in minors.

JOHN BURNSON

Pedroia,Dustin

			AB	R	H	HR	RBI	SB	Avg	vL	vR	OB	Slg	OPS	bb%	ct%	h%	Eye	xBA	G	L	F	PX	hr/f	SX	SBO	RC/G	RAR	R$
Pos	4	03	0	0	0	0	0	0	0							0									0				
Age	24	04	0	0	0	0	0	0	0							0									0				
Growth		05 a/a	453	63	125	10	52	7	276			343	415	758	9	92	28	1.35					85		84	8%	5.12	10.1	$13
Bats	Right	06 BOS	* 512	56	145	7	53	1	283	162	212	349	404	754	9	94	29	1.68	308	48	23	30	75	5%	39	4%	5.16	15.1	$10
Reliability	51	07 BOS	520	86	165	8	50	7	317	348	303	374	442	816	8	92	33	1.12	290	43	18	38	83	4%	80	5%	5.70	22.0	$17
BAvg Potl	55%	1st Half	205	30	66	3	23	1	322			393	449	842	10	91	34	1.33	286	42	19	39	87	4%	43	1%	6.14	11.0	$7
LIMA Plan	A	2nd Half	315	56	99	5	27	6	314			361	438	799	7	92	33	0.96	291	44	18	37	80	5%	93	7%	5.41	10.9	$11
+/- Score	-11	08 Proj	**543**	**97**	**162**	**10**	**55**	**9**	**298**			**360**	**430**	**790**	**9**	**93**	**31**	**1.32**	**295**	**44**	**19**	**37**	**83**	**5%**	**98**	**7%**	**5.46**	**20.2**	**$18**

A lesson in patience and trusting the skills. Hit .188 in first 144 career AB, but owners who stuck it out got a .333 BA after May 1. Not much power or speed yet, but ct% and Eye will keep him around .300.

Pena,Carlos

			AB	R	H	HR	RBI	SB	Avg	vL	vR	OB	Slg	OPS	bb%	ct%	h%	Eye	xBA	G	L	F	PX	hr/f	SX	SBO	RC/G	RAR	R$
Pos	3	03 DET	452	51	112	18	50	4	248	208	267	327	440	767	10	73	30	0.43	256	37	21	42	128	13%	84	8%	5.13	-3.4	$10
Age	29	04 DET	481	89	116	27	82	7	241	245	240	338	472	810	13	70	29	0.48	256	40	16	44	153	18%	112	6%	5.80	11.7	$17
Peak		05 DET	* 517	73	131	28	82	3	254	146	255	342	462	804	12	70	31	0.45	253	38	18	45	146	17%	47	5%	5.66	8.7	$17
Bats	Left	06 BOS	* 451	66	112	21	68	4	249	273	273	339	433	772	12	76	28	0.57	264	48	17	35	115	18%	58	3%	5.13	-3.8	$12
Reliability	14	07 TAM	490	99	138	46	121	1	282	271	286	406	627	1033	17	71	30	0.73	315	37	18	45	233	30%	46	1%	8.96	53.4	$28
BAvg Potl	55%	1st Half	195	39	57	17	45	0	292			389	621	1010	14	72	33	0.56	317	40	20	40	224	30%	28	0%	8.46	18.2	$11
LIMA Plan	C+	2nd Half	295	60	81	29	76	1	275			417	631	1047	20	71	29	0.83	313	36	17	48	239	29%	49	1%	9.27	35.0	$17
+/- Score	21	08 Proj	**538**	**94**	**143**	**37**	**107**	**1**	**266**			**373**	**525**	**898**	**15**	**72**	**30**	**0.61**	**279**	**38**	**18**	**44**	**173**	**21%**	**42**	**1%**	**6.98**	**27.9**	**$22**

Age, opportunity and resurgent FB% collided in a big way, but what does he do for an encore? PX, hr/f were off the charts, so some power regression is likely, taking some BA points with it. Still, this was not a fluke. Enjoy.

Pena,Tony

			AB	R	H	HR	RBI	SB	Avg	vL	vR	OB	Slg	OPS	bb%	ct%	h%	Eye	xBA	G	L	F	PX	hr/f	SX	SBO	RC/G	RAR	R$
Pos	6	03	0	0	0	0	0	0	0							0									0				
Age	26	04 aa	495	56	113	10	29	21	229			250	327	577	3	81	27	0.14					64		99	36%	2.32	-30.6	$9
Pre-Peak		05 aaa	485	41	109	4	35	15	225			251	309	560	3	79	28	0.17					63		95	32%	2.21	-31.5	$6
Bats	Right	06 ATL	* 344	48	91	2	25	11	265			293	340	633	4	81	32	0.22	264	53	22	25	50	3%	122	16%	3.16	-12.0	$8
Reliability	45	07 KC	509	58	136	2	47	5	267	271	266	281	356	637	2	85	31	0.13	276	57	19	25	60	2%	100	10%	3.18	-20.5	$8
BAvg Potl	45%	1st Half	277	33	75	1	21	3	271			286	354	640	2	83	32	0.13	272	59	19	22	54	2%	109	8%	3.18	-11.0	$4
LIMA Plan	D	2nd Half	232	25	61	1	26	2	263			275	358	633	2	87	30	0.13	280	54	18	28	68	2%	81	13%	3.18	-9.4	$4
+/- Score	5	08 Proj	**496**	**57**	**132**	**3**	**41**	**9**	**266**			**286**	**355**	**641**	**3**	**83**	**32**	**0.16**	**269**	**56**	**19**	**26**	**61**	**3%**	**100**	**15%**	**3.21**	**-18.9**	**$9**

Needs to run more if he's going to generate real value, but low bb% and OBA make it awfully hard. And despite rising ct%, poor Eye doesn't bode well for the future of his BA. This is not a skill set worthy of full-time AB.

Pena,Wily Mo

			AB	R	H	HR	RBI	SB	Avg	vL	vR	OB	Slg	OPS	bb%	ct%	h%	Eye	xBA	G	L	F	PX	hr/f	SX	SBO	RC/G	RAR	R$
Pos	79	03 CIN	* 216	34	56	9	28	3	259	204	225	310	435	746	7	71	32	0.26	262	46	21	32	121	18%	93	9%	4.65	-6.0	$7
Age	26	04 CIN	336	45	87	26	66	5	259	302	244	304	527	831	6	68	30	0.20	274	50	16	33	174	34%	72	10%	5.79	3.4	$15
Pre-Peak		05 CIN	311	42	79	19	51	2	254	291	234	299	492	791	6	63	34	0.17	265	48	20	32	189	31%	50	5%	5.63	2.7	$11
Bats	Right	06 BOS	276	36	83	11	42	0	301	260	326	348	489	837	7	67	41	0.22	247	40	21	39	137	15%	57	1%	6.16	7.5	$9
Reliability	25	07 2TM	289	42	73	13	39	2	253	330	203	305	439	745	7	67	33	0.23	254	48	20	32	136	21%	69	4%	4.76	-2.3	$8
BAvg Potl	35%	1st Half	103	14	23	4	11	0	223			292	388	680	9	61	32	0.25	222	48	17	35	137	18%	41	4%	4.14	-2.8	$2
LIMA Plan	C	2nd Half	186	28	50	9	28	2	269			313	468	781	6	71	33	0.22	270	48	21	31	135	22%	85	5%	5.09	0.3	$6
+/- Score	17	08 Proj	**424**	**59**	**112**	**20**	**62**	**2**	**264**			**314**	**463**	**777**	**7**	**67**	**35**	**0.22**	**254**	**46**	**20**	**34**	**144**	**21%**	**69**	**4%**	**5.26**	**1.9**	**$13**

63% contact as a part-timer in BOS, 73% as a regular in WAS; perhaps full-time play suits him. Batting eye, injuries, BA vs. RH are red flags, but it's the power skills that keep us coming back. At 26, time is right to speculate.

Pence,Hunter

			AB	R	H	HR	RBI	SB	Avg	vL	vR	OB	Slg	OPS	bb%	ct%	h%	Eye	xBA	G	L	F	PX	hr/f	SX	SBO	RC/G	RAR	R$
Pos	8	03	0	0	0	0	0	0	0							0									0				
Age	25	04	0	0	0	0	0	0	0							0									0				
Pre-Peak		05	0	0	0	0	0	0	0							0									0				
Bats	Right	06 aa	523	81	133	24	79	15	254			317	471	788	8	82	27	0.51					124		126	16%	5.19	10.0	$18
Reliability	0	07 HOU	* 551	70	174	20	86	13	315	354	314	354	531	885	6	80	36	0.31	305	49	19	32	135	14%	116	13%	6.31	26.3	$24
BAvg Potl	35%	1st Half	303	40	102	11	51	9	337			370	578	947	5	82	38	0.29	323	49	19	32	153	14%	119	16%	7.02	19.7	$15
LIMA Plan	C+	2nd Half	248	30	72	9	35	4	289			336	474	810	7	78	34	0.33	282	49	20	31	113	15%	97	9%	5.42	6.0	$8
+/- Score	2	08 Proj	**586**	**80**	**172**	**24**	**89**	**14**	**294**			**343**	**504**	**847**	**7**	**81**	**33**	**0.39**	**301**	**49**	**19**	**31**	**128**	**16%**	**118**	**13%**	**5.87**	**21.6**	**$24**

17-69-.322 in 456 AB at HOU. 2H declines likely caused by wrist fracture on July 22. Prior: 81% ct, 147 PX, .315 xBA After: 76% ct, 110 PX, .275 xBA Healthy, he was on a $30 pace. Consider that his upside.

Peralta,Jhonny

			AB	R	H	HR	RBI	SB	Avg	vL	vR	OB	Slg	OPS	bb%	ct%	h%	Eye	xBA	G	L	F	PX	hr/f	SX	SBO	RC/G	RAR	R$
Pos	6	03 aaa	237	25	64	1	21	1	269			311	348	659	6	84	32	0.37					59		58	7%	3.63	-4.4	$4
Age	25	04 aaa	556	88	166	12	69	6	298			349	440	789	7	82	35	0.44					97		77	7%	5.22	14.3	$18
Pre-Peak		05 CLE	504	82	147	24	78	0	292	305	288	365	520	885	10	75	35	0.45	291	46	19	35	158	18%	59	1%	6.65	29.4	$19
Bats	Right	06 CLE	569	84	146	13	68	0	257	267	252	323	385	708	9	73	33	0.37	241	48	19	34	91	9%	57	1%	4.30	-1.9	$11
Reliability	39	07 CLE	574	87	155	21	72	4	270	275	269	340	430	770	10	75	33	0.42	258	47	19	35	111	14%	60	5%	5.07	8.5	$17
BAvg Potl	40%	1st Half	279	48	79	13	45	3	283			359	480	839	11	78	32	0.53	272	49	14	37	127	16%	72	6%	5.94	10.9	$11
LIMA Plan	C	2nd Half	295	39	76	8	27	1	258			322	383	705	9	72	33	0.33	247	44	24	32	94	12%	40	4%	4.21	-3.0	$6
+/- Score	3	08 Proj	**572**	**85**	**153**	**18**	**68**	**2**	**267**			**335**	**422**	**756**	**9**	**75**	**33**	**0.40**	**258**	**47**	**19**	**34**	**107**	**12%**	**60**	**3%**	**4.89**	**6.3**	**$15**

On the surface, looks like he bounced back to '05 form, but PX and xBA beg to differ. And 2H slump looked a lot like 2006. So it's 1.5 seasons of good vs. 1.5 seasons of so-so. Split the difference, and don't overbid.

Phelps,Josh

			AB	R	H	HR	RBI	SB	Avg	vL	vR	OB	Slg	OPS	bb%	ct%	h%	Eye	xBA	G	L	F	PX	hr/f	SX	SBO	RC/G	RAR	R$
Pos	3	03 TOR	396	57	106	20	66	1	268	317	239	333	470	803	9	71	33	0.34	274	43	25	32	138	22%	46	3%	5.51	1.6	$13
Age	29	04 2AL	371	51	93	17	61	0	251	309	210	293	450	743	6	75	29	0.24	279	53	19	28	127	22%	54	0%	4.48	-5.5	$10
Peak		05 TAM	* 380	45	90	14	49	0	237	217	286	279	413	692	5	77	27	0.25	278	47	21	32	120	15%	53	1%	3.85	-14.2	$7
Bats	Right	06 aaa	464	52	126	20	78	6	273			322	467	789	7	74	33	0.27					124		86	6%	5.18	-7.0	$15
Reliability	17	07 2TM	157	21	48	7	31	0	306	314	296	384	503	887	11	73	38	0.48	264	34	24	41	127	15%	57	0%	6.77	6.1	$6
BAvg Potl	25%	1st Half	87	9	24	2	12	0	276			330	368	698	7	74	35	0.30	217	36	22	42	62	7%	20	0%	4.00	-3.3	$2
LIMA Plan	F	2nd Half	70	12	24	5	19	0	343			446	671	1117	16	73	41	0.68	318	33	27	40	208	24%	65	0%	10.17	8.7	$4
+/- Score	-47	08 Proj	**190**	**25**	**52**	**9**	**36**	**1**	**274**			**342**	**484**	**826**	**9**	**74**	**33**	**0.40**	**275**	**37**	**24**	**39**	**137**	**17%**	**68**	**2%**	**5.82**	**2.0**	**$7**

PX has stayed remarkably consistent for a guy who has played for five teams in four years. Impressive work w/PIT in 2H, and if some team gave him a shot, could pop 25 HR easy. But that's a big if.

Phillips,Andy

			AB	R	H	HR	RBI	SB	Avg	vL	vR	OB	Slg	OPS	bb%	ct%	h%	Eye	xBA	G	L	F	PX	hr/f	SX	SBO	RC/G	RAR	R$
Pos	3	03 aaa	67	6	13	2	4	0	188			233	333	566	5	78	21	0.27					100		24	0%	2.29	-6.7	($0)
Age	31	04 a/a	476	67	121	23	75	3	254			311	450	760	8	87	25	0.64					102		90	4%	4.81	-9.3	$14
Past Peak		05 NYY	* 340	54	81	18	46	2	239			297	446	743	8	80	25	0.41					127		73	2%	4.51	-5.9	$10
Bats	Right	06 NYY	246	30	59	7	29	3	240	195	262	284	394	678	6	77	28	0.27	261	44	20	35	97	10%	102	9%	3.72	-12.6	$4
Reliability	19	07 NYY	* 434	58	118	11	55	2	272	280	296	329	394	723	8	84	30	0.53	258	44	19	38	75	8%	55	5%	4.41	-8.5	$11
BAvg Potl	45%	1st Half	257	34	72	10	34	2	280			353	444	797	10	83	30	0.67		40	40	20	98	23%	57	4%	5.37	2.0	$8
LIMA Plan	F	2nd Half	177	24	46	1	21	0	260			292	322	614	4	85	30	0.30	234	44	18	38	43	2%	68	7%	3.00	-11.0	$3
+/- Score	-42	08 Proj	**168**	**23**	**43**	**5**	**21**	**1**	**256**			**306**	**397**	**703**	**7**	**82**	**29**	**0.40**	**264**	**44**	**19**	**37**	**87**	**10%**	**71**	**6%**	**4.07**	**-5.5**	**$4**

2-25-.292 in 185 AB at NYY. Needs to learn a new position, because a 75 PX and .257 xBA isn't cutting it at 1B. Now past his peak, and his peak wasn't that great to begin with. Sept wrist surgery won't help either.

Phillips,Brandon

			AB	R	H	HR	RBI	SB	Avg	vL	vR	OB	Slg	OPS	bb%	ct%	h%	Eye	xBA	G	L	F	PX	hr/f	SX	SBO	RC/G	RAR	R$
Pos	4	03 CLE	* 524	50	104	9	46	10	198	179	218	236	302	538	5	82	23	0.27	253	45	19	36	70	6%	83	19%	2.03	-35.4	$4
Age	26	04 CLE	* 543	65	141	6	39	11	260	167	188	306	361	667	6	91	28	0.71	274	35	24	41	65	3%	80	20%	3.91	-2.9	$10
Pre-Peak		05 aaa	459	60	102	10	35	5	222			270	340	610	6	85	24	0.42					76		78	11%	3.02	-18.8	$6
Bats	Right	06 CIN	536	65	148	17	75	25	276	299	268	320	427	748	6	84	30	0.40	277	46	19	35	90	11%	102	20%	4.58	-0.2	$20
Reliability	23	07 CIN	650	107	187	30	94	32	288	341	262	322	485	807	5	83	31	0.30	292	47	18	35	111	16%	133	25%	5.15	10.9	$31
BAvg Potl	45%	1st Half	309	47	85	14	39	15	275			311	476	786	5	83	29	0.31	294	47	19	34	112	16%	136	27%	4.93	3.3	$13
LIMA Plan	C+	2nd Half	341	60	102	16	55	17	299			332	493	825	5	83	32	0.30	290	46	18	35	110	16%	123	24%	5.34	7.5	$18
+/- Score	-10	08 Proj	**610**	**103**	**175**	**28**	**88**	**24**	**287**			**325**	**479**	**805**	**5**	**84**	**30**	**0.35**	**293**	**46**	**19**	**35**	**110**	**16%**	**121**	**21%**	**5.16**	**10.3**	**$28**

Followed up his breakout with... another breakout. Hit the same number of FB, but more over the fence, turning doubles into HR. At 26, further growth could fuel a repeat by itself; however, a small drop-off is a better bet.

BRANDON KRUSE

Piazza,Mike			AB	R	H	HR	RBI	SB	Avg	vL	vR	OB	Slg	OPS	bb%	ct%	h%	Eye	xBA	G	L	F	PX	hr/f	SX	SBO	RC/G	RAR	R$
Pos	0	03 NYM	234	37	67	11	34	0	286	265	292	379	483	862	13	83	31	0.88	280	44	18	39	120	15%	27	0%	6.32	11.1	$9
Age	39	04 NYM	455	47	121	20	54	0	266	303	257	361	444	805	13	83	28	0.87	268	41	20	39	104	14%	11	0%	5.62	4.2	$12
Decline		05 NYM	398	41	100	19	62	0	251	269	248	321	452	773	9	83	26	0.61	285	45	19	36	124	16%	13	0%	5.03	-11.6	$11
Bats	Right	06 SD	399	39	113	22	68	0	283	359	257	339	501	841	8	83	29	0.52	292	40	21	39	121	17%	16	0%	5.70	-8.2	$14
Reliability	0	07 OAK	309	33	85	8	44	0	275	292	268	315	414	729	6	80	32	0.30	262	39	21	40	95	8%	37	0%	4.34	-14.7	$7
BAvg Potl	40%	1st Half	103	14	29	1	8	0	282			339	379	718	8	82	34	0.47	255	49	19	32	76	4%	33	0%	4.43	-4.6	$2
LIMA Plan	D	2nd Half	206	19	56	7	36	0	272			302	432	734	4	80	31	0.21	265	34	22	43	104	10%	35	0%	4.29	-10.2	$5
+/- Score	-27	08 Proj	**375**	**40**	**99**	**12**	**55**	**0**	**264**			**310**	**420**	**730**	**6**	**81**	**30**	**0.35**	**268**	**41**	**21**	**38**	**101**	**10%**	**31**	**0%**	**4.37**	**-17.9**	**$9**

Drops in ct%, Eye, xBA and PX all paint picture of a player in decline. Even as he swung for the fences in 2H, 104 PX was a far cry from his salad days. Reputation will buy him another shot, but DH-only limits value.

Pierre,Juan			AB	R	H	HR	RBI	SB	Avg	vL	vR	OB	Slg	OPS	bb%	ct%	h%	Eye	xBA	G	L	F	PX	hr/f	SX	SBO	RC/G	RAR	R$
Pos	8	03 FLA	668	100	204	1	41	65	305	311	303	358	373	731	8	95	32	1.57	334	52	31	17	42	1%	150	38%	4.84	-2.7	$32
Age	30	04 FLA	678	100	221	3	49	45	326	305	334	368	407	775	6	95	34	1.29	305	56	21	23	43	2%	138	30%	5.19	10.1	$30
Peak		05 FLA	656	96	181	2	47	57	276	284	267	319	354	672	6	93	29	0.91	315	55	25	20	43	2%	170	39%	4.05	-9.9	$27
Bats	Left	06 CHC	699	87	204	3	40	58	292	293	291	323	388	711	4	95	31	0.84	311	55	21	24	52	2%	147	41%	4.40	-0.8	$26
Reliability	98	07 LA	668	96	196	0	41	64	293	274	301	327	353	680	5	94	31	0.89	291	53	21	26	36	0%	147	40%	4.08	-9.2	$27
BAvg Potl	60%	1st Half	321	42	87	0	17	26	271			301	321	622	4	93	29	0.64	278	51	21	28	31	0%	134	39%	3.38	-11.2	$10
LIMA Plan	B	2nd Half	347	54	109	0	24	38	314			350	383	733	5	96	33	1.27	303	55	20	24	41	0%	154	41%	4.71	1.5	$18
+/- Score	-5	08 Proj	**669**	**94**	**197**	**1**	**42**	**61**	**294**			**330**	**367**	**697**	**5**	**94**	**31**	**0.96**	**303**	**54**	**22**	**24**	**42**	**1%**	**156**	**40%**	**4.29**	**-5.0**	**$28**

Overpaid in real life, but money in the bank here. Eye, xBA have been slowly eroding, though he restored both in 2H. Greater worry might be sliding BA vs. LH. For now, these are minor issues; looks good to go for '08.

Pierzynski,A.J.			AB	R	H	HR	RBI	SB	Avg	vL	vR	OB	Slg	OPS	bb%	ct%	h%	Eye	xBA	G	L	F	PX	hr/f	SX	SBO	RC/G	RAR	R$
Pos	2	03 MIN	487	63	152	11	74	3	312	312	324	344	464	808	5	89	33	0.44	312	47	23	30	95	9%	74	3%	5.30	15.9	$17
Age	31	04 SF	471	45	128	11	77	0	272	227	283	300	410	710	4	94	27	0.70	293	47	19	35	78	7%	39	1%	4.27	6.2	$11
Past Peak		05 CHW	460	61	118	18	56	0	257	230	262	292	420	711	5	85	27	0.34	291	46	22	32	98	14%	35	2%	4.05	0.5	$11
Bats	Left	06 CHW	509	65	150	16	64	1	295	270	304	324	436	760	4	86	32	0.31	285	44	23	33	84	11%	43	1%	4.60	2.7	$14
Reliability	71	07 CHW	472	54	124	14	50	1	263	252	266	300	403	702	5	86	28	0.38	267	43	18	39	88	9%	37	2%	4.02	-0.0	$10
BAvg Potl	50%	1st Half	229	24	58	8	26	0	253			296	402	698	6	92	25	0.74	273	39	18	43	84	9%	25	2%	4.13	0.7	$4
LIMA Plan	D	2nd Half	243	30	66	6	24	1	272			303	403	706	4	81	32	0.23	262	48	18	34	92	9%	48	2%	3.99	-0.2	$5
+/- Score	4	08 Proj	**477**	**58**	**125**	**13**	**56**	**1**	**262**			**296**	**391**	**687**	**5**	**86**	**28**	**0.35**	**273**	**45**	**20**	**35**	**81**	**9%**	**43**	**2%**	**3.83**	**-4.2**	**$10**

hr/f shows what little power he had is trickling away, while xBA is on a steady downward trend. There's not a single skill left to point to as a strength; he could go downhill quickly in his 30s. Tread cautiously.

Pie,Felix			AB	R	H	HR	RBI	SB	Avg	vL	vR	OB	Slg	OPS	bb%	ct%	h%	Eye	xBA	G	L	F	PX	hr/f	SX	SBO	RC/G	RAR	R$
Pos	8	03	0	0	0	0	0	0	0							0									0				
Age	23	04	0	0	0	0	0	0	0							0									0				
Growth		05 aa	240	39	71	12	23	13	298			341	538	879	6	81	33	0.34					152		133	42%	6.19	12.4	$12
Bats	Left	06 aaa	559	78	165	17	57	18	295			350	468	818	8	81	34	0.44					107		107	20%	5.60	16.7	$20
Reliability	15	07 CHC *	406	69	115	10	57	16	283	111	241	333	436	769	7	81	33	0.39	276	48	20	32	92	9%	137	22%	4.94	4.5	$16
BAvg Potl	40%	1st Half	258	44	76	5	38	10	295			348	442	790	8	84	34	0.50	283	49	20	31	85	7%	135	21%	5.27	5.2	$11
LIMA Plan	C+	2nd Half	148	25	39	5	19	6	264			306	426	731	6	76	31	0.26	261	46	18	36	105	12%	120	23%	4.37	-0.8	$5
+/- Score	-3	08 Proj	**456**	**72**	**130**	**14**	**54**	**18**	**285**			**334**	**461**	**795**	**7**	**80**	**33**	**0.37**	**283**	**48**	**19**	**33**	**109**	**12%**	**127**	**24%**	**5.25**	**9.2**	**$18**

2-20-.215 in 177 AB at CHC. Terrific power/speed potential, but a year of AAA/MLB shuttling and sitting on the bench (why?) set him back a bit. Relocated power stroke in 2H, but at the expense of ct%. Give him time.

Podsednik,Scott			AB	R	H	HR	RBI	SB	Avg	vL	vR	OB	Slg	OPS	bb%	ct%	h%	Eye	xBA	G	L	F	PX	hr/f	SX	SBO	RC/G	RAR	R$
Pos	7	03 MIL	558	100	174	9	58	43	312	270	329	375	441	815	9	84	36	0.62	289	43	27	30	82	6%	160	29%	5.68	1.4	$30
Age	32	04 MIL	645	86	157	12	39	70	243	224	249	306	363	669	8	84	27	0.55	261	48	17	35	71	6%	162	49%	3.85	-31.3	$26
Past Peak		05 CHW	507	80	147	0	25	59	290	330	284	350	349	699	8	85	34	0.63	277	56	20	23	49	0%	129	50%	4.31	-6.2	$24
Bats	Left	06 CHW	524	86	137	3	45	40	261	216	278	330	353	684	9	82	32	0.56	269	49	23	28	63	2%	146	38%	4.12	-16.9	$18
Reliability	53	07 CHW *	287	40	70	3	16	14	244	279	229	296	363	659	7	82	29	0.41	280	53	19	28	83	4%	135	32%	3.69	-9.0	$6
BAvg Potl	55%	1st Half	107	21	31	2	7	6	290			372	439	811	12	82	34	0.74	318	45	32	23	104	10%	122	26%	5.79	3.3	$4
LIMA Plan	D	2nd Half	180	19	39	1	9	8	217			246	318	564	4	82	26	0.22	263	56	14	30	70	2%	137	38%	2.40	-13.2	$2
+/- Score	16	08 Proj	**285**	**43**	**74**	**2**	**18**	**15**	**260**			**318**	**362**	**680**	**8**	**83**	**31**	**0.50**	**276**	**52**	**21**	**28**	**71**	**4%**	**126**	**31%**	**4.01**	**-7.5**	**$7**

2-11-.243 in 214 AB at CHW. R$ highlights his plummet from must-own player to afterthought. Skills aren't far off from '03, but the truth is, they were never that great. And now opportunity and health are working against him.

Polanco,Placido			AB	R	H	HR	RBI	SB	Avg	vL	vR	OB	Slg	OPS	bb%	ct%	h%	Eye	xBA	G	L	F	PX	hr/f	SX	SBO	RC/G	RAR	R$
Pos	4	03 PHI	492	87	142	14	63	14	289	292	288	345	447	792	8	92	29	1.11	323	50	21	29	92	11%	125	12%	5.36	13.2	$20
Age	32	04 PHI	503	74	150	17	55	7	298	327	287	334	441	775	5	92	30	0.69	310	48	23	29	77	13%	69	8%	4.91	4.3	$18
Past Peak		05 2TM	501	84	166	9	56	4	331	348	324	373	447	820	6	95	34	1.32	330	48	27	25	69	8%	78	4%	5.60	16.6	$20
Bats	Right	06 DET	461	58	136	4	52	1	295	272	305	320	364	685	4	94	31	0.63	284	51	21	28	42	3%	53	2%	3.98	-1.8	$10
Reliability	32	07 DET	587	105	200	9	67	7	341	326	345	380	458	838	6	95	35	1.23	314	45	24	31	72	5%	87	5%	5.79	25.4	$23
BAvg Potl	55%	1st Half	293	52	95	1	35	2	324			363	406	769	6	95	34	1.29	302	43	25	32	54	1%	84	3%	5.12	7.7	$10
LIMA Plan	B	2nd Half	294	53	105	8	32	5	357			396	510	906	6	95	36	1.19	325	46	23	31	90	9%	80	7%	6.47	17.5	$14
+/- Score	-6	08 Proj	**501**	**81**	**158**	**8**	**57**	**5**	**315**			**353**	**428**	**780**	**5**	**94**	**32**	**1.03**	**311**	**47**	**23**	**29**	**67**	**6%**	**84**	**5%**	**5.13**	**13.6**	**$17**

PX, SX and LD% bounced back, driving up BA, but it was career-high AB total that made this his most valuable season. That and a 27-point xBA variance means there's more room to go down than up in 2008.

Posada,Jorge			AB	R	H	HR	RBI	SB	Avg	vL	vR	OB	Slg	OPS	bb%	ct%	h%	Eye	xBA	G	L	F	PX	hr/f	SX	SBO	RC/G	RAR	R$
Pos	2	03 NYY	481	83	135	30	101	1	281	295	276	397	518	915	16	77	31	0.85	290	43	21	36	148	22%	25	3%	7.16	42.2	$21
Age	36	04 NYY	449	72	122	21	81	1	272	275	270	391	481	872	16	80	30	0.96	284	52	17	31	133	19%	29	3%	6.68	30.4	$15
Decline		05 NYY	474	67	124	19	71	1	262	281	246	352	430	782	12	80	29	0.70	264	43	17	39	108	13%	39	1%	5.30	17.6	$14
Bats	Both	06 NYY	465	65	129	23	93	3	277	263	284	365	492	857	12	79	31	0.66	282	38	20	42	132	15%	63	2%	6.24	24.1	$17
Reliability	20	07 NYY	506	91	171	20	90	2	338	331	341	422	543	966	13	81	39	0.76	302	40	22	37	140	13%	58	1%	7.70	48.4	$24
BAvg Potl	35%	1st Half	252	40	85	9	44	1	337			401	536	937	10	80	40	0.53	299	42	22	37	141	12%	42	1%	7.19	20.8	$12
LIMA Plan	C+	2nd Half	254	51	86	11	46	1	339			442	551	993	16	81	38	1.00	304	39	23	38	139	14%	59	1%	8.18	27.4	$13
+/- Score	-38	08 Proj	**456**	**75**	**130**	**19**	**83**	**2**	**285**			**379**	**483**	**862**	**13**	**80**	**32**	**0.76**	**288**	**41**	**21**	**39**	**129**	**14%**	**57**	**2%**	**6.39**	**28.8**	**$17**

Posted his first .300 season at age 36, but it was aided by inflated h%. At 2006's 31% rate, he'd have only hit .280. Power skills are worth owning, but if BA drives bidding up, think twice. At his age, every extra $ adds risk.

Pujols,Albert			AB	R	H	HR	RBI	SB	Avg	vL	vR	OB	Slg	OPS	bb%	ct%	h%	Eye	xBA	G	L	F	PX	hr/f	SX	SBO	RC/G	RAR	R$
Pos	3	03 STL	591	137	212	43	124	5	359	387	350	434	667	1101	12	89	35	1.22	363	42	22	36	175	23%	77	3%	8.91	50.7	$42
Age	28	04 STL	592	133	196	46	123	5	331	379	319	414	657	1071	12	91	30	1.62	358	41	17	41	174	21%	74	6%	8.58	41.4	$38
Peak		05 STL	591	129	195	41	117	16	330	300	340	424	609	1034	14	89	32	1.49	343	42	20	38	156	21%	106	9%	8.30	42.2	$41
Bats	Right	06 STL	535	119	177	49	137	7	331	336	329	429	671	1100	15	91	29	1.84	348	37	18	45	170	23%	67	5%	8.98	42.0	$38
Reliability	74	07 STL	565	99	185	32	103	2	327	367	313	428	568	996	15	90	32	1.71	318	42	19	39	133	16%	32	4%	7.98	36.1	$29
BAvg Potl	65%	1st Half	275	44	82	16	48	1	298			399	527	926	14	88	29	1.35	310	42	20	38	127	17%	26	6%	7.11	11.7	$12
LIMA Plan	C	2nd Half	290	55	103	16	55	1	355			455	607	1062	15	92	35	2.21	328	43	17	40	139	15%	49	2%	8.79	23.5	$17
+/- Score	-25	08 Proj	**569**	**114**	**189**	**41**	**117**	**6**	**332**			**429**	**622**	**1051**	**14**	**90**	**31**	**1.71**	**340**	**41**	**19**	**40**	**155**	**20%**	**57**	**5%**	**8.51**	**42.0**	**$35**

Sizeable drops in PX, SX, hr/f, but other skills held strong. Given sheer number of ailing parts (oblique, knee, hamstring, elbow, calf), we can probably blame this on injury. Consider this a rare buying opportunity.

Punto,Nick			AB	R	H	HR	RBI	SB	Avg	vL	vR	OB	Slg	OPS	bb%	ct%	h%	Eye	xBA	G	L	F	PX	hr/f	SX	SBO	RC/G	RAR	R$
Pos	564	03 PHI *	203	31	53	1	12	8	261	278	179	306	330	636	6	83	31	0.38	283	56	24	20	50	3%	125	18%	3.34	-5.4	$5
Age	30	04 MIN	91	17	23	2	12	6	253	250	254	340	319	658	12	79	30	0.63	229	32	29	39	34	7%	105	18%	3.70	-3.2	$4
Peak		05 MIN	394	45	94	4	26	13	239	210	246	302	335	637	8	78	30	0.42	260	51	21	28	69	5%	113	20%	3.41	-13.1	$7
Bats	Both	06 MIN	459	73	133	1	45	17	290	331	267	356	373	728	9	85	34	0.69	270	46	24	30	53	1%	133	15%	4.72	-3.7	$13
Reliability	32	07 MIN	472	53	99	1	25	16	210	175	226	292	271	563	10	81	26	0.61	229	51	15	35	46	1%	106	17%	2.67	-27.2	$3
BAvg Potl	60%	1st Half	244	30	53	1	14	13	217			313	279	592	12	83	26	0.83	237	50	16	34	42	1%	113	21%	3.17	-10.1	$3
LIMA Plan	D	2nd Half	228	23	46	0	11	3	202			269	263	532	8	79	26	0.43	218	52	13	35	49	0%	87	11%	2.13	-17.2	($1)
+/- Score	15	08 Proj	**418**	**53**	**100**	**1**	**28**	**14**	**239**			**309**	**312**	**620**	**9**	**82**	**29**	**0.55**	**247**	**50**	**18**	**32**	**52**	**1%**	**114**	**16%**	**3.33**	**-16.8**	**$6**

xBA shows this wasn't just about h%; he was truly awful. LD% should rebound, but with no power, there's not much upside here. If the powers that be finally figure that out...
DN: A seat on the bench.

BRANDON KRUSE

Quentin,Carlos			AB	R	H	HR	RBI	SB	Avg	vL	vR	OB	Slg	OPS	bb%	ct%	h%	Eye	xBA	G	L	F	PX	hr/f	SX	SBO	RC/G	RAR	R$
Pos	9	03	0	0	0	0	0	0	0							0									0				
Age	25	04 aa	210	29	68	5	28	0	324			366	486	852	6	92	34	0.82					101		34	14%	5.92	5.5	$8
Pre-Peak		05 aaa	452	68	121	16	62	6	268			345	445	789	10	89	27	1.08					104		91	5%	5.43	5.9	$15
Bats	Right	06 ARI	* 484	74	127	16	72	5	262	171	280	331	469	800	9	86	28	0.72	302	46	16	38	125	10%	99	4%	5.51	10.3	$14
Reliability	14	07 ARI	* 344	52	83	9	52	2	242	172	230	294	400	694	7	80	28	0.37	266	43	16	41	110	8%	69	7%	4.03	-12.6	$7
BAvg Potl	50%	1st Half	190	28	42	5	28	2	221			288	368	657	9	78	26	0.44	250	42	15	43	104	8%	66	7%	3.62	-9.5	$3
LIMA Plan	C	2nd Half	154	24	41	4	24	0	268			300	439	739	4	83	30	0.27	299	47	21	32	117	9%	72	6%	4.49	-3.4	$4
+/- Score	1	08 Proj	**416**	**62**	**109**	**12**	**61**	**3**	**262**			**318**	**436**	**754**	**8**	**82**	**29**	**0.46**	**279**	**44**	**17**	**39**	**115**	**9%**	**76**	**7%**	**4.81**	**-4.1**	**$11**

5-31-.214 in 229 AB at ARI. Rapidly fading ct% is becoming a concern, especially in majors, where it dropped to 76% last year. But he still has that .315 xBA and 153 PX from 2H of '06. Talent is there. Don't give up.

Quinlan,Robb			AB	R	H	HR	RBI	SB	Avg	vL	vR	OB	Slg	OPS	bb%	ct%	h%	Eye	xBA	G	L	F	PX	hr/f	SX	SBO	RC/G	RAR	R$
Pos	37	03 ANA	* 487	56	133	7	56	9	273	286	288	309	374	682	5	87	30	0.40	289	49	24	27	61	6%	92	12%	3.86	-21.4	$12
Age	31	04 ANA	* 268	33	81	6	34	4	302	390	317	360	459	819	8	86	33	0.65	302	47	22	31	101	8%	71	8%	5.65	4.9	$8
Past Peak		05 ANA	134	17	31	5	14	0	231	289	137	270	403	672	5	81	25	0.27	283	51	18	30	114	15%	45	4%	3.58	-6.1	$2
Bats	Right	06 LAA	234	28	75	9	32	2	321	326	313	340	491	832	3	88	34	0.25	294	53	17	30	95	14%	60	5%	5.32	-0.6	$9
Reliability	8	07 LAA	178	21	44	3	21	3	247	269	203	302	348	650	7	85	28	0.52	246	48	14	38	69	5%	60	11%	3.58	-8.0	$3
BAvg Potl	50%	1st Half	89	10	25	3	14	1	281			333	449	783	7	87	30	0.58	282	47	15	37	107	10%	42	9%	5.11	0.0	$3
LIMA Plan	F	2nd Half	89	11	19	0	7	2	213			271	247	518	7	83	26	0.47	207	49	12	38	30	0%	74	13%	2.01	-8.6	$1
+/- Score	11	08 Proj	**165**	**20**	**44**	**4**	**19**	**2**	**267**			**309**	**387**	**695**	**6**	**85**	**29**	**0.41**	**260**	**50**	**16**	**34**	**77**	**8%**	**55**	**8%**	**3.99**	**-5.7**	**$4**

Power has come and gone, and LD% is in five-year freefall. xBA shows that without those two skills, there's nothing worth sticking around for. Not that you were planning on doing that anyway.

Quintanilla,Omar			AB	R	H	HR	RBI	SB	Avg	vL	vR	OB	Slg	OPS	bb%	ct%	h%	Eye	xBA	G	L	F	PX	hr/f	SX	SBO	RC/G	RAR	R$
Pos	4	03	0	0	0	0	0	0	0							0									0				
Age	26	04	0	0	0	0	0	0	0							0									0				
Pre-Peak		05 COL	* 474	59	123	4	30	3	259	67	239	299	338	637	5	90	28	0.57	283	42	26	32	48	3%	80	6%	3.49	-14.9	$7
Bats	Left	06 COL	* 342	39	85	3	25	4	249	250	167	298	360	657	7	86	28	0.51	285	52	20	28	73	4%	84	8%	3.74	-8.7	$4
Reliability	30	07 COL	* 418	47	112	3	37	2	269	100	250	315	373	688	6	83	32	0.40	310	55	29	16	77	5%	66	3%	4.03	-6.4	$6
BAvg Potl	50%	1st Half	210	24	61	0	19	1	290			326	386	712	5	85	34	0.35	309	46	31	23	71	0%	76	2%	4.29	-1.6	$4
LIMA Plan	F	2nd Half	208	23	51	3	18	1	247			305	360	665	8	80	30	0.43	311	70	25	5	83	32%	55	3%	3.76	-5.0	$2
+/- Score	-1	08 Proj	**229**	**26**	**59**	**2**	**18**	**2**	**258**			**305**	**365**	**671**	**6**	**85**	**30**	**0.45**	**293**	**56**	**22**	**22**	**74**	**4%**	**76**	**5%**	**3.85**	**-4.8**	**$3**

0-5-.229 in 70 AB at COL. Gradually trading ct% for what? More GB? Slightly more below-average power? xBA grabs your attention, but it's being driven by LD% that feels more like small MLB sample size than real skill.

Raburn,Ryan			AB	R	H	HR	RBI	SB	Avg	vL	vR	OB	Slg	OPS	bb%	ct%	h%	Eye	xBA	G	L	F	PX	hr/f	SX	SBO	RC/G	RAR	R$
Pos	9	03	0	0	0	0	0	0	0							0									0				
Age	27	04 aa	395	59	99	13	54	4	251			319	428	747	9	75	30	0.40					119		108	4%	4.81	-2.1	$10
Peak		05 aaa	466	53	109	16	57	7	234			294	399	694	8	81	26	0.44					101		99	9%	4.02	-13.5	$10
Bats	Right	06 aaa	451	62	116	18	73	15	257			328	454	782	10	75	30	0.43					127		118	16%	5.25	0.5	$15
Reliability	10	07 DET	* 453	81	125	19	84	14	277	259	338	353	489	842	11	78	32	0.54	287	41	19	39	141	13%	122	14%	6.05	17.6	$20
BAvg Potl	45%	1st Half	297	53	82	14	56	11	276			373	502	875	13	79	31	0.73					146		114	16%	6.58	16.2	$14
LIMA Plan	D	2nd Half	156	28	43	5	28	3	278			312	464	775	5	76	34	0.21	274	41	19	39	131	10%	126	8%	4.97	1.2	$6
+/- Score	12	08 Proj	**258**	**40**	**70**	**9**	**42**	**6**	**271**			**328**	**466**	**794**	**8**	**77**	**32**	**0.37**	**275**	**41**	**19**	**39**	**129**	**12%**	**120**	**12%**	**5.32**	**2.6**	**$9**

4-27-.304 in 138 AB at DET. Late bloomer or just a fluke?
PRO: Recent PX and SX growth, solid FB%, good xBA
CON: 2nd half slide in most skills, 0.24 Eye in majors
Call it late bloomer by a nose.

Ramirez,Aramis			AB	R	H	HR	RBI	SB	Avg	vL	vR	OB	Slg	OPS	bb%	ct%	h%	Eye	xBA	G	L	F	PX	hr/f	SX	SBO	RC/G	RAR	R$
Pos	5	03 2NL	607	75	165	27	106	2	272	285	268	319	465	784	6	84	29	0.42	276	36	18	46	116	12%	55	3%	4.99	12.8	$21
Age	29	04 CHC	547	99	174	36	103	0	318	267	328	374	578	952	8	89	31	0.79	325	34	23	43	139	17%	37	1%	6.96	28.0	$29
Peak		05 CHC	463	72	140	31	92	0	302	355	284	351	568	919	7	87	29	0.58	327	39	20	41	153	19%	28	1%	6.52	22.1	$23
Bats	Right	06 CHC	594	93	173	38	119	2	291	261	301	346	561	907	8	89	27	0.79	316	35	18	47	141	15%	66	2%	6.46	16.1	$27
Reliability	89	07 CHC	506	72	157	26	101	0	310	395	286	364	549	914	8	87	32	0.65	305	39	18	44	136	13%	47	0%	6.60	24.9	$22
BAvg Potl	55%	1st Half	232	32	69	14	42	0	297			348	539	887	7	85	30	0.53	301	43	18	40	131	18%	49	0%	6.18	9.0	$10
LIMA Plan	C+	2nd Half	274	40	88	12	59	0	321			378	558	936	8	88	33	0.78	310	35	17	47	141	11%	48	0%	6.95	15.8	$13
+/- Score	-12	08 Proj	**568**	**85**	**172**	**33**	**113**	**1**	**303**			**356**	**556**	**912**	**8**	**88**	**30**	**0.67**	**313**	**37**	**18**	**44**	**141**	**15%**	**51**	**1%**	**6.53**	**24.7**	**$26**

Hit just 6 HR in June/July/Aug, with hr/f of 7%; rest of the year, 20 HR with 19% hr/f. What else happened over the summer? Patellar tendinitis and fluid in his right wrist. If healthy, another 35-HR season is within reach.

Ramirez,Hanley			AB	R	H	HR	RBI	SB	Avg	vL	vR	OB	Slg	OPS	bb%	ct%	h%	Eye	xBA	G	L	F	PX	hr/f	SX	SBO	RC/G	RAR	R$
Pos	6	03	0	0	0	0	0	0	0							0									0				
Age	24	04 aa	129	23	39	4	13	11	301			344	472	816	6	84	33	0.42					101		140	39%	5.41	4.1	$7
Growth		05 aa	461	57	119	5	45	22	258			308	360	668	7	89	28	0.65					64		122	29%	3.90	-5.0	$13
Bats	Right	06 FLA	633	119	185	17	59	51	292	307	288	350	480	830	8	80	34	0.44	286	44	21	35	118	10%	164	40%	5.83	26.6	$31
Reliability	26	07 FLA	639	125	212	29	81	51	332	399	312	382	562	944	8	85	36	0.55	305	40	18	42	137	13%	141	36%	6.98	52.2	$41
BAvg Potl	40%	1st Half	312	63	99	11	26	22	317			366	500	866	7	84	35	0.47	291	45	19	36	110	12%	141	31%	6.07	18.1	$17
LIMA Plan	D+	2nd Half	327	62	113	18	55	29	346			397	621	1018	8	87	36	0.64	319	35	17	48	162	13%	136	41%	7.83	33.7	$25
+/- Score	-3	08 Proj	**616**	**111**	**190**	**27**	**76**	**47**	**308**			**360**	**531**	**891**	**7**	**84**	**33**	**0.52**	**301**	**41**	**19**	**41**	**132**	**13%**	**147**	**38%**	**6.37**	**39.6**	**$36**

2nd straight year with FB%, PX and ct% gains in 2nd half, and this time while playing with torn labrum tissue in left shoulder. Had surgery, but shoulder may not be full strength by spring. Still... UP: 35 HR.

Ramirez,Manny			AB	R	H	HR	RBI	SB	Avg	vL	vR	OB	Slg	OPS	bb%	ct%	h%	Eye	xBA	G	L	F	PX	hr/f	SX	SBO	RC/G	RAR	R$
Pos	7	03 BOS	569	117	185	37	104	3	325	385	305	423	587	1010	15	83	34	1.03	322	36	24	40	154	19%	58	2%	8.16	42.6	$31
Age	35	04 BOS	568	108	175	43	130	2	308	306	309	395	613	1008	13	78	33	0.66	309	41	15	43	188	22%	38	4%	8.13	49.6	$31
Decline		05 BOS	554	112	162	45	144	1	292	236	313	382	594	976	13	79	30	0.67	326	37	24	39	185	27%	56	1%	7.63	44.8	$32
Bats	Right	06 BOS	449	79	144	35	102	0	321	326	319	444	619	1064	18	77	35	0.98	313	36	22	42	181	24%	26	1%	9.19	48.1	$24
Reliability	13	07 BOS	483	84	143	20	88	0	296	344	279	386	493	879	13	81	33	0.77	290	38	22	41	129	13%	40	0%	6.58	24.8	$19
BAvg Potl	50%	1st Half	273	39	79	11	42	0	289			386	476	862	14	82	32	0.90	290	37	23	40	118	12%	36	0%	6.40	12.8	$9
LIMA Plan	C	2nd Half	210	45	64	9	46	0	305			387	514	901	12	79	35	0.64	290	39	20	42	145	13%	43	0%	6.83	12.1	$10
+/- Score	-8	08 Proj	**490**	**82**	**147**	**27**	**94**	**0**	**300**			**398**	**536**	**934**	**14**	**79**	**33**	**0.79**	**299**	**37**	**22**	**41**	**150**	**17%**	**39**	**1%**	**7.31**	**32.8**	**$21**

Sudden power decline makes us ask the question: Was it age, injuries, or both? Hit more 2B than HR for first time since '97. 2nd half PX gain gives hope for a decent rebound, but $30 days may be gone for good.

Ransom,Cody			AB	R	H	HR	RBI	SB	Avg	vL	vR	OB	Slg	OPS	bb%	ct%	h%	Eye	xBA	G	L	F	PX	hr/f	SX	SBO	RC/G	RAR	R$
Pos	6	03 aaa	423	50	88	9	39	10	207			267	320	587	7	79	24	0.39					71		114	16%	2.69	-21.0	$5
Age	32	04 SF	* 204	33	50	7	26	8	247			312	415	726	9	79	29	0.44					105		128	19%	4.47	2.1	$7
Past Peak		05 aaa	262	25	50	5	23	5	191			236	292	528	6	71	25	0.20					73		88	11%	1.66	-21.7	$1
Bats	Right	06 aaa	380	48	77	16	46	2	201			277	381	658	9	75	22	0.42					115		59	3%	3.54	-10.1	$5
Reliability	10	07 HOU	* 538	53	101	19	56	13	188	333	192	241	338	580	7	69	23	0.23	215	35	15	50	109	10%	77	18%	2.36	-27.7	$6
BAvg Potl	50%	1st Half	275	32	63	10	40	13	229			293	411	704	8	78	26	0.41					125		82	33%	4.17	1.8	$8
LIMA Plan	F	2nd Half	263	21	38	9	16	0	144			185	262	447	5	60	19	0.12	161	35	15	50	89	11%		-5%	0.26	-32.4	($3
+/- Score	7	08 Proj	**93**	**10**	**19**	**3**	**9**	**2**	**204**			**261**	**349**	**610**	**7**	**71**	**25**	**0.26**	**216**	**35**	**15**	**50**	**102**	**10%**	**57**	**10%**	**2.80**	**-3.7**	**$1**

1-3-.229 in 35 AB at HOU. He's the baseball equivalent of a thousand monkeys working at a thousand typewriters. Let him hack away, he'll eventually hit some out, but the overall results are messy and disturbing.

Redman,Tike			AB	R	H	HR	RBI	SB	Avg	vL	vR	OB	Slg	OPS	bb%	ct%	h%	Eye	xBA	G	L	F	PX	hr/f	SX	SBO	RC/G	RAR	R$
Pos	8	03 PIT	* 590	86	171	6	43	42	290	329	331	339	397	736	7	92	31	0.98	313	49	25	25	62	4%	154	32%	4.76	-3.6	$24
Age	31	04 PIT	546	65	153	8	51	18	280	266	284	309	374	683	4	90	30	0.44	280	55	17	28	53	6%	114	17%	3.88	-12.0	$16
Past Peak		05 PIT	319	33	80	2	26	4	251	260	249	293	332	625	6	92	27	0.70	284	52	20	28	49	2%	101	6%	3.46	-10.4	$5
Bats	Left	06 a/a	403	56	84	2	15	12	210			251	262	513	5	89	23	0.48					34		97	19%	2.06	-31.6	$1
Reliability	11	07 BAL	* 428	70	120	4	39	30	281	133	373	334	384	718	7	90	31	0.78	277	47	18	35	65	3%	145	31%	4.54	3.2	$16
BAvg Potl	55%	1st Half	172	29	48	2	14	10	279			358	390	747	11	89	30	1.11					65		137	23%	5.07	4.0	$6
LIMA Plan	D	2nd Half	256	41	72	2	25	20	282			317	381	697	5	90	31	0.52	278	47	18	35	64	2%	146	37%	4.16	-0.9	$10
+/- Score	11	08 Proj	**328**	**49**	**88**	**3**	**25**	**16**	**268**			**314**	**352**	**667**	**6**	**90**	**29**	**0.67**	**277**	**50**	**19**	**31**	**52**	**3%**	**127**	**23%**	**3.89**	**-5.1**	**$9**

2-16-.318 in 132 AB at BAL. .330 OBA, 7% walk rate seem to be the dividing line between elite and above-average SBO. .373 BA, .935 OPS vs. RH last year may buy him a platoon job; if that happens, could steal 20.

BRANDON KRUSE

Redmond,Mike

			AB	R	H	HR	RBI	SB	Avg	vL	vR	OB	Slg	OPS	bb%	ct%	h%	Eye	xBA	G	L	F	PX	hr/f	SX	SBO	RC/G	RAR	R$
Pos	2	03 FLA	125	12	30	0	11	0	240	314	211	280	312	592	5	87	28	0.44	275	49	23	28	53	0%	58	0%	2.96	-5.0	$1
Age	37	04 FLA	246	19	63	2	25	1	256	179	279	296	341	638	5	89	28	0.50	272	47	21	32	60	3%	36	2%	3.47	-2.5	$3
Decline		05 MIN	148	17	46	1	26	0	311	345	289	338	392	730	4	91	34	0.43	295	53	24	23	59	3%	30	0%	4.41	1.6	$5
Bats	Right	06 MIN	179	20	61	0	23	0	341	443	275	355	413	769	2	90	38	0.22	297	46	27	27	57	0%	29	0%	4.73	1.5	$5
Reliability	21	07 MIN	272	23	80	1	38	0	294	330	277	338	353	691	6	92	32	0.78	256	44	21	35	43	1%	18	0%	4.18	1.2	$5
BAvg Potl	50%	1st Half	180	14	52	1	23	0	289			326	356	682	5	91	31	0.59	259	40	22	38	48	2%	16	0%	3.99	-0.2	$3
LIMA Plan	F	2nd Half	92	9	28	0	15	0	304			360	348	708	8	93	33	1.33	252	53	18	28	34	0%	21	0%	4.56	1.3	$2
+/- Score	-41	08 Proj	199	20	56	1	28	0	281			318	344	663	5	91	31	0.60	274	48	22	29	47	1%	28	0%	3.80	-1.9	$4

Continues to be the master of wild BA and h% fluctuations. And now xBA has joined in, with a 43-point collapse brought on by drops in LD% and PX. They might bounce back, but don't ignore the risk. DN: .250 BA.

Renteria,Edgar

			AB	R	H	HR	RBI	SB	Avg	vL	vR	OB	Slg	OPS	bb%	ct%	h%	Eye	xBA	G	L	F	PX	hr/f	SX	SBO	RC/G	RAR	R$
Pos	6	03 STL	587	96	194	13	100	34	330	391	316	397	480	878	10	91	35	1.20	316	44	23	32	96	8%	109	21%	6.46	36.9	$34
Age	32	04 STL	586	84	168	10	72	17	287	366	264	331	401	732	6	87	32	0.50	287	47	22	31	75	6%	83	18%	4.51	6.4	$20
Past Peak		05 BOS	623	100	172	8	70	9	276	326	253	335	385	720	8	84	32	0.55	284	47	24	29	76	5%	99	7%	4.48	-1.4	$17
Bats	Right	06 ATL	598	100	175	14	70	17	293	333	281	359	436	796	9	85	33	0.70	294	47	22	31	90	9%	97	13%	5.43	18.0	$22
Reliability	66	07 ATL	494	87	164	12	57	11	332	349	323	389	470	859	9	84	38	0.60	290	46	23	31	89	9%	91	8%	6.09	27.7	$22
BAvg Potl	35%	1st Half	293	52	96	10	38	6	328			384	502	886	8	85	36	0.60	301	44	23	33	107	12%	89	8%	6.38	18.8	$14
LIMA Plan	C+	2nd Half	201	35	68	2	19	5	338			395	423	818	9	84	40	0.59	273	48	23	29	61	4%	75	8%	5.66	8.9	$8
+/- Score	-49	08 Proj	512	87	152	10	59	13	297			358	422	780	9	85	33	0.63	288	47	23	30	82	8%	97	11%	5.19	15.9	$19

Bad Aug ankle sprain explains some of the 2H drops, but even in July, had a 66 PX, 0% hr/f and .279 xBA. OPS says best year since '03, but subtract out 42-pt xBA gap, and it looks like 2006. Skills concur. Bid accordingly.

Reyes,Jose

			AB	R	H	HR	RBI	SB	Avg	vL	vR	OB	Slg	OPS	bb%	ct%	h%	Eye	xBA	G	L	F	PX	hr/f	SX	SBO	RC/G	RAR	R$
Pos	6	03 NYM	* 434	77	129	5	46	41	297	225	340	340	406	745	6	87	33	0.50	289	47	25	29	65	5%	176	39%	4.69	7.1	$23
Age	24	04 NYM	220	33	56	2	14	19	255	326	237	271	373	644	2	86	29	0.16	271	43	19	38	80	3%	176	51%	3.32	-5.3	$8
Growth		05 NYM	696	99	190	7	58	60	273	288	269	300	386	687	4	89	30	0.35	278	47	20	33	63	3%	182	44%	3.93	-0.5	$29
Bats	Both	06 NYM	647	122	194	19	81	64	300	330	288	353	487	840	8	87	32	0.65	300	45	21	34	98	10%	168	45%	5.85	27.4	$37
Reliability	26	07 NYM	681	119	191	12	57	78	280	318	266	354	421	775	10	89	30	0.99	275	42	18	40	81	5%	164	48%	5.33	27.4	$35
BAvg Potl	55%	1st Half	309	53	97	3	33	38	314			396	447	843	12	87	35	1.08	276	43	20	37	77	3%	159	43%	6.27	20.1	$19
LIMA Plan	C	2nd Half	372	66	94	9	24	40	253			317	401	717	9	90	26	0.90	275	41	17	42	85	6%	157	53%	4.56	6.8	$16
+/- Score	4	08 Proj	608	105	172	15	57	65	283			344	444	788	9	88	30	0.79	284	42	19	38	89	7%	174	47%	5.34	22.5	$32

You can see the impact bb% growth has had on his running game. 2H slump was simple h% correction; xBA shows that .280 is right on. FB, Eye growth could be setting the stage for more power... UP: 20 HR.

Reynolds,Mark

			AB	R	H	HR	RBI	SB	Avg	vL	vR	OB	Slg	OPS	bb%	ct%	h%	Eye	xBA	G	L	F	PX	hr/f	SX	SBO	RC/G	RAR	R$
Pos	5	03	0	0	0	0	0	0	0							0									0				
Age	24	04	0	0	0	0	0	0	0							0									0				
Growth		05	0	0	0	0	0	0	0							0									0				
Bats	Right	06 aa	114	20	30	8	18	0	264			322	528	849	8	70	31	0.29					177		48	4%	6.08	2.8	$4
Reliability	0	07 ARI	* 500	84	139	23	79	3	278	278	279	347	498	845	10	69	36	0.34	257	36	20	44	155	15%	93	4%	6.32	22.0	$18
BAvg Potl	25%	1st Half	253	44	73	11	39	3	289			364	530	894	11	77	34	0.51	287	36	20	43	155	13%	107	7%	6.78	14.3	$10
LIMA Plan	D+	2nd Half	247	40	66	12	40	0	267			330	466	795	9	61	39	0.24	227	36	20	44	156	18%	54	0%	5.99	8.6	$8
+/- Score	2	08 Proj	319	55	83	14	51	1	260			325	457	782	9	68	34	0.31	248	36	20	44	142	14%	77	3%	5.38	4.0	$10

17-62-.279 in 366 AB at ARI. Power is legitimate, BA is not. Ct% and Eye deteriorated in 2H, but high h% hid the damage. Must address holes in swing to continue growth. Don't overpay for likely period of adjustment.

Richar,Danny

			AB	R	H	HR	RBI	SB	Avg	vL	vR	OB	Slg	OPS	bb%	ct%	h%	Eye	xBA	G	L	F	PX	hr/f	SX	SBO	RC/G	RAR	R$
Pos	4	03	0	0	0	0	0	0	0							0									0				
Age	24	04	0	0	0	0	0	0	0							0									0				
Growth		05	0	0	0	0	0	0	0							0									0				
Bats	Left	06 aa	480	71	134	8	38	14	279			344	400	744	9	85	32	0.66					74		113	13%	4.82	6.4	$13
Reliability	0	07 CHW	* 585	83	156	20	69	7	266	205	236	324	450	774	8	83	29	0.50	287	45	18	36	112	11%	100	10%	5.04	15.6	$16
BAvg Potl	55%	1st Half	305	42	84	10	46	5	275			332	472	804	8	83	30	0.50					123		102	13%	5.44	11.6	$10
LIMA Plan	B	2nd Half	280	41	72	10	23	2	255			314	426	740	8	83	28	0.50	278	45	18	36	101	11%	90	7%	4.61	3.9	$6
+/- Score	21	08 Proj	513	74	138	15	50	9	269			330	433	763	8	84	30	0.56	280	45	18	36	99	9%	108	11%	4.95	12.3	$14

6-15-.230 in 187 AB at CHW. Skills held up well in majors, and .230 BA was due to 25% MLB hit rate. Power and speed are only average, but at 2b, that has value with full-time AB. Nice profit potential here.

Rios,Alex

			AB	R	H	HR	RBI	SB	Avg	vL	vR	OB	Slg	OPS	bb%	ct%	h%	Eye	xBA	G	L	F	PX	hr/f	SX	SBO	RC/G	RAR	R$
Pos	98	03 aa	514	71	168	9	68	9	327			367	469	836	6	86	37	0.47					89		113	8%	5.72	4.7	$20
Age	27	04 TOR	* 611	67	168	4	47	17	275	287	286	318	376	695	6	82	33	0.36	280	57	20	23	68	3%	125	13%	4.07	-11.0	$13
Peak		05 TOR	481	71	126	10	59	14	262	249	271	303	397	700	6	79	31	0.28	269	49	19	31	90	8%	129	20%	4.02	-9.8	$14
Bats	Right	06 TOR	450	68	136	17	82	15	302	295	305	353	516	868	7	80	35	0.39	288	37	22	42	134	11%	123	18%	6.18	6.5	$20
Reliability	26	07 TOR	643	114	191	24	85	17	297	345	283	352	498	850	8	84	32	0.53	289	36	20	44	125	10%	125	12%	5.94	22.2	$27
BAvg Potl	45%	1st Half	312	55	90	17	45	7	288			335	526	861	7	85	29	0.48	293	34	17	49	140	13%	109	11%	5.89	10.4	$14
LIMA Plan	B	2nd Half	331	59	101	7	40	10	305			368	471	839	9	83	35	0.58	286	38	23	39	110	7%	126	13%	5.98	11.7	$13
+/- Score	0	08 Proj	612	99	180	22	90	17	294			351	493	844	8	83	33	0.51	292	39	21	40	123	11%	124	14%	5.89	16.0	$25

For two straight seasons, he's been on 30-HR pace in 1H, only to see FB%, PX and hr/f drop significantly in 2H. At the same time, he's been quietly raising bb% and ct%. If he finally puts it all together, he's a $30 player.

Rivera,Juan

			AB	R	H	HR	RBI	SB	Avg	vL	vR	OB	Slg	OPS	bb%	ct%	h%	Eye	xBA	G	L	F	PX	hr/f	SX	SBO	RC/G	RAR	R$
Pos	9	03 NYY	* 481	62	136	13	58	1	283	340	236	327	432	760	6	88	30	0.54	304	47	23	30	95	10%	36	3%	4.82	-4.6	$13
Age	29	04 MON	394	49	121	12	49	6	307	276	328	362	464	827	8	89	32	0.76	301	49	20	31	93	11%	70	7%	5.67	4.1	$14
Peak		05 ANA	350	46	95	15	59	1	271	252	286	316	454	771	6	87	27	0.52	288	46	17	37	106	13%	43	12%	4.85	1.6	$11
Bats	Right	06 LAA	448	65	139	23	85	0	310	351	293	358	525	882	7	87	32	0.56	293	51	16	33	121	18%	23	3%	6.13	5.8	$18
Reliability	4	07 LAA	* 104	6	23	2	19	0	224	276	286	247	341	588	3	90	23	0.30	246	44	15	41	77	5%	10	0%	2.78	-6.1	$1
BAvg Potl	60%	1st Half	0	0	0	0	0	0	0														0						
LIMA Plan	D+	2nd Half	104	6	23	2	19	0	224			247	341	588	3	90	23	0.30	246	44	15	41	77	5%	10	0%	2.78	-6.1	$1
+/- Score	30	08 Proj	363	40	105	14	60	1	289			329	466	795	6	88	30	0.51	288	48	17	35	104	13%	28	5%	5.11	1.5	$12

2-8-.279 in 43 AB at LAA. Broken leg, broken season. Going back to 2006, had rising trends in PX and hr/f, but bad GB/FB mix raised questions about his ability to sustain the power. Hedge your bets.

Roberts,Brian

			AB	R	H	HR	RBI	SB	Avg	vL	vR	OB	Slg	OPS	bb%	ct%	h%	Eye	xBA	G	L	F	PX	hr/f	SX	SBO	RC/G	RAR	R$
Pos	4	03 BAL	* 638	99	174	5	55	41	273	264	272	346	364	709	10	89	30	1.03	302	40	32	28	59	3%	130	27%	4.60	8.6	$22
Age	30	04 BAL	641	107	175	4	53	29	273	215	299	346	376	721	10	85	32	0.75	265	39	21	39	75	2%	112	22%	4.68	11.3	$19
Peak		05 BAL	561	92	176	18	73	27	314	273	332	387	515	902	11	85	34	0.81	314	35	27	37	128	10%	125	21%	6.78	41.0	$28
Bats	Both	06 BAL	563	85	161	10	55	36	286	235	308	350	410	760	9	88	31	0.83	283	44	21	35	77	6%	126	25%	5.04	14.8	$21
Reliability	50	07 BAL	621	103	180	12	57	50	290	268	299	379	432	810	13	84	33	0.90	264	36	20	45	95	5%	132	27%	5.83	29.9	$28
BAvg Potl	50%	1st Half	301	46	97	4	22	25	322			409	445	854	13	87	36	1.10	269	37	22	41	79	4%	130	25%	6.40	18.5	$15
LIMA Plan	B	2nd Half	320	57	83	8	35	25	259			351	419	769	12	82	30	0.76	260	35	17	48	112	6%	128	30%	5.28	10.8	$13
+/- Score	-16	08 Proj	591	96	170	12	59	41	288			367	429	796	11	85	32	0.85	276	38	21	41	93	6%	131	26%	5.57	24.2	$25

2H FB% surge just resulted in a lot more doubles and outs, so maybe it's time to put those '05 memories out of our heads. He needs to be careful, as this new approach could hurt BA and SB, and nobody wants that.

Roberts,Dave

			AB	R	H	HR	RBI	SB	Avg	vL	vR	OB	Slg	OPS	bb%	ct%	h%	Eye	xBA	G	L	F	PX	hr/f	SX	SBO	RC/G	RAR	R$
Pos	87	03 LA	388	56	97	2	16	40	250	265	246	325	307	632	10	90	27	1.10	294	50	28	22	30	3%	155	43%	3.72	-15.0	$14
Age	35	04 2TM	319	64	81	4	35	38	254	179	270	333	379	713	11	85	29	0.79	266	50	16	35	72	4%	198	44%	4.60	-0.8	$16
Decline		05 SD	411	65	113	8	38	23	275	258	278	358	428	786	11	86	31	0.90	302	50	22	28	89	8%	146	27%	5.50	11.4	$16
Bats	Left	06 SD	499	80	146	2	44	49	293	292	293	358	393	751	9	88	33	0.84	287	56	19	25	54	2%	164	34%	5.04	8.4	$23
Reliability	51	07 SF	396	61	103	2	23	31	260	156	285	331	364	695	10	83	31	0.64	266	48	21	32	64	2%	162	31%	4.32	-2.8	$13
BAvg Potl	55%	1st Half	156	22	34	2	9	13	218			291	333	624	9	83	25	0.59	264	51	18	30	63	5%	160	38%	3.39	-5.7	$4
LIMA Plan	B	2nd Half	240	39	69	0	14	18	287			357	383	740	10	84	34	0.67	267	46	22	32	64	0%	155	27%	4.92	2.5	$9
+/- Score	-12	08 Proj	419	66	113	3	30	35	270			342	380	722	10	85	31	0.74	278	50	21	29	64	3%	164	32%	4.68	1.6	$16

A 5-point drop in ct% and a .156 BA vs. LH are worrisome at his age, as is a 7-point jump in FB% with no power to back it up. But the wheels keep turning, so he should maintain modest one-category value for another year.

BRANDON KRUSE

Rodriguez,Alex		AB	R	H	HR	RBI	SB	Avg	vL	vR	OB	Slg	OPS	bb%	ct%	h%	Eye	xBA	G	L	F	PX	hr/f	SX	SBO	RC/G	RAR	R$
Pos 5	03 TEX	607	124	181	47	118	17	298	305	295	386	600	986	13	79	31	0.69	320	39	22	39	176	25%	124	11%	7.77	54.9	$36
Age 32	04 NYY	601	112	172	36	106	28	286	311	279	370	512	883	12	78	31	0.61	280	46	16	39	132	20%	117	17%	6.48	26.6	$32
Past Peak	05 NYY	605	124	194	48	130	21	321	300	330	409	610	1019	13	77	35	0.65	308	45	16	40	179	26%	94	13%	8.29	61.9	$41
Bats Right	06 NYY	572	113	166	35	121	15	290	294	289	387	523	909	14	76	33	0.65	279	42	18	40	143	20%	93	10%	6.99	31.9	$29
Reliability 52	07 NYY	583	143	183	54	156	24	314	272	327	410	645	1055	14	79	32	0.79	330	41	17	42	199	28%	98	15%	8.64	65.6	$45
BAvg Potl 50%	1st Half	281	72	93	28	77	9	331			418	694	1112	13	79	34	0.70	349	43	18	39	222	33%	88	12%	9.33	36.0	$23
LIMA Plan C	2nd Half	302	71	90	26	79	15	298			403	599	1002	15	80	30	0.88	312	39	16	45	177	24%	96	16%	8.01	29.5	$22
+/- Score 8	08 Proj	**574**	**127**	**175**	**46**	**136**	**21**	**305**			**400**	**597**	**996**	**14**	**78**	**32**	**0.72**	**309**	**42**	**17**	**41**	**176**	**25%**	**103**	**13%**	**7.98**	**52.6**	**$38**

A season for the ages, but as Reliability score reflects, there's still inconsistency. PX, hr/f keep fluctuating, and as a result, so does xBA. No pattern to SB totals either. Hope for $40 value, know that you could get $30.

Rodriguez,Ivan		AB	R	H	HR	RBI	SB	Avg	vL	vR	OB	Slg	OPS	bb%	ct%	h%	Eye	xBA	G	L	F	PX	hr/f	SX	SBO	RC/G	RAR	R$
Pos 2	03 FLA	511	90	152	16	85	10	297	376	274	366	474	839	10	82	34	0.60	313	47	27	26	116	14%	100	11%	5.95	23.8	$22
Age 36	04 DET	527	72	176	19	86	7	334	343	330	382	510	892	7	83	38	0.45	291	45	22	33	108	13%	71	7%	6.38	28.5	$23
Decline	05 DET	504	71	139	14	50	7	276	294	271	291	444	736	2	82	31	0.12	298	48	22	30	111	11%	112	10%	4.26	3.4	$14
Bats Right	06 DET	547	74	164	13	69	8	300	340	284	332	437	769	5	84	34	0.30	289	50	21	28	83	10%	96	8%	4.77	5.5	$17
Reliability 69	07 DET	502	50	141	11	63	2	281	302	274	294	420	714	2	81	33	0.09	279	52	19	28	96	10%	60	4%	3.97	-0.8	$11
BAvg Potl 40%	1st Half	260	31	74	7	42	0	285			295	446	742	2	85	31	0.11	295	54	17	29	106	11%	51	4%	4.29	2.0	$7
LIMA Plan D	2nd Half	242	19	67	4	21	2	277			291	393	684	2	76	35	0.09	261	51	22	27	84	8%	72	4%	3.63	-2.7	$4
+/- Score -26	08 Proj	**494**	**53**	**134**	**9**	**55**	**2**	**271**			**295**	**395**	**690**	**3**	**81**	**32**	**0.18**	**276**	**50**	**21**	**29**	**85**	**8%**	**63**	**4%**	**3.78**	**-5.1**	**$10**

Fell just below replacement level for the first time in his career. PX bounced back, but hr/f shows that it was doubles, not HR. GB% keeps going up, speed, Eye keep going down. And 2H says it could get worse.

Rodriguez,Luis		AB	R	H	HR	RBI	SB	Avg	vL	vR	OB	Slg	OPS	bb%	ct%	h%	Eye	xBA	G	L	F	PX	hr/f	SX	SBO	RC/G	RAR	R$
Pos 54	03 aaa	199	18	40	2	8	2	201			264	271	535	8	78	25	0.40					48		76	4%	2.05	-14.5	($0)
Age 27	04 aaa	486	56	116	4	40	3	239			300	326	626	8	90	26	0.89					59		56	4%	3.57	-20.7	$5
Peak	05 MIN	* 305	34	79	3	34	2	260	233	276	328	358	686	9	88	29	0.84	271	43	21	36	66	3%	62	6%	4.25	-2.3	$5
Bats Both	06 MIN	115	11	27	2	6	0	235	250	231	318	322	640	11	86	26	0.88	244	46	19	34	53	6%	19	0%	3.68	-4.6	$1
Reliability 21	07 MIN	155	18	34	2	12	1	219	226	218	275	303	579	7	91	23	0.86	253	54	13	34	49	4%	72	3%	2.99	-7.2	$1
BAvg Potl 80%	1st Half	79	8	14	1	5	0	177			253	241	493	9	94	18	1.60	227	50	12	38	37	4%	31	0%	2.30	-5.6	($1)
LIMA Plan F	2nd Half	76	10	20	1	7	1	263			300	368	668	5	88	29	0.44	270	58	13	29	63	5%	95	5%	3.76	-1.6	$1
+/- Score 41	08 Proj	**129**	**14**	**30**	**2**	**10**	**1**	**233**			**295**	**326**	**622**	**8**	**88**	**25**	**0.76**	**258**	**51**	**15**	**33**	**57**	**4%**	**70**	**3%**	**3.43**	**-4.7**	**$1**

With this skill set, how did he manage to coax 445 AB out of MIN over 3 years? Is he related to the team owner? Does he have indiscreet 8x10s of Ron Gardenhire? Did he make a blood pact with Satan?

Rolen,Scott		AB	R	H	HR	RBI	SB	Avg	vL	vR	OB	Slg	OPS	bb%	ct%	h%	Eye	xBA	G	L	F	PX	hr/f	SX	SBO	RC/G	RAR	R$
Pos 5	03 STL	559	98	160	28	104	13	286	283	287	378	528	905	13	81	31	0.79	313	33	25	42	157	15%	94	10%	6.89	41.5	$27
Age 33	04 STL	500	109	157	34	124	4	314	371	302	400	598	998	13	82	33	0.78	305	30	21	49	164	17%	92	4%	7.93	38.9	$31
Past Peak	05 STL	196	28	46	5	28	1	235	237	234	321	383	704	11	86	25	0.89	280	35	23	42	95	7%	70	6%	4.47	-1.9	$4
Bats Right	06 STL	521	94	154	22	95	7	296	259	310	364	518	882	10	87	31	0.81	301	33	20	48	133	10%	77	8%	6.42	13.6	$23
Reliability 10	07 STL	392	55	104	8	58	5	265	204	287	329	398	727	9	86	29	0.66	265	38	20	42	85	6%	81	7%	4.59	-2.2	$10
BAvg Potl 55%	1st Half	220	28	59	4	30	4	268			343	386	729	10	85	30	0.76	255	40	18	42	76	5%	72	9%	4.70	-0.5	$6
LIMA Plan C+	2nd Half	172	27	45	4	28	1	262			310	413	723	7	87	28	0.52	278	35	21	44	95	6%	79	5%	4.43	-1.7	$5
+/- Score -8	08 Proj	**462**	**73**	**130**	**16**	**76**	**5**	**281**			**349**	**467**	**816**	**9**	**86**	**30**	**0.72**	**287**	**35**	**21**	**44**	**114**	**9%**	**76**	**7%**	**5.63**	**9.1**	**$17**

Injuries have sapped his power, but other skills have remained intact. If September surgery finally fixed his problematic left shoulder, he could repeat '05 performance. Still, heed age and Reliability; bid cautiously.

Rollins,Jimmy		AB	R	H	HR	RBI	SB	Avg	vL	vR	OB	Slg	OPS	bb%	ct%	h%	Eye	xBA	G	L	F	PX	hr/f	SX	SBO	RC/G	RAR	R$
Pos 6	03 PHI	628	85	165	8	62	20	263	262	263	321	387	708	8	82	31	0.48	280	39	27	34	87	5%	119	20%	4.33	4.1	$17
Age 29	04 PHI	657	119	190	14	73	30	289	303	285	346	455	801	8	89	31	0.78	299	43	21	36	96	7%	157	22%	5.49	25.3	$27
Peak	05 PHI	677	115	196	12	54	41	290	278	292	336	431	767	6	90	31	0.66	303	44	24	32	85	6%	166	26%	5.01	20.0	$29
Bats Both	06 PHI	689	127	191	25	83	36	277	277	277	332	478	810	8	88	28	0.71	306	44	19	37	111	11%	149	24%	5.49	22.2	$30
Reliability 88	07 PHI	716	139	212	30	94	41	296	321	286	341	531	872	6	88	30	0.58	300	36	20	44	124	11%	169	27%	6.10	42.9	$37
BAvg Potl 50%	1st Half	336	62	95	13	45	14	283			323	506	829	6	87	29	0.45	291	34	20	45	121	10%	156	23%	5.57	15.5	$15
LIMA Plan C	2nd Half	380	77	117	17	49	27	308			357	553	910	7	89	31	0.71	308	37	20	43	127	12%	170	31%	6.56	27.2	$22
+/- Score 6	08 Proj	**675**	**125**	**198**	**26**	**85**	**38**	**293**			**342**	**510**	**852**	**7**	**88**	**30**	**0.63**	**306**	**40**	**21**	**40**	**118**	**11%**	**167**	**26%**	**5.91**	**34.7**	**$33**

Carried his 2006 2H power breakout over to a full season, and the results were fantastic. With all other skills holding stable, this looks like it may be his peak. Huge AB total makes R$ tough to repeat.

Ross,Cody		AB	R	H	HR	RBI	SB	Avg	vL	vR	OB	Slg	OPS	bb%	ct%	h%	Eye	xBA	G	L	F	PX	hr/f	SX	SBO	RC/G	RAR	R$
Pos 8	03 aaa	470	75	132	17	61	15	281			328	494	822	6	84	30	0.44					128		139	20%	5.55	9.3	$19
Age 27	04 aaa	238	30	52	10	34	1	218			256	408	664	5	87	21	0.39					107		71	3%	3.58	-8.1	$4
Peak	05 aaa	388	49	78	14	40	3	201			258	353	611	7	83	21	0.45					92		71	8%	2.99	-17.5	$5
Bats Right	06 2NL	* 319	45	78	16	52	1	244	245	216	317	447	764	10	76	27	0.45	264	36	21	43	122	15%	59	5%	4.91	4.5	$9
Reliability 2	07 FLA	173	35	58	12	39	2	335	385	306	404	653	1057	10	78	37	0.53	339	41	21	38	211	23%	59	4%	8.71	18.7	$11
BAvg Potl 40%	1st Half	53	12	16	4	14	1	302			383	642	1025	12	74	34	0.50	346	46	23	31	237	33%	67	8%	8.59	5.8	$3
LIMA Plan D+	2nd Half	120	23	42	8	25	1	350			414	658	1072	10	80	39	0.54	335	39	20	41	200	20%	48	3%	8.77	12.9	$8
+/- Score -0	08 Proj	**254**	**43**	**70**	**13**	**47**	**3**	**276**			**343**	**521**	**864**	**9**	**79**	**30**	**0.48**	**304**	**40**	**21**	**39**	**158**	**17%**	**76**	**6%**	**6.19**	**11.9**	**$11**

PRO: bb% growth, strong xBA, .974 OPS, 226 PX vs RH in '07. CON: PX, hr/f and xBA likely to regress, career 1.009 OPS vs. LH, .720 vs RH, role uncertainty. Verdict: Power upside is worth a flyer.

Ross,Dave		AB	R	H	HR	RBI	SB	Avg	vL	vR	OB	Slg	OPS	bb%	ct%	h%	Eye	xBA	G	L	F	PX	hr/f	SX	SBO	RC/G	RAR	R$
Pos 2	03 LA	* 210	28	48	14	30	0	229	258	258	302	476	778	9	69	26	0.34	262	33	18	49	172	20%	28	4%	5.17	5.6	$6
Age 31	04 LA	165	13	28	5	15	0	170	125	198	239	291	530	8	62	23	0.24	176	33	15	52	87	9%	42	0%	1.68	-11.5	($1)
Past Peak	05 2NL	125	11	30	3	15	0	240	200	253	275	392	667	5	78	29	0.21	243	38	15	47	108	7%	52	0%	3.56	-0.9	$2
Bats Right	06 CIN	247	37	63	21	52	0	255	316	228	352	579	931	13	70	28	0.49	287	32	17	51	211	24%	34	0%	7.44	22.4	$10
Reliability 6	07 CIN	311	32	63	17	39	0	203	248	175	273	399	671	9	70	29	0.33	238	34	19	48	129	16%	14	0%	3.61	-1.7	$4
BAvg Potl 55%	1st Half	182	19	36	11	28	0	198			255	390	645	7	66	23	0.23	221	36	18	46	126	20%	15	0%	3.18	-3.5	$3
LIMA Plan D	2nd Half	129	13	27	6	11	0	209			297	411	707	11	77	23	0.53	262	33	18	49	133	12%	13	0%	4.27	1.9	$1
+/- Score -15	08 Proj	**335**	**38**	**79**	**19**	**46**	**0**	**236**			**309**	**457**	**766**	**10**	**72**	**27**	**0.38**	**253**	**34**	**17**	**49**	**146**	**16%**	**32**	**0%**	**4.98**	**10.3**	**$8**

Failed to match '06 power and everything fell apart. PX, xBA comparison shows how BA is entirely dependent upon power, due to poor ct%. Hit .258 with the Dodgers in '03; that might be as high as he ever gets.

Rowand,Aaron		AB	R	H	HR	RBI	SB	Avg	vL	vR	OB	Slg	OPS	bb%	ct%	h%	Eye	xBA	G	L	F	PX	hr/f	SX	SBO	RC/G	RAR	R$
Pos 8	03 CHW	* 277	35	71	9	35	0	256	338	250	299	412	711	6	89	26	0.55	308	43	25	32	93	11%	31	0%	4.23	-4.2	$6
Age 30	04 CHW	487	94	151	24	69	17	310	302	315	350	544	894	6	81	34	0.33	309	46	19	35	145	17%	120	19%	6.32	21.5	$25
Peak	05 CHW	578	77	156	13	69	16	270	303	259	308	407	715	5	80	32	0.28	281	52	21	28	92	10%	119	15%	4.18	-1.7	$17
Bats Right	06 PHI	405	59	106	12	47	10	262	222	275	293	425	718	4	81	30	0.24	282	44	22	34	101	11%	110	16%	4.15	-3.5	$12
Reliability 25	07 PHI	612	105	189	27	89	6	309	315	306	358	515	873	7	81	35	0.39	293	43	20	38	133	15%	65	5%	6.15	26.5	$26
BAvg Potl 35%	1st Half	283	47	89	10	40	5	314			374	481	855	9	84	34	0.61	290	43	21	36	103	12%	69	7%	6.01	11.1	$12
LIMA Plan C	2nd Half	329	58	100	17	49	1	304			344	544	888	6	77	35	0.27	296	43	18	39	162	17%	50	4%	6.33	16.0	$14
+/- Score -25	08 Proj	**541**	**86**	**156**	**20**	**72**	**9**	**288**			**330**	**475**	**805**	**6**	**81**	**33**	**0.33**	**290**	**45**	**20**	**35**	**119**	**13%**	**92**	**10%**	**5.27**	**10.8**	**$20**

Let 'er rip in 2H, perhaps eyeing all that free agent cash. Power returned to '04 levels, but history questions his ability to sustain it. Needs to re-start running game to offset potential losses from HR and AB totals.

Ruiz,Carlos		AB	R	H	HR	RBI	SB	Avg	vL	vR	OB	Slg	OPS	bb%	ct%	h%	Eye	xBA	G	L	F	PX	hr/f	SX	SBO	RC/G	RAR	R$
Pos 2	03 aa	169	17	38	2	12	1	225			266	292	558	5	92	24	0.69					42		50	5%	2.67	-7.9	$1
Age 29	04 aa	349	33	77	12	37	6	222			256	361	617	4	89	22	0.44					74		72	16%	3.10	-10.5	$5
Peak	05 aaa	339	37	89	4	30	3	263			307	401	707	6	89	29	0.56					85		99	11%	4.34	4.4	$6
Bats Right	06 PHI	* 437	58	126	20	76	4	289	263	260	354	488	842	9	85	30	0.68	297	47	19	34	113	16%	53	5%	5.85	18.5	$17
Reliability 23	07 PHI	374	42	97	6	54	6	259	189	282	334	396	730	10	87	30	0.86	284	46	18	36	91	5%	81	7%	4.79	10.9	$8
BAvg Potl 65%	1st Half	180	24	50	3	26	2	278			333	411	744	8	85	31	0.56	287	48	20	32	94	6%	56	6%	4.76	5.0	$5
LIMA Plan C	2nd Half	194	18	47	3	28	4	242			335	381	716	12	89	26	1.23	279	44	17	39	88	4%	84	7%	4.81	5.9	$4
+/- Score 5	08 Proj	**392**	**45**	**107**	**11**	**54**	**5**	**273**			**337**	**440**	**778**	**9**	**87**	**29**	**0.76**	**292**	**46**	**18**	**36**	**101**	**9%**	**78**	**7%**	**5.20**	**14.1**	**$11**

Minor-league PX has yet to translate into major-league HR. However, FB% and Eye growth are good signs, and he did hit a lot of doubles. xBA indicates that there's some BA upside. Give him another chance.

BRANDON KRUSE

Ryan,Brendan

			AB	R	H	HR	RBI	SB	Avg	vL	vR	OB	Slg	OPS	bb%	ct%	h%	Eye	xBA	G	L	F	PX	hr/f	SX	SBO	RC/G	RAR	R$
Pos	65	03	0	0	0	0	0	0	0							0									0				
Age	26	04	0	0	0	0	0	0	0							0									0				
Pre-Peak		05 aa	154	20	35	1	7	4	227			277	302	579	6	91	24	0.74					50		110	11%	2.97	-6.0	$2
Bats	Right	06 a/a	69	9	15	1	8	1	217			250	275	525	4	86	24	0.30					32		76	13%	1.92	-5.3	$1
Reliability	4	07 STL	* 501	71	120	5	23	20	240	354	238	288	311	599	6	89	26	0.64	258	47	19	34	42	3%	120	20%	3.10	-13.1	$9
BAvg Potl	65%	1st Half	279	38	65	2	15	10	233			275	297	572	5	89	26	0.53	229	52	10	38	36	2%	120	23%	2.74	-10.5	$4
LIMA Plan	D	2nd Half	222	33	55	3	8	10	248			304	329	633	7	90	27	0.78	269	46	20	34	51	4%	103	16%	3.54	-2.8	$5
+/- Score	18	08 Proj	**262**	**36**	**66**	**2**	**11**	**9**	**252**			**301**	**325**	**626**	**7**	**90**	**27**	**0.70**	**264**	**47**	**19**	**34**	**46**	**3%**	**109**	**15%**	**3.43**	**-5.0**	**$5**

4-12-.289 in 180 AB at STL. Solid base skills in MLB debut. Showed some SB upside too. But as a GB hitter with a PX that's MIA, he's unlikely to develop into a MLB regular. Murdered LHPs in 79 AB.

Salazar,Jeff

			AB	R	H	HR	RBI	SB	Avg	vL	vR	OB	Slg	OPS	bb%	ct%	h%	Eye	xBA	G	L	F	PX	hr/f	SX	SBO	RC/G	RAR	R$
Pos	9	03	0	0	0	0	0	0	0							0									0				
Age	27	04 aa	224	33	48	1	15	9	212			300	299	599	11	88	24	1.09					57		122	19%	3.43	-11.0	$3
Peak		05 a/a	497	59	117	8	40	11	236			308	353	661	9	85	26	0.71					77		89	18%	3.89	-16.7	$8
Bats	Left	06 COL	* 381	59	96	8	37	11	252		294	331	390	721	10	84	28	0.73	247	32	21	47	79	5%	120	15%	4.62	-1.8	$9
Reliability	36	07 ARI	* 494	68	124	9	59	14	252	300	274	321	402	724	9	85	28	0.71	278	35	24	41	93	5%	125	15%	4.65	-8.8	$12
BAvg Potl	60%	1st Half	300	49	87	7	39	10	290			362	463	826	10	88	31	0.92					103		122	17%	5.90	5.5	$11
LIMA Plan	D	2nd Half	194	19	37	2	20	4	192			257	308	565	8	82	23	0.48	256	35	24	41	77	3%	111	12%	2.63	-16.1	$1
+/- Score	25	08 Proj	**158**	**21**	**41**	**2**	**16**	**7**	**259**			**330**	**388**	**719**	**10**	**85**	**29**	**0.70**	**265**	**34**	**24**	**42**	**81**	**4%**	**119**	**21%**	**4.58**	**-2.7**	**$4**

1-10-.277 in 94 AB at ARI. Decent base skills and SX could make him a hidden SB source. But at age 27 and with no outstanding offensive skills otherwise, his window of opportunity will close fast.

Saltalamacchia,Jar

			AB	R	H	HR	RBI	SB	Avg	vL	vR	OB	Slg	OPS	bb%	ct%	h%	Eye	xBA	G	L	F	PX	hr/f	SX	SBO	RC/G	RAR	R$
Pos	23	03	0	0	0	0	0	0	0							0									0				
Age	23	04	0	0	0	0	0	0	0							0									0				
Growth		05	0	0	0	0	0	0	0							0									0				
Bats	Both	06 aa	313	29	69	8	38	0	220			335	358	693	15	78	26	0.78					91		30	1%	4.36	-0.2	$3
Reliability	0	07 2TM	* 389	55	105	16	44	2	270	226	290	322	450	772	7	77	31	0.33	262	44	17	39	118	14%	62	2%	4.92	11.3	$11
BAvg Potl	40%	1st Half	164	26	50	9	21	2	305			367	537	903	9	80	33	0.50	285	26	21	53	146	13%	53	4%	6.58	12.0	$7
LIMA Plan	D+	2nd Half	225	29	55	7	23	0	244			289	387	675	6	74	30	0.24	240	51	15	34	96	12%	53	0%	3.65	-1.7	$4
+/- Score	6	08 Proj	**476**	**58**	**123**	**19**	**55**	**1**	**258**			**334**	**432**	**766**	**10**	**77**	**30**	**0.50**	**258**	**44**	**17**	**39**	**114**	**13%**	**46**	**2%**	**5.01**	**13.4**	**$11**

11-33-.266 in 308 AB at ATL and TEX. Mid-season trade to TEX didn't light a fire in his bat. But his power upside is huge, and playing in Arlington will only help. Remains a top keeper league investment.

Sanchez,Freddy

			AB	R	H	HR	RBI	SB	Avg	vL	vR	OB	Slg	OPS	bb%	ct%	h%	Eye	xBA	G	L	F	PX	hr/f	SX	SBO	RC/G	RAR	R$
Pos	4	03 aaa	216	40	68	4	21	7	315			388	449	838	11	87	35	0.90					92		93	10%	6.04	10.3	$9
Age	30	04 PIT	* 144	10	32	1	11	3	222		176	263	306	569	5	90	24	0.53	269	63	13	25	53	3%	78	13%	2.75	-8.3	$1
Peak		05 PIT	453	54	132	5	35	2	291	326	278	331	400	731	6	92	31	0.75	300	46	23	31	68	4%	73	3%	4.60	0.5	$11
Bats	Right	06 PIT	582	85	200	6	85	3	344	442	316	377	473	849	5	91	37	0.60	311	37	28	36	85	3%	60	3%	5.85	18.8	$23
Reliability	29	07 PIT	602	77	183	11	81	0	304	364	282	339	442	781	5	87	33	0.42	286	39	22	39	88	5%	49	1%	5.02	7.6	$17
BAvg Potl	45%	1st Half	279	26	83	1	25	0	297			326	369	696	4	89	33	0.38	259	43	21	36	51	1%	37	0%	4.03	-4.1	$5
LIMA Plan	C	2nd Half	323	51	100	10	56	0	310			350	505	854	6	86	33	0.45	307	36	24	40	121	9%	67	1%	5.89	11.7	$12
+/- Score	-36	08 Proj	**591**	**79**	**173**	**16**	**85**	**1**	**293**			**331**	**461**	**793**	**5**	**89**	**31**	**0.53**	**299**	**39**	**22**	**39**	**101**	**8%**	**56**	**2%**	**5.17**	**10.0**	**$18**

Dialed it up a notch in 2nd half. Why 20 HR might not be a reach...
- Rising FB and PX trends
- 140+ PX in Aug and Sept

Just be wary of a BA decline given his ct% and Eye trends.

Sanders,Reggie

			AB	R	H	HR	RBI	SB	Avg	vL	vR	OB	Slg	OPS	bb%	ct%	h%	Eye	xBA	G	L	F	PX	hr/f	SX	SBO	RC/G	RAR	R$
Pos	7	03 PIT	453	74	129	31	87	15	285	301	278	340	567	907	8	76	31	0.35	306	37	23	40	180	22%	120	19%	6.67	13.9	$25
Age	40	04 STL	446	64	116	22	67	21	260	230	270	311	482	793	7	74	31	0.28	274	37	22	40	147	17%	126	27%	5.25	-2.4	$19
Decline		05 STL	295	49	80	21	54	14	271	245	281	334	546	880	9	75	30	0.37	281	36	14	50	176	19%	126	21%	6.35	8.6	$17
Bats	Right	06 KC	325	45	80	11	49	7	246	268	237	306	425	731	8	74	30	0.33	261	43	19	39	127	12%	85	19%	4.54	-6.4	$8
Reliability	0	07 KC	73	12	23	2	11	0	315	346	298	405	493	898	13	79	38	0.73	281	40	19	41	133	8%	37	4%	6.96	4.5	$3
BAvg Potl	35%	1st Half	49	6	18	2	8	0	367			436	612	1049	11	78	44	0.55	311	34	21	45	183	12%	25	6%	8.81	5.1	$2
LIMA Plan	D	2nd Half	24	6	5	0	3	0	208			345	250	595	17	83	25	1.25	223	50	15	35	37	0%	63	0%	3.48	-0.9	$0
+/- Score	-62	08 Proj	**217**	**32**	**57**	**8**	**35**	**2**	**263**			**319**	**446**	**765**	**8**	**74**	**32**	**0.32**	**261**	**39**	**20**	**42**	**128**	**12%**	**76**	**9%**	**4.95**	**0.4**	**$7**

Hamstring woes cost him most of the season. Still can provide some pop in bursts, but his playing days are numbered. He won't turn into a new player at age 40, just an even more brittle one. But a good end-game pick.

Santiago,Ramon

			AB	R	H	HR	RBI	SB	Avg	vL	vR	OB	Slg	OPS	bb%	ct%	h%	Eye	xBA	G	L	F	PX	hr/f	SX	SBO	RC/G	RAR	R$
Pos	6	03 DET	444	41	100	2	29	10	225			279	284	563	7	85	26	0.50					43		82	13%	2.59	-25.1	$4
Age	28	04 SEA	* 282	37	48	1	22	7	169			233	218	451	8	90	19	0.81					29		114	23%	1.58	-27.2	($0)
Peak		05 aaa	441	54	93	8	40	15	211			265	315	579	7	88	23	0.59					64		108	23%	2.82	-20.1	$7
Bats	Both	06 DET	* 163	20	37	1	14	3	227			267	294	562	5	80	28	0.27	241	58	15	27	47	3%	97	11%	2.32	-10.4	$1
Reliability	26	07 DET	* 432	44	104	3	33	10	241	300	281	266	333	600	3	84	28	0.22	268	39	26	35	63	2%	106	21%	2.81	-23.1	$5
BAvg Potl	50%	1st Half	316	33	81	3	26	6	256			284	354	638	4	85	29	0.25					64		95	21%	3.27	-12.3	$5
LIMA Plan	F	2nd Half	116	11	23	0	7	4	198			218	276	494	3	83	24	0.15	261	39	26	35	61	0%	119	22%	1.54	-11.0	$0
+/- Score	7	08 Proj	**167**	**18**	**40**	**1**	**13**	**4**	**240**			**274**	**319**	**593**	**5**	**84**	**28**	**0.29**	**260**	**47**	**22**	**32**	**56**	**2%**	**96**	**17%**	**2.77**	**-8.8**	**$2**

0-7-.284 in 67 AB at DET. A poor man's Esix Snead but without as much speed. He'll keep riding the MLB-AAA train if he can't produce an OPS above .600.

Schierholtz,Nathan

			AB	R	H	HR	RBI	SB	Avg	vL	vR	OB	Slg	OPS	bb%	ct%	h%	Eye	xBA	G	L	F	PX	hr/f	SX	SBO	RC/G	RAR	R$
Pos	9	03	0	0	0	0	0	0	0							0									0				
Age	24	04	0	0	0	0	0	0	0							0									0				
Growth		05	0	0	0	0	0	0	0							0									0				
Bats	Left	06 aa	470	56	127	14	55	8	270			310	445	755	5	83	30	0.33					103		108	10%	4.68	-7.3	$12
Reliability	0	07 SF	* 523	63	156	12	65	11	299	500	266	319	463	782	3	87	33	0.23	277	44	15	41	97	6%	114	14%	4.89	-5.3	$17
BAvg Potl	40%	1st Half	260	33	84	3	31	5	323			343	458	801	3	89	35	0.29	285	53	13	34	87	4%	107	8%	5.16	-0.6	$9
LIMA Plan	D	2nd Half	263	30	72	9	34	6	275			295	467	762	3	85	30	0.19	274	40	16	44	109	9%	112	22%	4.62	-4.9	$8
+/- Score	1	08 Proj	**202**	**24**	**55**	**5**	**25**	**4**	**272**			**301**	**440**	**741**	**4**	**85**	**30**	**0.27**	**272**	**43**	**15**	**42**	**100**	**7%**	**107**	**14%**	**4.46**	**-4.1**	**$6**

0-10-.304 in 112 AB at SF. Managed a .300 BA with SF despite a 2% bb%. A ditty:
A little pop / a little speed,
A batting eye / is all you need.

Burma Shave.

Schneider,Brian

			AB	R	H	HR	RBI	SB	Avg	vL	vR	OB	Slg	OPS	bb%	ct%	h%	Eye	xBA	G	L	F	PX	hr/f	SX	SBO	RC/G	RAR	R$
Pos	2	03 MON	335	34	77	9	46	0	230	179	243	306	394	700	10	78	27	0.50	272	51	18	32	118	11%	39	3%	4.26	-0.4	$5
Age	31	04 MON	436	40	112	12	49	0	257	244	260	322	399	721	9	86	28	0.67	277	49	20	32	83	10%	42	1%	4.49	8.7	$8
Past Peak		05 WAS	369	38	99	10	44	1	268	265	269	322	409	731	7	87	29	0.60	287	47	21	33	88	10%	46	1%	4.53	7.8	$9
Bats	Left	06 WAS	410	30	105	4	55	2	256	271	251	319	329	648	8	84	30	0.57	255	47	23	30	50	4%	28	3%	3.62	-8.7	$6
Reliability	58	07 WAS	408	33	96	6	54	0	235	212	244	328	336	663	12	86	26	1.00	241	48	15	36	66	5%	23	0%	4.08	3.5	$4
BAvg Potl	65%	1st Half	230	18	57	4	31	0	248			319	339	658	9	86	27	0.75	221	53	14	33	57	6%	13	0%	3.81	0.2	$3
LIMA Plan	D	2nd Half	178	15	39	2	23	0	219			338	331	670	15	87	24	1.33	256	42	17	40	76	3%	33	0%	4.38	3.2	$1
+/- Score	11	08 Proj	**407**	**34**	**106**	**7**	**53**	**1**	**260**			**339**	**368**	**706**	**11**	**85**	**29**	**0.81**	**258**	**47**	**19**	**34**	**70**	**5%**	**32**	**1%**	**4.47**	**6.1**	**$7**

End results weren't pretty, but 2nd half gave a glimmer of hope (despite .219 BA). If he can build on 2H BPI surge and regain some of his lost power skilll s, bat could re-emerge. Still a good $1 end-gamer.

Schumaker,Skip

			AB	R	H	HR	RBI	SB	Avg	vL	vR	OB	Slg	OPS	bb%	ct%	h%	Eye	xBA	G	L	F	PX	hr/f	SX	SBO	RC/G	RAR	R$
Pos	97	03 aa	342	39	79	2	19	6	230			301	312	613	9	85	27	0.66					59		83	13%	3.32	-21.7	$3
Age	28	04 aa	516	62	140	3	34	15	271			333	350	683	9	90	30	0.90					52		89	20%	4.22	-11.8	$11
Peak		05 aaa	440	51	111	4	26	10	252			290	340	630	5	90	27	0.55					59		97	13%	3.41	-20.4	$7
Bats	Left	06 aaa	369	42	104	3	23	10	281			319	350	668	5	88	31	0.46					42		94	13%	3.75	-15.4	$8
Reliability	28	07 STL	* 409	42	111	6	40	3	272	375	327	317	385	702	6	86	30	0.48	279	54	19	27	73	6%	53	7%	4.18	-12.7	$8
BAvg Potl	50%	1st Half	169	15	44	4	15	1	260			317	379	696	8	88	28	0.70	271	50	19	31	72	9%	30	7%	4.17	-5.4	$3
LIMA Plan	F	2nd Half	240	27	67	2	25	2	280			318	389	707	5	85	32	0.36	282	55	19	26	75	4%	71	7%	4.18	-7.3	$5
+/- Score	-5	08 Proj	**132**	**14**	**36**	**1**	**10**	**2**	**273**			**317**	**375**	**691**	**6**	**87**	**30**	**0.51**	**281**	**54**	**19**	**27**	**65**	**5%**	**80**	**10%**	**4.08**	**-4.1**	**$3**

2-19-.333 in 177 AB at STL. Great glove, but zero power and below average speed. Only strength is a BA that won't hurt you. It won't help much either but at least it won't hurt. Much.

STEPHEN NICKRAND

Scott,Luke			AB	R	H	HR	RBI	SB	Avg	vL	vR	OB	Slg	OPS	bb%	ct%	h%	Eye	xBA	G	L	F	PX	hr/f	SX	SBO	RC/G	RAR	R$
Pos	9	03 aa	183	17	43	6	31	0	235			271	410	681	5	79	27	0.24					117		48	3%	3.71	-9.2	$3
Age	29	04 aa	208	31	49	14	44	0	236			312	500	812	10	81	23	0.59					155		33	4%	5.45	2.9	$7
Peak		05 HOU	* 478	56	110	23	67	3	230	286	178	287	446	733	7	79	24	0.39	267	43	11	46	134	13%	82	6%	4.44	-11.8	$12
Bats	Left	06 HOU	* 532	79	153	26	85	7	287	240	366	369	517	887	11	81	31	0.68	297	36	24	40	133	15%	95	5%	6.58	27.1	$21
Reliability	18	07 HOU	369	49	94	18	64	3	255	271	252	348	504	852	13	74	30	0.56	290	41	19	40	167	16%	88	4%	6.36	12.1	$12
BAvg Potl	50%	1st Half	197	23	48	9	35	1	244			332	472	804	12	78	27	0.60	289	43	17	39	147	15%	66	4%	5.60	2.1	$5
LIMA Plan	B	2nd Half	172	26	46	9	29	2	267			367	541	908	14	70	33	0.52	289	38	20	42	194	18%	97	4%	7.38	10.5	$6
+/- Score	9	08 Proj	**462**	**63**	**125**	**23**	**77**	**4**	**271**			**352**	**511**	**863**	**11**	**77**	**31**	**0.54**	**290**	**40**	**20**	**41**	**153**	**16%**	**88**	**5%**	**6.35**	**15.9**	**$16**

Four straight years with a 130+ PX, and a 2nd half elite level that foretells a major power surge. Good ct% also bodes well for a BA rebound. Don't be frugal here.
UP: 30 HR, .300 BA

Scutaro,Marco			AB	R	H	HR	RBI	SB	Avg	vL	vR	OB	Slg	OPS	bb%	ct%	h%	Eye	xBA	G	L	F	PX	hr/f	SX	SBO	RC/G	RAR	R$
Pos	65	03 NYM	* 319	46	83	10	34	12	260	95	259	344	426	771	11	85	28	0.85	262	46	10	44	103	8%	101	20%	5.22	10.6	$11
Age	32	04 OAK	455	50	124	7	43	0	273	276	271	297	393	691	3	87	30	0.28	276	43	20	36	80	5%	41	0%	3.89	-7.4	$8
Past Peak		05 OAK	381	48	94	9	37	5	247	171	262	312	391	703	9	87	26	0.75	288	43	21	36	90	7%	89	7%	4.34	-2.4	$8
Bats	Right	06 OAK	365	52	97	5	41	5	266	218	279	354	397	751	12	82	31	0.76	268	44	21	36	84	5%	111	5%	5.11	7.3	$8
Reliability	48	07 OAK	338	49	88	7	41	2	260	309	245	330	361	691	9	88	28	0.88	258	39	20	41	62	6%	53	3%	4.23	-3.3	$7
BAvg Potl	60%	1st Half	116	16	28	4	11	1	241			285	371	655	6	86	25	0.44	264	43	19	38	73	11%	57	4%	3.47	-3.8	$2
LIMA Plan	D	2nd Half	222	33	60	3	30	1	270			352	356	708	11	89	29	1.17	256	38	21	42	56	4%	46	3%	4.61	0.3	$5
+/- Score	-32	08 Proj	**317**	**44**	**82**	**6**	**36**	**3**	**259**			**329**	**379**	**709**	**10**	**86**	**28**	**0.76**	**267**	**41**	**20**	**38**	**75**	**6%**	**80**	**5%**	**4.43**	**-0.7**	**$7**

If we ignore the small year to year fluctuations, what you see is what you get: a handful of HR, a handful of SB, and a BA liability. In short, roster worthy only in the deepest of leagues.

Sexson,Richie			AB	R	H	HR	RBI	SB	Avg	vL	vR	OB	Slg	OPS	bb%	ct%	h%	Eye	xBA	G	L	F	PX	hr/f	SX	SBO	RC/G	RAR	R$
Pos	3	03 MIL	606	97	165	45	124	2	272	279	271	374	548	921	14	75	29	0.65	302	47	19	34	173	29%	48	3%	7.13	28.1	$28
Age	33	04 ARI	90	20	21	9	23	0	233	222	236	337	578	914	13	77	20	0.67	318	48	14	38	201	35%	44	0%	6.81	2.3	$5
Past Peak		05 SEA	558	99	147	39	121	1	263	333	244	365	541	906	14	70	31	0.53	292	40	19	41	197	25%	48	1%	7.16	33.5	$25
Bats	Right	06 SEA	591	75	156	34	107	1	264	204	282	336	504	840	10	74	30	0.42	278	42	18	40	160	19%	28	1%	5.97	9.4	$19
Reliability	37	07 SEA	434	58	89	21	63	1	205	238	195	289	399	687	11	77	22	0.51	264	47	15	38	127	17%	42	1%	3.95	-15.4	$8
BAvg Potl	65%	1st Half	258	38	54	15	46	0	209			289	434	723	10	78	21	0.51	275	47	14	38	143	19%	32	0%	4.36	-5.8	$6
LIMA Plan	C	2nd Half	176	20	35	6	17	1	199			288	347	634	11	76	23	0.51	244	48	16	37	102	12%	41	2%	3.33	-9.7	$1
+/- Score	43	08 Proj	**519**	**72**	**137**	**25**	**85**	**1**	**264**			**347**	**465**	**812**	**11**	**75**	**31**	**0.50**	**265**	**45**	**17**	**38**	**136**	**17%**	**37**	**1%**	**5.66**	**7.2**	**$16**

His power is in a tailspin and nagging injuries have zapped his consistency. Still, buy low. A 22% hit rate means his BA will rebound. You know you can bank at least 20 HRs. Odds are you can get him for under $10.

Shealy,Ryan			AB	R	H	HR	RBI	SB	Avg	vL	vR	OB	Slg	OPS	bb%	ct%	h%	Eye	xBA	G	L	F	PX	hr/f	SX	SBO	RC/G	RAR	R$
Pos	3	03	0	0	0	0	0	0	0							0									0				
Age	28	04 aa	469	68	134	27	77	1	286			350	532	881	9	77	32	0.42					154		60	1%	6.40	12.2	$18
Peak		05 COL	* 498	65	143	21	69	4	286	125	373	336	484	820	7	86	30	0.52	321	45	25	30	121	16%	70	3%	5.47	-1.8	$18
Bats	Right	06 2TM	* 424	58	112	19	76	1	264	185	311	312	472	784	6	81	28	0.37	276	37	18	45	125	12%	61	2%	5.01	-8.6	$13
Reliability	9	07 KC	* 294	28	61	7	38	0	208	125	258	267	319	586	7	72	26	0.29	222	35	21	44	82	7%	23	0%	2.52	-23.5	$2
BAvg Potl	45%	1st Half	179	18	39	3	21	0	218			271	307	578	7	69	30	0.24	207	35	21	44	72	5%	28	0%	2.41	-14.7	$1
LIMA Plan	F	2nd Half	115	10	22	4	17	0	193			260	337	597	8	77	22	0.39					96		14	0%	2.73	-8.6	$1
+/- Score	-12	08 Proj	**222**	**25**	**58**	**8**	**33**	**0**	**261**			**316**	**423**	**739**	**7**	**78**	**30**	**0.36**	**256**	**37**	**20**	**43**	**107**	**11%**	**31**	**1%**	**4.51**	**-4.3**	**$5**

3-21-.221 in 172 AB at KC. Can't hit LHPs. Middling BPIs. Power slide. BA nosediving, etc, etc. In '07, hamstring woes made him unrosterworthy (is that a word?), but he might still have some latent value in '08.

Sheffield,Gary			AB	R	H	HR	RBI	SB	Avg	vL	vR	OB	Slg	OPS	bb%	ct%	h%	Eye	xBA	G	L	F	PX	hr/f	SX	SBO	RC/G	RAR	R$
Pos	0	03 ATL	576	126	190	39	132	18	330	341	327	417	604	1021	13	90	31	1.56	348	47	18	35	149	22%	109	11%	8.08	52.9	$40
Age	39	04 NYY	573	117	166	36	121	5	290	314	282	388	534	922	14	86	29	1.11	302	42	17	41	134	18%	60	6%	7.01	27.7	$28
Decline		05 NYY	584	104	170	34	123	10	291	359	266	375	512	887	12	87	29	1.03	302	42	17	41	125	16%	75	6%	6.47	7.3	$29
Bats	Right	06 NYY	151	22	45	6	25	5	298	344	286	354	450	804	8	89	30	0.81	274	49	15	37	81	12%	73	13%	5.34	-4.6	$6
Reliability	18	07 DET	494	107	131	25	75	22	265	245	271	372	462	834	15	86	27	1.18	284	41	17	42	112	14%	110	16%	6.04	0.3	$23
BAvg Potl	65%	1st Half	277	67	80	17	50	9	289			394	523	917	15	88	28	1.45	306	43	15	42	128	17%	101	13%	7.02	7.9	$15
LIMA Plan	B	2nd Half	217	40	51	8	25	13	235			344	382	726	14	82	25	0.95	257	38	19	44	90	10%	103	20%	4.73	-8.4	$8
+/- Score	17	08 Proj	**403**	**76**	**107**	**18**	**67**	**7**	**266**			**356**	**436**	**792**	**12**	**87**	**27**	**1.05**	**277**	**43**	**17**	**40**	**97**	**12%**	**75**	**8%**	**5.45**	**-6.6**	**$15**

Looked like his vintage self in 1H, then injuries nailed him... again. Off-season shoulder surgery, injury trend in general and unrelenting advancing age cloud his '08 outlook.
DN: 2006 is always possible.

Shoppach,Kelly			AB	R	H	HR	RBI	SB	Avg	vL	vR	OB	Slg	OPS	bb%	ct%	h%	Eye	xBA	G	L	F	PX	hr/f	SX	SBO	RC/G	RAR	R$
Pos	2	03 aa	340	38	88	10	50	0	260			318	442	760	8	78	31	0.39					131		44	0%	4.93	7.3	$8
Age	28	04 aaa	399	50	85	17	52	0	213			280	404	683	8	73	25	0.34					132		30	0%	3.86	-2.6	$6
Peak		05 aaa	370	46	84	19	57	0	227			294	423	716	9	76	25	0.39					127		24	0%	4.22	3.5	$9
Bats	Right	06 CLE	* 188	18	46	6	25	0	247	314	213	298	409	708	7	63	36	0.20	216	43	15	42	137	12%	23	2%	4.51	0.6	$3
Reliability	20	07 CLE	161	26	42	7	30	0	261	265	260	308	472	780	6	65	36	0.20	254	46	15	39	176	17%	41	0%	5.45	6.7	$5
BAvg Potl	25%	1st Half	68	18	26	4	16	0	382			455	676	1131	12	74	48	0.50	318	44	16	40	220	20%	45	0%	10.14	10.1	$5
LIMA Plan	F	2nd Half	93	8	16	3	14	0	172			189	323	512	2	59	25	0.05	205	48	14	38	137	15%	31	0%	1.42	-7.9	$0
+/- Score	-3	08 Proj	**186**	**25**	**47**	**10**	**30**	**0**	**253**			**303**	**476**	**780**	**7**	**67**	**32**	**0.22**	**256**	**46**	**15**	**39**	**172**	**19%**	**31**	**1%**	**5.29**	**6.3**	**$5**

Tiny sample size, but how about that first half? Big-time hacker power. Small-time BA downside (63% contact rate - yikes!). But he just needs an opportunity. An end-game bid could provide big dividends.

Sizemore,Grady			AB	R	H	HR	RBI	SB	Avg	vL	vR	OB	Slg	OPS	bb%	ct%	h%	Eye	xBA	G	L	F	PX	hr/f	SX	SBO	RC/G	RAR	R$
Pos	8	03 aa	496	88	143	12	71	9	288			344	442	785	8	86	31	0.62					91		117	14%	5.22	5.2	$18
Age	25	04 CLE	* 556	74	142	10	65	15	255	178	280	315	381	696	8	84	29	0.53	261	47	16	37	77	6%	111	19%	4.17	-9.1	$13
Pre-Peak		05 CLE	640	111	185	22	81	22	289	245	308	342	484	827	8	79	34	0.39	298	44	24	31	125	14%	145	19%	5.70	25.8	$27
Bats	Left	06 CLE	655	134	190	28	76	22	290	214	329	366	533	898	11	77	34	0.51	281	33	20	47	158	12%	152	16%	6.86	40.6	$28
Reliability	72	07 CLE	628	118	174	24	78	33	277	284	274	377	462	839	14	75	33	0.65	256	33	21	47	125	11%	124	20%	6.22	35.3	$28
BAvg Potl	40%	1st Half	302	65	85	13	36	22	281			378	470	848	13	73	35	0.58	248	33	20	47	128	12%	138	23%	6.34	17.7	$16
LIMA Plan	B+	2nd Half	326	53	89	11	42	11	273			376	454	830	14	77	32	0.73	263	33	21	46	123	10%	98	17%	6.13	17.7	$12
+/- Score	-22	08 Proj	**619**	**114**	**169**	**28**	**76**	**25**	**273**			**357**	**491**	**848**	**12**	**77**	**31**	**0.58**	**278**	**35**	**21**	**44**	**141**	**13%**	**128**	**20%**	**6.17**	**31.6**	**$26**

Got the green light a little more and poof -- 33 SB! He hasn't reached his ceiling yet, which means 30 HR is next. A caveat: His ct% slide is hurting BA, which will further zap PX if not reversed.

Sledge,Terrmel			AB	R	H	HR	RBI	SB	Avg	vL	vR	OB	Slg	OPS	bb%	ct%	h%	Eye	xBA	G	L	F	PX	hr/f	SX	SBO	RC/G	RAR	R$
Pos	7	03 aaa	497	70	139	16	68	10	280			338	445	783	8	86	30	0.61					97		101	12%	5.16	-4.3	$17
Age	31	04 MON	402	46	108	15	63	3	269	241	277	335	460	795	9	84	29	0.61	280	42	18	40	109	11%	81	6%	5.35	-1.1	$12
Past Peak		05 WAS	37	7	9	1	8	2	243		250	364	378	742	16	78	29	0.88	235	35	23	42	69	8%	134	21%	5.04	-0.3	$2
Bats	Left	06 SD	* 437	56	103	17	59	4	237	400	215	316	405	721	10	81	26	0.60	274	53	17	30	96	16%	74	6%	4.46	-10.4	$9
Reliability	0	07 SD	200	22	42	7	23	1	210	111	225	304	360	664	12	70	26	0.45	226	41	17	42	108	12%	33	6%	3.74	-10.0	$2
BAvg Potl	50%	1st Half	143	17	32	6	16	1	224			315	392	706	12	71	27	0.45	238	42	18	40	116	15%	37	5%	4.30	-4.6	$2
LIMA Plan	F	2nd Half	57	5	10	1	7	0	175			277	281	558	12	68	24	0.44	197	38	15	48	87	5%	32	7%	2.31	-5.7	($0)
+/- Score	-27	08 Proj	**250**	**28**	**58**	**8**	**33**	**2**	**232**			**315**	**380**	**695**	**11**	**76**	**28**	**0.50**	**238**	**41**	**17**	**43**	**97**	**10%**	**52**	**6%**	**4.14**	**-9.1**	**$4**

He's shown flashes of skill in the past... .364 OBA (2005), 86% contact rate (2003), 16% walk rate (2005), .280 xBA (2004), 116 PX (1st half 2007), 134 SX (2005)... Assembled, it would be a heckuva player.

Smith,Jason			AB	R	H	HR	RBI	SB	Avg	vL	vR	OB	Slg	OPS	bb%	ct%	h%	Eye	xBA	G	L	F	PX	hr/f	SX	SBO	RC/G	RAR	R$
Pos	6	03 aaa	515	65	135	13	61	12	262			276	425	701	2	77	32	0.08					100		135	22%	3.86	-6.2	$14
Age	30	04 DET	* 277	35	66	7	29	5	238	242	238	272	408	680	4	78	28	0.22	263	42	19	39	104	8%	129	15%	3.75	-6.0	$5
Peak		05 aaa	180	19	34	5	20	7	191			231	336	567	5	74	23	0.20					101		128	32%	2.23	-11.8	$2
Bats	Left	06 COL	* 240	26	61	8	28	5	256	400	255	305	418	723	11	75	31	0.28	247	43	19	38	98	11%	103	10%	4.34	-0.1	$6
Reliability	4	07 2TM	* 200	22	40	8	24	0	200	67	214	223	375	598	3	62	28	0.08	216	37	20	44	128	15%	91	3%	2.67	-10.0	$2
BAvg Potl	35%	1st Half	88	11	22	2	9	0	250			275	386	661	3	61	38	0.09	235	37	37	27	100	14%	99	11%	3.80	-1.2	$1
LIMA Plan	F	2nd Half	112	11	18	6	15	0	161			183	366	549	3	63	19	0.07		37	11	53	149	16%			1.81	-9.0	$0
+/- Score	-36	08 Proj	**101**	**11**	**22**	**4**	**12**	**1**	**218**			**250**	**392**	**643**	**4**	**68**	**28**	**0.14**	**231**	**38**	**19**	**43**	**116**	**12%**	**108**	**11%**	**3.23**	**-3.3**	**$2**

6-18-.199 in 141 AB at KC and ARI. PX and SX history gives a little optimism until you look at his aggregate OBA from the past three years... (Look away if you're sqeamish) .257 !! That's OBA, not BA.

STEPHEN NICKRAND

Snelling,Chris			AB	R	H	HR	RBI	SB	Avg	vL	vR	OB	Slg	OPS	bb%	ct%	h%	Eye	xBA	G	L	F	PX	hr/f	SX	SBO	RC/G	RAR	R$
Pos	8	03 a/a	253	35	78	5	35	2	307			343	432	774	5	85	35	0.36					80		63	15%	4.88	0.2	$9
Age	26	04	0	0	0	0	0	0	0							0									0				
Pre-Peak		05 aaa	246	42	81	7	38	2	329			406	484	890	12	85	37	0.84					99		62	7%	6.66	14.8	$11
Bats	Left	06 SEA	* 337	44	70	7	41	5	208	91	271	292	335	627	11	73	26	0.44	234	38	21	41	92	7%	92	10%	3.28	-14.6	$4
Reliability	0	07 2TM	69	10	17	1	7	0	246	235	250	373	333	707	17	78	30	0.93	241	42	25	34	50	5%	73	4%	4.68	0.5	$1
BAvg Potl	50%	1st Half	69	10	17	1	7	0	246			373	333	707	17	78	30	0.93	241	42	25	34	50	5%	73	4%	4.68	0.5	$1
LIMA Plan	F	2nd Half	0	0	0	0	0	0	0							0													
+/- Score	-11	08 Proj	119	18	33	3	15	1	277			364	401	765	12	80	33	0.69	264	41	24	35	78	8%	75	7%	5.17	2.4	$3

Year	Injury	DL Days
'03	Knee	188
'04	Wrist	182
'05	Knee	62
'06	Shoulder	69
'07	Knee	143

All of this *before* age 26.

Snyder,Chris			AB	R	H	HR	RBI	SB	Avg	vL	vR	OB	Slg	OPS	bb%	ct%	h%	Eye	xBA	G	L	F	PX	hr/f	SX	SBO	RC/G	RAR	R$
Pos	2	03 aa	188	15	34	3	19	0	181			238	298	535	7	89	19	0.67					79		24	0%	2.43	-10.6	($1)
Age	27	04 ARI	* 442	57	114	16	55	2	258	250	234	331	446	776	10	85	27	0.72	292	38	21	42	118	10%	45	3%	5.18	17.7	$11
Peak		05 ARI	326	24	66	6	28	0	202	260	185	290	301	590	11	73	26	0.46	224	51	19	29	75	9%	16	1%	2.76	-10.5	$0
Bats	Right	06 ARI	184	19	51	6	32	0	277	246	294	354	424	778	11	79	32	0.56	260	45	22	33	93	13%	14	0%	5.20	4.5	$5
Reliability	27	07 ARI	326	37	82	13	47	0	252	316	215	333	433	766	11	79	28	0.60	253	40	15	45	117	11%	19	1%	5.05	12.1	$7
BAvg Potl	50%	1st Half	151	17	33	6	15	0	219			298	364	662	10	79	24	0.55	221	40	13	47	86	11%	21	0%	3.64	-0.7	$2
LIMA Plan	D	2nd Half	175	20	49	7	32	0	280			364	491	855	12	79	32	0.64	280	40	17	43	144	12%	19	2%	6.26	12.3	$6
+/- Score	13	08 Proj	348	36	91	17	60	0	261			340	462	803	11	79	29	0.57	268	43	18	39	126	16%	14	1%	5.46	15.2	$10

A stable, 2nd catcher-type skill set on the surface. But a scan of his concurrent FB and PX trends points to further power upside.
UP: 20-25 HRs

Soriano,Alfonso			AB	R	H	HR	RBI	SB	Avg	vL	vR	OB	Slg	OPS	bb%	ct%	h%	Eye	xBA	G	L	F	PX	hr/f	SX	SBO	RC/G	RAR	R$
Pos	7	03 NYY	682	114	198	38	91	35	290	312	285	328	525	853	5	81	31	0.29	289	34	22	45	140	15%	134	27%	5.73	7.7	$35
Age	32	04 TEX	613	77	170	28	91	18	277	266	284	314	480	794	5	80	31	0.27	264	33	19	48	121	12%	108	17%	5.05	1.9	$23
Past Peak		05 TEX	637	102	171	36	104	30	268	257	272	304	512	816	5	80	28	0.26	293	34	19	47	155	15%	133	26%	5.29	10.4	$31
Bats	Right	06 WAS	647	119	179	46	95	41	277	293	271	345	560	904	9	75	30	0.42	283	29	20	51	175	18%	113	37%	6.70	27.6	$36
Reliability	71	07 CHC	579	97	173	33	70	19	299	254	311	334	560	894	5	78	34	0.24	293	34	20	46	166	16%	120	20%	6.35	16.3	$27
BAvg Potl	35%	1st Half	305	51	93	15	30	10	305			348	551	899	6	80	34	0.32	303	39	21	40	153	16%	124	18%	6.45	9.4	$14
LIMA Plan	B	2nd Half	274	46	80	18	40	9	292			319	569	889	4	75	33	0.16	283	28	18	54	181	16%	104	23%	6.24	7.0	$14
+/- Score	-25	08 Proj	616	104	171	37	85	27	278			321	538	859	6	77	30	0.28	287	32	20	49	164	16%	122	27%	5.92	10.5	$30

PRO:
- Elite PX/SX combo continues
- PX, FB rebound in 2H
- Stable xBA

CON:
- BA surge came from h%
- Running less with CHC

Sosa,Sammy			AB	R	H	HR	RBI	SB	Avg	vL	vR	OB	Slg	OPS	bb%	ct%	h%	Eye	xBA	G	L	F	PX	hr/f	SX	SBO	RC/G	RAR	R$
Pos	0	03 CHC	517	99	144	40	103	0	279	333	265	356	553	909	11	72	31	0.43	288	42	19	39	178	28%	37	1%	6.87	33.1	$26
Age	39	04 CHC	478	69	121	35	80	0	253	253	253	331	517	848	10	72	28	0.42	279	43	19	38	167	27%	21	0%	6.05	10.5	$17
Decline		05 BAL	380	39	84	14	45	1	221	288	196	294	376	670	9	78	25	0.46	247	44	16	40	100	12%	41	2%	3.72	-26.8	$6
Bats	Right	06	0	0	0	0	0	0	0							0									0				
Reliability	21	07 TEX	412	53	104	21	92	0	252	328	222	309	468	778	8	73	30	0.30	259	39	15	46	151	15%	33	0%	5.07	-11.4	$13
BAvg Potl	40%	1st Half	252	31	64	13	61	0	254			311	476	788	8	72	30	0.30	260	36	16	48	160	15%	21	0%	5.23	-5.8	$8
LIMA Plan	D	2nd Half	160	22	40	8	31	0	250			306	456	763	8	74	29	0.31	256	42	15	43	137	16%	52	0%	4.83	-5.6	$5
+/- Score	-59	08 Proj	315	42	78	16	57	0	248			314	452	765	9	74	29	0.37	259	42	16	42	135	16%	45	1%	4.92	-10.2	$9

Still a premium power source when he gets the AB. But that will be the problem. Age and two straight years of not hitting RHers will keep him on the bench more often than not, even if he does return.

Soto,Geovany			AB	R	H	HR	RBI	SB	Avg	vL	vR	OB	Slg	OPS	bb%	ct%	h%	Eye	xBA	G	L	F	PX	hr/f	SX	SBO	RC/G	RAR	R$
Pos	2	03	0	0	0	0	0	0	0							0									0				
Age	25	04 aa	332	41	81	8	41	1	244			318	358	676	10	80	28	0.55					73		39	3%	3.91	-1.6	$6
Pre-Peak		05 aaa	288	24	66	3	32	0	230			323	306	630	12	80	28	0.69					58		18	1%	3.50	-3.6	$2
Bats	Right	06 aaa	367	32	93	6	37	0	253			323	360	683	9	80	30	0.52	193	60	5	35	75	6%	18	1%	4.02	-3.8	$4
Reliability	1	07 CHC	* 439	73	143	26	95	0	325	444	333	390	588	978	10	78	37	0.48	311	41	22	37	170	21%	45	0%	7.68	45.2	$23
BAvg Potl	35%	1st Half	205	25	63	10	41	0	307			374	532	906	10	79	35	0.50					148		15	0%	6.76	16.5	$9
LIMA Plan	D+	2nd Half	234	48	80	16	54	0	340			403	638	1041	10	77	39	0.46	323	41	22	37	190	24%	63	0%	8.51	28.6	$15
+/- Score	18	08 Proj	342	45	93	13	56	0	272			344	457	801	10	79	31	0.52	274	45	18	36	120	13%	38	1%	5.47	14.8	$10

3-8-.389 in 54 AB at CHC. Where did this come from? A 37% h% deserves some credit. And while HR spike is confirmed by PX, inflated hr/f and low FB give reason for caution. Don't overbid.

Spiezio,Scott			AB	R	H	HR	RBI	SB	Avg	vL	vR	OB	Slg	OPS	bb%	ct%	h%	Eye	xBA	G	L	F	PX	hr/f	SX	SBO	RC/G	RAR	R$
Pos	5	03 ANA	521	69	138	16	83	6	265	223	282	325	453	777	8	87	28	0.70	303	38	23	39	112	9%	102	7%	5.17	10.0	$15
Age	35	04 SEA	367	38	79	10	41	4	215	203	218	285	346	631	9	84	23	0.60	236	33	18	49	74	7%	82	6%	3.38	-17.3	$4
Decline		05 SEA	* 105	12	20	2	9	0	190		100	227	276	503	5	73	24	0.18	151	14	10	76	62	3%	45	0%	1.31	-10.6	$0
Bats	Both	06 STL	276	44	75	13	52	1	272	318	251	358	496	854	12	76	31	0.56	269	34	20	46	137	14%	85	1%	6.28	6.2	$10
Reliability	0	07 STL	223	31	60	4	31	0	269	310	250	348	386	734	11	82	31	0.68	268	36	25	39	82	6%	33	1%	4.75	-0.2	$5
BAvg Potl	50%	1st Half	165	24	46	3	26	0	279			350	412	762	10	82	33	0.60	286	35	27	38	96	6%	32	0%	5.06	1.3	$4
LIMA Plan	F	2nd Half	58	7	14	1	5	0	241			343	310	654	13	83	28	0.90	215	37	18	45	41	5%	33	5%	3.87	-1.6	$1
+/- Score	-37	08 Proj	260	35	70	7	34	1	269			346	398	744	10	80	31	0.58	244	34	21	45	82	7%	50	2%	4.79	-1.2	$6

Switch-hitter swings much better against southpaws, which is really the only thing keeping him gainfully employed at this point. Aside from isolated PX outburst in '06, BPIs don't support much more than he's been doing.

Spilborghs,Ryan			AB	R	H	HR	RBI	SB	Avg	vL	vR	OB	Slg	OPS	bb%	ct%	h%	Eye	xBA	G	L	F	PX	hr/f	SX	SBO	RC/G	RAR	R$
Pos	89	03	0	0	0	0	0	0	0							0									0				
Age	28	04	0	0	0	0	0	0	0							0									0				
Peak		05 a/a	478	63	134	7	51	11	281			337	429	766	8	85	32	0.55					103		108	15%	5.06	8.8	$14
Bats	Right	06 COL	* 436	62	129	8	46	11	295	323	267	348	422	770	7	85	33	0.53	285	51	21	29	78	7%	103	11%	5.01	7.0	$14
Reliability	38	07 COL	* 388	57	109	14	62	6	282	356	271	349	452	801	9	84	31	0.63	295	50	21	30	101	15%	81	9%	5.40	9.3	$14
BAvg Potl	55%	1st Half	190	29	57	6	29	4	300			367	468	835	10	86	32	0.77	301	39	25	36	102	10%	80	12%	5.87	7.0	$8
LIMA Plan	D	2nd Half	198	28	52	8	33	2	265			332	435	767	9	81	29	0.53	285	53	19	28	101	19%	69	5%	4.94	2.2	$6
+/- Score	4	08 Proj	252	36	72	7	34	5	286			346	439	785	8	84	32	0.57	292	51	20	29	94	11%	91	10%	5.21	4.7	$9

11-51-.299 in 264 AB at COL. On the surface, a nice surge from '06, but there is limited upside for a GB hitter with barely decent speed. For an OFer, not enough talent to unseat an incumbent on most clubs.

Stairs,Matt			AB	R	H	HR	RBI	SB	Avg	vL	vR	OB	Slg	OPS	bb%	ct%	h%	Eye	xBA	G	L	F	PX	hr/f	SX	SBO	RC/G	RAR	R$
Pos	37	03 PIT	305	49	89	20	57	0	292	188	304	383	561	944	13	79	31	0.70	304	35	20	45	168	19%	41	1%	7.32	15.4	$14
Age	40	04 KC	439	48	117	18	66	1	267	223	278	340	451	791	10	79	30	0.53	260	50	13	37	112	14%	55	1%	5.32	4.1	$11
Decline		05 KC	396	55	109	13	66	1	275	259	278	371	444	815	13	83	31	0.87	275	40	19	42	111	10%	42	2%	5.84	8.5	$12
Bats	Left	06 2AL	348	42	86	13	51	0	247	217	252	325	420	744	10	75	29	0.47	250	43	17	39	117	13%	22	0%	4.76	-6.8	$7
Reliability	7	07 TOR	357	58	103	21	64	2	289	289	288	367	549	916	11	82	30	0.67	312	40	18	42	166	17%	55	3%	6.86	17.7	$15
BAvg Potl	55%	1st Half	167	26	48	12	28	1	287			350	551	901	9	81	29	0.50	297	40	16	44	157	20%	40	5%	6.43	6.3	$7
LIMA Plan	C	2nd Half	190	32	55	9	36	1	289			381	547	928	13	82	31	0.82	323	40	19	41	173	14%	64	2%	7.22	11.3	$8
+/- Score	5	08 Proj	342	50	94	16	58	1	275			357	498	855	11	80	30	0.63	290	41	18	41	145	15%	48	2%	6.18	9.7	$12

Made some adjustments vs. LHers, and had his best season in five years. At age 40, this was probably his last hurrah. But his base skills are strong enough to keep him a good part-timer.

Stewart,Ian			AB	R	H	HR	RBI	SB	Avg	vL	vR	OB	Slg	OPS	bb%	ct%	h%	Eye	xBA	G	L	F	PX	hr/f	SX	SBO	RC/G	RAR	R$
Pos	5	03	0	0	0	0	0	0	0							0									0				
Age	23	04	0	0	0	0	0	0	0							0									0				
Growth		05	0	0	0	0	0	0	0							0									0				
Bats	Left	06 aa	462	58	118	9	55	2	255			312	424	736	8	84	29	0.51					109		80	11%	4.69	-7.8	$8
Reliability	0	07 COL	* 457	63	130	14	63	9	284	100	242	346	442	788	9	81	33	0.48	274	46	19	35	101	11%	85	8%	5.24	5.9	$15
BAvg Potl	45%	1st Half	280	43	80	9	38	2	286			353	450	803	9	82	32	0.58					101		73	5%	5.46	5.4	$9
LIMA Plan	F	2nd Half	177	20	50	5	25	7	282			335	429	764	7	78	34	0.36	265	46	19	35	102	10%	75	15%	4.89	0.5	$6
+/- Score	-1	08 Proj	175	22	48	5	23	3	274			332	431	763	8	81	32	0.46	279	46	19	35	104	9%	79	10%	4.94	-0.0	$5

1-9-.209 in 43 AB at COL. Showed 30 HR power in the low minors a few years ago. But the pop in his bat hasn't returned, and as a GB hitter, it won't unless he adjusts. Expect another year in AAA.

STEPHEN NICKRAND

Stewart,Shannon			AB	R	H	HR	RBI	SB	Avg	vL	vR	OB	Slg	OPS	bb%	ct%	h%	Eye	xBA	G	L	F	PX	hr/f	SX	SBO	RC/G	RAR	R$
Pos	7	03 2AL	573	90	176	13	73	4	307	331	300	365	459	824	8	88	33	0.79	307	44	23	33	97	8%	66	6%	5.72	6.2	$20
Age	34	04 MIN	378	46	115	11	47	6	304	257	325	381	447	828	11	88	32	1.07	284	42	22	37	80	9%	72	7%	5.90	10.0	$13
Past Peak		05 MIN	551	69	151	10	56	7	274	244	283	316	388	705	6	87	30	0.47	274	46	20	35	73	6%	83	8%	4.16	-8.8	$13
Bats	Right	06 MIN	174	21	51	2	21	3	293	288	295	346	368	714	7	89	32	0.74	236	48	14	39	43	3%	78	7%	4.41	-3.7	$5
Reliability	50	07 OAK	576	79	167	12	48	11	290	269	298	343	394	738	8	90	31	0.78	278	45	21	34	62	7%	78	8%	4.67	-0.9	$16
BAvg Potl	50%	1st Half	253	39	74	6	24	6	292			356	395	751	9	91	30	1.04	289	47	23	30	59	9%	77	7%	4.91	1.4	$8
LIMA Plan	D+	2nd Half	323	40	93	6	24	5	288			333	393	727	6	89	31	0.61	270	42	20	37	65	6%	68	9%	4.47	-2.3	$8
+/- Score	-13	08 Proj	417	55	116	8	41	7	278			332	384	716	7	89	30	0.72	270	45	19	36	63	6%	82	8%	4.42	-5.4	$10

Based on history of alternating 400+ AB seasons, '08 won't be the prime time to bid. Power and wheels are both long gone, so the impact of 500 AB here is a red herring anyway.

Sullivan,Cory			AB	R	H	HR	RBI	SB	Avg	vL	vR	OB	Slg	OPS	bb%	ct%	h%	Eye	xBA	G	L	F	PX	hr/f	SX	SBO	RC/G	RAR	R$
Pos	8	03 aa	557	61	155	5	46	13	278			314	384	698	5	88	31	0.46					68		102	19%	4.14	-11.8	$13
Age	28	04 COL	0	0	0	0	0	0	0							0									0				
Peak		05 COL	378	64	111	4	30	12	294	250	301	342	386	729	7	78	37	0.34	276	44	32	24	65	6%	136	13%	4.47	-0.9	$13
Bats	Left	06 COL	386	47	103	2	30	10	267	280	266	323	402	725	8	74	36	0.32	265	36	32	33	95	2%	119	16%	4.64	2.2	$8
Reliability	18	07 COL	* 346	38	82	3	28	4	236	353	276	280	313	593	6	80	29	0.31	246	40	24	36	53	3%	87	8%	2.74	-19.0	$3
BAvg Potl	50%	1st Half	214	25	56	1	18	3	262			310	336	646	7	83	31	0.41					51		86	10%	3.51	-6.6	$3
LIMA Plan	F	2nd Half	132	13	26	2	10	1	194			229	276	505	4	77	24	0.20	233	41	23	36	56	5%	81	3%	1.45	-12.9	($0)
+/- Score	3	08 Proj	164	20	41	1	13	3	250			296	349	645	6	79	31	0.30	265	41	28	31	69	4%	104	12%	3.41	-5.6	$3

2-14-.286 in 140 AB at COL. He'll be overrated based on his BA at COL. No power, no speed, and no signs of either emerging anytime soon. At 28, OBA and SX should not be in a '3-year plummet.

Suzuki,Ichiro			AB	R	H	HR	RBI	SB	Avg	vL	vR	OB	Slg	OPS	bb%	ct%	h%	Eye	xBA	G	L	F	PX	hr/f	SX	SBO	RC/G	RAR	R$
Pos	8	03 SEA	679	111	212	13	62	34	312	359	291	347	436	783	5	90	33	0.52	307	49	24	27	70	8%	143	21%	5.03	5.5	$29
Age	34	04 SEA	704	101	262	8	60	36	372	404	359	413	455	868	7	91	40	0.78	301	64	18	18	47	7%	109	17%	6.07	24.1	$35
Past Peak		05 SEA	679	111	206	15	68	33	303	352	284	349	436	785	7	90	32	0.73	311	54	21	24	71	10%	150	20%	5.17	16.9	$29
Bats	Left	06 SEA	695	110	224	9	49	45	322	352	312	367	416	783	7	90	35	0.69	285	51	22	28	50	5%	150	20%	5.15	9.0	$30
Reliability	94	07 SEA	678	111	238	6	68	37	351	331	358	395	431	825	7	89	39	0.64	286	56	20	24	48	4%	127	18%	5.62	23.6	$33
BAvg Potl	35%	1st Half	313	54	114	5	39	22	364			418	466	885	8	90	39	0.91	292	54	20	27	59	7%	130	19%	6.40	16.7	$19
LIMA Plan	C	2nd Half	365	57	124	1	29	15	340			374	400	774	5	88	39	0.44	281	59	20	21	38	1%	116	16%	4.94	6.4	$15
+/- Score	-57	08 Proj	655	105	209	5	59	31	319			363	398	761	6	89	35	0.65	287	55	21	24	46	3%	136	17%	4.91	8.8	$26

Sub-.290 xBAs are not a flaw in the formula; that was corrected pre-2006. Drops in PX, hr/f, 2nd half ct% are all early signs that he's not ageless. This may be the last year you'll want to sign him to a multi-year contract.

Suzuki,Kurt			AB	R	H	HR	RBI	SB	Avg	vL	vR	OB	Slg	OPS	bb%	ct%	h%	Eye	xBA	G	L	F	PX	hr/f	SX	SBO	RC/G	RAR	R$
Pos	2	03	0	0	0	0	0	0	0							0									0				
Age	24	04	0	0	0	0	0	0	0							0									0				
Growth		05	0	0	0	0	0	0	0							0									0				
Bats	Right	06 aa	376	52	94	6	45	4	250			333	366	699	11	89	27	1.10					74		68	6%	4.51	1.5	$7
Reliability	0	07 OAK	* 424	53	105	9	61	0	249	151	281	315	363	679	9	83	28	0.57	236	39	16	45	78	6%	29	0%	3.95	-0.8	$8
BAvg Potl	45%	1st Half	224	29	59	4	26	0	263			321	362	683	8	84	30	0.54		55	9	36	66	6%	32	0%	3.97	-0.3	$4
LIMA Plan	D	2nd Half	200	24	46	5	35	0	232			309	365	674	10	81	26	0.59	243	38	16	45	92	7%	27	0%	3.93	-0.5	$3
+/- Score	-3	08 Proj	360	47	89	7	50	1	247			322	363	685	10	85	27	0.73	246	39	16	45	78	5%	46	3%	4.15	0.2	$7

7-39-.249 in 213 AB at OAK. May not have enough pop in his bat to warrant everyday work. But he's just 24, has shown a better Eye in the past, and had a bit of a 2H PX/FB surge. Patience is warranted.

Sweeney,Mark			AB	R	H	HR	RBI	SB	Avg	vL	vR	OB	Slg	OPS	bb%	ct%	h%	Eye	xBA	G	L	F	PX	hr/f	SX	SBO	RC/G	RAR	R$
Pos	3	03 COL	* 262	29	67	7	37	1	256		275	337	408	745	11	81	29	0.63	274	26	27	47	104	7%	45	9%	4.87	-5.1	$6
Age	38	04 COL	177	25	47	9	40	1	266	556	250	378	508	886	15	71	32	0.63	267	39	15	45	166	16%	77	2%	7.04	5.6	$7
Decline		05 SD	221	31	65	8	40	4	294	200	302	402	466	868	15	74	37	0.69	266	37	25	38	121	13%	79	5%	6.74	7.0	$10
Bats	Left	06 SF	259	32	65	5	37	0	251	135	270	324	382	706	10	81	29	0.56	265	42	22	36	85	7%	54	1%	4.35	-12.6	$5
Reliability	2	07 2NL	123	20	32	2	13	2	260	250	261	336	382	718	10	76	33	0.48	248	32	24	44	95	5%	69	6%	4.52	-3.8	$3
BAvg Potl	40%	1st Half	64	13	12	1	5	1	188			278	313	590	11	78	22	0.57	226	29	16	55	96	4%	92	7%	2.94	-5.4	$1
LIMA Plan	F	2nd Half	59	7	20	1	8	1	339			400	458	858	9	75	44	0.40	274	36	32	32	93	7%	41	5%	6.33	1.1	$2
+/- Score	-12	08 Proj	107	15	27	2	15	1	252			335	385	719	11	77	31	0.53	258	36	24	40	96	7%	54	5%	4.54	-3.7	$2

Hasn't done anything with his bat in two years. Used to show good power in bursts. Those are few and far between now. BPI trends confirms that his MLB days are probably numbered.

Sweeney,Mike			AB	R	H	HR	RBI	SB	Avg	vL	vR	OB	Slg	OPS	bb%	ct%	h%	Eye	xBA	G	L	F	PX	hr/f	SX	SBO	RC/G	RAR	R$
Pos	0	03 KC	392	62	115	16	83	3	293	277	300	393	467	859	14	86	31	1.14	290	42	21	37	100	13%	56	3%	6.38	19.2	$16
Age	34	04 KC	411	56	118	22	79	3	287	221	312	340	504	844	7	89	28	0.75	288	37	15	47	117	13%	47	5%	5.74	5.1	$16
Past Peak		05 KC	470	63	141	21	83	3	300	279	308	346	517	863	7	87	31	0.54	300	36	17	47	136	11%	54	3%	5.96	-0.8	$19
Bats	Right	06 KC	217	23	56	8	33	2	258	266	255	343	438	781	11	78	30	0.58	268	35	21	44	121	11%	40	3%	5.29	-7.2	$5
Reliability	12	07 KC	265	26	69	7	38	0	260	301	242	305	404	709	6	89	27	0.59	276	35	20	45	88	7%	34	0%	4.25	-13.6	$5
BAvg Potl	55%	1st Half	204	20	50	7	31	0	245			297	407	704	7	89	25	0.68	283	34	21	45	94	9%	32	0%	4.22	-10.9	$4
LIMA Plan	F	2nd Half	61	6	19	0	7	0	311			333	393	727	3	89	35	0.29	250	35	19	46	68	0%	25	0%	4.35	-2.7	$1
+/- Score	-2	08 Proj	246	27	65	5	37	0	264			317	391	709	7	86	29	0.54	262	35	19	45	87	5%	35	1%	4.30	-12.2	$5

Only spent 74 days on the DL in 2007, a 25% improvement from '06. That's the good news. The bad news is that, despite all his injuries, he had always been able to maintain solid BPIs. That stopped in '07. The end is near.

Swisher,Nick			AB	R	H	HR	RBI	SB	Avg	vL	vR	OB	Slg	OPS	bb%	ct%	h%	Eye	xBA	G	L	F	PX	hr/f	SX	SBO	RC/G	RAR	R$
Pos	893	03 aa	287	29	57	4	35	0	199			274	321	595	9	78	24	0.48					93		48	2%	2.94	-17.4	$1
Age	27	04 aaa	443	83	105	23	70	2	237			350	456	806	15	81	25	0.90					132		59	5%	5.71	13.8	$14
Peak		05 OAK	* 485	69	117	21	75	0	241	197	248	321	447	768	11	76	28	0.49	276	38	19	43	144	13%	39	2%	5.09	11.7	$12
Bats	Both	06 OAK	556	106	141	35	95	1	254	291	241	364	493	857	15	73	29	0.64	264	33	19	48	152	18%	55	2%	6.42	28.7	$20
Reliability	58	07 OAK	539	84	141	22	78	3	262	291	250	377	455	832	16	76	31	0.76	264	37	18	46	136	12%	53	3%	6.19	29.9	$16
BAvg Potl	50%	1st Half	254	33	71	10	42	1	280			408	461	868	18	77	33	0.95	267	38	20	42	125	12%	26	2%	6.77	17.9	$8
LIMA Plan	B	2nd Half	285	51	70	12	36	2	246			348	449	798	14	74	29	0.62	260	36	16	49	145	12%	71	4%	5.65	11.6	$8
+/- Score	3	08 Proj	541	88	136	27	82	2	251			357	465	823	14	75	29	0.67	268	36	18	46	144	14%	51	2%	5.94	24.3	$16

On the surface, a big decline from '06. But PX and FB remain solid, so HR should bounce back. Poor ct% will keep limiting his BA. Expect a rebound to somewhere between 2006 and 2007.

Taguchi,So			AB	R	H	HR	RBI	SB	Avg	vL	vR	OB	Slg	OPS	bb%	ct%	h%	Eye	xBA	G	L	F	PX	hr/f	SX	SBO	RC/G	RAR	R$
Pos	87	03 STL	* 312	35	70	5	33	12	224	259	259	280	317	597	7	84	25	0.49	275	53	21	26	57	7%	110	22%	2.93	-19.8	$6
Age	38	04 STL	* 234	30	66	4	31	11	282	266	318	320	406	726	5	85	32	0.37	279	48	20	32	78	6%	119	23%	4.37	-1.9	$9
Decline		05 STL	396	45	114	8	53	11	288	277	294	322	412	734	5	84	33	0.32	288	46	24	30	81	8%	102	13%	4.39	-1.8	$14
Bats	Right	06 STL	316	46	84	2	31	11	266	280	252	333	351	685	9	85	31	0.67	269	48	21	30	60	2%	95	15%	4.16	-2.5	$8
Reliability	49	07 STL	307	48	89	3	30	7	290	314	264	339	368	707	7	90	32	0.72	275	50	20	30	52	4%	76	12%	4.34	-1.9	$9
BAvg Potl	50%	1st Half	163	25	47	2	14	4	288			326	387	712	5	90	31	0.53	275	47	19	34	66	4%	78	14%	4.29	-1.3	$5
LIMA Plan	F	2nd Half	144	23	42	1	16	3	292			354	347	702	9	90	32	0.93	275	53	22	25	37	3%	67	10%	4.40	-0.7	$4
+/- Score	-33	08 Proj	259	37	72	2	28	6	278			331	357	688	7	87	31	0.62	273	49	21	29	54	3%	92	12%	4.12	-3.3	$7

His ct% and Eye are both surging, but those gains are offset by declingin PX and SX. Since he's a 300 AB guy, his improving plate control will have very little impact.

Taveras,Willy			AB	R	H	HR	RBI	SB	Avg	vL	vR	OB	Slg	OPS	bb%	ct%	h%	Eye	xBA	G	L	F	PX	hr/f	SX	SBO	RC/G	RAR	R$
Pos	8	03	0	0	0	0	0	0	0							0									0				
Age	26	04 aa	409	62	126	2	22	45	308			355	357	712	7	85	36	0.50					33		128	41%	4.29	-4.5	$21
Pre-Peak		05 HOU	592	82	172	3	29	34	291	233	311	319	341	661	4	83	35	0.24	249	55	19	26	33	2%	134	25%	3.46	-18.6	$20
Bats	Right	06 HOU	529	83	147	1	30	33	278	254	285	321	338	660	6	83	33	0.39	254	56	18	27	40	1%	137	27%	3.64	-12.2	$16
Reliability	73	07 COL	372	64	119	2	24	33	320	371	304	356	382	738	5	85	37	0.38	249	52	17	32	41	2%	134	34%	4.50	-0.6	$18
BAvg Potl	30%	1st Half	247	41	77	2	17	18	312			351	377	728	6	83	37	0.37	245	51	18	32	43	3%	116	32%	4.37	-1.3	$11
LIMA Plan	D+	2nd Half	125	23	42	0	7	15	336			366	392	758	5	89	38	0.43	256	53	16	32	38	0%	149	38%	4.76	0.6	$7
+/- Score	-38	08 Proj	511	84	149	4	29	44	292			329	358	688	5	85	34	0.38	256	53	17	29	43	3%	142	35%	3.91	-9.4	$22

BA was a fluke, but there are reasons to believe his wheels have plenty of upside:
- SX consistency
- ct% in 2H
- Mile high SBO in COL

UP: 50 SB

STEPHEN NICKRAND

Teahen,Mark			AB	R	H	HR	RBI	SB	Avg	vL	vR	OB	Slg	OPS	bb%	ct%	h%	Eye	xBA	G	L	F	PX	hr/f	SX	SBO	RC/G	RAR	R$
Pos	9	03	0	0	0	0	0	0	0							0									0				
Age	26	04 a/a	512	55	140	12	58	0	273			333	422	756	8	81	32	0.48					100		43	1%	4.89	-1.6	$11
Pre-Peak		05 KC	*474	63	116	7	58	7	245	200	263	310	371	682	9	76	31	0.39	279	53	23	24	96	8%	105	8%	3.99	-10.0	$9
Bats	Left	06 KC	*472	83	141	20	82	10	298	274	296	374	527	900	11	80	34	0.60	296	49	16	35	136	15%	136	7%	6.78	14.6	$20
Reliability	10	07 KC	544	78	155	7	60	13	285	255	297	351	410	761	9	77	36	0.43	266	50	21	29	90	6%	120	11%	5.06	5.6	$15
BAvg Potl	35%	1st Half	290	39	85	5	42	8	293			367	424	791	10	76	37	0.49	253	50	18	33	89	7%	116	11%	5.52	6.7	$10
LIMA Plan	B	2nd Half	254	39	70	2	18	5	276			331	394	725	8	78	35	0.37	279	51	24	26	91	4%	111	10%	4.54	-1.1	$6
+/- Score	-13	08 Proj	540	80	150	10	67	10	278			344	426	770	9	78	34	0.46	276	50	20	30	101	8%	122	9%	5.15	3.0	$15

It's tough for GB hitters to sustain power surges. Now 2006 stands out as the anomaly. But power also feeds xBA, so if he can't bump PX back up, he'll also find it hard to maintain a 0.280 BA.

Teixeira,Mark			AB	R	H	HR	RBI	SB	Avg	vL	vR	OB	Slg	OPS	bb%	ct%	h%	Eye	xBA	G	L	F	PX	hr/f	SX	SBO	RC/G	RAR	R$
Pos	3	03 TEX	529	66	137	26	84	1	259	295	242	316	480	796	8	77	29	0.37	299	36	28	36	140	18%	66	2%	5.26	-1.9	$16
Age	28	04 TEX	549	102	154	38	112	4	281	313	267	360	557	917	11	79	29	0.58	309	40	21	40	166	22%	78	3%	6.87	29.1	$25
Peak		05 TEX	644	112	194	43	144	4	301	292	301	372	575	946	10	81	32	0.58	321	40	21	38	168	22%	81	2%	7.14	36.1	$34
Bats	Both	06 TEX	628	99	177	33	110	2	282	302	275	371	514	885	12	80	31	0.70	294	39	20	41	146	16%	51	1%	6.61	21.0	$23
Reliability	83	07 2TM	494	86	151	30	105	0	306	357	282	394	563	957	13	77	34	0.64	299	39	20	41	165	19%	40	0%	7.56	29.8	$24
BAvg Potl	45%	1st Half	222	41	67	12	41	0	302			402	554	956	14	75	35	0.67	305	42	22	36	173	20%	48	0%	7.77	14.8	$10
LIMA Plan	D	2nd Half	272	45	84	18	64	0	309			388	570	957	11	79	34	0.61	294	37	18	45	159	19%	37	0%	7.39	15.1	$14
+/- Score	-19	08 Proj	630	106	191	42	138	0	303			386	574	960	12	79	33	0.63	308	39	20	40	169	21%	45	0%	7.48	35.1	$31

Minor changes to his approach in the NL hold hope that the big mega-breakout is coming. More aggression at plate (lower bb%) and higher FB rate added to already superb power skills =. UP: 50-150-.320

Tejada,Miguel			AB	R	H	HR	RBI	SB	Avg	vL	vR	OB	Slg	OPS	bb%	ct%	h%	Eye	xBA	G	L	F	PX	hr/f	SX	SBO	RC/G	RAR	R$
Pos	6	03 OAK	636	98	177	27	106	10	278	269	281	334	472	806	8	90	28	0.82	314	45	20	36	112	13%	85	6%	5.40	17.5	$24
Age	31	04 BAL	653	107	203	34	150	4	311	327	306	358	534	893	7	89	31	0.66	319	47	19	34	122	17%	71	3%	6.26	31.8	$31
Past Peak		05 BAL	654	89	199	26	98	5	304	293	309	344	515	860	6	87	32	0.48	322	48	19	33	129	14%	85	4%	5.90	23.9	$25
Bats	Right	06 BAL	648	99	214	24	100	6	330	335	329	375	498	873	7	88	35	0.58	312	51	22	27	98	16%	61	4%	6.06	28.1	$27
Reliability	80	07 BAL	514	72	152	18	81	2	296	323	287	348	442	789	7	89	30	0.75	285	52	17	31	82	13%	49	2%	5.17	8.7	$18
BAvg Potl	50%	1st Half	284	39	87	7	41	2	306			352	423	775	7	89	32	0.67	288	52	20	28	70	10%	52	2%	4.99	3.3	$10
LIMA Plan	D+	2nd Half	230	33	65	11	40	0	283			343	465	808	8	89	28	0.84	281	52	13	34	97	16%	44	1%	5.39	5.4	$8
+/- Score	-13	08 Proj	632	92	186	22	92	3	294			344	453	797	7	89	31	0.67	295	51	18	31	92	13%	60	2%	5.25	13.1	$21

PX trend would normally be a huge warning sign, but a fractured wrist deserves some of the blame in '07... at least in the 2nd half when he returned from the DL. But who will explain the first half power debacle?

Terrero,Luis			AB	R	H	HR	RBI	SB	Avg	vL	vR	OB	Slg	OPS	bb%	ct%	h%	Eye	xBA	G	L	F	PX	hr/f	SX	SBO	RC/G	RAR	R$
Pos	8	03 aaa	467	64	125	2	35	18	268			303	373	676	5	84	32	0.31					64		139	35%	3.83	-14.8	$12
Age	27	04 ARI	*446	46	117	10	38	20	262			313	404	717	7	75	33	0.30					95		121	23%	4.32	-4.3	$13
Peak		05 ARI	*191	27	44	4	21	4	230			286	340	627	7	74	29	0.30	236	47	19	34	78	8%	102	13%	3.10	-8.5	$4
Bats	Right	06 BAL	*342	54	99	17	49	17	290			325	500	825	5	80	32	0.26	288	48	15	36	129	17%	104	37%	5.40	7.4	$16
Reliability	4	07 CHW	*182	24	41	9	20	7	225	196	258	277	407	684	7	73	26	0.26	258	51	16	33	121	20%	80	28%	3.70	-3.3	$5
BAvg Potl	50%	1st Half	136	16	31	9	17	4	228			266	456	722	5	76	23	0.21	267	46	13	41	141	21%	63	28%	4.02	-1.1	$4
LIMA Plan	F	2nd Half	46	8	10	0	3	3	217			308	261	569	12	63	34	0.35	208	59	21	21	51	0%	99	29%	2.54	-2.5	$1
+/- Score	5	08 Proj	113	15	28	4	13	4	248			291	425	717	6	77	29	0.27	264	46	16	37	113	14%	107	27%	4.16	-0.9	$3

5-12-.231 in 117 AB at CHW. Showed a pretty good power/ speed combo early on with CHW. But AL pitchers found a huge hole in his swing late in the year. And with high GB%, HR won't be sustained.

Thames,Marcus			AB	R	H	HR	RBI	SB	Avg	vL	vR	OB	Slg	OPS	bb%	ct%	h%	Eye	xBA	G	L	F	PX	hr/f	SX	SBO	RC/G	RAR	R$
Pos	73	03 TEX	*333	42	78	5	34	4	234	250	95	296	342	638	8	78	29	0.39	239	42	18	40	80	5%	75	11%	3.37	-20.0	$5
Age	31	04 DET	*399	72	107	29	83	4	268	284	226	339	564	903	10	80	27	0.54	310	33	19	48	176	19%	75	7%	6.58	18.9	$18
Past Peak		05 DET	*364	54	95	24	63	4	262	212	186	341	522	863	11	75	29	0.47	262	27	14	59	165	15%	89	5%	6.25	16.2	$14
Bats	Right	06 DET	348	61	89	26	60	1	256	238	266	327	549	876	10	74	27	0.40	274	26	15	59	185	17%	72	3%	6.38	12.3	$13
Reliability	32	07 DET	269	37	65	18	54	2	242	310	209	277	498	775	5	73	26	0.18	279	38	16	46	173	20%	54	7%	4.80	0.7	$9
BAvg Potl	45%	1st Half	105	16	25	6	19	1	238			279	457	736	5	72	27	0.21	266	38	18	43	149	18%	62	10%	4.36	-1.1	$3
LIMA Plan	C	2nd Half	164	21	40	12	35	1	244			275	524	799	4	74	26	0.16	287	39	14	48	188	21%	43	4%	5.08	1.7	$6
+/- Score	-9	08 Proj	334	50	86	22	62	2	257			311	516	827	7	74	28	0.30	274	34	16	51	168	18%	67	5%	5.61	7.1	$12

Not many guys can boast a 160+ PX in four straight years. But there's a reason he can't play every day: he can't hit RHers. With these base skill trends, he'd get exposed in regular work anyway.

Theriot,Ryan			AB	R	H	HR	RBI	SB	Avg	vL	vR	OB	Slg	OPS	bb%	ct%	h%	Eye	xBA	G	L	F	PX	hr/f	SX	SBO	RC/G	RAR	R$
Pos	64	03 aa	178	18	38	1	8	8	213			317	245	562	13	88	24	1.25					21		67	25%	3.01	-7.3	$2
Age	28	04	0	0	0	0	0	0	0							0									0				
Peak		05 aa	445	41	113	1	43	19	253			309	324	632	7	91	28	0.93					50		99	24%	3.67	-8.0	$9
Bats	Right	06 CHC	*414	71	122	3	35	26	294	346	317	358	399	756	9	88	33	0.81	302	50	27	24	62	3%	148	23%	5.06	8.2	$16
Reliability	18	07 CHC	537	80	143	3	45	28	266	286	260	328	346	674	8	91	29	0.98	284	49	21	30	54	2%	121	20%	4.14	2.9	$15
BAvg Potl	65%	1st Half	230	32	59	1	23	14	257			316	326	642	8	89	29	0.77	285	51	23	26	48	2%	117	24%	3.70	-1.8	$7
LIMA Plan	B	2nd Half	307	48	84	2	22	14	274			336	362	698	9	92	29	1.21	282	47	20	34	59	2%	109	18%	4.47	4.5	$9
+/- Score	11	08 Proj	574	81	153	3	47	35	267			332	347	679	9	90	29	0.96	282	49	22	30	53	2%	124	25%	4.21	2.3	$18

Scrappy player had a very strong first full MLB season. Nice base skill growth in 2H. The power he showed late in '06 turned out to be a fluke, but the speed is here to stay. Good bet for 30+ SB.

Thigpen,Curtis			AB	R	H	HR	RBI	SB	Avg	vL	vR	OB	Slg	OPS	bb%	ct%	h%	Eye	xBA	G	L	F	PX	hr/f	SX	SBO	RC/G	RAR	R$
Pos	2	03	0	0	0	0	0	0	0							0									0				
Age	25	04	0	0	0	0	0	0	0							0									0				
Pre-Peak		05 aa	138	18	38	4	15	0	275			315	420	735	5	86	30	0.42					92		33	0%	4.44	2.1	$4
Bats	Right	06 a/a	362	48	92	6	42	5	254			345	406	751	12	82	30	0.76					102		96	7%	5.11	7.8	$7
Reliability	1	07 TOR	*280	30	72	3	28	3	257	256	224	311	343	654	7	87	29	0.59	276	43	24	33	61	4%	57	4%	3.70	-2.6	$4
BAvg Potl	55%	1st Half	177	20	51	3	16	1	288			340	395	736	7	88	31	0.67	316	42	32	26	72	7%	40	2%	4.64	3.1	$4
LIMA Plan	F	2nd Half	103	10	21	0	12	2	204			261	252	514	7	84	24	0.50	247	44	22	34	42	0%	65	8%	2.03	-6.4	$0
+/- Score	3	08 Proj	256	30	64	3	28	1	250			315	361	676	9	85	28	0.61	276	44	23	34	77	5%	59	2%	4.01	-1.0	$4

0-11-.238 in 101 AB at TOR. Marginal prospect was over-matched at MLB level. As a backstop at age 25, he's got time to grow. Solid control of plate will help but upside is only as a #2 end-game catcher.

Thomas,Frank			AB	R	H	HR	RBI	SB	Avg	vL	vR	OB	Slg	OPS	bb%	ct%	h%	Eye	xBA	G	L	F	PX	hr/f	SX	SBO	RC/G	RAR	R$
Pos	0	03 CHW	546	87	146	42	105	0	267	315	249	381	562	943	15	79	27	0.87	307	24	20	55	181	18%	18	0%	7.39	43.5	$23
Age	39	04 CHW	240	53	65	18	49	0	271	200	289	424	563	987	21	76	28	1.12	293	28	18	53	181	18%	31	2%	8.34	21.1	$11
Decline		05 CHW	*147	21	29	13	29	0	199	281	192	290	489	779	11	74	17	0.48	287	25	21	55	179	22%	19	0%	4.99	-4.8	$4
Bats	Right	06 OAK	466	77	126	39	114	0	270	245	278	378	545	923	15	83	25	1.00	288	24	19	57	145	18%	19	0%	6.96	7.0	$22
Reliability	2	07 TOR	531	63	147	26	95	0	277	336	259	373	480	853	13	82	29	0.86	268	30	17	53	127	11%	13	0%	6.21	2.9	$18
BAvg Potl	55%	1st Half	240	31	57	12	34	0	238			367	425	792	17	81	25	1.07	250	29	16	54	113	11%	15	0%	5.61	-2.9	$6
LIMA Plan	D+	2nd Half	291	32	90	14	61	0	309			378	526	903	10	84	33	0.67	282	30	17	52	137	11%	11	0%	6.64	4.9	$12
+/- Score	-34	08 Proj	449	53	119	24	85	0	265			365	468	833	14	81	28	0.81	263	27	18	54	123	12%	14	0%	5.95	-0.9	$14

Another strong finish, and skills are holding together reasonably well for a 40 year old. But as his PX, FB and hr/f continue to decline, so should his HR output. $20 will likely be a longshot in 2008.

Thome,Jim			AB	R	H	HR	RBI	SB	Avg	vL	vR	OB	Slg	OPS	bb%	ct%	h%	Eye	xBA	G	L	F	PX	hr/f	SX	SBO	RC/G	RAR	R$
Pos	0	03 PHI	578	111	154	47	131	0	266	254	272	385	573	957	16	69	31	0.61	298	38	22	39	210	30%	50	2%	8.03	57.1	$29
Age	37	04 PHI	508	97	139	42	105	0	274	239	294	397	581	978	17	72	30	0.72	292	38	18	45	198	26%	33	1%	8.17	41.7	$25
Decline		05 PHI	193	26	40	7	30	0	207	164	233	357	352	709	19	69	26	0.76	227	45	18	37	105	14%	21	0%	4.62	-8.4	$3
Bats	Left	06 CHW	490	108	141	42	109	0	288	236	321	415	598	1013	18	70	33	0.73	293	37	20	43	204	28%	30	0%	8.80	32.4	$26
Reliability	0	07 CHW	432	79	119	35	96	0	275	196	315	406	563	969	18	69	32	0.71	282	43	18	39	197	30%	21	1%	8.22	27.0	$21
BAvg Potl	45%	1st Half	145	25	41	10	30	0	283			455	531	987	24	67	36	0.96	272	48	22	30	178	34%	14	0%	8.94	11.9	$7
LIMA Plan	C	2nd Half	287	54	78	25	66	0	272			378	578	956	15	70	30	0.57	288	40	16	44	207	28%	27	1%	7.80	14.6	$14
+/- Score	-35	08 Proj	458	85	123	34	97	0	269			401	539	941	18	69	31	0.72	278	41	19	40	185	27%	24	0%	7.83	23.9	$20

Power outburst in 2H netted him 500th career HR. One of the more stable skill sets around. Pretty hapless vs LHPs and you have to wonder if that'll be the vulnerablity that starts cutting into this 37 y/o's PT.

STEPHEN NICKRAND

Thorman,Scott			AB	R	H	HR	RBI	SB	Avg	vL	vR	OB	Slg	OPS	bb%	ct%	h%	Eye	xBA	G	L	F	PX	hr/f	SX	SBO	RC/G	RAR	R$
Pos	3	03	0	0	0	0	0	0	0							0									0				
Age	26	04 aa	345	28	81	10	45	4	235			305	371	676	9	82	26	0.56					81		59	8%	3.89	-16.6	$6
Pre-Peak		05 a/a	550	63	149	19	81	2	271			312	440	752	6	81	30	0.32					107		65	3%	4.61	-11.6	$16
Bats	Left	06 ATL *	437	49	118	19	60	5	270	189	253	324	469	793	7	85	28	0.52	280	40	17	43	114	12%	62	7%	5.19	-10.2	$13
Reliability	20	07 ATL	287	37	62	11	36	1	216	176	228	252	394	646	5	76	25	0.20	248	41	14	45	122	11%	55	4%	3.21	-21.2	$4
BAvg Potl	55%	1st Half	215	26	49	9	30	1	228			256	414	670	4	80	25	0.19	258	38	15	47	119	11%	51	6%	3.45	-14.1	$4
LIMA Plan	F	2nd Half	72	11	13	2	6	0	181			244	333	577	8	63	26	0.22	215	50	11	39	134	11%	54	0%	2.52	-7.1	$0
+/- Score	21	08 Proj	205	25	52	7	25	1	254			303	429	732	7	76	30	0.30	250	44	13	43	117	11%	65	4%	4.44	-7.7	$5

Struggles prompted ATL to sell the farm for Teixeira. The news isn't all bad; FB% hints at PX upside, MLEs too. Now needs to at least show up to the ballpark vs LHPs. But this is it. Next year, prospect becomes suspect.

Torrealba,Yorvit			AB	R	H	HR	RBI	SB	Avg	vL	vR	OB	Slg	OPS	bb%	ct%	h%	Eye	xBA	G	L	F	PX	hr/f	SX	SBO	RC/G	RAR	R$
Pos	2	03 SF	200	22	52	4	29	1	260	212	269	308	390	698	7	81	31	0.36	285	55	22	23	85	11%	77	2%	4.07	-1.3	$4
Age	29	04 SF	172	19	39	6	23	2	227	286	170	296	407	703	9	82	24	0.55	276	59	10	31	102	14%	98	5%	4.23	2.2	$3
Peak		05 2TM	201	32	47	3	15	1	234	314	209	290	338	629	7	75	30	0.32	247	60	14	26	84	8%	69	2%	3.19	-4.3	$3
Bats	Right	06 COL *	259	23	61	7	44	4	234	246	247	273	407	680	5	79	27	0.25	282	63	13	25	112	14%	85	15%	3.76	-4.6	$5
Reliability	26	07 COL	396	47	101	8	47	2	255	264	252	314	376	690	8	82	30	0.47	265	53	18	29	81	8%	56	3%	4.04	2.9	$7
BAvg Potl	55%	1st Half	174	11	42	3	21	0	241			290	328	618	6	83	28	0.40	223	60	15	25	56	8%	15	2%	3.07	-3.8	$2
LIMA Plan	D	2nd Half	222	36	59	5	26	2	266			332	414	746	9	81	31	0.51	280	47	20	33	102	9%	79	3%	4.81	6.5	$6
+/- Score	-1	08 Proj	376	45	98	10	48	3	261			313	412	725	7	80	30	0.38	275	56	16	28	99	12%	71	5%	4.39	4.8	$9

Improvement has been hinted at sporadically in the past, in xBA and PX. Offense at CA matures late so there's still likely another burst to come. The only Yorvit in MLB history, but not the only Torrealba. (His brother is Steve.)

Towles,J.R.			AB	R	H	HR	RBI	SB	Avg	vL	vR	OB	Slg	OPS	bb%	ct%	h%	Eye	xBA	G	L	F	PX	hr/f	SX	SBO	RC/G	RAR	R$
Pos	2	03	0	0	0	0	0	0	0							0									0				
Age	24	04	0	0	0	0	0	0	0							0									0				
Growth		05	0	0	0	0	0	0	0							0									0				
Bats	Right	06	0	0	0	0	0	0	0							0									0				
Reliability	3	07 HOU *	299	52	88	11	54	9	293	333	387	347	466	813	8	87	31	0.64	289	34	24	42	99	10%	94	22%	5.46	14.5	$13
BAvg Potl	55%	1st Half	105	21	31	4	13	3	295			351	476	827	8	83	33	0.45					117		83	17%	5.64	5.5	$5
LIMA Plan	D+	2nd Half	194	31	57	7	41	6	293			344	461	805	7	91	30	0.85	293	34	24	42	90	9%	98	25%	5.40	9.2	$9
+/- Score	6	08 Proj	388	58	109	11	63	9	281			335	430	765	8	87	30	0.62	280	34	24	42	89	8%	87	20%	4.94	11.3	$14

1-12-.375 in 40 AB at HOU. Went from A-ball to latest heir apparent CA in one season. Solid ct%, double-digit SB at all stops. Caveat here is the lack of high minors time, but the skills are promising.

Tracy,Chad			AB	R	H	HR	RBI	SB	Avg	vL	vR	OB	Slg	OPS	bb%	ct%	h%	Eye	xBA	G	L	F	PX	hr/f	SX	SBO	RC/G	RAR	R$
Pos	5	03 aaa	522	71	156	8	62	0	299			339	412	751	6	93	31	0.82					69		54	1%	4.82	6.2	$14
Age	27	04 ARI *	521	51	150	10	62	4	288	215	305	351	418	770	9	87	31	0.77	266	36	20	44	81	5%	60	4%	5.14	1.1	$13
Peak		05 ARI	503	73	155	27	72	3	308	236	324	353	553	906	7	84	32	0.45	317	33	24	42	147	15%	77	3%	6.43	22.6	$23
Bats	Left	06 ARI	597	91	168	20	80	5	281	231	304	341	451	792	8	78	33	0.42	265	36	21	43	112	10%	63	4%	5.27	-3.7	$19
Reliability	57	07 ARI	227	30	60	7	35	0	264	174	287	348	454	801	11	81	30	0.67	274	37	18	45	125	8%	53	0%	5.61	5.5	$6
BAvg Potl	55%	1st Half	151	25	43	5	24	0	285			379	503	883	13	81	32	0.79	281	30	18	52	144	8%	69	0%	6.76	8.4	$5
LIMA Plan	C	2nd Half	76	5	17	2	11	0	224			280	355	636	7	82	25	0.43	235	52	16	32	86	10%	8	0%	3.31	-3.4	$1
+/- Score	7	08 Proj	480	60	135	21	68	2	281			343	486	829	9	82	31	0.52	287	39	19	41	126	13%	52	2%	5.70	10.2	$15

Chronic knee pain eventually resulted in surgery, leaving early '08 in doubt. Despite HR drought, 1H PX and FB% trend hint at a power spike. If the microfracture surgery works...
UP: 30 HR

Treanor,Matt			AB	R	H	HR	RBI	SB	Avg	vL	vR	OB	Slg	OPS	bb%	ct%	h%	Eye	xBA	G	L	F	PX	hr/f	SX	SBO	RC/G	RAR	R$
Pos	2	03 aaa	315	32	70	8	29	7	222			288	352	640	8	88	23	0.78					78		73	16%	3.61	-5.7	$5
Age	32	04 FLA *	253	27	52	5	25	1	206	182	250	282	300	583	10	81	23	0.57	276	56	24	20	60	12%	44	2%	2.77	-8.2	$1
Past Peak		05 FLA	134	10	27	0	13	0	201	120	215	287	261	548	11	79	25	0.57	229	49	19	32	55	0%	20	0%	2.44	-5.6	($0)
Bats	Right	06 FLA	157	12	36	2	14	0	229	268	216	313	318	631	11	78	28	0.56	224	44	18	38	59	4%	42	2%	3.42	-4.4	$1
Reliability	5	07 FLA	171	16	46	4	19	0	269	245	280	342	392	734	10	83	30	0.66	271	42	24	34	75	8%	34	0%	4.68	4.4	$3
BAvg Potl	55%	1st Half	51	3	13	0	1	0	255			321	333	655	9	86	30	0.71	263	44	23	33	48	0%	59	0%	3.88	0.1	$0
LIMA Plan	F	2nd Half	120	13	33	4	18	0	275			351	417	767	10	82	31	0.64	265	41	24	35	87	12%	1	0%	5.04	4.3	$3
+/- Score	-17	08 Proj	157	13	38	2	15	0	242			319	346	665	10	82	28	0.62	255	44	22	34	68	5%	43	1%	3.87	-0.4	$2

Overcame nagging injuries to net little gains here and there, especially in ct%. It all means he should keep his backup CA job for a while, which means a lot to his family. Means a bit less to you and your family.

Tulowitzki,Troy			AB	R	H	HR	RBI	SB	Avg	vL	vR	OB	Slg	OPS	bb%	ct%	h%	Eye	xBA	G	L	F	PX	hr/f	SX	SBO	RC/G	RAR	R$
Pos	6	03	0	0	0	0	0	0	0							0									0				
Age	23	04	0	0	0	0	0	0	0							0									0				
Growth		05	0	0	0	0	0	0	0							0									0				
Bats	Right	06 COL *	519	73	139	12	53	8	268	150	263	326	410	737	8	85	29	0.59	292	49	21	30	89	9%	78	10%	4.65	4.4	$13
Reliability	1	07 COL	609	104	177	24	99	7	291	333	278	351	479	831	9	79	34	0.44	276	42	20	38	119	13%	91	8%	5.76	30.9	$24
BAvg Potl	40%	1st Half	277	42	75	7	35	3	271			336	412	747	9	77	33	0.42	261	45	22	33	91	10%	91	8%	4.78	6.6	$8
LIMA Plan	C+	2nd Half	332	62	102	17	64	4	307			365	536	901	8	80	34	0.46	290	39	18	42	140	15%	83	8%	6.54	23.6	$16
+/- Score	-1	08 Proj	610	107	172	27	95	8	282			342	489	831	8	81	31	0.49	292	42	20	38	125	15%	94	9%	5.69	28.1	$24

His ct% isn't great, and the road splits are a little scary. (.326/.256) But critical rookie-year 2H was impressive; so is 24 HR. xBA foretells avg dip, and ct% says growth may be unsteady. Still, expect a solid follow-up.

Tyner,Jason			AB	R	H	HR	RBI	SB	Avg	vL	vR	OB	Slg	OPS	bb%	ct%	h%	Eye	xBA	G	L	F	PX	hr/f	SX	SBO	RC/G	RAR	R$
Pos	70	03 TAM *	365	41	107	0	26	11	293	167	295	344	370	713	7	90	33	0.78					50		102	18%	4.51	-8.6	$9
Age	31	04 aaa	382	58	105	1	29	21	276			328	328	656	7	90	31	0.76					36		118	23%	3.82	-15.2	$12
Past Peak		05 MIN *	580	72	146	1	34	16	252	333	318	303	296	599	7	90	28	0.73	277	57	20	22	30	1%	101	13%	3.17	-26.8	$9
Bats	Left	06 MIN *	534	76	161	0	38	11	301	269	325	342	356	697	6	88	34	0.52	291	52	27	21	35	0%	112	9%	4.16	-15.1	$13
Reliability	42	07 MIN	304	42	87	1	22	8	286	233	299	322	355	677	5	91	31	0.62	290	60	18	22	47	2%	101	13%	3.97	-6.5	$7
BAvg Potl	60%	1st Half	123	19	34	0	13	5	276			310	333	643	5	92	30	0.60	280	60	15	25	45	0%	96	18%	3.60	-3.9	$3
LIMA Plan	F	2nd Half	181	23	53	1	9	3	293			330	370	700	5	91	32	0.63	295	60	19	21	48	3%	91	9%	4.21	-2.6	$4
+/- Score	-6	08 Proj	292	40	83	1	20	9	284			325	345	670	6	90	31	0.62	286	59	19	22	41	1%	104	14%	3.90	-8.1	$7

If that "07" was 1907, he'd fit right in. This isn't the dead ball era though, and his empty BA was a poor use of 300 AB by MIN. In Roto, the BA and SB help a bit; in sim, his output is as wanting as in real life.

Uggla,Dan			AB	R	H	HR	RBI	SB	Avg	vL	vR	OB	Slg	OPS	bb%	ct%	h%	Eye	xBA	G	L	F	PX	hr/f	SX	SBO	RC/G	RAR	R$
Pos	4	03	0	0	0	0	0	0	0							0									0				
Age	28	04 aa	294	20	65	3	21	7	220			249	301	549	4	86	25	0.28					51		77	25%	2.27	-19.3	$2
Peak		05 aa	495	62	124	16	61	11	251			305	420	725	7	82	28	0.44					110		90	17%	4.40	0.8	$14
Bats	Right	06 FLA	611	105	172	27	90	6	282	307	273	334	480	813	7	80	31	0.39	266	41	17	42	113	13%	95	8%	5.42	14.4	$23
Reliability	68	07 FLA	632	113	155	31	88	2	245	245	245	319	479	798	10	74	29	0.41	268	34	16	51	162	13%	78	2%	5.48	17.3	$19
BAvg Potl	50%	1st Half	312	61	81	16	48	2	260			330	519	850	10	73	31	0.40	281	33	15	51	183	14%	94	3%	6.21	14.9	$11
LIMA Plan	C+	2nd Half	320	52	74	15	40	0	231			307	441	748	10	74	27	0.42	255	34	16	50	142	13%	55	1%	4.78	2.1	$7
+/- Score	22	08 Proj	602	94	151	29	79	3	251			312	469	781	8	78	28	0.40	269	36	16	48	139	13%	73	6%	5.09	9.4	$17

All the warning signs from his rookie 2nd half came to pass, save one: FB%. So the big PX spike offset the other losses. But that ct% still leaves him on a precipice: if the lofty FB rate recedes, the HR will dip too.

Upton,B.J.			AB	R	H	HR	RBI	SB	Avg	vL	vR	OB	Slg	OPS	bb%	ct%	h%	Eye	xBA	G	L	F	PX	hr/f	SX	SBO	RC/G	RAR	R$
Pos	84	03 aa	105	14	31	1	17	2	295			393	410	803	14	79	37	0.77					93		50	16%	5.87	3.1	$4
Age	23	04 TAM *	527	104	159	16	63	24	302	410	163	385	469	853	12	75	38	0.55	268	56	13	31	113	13%	125	18%	6.36	24.3	$24
Growth		05 aaa	536	75	147	13	56	35	275			349	425	773	10	84	31	0.72					96		118	34%	5.21	12.5	$22
Bats	Right	06 TAM *	573	90	148	8	50	56	258	298	227	345	357	702	12	79	31	0.63	259	54	19	27	65	7%	135	41%	4.38	-5.0	$23
Reliability	8	07 TAM	474	86	142	24	82	22	300	281	306	384	508	892	12	68	40	0.42	260	43	20	38	156	20%	95	19%	7.13	38.0	$25
BAvg Potl	20%	1st Half	200	36	64	9	31	13	320			387	545	932	10	66	45	0.32	273	46	18	35	182	19%	116	30%	7.85	19.7	$12
LIMA Plan	C+	2nd Half	274	50	78	15	51	9	285			382	482	863	14	69	36	0.50	252	41	20	39	137	20%	75	12%	6.63	18.3	$13
+/- Score	-52	08 Proj	534	90	147	19	74	22	275			361	439	800	12	74	34	0.51	259	45	19	36	114	13%	97	21%	5.62	18.9	$21

Underlying skills do not support this output at all; low ct%, low xBA, high hr/f, and inflated h% all say there's little chance he repeats '07 in '08. So look for stat drop-off, even as skills potentially improve.

ROD TRUESDELL

Upton,Justin

		Year	AB	R	H	HR	RBI	SB	Avg	vL	vR	OB	Slg	OPS	bb%	ct%	h%	Eye	xBA	G	L	F	PX	hr/f	SX	SBO	RC/G	RAR	R$
Pos	9	03	0	0	0	0	0	0	0							0									0				
Age	20	04	0	0	0	0	0	0	0							0									0				
Green		05	0	0	0	0	0	0	0							0									0				
Bats	Right	06	0	0	0	0	0	0	0							0									0				
Reliability	0	07 ARI	* 399	59	111	15	57	10	278	200	230	350	486	836	10	81	31	0.58	269	36	16	48	127	9%	114	17%	5.95	8.1	$15
BAvg Potl	45%	1st Half	170	28	50	7	28	6	294			351	518	869	8	82	32	0.50					133		126	20%	6.20	4.6	$8
LIMA Plan	D	2nd Half	229	31	61	8	29	4	266			350	462	812	11	79	31	0.63	262	36	16	48	122	9%	101	15%	5.74	3.4	$7
+/- Score	14	08 Proj	274	40	74	9	39	4	270			344	467	811	10	81	31	0.58	264	36	16	48	121	8%	105	13%	5.66	4.1	$9

2-11-.221 in 140 AB at ARI. Showed flashes of his huge promise -- and that he needs more time. BPIs took a tumble at ARI. Be wary if he starts '08 in majors; grab him after more AB in minors. Uber-prospect.

Uribe,Juan

		Year	AB	R	H	HR	RBI	SB	Avg	vL	vR	OB	Slg	OPS	bb%	ct%	h%	Eye	xBA	G	L	F	PX	hr/f	SX	SBO	RC/G	RAR	R$
Pos	6	03 COL	316	45	80	10	33	7	253	301	236	291	427	719	5	81	28	0.28	286	37	26	37	111	11%	122	14%	4.21	0.9	$9
Age	29	04 CHW	502	82	142	23	74	9	283	264	293	326	506	832	6	81	31	0.33	281	38	18	45	133	13%	107	18%	5.59	16.5	$19
Peak		05 CHW	481	58	121	16	71	4	252	311	234	301	412	713	7	84	27	0.44	271	38	19	42	98	9%	68	9%	4.21	-5.0	$12
Bats	Right	06 CHW	463	53	109	21	71	1	235	224	244	256	441	697	3	82	24	0.16	277	38	17	45	123	12%	58	3%	3.76	-9.1	$10
Reliability	83	07 CHW	513	55	120	20	68	1	234	257	225	282	394	675	6	78	26	0.30	235	35	15	50	101	10%	39	9%	3.62	-14.8	$9
BAvg Potl	45%	1st Half	216	20	50	6	26	1	231			284	347	632	7	75	28	0.30	217	33	19	48	75	8%	53	4%	3.10	-9.6	$3
LIMA Plan	C	2nd Half	297	35	70	14	42	0	236			279	428	707	6	80	25	0.31	250	37	13	50	118	12%	43	13%	3.99	-5.3	$6
+/- Score	-8	08 Proj	530	61	127	22	74	1	240			280	422	702	5	80	26	0.29	259	37	17	46	111	11%	46	7%	3.93	-9.3	$11

The bad: Unlike 2006, this poor BA was "earned," with ominous skills slide continuing.
The better: 2nd half ct%+FB%= possible PX spike. Family health issues may have been a distraction early.

Utley,Chase

		Year	AB	R	H	HR	RBI	SB	Avg	vL	vR	OB	Slg	OPS	bb%	ct%	h%	Eye	xBA	G	L	F	PX	hr/f	SX	SBO	RC/G	RAR	R$
Pos	4	03 PHI	* 565	85	162	18	90	11	287	333	230	344	457	800	8	83	32	0.52	291	40	23	37	108	10%	101	10%	5.35	15.1	$22
Age	29	04 PHI	* 390	55	102	18	78	7	262	200	279	314	462	776	7	83	27	0.45	297	44	22	34	114	16%	97	11%	4.94	3.7	$15
Peak		05 PHI	543	93	158	28	105	16	291	220	313	371	540	911	11	80	32	0.63	305	35	23	42	159	15%	125	12%	6.89	35.4	$29
Bats	Left	06 PHI	658	131	203	32	102	15	309	301	312	369	527	896	9	80	35	0.48	280	37	20	43	131	14%	111	10%	6.53	34.8	$32
Reliability	83	07 PHI	530	104	176	22	103	9	332	318	340	390	566	956	9	83	37	0.56	307	38	20	42	147	12%	112	7%	7.27	37.8	$29
BAvg Potl	35%	1st Half	297	56	97	13	60	5	327			388	566	954	9	82	36	0.57	311	38	20	42	157	13%	87	7%	7.30	21.6	$16
LIMA Plan	D+	2nd Half	233	48	79	9	43	4	339			391	567	958	8	85	37	0.56	301	38	20	42	136	11%	123	6%	7.24	16.2	$13
+/- Score	-16	08 Proj	606	115	186	32	110	12	307			368	558	926	9	82	33	0.54	306	37	20	42	152	15%	117	9%	6.89	38.5	$31

PX fell after return from broken hand - showing how terrific it was before the injury. 330 BA over his head, but .300+ isn't. HR should return; skills superb. Fanalytic gold, if he keeps his hands away from pitches.

Valentin,Javier

		Year	AB	R	H	HR	RBI	SB	Avg	vL	vR	OB	Slg	OPS	bb%	ct%	h%	Eye	xBA	G	L	F	PX	hr/f	SX	SBO	RC/G	RAR	R$
Pos	2	03 TAM	135	13	30	3	15	0	222	231	221	250	356	606	4	77	27	0.16	242	38	19	43	91	7%	54	0%	2.71	-5.7	$1
Age	32	04 CIN	202	18	47	6	20	0	233	109	269	292	381	673	8	82	26	0.47	265	35	22	43	91	9%	37	0%	3.80	-0.1	$2
Past Peak		05 CIN	221	36	62	14	50	0	281	184	298	367	520	887	12	83	28	0.81	308	34	23	43	141	18%	26	0%	6.47	16.7	$11
Bats	Both	06 CIN	186	24	50	8	27	0	269	111	286	317	441	757	7	84	28	0.45	274	33	23	43	92	12%	44	0%	4.67	1.7	$5
Reliability	27	07 CIN	243	19	67	2	34	0	276	290	274	328	387	715	7	90	30	0.76	266	40	19	42	80	2%	15	0%	4.52	5.0	$4
BAvg Potl	55%	1st Half	74	6	20	1	14	0	270			341	405	747	10	96	27	2.67	310	33	23	44	88	3%	13	0%	5.21	3.0	$2
LIMA Plan	F	2nd Half	169	13	47	1	20	0	278			322	379	701	6	87	32	0.50	247	43	16	41	76	2%	16	0%	4.23	2.1	$3
+/- Score	-12	08 Proj	258	27	69	5	40	0	267			324	400	724	8	87	29	0.64	272	36	21	43	85	5%	37	0%	4.54	4.3	$6

Did someone tell him chicks dig contact hitters? Sacrificed all production to just put it in play. Look at that hr/f collapse! Needs to be reminded that he was far more valuable when he took a real rip once in awhile.

Valentin,Jose

		Year	AB	R	H	HR	RBI	SB	Avg	vL	vR	OB	Slg	OPS	bb%	ct%	h%	Eye	xBA	G	L	F	PX	hr/f	SX	SBO	RC/G	RAR	R$
Pos	4	03 CHW	503	79	119	28	74	8	237	131	265	311	463	774	10	77	25	0.47	278	32	22	46	142	16%	89	9%	5.02	13.4	$16
Age	38	04 CHW	450	73	97	30	70	8	216	191	226	284	473	757	9	69	24	0.31	247	29	14	56	170	17%	109	16%	4.86	11.0	$13
Decline		05 LA	147	17	25	2	14	3	170	316	148	315	265	580	17	74	21	0.82	200	40	14	47	64	4%	100	8%	2.91	-7.9	$0
Bats	Both	06 NYM	384	56	104	18	62	6	271	219	288	335	490	825	9	82	29	0.52	265	31	16	53	129	11%	87	8%	5.65	11.6	$14
Reliability	0	07 NYM	166	18	40	3	18	2	241	275	226	304	373	677	8	83	27	0.54	262	32	23	45	89	5%	70	8%	3.97	-2.9	$2
BAvg Potl	55%	1st Half	123	13	34	3	17	0	276			331	447	778	8	85	31	0.53	294	32	25	43	111	7%	52	3%	5.14	2.0	$3
LIMA Plan	D	2nd Half	43	5	6	0	1	2	140			229	163	392	10	79	18	0.56	170	32	15	53	21	0%	88	20%	0.39	-6.0	($0)
+/- Score	-14	08 Proj	250	32	59	9	34	3	236			317	415	732	11	78	27	0.55	255	33	19	48	114	9%	84	8%	4.64	0.6	$6

The Jose Valentin career path took another injury-related turn in 2007. Was rebounding before ACL tear, but now he's coming off surgery and a tough rehab at age 38. Reliability score says it all.

Varitek,Jason

		Year	AB	R	H	HR	RBI	SB	Avg	vL	vR	OB	Slg	OPS	bb%	ct%	h%	Eye	xBA	G	L	F	PX	hr/f	SX	SBO	RC/G	RAR	R$
Pos	2	03 BOS	451	63	123	25	85	3	273	309	257	347	512	859	10	76	31	0.48	301	42	23	35	158	20%	54	4%	6.19	27.1	$17
Age	36	04 BOS	467	68	139	19	76	10	298	350	273	380	488	868	12	73	37	0.49	267	42	21	37	132	15%	78	9%	6.56	29.0	$19
Decline		05 BOS	470	70	132	22	70	2	281	320	267	365	489	854	12	75	33	0.53	291	45	23	32	144	20%	57	1%	6.27	29.8	$17
Bats	Both	06 BOS	365	46	87	12	55	1	238	229	244	324	400	724	11	76	28	0.53	252	45	17	38	106	11%	55	3%	4.55	1.6	$7
Reliability	30	07 BOS	435	57	111	17	68	1	255	264	252	360	421	780	14	72	32	0.58	241	42	18	40	112	14%	51	2%	5.45	18.2	$11
BAvg Potl	40%	1st Half	214	29	57	8	33	1	266			351	444	795	12	76	32	0.54	256	41	18	41	113	12%	83	2%	5.51	9.1	$6
LIMA Plan	D	2nd Half	221	28	54	9	35	0	244			367	398	766	16	68	32	0.61	222	43	18	40	110	15%	18	2%	5.36	8.9	$5
+/- Score	-19	08 Proj	427	57	105	16	67	1	246			343	414	757	13	73	30	0.55	252	43	19	38	115	13%	48	2%	5.07	11.8	$10

Bounced back from '06 injuries, but only part way. 2nd half ct% the most telling indicator of the skills deterioration. Still has value, especially in formats in which his walks count. It's just not 2005 value anymore.

Vazquez,Ramon

		Year	AB	R	H	HR	RBI	SB	Avg	vL	vR	OB	Slg	OPS	bb%	ct%	h%	Eye	xBA	G	L	F	PX	hr/f	SX	SBO	RC/G	RAR	R$
Pos	5	03 SD	422	56	110	3	30	10	261	224	275	342	341	683	11	79	32	0.59	258	46	25	29	57	3%	111	9%	4.14	-1.4	$9
Age	31	04 SD	* 299	40	72	7	39	3	241	143	248	322	398	720	11	84	27	0.73	300	53	21	26	99	11%	91	5%	4.63	-3.9	$6
Past Peak		05 2AL	* 169	18	34	0	9	1	201	250	203	250	254	504	6	80	25	0.32	241	53	19	28	43	0%	79	5%	1.70	-15.0	($0)
Bats	Left	06 CLE	* 166	29	36	2	18	2	217	286	200	323	289	612	14	72	29	0.55	194	40	17	43	50	4%	95	5%	3.17	-9.5	$2
Reliability	18	07 TEX	* 432	58	91	9	36	4	211	184	246	282	338	620	9	76	26	0.42	252	43	21	36	89	8%	97	5%	3.15	-18.1	$4
BAvg Potl	60%	1st Half	228	39	56	6	23	4	246			336	404	739	12	79	29	0.63	289	46	25	29	108	12%	103	8%	4.86	2.4	$5
LIMA Plan	F	2nd Half	204	19	35	3	13	0	172			218	265	482	6	72	22	0.22	220	42	20	39	65	5%	69	0%	1.13	-22.3	($2)
+/- Score	26	08 Proj	158	21	35	2	13	1	222			295	315	610	9	76	28	0.43	231	44	20	37	66	5%	84	5%	3.04	-7.8	$1

8-28-.230 in 300 AB at TEX. Homered thrice in first week up, netting him way more AB than skills warranted. All told, a lot like the previous few years, except the more he plays, the worse it all looks.

Victorino,Shane

		Year	AB	R	H	HR	RBI	SB	Avg	vL	vR	OB	Slg	OPS	bb%	ct%	h%	Eye	xBA	G	L	F	PX	hr/f	SX	SBO	RC/G	RAR	R$
Pos	9	03 a/a	307	37	80	3	21	14	261			306	345	651	6	87	29	0.49					49		123	27%	3.60	-16.5	$8
Age	27	04 a/a	493	77	121	15	50	13	245			280	389	670	5	83	27	0.29					82		119	22%	3.58	-21.3	$13
Peak		05 aaa	494	73	138	16	55	13	279			332	468	800	7	88	29	0.68					102		126	19%	5.37	5.6	$18
Bats	Both	06 PHI	415	70	119	6	46	4	287	273	293	326	414	740	5	87	32	0.44	277	45	21	34	72	5%	117	6%	4.60	-2.0	$12
Reliability	53	07 PHI	456	78	128	12	46	37	281	291	276	335	423	758	8	86	30	0.60	277	47	17	36	85	8%	140	32%	4.85	-5.2	$21
BAvg Potl	50%	1st Half	295	50	80	8	33	22	271			330	407	737	8	86	29	0.63	272	46	17	37	81	9%	130	29%	4.63	-5.3	$13
LIMA Plan	B	2nd Half	161	28	48	4	13	15	298			343	453	796	6	87	32	0.52	286	49	16	35	91	8%	151	39%	5.26	0.0	$8
+/- Score	6	08 Proj	551	90	156	13	55	40	283			330	429	759	7	87	31	0.53	281	47	18	35	84	8%	159	32%	4.85	-4.8	$24

And to think he missed time with LEG trouble. Long-lost speed skills returned via SBO, better bb%, and a legendary baserunning coach. Value highly dependent on SX, so be sure the wheels are sound.

Vidro,Jose

		Year	AB	R	H	HR	RBI	SB	Avg	vL	vR	OB	Slg	OPS	bb%	ct%	h%	Eye	xBA	G	L	F	PX	hr/f	SX	SBO	RC/G	RAR	R$
Pos	0	03 MON	509	77	158	15	65	3	310	315	309	393	470	862	12	90	32	1.38	313	52	20	28	98	12%	48	3%	6.38	24.4	$19
Age	33	04 MON	416	51	121	14	60	3	291	267	306	366	450	815	11	89	30	1.11	298	51	19	30	92	12%	45	3%	5.71	4.8	$14
Past Peak		05 WAS	309	38	85	7	32	0	275	258	280	341	424	765	9	90	29	1.03	315	44	25	31	92	8%	47	0%	5.15	-7.6	$7
Bats	Both	06 WAS	463	52	134	7	47	1	289	323	276	347	395	742	8	90	31	0.85	282	46	22	32	65	5%	45	1%	4.81	-20.0	$10
Reliability	59	07 SEA	548	78	172	6	59	0	314	328	309	385	394	779	10	90	34	1.11	266	51	19	30	54	4%	29	0%	5.36	-9.7	$15
BAvg Potl	45%	1st Half	271	36	80	3	22	0	295			357	362	719	9	92	31	1.18	256	53	18	30	42	4%	29	0%	4.62	-10.5	$6
LIMA Plan	C+	2nd Half	277	42	92	3	37	0	332			411	426	837	12	87	37	1.06	275	49	21	30	67	4%	28	0%	6.12	0.7	$9
+/- Score	-45	08 Proj	505	67	141	8	56	1	279			350	386	736	10	90	30	1.04	285	49	21	30	69	6%	42	0%	4.85	-16.7	$11

DH role helped, but so did a hit rate unsupported by skills. No speed, little power, and when (not if) h% regresses, the stats will look hauntingly like '05/'06. Isn't a DH with a negative RAR an oxymoron?

ROD TRUESDELL

Vizquel, Omar

Pos 6 · Age 41 · Decline · Bats Both · Reliability 8 · BAvg Potl 65% · LIMA Plan D+ · +/- Score -25

Yr/Tm	AB	R	H	HR	RBI	SB	Avg	vL	vR	OB	Slg	OPS	bb%	ct%	h%	Eye	xBA	G	L	F	PX	hr/f	SX	SBO	RC/G	RAR	R$
03 CLE	250	43	61	2	19	8	244	224	251	323	336	659	10	92	26	1.45	291	41	26	33	58	3%	120	15%	4.16	-2.0	$5
04 CLE	567	82	165	7	59	19	291	258	308	356	388	744	9	89	32	0.92	271	43	21	36	60	4%	108	14%	4.89	6.9	$18
05 SF	568	66	154	3	45	24	271	253	279	337	350	687	9	90	30	0.97	281	44	24	32	53	2%	106	19%	4.30	5.7	$15
06 SF	579	88	171	4	58	24	295	340	281	357	389	746	9	91	32	1.10	268	40	22	38	51	2%	132	16%	4.99	10.2	$19
07 SF	513	54	126	4	51	14	246	243	247	305	316	621	8	91	26	0.92	248	41	18	40	43	2%	91	14%	3.50	-7.1	$9
1st Half	254	28	60	2	22	6	236			287	303	590	7	87	24	0.53	243	42	19	38	44	2%	85	14%	2.92	-8.1	$3
2nd Half	259	26	66	2	29	8	255			323	328	651	9	95	26	1.86	252	40	17	42	42	2%	90	14%	4.06	0.8	$5
08 Proj	484	45	123	3	42	13	254			318	326	644	9	91	27	1.05	259	41	21	38	44	2%	91	14%	3.83	-3.5	$8

In retrospect, '06 xBA was the first sign. Now, all the skills are in decline. Even better 2nd half ct% didn't help much, with those FB hitting gloves. Wasn't pretty, could get worse. DN: 150 AB, loses job

Votto, Joey

Pos 3 · Age 24 · Growth · Bats Left · Reliability (07 CIN) · BAvg Potl 45% · LIMA Plan C+ · +/- Score 2

Yr/Tm	AB	R	H	HR	RBI	SB	Avg	vL	vR	OB	Slg	OPS	bb%	ct%	h%	Eye	xBA	G	L	F	PX	hr/f	SX	SBO	RC/G	RAR	R$
03	0	0	0	0	0	0	0							0							0		0				
04	0	0	0	0	0	0	0							0							0		0				
05	0	0	0	0	0	0	0							0							0						
06 aa	508	78	152	21	71	22	300			383	517	901	12	79	34	0.65					143		93	19%	6.86	16.3	$23
07 CIN	*580	77	165	26	99	16	284	269	345	359	469	828	10	81	32	0.59	275	28	26	46	112	12%	65	15%	5.74	2.4	$24
1st Half	284	37	84	10	40	7	296			388	451	839	13	80	34	0.77					95		64	13%	6.10	4.0	$11
2nd Half	296	40	81	16	59	9	274			328	486	815	7	81	29	0.42	287	28	26	46	128	14%	67	19%	5.38	-1.9	$13
08 Proj	406	57	115	18	65	14	283			360	486	846	11	80	32	0.60	283	28	26	46	128	12%	81	17%	6.03	3.7	$17

4-17-.321 in 84 AB at CIN. Intriguing multi-skilled prospect has risen steadily through the minors, hitting at most every stop. Impressed in September. If ct% gains continue and he gets a shot, could really shine.

Weeks, Rickie

Pos 4 · Age 25 · Pre-Peak · Bats Right · Reliability 34 · BAvg Potl 50% · LIMA Plan B+ · +/- Score 43

Yr/Tm	AB	R	H	HR	RBI	SB	Avg	vL	vR	OB	Slg	OPS	bb%	ct%	h%	Eye	xBA	G	L	F	PX	hr/f	SX	SBO	RC/G	RAR	R$
03	0	0	0	0	0	0	0							0									0				
04 aa	479	66	121	8	41	11	253			327	397	724	10	78	31	0.50					101		105	18%	4.62	4.0	$10
05 MIL	*563	88	143	22	78	23	254	229	244	327	446	773	10	76	30	0.45	284	49	20	31	124	17%	151	18%	5.12	9.3	$22
06 MIL	359	73	100	8	34	19	279	271	280	334	404	738	8	74	36	0.33	246	46	20	33	83	9%	141	23%	4.62	0.2	$14
07 MIL	409	87	96	16	36	25	235	258	225	357	433	790	16	72	29	0.67	254	42	17	41	133	13%	157	21%	5.72	14.3	$15
1st Half	195	38	48	5	19	8	246			341	441	782	13	76	30	0.60	268	40	18	43	133	8%	146	19%	5.52	5.6	$6
2nd Half	214	49	48	11	17	17	224			371	425	796	19	68	28	0.72	243	43	17	40	134	19%	148	22%	5.88	8.6	$9
08 Proj	459	90	120	20	44	25	261			354	469	824	13	73	31	0.54	268	44	18	38	134	16%	153	21%	5.97	18.9	$20

Better year than stats suggest. xBA better gauge of progress. He won't take that next step until ct% turns around, but the rest of his BPIs are headed the right way. Good candidate for those who like to speculate.

Wells, Vernon

Pos 8 · Age 29 · Peak · Bats Right · Reliability 33 · BAvg Potl — · LIMA Plan C+ · +/- Score 23

Yr/Tm	AB	R	H	HR	RBI	SB	Avg	vL	vR	OB	Slg	OPS	bb%	ct%	h%	Eye	xBA	G	L	F	PX	hr/f	SX	SBO	RC/G	RAR	R$
03 TOR	678	118	215	33	117	4	317	347	307	357	550	907	6	88	32	0.53	319	39	21	40	134	14%	90	3%	6.39	30.1	$31
04 TOR	536	82	146	23	67	9	272	287	267	336	472	808	9	85	29	0.61	293	45	17	38	118	13%	93	8%	5.44	11.2	$18
05 TOR	620	78	167	28	97	8	269	347	243	315	463	784	7	86	27	0.55	293	41	19	40	113	13%	82	7%	5.03	2.4	$18
06 TOR	611	91	185	32	106	17	303	333	292	359	542	901	8	85	31	0.60	308	42	18	40	136	15%	105	13%	6.48	30.7	$28
07 TOR	584	85	143	16	80	10	245	311	226	303	402	706	8	85	27	0.55	269	39	17	44	101	7%	103	10%	4.26	-0.4	$14
1st Half	292	42	73	9	43	5	250			303	418	720	7	84	27	0.47	270	39	16	46	110	8%	86	12%	4.36	0.7	$8
2nd Half	292	43	70	7	37	5	240			304	387	691	8	86	26	0.64	269	40	18	42	92	7%	106	8%	4.16	-1.0	$6
08 Proj	613	89	179	28	91	11	292			347	503	850	8	85	30	0.57	296	40	18	42	125	13%	96	9%	5.87	24.9	$24

It's clear from PX and hr/f collapse that something was amiss. Assuming it was the shoulder, and surgery fixes it, FB% gains suggest he could even improve on '06 PX. Now he's a buy-low candidate.

Werth, Jayson

Pos 97 · Age 28 · Peak · Bats Right · Reliability 11 · BAvg Potl 60% · LIMA Plan C · +/- Score -23

Yr/Tm	AB	R	H	HR	RBI	SB	Avg	vL	vR	OB	Slg	OPS	bb%	ct%	h%	Eye	xBA	G	L	F	PX	hr/f	SX	SBO	RC/G	RAR	R$
03 TOR	*284	39	64	10	40	11	225	56	300	267	419	686	5	71	28	0.20	269	42	19	38	147	13%	124	26%	3.86	-11.1	$8
04 LA	*341	66	93	20	63	6	273	290	249	342	510	852	10	72	33	0.37	266	32	25	43	150	19%	126	8%	6.19	8.8	$16
05 LA	*386	52	94	9	50	15	242	239	237	338	379	717	13	68	34	0.44	231	41	20	39	111	9%	109	15%	4.70	-6.4	$11
06	0	0	0	0	0	0	0							0									0				
07 PHI	255	43	76	8	49	7	298	375	257	401	459	860	15	71	39	0.60	260	40	27	33	109	13%	109	8%	6.71	10.3	$11
1st Half	85	12	20	3	10	0	235			337	353	690	13	74	28	0.59	230	36	23	41	71	12%	34	3%	4.09	-3.0	$2
2nd Half	170	31	56	5	39	7	329			433	512	945	17	70	45	0.61	274	42	29	30	130	15%	126	10%	8.09	12.7	$10
08 Proj	307	49	83	10	51	9	270			361	441	801	12	71	35	0.48	254	39	25	36	119	13%	113	11%	5.77	5.5	$12

PRO:
- Great bb%, some HR & SB
CON:
- Injured every year
- Lousy ct%
- Big drop-off vs RHP
H% regression means BA dip.

White, Rondell

Pos 0 · Age 36 · Decline · Bats Right · Reliability 0 · BAvg Potl 60% · LIMA Plan F · +/- Score 25

Yr/Tm	AB	R	H	HR	RBI	SB	Avg	vL	vR	OB	Slg	OPS	bb%	ct%	h%	Eye	xBA	G	L	F	PX	hr/f	SX	SBO	RC/G	RAR	R$
03 2TM	488	62	141	22	87	1	289	299	285	331	488	819	6	84	31	0.39	294	45	20	35	115	15%	55	4%	5.38	10.5	$18
04 DET	448	76	121	19	67	1	270	293	258	329	453	782	8	83	29	0.51	269	49	13	38	106	14%	65	3%	5.06	-3.1	$14
05 DET	374	49	117	12	53	1	313	325	309	343	489	832	4	87	33	0.35	306	55	17	29	108	13%	68	1%	5.49	-5.3	$14
06 MIN	337	32	83	7	38	1	246	271	235	270	365	635	3	84	28	0.20	268	44	21	34	75	7%	50	3%	4.33	-33.0	$4
07 MIN	109	8	19	4	20	0	174	143	194	217	321	538	5	83	17	0.32	230	51	12	37	90	12%	14	0%	2.00	-14.2	$1
1st Half	9	1	1	0	2	0	111			273	111	384	18	89	13	2.00		50	0	50	31	0%			1.25	-1.5	($0)
2nd Half	100	7	18	4	18	0	180			212	340	552	4	82	18	0.22	237	51	13	36	98	13%	11	0%	2.06	-12.7	$1
08 Proj	153	17	37	4	23	0	242			277	393	670	5	84	26	0.31	274	50	16	34	94	10%	64	2%	3.62	-10.9	$3

Spent four months on - yes - the DL, and stated after the season, "My body hurts." At this writing, he was leaning toward retirement. For his sake, and to curb spiraling medical insurance costs, let's hope so.

Wigginton, Ty

Pos 54 · Age 30 · Peak · Bats Right · Reliability 57 · BAvg Potl 40% · LIMA Plan C · +/- Score -23

Yr/Tm	AB	R	H	HR	RBI	SB	Avg	vL	vR	OB	Slg	OPS	bb%	ct%	h%	Eye	xBA	G	L	F	PX	hr/f	SX	SBO	RC/G	RAR	R$
03 NYM	573	73	146	11	71	12	255	297	239	310	396	706	7	78	31	0.34	269	45	20	34	99	7%	124	10%	4.23	-3.8	$14
04 2NL	494	63	129	17	66	7	261	222	272	323	426	750	8	83	28	0.55	284	45	19	36	105	11%	85	6%	4.83	-3.3	$14
05 PIT	*435	58	109	17	62	6	251	247	268	322	428	750	9	83	27	0.63	293	42	22	36	111	13%	66	11%	4.80	0.2	$13
06 TAM	444	55	122	24	79	4	275	316	260	303	498	821	7	78	30	0.33	283	40	19	41	138	17%	55	7%	5.46	5.8	$15
07 2TM	547	71	152	22	67	3	278	284	276	328	459	787	7	79	32	0.36	271	44	18	38	119	13%	41	5%	5.09	7.0	$16
1st Half	293	36	79	13	39	1	270			316	461	777	6	82	29	0.37	281	43	18	38	120	14%	32	7%	4.90	2.2	$8
2nd Half	254	35	73	9	28	2	287			342	457	799	8	77	34	0.36	259	45	16	39	117	12%	52	3%	5.31	4.9	$8
08 Proj	551	76	150	27	86	2	272			326	482	808	7	79	30	0.39	284	43	18	39	132	16%	47	4%	5.35	8.8	$18

Slugged .539 at HR-haven Minute Maid; his six HR there in 89 AB equates to 20 bombs in 275. FB dip not significant, and his skills are stable. A bargain power source (again). UP: 30+ HR

Wilkerson, Brad

Pos 37 · Age 30 · Peak · Bats Left · Reliability 52 · BAvg Potl 45% · LIMA Plan C · +/- Score 1

Yr/Tm	AB	R	H	HR	RBI	SB	Avg	vL	vR	OB	Slg	OPS	bb%	ct%	h%	Eye	xBA	G	L	F	PX	hr/f	SX	SBO	RC/G	RAR	R$
03 MON	504	78	135	19	77	13	268	281	263	378	464	842	15	69	35	0.57	267	40	24	36	147	15%	97	14%	6.53	15.1	$19
04 MON	573	112	146	32	67	13	255	278	245	371	497	869	16	73	30	0.70	275	31	21	47	162	16%	94	11%	6.66	12.1	$22
05 WAS	565	76	140	11	57	8	248	296	228	345	405	750	13	74	32	0.57	254	31	24	45	120	6%	96	11%	5.14	-7.9	$12
06 TEX	320	55	73	15	44	3	222	190	233	303	422	724	10	64	30	0.32	224	35	15	50	149	15%	100	7%	4.73	-6.8	$7
07 TEX	338	54	79	20	62	4	234	258	224	320	467	788	11	68	28	0.40	260	39	17	45	168	19%	77	6%	5.45	3.7	$11
1st Half	144	22	32	9	27	2	222			317	458	775	12	70	25	0.47	263	42	15	43	165	21%	54	8%	5.22	0.6	$4
2nd Half	194	32	47	11	35	2	242			323	474	797	11	67	30	0.36	256	36	18	46	171	18%	84	4%	5.65	3.2	$6
08 Proj	433	70	112	24	67	5	259			345	491	836	12	68	31	0.42	259	36	18	46	167	18%	75	6%	6.21	13.1	$15

5 steps to achieve success:
1. Raise ct% to mediocre.
2. Learn to hit right-handers.
3. Stay off the DL for a full season.
4. Play for team in hitter's park.
5. Only play in home games.
It's not asking a lot. Really.

Willingham, Josh

Pos 7 · Age 29 · Peak · Bats Right · Reliability 68 · BAvg Potl 45% · LIMA Plan B · +/- Score -5

Yr/Tm	AB	R	H	HR	RBI	SB	Avg	vL	vR	OB	Slg	OPS	bb%	ct%	h%	Eye	xBA	G	L	F	PX	hr/f	SX	SBO	RC/G	RAR	R$
03 aa	67	12	17	4	11	0	255			364	482	846	15	72	30	0.60					142		80	0%	6.31	1.7	$2
04 aa	338	60	75	15	57	6	221			356	413	769	17	75	25	0.85					126		63	3%	5.36	1.8	$9
05 aaa	219	39	57	12	37	4	261			360	492	852	13	81	27	0.82					140		99	7%	6.22	7.6	$9
06 FLA	502	62	139	26	74	2	277	299	269	347	496	843	10	78	31	0.50	273	43	16	41	132	16%	51	3%	5.92	9.6	$17
07 FLA	521	75	138	21	89	8	265	218	281	348	486	810	11	77	31	0.54	269	36	21	43	130	12%	97	6%	5.68	5.1	$18
1st Half	273	38	70	9	47	4	256			345	447	792	12	77	30	0.59	264	37	18	45	128	10%	96	5%	5.53	1.5	$8
2nd Half	248	37	68	12	42	4	274			350	480	830	10	76	32	0.49	276	35	23	41	132	15%	74	7%	5.84	3.6	$9
08 Proj	525	78	139	24	86	7	265			351	473	824	12	78	30	0.59	275	38	19	42	132	14%	83	5%	5.83	7.5	$18

July/Aug PX was 147; disk problem wrecked Sept. Still owns the skills and PX history to take power up a notch. Consistent .270-ish BA won't hurt you. Just hope he avoids dreaded "lingering back woes."

ROD TRUESDELL

Willits,Reggie			AB	R	H	HR	RBI	SB	Avg	vL	vR	OB	Slg	OPS	bb%	ct%	h%	Eye	xBA	G	L	F	PX	hr/f	SX	SBO	RC/G	RAR	R$
Pos	798	03	0	0	0	0	0	0	0							0									0				
Age	26	04	0	0	0	0	0	0	0							0									0				
Pre-Peak		05 aa	487	55	124	1	34	29	254			308	310	618	7	87	29	0.59					41		114	33%	3.31	-25.6	$12
Bats	Both	06 LAA	* 397	78	113	2	33	28	285			391	352	743	15	88	32	1.41	300	39	35	26	45	2%	109	30%	5.25	0.9	$15
Reliability	14	07 LAA	430	74	126	0	34	27	293	333	276	391	344	735	14	81	36	0.83	251	49	23	28	44	0%	105	20%	5.00	3.4	$15
BAvg Potl	40%	1st Half	208	39	70	0	24	18	337			434	399	833	15	84	40	1.09	254	47	20	33	50	0%	115	21%	6.32	8.8	$11
LIMA Plan	D+	2nd Half	222	35	56	0	10	9	252			349	293	642	13	77	33	0.66	248	52	25	23	38	0%	79	19%	3.69	-6.9	$4
+/- Score	-36	08 Proj	**325**	**56**	**86**	**1**	**25**	**20**	**265**			**371**	**320**	**691**	**14**	**84**	**31**	**1.04**	**263**	**49**	**24**	**27**	**43**	**1%**	**102**	**25%**	**4.52**	**-3.5**	**$10**

Rode aberrant h% to 1st half success, but landed with a thud. 2H slides in ct% and SX suggest he's better suited for part-time duty. There's value in what he does well (bb%, SB), but there's also little upside.

Wilson,Jack			AB	R	H	HR	RBI	SB	Avg	vL	vR	OB	Slg	OPS	bb%	ct%	h%	Eye	xBA	G	L	F	PX	hr/f	SX	SBO	RC/G	RAR	R$
Pos	6	03 PIT	558	58	143	9	62	5	256	261	255	301	357	658	6	87	28	0.49	277	42	25	33	61	6%	77	7%	3.65	-7.7	$11
Age	30	04 PIT	652	82	201	11	59	8	308	261	318	335	459	793	4	89	33	0.37	292	45	20	36	87	5%	113	7%	5.12	17.7	$20
Peak		05 PIT	587	60	151	8	52	7	257	255	256	294	363	657	5	90	27	0.53	275	48	18	34	62	4%	100	7%	3.69	-4.6	$11
Bats	Right	06 PIT	543	70	148	8	35	4	273	301	262	314	370	684	6	88	30	0.51	281	47	23	30	61	6%	60	5%	3.96	-6.3	$10
Reliability	72	07 PIT	477	67	141	12	56	2	296	320	289	348	440	788	7	90	31	0.83	280	39	19	42	86	7%	54	5%	5.25	17.3	$14
BAvg Potl	60%	1st Half	268	36	70	4	20	0	261			308	366	673	6	91	27	0.78	255	43	15	42	64	4%	53	4%	3.98	0.2	$4
LIMA Plan	C	2nd Half	209	31	71	8	36	2	340			397	536	933	9	89	35	0.87	310	35	23	41	115	10%	58	6%	6.92	16.3	$10
+/- Score	-14	08 Proj	**514**	**67**	**144**	**11**	**55**	**2**	**280**			**327**	**414**	**741**	**7**	**89**	**30**	**0.66**	**284**	**42**	**21**	**37**	**80**	**7%**	**60**	**4%**	**4.67**	**8.8**	**$13**

Fought through injuries and saved his season with huge PX-driven Aug/Sept. Suddenly, GB became LD. Tempting to say "fluke," but FB% was up all year. I'm still not buying that it'll stick. Watch '08 G/L/F for clues.

Wilson,Josh			AB	R	H	HR	RBI	SB	Avg	vL	vR	OB	Slg	OPS	bb%	ct%	h%	Eye	xBA	G	L	F	PX	hr/f	SX	SBO	RC/G	RAR	R$
Pos	64	03 aa	434	46	102	2	50	5	235			275	341	616	5	85	27	0.38					73		103	12%	3.19	-14.3	$5
Age	27	04 a/a	551	71	142	10	48	11	258			317	374	691	8	85	29	0.60					72		94	11%	4.13	-2.7	$12
Peak		05 aaa	521	61	111	11	57	12	213			263	342	604	6	84	23	0.43					82		106	20%	2.99	-20.9	$8
Bats	Right	06 aaa	335	46	96	8	34	11	287			341	426	767	8	91	30	0.95					77		102	16%	5.06	6.5	$11
Reliability	6	07 2TM	282	28	67	2	24	6	238	256	230	281	333	614	6	80	29	0.30	223	43	13	44	69	2%	104	13%	3.03	-10.4	$3
BAvg Potl	40%	1st Half	64	9	14	0	3	3	219			296	281	577	10	80	27	0.54	226	42	17	40	57	0%	88	18%	2.80	-2.9	$1
LIMA Plan	F	2nd Half	218	19	53	2	21	3	243			276	349	625	4	80	30	0.23	221	43	11	45	73	3%	92	11%	3.09	-7.6	$2
+/- Score	-19	08 Proj	**210**	**25**	**49**	**3**	**19**	**6**	**233**			**285**	**344**	**629**	**7**	**84**	**27**	**0.45**	**240**	**43**	**14**	**43**	**72**	**4%**	**107**	**16%**	**3.33**	**-6.1**	**$3**

AAA three-peater's BPIs tanked at ML level. Looks like '06 ct% is the outlier; even with pre-2006 ct% levels; just-okay SX isn't enough to boost the BA. Don't count on him keeping job long enough to pad SB total.

Wilson,Preston			AB	R	H	HR	RBI	SB	Avg	vL	vR	OB	Slg	OPS	bb%	ct%	h%	Eye	xBA	G	L	F	PX	hr/f	SX	SBO	RC/G	RAR	R$
Pos	9	03 COL	600	94	169	36	141	14	282	274	285	341	537	878	8	77	31	0.39	307	41	22	37	168	21%	88	15%	6.30	11.9	$31
Age	33	04 COL	202	24	50	6	29	2	248	290	226	306	391	697	8	76	30	0.35	258	44	22	35	99	11%	53	6%	4.04	-7.5	$5
Past Peak		05 2NL	520	73	135	25	90	6	260	262	259	319	467	786	8	72	32	0.30	284	52	21	27	147	25%	73	10%	5.25	-0.0	$19
Bats	Right	06 2NL	501	58	132	17	72	12	263	292	255	304	423	727	5	76	32	0.24	271	55	18	27	103	17%	89	12%	4.29	-6.9	$15
Reliability	17	07 STL	64	6	14	1	5	2	219	208	225	265	313	577	6	73	28	0.24	218	57	11	32	72	7%	65	21%	2.40	-5.7	$1
BAvg Potl	40%	1st Half	64	6	14	1	5	2	219			265	313	577	6	73	28	0.24	218	57	11	32	72	7%	65	21%	2.40	-5.7	$1
LIMA Plan	D	2nd Half	0	0	0	0	0	0	0							0													
+/- Score	1	08 Proj	**363**	**44**	**94**	**12**	**51**	**1**	**259**			**310**	**419**	**728**	**7**	**74**	**32**	**0.28**	**254**	**52**	**18**	**31**	**109**	**15%**	**40**	**5%**	**4.40**	**-8.0**	**$9**

Another season-ending knee surgery. Now 33, with the knees of a much older man. Club officials are unsure how he came into possession of these knees but there's one angry geezer up in Peoria.

Winn,Randy			AB	R	H	HR	RBI	SB	Avg	vL	vR	OB	Slg	OPS	bb%	ct%	h%	Eye	xBA	G	L	F	PX	hr/f	SX	SBO	RC/G	RAR	R$
Pos	987	03 SEA	600	103	177	11	75	23	295	314	288	340	425	765	6	82	35	0.38	283	51	20	29	88	8%	132	17%	4.88	-4.5	$24
Age	33	04 SEA	626	84	179	14	81	21	286	257	299	342	427	768	8	84	32	0.54	285	53	18	29	85	9%	116	16%	5.00	5.4	$21
Past Peak		05 2TM	617	85	189	20	63	19	306	269	317	356	499	856	7	85	33	0.53	320	50	21	29	123	13%	107	18%	5.99	17.4	$25
Bats	Both	06 SF	573	82	150	11	56	10	262	219	278	319	396	715	8	89	28	0.76	284	50	17	33	79	6%	92	12%	4.48	-4.9	$13
Reliability	29	07 SF	593	73	178	14	65	15	300	351	277	349	445	794	7	86	33	0.52	292	51	19	31	94	9%	80	11%	5.24	-0.1	$20
BAvg Potl	50%	1st Half	290	34	83	5	23	6	286			330	410	740	6	83	33	0.40	280	52	19	29	84	7%	78	12%	4.58	-5.5	$7
LIMA Plan	C+	2nd Half	303	39	95	9	42	9	314			366	479	844	8	88	33	0.68	302	50	18	32	104	10%	76	10%	5.86	5.0	$13
+/- Score	-30	08 Proj	**552**	**74**	**156**	**12**	**61**	**10**	**283**			**335**	**429**	**764**	**7**	**86**	**31**	**0.57**	**293**	**50**	**19**	**31**	**93**	**8%**	**90**	**10%**	**4.94**	**-3.2**	**$16**

The good:
- Strong 2nd half skills rebound
- ct% keeps BA respectable

The not-so-good:
- SX freefall continues
- RAR falling into the red
- Wrong side of 30

Woodward,Chris			AB	R	H	HR	RBI	SB	Avg	vL	vR	OB	Slg	OPS	bb%	ct%	h%	Eye	xBA	G	L	F	PX	hr/f	SX	SBO	RC/G	RAR	R$
Pos	5	03 TOR	349	49	91	7	45	1	261	307	242	316	395	711	7	79	31	0.39	256	31	23	45	94	6%	68	3%	4.27	-2.4	$8
Age	31	04 TOR	213	21	50	1	24	1	235	254	227	282	347	629	6	78	30	0.30	246	39	21	40	78	2%	97	7%	3.29	-10.5	$2
Past Peak		05 NYM	173	16	49	3	18	0	283	260	316	333	393	726	7	73	37	0.28	271	35	32	33	88	7%	18	0%	4.46	-1.5	$4
Bats	Right	06 NYM	222	25	48	3	25	1	216	226	209	290	311	601	9	75	27	0.42	225	44	18	38	67	5%	62	4%	2.91	-17.7	$2
Reliability	8	07 ATL	136	16	27	1	8	1	199	229	167	253	279	533	7	79	25	0.34	212	35	17	48	58	2%	85	3%	2.03	-11.8	($0)
BAvg Potl	55%	1st Half	93	10	20	1	7	1	215			240	301	541	3	76	27	0.14	200	35	15	49	58	3%	97	6%	1.87	-8.3	$0
LIMA Plan	F	2nd Half	43	6	7	0	1	0	163			280	233	513	14	84	19	1.00	239	35	21	44	59	0%	42	0%	2.36	-3.4	($1)
+/- Score	33	08 Proj	**103**	**11**	**24**	**1**	**10**	**1**	**233**			**281**	**340**	**621**	**6**	**76**	**29**	**0.28**	**235**	**37**	**22**	**41**	**75**	**4%**	**76**	**4%**	**3.06**	**-5.9**	**$1**

Fanalytically irrelevant since crash-and-burn with TOR, '07's little debacle does nothing to remedy that. The clubhouse leader in a spirited competition for the title "worst player on this talent-starved page."

Wood,Brandon			AB	R	H	HR	RBI	SB	Avg	vL	vR	OB	Slg	OPS	bb%	ct%	h%	Eye	xBA	G	L	F	PX	hr/f	SX	SBO	RC/G	RAR	R$
Pos	5	03	0	0	0	0	0	0	0							0									0				
Age	23	04	0	0	0	0	0	0	0							0									0				
Growth		05 aaa	19	1	5	0	1	0	263			263	421	684	0	58	45	0.00					133		54	0%	4.70	0.0	$0
Bats	Right	06 aa	453	55	107	18	61	14	236			297	446	743	8	76	27	0.35					143		103	20%	4.67	-8.0	$12
Reliability	16	07 LAA	* 470	68	116	21	73	9	247			306	440	746	8	74	29	0.33	261	52	10	38	134	16%	90	9%	4.65	2.1	$14
BAvg Potl	40%	1st Half	287	40	68	12	44	7	237			309	429	738	9	75	27	0.42		50	17	33	132	17%	91	12%	4.63	1.1	$8
LIMA Plan	D	2nd Half	183	28	48	9	29	2	262			301	459	760	5	73	31	0.20	247	53	7	40	136	17%	65	5%	4.69	1.0	$6
+/- Score	45	08 Proj	**315**	**43**	**81**	**12**	**47**	**5**	**257**			**312**	**439**	**750**	**7**	**75**	**31**	**0.31**	**254**	**53**	**8**	**39**	**128**	**13%**	**84**	**9%**	**4.73**	**0.7**	**$9**

1-3-.152 in 33 AB at LAA. Already studly PX shows a player with upside. That said, ct% keeps BA and HR totals in check, and will cause some agonizing growing pains. Keeper league work in progress.

Wood,Jason			AB	R	H	HR	RBI	SB	Avg	vL	vR	OB	Slg	OPS	bb%	ct%	h%	Eye	xBA	G	L	F	PX	hr/f	SX	SBO	RC/G	RAR	R$
Pos	3	03 aaa	473	54	109	10	57	4	230			278	348	626	6	82	26	0.37					75		84	4%	3.17	-32.5	$7
Age	38	04 aaa	375	27	68	5	31	1	180			233	266	500	7	84	20	0.44					55		50	3%	1.79	-44.6	($2)
Decline		05 aaa	447	47	101	13	49	4	226			276	348	625	7	85	24	0.47					72		64	7%	3.19	-29.6	$7
Bats	Right	06 aaa	441	45	99	7	54	1	224			276	320	597	7	81	26	0.37					62		54	2%	2.80	-39.1	$4
Reliability	5	07 FLA	117	11	28	3	26	0	239	244	236	288	368	656	6	68	33	0.21	224	39	22	39	101	10%	20	0%	3.52	-7.3	$2
BAvg Potl	30%	1st Half	61	5	15	2	16	0	246			292	426	719	6	64	35	0.18	238	36	21	44	155	12%	12	0%	4.63	-1.7	$2
LIMA Plan	F	2nd Half	56	6	13	1	10	0	232			283	304	587	7	71	31	0.25	211	43	23	35	49	7%	28	0%	2.48	-5.3	$1
+/- Score	-59	08 Proj	**51**	**5**	**12**	**1**	**8**	**0**	**235**			**286**	**340**	**626**	**7**	**75**	**29**	**0.29**	**234**	**40**	**22**	**38**	**73**	**8%**	**34**	**2%**	**3.05**	**-4.1**	**$1**

No, HE'S the worst player on the page. 5th MLB cup of coffee in his 17-year pro career, (11 years in AAA) and he beat his previous PT high by 73 AB. Shows how one hot spring can trump 17 years of winter.

Wright,David			AB	R	H	HR	RBI	SB	Avg	vL	vR	OB	Slg	OPS	bb%	ct%	h%	Eye	xBA	G	L	F	PX	hr/f	SX	SBO	RC/G	RAR	R$
Pos	5	03	0	0	0	0	0	0	0							0									0				
Age	25	04 NYM	* 600	97	188	31	91	26	313	309	288	378	557	934	9	85	33	0.69	308	35	20	46	146	13%	90	23%	6.97	31.7	$33
Pre-Peak		05 NYM	575	99	176	27	102	17	306	336	300	383	523	907	11	80	34	0.64	310	39	25	35	143	17%	86	13%	6.82	32.4	$31
Bats	Right	06 NYM	582	96	181	26	116	20	311	285	321	381	531	912	10	81	35	0.58	283	36	19	44	133	13%	110	14%	6.85	21.6	$30
Reliability	94	07 NYM	604	113	196	30	107	34	325	361	311	415	546	962	13	81	36	0.82	303	39	23	38	139	16%	99	18%	7.62	46.0	$37
BAvg Potl	45%	1st Half	285	43	82	13	42	16	288			372	495	866	12	78	33	0.59	279	40	20	41	134	15%	104	19%	6.39	12.9	$14
LIMA Plan	D+	2nd Half	319	70	114	17	65	18	357			453	592	1046	15	84	39	1.10	324	39	26	35	143	18%	89	17%	8.67	31.9	$24
+/- Score	-13	08 Proj	**607**	**119**	**194**	**34**	**111**	**28**	**320**			**401**	**569**	**970**	**12**	**81**	**35**	**0.73**	**311**	**38**	**23**	**39**	**152**	**18%**	**109**	**17%**	**7.60**	**43.6**	**$37**

After a 0 HR, .244 April, went on a 5-month tear and improved on almost every measurable skill. Just got better as the year went on. (The Mets' September wasn't his fault.)
UP: batting title, 35 HR, 35 SB

ROD TRUESDELL

Youkilis, Kevin

Pos 3 · Age 29 · Bats Right · Reliability 73 · BAvg Potl 45% · LIMA Plan B · +/- Score -18

	AB	R	H	HR	RBI	SB	Avg	vL	vR	OB	Slg	OPS	bb%	ct%	h%	Eye	xBA	G	L	F	PX	hr/f	SX	SBO	RC/G	RAR	R$
03 a/a	421	70	111	6	44	6	264			389	371	759	17	87	29	1.54					72		80	4%	5.52	0.9	$10
04 BOS	*365	58	92	9	50	2	252	250	265	342	389	731	12	82	29	0.75	260	37	21	42	91	7%	56	3%	4.76	-2.5	$8
05 BOS	*231	33	66	7	29	1	284	300	265	390	474	865	15	82	32	0.96	310	32	28	40	133	9%	49	5%	6.61	10.1	$7
06 BOS	569	100	159	13	72	5	279	270	283	379	429	808	14	79	33	0.76	262	31	24	45	104	6%	79	4%	5.85	6.9	$16
07 BOS	528	85	152	16	83	4	288	290	287	379	453	831	13	80	33	0.78	268	34	21	45	113	8%	68	3%	6.04	14.0	$18
1st Half	279	45	92	8	41	2	330			404	498	903	11	86	36	0.92	285	37	19	44	109	8%	65	2%	6.79	12.5	$12
2nd Half	249	40	60	8	42	2	241			351	402	752	14	73	30	0.63	249	32	23	46	117	10%	64	5%	5.11	0.2	$6
08 Proj	544	88	150	18	78	4	276			375	452	827	14	80	32	0.78	274	33	23	45	119	9%	67	4%	6.03	13.2	$17

Yet another 2nd half fade, as ct% plunged. FB% begs for more PX. But hr/f, 2H woes, and his Mgr all say wrist pain from HBP sapped his strength. He gets hit & hurt a lot, so we'll assume more aches & pains.

Young, Chris

Pos 8 · Age 24 · Growth · Bats Right · Reliability 29 · BAvg Potl 50% · LIMA Plan B · +/- Score 20

	AB	R	H	HR	RBI	SB	Avg	vL	vR	OB	Slg	OPS	bb%	ct%	h%	Eye	xBA	G	L	F	PX	hr/f	SX	SBO	RC/G	RAR	R$
03	0	0	0	0	0	0	0						0										0				
04	0	0	0	0	0	0	0						0										0				
05 aa	462	78	115	24	61	25	249			330	489	819	11	78	27	0.54					161		126	29%	5.72	18.1	$20
06 ARI	*472	67	114	18	66	14	241	360	178	307	440	747	9	86	25	0.66	301	42	20	37	116	12%	99	20%	4.78	4.9	$14
07 ARI	569	85	135	32	68	27	237	246	234	311	467	758	7	75	26	0.30	264	37	15	48	146	15%	122	29%	4.71	2.6	$21
1st Half	248	33	60	11	29	8	242			274	435	710	4	81	26	0.23	260	37	14	49	118	11%	107	17%	3.97	-4.3	$7
2nd Half	321	52	75	21	39	19	234			303	492	795	9	71	26	0.34	266	36	16	48	171	19%	125	37%	5.38	8.1	$13
08 Proj	546	82	141	29	70	23	258			319	492	811	8	79	28	0.43	278	37	16	47	144	14%	113	25%	5.44	14.2	$22

You can see him learning on the job in those Eye ratios: took more 2H pitches, but not always the right pitches. But except for that ct%, skills took a step up. Still owns '06 ct%; add that, and he's in the elite.

Young, Delmon

Pos 98 · Age 22 · Growth · Bats Right · Reliability 41 · BAvg Potl 35% · LIMA Plan D+ · +/- Score -30

	AB	R	H	HR	RBI	SB	Avg	vL	vR	OB	Slg	OPS	bb%	ct%	h%	Eye	xBA	G	L	F	PX	hr/f	SX	SBO	RC/G	RAR	R$
03	0	0	0	0	0	0	0						0										0				
04	0	0	0	0	0	0	0						0										0				
05 a/a	558	75	163	21	81	28	292			321	463	784	4	88	30	0.35					96		120	32%	4.90	-1.3	$26
06 TAM	*468	68	152	11	71	25	325	379	299	348	485	834	3	83	38	0.20	305	47	26	27	102	10%	136	26%	5.51	-2.0	$22
07 TAM	645	65	186	13	93	10	288	299	285	316	408	724	4	80	34	0.20	267	46	21	33	86	8%	63	8%	4.19	-9.3	$18
1st Half	303	38	84	9	43	6	277			307	416	723	4	80	32	0.22	269	45	21	34	93	11%	70	11%	4.14	-4.8	$9
2nd Half	342	27	102	4	50	4	298			324	401	725	4	80	36	0.19	264	48	21	31	80	5%	47	6%	4.23	-4.5	$9
08 Proj	626	75	179	16	92	16	286			313	435	748	4	82	33	0.22	287	46	22	32	98	10%	96	16%	4.47	-8.8	$21

High AB total hides fact that skills took a step back. Still, he's only 22, with great BA (see LD) and speed upside. But Eye ratios limiting both, GB hurting PX and TAM needs to restore his green light. No breakout yet.

Young, Delwyn

Pos 7 · Age 25 · Pre-Peak · Bats Both · Reliability 23 · BAvg Potl 35% · LIMA Plan F · +/- Score 16

	AB	R	H	HR	RBI	SB	Avg	vL	vR	OB	Slg	OPS	bb%	ct%	h%	Eye	xBA	G	L	F	PX	hr/f	SX	SBO	RC/G	RAR	R$
03	0	0	0	0	0	0	0						0										0				
04	0	0	0	0	0	0	0						0										0				
05 a/a	526	54	133	15	55	1	253			285	394	679	4	84	28	0.28					92		31	4%	3.68	-21.0	$10
06 aaa	532	58	124	14	75	2	233			277	378	654	6	85	25	0.39					92		40	7%	3.52	-27.4	$8
07 LA	*524	85	147	16	77	4	281	333	421	322	470	791	6	80	33	0.30	279	34	21	45	129	8%	87	6%	5.18	-2.4	$17
1st Half	300	49	90	11	50	3	300			346	517	862	7	79	35	0.34					147		82	10%	6.10	6.4	$12
2nd Half	224	36	57	5	27	1	255			289	407	696	5	81	30	0.25	263	34	21	45	105	6%	88	1%	3.96	-9.0	$5
08 Proj	170	23	46	5	23	1	271			309	433	743	5	82	31	0.32	270	34	21	45	106	7%	70	5%	4.54	-3.9	$4

2-3-.382 in 34 AB at LA. Which is more telling, overall step up or the 2H regression? Since the drop wasn't all the way back down, we'll say it's a push. Either way, don't expect much from him in '08.

Young, Dmitri

Pos 3 · Age 34 · Past Peak · Bats Both · Reliability 17 · BAvg Potl 35% · LIMA Plan D+ · +/- Score -28

	AB	R	H	HR	RBI	SB	Avg	vL	vR	OB	Slg	OPS	bb%	ct%	h%	Eye	xBA	G	L	F	PX	hr/f	SX	SBO	RC/G	RAR	R$
03 DET	562	78	167	29	85	2	297	293	299	363	537	900	9	77	34	0.45	312	44	27	29	152	23%	79	2%	6.71	20.7	$22
04 DET	389	72	106	18	60	0	272	248	286	329	481	810	8	82	29	0.46	296	46	20	34	124	16%	69	1%	5.40	4.6	$13
05 DET	469	61	127	21	72	1	271	277	269	331	470	784	6	79	30	0.30	291	47	20	33	129	18%	67	1%	4.99	-1.3	$15
06 DET	172	19	43	7	23	1	250	136	267	295	407	702	6	77	29	0.28	247	52	14	34	91	16%	59	5%	3.93	-7.6	$4
07 WAS	460	57	147	13	74	0	320	301	327	379	491	870	9	84	36	0.59	293	43	22	36	114	9%	30	0%	6.27	8.2	$17
1st Half	247	36	83	7	36	0	336			390	506	896	8	84	38	0.55	294	39	22	38	114	9%	26	0%	6.53	6.0	$10
2nd Half	213	21	64	6	38	0	300			366	474	840	9	84	34	0.63	294	47	21	32	114	10%	33	0%	5.96	2.1	$7
08 Proj	452	55	131	19	70	0	290			344	486	830	8	81	32	0.44	288	46	20	34	121	16%	40	1%	5.66	-0.7	$15

Batting average was over his head, but throw out troubled '06, and xBA shows it wasn't that much of a fluke. Of course, health remains a big question. But not skills.

Young, Michael

Pos 6 · Age 31 · Past Peak · Bats Right · Reliability 86 · BAvg Potl 35% · LIMA Plan D+ · +/- Score -22

	AB	R	H	HR	RBI	SB	Avg	vL	vR	OB	Slg	OPS	bb%	ct%	h%	Eye	xBA	G	L	F	PX	hr/f	SX	SBO	RC/G	RAR	R$
03 TEX	666	106	204	14	72	13	306	308	306	342	446	788	5	85	35	0.35	298	44	27	29	85	9%	131	8%	5.06	11.6	$24
04 TEX	693	115	216	22	100	12	312	330	307	355	481	835	6	87	33	0.52	292	38	25	38	93	10%	120	8%	5.65	22.3	$28
05 TEX	668	114	221	24	91	5	331	340	327	384	513	898	8	86	36	0.64	320	45	26	29	111	14%	87	3%	6.47	33.6	$30
06 TEX	691	93	217	14	103	7	314	295	320	359	459	817	6	86	35	0.50	310	48	25	27	94	9%	76	5%	5.52	20.7	$23
07 TEX	639	80	201	9	94	13	315	309	316	362	418	779	7	83	37	0.44	294	48	27	24	74	7%	77	8%	5.07	8.9	$22
1st Half	318	45	94	4	47	6	296			343	409	752	7	84	34	0.45	298	46	27	27	82	6%	81	9%	4.78	1.9	$10
2nd Half	321	35	107	5	47	7	333			380	427	806	7	83	39	0.43	289	51	27	22	66	9%	61	7%	5.37	6.8	$12
08 Proj	629	86	192	12	90	10	305			353	431	784	7	85	35	0.48	300	47	26	26	84	8%	87	7%	5.13	10.7	$21

Some definite skills erosion, but LD stroke as reliable as ever. Few provide his annual AB and BA levels. xBA says Avg may start down, and he's basically a one-trick pony now. But it's a pretty good trick.

Zaun, Gregg

Pos 2 · Age 37 · Decline · Bats Both · Reliability 28 · BAvg Potl 65% · LIMA Plan D · +/- Score 6

	AB	R	H	HR	RBI	SB	Avg	vL	vR	OB	Slg	OPS	bb%	ct%	h%	Eye	xBA	G	L	F	PX	hr/f	SX	SBO	RC/G	RAR	R$
03 2NL	166	15	38	4	21	1	229	308	205	308	349	658	10	87	24	0.90	276	43	21	35	75	8%	34	4%	3.88	-2.1	$2
04 TOR	338	46	91	6	36	0	269	272	268	358	393	752	12	82	31	0.77	277	45	24	32	87	7%	29	3%	5.07	7.2	$7
05 TOR	434	61	109	11	61	2	251	278	241	359	373	732	14	84	28	1.04	263	46	19	35	77	9%	49	3%	4.91	11.5	$10
06 TOR	290	39	79	12	40	0	272	373	251	363	462	825	12	86	28	0.98	287	38	20	42	113	11%	23	0%	5.88	12.2	$7
07 TOR	331	43	80	10	52	0	242	290	229	343	411	754	13	84	26	0.93	275	42	17	41	113	9%	33	0%	5.13	10.9	$7
1st Half	97	13	22	3	19	0	227			330	402	732	13	82	25	0.88	280	42	19	39	112	10%	55	0%	4.86	2.5	$2
2nd Half	234	30	58	7	33	0	248			348	415	763	13	84	27	0.95	271	42	17	42	113	9%	23	0%	5.24	8.4	$5
08 Proj	374	49	94	13	56	0	251			349	423	772	13	84	27	0.94	280	41	19	40	109	10%	38	1%	5.31	13.0	$9

Almost a skills repeat of '06, but bad h% luck and a little less contact did stats damage. The odds of him being able to get those numbers back up are reduced given that he's 37.

Zimmerman, Ryan

Pos 5 · Age 23 · Growth · Bats Right · Reliability 64 · BAvg Potl 55% · LIMA Plan C · +/- Score 31

	AB	R	H	HR	RBI	SB	Avg	vL	vR	OB	Slg	OPS	bb%	ct%	h%	Eye	xBA	G	L	F	PX	hr/f	SX	SBO	RC/G	RAR	R$
03	0	0	0	0	0	0	0						0										0				
04	0	0	0	0	0	0	0						0										0				
05 WAS	*291	39	90	7	32	1	309	400	395	343	481	824	5	86	34	0.38	365	43	38	19	120	15%	41	10%	5.50	5.9	$10
06 WAS	614	84	176	20	110	11	287	280	289	351	471	822	9	80	33	0.51	288	42	22	36	119	11%	78	11%	5.73	3.8	$23
07 WAS	653	99	174	24	91	6	266	374	235	329	458	787	8	81	30	0.49	288	44	17	40	121	11%	85	3%	5.22	8.4	$19
1st Half	319	48	78	12	43	3	245			293	423	716	8	83	26	0.40	264	43	14	44	108	10%	80	4%	4.23	-5.2	$7
2nd Half	334	50	96	12	49	1	287			362	490	853	10	79	34	0.56	293	44	20	35	135	13%	76	2%	6.20	13.3	$12
08 Proj	610	94	177	23	96	6	290			349	490	839	8	81	32	0.49	294	43	20	37	128	13%	76	7%	5.85	15.5	$23

LD and H% rebounded to prior levels in 2H, and his numbers came with them. 2H PX spike fueled by 25 doubles, a good sign for both BA and power upside. Exciting skills for such a young player. Invest.

Zobrist, Ben

Pos 6 · Age 26 · Pre-Peak · Bats Both · Reliability 2 · BAvg Potl 65% · LIMA Plan D · +/- Score 24

	AB	R	H	HR	RBI	SB	Avg	vL	vR	OB	Slg	OPS	bb%	ct%	h%	Eye	xBA	G	L	F	PX	hr/f	SX	SBO	RC/G	RAR	R$
03	0	0	0	0	0	0	0						0										0				
04	0	0	0	0	0	0	0						0										0				
05	0	0	0	0	0	0	0						0										0				
06 TAM	*567	65	150	5	48	12	265	212	229	340	372	712	10	86	30	0.82	281	47	22	30	67	3%	103	13%	4.58	2.9	$10
07 TAM	*319	47	72	6	29	10	226	182	147	320	361	680	12	82	25	0.75	264	43	20	37	87	8%	101	14%	4.12	-4.3	$6
1st Half	213	25	47	6	19	5	221			305	371	676	11	81	25	0.65	279	46	22	33	95	11%	91	15%	4.00	-3.7	$3
2nd Half	106	22	25	0	10	5	236			347	340	686	15	82	27	0.95	237	38	17	45	72	5%	98	14%	4.35	-0.7	$3
08 Proj	185	28	45	3	17	6	243			333	354	687	12	83	28	0.82	262	44	20	36	73	6%	98	14%	4.27	-1.4	$4

1-9-.155 in 97 AB at TAM. Small signs of potential that might be assembled some day into a usable skill set. But he's already 26 and his BPIs are at a better stage for a 23-year-old. Timing is everything.

ROD TRUESDELL

The Pitchers

QUALIFICATION: All pitchers who accumulated at least 40 IP in the majors in 2007 are included. Some select players with fewer than 40 IP are included if we believe they will have an impact in 2008. Players who may have a role in 2008 but have spent several years battling injuries are often not included, though an injury status update appears on page 178. All of these players will appear on BaseballHQ.com over the winter as their 2008 roles and projected impacts become clearer.

THROWS: How he throws — right (RH) or left (LH).

ROLE: Pitchers are classified as Starters (projected 18+ batters faced per game) or Relievers (under 18 BF/G).

AGE: Each pitcher's current age is shown, along with a description of the associated stage in his career.

TYPE evaluates the extent to which a pitcher allows the ball to be put into play and his ground ball or flyball tendency. CON (contact) represents pitchers who allow the ball to be put into play a great deal. PWR (power) represents those with high strikeout and/or walk totals who keep the ball out of play. GB are those who have a ground ball rate of over 50%; xGB are those who have a GB rate over 55%. FB are those who have a fly ball rate of over 40%; xFB are those who have a FB rate over 45%.

RELIABILITY SCORE: An analysis of each player's forecast risk, on a 0-100 scale. High scores go those pitchers who throw many innings, are healthy (and have not been overused at a young age), are in a stable age range and have displayed consistent performance over the past two years (using xERA).

ERA POTENTIAL (ERA Potl): The probability that a pitcher will improve his ERA in 2008 over 2007, based on an evaluation of strand rate, hit rate, xERA variance and base performance value. These percentages are in 5% increments, ranging from 10% to 90%, though most will be centered closer to the mean. If a pitcher's ERA Potl says 60%, for instance, it means that he has a 60% chance of improving his ERA in 2008.

LIMA PLAN GRADE: Rating that evaluates how well that pitcher would be a good fit for a team employing the LIMA Plan. Best grades will go to pitchers who have excellent base skills and had a 2007 Roto value under $20. Lowest grades will go to poor skills and values over $20.

+/- SCORE: A score that measures the probability that a pitcher's 2008 performance will exceed or fall short 2007's numbers. Two types of variables are tracked: 1) Multi-year trends in BPV, and 2) Outlying 2007 levels for h%, s%, xERA, hr/f and LH/RH variance. Positive scores indicate both rebounds and potential breakouts. Negative scores indicate both corrections and breakdowns.

PLAYER STAT LINES: The past five year's statistics represent the total accumulated in the majors as well as in Triple-A, Double-A ball and various foreign leagues during each year. All non-major league stats used have been converted to their equivalent major league performance level. Minor league levels below AA are not included.

Bill James has proven that minor league statistics, at Double-A level or above, are accurate indicators of future potential. Other researchers have also devised conversion factors for foreign leagues that place them on a comparable playing field as MLB stats. Since these conversions are accurate barometers of potential performance, then we should be including them in the pool of historical data.

TEAM DESIGNATIONS: An asterisk (*) appearing with a team name means that major league equivalent Triple-A and/or Double-A numbers are included in that year's stat line. A designation of "a/a" means the stats were accumulated at both levels that year. "JPN" means Japan, "MEX" means Mexico, "KOR" means Korea, "TWN" means Taiwan, "CUB" means Cuba and "ind" means independent league. All stats that appear with these designations are converted to major league equivalents.

The designation "2TM" appears whenever a player was on more than one major league team, crossing leagues, in a season. "2AL" and "2NL" represent more than one team in the same league. Complete season stats are presented for players who crossed leagues during the season.

SABERMETRIC CATEGORIES: Descriptions of all the sabermetric categories appear in the glossary. The decimal point has been suppressed on several categories to conserve space. *Notes:*

° Platoon data (vL, vR) and Ball-in-play data (G/L/F) are for major league performance only.

° The xERA2 formula is used for years in which G/L/F data is available. The old formula is used otherwise.

2008 FORECASTS: It is far too early to be making definitive projections for 2008, especially on playing time. Focus on the skill levels and trends, then consult Baseball HQ for playing time revisions as players change teams and roles become finalized. A free projections update will also be available online in March.

Forecasts are computed from a player's trends over the past five years. Adjustments were made for leading indicators and variances between skill and statistical output. After reviewing the leading indicators, you might opt to make further adjustments.

Although each year's numbers include all playing time at the Double-A level or above, the 2008 forecast only represents potential playing time at the major league level, and again is highly preliminary.

CAPSULE COMMENTARIES: For each player, a brief analysis of their BPIs and the potential impact on performance in 2008 is provided. For those who played only a portion of 2007 at the major league level, and whose isolated MLB stats are significantly different from their full-season total, their MLB stats are listed here. Note that these commentaries generally look at performance related issues only. Playing time expectations may impact these analyses, so you will have to adjust accordingly, especially as we get closer to Opening Day. Upside (UP) and downside (DN) statistical potential appears for some players. These are less grounded in hard data and more speculative of skills potential.

Accardo,Jeremy			W	L	Sv	IP	K	ERA	WHIP	OBA	vL	vR	BF/G	H%	S%	xERA	G	L	F	Ctl	Dom	Cmd	hr/f	hr/9	RAR	BPV	R$
RH Reliever	03		0	0	0	0	0	0.00	0.00											0.0	0.0						
Age 26	04	a/a	3	0	7	42	38	1.71	1.07	228			5.1	30%	82%	2.11				2.1	8.1	3.8		0.0	13.6	138	$9
Growth	05	SF *	4	5	7	73	59	3.45	1.19	234	182	265	4.9	29%	71%	4.03	39	23	38	3.0	7.3	2.5	5%	0.5	7.1	89	$10
Type	06	2TM	2	4	3	69	54	5.35	1.39	281	241	307	4.6	33%	62%	3.98	42	25	32	2.6	7.0	2.7	10%	0.9	-7.0	70	$4
Reliability 39	07	TOR	4	4	30	67	57	2.14	1.11	212	161	250	4.2	26%	83%	3.53	49	20	30	3.2	7.6	2.4	7%	0.5	19.6	92	$21
ERA Potl 40%	1st Half		1	2	10	33	35	2.45	1.12	205			4.3	27%	80%	2.87	52	26	22	3.5	9.5	2.7	11%	0.5	8.3	111	$8
LIMA Plan D+	2nd Half		3	2	20	34	22	1.84	1.11	218			4.2	25%	86%	4.17	47	16	37	2.9	5.8	2.0	5%	0.5	11.3	72	$13
+/- Score -34	08	Proj	3	3	15	58	45	3.57	1.24	245			4.6	29%	72%	3.88	45	22	32	2.9	7.0	2.4	7%	0.6	4.4	79	$11

H%, S% luck pendulum swung the other way, and voila! xERA shows the overswing. ERA will now go up again. More troubling is another 2H Dom collapse, and reports of a "tired arm." Monitor both health and role.

Affeldt,Jeremy			W	L	Sv	IP	K	ERA	WHIP	OBA	vL	vR	BF/G	H%	S%	xERA	G	L	F	Ctl	Dom	Cmd	hr/f	hr/9	RAR	BPV	R$
LH Reliever	03	KC	7	6	4	126	98	3.93	1.30	262	223	272	14.8	31%	72%	4.08	43	20	37	2.7	7.0	2.6	8%	0.9	9.3	73	$13
Age 28	04	KC	3	4	13	76	49	4.97	1.62	298	271	312	9.1	34%	69%	4.79	46	21	33	3.8	5.8	1.5	7%	0.7	-5.0	41	$6
Pre-Peak	05	KC	0	2	0	49	39	5.30	1.73	288	263	283	4.7	35%	68%	4.47	53	22	25	5.3	7.1	1.3	8%	0.5	-5.7	52	($1)
Type Pwr GB	06	2TM	8	8	1	97	48	6.21	1.62	271	212	289	8.2	28%	63%	5.38	50	17	33	5.1	4.4	0.9	12%	1.2	-20.2	10	$1
Reliability 11	07	COL	4	3	0	59	46	3.51	1.36	220	250	211	3.4	27%	74%	4.33	53	14	33	5.0	7.0	1.4	6%	0.5	6.7	69	$6
ERA Potl 45%	1st Half		4	1	0	31	23	2.90	1.35	201			3.6	25%	76%	4.77	49	16	34	5.8	6.7	1.2	0%	0.0	5.8	79	$4
LIMA Plan C+	2nd Half		0	2	0	28	23	4.18	1.36	240			3.2	28%	71%	3.87	57	12	31	4.2	7.4	1.8	12%	1.0	0.9	59	$1
+/- Score -34	08	Proj	3	3	0	58	45	4.50	1.47	252			4.5	30%	70%	4.33	52	17	32	4.7	7.0	1.5	9%	0.8	0.5	55	$3

Nine of his 33 walks were intentional; take out those and his Ctl is 3.7. Still, value in setup role is limited and skills aren't quite LIMA-worthy. But they could get there if teams will just leave him in the pen.

Albers,Matt			W	L	Sv	IP	K	ERA	WHIP	OBA	vL	vR	BF/G	H%	S%	xERA	G	L	F	Ctl	Dom	Cmd	hr/f	hr/9	RAR	BPV	R$
RH Starter	03		0	0	0	0	0	0.00	0.00																		
Age 25	04		0	0	0	0	0	0.00	0.00																		
Growth	05		0	0	0	0	0	0.00	0.00																		
Type	06	HOU *	12	5	0	156	113	3.23	1.38	258	333	267	24.9	31%	77%	4.28	43	26	30	3.6	6.5	1.8	5%	0.5	24.2	66	$15
Reliability 0	07	HOU *	6	14	0	164	105	5.43	1.59	288	280	298	18.5	31%	69%	4.77	48	17	35	4.0	5.8	1.4	13%	1.4	-20.4	21	$1
ERA Potl 50%	1st Half		3	7	0	87	53	5.17	1.53	283			24.2	30%	70%	4.79	46	19	36	3.7	5.5	1.5	14%	1.6	-8.0	16	$1
LIMA Plan C	2nd Half		3	7	0	77	52	5.73	1.65	293			14.7	33%	67%	4.80	49	17	34	4.3	6.1	1.4	12%	1.2	-12.4	27	($0)
+/- Score 21	08	Proj	7	8	0	131	89	4.62	1.52	277			20.0	31%	71%	4.59	48	18	34	3.9	6.1	1.6	10%	1.0	-3.1	40	$5

4-11, 5.86 in 111 IP at HOU. Despite reputation as GBer, GB% not that extreme. Couple that with poor Cmd and, well, he could've used more Triple-A time. He's shown better, but let others take the lumps now.

Alfonseca,Antonio			W	L	Sv	IP	K	ERA	WHIP	OBA	vL	vR	BF/G	H%	S%	xERA	G	L	F	Ctl	Dom	Cmd	hr/f	hr/9	RAR	BPV	R$
RH Reliever	03	CHC	3	1	0	66	51	5.86	1.56	290	340	259	4.9	34%	63%	3.87	55	20	24	3.7	7.0	1.9	14%	1.0	-12.9	50	$0
Age 36	04	ATL	6	4	0	73	45	2.58	1.35	256	248	261	4.0	29%	83%	3.72	61	18	21	3.4	5.5	1.6	10%	0.6	15.2	52	$8
Decline	05	FLA	1	1	0	27	16	4.98	1.59	275	244	346	3.7	31%	68%	4.31	61	17	22	4.6	5.3	1.1	10%	0.7	-2.5	36	$0
Type GB	06	TEX	0	0	0	16	5	5.63	1.88	338	452	257	4.0	33%	74%	5.48	51	23	26	3.9	2.8	0.7	18%	1.7	-2.1	-31	($1)
Reliability 0	07	PHI	5	2	8	50	24	5.43	1.85	317	370	278	3.9	35%	70%	5.41	53	19	28	4.9	4.3	0.9	6%	0.5	-6.2	20	$3
ERA Potl 50%	1st Half		3	1	5	31	12	3.77	1.65	314			4.4	34%	76%	4.87	53	22	25	3.2	3.5	1.1	3%	0.3	2.5	27	$3
LIMA Plan C+	2nd Half		2	1	3	19	12	8.18	2.19	322			3.3	36%	62%	6.40	52	13	34	7.7	5.8	0.8	9%	1.0	-8.7	12	($1)
+/- Score -39	08	Proj	2	4	0	44	22	5.17	1.70	294			3.9	32%	69%	5.09	54	19	28	4.8	4.6	1.0	7%	0.6	-3.7	25	($0)

Fooled the unwary with 1st half ERA, but you saw those base skills and stayed away (we hope). Now, may not even be able to fool the MLB GMs who keep signing him. Certainly, he's not fooling any MLB hitters.

Armas Jr.,Tony			W	L	Sv	IP	K	ERA	WHIP	OBA	vL	vR	BF/G	H%	S%	xERA	G	L	F	Ctl	Dom	Cmd	hr/f	hr/9	RAR	BPV	R$
RH Reliever	03	MON	2	1	0	31	23	2.61	1.06	222	250	209	24.7	25%	83%	4.28	33	17	50	2.3	6.7	2.9	9%	1.2	6.4	76	$4
Age 30	04	MON	2	4	0	72	54	4.88	1.54	245	231	258	20.1	26%	73%	5.29	35	23	42	5.6	6.8	1.2	14%	1.6	-5.4	23	$1
Peak	05	WAS *	8	9	0	125	76	4.93	1.53	267	276	241	23.2	28%	71%	5.39	36	21	43	4.6	5.5	1.2	11%	1.4	-10.6	18	$4
Type FB	06	WAS	9	12	0	154	97	5.03	1.50	278	274	284	22.7	30%	68%	4.99	39	22	40	3.7	5.7	1.5	10%	1.1	-10.2	32	$6
Reliability 31	07	PIT	4	5	0	97	73	6.03	1.54	289	280	294	13.9	32%	64%	4.76	37	20	43	3.5	6.8	1.9	13%	1.7	-19.2	28	$1
ERA Potl 50%	1st Half		0	3	0	35	24	9.00	2.17	366			13.7	40%	60%	6.02	34	24	42	4.9	6.2	1.3	14%	2.1	-19.7	-16	($6)
LIMA Plan C+	2nd Half		4	2	0	62	49	4.35	1.18	236			14.1	26%	68%	4.10	39	17	44	2.8	7.1	2.6	13%	1.5	0.5	61	$6
+/- Score 22	08	Proj	6	8	0	131	91	4.97	1.51	280			17.0	31%	71%	4.91	37	21	42	3.7	6.3	1.7	12%	1.4	-8.3	29	$4

Just when we were ready to call him a lost cause, he reels us back in. 2nd half Cmd recalls days of promise. But can he do it over an entire season -- and stay healthy? Risk-averse money says no.

Arroyo,Bronson			W	L	Sv	IP	K	ERA	WHIP	OBA	vL	vR	BF/G	H%	S%	xERA	G	L	F	Ctl	Dom	Cmd	hr/f	hr/9	RAR	BPV	R$
RH Starter	03	aaa	12	6	0	149	127	4.46	1.36	297			26.6	36%	67%	4.34				1.5	7.7	5.1		0.6	-1.3	130	$13
Age 31	04	BOS	10	9	0	178	142	4.04	1.22	254	269	227	23.1	30%	69%	3.94	41	20	39	2.4	7.2	3.0	8%	0.9	8.6	85	$16
Peak	05	BOS	14	10	0	205	100	4.52	1.30	269	286	234	24.7	29%	67%	4.97	38	18	44	2.4	4.4	1.9	7%	1.0	-3.7	37	$14
Type FB	06	CIN	14	11	0	240	184	3.30	1.19	247	282	206	28.2	28%	78%	4.05	38	21	41	2.4	6.9	2.9	11%	1.2	35.3	73	$26
Reliability 80	07	CIN	9	15	0	211	156	4.23	1.40	281	274	285	26.8	32%	73%	4.55	35	21	44	2.7	6.7	2.5	10%	1.2	5.1	55	$12
ERA Potl 50%	1st Half		2	9	0	98	66	5.14	1.52	292			27.2	33%	66%	5.05	33	22	44	3.2	6.1	1.9	6%	0.8	-8.7	48	$1
LIMA Plan C+	2nd Half		7	6	0	113	90	3.43	1.30	271			26.4	30%	81%	4.13	37	20	43	2.2	7.2	3.2	13%	1.5	13.8	66	$11
+/- Score -1	08	Proj	11	12	0	203	151	3.77	1.31	269			26.8	31%	75%	4.33	37	20	42	2.4	6.7	2.7	9%	1.1	1.8	66	$17

Throw out his last three starts in May, and his ERA is 3.56 and BPV is 69. But that's just it; every time he seems ready to take the next step, stuff happens. His owners relate to his May line: "I'm going through a spell."

Ayala,Luis			W	L	Sv	IP	K	ERA	WHIP	OBA	vL	vR	BF/G	H%	S%	xERA	G	L	F	Ctl	Dom	Cmd	hr/f	hr/9	RAR	BPV	R$
RH Reliever	03	MON	10	3	5	71	46	2.92	1.10	245	337	188	4.4	27%	79%	3.28	58	17	25	1.6	5.8	3.5	14%	1.0	11.9	85	$13
Age 30	04	MON	6	12	2	90	63	2.70	1.19	266	246	282	4.6	31%	79%	3.36	54	19	26	1.5	6.3	4.2	8%	0.6	17.4	110	$11
Peak	05	WAS	8	7	1	71	40	2.66	1.25	273	350	230	4.4	30%	83%	4.21	43	23	34	1.8	5.1	2.9	9%	0.9	13.9	64	$10
Type Con	06	WAS	0	0	0	0	0	0.00	0.00																		
Reliability 0	07	WAS	2	2	1	42	28	3.19	1.30	265	243	286	4.1	29%	80%	4.45	39	21	40	2.6	6.0	2.3	9%	1.1	6.4	55	$4
ERA Potl 40%	1st Half		0	0	0	2	0	4.50	2.00	415			3.3	41%	75%	5.56	44	33	22	0.0	0.0		0%	0.0	-0.0	-28	($0)
LIMA Plan B+	2nd Half		2	2	1	40	28	3.13	1.27	255			4.1	28%	80%	4.39	39	20	42	2.7	6.3	2.3	10%	1.1	6.5	57	$4
+/- Score -23	08	Proj	6	6	5	73	50	2.86	1.21	260			4.3	30%	80%	3.81	48	20	33	2.0	6.2	3.1	10%	0.9	5.3	80	$11

July-Sept BPVs after return from TJ surgery: 38 / 52 / 70. Given that most pitchers are better in Year 2 after TJ, there is hope he can return to something close to prior form. If so, a solid LIMA performer.

Backe,Brandon			W	L	Sv	IP	K	ERA	WHIP	OBA	vL	vR	BF/G	H%	S%	xERA	G	L	F	Ctl	Dom	Cmd	hr/f	hr/9	RAR	BPV	R$
RH Starter	03	TAM	3	2	0	77	59	5.73	1.53	267	302	220	7.8	31%	62%	4.81	26	42	32	4.6	6.9	1.5	9%	0.8	-11.4	50	$2
Age 30	04	HOU *	11	8	0	131	114	3.84	1.48	276	347	253	11.1	32%	78%	4.29	40	21	39	3.6	7.8	2.2	12%	1.2	6.8	55	$10
Peak	05	HOU	10	8	0	149	97	4.77	1.46	264	260	266	25.1	29%	70%	4.87	42	20	38	4.0	5.9	1.4	10%	1.1	-9.6	33	$7
Type FB	06	HOU	3	2	0	43	19	3.77	1.42	262	317	205	23.3	28%	75%	5.60	36	20	44	3.8	4.0	1.1	6%	0.8	3.8	24	$3
Reliability 0	07	HOU *	7	3	0	59	30	5.52	1.76	312	245	250	25.0	32%	74%	5.90	42	11	46	4.3	4.6	1.1	12%	1.8	-7.9	-13	$1
ERA Potl 35%	1st Half		0	0	0	0	0	0.00	0.00																		
LIMA Plan C	2nd Half		7	3	0	59	30	5.52	1.76	312			25.0	32%	74%	5.90	42	11	46	4.3	4.6	1.1	12%	1.8	-7.9	-13	$1
+/- Score -21	08	Proj	9	8	0	131	80	4.76	1.56	281			17.7	30%	72%	5.21	39	20	41	4.1	5.5	1.4	10%	1.2	-13.1	23	$5

3-1, 3.77 in 29 IP at HOU. Another TJ surgery returnee, only this one's skills were nothing special before. Still... prior to '05, he actually struck guys out. Watch Dom; if it returns, could be interesting.

Bacsik,Mike			W	L	Sv	IP	K	ERA	WHIP	OBA	vL	vR	BF/G	H%	S%	xERA	G	L	F	Ctl	Dom	Cmd	hr/f	hr/9	RAR	BPV	R$
LH Reliever	03	NYM *	3	11	0	134	63	6.75	1.65	320			22.8	34%	60%	6.08				2.9	4.3	1.5		1.3	-41.0	9	($6)
Age 30	04	TEX *	9	7	0	110	48	5.54	1.50	312			13.2	31%	69%	6.31				2.0	3.9	1.9		1.9	-15.0	-1	$3
Peak	05	aaa	7	10	0	160	90	5.56	1.62	324			24.2	34%	69%	6.36				2.4	5.1	2.1		1.6	-24.8	18	($0)
Type Con FB	06	aaa	11	0	0	87	47	3.45	1.35	285			13.3	31%	78%	4.49				2.0	4.8	2.4		1.0	11.5	47	$11
Reliability 4	07	WAS *	6	11	0	154	66	5.20	1.47	306	287	297	17.8	30%	71%	5.04	41	18	41	2.1	3.9	1.9	14%	1.9	-14.7	-1	$2
ERA Potl 35%	1st Half		2	8	0	80	38	5.06	1.51	311			20.9	32%	72%	4.93	42	19	39	2.1	4.3	2.0	13%	1.7	-6.3	10	$1
LIMA Plan C	2nd Half		4	3	0	74	28	5.35	1.43	300			15.3	28%	70%	5.13	40	18	42	2.0	3.4	1.7	16%	2.1	-8.4	-14	$2
+/- Score -6	08	Proj	3	2	0	44	21	5.17	1.47	306			17.4	31%	71%	4.91	41	18	41	2.1	4.3	2.1	14%	1.9	-2.8	8	$1

5-8, 5.11 ERA in 118 IP at WAS. Soft-tossing lefty bought himself some life after going 11-0 in AAA in '06. But giving up a HR for every two K's just doesn't cut it. At least he'll be in the Hall of Fame for one of those HRs.

ROD TRUESDELL

Baek,Cha Seung

	Yr	Tm	W	L	Sv	IP	K	ERA	WHIP	OBA	vL	vR	BF/G	H%	S%	xERA	G	L	F	Ctl	Dom	Cmd	hr/f	hr/9	RAR	BPV	R$
RH Starter	03	aa	3	3	0	56	40	3.31	1.36	268			26.6	32%	75%	3.67				3.0	6.4	2.1		0.3	7.5	75	$5
Age 27	04	aaa	5	4	0	72	52	4.74	1.62	314			23.4	36%	72%	5.54				3.0	6.5	2.2		0.9	-3.5	51	$2
Pre-Peak	05	aaa	8	8	0	112	65	7.05	1.73	334			21.7	36%	61%	6.74				2.8	5.2	1.8		1.5	-38.0	12	($3)
Type Con FB	06	SEA	* 16	5	0	181	113	3.62	1.28	260	211	206	25.4	28%	77%	4.44	43	17	40	2.6	5.6	2.2	11%	1.2	21.0	46	$20
Reliability 0	07	SEA	* 5	4	0	104	62	4.98	1.52	309	267	305	23.2	35%	67%	5.00	34	24	42	2.4	5.4	2.3	5%	0.6	-6.1	55	$3
ERA Potl 55%	1st Half		4	3	0	81	56	5.21	1.43	295			25.2	34%	63%	4.56	35	25	41	2.2	6.2	2.8	5%	0.7	-7.1	72	$4
LIMA Plan C+	2nd Half		1	1	0	23	6	4.15	1.85	353			18.4	37%	77%	6.97	28	19	53	2.8	2.4	0.9	2%	0.5	1.0	3	($0)
+/- Score 1	08	Proj	6	4	0	102	62	4.34	1.55	311			21.6	35%	73%	5.10	34	21	45	2.5	5.5	2.2	6%	0.9	-7.5	46	$5

4-3, 5.15 in 73 IP at SEA. Upward skills trend continued until shoulder started hurting. But FB% is foreboding: contact flyball pitchers are notoriously flammable. That and more role uncertainty temper enthusiasm.

Baez,Danys

	Yr	Tm	W	L	Sv	IP	K	ERA	WHIP	OBA	vL	vR	BF/G	H%	S%	xERA	G	L	F	Ctl	Dom	Cmd	hr/f	hr/9	RAR	BPV	R$
RH Reliever	03	CLE	2	9	25	75	66	3.84	1.17	235	285	165	4.2	28%	71%	3.65	44	19	37	2.8	7.9	2.9	12%	1.1	6.3	83	$16
Age 30	04	TAM	4	4	30	68	52	3.57	1.31	238	252	223	4.6	28%	75%	4.53	42	16	43	3.8	6.9	1.8	7%	0.8	7.2	62	$17
Peak	05	TAM	5	4	41	72	51	2.87	1.33	245	268	215	4.6	28%	82%	4.29	47	20	33	3.7	6.4	1.7	10%	0.9	13.3	54	$21
Type	06	2NL	5	6	9	59	39	4.56	1.30	264	295	244	4.4	31%	64%	4.58	40	17	43	2.6	5.9	2.3	4%	0.5	-0.5	72	$8
Reliability 28	07	BAL	0	6	3	50	29	6.44	1.57	261	346	200	4.3	27%	61%	5.03	51	17	32	5.2	5.2	1.0	15%	1.4	-12.0	12	($0)
ERA Potl 60%	1st Half		0	4	0	29	17	6.52	1.48	248			4.1	24%	59%	4.92	50	16	34	5.0	5.3	1.1	19%	1.9	-7.2	3	($1)
LIMA Plan D	2nd Half		0	2	3	21	12	6.34	1.69	277			4.5	30%	62%	5.17	53	19	29	5.5	5.1	0.9	10%	0.8	-4.8	24	$0
+/- Score 28	08	Proj	0	1	0	11	7	4.97	1.47	264			4.3	30%	67%	4.74	47	18	35	4.1	5.8	1.4	8%	0.8	-0.3	42	$0

So the Orioles lost two closers to Tommy John surgery this year. Not exactly what Leo Mazzone envisioned. If Baez returns at all in '08, it will be a few IP. Under contract through '09, so the O's will wait him out.

Bailey,Homer

	Yr	Tm	W	L	Sv	IP	K	ERA	WHIP	OBA	vL	vR	BF/G	H%	S%	xERA	G	L	F	Ctl	Dom	Cmd	hr/f	hr/9	RAR	BPV	R$
RH Starter	03		0	0	0	0	0	0.00	0.00																		
Age 22	04		0	0	0	0	0	0.00	0.00																		
Green	05		0	0	0	0	0	0.00	0.00																		
Type Pwr	06	aa	7	1	0	68	68	2.02	1.25	230			21.8	31%	83%	2.62				3.7	9.0	2.5		0.1	21.0	111	$12
Reliability 0	07	CIN	* 10	5	0	112	83	4.51	1.37	232	284	233	22.9	27%	67%	4.55	47	18	35	4.6	6.6	1.4	6%	0.6	-1.1	60	$9
ERA Potl 65%	1st Half		8	2	0	78	52	3.92	1.34	231			23.8	27%	71%	4.36	51	21	29	4.5	6.0	1.3	7%	0.6	4.9	56	$8
LIMA Plan B	2nd Half		2	3	0	34	31	5.84	1.42	235			21.3	29%	57%	4.49	43	16	41	5.0	8.1	1.6	7%	0.7	-6.0	71	$1
+/- Score 10	08	Proj	10	9	0	145	129	3.97	1.30	231			21.8	29%	69%	4.11	45	17	38	4.0	8.0	2.0	6%	0.6	5.2	82	$14

2-2, 5.76 in 45 IP at CIN. Battled a strained groin most all year, a likely reason for this step back. Arm was fine, still owns '06 skills, and got feet wet. Now let's just hope Dusty doesn't do a Wood/Prior on him.

Baker,Scott

	Yr	Tm	W	L	Sv	IP	K	ERA	WHIP	OBA	vL	vR	BF/G	H%	S%	xERA	G	L	F	Ctl	Dom	Cmd	hr/f	hr/9	RAR	BPV	R$
RH Starter	03		0	0	0	0	0	0.00	0.00											0.0	0.0						
Age 26	04	a/a	6	6	0	124	96	4.42	1.26	266			27.3	32%	63%	3.43				2.1	7.0	3.3		0.4	-1.2	102	$9
Growth	05	MIN	* 8	11	0	187	125	3.60	1.23	263	221	257	24.3	29%	74%	4.25	40	19	41	2.0	6.0	3.0	9%	1.0	17.8	72	$17
Type FB	06	MIN	* 10	12	0	167	119	5.19	1.54	310	349	299	26.6	35%	68%	4.86	34	19	47	2.4	6.4	2.6	8%	1.2	-13.0	51	$7
Reliability 17	07	MIN	* 12	11	1	186	134	4.39	1.29	282	323	257	25.3	32%	68%	4.28	35	22	43	1.7	6.5	3.9	7%	0.9	2.6	92	$16
ERA Potl 60%	1st Half		5	4	1	81	65	5.21	1.29	282			24.4	33%	61%	3.76	40	25	35	1.7	7.2	4.3	11%	1.1	-7.1	100	$6
LIMA Plan C+	2nd Half		7	7	0	105	69	3.75	1.29	283			26.0	32%	73%	4.55	33	21	46	1.6	5.9	3.6	6%	0.8	9.7	86	$10
+/- Score 19	08	Proj	10	11	0	174	124	4.19	1.34	285			25.6	33%	71%	4.46	35	21	44	2.0	6.4	3.3	7%	0.9	0.8	77	$14

9-9, 4.26 in 144 IP at MIN. Solid growth season. Dom held steady overall even with Ctl gains, a good sign. Still fairly hittable, and FB style means some HR. But you could do worse filling out your staff.

Bannister,Brian

	Yr	Tm	W	L	Sv	IP	K	ERA	WHIP	OBA	vL	vR	BF/G	H%	S%	xERA	G	L	F	Ctl	Dom	Cmd	hr/f	hr/9	RAR	BPV	R$
RH Starter	03		0	0	0	0	0	0.00	0.00																		
Age 27	04	aa	3	3	0	44	23	4.84	1.57	293			24.7	33%	68%	4.68				3.6	4.8	1.3		0.4	-2.7	40	$1
Growth	05	a/a	13	5	0	154	115	3.19	1.29	266			25.0	31%	77%	3.77				2.4	6.7	2.8		0.7	21.2	81	$17
Type Con FB	06	NYM	* 5	4	0	68	40	4.78	1.52	285	286	185	21.6	31%	71%	5.25	40	15	45	3.6	5.3	1.5	9%	1.2	-2.5	25	$3
Reliability 0	07	KC	* 13	10	0	185	87	3.84	1.22	254	281	219	24.7	27%	71%	4.74	41	19	40	2.4	4.2	1.8	8%	1.0	15.2	39	$18
ERA Potl 40%	1st Half		5	5	0	87	48	3.61	1.20	252			24.0	27%	72%	4.65	40	17	43	2.3	5.0	2.2	7%	0.8	9.6	55	$9
LIMA Plan D+	2nd Half		8	5	0	98	39	4.04	1.24	255			25.5	26%	70%	4.85	42	21	38	2.4	3.6	1.5	9%	1.1	5.6	25	$9
+/- Score -39	08	Proj	10	14	0	189	102	4.58	1.34	267			23.6	29%	67%	4.86	41	18	41	2.8	4.9	1.7	8%	1.0	-8.4	38	$12

12-9, 3.87 in 165 IP at KC. Decent June/July (BPV 66, 65) sandwiched inside four awful months (14, 4, 29, -8), but H% saved the day. As usual, xERA tells the true story. Overvalued. DN: 5.00+ ERA.

Batista,Miguel

	Yr	Tm	W	L	Sv	IP	K	ERA	WHIP	OBA	vL	vR	BF/G	H%	S%	xERA	G	L	F	Ctl	Dom	Cmd	hr/f	hr/9	RAR	BPV	R$
RH Starter	03	ARI	10	9	0	193	142	3.54	1.33	266	297	241	22.8	31%	74%	3.74	53	19	27	2.8	6.6	2.4	8%	0.6	17.5	73	$15
Age 37	04	TOR	10	13	5	198	104	4.81	1.52	269	264	285	23.2	29%	70%	4.81	52	18	29	4.4	4.7	1.1	11%	1.0	-9.3	22	$7
Decline	05	TOR	5	8	31	74	54	4.12	1.44	277	256	282	4.6	31%	74%	4.23	48	19	33	3.3	6.5	2.0	12%	1.1	2.3	48	$15
Type	06	ARI	11	8	0	206	110	4.59	1.53	284	321	257	27.0	31%	71%	4.63	52	20	28	3.7	4.8	1.3	9%	0.8	-2.5	31	$7
Reliability 75	07	SEA	16	11	0	193	133	4.29	1.52	277	295	258	26.0	32%	73%	4.85	44	17	39	4.0	6.2	1.6	7%	0.8	5.1	44	$13
ERA Potl 50%	1st Half		7	6	0	89	61	4.85	1.61	299			25.2	34%	71%	4.79	46	16	38	3.6	6.2	1.7	8%	0.9	-3.8	41	$4
LIMA Plan D+	2nd Half		9	5	0	104	72	3.81	1.45	258			26.7	30%	75%	4.90	42	17	41	4.2	6.2	1.5	7%	0.8	9.0	48	$9
+/- Score -35	08	Proj	13	11	0	189	123	4.54	1.50	277			26.9	31%	71%	4.65	47	18	35	3.8	5.9	1.6	9%	0.9	-3.6	42	$11

It was 2nd-half S% luck that propped up his ERA, but 47/9 DOM/DIS did keep SEA in his starts. Despite fluctuations in skill components, he always nets out roughly the same. He's reliably halfway-decent.

Bazardo,Yorman

	Yr	Tm	W	L	Sv	IP	K	ERA	WHIP	OBA	vL	vR	BF/G	H%	S%	xERA	G	L	F	Ctl	Dom	Cmd	hr/f	hr/9	RAR	BPV	R$
RH Starter	03		0	0	0	0	0	0.00	0.00																		
Age 23	04		0	0	0	0	0	0.00	0.00																		
Growth	05	aa	11	8	0	142	91	5.20	1.57	300			25.5	33%	68%	5.37				3.2	5.8	1.8		1.1	-15.6	35	$4
Type Con	06	aa	6	5	0	138	72	4.76	1.59	305			24.9	33%	71%	5.21				3.2	4.7	1.5		0.8	-4.0	30	$3
Reliability 4	07	DET	* 12	7	0	160	75	4.50	1.41	283	289	143	20.4	31%	68%	4.79	47	18	35	2.7	4.2	1.6	6%	0.6	0.1	38	$10
ERA Potl 50%	1st Half		7	3	0	84	46	4.50	1.48	288			20.5	33%	67%	5.59	38	8	54	3.0	4.9	1.6	1%	0.2	0.1	55	$5
LIMA Plan C+	2nd Half		5	4	0	76	29	4.51	1.34	277			20.2	28%	69%	4.61	49	20	31	2.4	3.4	1.5	11%	1.1	-0.0	19	$5
+/- Score -21	08	Proj	6	4	0	87	44	4.66	1.49	294			22.6	32%	70%	4.75	48	19	33	2.9	4.6	1.6	8%	0.8	-2.7	32	$4

2-1, 2.28 in 24 IP at DET. Mysteriously conjured 3.0 Cmd in his DET stint. Overall skills peg that as sample size fluke. Some upside as a GB specialist, so watch for growth. But ignore the sleeper talk for now.

Beckett,Josh

	Yr	Tm	W	L	Sv	IP	K	ERA	WHIP	OBA	vL	vR	BF/G	H%	S%	xERA	G	L	F	Ctl	Dom	Cmd	hr/f	hr/9	RAR	BPV	R$
RH Starter	03	FLA	9	8	0	142	152	3.04	1.32	248	220	267	25.1	33%	78%	3.47	44	24	32	3.5	9.6	2.7	7%	0.6	21.7	103	$16
Age 27	04	FLA	9	9	0	156	152	3.80	1.22	237	281	192	24.9	30%	71%	3.57	46	17	37	3.1	8.8	2.8	10%	0.9	8.8	92	$16
Pre-Peak	05	FLA	15	8	0	178	166	3.38	1.18	233	217	252	25.2	29%	73%	3.61	43	22	36	2.9	8.4	2.9	8%	0.7	18.9	98	$22
Type Pwr	06	BOS	16	11	0	204	158	5.02	1.30	249	251	238	26.1	27%	66%	4.10	45	17	38	3.3	7.0	2.1	16%	1.6	-11.8	44	$18
Reliability 61	07	BOS	20	7	0	201	194	3.27	1.14	250	255	235	27.2	32%	74%	3.26	47	16	37	1.8	8.7	4.9	8%	0.8	30.5	136	$31
ERA Potl 60%	1st Half		11	1	0	91	79	3.07	1.05	228			25.8	29%	71%	3.35	50	15	35	2.0	7.8	4.0	6%	0.5	16.2	124	$16
LIMA Plan C	2nd Half		9	6	0	110	115	3.45	1.21	268			28.3	34%	75%	3.20	45	16	38	1.6	9.4	5.8	10%	1.0	14.3	149	$15
+/- Score 19	08	Proj	18	9	0	203	198	3.55	1.21	248			26.2	31%	74%	3.43	46	17	37	2.5	8.8	3.5	11%	1.0	26.7	103	$28

Every skill that had been in decline turned around, and in spectacular fashion. Ctl gains may be the most impressive. Now health, especially perhaps lingering eczema problem, is the only remaining concern.

Bedard,Erik

	Yr	Tm	W	L	Sv	IP	K	ERA	WHIP	OBA	vL	vR	BF/G	H%	S%	xERA	G	L	F	Ctl	Dom	Cmd	hr/f	hr/9	RAR	BPV	R$
LH Starter	03		0	0	0	0	0	0.00	0.00											0.0	0.0						
Age 29	04	BAL	6	10	0	137	121	4.60	1.60	278	277	269	23.0	34%	72%	4.80	38	19	42	4.7	7.9	1.7	7%	0.9	-2.8	57	$5
Pre-Peak	05	BAL	6	8	0	141	125	4.02	1.39	259	252	263	25.3	32%	72%	4.15	40	23	37	3.6	8.0	2.2	7%	0.6	6.2	78	$11
Type Pwr	06	BAL	15	11	0	196	171	3.76	1.35	262	200	272	25.4	32%	73%	3.69	49	21	30	3.2	7.8	2.5	9%	0.7	19.2	80	$21
Reliability 50	07	BAL	13	5	0	182	221	3.16	1.09	216	229	208	26.1	29%	75%	2.81	48	17	35	2.8	10.9	3.9	13%	0.9	30.1	131	$29
ERA Potl 60%	1st Half		6	4	0	107	129	3.36	1.18	238			25.8	32%	75%	2.94	46	18	36	2.7	10.9	4.0	12%	0.9	15.1	129	$15
LIMA Plan C+	2nd Half		7	1	0	75	92	2.88	0.96	182			26.5	25%	75%	2.63	50	16	33	3.0	11.0	3.7	14%	1.0	15.0	133	$15
+/- Score 31	08	Proj	15	9	0	218	238	3.35	1.23	236			25.8	31%	75%	3.27	46	19	34	3.2	9.8	3.1	10%	0.8	32.8	106	$29

Was on his way to a season every bit as good as Beckett's until late-August oblique strain. Built on '06 2nd-half breakout with PQS 4/5 DOMinance in 75% of starts, and no DISasters after April. He's arrived.

ROD TRUESDELL

Beimel,Joe

			W	L	Sv	IP	K	ERA	WHIP	OBA	vL	vR	BF/G	H%	S%	xERA	G	L	F	Ctl	Dom	Cmd	hr/f	hr/9	RAR	BPV	R$
LH Reliever	03	PIT	1	3	0	62	42	5.07	1.64	283	311	288	4.1	32%	71%	4.97	35	36	29	4.8	6.1	1.3	12%	1.0	-6.1	31	($1)
Age 31	04	aaa	2	4	2	62	37	8.71	2.02	361			6.3	39%	58%	8.28				3.8	5.4	1.4		1.8	-33.4	-10	($7)
Peak	05	aaa	1	2	0	52	29	4.08	1.61	301			4.9	34%	74%	4.82				3.5	5.0	1.4		0.4	1.5	43	$1
Type Con	06	LA *	5	1	2	83	37	2.73	1.26	252	234	277	4.8	27%	81%	4.37	57	11	32	2.8	4.0	1.5	8%	0.8	18.0	37	$9
Reliability 21	07	LA	4	2	1	67	39	3.88	1.29	249	188	294	3.4	29%	67%	4.53	48	18	35	3.2	5.2	1.6	1%	0.1	4.5	67	$6
ERA Potl 50%	1st Half		1	1	1	31	15	4.65	1.19	236			3.4	27%	57%	4.76	44	18	38	2.9	4.4	1.5	0%	0.0	-0.8	65	$2
LIMA Plan C	2nd Half		3	1	0	36	24	3.22	1.38	260			3.5	31%	76%	4.32	51	17	32	3.5	6.0	1.7	3%	0.2	5.4	67	$4
+/- Score -39	08	Proj	3	2	0	64	35	4.39	1.39	266			4.0	29%	70%	4.55	49	19	32	3.3	5.0	1.5	9%	0.9	-1.2	38	$3

Last year, superb infield defense bailed him out. This year, he somehow surrendered only one homer out of 72 FB allowed. Unless he truly has struck a deal with a higher power, his luck will run out eventually.

Belisle,Matt

			W	L	Sv	IP	K	ERA	WHIP	OBA	vL	vR	BF/G	H%	S%	xERA	G	L	F	Ctl	Dom	Cmd	hr/f	hr/9	RAR	BPV	R$
RH Starter	03	a/a	8	12	0	171	102	5.21	1.62	319			27.7	36%	67%	5.33				2.7	5.4	2.0		0.6	-17.2	48	$2
Age 27	04	aaa	9	11	0	162	89	5.88	1.60	316			26.2	34%	64%	5.66				2.7	4.9	1.8		1.0	-30.8	30	($0)
Pre-Peak	05	CIN	4	8	1	85	59	4.44	1.49	296	331	273	6.3	33%	73%	3.89	52	21	26	2.7	6.2	2.3	15%	1.2	-2.0	46	$4
Type	06	CIN	2	0	0	40	26	3.60	1.55	276	240	295	6.0	30%	81%	4.80	48	17	35	4.3	5.9	1.4	11%	1.1	4.3	30	$2
Reliability 28	07	CIN	8	9	0	178	125	5.32	1.44	297	298	303	25.8	33%	66%	4.23	42	22	36	2.2	6.3	2.9	12%	1.3	-19.6	55	$6
ERA Potl 55%	1st Half		5	5	0	93	61	4.74	1.35	286			26.5	32%	67%	4.15	44	22	34	2.0	5.9	2.9	10%	1.1	-3.6	62	$5
LIMA Plan C	2nd Half		3	4	0	85	64	5.95	1.52	309			25.1	34%	64%	4.32	39	22	38	2.3	6.8	2.9	14%	1.6	-15.9	47	$1
+/- Score 32	08	Proj	6	6	0	131	89	4.83	1.48	295			26.1	33%	70%	4.32	45	20	34	2.7	6.1	2.3	12%	1.2	1.3	44	$5

Declining GB% hardly a cure for crippling gopheritis. If not for that, we'd be talking about a Cmd spike, and his best skills ever. For now, though, 100+ IP jump means a burnout risk, and he's still an iffy play.

Bell,Heath

			W	L	Sv	IP	K	ERA	WHIP	OBA	vL	vR	BF/G	H%	S%	xERA	G	L	F	Ctl	Dom	Cmd	hr/f	hr/9	RAR	BPV	R$
RH Reliever	03	aaa	2	3	3	49	44	6.03	1.47	315			5.4	39%	58%	5.03				1.5	8.0	5.3		0.8	-10.0	128	$2
Age 30	04	a/a	3	1	16	57	50	4.34	1.49	263			5.5	32%	71%	4.29				4.3	7.9	1.8		0.7	0.0	67	$8
Peak	05	NYM	1	3	0	46	43	5.65	1.49	301	303	288	4.9	38%	61%	3.69	45	24	31	2.5	8.4	3.3	7%	0.6	-8.0	97	$0
Type Pwr GB	06	NYM *	3	3	12	72	79	3.59	1.49	301	308	348	6.1	39%	78%	2.95	51	26	23	2.5	9.8	4.0	15%	0.9	8.0	111	$10
Reliability 27	07	SD	6	4	2	94	102	2.02	0.96	185	216	157	4.5	26%	79%	2.50	59	19	23	2.9	9.8	3.4	6%	0.3	27.8	140	$18
ERA Potl 50%	1st Half		1	2	0	46	49	1.57	0.89	178			4.6	25%	83%	2.44	59	18	23	2.5	9.6	3.8	4%	0.2	16.2	150	$8
LIMA Plan B	2nd Half		5	2	2	48	53	2.45	1.03	192			4.4	27%	77%	2.55	58	19	22	3.2	10.0	3.1	8%	0.4	11.6	131	$10
+/- Score -8	08	Proj	4	3	0	73	76	2.96	1.22	246			5.0	33%	76%	2.89	54	22	24	2.7	9.4	3.5	8%	0.5	13.6	120	$9

The skills he'd been flashing for years finally bore fruit in pitching-fertile Petco. These are closer-worthy BPIs, and with Trevor Hoffman showing all the skills signs of a collapse: UP: Double-digit Saves

Benitez,Armando

			W	L	Sv	IP	K	ERA	WHIP	OBA	vL	vR	BF/G	H%	S%	xERA	G	L	F	Ctl	Dom	Cmd	hr/f	hr/9	RAR	BPV	R$
RH Reliever	03	2TM	4	4	21	73	75	2.96	1.37	223	214	221	4.5	29%	81%	4.33	35	22	43	5.1	9.2	1.8	7%	0.7	12.9	82	$15
Age 35	04	FLA	2	2	47	69	62	1.30	0.82	156	168	140	4.0	18%	92%	3.83	30	17	53	2.7	8.1	3.0	7%	0.8	25.3	111	$27
Decline	05	SF	2	3	19	30	23	4.50	1.37	228	212	246	4.3	25%	72%	5.10	32	18	50	4.8	6.9	1.4	12%	1.5	-0.9	36	$8
Type Pwr xFB	06	SF	2	2	17	38	31	3.54	1.57	266	270	265	4.2	30%	83%	5.18	32	21	47	5.0	7.3	1.5	11%	1.4	4.4	34	$9
Reliability 0	07	2NL	2	8	9	50	57	5.37	1.55	257	273	243	4.1	33%	69%	4.42	33	18	49	5.2	10.2	2.0	12%	1.4	-5.8	63	$5
ERA Potl 55%	1st Half		2	3	9	28	28	3.54	1.29	233			4.1	28%	78%	4.18	36	14	50	3.9	9.0	2.3	11%	1.3	3.1	73	$6
LIMA Plan B	2nd Half		0	5	0	22	29	7.67	1.88	284			4.1	38%	61%	4.74	29	24	47	6.9	11.7	1.7	14%	1.6	-8.9	56	($2)
+/- Score 16	08	Proj	2	5	3	44	44	4.76	1.54	255			4.1	31%	73%	4.71	32	20	48	5.2	9.1	1.8	12%	1.4	-1.7	52	$3

Ironically, best skills in years, but it was his turn for some bad luck. Injuries mount: that Reliability score is dead on. Sure, he could surprise us with a rebound. But as Magic 8-ball says, "outlook not so good."

Benoit,Joaquin

			W	L	Sv	IP	K	ERA	WHIP	OBA	vL	vR	BF/G	H%	S%	xERA	G	L	F	Ctl	Dom	Cmd	hr/f	hr/9	RAR	BPV	R$
RH Reliever	03	TEX *	10	6	0	138	113	5.48	1.42	256	222	272	19.3	28%	66%	4.63	35	20	44	4.0	7.4	1.8	15%	1.8	-16.2	33	$8
Age 30	04	TEX	3	5	0	103	95	5.68	1.40	280	249	311	15.9	32%	63%	4.19	34	19	47	2.7	8.3	3.1	13%	1.7	-15.8	63	$4
Peak	05	TEX	4	4	0	87	78	3.72	1.23	220	227	196	11.3	26%	72%	4.39	33	19	48	3.9	8.1	2.1	8%	0.9	6.9	75	$9
Type Pwr FB	06	TEX	1	1	0	79	85	4.89	1.34	233	191	245	6.0	31%	62%	4.04	37	19	44	4.3	9.7	2.2	5%	0.6	-3.2	96	$5
Reliability 31	07	TEX	7	4	6	82	87	2.85	1.17	227	172	268	4.8	30%	78%	3.51	37	24	39	3.1	9.5	3.1	7%	0.7	16.7	112	$15
ERA Potl 55%	1st Half		2	2	1	39	41	3.69	1.38	267			5.1	34%	76%	3.68	38	25	36	3.2	9.5	2.9	10%	0.9	3.9	92	$4
LIMA Plan B	2nd Half		5	2	5	43	46	2.09	0.98	188			4.5	26%	80%	3.36	36	21	42	2.9	9.6	3.3	5%	0.4	12.8	132	$11
+/- Score -1	08	Proj	5	3	5	83	84	3.49	1.22	229			6.1	29%	73%	3.84	36	21	43	3.5	9.2	2.6	8%	0.8	6.7	96	$12

Better S% luck and better Ctl coincided, and eureka! So can he take the big step to the 9th? Justified or not, disappointments of the past work against him. So don't bet on big Sv totals, nor on another sub-3 ERA, xERA says.

Benson,Kris

			W	L	Sv	IP	K	ERA	WHIP	OBA	vL	vR	BF/G	H%	S%	xERA	G	L	F	Ctl	Dom	Cmd	hr/f	hr/9	RAR	BPV	R$
RH Reliever	03	PIT	5	9	0	105	68	4.97	1.55	300	339	260	26.1	33%	70%	5.16	34	20	47	3.1	5.8	1.9	8%	1.2	-9.0	34	$2
Age 33	04	2NL	12	12	0	200	134	4.32	1.31	264	276	251	27.3	30%	67%	4.39	42	20	38	2.7	6.0	2.2	6%	0.7	-1.4	64	$13
Peak	05	NYM	10	8	0	174	95	4.14	1.26	258	268	240	26.0	27%	71%	4.46	44	19	37	2.5	4.9	1.9	12%	1.2	2.4	36	$12
Type Con	06	BAL	11	12	0	183	88	4.82	1.40	278	303	270	26.4	28%	71%	4.96	41	19	39	2.9	4.3	1.5	13%	1.6	-5.9	8	$10
Reliability 0	07	BAL	0	0	0	0	0	0.00	0.00																		
ERA Potl	1st Half		0	0	0	0	0	0.00	0.00																		
LIMA Plan	2nd Half		0	0	0	0	0	0.00	0.00																		
+/- Score	08	Proj	7	7	0	116	61	4.66	1.37	273			26.2	29%	69%	4.83	41	19	39	2.8	4.7	1.7	10%	1.2	-4.8	29	$7

Missed all of '07 after labrum surgery, which can be much dicier than TJ surgery. Given this fact, and an already morose skills set, the only Benson worth an Internet search is Anna. Or even Robert Guillaume.

Bergmann,Jason

			W	L	Sv	IP	K	ERA	WHIP	OBA	vL	vR	BF/G	H%	S%	xERA	G	L	F	Ctl	Dom	Cmd	hr/f	hr/9	RAR	BPV	R$
RH Starter	03		0	0	0	0	0	0.00	0.00																		
Age 26	04		0	0	0	0	0	0.00	0.00																		
Growth	05	a/a	5	2	7	74	66	2.31	1.12	212			7.3	26%	84%	2.80				3.3	8.0	2.4		0.9	18.2	87	$13
Type Pwr xFB	06	WAS *	8	4	4	124	105	5.38	1.54	289	255	353	10.1	34%	67%	4.68	32	24	45	3.5	7.6	2.2	10%	1.2	-13.6	52	$6
Reliability 1	07	WAS *	8	7	0	139	103	4.02	1.23	238	263	200	22.2	27%	71%	4.64	33	16	50	3.1	6.7	2.1	9%	1.2	7.0	58	$13
ERA Potl 50%	1st Half		1	4	0	60	49	2.55	1.02	183			21.5	22%	79%	4.36	34	13	53	3.5	7.4	2.1	6%	0.8	13.9	85	$8
LIMA Plan C	2nd Half		7	3	0	79	54	5.12	1.39	275			22.8	30%	67%	4.85	33	19	49	2.9	6.2	2.2	11%	1.5	-6.8	38	$5
+/- Score -17	08	Proj	8	10	0	174	139	4.45	1.32	254			22.4	29%	69%	4.61	33	19	49	3.3	7.2	2.2	9%	1.1	-4.5	60	$12

6-6, 4.45 in 115 IP at WAS. Feast or famine: 43% DOMinant starts, 38% DISasters. But that's the kind of profile from which upside shines. If speculating is your thing, here's your man. But know the risk.

Betancourt,Rafael

			W	L	Sv	IP	K	ERA	WHIP	OBA	vL	vR	BF/G	H%	S%	xERA	G	L	F	Ctl	Dom	Cmd	hr/f	hr/9	RAR	BPV	R$
RH Reliever	03	CLE *	2	2	18	90	95	2.40	1.27	244	270	133	5.5	32%	83%	4.34	21	19	59	3.2	9.5	3.0	4%	0.6	23.6	108	$18
Age 33	04	CLE	5	6	4	66	76	3.94	1.34	276	272	264	4.2	37%	73%	3.50	38	19	44	2.4	10.3	4.2	9%	1.0	4.0	122	$9
Peak	05	CLE	4	3	1	67	73	2.81	1.10	231	264	204	5.0	31%	77%	3.42	33	22	44	2.3	9.8	4.3	6%	0.7	12.9	138	$11
Type Pwr xFB	06	CLE	3	4	3	56	48	3.84	1.12	247	221	254	4.5	29%	70%	4.12	23	25	51	1.8	7.7	4.4	8%	1.1	5.0	110	$8
Reliability 20	07	CLE	5	1	3	79	80	1.48	0.76	186	241	147	4.3	25%	84%	3.31	27	20	54	1.0	9.1	8.9	4%	0.5	29.6	245	$19
ERA Potl 40%	1st Half		1	0	0	33	32	1.36	0.73	184			4.0	25%	83%	3.41	22	21	56	0.8	8.7	10.7	2%	0.3	12.8	286	$7
LIMA Plan B	2nd Half		4	1	3	46	48	1.56	0.78	187			4.5	25%	85%	3.19	30	19	51	1.2	9.3	8.0	5%	0.6	16.8	224	$12
+/- Score -63	08	Proj	4	3	5	73	72	2.86	1.01	224			4.6	29%	75%	3.65	27	22	51	1.7	8.9	5.1	6%	0.7	7.6	149	$13

"Raffy Righty" took his closer-worthy skills and forayed into Vintage Eck Territory. H%, hr/f and history, say his ERA can't stay this low. But it won't have to for him to be valuable. Role becomes crucial here.

Billingsley,Chad

			W	L	Sv	IP	K	ERA	WHIP	OBA	vL	vR	BF/G	H%	S%	xERA	G	L	F	Ctl	Dom	Cmd	hr/f	hr/9	RAR	BPV	R$
RH Reliever	03		0	0	0	0	0	0.00	0.00																		
Age 23	04	aa	4	1	0	42	42	3.26	1.31	224			22.3	30%	74%	2.85				4.5	9.0	2.0		0.2	5.6	100	$5
Growth	05	aa	13	6	0	146	136	3.64	1.16	229			21.3	29%	70%	2.99				2.9	8.4	2.9		0.7	12.0	98	$19
Type Pwr	06	LA *	13	7	0	160	128	3.79	1.47	247	328	213	22.7	29%	76%	4.53	48	16	36	4.9	7.2	1.5	8%	0.8	13.7	57	$13
Reliability 0	07	LA	12	5	0	147	141	3.31	1.33	240	277	210	14.5	30%	78%	3.99	41	20	39	3.9	8.6	2.2	10%	0.9	20.3	77	$17
ERA Potl 50%	1st Half		4	0	0	43	44	3.98	1.26	224			7.2	28%	71%	3.80	42	17	41	4.0	9.2	2.3	11%	1.0	2.4	83	$5
LIMA Plan C	2nd Half		8	5	0	104	97	3.03	1.36	247			24.7	30%	81%	4.07	41	21	38	3.9	8.4	2.2	9%	0.9	17.9	75	$12
+/- Score 5	08	Proj	13	9	0	189	174	3.53	1.33	237			25.0	29%	76%	4.06	43	19	38	4.1	8.3	2.0	9%	0.8	8.0	76	$19

BPV in three months as starter: (Jul-Sep): 60, 78, 84. Dom in those months: 7.4, 8.6, 9.2. Still just 23, and Ctl is shaky enough that it won't always be a luxurious ride. But keeper leaguers best hop aboard now.

ROD TRUESDELL

Blanton,Joe				W	L	Sv	IP	K	ERA	WHIP	OBA	vL	vR	BF/G	H%	S%	xERA	G	L	F	Ctl	Dom	Cmd	hr/f	hr/9	RAR	BPV	R$
RH	Starter	03	aa	3	1	1	35	26	1.53	0.85	188			19.0	23%	83%	1.31				1.8	6.6	**3.7**		0.3	12.4	128	$8
Age	27	04	aaa	11	8	0	176	121	4.40	1.39	299			27.1	35%	69%	4.54				1.7	6.2	**3.7**		0.7	-1.1	89	$11
Growth		05	OAK	12	12	0	201	116	3.54	1.22	239	228	246	25.2	26%	75%	4.45	46	17	38	3.0	5.2	**1.7**	10%	1.0	20.7	44	$19
Type	Con	06	OAK	16	12	0	194	107	4.82	1.54	306	314	304	27.1	34%	69%	4.87	43	20	37	2.7	5.0	**1.8**	7%	0.8	-6.3	39	$10
Reliability	66	07	OAK	14	10	0	230	140	3.95	1.22	270	291	248	28.0	31%	68%	3.93	47	21	32	1.6	5.5	**3.5**	7%	0.6	15.7	89	$22
ERA Potl	55%	1st Half		7	4	0	113	77	3.19	1.08	239			28.2	27%	73%	3.69	48	18	34	1.8	6.1	**3.5**	9%	0.8	18.4	94	$15
LIMA Plan	D	2nd Half		7	6	0	117	63	4.69	1.35	298			27.8	33%	64%	4.18	46	23	31	1.4	4.8	**3.5**	5%	0.5	-2.7	84	$7
+/- Score	7	08	Proj	**15**	**11**	**0**	**218**	**129**	**4.10**	**1.30**	**275**			**27.0**	**31%**	**70%**	**4.25**	**45**	**20**	**35**	**2.1**	**5.3**	**2.6**	**8%**	**0.8**	**6.5**	**63**	**$19**

A notable demonstration of the difference between a sub-2.0 and 3.5 Cmd. Other skills were mostly unchanged. Even Greg Maddux's career Ctl isn't this good -- and he's no Maddux. So expect a small regression.

Bonderman,Jeremy				W	L	Sv	IP	K	ERA	WHIP	OBA	vL	vR	BF/G	H%	S%	xERA	G	L	F	Ctl	Dom	Cmd	hr/f	hr/9	RAR	BPV	R$
RH	Starter	03	DET	6	19	0	162	108	5.56	1.55	297	306	277	21.9	33%	66%	4.57	45	20	35	3.2	6.0	**1.9**	12%	1.3	-20.6	32	$3
Age	25	04	DET	11	13	0	184	168	4.89	1.31	245	255	223	23.6	29%	65%	3.73	48	18	34	3.6	8.2	**2.3**	14%	1.2	-10.4	68	$14
Growth		05	DET	14	13	0	189	145	4.57	1.35	272	287	249	27.9	31%	68%	3.94	48	19	33	2.7	6.9	**2.5**	11%	1.0	-4.7	65	$15
Type	Pwr	06	DET	14	8	0	214	202	4.08	1.30	262	284	235	26.6	33%	70%	3.47	48	20	32	2.7	8.5	**3.2**	9%	0.8	12.6	97	$23
Reliability	59	07	DET	11	9	0	174	145	5.01	1.38	282	268	291	26.8	33%	66%	3.80	48	18	34	2.5	7.5	**3.0**	12%	1.2	-10.8	71	$12
ERA Potl	60%	1st Half		8	1	0	90	82	3.90	1.21	260			26.6	32%	70%	3.54	45	16	38	2.0	8.2	**4.1**	9%	0.9	6.7	111	$12
LIMA Plan	B	2nd Half		3	8	0	84	63	6.19	1.57	304			27.0	34%	63%	4.09	50	19	31	3.0	6.7	**2.3**	16%	1.5	-17.5	37	$0
+/- Score	54	08	Proj	**13**	**8**	**0**	**174**	**151**	**3.98**	**1.30**	**266**			**26.2**	**32%**	**72%**	**3.62**	**48**	**19**	**33**	**2.5**	**7.8**	**3.1**	**10%**	**0.9**	**18.9**	**87**	**$18**

Despite another year of skills exceeding stats, we'd still be bullish. But with lingering elbow soreness in the mix, things are dicier. The huge upside is still there, we must hope that the doctors don't have to intervene.

Bonser,Boof				W	L	Sv	IP	K	ERA	WHIP	OBA	vL	vR	BF/G	H%	S%	xERA	G	L	F	Ctl	Dom	Cmd	hr/f	hr/9	RAR	BPV	R$
RH	Starter	03	a/a	8	12	0	158	117	3.91	1.31	240			23.9	28%	70%	3.41				3.7	6.6	**1.8**		0.6	9.5	66	$13
Age	26	04	a/a	13	10	0	161	136	5.31	1.56	297			25.8	35%	69%	5.57				3.4	7.6	**2.3**		1.3	-19.2	49	$7
Growth		05	aaa	11	9	0	160	147	4.89	1.47	280			25.1	33%	70%	4.99				3.3	8.3	**2.5**		1.3	-11.6	62	$9
Type	Pwr	06	MIN *	13	10	0	186	154	4.21	1.37	266	251	280	25.0	31%	72%	4.30	42	15	43	3.1	7.4	**2.4**	9%	1.1	8.1	63	$17
Reliability	38	07	MIN	8	12	0	173	136	5.10	1.53	290	349	214	24.8	33%	70%	4.37	45	17	38	3.4	7.1	**2.1**	13%	1.4	-12.7	41	$7
ERA Potl	50%	1st Half		5	4	0	91	85	4.65	1.49	280			25.1	34%	72%	4.08	45	16	39	3.6	8.4	**2.4**	12%	1.3	-1.6	60	$6
LIMA Plan	C+	2nd Half		3	8	0	82	51	5.60	1.56	300			24.5	32%	68%	4.71	45	18	37	3.2	5.6	**1.8**	14%	1.5	-11.0	19	$1
+/- Score	22	08	Proj	**9**	**11**	**0**	**162**	**129**	**4.56**	**1.41**	**270**			**24.2**	**31%**	**71%**	**4.26**	**44**	**17**	**39**	**3.3**	**7.2**	**2.2**	**11%**	**1.2**	**4.6**	**53**	**$11**

BPIs declined each month after May. Skills awful over innings 4-6 overall. These indicators support MIN's belief that he was out of shape. With his stuff, word of a new training regimen may be news, not noise.

Bootcheck,Chris				W	L	Sv	IP	K	ERA	WHIP	OBA	vL	vR	BF/G	H%	S%	xERA	G	L	F	Ctl	Dom	Cmd	hr/f	hr/9	RAR	BPV	R$
RH	Reliever	03	aaa	8	10	0	181	77	5.07	1.53	310			25.2	32%	69%	5.61				2.3	3.8	**1.6**		1.2	-15.0	13	$3
Age	29	04	aaa	11	9	0	163	88	5.02	1.62	313			26.4	34%	70%	5.65				3.0	4.9	**1.6**		1.0	-13.6	25	$3
Peak		05	aaa	7	5	1	134	81	5.10	1.65	310			23.6	35%	69%	5.18	40	19	40	3.4	5.4	**1.6**	7%	0.8	-13.1	34	$2
Type		06	aaa	4	4	1	75	41	7.85	2.02	341			7.9	36%	62%	6.47	35	19	46	5.1	4.9	**1.0**	10%	1.5	-30.9	-8	($6)
Reliability	7	07	LAA	3	3	0	77	56	4.77	1.36	271	302	253	6.5	31%	65%	4.26	44	19	37	2.8	6.5	**2.3**	8%	0.8	-2.6	64	$5
ERA Potl	55%	1st Half		2	1	0	34	16	4.24	1.06	226			6.8	25%	59%	4.56	44	14	42	2.1	4.2	**2.0**	4%	0.5	1.1	61	$4
LIMA Plan	C+	2nd Half		1	2	0	43	40	5.20	1.59	303			6.3	37%	69%	4.00	43	24	33	3.3	8.3	**2.5**	11%	1.0	-3.7	66	$1
+/- Score	2	08	Proj	**3**	**3**	**0**	**68**	**49**	**4.90**	**1.47**	**281**			**8.3**	**32%**	**69%**	**4.50**	**43**	**20**	**38**	**3.3**	**6.5**	**2.0**	**11%**	**1.2**	**-0.1**	**43**	**$3**

Took the way-back machine to find pre-injury Dom. Wild H% and S% swings cloud overall ERA picture, but the skills revival is real. That said, they aren't amazing skills, and it's not like he's going to replace K-Rod.

Borkowski,Dave				W	L	Sv	IP	K	ERA	WHIP	OBA	vL	vR	BF/G	H%	S%	xERA	G	L	F	Ctl	Dom	Cmd	hr/f	hr/9	RAR	BPV	R$
RH	Reliever	03	aa	6	8	0	128	53	4.71	1.62	333			19.4	35%	72%	5.90				2.0	3.7	**1.9**		0.9	-5.0	23	$1
Age	31	04	BAL *	9	13	0	141	93	5.80	1.60	316	270	307	19.3	36%	63%	4.55	44	22	34	2.7	5.9	**2.2**	8%	0.8	-23.9	49	$2
Peak		05	aaa	10	10	0	182	85	5.74	1.69	343			29.0	36%	67%	6.43				2.0	4.2	**2.1**		1.1	-32.2	23	($2)
Type	Pwr	06	HOU	3	2	0	71	52	4.69	1.31	259	262	255	7.5	29%	66%	4.12	47	17	36	2.9	6.6	**2.3**	10%	1.0	-1.8	60	$4
Reliability	17	07	HOU	5	3	1	72	63	5.15	1.53	273	300	256	5.0	33%	68%	4.40	43	19	38	4.3	7.9	**1.9**	10%	1.0	-6.4	57	$4
ERA Potl	50%	1st Half		1	3	0	32	29	5.06	1.47	250			5.2	29%	69%	4.49	42	16	42	4.8	8.2	**1.7**	13%	1.4	-2.5	48	$1
LIMA Plan	C+	2nd Half		4	0	1	40	34	5.21	1.59	291			4.8	36%	67%	4.34	44	21	35	3.9	7.7	**2.0**	7%	0.7	-3.9	65	$3
+/- Score	18	08	Proj	**4**	**3**	**0**	**73**	**55**	**4.81**	**1.47**	**277**			**7.0**	**32%**	**69%**	**4.39**	**45**	**19**	**37**	**3.5**	**6.8**	**2.0**	**11%**	**1.1**	**0.1**	**48**	**$3**

If this Dom trend keeps up, we might be tempted to think about possibly being interested. Maybe. Except, when he dials it up he loses Ctl, '06 was his "best" year ever, and he's passing peak. Nevermind.

Borowski,Joe				W	L	Sv	IP	K	ERA	WHIP	OBA	vL	vR	BF/G	H%	S%	xERA	G	L	F	Ctl	Dom	Cmd	hr/f	hr/9	RAR	BPV	R$
RH	Reliever	03	CHC	2	2	33	68	66	2.65	1.06	217	212	204	4.0	28%	78%	3.54	38	20	42	2.5	8.7	**3.5**	7%	0.7	13.7	117	$20
Age	37	04	CHC	2	4	9	21	17	8.10	1.99	312	344	281	4.7	36%	59%	6.07	33	21	46	6.4	7.3	**1.1**	9%	1.3	-10.0	21	$1
Decline		05	2TM	1	5	0	46	27	4.49	1.08	226	192	244	4.3	23%	64%	4.03	47	17	36	2.3	5.3	**2.3**	16%	1.6	-1.1	42	$3
Type	Pwr FB	06	FLA	3	3	36	69	64	3.77	1.59	244	167	291	4.1	30%	75%	4.63	33	18	50	4.3	8.3	**1.9**	7%	0.9	6.1	70	$18
Reliability	45	07	CLE	4	5	45	66	58	5.07	1.43	294	293	286	4.1	35%	67%	4.24	34	21	45	2.3	7.9	**3.4**	10%	1.2	-4.6	79	$19
ERA Potl	65%	1st Half		0	3	21	28	25	6.11	1.57	313			4.2	38%	61%	4.65	27	23	49	2.6	8.0	**3.1**	7%	1.0	-5.5	77	$7
LIMA Plan	C	2nd Half		4	2	24	38	33	4.30	1.33	278			4.1	32%	73%	3.93	39	19	42	2.1	7.9	**3.7**	12%	1.4	1.0	81	$12
+/- Score	20	08	Proj	**3**	**5**	**35**	**68**	**58**	**4.37**	**1.32**	**265**			**4.1**	**31%**	**70%**	**4.23**	**36**	**20**	**45**	**2.8**	**7.7**	**2.8**	**10%**	**1.2**	**2.2**	**70**	**$17**

PRO: xERA better than ERA, best skills since '03... and 45 Sv!
CON: Unreliable Cmd, risky FB, skills marginally closer-worthy, better options in wings.
But he's still the incumbent.
UP: 2007 DN: 10 Sv, loses job

Bowie,Micah				W	L	Sv	IP	K	ERA	WHIP	OBA	vL	vR	BF/G	H%	S%	xERA	G	L	F	Ctl	Dom	Cmd	hr/f	hr/9	RAR	BPV	R$
LH	Reliever	03	OAK *	0	1	2	12	7	5.21	1.51	307			4.9	34%	65%	5.05				2.3	5.1	**2.2**		0.7	-1.0	48	$1
Age	33	04		0	0	0	0	0	0.00	0.00																		
Past Peak		05	aa	1	1	1	16	16	4.50	1.38	274			6.9	34%	70%	4.49				2.8	9.0	**3.2**		1.1	-0.4	88	$2
Type	Pwr FB	06	WAS *	2	1	1	61	57	3.69	1.36	224			5.7	30%	71%	4.78	36	13	51	4.9	8.3	**1.7**	1%	0.1	6.1	91	$5
Reliability	0	07	WAS *	4	5	0	71	49	4.78	1.45	260	250	266	9.3	29%	69%	4.81	43	18	40	4.1	6.2	**1.5**	9%	1.0	-3.1	41	$3
ERA Potl	55%	1st Half		4	3	0	55	42	4.42	1.35	244			8.4	28%	70%	4.50	42	17	41	3.9	6.9	**1.8**	11%	1.1	0.1	50	$4
LIMA Plan	B	2nd Half		0	2	0	16	7	6.05	1.81	311			14.7	34%	65%	5.12	56	22	22	4.8	3.9	**0.8**	8%	0.6	-3.1	15	($1)
+/- Score	-9	08	Proj	**1**	**2**	**0**	**29**	**21**	**4.66**	**1.52**	**262**			**8.0**	**31%**	**69%**	**5.00**	**43**	**17**	**41**	**4.7**	**6.5**	**1.4**	**5%**	**0.6**	**-2.2**	**53**	**$1**

4-3, 4.55 ERA in 57 IP at WAS. Newsflash: missed three months with more injuries. He's NEVER healthy. Skills can be tempting... so to be safe, get a restraining order that keeps him at least 100 yards away from your roster.

Braden,Dallas				W	L	Sv	IP	K	ERA	WHIP	OBA	vL	vR	BF/G	H%	S%	xERA	G	L	F	Ctl	Dom	Cmd	hr/f	hr/9	RAR	BPV	R$
LH	Starter	03		0	0	0	0	0	0.00	0.00																		
Age	24	04		0	0	0	0	0	0.00	0.00																		
Growth		05	aa	9	5	0	97	61	4.08	1.45	289			26.5	33%	71%	4.32				2.8	5.7	**2.0**		0.5	2.7	60	$7
Type	FB	06	aa	0	0	0	3	2	18.00	3.00	515			17.8	55%	38%	15.50				0.0	6.0			3.0	-5.0	-102	($1)
Reliability	0	07	OAK *	4	11	0	148	125	5.13	1.39	275	214	324	19.3	33%	64%	4.35	37	18	45	2.9	7.6	**2.7**	8%	0.9	-11.4	74	$7
ERA Potl	65%	1st Half		2	4	0	62	50	5.08	1.34	265			20.3	30%	65%	4.45	35	18	47	2.9	7.3	**2.5**	10%	1.3	-4.4	59	$3
LIMA Plan	B	2nd Half		2	7	0	86	75	5.16	1.42	282			18.7	35%	63%	4.30	38	18	44	2.8	7.9	**2.8**	5%	0.7	-7.0	85	$4
+/- Score	25	08	Proj	**5**	**6**	**0**	**94**	**74**	**4.43**	**1.36**	**271**			**23.5**	**32%**	**68%**	**4.44**	**37**	**18**	**45**	**2.8**	**7.1**	**2.6**	**6%**	**0.8**	**0.6**	**74**	**$7**

1-8, 6.72 ERA in 72 IP at OAK. Fared better at AAA, with a 17-K game on his resume. FB% could be an issue, but this isn't a "AAAA" skills set. Don't be surprised if he gets another shot, and does better.

Bradford,Chad				W	L	Sv	IP	K	ERA	WHIP	OBA	vL	vR	BF/G	H%	S%	xERA	G	L	F	Ctl	Dom	Cmd	hr/f	hr/9	RAR	BPV	R$
RH	Reliever	03	OAK	7	4	2	77	62	3.04	1.26	236	326	190	4.5	28%	79%	3.03	64	19	17	3.5	7.2	**2.1**	18%	0.8	14.1	70	$11
Age	33	04	OAK	5	7	1	59	34	4.42	1.27	235	298	211	3.6	26%	66%	3.89	61	16	23	3.7	5.2	**1.4**	12%	0.8	0.1	46	$5
Past Peak		05	BOS	2	1	0	23	10	3.90	1.43	308	409	282	3.2	34%	72%	3.19	65	23	12	1.6	3.9	**2.5**	10%	0.4	1.4	58	$2
Type	Con xGB	06	NYM	4	2	2	62	45	2.90	1.16	252	250	256	3.6	31%	73%	3.02	63	16	21	1.9	6.5	**3.5**	3%	0.1	12.1	112	$9
Reliability	5	07	BAL	4	7	2	65	29	3.34	1.44	297	321	282	3.6	33%	75%	4.03	62	15	23	2.2	4.0	**1.8**	2%	0.1	9.3	54	$6
ERA Potl	45%	1st Half		0	4	0	30	18	3.30	1.40	299			3.1	35%	74%	3.11	70	14	17	1.8	5.4	**3.0**	0%	0.0	4.5	91	$2
LIMA Plan	C+	2nd Half		4	3	2	35	11	3.37	1.47	295			4.2	32%	76%	4.81	56	16	28	2.6	2.9	**1.1**	3%	0.3	4.9	28	$4
+/- Score	-23	08	Proj	**4**	**5**	**13**	**58**	**33**	**3.88**	**1.33**	**272**			**3.7**	**31%**	**70%**	**3.59**	**62**	**17**	**21**	**2.5**	**5.1**	**2.1**	**7%**	**0.5**	**6.5**	**61**	**$9**

Red flags: Skills collapsed as year progressed; just 2 K in 11 Sept IP (1.7 Dom). 2nd half GB, Ctl also off. Injury past makes dismissing this as a fluke seem foolhardy. It's scary how much it looks like 2004-05. Caution.

ROD TRUESDELL

Bray,Bill

		Yr	Tm	W	L	Sv	IP	K	ERA	WHIP	OBA	vL	vR	BF/G	H%	S%	xERA	G	L	F	Ctl	Dom	Cmd	hr/f	hr/9	RAR	BPV	R$
LH	Reliever	03		0	0	0	0	0	0.00	0.00																		
Age	24	04		0	0	0	0	0	0.00	0.00																		
Growth		05		0	0	0	0	0	0.00	0.00																		
Type	Pwr	06	2NL *	7	3	7	81	77	4.42	1.39	273	333	252	5.1	33%	71%	3.62	44	25	31	3.0	8.5	2.9	13%	1.1	0.7	78	$10
Reliability	0	07	CIN *	4	5	1	33	39	5.95	1.50	293	158	342	4.0	40%	58%	3.62	37	23	40	3.0	10.5	3.5	5%	0.5	-6.2	118	$3
ERA Potl	85%	1st Half		0	0	0	1	1	30.00	4.17	596			4.3	68%	20%					0.0	7.5			0.0	-3.8	-19	($1)
LIMA Plan	A	2nd Half		4	5	1	32	38	5.05	1.40	273			4.0	38%	63%	3.51	37	23	40	3.1	10.7	3.5	6%	0.6	-2.5	120	$4
+/- Score	100	08	Proj	6	6	3	58	63	3.88	1.31	255			4.2	33%	73%	3.45	41	24	36	3.1	9.8	3.2	11%	0.9	6.8	101	$8

3-3, 6.28 ERA in 14 IP at CIN. Basically injured all year (broken pinkie, shoulder tendinitis), so it's encouraging to see him put up these skills. Ignore sample-size skewed ERA. Should again be near the top of LIMA picks.

Brazoban,Yhency

		Yr	Tm	W	L	Sv	IP	K	ERA	WHIP	OBA	vL	vR	BF/G	H%	S%	xERA	G	L	F	Ctl	Dom	Cmd	hr/f	hr/9	RAR	BPV	R$
RH	Reliever	03	aa	2	2	3	27	16	9.26	1.88	325			6.5	34%	51%	7.41				4.6	5.3	1.1		2.0	-16.3	-14	($2)
Age	27	04	a/a	6	5	14	63	65	2.65	1.23	238			5.6	31%	81%	3.31				3.1	9.3	3.0		0.7	13.2	104	$14
Pre-Peak		05	LA	4	10	21	72	61	5.36	1.41	256	267	250	4.2	29%	65%	4.37	39	22	39	4.0	7.6	1.9	13%	1.4	-9.9	48	$10
Type	Pwr	06	LA	0	0	0	5	4	5.40	1.80	332	333	364	4.7	41%	67%	5.89	18	24	59	3.6	7.2	2.0	0%	0.0	-0.6	74	($0)
Reliability	0	07	LA *	0	0	3	15	15	3.97	1.20	213			4.1	25%	73%	3.60				4.0	9.0	2.3		1.4	0.9	70	$2
ERA Potl	45%	1st Half		0	0	3	15	15	3.97	1.20	213			4.1	25%	73%					4.0	9.0	2.3		1.4	0.9	70	$2
LIMA Plan	B+	2nd Half		0	0	0	0	0	0.00	0.00																		
+/- Score	-16	08	Proj	2	3	0	44	37	4.14	1.31	246			4.7	29%	71%	4.17	39	22	39	3.5	7.7	2.2	10%	1.0	1.2	66	$3

0-0, 16.20 ERA in 2 IP at LA. Tore a labrum just after he returned from TJ surgery. Expected to be ready in '08, but now it's almost no action in two years, it's a shoulder, and 2004 seems so long ago.

Britton,Chris

		Yr	Tm	W	L	Sv	IP	K	ERA	WHIP	OBA	vL	vR	BF/G	H%	S%	xERA	G	L	F	Ctl	Dom	Cmd	hr/f	hr/9	RAR	BPV	R$
RH	Reliever	03		0	0	0	0	0	0.00	0.00																		
Age	25	04		0	0	0	0	0	0.00	0.00																		
Growth		05		0	0	0	0	0	0.00	0.00																		
Type	xFB	06	BAL *	1	2	3	69	62	3.38	1.23	238	301	186	4.4	30%	73%	4.35	31	19	50	3.1	8.1	2.6	4%	0.5	10.0	94	$8
Reliability	0	07	NYY *	4	3	8	70	54	3.34	1.26	259			6.1	31%	76%	4.63	32	15	54	2.4	6.9	2.8	5%	0.8	10.0	81	$11
ERA Potl	50%	1st Half		2	0	8	43	39	2.72	1.26	257			7.2	32%	80%	4.45	29	14	57	2.5	8.2	3.3	4%	0.6	9.5	102	$8
LIMA Plan	B+	2nd Half		2	3	0	27	15	4.33	1.26	262			4.9	28%	68%	5.06	33	15	52	2.3	5.0	2.1	7%	1.0	0.6	48	$2
+/- Score	-4	08	Proj	2	2	0	49	38	4.04	1.27	254			5.1	30%	70%	4.59	32	17	51	2.8	7.0	2.5	7%	0.9	-0.6	72	$4

0-1, 3.55 ERA in 13 IP at NYY. 3.6 Dom with NYY is a head-scratcher, but with no apparent injury, go with the overall skills. Those speak of a power arm with upside. He does need K's to offset FB%, so watch Dom.

Brocail,Doug

		Yr	Tm	W	L	Sv	IP	K	ERA	WHIP	OBA	vL	vR	BF/G	H%	S%	xERA	G	L	F	Ctl	Dom	Cmd	hr/f	hr/9	RAR	BPV	R$
RH	Reliever	03		0	0	0	0	0	0.00	0.00											0.0	0.0						
Age	41	04	TEX *	6	2	1	72	59	4.36	1.44	282	190	320	5.7	35%	68%	3.63	55	19	26	3.0	7.4	2.5	5%	0.4	0.6	83	$6
Decline		05	TEX	5	3	1	73	61	5.54	1.70	304	346	267	5.5	38%	65%	4.26	49	23	27	4.2	7.5	1.8	3%	0.2	-10.5	70	$2
Type		06	SD	2	2	0	28	19	4.82	1.25	255	280	228	4.7	30%	59%	4.17	40	26	33	2.6	6.1	2.4	3%	0.3	-1.2	81	$2
Reliability	0	07	SD	5	1	0	77	43	3.05	1.17	234	182	268	4.7	25%	78%	4.53	42	18	40	2.8	5.0	1.8	8%	0.9	13.0	48	$9
ERA Potl	40%	1st Half		2	1	0	33	20	3.27	1.09	212			4.6	23%	73%	4.54	38	19	43	3.0	5.5	1.8	7%	0.8	4.7	59	$4
LIMA Plan	C	2nd Half		3	0	0	44	23	2.88	1.24	250			4.8	26%	82%	4.52	46	17	37	2.7	4.7	1.8	10%	1.0	8.3	40	$5
+/- Score	-65	08	Proj	2	3	0	58	35	4.34	1.40	268			5.1	30%	71%	4.60	44	21	35	3.3	5.4	1.7	9%	0.9	-1.5	41	$3

Ah, the fickle fingers of H% and S%. One year they bring comfort, peace, love, and a suppressed ERA. Then they turn around, and reality strikes. Truth here is that skills were off; at 40, this is not a positive.

Brown,Andrew

		Yr	Tm	W	L	Sv	IP	K	ERA	WHIP	OBA	vL	vR	BF/G	H%	S%	xERA	G	L	F	Ctl	Dom	Cmd	hr/f	hr/9	RAR	BPV	R$
RH	Reliever	03	aa	0	0	0	1	1	0.00	0.00	0			2.9	0%		-2.83				0.0	9.0				0.5	109	$0
Age	27	04	a/a	5	10	0	122	110	4.86	1.42	255			20.4	31%	67%	4.23				4.1	8.1	2.0		1.0	-7.8	66	$6
Growth		05	aaa	4	2	4	69	71	3.51	1.05	220			5.6	28%	69%	2.65				2.3	9.2	3.9		0.8	6.8	126	$11
Type	Pwr FB	06	CLE *	5	4	5	72	54	3.40	1.58	250	286	95	6.8	29%	80%	5.44	39	18	43	5.8	6.7	1.2	5%	0.6	10.3	51	$7
Reliability	0	07	OAK *	5	6	4	82	80	4.33	1.39	259	242	247	5.0	33%	69%	4.06	41	19	41	3.6	8.7	2.4	6%	0.6	1.8	88	$9
ERA Potl	60%	1st Half		2	3	1	37	38	3.40	1.21	229			4.5	29%	76%					3.4	9.2	2.7		1.0	5.1	92	$5
LIMA Plan	B	2nd Half		3	3	3	45	42	5.10	1.53	282			5.5	36%	65%	4.38	41	19	41	3.8	8.3	2.2	3%	0.3	-3.3	85	$3
+/- Score	17	08	Proj	4	4	0	58	53	4.03	1.40	252			6.0	31%	72%	4.28	41	19	41	4.0	8.2	2.0	7%	0.8	1.6	74	$5

3-3, 4.54 ERA in 42 IP at OAK. Cmd rebounded, and he was able to carry the surge to OAK. That rebound, though, only elevated him to "serviceable," as Ctl remains tremulous. Still, as always, he's worth watching.

Broxton,Jonathan

		Yr	Tm	W	L	Sv	IP	K	ERA	WHIP	OBA	vL	vR	BF/G	H%	S%	xERA	G	L	F	Ctl	Dom	Cmd	hr/f	hr/9	RAR	BPV	R$
RH	Reliever	03		0	0	0	0	0	0.00	0.00																		
Age	23	04		0	0	0	0	0	0.00	0.00																		
Growth		05	aa	5	3	5	96	90	3.27	1.16	234			11.9	30%	71%	2.73				2.7	8.4	3.1		0.4	12.2	113	$13
Type	Pwr	06	LA *	5	1	8	87	113	2.27	1.18	213	244	196	4.5	31%	84%	3.13	39	20	40	3.7	11.6	3.1	9%	0.7	23.8	126	$16
Reliability	11	07	LA	4	4	2	82	99	2.85	1.15	230	200	247	4.0	32%	77%	2.73	49	22	29	2.7	10.9	4.0	10%	0.7	15.9	138	$12
ERA Potl	55%	1st Half		3	2	1	40	47	3.15	1.23	221			4.3	33%	71%	3.02	50	22	28	3.8	10.6	2.8	0%	0.0	6.3	132	$6
LIMA Plan	B+	2nd Half		1	2	1	42	52	2.57	1.07	238			3.8	32%	85%	2.48	47	22	31	1.7	11.1	6.5	19%	1.3	9.6	172	$6
+/- Score	41	08	Proj	4	3	10	83	100	2.71	1.12	223			4.6	31%	78%	2.88	45	21	34	2.8	10.8	3.8	9%	0.7	15.5	137	$15

Cmd gains have taken him from just "really good" to "dominant." Impressive growth across the board. In fact, the only thing NOT to like is his continuing role as caddy. But just like '07... UP: 40 saves

Bruney,Brian

		Yr	Tm	W	L	Sv	IP	K	ERA	WHIP	OBA	vL	vR	BF/G	H%	S%	xERA	G	L	F	Ctl	Dom	Cmd	hr/f	hr/9	RAR	BPV	R$
RH	Reliever	03	a/a	3	3	26	63	56	3.00	1.33	239			4.5	31%	76%	3.02				4.0	8.0	2.0		0.1	10.9	93	$15
Age	26	04	ARI *	5	5	5	69	75	2.87	1.20	163	214	172	4.7	23%	76%	4.19	33	26	41	5.9	9.8	1.7	5%	0.4	11.9	104	$11
Growth		05	ARI	1	3	12	46	51	7.43	1.98	302	280	314	4.8	39%	62%	4.90	41	22	37	6.8	10.0	1.5	12%	1.2	-18.1	50	$0
Type	Pwr xFB	06	NYY *	2	3	3	37	48	4.84	1.69	245	115	229	5.0	34%	74%	4.54	35	18	47	7.0	11.6	1.7	12%	1.2	-1.3	74	$3
Reliability	5	07	NYY	3	2	0	50	39	4.68	1.62	238	303	209	3.9	28%	72%	6.00	31	17	52	6.7	7.0	1.1	7%	0.9	-1.1	45	$2
ERA Potl	45%	1st Half		2	1	0	33	26	1.91	1.45	205			3.9	26%	87%	5.83	30	17	53	6.5	7.1	1.1	2%	0.3	10.6	71	$4
LIMA Plan	C+	2nd Half		1	1	0	17	13	10.06	1.94	294			3.9	31%	48%	6.34	32	18	50	6.9	6.9	1.0	15%	2.1	-11.6	-5	($2)
+/- Score	-35	08	Proj	2	3	0	44	38	5.59	1.72	260			4.4	30%	70%	5.64	34	19	48	6.6	7.9	1.2	10%	1.2	-6.2	38	$0

Home plate continues to be an elusive concept. Luck finally gave way, and NYY just quit using him. We can talk all day about his "stuff," but any pitcher who can't manage fewer than 6 BBs per 9 IP is unrosterable.

Buchholz,Clay

		Yr	Tm	W	L	Sv	IP	K	ERA	WHIP	OBA	vL	vR	BF/G	H%	S%	xERA	G	L	F	Ctl	Dom	Cmd	hr/f	hr/9	RAR	BPV	R$
RH	Starter	03		0	0	0	0	0	0.00	0.00																		
Age	23	04		0	0	0	0	0	0.00	0.00																		
Growth		05		0	0	0	0	0	0.00	0.00																		
Type	Pwr	06	aa	9	4	0	103	70	4.62	1.65	307			22.4	34%	75%	5.80				3.6	6.1	1.7		1.2	-1.3	28	$5
Reliability	0	07	BOS *	11	6	0	148	168	2.92	1.10	219	217	133	21.2	30%	75%	3.06	38	29	33	2.8	10.2	3.7	8%	0.6	28.9	131	$24
ERA Potl	55%	1st Half		6	2	0	85	98	2.12	0.96	203			22.0	29%	79%					2.2	10.4	4.7		0.4	25.1	162	$17
LIMA Plan	B	2nd Half		5	4	0	63	70	4.02	1.29	241			20.3	32%	71%	3.41	38	29	33	3.6	10.0	2.8	11%	0.9	3.8	100	$8
+/- Score	15	08	Proj	11	6	0	136	129	3.97	1.35	260			24.2	32%	73%	3.76	38	29	33	3.2	8.5	2.6	11%	0.9	12.3	82	$15

3-1, 1.59 ERA in 23 IP at BOS. Oh yeah, and a no-hitter. It took guts for BOS to stick to the program and limit his IP, but keeper league owners, rejoice. May yet be asked to serve more AAA time, but a future ace.

Buchholz,Taylor

		Yr	Tm	W	L	Sv	IP	K	ERA	WHIP	OBA	vL	vR	BF/G	H%	S%	xERA	G	L	F	Ctl	Dom	Cmd	hr/f	hr/9	RAR	BPV	R$
RH	Reliever	03	aa	9	11	0	144	100	3.93	1.26	267			24.1	30%	71%	3.92				2.1	6.2	2.9		0.9	8.2	75	$13
Age	26	04	aaa	6	7	0	98	62	6.15	1.51	303			21.7	32%	62%	5.75				2.6	5.7	2.2		1.6	-21.9	28	$1
Growth		05	aaa	6	0	0	74	36	5.46	1.46	286			17.1	29%	67%	5.47				2.9	4.4	1.5		1.7	-10.6	4	$2
Type	Con	06	HOU *	7	13	0	157	108	5.85	1.34	265	249	248	23.1	29%	58%	4.35	44	18	38	2.9	6.2	2.1	12%	1.3	-26.3	44	$5
Reliability	16	07	COL	6	5	0	94	61	4.23	1.33	284	268	306	9.7	32%	69%	4.27	44	17	38	1.9	5.9	3.1	7%	0.8	2.3	74	$7
ERA Potl	55%	1st Half		4	3	0	57	34	4.74	1.32	285			13.4	32%	64%	4.33	47	14	39	1.7	5.4	3.1	7%	0.8	-2.2	71	$4
LIMA Plan	C+	2nd Half		2	2	0	37	27	3.43	1.36	284			6.8	33%	77%	4.17	41	22	37	2.2	6.6	3.0	7%	0.7	4.5	79	$3
+/- Score	9	08	Proj	5	5	0	87	57	4.55	1.36	279			9.1	31%	69%	4.35	43	19	38	2.4	5.9	2.5	10%	1.1	0.6	52	$5

Finally regained top-notch, pre-injury Cmd. Despite ERA splits, there's only one skills difference:
Career hr/9: as reliever - 0.5
as starter - 1.4
May be hr/f luck, but chances to prove otherwise are dimming.

ROD TRUESDELL

Buehrle, Mark

LH Starter — Age 29 — Pre-Peak — Type Con — Reliability 70 — ERA Potl 45% — LIMA Plan D — +/- Score -23

Yr	Tm	W	L	Sv	IP	K	ERA	WHIP	OBA	vL	vR	BF/G	H%	S%	xERA	G	L	F	Ctl	Dom	Cmd	hr/f	hr/9	RAR	BPV	R$
03	CHW	14	14	0	230	119	4.15	1.35	278	263	285	28.1	30%	71%	4.63	46	17	37	2.4	4.7	2.0	8%	0.9	10.7	42	$16
04	CHW	16	10	0	245	165	3.89	1.26	271	271	267	29.2	30%	73%	3.81	49	19	32	1.9	6.1	3.2	13%	1.2	16.3	69	$22
05	CHW	16	8	0	236	149	3.12	1.19	265	271	260	29.4	30%	76%	3.86	46	21	33	1.5	5.7	3.7	8%	0.8	36.3	91	$27
06	CHW	12	13	0	204	98	4.99	1.45	300	238	322	27.8	31%	70%	4.72	44	19	37	2.1	4.3	2.0	13%	1.6	-10.8	16	$9
07	CHW	10	9	0	201	115	3.63	1.26	268	314	258	28.0	29%	74%	4.39	43	18	39	2.0	5.1	2.6	9%	1.0	21.8	56	$18
1st Half		5	4	0	100	66	3.33	1.10	242			26.8	26%	75%	3.90	46	16	38	1.8	5.9	3.3	11%	1.2	14.5	76	$12
2nd Half		5	5	0	101	49	3.92	1.42	293			29.2	32%	74%	4.89	41	20	39	2.2	4.4	2.0	7%	0.8	7.3	40	$6
08	Proj	11	10	0	203	112	4.17	1.33	279			28.7	30%	72%	4.45	44	19	37	2.1	5.0	2.4	10%	1.1	1.2	46	$15

Not the rebound it appears. Skills faded under ever-higher workload as season went on, and 2H Dom shows the wear. xERA 4.00+ in every month but April, but S% saved the day. ERA *will* be back over 4.00.

Burnett, A.J.

RH Starter — Age 31 — Peak — Type Pwr GB — Reliability 49 — ERA Potl 55% — LIMA Plan C — +/- Score 39

Yr	Tm	W	L	Sv	IP	K	ERA	WHIP	OBA	vL	vR	BF/G	H%	S%	xERA	G	L	F	Ctl	Dom	Cmd	hr/f	hr/9	RAR	BPV	R$
03	FLA	0	2	0	23	21	4.70	1.57	217	234	194	25.8	27%	71%	4.82	47	20	33	7.0	8.2	1.2	10%	0.8	-1.2	62	$0
04	FLA	7	6	0	120	113	3.68	1.17	232	247	211	24.5	29%	69%	3.36	50	17	33	2.9	8.5	3.0	8%	0.7	8.7	102	$13
05	FLA	12	12	0	209	198	3.44	1.26	238	226	249	27.3	31%	73%	3.07	58	19	22	3.4	8.5	2.5	9%	0.5	20.6	96	$21
06	TOR	10	8	0	135	118	3.99	1.31	266	261	267	27.2	32%	72%	3.47	50	20	29	2.6	7.9	3.0	12%	0.9	9.4	85	$15
07	TOR	10	8	0	166	176	3.75	1.19	219	200	231	27.2	27%	74%	3.07	55	15	30	3.6	9.6	2.7	18%	1.2	15.5	87	$21
1st Half		5	6	0	90	100	4.00	1.26	223			26.8	28%	73%	3.17	54	15	31	4.0	10.0	2.5	18%	1.3	5.6	84	$10
2nd Half		5	2	0	76	76	3.45	1.11	214			27.7	26%	74%	2.96	56	16	28	3.1	9.0	2.9	18%	1.1	9.9	92	$11
08	Proj	11	9	0	174	170	3.57	1.21	234			26.6	29%	73%	3.20	54	18	29	3.2	8.8	2.8	12%	0.8	27.9	95	$21

Missed more time with injury, and got ripped by his GM. But no one can fault the skills when (he decides?) he's healthy. Few possess his Pwr/GB profile, or BPIs this consistently solid. Just don't count on 200 IP.

Burres, Brian

LH Reliever — Age 27 — Growth — Type Pwr — Reliability 28 — ERA Potl 50% — LIMA Plan C+ — +/- Score 15

Yr	Tm	W	L	Sv	IP	K	ERA	WHIP	OBA	vL	vR	BF/G	H%	S%	xERA	G	L	F	Ctl	Dom	Cmd	hr/f	hr/9	RAR	BPV	R$
03		0	0	0	0	0	0.00	0.00																		
04		0	0	0	0	0	0.00	0.00																		
05	aa	9	6	0	128	85	5.25	1.67	300			22.6	34%	69%	5.42				4.1	5.9	1.4		0.9	-14.9	34	$2
06	aa	10	6	0	139	98	5.43	1.64	298			24.4	33%	66%	5.62				4.4	6.3	1.6		1.2	-15.6	30	$4
07	BAL	6	8	0	121	96	5.95	1.70	291	306	281	15.1	34%	66%	5.11	38	22	40	4.9	7.1	1.5	9%	1.0	-21.6	39	$0
1st Half		3	2	0	56	49	3.38	1.52	244			16.6	30%	79%	4.81	42	17	41	5.5	7.9	1.4	6%	0.6	7.8	64	$5
2nd Half		3	6	0	65	47	8.17	1.86	327			14.1	37%	56%	5.36	35	26	39	4.4	6.5	1.5	11%	1.4	-29.4	18	($4)
08	Proj	4	7	0	95	70	5.31	1.63	287			18.0	33%	69%	5.06	37	23	40	4.5	6.6	1.5	10%	1.1	-6.6	34	$2

Elevated S% made his 1st half look far better than it was, and by time BAL realized he really had no skill, the season was over. Doesn't anyone at BAL know about MLEs? Even his xERAs never cracked 5.00.

Burton, Jared

RH Reliever — Age 26 — Growth — Type Pwr — Reliability 0 — ERA Potl 40% — LIMA Plan C — +/- Score -31

Yr	Tm	W	L	Sv	IP	K	ERA	WHIP	OBA	vL	vR	BF/G	H%	S%	xERA	G	L	F	Ctl	Dom	Cmd	hr/f	hr/9	RAR	BPV	R$
03		0	0	0	0	0	0.00	0.00																		
04		0	0	0	0	0	0.00	0.00																		
05		0	0	0	0	0	0.00	0.00																		
06	aa	0	0	0	74	50	5.27	1.58	296			6.3	34%	67%	5.17				3.5	6.1	1.7		0.9	-6.8	41	$3
07	CIN *	5	3	1	62	49	3.35	1.41	242	130	219	4.4	30%	75%	4.69	45	15	40	4.6	7.0	1.5	3%	0.3	8.2	72	$6
1st Half		0	1	1	15	11	5.96	2.05	351			6.3	42%	68%					4.8	6.6	1.4		0.0	-2.9	53	($1)
2nd Half		5	2	0	47	38	2.51	1.21	198			4.0	24%	80%	4.39	45	15	40	4.6	7.2	1.6	4%	0.4	11.1	80	$7
08	Proj	4	3	8	58	43	4.50	1.57	281			5.3	33%	72%	4.83	45	15	40	4.2	6.7	1.6	7%	0.8	-3.1	49	$5

4-2, 2.51 ERA in 43 IP at CIN. Saves coming here? Um, no. Just another hard-thrower with poor control. Lucked his way to prominent role with a miniscule H%, which won't last. Some upside, but a long way to go.

Bush, David

RH Starter — Age 28 — Pre-Peak — Type — Reliability 63 — ERA Potl 60% — LIMA Plan B — +/- Score 36

Yr	Tm	W	L	Sv	IP	K	ERA	WHIP	OBA	vL	vR	BF/G	H%	S%	xERA	G	L	F	Ctl	Dom	Cmd	hr/f	hr/9	RAR	BPV	R$
03	aa	7	3	0	81	62	3.44	1.31	274			24.5	33%	74%	3.72				2.2	6.9	3.1		0.4	9.5	93	$9
04	TOR *	11	10	0	196	141	4.45	1.36	286	289	206	26.3	33%	69%	4.33	42	16	42	2.1	6.5	3.1	7%	0.9	-0.3	73	$13
05	TOR *	7	13	0	191	110	4.77	1.33	287	269	269	23.9	31%	67%	4.23	46	19	35	1.8	5.2	2.9	12%	1.3	-9.4	51	$9
06	MIL	12	11	0	210	166	4.41	1.14	253	258	246	25.1	29%	64%	3.49	47	19	34	1.6	7.1	4.4	12%	1.1	1.9	105	$20
07	MIL	12	10	0	186	134	5.12	1.40	292	246	324	24.4	33%	66%	4.18	43	19	38	2.1	6.5	3.0	12%	1.3	-16.0	60	$10
1st Half		6	6	0	94	68	5.07	1.34	286			25.0	33%	62%	3.88	45	23	32	1.9	6.5	3.4	9%	0.9	-7.5	82	$6
2nd Half		6	4	0	92	66	5.17	1.46	299			23.8	32%	70%	4.47	42	15	43	2.3	6.4	2.8	14%	1.8	-8.4	39	$4
08	Proj	12	11	0	203	146	4.34	1.28	272			24.3	30%	70%	3.99	44	18	37	2.0	6.5	3.2	12%	1.2	10.2	70	$16

"The probability of a player correcting a deficiency declines with each year he allows the deficiency to continue to exist." For him, it's the inability to pitch out of the stretch (S%). Can he fix it? Sure... but see the above.

Byrd, Paul

RH Starter — Age 37 — Decline — Type Con FB — Reliability 85 — ERA Potl 45% — LIMA Plan D+ — +/- Score -28

Yr	Tm	W	L	Sv	IP	K	ERA	WHIP	OBA	vL	vR	BF/G	H%	S%	xERA	G	L	F	Ctl	Dom	Cmd	hr/f	hr/9	RAR	BPV	R$
03	aa	0	0	0	4	3	13.17	3.17	509			25.0	56%	58%	15.01				2.2	6.6	3.0		2.2	-4.4	-10	($2)
04	ATL *	9	8	0	126	85	4.43	1.30	281	329	219	24.2	31%	71%	4.45	36	18	46	1.8	6.1	3.4	11%	1.4	-2.5	64	$9
05	ANA	12	11	0	204	102	3.75	1.20	273	306	234	27.1	29%	72%	4.53	38	20	42	1.2	4.5	3.6	8%	1.0	15.7	75	$18
06	CLE	10	9	0	179	88	4.88	1.51	315	369	256	25.6	33%	71%	4.84	39	24	37	1.9	4.4	2.3	11%	1.3	-7.1	28	$7
07	CLE	15	8	0	192	88	4.59	1.39	306	322	280	26.7	32%	70%	4.79	38	21	41	1.3	4.1	3.1	10%	1.3	-1.9	47	$13
1st Half		6	3	0	80	46	4.73	1.44	328			26.8	35%	71%	4.48	38	20	42	0.6	5.2	9.0	10%	1.4	-2.2	173	$5
2nd Half		9	5	0	112	42	4.49	1.35	289			26.7	29%	70%	5.02	39	22	39	1.8	3.4	1.8	9%	1.2	0.2	20	$8
08	Proj	12	10	0	189	93	4.54	1.39	297			26.2	31%	71%	4.79	38	22	40	1.8	4.4	2.5	10%	1.2	-6.9	38	$11

In this case, "HGH" is a less important abbreviation than "xERA," which defines where his pitching lies. Expect an ERA between 4.50 and 5.00, and double-digit wins, regardless of any HGH noise.

Cabrera, Daniel

RH Starter — Age 26 — Growth — Type Pwr — Reliability 61 — ERA Potl 60% — LIMA Plan C+ — +/- Score 26

Yr	Tm	W	L	Sv	IP	K	ERA	WHIP	OBA	vL	vR	BF/G	H%	S%	xERA	G	L	F	Ctl	Dom	Cmd	hr/f	hr/9	RAR	BPV	R$
03		0	0	0	0	0	0.00	0.00											0.0	0.0						
04	BAL *	12	9	1	174	104	4.75	1.50	243	249	270	23.3	27%	69%	5.45	43	17	40	5.3	5.4	1.0	7%	0.8	-6.9	37	$8
05	BAL	10	13	0	161	157	4.53	1.43	241	285	174	24.2	30%	69%	3.80	53	18	30	4.9	8.8	1.8	11%	0.8	-3.1	74	$12
06	BAL	9	10	0	148	157	4.74	1.58	238	231	251	25.6	31%	70%	4.53	41	22	37	6.3	9.5	1.5	8%	0.7	-3.4	76	$10
07	BAL	9	18	0	204	166	5.55	1.54	264	294	236	26.8	31%	65%	4.46	50	16	35	4.8	7.3	1.5	12%	1.1	-26.3	45	$6
1st Half		6	8	0	103	83	4.98	1.39	244			27.7	28%	67%	4.27	49	14	37	4.3	7.3	1.7	13%	1.2	-6.0	48	$7
2nd Half		3	10	0	101	83	6.13	1.70	283			26.0	33%	64%	4.66	50	17	33	5.2	7.4	1.4	11%	1.0	-20.3	43	($1)
08	Proj	10	15	0	189	166	4.68	1.46	249			25.0	30%	69%	4.28	47	18	35	4.8	7.9	1.7	10%	0.9	5.0	60	$12

No Mazzone magic, but not even David Copperfield could make these bad numbers disappear. Fewer implosions (50/15 DOM/DIS), but each step forward (Ctl) has a step back (Dom). Just 26, he still has stuff, still not there.

Cabrera, Fernando

RH Reliever — Age 26 — Growth — Type Pwr FB — Reliability 2 — ERA Potl 70% — LIMA Plan C — +/- Score 63

Yr	Tm	W	L	Sv	IP	K	ERA	WHIP	OBA	vL	vR	BF/G	H%	S%	xERA	G	L	F	Ctl	Dom	Cmd	hr/f	hr/9	RAR	BPV	R$
03	aa	9	4	5	109	98	3.96	1.45	272			13.2	33%	74%	4.40				3.6	8.1	2.3		0.8	5.8	72	$11
04	aaa	4	3	5	75	64	3.77	1.30	213			7.2	28%	73%	3.32				4.8	10.0	2.1		0.9	5.3	88	$9
05	CLE *	8	2	3	81	88	1.33	1.03	213	196	224	7.1	29%	90%	3.17	35	29	36	2.4	9.7	4.0	5%	0.4	30.5	142	$18
06	CLE	3	3	0	60	77	5.23	1.41	238	235	248	5.1	29%	68%	3.89	33	23	43	4.8	10.6	2.2	18%	1.8	-5.0	64	$5
07	2AL	1	2	1	44	48	7.21	1.85	289	319	267	6.3	35%	64%	5.08	31	22	47	6.4	9.9	1.5	15%	1.9	-14.6	33	($1)
1st Half		1	2	0	28	35	4.82	1.68	262			6.8	33%	78%	4.42	32	20	48	6.1	11.3	1.8	17%	1.9	-1.1	51	$1
2nd Half		0	0	1	16	13	11.46	2.17	332			5.7	38%	45%	6.35	30	25	45	6.9	7.5	1.1	12%	1.7	-13.5	4	($3)
08	Proj	2	2	8	58	61	4.81	1.41	238			5.8	30%	69%	4.30	32	23	45	4.8	9.5	2.0	12%	1.2	1.4	68	$6

Mentioned as a candidate to fill BAL closer void, but that's a very long shot. Ctl is the key, and it's getting way out of hand. Still owns pre-'06 skills, and those are darn good. But hope for baby steps now, not saves.

Cain, Matt

RH Starter — Age 23 — Growth — Type Pwr xFB — Reliability 54 — ERA Potl 55% — LIMA Plan C — +/- Score 0

Yr	Tm	W	L	Sv	IP	K	ERA	WHIP	OBA	vL	vR	BF/G	H%	S%	xERA	G	L	F	Ctl	Dom	Cmd	hr/f	hr/9	RAR	BPV	R$
03		0	0	0	0	0	0.00	0.00											0.0	0.0						
04	aa	8	6	0	86	64	3.99	1.38	250			24.7	29%	72%	3.85				4.0	6.7	1.7		0.7	3.8	60	$7
05	SF *	12	6	0	191	201	3.35	1.06	192	160	143	23.1	24%	72%	3.89	29	18	53	3.5	9.5	2.7	8%	0.9	21.2	104	$25
06	SF	13	12	0	190	179	4.16	1.28	226	217	227	25.0	28%	69%	4.34	36	16	48	4.1	8.5	2.1	7%	0.9	7.6	78	$18
07	SF	7	16	0	200	163	3.65	1.26	235	248	224	26.1	28%	72%	4.39	39	16	45	3.6	7.3	2.1	5%	0.6	19.3	76	$17
1st Half		2	9	0	104	76	3.38	1.30	227			27.4	26%	75%	4.87	37	17	45	4.3	6.6	1.5	5%	0.6	13.5	63	$9
2nd Half		5	7	0	96	87	3.94	1.22	245			24.8	31%	68%	3.91	42	15	44	2.7	8.2	3.0	6%	0.7	5.8	98	$9
08	Proj	11	13	0	203	180	3.81	1.29	239			25.1	29%	73%	4.31	38	16	46	3.6	8.0	2.2	8%	0.9	2.3	73	$18

Record aside, not a bad year for a 22-year-old. Was again better in 2H, excellent from August on (100+ BPV, 4.8 Cmd in Aug/Sept). He's inconsistent, so this is a low-chance "up", but: UP: 15 Wins, 3.25 ERA

ROD TRUESDELL

Calero,Kiko

		Yr	Tm	W	L	Sv	IP	K	ERA	WHIP	OBA	vL	vR	BF/G	H%	S%	xERA	G	L	F	Ctl	Dom	Cmd	hr/f	hr/9	RAR	BPV	R$
RH	Reliever	03	STL	1	1	1	38	51	2.84	1.29	213	222	205	6.2	30%	84%	3.61	24	29	48	4.7	12.1	2.6	12%	1.2	6.7	103	$5
Age	33	04	STL *	3	1	3	70	73	2.82	1.06	205	175	177	5.3	25%	80%	3.32	44	16	40	3.0	9.4	3.2	13%	1.2	12.4	102	$10
Peak		05	OAK	4	1	1	55	52	3.26	1.14	224	319	162	3.9	27%	75%	3.93	34	19	47	2.9	8.5	2.9	9%	1.0	7.6	92	$8
Type	Pwr FB	06	OAK	3	2	2	58	67	3.41	1.28	234	278	208	3.5	32%	74%	3.70	35	21	44	3.7	10.4	2.8	6%	0.6	8.2	111	$8
Reliability	11	07	OAK	1	5	1	41	31	5.75	1.65	286	245	315	4.0	34%	64%	5.38	34	20	47	4.6	6.9	1.5	5%	0.7	-6.2	50	$0
ERA Potl	0%	1st Half		1	4	0	25	21	6.48	1.40	269			3.5	32%	53%	4.79	26	21	53	3.2	7.6	2.3	8%	1.1	-6.1	63	$1
LIMA Plan	A	2nd Half		0	1	1	16	10	4.59	2.04	311			5.2	37%	75%	6.35	45	18	37	6.9	5.7	0.8	0%	0.0	-0.2	45	($0)
+/- Score	4	08	Proj	2	3	0	44	41	3.93	1.40	255			4.1	32%	72%	4.36	36	20	44	3.9	8.5	2.2	6%	0.6	0.7	82	$4

Said his shoulder began hurting in May, and skills back that up: April: 0.8 Ctl, 9.0 Cmd, 184 BPV Rest: 6.0 Ctl, 1.1 Cmd, 25 BPV So we'll chalk this season up to injury, but at 33, don't expect a return to full value.

Cali,Carmen

		Yr	Tm	W	L	Sv	IP	K	ERA	WHIP	OBA	vL	vR	BF/G	H%	S%	xERA	G	L	F	Ctl	Dom	Cmd	hr/f	hr/9	RAR	BPV	R$
LH	Reliever	03		0	0	0	0	0	0.00	0.00																		
Age	29	04	a/a	2	3	17	66	56	3.30	1.39	269			5.2	32%	80%	4.38				3.2	7.6	2.4		1.0	8.5	68	$10
Peak		05	aaa	4	5	2	58	39	6.08	1.88	335			5.7	38%	67%	6.46				4.2	6.0	1.4		0.8	-12.7	30	($1)
Type	Pwr GB	06	a/a	1	6	1	66	41	5.63	2.16	357			6.7	40%	74%	7.48				5.3	5.6	1.0		0.8	-9.1	16	($5)
Reliability	3	07	MIN *	5	2	1	68	35	4.15	1.65	291	255	278	5.7	33%	74%	4.98	54	17	29	4.4	4.7	1.1	4%	0.4	3.0	35	$3
ERA Potl	45%	1st Half		3	0	1	34	13	3.95	1.37	272			5.6	30%	70%	4.73	56	13	31	2.9	3.4	1.2	3%	0.3	2.4	38	$3
LIMA Plan	C+	2nd Half		2	2	0	34	22	4.35	1.92	310			5.7	36%	77%	5.28	53	19	28	5.9	5.9	1.0	6%	0.5	0.7	33	$0
+/- Score	-32	08	Proj	2	2	0	29	18	4.66	1.83	317			6.0	36%	75%	4.96	53	18	29	4.7	5.6	1.2	7%	0.6	-1.7	32	$0

0-1, 4.71 ERA in 21 IP at MIN. Another journeyman gets his introduction to the career benefits of pitching from the left side. Somewhere Terry Mulholland is smiling.

Cameron,Kevin

		Yr	Tm	W	L	Sv	IP	K	ERA	WHIP	OBA	vL	vR	BF/G	H%	S%	xERA	G	L	F	Ctl	Dom	Cmd	hr/f	hr/9	RAR	BPV	R$
RH	Reliever	03		0	0	0	0	0	0.00	0.00																		
Age	28	04	aa	1	3	3	46	40	3.29	1.78	312			8.3	39%	81%	5.28				4.5	7.8	1.7		0.2	6.0	69	$2
Pre-Peak		05	aa	6	2	6	79	47	3.67	1.62	302			8.3	33%	80%	5.45				3.5	5.3	1.5		1.0	6.2	28	$6
Type	Pwr	06	aaa	6	4	9	66	53	4.49	1.51	270			7.3	33%	69%	4.13				4.2	7.3	1.7		0.4	0.2	68	$8
Reliability	10	07	SD	2	0	0	58	50	2.79	1.57	252	255	243	5.4	33%	80%	4.60	49	19	32	5.6	7.8	1.4	0%	0.0	11.7	80	$4
ERA Potl	40%	1st Half		0	0	0	25	20	0.36	1.24	175			6.1	23%	97%	4.13	57	15	28	5.8	7.2	1.3	0%	0.0	12.5	89	$3
LIMA Plan	B	2nd Half		2	0	0	33	30	4.64	1.82	301			5.0	39%	72%	4.90	43	22	35	5.5	8.2	1.5	0%	0.0	-0.9	75	$1
+/- Score	-28	08	Proj	2	2	0	58	47	4.03	1.59	272			6.4	33%	74%	4.55	48	19	33	4.8	7.3	1.5	5%	0.5	-1.1	62	$2

Major ERA downside. Zero HR is unrealistic, even for a GB pitcher, even in Petco. That high GB/low HR combo has also led to high strand rates. If luck turns against him (as in '06), he could double his '07 ERA.

Capps,Matt

		Yr	Tm	W	L	Sv	IP	K	ERA	WHIP	OBA	vL	vR	BF/G	H%	S%	xERA	G	L	F	Ctl	Dom	Cmd	hr/f	hr/9	RAR	BPV	R$
RH	Reliever	03		0	0	0	0	0	0.00	0.00																		
Age	24	04		0	0	0	0	0	0.00	0.00																		
Growth		05	aa	0	2	7	24	23	3.75	1.29	293			4.8	37%	72%	4.21				1.1	8.6	7.7		0.8	1.6	187	$4
Type	FB	06	PIT	9	1	1	80	56	3.82	1.16	264	250	275	3.8	29%	73%	3.90	41	20	40	1.3	6.3	4.7	12%	1.3	6.6	98	$11
Reliability	33	07	PIT	4	7	18	79	64	2.28	1.01	223	281	181	4.1	27%	80%	4.04	31	19	50	1.8	7.3	4.0	4%	0.6	20.9	121	$18
ERA Potl	50%	1st Half		3	4	7	44	32	2.66	1.07	230			4.2	28%	76%	4.51	29	16	55	2.0	6.5	3.2	3%	0.4	9.6	103	$9
LIMA Plan	B	2nd Half		1	3	11	35	32	1.80	0.94	215			4.0	26%	87%	3.45	34	22	44	1.5	8.2	5.3	7%	0.8	11.3	150	$9
+/- Score	-19	08	Proj	5	4	33	73	60	2.98	1.09	244			4.0	29%	76%	3.84	36	19	45	1.6	7.4	4.6	7%	0.9	5.0	122	$21

PRO: Stellar Ctl and Cmd history, closer-worthy BPVs, 2nd half skills breakout CON: Large xERA variance, high FB%, PIT ranked 27th in MLB save opps in 2007 Heed the cons, don't overbid.

Capuano,Chris

		Yr	Tm	W	L	Sv	IP	K	ERA	WHIP	OBA	vL	vR	BF/G	H%	S%	xERA	G	L	F	Ctl	Dom	Cmd	hr/f	hr/9	RAR	BPV	R$
LH	Starter	03	aaa	9	5	0	142	94	4.05	1.36	275			26.4	32%	70%	4.05				2.6	5.9	2.3		0.6	6.0	65	$11
Age	29	04	MIL	6	8	0	88	80	5.01	1.45	268	207	282	22.7	30%	72%	4.30	38	19	43	3.8	8.2	2.2	16%	1.8	-8.1	41	$5
Peak		05	MIL	18	12	0	219	176	3.99	1.38	256	201	270	26.9	29%	76%	4.47	38	21	41	3.7	7.2	1.9	12%	1.3	7.0	50	$18
Type	Pwr	06	MIL	11	12	0	221	174	4.03	1.25	269	273	264	27.1	31%	72%	3.94	40	20	40	1.9	7.1	3.7	11%	1.2	12.5	86	$19
Reliability	77	07	MIL	5	12	0	150	132	5.10	1.49	287	259	293	22.8	34%	68%	4.16	43	18	39	3.2	7.9	2.4	11%	1.2	-12.5	61	$5
ERA Potl	60%	1st Half		5	5	0	70	60	4.37	1.41	265			23.3	32%	71%	4.16	44	19	37	3.6	7.7	2.1	9%	0.9	0.5	66	$5
LIMA Plan	B	2nd Half		0	7	0	80	72	5.74	1.56	305			22.4	36%	66%	4.17	42	18	40	2.9	8.1	2.8	13%	1.5	-12.9	57	($1)
+/- Score	37	08	Proj	11	8	0	166	139	4.28	1.36	266			24.5	31%	72%	4.13	41	19	40	3.0	7.5	2.5	11%	1.2	5.6	64	$13

H% and S% tanked in the 2nd half. Went 0-10 after May 13 and lost rotation spot. All that means is you can now buy a reliable pitcher with decent skills at a discount price.

Carlyle,Buddy

		Yr	Tm	W	L	Sv	IP	K	ERA	WHIP	OBA	vL	vR	BF/G	H%	S%	xERA	G	L	F	Ctl	Dom	Cmd	hr/f	hr/9	RAR	BPV	R$
RH	Starter	03	a/a	3	3	3	32	35	3.54	1.18	246			7.7	32%	73%	3.40				2.4	9.9	4.2		0.9	3.4	126	$6
Age	30	04	a/a	12	6	0	144	105	4.10	1.37	295			22.9	34%	73%	4.79				1.7	6.6	3.8		1.0	4.4	84	$12
Peak		05	LA *	1	2	2	62	55	5.10	1.41	272			8.9	32%	67%	4.72	26	19	55	3.2	8.0	2.5	9%	1.3	-6.5	60	$2
Type	xFB	06	aaa	3	1	0	28	18	2.14	0.91	193			8.3	21%	81%	1.92				2.1	5.8	2.7		0.7	8.2	86	$6
Reliability	3	07	ATL *	13	9	0	155	118	4.74	1.36	278	343	229	21.4	31%	70%	4.45	32	23	44	2.5	6.8	2.7	12%	1.5	-6.1	53	$12
ERA Potl	50%	1st Half		7	4	0	83	73	4.11	1.25	259			21.7	30%	72%	4.07	33	21	46	2.4	7.9	3.3	11%	1.3	3.2	81	$9
LIMA Plan	C	2nd Half		6	5	0	72	45	5.47	1.49	299			21.2	32%	68%	4.94	32	24	44	2.6	5.6	2.1	13%	1.7	-9.3	22	$3
+/- Score	11	08	Proj	7	5	0	102	71	4.70	1.38	279			20.8	31%	70%	4.70	31	23	46	2.6	6.3	2.4	10%	1.3	-3.8	48	$6

8-7, 5.21 ERA in 107 IP at ATL. Long history of good Cmd skill, but it's offset by FB tendencies. Upside is league average, so value comes down to role. If starting, he's worth a look; if not, pen volatility is too dangerous.

Carmona,Fausto

		Yr	Tm	W	L	Sv	IP	K	ERA	WHIP	OBA	vL	vR	BF/G	H%	S%	xERA	G	L	F	Ctl	Dom	Cmd	hr/f	hr/9	RAR	BPV	R$
RH	Starter	03	aa	0	0	0	6	3	5.45	1.52	350			26.6	38%	67%	6.33				0.0	5.0			1.4	-0.8	-26	($0)
Age	24	04	a/a	5	9	0	93	62	5.01	1.52	312			25.8	37%	64%	4.68				2.1	6.0	2.8		0.3	-7.7	80	$3
Growth		05	a/a	13	9	0	173	97	3.86	1.25	272			26.7	30%	70%	3.84				1.7	5.0	2.9		0.7	9.5	69	$15
Type	xGB	06	CLE *	2	13	0	102	85	5.75	1.55	294	299	298	10.4	35%	63%	3.69	60	13	27	3.4	7.5	2.2	12%	1.0	-15.0	58	$2
Reliability	36	07	CLE	19	8	0	215	137	3.06	1.21	247	275	216	27.7	28%	77%	3.34	64	14	22	2.6	5.7	2.2	11%	0.7	38.4	67	$27
ERA Potl	50%	1st Half		8	4	0	96	48	3.94	1.33	278			27.2	30%	73%	3.73	63	14	23	2.3	4.5	2.0	13%	0.9	6.7	40	$9
LIMA Plan	D+	2nd Half		11	4	0	119	89	2.34	1.11	221			28.2	27%	80%	3.03	65	14	21	2.8	6.7	2.4	9%	0.5	31.7	88	$20
+/- Score	10	08	Proj	15	12	0	203	141	3.90	1.33	268			27.8	31%	72%	3.44	63	14	23	2.6	6.3	2.4	11%	0.7	26.5	68	$19

6.7 Dom after 6/1 pushed him over the top. Sustaining it for 4 months suggests he can do it again. But H%, S% regression may cause slight drop in value, and doubled IP means there's burnout risk. Bid judiciously.

Carpenter,Chris

		Yr	Tm	W	L	Sv	IP	K	ERA	WHIP	OBA	vL	vR	BF/G	H%	S%	xERA	G	L	F	Ctl	Dom	Cmd	hr/f	hr/9	RAR	BPV	R$
RH	Starter	03	a/a	0	1	0	11	4	12.05	2.77	452			15.9	48%	53%	11.12				4.0	3.2	0.8		0.8	-10.6	-23	($4)
Age	33	04	STL	15	5	0	182	152	3.46	1.14	248	268	226	26.4	29%	73%	3.21	52	18	29	1.9	7.5	4.0	15%	1.2	18.0	99	$22
Peak		05	STL	21	5	0	241	213	2.84	1.06	231	264	199	29.1	28%	76%	2.94	55	19	26	1.9	7.9	4.2	10%	0.7	41.9	124	$35
Type	GB	06	STL	15	8	0	221	184	3.09	1.07	237	266	210	27.6	28%	75%	3.10	53	18	28	1.7	7.5	4.3	12%	0.9	38.1	117	$30
Reliability	19	07	STL	0	1	0	6	3	7.50	1.67	347	375	300	27.5	39%	50%	2.93	65	26	9	1.5	4.5	3.0	0%	0.0	-2.3	76	($0)
ERA Potl	80%	1st Half		0	1	0	6	3	7.50	1.67	347			27.5	39%	50%	2.93	65	26	9	1.5	4.5	3.0	0%	0.0	-2.3	76	($0)
LIMA Plan	C	2nd Half		0	0	0	0	0	0.00	0.00																		
+/- Score	148	08	Proj	5	2	0	58	44	3.57	1.28	258			24.3	30%	75%	3.51	55	19	26	2.6	6.8	2.6	13%	0.9	6.4	71	$6

Tommy John surgery will keep him out until at least mid-2008. Even if he does pitch, may not be 100%, so any bid for his services must be a restrained one. Hope for bigger and better things in 2009.

Casilla,Santiago

		Yr	Tm	W	L	Sv	IP	K	ERA	WHIP	OBA	vL	vR	BF/G	H%	S%	xERA	G	L	F	Ctl	Dom	Cmd	hr/f	hr/9	RAR	BPV	R$
RH	Reliever	03		0	0	0	0	0	0.00	0.00																		
Age	27	04		0	0	0	0	0	0.00	0.00																		
Pre-Peak		05		0	0	0	0	0	0.00	0.00																		
Type	Pwr xFB	06	OAK *	2	0	4	35	29	4.10	1.14	227	400		5.3	28%	63%	3.33	40	40	20	2.8	7.4	2.6	10%	0.5	2.0	94	$5
Reliability	1	07	OAK *	5	2	5	75	73	4.75	1.38	235	212	230	4.7	29%	66%	4.62	33	16	51	4.7	8.8	1.9	7%	0.9	-2.3	74	$8
ERA Potl	60%	1st Half		4	2	5	40	43	2.93	1.13	193			4.6	27%	73%	4.28	19	22	58	4.1	9.7	2.4	2%	0.2	7.8	118	$9
LIMA Plan	B	2nd Half		1	0	0	35	30	6.86	1.68	278			4.8	32%	61%	5.25	38	13	49	5.4	7.7	1.4	12%	1.6	-10.1	28	($1)
+/- Score	13	08	Proj	3	2	0	73	65	4.72	1.32	238			5.0	29%	65%	4.55	35	15	50	4.0	8.1	2.0	7%	0.9	-0.5	72	$5

3-1, 4.44 ERA in 51 IP at OAK. 2nd half skill slide represents time spent in majors, so obviously there's some work to be done. Closer upside if he can work through Cmd, FB% issues; Keep him on your radar.

BRANDON KRUSE

Cassel,Jack

Cassel,Jack				W	L	Sv	IP	K	ERA	WHIP	OBA	vL	vR	BF/G	H%	S%	xERA	G	L	F	Ctl	Dom	Cmd	hr/f	hr/9	RAR	BPV	R$
RH	Starter	03		0	0	0	0	0	0.00	0.00																		
Age	27	04	aa	4	2	1	74	42	4.72	1.59	302			5.9	34%	69%	4.95				3.3	5.1	**1.5**		0.5	-3.5	42	$2
Pre-Peak		05	a/a	6	5	1	82	44	4.27	1.73	321			8.1	36%	74%	5.32				3.6	4.8	**1.3**		0.2	0.3	41	$2
Type	Con	06	a/a	9	8	0	155	95	5.29	1.59	309			23.3	35%	67%	5.31				3.0	5.5	**1.8**		0.8	-14.7	40	$4
Reliability	23	07	SD *	8	15	0	179	96	5.41	2.04	378	375	300	26.9	41%	74%	5.39	41	26	33	2.9	4.8	**1.6**	8%	0.9	-21.8	16	($8)
ERA Potl	45%	1st Half		6	7	0	90	58	4.19	1.69	333			24.4	38%	75%					2.5	5.8	**2.3**		0.6	2.6	54	$3
LIMA Plan	F	2nd Half		2	8	0	89	38	6.66	2.40	419			29.5	44%	73%	6.18	41	26	33	3.3	3.8	**1.1**	9%	1.2	-24.4	-18	($12)
+/- Score	6	08	Proj	**6**	**8**	**0**	**116**	**63**	**5.28**	**1.87**	**351**			**22.2**	**39%**	**72%**	**5.23**	**41**	**26**	**33**	**3.1**	**4.9**	**1.6**	**7%**	**0.8**	**-11.8**	**24**	**($3)**

1-1, 3.97 ERA in 23 IP at SD. Cmd, Dom, xERA and BPV all show why he didn't make his MLB debut until age 27. ERA with SD was nice, but don't confuse it with something that's within 2 runs of his skill level.

Chacin,Gustavo

Chacin,Gustavo				W	L	Sv	IP	K	ERA	WHIP	OBA	vL	vR	BF/G	H%	S%	xERA	G	L	F	Ctl	Dom	Cmd	hr/f	hr/9	RAR	BPV	R$
LH	Starter	03	aa	3	4	2	69	48	5.34	1.71	314			7.0	37%	66%	5.04				3.8	6.3	**1.7**		0.1	-8.1	61	$1
Age	27	04	a/a	18	3	0	153	107	3.88	1.38	267			24.4	30%	76%	4.53				3.2	6.3	**1.9**		1.2	8.7	45	$15
Growth		05	TOR	13	9	0	203	121	3.72	1.39	271	225	288	25.8	30%	76%	4.71	41	22	37	3.1	5.4	**1.7**	8%	0.9	16.2	43	$15
Type	Con FB	06	TOR	9	4	0	87	47	5.06	1.47	268	268	266	22.5	26%	72%	5.35	35	21	44	3.9	4.9	**1.2**	15%	2.0	-5.4	-2	$6
Reliability	0	07	TOR	2	1	0	27	11	5.60	1.32	274	269	265	23.1	26%	63%	4.96	40	19	41	2.3	3.6	**1.6**	15%	2.0	-3.7	-4	$1
ERA Potl	45%	1st Half		2	1	0	27	11	5.67	1.33	276			23.0	26%	63%	4.98	40	19	41	2.3	3.7	**1.6**	16%	2.0	-3.9	-5	$1
LIMA Plan	C	2nd Half		0	0	0	0	0	0.00	0.00																		
+/- Score	2	08	Proj	**6**	**3**	**0**	**73**	**40**	**4.72**	**1.42**	**276**			**18.5**	**29%**	**71%**	**4.94**	**39**	**21**	**40**	**3.1**	**5.0**	**1.6**	**11%**	**1.4**	**-4.0**	**22**	**$5**

Injuries have decimated his skills, which were already shaky to begin with. Even if September shoulder surgery gets him healthy again, the upside (an ERA barely under 5.00) is not worth the risk.

Chacon,Shawn

Chacon,Shawn				W	L	Sv	IP	K	ERA	WHIP	OBA	vL	vR	BF/G	H%	S%	xERA	G	L	F	Ctl	Dom	Cmd	hr/f	hr/9	RAR	BPV	R$
RH	Reliever	03	COL	11	8	0	137	93	4.60	1.33	243	254	230	25.3	28%	66%	4.79	40	17	43	3.8	6.1	**1.6**	7%	0.8	-5.4	53	$10
Age	30	04	COL	1	9	35	63	52	7.13	1.95	285	236	326	4.7	32%	66%	6.30	33	19	48	7.4	7.4	**1.0**	13%	1.7	-22.3	12	$6
Peak		05	2TM	8	10	0	151	79	3.45	1.33	240	232	252	23.8	26%	76%	5.10	40	21	39	3.9	4.7	**1.2**	7%	0.8	15.9	35	$11
Type	Pwr FB	06	2TM	7	6	0	109	62	6.36	1.72	287	305	274	19.4	29%	67%	6.15	33	18	50	5.2	5.1	**1.0**	13%	1.9	-24.7	-8	($1)
Reliability	19	07	PIT	5	4	1	96	79	3.94	1.49	260	317	236	6.6	31%	75%	4.58	44	17	39	4.5	7.4	**1.6**	8%	0.8	5.8	57	$6
ERA Potl	40%	1st Half		4	1	1	60	48	3.90	1.48	265			10.2	32%	75%	4.38	48	17	35	4.2	7.2	**1.7**	8%	0.8	3.9	59	$5
LIMA Plan	C	2nd Half		1	3	0	36	31	4.00	1.50	251			4.2	30%	76%	4.91	37	18	46	5.0	7.7	**1.6**	8%	1.0	1.9	54	$2
+/- Score	-22	08	Proj	**4**	**5**	**0**	**87**	**62**	**4.97**	**1.54**	**264**			**8.1**	**30%**	**70%**	**5.20**	**38**	**18**	**44**	**4.8**	**6.4**	**1.3**	**9%**	**1.1**	**-8.6**	**35**	**$2**

Skill-wise, this was actually his best season, if a 4.58 xERA and 57 BPV can actually be referred to as "best" with a straight face. Just like '04, high S% kept ERA under 4.00; and just like '05, he'll likely burn you if you buy in.

Chamberlain,Joba

Chamberlain,Joba				W	L	Sv	IP	K	ERA	WHIP	OBA	vL	vR	BF/G	H%	S%	xERA	G	L	F	Ctl	Dom	Cmd	hr/f	hr/9	RAR	BPV	R$
RH	Reliever	03		0	0	0	0	0	0.00	0.00																		
Age	22	04		0	0	0	0	0	0.00	0.00																		
Growth		05		0	0	0	0	0	0.00	0.00																		
Type	Pwr FB	06		0	0	0	0	0	0.00	0.00																		
Reliability	0	07	NYY *	7	2	1	72	104	2.62	1.11	219	132	156	9.7	34%	80%	2.68	37	22	41	2.9	13.0	**4.5**	9%	0.7	16.8	162	$15
ERA Potl	55%	1st Half		2	1	0	21	30	5.09	1.46	251			23.2	39%	63%					4.7	12.7	**2.7**		0.4	-1.5	126	$2
LIMA Plan	B	2nd Half		5	1	1	51	74	1.59	0.96	205			7.6	32%	91%	2.41	37	22	41	2.1	13.1	**6.2**	11%	0.9	18.3	195	$13
+/- Score	39	08	Proj	**12**	**8**	**0**	**158**	**172**	**4.16**	**1.37**	**251**			**27.1**	**33%**	**70%**	**3.85**	**37**	**22**	**41**	**3.8**	**9.8**	**2.6**	**7%**	**0.7**	**12.6**	**97**	**$17**

2-0, 0.38 ERA in 24 IP at NYY. As great as he was (and he was great), 3 things to keep in mind:
- Only 48 AA/AAA innings
- Only 24 MLB innings
- Not one pitch as MLB starter

Bid speculatively, not recklessly.

Chico,Matt

Chico,Matt				W	L	Sv	IP	K	ERA	WHIP	OBA	vL	vR	BF/G	H%	S%	xERA	G	L	F	Ctl	Dom	Cmd	hr/f	hr/9	RAR	BPV	R$
LH	Starter	03		0	0	0	0	0	0.00	0.00																		
Age	24	04	aa	3	7	0	62	55	6.68	2.03	342			21.9	41%	68%	7.31				5.1	8.0	**1.6**		1.2	-17.9	33	($4)
Growth		05	aa	1	7	0	53	32	7.30	1.91	365			25.6	39%	64%	7.89				2.5	5.4	**2.1**		1.7	-19.6	8	($5)
Type	xFB	06	aa	9	2	0	103	62	3.24	1.36	271			25.9	30%	80%	4.31				2.8	5.4	**1.9**		1.0	16.2	44	$11
Reliability	0	07	WAS *	8	10	0	178	100	4.60	1.53	278	273	283	24.0	29%	74%	5.56	33	20	47	4.0	5.1	**1.3**	10%	1.4	-3.8	15	$5
ERA Potl	40%	1st Half		3	5	0	83	45	5.10	1.57	284			23.3	30%	71%	5.66	33	21	46	4.0	4.9	**1.2**	10%	1.4	-6.9	11	$1
LIMA Plan	C	2nd Half		5	5	0	95	55	4.17	1.49	272			24.7	29%	77%	5.47	34	19	47	4.0	5.2	**1.3**	10%	1.3	3.0	20	$4
+/- Score	-22	08	Proj	**8**	**9**	**0**	**145**	**89**	**4.84**	**1.59**	**297**			**24.2**	**32%**	**73%**	**5.42**	**33**	**20**	**47**	**3.6**	**5.5**	**1.5**	**9%**	**1.3**	**-18.2**	**22**	**$4**

7-9, 4.64 ERA in 167 IP at WAS. Two years of Ctl growth failed him at the major-league level, leaving his low-Dom, high-FB approach exposed. S% hid the damage, but if he can't corral the walks, things could get uglier.

Chulk,Vinnie

Chulk,Vinnie				W	L	Sv	IP	K	ERA	WHIP	OBA	vL	vR	BF/G	H%	S%	xERA	G	L	F	Ctl	Dom	Cmd	hr/f	hr/9	RAR	BPV	R$
RH	Reliever	03	aaa	8	10	0	119	79	5.52	1.57	294			23.3	32%	67%	5.48				3.6	6.0	**1.7**		1.3	-16.5	29	$3
Age	29	04	TOR *	4	5	4	84	65	4.29	1.56	278	308	228	5.8	31%	76%	4.77	40	20	39	4.3	7.0	**1.6**	12%	1.3	1.5	37	$5
Pre-Peak		05	TOR	0	1	0	72	39	3.88	1.31	251	283	231	4.9	26%	74%	4.79	42	19	39	3.3	4.9	**1.5**	10%	1.1	4.4	32	$3
Type	Pwr FB	06	2TM *	4	5	1	78	78	4.45	1.37	244	206	282	5.0	30%	71%	3.92	43	18	39	4.1	9.0	**2.2**	14%	1.3	0.7	67	$7
Reliability	6	07	SF	5	4	0	53	41	3.57	1.26	262	290	250	3.9	32%	72%	4.49	31	21	48	2.4	7.0	**2.9**	4%	0.5	5.6	91	$6
ERA Potl	60%	1st Half		3	2	0	34	21	2.65	1.09	238			4.0	27%	77%	4.52	32	20	48	1.9	5.6	**3.0**	4%	0.5	7.5	88	$5
LIMA Plan	B+	2nd Half		2	2	0	19	20	5.21	1.58	300			3.7	40%	66%	4.41	28	23	48	3.3	9.5	**2.9**	4%	0.5	-1.8	98	$1
+/- Score	-9	08	Proj	**1**	**1**	**0**	**15**	**13**	**4.20**	**1.33**	**262**			**4.6**	**32%**	**68%**	**4.30**	**35**	**21**	**44**	**3.0**	**7.8**	**2.6**	**5%**	**0.6**	**0.2**	**86**	**$1**

Has made terrific gains in Cmd and BPV. But xERA shows how the leap in FB% undermined everything. With 10% hr/f, he'd have a 1.3 hr/9. LIMA skills if he works it out, but blood clot in hand may delay that opportunity.

Clemens,Roger

Clemens,Roger				W	L	Sv	IP	K	ERA	WHIP	OBA	vL	vR	BF/G	H%	S%	xERA	G	L	F	Ctl	Dom	Cmd	hr/f	hr/9	RAR	BPV	R$
RH	Starter	03	NYY	17	9	0	211	190	3.92	1.22	251	215	288	26.5	30%	71%	3.64	42	22	36	2.5	8.1	**3.3**	11%	1.0	15.6	92	$25
Age	45	04	HOU	18	4	0	214	218	2.98	1.16	219	218	217	26.5	29%	76%	3.32	49	18	33	3.3	9.2	**2.8**	8%	0.6	33.2	105	$29
Decline		05	HOU	13	8	0	211	185	1.88	1.01	202	195	202	25.9	25%	84%	3.25	50	20	30	2.6	7.9	**3.0**	7%	0.5	61.7	110	$33
Type		06	HOU	7	6	0	113	102	2.31	1.04	218	254	185	23.6	27%	80%	3.32	49	16	35	2.3	8.1	**3.5**	7%	0.6	30.4	117	$18
Reliability	37	07	NYY	6	6	0	99	68	4.18	1.31	262	233	282	23.3	30%	69%	4.15	46	20	34	2.8	6.2	**2.2**	9%	0.8	4.0	61	$8
ERA Potl	60%	1st Half		1	3	0	24	22	5.25	1.46	285			21.0	33%	68%	3.67	49	18	32	3.0	8.3	**2.8**	17%	1.5	-2.2	60	$1
LIMA Plan	B	2nd Half		5	3	0	75	46	3.84	1.27	254			24.2	29%	70%	4.30	45	21	34	2.8	5.5	**2.0**	6%	0.6	6.2	61	$7
+/- Score	-26	08	Proj	**6**	**6**	**0**	**96**	**74**	**4.03**	**1.26**	**254**			**23.6**	**30%**	**69%**	**3.86**	**48**	**19**	**33**	**2.7**	**6.9**	**2.6**	**8%**	**0.8**	**7.6**	**77**	**$10**

Lowest Dom of his career, and lowest Cmd since 1999. We can give some benefit of the doubt because of injuries, but it's not like they're going to go away at his age. If he returns, expect more '07 than '06.

Clement,Matt

Clement,Matt				W	L	Sv	IP	K	ERA	WHIP	OBA	vL	vR	BF/G	H%	S%	xERA	G	L	F	Ctl	Dom	Cmd	hr/f	hr/9	RAR	BPV	R$
RH	Reliever	03	CHC	14	12	0	201	171	4.12	1.23	230	246	209	26.1	27%	69%	3.52	53	19	28	3.5	7.7	**2.2**	14%	1.0	3.9	71	$19
Age	33	04	CHC	9	13	0	181	190	3.68	1.28	233	234	224	25.4	29%	76%	3.39	50	17	33	3.8	9.4	**2.5**	15%	1.1	13.0	83	$17
Past Peak		05	BOS	13	6	0	191	146	4.57	1.36	263	275	244	25.6	31%	67%	4.11	45	21	34	3.2	6.9	**2.1**	9%	0.8	-4.7	63	$14
Type	Pwr	06	BOS	5	5	0	65	43	6.64	1.77	295	307	272	25.4	33%	63%	5.25	49	16	35	5.3	5.9	**1.1**	10%	1.1	-16.7	22	($1)
Reliability	0	07	BOS	0	0	0	0	0	0.00	0.00																		
ERA Potl		1st Half		0	0	0	0	0	0.00	0.00																		
LIMA Plan		2nd Half		0	0	0	0	0	0.00	0.00																		
+/- Score		08	Proj	**5**	**5**	**0**	**73**	**61**	**4.84**	**1.43**	**258**			**26.3**	**31%**	**68%**	**4.10**	**49**	**18**	**33**	**4.1**	**7.6**	**1.8**	**11%**	**1.0**	**3.5**	**58**	**$5**

Rotator cuff and labrum surgery took away all of 2007, and his injuries probably ruined '05-'06. Pre-injury skills were good enough to merit a speculative flyer this spring; anything more might be overly optimistic.

Coffey,Todd

Coffey,Todd				W	L	Sv	IP	K	ERA	WHIP	OBA	vL	vR	BF/G	H%	S%	xERA	G	L	F	Ctl	Dom	Cmd	hr/f	hr/9	RAR	BPV	R$
RH	Reliever	03		0	0	0	0	0	0.00	0.00											0.0	0.0						
Age	27	04	a/a	5	2	24	59	52	3.77	1.10	261			4.3	32%	67%	3.36				0.9	8.0	**8.5**		0.8	4.1	205	$15
Pre-Peak		05	CIN	4	1	1	58	26	4.50	1.64	339	337	348	4.6	36%	73%	4.44	51	23	26	1.7	4.0	**2.4**	9%	0.8	-1.8	38	$1
Type	GB	06	CIN	6	7	8	78	60	3.58	1.44	279	347	242	4.2	33%	77%	3.82	52	21	27	3.1	6.9	**2.2**	10%	0.8	8.8	63	$10
Reliability	22	07	CIN *	4	1	1	78	63	4.41	1.48	293	343	313	4.5	33%	75%	3.56	58	16	27	2.8	7.3	**2.6**	18%	1.4	0.1	53	$4
ERA Potl	50%	1st Half		1	1	0	39	36	3.69	1.46	290			4.1	34%	82%	3.42	58	11	31	2.8	8.3	**3.0**	19%	1.6	3.5	61	$2
LIMA Plan	B+	2nd Half		3	0	1	39	27	5.14	1.50	295			4.9	33%	68%	3.60	57	23	20	2.8	6.2	**2.2**	19%	1.2	-3.4	45	$2
+/- Score	46	08	Proj	**3**	**1**	**0**	**44**	**32**	**3.72**	**1.38**	**281**			**4.3**	**33%**	**75%**	**3.65**	**54**	**20**	**26**	**2.5**	**6.6**	**2.7**	**11%**	**0.8**	**4.0**	**70**	**$4**

2-1, 5.82 ERA in 51 IP at CIN. hr/f explosion buried continued growth in Dom, Cmd, and xERA. And the resulting bloated ERA got him demoted. Saves potential is still there if he ever gets another shot. Sleeper.

BRANDON KRUSE

Colome,Jesus				W	L	Sv	IP	K	ERA	WHIP	OBA	vL	vR	BF/G	H%	S%	xERA	G	L	F	Ctl	Dom	Cmd	hr/f	hr/9	RAR	BPV	R$
RH	Reliever	03	TAM	3	7	2	74	69	4.50	1.55	248	218	269	6.1	30%	74%	5.07	30	22	48	5.6	8.4	**1.5**	9%	1.1	0.2	54	$5
Age	30	04	TAM *	4	3	5	71	55	3.66	1.32	230	245	163	5.9	28%	72%	4.91	33	20	47	4.3	6.9	**1.6**	4%	0.5	6.8	70	$8
Peak		05	TAM	2	3	0	45	28	4.59	1.60	298	291	276	5.7	32%	75%	4.89	42	21	36	3.6	5.6	**1.6**	13%	1.4	-1.2	20	$1
Type	FB	06	a/a	3	1	0	38	19	5.57	1.95	326			6.6	34%	74%	7.01				5.3	4.4	**0.8**		1.4	-4.9	-8	($1)
Reliability	0	07	WAS	5	1	1	66	43	3.82	1.38	256	311	218	4.7	29%	74%	5.04	36	19	45	3.7	5.9	**1.6**	6%	0.8	4.9	48	$6
ERA Potl	40%	1st Half		4	0	1	46	28	2.74	1.28	227			4.8	26%	80%	5.10	39	16	45	4.1	5.5	**1.3**	5%	0.6	9.6	53	$6
LIMA Plan	D+	2nd Half		1	1	0	20	15	6.30	1.60	316			4.3	36%	62%	4.90	29	26	46	2.7	6.7	**2.5**	10%	1.3	-4.6	44	($0)
+/- Score	-48	08	Proj	**3**	**2**	**0**	**44**	**28**	**4.97**	**1.61**	**294**			**5.2**	**32%**	**72%**	**5.29**	**35**	**22**	**43**	**3.9**	**5.8**	**1.5**	**10%**	**1.2**	**-4.8**	**25**	**$1**

ERA got a big boost from hr/f, which got a big boost from RFK (0.3 hr/9 at home, 1.5 on road). Poor skills leave him dependent on that kind of outside help, though 2nd half BPIs show minor signs of self-sufficiency.

Colon,Bartolo				W	L	Sv	IP	K	ERA	WHIP	OBA	vL	vR	BF/G	H%	S%	xERA	G	L	F	Ctl	Dom	Cmd	hr/f	hr/9	RAR	BPV	R$
RH	Starter	03	CHW	15	13	0	242	173	3.87	1.20	246	250	246	29.3	27%	72%	4.28	39	18	44	2.5	6.4	**2.6**	9%	1.1	19.6	65	$25
Age	34	04	ANA	18	12	0	208	158	5.02	1.37	268	273	256	26.3	29%	69%	4.49	39	17	45	3.1	6.8	**2.2**	13%	1.6	-15.0	40	$15
Past Peak		05	ANA	21	8	0	222	157	3.48	1.16	255	250	258	27.5	29%	74%	3.92	44	17	39	1.7	6.4	**3.7**	10%	1.1	24.3	87	$28
Type		06	LAA	1	5	0	56	31	5.13	1.46	310	354	261	24.6	32%	70%	4.52	41	22	37	1.8	5.0	**2.8**	15%	1.8	-4.0	29	$1
Reliability	10	07	LAA	6	8	0	99	76	6.34	1.62	320	313	325	23.7	36%	62%	4.51	42	18	40	2.6	6.9	**2.6**	11%	1.4	-22.5	47	$1
ERA Potl	65%	1st Half		6	3	0	72	51	5.88	1.53	312			26.7	34%	66%	4.56	40	17	43	2.3	6.4	**2.8**	14%	1.9	-12.2	34	$3
LIMA Plan	B	2nd Half		0	5	0	27	25	7.58	1.87	342			18.7	43%	55%	4.32	47	22	31	3.6	8.2	**2.3**	0%	0.0	-10.4	84	($2)
+/- Score	39	08	Proj	**9**	**10**	**0**	**131**	**96**	**4.62**	**1.39**	**281**			**22.5**	**32%**	**69%**	**4.21**	**43**	**20**	**37**	**2.6**	**6.6**	**2.6**	**10%**	**1.1**	**4.5**	**60**	**$10**

PRO: Resurgent Dom, xERA not as awful as ERA
CON: xERA still only average, continued refusal to undergo surgery means health risk will once again be an issue.
From Cy Young to flyer in 3 yrs.

Condrey,Clay				W	L	Sv	IP	K	ERA	WHIP	OBA	vL	vR	BF/G	H%	S%	xERA	G	L	F	Ctl	Dom	Cmd	hr/f	hr/9	RAR	BPV	R$
RH	Reliever	03	SD *	4	5	0	97	61	5.90	1.52	295			21.5	32%	62%	5.29				3.0	5.7	**1.9**		1.2	-19.4	32	$0
Age	32	04	aaa	9	9	0	155	58	6.31	1.78	352			27.0	36%	66%	7.02				2.2	3.3	**1.5**		1.3	-37.5	-3	($5)
Peak		05	aaa	7	8	0	132	57	5.32	1.71	344			24.5	36%	71%	6.51				2.1	3.9	**1.9**		1.1	-16.5	15	($1)
Type	Con	06	PHI *	6	4	6	79	37	3.28	1.52	296			5.9	32%	79%	4.54	48	29	23	3.0	4.2	**1.4**	8%	0.6	11.8	32	$8
Reliability	5	07	PHI *	6	0	3	72	36	4.55	1.48	296	299	302	6.5	33%	68%	4.58	46	25	28	2.7	4.4	**1.7**	6%	0.5	-1.1	43	$5
ERA Potl	50%	1st Half		3	0	0	29	17	6.47	1.68	316			7.1	36%	60%	4.69	46	27	27	3.4	5.2	**1.5**	7%	0.6	-7.4	37	$0
LIMA Plan	C+	2nd Half		3	0	3	43	19	3.24	1.34	281			6.1	31%	76%	4.49	47	24	29	2.2	3.9	**1.8**	5%	0.4	6.2	48	$5
+/- Score	-16	08	Proj	**2**	**2**	**0**	**44**	**21**	**4.55**	**1.54**	**306**			**6.5**	**33%**	**70%**	**4.62**	**48**	**24**	**28**	**2.7**	**4.3**	**1.6**	**7%**	**0.6**	**-1.2**	**35**	**$1**

5-0, 5.04 ERA in 50 IP at PHI. Poor Cmd, lousy Dom and he still manages back-to-back league average xERAs thanks to super-low FB%. But league average only has value for SPs, and he isn't one anymore.

Contreras,Jose				W	L	Sv	IP	K	ERA	WHIP	OBA	vL	vR	BF/G	H%	S%	xERA	G	L	F	Ctl	Dom	Cmd	hr/f	hr/9	RAR	BPV	R$
RH	Starter	03	NYY *	9	2	0	87	88	2.90	1.14	209	203	202	16.0	28%	76%	3.34	47	21	32	3.5	9.1	**2.6**	7%	0.5	17.5	107	$15
Age	36	04	2AL	13	9	0	170	150	5.50	1.47	257	251	254	24.1	29%	67%	4.37	44	16	40	4.4	7.9	**1.8**	16%	1.6	-22.5	39	$9
Decline		05	CHW	15	7	0	204	154	3.61	1.23	235	231	233	26.5	27%	74%	4.08	44	20	36	3.3	6.8	**2.1**	11%	1.0	19.1	61	$22
Type		06	CHW	13	9	0	196	134	4.27	1.27	260	267	248	27.4	29%	68%	4.24	45	16	39	2.5	6.2	**2.4**	8%	0.9	6.9	64	$18
Reliability	77	07	CHW	10	17	0	189	113	5.57	1.56	303	333	270	26.4	33%	65%	4.75	45	19	36	3.0	5.4	**1.8**	9%	1.0	-24.9	35	$4
ERA Potl	55%	1st Half		5	8	0	89	52	4.65	1.45	279			25.9	31%	67%	4.62	46	21	33	3.2	5.3	**1.6**	6%	0.6	-1.6	47	$5
LIMA Plan	C+	2nd Half		5	9	0	100	61	6.39	1.65	324			26.9	35%	63%	4.88	44	17	39	2.7	5.5	**2.0**	11%	1.3	-23.2	25	($1)
+/- Score	-3	08	Proj	**12**	**12**	**0**	**189**	**123**	**4.87**	**1.42**	**278**			**25.5**	**31%**	**67%**	**4.50**	**45**	**18**	**37**	**3.0**	**5.9**	**2.0**	**9%**	**1.0**	**-0.0**	**46**	**$11**

Plummeting Dom rate has put him on fast track to irrelevance, especially now that he's moved to the wrong side of the 5.6 line. H% and S% regression should help him bounce back a little, but buy only at a discount.

Cook,Aaron				W	L	Sv	IP	K	ERA	WHIP	OBA	vL	vR	BF/G	H%	S%	xERA	G	L	F	Ctl	Dom	Cmd	hr/f	hr/9	RAR	BPV	R$
RH	Starter	03	COL *	5	7	0	140	53	5.66	1.66	303	342	298	14.3	32%	65%	4.94	59	16	25	3.9	3.4	**0.9**	8%	0.7	-23.8	12	($3)
Age	29	04	COL *	9	5	0	142	61	3.92	1.37	271	267	324	26.5	29%	71%	4.32	58	16	26	2.9	3.9	**1.3**	6%	0.5	5.9	37	$8
Pre-Peak		05	COL	7	2	0	83	24	3.68	1.41	301	313	281	27.7	31%	76%	3.96	62	20	19	1.7	2.6	**1.5**	14%	0.9	5.8	16	$5
Type	Con xGB	06	COL	9	15	0	212	92	4.24	1.40	288	314	258	28.6	31%	70%	4.13	58	18	24	2.3	3.9	**1.7**	10%	0.7	6.4	34	$10
Reliability	41	07	COL	8	7	0	166	61	4.12	1.34	275	263	295	28.3	29%	71%	4.20	58	19	24	2.4	3.3	**1.4**	11%	0.8	6.3	24	$9
ERA Potl	45%	1st Half		4	5	0	104	33	4.93	1.41	280			28.2	29%	66%	4.54	57	19	24	2.9	2.9	**1.0**	11%	0.9	-6.5	11	$2
LIMA Plan	C	2nd Half		4	2	0	62	28	2.76	1.21	268			28.4	29%	80%	3.65	60	17	23	1.6	4.1	**2.5**	10%	0.7	12.8	57	$7
+/- Score	-17	08	Proj	**9**	**8**	**0**	**170**	**66**	**4.02**	**1.36**	**283**			**26.9**	**30%**	**71%**	**4.09**	**59**	**18**	**23**	**2.2**	**3.5**	**1.6**	**10%**	**0.7**	**6.5**	**30**	**$9**

Oblique strain shut him down just as skills were getting interesting. 2H line was a step up, but Dom is still microscopic. High BF/G could lead to more injury or burnout. More risk than upside here. Be wary.

Cordero,Chad				W	L	Sv	IP	K	ERA	WHIP	OBA	vL	vR	BF/G	H%	S%	xERA	G	L	F	Ctl	Dom	Cmd	hr/f	hr/9	RAR	BPV	R$
RH	Reliever	03	MON	1	0	1	11	12	1.64	0.64	114			3.3	14%	83%	0.47				2.5	9.8	**4.0**		0.8	3.6	151	$3
Age	26	04	MON	7	3	14	82	83	2.96	1.35	227	243	205	5.1	29%	82%	4.53	29	20	51	4.7	9.1	**1.9**	7%	0.9	13.2	78	$14
Growth		05	WAS	2	4	47	74	61	1.82	0.97	208	186	205	3.9	24%	90%	3.87	35	16	49	2.1	7.4	**3.6**	9%	1.1	22.2	100	$26
Type	Pwr xFB	06	WAS	7	4	29	73	69	3.20	1.11	223	219	212	4.3	25%	81%	3.91	35	13	52	2.7	8.5	**3.1**	13%	1.6	11.6	79	$21
Reliability	62	07	WAS	3	3	37	75	62	3.36	1.39	262	221	295	4.3	31%	79%	4.45	38	19	43	3.5	7.4	**2.1**	8%	1.0	9.9	63	$18
ERA Potl	45%	1st Half		1	2	13	37	29	3.16	1.43	262			4.4	30%	83%	4.65	39	18	43	3.9	7.1	**1.8**	10%	1.2	5.8	47	$7
LIMA Plan	C	2nd Half		2	1	24	38	33	3.55	1.34	262			4.2	32%	75%	4.27	37	19	44	3.1	7.8	**2.5**	6%	0.7	4.1	82	$11
+/- Score	-5	08	Proj	**4**	**3**	**33**	**73**	**64**	**3.23**	**1.31**	**255**			**4.3**	**30%**	**80%**	**4.27**	**36**	**17**	**47**	**3.1**	**7.9**	**2.6**	**9%**	**1.1**	**1.1**	**72**	**$18**

Walks and HR have become a real problem, and three-year skill slide has left him below the 75 BPV benchmark for closers. He's only 26, so perhaps this is fixable. 2H at least gives hope that he'll reverse the trends.

Cordero,Francisco				W	L	Sv	IP	K	ERA	WHIP	OBA	vL	vR	BF/G	H%	S%	xERA	G	L	F	Ctl	Dom	Cmd	hr/f	hr/9	RAR	BPV	R$
RH	Reliever	03	TEX	5	8	15	82	90	2.96	1.32	232	236	223	4.8	32%	78%	3.38	47	24	29	4.2	9.9	**2.4**	7%	0.4	15.8	104	$16
Age	32	04	TEX	3	4	49	71	79	2.15	1.29	230	235	216	4.5	33%	82%	3.70	42	18	40	4.0	10.0	**2.5**	1%	0.1	20.1	117	$26
Peak		05	TEX	3	1	37	69	79	3.39	1.32	239	250	214	4.2	33%	76%	3.53	43	19	38	3.9	10.3	**2.6**	7%	0.7	8.3	105	$19
Type	Pwr FB	06	2TM	10	5	22	75	84	3.72	1.34	246	286	219	4.2	33%	74%	3.65	40	21	39	3.8	10.1	**2.6**	9%	0.8	7.5	96	$18
Reliability	68	07	MIL	0	4	44	63	86	2.99	1.11	226	225	212	3.9	34%	74%	2.80	41	17	42	2.6	12.2	**4.8**	7%	0.6	11.2	167	$22
ERA Potl	65%	1st Half		0	1	27	33	47	2.18	1.00	184			3.7	31%	76%	2.55	43	21	36	3.3	12.8	**3.9**	0%	0.0	9.1	177	$14
LIMA Plan	C+	2nd Half		0	3	17	30	39	3.86	1.22	266			4.0	37%	73%	3.08	38	14	48	1.8	11.6	**6.5**	11%	1.2	2.1	172	$8
+/- Score	21	08	Proj	**5**	**3**	**45**	**73**	**91**	**3.23**	**1.21**	**238**			**4.1**	**34%**	**76%**	**3.12**	**41**	**18**	**41**	**3.0**	**11.3**	**3.8**	**8%**	**0.7**	**11.4**	**132**	**$25**

Turned in the best skills of his career by ramping up his Cmd. Really found Ctl in 2H, but throw strikes approach also turned him into FB pitcher. xERA likes 1H version better, but that's just nitpicking. Either way, he's good.

Corpas,Manuel				W	L	Sv	IP	K	ERA	WHIP	OBA	vL	vR	BF/G	H%	S%	xERA	G	L	F	Ctl	Dom	Cmd	hr/f	hr/9	RAR	BPV	R$
RH	Reliever	03		0	0	0	0	0	0.00	0.00																		
Age	25	04		0	0	0	0	0	0.00	0.00																		
Growth		05		0	0	0	0	0	0.00	0.00																		
Type	GB	06	COL *	3	3	19	77	63	2.22	1.06	238	281	290	4.0	29%	81%	3.43	45	20	34	1.6	7.3	**4.5**	5%	0.5	21.6	132	$17
Reliability	1	07	COL	4	2	19	78	58	2.08	1.06	223	234	214	4.0	26%	84%	3.31	57	14	28	2.3	6.7	**2.9**	9%	0.7	22.6	91	$18
ERA Potl	45%	1st Half		2	2	0	38	29	2.84	1.24	241			4.1	29%	78%	3.45	59	15	25	3.1	6.9	**2.2**	7%	0.5	7.4	81	$4
LIMA Plan	B	2nd Half		2	0	19	40	29	1.35	0.90	205			3.9	23%	94%	3.17	55	13	31	1.6	6.5	**4.1**	11%	0.9	15.2	113	$14
+/- Score	-20	08	Proj	**3**	**2**	**33**	**73**	**56**	**2.48**	**1.12**	**241**			**4.1**	**29%**	**80%**	**3.36**	**54**	**16**	**30**	**2.0**	**7.0**	**3.5**	**8%**	**0.6**	**9.3**	**103**	**$20**

Dom rate isn't as overpowering as you'd like to see in a closer, but he makes up for it with elite Cmd (particularly in 2H) and a high GB%. Low H% means ERA and WHIP are likely heading up a little though.

Correia,Kevin				W	L	Sv	IP	K	ERA	WHIP	OBA	vL	vR	BF/G	H%	S%	xERA	G	L	F	Ctl	Dom	Cmd	hr/f	hr/9	RAR	BPV	R$
RH	Reliever	03	a/a	6	7	0	105	81	3.68	1.26	256			23.1	31%	70%	3.33				2.6	6.9	**2.7**		0.4	9.2	89	$10
Age	27	04	aaa	3	7	0	105	59	4.54	1.46	292			15.9	32%	69%	4.70				2.7	5.1	**1.9**		0.8	-2.5	44	$3
Pre-Peak		05	SF *	5	7	7	104	74	5.21	1.57	277	311	242	10.0	30%	71%	5.01	37	24	39	4.4	6.4	**1.4**	13%	1.5	-12.4	24	$4
Type		06	SF	2	0	0	69	57	3.51	1.24	247	275	218	6.0	30%	73%	4.27	34	22	44	2.9	7.4	**2.6**	6%	0.7	8.3	85	$6
Reliability	29	07	SF	4	7	0	102	80	3.45	1.32	247	217	257	7.3	29%	76%	4.30	45	15	40	3.5	7.1	**2.0**	7%	0.8	12.2	66	$9
ERA Potl	50%	1st Half		1	3	0	34	27	3.18	1.26	226			4.6	26%	79%	4.57	41	12	48	4.0	7.1	**1.8**	9%	1.1	5.2	59	$3
LIMA Plan	B	2nd Half		3	4	0	68	53	3.59	1.34	257			10.3	31%	74%	4.16	47	16	37	3.3	7.0	**2.1**	7%	0.7	7.0	70	$5
+/- Score	-8	08	Proj	**8**	**10**	**0**	**156**	**120**	**4.05**	**1.31**	**254**			**25.3**	**30%**	**71%**	**4.18**	**44**	**18**	**38**	**3.2**	**6.9**	**2.2**	**9%**	**0.9**	**4.2**	**66**	**$12**

Moved to rotation on 8/14:
As SP - 2.5 Ctl, 3.71 xERA
As RP - 4.4 Ctl, 4.65 xERA
Also raised his GB rate to 49% as a starter. Should be a nice sleeper candidate. Watch his role this spring.

BRANDON KRUSE

Coutlangus,Jon

Coutlangus,Jon		Yr	W	L	Sv	IP	K	ERA	WHIP	OBA	vL	vR	BF/G	H%	S%	xERA	G	L	F	Ctl	Dom	Cmd	hr/f	hr/9	RAR	BPV	R$
LH	Reliever	03	0	0	0	0	0	0.00	0.00																		
Age	27	04	0	0	0	0	0	0.00	0.00																		
Pre-Peak		05	0	0	0	0	0	0.00	0.00																		
Type | Pwr		06 a/a	1	3	9	65	47	3.92	1.39	226			5.5	28%	69%	2.84				5.1	6.4	**1.3**		0.0	4.8	75	$7
Reliability	1	07 CIN *	6	2	0	52	50	5.24	1.72	274	231	264	3.3	33%	72%	4.63	48	17	35	5.9	8.6	**1.5**	13%	1.2	-5.2	45	$2
ERA Potl	50%	1st Half	3	1	0	25	21	4.68	1.52	230			2.9	27%	71%	4.92	44	17	39	6.1	7.6	**1.2**	11%	1.1	-0.8	48	$2
LIMA Plan	C+	2nd Half	3	1	0	27	29	5.75	1.91	311			3.7	39%	72%	4.21	53	16	30	5.7	9.5	**1.7**	17%	1.4	-4.4	44	$0
+/- Score	29	08 Proj	**3**	**2**	**0**	**44**	**38**	**4.76**	**1.61**	**260**			**3.9**	**31%**	**72%**	**4.61**	**49**	**17**	**35**	**5.6**	**7.9**	**1.4**	**11%**	**1.0**	**-1.1**	**49**	**$2**

4-2, 4.39 ERA in 41 IP at CIN. With Dom and GB%, he's got two-thirds of the makings of a good pitcher. But abysmal Ctl ruins the whole deal. Needs to cut walks in half to really make this work, and that's a tall order.

Crain,Jesse

Crain,Jesse		Yr	W	L	Sv	IP	K	ERA	WHIP	OBA	vL	vR	BF/G	H%	S%	xERA	G	L	F	Ctl	Dom	Cmd	hr/f	hr/9	RAR	BPV	R$
RH	Reliever	03 a/a	4	2	19	65	75	2.08	1.20	194			5.7	29%	77%	1.47				2.9	10.4	**3.6**		0.0	18.6	154	$18
Age	26	04 aaa	3	2	19	50	57	3.05	1.20	233			5.0	31%	78%	3.30				3.0	10.2	**3.4**		0.9	8.0	113	$13
Growth		05 MIN	12	5	1	79	25	2.73	1.14	215	194	225	4.3	22%	79%	5.08	46	16	37	3.3	2.8	**0.9**	6%	0.7	16.1	27	$13
Type		06 MIN	4	5	1	76	60	3.54	1.27	269	259	263	4.7	32%	74%	3.28	55	21	24	2.1	7.1	**3.3**	11%	0.7	9.5	92	$9
Reliability	0	07 MIN	1	2	0	16	10	5.52	1.41	292	269	308	3.9	29%	68%	4.28	48	14	38	2.2	5.5	**2.5**	19%	2.2	-2.0	16	$1
ERA Potl	55%	1st Half	1	2	0	16	10	5.63	1.44	296			3.9	30%	68%	4.29	48	14	38	2.3	5.6	**2.5**	20%	2.3	-2.2	14	$1
LIMA Plan	B	2nd Half	0	0	0	0	0	0.00	0.00																		
+/- Score	38	08 Proj	**4**	**3**	**0**	**44**	**31**	**3.72**	**1.24**	**251**			**4.4**	**28%**	**73%**	**3.94**	**49**	**17**	**34**	**2.7**	**6.4**	**2.4**	**11%**	**1.0**	**3.0**	**62**	**$5**

Shut down in late May for rotator cuff and labrum surgery. Might be back by spring, might not be. What this does to unpredictable Dom rate is anybody's guess. Given inconsistent skill history, might be best to sit this one out.

Cruz,Juan

Cruz,Juan		Yr	W	L	Sv	IP	K	ERA	WHIP	OBA	vL	vR	BF/G	H%	S%	xERA	G	L	F	Ctl	Dom	Cmd	hr/f	hr/9	RAR	BPV	R$
RH	Reliever	03 CHC *	6	7	0	111	106	4.38	1.32	255	292	265	13.8	32%	67%	3.67	42	25	33	3.2	8.6	**2.7**	8%	0.6	-1.4	93	$9
Age	29	04 ATL	6	2	0	72	70	2.75	1.24	225	239	214	6.0	28%	82%	3.68	45	20	35	3.8	8.8	**2.3**	10%	0.9	13.4	85	$10
Peak		05 OAK *	5	4	0	107	111	4.03	1.32	235	283	296	11.1	31%	70%	3.67	45	19	35	4.0	9.3	**2.3**	9%	0.8	4.5	90	$10
Type | Pwr FB		06 ARI	5	6	0	94	88	4.20	1.35	231	263	199	13.0	29%	69%	4.18	40	23	37	4.5	8.4	**1.9**	7%	0.7	3.3	78	$8
Reliability	18	07 ARI	6	1	0	61	87	3.10	1.26	207	269	143	4.8	31%	80%	3.28	35	19	47	4.7	12.8	**2.7**	12%	1.0	10.0	117	$10
ERA Potl	50%	1st Half	3	1	0	29	36	3.41	1.38	241			5.2	32%	81%	3.53	36	25	39	4.3	11.2	**2.6**	14%	1.2	3.6	91	$4
LIMA Plan	A	2nd Half	3	0	0	32	51	2.81	1.16	174			4.5	29%	79%	3.07	33	10	57	5.1	14.3	**2.8**	9%	0.8	6.4	140	$6
+/- Score	16	08 Proj	**5**	**2**	**0**	**64**	**79**	**3.54**	**1.28**	**218**			**4.8**	**31%**	**75%**	**3.52**	**38**	**20**	**42**	**4.4**	**11.2**	**2.5**	**9%**	**0.9**	**6.9**	**107**	**$8**

Spent the year in one place with one role and it paid off in career-best skills. Had 10.4 Dom as RP in '06, so '07 leap was more gradual than it looked. But rising Ctl and FB% mean that if Dom ever drops, ERA skyrockets.

Danks,John

Danks,John		Yr	W	L	Sv	IP	K	ERA	WHIP	OBA	vL	vR	BF/G	H%	S%	xERA	G	L	F	Ctl	Dom	Cmd	hr/f	hr/9	RAR	BPV	R$
LH	Starter	03	0	0	0	0	0	0.00	0.00																		
Age	23	04	0	0	0	0	0	0.00	0.00																		
Growth		05 aa	4	10	0	98	77	6.82	1.67	322			25.0	37%	60%	6.25				3.0	7.0	**2.4**		1.4	-30.4	41	($3)
Type | Pwr xFB		06 a/a	9	9	0	140	140	5.69	1.59	296			23.4	35%	69%	6.05				3.6	9.0	**2.5**		1.9	-20.3	45	$5
Reliability	14	07 CHW	6	13	0	139	109	5.50	1.54	290	281	292	23.8	32%	69%	4.79	35	19	46	3.5	7.1	**2.0**	14%	1.8	-17.1	27	$4
ERA Potl	50%	1st Half	4	6	0	75	59	4.80	1.60	289			24.2	32%	75%	5.06	33	20	47	4.1	7.1	**1.7**	13%	1.7	-2.7	26	$3
LIMA Plan	C+	2nd Half	2	7	0	64	50	6.33	1.47	291			23.4	31%	61%	4.49	37	18	45	2.8	7.0	**2.5**	15%	2.0	-14.4	32	$1
+/- Score	27	08 Proj	**9**	**12**	**0**	**156**	**133**	**4.86**	**1.42**	**273**			**23.3**	**31%**	**71%**	**4.43**	**35**	**19**	**45**	**3.2**	**7.7**	**2.4**	**13%**	**1.6**	**1.3**	**50**	**$10**

Low S% inflated his 2H ERA and overshadowed some nice Ctl growth. The next step is getting his gopheritis in check. The seeds of something pretty good are here, but it may take a while to get there.

Davies,Kyle

Davies,Kyle		Yr	W	L	Sv	IP	K	ERA	WHIP	OBA	vL	vR	BF/G	H%	S%	xERA	G	L	F	Ctl	Dom	Cmd	hr/f	hr/9	RAR	BPV	R$
RH	Starter	03	0	0	0	0	0	0.00	0.00											0.0	0.0						
Age	24	04 a/a	4	2	0	67	70	3.33	1.09	208			22.4	25%	76%	3.11				3.2	9.5	**3.0**		1.3	8.4	94	$9
Growth		05 ATL *	12	8	0	160	119	4.57	1.57	274	264	295	21.2	32%	72%	5.13	34	25	41	4.6	6.7	**1.5**	7%	0.8	-6.3	46	$7
Type | Pwr FB		06 ATL	3	7	0	63	51	8.42	1.95	336	333	331	21.9	37%	59%	5.19	37	24	39	4.7	7.3	**1.5**	17%	2.0	-30.6	4	($5)
Reliability	13	07 2TM	7	15	0	136	99	6.09	1.65	288	275	293	22.2	32%	66%	5.13	39	21	41	4.6	6.6	**1.4**	12%	1.5	-27.3	23	$0
ERA Potl	50%	1st Half	3	7	0	78	51	5.42	1.50	267			24.6	29%	66%	5.00	41	19	40	4.3	5.9	**1.4**	11%	1.3	-9.2	28	$2
LIMA Plan	C+	2nd Half	4	8	0	58	48	6.98	1.86	314			19.8	36%	65%	5.30	36	23	42	5.1	7.4	**1.5**	14%	1.7	-18.0	16	($2)
+/- Score	17	08 Proj	**3**	**6**	**0**	**58**	**46**	**5.43**	**1.60**	**281**			**21.9**	**32%**	**69%**	**4.88**	**37**	**23**	**40**	**4.5**	**7.1**	**1.6**	**12%**	**1.4**	**-3.2**	**33**	**$1**

An ERA in the low fives is not what you want to hear when asking the question, "What's his skill upside?" Too many walks, above-average LD% and excessive HRs indicate he's not fooling anybody. Stay away.

Davis,Doug

Davis,Doug		Yr	W	L	Sv	IP	K	ERA	WHIP	OBA	vL	vR	BF/G	H%	S%	xERA	G	L	F	Ctl	Dom	Cmd	hr/f	hr/9	RAR	BPV	R$
LH	Starter	03 MIL *	12	10	0	177	93	4.47	1.57	297	293	283	25.6	32%	75%	5.23	42	18	40	3.4	4.7	**1.4**	9%	1.2	-4.3	18	$6
Age	32	04 MIL	12	12	0	215	168	3.26	1.28	243	259	244	26.6	29%	75%	4.02	47	19	34	3.3	7.0	**2.1**	6%	0.6	26.5	75	$20
Peak		05 MIL	11	11	0	222	208	3.85	1.30	238	259	228	26.8	29%	74%	3.85	44	20	36	3.8	8.4	**2.2**	12%	1.1	10.9	73	$19
Type | Pwr		06 MIL	11	11	0	203	159	4.92	1.52	265	307	253	26.5	31%	68%	4.61	44	20	36	4.5	7.0	**1.6**	9%	0.8	-10.8	52	$8
Reliability	89	07 ARI	13	12	0	193	144	4.25	1.59	280	252	290	26.3	32%	75%	4.62	47	19	34	4.4	6.7	**1.5**	10%	1.0	4.2	42	$10
ERA Potl	40%	1st Half	5	8	0	93	68	4.16	1.72	299			27.0	35%	77%	4.88	46	21	33	4.6	6.6	**1.4**	9%	0.9	3.0	38	$3
LIMA Plan	C	2nd Half	8	4	0	100	76	4.33	1.46	260			25.7	30%	73%	4.38	49	18	34	4.2	6.9	**1.6**	12%	1.1	1.1	46	$7
+/- Score	-11	08 Proj	**13**	**11**	**0**	**203**	**153**	**4.34**	**1.50**	**267**			**26.4**	**31%**	**73%**	**4.53**	**46**	**19**	**35**	**4.3**	**6.8**	**1.6**	**10%**	**1.0**	**-3.3**	**46**	**$11**

Had a nice two-year peak driven by a brief period of acceptable Cmd, but it appears to be over. Did manage to post a 2.2 Cmd and 4.02 xERA in Aug/Sept, but moments like that are now the exception rather than the norm.

Davis,Wade

Davis,Wade		Yr	W	L	Sv	IP	K	ERA	WHIP	OBA	vL	vR	BF/G	H%	S%	xERA	G	L	F	Ctl	Dom	Cmd	hr/f	hr/9	RAR	BPV	R$
RH	Starter	03	0	0	0	0	0	0.00	0.00																		
Age	22	04	0	0	0	0	0	0.00	0.00																		
Growth		05	0	0	0	0	0	0.00	0.00																		
Type | Pwr		06	0	0	0	0	0	0.00	0.00																		
Reliability	0	07 aa	7	3	0	80	71	3.83	1.44	271			24.9	34%	72%	3.92				3.5	8.0	**2.3**		0.3	6.3	87	$8
ERA Potl	60%	1st Half	1	0	0	11	14	3.21	1.43	307			24.4	43%	80%					1.6	11.3	**7.0**		0.8	1.7	184	$1
LIMA Plan	B	2nd Half	6	3	0	69	57	3.92	1.44	265			25.0	33%	71%					3.8	7.5	**2.0**		0.3	4.6	80	$6
+/- Score	14	08 Proj	**4**	**2**	**0**	**44**	**40**	**4.34**	**1.54**	**277**			**24.3**	**34%**	**73%**	**4.70**				**4.1**	**8.3**	**2.0**		**0.8**	**-1.4**	**66**	**$3**

Promoted to Double-A in mid-season and looked incredible in his first two starts, but hitters adjusted in the 2H. MLEs are encouraging, but he'll need more time in the minors. Tuck him away for late-season 2008.

de la Rosa,Jorge

de la Rosa,Jorge		Yr	W	L	Sv	IP	K	ERA	WHIP	OBA	vL	vR	BF/G	H%	S%	xERA	G	L	F	Ctl	Dom	Cmd	hr/f	hr/9	RAR	BPV	R$
LH	Starter	03 aa	7	5	1	124	101	3.77	1.48	276			20.2	34%	74%	4.16				3.6	7.3	**2.0**		0.4	9.5	73	$9
Age	27	04 MIL *	5	9	0	109	78	5.45	1.54	279			19.5	32%	65%	4.78				4.0	6.4	**1.6**		0.9	-16.0	44	$1
Growth		05 MIL	2	2	0	42	42	4.49	2.04	288	321	273	5.5	38%	76%	5.24	49	23	28	8.1	9.0	**1.1**	3%	0.2	-1.3	68	($1)
Type | Pwr		06 2TM *	8	7	0	109	85	5.72	1.66	286	250	269	14.7	33%	67%	4.95	41	20	39	4.7	7.0	**1.5**	11%	1.2	-16.1	34	$3
Reliability	16	07 KC	8	12	0	130	82	5.82	1.64	304	234	321	22.8	33%	67%	5.07	41	20	39	3.7	5.7	**1.5**	12%	1.4	-21.0	19	$2
ERA Potl	50%	1st Half	5	9	0	94	56	5.36	1.57	304			24.9	33%	68%	4.97	41	20	40	3.1	5.4	**1.8**	10%	1.2	-9.9	26	$2
LIMA Plan	C+	2nd Half	3	3	0	36	26	7.00	1.81	302			18.9	33%	64%	5.33	40	22	38	5.2	6.5	**1.2**	16%	1.7	-11.1	7	($1)
+/- Score	6	08 Proj	**9**	**10**	**0**	**131**	**91**	**5.72**	**1.62**	**294**			**23.7**	**33%**	**66%**	**4.87**	**42**	**21**	**37**	**4.0**	**6.3**	**1.6**	**11%**	**1.2**	**-6.0**	**32**	**$3**

1.9 Ctl in first 9 GS, then 5.1 Ctl thereafter, though that may have been related to a mid-season elbow strain. Overall, Ctl growth has come at the expense of other skills, leaving him as unrosterable as ever.

Delcarmen,Manny

Delcarmen,Manny		Yr	W	L	Sv	IP	K	ERA	WHIP	OBA	vL	vR	BF/G	H%	S%	xERA	G	L	F	Ctl	Dom	Cmd	hr/f	hr/9	RAR	BPV	R$
RH	Reliever	03	0	0	0	0	0	0.00	0.00																		
Age	26	04	0	0	0	0	0	0.00	0.00																		
Growth		05 a/a	7	5	5	59	62	3.20	1.44	248			5.7	33%	78%	3.68				4.6	9.5	**2.1**		0.5	8.0	92	$9
Type | Pwr		06 BOS *	2	1	0	70	62	4.62	1.44	283	319	302	5.1	36%	66%	3.80	45	26	30	3.0	8.0	**2.7**	3%	0.3	-0.6	95	$4
Reliability	4	07 BOS *	3	2	1	73	73	3.10	1.29	232	167	194	4.8	30%	77%	3.84	45	17	38	4.0	8.9	**2.3**	7%	0.6	12.7	91	$9
ERA Potl	55%	1st Half	3	2	0	34	33	4.49	1.55	272			6.1	36%	69%	3.87	60	7	33	4.5	8.7	**1.9**	3%	0.3	0.1	86	$3
LIMA Plan	B+	2nd Half	0	0	1	39	40	1.88	1.06	193			4.0	24%	89%	3.49	42	19	39	3.5	9.2	**2.6**	11%	0.9	12.6	99	$6
+/- Score	9	08 Proj	**3**	**2**	**0**	**58**	**56**	**3.57**	**1.33**	**252**			**4.9**	**32%**	**75%**	**3.70**	**44**	**22**	**34**	**3.4**	**8.7**	**2.5**	**9%**	**0.8**	**5.7**	**87**	**$6**

0-0, 2.05 ERA in 44 IP at BOS. Awfully close to becoming a dominant force in the pen. Just needs to find better Ctl. Owns a 2.5 Ctl mark from 2H of '06, so there's hope. Good LIMA option now, great if he improves Cmd.

BRANDON KRUSE

Dempster,Ryan

	Yr	Tm	W	L	Sv	IP	K	ERA	WHIP	OBA	vL	vR	BF/G	H%	S%	xERA	G	L	F	Ctl	Dom	Cmd	hr/f	hr/9	RAR	BPV	R$
RH Reliever	03	CIN	3	7	0	115	84	6.57	1.77	292	300	288	24.5	33%	63%	5.28	44	20	36	5.5	6.6	**1.2**	10%	1.1	-32.6	28	($5)
Age 31	04	CHC *	2	2	2	41	34	4.37	1.55	251	222	200	6.4	31%	71%	4.38	52	21	28	5.5	7.4	**1.4**	6%	0.4	-0.5	65	$2
Peak	05	CHC	5	3	33	92	89	3.13	1.43	242	278	216	6.4	32%	78%	3.44	58	21	21	4.8	8.7	**1.8**	7%	0.4	12.7	85	$19
Type Pwr	06	CHC	1	9	24	75	67	4.80	1.51	267	310	226	4.5	33%	68%	4.00	52	18	30	4.3	8.0	**1.9**	7%	0.6	-2.9	71	$10
Reliability 59	07	CHC	2	7	28	67	55	4.72	1.33	239	259	224	4.3	28%	67%	4.03	47	20	32	4.0	7.4	**1.8**	13%	1.1	-2.4	58	$13
ERA Potl 55%	1st Half		1	3	16	35	33	3.34	1.00	175			4.2	23%	65%	3.34	48	21	31	3.6	8.5	**2.4**	4%	0.3	4.7	113	$10
LIMA Plan C	2nd Half		1	4	12	32	22	6.25	1.70	298			4.4	32%	68%	4.85	46	20	34	4.5	6.2	**1.4**	20%	2.0	-7.1	2	$3
+/- Score 13	08	Proj	**2**	**7**	**25**	**73**	**61**	**4.72**	**1.48**	**258**			**4.6**	**31%**	**70%**	**4.21**	**48**	**20**	**32**	**4.5**	**7.6**	**1.7**	**12%**	**1.0**	**1.7**	**55**	**$11**

Raised hopes with strong 1H, then dashed them with an ugly finish. Talk of moving him back to rotation, though with spotty Cmd, rising FB% and sinking BPV, he's a questionable option no matter what the role.

Devine,Joey

	Yr	Tm	W	L	Sv	IP	K	ERA	WHIP	OBA	vL	vR	BF/G	H%	S%	xERA	G	L	F	Ctl	Dom	Cmd	hr/f	hr/9	RAR	BPV	R$
RH Reliever	03		0	0	0	0	0	0.00	0.00																		
Age 24	04		0	0	0	0	0	0.00	0.00																		
Growth	05	ATL *	1	2	5	26	28	5.88	1.96	297			5.3	36%	74%	6.91				6.9	9.7	**1.4**		1.7	-5.3	31	$1
Type Pwr GB	06	ATL *	2	0	0	17	28	5.26	1.64	212	333	286	4.6	35%	69%	4.08	13	38	50	7.9	14.7	**1.9**	12%	1.1	-1.6	109	$1
Reliability 0	07	ATL *	6	4	20	65	72	2.27	1.30	235	300	211	4.6	33%	83%	3.34	57	9	35	3.9	9.9	**2.5**	4%	0.3	17.4	112	$17
ERA Potl 40%	1st Half		2	4	16	35	45	2.57	1.29	239			4.5	36%	80%	3.17	33	33	33	3.6	11.6	**3.2**	4%	0.3	8.0	136	$10
LIMA Plan B	2nd Half		4	0	4	30	27	1.92	1.32	230			4.8	29%	86%	3.83	60	5	35	4.3	8.0	**1.8**	4%	0.3	9.4	86	$6
+/- Score -10	08	Proj	**4**	**2**	**3**	**44**	**41**	**4.34**	**1.54**	**255**			**4.9**	**32%**	**73%**	**4.27**	**52**	**12**	**36**	**5.2**	**8.5**	**1.6**	**9%**	**0.8**	**0.7**	**64**	**$4**

1-0, 1.08 ERA in 8 IP at ATL. Three years of steady Cmd growth is promising, though 2H was hurt by 8 walks with ATL. MLB save opps won't come until he improves on career 10.1 Ctl, 0.9 Cmd in majors. Be patient.

Dinardo,Lenny

	Yr	Tm	W	L	Sv	IP	K	ERA	WHIP	OBA	vL	vR	BF/G	H%	S%	xERA	G	L	F	Ctl	Dom	Cmd	hr/f	hr/9	RAR	BPV	R$
LH Reliever	03	aa	1	3	0	40	29	4.03	1.34	262			24.4	30%	71%	3.90				3.1	6.4	**2.1**		0.7	1.8	64	$2
Age 28	04	BOS	0	0	0	27	21	4.30	1.69	307			5.7	37%	73%	5.18				4.0	6.9	**1.8**		0.3	0.4	62	$0
Pre-Peak	05	BOS *	6	4	0	122	93	3.48	1.44	285			17.2	34%	77%	3.63	66	5	29	2.9	6.8	**2.4**	7%	0.6	13.5	71	$9
Type Con xGB	06	BOS	1	2	0	39	17	7.85	2.08	357	375	358	15.0	37%	63%	4.93	61	20	19	4.6	3.9	**0.9**	20%	1.4	-15.8	-17	($4)
Reliability 15	07	OAK	8	10	0	131	59	4.11	1.42	269	304	271	16.3	28%	73%	4.46	56	18	26	3.4	4.0	**1.2**	11%	0.9	6.4	24	$8
ERA Potl 40%	1st Half		3	4	0	51	24	2.47	1.25	234			12.5	25%	82%	3.95	62	17	21	3.5	4.2	**1.2**	9%	0.5	12.8	43	$6
LIMA Plan D+	2nd Half		5	6	0	80	35	5.16	1.52	289			19.8	30%	68%	4.76	53	18	29	3.4	3.9	**1.2**	12%	1.1	-6.4	12	$2
+/- Score -24	08	Proj	**5**	**6**	**0**	**102**	**53**	**4.97**	**1.58**	**294**			**16.3**	**32%**	**70%**	**4.31**	**59**	**18**	**23**	**3.6**	**4.7**	**1.3**	**14%**	**1.0**	**2.4**	**22**	**$2**

High GB% is the main thing keeping him from disaster, though '07 role had impact too: As SP - 3.4 Dom, 0.9 Cmd As RP - 5.7 Dom, 3.1 Cmd Still, there's not much value in a soft-tossing RP. Pass.

Donnelly,Brendan

	Yr	Tm	W	L	Sv	IP	K	ERA	WHIP	OBA	vL	vR	BF/G	H%	S%	xERA	G	L	F	Ctl	Dom	Cmd	hr/f	hr/9	RAR	BPV	R$
RH Reliever	03	ANA	2	2	3	74	79	1.58	1.07	209	199	202	4.7	29%	86%	3.75	28	22	50	2.9	9.6	**3.3**	2%	0.2	26.9	133	$14
Age 36	04	ANA	5	2	0	42	56	3.00	1.17	223	211	237	4.3	32%	80%	3.21	34	16	50	3.2	12.0	**3.7**	10%	1.1	7.4	129	$8
Decline	05	ANA	9	3	0	65	53	3.73	1.21	246	213	274	4.1	28%	74%	4.23	34	20	46	2.6	7.3	**2.8**	10%	1.2	5.1	71	$10
Type xFB	06	LAA	6	0	0	64	53	3.94	1.34	243	290	204	4.4	28%	74%	4.21	44	18	37	3.9	7.5	**1.9**	12%	1.1	4.9	57	$7
Reliability 0	07	BOS	2	1	0	21	15	3.00	1.14	243	212	250	3.2	30%	71%	4.48	34	17	49	2.1	6.4	**3.0**	0%	0.0	3.9	108	$3
ERA Potl 50%	1st Half		2	1	0	21	15	3.00	1.14	243			3.2	30%	71%	4.48	34	17	49	2.1	6.4	**3.0**	0%	0.0	3.9	108	$3
LIMA Plan C+	2nd Half		0	0	0	0	0	0.00	0.00																		
+/- Score -46	08	Proj	**1**	**1**	**0**	**15**	**10**	**4.34**	**1.24**	**241**			**4.0**	**26%**	**69%**	**4.63**	**35**	**18**	**46**	**3.1**	**6.2**	**2.0**	**10%**	**1.2**	**-0.2**	**49**	**$1**

On the surface, a nice rebound, but lack of HR artificially skewed the results. Mid-season Tommy John surgery will keep him out until 2H of 2008, and given his age and xERA, he's not worth waiting around for.

Dotel,Octavio

	Yr	Tm	W	L	Sv	IP	K	ERA	WHIP	OBA	vL	vR	BF/G	H%	S%	xERA	G	L	F	Ctl	Dom	Cmd	hr/f	hr/9	RAR	BPV	R$
RH Reliever	03	HOU	6	4	4	87	97	2.48	0.97	178	152	186	4.4	23%	80%	3.29	35	22	43	3.2	10.0	**3.1**	10%	0.9	19.3	117	$16
Age 34	04	2TM	6	6	36	85	122	3.70	1.19	221	245	188	4.5	32%	75%	3.19	28	19	54	3.5	12.9	**3.7**	13%	1.4	6.7	125	$24
Past Peak	05	OAK	1	2	7	15	16	3.58	1.39	190	269	107	4.3	23%	79%	4.89	24	26	50	6.6	9.5	**1.5**	11%	1.2	1.5	69	$4
Type Pwr xFB	06	NYY	0	0	0	10	7	10.80	2.90	390	333	414	4.2	43%	63%	8.61	37	20	44	9.9	6.3	**0.6**	12%	1.8	-7.7	-26	($3)
Reliability 0	07	2TM	2	1	11	31	41	4.10	1.34	251	265	225	4.0	35%	73%	3.29	38	16	46	3.5	12.0	**3.4**	12%	1.2	1.4	114	$7
ERA Potl 65%	1st Half		0	0	8	14	14	3.21	1.29	248			3.9	30%	81%	3.41	54	10	36	3.2	9.0	**2.8**	14%	1.3	2.2	80	$4
LIMA Plan A	2nd Half		2	1	3	17	27	4.85	1.38	254			4.0	41%	67%	3.13	23	23	55	3.8	14.6	**3.9**	10%	1.1	-0.8	140	$3
+/- Score 27	08	Proj	**4**	**2**	**5**	**44**	**55**	**3.52**	**1.17**	**217**			**4.3**	**30%**	**74%**	**3.32**	**35**	**18**	**46**	**3.5**	**11.4**	**3.2**	**11%**	**1.0**	**6.0**	**117**	**$8**

Finally looked all the way back from TJS, as Dom and Cmd reached pre-injury levels. FB% is still an issue, but BPIs remain suited to closing. Just needs health (366 DL days since '05) and opportunity. UP: 30 SV.

Downs,Scott

	Yr	Tm	W	L	Sv	IP	K	ERA	WHIP	OBA	vL	vR	BF/G	H%	S%	xERA	G	L	F	Ctl	Dom	Cmd	hr/f	hr/9	RAR	BPV	R$
LH Reliever	03	aaa	8	9	0	121	43	4.90	1.44	285			25.2	29%	68%	4.82				2.9	3.2	**1.1**		1.0	-7.6	9	$4
Age 32	04	MON *	13	12	0	198	90	4.68	1.52	311	286	315	25.9	32%	73%	4.46	53	18	29	2.3	4.1	**1.8**	13%	1.3	-10.2	17	$6
Peak	05	TOR *	6	6	0	133	104	4.82	1.38	281	234	262	17.3	32%	68%	3.43	54	22	24	2.5	7.1	**2.8**	18%	1.2	-7.4	63	$7
Type Pwr xGB	06	TOR	6	2	1	77	61	4.09	1.34	252	232	258	5.6	29%	72%	3.64	56	18	26	3.5	7.1	**2.0**	15%	1.1	4.4	59	$8
Reliability 29	07	TOR	4	2	1	58	57	2.17	1.22	223	209	238	3.0	29%	84%	3.02	60	18	22	3.7	8.8	**2.4**	9%	0.5	16.7	99	$9
ERA Potl 45%	1st Half		1	1	0	31	36	2.61	1.32	194			3.3	26%	84%	2.88	67	13	20	5.8	10.5	**1.8**	21%	0.9	7.2	91	$4
LIMA Plan B+	2nd Half		3	1	1	27	21	1.67	1.11	255			2.7	32%	83%	3.10	54	22	24	1.3	7.0	**5.3**	0%	0.0	9.5	156	$6
+/- Score -26	08	Proj	**5**	**3**	**0**	**73**	**60**	**3.72**	**1.27**	**252**			**4.3**	**30%**	**72%**	**3.31**	**57**	**19**	**24**	**2.9**	**7.4**	**2.6**	**12%**	**0.7**	**10.6**	**82**	**$8**

First season of full-time relief brought out the best in his Dom and GB%, leading to career-low ERA (with help from S%). Lefty bias may keep him from save opps, but these are LIMA skills, especially if he builds on 2H Ctl.

Duchscherer,Justin

	Yr	Tm	W	L	Sv	IP	K	ERA	WHIP	OBA	vL	vR	BF/G	H%	S%	xERA	G	L	F	Ctl	Dom	Cmd	hr/f	hr/9	RAR	BPV	R$
RH Reliever	03	aaa	14	2	0	155	99	3.60	1.18	274			26.5	31%	71%	3.65				1.0	5.7	**5.5**		0.7	15.2	129	$18
Age 30	04	OAK	7	6	0	96	59	3.28	1.22	239	247	235	7.5	25%	79%	4.48	43	17	40	3.0	5.5	**1.8**	11%	1.2	13.7	43	$10
Peak	05	OAK	7	4	5	85	85	2.22	1.01	218	225	208	5.2	28%	82%	3.14	44	19	37	2.0	9.0	**4.5**	9%	0.7	22.6	137	$17
Type	06	OAK	2	1	9	55	51	2.93	1.11	250	248	241	4.2	31%	75%	3.41	37	26	38	1.5	8.3	**5.7**	7%	0.7	11.1	154	$11
Reliability 0	07	OAK	3	3	0	16	13	4.97	1.60	281	400	176	4.3	31%	74%	4.52	47	17	36	4.4	7.2	**1.6**	16%	1.7	-0.9	26	$2
ERA Potl 60%	1st Half		3	3	0	16	13	5.06	1.63	285			4.3	32%	74%	4.53	47	17	36	4.5	7.3	**1.6**	17%	1.7	-1.1	25	$2
LIMA Plan A+	2nd Half		0	0	0	0	0	0.00	0.00																		
+/- Score 23	08	Proj	**5**	**4**	**5**	**44**	**39**	**3.52**	**1.20**	**255**			**5.1**	**31%**	**73%**	**3.56**	**44**	**19**	**37**	**2.1**	**8.1**	**3.9**	**9%**	**0.8**	**5.0**	**109**	**$8**

Arthritic hip ruined his season. Prior to that, Ctl, Cmd and BPV were well into elite territory. Some talk of moving him back to SP; hasn't done it since '03, but skills show he did it well. Watch role, health this spring.

Duckworth,Brandon

	Yr	Tm	W	L	Sv	IP	K	ERA	WHIP	OBA	vL	vR	BF/G	H%	S%	xERA	G	L	F	Ctl	Dom	Cmd	hr/f	hr/9	RAR	BPV	R$
RH Reliever	03	PHI *	6	8	0	113	80	4.85	1.55	285	246	297	18.1	31%	72%	5.33				3.9	6.4	**1.6**		1.4	-8.0	30	$3
Age 32	04	aaa	5	5	0	70	49	6.91	1.81	331			23.7	37%	64%	6.92				3.7	6.3	**1.7**		1.5	-22.2	17	($2)
Peak	05	aaa	8	6	0	115	67	5.50	1.77	337			27.0	36%	72%	6.82				3.0	5.3	**1.8**		1.5	-17.0	12	($1)
Type	06	KC *	9	8	0	119	70	4.69	1.72	314	232	390	25.1	35%	73%	5.00	47	21	32	3.8	5.3	**1.4**	6%	0.6	-1.9	34	$4
Reliability 0	07	KC	3	5	1	47	21	4.63	1.58	279	266	283	8.1	30%	70%	5.45	45	21	34	4.4	4.0	**0.9**	6%	0.6	-0.7	25	$2
ERA Potl 45%	1st Half		2	3	1	34	15	2.91	1.50	250			8.3	27%	82%	5.66	46	17	37	5.0	4.0	**0.8**	5%	0.5	6.7	29	$3
LIMA Plan C+	2nd Half		1	2	0	13	6	9.21	1.81	347			7.5	38%	45%	4.95	43	31	25	2.8	4.3	**1.5**	8%	0.7	-7.4	21	($1)
+/- Score -46	08	Proj	**3**	**4**	**0**	**44**	**23**	**4.97**	**1.56**	**290**			**11.5**	**32%**	**69%**	**4.91**	**45**	**25**	**30**	**3.7**	**4.8**	**1.3**	**9%**	**0.8**	**-2.2**	**28**	**$1**

Cmd has crashed so badly, it's getting hard to remember that he once had some promising skills. Now all he has is a five-year streak of not being worth owning. He's the Cal Ripken of unrosterability.

Duke,Zach

	Yr	Tm	W	L	Sv	IP	K	ERA	WHIP	OBA	vL	vR	BF/G	H%	S%	xERA	G	L	F	Ctl	Dom	Cmd	hr/f	hr/9	RAR	BPV	R$
LH Starter	03		0	0	0	0	0	0.00	0.00											0.0	0.0						
Age 25	04	aa	5	1	0	51	30	1.94	1.08	242			22.7	28%	83%	2.66				1.6	5.3	**3.3**		0.4	15.2	98	$8
Growth	05	PIT *	20	5	0	192	117	2.49	1.21	260	150	273	26.5	30%	81%	3.78	48	26	26	2.0	5.5	**2.7**	7%	0.5	41.6	78	$26
Type Con	06	PIT	10	15	0	215	117	4.48	1.50	296	264	310	28.0	33%	71%	4.43	51	20	29	2.8	4.9	**1.7**	8%	0.7	0.3	40	$8
Reliability 20	07	PIT	3	8	0	107	41	5.54	1.73	347	341	363	25.0	36%	70%	4.89	51	20	29	2.1	3.4	**1.6**	11%	1.2	-14.7	5	($3)
ERA Potl 50%	1st Half		3	6	0	89	29	5.46	1.69	339			25.6	35%	69%	4.94	52	20	29	2.1	2.9	**1.4**	10%	1.1	-11.4	3	($2)
LIMA Plan D	2nd Half		0	2	0	18	12	5.90	1.97	383			22.4	41%	75%	4.64	46	21	33	2.0	5.9	**3.0**	17%	2.0	-3.3	18	($1)
+/- Score 15	08	Proj	**6**	**9**	**0**	**131**	**71**	**4.55**	**1.59**	**324**			**24.5**	**35%**	**74%**	**4.44**	**49**	**21**	**30**	**2.2**	**4.9**	**2.2**	**11%**	**1.1**	**-0.7**	**33**	**$3**

Diagnosed at mid-season with elbow tendinitis; that likely explains 1H Dom drop. Looked better in return, but it was only 18 IP. Needs to prove he can maintain at least a mid-5 Dom rate before you can buy back in.

BRANDON KRUSE

Durbin,Chad

		Yr	Tm	W	L	Sv	IP	K	ERA	WHIP	OBA	vL	vR	BF/G	H%	S%	xERA	G	L	F	Ctl	Dom	Cmd	hr/f	hr/9	RAR	BPV	R$
RH	Reliever	03	a/a	5	6	0	70	61	5.80	1.30	268			22.8	30%	59%	4.86				2.4	7.8	3.2		1.8	-12.2	63	$4
Age	30	04	ARI *	9	10	0	112	81	5.51	1.63	294			15.5	33%	69%	5.67				4.1	6.5	1.6		1.4	-17.2	27	$2
Peak		05	aaa	4	5	0	115	82	5.93	1.53	287			19.7	31%	65%	5.58				3.5	6.4	1.8		1.6	-23.0	24	$0
Type	FB	06	aaa	11	8	0	185	120	4.34	1.44	292			28.8	33%	72%	4.80				2.5	5.8	2.4		1.0	4.1	52	$12
Reliability	33	07	DET	8	7	1	128	66	4.72	1.43	270	281	255	15.4	28%	71%	5.04	44	16	40	3.5	4.7	1.3	12%	1.5	-3.4	13	$7
ERA Potl	40%	1st Half		6	3	1	81	44	4.22	1.40	264			23.3	28%	74%	4.86	47	14	39	3.4	4.9	1.4	11%	1.3	2.8	21	$6
LIMA Plan	D+	2nd Half		2	4	0	47	22	5.59	1.48	279			9.8	28%	67%	5.34	39	18	42	3.5	4.2	1.2	13%	1.7	-6.2	-2	$1
+/- Score	-20	08	Proj	4	5	0	77	46	4.94	1.45	280			9.6	30%	70%	4.85	42	17	41	3.2	5.4	1.7	11%	1.4	-3.4	25	$3

Fading Dom, lousy xERAs, an inability to keep the ball in the park... there's not much to like here. Swingman flexibility may be nice for MLB teams, but in his case, it just means more ways to disappoint.

Durbin,J.D.

		Yr	Tm	W	L	Sv	IP	K	ERA	WHIP	OBA	vL	vR	BF/G	H%	S%	xERA	G	L	F	Ctl	Dom	Cmd	hr/f	hr/9	RAR	BPV	R$
RH	Starter	03	aa	6	3	0	94	59	3.92	1.57	308			30.2	34%	78%	5.38				2.9	5.6	2.0		1.0	5.5	40	$5
Age	26	04	a/a	7	3	0	100	81	4.05	1.69	314			23.1	38%	77%	5.57				3.6	7.3	2.0		0.7	3.6	57	$4
Growth		05	aaa	5	5	0	104	79	5.28	1.58	275			21.3	32%	66%	4.63				4.6	6.8	1.5		0.7	-12.5	52	$2
Type	Pwr	06	aaa	4	3	0	89	69	3.44	1.60	251			25.1	31%	78%	4.05				5.9	7.0	1.2		0.4	11.9	60	$5
Reliability	0	07	2NL *	8	9	1	124	78	5.96	1.74	309	301	297	20.0	34%	68%	5.10	48	15	36	4.3	5.6	1.3	12%	1.3	-23.5	15	($1)
ERA Potl	50%	1st Half		2	4	0	60	39	6.74	1.80	334			25.8	36%	66%	4.82	25	50	25	3.4	5.8	1.7	22%	1.8	-17.1	5	($3)
LIMA Plan	C+	2nd Half		6	5	1	64	39	5.23	1.68	284			16.4	32%	69%	5.33	49	14	37	5.1	5.4	1.1	8%	0.9	-6.4	27	$2
+/- Score	22	08	Proj	4	4	0	73	50	4.97	1.67	289			20.8	33%	71%	5.04	47	16	37	4.7	6.2	1.3	8%	0.9	-5.7	36	$1

6-5, 6.06 ERA in 65 IP at AZ/PHI. Self-proclaimed "Real Deal" finally got a shot at the majors and flopped, though S% bought him a 3.37 ERA in July/August. Ctl, Cmd offer little hope at this point. Time for a new nickname.

Eaton,Adam

		Yr	Tm	W	L	Sv	IP	K	ERA	WHIP	OBA	vL	vR	BF/G	H%	S%	xERA	G	L	F	Ctl	Dom	Cmd	hr/f	hr/9	RAR	BPV	R$
RH	Starter	03	SD	9	12	0	183	146	4.08	1.32	251	276	222	25.0	29%	71%	4.10	45	19	36	3.3	7.2	2.1	10%	1.0	4.4	63	$13
Age	30	04	SD	10	14	0	199	153	4.61	1.29	267	260	272	25.4	30%	68%	4.18	40	18	42	2.4	6.9	2.9	11%	1.3	-8.6	67	$13
Peak		05	SD	11	5	0	128	100	4.28	1.44	279	309	255	23.3	33%	72%	4.25	41	24	35	3.1	7.0	2.3	10%	1.0	-0.6	60	$9
Type	FB	06	TEX	7	4	0	65	43	5.12	1.57	299	320	279	22.4	32%	71%	4.84	37	24	38	3.0	6.0	1.8	13%	1.5	-4.5	23	$4
Reliability	15	07	PHI	10	10	0	162	97	6.29	1.63	296	321	284	24.5	31%	64%	5.29	39	19	42	4.0	5.4	1.4	13%	1.7	-37.2	7	($0)
ERA Potl	50%	1st Half		7	5	0	86	55	5.65	1.51	271			25.4	29%	65%	5.07	40	19	41	4.2	5.8	1.4	12%	1.4	-13.0	23	$3
LIMA Plan	F	2nd Half		3	5	0	76	42	7.01	1.76	323			23.6	33%	64%	5.54	38	18	43	3.7	5.0	1.4	14%	2.0	-24.2	-12	($4)
+/- Score	3	08	Proj	9	12	0	160	99	5.02	1.57	295			23.9	31%	72%	5.01	39	21	40	3.5	5.6	1.6	13%	1.5	-12.1	17	$4

Cmd in four-year freefall, xERA keeps getting worse, and rising FB% not a good match for last two home parks. Hasn't been rosterable since '05 finger injury:
Before: 7.0 Dom, 2.2 Cmd
After: 5.8 Dom, 1.6 Cmd

Embree,Alan

		Yr	Tm	W	L	Sv	IP	K	ERA	WHIP	OBA	vL	vR	BF/G	H%	S%	xERA	G	L	F	Ctl	Dom	Cmd	hr/f	hr/9	RAR	BPV	R$
LH	Reliever	03	BOS	4	1	1	55	45	4.25	1.18	240	263	221	3.5	29%	65%	3.81	44	20	37	2.6	7.4	2.8	9%	0.8	1.8	86	$7
Age	38	04	BOS	2	2	0	53	37	4.07	1.15	250	240	247	3.0	28%	69%	3.99	38	24	38	1.9	6.3	3.4	11%	1.2	2.4	78	$5
Decline		05	2AL	2	5	1	52	38	7.62	1.46	297	320	278	3.4	32%	48%	4.23	40	23	36	2.4	6.6	2.7	16%	1.7	-20.8	40	($1)
Type	FB	06	SD	4	3	0	52	53	3.28	1.25	254	240	258	3.0	33%	75%	3.47	43	20	37	2.6	9.2	3.5	8%	0.7	7.7	113	$7
Reliability	13	07	OAK	1	2	17	68	51	3.97	1.26	259	205	278	4.2	31%	69%	4.44	34	20	45	2.5	6.8	2.7	5%	0.7	4.5	80	$11
ERA Potl	60%	1st Half		1	1	8	36	28	4.25	1.33	272			4.1	33%	67%	4.55	27	27	46	2.5	7.0	2.8	4%	0.5	1.1	86	$5
LIMA Plan	C+	2nd Half		0	1	9	32	23	3.66	1.19	243			4.2	28%	71%	4.30	42	12	45	2.5	6.5	2.6	7%	0.8	3.4	74	$6
+/- Score	-19	08	Proj	2	3	5	63	48	3.60	1.26	260			3.6	30%	75%	4.17	39	20	41	2.4	6.9	2.8	9%	1.0	2.5	73	$7

Has long had the Cmd and BPV to close, and finally got the chance to prove it. FB% spike was caused by facing more RH (1.30 G/F vs. LH, 0.50 vs. RH); should regress with return to setup, keeping him LIMA-worthy.

Escobar,Kelvim

		Yr	Tm	W	L	Sv	IP	K	ERA	WHIP	OBA	vL	vR	BF/G	H%	S%	xERA	G	L	F	Ctl	Dom	Cmd	hr/f	hr/9	RAR	BPV	R$
RH	Starter	03	TOR	13	9	4	180	159	4.30	1.48	271	233	308	19.3	33%	72%	4.01	47	22	31	3.9	8.0	2.0	9%	0.8	5.0	69	$16
Age	32	04	ANA	11	12	0	208	191	3.94	1.29	247	252	236	26.5	30%	72%	3.93	43	17	40	3.3	8.3	2.5	9%	0.9	12.7	81	$19
Peak		05	ANA	3	2	1	59	63	3.04	1.11	212	278	138	14.9	28%	74%	3.31	47	15	38	3.2	9.6	3.0	7%	0.6	9.7	115	$9
Type	Pwr	06	LAA	11	14	0	189	147	3.62	1.28	265	258	270	26.5	31%	74%	3.93	45	19	36	2.4	7.0	2.9	8%	0.8	21.9	81	$20
Reliability	47	07	LAA	18	7	0	196	160	3.40	1.27	248	264	233	27.3	30%	73%	4.06	44	17	39	3.0	7.4	2.4	5%	0.5	26.6	85	$25
ERA Potl	55%	1st Half		9	3	0	96	78	2.81	1.11	228			27.7	28%	75%	3.69	47	17	36	2.5	7.3	2.9	4%	0.4	20.0	103	$15
LIMA Plan	C	2nd Half		9	4	0	100	82	3.97	1.41	266			27.0	32%	72%	4.42	41	18	41	3.5	7.4	2.1	6%	0.6	6.6	71	$10
+/- Score	-8	08	Proj	14	9	0	189	156	3.63	1.25	250			23.8	30%	73%	3.91	44	18	38	2.8	7.4	2.7	8%	0.8	13.6	82	$22

Jump in R$ was about better run support, not better skills. Sharp 2H decline likely caused by knee and shoulder ailments, so he should bounce back. But it's a reminder that health is always an issue with him.

Eyre,Scott

		Yr	Tm	W	L	Sv	IP	K	ERA	WHIP	OBA	vL	vR	BF/G	H%	S%	xERA	G	L	F	Ctl	Dom	Cmd	hr/f	hr/9	RAR	BPV	R$
LH	Reliever	03	SF	2	1	1	57	35	3.32	1.51	272	219	305	3.4	31%	79%	5.03	44	18	38	4.1	5.5	1.3	6%	0.6	6.8	43	$3
Age	35	04	SF	2	2	1	52	49	4.14	1.34	226	200	240	2.7	26%	74%	4.36	41	13	46	4.7	8.4	1.8	12%	1.4	0.8	57	$4
Decline		05	SF	2	2	0	68	65	2.64	1.09	200	182	213	3.2	26%	76%	3.84	38	18	43	3.4	8.6	2.5	4%	0.4	13.5	107	$9
Type	Pwr	06	CHC	1	3	0	61	73	3.39	1.49	261	273	261	3.6	33%	85%	3.63	42	20	38	4.4	10.8	2.4	18%	1.6	8.3	70	$4
Reliability	11	07	CHC	2	1	0	52	45	4.13	1.80	286	253	317	4.5	35%	77%	5.28	39	24	38	6.0	7.7	1.3	5%	0.5	1.9	56	$1
ERA Potl	50%	1st Half		0	1	0	26	25	6.92	2.19	347			5.5	43%	69%	5.52	33	31	36	6.2	8.7	1.4	9%	1.0	-8.0	35	($3)
LIMA Plan	B+	2nd Half		2	0	0	26	20	1.37	1.41	212			3.7	27%	89%	5.00	46	15	39	5.8	6.8	1.2	0%	0.0	9.9	78	$4
+/- Score	-26	08	Proj	2	2	0	58	53	3.57	1.52	258			3.8	32%	78%	4.52	40	20	39	4.8	8.2	1.7	8%	0.8	-0.9	65	$3

Dom regression hurt, but it was career-worst Ctl rate that really doomed him. His worst trait is inconsistency, particularly his yo-yoing Cmd. He's only posted 2+ Cmd three times in 11 years; don't bet on a fourth in 2008.

Eyre,Willie

		Yr	Tm	W	L	Sv	IP	K	ERA	WHIP	OBA	vL	vR	BF/G	H%	S%	xERA	G	L	F	Ctl	Dom	Cmd	hr/f	hr/9	RAR	BPV	R$
RH	Reliever	03	a/a	6	7	0	120	71	5.36	1.77	311			16.1	35%	69%	5.71				4.5	5.3	1.2		0.7	-14.4	29	($1)
Age	29	04	aaa	6	7	4	136	79	4.50	1.54	286			16.8	31%	72%	4.94				3.7	5.2	1.4		0.9	-2.7	32	$5
Peak		05	aaa	1	3	7	82	62	3.57	1.54	292			6.5	35%	76%	4.47				3.3	6.8	2.0		0.3	7.4	69	$5
Type		06	MIN	1	0	0	59	26	5.33	1.64	310	379	257	6.4	32%	70%	5.32	46	18	36	3.4	4.0	1.2	10%	1.2	-5.6	5	($1)
Reliability	21	07	TEX	4	6	1	68	42	5.16	1.62	289	248	323	9.4	32%	70%	5.04	45	19	36	4.2	5.6	1.3	10%	1.1	-5.5	26	$2
ERA Potl	50%	1st Half		2	3	1	41	27	3.29	1.24	242			8.5	27%	78%	4.32	47	15	38	3.1	5.9	1.9	10%	1.1	6.1	50	$5
LIMA Plan	C+	2nd Half		2	3	0	27	15	8.00	2.19	350			10.6	38%	63%	6.24	43	25	32	6.0	5.0	0.8	9%	1.0	-11.6	2	($3)
+/- Score	-19	08	Proj	0	1	0	10	6	5.40	1.70	299			9.2	33%	69%	5.25	45	20	35	4.5	5.4	1.2	8%	0.9	-0.9	26	($0)

Expected to miss all of 2008 after Tommy John surgery.

Farnsworth,Kyle

		Yr	Tm	W	L	Sv	IP	K	ERA	WHIP	OBA	vL	vR	BF/G	H%	S%	xERA	G	L	F	Ctl	Dom	Cmd	hr/f	hr/9	RAR	BPV	R$
RH	Reliever	03	CHC	3	2	0	76	92	3.32	1.17	198	189	199	4.0	28%	73%	3.11	44	25	31	4.3	10.9	2.6	11%	0.7	9.0	113	$9
Age	32	04	CHC	4	5	0	66	78	4.76	1.51	264	267	255	4.1	34%	72%	3.85	40	19	41	4.5	10.6	2.4	14%	1.4	-4.1	75	$4
Peak		05	2TM	1	1	16	70	87	2.19	1.01	182	198	165	3.8	26%	82%	2.91	43	21	36	3.5	11.2	3.2	9%	0.6	18.3	134	$16
Type	Pwr xFB	06	NYY	3	6	6	66	75	4.36	1.36	250	215	264	3.9	33%	71%	3.81	34	22	44	3.8	10.2	2.7	11%	1.1	1.6	90	$8
Reliability	11	07	NYY	2	1	0	60	48	4.80	1.45	262	273	242	4.1	30%	71%	5.02	30	19	51	4.1	7.2	1.8	10%	1.4	-2.2	43	$3
ERA Potl	55%	1st Half		0	1	0	31	20	4.94	1.61	280			4.3	31%	70%	5.72	32	19	49	4.6	5.8	1.3	6%	0.9	-1.6	34	($0)
LIMA Plan	B+	2nd Half		2	0	0	29	28	4.66	1.28	241			3.9	27%	71%	4.32	28	18	54	3.4	8.7	2.5	14%	1.9	-0.5	56	$3
+/- Score	-9	08	Proj	2	2	0	58	57	4.19	1.33	241			4.0	29%	72%	4.21	33	20	47	3.9	8.8	2.3	11%	1.2	2.0	70	$5

Recipe for losing your setup job: Mix declining Cmd with liberal number of fly balls. Watch ERA rise. Dom loss is most alarming part. Has averaged 71 G per year since '03; maybe he's just gassed. Bid cautiously, if at all.

Feliciano,Pedro

		Yr	Tm	W	L	Sv	IP	K	ERA	WHIP	OBA	vL	vR	BF/G	H%	S%	xERA	G	L	F	Ctl	Dom	Cmd	hr/f	hr/9	RAR	BPV	R$
LH	Reliever	03	NYM *	3	2	1	70	57	3.97	1.47	277	304	259	8.1	32%	76%	4.68				3.5	7.3	2.1		1.0	2.7	57	$4
Age	31	04	NYM *	5	4	2	53	34	6.79	1.62	280			4.5	31%	58%	5.26				4.8	5.8	1.2		1.2	-16.5	24	$0
Peak		05	JPN	3	2	0	37	38	4.83	1.31	236			4.2	26%	71%	4.64				3.9	9.2	2.4		2.0	-2.4	52	$3
Type	Pwr GB	06	NYM	7	2	0	60	54	2.10	1.26	248	231	266	3.9	31%	86%	3.49	49	21	29	3.0	8.1	2.7	8%	0.6	17.7	93	$10
Reliability	24	07	NYM	2	2	2	64	61	3.09	1.22	207	168	221	3.4	27%	75%	3.43	56	17	27	4.4	8.6	2.0	7%	0.4	10.5	94	$7
ERA Potl	55%	1st Half		1	1	0	28	24	1.61	1.07	168			3.2	21%	86%	3.51	59	13	28	4.5	7.7	1.7	5%	0.3	9.7	94	$4
LIMA Plan	B+	2nd Half		1	1	2	36	37	4.25	1.33	234			3.6	31%	67%	3.36	53	21	26	4.2	9.2	2.2	8%	0.5	0.8	94	$3
+/- Score	-6	08	Proj	4	2	0	63	59	3.43	1.27	230			3.8	29%	74%	3.48	53	19	28	3.9	8.4	2.2	8%	0.6	7.2	88	$7

The GB% growth was nice, the Ctl slide was not. But the net effect is a wash, as consistent back-to-back xERAs and BPVs show. Given history, walks aren't going away, so be careful in case the grounders do.

BRANDON KRUSE

Flores,Randy	Yr	Tm	W	L	Sv	IP	K	ERA	WHIP	OBA	vL	vR	BF/G	H%	S%	xERA	G	L	F	Ctl	Dom	Cmd	hr/f	hr/9	RAR	BPV	R$
LH Reliever	03	aaa	10	8	0	142	94	7.28	1.92	335			24.6	36%	64%	7.41				4.5	5.9	1.3		1.7	-50.7	0	($7)
Age 32	04	STL *	6	7	2	136	86	4.10	1.43	276			13.2	31%	72%	4.23				3.2	5.7	1.8		0.7	2.7	51	$7
Peak	05	STL	3	1	1	41	43	3.50	1.21	242	173	304	3.4	30%	76%	3.34	43	22	35	2.8	9.4	3.3	13%	1.1	3.8	100	$5
Type Pwr	06	STL	1	1	0	41	40	5.68	1.72	297	258	329	2.9	37%	68%	4.61	39	22	39	4.8	8.7	1.8	10%	1.1	-6.1	54	($0)
Reliability 14	07	STL	3	0	1	55	47	4.25	1.56	314	326	299	3.5	39%	71%	4.19	41	23	37	2.5	7.7	3.1	3%	0.3	1.2	94	$3
ERA Potl 60%	1st Half		1	0	1	28	24	5.14	1.61	325			3.5	40%	67%	4.09	41	25	34	2.3	7.7	3.4	6%	0.6	-2.5	89	$1
LIMA Plan B+	2nd Half		2	0	0	27	23	3.33	1.52	302			3.5	38%	76%	4.30	40	20	39	2.7	7.7	2.9	0%	0.0	3.6	101	$2
+/- Score 14	08	Proj	3	1	0	58	52	4.50	1.55	297			3.6	37%	71%	4.24	40	22	38	3.3	8.1	2.5	6%	0.6	1.1	77	$3

These are not trends you want in a LH reliever's stats vs. LHB: '05: .173 BA, 11 Dom, 3.7 Cmd '06: .258 BA, 8.4 Dom, 2.3 Cmd '07: .326 BA, 6.1 Dom, 2.1 Cmd H% regression will help, but he's simply too volatile to roster.

Floyd,Gavin	Yr	Tm	W	L	Sv	IP	K	ERA	WHIP	OBA	vL	vR	BF/G	H%	S%	xERA	G	L	F	Ctl	Dom	Cmd	hr/f	hr/9	RAR	BPV	R$
RH Starter	03		0	0	0	0	0	0.00	0.00											0.0	0.0						
Age 25	04	a/a	7	9	0	149	104	3.16	1.26	243			25.0	29%	75%	3.24				3.2	6.3	1.9		0.5	21.8	71	$14
Growth	05	PHI *	7	11	0	163	103	7.33	1.67	297	283	283	24.1	33%	55%	5.26	42	19	39	4.2	5.7	1.3	8%	1.0	-62.0	29	($7)
Type	06	PHI *	11	7	0	169	105	6.81	1.74	317	306	323	28.1	34%	62%	5.19	39	24	37	3.9	5.6	1.4	13%	1.5	-48.5	11	($4)
Reliability 11	07	CHW *	8	8	0	176	134	4.70	1.44	285	314	286	23.3	32%	72%	4.35	42	17	41	2.8	6.8	2.4	13%	1.5	-4.2	44	$10
ERA Potl 45%	1st Half		6	3	0	88	66	4.19	1.44	289			27.4	33%	74%					2.7	6.8	2.5		1.0	3.4	60	$7
LIMA Plan C+	2nd Half		2	5	0	88	68	5.20	1.43	281			20.2	30%	71%	4.30	42	17	41	3.0	6.9	2.3	18%	2.0	-7.6	29	$3
+/- Score 16	08	Proj	6	6	0	122	88	5.53	1.48	291			24.4	32%	65%	4.51	41	19	40	3.0	6.5	2.2	12%	1.4	-0.3	40	$4

1-5, 5.27 ERA in 70 IP at CHW. For years, we've been harping on Cmd, Cmd, Cmd; he finally delivered, and ERA dropped two runs. Now we'll start harping on FB%. Needs to fix that to become rosterable, but worth a late flyer.

Fogg,Josh	Yr	Tm	W	L	Sv	IP	K	ERA	WHIP	OBA	vL	vR	BF/G	H%	S%	xERA	G	L	F	Ctl	Dom	Cmd	hr/f	hr/9	RAR	BPV	R$
RH Starter	03	PIT	10	9	0	142	71	5.26	1.45	293	320	273	23.0	30%	67%	4.73	46	17	37	2.5	4.5	1.8	12%	1.4	-17.2	19	$5
Age 31	04	PIT	11	10	0	178	82	4.65	1.45	278	282	285	24.3	30%	69%	4.94	48	18	34	3.3	4.1	1.2	8%	0.9	-8.5	25	$7
Peak	05	PIT	6	11	0	169	85	5.06	1.47	291	340	249	21.8	30%	69%	4.97	41	21	38	2.8	4.5	1.6	12%	1.4	-16.9	14	$2
Type Con	06	COL	11	9	0	172	93	5.49	1.55	298	309	291	24.8	32%	67%	4.98	43	20	37	3.1	4.9	1.6	11%	1.3	-21.4	19	$4
Reliability 81	07	COL	10	9	0	166	94	4.94	1.53	293	279	305	24.6	31%	70%	5.05	40	20	40	3.2	5.1	1.6	10%	1.2	-10.6	23	$5
ERA Potl 40%	1st Half		3	6	0	77	48	4.79	1.52	293			24.4	32%	71%	4.95	36	24	40	3.2	5.6	1.8	10%	1.2	-3.5	32	$2
LIMA Plan D+	2nd Half		7	3	0	89	46	5.07	1.53	294			24.7	31%	70%	5.13	43	16	40	3.2	4.7	1.4	11%	1.3	-7.1	15	$3
+/- Score -18	08	Proj	7	10	0	153	82	5.12	1.52	293			24.2	31%	69%	5.01	42	20	39	3.1	4.8	1.5	11%	1.3	-11.6	19	$3

Amazingly reliable, with xERAs flat-lining in more ways than one. No longer has the GB profile to offset his low Dom, and while he hasn't imploded thus far, it wouldn't take much for it to happen. Duck and cover.

Fossum,Casey	Yr	Tm	W	L	Sv	IP	K	ERA	WHIP	OBA	vL	vR	BF/G	H%	S%	xERA	G	L	F	Ctl	Dom	Cmd	hr/f	hr/9	RAR	BPV	R$
LH Reliever	03	BOS *	7	6	2	96	80	5.53	1.50	274	230	286	15.7	32%	64%	4.82	33	21	46	3.9	7.5	1.9	8%	1.0	-11.9	54	$5
Age 30	04	ARI *	6	16	0	161	134	5.98	1.60	293	257	316	22.8	33%	67%	4.49	41	21	38	3.9	7.5	1.9	16%	1.7	-34.1	30	($0)
Peak	05	TAM	8	12	0	162	128	4.94	1.42	271	234	278	19.5	31%	67%	4.37	39	22	39	3.3	7.1	2.1	11%	1.2	-11.3	53	$8
Type	06	TAM	6	6	0	130	88	5.33	1.53	271	271	263	23.1	30%	67%	4.68	46	21	33	4.4	6.1	1.4	13%	1.2	-12.4	29	$4
Reliability 50	07	TAM	5	8	0	76	53	7.70	1.79	337	320	336	8.9	37%	59%	4.61	45	23	32	3.2	6.3	2.0	17%	1.8	-29.9	13	($3)
ERA Potl 60%	1st Half		5	7	0	62	39	7.40	1.74	337			12.6	36%	59%	4.60	46	22	32	2.8	5.7	2.1	15%	1.6	-22.2	17	($2)
LIMA Plan D	2nd Half		0	1	0	14	14	9.00	2.00	336			4.1	39%	58%	4.67	36	30	34	5.1	9.0	1.8	26%	2.6	-7.8	1	($2)
+/- Score 94	08	Proj	1	3	0	29	21	5.59	1.55	294			9.3	33%	66%	4.51	41	24	34	3.4	6.5	1.9	12%	1.2	-0.1	38	$0

Bad luck season capped off a long fall from 2002 glory days. Still a few signs of hope: Cmd isn't awful, FB% is down, and xERA is close to average. But when that's the best you can say, you're scraping bottom.

Francisco,Frank	Yr	Tm	W	L	Sv	IP	K	ERA	WHIP	OBA	vL	vR	BF/G	H%	S%	xERA	G	L	F	Ctl	Dom	Cmd	hr/f	hr/9	RAR	BPV	R$
RH Reliever	03	aa	2	3	0	35	18	11.79	2.11	357			25.2	37%	42%	8.37				4.9	4.6	0.9		1.8	-32.0	-23	($7)
Age 28	04	TEX *	6	5	6	68	84	3.30	1.23	186	247	165	4.7	27%	75%	4.05	28	19	54	5.3	11.1	2.1	6%	0.7	9.5	109	$12
Pre-Peak	05	TEX	0	0	0	0	0	0.00	0.00											0.0	0.0						
Type Pwr FB	06	TEX *	0	1	0	22	25	3.26	1.22	243		444	4.4	31%	79%	3.13	50	13	38	2.9	10.2	3.6	14%	1.2	3.5	106	$2
Reliability 0	07	TEX	1	1	0	59	49	4.55	1.60	254	221	286	4.5	31%	71%	5.30	35	22	43	5.8	7.4	1.3	4%	0.5	-0.3	62	$2
ERA Potl 55%	1st Half		1	0	0	29	19	4.03	1.34	248			4.6	28%	70%	4.93	37	19	44	3.7	5.9	1.6	5%	0.6	1.7	55	$2
LIMA Plan B	2nd Half		0	1	0	30	30	5.05	1.85	260			4.5	34%	71%	5.70	33	25	42	7.7	8.9	1.2	3%	0.3	-2.0	72	($0)
+/- Score -11	08	Proj	3	3	0	58	54	4.81	1.57	252			4.6	31%	70%	4.90	37	20	43	5.6	8.4	1.5	7%	0.8	-2.9	63	$3

2006 Ctl, Cmd look like outliers (especially since it was only 22 IP). And without the Ctl, he's just another hard thrower with no idea where the ball's actually going. Reliability score, xERA are like big "Keep Out" signs.

Francis,Jeff	Yr	Tm	W	L	Sv	IP	K	ERA	WHIP	OBA	vL	vR	BF/G	H%	S%	xERA	G	L	F	Ctl	Dom	Cmd	hr/f	hr/9	RAR	BPV	R$
LH Starter	03		0	0	0	0	0	0.00	0.00											0.0	0.0						
Age 27	04	a/a	16	3	0	154	164	2.80	1.00	225			25.2	29%	77%	2.80				1.6	9.6	5.9		1.0	29.3	161	$27
Growth	05	COL	14	12	0	183	128	5.70	1.51	306	285	317	25.2	34%	67%	4.81	40	22	38	3.4	6.3	1.8	11%	1.3	-32.8	32	$3
Type	06	COL	13	11	0	199	117	4.16	1.29	250	241	252	26.2	28%	69%	4.53	45	19	36	3.1	5.3	1.7	8%	0.8	8.0	48	$16
Reliability 79	07	COL	17	9	0	215	165	4.22	1.38	278	242	289	27.2	32%	72%	4.13	44	18	37	2.6	6.9	2.6	10%	1.0	5.4	64	$18
ERA Potl 55%	1st Half		7	5	0	104	72	3.81	1.35	275			27.7	31%	74%	4.24	45	18	37	2.5	6.2	2.5	8%	0.9	7.9	64	$9
LIMA Plan C	2nd Half		10	4	0	111	93	4.61	1.41	282			26.8	33%	70%	4.03	44	19	37	2.7	7.5	2.7	12%	1.2	-2.5	65	$9
+/- Score 13	08	Proj	17	10	0	218	168	4.10	1.35	271			26.5	31%	72%	4.09	44	19	37	2.7	7.0	2.6	10%	1.0	8.2	66	$19

Four reasons to feel optimistic:
- Three years of Ctl growth
- Strong Dom rebound
- Best Cmd in his ML career
- xERA trend, including 2H mark that almost edged under 4.00

UP: Actual ERA under 4.00.

Franklin,Ryan	Yr	Tm	W	L	Sv	IP	K	ERA	WHIP	OBA	vL	vR	BF/G	H%	S%	xERA	G	L	F	Ctl	Dom	Cmd	hr/f	hr/9	RAR	BPV	R$
RH Reliever	03	SEA	11	13	0	212	99	3.57	1.23	250	267	233	27.5	25%	78%	5.20	35	15	51	2.6	4.2	1.6	10%	1.4	25.1	21	$19
Age 35	04	SEA	4	16	0	200	104	4.90	1.42	284	275	297	27.2	29%	70%	5.16	35	20	45	2.7	4.7	1.7	11%	1.5	-11.6	18	$4
Past Peak	05	SEA	8	15	0	190	93	5.11	1.44	283	266	295	25.9	29%	67%	5.10	42	16	42	2.9	4.4	1.5	10%	1.3	-17.3	16	$5
Type Con	06	2NL	6	7	0	77	43	4.55	1.54	283	265	294	5.2	30%	75%	4.91	47	18	35	3.9	5.0	1.3	14%	1.5	-0.6	10	$4
Reliability 36	07	STL	4	4	1	80	44	3.04	1.01	237	238	231	4.6	25%	74%	3.77	48	18	34	1.2	5.0	4.0	9%	0.9	13.7	94	$10
ERA Potl 40%	1st Half		2	0	0	38	13	1.42	0.87	219			4.4	23%	87%	3.90	50	18	32	0.7	3.1	4.3	5%	0.5	14.1	107	$6
LIMA Plan D+	2nd Half		2	4	1	42	31	4.50	1.14	252			4.7	28%	64%	3.64	47	18	35	1.7	6.6	3.9	13%	1.3	-0.4	87	$4
+/- Score -25	08	Proj	4	5	0	73	40	3.97	1.26	260			6.1	27%	73%	4.37	46	18	37	2.4	5.0	2.1	12%	1.2	0.2	40	$6

Couldn't raise his Dom, so he lowered his Ctl. But the third-lowest Ctl rate among full-time pitchers?? LaRussa/Duncan may be miracle workers, but even they can't maintain this. Expect regression.

Frasor,Jason	Yr	Tm	W	L	Sv	IP	K	ERA	WHIP	OBA	vL	vR	BF/G	H%	S%	xERA	G	L	F	Ctl	Dom	Cmd	hr/f	hr/9	RAR	BPV	R$
RH Reliever	03	aa	1	0	17	36	38	4.23	1.69	301			4.8	40%	75%	5.10				4.2	9.4	2.2		0.5	0.7	83	$7
Age 30	04	TOR	4	6	17	68	54	4.10	1.47	250	232	274	4.7	30%	72%	4.54	47	19	35	4.8	7.1	1.5	6%	0.5	2.8	63	$10
Peak	05	TOR	3	5	1	74	62	3.27	1.28	243	236	257	4.7	29%	78%	3.77	50	18	32	3.4	7.5	2.2	12%	1.0	10.0	69	$8
Type Pwr	06	TOR *	6	3	1	70	81	4.50	1.49	265	211	262	4.5	34%	73%	3.59	43	23	34	4.2	10.4	2.5	16%	1.3	0.5	78	$7
Reliability 28	07	TOR	1	5	3	57	59	4.58	1.23	226	245	200	4.6	30%	61%	3.54	45	19	36	3.6	9.3	2.6	6%	0.5	-0.5	105	$6
ERA Potl 75%	1st Half		1	2	2	34	34	2.91	1.06	187			4.8	24%	74%	3.40	50	14	36	3.7	9.0	2.4	7%	0.5	6.7	107	$6
LIMA Plan B+	2nd Half		0	3	1	23	25	7.04	1.48	278			4.4	38%	48%	3.74	40	25	35	3.5	9.8	2.8	4%	0.4	-7.2	105	$0
+/- Score 41	08	Proj	3	3	5	58	60	3.72	1.29	234			4.4	30%	73%	3.62	45	21	35	3.9	9.3	2.4	9%	0.8	6.3	91	$8

ERA says this was his worst season, skills say it was his best. Guess which one we believe? 2nd half bad luck means you can probably get a LIMA reliever with closer experience for a buck.

Fuentes,Brian	Yr	Tm	W	L	Sv	IP	K	ERA	WHIP	OBA	vL	vR	BF/G	H%	S%	xERA	G	L	F	Ctl	Dom	Cmd	hr/f	hr/9	RAR	BPV	R$
LH Reliever	03	COL	3	3	4	75	82	2.76	1.31	232	238	227	4.2	31%	82%	3.92	32	25	43	4.1	9.8	2.4	8%	0.8	14.0	93	$10
Age 32	04	COL	2	4	0	44	48	5.70	1.47	270	213	300	4.1	35%	62%	4.06	34	23	44	3.9	9.8	2.5	9%	1.0	-7.8	82	$1
Peak	05	COL	2	5	31	74	91	2.91	1.26	220	167	236	4.0	31%	79%	3.33	38	26	36	4.1	11.1	2.7	9%	0.7	12.2	112	$18
Type Pwr FB	06	COL	3	4	30	65	73	3.46	1.17	214	186	217	4.0	28%	75%	3.73	35	16	50	3.6	10.1	2.8	10%	1.1	8.3	99	$18
Reliability 48	07	COL	3	5	20	61	56	3.08	1.13	210	204	207	3.9	25%	76%	3.95	36	21	43	3.4	8.2	2.4	9%	0.9	10.2	87	$14
ERA Potl 50%	1st Half		0	2	20	34	26	2.38	1.03	220			3.7	25%	84%	3.98	33	23	44	2.1	6.9	3.3	9%	1.1	8.6	89	$11
LIMA Plan B	2nd Half		3	3	0	27	30	3.96	1.25	198			4.1	27%	69%	3.89	40	18	42	4.9	9.9	2.0	7%	0.7	1.6	97	$4
+/- Score -13	08	Proj	4	6	8	73	76	3.35	1.20	215			4.0	28%	75%	3.82	36	20	44	3.8	9.4	2.5	9%	0.9	5.1	94	$11

Three-year slides in Dom, xERA and BPV, but biggest crime was simply being less skilled than Manny Corpas (and maybe being a lefty). This is still a closer-worthy skill set, albeit one fraying around the edges.

BRANDON KRUSE

Fultz,Aaron		Yr	Tm	W	L	Sv	IP	K	ERA	WHIP	OBA	vL	vR	BF/G	H%	S%	xERA	G	L	F	Ctl	Dom	Cmd	hr/f	hr/9	RAR	BPV	R$
LH Reliever		03	TEX	1	3	0	67	53	5.24	1.52	284	218	345	4.7	33%	68%	4.22	46	21	32	3.6	7.1	**2.0**	13%	1.2	-5.9	46	$1
Age	34	04	MIN	3	3	1	50	37	5.04	1.46	262	212	314	4.0	30%	66%	4.73	42	18	40	4.1	6.7	**1.6**	8%	0.9	-3.7	49	$3
Past Peak		05	PHI	4	0	0	72	54	2.25	0.97	188	220	170	4.5	22%	81%	3.89	40	22	39	2.9	6.7	**2.3**	8%	0.7	17.8	85	$11
Type	Pwr	06	PHI	3	1	0	71	62	4.56	1.52	285	277	293	4.8	35%	71%	4.38	38	23	39	3.5	7.8	**2.2**	8%	0.9	-0.6	65	$3
Reliability	13	07	CLE	4	3	0	37	28	2.92	1.32	229	191	265	3.2	28%	79%	4.83	35	22	43	4.4	6.8	**1.6**	4%	0.5	7.2	68	$5
ERA Potl	45%	1st Half		3	1	0	21	17	1.71	1.00	157			2.6	19%	85%	4.56	28	21	51	4.3	7.3	**1.7**	4%	0.4	7.2	90	$5
LIMA Plan	C+	2nd Half		1	2	0	16	11	4.50	1.75	307			4.4	36%	74%	5.15	43	22	35	4.5	6.2	**1.4**	5%	0.6	0.0	43	$0
+/- Score	-54	08	Proj	**3**	**2**	**0**	**44**	**32**	**4.14**	**1.43**	**255**			**4.0**	**30%**	**71%**	**4.77**	**39**	**22**	**40**	**4.1**	**6.6**	**1.6**	**6%**	**0.6**	**-1.5**	**59**	**$3**

Manager's refusal to use him in post-season spoke volumes. High strand rate hiding skill erosion. 3 year Ctl trend limiting effectiveness. Falling GB rate also portends more struggles ahead.

Gabbard,Kason		Yr	Tm	W	L	Sv	IP	K	ERA	WHIP	OBA	vL	vR	BF/G	H%	S%	xERA	G	L	F	Ctl	Dom	Cmd	hr/f	hr/9	RAR	BPV	R$
LH Starter		03		0	0	0	0	0	0.00	0.00																		
Age	26	04	aa	3	6	0	53	30	7.47	1.77	316			17.8	35%	56%	5.95				4.2	5.1	**1.2**		0.8	-20.5	22	($3)
Growth		05	aa	9	11	0	132	80	6.18	1.69	295			22.6	33%	63%	5.30				4.6	5.4	**1.2**		0.8	-30.5	30	($1)
Type	Pwr xGB	06	BOS	* 11	12	0	150	113	4.98	1.49	265			22.8	31%	67%	3.92	58	18	24	4.2	6.8	**1.6**	14%	0.9	-7.9	48	$9
Reliability	5	07	2AL	* 13	3	0	156	109	4.57	1.38	252	236	230	23.2	28%	69%	4.09	55	16	30	3.9	6.3	**1.6**	13%	1.1	-1.3	43	$13
ERA Potl	50%	1st Half		8	2	0	83	64	4.66	1.51	282			23.0	32%	73%	4.31	46	19	35	3.6	6.9	**1.9**	13%	1.3	-1.6	42	$6
LIMA Plan	C	2nd Half		5	1	0	73	45	4.47	1.24	216			23.5	24%	65%	4.18	56	15	29	4.2	5.6	**1.3**	11%	0.9	0.4	47	$6
+/- Score	15	08	Proj	**11**	**11**	**0**	**174**	**117**	**4.76**	**1.48**	**265**			**23.9**	**30%**	**69%**	**4.27**	**56**	**16**	**29**	**4.1**	**6.1**	**1.5**	**11%**	**0.9**	**4.8**	**41**	**$10**

6-1, 4.65 ERA in 81 IP at BOS and TEX. 2nd half's 1.3 Cmd eerily like AA, but nobody said pitching in TEX would be easy. With 1H Cmd, 2H GB%, and health, he would do fine. Odds are he won't get all three.

Gagne,Eric		Yr	Tm	W	L	Sv	IP	K	ERA	WHIP	OBA	vL	vR	BF/G	H%	S%	xERA	G	L	F	Ctl	Dom	Cmd	hr/f	hr/9	RAR	BPV	R$
RH Reliever		03	LA	2	3	55	82	137	1.21	0.70	138	130	135	3.8	27%	84%	1.64	38	33	29	2.2	15.0	**6.9**	5%	0.2	31.1	255	$37
Age	32	04	LA	7	3	45	82	114	2.19	0.91	186	233	129	4.5	29%	79%	2.47	42	18	40	2.4	12.5	**5.2**	7%	0.5	21.0	185	$30
Peak		05	LA	1	0	8	13	22	2.75	0.99	213	217	185	3.7	35%	82%	1.80	52	11	37	2.1	15.1	**7.3**	22%	1.4	2.4	216	$5
Type	Pwr	06	LA	0	0	1	2	3	0.00	0.50	0			3.4	0%		2.64	33	0	67	4.5	13.5	**3.0**	0%		1.1	199	$1
Reliability	0	07	2AL	4	2	16	52	51	3.81	1.35	250	224	265	4.1	32%	72%	3.98	39	22	39	3.6	8.8	**2.4**	5%	0.5	4.5	93	$11
ERA Potl	60%	1st Half		2	0	8	22	20	1.23	1.00	162			3.7	21%	90%	3.90	39	20	41	4.1	8.2	**2.0**	5%	0.4	8.9	101	$7
LIMA Plan	B	2nd Half		2	2	8	30	31	5.70	1.60	304			4.4	40%	63%	4.03	38	24	38	3.3	9.3	**2.8**	6%	0.6	-4.4	91	$4
+/- Score	9	08	Proj	**3**	**3**	**23**	**58**	**58**	**3.72**	**1.28**	**234**			**4.3**	**30%**	**72%**	**3.78**	**42**	**20**	**38**	**3.7**	**9.0**	**2.4**	**8%**	**0.8**	**5.1**	**90**	**$14**

BOS collapse and shoulder woes will depress his draft value. Dom shows that this is not the same pitcher, but BPV is still elite. Minimal investment could pay dividends, especially if he lands a closer's job.

Gallardo,Yovani		Yr	Tm	W	L	Sv	IP	K	ERA	WHIP	OBA	vL	vR	BF/G	H%	S%	xERA	G	L	F	Ctl	Dom	Cmd	hr/f	hr/9	RAR	BPV	R$
RH Starter		03		0	0	0	0	0	0.00	0.00																		
Age	22	04		0	0	0	0	0	0.00	0.00																		
Green		05		0	0	0	0	0	0.00	0.00																		
Type	Pwr	06	aa	5	2	0	77	80	2.22	1.15	214			24.1	29%	81%	2.36				3.4	9.3	**2.7**		0.3	21.8	115	$12
Reliability	0	07	MIL	* 17	8	0	188	211	3.56	1.19	232	247	244	23.4	32%	71%	3.37	38	24	38	3.1	10.1	**3.3**	7%	0.6	20.1	120	$26
ERA Potl	60%	1st Half		9	3	0	90	112	3.59	1.18	218			24.6	31%	70%	3.06	35	32	32	3.5	11.2	**3.2**	9%	0.6	9.3	128	$14
LIMA Plan	C+	2nd Half		8	5	0	97	99	3.52	1.21	244			22.3	32%	72%	3.56	39	23	39	2.7	9.2	**3.4**	6%	0.6	10.8	114	$12
+/- Score	40	08	Proj	**14**	**6**	**0**	**174**	**191**	**3.47**	**1.18**	**226**			**23.8**	**30%**	**73%**	**3.42**	**38**	**23**	**38**	**3.2**	**9.9**	**3.1**	**9%**	**0.8**	**21.0**	**111**	**$23**

9-5, 3.67 ERA in 110 IP at MIL. Effective Cmd at every level. Skills support '07 and indicate even better future. Turn a few FB to GB and he could be a future ace.
UP: 20 wins, sub-3.00 ERA

Garcia,Freddy		Yr	Tm	W	L	Sv	IP	K	ERA	WHIP	OBA	vL	vR	BF/G	H%	S%	xERA	G	L	F	Ctl	Dom	Cmd	hr/f	hr/9	RAR	BPV	R$
RH Starter		03	SEA	12	14	0	201	144	4.52	1.33	257	281	223	25.9	28%	70%	4.42	41	18	41	3.2	6.4	**2.0**	12%	1.4	0.1	43	$15
Age	31	04	2AL	13	11	0	210	184	3.81	1.22	245	236	248	28.0	29%	71%	3.82	43	17	40	2.7	7.9	**2.9**	9%	0.9	16.0	85	$21
Peak		05	CHW	14	8	0	228	146	3.87	1.25	259	268	249	28.8	29%	72%	3.93	49	21	31	2.4	5.8	**2.4**	12%	1.0	14.2	58	$20
Type		06	CHW	17	9	0	216	135	4.54	1.28	272	262	271	27.5	29%	68%	4.35	41	18	41	2.0	5.6	**2.8**	11%	1.3	0.5	53	$20
Reliability	43	07	PHI	1	5	0	58	50	5.90	1.60	312	292	339	23.9	35%	68%	4.28	36	27	38	2.9	7.8	**2.6**	17%	1.9	-10.5	39	($0)
ERA Potl	55%	1st Half		1	5	0	58	50	5.90	1.60	312			23.9	35%	68%	4.28	36	27	38	2.9	7.8	**2.6**	17%	1.9	-10.5	39	($0)
LIMA Plan	D	2nd Half		0	0	0	0	0	0.00	0.00																		
+/- Score	43	08	Proj	**1**	**2**	**0**	**29**	**18**	**4.66**	**1.38**	**275**			**24.9**	**30%**	**69%**	**4.52**	**42**	**21**	**37**	**2.8**	**5.6**	**2.0**	**11%**	**1.2**	**-0.4**	**38**	**$1**

Skills holding up well before labrum surgery. High h%, LD%, and hr/f ratio exacerbated problems. Expect him to pull a Pedro, returning in time for a September surge. May be worth a flyer if healthy.

Gardner,Lee		Yr	Tm	W	L	Sv	IP	K	ERA	WHIP	OBA	vL	vR	BF/G	H%	S%	xERA	G	L	F	Ctl	Dom	Cmd	hr/f	hr/9	RAR	BPV	R$
RH Reliever		03	aaa	3	7	30	62	45	5.13	1.64	329			5.0	37%	73%	6.46				2.3	6.5	**2.8**		1.6	-5.7	39	$11
Age	33	04	aaa	7	4	1	70	33	4.93	1.60	313			5.6	34%	70%	5.46				2.8	4.2	**1.5**		0.8	-5.1	24	$3
Peak		05	aaa	4	3	15	52	27	3.46	1.52	302			4.8	32%	83%	5.52				2.7	4.7	**1.7**		1.3	5.4	19	$8
Type	Con	06	aaa	5	5	30	61	37	4.02	1.24	251			4.4	29%	67%	3.23				2.6	5.4	**2.1**		0.5	3.7	67	$16
Reliability	4	07	FLA	* 3	6	3	87	59	2.62	1.20	256	308	208	5.1	31%	77%	4.22	43	18	40	2.1	6.1	**2.9**	2%	0.2	19.5	95	$10
ERA Potl	50%	1st Half		1	4	2	41	27	4.38	1.41	284			5.6	34%	67%	4.57	41	21	38	2.6	5.9	**2.3**	2%	0.2	0.2	74	$2
LIMA Plan	B	2nd Half		2	2	1	46	32	1.05	1.02	230			4.7	28%	90%	3.91	44	16	41	1.6	6.2	**3.8**	2%	0.2	19.3	120	$8
+/- Score	-37	08	Proj	**3**	**4**	**0**	**58**	**36**	**3.57**	**1.29**	**268**			**4.9**	**30%**	**74%**	**4.44**	**43**	**18**	**40**	**2.3**	**5.6**	**2.4**	**7%**	**0.8**	**-0.3**	**62**	**$5**

3-4, 1.94 ERA in 74 IP at FLA And there are post-Bull Durham prospects. This was his 3rd cup of coffee in 10-year pro career but this time he stuck around for some danish. Expect a shorter MLB stint than Jesse Orosco.

Garland,Jon		Yr	Tm	W	L	Sv	IP	K	ERA	WHIP	OBA	vL	vR	BF/G	H%	S%	xERA	G	L	F	Ctl	Dom	Cmd	hr/f	hr/9	RAR	BPV	R$
RH Starter		03	CHW	12	13	0	191	108	4.52	1.37	259	278	234	25.6	27%	71%	4.65	48	16	36	3.5	5.1	**1.5**	13%	1.3	0.0	25	$12
Age	28	04	CHW	12	11	0	217	113	4.89	1.38	267	269	277	27.4	27%	68%	4.79	46	17	38	3.2	4.7	**1.5**	12%	1.4	-12.4	19	$10
Pre-Peak		05	CHW	18	10	0	221	115	3.50	1.17	254	267	242	28.3	27%	74%	4.08	47	21	32	1.9	4.7	**2.4**	11%	1.1	23.7	52	$24
Type	Con	06	CHW	18	7	0	211	112	4.52	1.36	293	290	297	27.4	31%	69%	4.53	42	20	38	1.7	4.8	**2.7**	9%	1.1	1.0	49	$17
Reliability	82	07	CHW	10	13	0	208	98	4.23	1.33	272	259	281	27.6	29%	69%	4.85	39	23	38	2.5	4.2	**1.7**	7%	0.8	7.0	38	$13
ERA Potl	50%	1st Half		5	5	0	104	46	3.38	1.16	239			28.3	26%	72%	4.63	42	23	35	2.5	4.0	**1.6**	6%	0.6	14.5	46	$10
LIMA Plan	D+	2nd Half		5	8	0	104	52	5.09	1.49	302			27.0	32%	67%	5.05	37	23	40	2.4	4.5	**1.9**	8%	1.0	-7.5	30	$3
+/- Score	-25	08	Proj	**11**	**13**	**0**	**203**	**100**	**4.52**	**1.40**	**287**			**28.3**	**30%**	**70%**	**4.79**	**42**	**21**	**37**	**2.4**	**4.4**	**1.9**	**9%**	**1.0**	**-7.3**	**33**	**$11**

xERA trend tells the story of rising Ctl and declining GB%. Could have been worse, but increasingly lucky hr/9 hid the decline. Some will yearn for the return of '05's promise. You just stare at his 2nd half reality.

Garza,Matt		Yr	Tm	W	L	Sv	IP	K	ERA	WHIP	OBA	vL	vR	BF/G	H%	S%	xERA	G	L	F	Ctl	Dom	Cmd	hr/f	hr/9	RAR	BPV	R$
RH Starter		03		0	0	0	0	0	0.00	0.00																		
Age	24	04		0	0	0	0	0	0.00	0.00																		
Growth		05		0	0	0	0	0	0.00	0.00																		
Type	Pwr	06	MIN	* 12	9	0	141	123	4.15	1.30	255	245	356	23.8	31%	68%	4.12	35	25	40	3.0	7.8	**2.6**	6%	0.6	7.2	87	$16
Reliability	0	07	MIN	* 9	13	0	175	144	4.53	1.59	300	314	276	24.7	36%	72%	4.38	48	15	38	3.4	7.4	**2.1**	7%	0.7	-0.4	63	$8
ERA Potl	60%	1st Half		4	6	0	92	77	5.28	1.64	309			26.2	38%	67%					3.4	7.5	**2.2**		0.6	-8.8	67	$2
LIMA Plan	C+	2nd Half		5	7	0	83	67	3.69	1.54	291			23.1	35%	78%	4.36	48	15	38	3.5	7.3	**2.1**	8%	0.9	8.4	58	$6
+/- Score	26	08	Proj	**12**	**13**	**0**	**189**	**158**	**4.25**	**1.46**	**281**			**24.3**	**34%**	**72%**	**4.22**	**45**	**17**	**38**	**3.2**	**7.5**	**2.3**	**7%**	**0.7**	**6.3**	**71**	**$14**

3-7, 3.69 ERA in 83 IP at MIN. A solid debut, though his 3-7 record will cost him a few bid dollars this March. BPIs are not overwhelming, but serviceable, and there is upside.

Gaudin,Chad		Yr	Tm	W	L	Sv	IP	K	ERA	WHIP	OBA	vL	vR	BF/G	H%	S%	xERA	G	L	F	Ctl	Dom	Cmd	hr/f	hr/9	RAR	BPV	R$
RH Starter		03	TAM	* 4	0	0	59	44	2.59	1.12	220	269	218	13.2	26%	79%	4.38	28	28	44	2.9	6.7	**2.3**	5%	0.6	14.1	82	$9
Age	25	04	TAM	* 2	5	2	90	80	5.00	1.54	299	403	301	9.3	36%	70%	4.35	36	23	41	3.1	8.0	**2.6**	10%	1.1	-6.3	64	$3
Growth		05	TOR	* 10	11	0	163	117	4.64	1.36	285	481	462	24.9	32%	68%	3.97	40	29	31	2.2	6.5	**3.0**	12%	1.0	-5.4	68	$11
Type	Pwr	06	OAK	* 7	2	2	88	58	2.45	1.31	210	253	201	6.3	25%	81%	5.20	39	16	45	5.0	5.9	**1.2**	3%	0.3	22.9	64	$12
Reliability	0	07	OAK	11	13	0	199	154	4.43	1.53	267	282	250	26.1	31%	73%	4.31	51	19	30	4.5	7.0	**1.5**	12%	0.9	2.0	47	$11
ERA Potl	50%	1st Half		6	3	0	95	61	3.13	1.41	258			25.7	30%	78%	4.38	51	19	29	3.9	5.8	**1.5**	6%	0.5	16.2	55	$9
LIMA Plan	C	2nd Half		5	10	0	104	93	5.61	1.64	276			26.4	32%	68%	4.25	51	19	30	5.1	8.0	**1.6**	17%	1.4	-14.2	40	$2
+/- Score	14	08	Proj	**11**	**10**	**0**	**189**	**141**	**4.25**	**1.44**	**256**			**25.7**	**30%**	**72%**	**4.45**	**47**	**19**	**34**	**4.2**	**6.7**	**1.6**	**9%**	**0.8**	**1.0**	**53**	**$13**

4 reasons to avoid on draft day:
1. BPI decline at 25 is not good.
2. Workload spike from '06 may have taken its toll in the 2nd half.
3. Inconsistent: 35/35 DOM/DIS
4. Starter? Reliever? Pick a role and stick with it.

MATT BEAGLE

Geary,Geoff

	Yr	W	L	Sv	IP	K	ERA	WHIP	OBA	vL	vR	BF/G	H%	S%	xERA	G	L	F	Ctl	Dom	Cmd	hr/f	hr/9	RAR	BPV	R$
RH Reliever	03 aaa	9	4	5	87	67	2.79	1.19	266			7.8	32%	76%	3.19				1.5	6.9	4.5		0.3	17.3	128	$14
Age 31	04 PHI *	2	2	8	67	48	4.55	1.61	286	322	261	5.6	32%	75%	5.15	39	17	44	4.3	6.4	1.5	9%	1.2	-2.4	32	$3
Peak	05 PHI	2	1	0	58	42	3.72	1.29	248	192	294	6.1	29%	73%	4.13	44	23	32	3.3	6.5	2.0	9%	0.8	3.7	63	$4
Type Con	06 PHI	7	1	1	91	60	2.96	1.35	286	348	249	4.8	33%	79%	3.95	50	19	31	2.0	5.9	3.0	6%	0.6	17.1	79	$10
Reliability 23	07 PHI *	5	3	0	92	55	4.14	1.44	291	248	309	5.7	32%	72%	4.32	49	19	32	2.5	5.4	2.1	8%	0.8	3.2	50	$5
ERA Potl 45%	1st Half	1	2	0	37	23	5.11	1.49	272			4.5	29%	69%	4.77	47	16	37	3.9	5.6	1.4	13%	1.5	-3.1	21	$1
LIMA Plan C+	2nd Half	4	1	0	55	32	3.49	1.41	303			6.8	35%	74%	3.91	52	23	26	1.6	5.2	3.2	4%	0.3	6.4	83	$5
+/- Score -5	08 Proj	4	3	0	78	46	4.15	1.41	286			5.5	32%	72%	4.36	48	20	33	2.5	5.3	2.1	8%	0.8	0.3	49	$4

3-2, 4.43 ERA in 67.3 IP in PHI. When you're 31, being sent down twice to work out problems is not a good sign. Ctl surge helped spur 2nd half rebound, but Dom trend really tells the whole story.

Germano,Justin

	Yr	W	L	Sv	IP	K	ERA	WHIP	OBA	vL	vR	BF/G	H%	S%	xERA	G	L	F	Ctl	Dom	Cmd	hr/f	hr/9	RAR	BPV	R$
RH Starter	03 aa	2	5	0	58	36	5.12	1.40	294			27.8	33%	64%	4.71				2.0	5.6	2.8		0.9	-5.2	60	$2
Age 25	04 SD *	12	8	0	176	116	4.19	1.32	276			23.4	31%	70%	4.10				2.2	5.9	2.6		0.8	1.5	66	$13
Growth	05 aaa	10	8	0	161	116	3.97	1.36	288			25.5	33%	73%	4.47				2.0	6.5	3.3		0.9	6.7	79	$12
Type Con	06 aaa	10	6	0	155	77	5.11	1.50	321			27.4	34%	68%	5.52				1.5	4.5	3.1		1.1	-11.2	49	$6
Reliability 0	07 SD *	11	10	0	165	93	4.02	1.24	258	244	272	22.2	28%	69%	4.20	49	17	33	2.4	5.1	2.2	8%	0.8	8.3	56	$14
ERA Potl 55%	1st Half	9	1	0	86	45	2.41	0.92	219			23.6	24%	75%	3.71	51	15	34	1.2	4.7	4.1	4%	0.4	21.4	113	$15
LIMA Plan B	2nd Half	2	9	0	79	48	5.76	1.59	296			21.0	32%	65%	4.75	48	19	33	3.7	5.5	1.5	11%	1.1	-13.1	26	($1)
+/- Score -3	08 Proj	5	5	0	87	51	4.55	1.37	285			23.3	31%	68%	4.24	49	18	33	2.2	5.3	2.4	9%	0.9	1.7	53	$5

7-10, 4.46 ERA in 133 IP at SD. Lost Ctl for first time in career in 2nd half. With a Dom well below 6.0, less room for error. Past BPI's suggest he can be an average starter, just never a staff anchor.

Glavine,Tom

	Yr	W	L	Sv	IP	K	ERA	WHIP	OBA	vL	vR	BF/G	H%	S%	xERA	G	L	F	Ctl	Dom	Cmd	hr/f	hr/9	RAR	BPV	R$
LH Starter	03 NYM	9	14	0	183	82	4.52	1.48	284	285	289	25.2	30%	72%	5.05	48	16	36	3.2	4.0	1.2	9%	1.0	-5.6	17	$6
Age 42	04 NYM	11	14	0	212	109	3.61	1.29	254	242	255	27.1	27%	74%	4.33	51	19	30	3.0	4.6	1.6	10%	0.8	17.1	39	$15
Decline	05 NYM	13	13	0	211	105	3.54	1.36	276	323	267	27.4	30%	74%	4.49	47	23	30	2.6	4.5	1.7	6%	0.5	18.4	47	$15
Type Con	06 NYM	15	7	0	198	131	3.82	1.33	266	200	287	26.3	30%	74%	4.20	44	23	32	2.8	6.0	2.1	11%	1.0	16.3	52	$18
Reliability 60	07 NYM	13	8	0	200	89	4.45	1.41	279	326	266	25.5	29%	71%	5.02	42	21	37	2.9	4.0	1.4	9%	1.0	-0.6	21	$10
ERA Potl 40%	1st Half	7	5	0	103	49	4.11	1.35	266			25.9	28%	73%	4.88	43	20	37	3.0	4.3	1.4	10%	1.1	4.1	24	$7
LIMA Plan D	2nd Half	6	3	0	97	40	4.81	1.48	294			25.2	31%	69%	5.17	41	23	36	2.8	3.7	1.3	8%	0.9	-4.6	19	$3
+/- Score -53	08 Proj	11	7	0	164	78	4.62	1.47	287			24.7	30%	71%	4.90	44	22	34	3.0	4.3	1.4	10%	1.0	-10.1	22	$7

2nd half decline forebodes things to come. Can't remember how many times I've written that about him recently, and yet he's still here. One day, though, he WILL retire. Even crafty lefties eventually wear out.

Glover,Gary

	Yr	W	L	Sv	IP	K	ERA	WHIP	OBA	vL	vR	BF/G	H%	S%	xERA	G	L	F	Ctl	Dom	Cmd	hr/f	hr/9	RAR	BPV	R$
RH Reliever	03 2AL	2	0	0	62	37	4.77	1.59	305	360	258	6.7	34%	71%	4.95	34	32	34	3.2	5.4	1.7	8%	0.9	-1.9	35	$1
Age 31	04 MIL *	8	7	0	105	43	6.26	1.77	335	273	257	13.3	34%	67%	6.85				3.2	3.7	1.2		1.5	-25.8	-12	($3)
Peak	05 MIL *	11	8	1	156	118	4.29	1.46	288	256	318	21.4	33%	74%	4.27	42	22	37	2.8	6.8	2.4	11%	1.1	-0.8	55	$10
Type FB	06 JPN	5	7	0	96	60	6.17	1.69	331			22.2	35%	69%	7.04				2.7	5.6	2.1		2.0	-19.6	6	($1)
Reliability 8	07 TAM	6	5	2	77	51	4.89	1.47	285	286	290	5.1	31%	71%	5.02	38	14	48	3.1	5.9	1.9	10%	1.4	-3.7	31	$5
ERA Potl 45%	1st Half	3	3	0	39	22	5.31	1.49	290			5.7	32%	65%	5.28	40	11	49	3.0	5.1	1.7	6%	0.9	-3.9	35	$2
LIMA Plan C	2nd Half	3	2	2	38	29	4.46	1.46	280			4.5	30%	77%	4.77	36	16	48	3.3	6.8	2.1	14%	1.9	0.2	27	$4
+/- Score -17	08 Proj	3	6	0	73	47	4.97	1.50	289			7.6	31%	71%	4.94	38	19	43	3.2	5.8	1.8	12%	1.5	-3.9	26	$2

Amazing how 30-something relievers with mediocre skills continually find and keep jobs. He even got a few saves despite gopherball tendencies. If LD normalization comes from GB, this could get ugly.

Gobble,Jimmy

	Yr	W	L	Sv	IP	K	ERA	WHIP	OBA	vL	vR	BF/G	H%	S%	xERA	G	L	F	Ctl	Dom	Cmd	hr/f	hr/9	RAR	BPV	R$
LH Reliever	03 KC *	16	13	0	184	114	4.45	1.45	289	263	273	25.9	32%	72%	5.27	30	17	53	2.7	5.6	2.1	7%	1.1	1.7	40	$13
Age 26	04 KC *	11	9	0	167	61	5.39	1.43	284	317	255	25.0	28%	66%	5.48	38	18	44	2.7	3.3	1.2	11%	1.6	-19.7	-6	$5
Growth	05 KC *	3	8	0	111	77	6.39	1.74	316	304	294	13.0	35%	65%	5.23	40	18	42	4.0	6.2	1.6	10%	1.3	-27.7	23	($4)
Type Pwr FB	06 KC	4	6	2	84	80	5.14	1.48	286	255	294	6.2	35%	68%	4.07	38	22	40	3.1	8.6	2.8	12%	1.3	-6.1	69	$5
Reliability 9	07 KC	4	1	1	54	50	3.02	1.47	270	241	319	3.2	33%	84%	4.43	35	21	44	3.9	8.4	2.2	9%	1.0	9.9	67	$6
ERA Potl 35%	1st Half	3	1	1	26	20	2.77	1.69	297			3.2	35%	86%	5.12	34	27	39	4.5	6.9	1.5	6%	0.7	5.6	49	$3
LIMA Plan B	2nd Half	1	0	0	28	30	3.25	1.26	242			3.2	30%	81%	3.85	36	14	50	3.2	9.7	3.0	11%	1.3	4.3	89	$3
+/- Score -24	08 Proj	3	2	0	58	55	4.19	1.41	272			3.6	33%	74%	4.15	37	20	43	3.3	8.5	2.6	11%	1.2	2.5	70	$5

Got off to a slow start after all those '06 gains. But something seemed to quietly click in 2nd half, and took the next logical step we were expecting. Still some problems - FB%, BA vs RHP - but intriguing nonetheless.

Gonzalez,Edgar

	Yr	W	L	Sv	IP	K	ERA	WHIP	OBA	vL	vR	BF/G	H%	S%	xERA	G	L	F	Ctl	Dom	Cmd	hr/f	hr/9	RAR	BPV	R$
RH Reliever	03 a/a	10	9	0	165	96	3.86	1.22	265			26.3	31%	67%	3.26				1.8	5.2	2.8		0.3	10.8	84	$15
Age 25	04 aaa	5	5	0	94	67	4.79	1.26	268			26.2	30%	65%	4.36				2.0	6.4	3.2		1.3	-5.2	68	$6
Growth	05 aaa	1	5	0	160	100	4.50	1.36	289			25.3	32%	69%	4.61				1.9	5.6	3.0		1.0	-3.9	63	$5
Type FB	06 ARI *	6	12	0	180	122	4.49	1.33	286	259	288	21.9	32%	68%	4.54	38	15	47	1.7	6.1	3.5	7%	0.9	-0.1	79	$10
Reliability 20	07 ARI	8	4	0	102	62	5.03	1.35	277	313	237	13.6	29%	68%	4.48	45	15	40	2.5	5.5	2.2	13%	1.6	-7.6	31	$6
ERA Potl 55%	1st Half	3	2	0	56	43	4.82	1.25	262			16.7	28%	68%	3.99	45	13	42	2.3	6.9	3.1	15%	1.8	-2.7	56	$4
LIMA Plan C+	2nd Half	5	2	0	46	19	5.28	1.48	294			11.2	30%	67%	5.12	44	18	38	2.7	3.7	1.4	11%	1.4	-4.9	6	$2
+/- Score 16	08 Proj	8	6	0	131	89	4.55	1.34	276			16.4	30%	69%	4.34	44	16	41	2.4	6.1	2.5	11%	1.2	0.9	53	$9

Was cruising along skillswise, then everything fell apart in the 2nd half. Dom collapse is the most alarming - it fell each month down the stretch. This suggests a hidden injury. If healthy, he should rebound.

Gonzalez,Gio

	Yr	W	L	Sv	IP	K	ERA	WHIP	OBA	vL	vR	BF/G	H%	S%	xERA	G	L	F	Ctl	Dom	Cmd	hr/f	hr/9	RAR	BPV	R$
LH Starter	03	0	0	0	0	0	0.00	0.00																		
Age 22	04	0	0	0	0	0	0.00	0.00																		
Growth	05	0	0	0	0	0	0.00	0.00																		
Type Pwr	06 aa	7	12	0	154	139	6.36	1.64	281			26.0	32%	65%	6.01				4.8	8.1	1.7		1.9	-35.0	25	$1
Reliability 0	07 aa	9	7	0	150	165	4.44	1.35	251			23.7	33%	69%	3.94				3.7	9.9	2.7		0.9	0.4	94	$13
ERA Potl 60%	1st Half	6	3	0	86	94	4.08	1.38	262			23.1	34%	74%					3.5	9.8	2.8		1.2	4.0	87	$8
LIMA Plan C+	2nd Half	3	4	0	64	71	4.92	1.31	237			24.6	32%	61%					3.9	10.0	2.5		0.6	-3.6	104	$5
+/- Score 17	08 Proj	5	6	0	94	96	5.29	1.45	261			24.1	32%	66%	4.64				4.1	9.2	2.2		1.3	-2.3	68	$5

Major step forward in Cmd. Low S% creates appearance of regression, when BPV actually grew. A LHP with this type of Dom and Cmd will not stay in the minors for long. At 22, plenty of time to grow.

Gonzalez,Mike

	Yr	W	L	Sv	IP	K	ERA	WHIP	OBA	vL	vR	BF/G	H%	S%	xERA	G	L	F	Ctl	Dom	Cmd	hr/f	hr/9	RAR	BPV	R$
LH Reliever	03 PIT *	0	1	3	25	22	5.40	1.44	254	222	238	3.9	28%	68%	5.02				4.3	7.9	1.8		1.8	-3.5	36	$1
Age 29	04 PIT *	5	2	3	63	83	1.14	0.95	205	213	194	4.0	32%	90%	2.29	50	19	31	2.0	11.8	5.9	5%	0.3	24.3	201	$14
Peak	05 PIT	1	3	3	50	58	2.70	1.32	199	156	223	4.2	28%	80%	3.47	53	18	30	5.6	10.4	1.9	6%	0.4	9.5	106	$6
Type Pwr	06 PIT	3	4	24	54	64	2.17	1.35	216	163	227	4.3	32%	83%	3.79	37	27	36	5.2	10.7	2.1	2%	0.2	15.5	114	$16
Reliability 0	07 ATL	2	0	2	17	13	1.59	1.35	238	333	189	4.0	30%	87%	4.73	39	20	41	4.2	6.9	1.6	0%	0.0	6.0	83	$3
ERA Potl 35%	1st Half	2	0	2	17	13	1.59	1.35	238			4.0	30%	87%	4.73	39	20	41	4.2	6.9	1.6	0%	0.0	6.0	83	$3
LIMA Plan B+	2nd Half	0	0	0	0	0	0.00	0.00																		
+/- Score -98	08 Proj	1	1	0	15	12	3.72	1.38	227			4.2	28%	74%	4.45	44	21	35	5.0	7.4	1.5	7%	0.6	-0.1	67	$1

Failed to outproduce Adam LaRoche. Tommy John surgery means an All Star break return if all goes well. Full health and return of Ctl unlikely until 2009. Hopefully, Dom returns before then.

Gordon,Tom

	Yr	W	L	Sv	IP	K	ERA	WHIP	OBA	vL	vR	BF/G	H%	S%	xERA	G	L	F	Ctl	Dom	Cmd	hr/f	hr/9	RAR	BPV	R$
RH Reliever	03 CHW	7	6	12	74	91	3.16	1.19	215	231	196	4.6	31%	74%	3.15	40	26	34	3.8	11.1	2.9	7%	0.5	12.4	126	$16
Age 40	04 NYY	9	4	4	89	96	2.22	0.89	182	185	174	4.2	25%	77%	2.91	47	16	38	2.3	9.7	4.2	6%	0.5	24.3	149	$20
Decline	05 NYY	5	4	2	80	69	2.58	1.10	207	187	217	4.1	24%	81%	3.55	53	12	35	3.3	7.7	2.4	10%	0.9	17.7	83	$13
Type Pwr	06 PHI	3	4	34	59	68	3.35	1.27	241	185	277	4.2	31%	80%	3.11	45	23	31	3.4	10.4	3.1	19%	1.4	8.3	93	$19
Reliability 2	07 PHI	3	2	6	40	32	4.73	1.33	262	310	222	3.9	29%	70%	3.87	49	16	35	2.9	7.2	2.5	16%	1.6	-1.5	50	$5
ERA Potl 55%	1st Half	1	1	5	9	11	5.00	1.78	321			4.7	41%	79%	3.14	59	14	28	4.0	11.0	2.8	27%	2.0	-0.6	55	$2
LIMA Plan C+	2nd Half	2	1	1	31	21	4.65	1.19	243			3.6	26%	66%	4.07	46	16	38	2.6	6.1	2.3	14%	1.5	-0.8	49	$3
+/- Score 6	08 Proj	4	3	5	58	45	4.34	1.36	258			4.3	30%	71%	4.03	50	17	33	3.4	7.0	2.0	12%	1.1	2.6	56	$6

Longball remains Flash's Ming the Merciless. If he can figure out how to keep the ball in the park, his skills are still solid. That is, if his 2nd half Dom can rebound despite a torn labrum and back pain.

MATT BEAGLE

Gorzelanny,Tom

Gorzelanny,Tom		W	L	Sv	IP	K	ERA	WHIP	OBA	vL	vR	BF/G	H%	S%	xERA	G	L	F	Ctl	Dom	Cmd	hr/f	hr/9	RAR	BPV	R$
LH Starter	03	0	0	0	0	0	0.00	0.00																		
Age 25	04	0	0	0	0	0	0.00	0.00																		
Growth	05 aa	8	5	0	129	102	3.88	1.36	264			24.0	32%	71%	3.68				3.1	7.1	**2.3**		0.4	6.8	80	$11
Type	06 PIT *	8	10	0	160	120	3.53	1.20	227	239	223	24.5	27%	70%	3.97	49	18	33	3.4	6.7	**2.0**	5%	0.4	18.8	78	$16
Reliability 39	07 PIT	14	10	0	202	135	3.88	1.40	273	217	284	27.2	31%	74%	4.60	42	18	40	3.0	6.0	**2.0**	7%	0.8	13.5	54	$15
ERA Potl 55%	1st Half	7	4	0	105	64	3.09	1.28	260			27.5	29%	77%	4.51	43	18	40	2.6	5.5	**2.1**	5%	0.6	17.4	63	$11
LIMA Plan D+	2nd Half	7	6	0	97	71	4.75	1.53	287			26.9	33%	71%	4.68	41	19	40	3.5	6.6	**1.9**	9%	1.0	-3.8	46	$5
+/- Score -5	08 Proj	**13**	**11**	**0**	**203**	**147**	**3.99**	**1.34**	**258**			**25.4**	**30%**	**72%**	**4.38**	**43**	**18**	**38**	**3.2**	**6.5**	**2.0**	**8%**	**0.8**	**0.5**	**61**	**$16**

Yes, it's better than the 1.3 Cmd posted in his 62 IP stint in PIT last year. Still, he's living on the edge: Cmd is on the edge of decency, FB rate the edge of danger. Lefties can take a while. Patience.

Grabow,John

Grabow,John		W	L	Sv	IP	K	ERA	WHIP	OBA	vL	vR	BF/G	H%	S%	xERA	G	L	F	Ctl	Dom	Cmd	hr/f	hr/9	RAR	BPV	R$
LH Reliever	03 a/a	6	3	1	107	82	5.12	1.61	326			11.9	38%	69%	5.66				2.3	6.9	**3.0**		0.8	-9.6	70	$3
Age 29	04 PIT	2	5	1	61	64	5.15	1.78	319	327	319	4.2	40%	73%	3.85	48	23	29	4.1	9.4	**2.3**	15%	1.2	-6.7	60	$0
Peak	05 PIT	2	3	0	52	42	4.85	1.37	239	219	250	3.5	28%	66%	4.18	47	20	33	4.3	7.3	**1.7**	12%	1.0	-3.9	55	$2
Type Pwr	06 PIT	4	2	0	69	66	4.16	1.42	258	275	251	4.2	32%	73%	3.81	49	18	34	3.9	8.6	**2.2**	11%	0.9	2.8	74	$5
Reliability 20	07 PIT	3	2	1	52	42	4.53	1.45	278	238	303	3.6	33%	71%	4.01	50	17	33	3.3	7.3	**2.2**	11%	1.0	-0.6	58	$3
ERA Potl 55%	1st Half	1	1	1	19	13	6.16	1.84	309			3.4	34%	69%	5.69	43	12	45	5.2	6.2	**1.2**	10%	1.4	-4.1	12	($0)
LIMA Plan B	2nd Half	2	1	0	33	29	3.58	1.22	258			3.8	31%	73%	3.09	54	21	25	2.2	8.0	**3.6**	13%	0.8	3.4	103	$4
+/- Score 21	08 Proj	**3**	**2**	**0**	**54**	**46**	**4.17**	**1.43**	**272**			**3.8**	**32%**	**73%**	**3.92**	**49**	**18**	**33**	**3.3**	**7.7**	**2.3**	**11%**	**1.0**	**3.2**	**65**	**$4**

Quietly put it all together in the 2nd half despite bone chips in elbow (which were removed in off-season). Nice Ctl trend if he can avoid relapses like 1H. We saw similar performance 2H '06, so needs consistency.

Green,Sean

Green,Sean		W	L	Sv	IP	K	ERA	WHIP	OBA	vL	vR	BF/G	H%	S%	xERA	G	L	F	Ctl	Dom	Cmd	hr/f	hr/9	RAR	BPV	R$
RH Reliever	03	0	0	0	0	0	0.00	0.00																		
Age 29	04 aa	4	3	2	77	38	4.93	1.57	288			6.7	31%	70%	5.19				3.9	4.4	**1.1**		1.0	-5.6	17	$2
Pre-Peak	05 a/a	4	3	15	73	51	4.37	1.53	253			6.0	30%	70%	3.84				5.2	6.3	**1.2**		0.3	-0.6	60	$8
Type xGB	06 SEA	0	0	0	32	15	4.50	1.47	274			5.9	30%	69%	4.42	58	19	24	3.7	4.2	**1.2**	8%	0.6	0.2	33	$1
Reliability 11	07 SEA *	7	3	1	85	60	3.73	1.64	285	329	286	5.2	34%	76%	3.99	61	20	19	4.7	6.4	**1.4**	4%	0.2	8.2	59	$6
ERA Potl 45%	1st Half	3	2	1	45	35	2.59	1.60	266			6.6	33%	83%	3.97	56	27	17	5.2	7.0	**1.3**	4%	0.2	10.6	66	$4
LIMA Plan C+	2nd Half	4	1	0	40	25	5.01	1.69	306			4.3	36%	68%	4.03	64	16	20	4.0	5.7	**1.4**	4%	0.2	-2.5	50	$2
+/- Score -8	08 Proj	**2**	**3**	**0**	**58**	**36**	**4.34**	**1.59**	**281**			**5.4**	**32%**	**72%**	**4.18**	**60**	**19**	**21**	**4.3**	**5.6**	**1.3**	**7%**	**0.5**	**2.3**	**45**	**$2**

5-2, 3.84 ERA in 68 IP at SEA. Extreme GB pitchers can find success, but 4.7 Ctl always scary. No sign of success in past to warrant '07 callup. If he faced Shawn, would every ball in play be a groundball?

Gregg,Kevin

Gregg,Kevin		W	L	Sv	IP	K	ERA	WHIP	OBA	vL	vR	BF/G	H%	S%	xERA	G	L	F	Ctl	Dom	Cmd	hr/f	hr/9	RAR	BPV	R$
RH Reliever	03 a/a	11	7	0	158	109	4.78	1.37	287			22.6	33%	66%	4.41				2.2	6.2	**2.9**		0.8	-7.6	71	$10
Age 29	04 ANA	5	2	1	87	84	4.23	1.31	259	260	250	6.7	33%	68%	3.74	44	18	38	2.9	8.7	**3.0**	6%	0.6	2.2	100	$8
Peak	05 ANA *	4	3	0	98	81	4.65	1.50	282	267	279	10.9	33%	70%	4.13	48	19	33	3.5	7.4	**2.1**	10%	0.9	-3.3	59	$4
Type Pwr xFB	06 LAA	3	4	0	78	71	4.15	1.40	285	298	268	10.5	34%	74%	4.17	36	18	46	2.4	8.2	**3.4**	9%	1.2	3.9	83	$6
Reliability 53	07 FLA	0	5	32	84	87	3.54	1.23	210	162	247	4.7	27%	73%	4.34	29	16	55	4.3	9.3	**2.2**	6%	0.8	9.2	92	$18
ERA Potl 55%	1st Half	0	3	14	45	41	3.00	1.18	211			4.9	25%	79%	4.53	30	13	57	3.8	8.2	**2.2**	7%	1.0	7.9	77	$9
LIMA Plan C+	2nd Half	0	2	18	39	46	4.15	1.28	209			4.6	30%	67%	4.14	28	20	52	4.8	10.6	**2.2**	4%	0.5	1.3	109	$9
+/- Score -14	08 Proj	**2**	**4**	**35**	**88**	**85**	**4.01**	**1.33**	**247**			**4.5**	**31%**	**71%**	**4.24**	**35**	**18**	**48**	**3.6**	**8.7**	**2.4**	**7%**	**0.8**	**1.7**	**84**	**$18**

PRO: Rising Dom, BPV, saves
CON: Rise in FB% to extreme levels, high Ctl, S% in 2nd half, xERA, lucky hr/f given FB rate... So much to like, so much to be terrified of. Be thankful he doesn't pitch in a bandbox.

Greinke,Zack

Greinke,Zack		W	L	Sv	IP	K	ERA	WHIP	OBA	vL	vR	BF/G	H%	S%	xERA	G	L	F	Ctl	Dom	Cmd	hr/f	hr/9	RAR	BPV	R$
RH Reliever	03 aa	4	3	0	53	31	4.08	1.30	300			24.9	33%	71%	4.65				0.8	5.3	**6.2**		1.0	2.1	126	$5
Age 24	04 KC *	9	12	0	173	118	3.85	1.19	262	251	262	23.7	28%	74%	4.25	35	20	45	1.7	6.1	**3.6**	12%	1.5	12.4	71	$16
Growth	05 KC	5	17	0	183	114	5.80	1.56	311	340	279	24.9	34%	64%	4.75	39	23	37	2.6	5.6	**2.2**	10%	1.1	-32.3	38	($0)
Type FB	06 KC *	9	3	0	111	87	4.69	1.23	260	400	200	22.0	30%	63%	3.75	35	35	30	2.2	7.0	**3.2**	11%	0.9	-1.8	86	$12
Reliability 25	07 KC	7	7	1	122	106	3.69	1.30	262	266	263	9.9	32%	74%	4.23	32	22	46	2.7	7.8	**2.9**	7%	0.9	12.3	85	$13
ERA Potl 55%	1st Half	4	4	0	63	52	4.86	1.48	297			11.1	35%	69%	4.46	32	25	44	2.6	7.4	**2.9**	9%	1.1	-2.7	67	$4
LIMA Plan C+	2nd Half	3	3	1	59	54	2.44	1.10	220			8.8	28%	80%	3.98	33	19	48	2.7	8.2	**3.0**	5%	0.6	15.0	105	$9
+/- Score 13	08 Proj	**11**	**10**	**0**	**189**	**154**	**3.92**	**1.29**	**266**			**24.8**	**31%**	**73%**	**4.14**	**35**	**22**	**42**	**2.4**	**7.4**	**3.1**	**10%**	**1.1**	**8.3**	**78**	**$18**

2H breakthrough supported by BPI's, but accentuated by high S%. Cmd always solid, but rise in Dom shows upside. Only FB holding him back. With 2+ years experience, expect progress.
UP: 12-15 Wins, 3.50- ERA

Grilli,Jason

Grilli,Jason		W	L	Sv	IP	K	ERA	WHIP	OBA	vL	vR	BF/G	H%	S%	xERA	G	L	F	Ctl	Dom	Cmd	hr/f	hr/9	RAR	BPV	R$
RH Reliever	03 aaa	6	2	0	66	33	3.53	1.50	270			24.4	30%	76%	4.13				4.1	4.5	**1.1**		0.4	7.0	39	$5
Age 31	04 CHW *	11	12	0	197	108	6.66	1.69	312	292	296	27.6	32%	64%	5.46	40	17	43	3.7	4.9	**1.3**	14%	1.9	-54.3	-8	($4)
Peak	05 aaa	1	9	0	160	86	5.38	1.63	308			27.0	33%	69%	5.76				3.3	4.9	**1.5**		1.2	-21.2	17	($3)
Type	06 DET	2	3	0	62	31	4.21	1.39	259	292	249	5.2	28%	71%	5.00	47	15	38	3.6	4.5	**1.2**	8%	0.9	2.7	30	$3
Reliability 27	07 DET	5	3	0	80	62	4.74	1.42	265	237	275	6.1	32%	66%	4.44	45	16	39	3.6	7.0	**1.9**	5%	0.6	-2.3	68	$5
ERA Potl 55%	1st Half	2	2	0	35	25	5.91	1.57	303			5.8	35%	62%	4.68	41	21	38	3.1	6.4	**2.1**	7%	0.8	-6.1	53	$1
LIMA Plan C	2nd Half	3	1	0	45	37	3.83	1.30	232			6.3	29%	70%	4.25	48	12	40	4.0	7.4	**1.9**	4%	0.4	3.7	80	$5
+/- Score -5	08 Proj	**3**	**3**	**0**	**73**	**47**	**4.72**	**1.45**	**271**			**7.2**	**31%**	**68%**	**4.75**	**46**	**15**	**39**	**3.6**	**5.8**	**1.6**	**7%**	**0.7**	**-2.3**	**47**	**$3**

Where did this strikeout rate come from? In the spring, he started setting up on the 1B side of the pitching rubber to improve his sinker. More K's, but also more walks and hits. At 31, it's tough to learn new tricks.

Guardado,Eddie

Guardado,Eddie		W	L	Sv	IP	K	ERA	WHIP	OBA	vL	vR	BF/G	H%	S%	xERA	G	L	F	Ctl	Dom	Cmd	hr/f	hr/9	RAR	BPV	R$
LH Reliever	03 MIN	3	5	41	65	60	2.91	0.98	214	175	219	3.8	26%	75%	3.81	29	19	52	1.9	8.3	**4.3**	8%	1.0	13.0	123	$24
Age 37	04 SEA	2	2	18	45	45	2.79	1.00	196	109	228	4.3	22%	84%	3.82	28	17	55	2.8	9.0	**3.2**	13%	1.6	9.1	89	$13
Decline	05 SEA	2	3	36	56	48	2.73	1.19	247	231	242	4.0	29%	83%	4.05	35	19	46	2.4	7.7	**3.2**	9%	1.1	11.4	85	$18
Type xFB	06 2TM	1	3	13	37	39	3.89	1.54	297	239	324	3.8	34%	87%	4.28	33	14	54	3.2	9.5	**3.0**	17%	2.4	2.9	43	$7
Reliability 0	07 CIN	0	0	0	14	8	7.23	1.46	293	333	273	4.0	31%	50%	5.27	23	29	48	2.6	5.3	**2.0**	9%	1.3	-4.7	31	($1)
ERA Potl 60%	1st Half	0	0	0	0	0	0.00	0.00																		
LIMA Plan D	2nd Half	0	0	0	14	8	7.23	1.46	293			4.0	31%	50%	5.27	23	29	48	2.6	5.3	**2.0**	9%	1.3	-4.7	31	($1)
+/- Score 76	08 Proj	**1**	**2**	**8**	**38**	**27**	**4.26**	**1.53**	**291**			**4.3**	**32%**	**78%**	**5.14**	**29**	**21**	**50**	**3.3**	**6.4**	**1.9**	**11%**	**1.7**	**-3.5**	**26**	**$4**

Been a while since he's been appearing "every day." He may not live up to that moniker again. Marginal cmd remains, but can he regain Dom to offset FB tendencies? At 37, it's a longshot.

Guerrier,Matt

Guerrier,Matt		W	L	Sv	IP	K	ERA	WHIP	OBA	vL	vR	BF/G	H%	S%	xERA	G	L	F	Ctl	Dom	Cmd	hr/f	hr/9	RAR	BPV	R$
RH Reliever	03 aaa	4	6	0	105	66	5.97	1.40	304			22.7	33%	60%	5.38				1.6	5.7	**3.6**		1.5	-20.4	61	$2
Age 29	04 aaa	5	10	0	144	83	3.93	1.28	280			25.2	31%	72%	4.27				1.7	5.2	**3.1**		1.0	7.3	67	$9
Peak	05 MIN	0	3	0	71	46	3.41	1.33	261	279	247	7.0	30%	76%	4.30	47	19	34	3.0	5.8	**1.9**	8%	0.8	8.4	55	$4
Type Con	06 MIN	1	0	1	69	37	3.38	1.43	286	333	256	7.7	30%	81%	4.71	45	18	37	2.7	4.8	**1.8**	10%	1.2	10.0	29	$4
Reliability 26	07 MIN	2	4	1	88	68	2.35	1.05	222	264	187	4.8	26%	83%	3.60	47	16	36	2.1	7.0	**3.2**	10%	0.9	23.4	93	$13
ERA Potl 35%	1st Half	1	3	0	47	34	1.91	0.89	185			5.3	22%	80%	3.59	49	15	36	2.3	6.5	**2.8**	4%	0.4	15.0	105	$8
LIMA Plan C	2nd Half	1	1	1	41	34	2.85	1.22	262			4.4	29%	86%	3.61	46	17	37	2.0	7.5	**3.8**	16%	1.5	8.4	81	$5
+/- Score -41	08 Proj	**1**	**2**	**0**	**73**	**48**	**3.48**	**1.27**	**266**			**6.2**	**29%**	**77%**	**4.09**	**46**	**18**	**36**	**2.2**	**6.0**	**2.7**	**11%**	**1.1**	**3.6**	**60**	**$6**

Low H% and high S% make solid season look better than it was. It WAS good, though, but kinda out of the blue, given his track record. Inability to retire LHB may limit his potential to repeat. Expect a regression.

Guthrie,Jeremy

Guthrie,Jeremy		W	L	Sv	IP	K	ERA	WHIP	OBA	vL	vR	BF/G	H%	S%	xERA	G	L	F	Ctl	Dom	Cmd	hr/f	hr/9	RAR	BPV	R$
RH Starter	03 a/a	10	11	0	159	81	6.18	1.65	322			25.9	34%	63%	5.96				2.7	4.6	**1.7**		1.1	-35.1	20	($1)
Age 29	04 a/a	9	10	0	149	85	5.46	1.72	314			25.6	34%	69%	5.89				3.9	5.1	**1.3**		1.0	-20.6	22	($0)
Pre-Peak	05 aaa	12	10	0	136	84	5.39	1.57	301			24.4	34%	66%	5.19				3.2	5.6	**1.7**		0.9	-18.2	38	$4
Type	06 CLE *	9	5	0	142	88	4.61	1.55	275			21.2	32%	70%	4.73	50	19	31	4.3	5.6	**1.3**	6%	0.5	-1.0	45	$7
Reliability 39	07 BAL	7	5	0	175	123	3.70	1.21	250	255	243	22.6	28%	74%	4.09	42	19	40	2.4	6.3	**2.6**	11%	1.2	17.5	62	$17
ERA Potl 45%	1st Half	4	1	0	88	62	2.45	0.92	210			19.9	24%	76%	3.46	48	18	35	1.5	6.3	**4.1**	7%	0.6	22.3	119	$14
LIMA Plan D	2nd Half	3	4	0	87	61	4.95	1.50	287			25.7	31%	73%	4.74	38	21	41	3.3	6.3	**1.9**	14%	1.8	-4.8	23	$3
+/- Score -3	08 Proj	**9**	**9**	**0**	**189**	**125**	**4.54**	**1.43**	**275**			**23.4**	**31%**	**71%**	**4.60**	**42**	**20**	**38**	**3.2**	**6.0**	**1.9**	**10%**	**1.1**	**-2.4**	**42**	**$11**

Second time around revealed truer skills, without the lucky H% and sudden pinpoint ctl. Nice BPI trends, though far from elite. At 29, it's more likely he'll revert to previous levels than find a new one.

MATT BEAGLE

Halladay,Roy

Halladay,Roy			W	L	Sv	IP	K	ERA	WHIP	OBA	vL	vR	BF/G	H%	S%	xERA	G	L	F	Ctl	Dom	Cmd	hr/f	hr/9	RAR	BPV	R$
RH Starter	03	TOR	22	7	0	266	204	3.25	1.07	252	262	224	29.5	29%	73%	2.85	58	19	23	1.1	6.9	6.4	14%	0.9	41.9	153	$37
Age 31	04	TOR	8	8	0	133	95	4.20	1.35	272	285	258	27.0	31%	70%	3.60	60	13	27	2.6	6.4	2.4	11%	0.9	3.9	64	$10
Peak	05	TOR	12	4	0	141	108	2.42	0.96	229	217	235	28.9	27%	78%	2.69	61	18	21	1.1	6.9	6.0	13%	0.7	34.0	156	$24
Type Con GB	06	TOR	16	5	0	220	132	3.19	1.10	251	259	244	27.6	28%	74%	3.23	57	21	22	1.4	5.4	3.9	12%	0.8	37.1	95	$29
Reliability 66	07	TOR	16	7	0	225	139	3.72	1.24	267	265	270	30.3	30%	71%	3.79	53	18	29	1.9	5.6	2.9	7%	0.6	22.0	78	$23
ERA Potl 55%	1st Half		9	2	0	97	62	4.27	1.22	268			28.7	30%	65%	3.53	56	17	27	1.7	5.8	3.4	9%	0.7	2.8	86	$11
LIMA Plan D+	2nd Half		7	5	0	128	77	3.30	1.26	267			31.6	31%	74%	3.98	51	19	30	2.1	5.4	2.6	6%	0.5	19.1	73	$13
+/- Score 8	08	Proj	15	8	0	218	136	3.81	1.27	270			29.4	30%	72%	3.72	54	18	27	2.0	5.6	2.8	10%	0.8	20.8	69	$21

Some reasons for caution...
- OBA going up
- Cmd going down

The end result is an ominous ERA/xERA trend. In fact, only a low hr/f kept his ERA below 4.00 in '07. Elite status now at risk.

Hamels,Cole

Hamels,Cole			W	L	Sv	IP	K	ERA	WHIP	OBA	vL	vR	BF/G	H%	S%	xERA	G	L	F	Ctl	Dom	Cmd	hr/f	hr/9	RAR	BPV	R$
LH Starter	03		0	0	0	0	0	0.00	0.00																		
Age 24	04		0	0	0	0	0	0.00	0.00																		
Growth	05	aa	2	0	0	19	18	2.84	1.32	183			26.8	22%	83%	3.04				6.2	8.5	1.4		0.9	3.4	70	$3
Type Pwr	06	PHI	* 11	8	0	155	177	3.59	1.15	228	207	244	24.3	30%	73%	3.34	39	18	43	2.8	10.2	3.6	11%	1.1	17.1	113	$21
Reliability 29	07	PHI	15	5	0	183	177	3.39	1.12	240	247	236	26.5	29%	76%	3.38	42	19	39	2.1	8.7	4.1	13%	1.2	23.5	109	$25
ERA Potl 55%	1st Half		9	3	0	107	111	3.79	1.18	253			27.4	31%	74%	3.40	39	19	42	2.0	9.3	4.6	14%	1.4	8.5	115	$14
LIMA Plan C+	2nd Half		6	2	0	76	66	2.83	1.05	221			25.2	26%	78%	3.37	46	20	34	2.2	7.8	3.5	11%	0.9	15.0	102	$12
+/- Score 40	08	Proj	12	6	0	160	163	3.38	1.12	232			25.8	29%	75%	3.35	42	19	39	2.4	9.2	3.8	12%	1.1	20.7	110	$22

H% and GB% combined to give him an elite 2nd half ERA. Stable xERA confirms he can keeping producing at a sub-3.50 ERA level. But late season elbow discomfort makes him a riskier play in '08.

Hammel,Jason

Hammel,Jason			W	L	Sv	IP	K	ERA	WHIP	OBA	vL	vR	BF/G	H%	S%	xERA	G	L	F	Ctl	Dom	Cmd	hr/f	hr/9	RAR	BPV	R$
RH Starter	03		0	0	0	0	0	0.00	0.00																		
Age 25	04		0	0	0	0	0	0.00	0.00																		
Growth	05	a/a	11	4	0	136	106	3.38	1.32	260			26.2	31%	76%	3.81				2.9	7.0	2.4		0.7	15.6	74	$14
Type Pwr FB	06	TAM	* 5	15	0	171	132	6.10	1.62	311	372	299	23.5	36%	62%	4.51	44	19	38	3.1	6.9	2.2	9%	1.0	-32.5	51	$1
Reliability 13	07	TAM	* 7	10	0	161	129	5.50	1.52	278	310	277	19.3	33%	64%	4.73	41	16	43	3.9	7.2	1.8	7%	0.9	-19.7	55	$5
ERA Potl 60%	1st Half		5	5	0	86	77	4.70	1.35	252			23.0	32%	64%	4.84	27	15	58	3.6	8.0	2.3	3%	0.5	-2.1	85	$7
LIMA Plan C+	2nd Half		2	5	0	75	52	6.41	1.72	305			16.6	34%	64%	5.23	42	16	42	4.4	6.3	1.4	10%	1.3	-17.6	22	($2)
+/- Score 24	08	Proj	6	10	0	145	112	4.90	1.45	272			22.6	32%	68%	4.56	42	16	42	3.5	7.0	2.0	9%	1.0	-1.2	54	$7

3-5, 6.14 ERA in 85 IP at TAM.

PRO:
- Dom rate in 1st half
- September rebound (74 BPV)

CON:
- Cmd deterioration
- Struggles vs. LHers continue

Hampson,Justin

Hampson,Justin			W	L	Sv	IP	K	ERA	WHIP	OBA	vL	vR	BF/G	H%	S%	xERA	G	L	F	Ctl	Dom	Cmd	hr/f	hr/9	RAR	BPV	R$
LH Reliever	03	aa	0	1	0	4	0	20.88	3.35	478			25.1	48%	31%	12.54				7.0	0.0	0.0		0.0	-8.1	-41	($2)
Age 27	04	aa	10	9	0	170	83	5.40	1.78	328			29.6	33%	76%	7.24				3.6	4.4	1.2		2.0	-22.2	-19	($2)
Pre-Peak	05	aaa	5	13	0	144	79	6.37	1.67	306			24.5	33%	63%	5.88				3.8	4.9	1.3		1.3	-36.7	13	($4)
Type	06	COL	* 9	4	0	133	88	4.65	1.56	304			16.6	34%	73%	4.90	33	27	40	2.9	5.9	2.0	9%	1.1	-2.6	39	$6
Reliability 7	07	SD	* 3	4	0	66	42	3.19	1.38	260	213	255	5.8	30%	78%	4.62	47	15	38	3.5	5.8	1.6	6%	0.6	10.0	54	$5
ERA Potl 40%	1st Half		3	2	0	30	16	2.40	1.33	255			6.1	29%	82%	4.96	43	17	40	3.3	4.8	1.5	3%	0.3	7.5	54	$4
LIMA Plan C+	2nd Half		0	2	0	36	26	3.86	1.42	264			5.5	30%	75%	4.33	51	13	36	3.7	6.7	1.8	9%	0.9	2.5	52	$1
+/- Score -32	08	Proj	2	2	0	44	27	4.34	1.52	285			9.2	32%	74%	4.82	46	16	38	3.5	5.6	1.6	9%	1.0	-2.3	34	$2

2-3, 2.70 ERA in 53 IP at SD. ERA at SD will draw attention to him, but xERA paints the true picture. Just doesn't have enough upside to bet on a repeat, even with slight Dom spike in 2nd half.

Hanrahan,Joel

Hanrahan,Joel			W	L	Sv	IP	K	ERA	WHIP	OBA	vL	vR	BF/G	H%	S%	xERA	G	L	F	Ctl	Dom	Cmd	hr/f	hr/9	RAR	BPV	R$
RH Starter	03	a/a	11	6	0	158	127	4.04	1.51	273			25.0	33%	72%	4.17				4.1	7.2	1.8		0.4	6.9	69	$11
Age 26	04	aaa	7	7	0	119	83	4.38	1.58	268			21.4	29%	76%	5.21				4.9	6.3	1.3		1.4	-0.6	25	$5
Growth	05	aa	9	8	0	111	82	5.26	1.64	291			22.1	33%	71%	5.64				4.3	6.7	1.5		1.3	-13.1	29	$3
Type Pwr FB	06	a/a	11	5	0	140	91	4.32	1.57	260			24.2	29%	74%	4.51				5.2	5.9	1.1		0.8	3.4	37	$8
Reliability 0	07	WAS	* 10	7	0	126	101	5.24	1.67	276	267	305	21.5	31%	72%	5.38	31	25	44	5.4	7.2	1.3	12%	1.4	-12.6	28	$4
ERA Potl 45%	1st Half		3	2	0	53	40	3.39	1.51	261			21.4	30%	81%					4.6	6.8	1.5		1.0	6.8	44	$4
LIMA Plan C+	2nd Half		7	5	0	73	61	6.58	1.80	287			21.5	32%	66%	5.55	31	25	44	6.0	7.6	1.3	14%	1.7	-19.4	18	($0)
+/- Score -3	08	Proj	8	9	0	131	98	5.03	1.63	274			22.0	31%	72%	5.42	31	25	44	5.1	6.8	1.3	10%	1.2	-16.5	31	$3

5-3, 6.00 ERA in 51 IP at WAS. Yep, this was the guy holding the "Keep RFK in '08" signs around town. With a 3.80/7.90 ERA home/road split and growing Ctl issues, he needs all the help he can get.

Harang,Aaron

Harang,Aaron			W	L	Sv	IP	K	ERA	WHIP	OBA	vL	vR	BF/G	H%	S%	xERA	G	L	F	Ctl	Dom	Cmd	hr/f	hr/9	RAR	BPV	R$
RH Starter	03	2TM	* 13	9	0	148	96	4.62	1.37	285	272	322	21.9	32%	69%	4.43	42	18	40	2.3	5.8	2.6	9%	1.1	-4.2	55	$11
Age 30	04	CIN	10	9	0	161	125	4.86	1.43	280	262	292	25.0	31%	70%	4.26	42	19	38	3.0	7.0	2.4	13%	1.5	-11.9	47	$8
Peak	05	CIN	11	13	0	211	163	3.84	1.27	267	253	279	27.6	31%	72%	4.04	39	22	39	2.2	6.9	3.2	9%	0.9	10.7	82	$17
Type FB	06	CIN	16	11	0	234	216	3.77	1.27	268	267	270	27.3	33%	74%	3.72	39	22	40	2.2	8.3	3.9	10%	1.1	20.8	100	$24
Reliability 97	07	CIN	16	6	0	232	218	3.73	1.14	246	237	246	27.7	30%	71%	3.56	40	18	42	2.0	8.5	4.2	10%	1.1	19.9	112	$27
ERA Potl 55%	1st Half		8	2	0	114	100	3.79	1.18	248			27.5	30%	69%	3.70	42	18	39	2.2	7.9	3.6	7%	0.7	9.0	106	$13
LIMA Plan C+	2nd Half		8	4	0	118	118	3.67	1.11	244			27.9	29%	74%	3.43	38	18	44	1.8	9.0	4.9	13%	1.5	11.0	120	$15
+/- Score 27	08	Proj	15	9	0	218	194	3.64	1.22	259			27.3	31%	74%	3.74	40	20	41	2.1	8.0	3.8	10%	1.1	17.7	98	$24

If history is any indicator, his growth ain't done yet. Note his Cmd, BPV, and xERA trends. Only reason for concern is his increasing FB%, which helped to elevate his hr/9 in the 2nd half.

Harden,Rich

Harden,Rich			W	L	Sv	IP	K	ERA	WHIP	OBA	vL	vR	BF/G	H%	S%	xERA	G	L	F	Ctl	Dom	Cmd	hr/f	hr/9	RAR	BPV	R$
RH Reliever	03	OAK	* 16	8	0	175	164	3.55	1.25	228	271	241	22.1	29%	72%	3.57	49	21	30	3.7	8.4	2.3	8%	0.6	21.1	91	$23
Age 26	04	OAK	11	7	0	189	167	4.00	1.33	243	254	227	26.0	30%	71%	4.07	45	18	37	3.9	7.9	2.1	8%	0.8	10.2	75	$16
Growth	05	OAK	10	5	0	128	121	2.53	1.06	205	179	221	23.2	26%	78%	3.35	43	26	31	3.0	8.5	2.8	7%	0.5	29.1	109	$21
Type Pwr	06	OAK	4	0	0	46	49	4.29	1.23	192	176	211	21.3	24%	67%	3.67	43	24	32	5.1	9.5	1.9	14%	1.0	1.6	84	$6
Reliability 0	07	OAK	1	2	0	26	27	2.45	1.13	199	292	98	14.9	25%	85%	3.65	39	19	42	3.9	9.5	2.5	11%	1.1	6.5	92	$4
ERA Potl 35%	1st Half		1	1	0	21	24	1.29	0.90	180			16.1	24%	94%	2.96	40	19	40	2.6	10.3	4.0	10%	0.9	8.3	139	$4
LIMA Plan B+	2nd Half		0	1	0	5	3	7.66	2.13	274			11.9	28%	67%	7.79	33	20	47	9.6	5.7	0.6	14%	1.9	-1.8	-10	($1)
+/- Score -36	08	Proj	6	3	0	81	77	3.80	1.28	228			24.1	28%	73%	3.98	39	22	39	4.0	8.6	2.1	11%	1.0	5.1	76	$9

In '06, it was his elbow. In '07, it was his shoulder. BPIs are excellent but injuries have been playing games -- Ctl in '06, FB% in '07 -- and there's no telling what's in store for 2008. A high risk, high reward investment.

Haren,Dan

Haren,Dan			W	L	Sv	IP	K	ERA	WHIP	OBA	vL	vR	BF/G	H%	S%	xERA	G	L	F	Ctl	Dom	Cmd	hr/f	hr/9	RAR	BPV	R$
RH Starter	03	STL	* 11	8	0	172	120	4.24	1.30	278	278	304	24.2	32%	70%	4.30	40	18	42	1.9	6.3	3.2	8%	1.0	0.8	75	$13
Age 27	04	STL	* 14	7	0	174	164	4.34	1.35	277	190	330	21.2	34%	71%	3.72	45	16	39	2.4	8.5	3.5	10%	1.1	-1.8	91	$15
Pre-Peak	05	OAK	14	12	0	217	163	3.73	1.22	257	252	258	26.4	29%	73%	3.66	48	20	32	2.2	6.8	3.1	12%	1.1	17.1	76	$22
Type	06	OAK	14	13	0	223	176	4.12	1.21	263	246	268	27.1	30%	70%	3.66	45	19	36	1.8	7.1	3.9	13%	1.3	12.1	90	$24
Reliability 88	07	OAK	15	9	0	223	192	3.07	1.21	254	230	264	27.0	30%	79%	3.68	44	17	38	2.2	7.8	3.5	10%	1.0	39.4	95	$28
ERA Potl 55%	1st Half		9	2	0	118	93	1.91	0.94	198			26.8	23%	85%	3.75	42	15	44	2.2	7.1	3.2	7%	0.8	37.8	102	$22
LIMA Plan C+	2nd Half		6	7	0	105	99	4.38	1.51	309			27.3	38%	74%	3.60	47	20	33	2.2	8.5	3.8	13%	1.2	1.6	88	$7
+/- Score 15	08	Proj	17	8	0	218	191	3.31	1.21	258			26.4	31%	77%	3.54	46	19	36	2.1	7.9	3.7	11%	1.1	25.6	97	$28

On the surface, went from a Cy Young front-runner in 1st half to average pitcher in 2nd half. But it was a case of wild H% and S% swings. Use stable xERA trend to guide your expectations and BPV to seal the deal.

Hawkins,LaTroy

Hawkins,LaTroy			W	L	Sv	IP	K	ERA	WHIP	OBA	vL	vR	BF/G	H%	S%	xERA	G	L	F	Ctl	Dom	Cmd	hr/f	hr/9	RAR	BPV	R$
RH Reliever	03	MIN	9	3	2	77	75	1.87	1.09	241	205	263	4.2	31%	85%	3.43	37	22	40	1.8	8.8	5.0	5%	0.5	25.2	150	$16
Age 35	04	CHC	5	4	25	82	69	2.63	1.05	237	230	236	4.2	28%	82%	3.58	38	21	41	1.5	7.6	4.9	10%	1.1	16.5	124	$19
Past Peak	05	2NL	2	8	6	56	43	3.85	1.46	268	228	297	3.7	31%	77%	4.51	44	17	39	3.9	6.9	1.8	10%	1.1	2.7	47	$5
Type Con GB	06	BAL	3	2	0	60	27	4.49	1.46	301	323	285	4.4	33%	69%	4.85	44	21	35	2.2	4.0	1.8	5%	0.6	0.5	39	$3
Reliability 9	07	COL	2	5	0	55	29	3.42	1.23	250	237	266	3.7	27%	76%	3.56	63	16	21	2.6	4.7	1.8	16%	1.0	6.9	42	$5
ERA Potl 40%	1st Half		0	3	0	20	11	3.60	1.15	252			3.5	27%	71%	3.61	59	14	27	1.8	5.0	2.8	12%	0.9	2.0	65	$1
LIMA Plan C+	2nd Half		2	2	0	35	18	3.31	1.27	249			3.8	26%	78%	3.50	66	17	18	3.1	4.6	1.5	20%	1.0	4.8	34	$3
+/- Score -15	08	Proj	2	4	0	44	24	3.93	1.33	273			3.9	30%	72%	4.12	53	18	29	2.5	5.0	2.0	10%	0.8	1.5	47	$3

Has morphed from an electric, flammable reliever to a finesse GB type. That approach worked well in '07, but with a razor thin margin of error, betting on a repeat is a risky venture.

STEPHEN NICKRAND

Heilman,Aaron

Heilman,Aaron		Yr	Tm	W	L	Sv	IP	K	ERA	WHIP	OBA	vL	vR	BF/G	H%	S%	xERA	G	L	F	Ctl	Dom	Cmd	hr/f	hr/9	RAR	BPV	R$
RH	Reliever	03	NYM *	8	11	0	159	110	5.15	1.68	301	299	301	24.4	34%	71%	4.79	46	21	33	4.2	6.2	1.5	10%	1.0	-17.1	33	$1
Age	29	04	NYM *	8	13	0	179	125	5.52	1.64	295	232	286	26.3	33%	68%	4.45	51	20	29	4.1	6.3	1.5	13%	1.1	-27.9	33	$0
Peak		05	NYM	5	3	5	108	106	3.17	1.15	222	208	236	8.3	29%	73%	3.32	46	24	31	3.1	8.8	2.9	7%	0.5	14.4	109	$14
Type		06	NYM	4	5	0	87	73	3.62	1.16	229	231	231	4.8	28%	69%	3.83	45	17	38	2.9	7.6	2.6	5%	0.5	9.3	94	$9
Reliability	39	07	NYM	7	7	1	86	63	3.03	1.07	229	234	218	4.2	26%	75%	3.68	45	21	34	2.1	6.6	3.2	9%	0.8	14.8	90	$13
ERA Potl	50%	1st Half		6	3	0	36	25	4.00	1.06	234			4.1	25%	67%	4.08	38	17	46	1.8	6.3	3.6	10%	1.3	1.9	83	$6
LIMA Plan	B	2nd Half		1	4	1	50	38	2.34	1.08	225			4.3	27%	80%	3.34	51	24	26	2.3	6.8	2.9	8%	0.5	12.9	96	$7
+/- Score	1	08	Proj	5	5	3	73	58	3.48	1.16	236			5.3	28%	72%	3.73	45	20	34	2.6	7.2	2.8	8%	0.7	6.0	87	$9

Has found a home in relief. Net effect of improved Ctl, reduced Dom is a higher Cmd. Tapped into a dormant GB approach in the 2nd half. H% correction should send his ERA north, but just a touch.

Hendrickson,Mark

Hendrickson,Mark		Yr	Tm	W	L	Sv	IP	K	ERA	WHIP	OBA	vL	vR	BF/G	H%	S%	xERA	G	L	F	Ctl	Dom	Cmd	hr/f	hr/9	RAR	BPV	R$
LH	Reliever	03	TOR	9	9	0	158	76	5.53	1.56	317	269	333	23.6	33%	67%	4.90	45	18	37	2.3	4.3	1.9	11%	1.4	-19.5	16	$3
Age	33	04	TAM	10	15	0	183	87	4.82	1.40	290	291	295	24.7	31%	67%	4.69	46	19	36	2.3	4.3	1.9	9%	1.0	-8.7	31	$7
Past Peak		05	TAM	11	8	0	178	89	5.91	1.55	311	258	328	25.7	33%	63%	4.67	46	22	32	2.5	4.5	1.8	12%	1.2	-33.8	21	$2
Type	Con	06	2TM	6	15	0	164	99	4.22	1.43	272	287	264	23.0	30%	72%	4.65	48	16	36	3.4	5.4	1.6	9%	0.9	6.1	39	$8
Reliability	58	07	LA	4	8	0	123	92	5.21	1.39	291	258	300	13.6	33%	64%	3.94	44	23	33	2.1	6.7	3.2	12%	1.1	-11.8	71	$4
ERA Potl	60%	1st Half		2	3	0	65	52	4.29	1.32	262			15.3	30%	71%	3.83	46	22	32	2.9	7.2	2.5	14%	1.2	1.1	60	$4
LIMA Plan	B	2nd Half		2	5	0	58	40	6.24	1.47	321			12.1	37%	57%	4.05	42	24	34	1.2	6.2	5.0	9%	0.9	-12.9	105	$0
+/- Score	31	08	Proj	2	3	0	44	28	4.55	1.38	281			11.7	31%	69%	4.26	45	21	34	2.5	5.8	2.3	10%	1.0	0.8	51	$2

If he were 10 years younger, these skill trends would signal a breakout. As it stands, he just needs the right use:

	Dom	OBA	ERA
RP	8.0	.240	3.69
SP	6.0	.321	6.13

Hennessey,Brad

Hennessey,Brad		Yr	Tm	W	L	Sv	IP	K	ERA	WHIP	OBA	vL	vR	BF/G	H%	S%	xERA	G	L	F	Ctl	Dom	Cmd	hr/f	hr/9	RAR	BPV	R$
RH	Reliever	03		0	0	0	0	0	0.00	0.00											0.0	0.0						
Age	28	04	a/a	9	6	0	136	58	3.61	1.44	279			25.8	30%	75%	4.27				3.1	3.8	1.2		0.5	12.3	32	$8
Pre-Peak		05	SF *	9	10	0	185	103	4.78	1.48	281	320	244	25.5	30%	69%	4.67	48	20	32	3.5	5.0	1.4	10%	1.0	-12.2	30	$5
Type	Con	06	SF	5	6	1	99	42	4.27	1.35	248	230	265	12.5	25%	71%	5.20	44	19	37	3.8	3.8	1.0	10%	1.1	2.7	17	$6
Reliability	33	07	SF	4	5	19	68	40	3.43	1.30	255	245	265	4.2	28%	77%	4.42	46	20	34	3.0	5.3	1.7	9%	0.9	8.4	44	$12
ERA Potl	35%	1st Half		1	2	3	33	22	3.27	1.12	250			4.3	28%	74%	3.75	50	16	35	1.6	6.0	3.7	8%	0.8	4.7	93	$4
LIMA Plan	D+	2nd Half		3	3	16	35	18	3.57	1.47	260			4.1	28%	79%	5.13	43	23	33	4.3	4.6	1.1	10%	1.0	3.7	22	$8
+/- Score	-29	08	Proj	3	4	8	58	30	4.03	1.43	272			6.8	29%	74%	4.87	45	20	35	3.4	4.7	1.4	9%	0.9	-3.4	29	$6

Earned a shot to close after an impressive 1st half, then gave away all those gains in the 2nd half. What's real? Given his history, believe the second half. Not a viable closer option over the long haul.

Hensley,Clay

Hensley,Clay		Yr	Tm	W	L	Sv	IP	K	ERA	WHIP	OBA	vL	vR	BF/G	H%	S%	xERA	G	L	F	Ctl	Dom	Cmd	hr/f	hr/9	RAR	BPV	R$
RH	Starter	03		0	0	0	0	0	0.00	0.00											0.0	0.0						
Age	28	04	aa	11	10	0	159	95	5.66	1.65	319			26.9	36%	66%	5.71				3.0	5.4	1.8		0.9	-25.8	36	$1
Pre-Peak		05	SD *	3	3	0	137	91	2.62	1.00	205	275	103	13.8	24%	74%	3.33	59	16	25	2.5	6.0	2.4	6%	0.4	27.6	88	$16
Type	GB	06	SD	11	12	0	187	122	3.71	1.34	248	263	239	21.5	28%	74%	4.16	54	17	30	3.7	5.9	1.6	9%	0.7	18.0	53	$15
Reliability	8	07	SD *	3	10	0	121	65	8.68	2.34	378	287	324	24.5	41%	63%	6.37	49	15	36	5.6	4.8	0.9	11%	1.4	-63.5	-15	($19)
ERA Potl	60%	1st Half		2	7	0	71	38	7.97	2.17	369			25.8	40%	63%	5.88	50	14	36	4.7	4.8	1.0	10%	1.3	-31.1	-6	($9)
LIMA Plan	F	2nd Half		1	3	0	50	27	9.69	2.58	390			22.9	42%	63%	7.13	46	17	37	7.0	4.9	0.7	12%	1.6	-32.4	-26	($11)
+/- Score	57	08	Proj	3	5	0	77	45	5.53	1.73	301			20.9	33%	69%	5.03	52	16	32	4.6	5.3	1.2	11%	1.1	-5.9	19	($1)

2-3, 6.84 ERA in 50 IP at SD. Even as a GB hurler, he can't afford to issue BBs at this rate. Sure, H% and S% hurt too, but he seems perfectly capable of putting up ugly numbers even without the benefit of bad luck.

Herges,Matt

Herges,Matt		Yr	Tm	W	L	Sv	IP	K	ERA	WHIP	OBA	vL	vR	BF/G	H%	S%	xERA	G	L	F	Ctl	Dom	Cmd	hr/f	hr/9	RAR	BPV	R$
RH	Reliever	03	2NL	3	2	3	79	68	2.62	1.23	234	209	249	4.9	30%	79%	3.98	43	20	38	3.3	7.7	2.3	4%	0.3	16.2	94	$10
Age	38	04	SF	4	5	23	65	39	5.25	1.71	329	366	318	4.3	36%	71%	5.01	44	18	39	2.9	5.4	1.9	9%	1.1	-8.0	27	$7
Decline		05	2NL *	2	3	0	58	35	3.88	1.71	320	256	333	5.0	34%	83%	5.17	39	22	39	3.4	5.4	1.6	12%	1.6	2.6	10	$1
Type		06	FLA	2	3	0	71	36	4.31	1.72	319	300	340	5.0	35%	75%	5.11	47	22	31	3.5	4.6	1.3	6%	0.6	1.6	26	$0
Reliability	6	07	COL *	7	2	1	84	55	2.60	1.13	224	216	184	5.1	25%	81%	4.18	46	15	38	2.9	5.9	2.0	8%	0.8	18.8	64	$12
ERA Potl	30%	1st Half		2	1	1	37	33	2.43	1.24	240			4.7	30%	84%	3.18	50	30	20	3.2	8.0	2.5	14%	0.7	9.2	87	$5
LIMA Plan	C+	2nd Half		5	1	0	47	22	2.74	1.05	211			5.4	22%	78%	4.52	46	14	39	2.7	4.2	1.6	8%	0.9	9.7	45	$7
+/- Score	-64	08	Proj	3	2	0	44	26	3.93	1.43	277			5.0	30%	75%	4.61	45	19	36	3.1	5.4	1.7	10%	1.0	-1.1	37	$3

5-1, 2.96 ERA in 48 IP at COL. Journeyman dominated AAA in the 1st half. At first glance, that success continued with COL. But a depressed H% gets most of the credit. He's not a new pitcher.

Hernandez,Felix

Hernandez,Felix		Yr	Tm	W	L	Sv	IP	K	ERA	WHIP	OBA	vL	vR	BF/G	H%	S%	xERA	G	L	F	Ctl	Dom	Cmd	hr/f	hr/9	RAR	BPV	R$
RH	Starter	03		0	0	0	0	0	0.00	0.00											0.0	0.0						
Age	22	04	aa	5	1	0	57	62	3.56	1.16	226			23.3	31%	68%	2.67				3.0	9.8	3.2		0.4	5.5	124	$8
Green		05	SEA *	13	8	0	172	187	2.35	1.04	194	164	224	22.0	27%	78%	2.36	67	14	19	3.3	9.8	3.0	10%	0.4	42.8	126	$30
Type	Pwr xGB	06	SEA	12	14	0	191	176	4.52	1.34	266	281	241	26.2	32%	69%	3.14	58	18	25	2.8	8.3	2.9	17%	1.1	0.8	81	$18
Reliability	42	07	SEA	14	7	0	190	165	3.93	1.38	280	299	262	27.3	34%	74%	3.12	61	16	23	2.5	7.8	3.1	15%	0.9	13.6	83	$19
ERA Potl	60%	1st Half		4	4	0	69	73	4.30	1.52	302			25.5	39%	73%	2.97	58	19	23	2.7	9.5	3.5	15%	0.9	1.7	97	$5
LIMA Plan	B	2nd Half		10	3	0	121	92	3.71	1.29	268			28.4	31%	74%	3.21	62	15	23	2.4	6.8	2.9	15%	1.0	11.9	74	$13
+/- Score	64	08	Proj	17	8	0	214	201	3.58	1.26	256			25.5	32%	74%	2.92	60	17	23	2.6	8.5	3.3	14%	0.8	41.5	99	$26

The only thing keeping him from a breakout was some bad luck (h% and hr/f). Not only does he have premium Dom upside, but few SPs induce more GB than he does. A stud if healthy.
UP: 18-20 wins, 3.00 ERA

Hernandez,Livan

Hernandez,Livan		Yr	Tm	W	L	Sv	IP	K	ERA	WHIP	OBA	vL	vR	BF/G	H%	S%	xERA	G	L	F	Ctl	Dom	Cmd	hr/f	hr/9	RAR	BPV	R$
RH	Starter	03	MON	15	10	0	233	178	3.21	1.21	255	278	233	29.2	29%	78%	3.74	47	19	34	2.2	6.9	3.1	11%	1.0	30.8	80	$25
Age	33	04	MON	11	15	0	255	186	3.60	1.24	246	258	238	30.3	28%	74%	4.04	46	19	35	2.9	6.6	2.2	10%	0.9	20.8	65	$21
Peak		05	WAS	15	10	0	246	147	3.99	1.43	279	290	278	30.6	31%	74%	4.65	40	26	34	3.1	5.4	1.8	9%	0.9	7.9	41	$14
Type	Con	06	2NL	13	13	0	216	128	4.83	1.50	288	302	275	28.1	31%	71%	5.13	37	20	44	3.3	5.3	1.6	9%	1.2	-9.2	28	$9
Reliability	89	07	ARI	11	11	0	204	90	4.93	1.60	300	295	320	28.0	30%	73%	5.55	38	21	41	3.5	4.0	1.1	11%	1.5	-12.8	-2	$3
ERA Potl	40%	1st Half		5	5	0	100	50	4.68	1.64	291			28.5	31%	74%	5.68	38	22	40	4.3	4.5	1.0	9%	1.1	-3.1	13	$1
LIMA Plan	C	2nd Half		6	6	0	104	40	5.18	1.55	308			27.4	30%	73%	5.42	39	20	41	2.7	3.5	1.3	14%	1.9	-9.7	-16	$1
+/- Score	-34	08	Proj	7	12	0	168	83	5.00	1.53	290			28.7	30%	71%	5.30	39	21	40	3.4	4.5	1.3	11%	1.3	-18.6	11	$3

It's all smoke and mirrors now. Just by virtue of sheer willpower has his ERA managed to stay under 5.00, but with 4 years of plummeting BPIs, that's the next barrier to fall. DN: ERA well over 5; IP well under 200.

Hernandez,Orlando

Hernandez,Orlando		Yr	Tm	W	L	Sv	IP	K	ERA	WHIP	OBA	vL	vR	BF/G	H%	S%	xERA	G	L	F	Ctl	Dom	Cmd	hr/f	hr/9	RAR	BPV	R$
RH	Starter	03	NYY	0	0	0	0	0	0.00	0.00											0.0	0.0						
Age	38	04	NYY	8	2	0	84	84	3.31	1.29	235	255	194	23.7	29%	78%	4.07	35	21	44	3.8	9.0	2.3	9%	1.0	11.6	82	$11
Decline		05	CHW	9	9	1	128	91	5.13	1.46	275	295	257	23.4	31%	67%	4.65	39	22	39	3.5	6.4	1.8	11%	1.3	-12.0	39	$7
Type	Pwr xFB	06	2NL	11	11	0	162	164	4.66	1.33	253	300	199	23.8	31%	68%	4.06	34	19	47	3.4	9.1	2.7	10%	1.2	-3.5	79	$14
Reliability	36	07	NYM	9	5	0	148	128	3.72	1.17	207	245	167	22.4	23%	75%	4.35	38	12	51	3.9	7.8	2.0	11%	1.4	12.9	60	$16
ERA Potl	40%	1st Half		3	3	0	68	52	2.78	1.06	204			24.6	23%	78%	4.12	42	12	45	3.0	6.9	2.3	8%	0.9	13.8	75	$9
LIMA Plan	D	2nd Half		6	2	0	80	76	4.52	1.27	211			20.9	23%	72%	4.54	34	11	55	4.6	8.6	1.9	14%	1.8	-0.9	49	$8
+/- Score	-38	08	Proj	6	7	0	116	94	4.58	1.46	267			24.2	30%	72%	4.77	37	16	47	3.9	7.3	1.9	10%	1.3	-5.3	45	$6

His best season in recent memory, at first glance. But a closer look shows that a tiny h% deserves most of the credit. And with his FB% trend, he needs a pitcher-friendly park to succeed. Heed the xERA.

Hill,Rich

Hill,Rich		Yr	Tm	W	L	Sv	IP	K	ERA	WHIP	OBA	vL	vR	BF/G	H%	S%	xERA	G	L	F	Ctl	Dom	Cmd	hr/f	hr/9	RAR	BPV	R$
LH	Starter	03		0	0	0	0	0	0.00	0.00																		
Age	28	04		0	0	0	0	0	0.00	0.00																		
Pre-Peak		05	a/a	10	4	0	122	152	4.34	1.23	246			24.2	31%	73%	4.36				2.8	11.2	4.0		1.8	-0.6	104	$15
Type	Pwr xFB	06	CHC *	13	8	0	199	205	3.34	1.12	222	262	220	25.1	28%	74%	3.86	30	18	52	2.8	9.3	3.3	8%	0.9	28.2	108	$26
Reliability	54	07	CHC	11	8	0	195	183	3.92	1.19	236	191	247	25.1	28%	72%	3.85	36	21	43	2.9	8.4	2.9	12%	1.2	12.1	82	$20
ERA Potl	55%	1st Half		5	5	0	95	85	3.13	1.06	212			25.2	24%	79%	3.75	36	22	43	2.7	8.1	2.9	14%	1.4	15.2	80	$13
LIMA Plan	C	2nd Half		6	3	0	100	98	4.68	1.32	258			24.9	32%	67%	3.93	36	21	43	3.1	8.8	2.9	10%	1.1	-3.1	84	$8
+/- Score	20	08	Proj	13	8	0	201	205	3.63	1.21	240			25.1	30%	75%	3.75	35	20	45	2.9	9.2	3.2	11%	1.2	16.0	93	$23

First half was aided by a friendly H% and S% yet base skills remained strong all season long. If he can keep the ball down a little better, he'd have room for more growth.

STEPHEN NICKRAND

Hill,Shawn

Hill,Shawn		Yr	Tm	W	L	Sv	IP	K	ERA	WHIP	OBA	vL	vR	BF/G	H%	S%	xERA	G	L	F	Ctl	Dom	Cmd	hr/f	hr/9	RAR	BPV	R$
RH Starter		03	aa	3	1	0	20	10	4.03	1.84	314			23.9	36%	76%	5.28				4.9	4.5	**0.9**		0.0	0.9	38	$1
Age	27	04	aa	5	7	0	87	43	4.58	1.50	310			22.7	34%	69%	4.88				2.1	4.4	**2.1**		0.5	-2.5	47	$3
Growth		05		0	0	0	0	0	0.00	0.00																		
Type	Con GB	06	WAS *	4	6	0	91	44	3.95	1.36	290			23.0	32%	70%	4.36	50	19	31	1.9	4.3	**2.2**	4%	0.4	6.1	58	$5
Reliability	0	07	WAS	4	5	0	97	65	3.42	1.14	239	288	189	24.7	27%	73%	3.58	55	17	28	2.3	6.0	**2.6**	11%	0.8	12.0	73	$10
ERA Potl	50%	1st Half		3	3	0	50	33	2.70	1.06	208			24.9	24%	75%	3.56	59	14	27	2.9	5.9	**2.1**	5%	0.4	10.6	82	$7
LIMA Plan	C+	2nd Half		1	2	0	47	32	4.19	1.23	269			24.5	29%	71%	3.60	51	20	29	1.7	6.1	**3.6**	16%	1.3	1.4	73	$3
+/- Score	2	08	Proj	**5**	**7**	**0**	**116**	**67**	**3.88**	**1.28**	**272**			**23.2**	**30%**	**71%**	**3.95**	**53**	**18**	**29**	**2.1**	**5.2**	**2.5**	**8%**	**0.7**	**6.5**	**63**	**$8**

Chronic arm problems aside, this is a skill set you want to own. And it's getting better; note the xERA. Blame an inflated hr/f for his 2nd half ERA. You'll probably never get 200 IP here, but the gamble's worth it.

Hirsh,Jason

Hirsh,Jason		Yr	Tm	W	L	Sv	IP	K	ERA	WHIP	OBA	vL	vR	BF/G	H%	S%	xERA	G	L	F	Ctl	Dom	Cmd	hr/f	hr/9	RAR	BPV	R$
RH Starter		03		0	0	0	0	0	0.00	0.00																		
Age	26	04		0	0	0	0	0	0.00	0.00																		
Growth		05	aa	1	8	0	172	133	4.15	1.28	263			24.9	31%	69%	3.82				2.4	6.9	**2.9**		0.8	3.3	80	$9
Type	xFB	06	HOU *	16	6	0	181	129	3.33	1.25	231	211	303	23.6	27%	76%	4.96	30	18	52	3.6	6.4	**1.8**	6%	0.8	26.0	61	$21
Reliability	7	07	COL	5	7	0	112	75	4.81	1.34	245	236	250	25.2	26%	68%	5.18	30	18	51	3.8	6.0	**1.6**	10%	1.4	-5.3	32	$6
ERA Potl	45%	1st Half		3	7	0	95	64	5.21	1.39	254			25.6	27%	66%	5.24	30	18	52	3.9	6.1	**1.6**	10%	1.5	-9.2	28	$3
LIMA Plan	C	2nd Half		2	0	0	17	11	2.60	1.10	197			23.2	21%	82%	4.87	32	18	50	3.6	5.7	**1.6**	8%	1.0	3.9	52	$3
+/- Score	-15	08	Proj	**9**	**8**	**0**	**160**	**110**	**4.91**	**1.39**	**262**			**24.6**	**29%**	**68%**	**5.10**	**31**	**18**	**51**	**3.5**	**6.2**	**1.8**	**9%**	**1.3**	**-13.9**	**38**	**$8**

Three reasons why 2008 may only get worse...
1. Deteriorating Cmd
2. Extreme FB approach in COL
3. Lucky 2nd half h%
Low upside, high risk play here.

Hochevar,Luke

Hochevar,Luke		Yr	Tm	W	L	Sv	IP	K	ERA	WHIP	OBA	vL	vR	BF/G	H%	S%	xERA	G	L	F	Ctl	Dom	Cmd	hr/f	hr/9	RAR	BPV	R$
RH Starter		03		0	0	0	0	0	0.00	0.00																		
Age	24	04		0	0	0	0	0	0.00	0.00																		
Growth		05		0	0	0	0	0	0.00	0.00																		
Type	xGB	06		0	0	0	0	0	0.00	0.00																		
Reliability	6	07	KC *	4	10	0	165	121	6.03	1.59	310	273	208	23.9	35%	64%	3.70	63	10	27	2.9	6.6	**2.3**	18%	1.4	-31.0	38	$0
ERA Potl	60%	1st Half		3	6	0	90	78	5.50	1.59	319			25.4	38%	67%					2.4	7.8	**3.3**		1.2	-11.0	70	$2
LIMA Plan	B	2nd Half		1	4	0	75	43	6.67	1.58	299			22.4	31%	60%	4.14	63	10	27	3.4	5.2	**1.5**	21%	1.7	-20.0	6	($2)
+/- Score	70	08	Proj	**1**	**3**	**0**	**44**	**30**	**4.76**	**1.43**	**277**			**23.6**	**32%**	**67%**	**3.74**	**63**	**10**	**27**	**3.1**	**6.2**	**2.0**	**11%**	**0.8**	**4.0**	**54**	**$2**

0-1, 2.13 ERA in 12 IP at KC. Top pick from a couple years ago had a pretty quick ascent through the high minors. GB profile and Dom upside make him a young prospect worth watching.

Hoey,James

Hoey,James		Yr	Tm	W	L	Sv	IP	K	ERA	WHIP	OBA	vL	vR	BF/G	H%	S%	xERA	G	L	F	Ctl	Dom	Cmd	hr/f	hr/9	RAR	BPV	R$
RH Reliever		03		0	0	0	0	0	0.00	0.00																		
Age	25	04		0	0	0	0	0	0.00	0.00																		
Growth		05		0	0	0	0	0	0.00	0.00																		
Type	Pwr	06	BAL	0	1	0	9	6	10.76	2.07	350			3.8	39%	44%	5.32	51	17	31	4.9	5.9	**1.2**	9%	1.0	-7.0	16	($2)
Reliability	0	07	BAL *	6	4	16	70	76	3.24	1.31	230	351	218	4.7	32%	75%	3.89	38	19	42	4.2	9.8	**2.3**	4%	0.4	10.9	105	$15
ERA Potl	60%	1st Half		1	0	15	32	41	1.96	1.00	203			4.1	31%	81%	2.73	33	33	33	2.5	11.5	**4.6**	4%	0.3	10.1	171	$11
LIMA Plan	A	2nd Half		5	4	1	38	35	4.32	1.57	253			5.3	32%	72%	4.88	39	19	43	5.6	8.4	**1.5**	4%	0.5	0.9	72	$4
+/- Score	-8	08	Proj	**4**	**3**	**5**	**44**	**47**	**3.72**	**1.33**	**232**			**4.7**	**31%**	**73%**	**3.69**	**46**	**18**	**36**	**4.3**	**9.7**	**2.2**	**7%**	**0.6**	**4.3**	**95**	**$7**

3-4, 7.30 ERA in 24 IP at BAL. One of the game's better RP prospects. Turning his electric skills from the minors into MLB results has been a big obstacle, but BAL may need a closer. Deep-sleeper for Saves.

Hoffman,Trevor

Hoffman,Trevor		Yr	Tm	W	L	Sv	IP	K	ERA	WHIP	OBA	vL	vR	BF/G	H%	S%	xERA	G	L	F	Ctl	Dom	Cmd	hr/f	hr/9	RAR	BPV	R$
RH Reliever		03	SD	0	0	0	9	11	2.00	1.11	216	182	273	4.0	29%	89%	2.90	41	25	34	3.0	11.0	**3.7**	14%	1.0	2.5	125	$1
Age	40	04	SD	3	3	40	54	53	2.32	0.92	216	255	161	3.8	27%	80%	3.38	31	22	47	1.3	8.8	**6.6**	7%	0.8	13.0	179	$21
Decline		05	SD	1	6	43	57	54	2.99	1.12	244	291	179	3.9	31%	74%	3.60	37	21	42	1.9	8.5	**4.5**	4%	0.5	8.9	138	$20
Type	xFB	06	SD	0	2	46	63	50	2.14	0.97	213	194	214	3.8	25%	84%	3.85	32	22	45	1.9	7.1	**3.8**	8%	0.9	18.2	110	$24
Reliability	53	07	SD	4	5	42	57	44	2.98	1.12	233	299	169	3.8	29%	73%	4.44	31	18	52	2.4	6.9	**2.9**	2%	0.3	10.2	102	$22
ERA Potl	50%	1st Half		2	3	21	29	18	1.86	0.79	172			3.5	20%	77%	4.31	34	12	54	1.9	5.6	**3.0**	2%	0.3	9.2	108	$13
LIMA Plan	D+	2nd Half		2	2	21	28	26	4.13	1.45	286			4.1	37%	70%	4.55	28	23	49	2.9	8.3	**2.9**	2%	0.3	1.0	98	$9
+/- Score	-50	08	Proj	**3**	**4**	**33**	**58**	**44**	**3.88**	**1.33**	**268**			**4.0**	**31%**	**73%**	**4.61**	**32**	**20**	**48**	**2.6**	**6.8**	**2.6**	**7%**	**0.9**	**-1.5**	**69**	**$15**

The skill decline is evident across the board. Dom is diving and he can't keep the ball down anymore. Only a friendly hr/f kept his ERA from shooting north. 2007 may have been his final triple-digit BPV.

Howell,J.P.

Howell,J.P.		Yr	Tm	W	L	Sv	IP	K	ERA	WHIP	OBA	vL	vR	BF/G	H%	S%	xERA	G	L	F	Ctl	Dom	Cmd	hr/f	hr/9	RAR	BPV	R$
LH Starter		03		0	0	0	0	0	0.00	0.00											0.0	0.0						
Age	25	04		0	0	0	0	0	0.00	0.00											0.0	0.0						
Growth		05	KC *	8	6	0	127	99	5.16	1.48	263	229	271	22.4	31%	65%	3.86	58	19	24	4.3	7.0	**1.6**	12%	0.8	-12.3	55	$6
Type	Pwr	06	TAM *	9	8	0	133	103	4.60	1.53	298	400	281	22.8	36%	70%	4.08	45	26	29	3.0	7.0	**2.3**	7%	0.6	-0.7	68	$8
Reliability	12	07	TAM *	8	14	0	179	177	5.43	1.45	286	296	325	25.2	35%	66%	3.51	46	23	31	2.9	8.9	**3.1**	17%	1.4	-20.4	73	$9
ERA Potl	65%	1st Half		4	6	0	93	85	5.12	1.51	293			25.8	35%	69%	3.68	49	22	29	3.1	8.2	**2.7**	15%	1.3	-7.0	64	$4
LIMA Plan	B	2nd Half		4	8	0	86	92	5.77	1.39	278			24.6	34%	62%	3.35	43	24	33	2.7	9.7	**3.5**	19%	1.6	-13.4	84	$5
+/- Score	75	08	Proj	**8**	**10**	**0**	**145**	**139**	**4.53**	**1.34**	**267**			**22.9**	**33%**	**68%**	**3.38**	**48**	**23**	**29**	**2.8**	**8.6**	**3.1**	**12%**	**0.9**	**20.0**	**90**	**$12**

1-6, 7.59 ERA in 51 IP at TAM. His surface stats scream stay away, but there's something good lurking here. Skills are growing nicely. He just needs some hr/f and h% fortune.
UP: Sub-4.00 ERA

Howry,Bob

Howry,Bob		Yr	Tm	W	L	Sv	IP	K	ERA	WHIP	OBA	vL	vR	BF/G	H%	S%	xERA	G	L	F	Ctl	Dom	Cmd	hr/f	hr/9	RAR	BPV	R$
RH Reliever		03	aaa	2	0	0	17	7	1.59	1.12	273			5.3	29%	89%	3.34				0.5	3.7	**7.0**		0.5	5.9	154	$3
Age	34	04	CLE *	5	3	0	68	58	4.09	1.20	247	291	169	5.1	29%	70%	3.94	33	28	40	2.5	7.7	**3.1**	11%	1.2	2.9	80	$7
Past Peak		05	CLE	7	4	3	73	48	2.47	0.89	192	186	198	3.5	22%	74%	3.92	40	19	41	2.0	5.9	**3.0**	5%	0.5	17.2	100	$14
Type	xFB	06	CHC	4	5	5	76	71	3.19	1.14	246	247	244	3.7	30%	76%	3.68	38	18	44	2.0	8.4	**4.2**	8%	0.9	12.2	116	$11
Reliability	37	07	CHC	6	7	8	81	72	3.32	1.17	249	192	283	4.3	30%	75%	4.00	32	20	48	2.1	8.0	**3.8**	7%	0.9	11.1	106	$13
ERA Potl	60%	1st Half		4	4	2	38	29	4.26	1.32	272			4.7	32%	70%	4.48	34	19	47	2.4	6.9	**2.9**	7%	0.9	0.8	74	$5
LIMA Plan	B+	2nd Half		2	3	6	43	43	2.49	1.04	228			3.9	29%	80%	3.60	31	21	48	1.9	8.9	**4.8**	7%	0.8	10.3	138	$9
+/- Score	-7	08	Proj	**4**	**4**	**5**	**58**	**50**	**3.26**	**1.16**	**248**			**4.1**	**30%**	**75%**	**3.92**	**35**	**20**	**45**	**2.0**	**7.8**	**3.8**	**8%**	**0.9**	**3.4**	**105**	**$9**

Has developed into a reliable setup man. But two reasons why his role is unlikely to expand:
- RHers are figuring him out
- Extreme flyballer

Good LIMA stash, but mine for saves elsewhere.

Hudson,Tim

Hudson,Tim		Yr	Tm	W	L	Sv	IP	K	ERA	WHIP	OBA	vL	vR	BF/G	H%	S%	xERA	G	L	F	Ctl	Dom	Cmd	hr/f	hr/9	RAR	BPV	R$
RH Starter		03	OAK	16	7	0	240	162	2.70	1.08	225	229	214	28.2	26%	77%	3.39	58	16	26	2.3	6.1	**2.7**	8%	0.6	54.0	85	$33
Age	32	04	OAK	12	6	0	188	103	3.54	1.26	268	298	229	29.2	30%	71%	3.65	60	17	23	2.1	4.9	**2.3**	6%	0.4	20.7	69	$16
Peak		05	ATL	14	9	0	192	115	3.52	1.35	264	285	240	28.3	29%	77%	3.69	59	21	21	3.0	5.4	**1.8**	16%	0.9	17.3	44	$16
Type	Con xGB	06	ATL	13	12	0	218	141	4.87	1.44	276	281	265	27.2	31%	68%	3.88	58	18	24	3.3	5.8	**1.8**	15%	1.0	-10.3	41	$10
Reliability	84	07	ATL	16	10	0	224	132	3.33	1.22	259	261	261	27.3	30%	72%	3.43	62	17	22	2.1	5.3	**2.5**	6%	0.4	30.3	75	$23
ERA Potl	50%	1st Half		7	5	0	112	67	3.29	1.14	244			26.8	28%	70%	3.33	62	17	21	2.1	5.4	**2.6**	5%	0.3	15.6	83	$12
LIMA Plan	D	2nd Half		9	5	0	112	65	3.37	1.30	273			27.9	31%	74%	3.52	62	16	22	2.2	5.2	**2.4**	7%	0.5	14.7	68	$11
+/- Score	-7	08	Proj	**15**	**11**	**0**	**218**	**132**	**3.72**	**1.30**	**264**			**27.8**	**30%**	**72%**	**3.59**	**60**	**18**	**22**	**2.6**	**5.5**	**2.1**	**10%**	**0.7**	**21.6**	**60**	**$19**

It took three years for his BPIs in Atlanta to return to Oakland levels. But that's the thin line that contact GB pitchers often have to navigate. A few walks, a few wind-blown HRs, can slam ERA. Still tread carefully.

Hughes,Philip

Hughes,Philip		Yr	Tm	W	L	Sv	IP	K	ERA	WHIP	OBA	vL	vR	BF/G	H%	S%	xERA	G	L	F	Ctl	Dom	Cmd	hr/f	hr/9	RAR	BPV	R$
RH Starter		03		0	0	0	0	0	0.00	0.00																		
Age	21	04		0	0	0	0	0	0.00	0.00																		
Green		05		0	0	0	0	0	0.00	0.00																		
Type	Pwr FB	06	aa	10	3	0	116	120	2.96	1.02	206			21.8	28%	71%	2.05				2.6	9.3	**3.6**		0.4	22.4	132	$20
Reliability	0	07	NYY *	9	4	0	108	93	3.88	1.18	224	264	210	22.1	27%	68%	4.18	37	18	45	3.3	7.7	**2.3**	6%	0.7	8.4	86	$11
ERA Potl	60%	1st Half		3	2	0	27	25	4.33	1.04	208			21.4	28%	54%	3.00	58	15	27	2.7	8.3	**3.1**	0%	0.0	0.6	129	$4
LIMA Plan	C	2nd Half		6	2	0	81	68	3.72	1.23	229			22.4	27%	72%	4.42	34	19	47	3.5	7.5	**2.1**	7%	0.9	7.8	73	$10
+/- Score	14	08	Proj	**12**	**8**	**0**	**160**	**144**	**4.12**	**1.29**	**248**			**23.1**	**30%**	**71%**	**4.07**	**39**	**18**	**43**	**3.2**	**8.1**	**2.5**	**9%**	**1.0**	**8.4**	**77**	**$17**

5-3, 4.46 ERA in 72 IP at NYY. Top SP prospect flaunted upside late in season in NY. Skills eroded a bit in the high minors, but it's hard to argue with these results at age 21. He could emerge quickly.

STEPHEN NICKRAND

Humber,Philip				W	L	Sv	IP	K	ERA	WHIP	OBA	vL	vR	BF/G	H%	S%	xERA	G	L	F	Ctl	Dom	Cmd	hr/f	hr/9	RAR	BPV	R$
RH Starter		03		0	0	0	0	0	0.00	0.00																		
Age	25	04		0	0	0	0	0	0.00	0.00																		
Growth		05		0	0	0	0	0	0.00	0.00																		
Type	xFB	06	aa	2	2	0	34	30	4.08	1.24	249			23.6	29%	72%	4.03				2.7	7.9	2.9		1.4	1.8	73	$4
Reliability	0	07	NYM	* 11	9	0	146	101	5.37	1.42	281	375	214	22.6	31%	65%	4.89	29	25	46	2.9	6.2	2.1	11%	1.4	-16.9	38	$7
ERA Potl	50%	1st Half		9	5	0	91	64	5.13	1.39	294			24.6	33%	66%					2.0	6.3	3.2		1.3	-7.9	63	$6
LIMA Plan	C+	2nd Half		2	4	0	55	37	5.76	1.48	257			20.1	27%	65%	5.34	29	25	46	4.5	6.0	1.3	13%	1.7	-9.0	18	$1
+/- Score	6	08	Proj	4	5	0	73	55	4.97	1.35	263			22.1	29%	67%	4.66	29	25	46	3.1	6.8	2.2	12%	1.5	-2.4	45	$4

0-0, 7.71 ERA in 7 IP at NYM. Held his own in the PCL before fading late. If he can carry those 1st half skills with him to MLB, we'll have something here. As it stands, the risk averse should bid with caution.

Igawa,Kei				W	L	Sv	IP	K	ERA	WHIP	OBA	vL	vR	BF/G	H%	S%	xERA	G	L	F	Ctl	Dom	Cmd	hr/f	hr/9	RAR	BPV	R$
LH Starter		03	JPN	20	5	0	206	189	3.47	1.31	254			30.0	31%	78%	4.03				3.1	8.2	2.6		1.1	23.4	76	$25
Age	28	04	JPN	14	11	0	200	240	4.64	1.35	266			29.5	32%	75%	5.32				3.0	10.8	3.6		2.2	-7.3	77	$18
Pre-Peak		05	JPN	13	9	0	172	153	4.81	1.67	306			29.3	35%	78%	6.55				3.9	8.0	2.1		2.0	-10.7	25	$7
Type	Pwr xFB	06	JPN	14	9	0	209	204	3.69	1.22	247			29.8	30%	75%	3.78				2.6	8.8	3.4		1.2	21.4	93	$25
Reliability	4	07	NYY	* 7	7	0	136	108	5.68	1.59	297	320	264	24.5	33%	69%	5.06	30	20	50	3.6	7.1	2.0	13%	1.8	-19.7	25	$3
ERA Potl	50%	1st Half		4	3	0	60	49	5.70	1.52	284			24.2	31%	67%	4.85	31	19	49	3.6	7.4	2.0	13%	1.8	-8.8	31	$2
LIMA Plan	C	2nd Half		3	4	0	76	59	5.66	1.65	308			24.8	34%	71%	5.25	28	20	52	3.6	7.0	1.9	12%	1.9	-10.8	20	$1
+/- Score	19	08	Proj	5	4	0	79	70	4.78	1.42	271			26.4	31%	72%	4.56	30	20	51	3.3	8.0	2.4	13%	1.7	-0.7	48	$6

2-3, 6.25 ERA in 67 IP at NYY. Came over in Dice-K's shadow but still crumbled under the NY media glare. Fared better in AAA, but MLB hitters just kept raking him after recall. Shaky Ctl and high FB% are the problems.

Isringhausen,Jason				W	L	Sv	IP	K	ERA	WHIP	OBA	vL	vR	BF/G	H%	S%	xERA	G	L	F	Ctl	Dom	Cmd	hr/f	hr/9	RAR	BPV	R$
RH Reliever		03	STL	0	1	22	42	41	2.36	1.17	207	254	159	4.3	27%	81%	3.51	48	19	32	3.9	8.8	2.3	6%	0.4	10.0	101	$12
Age	35	04	STL	4	2	47	75	71	2.88	1.04	206	205	195	4.0	26%	74%	3.41	44	19	37	2.8	8.5	3.1	7%	0.6	12.8	112	$25
Decline		05	STL	1	2	39	59	51	2.14	1.19	205	170	229	3.8	25%	85%	3.67	51	20	29	4.1	7.8	1.9	9%	0.6	15.4	82	$19
Type	Pwr	06	STL	4	8	33	58	52	3.56	1.46	223	270	187	4.3	25%	83%	4.62	44	18	38	5.9	8.1	1.4	16%	1.5	6.6	41	$16
Reliability	38	07	STL	4	0	32	65	54	2.48	1.07	186	196	167	4.1	23%	79%	3.94	45	18	37	3.9	7.4	1.9	6%	0.6	15.7	86	$20
ERA Potl	40%	1st Half		3	0	14	31	23	1.74	0.84	155			3.9	18%	83%	3.45	54	12	34	2.9	6.7	2.3	7%	0.6	10.3	95	$11
LIMA Plan	D+	2nd Half		1	0	18	34	31	3.15	1.28	212			4.4	27%	76%	4.38	36	24	40	4.7	8.1	1.7	5%	0.5	5.4	82	$9
+/- Score	-52	08	Proj	3	2	30	58	50	3.44	1.30	225			4.3	27%	77%	4.14	45	19	36	4.4	7.8	1.8	10%	0.9	1.9	66	$15

Bounced back nicely after it looked like his elite days were over. But concerns remain. Lucky H% drove his 1st half success, and from there he essentially coasted. 2nd half xERA is a realistic downside.

Jackson,Edwin				W	L	Sv	IP	K	ERA	WHIP	OBA	vL	vR	BF/G	H%	S%	xERA	G	L	F	Ctl	Dom	Cmd	hr/f	hr/9	RAR	BPV	R$
RH Starter		03	aa	7	7	0	148	147	4.40	1.25	242			22.9	31%	64%	3.26				3.2	8.9	2.8		0.6	-0.1	102	$13
Age	24	04	aaa	6	4	0	90	66	4.63	1.36	237			20.3	29%	64%	3.22				4.4	6.6	1.5		0.3	-3.2	71	$6
Growth		05	LA	* 11	13	0	145	78	5.57	1.53	277	333	236	21.5	29%	65%	5.58	36	19	46	4.0	4.8	1.2	9%	1.2	-23.8	16	$3
Type	Pwr	06	TAM	* 3	7	5	109	83	6.60	1.86	314	233	333	11.6	37%	64%	4.86	52	17	31	5.1	6.8	1.3	9%	0.8	-27.5	37	($2)
Reliability	27	07	TAM	5	15	0	161	128	5.76	1.76	300	313	285	23.5	35%	68%	4.90	45	19	36	4.9	7.2	1.5	10%	1.1	-24.9	37	($1)
ERA Potl	60%	1st Half		1	8	0	63	54	7.43	1.94	321			21.9	37%	63%	5.15	42	20	38	5.4	7.7	1.4	13%	1.4	-22.7	24	($4)
LIMA Plan	D	2nd Half		4	7	0	98	74	4.68	1.64	287			24.8	34%	72%	4.74	47	19	34	4.6	6.8	1.5	8%	0.8	-2.2	45	$3
+/- Score	23	08	Proj	8	13	0	174	136	4.81	1.55	268			22.9	31%	70%	4.61	46	19	35	4.6	7.0	1.5	10%	1.0	-2.4	46	$7

The stat scan does not tell the whole story. Behind the 5.76 ERA are more encouraging BPIs. He had a streak with 4 of 6 PQS DOM starts. There was 2nd half improvement. And he's only 24. Deep, deep sleeper.

James,Chuck				W	L	Sv	IP	K	ERA	WHIP	OBA	vL	vR	BF/G	H%	S%	xERA	G	L	F	Ctl	Dom	Cmd	hr/f	hr/9	RAR	BPV	R$
LH Starter		03		0	0	0	0	0	0.00	0.00																		
Age	26	04		0	0	0	0	0	0.00	0.00																		
Growth		05	a/a	10	4	0	119	117	3.10	1.04	222			21.5	28%	72%	2.55				2.1	8.8	4.2		0.7	17.8	131	$19
Type	xFB	06	ATL	* 12	4	0	152	113	3.78	1.25	243	297	215	19.9	26%	76%	4.80	28	19	53	3.1	6.7	2.1	10%	1.4	13.2	49	$16
Reliability	6	07	ATL	11	10	0	161	116	4.24	1.38	265	252	268	23.1	28%	77%	4.86	31	20	49	3.2	6.5	2.0	13%	1.8	3.7	29	$12
ERA Potl	40%	1st Half		6	7	0	86	64	4.29	1.53	281			23.9	31%	77%	5.12	32	19	49	3.9	6.7	1.7	11%	1.5	1.4	31	$5
LIMA Plan	D+	2nd Half		5	3	0	75	52	4.18	1.20	245			22.1	24%	76%	4.55	30	20	50	2.5	6.2	2.5	16%	2.2	2.3	31	$7
+/- Score	-14	08	Proj	13	7	0	174	133	4.29	1.33	261			23.1	29%	74%	4.73	30	20	51	3.1	6.9	2.3	11%	1.6	-7.0	45	$14

An up-and-comer, but there are warning signs. Dom is sliding, Ctl is marginal, and FB% remains way too high. He's young enough to fix these issues, but if he doesn't, xERA paints a gloomy picture.

Janssen,Casey				W	L	Sv	IP	K	ERA	WHIP	OBA	vL	vR	BF/G	H%	S%	xERA	G	L	F	Ctl	Dom	Cmd	hr/f	hr/9	RAR	BPV	R$
RH Reliever		03		0	0	0	0	0	0.00	0.00																		
Age	26	04		0	0	0	0	0	0.00	0.00																		
Growth		05	aa	3	3	0	43	39	4.63	1.62	350			21.7	43%	73%	6.09				0.9	8.2	9.3		0.9	-1.7	202	$2
Type	Con GB	06	TOR	* 7	15	0	136	72	5.64	1.40	295	292	261	21.0	32%	60%	4.22	53	16	31	2.0	4.7	2.4	11%	1.1	-18.2	43	$5
Reliability	16	07	TOR	2	3	6	73	39	2.35	1.20	246	257	241	4.3	28%	82%	4.24	49	18	33	2.5	4.8	2.0	5%	0.5	19.3	61	$10
ERA Potl	30%	1st Half		2	1	3	41	18	2.20	1.07	242			4.7	27%	79%	4.26	46	20	34	1.5	4.0	2.6	2%	0.2	11.7	78	$7
LIMA Plan	D+	2nd Half		0	2	3	32	21	2.56	1.36	251			3.9	28%	85%	4.21	53	16	31	3.7	6.0	1.6	10%	0.9	7.6	49	$4
+/- Score	-47	08	Proj	3	5	8	73	40	3.97	1.35	281			7.0	31%	73%	4.23	51	17	32	2.2	5.0	2.2	9%	0.9	2.4	49	$7

Looks like a top flight reliever on the surface. In reality, career year was fueled by a friendly S% and hr/f. GB ability reduces his risk, but he'll need better command to sustain these levels. Dom, BPV unimpressive.

Jenks,Bobby				W	L	Sv	IP	K	ERA	WHIP	OBA	vL	vR	BF/G	H%	S%	xERA	G	L	F	Ctl	Dom	Cmd	hr/f	hr/9	RAR	BPV	R$
RH Reliever		03	aa	7	2	0	83	88	2.71	1.40	217			22.4	30%	80%	2.97				5.5	9.5	1.7		0.2	17.2	99	$11
Age	27	04	aaa	0	1	0	12	12	9.75	2.25	360			20.7	44%	56%	8.47				6.0	9.0	1.5		1.5	-8.0	24	($2)
Growth		05	CHW	* 2	3	25	80	89	3.12	1.37	247	105	298	5.1	34%	78%	3.45	45	26	30	4.1	10.0	2.5	6%	0.5	12.3	104	$16
Type	Pwr xGB	06	CHW	3	4	41	69	80	4.03	1.40	253	227	268	4.5	35%	72%	2.87	59	19	22	4.0	10.4	2.6	13%	0.7	4.5	102	$20
Reliability	55	07	CHW	3	5	40	65	56	2.77	0.89	197	237	169	3.8	25%	68%	2.99	54	16	30	1.8	7.8	4.3	4%	0.3	13.9	144	$24
ERA Potl	65%	1st Half		2	3	20	31	29	2.90	1.10	215			3.9	28%	73%	3.40	46	21	33	2.9	8.4	2.9	4%	0.3	6.1	115	$12
LIMA Plan	C+	2nd Half		1	2	20	34	27	2.65	0.71	180			3.6	23%	61%	2.64	60	11	29	0.8	7.1	9.0	4%	0.3	7.8	243	$13
+/- Score	-5	08	Proj	3	4	48	68	62	3.44	1.19	238			4.6	30%	72%	3.18	56	17	27	2.8	8.2	3.0	10%	0.7	11.0	99	$24

He has been a draft day bargain the last two years due to poor springs. This year he dialed down the heat, but Ctl gains made it well worth the tradeoff. H% correction will raise ERA, but he's solid.

Jennings,Jason				W	L	Sv	IP	K	ERA	WHIP	OBA	vL	vR	BF/G	H%	S%	xERA	G	L	F	Ctl	Dom	Cmd	hr/f	hr/9	RAR	BPV	R$
RH Starter		03	COL	12	13	0	181	119	5.12	1.66	293	323	271	25.9	33%	70%	4.84	48	20	32	4.4	5.9	1.4	10%	1.0	-18.8	30	$3
Age	29	04	COL	11	11	0	201	133	5.51	1.70	298	340	261	28.1	33%	70%	4.81	48	22	30	4.5	6.0	1.3	13%	1.2	-30.9	22	($0)
Peak		05	COL	6	9	0	122	75	5.02	1.57	274	269	279	27.4	31%	69%	4.72	48	25	27	4.6	5.5	1.2	10%	0.8	-11.6	34	$2
Type		06	COL	9	13	0	212	142	3.78	1.37	256	254	261	28.4	29%	74%	4.58	44	19	37	3.6	6.0	1.7	7%	0.7	18.5	53	$14
Reliability	36	07	HOU	2	9	0	99	71	6.45	1.55	299	309	295	23.3	32%	61%	4.82	35	21	44	3.1	6.5	2.1	13%	1.7	-24.8	26	($2)
ERA Potl	55%	1st Half		1	2	0	47	33	3.64	1.30	262			24.8	29%	76%	4.30	39	22	38	2.7	6.3	2.4	11%	1.1	4.6	56	$3
LIMA Plan	D	2nd Half		1	7	0	52	38	9.00	1.77	329			22.2	35%	51%	5.28	32	20	48	3.5	6.6	1.9	15%	2.2	-29.3	1	($5)
+/- Score	48	08	Proj	5	11	0	140	96	4.84	1.51	281			24.7	31%	71%	4.76	40	21	39	3.6	6.2	1.7	11%	1.3	-6.3	33	$4

H% and S% doomed him during 2nd half collapse. Torn flexor tendon ended season early. If he can go back to his GB ways, he'll shave a few ER from that ERA. But he'll still be mediocre.

Jimenez,Ubaldo				W	L	Sv	IP	K	ERA	WHIP	OBA	vL	vR	BF/G	H%	S%	xERA	G	L	F	Ctl	Dom	Cmd	hr/f	hr/9	RAR	BPV	R$
RH Starter		03		0	0	0	0	0	0.00	0.00																		
Age	24	04		0	0	0	0	0	0.00	0.00																		
Growth		05	aa	2	5	0	63	45	7.43	1.60	283			23.7	28%	59%	6.58				4.4	6.4	1.5		2.6	-24.3	-10	($3)
Type	Pwr	06	a/a	14	4	0	151	128	4.88	1.48	254			25.6	31%	67%	4.09				4.7	7.6	1.6		0.7	-6.7	63	$11
Reliability	0	07	COL	* 12	9	0	185	145	6.51	1.67	285	244	212	25.0	33%	61%	4.85	46	17	37	4.9	7.0	1.4	10%	1.1	-47.6	38	($0)
ERA Potl	60%	1st Half		5	5	0	84	65	8.88	1.97	323			25.7	37%	54%					5.7	7.0	1.2		1.3	-46.2	19	($8)
LIMA Plan	C	2nd Half		7	4	0	101	80	4.54	1.42	251			24.3	29%	69%	4.42	46	17	37	4.3	7.1	1.7	9%	0.9	-1.4	55	$7
+/- Score	58	08	Proj	11	10	0	183	145	4.92	1.52	267			24.6	31%	69%	4.56	46	17	37	4.5	7.1	1.6	10%	1.0	-3.7	47	$8

4-4, 4.28 ERA in 82 IP at COL. Showed late-season flashes of skill when he posted a 94 BPV in August. Good GB% will help him in sophomore campaign. If he knocks his Ctl down a bit, watch out.

STEPHEN NICKRAND

134

Johnson,Josh		Yr	W	L	Sv	IP	K	ERA	WHIP	OBA	vL	vR	BF/G	H%	S%	xERA	G	L	F	Ctl	Dom	Cmd	hr/f	hr/9	RAR	BPV	R$
RH Starter		03	0	0	0	0	0	0.00	0.00																		
Age	24	04	0	0	0	0	0	0.00	0.00																		
Growth		05 FLA *	1	4	0	151	112	4.71	1.56	288			22.5	35%	68%	4.38				3.8	6.7	1.8		0.2	-8.6	68	$1
Type	Pwr	06 FLA	12	7	0	157	133	3.10	1.30	235	246	227	21.4	28%	79%	4.06	46	19	36	3.9	7.6	2.0	9%	0.8	27.0	71	$18
Reliability	0	07 FLA	0	3	0	16	14	7.45	2.42	370	419	361	21.0	45%	68%	5.38	44	33	22	6.9	8.0	1.2	8%	0.6	-5.9	36	($2)
ERA Potl	65%	1st Half	0	2	0	7	5	14.14	3.43	463			22.2	52%	57%	7.26	45	38	17	9.0	6.4	0.7	18%	1.3	-8.4	-23	($3)
LIMA Plan	C	2nd Half	0	1	0	9	9	2.07	1.61	268			19.7	37%	86%	4.07	44	28	28	5.2	9.3	1.8	0%	0.0	2.5	95	$1
+/- Score	69	08 Proj	1	1	0	15	12	3.72	1.38	255			20.8	31%	74%	3.91	45	28	27	3.7	7.4	2.0	9%	0.6	0.9	72	$1

Tried to rehab forearm pain, but eventually underwent Tommy John surgery in August. Likely out until early 2009. Check back next year.

Johnson,Randy		Yr	W	L	Sv	IP	K	ERA	WHIP	OBA	vL	vR	BF/G	H%	S%	xERA	G	L	F	Ctl	Dom	Cmd	hr/f	hr/9	RAR	BPV	R$
LH Starter		03 ARI	6	8	0	114	125	4.26	1.33	280	303	276	26.9	36%	72%	3.17	40	27	32	2.1	9.9	4.6	15%	1.3	0.2	118	$9
Age	44	04 ARI	16	14	0	245	290	2.61	0.90	204	163	204	26.8	28%	74%	2.63	45	18	37	1.6	10.6	6.6	8%	0.7	50.1	197	$41
Decline		05 NYY	17	8	0	225	211	3.80	1.13	246	185	257	26.8	29%	72%	3.35	45	17	38	1.9	8.4	4.5	13%	1.3	16.0	112	$29
Type	Pwr	06 NYY	17	11	0	205	172	5.00	1.24	251	194	259	25.8	29%	62%	3.99	42	16	43	2.6	7.6	2.9	11%	1.2	-11.3	73	$20
Reliability	9	07 ARI	4	3	0	57	72	3.81	1.15	245	182	257	23.1	34%	71%	2.86	40	19	40	2.1	11.4	5.5	12%	1.1	4.3	157	$8
ERA Potl	55%	1st Half	4	2	0	54	70	3.50	1.06	232			23.9	33%	71%	2.66	42	18	40	1.8	11.7	6.4	12%	1.0	6.2	182	$8
LIMA Plan	C+	2nd Half	0	1	0	3	2	10.00	2.96	441			15.9	47%	71%	7.58	23	31	46	6.7	6.7	1.0	19%	3.3	-1.9	-72	($1)
+/- Score	16	08 Proj	10	8	0	149	121	4.41	1.42	273			28.1	32%	72%	4.24	43	18	39	3.2	7.3	2.3	11%	1.2	3.0	56	$10

Looked like his vintage self in the 1st half before undergoing another back surgery. But as he enters his mid 40s, his fantasy roster-worthiness is living on borrowed time. It's best to take out a month-to-month lease.

Jones,Todd		Yr	W	L	Sv	IP	K	ERA	WHIP	OBA	vL	vR	BF/G	H%	S%	xERA	G	L	F	Ctl	Dom	Cmd	hr/f	hr/9	RAR	BPV	R$
RH Reliever		03 2TM	3	5	0	68	59	7.15	1.82	327	323	323	5.5	38%	61%	4.43	45	24	31	4.1	7.8	1.9	14%	1.3	-23.1	37	($3)
Age	40	04 2NL	11	5	2	82	59	4.17	1.43	266	221	290	4.6	31%	72%	4.59	41	21	38	3.6	6.5	1.8	7%	0.8	1.0	55	$9
Decline		05 FLA	1	5	40	73	62	2.10	1.03	229	211	229	4.2	29%	79%	3.04	53	21	27	1.7	7.6	4.4	4%	0.2	19.4	141	$22
Type	Con	06 DET	2	6	37	64	28	3.94	1.27	279	264	284	4.3	30%	69%	4.16	53	18	29	1.5	3.9	2.5	6%	0.6	4.9	59	$16
Reliability	34	07 DET	1	4	38	61	33	4.26	1.42	270	265	269	4.2	30%	69%	4.75	46	21	33	3.4	4.8	1.4	5%	0.4	1.9	47	$15
ERA Potl	50%	1st Half	1	4	18	30	16	6.30	1.73	310			4.2	35%	61%	5.59	39	25	36	4.2	4.8	1.1	3%	0.3	-6.6	37	$5
LIMA Plan	D	2nd Half	0	0	20	31	17	2.30	1.12	228			4.2	25%	82%	3.94	54	18	29	2.6	4.9	1.9	7%	0.6	8.5	61	$10
+/- Score	-42	08 Proj	1	4	25	58	29	4.66	1.45	281			4.4	31%	68%	4.67	49	20	31	3.1	4.5	1.5	7%	0.6	-1.2	38	$10

Why 2008 will be the year he finally loses the closer's job...
- Ominous xERA trend
- Ctl of '05-'06 is gone
- 1st half showed downside

He can't afford another like that. DN: 15 saves

Julio,Jorge		Yr	W	L	Sv	IP	K	ERA	WHIP	OBA	vL	vR	BF/G	H%	S%	xERA	G	L	F	Ctl	Dom	Cmd	hr/f	hr/9	RAR	BPV	R$
RH Reliever		03 BAL	0	7	36	61	52	4.43	1.54	259	273	239	4.3	29%	76%	4.58	43	20	37	5.0	7.7	1.5	15%	1.5	0.7	37	$14
Age	29	04 BAL	2	5	22	69	70	4.57	1.42	233	234	221	4.6	28%	72%	4.31	41	14	45	5.1	9.1	1.8	13%	1.4	-1.1	58	$12
Pre-Peak		05 BAL	3	5	0	71	58	5.94	1.40	275	281	257	4.6	30%	62%	4.25	40	18	41	3.0	7.3	2.4	16%	1.8	-13.8	42	$2
Type	Pwr	06 2NL	2	4	16	66	88	4.23	1.32	218	185	234	4.5	30%	73%	3.29	40	21	39	4.8	12.0	2.5	17%	1.4	2.1	95	$11
Reliability	22	07 2NL	0	5	0	62	56	5.23	1.60	280	227	322	4.1	34%	69%	4.04	52	19	30	4.5	8.1	1.8	14%	1.2	-6.1	51	($0)
ERA Potl	60%	1st Half	0	2	0	23	16	6.26	1.91	294			4.3	33%	68%	5.80	46	18	36	6.7	6.3	0.9	11%	1.2	-5.2	18	($2)
LIMA Plan	D+	2nd Half	0	3	0	39	40	4.62	1.41	272			4.0	34%	70%	3.16	55	19	26	3.2	9.2	2.9	17%	1.2	-0.9	81	$2
+/- Score	41	08 Proj	1	3	0	44	43	4.76	1.45	251			4.2	31%	70%	3.96	46	19	35	4.6	8.9	2.0	14%	1.2	2.4	62	$2

Led the NL in most pitches over 95mph (thanks, Bill James 2008 Handbook) but he can't hold a job. 2nd half elite Dom and declining FB% give a hint of what could be. That's why he'll keep getting chances.

Jurrjens,Jair		Yr	W	L	Sv	IP	K	ERA	WHIP	OBA	vL	vR	BF/G	H%	S%	xERA	G	L	F	Ctl	Dom	Cmd	hr/f	hr/9	RAR	BPV	R$
RH Starter		03	0	0	0	0	0	0.00	0.00																		
Age	22	04	0	0	0	0	0	0.00	0.00																		
Green		05	0	0	0	0	0	0.00	0.00																		
Type	FB	06 aa	4	3	0	67	48	4.22	1.52	300			24.8	34%	75%	5.15				2.8	6.5	2.3		1.0	2.5	52	$4
Reliability	0	07 DET *	10	6	0	143	94	4.47	1.42	284	262	167	23.9	32%	69%	4.80	38	18	44	2.7	5.9	2.2	6%	0.8	0.6	57	$10
ERA Potl	50%	1st Half	3	3	0	73	47	4.92	1.63	315			25.6	37%	68%					3.0	5.8	2.0		0.2	-3.7	60	$1
LIMA Plan	C	2nd Half	7	3	0	70	47	4.00	1.21	249			22.1	27%	72%	4.40	38	18	44	2.5	6.1	2.5	11%	1.3	4.3	55	$8
+/- Score	4	08 Proj	6	4	0	87	60	4.45	1.44	288			23.7	32%	72%	4.70	38	18	44	2.7	6.2	2.3	9%	1.1	-2.2	49	$6

3-1, 4.70 ERA in 30 IP at DET. Fared well as a 21-year-old in AA, then held his own with DET. But MLB skills weren't good, so more seasoning in the high minors is needed. Risky in '08.

Kazmir,Scott		Yr	W	L	Sv	IP	K	ERA	WHIP	OBA	vL	vR	BF/G	H%	S%	xERA	G	L	F	Ctl	Dom	Cmd	hr/f	hr/9	RAR	BPV	R$
LH Starter		03	0	0	0	0	0	0.00	0.00											0.0	0.0						
Age	24	04 aa	3	3	0	51	48	1.85	1.01	184			25.0	25%	80%	1.42				3.4	8.5	2.5		0.0	15.7	123	$9
Growth		05 TAM	10	9	0	186	174	3.77	1.46	247	174	268	25.5	31%	75%	4.38	42	20	38	4.8	8.4	1.7	6%	0.6	13.7	75	$15
Type	Pwr FB	06 TAM	10	8	0	144	163	3.25	1.28	245	227	242	25.2	32%	78%	3.42	42	19	39	3.2	10.2	3.1	10%	0.9	23.3	105	$20
Reliability	43	07 TAM	13	9	0	207	239	3.48	1.38	252	217	263	26.1	34%	77%	3.64	43	16	41	3.9	10.4	2.7	8%	0.8	26.1	100	$24
ERA Potl	60%	1st Half	5	3	0	96	96	4.13	1.55	270			26.8	34%	76%	4.31	42	17	41	4.6	9.0	2.0	9%	0.9	4.5	68	$7
LIMA Plan	C+	2nd Half	8	6	0	111	143	2.93	1.23	235			25.5	34%	78%	3.10	44	14	42	3.3	11.6	3.6	7%	0.7	21.6	133	$17
+/- Score	35	08 Proj	15	10	0	203	229	3.19	1.27	237			25.0	32%	78%	3.50	43	17	40	3.5	10.2	2.9	9%	0.8	25.0	103	$28

On the surface, looks like a repeat of 2006. But check out that 2nd half. Posted a 125+ BPV in both Aug and Sept. Had a PQS-4/5 in all but two starts during that period. A legit ace. UP: 2.90 ERA, 250 K

Kendrick,Kyle		Yr	W	L	Sv	IP	K	ERA	WHIP	OBA	vL	vR	BF/G	H%	S%	xERA	G	L	F	Ctl	Dom	Cmd	hr/f	hr/9	RAR	BPV	R$
RH Starter		03	0	0	0	0	0	0.00	0.00																		
Age	23	04	0	0	0	0	0	0.00	0.00																		
Growth		05	0	0	0	0	0	0.00	0.00																		
Type	Con	06	0	0	0	0	0	0.00	0.00																		
Reliability	6	07 PHI *	14	11	0	202	91	3.88	1.33	283	321	241	26.8	30%	73%	4.45	47	21	32	1.9	4.0	2.1	9%	0.9	13.7	39	$15
ERA Potl	40%	1st Half	6	7	0	99	51	4.00	1.35	282			28.2	31%	71%	4.50	45	21	34	2.2	4.6	2.1	6%	0.6	5.3	52	$7
LIMA Plan	C	2nd Half	8	4	0	103	40	3.76	1.31	283			25.6	29%	75%	4.48	47	21	32	1.7	3.5	2.0	11%	1.1	8.4	27	$8
+/- Score	-10	08 Proj	10	11	0	174	77	4.29	1.36	283			26.6	30%	71%	4.53	47	21	32	2.2	4.0	1.8	10%	1.0	-2.8	31	$10

10-4, 3.87 ERA in 121 IP at PHI. He'll be overrated based on these surface stats. As a low Dom, control type, he puts his fate in the hands of his infield. Use his xERA as your baseline for '08.

Kennedy,Ian		Yr	W	L	Sv	IP	K	ERA	WHIP	OBA	vL	vR	BF/G	H%	S%	xERA	G	L	F	Ctl	Dom	Cmd	hr/f	hr/9	RAR	BPV	R$
RH Starter		03	0	0	0	0	0	0.00	0.00																		
Age	23	04	0	0	0	0	0	0.00	0.00																		
Growth		05	0	0	0	0	0	0.00	0.00																		
Type	Pwr xFB	06	0	0	0	0	0	0.00	0.00																		
Reliability	0	07 NYY *	7	2	0	102	91	3.00	1.13	209	161	216	23.0	26%	74%	4.36	26	23	51	3.4	8.0	2.3	4%	0.5	19.0	94	$15
ERA Potl	55%	1st Half	3	1	0	26	25	4.15	1.27	247			21.8	32%	66%					3.1	8.7	2.8		0.3	1.1	106	$3
LIMA Plan	C+	2nd Half	4	1	0	76	66	2.60	1.08	195			23.4	24%	78%	4.37	26	23	51	3.5	7.8	2.2	5%	0.6	17.9	91	$11
+/- Score	-18	08 Proj	9	5	0	145	126	4.16	1.36	252			23.9	31%	71%	4.73	26	23	51	3.7	7.8	2.1	6%	0.8	-4.1	72	$13

1-0, 1.89 ERA in 19 IP at NYY. Quickly ascended through the minors, then looked good in a September stint. Doesn't have the raw stuff of Joba or Hughes, but knows how to pitch. Worth a look.

Kennedy,Joe		Yr	W	L	Sv	IP	K	ERA	WHIP	OBA	vL	vR	BF/G	H%	S%	xERA	G	L	F	Ctl	Dom	Cmd	hr/f	hr/9	RAR	BPV	R$
LH Reliever		03 TAM	3	12	1	133	77	6.16	1.61	308	230	324	18.8	33%	63%	4.95	44	19	37	3.2	5.2	1.6	11%	1.3	-26.8	20	($2)
Age	28	04 COL	9	7	0	162	117	3.66	1.42	263	183	289	26.0	30%	77%	4.36	48	17	34	3.7	6.5	1.7	10%	0.9	11.9	50	$11
Pre-Peak		05 2TM	8	13	0	152	97	6.03	1.68	309	265	320	20.0	34%	65%	4.82	45	22	32	3.8	5.7	1.5	12%	1.2	-32.4	24	($2)
Type	Pwr	06 OAK	4	1	1	35	29	2.31	1.34	256	326	220	3.8	32%	83%	3.90	49	20	31	3.3	7.5	2.2	3%	0.3	9.7	88	$6
Reliability		07 2TM	4	9	0	111	51	4.80	1.57	276	204	306	12.7	30%	70%	5.38	49	16	35	4.5	4.1	0.9	7%	0.7	-4.6	22	$2
ERA Potl		1st Half	2	5	0	84	33	3.96	1.45	266			24.5	28%	75%	5.27	50	14	36	3.9	3.5	0.9	8%	0.9	5.2	16	$3
LIMA Plan		2nd Half	2	4	0	27	18	7.42	1.95	305			5.4	36%	59%	5.77	45	23	32	6.4	6.1	0.9	3%	0.3	-9.7	40	($2)
+/- Score		08 Proj																									

His career was marked with intermittent signs of solid skill, but he was never able to tie it all together. So sad. R.I.P.

STEPHEN NICKRAND

Kim,Byung-Hyun			W	L	Sv	IP	K	ERA	WHIP	OBA	vL	vR	BF/G	H%	S%	xERA	G	L	F	Ctl	Dom	Cmd	hr/f	hr/9	RAR	BPV	R$
RH Starter	03	2TM	9	10	16	122	102	3.32	1.12	232	221	227	8.8	28%	74%	3.54	47	19	34	2.4	7.5	3.1	10%	0.9	16.2	92	$21
Age 29	04	BOS	* 4	7	0	77	40	6.29	1.50	310	308	185	11.8	34%	57%	4.81	45	16	39	2.1	4.7	2.2	7%	0.8	-17.7	43	$0
Pre-Peak	05	COL	5	12	0	148	115	4.86	1.53	272	308	244	16.5	31%	70%	4.72	42	20	39	4.3	7.0	1.6	10%	1.0	-11.3	46	$3
Type Pwr	06	COL	8	12	0	155	129	5.57	1.55	291	325	265	25.7	34%	65%	4.33	42	23	35	3.5	7.5	2.1	10%	1.0	-20.8	55	$4
Reliability 32	07	2NL	* 11	9	0	142	129	5.93	1.72	289	316	242	20.0	34%	68%	4.83	40	20	40	5.2	8.2	1.6	14%	1.5	-26.3	34	$2
ERA Potl 55%	1st Half		4	5	0	70	65	5.14	1.63	264			19.9	31%	72%	4.70	45	15	41	5.5	8.3	1.5	13%	1.4	-6.1	42	$2
LIMA Plan B	2nd Half		7	4	0	72	64	6.69	1.82	312			20.1	36%	65%	4.93	37	23	40	4.8	8.0	1.7	14%	1.6	-20.2	28	($0)
+/- Score 24	08	Proj	5	7	0	87	74	5.07	1.56	277			21.7	33%	69%	4.58	41	21	38	4.3	7.7	1.8	10%	1.0	-1.9	51	$3

10-8, 6.08 ERA in 118 IP at ARI, COL, and FLA. Same old story. Sexy Dom, but spotty Ctl and struggles vs. LHers do him in. 2003 is gone; since then, he's accumulated lots of RAR baggage, and he's still only 29.

King,Ray			W	L	Sv	IP	K	ERA	WHIP	OBA	vL	vR	BF/G	H%	S%	xERA	G	L	F	Ctl	Dom	Cmd	hr/f	hr/9	RAR	BPV	R$
LH Reliever	03	ATL	3	4	0	59	43	3.51	1.24	217	200	223	3.1	26%	71%	3.95	55	17	29	4.1	6.6	1.6	6%	0.5	5.6	71	$5
Age 34	04	STL	5	2	0	62	40	2.61	1.08	197	150	248	2.9	24%	74%	4.01	51	19	31	3.5	5.8	1.7	2%	0.1	12.6	81	$9
Past Peak	05	STL	4	4	0	40	23	3.38	1.55	290	244	352	2.3	32%	81%	4.58	50	22	29	3.6	5.2	1.4	10%	0.9	4.3	31	$3
Type Pwr	06	COL	1	4	1	44	23	4.48	1.72	310	303	347	3.1	33%	77%	4.78	53	22	25	4.1	4.7	1.2	15%	1.2	0.0	9	$0
Reliability 14	07	2NL	1	1	0	40	25	4.76	1.49	248	187	311	2.6	26%	72%	5.13	41	22	37	5.0	5.7	1.1	13%	1.4	-1.6	22	$1
ERA Potl 40%	1st Half		0	0	0	19	8	6.16	1.58	291			2.9	27%	68%	5.10	39	32	29	3.8	3.8	1.0	26%	2.4	-4.1	-31	($1)
LIMA Plan C+	2nd Half		1	1	0	21	17	3.48	1.40	204			2.4	25%	75%	5.13	42	12	46	6.1	7.4	1.2	4%	0.4	2.4	71	$2
+/- Score -43	08	Proj	1	2	0	29	18	4.66	1.59	275			2.7	31%	72%	4.97	46	21	32	4.7	5.6	1.2	10%	0.9	-2.0	31	$0

This is why you should put a glove on your son's right hand immediately after birth. No matter what happens in the next 18 years, feel safe in knowing that he can always find gainful employment in the good ol' MLB.

Kline,Steve			W	L	Sv	IP	K	ERA	WHIP	OBA	vL	vR	BF/G	H%	S%	xERA	G	L	F	Ctl	Dom	Cmd	hr/f	hr/9	RAR	BPV	R$
LH Reliever	03	STL	5	5	3	63	31	3.86	1.37	240	243	233	3.5	26%	73%	4.95	52	14	35	4.3	4.4	1.0	7%	0.7	3.3	34	$6
Age 35	04	STL	2	2	3	50	35	1.80	1.08	208	143	269	3.0	24%	86%	3.56	58	14	28	3.1	6.3	2.1	7%	0.5	15.2	78	$8
Decline	05	BAL	2	4	0	61	36	4.28	1.46	255	317	209	4.0	26%	77%	4.44	56	16	28	4.4	5.3	1.2	20%	1.6	0.7	12	$2
Type	06	SF	4	3	1	51	33	3.69	1.54	269	261	287	3.2	31%	76%	4.92	47	19	34	4.6	5.8	1.3	5%	0.5	5.0	47	$4
Reliability 14	07	SF	1	2	2	46	17	4.70	1.65	309	318	287	3.1	33%	70%	5.47	48	19	33	3.5	3.3	0.9	4%	0.4	-1.5	21	$0
ERA Potl 50%	1st Half		0	1	1	22	6	4.50	1.77	326			3.7	34%	74%	5.81	49	20	31	3.7	2.5	0.7	4%	0.4	-0.2	6	($0)
LIMA Plan C+	2nd Half		1	1	1	24	11	4.87	1.54	293			2.7	32%	67%	5.17	47	18	35	3.4	4.1	1.2	3%	0.4	-1.3	36	$1
+/- Score -45	08	Proj	2	3	3	58	29	4.19	1.53	281			3.2	31%	73%	5.02	49	18	33	3.9	4.5	1.2	6%	0.6	-4.4	31	$2

More evidence that it doesn't matter if you can't hit the side of a barn with a handful of rice. As long as you're tossing with your left hand, MLB doors will be open.

Kuo,Hong-Chih			W	L	Sv	IP	K	ERA	WHIP	OBA	vL	vR	BF/G	H%	S%	xERA	G	L	F	Ctl	Dom	Cmd	hr/f	hr/9	RAR	BPV	R$
LH Reliever	03		0	0	0	0	0	0.00	0.00																		
Age 26	04		0	0	0	0	0	0.00	0.00																		
Growth	05	aa	1	2	3	33	49	3.82	1.48	250			5.6	40%	74%	3.86				4.9	13.4	2.7		0.5	2.0	126	$4
Type Pwr FB	06	LA	* 5	8	1	112	123	3.70	1.45	255	241	246	9.6	34%	75%	3.72	44	21	34	4.3	9.9	2.3	8%	0.6	10.8	92	$9
Reliability 0	07	LA	* 1	5	0	50	49	6.32	1.61	290	240	296	15.2	36%	60%	4.78	31	20	49	4.2	8.8	2.1	7%	0.9	-11.8	65	($1)
ERA Potl 80%	1st Half		1	4	0	47	49	5.36	1.45	270			14.7	35%	63%	4.27	31	20	48	3.6	9.4	2.6	6%	0.8	-5.4	88	$1
LIMA Plan A+	2nd Half		0	1	0	3	0	20.03	3.99	491			22.8	45%	49%	14.74	25	17	58	11.4	0.0	0.0	12%	3.5	-6.4	******	($2)
+/- Score 71	08	Proj	2	5	0	73	89	4.34	1.46	258			8.1	36%	70%	3.82	36	21	44	4.3	11.0	2.5	6%	0.6	5.2	105	$4

1-4, 7.42 ERA in 30 IP at LA. The ultimate high risk, high reward. Seemingly can't get through a season without some kind of arm injury. But he'll keep getting chances, and he's still too young to give up on.

Kuroda,Hiroki			W	L	Sv	IP	K	ERA	WHIP	OBA	vL	vR	BF/G	H%	S%	xERA	G	L	F	Ctl	Dom	Cmd	hr/f	hr/9	RAR	BPV	R$
RH Starter	03	JPN	13	9	0	206	130	3.85	1.30	267			31.0	29%	75%	4.42				2.4	5.7	2.3		1.3	13.7	45	$17
Age 33	04	JPN	7	9	0	147	131	5.78	1.61	326			31.7	38%	68%	6.50				2.2	8.0	3.6		1.7	-26.0	62	$2
Peak	05	JPN	15	12	0	213	157	3.94	1.17	246			30.0	27%	71%	3.68				2.2	6.6	3.0		1.2	9.7	73	$22
Type	06	JPN	13	6	1	189	137	2.31	1.10	254			29.2	29%	85%	3.35				1.2	6.5	5.2		0.9	51.6	125	$28
Reliability 66	07	JPN	12	8	0	180	117	4.41	1.34	271			29.5	28%	74%	4.93				2.6	5.8	2.2		1.7	1.2	33	$13
ERA Potl 45%	1st Half		0	0	0	0	0	0.00	0.00											0.0	0.0				0.0	55	
LIMA Plan D+	2nd Half		12	8	0	180	117	4.41	1.34	271			29.5	28%	74%					2.6	5.8	2.2		1.7	1.2	33	$13
+/- Score -17	08	Proj	9	7	0	145	99	4.34	1.35	276			26.9	30%	72%	4.74				2.5	6.1	2.5		1.4	-5.2	48	$11

Solid base skills, but at 33 and facing the typical one year adjustment period, odds are he's not going to provide much value in 2008. This projection may be a bit generous.

Lackey,John			W	L	Sv	IP	K	ERA	WHIP	OBA	vL	vR	BF/G	H%	S%	xERA	G	L	F	Ctl	Dom	Cmd	hr/f	hr/9	RAR	BPV	R$
RH Starter	03	ANA	10	16	0	204	151	4.63	1.42	279	286	269	26.8	31%	71%	4.37	41	21	39	2.9	6.7	2.3	12%	1.4	-2.7	46	$12
Age 29	04	ANA	14	13	0	198	144	4.68	1.39	278	303	248	25.9	32%	68%	4.34	44	16	40	2.7	6.5	2.4	9%	1.0	-6.0	59	$13
Peak	05	ANA	14	5	0	209	199	3.44	1.33	261	274	241	26.9	33%	75%	3.64	45	23	33	3.1	8.6	2.8	7%	0.6	23.9	96	$22
Type	06	LAA	13	11	0	217	190	3.56	1.27	249	263	231	27.6	31%	72%	3.93	43	18	39	3.0	7.9	2.6	6%	0.6	26.6	90	$25
Reliability 96	07	LAA	19	9	0	224	179	3.01	1.21	257	280	229	28.0	31%	77%	3.75	45	19	36	2.1	7.2	3.4	7%	0.7	41.2	97	$30
ERA Potl 55%	1st Half		10	5	0	105	82	3.00	1.21	249			27.1	29%	79%	3.91	42	21	37	2.5	7.0	2.8	9%	0.9	19.5	81	$15
LIMA Plan D+	2nd Half		9	4	0	119	97	3.03	1.21	265			28.9	32%	76%	3.62	47	17	36	1.7	7.3	4.2	6%	0.6	21.7	116	$16
+/- Score 4	08	Proj	17	7	0	203	170	3.37	1.27	259			27.4	31%	75%	3.83	44	19	37	2.5	7.5	3.0	8%	0.8	16.7	88	$25

Three straight years of 90-plus BPVs and he's only still peaking. Not only has he become an elite level pitcher but he also possesses one other hugely valuable asset... a 96 reliability score. Talented AND consistent.

Lannan,John			W	L	Sv	IP	K	ERA	WHIP	OBA	vL	vR	BF/G	H%	S%	xERA	G	L	F	Ctl	Dom	Cmd	hr/f	hr/9	RAR	BPV	R$
LH Starter	03		0	0	0	0	0	0.00	0.00																		
Age 23	04		0	0	0	0	0	0.00	0.00																		
Growth	05		0	0	0	0	0	0.00	0.00																		
Type Con GB	06		0	0	0	0	0	0.00	0.00																		
Reliability 0	07	WAS	* 8	5	0	109	43	3.31	1.38	257	273	273	24.6	28%	76%	5.11	51	14	35	3.6	3.6	1.0	5%	0.5	14.9	31	$9
ERA Potl 35%	1st Half		4	2	0	47	21	3.24	1.42	269			25.6	30%	77%					3.4	4.0	1.2		0.4	6.9	38	$4
LIMA Plan C	2nd Half		4	3	0	62	22	3.37	1.35	247			23.9	26%	76%	5.20	51	14	35	3.8	3.2	0.8	5%	0.6	8.0	25	$5
+/- Score -40	08	Proj	3	4	0	58	24	4.66	1.57	288			26.0	30%	72%	5.30	51	14	35	3.9	3.7	1.0	8%	0.9	-6.4	12	$1

2-2, 4.15 ERA in 34 IP at WAS. Another misleading ERA. Keeps ball on ground, but that's really his only strength. At age 23, he's got time to grow, but with little skill support, his short-term future looks bleak.

Ledezma,Wil			W	L	Sv	IP	K	ERA	WHIP	OBA	vL	vR	BF/G	H%	S%	xERA	G	L	F	Ctl	Dom	Cmd	hr/f	hr/9	RAR	BPV	R$
LH Reliever	03	DET	3	7	0	84	49	5.79	1.60	295	309	292	11.2	32%	66%	5.62	33	18	49	3.8	5.3	1.4	9%	1.3	-13.1	18	$0
Age 27	04	DET	* 14	6	0	164	107	3.40	1.25	261	227	285	21.4	30%	74%	4.27	46	14	39	2.3	5.9	2.5	5%	0.6	21.0	73	$18
Growth	05	DET	* 6	7	0	99	66	6.90	1.70	298	352	286	22.9	33%	60%	5.26	43	18	40	4.5	6.0	1.3	10%	1.2	-30.9	24	($2)
Type Pwr FB	06	DET	* 7	6	0	131	95	3.45	1.36	263	241	261	15.6	30%	77%	4.74	34	21	46	3.2	6.5	2.1	7%	0.8	18.0	60	$13
Reliability 10	07	2TM	3	3	0	59	47	5.62	1.82	295	312	288	6.4	34%	70%	5.48	39	20	41	5.8	7.1	1.2	9%	1.1	-8.4	33	($1)
ERA Potl 50%	1st Half		3	1	0	39	28	4.62	1.67	262			6.9	30%	74%	5.69	38	19	44	6.0	6.5	1.1	8%	0.9	-0.7	36	$2
LIMA Plan D	2nd Half		0	2	0	20	19	7.54	2.12	351			5.7	42%	65%	5.08	42	22	36	5.3	8.4	1.6	12%	1.3	-7.7	29	($2)
+/- Score 10	08	Proj	3	4	0	58	45	4.97	1.69	297			8.6	34%	73%	5.04	39	20	40	4.5	7.0	1.6	9%	1.1	-4.3	38	$1

Flopped for three different clubs in '07. Improving Dom would give optimism if not for spotty control. Has struggled vs. LHers in three of last five years, meaning his job security will continue to be an issue.

Lee,Cliff			W	L	Sv	IP	K	ERA	WHIP	OBA	vL	vR	BF/G	H%	S%	xERA	G	L	F	Ctl	Dom	Cmd	hr/f	hr/9	RAR	BPV	R$
LH Starter	03	CLE	* 10	4	0	127	104	3.97	1.47	263	278	197	25.4	31%	76%	4.75	37	19	44	4.2	7.4	1.8	8%	1.0	8.7	54	$11
Age 29	04	CLE	14	8	0	179	161	5.43	1.50	271	231	277	24.0	31%	67%	4.60	34	21	45	4.1	8.1	2.0	13%	1.5	-22.0	46	$9
Peak	05	CLE	18	5	0	202	143	3.79	1.22	254	293	237	26.1	29%	72%	4.35	35	21	44	2.3	6.4	2.8	8%	1.0	14.6	71	$23
Type xFB	06	CLE	14	11	0	200	129	4.41	1.41	284	261	282	26.3	31%	73%	4.95	33	19	48	2.6	5.8	2.2	9%	1.3	3.8	41	$15
Reliability 48	07	CLE	* 7	11	0	143	109	5.73	1.59	283	327	267	22.3	32%	65%	5.29	35	15	50	4.3	6.8	1.6	8%	1.1	-21.6	38	$3
ERA Potl 50%	1st Half		5	4	0	73	50	4.93	1.38	270			24.2	28%	70%	4.96	34	14	52	3.1	6.2	2.0	12%	1.7	-3.8	28	$5
LIMA Plan D+	2nd Half		2	7	0	70	59	6.55	1.81	297			20.8	36%	62%	5.57	37	17	46	5.6	7.5	1.3	4%	0.5	-17.7	53	($2)
+/- Score -4	08	Proj	10	10	0	162	120	4.56	1.44	279			23.6	31%	72%	4.82	35	18	48	3.2	6.7	2.1	9%	1.3	-6.5	45	$11

5-8, 6.29 ERA in 97 IP at CLE. A lost season. Abdominal strain came first, then H% and S% doomed him later. Has the skill history to bounce back, but as an extreme flyballer, 2005 will be tough to duplicate.

STEPHEN NICKRAND

Lester,Jon

Lester,Jon	Yr	Tm	W	L	Sv	IP	K	ERA	WHIP	OBA	vL	vR	BF/G	H%	S%	xERA	G	L	F	Ctl	Dom	Cmd	hr/f	hr/9	RAR	BPV	R$
LH Starter	03		0	0	0	0	0	0.00	0.00																		
Age 24	04		0	0	0	0	0	0.00	0.00																		
Growth	05	aa	1	6	0	148	139	3.40	1.30	244			24.1	31%	75%	3.49				3.5	8.4	**2.4**		0.7	16.5	87	$11
Type Pwr FB	06	BOS	* 10	6	0	127	100	4.39	1.64	283	397	271	22.3	33%	75%	4.93	41	22	38	4.8	7.1	**1.5**	8%	0.9	2.7	45	$8
Reliability 0	07	BOS	* 9	5	0	140	97	4.69	1.52	270	231	267	23.1	31%	70%	5.31	34	19	47	4.3	6.2	**1.4**	7%	0.9	-3.1	42	$7
ERA Potl 50%	1st Half		2	4	0	52	32	5.17	1.57	290			21.3	33%	65%					3.8	5.5	**1.5**		0.3	-4.3	50	$1
LIMA Plan C	2nd Half		7	1	0	88	65	4.40	1.49	257			24.2	29%	74%	5.18	34	19	47	4.6	6.6	**1.4**	10%	1.2	1.2	37	$6
+/- Score -15	08	Proj	**10**	**7**	**0**	**160**	**122**	**4.39**	**1.53**	**271**			**23.7**	**31%**	**74%**	**4.98**	**37**	**20**	**43**	**4.3**	**6.9**	**1.6**	**8%**	**1.0**	**-9.6**	**45**	**$10**

4-0, 4.57 ERA in 63 IP at BOS. Regardless of performance, has to be considered an incredibly successful return from lymphoma. Now he's just another young SP who needs to improve his Cmd to be successful.

Lidge,Brad

Lidge,Brad	Yr	Tm	W	L	Sv	IP	K	ERA	WHIP	OBA	vL	vR	BF/G	H%	S%	xERA	G	L	F	Ctl	Dom	Cmd	hr/f	hr/9	RAR	BPV	R$
RH Reliever	03	HOU	6	3	1	85	97	3.60	1.20	200	230	179	4.5	27%	71%	3.70	35	24	41	4.4	10.3	**2.3**	7%	0.6	7.1	106	$11
Age 31	04	HOU	6	5	29	94	157	1.91	0.92	177	191	155	4.5	31%	85%	2.24	32	21	47	2.9	15.0	**5.2**	10%	0.8	27.3	197	$28
Peak	05	HOU	4	4	42	70	103	2.31	1.15	227	244	202	4.1	36%	83%	2.35	47	23	30	2.9	13.2	**4.5**	11%	0.6	16.8	164	$25
Type Pwr	06	HOU	1	5	32	75	104	5.28	1.40	246	286	201	4.2	35%	64%	3.00	44	23	33	4.3	12.5	**2.9**	17%	1.2	-7.3	105	$15
Reliability 56	07	HOU	5	3	19	67	88	3.36	1.25	222	184	243	4.2	31%	79%	3.22	42	15	43	4.0	11.8	**2.9**	13%	1.2	8.8	107	$15
ERA Potl 55%	1st Half		2	1	0	35	44	2.31	1.26	221			4.3	31%	85%	3.39	42	15	43	4.1	11.3	**2.8**	8%	0.8	9.1	113	$5
LIMA Plan B	2nd Half		3	2	19	32	44	4.50	1.25	224			4.2	30%	71%	3.03	43	14	43	3.9	12.4	**3.1**	19%	1.7	-0.3	100	$10
+/- Score 29	08	Proj	**4**	**4**	**38**	**73**	**97**	**3.23**	**1.23**	**218**			**4.2**	**31%**	**78%**	**3.04**	**43**	**19**	**39**	**4.0**	**12.0**	**3.0**	**13%**	**1.0**	**12.2**	**118**	**$22**

Almost a carbon copy of 2006, just with better hit/strand rates. Skill set has stabilized and still remains closer-worthy. General perception is that he's volatile, which may create a discount buying opportunity.

Lieber,Jon

Lieber,Jon	Yr	Tm	W	L	Sv	IP	K	ERA	WHIP	OBA	vL	vR	BF/G	H%	S%	xERA	G	L	F	Ctl	Dom	Cmd	hr/f	hr/9	RAR	BPV	R$
RH Starter	03	NYY	0	0	0	0	0	0.00	0.00											0.0	0.0						
Age 38	04	NYY	14	8	0	176	102	4.34	1.33	303	346	250	27.7	33%	70%	3.90	52	15	33	0.9	5.2	**5.7**	10%	1.0	2.0	114	$13
Decline	05	PHI	17	13	0	218	149	4.21	1.21	266	305	223	25.7	29%	70%	3.75	46	22	33	1.7	6.1	**3.6**	15%	1.4	1.0	74	$20
Type Con	06	PHI	9	11	0	168	100	4.93	1.31	293	304	278	26.3	31%	66%	4.10	43	22	35	1.3	5.4	**4.2**	13%	1.4	-9.1	73	$9
Reliability 43	07	PHI	3	6	0	78	54	4.73	1.45	293	310	278	24.3	34%	68%	4.09	44	28	29	2.5	6.2	**2.5**	9%	0.8	-2.9	61	$3
ERA Potl 60%	1st Half		3	6	0	78	54	4.73	1.45	293			24.3	34%	68%	4.09	44	28	29	2.5	6.2	**2.5**	9%	0.8	-2.9	61	$3
LIMA Plan B	2nd Half		0	0	0	0	0	0.00	0.00																		
+/- Score 8	08	Proj	**10**	**10**	**0**	**158**	**103**	**4.50**	**1.35**	**285**			**25.9**	**32%**	**69%**	**4.03**	**46**	**22**	**32**	**2.0**	**5.9**	**2.9**	**11%**	**1.1**	**7.2**	**62**	**$10**

Ruptured tendon in his foot ended season in July. Before that, had traded a little Ctl for a Dom bump. At 38, that isn't likely sustainable. Should get back to eating innings in a rotation, but at 38 it's just downhill from here.

Lilly,Ted

Lilly,Ted	Yr	Tm	W	L	Sv	IP	K	ERA	WHIP	OBA	vL	vR	BF/G	H%	S%	xERA	G	L	F	Ctl	Dom	Cmd	hr/f	hr/9	RAR	BPV	R$
LH Starter	03	OAK	12	10	0	178	147	4.35	1.33	263	235	261	23.6	30%	71%	4.35	35	20	45	2.9	7.4	**2.5**	10%	1.2	3.9	64	$16
Age 32	04	TOR	12	10	0	197	168	4.06	1.32	235	196	238	26.1	27%	73%	4.52	36	18	46	4.1	7.7	**1.9**	10%	1.2	9.0	58	$17
Peak	05	TOR	10	11	0	126	96	5.57	1.53	275	336	248	22.4	30%	68%	4.82	37	22	41	4.1	6.9	**1.7**	14%	1.6	-18.6	27	$5
Type Pwr xFB	06	TOR	15	13	0	181	160	4.32	1.43	259	202	265	24.7	30%	75%	4.44	38	19	43	4.0	7.9	**2.0**	12%	1.4	5.3	51	$17
Reliability 72	07	CHC	15	8	0	207	174	3.83	1.14	237	258	230	24.7	27%	71%	4.11	34	17	49	2.4	7.6	**3.2**	10%	1.2	15.3	83	$24
ERA Potl 50%	1st Half		6	4	0	98	87	4.04	1.10	235			24.6	28%	67%	3.87	34	19	48	2.1	8.0	**3.8**	10%	1.2	4.7	100	$11
LIMA Plan D	2nd Half		9	4	0	109	87	3.63	1.17	238			24.8	27%	74%	4.34	34	16	50	2.6	7.2	**2.7**	9%	1.2	10.7	70	$13
+/- Score -7	08	Proj	**14**	**10**	**0**	**183**	**153**	**4.23**	**1.35**	**261**			**24.4**	**30%**	**73%**	**4.41**	**35**	**19**	**46**	**3.2**	**7.5**	**2.4**	**11%**	**1.3**	**-0.3**	**58**	**$16**

The latest AL-to-NL left-handed crossover to find success. Key driver was the Ctl improvement, which defies his long-term track record. A lot would need to go right for a repeat; regression is a better bet.

Lincecum,Tim

Lincecum,Tim	Yr	Tm	W	L	Sv	IP	K	ERA	WHIP	OBA	vL	vR	BF/G	H%	S%	xERA	G	L	F	Ctl	Dom	Cmd	hr/f	hr/9	RAR	BPV	R$
RH Starter	03		0	0	0	0	0	0.00	0.00																		
Age 23	04		0	0	0	0	0	0.00	0.00																		
Growth	05		0	0	0	0	0	0.00	0.00																		
Type Pwr	06		0	0	0	0	0	0.00	0.00																		
Reliability 4	07	SF	* 11	5	0	177	188	3.35	1.20	214	214	238	25.2	29%	73%	3.52	47	15	38	3.9	9.5	**2.5**	7%	0.6	23.5	103	$22
ERA Potl 60%	1st Half		6	2	0	90	101	3.50	1.14	199			24.4	27%	70%	3.39	46	16	38	4.0	10.1	**2.5**	7%	0.6	10.3	111	$12
LIMA Plan C+	2nd Half		5	3	0	87	87	3.20	1.26	230			26.0	30%	76%	3.67	48	15	37	3.7	9.0	**2.4**	7%	0.6	13.2	94	$10
+/- Score 16	08	Proj	**13**	**7**	**0**	**174**	**177**	**3.83**	**1.27**	**231**			**26.0**	**30%**	**71%**	**3.66**	**47**	**15**	**37**	**3.8**	**9.2**	**2.4**	**9%**	**0.8**	**15.9**	**91**	**$19**

7-5, 4.00 ERA in 146 IP at SF. Skill set is the stuff of dreams: high DOM, GB%, low hitter BAs. Ctl is tolerable now given lack of experience, but there will be bumps in the road, and the hype machine may overvalue him.

Lindstrom,Matt

Lindstrom,Matt	Yr	Tm	W	L	Sv	IP	K	ERA	WHIP	OBA	vL	vR	BF/G	H%	S%	xERA	G	L	F	Ctl	Dom	Cmd	hr/f	hr/9	RAR	BPV	R$
RH Reliever	03		0	0	0	0	0	0.00	0.00																		
Age 28	04		0	0	0	0	0	0.00	0.00																		
Pre-Peak	05	aa	2	5	0	73	44	6.43	2.26	341			10.8	37%	74%	8.18				7.3	5.4	**0.7**		1.5	-19.2	-10	($8)
Type Pwr	06	aa	2	4	11	40	40	6.18	1.89	341			5.5	43%	66%	6.24				3.9	9.0	**2.3**		0.5	-8.2	74	$3
Reliability 2	07	FLA	3	4	0	67	62	3.09	1.30	259	263	255	4.0	34%	75%	3.70	47	16	36	2.8	8.3	**3.0**	3%	0.3	11.0	107	$7
ERA Potl 55%	1st Half		1	2	0	32	29	3.38	1.25	237			3.9	31%	70%	4.03	46	11	43	3.4	8.2	**2.4**	0%	0.0	4.1	107	$3
LIMA Plan B+	2nd Half		2	2	0	35	33	2.83	1.34	278			4.0	35%	80%	3.41	49	21	30	2.3	8.5	**3.7**	6%	0.5	6.9	112	$4
+/- Score 7	08	Proj	**3**	**4**	**3**	**58**	**52**	**3.88**	**1.38**	**272**			**4.7**	**33%**	**73%**	**3.80**	**48**	**17**	**35**	**2.9**	**8.1**	**2.7**	**8%**	**0.8**	**4.3**	**83**	**$5**

Nice MLB debut, could have been even better with a normal h% (a recurring issue for him). Needs to sustain his Ctl gains. If he does, he's a great LIMA option and speculative saves source.

Linebrink,Scott

Linebrink,Scott	Yr	Tm	W	L	Sv	IP	K	ERA	WHIP	OBA	vL	vR	BF/G	H%	S%	xERA	G	L	F	Ctl	Dom	Cmd	hr/f	hr/9	RAR	BPV	R$
RH Reliever	03	2NL	3	2	0	92	68	3.33	1.40	264	275	265	7.6	30%	79%	4.80	35	20	45	3.5	6.7	**1.9**	7%	0.9	10.8	55	$6
Age 31	04	SD	7	3	0	84	83	2.14	1.04	205	178	236	4.6	26%	85%	3.68	33	21	46	2.8	8.9	**3.2**	8%	0.9	22.0	109	$14
Peak	05	SD	8	1	1	73	70	1.84	1.07	210	195	223	4.0	27%	85%	3.62	39	21	41	2.8	8.6	**3.0**	5%	0.5	21.7	114	$14
Type Pwr	06	SD	7	4	2	75	68	3.59	1.22	248	204	294	4.3	30%	75%	3.84	39	19	42	2.6	8.1	**3.1**	10%	1.1	8.3	87	$10
Reliability 34	07	2NL	5	6	1	70	50	3.71	1.32	255	215	284	4.2	27%	79%	4.29	42	21	37	3.2	6.4	**2.0**	15%	1.5	6.2	38	$7
ERA Potl 45%	1st Half		2	1	1	35	19	2.57	1.11	227			4.3	22%	88%	4.32	42	21	37	2.6	4.9	**1.9**	15%	1.5	8.0	33	$5
LIMA Plan B	2nd Half		3	5	0	35	31	4.84	1.53	281			4.1	32%	73%	4.25	42	21	37	3.8	7.9	**2.1**	15%	1.5	-1.8	44	$2
+/- Score -14	08	Proj	**6**	**5**	**3**	**73**	**60**	**3.85**	**1.31**	**255**			**4.3**	**30%**	**74%**	**4.12**	**40**	**20**	**39**	**3.1**	**7.4**	**2.4**	**11%**	**1.1**	**2.5**	**66**	**$8**

Both Ctl and Dom deteriorated badly, xERA shows the damage. RH batters having more success against him. Still owns the elite skills, but until further notice he's merely a mortal setup-type reliever.

Liriano,Francisco

Liriano,Francisco	Yr	Tm	W	L	Sv	IP	K	ERA	WHIP	OBA	vL	vR	BF/G	H%	S%	xERA	G	L	F	Ctl	Dom	Cmd	hr/f	hr/9	RAR	BPV	R$
LH Reliever	03		0	0	0	0	0	0.00	0.00											0.0	0.0						
Age 24	04	aa	3	2	0	39	46	3.94	1.72	313			26.0	42%	79%	5.76				3.9	10.6	**2.7**		0.9	2.0	86	$2
Growth	05	MIN	* 13	9	0	190	220	3.41	1.12	226	222	221	23.3	31%	71%	2.82	50	19	31	2.7	10.4	**3.9**	9%	0.6	22.6	135	$27
Type Pwr GB	06	MIN	12	3	1	121	144	2.16	1.00	207	202	206	16.9	29%	82%	2.33	55	21	23	2.4	10.7	**4.5**	13%	0.7	35.8	152	$26
Reliability 0	07	MIN	0	0	0	0	0	0.00	0.00																		
ERA Potl	1st Half		0	0	0	0	0	0.00	0.00																		
LIMA Plan	2nd Half		0	0	0	0	0	0.00	0.00																		
+/- Score	08	Proj	**14**	**7**	**0**	**166**	**180**	**3.74**	**1.32**	**251**			**22.0**	**33%**	**72%**	**2.96**	**55**	**21**	**24**	**3.4**	**9.8**	**2.9**	**11%**	**0.7**	**31.5**	**105**	**$21**

Rehab from TJ surgery has been smooth, appears on track to return to MIN rotation. Don't pay top dollar for him at the draft table, but do look to acquire him at a discount in-season if he starts slow in his return.

Litsch,Jesse

Litsch,Jesse	Yr	Tm	W	L	Sv	IP	K	ERA	WHIP	OBA	vL	vR	BF/G	H%	S%	xERA	G	L	F	Ctl	Dom	Cmd	hr/f	hr/9	RAR	BPV	R$
RH Starter	03		0	0	0	0	0	0.00	0.00																		
Age 23	04		0	0	0	0	0	0.00	0.00																		
Growth	05		0	0	0	0	0	0.00	0.00																		
Type Con	06	aa	3	4	0	69	47	7.29	1.74	352			26.8	40%	57%	6.58				1.8	6.1	**3.4**		1.0	-23.6	61	($3)
Reliability 0	07	TOR	* 15	11	0	187	98	3.42	1.29	264	308	229	24.6	28%	77%	4.43	48	18	34	2.5	4.7	**1.8**	9%	1.0	25.2	41	$19
ERA Potl 40%	1st Half		9	4	0	94	51	3.54	1.28	266			24.7	29%	75%	4.19	50	18	32	2.3	4.9	**2.1**	10%	1.0	11.2	47	$11
LIMA Plan D+	2nd Half		6	7	0	93	47	3.29	1.31	262			24.6	28%	79%	4.57	48	17	35	2.8	4.5	**1.6**	9%	1.0	13.9	35	$9
+/- Score -13	08	Proj	**9**	**8**	**0**	**136**	**79**	**4.30**	**1.33**	**276**			**25.1**	**30%**	**70%**	**4.29**	**48**	**18**	**34**	**2.3**	**5.2**	**2.3**	**10%**	**1.1**	**3.5**	**47**	**$10**

7-9, 3.81 ERA in 111 IP at TOR. Low-DOM GB specialist who outpitched his mediocre skill set, as xERA shows. 2006 MLEs show where his BPIs need to get to, but even then the low-DOM/high-CMD road is uphill.

RAY MURPHY

Littleton,Wes			W	L	Sv	IP	K	ERA	WHIP	OBA	vL	vR	BF/G	H%	S%	xERA	G	L	F	Ctl	Dom	Cmd	hr/f	hr/9	RAR	BPV	R$
RH Reliever	03		0	0	0	0	0	0.00	0.00																		
Age 25	04		0	0	0	0	0	0.00	0.00																		
Growth	05	aa	2	3	3	81	59	5.37	1.70	331			7.8	37%	71%	6.46				2.7	6.6	**2.4**		1.4	-10.7	37	($0)
Type Con xGB	06	TEX *	9	2	6	80	51	1.71	1.04	202	256	157	5.0	22%	91%	2.91	71	12	17	3.0	5.7	**1.9**	21%	0.9	28.1	62	$18
Reliability 0	07	TEX *	3	3	4	80	40	5.46	1.42	283	236	279	6.0	29%	65%	4.22	55	19	27	2.8	4.5	**1.6**	17%	1.4	-9.4	17	$3
ERA Potl 50%	1st Half		0	2	1	41	21	4.81	1.24	270			6.6	27%	66%	3.94	59	9	33	1.7	4.6	**2.6**	15%	1.5	-1.5	38	$2
LIMA Plan C+	2nd Half		3	1	3	39	19	6.14	1.62	296			5.5	31%	64%	4.61	52	24	23	3.9	4.4	**1.1**	18%	1.3	-7.9	7	$1
+/- Score 29	08	Proj	**4**	**2**	**0**	**58**	**34**	**4.50**	**1.40**	**275**			**5.8**	**30%**	**70%**	**3.84**	**59**	**18**	**23**	**2.9**	**5.3**	**1.8**	**16%**	**1.1**	**4.7**	**37**	**$4**

3-2, 4.31 ERA in 48 IP at TEX. Low-DOM, GB type who has not yet displayed the required CMD to succeed at the big league level. Still has time to develop, but let him do so in your free agent pool.

Livingston,Bobby			W	L	Sv	IP	K	ERA	WHIP	OBA	vL	vR	BF/G	H%	S%	xERA	G	L	F	Ctl	Dom	Cmd	hr/f	hr/9	RAR	BPV	R$
LH Starter	03		0	0	0	0	0	0.00	0.00																		
Age 25	04		0	0	0	0	0	0.00	0.00																		
Growth	05	a/a	14	6	0	168	109	3.91	1.29	267			25.2	31%	69%	3.61				2.3	5.8	**2.5**		0.5	8.2	75	$16
Type Con	06	aaa	8	11	0	135	62	5.33	1.64	326			26.8	34%	70%	6.10				2.5	4.1	**1.7**		1.3	-13.5	12	$2
Reliability 0	07	CIN *	6	7	0	160	80	5.08	1.56	332	341	321	26.6	36%	69%	4.68	42	23	35	1.5	4.5	**3.1**	8%	1.0	-13.0	52	$2
ERA Potl 55%	1st Half		4	4	0	101	51	4.81	1.54	329			28.2	36%	68%	4.37	52	17	31	1.4	4.5	**3.2**	5%	0.5	-4.8	67	$2
LIMA Plan C+	2nd Half		2	3	0	59	29	5.55	1.60	336			24.3	35%	70%	4.77	39	25	36	1.5	4.5	**2.9**	14%	1.7	-8.2	25	($0)
+/- Score 20	08	Proj	**3**	**3**	**0**	**58**	**29**	**5.12**	**1.55**	**320**			**25.9**	**34%**	**69%**	**4.83**	**40**	**24**	**36**	**2.0**	**4.5**	**2.2**	**9%**	**1.1**	**-3.1**	**32**	**$1**

3-3, 5.27 ERA in 56 IP at CIN. Some decent skills buried under the continued high h% here. Had surgery for torn labrum in Sept., likely impacting his start of 2008. Worth a flier only for patient owner in a deep league.

Liz,Radhames			W	L	Sv	IP	K	ERA	WHIP	OBA	vL	vR	BF/G	H%	S%	xERA	G	L	F	Ctl	Dom	Cmd	hr/f	hr/9	RAR	BPV	R$
RH Starter	03		0	0	0	0	0	0.00	0.00																		
Age 24	04		0	0	0	0	0	0.00	0.00																		
Growth	05		0	0	0	0	0	0.00	0.00																		
Type Pwr xFB	06	aa	3	1	0	50	48	7.59	2.04	328			24.8	38%	67%	8.01				5.9	8.5	**1.4**		2.2	-19.0	4	($3)
Reliability 0	07	BAL *	11	6	0	162	157	4.46	1.48	243	244	275	20.9	30%	72%	5.00	23	25	52	5.2	8.7	**1.7**	8%	1.0	1.0	65	$13
ERA Potl 50%	1st Half		5	4	0	85	82	4.65	1.41	240			23.0	30%	68%					4.6	8.7	**1.9**		0.8	-1.5	73	$7
LIMA Plan C	2nd Half		6	2	0	77	75	4.24	1.56	245			19.1	30%	76%	5.21	23	25	52	5.8	8.8	**1.5**	9%	1.1	2.5	56	$6
+/- Score -7	08	Proj	**5**	**5**	**0**	**102**	**98**	**4.97**	**1.55**	**261**			**23.9**	**31%**	**72%**	**5.00**	**23**	**25**	**52**	**5.0**	**8.7**	**1.8**	**11%**	**1.4**	**-6.3**	**49**	**$5**

0-2, 6.93 ERA in 25 IP at BAL. Throws hard with little idea where it's going. 1.95 WHIP in MLB was brutal. Still, one of BAL's top 10 prospects, which says a lot... about the state of the Orioles farm system.

Loaiza,Esteban			W	L	Sv	IP	K	ERA	WHIP	OBA	vL	vR	BF/G	H%	S%	xERA	G	L	F	Ctl	Dom	Cmd	hr/f	hr/9	RAR	BPV	R$
RH Starter	03	CHW	21	9	0	226	207	2.91	1.12	235	259	191	26.8	29%	76%	3.32	46	21	33	2.2	8.2	**3.7**	8%	0.7	45.1	115	$35
Age 36	04	2AL	10	7	0	183	117	5.70	1.57	296	298	293	26.5	32%	67%	4.94	41	18	40	3.5	5.8	**1.6**	13%	1.6	-28.7	18	$3
Decline	05	WAS	12	10	0	217	173	3.77	1.30	271	285	255	26.9	32%	72%	3.85	44	22	35	2.3	7.2	**3.1**	8%	0.7	12.6	88	$18
Type Con	06	OAK	11	9	0	154	97	4.90	1.42	292	319	265	25.7	32%	67%	4.49	42	20	38	2.3	5.7	**2.4**	9%	1.0	-6.6	52	$10
Reliability 0	07	2TM *	4	5	0	65	29	5.58	1.65	311	294	239	23.0	31%	71%	6.13	21	29	50	3.4	4.0	**1.2**	11%	1.9	-9.0	-14	$0
ERA Potl 40%	1st Half		0	1	0	6	2	8.71	1.94	386			15.1	39%	55%					1.5	2.9	**2.0**		1.5	-3.2	-6	($1)
LIMA Plan C	2nd Half		4	4	0	59	27	5.25	1.62	302			24.4	30%	74%	6.09	21	29	50	3.6	4.2	**1.2**	12%	1.9	-5.7	-13	$1
+/- Score -37	08	Proj	**6**	**9**	**0**	**124**	**66**	**4.94**	**1.51**	**289**			**23.9**	**31%**	**70%**	**5.14**	**38**	**22**	**40**	**3.3**	**4.8**	**1.5**	**10%**	**1.2**	**-10.7**	**20**	**$4**

2-1, 5.79 in 37 IP at OAK/LA. Shoulder and back problems the past two years have taken their toll, leaving 2003 and 2005 as distant memories. At 36, the odds of him making it all the way back are remote.

Loewen,Adam			W	L	Sv	IP	K	ERA	WHIP	OBA	vL	vR	BF/G	H%	S%	xERA	G	L	F	Ctl	Dom	Cmd	hr/f	hr/9	RAR	BPV	R$
LH Starter	03		0	0	0	0	0	0.00	0.00																		
Age 24	04		0	0	0	0	0	0.00	0.00																		
Growth	05		0	0	0	0	0	0.00	0.00																		
Type Pwr GB	06	BAL *	12	8	0	183	166	4.52	1.49	258	277	254	23.7	32%	69%	4.06	48	21	31	4.5	8.2	**1.8**	7%	0.6	0.8	72	$14
Reliability 0	07	BAL	2	0	0	30	22	3.56	1.75	240	227	242	23.6	29%	79%	5.56	52	18	30	7.7	6.5	**0.8**	4%	0.3	3.5	55	$1
ERA Potl 45%	1st Half		2	0	0	30	22	3.60	1.77	242			23.4	29%	79%	5.58	52	18	30	7.8	6.6	**0.8**	4%	0.3	3.4	55	$1
LIMA Plan B	2nd Half		0	0	0	0	0	0.00	0.00																		
+/- Score -30	08	Proj	**7**	**4**	**0**	**137**	**110**	**4.27**	**1.47**	**249**			**23.2**	**30%**	**71%**	**4.30**	**51**	**19**	**30**	**4.9**	**7.2**	**1.5**	**7%**	**0.6**	**3.3**	**62**	**$9**

Elbow injury shut him down in May, and likely contributed to ridiculous ctl problems before-hand. There was a lot to like in 2006 skills. Likely won't pick up right where he left off, but still a good longer-term play.

Loe,Kameron			W	L	Sv	IP	K	ERA	WHIP	OBA	vL	vR	BF/G	H%	S%	xERA	G	L	F	Ctl	Dom	Cmd	hr/f	hr/9	RAR	BPV	R$
RH Starter	03		0	0	0	0	0	0.00	0.00											0.0	0.0						
Age 26	04	a/a	12	9	0	157	115	4.24	1.54	311			26.9	36%	74%	5.27				2.4	6.6	**2.8**		0.9	1.9	65	$9
Growth	05	TEX *	11	7	1	120	65	3.97	1.37	268	284	223	9.7	29%	74%	3.82	61	16	22	3.0	4.9	**1.6**	15%	1.0	5.9	36	$11
Type xGB	06	TEX	3	6	0	78	34	5.88	1.63	323	313	321	23.7	34%	65%	4.79	51	19	30	2.5	3.9	**1.5**	11%	1.2	-12.7	12	($1)
Reliability 22	07	TEX	6	11	0	136	78	5.36	1.60	297	328	262	22.0	33%	67%	4.43	56	18	26	3.7	5.2	**1.4**	11%	0.9	-14.3	30	$2
ERA Potl 50%	1st Half		4	6	0	84	47	6.00	1.52	301			20.7	32%	62%	4.21	55	18	27	2.8	5.0	**1.8**	14%	1.2	-15.5	28	$1
LIMA Plan C+	2nd Half		2	5	0	52	31	4.33	1.73	290			24.2	33%	74%	4.81	58	16	25	5.2	5.4	**1.0**	5%	0.3	1.1	40	$1
+/- Score 12	08	Proj	**6**	**9**	**0**	**123**	**68**	**5.00**	**1.59**	**300**			**24.0**	**33%**	**69%**	**4.47**	**55**	**18**	**27**	**3.5**	**5.0**	**1.4**	**10%**	**0.9**	**0.4**	**29**	**$3**

Another GB specialist who does not appreciate the importance of Cmd. LH hitters pound him; 2H Ctl troubles heighten the risk. Quite a bit of work to be done just to get us interested. Oh, and he had Sept. elbow surgery.

Logan,Boone			W	L	Sv	IP	K	ERA	WHIP	OBA	vL	vR	BF/G	H%	S%	xERA	G	L	F	Ctl	Dom	Cmd	hr/f	hr/9	RAR	BPV	R$
LH Reliever	03		0	0	0	0	0	0.00	0.00																		
Age 23	04		0	0	0	0	0	0.00	0.00																		
Growth	05		0	0	0	0	0	0.00	0.00																		
Type Pwr	06	CHW *	3	1	12	59	66	5.46	1.49	267			4.4	37%	61%	3.83	44	17	39	4.2	10.1	**2.4**	5%	0.4	-6.6	100	$7
Reliability 0	07	CHW	2	1	0	51	35	4.97	1.56	292	221	357	3.3	33%	71%	4.48	51	14	35	3.6	6.2	**1.8**	12%	1.2	-2.9	33	$1
ERA Potl 55%	1st Half		1	0	0	21	15	4.29	1.29	262			3.0	31%	65%	3.62	55	18	27	2.6	6.4	**2.5**	6%	0.4	0.6	81	$2
LIMA Plan B	2nd Half		1	1	0	30	20	5.45	1.75	312			3.6	33%	74%	5.09	48	12	40	4.2	6.1	**1.4**	15%	1.8	-3.5	4	($0)
+/- Score 23	08	Proj	**2**	**1**	**0**	**44**	**38**	**4.55**	**1.45**	**268**			**3.7**	**32%**	**71%**	**4.03**	**50**	**15**	**35**	**3.7**	**7.9**	**2.1**	**11%**	**1.0**	**2.5**	**62**	**$3**

Didn't sustain his big DOM in first full MLB season, but there are seeds of something better here. Needs to figure out a way to handle RH hitters if he wants to be more than Mike Myers when he grows up.

Lohse,Kyle			W	L	Sv	IP	K	ERA	WHIP	OBA	vL	vR	BF/G	H%	S%	xERA	G	L	F	Ctl	Dom	Cmd	hr/f	hr/9	RAR	BPV	R$
RH Starter	03	MIN	14	11	0	201	130	4.61	1.27	271	283	249	25.5	30%	67%	4.41	39	18	43	2.0	5.8	**2.9**	10%	1.3	-2.2	59	$16
Age 29	04	MIN	9	13	0	194	111	5.34	1.63	305	290	324	25.2	33%	70%	5.03	45	18	37	3.5	5.1	**1.5**	11%	1.3	-21.6	17	$1
Peak	05	MIN	9	13	0	178	86	4.19	1.43	296	291	305	25.0	31%	74%	4.64	44	22	34	2.2	4.3	**2.0**	10%	1.1	3.9	30	$9
Type	06	2TM *	7	11	0	150	106	5.30	1.48	287	288	304	17.4	33%	65%	4.50	43	20	37	3.1	6.4	**2.1**	9%	1.0	-14.4	50	$5
Reliability 71	07	2NL	9	12	0	193	122	4.62	1.37	276	276	282	24.3	31%	68%	4.68	37	22	41	2.7	5.7	**2.1**	8%	1.0	-4.7	48	$10
ERA Potl 50%	1st Half		3	10	0	99	57	5.00	1.40	292			26.8	32%	66%	4.78	35	23	41	2.2	5.2	**2.4**	9%	1.1	-7.0	45	$3
LIMA Plan C	2nd Half		6	2	0	94	65	4.23	1.33	258			22.1	29%	70%	4.57	39	20	41	3.2	6.2	**2.0**	8%	1.0	2.3	53	$7
+/- Score -5	08	Proj	**9**	**11**	**0**	**185**	**117**	**4.67**	**1.41**	**281**			**24.3**	**31%**	**69%**	**4.63**	**40**	**21**	**39**	**2.8**	**5.7**	**2.1**	**9%**	**1.0**	**-5.3**	**45**	**$9**

Making some small strides against both LH and RH hitters. Also turning into more of an FB pitcher over time, so where he signs will influence his value. Upside of a league-average innings eater, nothing more.

Looper,Braden			W	L	Sv	IP	K	ERA	WHIP	OBA	vL	vR	BF/G	H%	S%	xERA	G	L	F	Ctl	Dom	Cmd	hr/f	hr/9	RAR	BPV	R$
RH Starter	03	FLA	6	4	28	80	56	3.71	1.39	267	280	250	4.7	32%	73%	4.05	53	18	29	3.3	6.3	**1.9**	5%	0.5	5.6	67	$16
Age 33	04	NYM	2	5	29	83	60	2.71	1.23	268	311	227	4.9	32%	79%	3.14	62	15	23	1.7	6.5	**3.8**	8%	0.5	15.9	103	$17
Past Peak	05	NYM	4	7	28	59	27	3.96	1.47	281	336	210	4.3	29%	76%	4.64	51	21	27	3.4	4.1	**1.2**	12%	1.1	2.1	17	$12
Type Con	06	STL	9	3	0	73	41	3.57	1.31	269	287	272	4.5	31%	72%	4.23	49	20	30	2.5	5.0	**2.1**	4%	0.4	8.3	63	$9
Reliability 56	07	STL	12	12	0	175	87	4.94	1.34	271	279	261	24.0	28%	65%	4.71	42	21	36	2.6	4.5	**1.7**	10%	1.1	-11.0	30	$10
ERA Potl 50%	1st Half		6	6	0	83	41	4.66	1.41	273			25.7	29%	68%	4.58	48	23	29	3.1	4.4	**1.4**	10%	0.9	-2.4	31	$4
LIMA Plan C	2nd Half		6	6	0	92	46	5.18	1.27	268			22.7	28%	62%	4.80	37	20	43	2.2	4.5	**2.1**	11%	1.4	-8.6	31	$5
+/- Score -16	08	Proj	**9**	**11**	**0**	**140**	**74**	**4.45**	**1.38**	**277**			**25.0**	**30%**	**70%**	**4.50**	**46**	**21**	**33**	**2.6**	**4.8**	**1.8**	**10%**	**1.0**	**-1.8**	**35**	**$8**

Brilliant in April (1.91 ERA, but xERA was a more sedate 3.93), then crashed hard. There's little reason to expect further growth at his age, and IP spike could have repercussions in 2008. Avoid.

RAY MURPHY

Lopez,Javier

Lopez,Javier	Yr	Tm	W	L	Sv	IP	K	ERA	WHIP	OBA	vL	vR	BF/G	H%	S%	xERA	G	L	F	Ctl	Dom	Cmd	hr/f	hr/9	RAR	BPV	R$
LH Reliever	03	COL	4	1	1	58	40	3.72	1.21	262	250	266	3.2	30%	71%	3.38	59	15	26	1.9	6.2	3.3	10%	0.8	4.0	87	$6
Age 30	04	COL	1	2	0	40	20	7.61	1.77	284	221	350	2.9	32%	53%	5.22	55	23	22	5.8	4.5	0.8	3%	0.2	-16.6	34	($3)
Peak	05	2NL *	1	2	4	40	29	6.30	1.80	294			3.2	34%	64%	5.50				5.6	6.5	1.2		0.7	-10.1	39	($1)
Type GB	06	BOS *	3	1	17	65	41	2.96	1.56	294	250	208	4.4	34%	82%	3.35	65	22	13	3.5	5.6	1.6	15%	0.6	12.9	46	$10
Reliability 4	07	BOS *	4	2	0	57	38	3.80	1.55	277	293	176	3.3	33%	75%	4.47	53	20	28	4.3	6.0	1.4	4%	0.3	5.0	55	$4
ERA Potl 50%	1st Half		2	1	0	31	21	4.06	1.58	280			3.9	33%	73%	4.51	55	16	29	4.4	6.1	1.4	3%	0.3	1.7	56	$2
LIMA Plan B	2nd Half		2	1	0	26	17	3.47	1.52	274			2.7	32%	77%	4.44	51	22	26	4.1	5.8	1.4	5%	0.3	3.3	54	$2
+/- Score -27	08	Proj	2	1	0	44	28	4.14	1.56	281			3.4	33%	73%	4.33	55	20	25	4.1	5.8	1.4	6%	0.4	0.9	50	$2

2-1, 3.10 ERA in 40 IP at BOS. Lefty specialist got pounded by LH hitters, but compensated by mowing down RHers. If he could ever get them both out, AND reduce his walk rate, he'd be much more valuable.

Lopez,Rodrigo

Lopez,Rodrigo	Yr	Tm	W	L	Sv	IP	K	ERA	WHIP	OBA	vL	vR	BF/G	H%	S%	xERA	G	L	F	Ctl	Dom	Cmd	hr/f	hr/9	RAR	BPV	R$
RH Starter	03	BAL	7	10	0	147	103	5.82	1.57	312	308	319	25.4	34%	66%	4.43	42	22	35	2.6	6.3	2.4	14%	1.5	-23.4	37	$2
Age 32	04	BAL	14	9	0	170	121	3.60	1.28	255	258	245	19.3	28%	76%	4.13	46	18	36	2.9	6.4	2.2	11%	1.1	17.6	56	$17
Peak	05	BAL	15	12	0	209	118	4.91	1.41	282	288	262	25.9	30%	68%	4.59	44	21	36	2.7	5.1	1.9	11%	1.2	-13.8	32	$11
Type	06	BAL	9	18	0	189	136	5.90	1.55	305	308	296	23.5	34%	65%	4.38	43	22	35	2.8	6.5	2.3	14%	1.5	-31.4	36	$4
Reliability 48	07	COL	5	4	0	79	43	4.43	1.31	271	270	276	24.0	29%	70%	4.55	47	13	40	2.4	4.9	2.0	10%	1.2	-0.0	36	$5
ERA Potl 40%	1st Half		4	1	0	51	26	4.06	1.39	291			24.4	31%	74%	4.45	51	14	35	2.1	4.6	2.2	10%	1.1	2.3	38	$4
LIMA Plan D+	2nd Half		1	3	0	28	17	5.09	1.17	231			23.1	23%	61%	4.73	39	11	49	2.9	5.4	1.9	12%	1.6	-2.3	33	$2
+/- Score -19	08	Proj	0	0	0	0	0	0.00	0.00																	0	

Had Tommy John surgery in August and will miss most or all of 2008. Check back here next year for continuing up-to-the-minute status reports.

Lowe,Derek

Lowe,Derek	Yr	Tm	W	L	Sv	IP	K	ERA	WHIP	OBA	vL	vR	BF/G	H%	S%	xERA	G	L	F	Ctl	Dom	Cmd	hr/f	hr/9	RAR	BPV	R$
RH Starter	03	BOS	17	7	0	203	110	4.48	1.42	274	276	266	26.7	30%	69%	3.70	65	16	19	3.2	4.9	1.5	13%	0.8	1.2	39	$14
Age 34	04	BOS	14	12	0	189	110	5.23	1.60	299	305	293	25.9	33%	67%	3.97	62	17	20	3.5	5.2	1.5	12%	0.8	-18.7	35	$5
Past Peak	05	LA	12	15	0	222	146	3.61	1.25	263	296	219	26.5	29%	76%	3.22	64	15	21	2.2	5.9	2.7	19%	1.1	17.5	60	$18
Type xGB	06	LA	16	8	0	218	123	3.63	1.27	264	270	255	26.1	30%	72%	3.22	67	16	17	2.3	5.1	2.2	11%	0.6	23.0	62	$20
Reliability 95	07	LA	12	14	0	199	147	3.88	1.27	257	271	239	25.3	30%	72%	3.08	65	16	19	2.7	6.6	2.5	17%	0.9	13.3	69	$18
ERA Potl 50%	1st Half		8	7	0	116	81	3.03	1.14	229			27.7	27%	74%	3.06	66	15	19	2.7	6.3	2.3	9%	0.5	20.0	82	$14
LIMA Plan D+	2nd Half		4	7	0	83	66	5.08	1.45	292			22.8	33%	69%	3.10	64	16	20	2.6	7.1	2.8	27%	1.5	-6.7	52	$3
+/- Score 26	08	Proj	14	13	0	218	143	3.85	1.32	268			25.6	31%	72%	3.26	65	16	19	2.6	5.9	2.3	13%	0.7	30.5	64	$18

Outwardly, this looked just like the last two years in LA. But he was unlucky on hr/f, and kicked up his DOM. Seems a little old to be showing growth, but xERA shows the upside if he can sustain new Dom level.

Lowry,Noah

Lowry,Noah	Yr	Tm	W	L	Sv	IP	K	ERA	WHIP	OBA	vL	vR	BF/G	H%	S%	xERA	G	L	F	Ctl	Dom	Cmd	hr/f	hr/9	RAR	BPV	R$
LH Starter	03	a/a	10	6	0	137	93	4.66	1.47	282			22.3	33%	66%	4.14				3.2	6.1	1.9		0.3	-4.5	65	$8
Age 27	04	SF *	13	5	0	181	134	3.98	1.35	273	338	238	23.4	32%	72%	4.32	42	17	41	2.6	6.7	2.5	7%	0.8	6.4	68	$14
Pre-Peak	05	SF	13	13	0	204	172	3.79	1.32	251	213	259	26.2	30%	74%	4.15	41	20	39	3.3	7.6	2.3	9%	0.9	11.5	70	$18
Type	06	SF	7	10	0	159	84	4.75	1.40	270	312	262	25.4	28%	69%	5.22	36	18	45	3.2	4.8	1.5	9%	1.2	-5.2	25	$7
Reliability 50	07	SF	14	8	0	156	87	3.92	1.55	261	216	277	26.8	29%	76%	5.35	45	20	36	5.0	5.0	1.0	7%	0.7	9.7	33	$10
ERA Potl 35%	1st Half		7	6	0	95	51	3.60	1.41	245			27.4	27%	75%	4.96	48	19	33	4.5	4.8	1.1	6%	0.6	9.7	41	$7
LIMA Plan D+	2nd Half		7	2	0	61	36	4.43	1.77	283			26.0	31%	76%	5.97	40	20	39	5.9	5.3	0.9	7%	0.9	-0.0	23	$3
+/- Score -44	08	Proj	8	10	0	145	89	4.53	1.53	274			25.8	30%	73%	5.16	41	19	40	4.2	5.5	1.3	9%	1.1	-13.6	29	$5

Others will look at 2007 and think he has come all the way back from injuries that have hampered him since his 2005 breakout. You see high Ctl, poor CMD, lofty xERA and know that he's not ready yet.

Lyon,Brandon

Lyon,Brandon	Yr	Tm	W	L	Sv	IP	K	ERA	WHIP	OBA	vL	vR	BF/G	H%	S%	xERA	G	L	F	Ctl	Dom	Cmd	hr/f	hr/9	RAR	BPV	R$
RH Reliever	03	BOS	4	6	9	59	50	4.12	1.56	305	317	276	5.4	37%	76%	4.51	35	23	43	2.9	7.6	2.6	7%	0.9	3.0	68	$7
Age 28	04	ARI	0	0	0	0	0	0.00	0.00											0.0	0.0						
Pre-Peak	05	ARI	0	2	14	29	17	6.49	1.86	349	317	364	4.3	37%	69%	5.06	42	23	35	3.1	5.3	1.7	16%	1.9	-8.1	-3	$2
Type	06	ARI	2	4	0	69	46	3.91	1.30	259	244	270	4.3	29%	72%	4.22	43	24	33	2.9	6.0	2.1	10%	0.9	4.9	56	$5
Reliability 13	07	ARI	6	4	2	74	40	2.68	1.24	251	233	267	4.2	29%	78%	4.64	43	19	38	2.7	4.9	1.8	2%	0.2	16.0	65	$10
ERA Potl 40%	1st Half		5	2	2	39	19	2.08	1.23	236			4.4	27%	81%	4.71	48	17	35	3.2	4.4	1.4	0%	0.0	11.3	63	$7
LIMA Plan C	2nd Half		1	2	0	35	21	3.34	1.26	267			4.1	30%	74%	4.55	37	22	41	2.1	5.4	2.6	4%	0.5	4.7	74	$3
+/- Score -45	08	Proj	3	4	0	58	37	4.03	1.33	268			4.4	30%	73%	4.40	41	22	37	2.6	5.7	2.2	10%	1.1	-0.0	49	$4

Good fortune on hr/f propped up his ERA. Recovered some Cmd in 2H, but xERA doesn't support even that performance. 2008 should look a lot more like 2006 than 2007, and even that may be optimistic.

MacDougal,Mike

MacDougal,Mike	Yr	Tm	W	L	Sv	IP	K	ERA	WHIP	OBA	vL	vR	BF/G	H%	S%	xERA	G	L	F	Ctl	Dom	Cmd	hr/f	hr/9	RAR	BPV	R$
RH Reliever	03	KC	3	5	27	64	57	4.08	1.50	262	230	314	4.2	33%	73%	3.72	55	21	24	4.5	8.0	1.8	9%	0.6	3.5	71	$14
Age 31	04	KC *	2	3	4	43	30	5.61	2.08	303	304	321	4.9	35%	72%	5.75	51	24	24	7.7	6.2	0.8	8%	0.6	-6.3	30	($1)
Peak	05	KC	5	6	21	70	72	3.34	1.33	259	240	270	4.4	33%	77%	3.13	57	15	28	3.1	9.2	3.0	11%	0.8	8.9	99	$15
Type Pwr xGB	06	2AL	1	1	1	29	21	1.55	0.93	204	281	171	3.9	25%	85%	2.55	64	21	15	1.9	6.5	3.5	8%	0.3	10.8	117	$6
Reliability 0	07	CHW	2	5	0	42	39	6.81	1.96	295	298	288	3.8	37%	64%	4.75	56	18	26	7.0	8.3	1.2	9%	0.6	-12.0	51	($2)
ERA Potl 0%	1st Half		1	3	0	20	20	6.75	2.25	307			3.4	40%	68%	5.21	62	14	25	9.0	9.0	1.0	7%	0.5	-5.5	55	($1)
LIMA Plan C	2nd Half		1	2	0	22	19	6.86	1.70	284			4.3	34%	58%	4.38	51	22	27	5.2	7.7	1.5	11%	0.8	-6.5	51	($0)
+/- Score 56	08	Proj	2	4	0	44	39	4.14	1.43	264			3.9	33%	71%	3.43	58	19	23	3.7	8.1	2.2	10%	0.6	5.7	77	$3

If you roll 2007 disaster with lucky 2006, you get normal hit/strand rates. His true skill level lies in that middle ground. Injuries likely drove his Ctl issues, but he must show he's over that before you roster him.

Maddux,Greg

Maddux,Greg	Yr	Tm	W	L	Sv	IP	K	ERA	WHIP	OBA	vL	vR	BF/G	H%	S%	xERA	G	L	F	Ctl	Dom	Cmd	hr/f	hr/9	RAR	BPV	R$
RH Starter	03	ATL	16	11	0	218	123	3.96	1.18	268	271	264	24.8	29%	69%	3.71	54	17	30	1.4	5.1	3.7	11%	1.0	8.5	80	$20
Age 42	04	CHC	16	11	0	212	151	4.03	1.18	267	271	268	26.4	29%	72%	3.41	51	20	29	1.4	6.4	4.6	18%	1.5	6.1	92	$21
Decline	05	CHC	13	15	0	225	136	4.24	1.22	274	283	270	26.6	30%	69%	3.59	52	22	27	1.4	5.4	3.8	15%	1.2	0.2	77	$17
Type Con GB	06	2NL	15	14	0	210	117	4.20	1.22	270	254	284	25.6	30%	67%	3.81	51	21	28	1.6	5.0	3.2	10%	0.9	7.4	72	$18
Reliability 80	07	SD	14	11	0	198	104	4.14	1.24	284	280	289	24.2	31%	67%	3.86	51	20	29	1.1	4.7	4.2	7%	0.6	7.1	95	$16
ERA Potl 60%	1st Half		7	4	0	98	52	3.67	1.23	275			25.4	31%	70%	4.00	50	20	31	1.5	4.8	3.3	6%	0.6	9.1	80	$9
LIMA Plan C	2nd Half		7	7	0	100	52	4.59	1.25	291			23.2	32%	63%	3.73	53	19	28	0.8	4.7	5.8	8%	0.7	-2.0	125	$7
+/- Score -5	08	Proj	12	11	0	173	91	4.02	1.24	278			23.9	30%	69%	3.86	52	20	28	1.4	4.7	3.4	10%	0.8	11.5	74	$15

Continues to successfully apply the same old formula: don't walk anyone, get ground balls. Now he has Petco to hold his FBs for him. BF/G trend will start to impact Wins, but he could well pitch until he's 50. Or even 51.

Madson,Ryan

Madson,Ryan	Yr	Tm	W	L	Sv	IP	K	ERA	WHIP	OBA	vL	vR	BF/G	H%	S%	xERA	G	L	F	Ctl	Dom	Cmd	hr/f	hr/9	RAR	BPV	R$
RH Reliever	03	aaa	12	8	0	157	122	4.36	1.45	291			26.4	35%	70%	4.46				2.6	7.0	2.7		0.6	0.7	77	$11
Age 27	04	PHI	9	3	1	77	55	2.34	1.13	238	252	227	6.0	28%	83%	3.47	54	18	28	2.2	6.4	2.9	9%	0.7	18.3	86	$13
Pre-Peak	05	PHI	6	5	0	87	79	4.14	1.25	255	292	233	4.7	31%	70%	3.29	48	25	27	2.6	8.2	3.2	16%	1.1	1.2	85	$8
Type	06	PHI	11	9	2	134	99	5.70	1.69	318	306	336	12.4	36%	68%	4.62	43	22	35	3.4	6.6	2.0	12%	1.3	-20.1	33	$3
Reliability 12	07	PHI	2	2	1	56	43	3.05	1.27	233	170	275	6.2	27%	79%	4.03	47	21	32	3.7	6.9	1.9	10%	0.8	9.5	65	$6
ERA Potl 45%	1st Half		1	2	0	37	31	3.65	1.27	223			6.0	27%	73%	3.80	52	18	30	4.1	7.5	1.8	10%	0.7	3.5	72	$3
LIMA Plan C+	2nd Half		1	0	1	19	12	1.89	1.26	251			6.6	28%	91%	4.43	38	25	37	2.8	5.7	2.0	9%	0.9	5.9	52	$3
+/- Score -23	08	Proj	4	3	0	64	47	4.11	1.40	266			6.9	31%	73%	4.22	45	22	33	3.4	6.7	2.0	11%	1.0	1.4	53	$4

Returned to the bullpen and found success again. Or did he? CON: H% and S% gains explain most of the ERA drop. Ctl trend is troubling. PRO: Solved LHers, which was a major issue. Has upside if CMD nudges up.

Mahay,Ron

Mahay,Ron	Yr	Tm	W	L	Sv	IP	K	ERA	WHIP	OBA	vL	vR	BF/G	H%	S%	xERA	G	L	F	Ctl	Dom	Cmd	hr/f	hr/9	RAR	BPV	R$
LH Reliever	03	TEX *	7	5	3	87	80	4.55	1.25	241	208	190	6.0	29%	66%	4.43	28	18	54	3.2	8.3	2.6	8%	1.0	-0.3	80	$10
Age 36	04	TEX	3	0	0	67	54	2.55	1.33	241	227	241	4.7	31%	83%	4.42	44	14	42	3.9	7.3	1.9	6%	0.7	15.5	69	$7
Decline	05	TEX *	1	5	1	59	52	7.02	1.73	308	302	322	7.2	36%	62%	4.16	48	23	29	4.3	7.9	1.9	20%	1.7	-19.3	30	($2)
Type Pwr	06	TEX	1	3	0	57	56	3.95	1.44	251	240	258	4.0	31%	76%	4.13	41	21	38	4.4	8.8	2.0	12%	1.1	4.3	67	$4
Reliability 0	07	2TM *	3	1	1	77	62	3.45	1.51	252	189	242	5.2	30%	78%	4.55	49	17	34	5.0	7.2	1.4	7%	0.6	9.6	60	$5
ERA Potl 45%	1st Half		0	1	0	34	28	4.22	1.61	261			6.4	31%	75%	4.90	49	11	40	5.5	7.4	1.3	7%	0.8	1.0	51	$1
LIMA Plan B	2nd Half		3	0	1	43	34	2.84	1.42	244			4.6	30%	81%	4.32	49	20	31	4.6	7.1	1.5	5%	0.5	8.6	67	$5
+/- Score -33	08	Proj	2	2	0	58	50	4.07	1.50	260			5.1	31%	75%	4.34	46	19	36	4.5	7.8	1.7	10%	0.9	0.7	58	$3

3-0, 2.55 in 67 IP at TEX/ATL. Still handles lefty hitters with ease, but ongoing Ctl issues make him volatile. Not bad as an end-gamer, but there are better LIMA options around if you have more than a buck to spend.

RAY MURPHY

Maholm,Paul		Yr	Tm	W	L	Sv	IP	K	ERA	WHIP	OBA	vL	vR	BF/G	H%	S%	xERA	G	L	F	Ctl	Dom	Cmd	hr/f	hr/9	RAR	BPV	R$
LH	Starter	03		0	0	0	0	0	0.00	0.00											0.0	0.0						
Age	25	04		0	0	0	0	0	0.00	0.00											0.0	0.0						
Growth		05	PIT *	10	4	0	158	107	3.30	1.31	258	87	232	23.9	30%	75%	3.74	55	20	25	3.0	6.1	**2.1**	7%	0.5	18.5	68	$14
Type	Con GB	06	PIT	8	10	0	176	117	4.76	1.61	289	233	313	26.6	33%	72%	4.39	53	20	27	4.1	6.0	**1.4**	12%	1.0	-5.8	34	$4
Reliability	54	07	PIT	10	15	0	178	105	5.01	1.42	289	238	305	26.6	31%	67%	4.12	53	17	30	2.5	5.3	**2.1**	12%	1.1	-12.9	41	$7
ERA Potl	55%	1st Half		4	10	0	99	58	4.82	1.34	271			26.4	29%	67%	4.13	55	13	32	2.6	5.3	**2.0**	13%	1.3	-4.8	36	$5
LIMA Plan	C+	2nd Half		6	5	0	79	47	5.26	1.52	311			26.9	34%	66%	4.11	51	22	27	2.3	5.4	**2.4**	11%	0.9	-8.1	47	$3
+/- Score	19	08	Proj	**10**	**11**	**0**	**176**	**111**	**4.40**	**1.38**	**278**			**25.2**	**31%**	**70%**	**3.96**	**53**	**19**	**28**	**2.6**	**5.7**	**2.2**	**11%**	**0.9**	**9.5**	**52**	**$10**

Traded off some Dom for better Ctl, netting slightly better BPIs but equally poor results. With a few more Ks, fewer HRs, and a better lineup, we might have something. These low-Dom guys make you say "if only" a lot.

Maine,John		Yr	Tm	W	L	Sv	IP	K	ERA	WHIP	OBA	vL	vR	BF/G	H%	S%	xERA	G	L	F	Ctl	Dom	Cmd	hr/f	hr/9	RAR	BPV	R$
RH	Starter	03		0	0	0	0	0	0.00	0.00											0.0	0.0						
Age	27	04	a/a	9	8	0	147	124	4.40	1.47	277			24.0	33%	72%	4.65				3.5	7.6	**2.1**		0.9	-1.1	62	$9
Growth		05	BAL *	8	14	0	168	121	5.78	1.50	283	227	275	22.5	32%	63%	4.38	46	21	34	3.5	6.5	**1.9**	13%	1.2	-29.2	39	$4
Type	Pwr FB	06	NYM *	9	10	0	146	112	4.14	1.31	250	231	191	23.8	29%	71%	4.60	38	15	47	3.3	6.9	**2.1**	8%	1.0	6.2	58	$12
Reliability	38	07	NYM	15	10	0	191	180	3.91	1.27	238	237	234	25.0	29%	73%	4.10	37	18	45	3.5	8.5	**2.4**	10%	1.1	12.1	76	$20
ERA Potl	50%	1st Half		8	4	0	94	78	2.87	1.20	221			25.8	26%	81%	4.33	37	18	45	3.6	7.5	**2.1**	8%	1.0	18.0	70	$13
LIMA Plan	D+	2nd Half		7	6	0	97	102	4.92	1.34	254			24.3	32%	66%	3.89	37	19	44	3.4	9.5	**2.8**	11%	1.2	-5.9	83	$8
+/- Score	11	08	Proj	**15**	**12**	**0**	**203**	**185**	**3.96**	**1.34**	**254**			**24.0**	**30%**	**74%**	**4.22**	**38**	**18**	**45**	**3.5**	**8.2**	**2.4**	**10%**	**1.2**	**4.4**	**69**	**$19**

Managed another step forward, showing nice Dom growth. 2nd half Dom spike suggests he may have yet another level on the growth curve within reach. If so: UP: 18 wins, 3.50 ERA.

Marcum,Shaun		Yr	Tm	W	L	Sv	IP	K	ERA	WHIP	OBA	vL	vR	BF/G	H%	S%	xERA	G	L	F	Ctl	Dom	Cmd	hr/f	hr/9	RAR	BPV	R$
RH	Reliever	03		0	0	0	0	0	0.00	0.00																		
Age	26	04		0	0	0	0	0	0.00	0.00																		
Growth		05	a/a	13	5	0	157	115	5.50	1.38	298			25.0	33%	64%	5.35				1.7	6.6	**4.0**		1.6	-23.2	70	$9
Type	FB	06	TOR *	7	4	0	130	117	4.90	1.48	283	303	256	14.7	33%	71%	4.43	36	18	46	3.3	8.1	**2.4**	12%	1.5	-5.6	52	$8
Reliability	28	07	TOR	12	6	1	159	122	4.13	1.25	249	259	237	17.4	27%	73%	4.17	40	18	42	2.8	6.9	**2.5**	13%	1.5	7.3	53	$17
ERA Potl	50%	1st Half		4	2	1	72	64	3.13	1.07	204			13.1	22%	80%	3.74	41	18	41	3.1	8.0	**2.6**	15%	1.5	12.3	71	$11
LIMA Plan	D+	2nd Half		8	4	0	87	58	4.97	1.39	283			23.4	30%	69%	4.54	40	18	43	2.5	6.0	**2.4**	12%	1.6	-4.9	39	$7
+/- Score	9	08	Proj	**11**	**7**	**0**	**174**	**140**	**4.24**	**1.33**	**265**			**24.6**	**30%**	**73%**	**4.25**	**39**	**18**	**43**	**2.8**	**7.2**	**2.6**	**12%**	**1.4**	**5.2**	**58**	**$15**

Joined rotation in May, had a terrific run (56% PQS-Dom) before wearing down in late August. Low BF/G means he'll have to show more durability, but the potential is there... UP: 16 wins, 3.75 ERA.

Marmol,Carlos		Yr	Tm	W	L	Sv	IP	K	ERA	WHIP	OBA	vL	vR	BF/G	H%	S%	xERA	G	L	F	Ctl	Dom	Cmd	hr/f	hr/9	RAR	BPV	R$
RH	Reliever	03		0	0	0	0	0	0.00	0.00																		
Age	25	04		0	0	0	0	0	0.00	0.00																		
Growth		05	aa	3	4	0	81	62	4.77	1.55	266			25.9	30%	73%	5.16				4.8	6.9	**1.4**		1.4	-4.7	30	$2
Type	Pwr xFB	06	CHC *	8	9	0	138	117	5.21	1.59	252	229	263	19.5	30%	68%	5.58	29	18	53	5.8	7.6	**1.3**	7%	1.0	-12.2	49	$4
Reliability	0	07	CHC *	9	2	1	110	134	2.87	1.14	200	209	146	6.7	28%	77%	3.66	31	16	52	3.9	10.9	**2.8**	6%	0.7	21.1	119	$18
ERA Potl	50%	1st Half		6	1	1	62	69	3.77	1.11	219			9.6	29%	68%	3.75	27	20	53	2.9	10.0	**3.5**	7%	0.9	5.0	118	$10
LIMA Plan	B	2nd Half		3	1	0	48	65	1.72	1.17	175			4.8	27%	87%	3.60	33	15	52	5.1	12.1	**2.4**	4%	0.4	16.1	129	$8
+/- Score	-5	08	Proj	**5**	**3**	**10**	**73**	**81**	**3.58**	**1.33**	**231**			**7.2**	**30%**	**76%**	**4.20**	**31**	**17**	**53**	**4.3**	**10.0**	**2.3**	**8%**	**1.0**	**1.8**	**88**	**$11**

5-1, 1.43 ERA in 69 IP at CHC. Flashed closer-worthy BPIs in breakout season, earning CHC's "closer in waiting" role. FB% tendency could cause issues, and 2H Ctl regression a concern. That said, a worthy investment.

Maroth,Mike		Yr	Tm	W	L	Sv	IP	K	ERA	WHIP	OBA	vL	vR	BF/G	H%	S%	xERA	G	L	F	Ctl	Dom	Cmd	hr/f	hr/9	RAR	BPV	R$
LH	Starter	03	DET	9	21	0	193	87	5.74	1.46	298	257	311	25.6	30%	64%	4.79	47	17	36	2.3	4.1	**1.7**	14%	1.6	-28.8	9	$4
Age	30	04	DET	11	13	0	217	108	4.31	1.40	285	288	294	28.4	30%	72%	4.69	46	18	36	2.4	4.5	**1.8**	9%	1.0	3.2	32	$11
Peak		05	DET	14	14	0	209	115	4.74	1.37	285	275	293	26.4	30%	69%	4.37	48	17	35	2.2	5.0	**2.3**	12%	1.3	-9.4	36	$12
Type	Con	06	DET	5	2	0	53	24	4.23	1.50	299	250	309	18.1	30%	80%	5.11	42	18	40	2.7	4.1	**1.5**	15%	1.9	2.2	-5	$4
Reliability	26	07	2TM	5	7	0	116	51	6.89	1.87	339	299	359	20.7	34%	67%	5.74	43	20	37	3.9	3.9	**1.0**	16%	2.0	-34.8	-28	($7)
ERA Potl	40%	1st Half		5	2	0	86	32	4.71	1.56	290			27.5	28%	75%	5.50	43	19	37	3.7	3.3	**0.9**	14%	1.7	-2.6	-14	$2
LIMA Plan	F	2nd Half		0	5	0	30	19	13.07	2.77	447			13.3	47%	54%	6.38	41	22	37	4.5	5.6	**1.3**	20%	3.0	-32.2	-63	($10)
+/- Score	10	08	Proj	**3**	**5**	**0**	**58**	**29**	**5.90**	**1.69**	**320**			**17.8**	**33%**	**69%**	**5.24**	**43**	**19**	**38**	**3.3**	**4.5**	**1.4**	**14%**	**1.7**	**-5.7**	**-4**	**($1)**

CAUTION: The publisher of this book takes no responsibility for any eye damage suffered by the reader when reviewing the "skills" in the box to the left. For safety's sake, look away. This is no joke, I'm serious. Don't look.

Marquis,Jason		Yr	Tm	W	L	Sv	IP	K	ERA	WHIP	OBA	vL	vR	BF/G	H%	S%	xERA	G	L	F	Ctl	Dom	Cmd	hr/f	hr/9	RAR	BPV	R$
RH	Starter	03	ATL *	8	4	1	134	82	4.97	1.57	295	250	287	16.7	33%	68%	4.65	52	15	33	3.6	5.5	**1.5**	6%	0.6	-11.4	43	$3
Age	29	04	STL	15	7	0	201	138	3.71	1.42	275	278	271	27.3	31%	78%	3.85	56	19	26	3.1	6.2	**2.0**	16%	1.2	13.6	44	$15
Peak		05	STL	13	14	0	207	100	4.13	1.33	261	238	280	26.6	27%	73%	4.44	52	17	31	3.0	4.3	**1.4**	14%	1.3	2.9	22	$13
Type	Con	06	STL	14	16	0	194	96	6.03	1.52	288	288	291	26.1	29%	64%	5.21	43	17	40	3.5	4.5	**1.3**	13%	1.6	-36.9	2	$3
Reliability	76	07	CHC	12	9	0	192	109	4.60	1.39	260	274	242	24.3	28%	69%	4.58	50	17	33	3.6	5.1	**1.4**	11%	1.0	-4.1	33	$11
ERA Potl	45%	1st Half		5	4	0	94	54	3.45	1.24	232			24.5	25%	75%	4.38	50	17	32	3.5	5.2	**1.5**	10%	0.9	11.4	44	$9
LIMA Plan	D	2nd Half		7	5	0	98	55	5.71	1.53	285			24.1	31%	64%	4.77	49	17	34	3.6	5.1	**1.4**	12%	1.2	-15.5	22	$2
+/- Score	-18	08	Proj	**10**	**13**	**0**	**189**	**103**	**4.87**	**1.46**	**277**			**25.0**	**30%**	**69%**	**4.74**	**48**	**17**	**34**	**3.4**	**4.9**	**1.4**	**11%**	**1.1**	**-7.9**	**25**	**$7**

2007's rebound was really just a reclaiming of 2005's mediocre skills. Wrigley helped the hr/f a bit, but this is still not the type of profile you want to invest in. A couple of small skill erosions mean another 2006.

Marshall,Jay		Yr	Tm	W	L	Sv	IP	K	ERA	WHIP	OBA	vL	vR	BF/G	H%	S%	xERA	G	L	F	Ctl	Dom	Cmd	hr/f	hr/9	RAR	BPV	R$
LH	Reliever	03		0	0	0	0	0	0.00	0.00																		
Age	25	04		0	0	0	0	0	0.00	0.00																		
Growth		05		0	0	0	0	0	0.00	0.00																		
Type	xGB	06		0	0	0	0	0	0.00	0.00																		
Reliability	3	07	OAK	1	2	0	42	18	6.43	1.71	297	296	299	3.8	32%	61%	4.99	58	19	23	4.7	3.9	**0.8**	9%	0.6	-10.0	17	($2)
ERA Potl	55%	1st Half		1	2	0	27	10	5.67	1.59	289			3.5	30%	65%	4.59	60	19	20	4.0	3.3	**0.8**	15%	1.0	-3.9	5	($0)
LIMA Plan	F	2nd Half		0	0	0	15	8	7.80	1.93	310			4.6	36%	55%	5.71	54	17	29	6.0	4.8	**0.8**	0%	0.0	-6.1	39	($2)
+/- Score	40	08	Proj	**0**	**0**	**0**	**15**	**7**	**5.40**	**1.80**	**299**			**4.2**	**33%**	**69%**	**5.30**	**56**	**18**	**25**	**5.4**	**4.2**	**0.8**	**7%**	**0.6**	**-1.5**	**19**	**($1)**

Rule 5 pick spent the full year in OAK bullpen, then claimed by BOS off waivers in October. High GB% is interesting, but lousy Cmd says he's a long way from making an impact, even as a situational lefty.

Marshall,Sean		Yr	Tm	W	L	Sv	IP	K	ERA	WHIP	OBA	vL	vR	BF/G	H%	S%	xERA	G	L	F	Ctl	Dom	Cmd	hr/f	hr/9	RAR	BPV	R$
LH	Starter	03		0	0	0	0	0	0.00	0.00																		
Age	25	04	aa	2	2	0	29	19	10.13	2.25	382			25.0	43%	53%	8.44				4.6	5.9	**1.3**		1.0	-20.7	12	($5)
Growth		05	aa	0	1	0	25	20	4.55	1.14	239			25.4	28%	60%	3.09				2.3	7.2	**3.2**		0.8	-0.7	94	$2
Type		06	CHC *	6	11	0	146	95	5.48	1.55	271	256	273	23.4	29%	67%	4.91	47	17	36	4.6	5.8	**1.3**	12%	1.3	-17.9	24	$2
Reliability	0	07	CHC *	9	8	0	128	79	3.65	1.36	264	203	280	21.8	29%	77%	4.44	48	16	36	3.1	5.6	**1.8**	11%	1.2	12.3	39	$11
ERA Potl	35%	1st Half		6	2	0	68	47	2.38	1.11	229			25.0	25%	87%	3.93	48	15	38	2.5	6.2	**2.5**	12%	1.2	17.3	63	$10
LIMA Plan	C+	2nd Half		3	6	0	59	32	5.11	1.64	302			19.3	32%	71%	5.08	49	16	35	3.8	4.8	**1.3**	10%	1.1	-5.0	17	$0
+/- Score	-20	08	Proj	**4**	**5**	**0**	**73**	**45**	**4.59**	**1.45**	**271**			**22.6**	**30%**	**71%**	**4.64**	**48**	**17**	**36**	**3.6**	**5.6**	**1.6**	**11%**	**1.1**	**-2.2**	**33**	**$3**

7-8, 3.92 ERA in 103 IP at CHC. Had a sudden bout of good Cmd in 1st half, but it left as quickly as it appeared. Good news is that he stayed healthy. Now the challenge is to mix in some sustained effectiveness.

Marte,Damaso		Yr	Tm	W	L	Sv	IP	K	ERA	WHIP	OBA	vL	vR	BF/G	H%	S%	xERA	G	L	F	Ctl	Dom	Cmd	hr/f	hr/9	RAR	BPV	R$
LH	Reliever	03	CHW	4	2	11	79	87	1.59	1.06	183	168	199	4.4	26%	86%	3.57	36	22	42	3.9	9.9	**2.6**	4%	0.3	28.5	121	$18
Age	33	04	CHW	6	5	6	73	68	3.44	1.23	213	143	263	4.1	25%	78%	4.25	36	17	46	4.2	8.4	**2.0**	11%	1.2	8.9	68	$11
Peak		05	CHW	3	4	4	45	54	3.79	1.73	261	267	244	3.2	35%	81%	4.43	40	21	39	6.6	10.8	**1.6**	11%	1.0	3.2	72	$4
Type	Pwr FB	06	PIT	1	7	0	58	63	3.72	1.41	237	225	258	3.4	31%	75%	4.13	34	25	41	4.8	9.8	**2.0**	8%	0.8	5.5	86	$4
Reliability	19	07	PIT	2	0	0	45	51	2.38	1.10	200	94	271	2.8	28%	79%	3.48	43	13	44	3.6	10.1	**2.8**	4%	0.4	11.4	123	$7
ERA Potl	55%	1st Half		0	0	0	23	26	1.96	1.13	198			2.8	29%	81%	3.50	47	10	43	3.9	10.2	**2.6**	0%	0.0	7.0	131	$3
LIMA Plan	B+	2nd Half		2	0	0	22	25	2.82	1.08	203			2.8	27%	77%	3.46	38	16	46	3.2	10.1	**3.1**	8%	0.8	4.4	116	$4
+/- Score	-31	08	Proj	**3**	**3**	**3**	**53**	**58**	**3.43**	**1.30**	**225**			**3.1**	**30%**	**76%**	**3.83**	**39**	**18**	**43**	**4.3**	**9.9**	**2.3**	**9%**	**0.9**	**3.7**	**93**	**$7**

Unlikely bounceback year at age 33: Incredible success vs LH hitters, best BPV since 2003. BA vs. RHers reminds us that he remains a poor candidate for an expanded role. But used correctly, he's a nice end-gamer.

RAY MURPHY

Martinez,Pedro			W	L	Sv	IP	K	ERA	WHIP	OBA	vL	vR	BF/G	H%	S%	xERA	G	L	F	Ctl	Dom	Cmd	hr/f	hr/9	RAR	BPV	R$
RH Starter	03	BOS	14	4	0	186	206	2.23	1.04	219	238	179	25.4	31%	79%	3.05	40	24	36	2.3	10.0	4.4	4%	0.3	52.7	153	$34
Age 36	04	BOS	16	9	0	217	227	3.90	1.17	240	236	240	26.9	30%	70%	3.50	38	19	43	2.5	9.4	3.7	10%	1.1	14.3	109	$26
Decline	05	NYM	15	8	0	217	208	2.82	0.95	206	215	192	27.1	26%	74%	3.43	38	17	45	1.9	8.6	4.4	8%	0.8	38.2	135	$33
Type Pwr FB	06	NYM	9	8	0	132	137	4.49	1.11	225	231	211	23.2	27%	63%	3.52	36	19	44	2.7	9.3	3.5	12%	1.3	-0.1	101	$15
Reliability 0	07	NYM	3	1	0	28	32	2.57	1.43	295	319	261	24.4	41%	80%	3.72	31	24	44	2.3	10.3	4.6	0%	0.0	6.4	154	$4
ERA Potl 50%	1st Half		0	0	0	0	0	0.00	0.00																		
LIMA Plan A+	2nd Half		3	1	0	28	32	2.57	1.43	295			24.3	41%	80%	3.72	31	24	44	2.3	10.3	4.6	0%	0.0	6.4	154	$4
+/- Score -6	08	Proj	13	6	0	160	159	3.50	1.20	245			25.3	31%	74%	3.71	36	21	44	2.6	9.0	3.5	9%	1.0	13.5	104	$20

Flashed vintage skills in Sept. return. But, these 28 IP do not absolve him of risk entering 2008. He still needs to show he can hold up physically for a full year. Someone else will bid on a full rebound; let them do so.

Mastny,Tom			W	L	Sv	IP	K	ERA	WHIP	OBA	vL	vR	BF/G	H%	S%	xERA	G	L	F	Ctl	Dom	Cmd	hr/f	hr/9	RAR	BPV	R$
RH Reliever	03		0	0	0	0	0	0.00	0.00																		
Age 27	04		0	0	0	0	0	0.00	0.00																		
Growth	05	aa	1	1	0	21	16	3.00	1.19	243			17.3	29%	75%	2.98				2.6	6.9	2.7		0.4	3.4	91	$2
Type Pwr FB	06	CLE	* 2	3	6	78	79	3.33	1.27	229	273	282	6.4	31%	72%	3.52	48	23	29	3.9	9.0	2.3	2%	0.1	11.9	108	$11
Reliability 10	07	CLE	7	2	0	58	52	4.68	1.65	279	282	283	5.2	34%	73%	4.79	40	19	41	5.0	8.1	1.6	8%	0.9	-1.2	54	$4
ERA Potl 55%	1st Half		5	2	0	31	28	5.23	1.68	280			4.6	34%	69%	4.68	44	19	37	5.2	8.1	1.6	9%	0.9	-2.8	54	$3
LIMA Plan B+	2nd Half		2	0	0	27	24	4.04	1.61	278			6.0	34%	78%	4.91	36	18	46	4.7	8.1	1.7	8%	1.0	1.5	54	$2
+/- Score 20	08	Proj	4	2	0	58	55	4.03	1.45	252			5.6	31%	74%	4.33	40	19	41	4.5	8.5	1.9	9%	0.9	1.2	68	$5

Couldn't sustain '06's breakout, and the culprit is home plate. It's been getting more and more blurry each year, and tougher to find. All other skills are intact; it's just that darn plate. Maybe he needs glasses.

Matsuzaka,Daisuke			W	L	Sv	IP	K	ERA	WHIP	OBA	vL	vR	BF/G	H%	S%	xERA	G	L	F	Ctl	Dom	Cmd	hr/f	hr/9	RAR	BPV	R$
RH Starter	03	JPN	16	7	0	194	227	3.51	1.32	244			28.3	33%	77%	3.83				3.6	10.5	2.9		1.0	21.0	100	$24
Age 27	04	JPN	10	6	0	146	134	3.60	1.29	249			26.7	31%	74%	3.60				3.2	8.3	2.6		0.7	13.4	87	$15
Pre-Peak	05	JPN	14	13	0	215	238	2.86	1.14	233			31.2	31%	79%	3.14				2.5	10.0	3.9		0.9	38.3	123	$30
Type Pwr FB	06	JPN	17	5	0	186	211	2.64	1.02	220			29.4	29%	80%	2.78				2.0	10.2	5.0		1.0	43.2	146	$34
Reliability 58	07	BOS	15	12	0	205	201	4.40	1.32	249	238	253	27.1	31%	70%	4.01	38	18	44	3.5	8.8	2.5	10%	1.1	2.7	78	$20
ERA Potl 65%	1st Half		9	5	0	107	110	3.79	1.23	241			27.8	31%	71%	3.70	39	19	42	3.0	9.3	3.1	7%	0.8	9.5	104	$14
LIMA Plan C+	2nd Half		6	7	0	98	91	5.07	1.42	256			26.5	30%	68%	4.37	38	17	45	4.1	8.4	2.1	13%	1.5	-6.8	53	$7
+/- Score 30	08	Proj	16	9	0	203	211	3.72	1.23	240			28.1	30%	73%	3.71	38	18	44	3.1	9.4	3.1	10%	1.1	19.7	95	$26

Much-hyped import delivered on expectations in 1H, then faded.
PRO: Dom translated well, 63% PQS-DOM starts.
CON: Ctl issues, Sept. collapse
His 1-year cultural adjustment is complete. He's a buy in 2008.

McCarthy,Brandon			W	L	Sv	IP	K	ERA	WHIP	OBA	vL	vR	BF/G	H%	S%	xERA	G	L	F	Ctl	Dom	Cmd	hr/f	hr/9	RAR	BPV	R$
RH Starter	03		0	0	0	0	0	0.00	0.00											0.0	0.0						
Age 24	04	aa	3	1	0	26	25	4.15	1.31	262			27.5	32%	71%	4.12				2.8	8.7	3.1		1.0	0.6	89	$3
Growth	05	CHW	* 10	9	0	186	165	4.31	1.19	249	182	276	23.9	28%	70%	3.80	35	23	42	2.3	8.0	3.5	14%	1.5	1.5	79	$18
Type xFB	06	CHW	4	7	0	84	69	4.70	1.31	245	197	270	6.7	26%	71%	4.40	38	15	47	3.5	7.4	2.1	15%	1.8	-1.5	40	$7
Reliability 10	07	TEX	5	10	0	102	59	4.87	1.56	279	292	263	19.8	31%	69%	5.64	36	17	47	4.2	5.2	1.2	6%	0.8	-4.5	32	$3
ERA Potl 50%	1st Half		4	4	0	50	31	5.94	1.58	277			18.8	31%	62%	5.77	33	16	51	4.5	5.6	1.2	6%	0.9	-8.8	32	$1
LIMA Plan C+	2nd Half		1	6	0	52	28	3.83	1.55	281			21.0	31%	76%	5.51	39	18	43	4.0	4.9	1.2	5%	0.7	4.3	33	$2
+/- Score -23	08	Proj	7	13	0	145	102	4.66	1.45	270			23.5	30%	71%	4.95	37	17	46	3.7	6.3	1.7	9%	1.2	-8.1	38	$8

Hit the trifecta of arm problems in 2007: shoulder, forearm, and blister issues all sidelined him at various times. Cmd trend, even amid injuries, is a red flag. 2005 promise is fading. Far more risk than reward, especially in TEX.

McGowan,Dustin			W	L	Sv	IP	K	ERA	WHIP	OBA	vL	vR	BF/G	H%	S%	xERA	G	L	F	Ctl	Dom	Cmd	hr/f	hr/9	RAR	BPV	R$
RH Starter	03	aa	7	0	0	76	63	3.78	1.42	293			23.6	37%	71%	3.96				2.2	7.4	3.3		0.1	5.8	107	$7
Age 26	04	aa	2	1	0	31	25	6.10	1.52	255			22.9	28%	63%	5.23				4.9	7.3	1.5		1.7	-6.7	26	$1
Growth	05	TOR	* 1	5	0	80	62	5.91	1.54	297	243	301	18.8	33%	66%	4.23	47	17	36	3.2	7.0	2.2	18%	1.8	-15.2	29	($0)
Type Pwr GB	06	TOR	* 5	7	1	111	96	6.32	1.76	292	327	283	13.3	35%	64%	4.76	43	26	31	5.4	7.8	1.4	10%	0.9	-24.1	47	($0)
Reliability 6	07	TOR	* 12	12	0	192	169	3.85	1.23	234	257	198	24.8	29%	69%	3.54	53	16	31	3.3	7.9	2.4	8%	0.7	15.4	87	$21
ERA Potl 60%	1st Half		4	5	0	82	74	4.06	1.29	242			23.0	31%	68%	3.74	49	18	33	3.5	8.1	2.3	5%	0.4	4.5	91	$8
LIMA Plan D+	2nd Half		8	7	0	110	95	3.70	1.18	228			26.4	27%	71%	3.41	55	15	30	3.1	7.8	2.5	11%	0.8	11.0	84	$14
+/- Score 14	08	Proj	13	9	0	199	175	3.98	1.29	244			26.2	30%	71%	3.66	51	18	32	3.4	7.9	2.3	11%	0.9	20.5	77	$20

12-10, 4.08 in 170 IP at TOR. One-time top prospect solved Ctl issues, driving major breakthru. Combo of GB% and Dom is a winner, Year-over-year IP spike is a concern for 2008, but this breakout is very real.

Meche,Gil			W	L	Sv	IP	K	ERA	WHIP	OBA	vL	vR	BF/G	H%	S%	xERA	G	L	F	Ctl	Dom	Cmd	hr/f	hr/9	RAR	BPV	R$
RH Starter	03	SEA	15	13	0	186	130	4.60	1.34	263	275	248	24.8	28%	70%	4.57	38	18	43	3.0	6.3	2.1	12%	1.5	-1.7	40	$15
Age 29	04	SEA	* 8	10	0	184	140	5.23	1.50	279	269	278	24.7	31%	68%	4.80	37	19	44	3.7	6.8	1.9	11%	1.4	-18.1	37	$6
Peak	05	SEA	10	8	0	143	83	5.09	1.57	275	266	285	22.2	30%	70%	5.40	40	20	40	4.5	5.2	1.2	9%	1.1	-12.8	22	$4
Type	06	SEA	11	8	0	186	156	4.50	1.43	258	240	271	25.3	30%	72%	4.36	43	18	38	4.1	7.5	1.9	11%	1.2	1.4	53	$14
Reliability 69	07	KC	9	13	0	216	156	3.67	1.30	264	242	284	26.8	30%	74%	4.04	47	18	35	2.6	6.5	2.5	9%	0.9	22.3	67	$19
ERA Potl 50%	1st Half		5	6	0	110	83	3.27	1.29	267			27.2	31%	78%	3.71	51	18	31	2.4	6.8	2.9	10%	0.9	16.7	75	$11
LIMA Plan D+	2nd Half		4	7	0	106	73	4.08	1.30	260			26.3	29%	71%	4.38	42	18	38	2.8	6.2	2.2	8%	0.9	5.6	59	$8
+/- Score -1	08	Proj	11	11	0	203	148	4.03	1.33	265			26.2	30%	73%	4.25	44	18	38	2.9	6.6	2.3	10%	1.1	6.1	57	$17

Justified KC's investment in him, as Ctl gains led to his best year. Skills eroded just a bit in 2H, but overall GB% and Cmd trends are enticing. A few more wins could push him over the $20 level, but again, this is Kansas City.

Meloan,Jonathan			W	L	Sv	IP	K	ERA	WHIP	OBA	vL	vR	BF/G	H%	S%	xERA	G	L	F	Ctl	Dom	Cmd	hr/f	hr/9	RAR	BPV	R$
RH Reliever	03		0	0	0	0	0	0.00	0.00																		
Age 23	04		0	0	0	0	0	0.00	0.00																		
Growth	05		0	0	0	0	0	0.00	0.00																		
Type Pwr xFB	06	aa	1	0	0	10	20	2.70	1.20	151			8.2	33%	82%	2.23				6.3	18.0	2.9		0.9	2.2	166	$2
Reliability 0	07	LA	* 7	2	20	74	85	3.25	1.16	192	231	333	5.5	26%	75%	3.77	33	19	48	4.4	10.4	2.4	9%	0.9	10.7	102	$18
ERA Potl 50%	1st Half		5	2	16	38	51	2.36	0.94	176			4.9	28%	74%					3.1	12.0	3.9		0.2	9.7	167	$14
LIMA Plan A	2nd Half		2	0	4	35	34	4.20	1.39	208			6.4	23%	76%	4.79	33	19	48	5.8	8.5	1.5	14%	1.6	1.0	48	$4
+/- Score 9	08	Proj	3	3	0	54	59	4.04	1.33	222			5.8	29%	72%	4.14	33	19	48	4.7	9.9	2.1	9%	1.0	1.7	84	$5

0-0, 11.05 ERA in 7 IP at LA. Attention-grabbing DOM levels in minors, had Ctl issues in brief MLB debut. Should be a factor in LA pen, could earn a setup role right away. Future closer material.

Meredith,Cla			W	L	Sv	IP	K	ERA	WHIP	OBA	vL	vR	BF/G	H%	S%	xERA	G	L	F	Ctl	Dom	Cmd	hr/f	hr/9	RAR	BPV	R$
RH Reliever	03		0	0	0	0	0	0.00	0.00																		
Age 24	04		0	0	0	0	0	0.00	0.00																		
Growth	05	a/a	3	5	19	61	46	5.16	1.46	300			5.2	35%	65%	4.89				2.2	6.8	3.1		0.9	-6.4	73	$8
Type xGB	06	SD	* 8	1	2	96	70	1.96	0.96	221	281	107	4.8	26%	83%	2.40	69	16	15	1.4	6.5	4.7	14%	0.6	29.9	131	$18
Reliability 2	07	SD	5	6	0	80	59	3.50	1.39	295	286	303	4.3	35%	76%	2.61	72	14	14	1.9	6.7	3.5	17%	0.7	9.1	89	$7
ERA Potl 55%	1st Half		3	5	0	37	29	3.41	1.41	301			4.6	36%	78%	2.65	69	17	15	1.7	7.1	4.1	17%	0.7	4.7	102	$4
LIMA Plan A	2nd Half		2	1	0	43	30	3.58	1.38	289			4.1	34%	75%	2.55	75	13	13	2.1	6.3	3.0	17%	0.6	4.4	79	$3
+/- Score 69	08	Proj	6	4	3	83	61	3.04	1.19	259			4.5	31%	76%	2.50	72	15	14	1.8	6.6	3.6	14%	0.5	19.4	102	$11

Another RP who sees his h% and s% normalize over a two-year period. GB rate is just obscene, and along with elite Cmd are a lethal combo. xERA for last two years show his true level. That's what you pay for.

Mesa,Jose			W	L	Sv	IP	K	ERA	WHIP	OBA	vL	vR	BF/G	H%	S%	xERA	G	L	F	Ctl	Dom	Cmd	hr/f	hr/9	RAR	BPV	R$
RH Reliever	03	PHI	5	7	24	58	45	6.52	1.76	303	213	349	4.4	35%	63%	4.85	45	21	34	4.8	7.0	1.5	11%	1.1	-16.0	34	$7
Age 41	04	PIT	5	2	43	69	37	3.26	1.42	286	331	255	4.3	31%	79%	4.69	46	17	37	2.6	4.8	1.9	7%	0.8	8.6	42	$18
Decline	05	PIT	2	8	27	56	37	4.80	1.55	278	309	265	4.6	31%	71%	5.01	43	18	40	4.2	5.9	1.4	10%	1.1	-3.9	31	$10
Type	06	COL	1	5	1	72	39	3.87	1.51	264	270	271	4.0	28%	78%	5.19	46	17	37	4.5	4.9	1.1	10%	1.1	5.5	20	$2
Reliability 14	07	2TM	2	3	1	51	29	7.10	1.54	270	263	280	4.0	28%	55%	5.20	46	16	38	4.4	5.1	1.2	14%	1.6	-16.5	8	($1)
ERA Potl 55%	1st Half		1	1	0	19	11	9.00	1.74	309			3.8	32%	48%	5.08	51	13	36	4.3	5.2	1.2	17%	1.9	-10.6	-7	($2)
LIMA Plan F	2nd Half		1	2	1	32	18	5.96	1.42	245			4.2	25%	60%	5.27	42	16	43	4.5	5.1	1.1	12%	1.4	-5.9	18	$1
+/- Score 35	08	Proj	1	4	0	45	25	5.46	1.64	285			4.2	30%	69%	5.39	46	16	39	4.7	5.1	1.1	10%	1.2	-5.2	15	($1)

All evidence of the once-dominant closer of the same name has apparently been destroyed. For the youngsters: He posted 46 Svs and a 1.13 ERA in his best season... way back in 1995.

RAY MURPHY

Messenger,Randy

	Yr	W	L	Sv	IP	K	ERA	WHIP	OBA	vL	vR	BF/G	H%	S%	xERA	G	L	F	Ctl	Dom	Cmd	hr/f	hr/9	RAR	BPV	R$
RH Reliever	03	0	0	0	0	0	0.00	0.00																		
Age 26	04 aa	6	3	21	69	62	3.08	1.56	284			5.4	35%	81%	4.61				4.0	8.1	**2.0**		0.5	10.7	73	$13
Growth	05 aaa	4	2	7	48	32	3.73	1.29	253			5.2	29%	72%	3.66				3.0	6.0	**2.0**		0.7	3.4	60	$7
Type	06 FLA	2	7	0	60	45	5.69	1.60	298	333	267	4.6	34%	66%	4.88	38	19	43	3.6	6.7	**1.9**	9%	1.2	-8.9	39	$0
Reliability 12	07 2NL	2	4	1	64	34	4.20	1.65	319	342	320	4.9	35%	75%	5.15	46	16	39	2.9	4.8	**1.6**	4%	0.6	1.8	37	$1
ERA Potl 50%	1st Half	1	2	0	38	21	2.37	1.42	277			4.9	32%	83%	4.95	47	12	41	3.1	5.0	**1.6**	2%	0.2	9.6	56	$3
LIMA Plan C+	2nd Half	1	2	1	26	13	6.84	1.98	372			5.0	40%	65%	5.44	44	20	36	2.7	4.4	**1.6**	8%	1.0	-7.8	11	($2)
+/- Score -20	08 Proj	**3**	**4**	**0**	**58**	**37**	**4.81**	**1.64**	**312**			**4.9**	**35%**	**71%**	**5.00**	**43**	**18**	**40**	**3.3**	**5.7**	**1.8**	**6%**	**0.8**	**-4.3**	**41**	**$1**

CON: Cmd remains sub-par due to drop in Dom. 3-year xERA trend tells the story. Missed time after breaking hand punching a cart in the clubhouse.
PRO: It wasn't his pitching hand.

Miller,Adam

	Yr	W	L	Sv	IP	K	ERA	WHIP	OBA	vL	vR	BF/G	H%	S%	xERA	G	L	F	Ctl	Dom	Cmd	hr/f	hr/9	RAR	BPV	R$
RH Reliever	03	0	0	0	0	0	0.00	0.00																		
Age 23	04	0	0	0	0	0	0.00	0.00																		
Growth	05	0	0	0	0	0	0.00	0.00																		
Type Pwr	06 a/a	15	6	0	158	150	3.42	1.22	248			24.2	32%	72%	3.12				2.6	8.5	**3.3**		0.5	21.5	111	$22
Reliability 0	07 aaa	5	4	0	65	65	5.53	1.43	285			14.9	37%	60%	4.28				2.8	9.0	**3.3**		0.5	-8.6	104	$4
ERA Potl 80%	1st Half	4	1	0	47	37	2.68	1.21	241			21.6	30%	78%					2.9	7.1	**2.5**		0.4	10.3	90	$7
LIMA Plan A	2nd Half	1	3	0	18	28	12.93	2.01	380			8.9	56%	30%					2.5	14.0	**5.6**		0.9	-18.9	154	($3)
+/- Score 77	08 Proj	**8**	**8**	**0**	**104**	**96**	**4.41**	**1.38**	**273**			**24.8**	**34%**	**69%**	**4.26**				**2.9**	**8.3**	**2.9**		**0.9**	**2.4**	**85**	**$9**

Injury plagued season pushed back arrival time for this top SP prospect, but he's still coming. Had arm problems but didn't require surgery. Appeared in AFL this fall, demonstrating health. Big upside, quick impact.

Miller,Andrew

	Yr	W	L	Sv	IP	K	ERA	WHIP	OBA	vL	vR	BF/G	H%	S%	xERA	G	L	F	Ctl	Dom	Cmd	hr/f	hr/9	RAR	BPV	R$
LH Starter	03	0	0	0	0	0	0.00	0.00																		
Age 22	04	0	0	0	0	0	0.00	0.00																		
Growth	05	0	0	0	0	0	0.00	0.00																		
Type Pwr xGB	06 DET	0	1	0	10	6	6.24	1.78	219			5.9	26%	61%	5.03	64	24	12	8.9	5.3	**0.6**	0%	0.0	-2.1	56	($0)
Reliability 0	07 DET *	7	5	0	100	85	4.67	1.56	275	175	312	23.6	33%	71%	4.18	49	21	30	4.4	7.6	**1.7**	11%	0.9	-2.0	55	$6
ERA Potl 55%	1st Half	5	1	0	53	36	1.86	1.18	239			27.3	27%	90%	4.04	45	21	34	2.7	6.1	**2.3**	9%	0.8	17.4	66	$9
LIMA Plan B	2nd Half	2	4	0	47	49	7.85	1.98	312			20.9	40%	59%	4.44	52	21	28	6.3	9.4	**1.5**	13%	1.0	-19.4	51	($3)
+/- Score 27	08 Proj	**7**	**6**	**0**	**104**	**93**	**4.59**	**1.41**	**256**			**21.5**	**32%**	**67%**	**3.39**	**57**	**22**	**21**	**4.0**	**8.0**	**2.0**	**11%**	**0.6**	**14.1**	**76**	**$8**

5-5, 5.63 ERA in 64 IP at DET. 2006 1st-round pick rushed to the majors, with predictable outcome. Combo of Dom/GB% is enticing, but needs to solve Ctl issues to find success. ETA for that is likely beyond 2008.

Miller,Justin

	Yr	W	L	Sv	IP	K	ERA	WHIP	OBA	vL	vR	BF/G	H%	S%	xERA	G	L	F	Ctl	Dom	Cmd	hr/f	hr/9	RAR	BPV	R$
RH Reliever	03	0	0	0	0	0	0.00	0.00																		
Age 30	04 TOR *	4	5	0	97	66	5.74	1.72	303			20.5	33%	70%	6.36				4.4	6.1	**1.4**		1.6	-15.7	13	($1)
Peak	05 aaa	3	1	2	50	46	3.09	1.27	255			7.5	32%	77%	3.46				2.7	8.2	**3.0**		0.6	7.5	99	$6
Type Pwr FB	06 JPN	0	1	0	12	10	13.04	2.64	363			5.6	38%	54%	11.58				9.3	7.8	**0.8**		3.7	-12.6	-65	($4)
Reliability 2	07 FLA *	5	0	6	76	90	3.41	1.36	248	324	184	4.3	35%	76%	3.63	43	14	43	3.9	10.7	**2.7**	6%	0.6	9.5	109	$10
ERA Potl 60%	1st Half	2	0	6	35	41	2.56	1.28	233			4.6	33%	80%	3.84	41	7	52	3.8	10.5	**2.7**	2%	0.3	8.1	121	$7
LIMA Plan B+	2nd Half	3	0	0	41	49	4.15	1.43	261			4.0	36%	73%	3.51	43	18	38	3.9	10.8	**2.8**	10%	0.9	1.4	99	$4
+/- Score -2	08 Proj	**3**	**2**	**0**	**58**	**59**	**3.88**	**1.34**	**252**			**5.8**	**32%**	**74%**	**3.89**	**43**	**15**	**42**	**3.6**	**9.2**	**2.6**	**9%**	**0.9**	**3.7**	**86**	**$5**

5-0, 3.65 ERA in 62 IP at FLA. Brought 2005's MLE skills to the majors. 2H fade was h% and s% betraying him; skills held up just fine. Troubles with lefties limit him to setup work, but this is a repeatable performance.

Miller,Trever

	Yr	W	L	Sv	IP	K	ERA	WHIP	OBA	vL	vR	BF/G	H%	S%	xERA	G	L	F	Ctl	Dom	Cmd	hr/f	hr/9	RAR	BPV	R$
LH Reliever	03 TOR	2	2	4	52	44	4.67	1.42	239	226	237	2.9	28%	70%	4.59	41	19	40	4.8	7.6	**1.6**	12%	1.2	-1.0	50	$4
Age 34	04 TAM	1	1	1	49	43	3.12	1.29	258	214	303	3.4	32%	77%	3.44	53	17	29	2.8	7.9	**2.9**	7%	0.6	7.9	94	$5
Past Peak	05 TAM	2	2	0	44	35	4.08	1.68	266	267	289	3.3	31%	77%	5.15	40	25	35	5.9	7.1	**1.2**	9%	0.8	1.6	46	$2
Type Pwr xFB	06 HOU	2	3	1	50	56	3.05	1.10	229	224	225	2.9	29%	79%	3.45	33	18	49	2.3	10.0	**4.3**	11%	1.3	8.9	122	$7
Reliability 3	07 HOU	0	0	1	46	46	4.86	1.47	256	209	289	2.7	32%	69%	4.52	34	18	48	4.5	8.9	**2.0**	10%	1.2	-2.5	64	$2
ERA Potl 60%	1st Half	0	0	0	19	24	7.58	2.16	309			2.4	43%	64%	5.42	31	24	44	8.1	11.4	**1.4**	8%	0.9	-7.4	63	($2)
LIMA Plan B+	2nd Half	0	0	1	27	22	2.97	0.99	214			3.0	24%	78%	3.94	36	14	51	2.0	7.3	**3.7**	10%	1.3	4.9	93	$3
+/- Score 6	08 Proj	**1**	**1**	**0**	**48**	**47**	**4.50**	**1.40**	**250**			**2.9**	**31%**	**70%**	**4.29**	**36**	**19**	**45**	**4.1**	**8.8**	**2.1**	**10%**	**1.1**	**0.7**	**69**	**$2**

For 2nd straight year, had no idea of the strike zone early in the season, then suddenly composed himself. The 2nd half version is intriguing, but you also have to live with the wild man each spring.

Millwood,Kevin

	Yr	W	L	Sv	IP	K	ERA	WHIP	OBA	vL	vR	BF/G	H%	S%	xERA	G	L	F	Ctl	Dom	Cmd	hr/f	hr/9	RAR	BPV	R$
RH Starter	03 PHI	14	12	0	222	169	4.01	1.25	251	246	253	26.5	29%	69%	4.24	40	19	41	2.8	6.9	**2.5**	7%	0.8	7.3	75	$19
Age 33	04 PHI	9	6	0	141	125	4.85	1.46	280	309	250	24.7	34%	68%	4.11	42	21	37	3.3	8.0	**2.5**	9%	0.9	-10.2	71	$7
Peak	05 CLE	9	11	0	192	146	2.86	1.22	252	269	227	26.5	29%	81%	3.78	46	21	33	2.4	6.8	**2.8**	10%	0.9	35.8	77	$21
Type	06 TEX	16	12	0	215	157	4.52	1.31	273	285	258	26.7	31%	67%	3.96	45	21	34	2.2	6.6	**3.0**	10%	1.0	1.0	73	$20
Reliability 75	07 TEX	10	14	0	173	123	5.16	1.62	304	288	311	25.3	35%	69%	4.49	46	21	32	3.5	6.4	**1.8**	10%	1.0	-13.9	41	$5
ERA Potl 60%	1st Half	4	6	0	60	46	7.35	1.85	342			23.9	38%	63%	4.72	43	21	36	3.5	6.9	**2.0**	17%	2.0	-21.1	11	($2)
LIMA Plan C+	2nd Half	6	8	0	113	77	3.99	1.50	282			26.2	33%	72%	4.36	49	21	30	3.5	6.1	**1.8**	5%	0.5	7.1	58	$7
+/- Score 14	08 Proj	**12**	**14**	**0**	**203**	**150**	**4.43**	**1.39**	**274**			**25.0**	**31%**	**70%**	**4.14**	**45**	**21**	**34**	**3.0**	**6.7**	**2.2**	**11%**	**1.0**	**8.8**	**57**	**$15**

Has the skills to return to a sub-4.00 ERA, but he's treading a thin line. Pushing him over the edge in '07 was the confluence of an extra bb/9, Dom erosion, 1H H%/S% bad luck, Texas, age 33, all reaching critical mass.

Milton,Eric

	Yr	W	L	Sv	IP	K	ERA	WHIP	OBA	vL	vR	BF/G	H%	S%	xERA	G	L	F	Ctl	Dom	Cmd	hr/f	hr/9	RAR	BPV	R$
LH Starter	03 MIN	1	0	0	17	7	2.65	0.94	238	389	174	21.9	24%	79%	4.87	27	15	58	0.5	3.7	**7.0**	6%	1.1	3.9	145	$3
Age 32	04 PHI	14	6	0	201	161	4.75	1.35	257	252	256	25.2	27%	72%	4.73	30	18	52	3.4	7.2	**2.1**	14%	1.9	-12.0	34	$13
Peak	05 CIN	8	15	0	186	123	6.48	1.55	311	284	307	24.5	33%	62%	4.94	33	21	46	2.5	5.9	**2.4**	14%	1.9	-51.3	20	($2)
Type xFB	06 CIN	8	8	0	152	90	5.20	1.35	275	216	286	25.0	28%	66%	5.03	31	19	50	2.5	5.3	**2.1**	11%	1.7	-13.4	25	$7
Reliability 11	07 CIN	0	4	0	31	18	5.18	1.53	306	300	297	23.2	33%	68%	5.44	26	24	50	2.6	5.2	**2.0**	7%	1.2	-2.9	32	($0)
ERA Potl 50%	1st Half	0	4	0	31	18	5.23	1.55	308			23.1	34%	68%	5.45	26	24	50	2.6	5.2	**2.0**	7%	1.2	-3.1	32	($0)
LIMA Plan D	2nd Half	0	0	0	0	0	0.00	0.00																		
+/- Score -21	08 Proj	**1**	**2**	**0**	**29**	**19**	**5.59**	**1.48**	**294**			**25.5**	**32%**	**66%**	**5.13**	**29**	**21**	**50**	**2.8**	**5.9**	**2.1**	**10%**	**1.6**	**-2.6**	**29**	**$0**

TJ surgery in June can only be described as a public service to the good, hard-working people of Cincinnti.

Remember... Never mix xFB and GAB. Ever.

Miner,Zach

	Yr	W	L	Sv	IP	K	ERA	WHIP	OBA	vL	vR	BF/G	H%	S%	xERA	G	L	F	Ctl	Dom	Cmd	hr/f	hr/9	RAR	BPV	R$
RH Reliever	03	0	0	0	0	0	0.00	0.00																		
Age 26	04 aa	6	10	0	129	96	6.55	1.61	297			21.7	34%	59%	5.49				3.8	6.7	**1.8**		1.1	-35.2	40	($1)
Growth	05 a/a	5	9	1	140	87	4.88	1.73	305			24.2	34%	72%	5.56				4.5	5.6	**1.2**		0.8	-10.0	31	($0)
Type GB	06 DET *	13	6	0	144	94	4.44	1.42	271	320	245	17.3	31%	70%	4.38	47	21	32	3.3	5.9	**1.8**	9%	0.8	2.1	49	$12
Reliability 0	07 DET *	4	8	0	107	63	4.97	1.51	276	207	317	10.1	31%	67%	4.42	56	16	27	3.9	5.3	**1.4**	8%	0.7	-6.1	39	$3
ERA Potl 50%	1st Half	1	5	0	64	39	5.89	1.48	276			15.7	31%	59%	4.90	38	27	35	3.6	5.5	**1.5**	7%	0.7	-10.9	43	$0
LIMA Plan C+	2nd Half	3	3	0	43	24	3.59	1.55	276			6.6	31%	78%	4.43	61	13	25	4.3	5.0	**1.2**	9%	0.7	4.8	33	$3
+/- Score -3	08 Proj	**5**	**5**	**0**	**83**	**51**	**4.77**	**1.54**	**282**			**11.9**	**32%**	**69%**	**4.48**	**54**	**17**	**29**	**3.9**	**5.5**	**1.4**	**9%**	**0.8**	**0.1**	**39**	**$3**

3-4, 3.02 ERA in 54 IP at DET. Decent MLB outcome full of warnings: RH hitters crush him, Cmd insufficient. A high GB% can mask some skill blemishes, but not this many, and not forever.

Mitre,Sergio

	Yr	W	L	Sv	IP	K	ERA	WHIP	OBA	vL	vR	BF/G	H%	S%	xERA	G	L	F	Ctl	Dom	Cmd	hr/f	hr/9	RAR	BPV	R$
RH Starter	03 aa	7	9	0	145	113	4.34	1.62	318			26.4	38%	72%	5.16				2.7	7.0	**2.6**		0.4	1.0	74	$5
Age 27	04 CHC *	8	7	1	153	122	4.28	1.51	286	408	261	22.6	34%	73%	3.66	59	16	25	3.4	7.2	**2.1**	12%	0.9	-0.4	59	$8
Growth	05 CHC *	7	11	0	130	85	5.04	1.42	276	294	235	16.6	31%	66%	3.54	66	11	22	3.1	5.9	**1.9**	17%	1.1	-12.8	42	$5
Type xGB	06 FLA	1	5	0	41	31	5.71	1.56	276	344	232	12.2	30%	67%	4.22	52	20	28	4.4	6.8	**1.6**	20%	1.5	-6.2	27	($0)
Reliability 14	07 FLA	5	8	0	149	80	4.65	1.48	300	271	332	24.3	33%	68%	3.94	60	17	23	2.5	4.8	**2.0**	8%	0.5	-4.1	49	$4
ERA Potl 55%	1st Half	2	3	0	75	50	2.76	1.25	269			24.1	31%	80%	3.34	60	17	23	1.9	6.0	**3.1**	9%	0.6	15.4	85	$7
LIMA Plan C+	2nd Half	3	5	0	74	30	6.57	1.72	328			24.5	35%	59%	4.60	60	17	23	3.0	3.6	**1.2**	6%	0.5	-19.5	22	($3)
+/- Score 4	08 Proj	**8**	**11**	**0**	**174**	**108**	**4.50**	**1.45**	**283**			**23.8**	**32%**	**69%**	**3.91**	**58**	**18**	**24**	**3.0**	**5.6**	**1.9**	**10%**	**0.7**	**10.4**	**49**	**$8**

Reasons to put him back on your radar screen:
- Brilliant 1st half.
- Full-year Cmd hit key 2.0 level.
- Pushed GB% to elite levels.

Still needs to recapture prior Dom levels, but the seeds are here.

RAY MURPHY

Moehler,Brian	Yr	Tm	W	L	Sv	IP	K	ERA	WHIP	OBA	vL	vR	BF/G	H%	S%	xERA	G	L	F	Ctl	Dom	Cmd	hr/f	hr/9	RAR	BPV	R$
RH Reliever	03	HOU *	0	0	0	16	8	7.31	1.94	357			19.4	36%	67%	8.33				3.4	4.5	1.3		2.3	-6.0	-29	($2)
Age 36	04	aa	3	9	0	108	42	5.83	1.63	321			24.6	34%	64%	5.75				2.7	3.5	1.3		0.9	-19.9	12	($3)
Decline	05	FLA	6	12	0	158	95	4.55	1.52	308	320	305	19.0	34%	71%	4.41	44	25	31	2.4	5.4	2.3	9%	0.9	-6.0	46	$4
Type Con	06	FLA	7	11	0	122	58	6.57	1.66	323	351	297	19.2	34%	62%	4.96	45	22	33	2.8	4.3	1.5	13%	1.4	-31.3	6	($2)
Reliability 28	07	HOU	1	4	1	60	36	4.07	1.41	285	303	268	6.2	31%	75%	4.18	52	16	32	2.6	5.4	2.1	13%	1.2	2.6	39	$3
ERA Potl 35%	1st Half		0	2	0	27	20	5.67	1.59	327			7.6	37%	67%	3.56	55	21	23	2.0	6.7	3.3	18%	1.3	-4.1	60	($0)
LIMA Plan C	2nd Half		1	2	1	33	16	2.75	1.25	245			5.2	25%	84%	4.68	50	11	39	3.0	4.4	1.5	10%	1.1	6.8	30	$3
+/- Score -23	08	Proj	2	4	0	58	31	4.81	1.50	300			6.9	32%	71%	4.55	48	19	32	2.6	4.8	1.8	12%	1.2	-1.1	25	$1

Results seemed to improve with move to bullpen. But despite Cmd gains, there's little to get excited about here. Struggles with LH hitters continue to limit his utility. Less disastrous than before, but still not rosterable.

Morales,Franklin	Yr	Tm	W	L	Sv	IP	K	ERA	WHIP	OBA	vL	vR	BF/G	H%	S%	xERA	G	L	F	Ctl	Dom	Cmd	hr/f	hr/9	RAR	BPV	R$
LH Starter	03		0	0	0	0	0	0.00	0.00																		
Age 22	04		0	0	0	0	0	0.00	0.00																		
Green	05		0	0	0	0	0	0.00	0.00																		
Type Pwr GB	06		0	0	0	0	0	0.00	0.00																		
Reliability 0	07	COL *	8	6	0	152	109	4.46	1.48	262	129	273	23.8	30%	71%	4.14	55	19	27	4.3	6.5	1.5	11%	0.8	-0.6	48	$8
ERA Potl 50%	1st Half		0	3	0	66	49	4.50	1.50	262			24.3	31%	70%					4.5	6.7	1.5		0.7	-0.6	53	$1
LIMA Plan C	2nd Half		8	3	0	86	60	4.42	1.46	263			23.4	30%	72%	4.12	55	19	27	4.1	6.3	1.5	13%	0.9	0.1	44	$6
+/- Score 11	08	Proj	8	6	0	146	104	4.33	1.47	262			23.7	30%	72%	4.13	55	19	27	4.2	6.4	1.5	11%	0.8	4.8	49	$8

3-2, 3.43 ERA in 39 IP at COL. Five of his eight COL starts were PQS-Dom, even improved Ctl (3.2) after callup. Still, he's an inexperienced, marginal Dom guy in Coors. In other words, risk easily outweighs reward.

Morris,Matt	Yr	Tm	W	L	Sv	IP	K	ERA	WHIP	OBA	vL	vR	BF/G	H%	S%	xERA	G	L	F	Ctl	Dom	Cmd	hr/f	hr/9	RAR	BPV	R$
RH Starter	03	STL	11	8	0	172	120	3.77	1.18	253	255	249	26.1	28%	72%	3.84	47	18	35	2.0	6.3	3.1	11%	1.0	10.8	75	$17
Age 33	04	STL	15	10	0	202	131	4.72	1.29	265	259	272	26.6	28%	69%	3.97	51	16	33	2.5	5.8	2.3	17%	1.6	-11.5	39	$14
Past Peak	05	STL	14	10	0	192	117	4.12	1.28	278	279	273	26.0	31%	71%	3.86	49	21	30	1.7	5.5	3.2	12%	1.0	3.0	68	$15
Type Con	06	SF	10	15	0	207	117	5.00	1.36	272	277	261	26.8	30%	64%	4.45	46	21	33	2.7	5.1	1.9	10%	1.0	-13.0	41	$9
Reliability 85	07	2NL	10	11	0	199	102	4.89	1.51	300	293	309	27.5	33%	68%	4.65	48	20	32	2.8	4.6	1.7	8%	0.8	-11.4	33	$5
ERA Potl 50%	1st Half		7	4	0	101	51	3.39	1.35	267			28.7	30%	75%	4.63	48	18	34	2.9	4.5	1.6	5%	0.5	13.0	46	$9
LIMA Plan C	2nd Half		3	7	0	98	51	6.45	1.69	330			26.5	36%	62%	4.67	49	22	29	2.7	4.7	1.8	11%	1.1	-24.4	21	($3)
+/- Score -11	08	Proj	9	10	0	174	95	4.66	1.44	290			27.1	31%	69%	4.46	48	20	32	2.6	4.9	1.9	10%	1.0	-1.3	36	$7

Five straight years of eroding Dom. BA against both LH and RH hitters on the rise. Cmd now well below 2.0 threshold. 1st half xERA shows ERA was a mirage. Obviously, former PIT mgmt not schooled in BPI analysis.

Morrow,Brandon	Yr	Tm	W	L	Sv	IP	K	ERA	WHIP	OBA	vL	vR	BF/G	H%	S%	xERA	G	L	F	Ctl	Dom	Cmd	hr/f	hr/9	RAR	BPV	R$
RH Reliever	03		0	0	0	0	0	0.00	0.00																		
Age 23	04		0	0	0	0	0	0.00	0.00																		
Growth	05		0	0	0	0	0	0.00	0.00																		
Type Pwr xFB	06		0	0	0	0	0	0.00	0.00																		
Reliability 5	07	SEA	3	4	0	63	66	4.12	1.67	239	278	221	4.8	32%	75%	5.28	35	18	47	7.1	9.4	1.3	4%	0.4	3.0	78	$3
ERA Potl 55%	1st Half		3	1	0	29	29	3.41	1.86	227			5.1	31%	80%	6.34	35	18	47	9.3	9.0	1.0	0%	0.0	3.9	84	$2
LIMA Plan B+	2nd Half		0	3	0	34	37	4.72	1.52	249			4.6	33%	69%	4.51	35	18	47	5.2	9.7	1.9	7%	0.8	-0.9	79	$1
+/- Score -8	08	Proj	5	8	0	127	132	4.98	1.58	241			22.8	31%	70%	4.89	35	18	47	6.2	9.4	1.5	8%	0.9	-6.1	67	$6

2006 draftee struggled through first pro season at MLB level. Dom is as exciting as the Ctl is frightening. Transition to SP role is planned for 2008. Nice longer-term target, but expect major growing pains in 2008.

Moseley,Dustin	Yr	Tm	W	L	Sv	IP	K	ERA	WHIP	OBA	vL	vR	BF/G	H%	S%	xERA	G	L	F	Ctl	Dom	Cmd	hr/f	hr/9	RAR	BPV	R$
RH Reliever	03	a/a	7	9	0	162	90	4.33	1.37	286			26.8	31%	71%	4.65				2.2	5.0	2.3		1.1	1.2	44	$8
Age 26	04	a/a	5	6	0	119	74	4.54	1.41	271			25.8	30%	70%	4.49				3.3	5.6	1.7		1.0	-2.9	41	$5
Growth	05	aaa	4	6	0	82	32	4.82	1.60	310			21.8	32%	71%	5.52				3.0	3.5	1.2		1.0	-5.3	9	$1
Type Con	06	aaa	13	8	0	149	96	4.95	1.49	294			25.3	33%	68%	5.00				2.9	5.8	2.0		1.0	-7.8	42	$9
Reliability 8	07	LAA	4	3	0	92	50	4.40	1.35	272	224	323	8.5	30%	68%	4.47	48	18	34	2.6	4.9	1.9	7%	0.7	1.2	48	$6
ERA Potl 50%	1st Half		4	1	0	41	15	2.41	1.07	232			6.5	25%	79%	4.14	55	17	29	2.0	3.3	1.7	5%	0.4	10.6	50	$6
LIMA Plan C	2nd Half		0	2	0	51	35	6.00	1.57	301			10.9	34%	61%	4.70	43	20	38	3.2	6.2	1.9	8%	0.9	-9.4	46	($1)
+/- Score -13	08	Proj	5	4	0	87	48	4.66	1.44	285			13.1	31%	68%	4.59	47	18	34	2.8	5.0	1.8	8%	0.8	-1.0	40	$5

Two very different halves, neither of which were all that successful. BA vs. RH batters a major concern. If he nudges that Cmd back over 2.0, he might be a marginal end-gamer. Until then, stay clear.

Mota,Guillermo	Yr	Tm	W	L	Sv	IP	K	ERA	WHIP	OBA	vL	vR	BF/G	H%	S%	xERA	G	L	F	Ctl	Dom	Cmd	hr/f	hr/9	RAR	BPV	R$
RH Reliever	03	LA	6	3	1	105	99	1.97	0.99	209	181	220	5.4	26%	84%	3.16	46	21	33	2.2	8.5	3.8	8%	0.6	29.9	126	$18
Age 34	04	2NL	9	8	4	96	85	2.99	1.16	217	196	236	5.0	26%	77%	3.72	47	17	36	3.5	8.0	2.3	9%	0.7	15.0	85	$15
Past Peak	05	FLA	2	2	2	67	60	4.70	1.45	256	243	262	5.2	32%	67%	4.43	41	19	41	4.3	8.1	1.9	6%	0.7	-3.8	71	$3
Type Pwr FB	06	2TM	4	3	0	55	46	4.57	1.43	261	252	261	4.6	29%	75%	4.71	34	18	48	3.9	7.5	1.9	14%	1.8	-0.3	34	$4
Reliability 9	07	NYM *	2	3	0	67	52	6.26	1.52	291	235	284	5.0	33%	60%	4.37	44	18	38	3.2	7.1	2.2	11%	1.2	-15.0	48	($0)
ERA Potl 60%	1st Half		0	1	0	22	18	6.08	1.67	301			5.4	36%	63%	4.15	52	21	27	4.1	7.3	1.8	10%	0.8	-4.5	52	($1)
LIMA Plan C+	2nd Half		2	2	0	44	34	6.35	1.44	286			4.8	32%	58%	4.37	41	17	41	2.8	6.9	2.5	12%	1.5	-10.5	47	$1
+/- Score 48	08	Proj	1	3	0	44	35	4.97	1.45	273			5.0	31%	68%	4.42	41	18	40	3.5	7.2	2.1	11%	1.2	-0.1	50	$1

2-2, 5.76 ERA in 59 IP at NYM. A more effective season than ERA portrays, but the point here is that the 2003-04 heyday is gone (and we have a good idea why <quack>).

Moyer,Jamie	Yr	Tm	W	L	Sv	IP	K	ERA	WHIP	OBA	vL	vR	BF/G	H%	S%	xERA	G	L	F	Ctl	Dom	Cmd	hr/f	hr/9	RAR	BPV	R$
LH Starter	03	SEA	21	7	0	215	129	3.27	1.23	247	275	233	27.1	27%	76%	4.73	39	16	45	2.8	5.4	2.0	6%	0.8	33.4	55	$26
Age 45	04	SEA	7	13	0	202	125	5.21	1.39	276	293	263	25.6	28%	69%	4.71	39	17	43	2.8	5.6	2.0	15%	2.0	-19.5	16	$7
Decline	05	SEA	13	7	0	200	102	4.28	1.39	285	294	278	26.9	30%	72%	4.92	37	22	41	2.3	4.6	2.0	8%	1.0	2.4	36	$12
Type	06	2TM	11	14	0	211	108	4.31	1.32	277	251	285	27.1	29%	72%	4.67	40	21	39	2.2	4.6	2.1	12%	1.4	5.6	30	$14
Reliability 80	07	PHI	14	12	0	199	133	5.01	1.45	283	309	279	26.4	31%	69%	4.63	39	21	39	3.0	6.0	2.0	12%	1.4	-14.4	36	$10
ERA Potl 50%	1st Half		7	5	0	102	62	4.15	1.24	250			26.5	27%	71%	4.59	38	19	43	2.6	5.5	2.1	10%	1.2	3.5	44	$9
LIMA Plan D+	2nd Half		7	7	0	97	71	5.92	1.66	315			26.2	35%	67%	4.66	40	24	36	3.3	6.6	2.0	13%	1.5	-17.9	28	$1
+/- Score -32	08	Proj	8	11	0	160	97	4.91	1.48	289			27.0	31%	71%	4.82	39	21	40	3.0	5.5	1.8	12%	1.4	-8.3	26	$5

Factoring in the AL-NL move, this was basically just more of the same from this ageless wonder. Clock will strike midnight sometime soon. Do you ever remember so many 40-plus arms pitching in the majors?

Moylan,Peter	Yr	Tm	W	L	Sv	IP	K	ERA	WHIP	OBA	vL	vR	BF/G	H%	S%	xERA	G	L	F	Ctl	Dom	Cmd	hr/f	hr/9	RAR	BPV	R$
RH Reliever	03		0	0	0	0	0	0.00	0.00																		
Age 29	04		0	0	0	0	0	0.00	0.00																		
Pre-Peak	05		0	0	0	0	0	0.00	0.00																		
Type Pwr xGB	06	ATL *	1	7	1	71	60	8.33	2.02	323			7.0	39%	57%	4.67	58	17	25	6.1	7.5	1.2	11%	0.8	-33.7	38	($7)
Reliability 5	07	ATL	5	3	1	90	63	1.80	1.07	204	242	184	4.5	24%	87%	3.37	62	13	25	3.1	6.3	2.0	9%	0.6	29.2	77	$14
ERA Potl 30%	1st Half		2	1	1	40	28	2.48	1.08	205			5.2	23%	82%	3.59	57	14	29	3.2	6.3	2.0	12%	0.9	9.6	67	$6
LIMA Plan C	2nd Half		3	2	0	50	35	1.26	1.06	203			4.1	24%	90%	3.17	66	11	22	3.1	6.3	2.1	6%	0.4	19.5	85	$8
+/- Score -69	08	Proj	3	4	3	73	55	3.72	1.38	255			5.3	30%	74%	3.64	62	13	25	3.7	6.8	1.8	11%	0.7	6.8	61	$6

With an 87% strand rate, 2007 performance is clearly not sustainable. But high GB% plus tolerable Dom make him a reasonable choice to fill out your staff. Just pay for an ERA that starts with a 3, rather than a 1.

Mulder,Mark	Yr	Tm	W	L	Sv	IP	K	ERA	WHIP	OBA	vL	vR	BF/G	H%	S%	xERA	G	L	F	Ctl	Dom	Cmd	hr/f	hr/9	RAR	BPV	R$
LH Starter	03	OAK	15	9	0	186	128	3.15	1.18	255	252	260	29.4	29%	76%	3.44	55	18	27	1.9	6.2	3.2	10%	0.7	31.7	86	$24
Age 30	04	OAK	17	8	0	225	140	4.44	1.36	260	264	263	29.2	29%	69%	4.04	56	17	27	3.3	5.6	1.7	13%	1.0	-0.1	42	$16
Peak	05	STL	16	8	0	205	111	3.64	1.38	268	201	289	27.5	29%	76%	3.83	61	18	21	3.1	4.9	1.6	13%	0.8	15.2	39	$16
Type Con	06	STL	6	7	0	93	50	7.15	1.71	321	241	351	25.3	33%	61%	4.38	55	22	24	3.4	4.8	1.4	24%	1.8	-30.6	-5	($3)
Reliability 0	07	STL	0	3	0	11	3	12.27	2.64	415	455	436	20.4	39%	56%	8.23	34	19	47	5.7	2.5	0.4	17%	3.3	-10.6	-102	($3)
ERA Potl 60%	1st Half		0	0	0	0	0	0.00	0.00																		
LIMA Plan D	2nd Half		0	3	0	11	3	12.28	2.64	415			20.4	39%	56%	8.23	34	19	47	5.7	2.5	0.4	17%	3.3	-10.7	-102	($3)
+/- Score 116	08	Proj	4	6	0	83	49	4.88	1.43	280			22.6	30%	69%	4.42	49	19	32	3.0	5.3	1.8	12%	1.2	-0.2	32	$3

Lost year due to recovery from labrum surgery, then had more surgery on rotator cuff in Sept. Expects to be ready for spring, but risk level is off the charts until he shows some combo of durability and effectiveness.

RAY MURPHY

Mussina,Mike				W	L	Sv	IP	K	ERA	WHIP	OBA	vL	vR	BF/G	H%	S%	xERA	G	L	F	Ctl	Dom	Cmd	hr/f	hr/9	RAR	BPV	R$
RH Starter		03	NYY	17	8	0	214	195	3.41	1.08	241	229	247	27.6	30%	72%	3.48	38	22	40	1.7	8.2	4.9	9%	0.9	29.5	132	$31
Age	39	04	NYY	12	9	0	164	132	4.60	1.33	278	254	299	25.8	32%	68%	3.85	44	21	36	2.2	7.2	3.3	12%	1.2	-3.5	76	$13
Decline		05	NYY	13	8	0	179	142	4.42	1.37	283	282	286	25.6	33%	71%	3.98	45	18	37	2.4	7.1	3.0	11%	1.2	-1.1	70	$14
Type		06	NYY	15	7	0	197	172	3.52	1.11	249	223	258	24.8	30%	72%	3.53	42	17	40	1.6	7.9	4.9	10%	1.0	25.3	125	$28
Reliability	47	07	NYY	11	10	0	152	91	5.15	1.47	305	315	307	23.8	34%	65%	4.54	42	22	36	2.1	5.4	2.6	7%	0.8	-12.1	56	$8
ERA Potl	60%	1st Half		3	5	0	65	41	4.98	1.35	282			23.2	31%	66%	4.41	40	22	38	2.2	5.7	2.6	11%	1.2	-3.8	49	$4
LIMA Plan	C+	2nd Half		8	5	0	87	50	5.28	1.55	321			24.3	36%	65%	4.64	43	22	35	2.0	5.2	2.6	5%	0.5	-8.3	62	$4
+/- Score	4	08	Proj	11	8	0	145	100	4.53	1.37	284			24.9	32%	70%	4.26	43	20	37	2.3	6.2	2.7	10%	1.1	4.2	59	$11

Gave back 2006's unlikely skill surge, and then some. Dom dip is particularly worrisome, and unlikely to return as he closes in on age 40. 2007 xERA is a good indicator of his new reality.

Myers,Brett				W	L	Sv	IP	K	ERA	WHIP	OBA	vL	vR	BF/G	H%	S%	xERA	G	L	F	Ctl	Dom	Cmd	hr/f	hr/9	RAR	BPV	R$
RH Starter		03	PHI	14	9	0	193	143	4.43	1.46	274	270	273	26.4	32%	71%	4.12	50	20	30	3.5	6.7	1.9	11%	0.9	-3.6	52	$12
Age	27	04	PHI	11	11	0	176	116	5.52	1.47	283	278	293	24.1	30%	66%	4.38	47	19	34	3.2	5.9	1.9	16%	1.6	-27.4	26	$5
Pre-Peak		05	PHI	13	8	0	215	208	3.72	1.21	241	241	233	26.1	29%	75%	3.30	46	23	31	2.8	8.7	3.1	17%	1.3	13.8	84	$22
Type	Pwr	06	PHI	12	7	0	198	189	3.91	1.30	258	259	254	26.9	31%	75%	3.59	46	18	36	2.9	8.6	3.0	14%	1.3	14.1	78	$19
Reliability	49	07	PHI	5	7	21	69	83	4.32	1.28	239	183	274	5.7	32%	70%	3.14	46	19	35	3.5	10.9	3.1	15%	1.2	0.9	102	$14
ERA Potl	60%	1st Half		1	2	6	36	51	5.50	1.47	256			7.5	36%	66%	3.16	41	22	38	4.5	12.8	2.8	19%	1.5	-4.8	95	$4
LIMA Plan	B	2nd Half		4	5	15	33	32	3.03	1.07	220			4.3	28%	75%	3.11	51	17	33	2.5	8.8	3.6	11%	0.8	5.6	114	$11
+/- Score	56	08	Proj	13	10	0	189	184	3.92	1.27	247			26.3	30%	72%	3.50	47	19	34	3.1	8.8	2.8	12%	1.1	20.9	86	$19

Skills translated well to closer role, although DL stint (elbow) leaves lingering questions about his durability. Slotted back into the 2008 rotation, but skills say he's a $20+ player no matter what his role.

Myers,Mike				W	L	Sv	IP	K	ERA	WHIP	OBA	vL	vR	BF/G	H%	S%	xERA	G	L	F	Ctl	Dom	Cmd	hr/f	hr/9	RAR	BPV	R$
LH Reliever		03	ARI	0	1	0	36	21	5.75	1.64	272	237	290	2.6	30%	65%	4.76	58	16	26	5.3	5.3	1.0	13%	1.0	-6.5	23	($1)
Age	38	04	2AL	5	1	0	42	32	4.69	1.61	274	233	344	2.5	31%	73%	4.64	51	16	33	4.9	6.8	1.4	11%	1.1	-1.4	38	$3
Decline		05	BOS	3	1	0	37	21	3.15	1.16	223	158	385	2.3	24%	75%	4.07	50	22	28	3.2	5.1	1.6	10%	0.7	5.6	53	$5
Type	GB	06	NYY	1	2	0	30	22	3.28	1.29	254	257	224	2.1	29%	78%	4.18	47	14	38	3.0	6.6	2.2	9%	0.9	4.8	63	$3
Reliability	4	07	2AL	4	0	0	54	27	4.81	1.51	278	295	259	3.3	30%	70%	4.62	56	16	28	3.8	4.5	1.2	11%	1.0	-2.0	21	$2
ERA Potl	45%	1st Half		0	0	0	30	13	2.70	1.20	228			3.3	24%	82%	3.98	63	15	23	3.3	3.9	1.2	14%	0.9	6.7	31	$3
LIMA Plan	C+	2nd Half		4	0	0	24	14	7.41	1.89	332			3.3	36%	60%	5.35	49	17	34	4.4	5.2	1.2	10%	1.1	-8.7	11	($0)
+/- Score	-23	08	Proj	2	2	0	43	24	4.60	1.51	275			2.7	30%	72%	4.73	52	17	32	4.0	5.0	1.3	11%	1.0	-1.2	25	$2

Trend of declining effectiveness vs LH hitters suggest that his career is nearing the end of its "useful" phase. That doesn't preclude the possibility that he'll kick around MLB for 13-14 more years, though.

Nathan,Joe				W	L	Sv	IP	K	ERA	WHIP	OBA	vL	vR	BF/G	H%	S%	xERA	G	L	F	Ctl	Dom	Cmd	hr/f	hr/9	RAR	BPV	R$
RH Reliever		03	SF	12	4	0	79	83	2.96	1.06	186	276	136	4.0	24%	75%	3.91	28	21	51	3.8	9.5	2.5	7%	0.8	12.8	103	$15
Age	33	04	MIN	1	2	44	72	89	1.62	0.98	191	212	160	3.9	28%	85%	3.18	35	16	49	2.9	11.1	3.9	4%	0.4	25.0	153	$28
Peak		05	MIN	7	4	43	70	94	2.70	0.97	189	160	206	3.9	28%	75%	2.93	37	12	50	2.8	12.1	4.3	7%	0.6	14.4	160	$28
Type	Pwr FB	06	MIN	7	0	36	68	95	1.59	0.79	165	193	130	4.0	27%	82%	2.42	36	22	42	2.1	12.6	5.9	5%	0.4	25.0	210	$29
Reliability	63	07	MIN	4	2	37	72	77	1.88	1.02	211	221	199	4.2	29%	84%	3.17	40	21	39	2.4	9.7	4.1	6%	0.5	23.2	141	$26
ERA Potl	50%	1st Half		3	1	14	33	37	2.45	1.33	273			4.4	38%	81%	3.22	40	29	31	2.5	10.1	4.1	4%	0.3	8.3	139	$10
LIMA Plan	C+	2nd Half		1	1	23	39	40	1.40	0.75	148			3.9	19%	88%	3.12	41	12	47	2.3	9.3	4.0	7%	0.7	14.8	144	$16
+/- Score	-38	08	Proj	5	2	40	73	78	2.59	1.07	220			4.2	29%	78%	3.37	38	19	43	2.5	9.6	3.9	6%	0.6	10.1	132	$26

2006 now looks like his peak in terms of skills, but he can still be a highly effective closer by replicating his 2004-05-07 skill set. Don't pay for another ERA under 2.00, but do bid as appropriate for a top-tier closer.

Neshek,Pat				W	L	Sv	IP	K	ERA	WHIP	OBA	vL	vR	BF/G	H%	S%	xERA	G	L	F	Ctl	Dom	Cmd	hr/f	hr/9	RAR	BPV	R$
RH Reliever		03		0	0	0	0	0	0.00	0.00																		
Age	27	04	aa	2	1	2	35	32	5.40	1.77	298			6.3	37%	68%	5.35				5.1	8.3	1.6		0.5	-4.6	63	$1
Pre-Peak		05	aa	6	4	24	82	75	2.92	1.37	275			6.4	33%	84%	4.47				2.7	8.2	3.1		1.1	14.0	80	$17
Type	Pwr xFB	06	MIN	* 10	4	14	97	125	2.65	1.02	219	244	140	5.9	29%	84%	3.08	32	14	54	2.1	11.6	5.5	13%	1.4	22.8	155	$25
Reliability	4	07	MIN	7	2	0	70	74	2.94	1.01	182	181	185	3.7	23%	75%	3.78	32	16	52	3.5	9.5	2.7	8%	0.9	13.5	106	$13
ERA Potl	40%	1st Half		3	0	0	38	45	1.18	0.71	123			3.7	16%	92%	3.07	30	18	53	2.8	10.7	3.8	7%	0.7	15.6	152	$10
LIMA Plan	C+	2nd Half		4	2	0	32	29	5.02	1.36	241			3.7	29%	65%	4.68	34	15	52	4.2	8.1	1.9	8%	1.1	-2.0	62	$3
+/- Score	-8	08	Proj	5	3	0	58	56	3.57	1.31	238			4.8	29%	78%	4.41	32	15	52	3.9	8.7	2.2	10%	1.2	0.6	69	$7

BPV by month tells the story of escalating elbow issues: 106-135-252-94-45-18. Return to elite form depends on the condition of that elbow, so...
UP: 2006.
DN: Long DL stint.

Nippert,Dustin				W	L	Sv	IP	K	ERA	WHIP	OBA	vL	vR	BF/G	H%	S%	xERA	G	L	F	Ctl	Dom	Cmd	hr/f	hr/9	RAR	BPV	R$
RH Reliever		03		0	0	0	0	0	0.00	0.00																		
Age	27	04	aa	2	5	0	71	65	4.30	1.81	306			24.1	40%	74%	5.06				5.1	8.2	1.6		0.0	0.4	77	$0
Growth		05	aa	8	3	0	117	84	3.07	1.36	258			27.8	31%	77%	3.58				3.4	6.4	1.9		0.4	17.8	70	$11
Type	Pwr	06	ARI	* 13	10	0	150	123	6.11	1.66	317	333	375	25.7	37%	64%	4.13	56	12	32	3.4	7.4	2.1	11%	1.0	-30.0	50	$2
Reliability	10	07	ARI	* 1	4	0	81	74	6.15	1.49	256	238	290	7.8	31%	59%	4.34	38	28	34	4.7	8.2	1.7	12%	1.1	-17.3	57	($0)
ERA Potl	70%	1st Half		1	3	0	48	50	5.44	1.29	210			10.1	27%	58%	4.03	33	29	38	4.9	9.4	1.9	11%	0.9	-6.0	81	$2
LIMA Plan	B	2nd Half		0	1	0	33	24	7.19	1.79	314			6.0	35%	60%	4.97	40	28	32	4.4	6.4	1.4	13%	1.2	-11.3	23	($2)
+/- Score	69	08	Proj	3	3	0	69	56	4.73	1.53	274			10.2	32%	70%	4.44	40	27	33	4.2	7.4	1.8	10%	0.9	-0.4	53	$2

1-1, 5.56 ERA in 45 IP at ARI. How to yank around a young arm: 3 round trips on the AAA shuttle; started in minors and relieved in majors. Skill set has intriguing elements, will need some stability to develop further.

Nolasco,Ricky				W	L	Sv	IP	K	ERA	WHIP	OBA	vL	vR	BF/G	H%	S%	xERA	G	L	F	Ctl	Dom	Cmd	hr/f	hr/9	RAR	BPV	R$
RH Starter		03		0	0	0	0	0	0.00	0.00																		
Age	25	04	a/a	8	7	0	147	134	5.53	1.57	301			23.6	36%	67%	5.52				3.1	8.2	2.6		1.2	-21.6	62	$4
Growth		05	aa	1	3	0	161	152	3.74	1.41	281			25.8	35%	76%	4.53				2.7	8.5	3.1		0.9	11.2	86	$9
Type	FB	06	FLA	11	11	0	140	99	4.82	1.41	285	338	240	17.3	32%	69%	4.46	39	21	40	2.6	6.4	2.4	11%	1.3	-5.8	48	$9
Reliability	0	07	FLA	* 1	5	0	39	26	10.18	1.96	361	293	350	19.2	39%	48%	5.44	37	19	44	3.3	6.0	1.8	14%	2.1	-28.0	-7	($6)
ERA Potl	75%	1st Half		1	2	0	21	11	5.57	1.67	305			19.3	32%	69%	5.67	37	19	44	3.9	4.7	1.2	9%	1.3	-3.0	9	($0)
LIMA Plan	C+	2nd Half		0	3	0	18	15	15.45	2.29	415			19.2	45%	29%					2.6	7.4	2.9		3.1	-25.0	-15	($6)
+/- Score	173	08	Proj	6	8	0	102	78	4.61	1.42	285			18.3	32%	71%	4.41	38	20	43	2.7	6.9	2.6	11%	1.3	-0.2	54	$6

1-2, 5.48 ERA in 21 IP at FLA. Elbow troubles ended season in May. No surgery required, increasing chances that pre-2007 skills can return fairly quickly. Could step up if health, role, h% all cooperate.

Nunez,Leo				W	L	Sv	IP	K	ERA	WHIP	OBA	vL	vR	BF/G	H%	S%	xERA	G	L	F	Ctl	Dom	Cmd	hr/f	hr/9	RAR	BPV	R$
RH Reliever		03		0	0	0	0	0	0.00	0.00											0.0	0.0						
Age	24	04		0	0	0	0	0	0.00	0.00											0.0	0.0						
Growth		05	KC	* 4	2	4	66	44	6.53	1.59	308	374	298	5.6	34%	61%	4.92	37	21	42	3.0	6.0	2.0	12%	1.5	-17.6	26	$1
Type	FB	06	KC	* 3	4	8	72	55	3.62	1.44	272	211	355	7.0	31%	79%	4.17	41	30	30	3.5	6.9	2.0	14%	1.1	8.3	49	$8
Reliability	0	07	KC	* 4	6	0	87	64	3.17	1.11	236	275	248	14.6	26%	78%	4.28	32	19	49	2.1	6.6	3.1	10%	1.3	14.3	75	$11
ERA Potl	40%	1st Half		1	0	0	26	17	1.37	0.84	169			14.1	20%	86%					2.4	5.8	2.4		0.3	10.1	97	$5
LIMA Plan	C+	2nd Half		3	6	0	61	47	3.94	1.22	261			14.8	28%	76%	4.28	32	19	49	2.0	6.9	3.4	12%	1.7	4.2	67	$6
+/- Score	-15	08	Proj	3	4	0	73	53	3.70	1.27	256			8.7	29%	76%	4.43	36	21	44	2.7	6.5	2.4	10%	1.2	0.6	57	$7

2-4, 3.92 ERA in 44 IP at KC. Took major step forward with skills that were even better in majors (3.7 Cmd, 86 BPV). FB style will lead to continued HR troubles, but developing into a future LIMA mainstay.

O'Flaherty,Eric				W	L	Sv	IP	K	ERA	WHIP	OBA	vL	vR	BF/G	H%	S%	xERA	G	L	F	Ctl	Dom	Cmd	hr/f	hr/9	RAR	BPV	R$
LH Reliever		03		0	0	0	0	0	0.00	0.00																		
Age	23	04		0	0	0	0	0	0.00	0.00																		
Growth		05		0	0	0	0	0	0.00	0.00																		
Type	Pwr	06	SEA	* 3	2	7	54	44	1.83	1.52	283			5.7	35%	89%	4.11				3.7	7.3	2.0		0.3	18.1	74	$9
Reliability	0	07	SEA	7	1	0	52	36	4.47	1.24	234	183	277	3.9	28%	61%	4.39	45	18	37	3.4	6.2	1.8	2%	0.2	0.2	78	$7
ERA Potl	65%	1st Half		5	0	0	26	16	2.08	0.96	188			4.4	22%	79%	4.22	44	14	42	2.8	5.5	2.0	3%	0.3	7.8	82	$6
LIMA Plan	C+	2nd Half		2	1	0	26	20	6.84	1.52	274			3.5	34%	50%	4.54	45	22	33	4.1	6.8	1.7	0%	0.0	-7.6	76	$0
+/- Score	19	08	Proj	4	4	0	58	43	4.19	1.38	258			4.5	30%	71%	4.36	45	19	36	3.6	6.7	1.9	8%	0.8	0.9	59	$5

Dominated LH batters in situational role (56 Gm, but only 52 IP). 23 is awfully young to typecast someone as a specialist, but L/R split suggests that he is not yet ready for a wider role.

RAY MURPHY

Obermueller,Wes

Obermueller,Wes		Yr	Tm	W	L	Sv	IP	K	ERA	WHIP	OBA	vL	vR	BF/G	H%	S%	xERA	G	L	F	Ctl	Dom	Cmd	hr/f	hr/9	RAR	BPV	R$
RH	Starter	03	MIL *	12	12	0	186	93	4.98	1.56	295	301	301	26.1	31%	70%	5.03	47	17	35	3.4	4.5	1.3	10%	1.1	-16.2	17	$4
Age	31	04	MIL *	6	12	0	144	73	5.88	1.56	300	286	296	22.2	32%	63%	4.75	50	19	32	3.1	4.6	1.5	12%	1.2	-28.7	17	($1)
Peak		05	MIL *	4	5	1	107	65	4.37	1.57	281	262	307	15.0	32%	73%	4.91	46	22	32	4.2	5.4	1.3	7%	0.7	-1.6	38	$3
Type	Pwr	06	JPN	1	6	0	42	26	6.65	2.03	294			14.9	32%	68%	6.40				7.7	5.5	0.7		1.1	-11.1	12	($3)
Reliability	16	07	FLA *	6	4	0	122	64	7.07	2.09	342	309	304	21.1	37%	66%	6.44	40	21	39	5.6	4.7	0.8	9%	1.1	-39.8	-2	($10)
ERA Potl	50%	1st Half		2	4	0	71	35	4.56	1.43	267			18.2	29%	69%	5.27	40	20	40	3.7	4.4	1.2	6%	0.8	-1.1	31	$2
LIMA Plan	F	2nd Half		4	0	0	51	29	10.56	3.00	425			25.2	46%	65%	8.08	36	32	32	8.3	5.1	0.6	14%	1.7	-38.6	-37	($13)
+/- Score	-2	08	Proj	1	2	0	29	16	6.21	1.93	306			17.6	33%	69%	6.06	44	21	35	6.2	5.0	0.8	11%	1.2	-6.0	3	($2)

2-3, 6.56 ERA in 59 IP at FLA. "Avoid at all costs" doesn't quite express the sentiment strongly enough. The 2H line belongs in the "Bad BPI Hall of Fame". It's no wonder that he didn't get a Sept. callup.

Ohka,Tomo

Ohka,Tomo		Yr	Tm	W	L	Sv	IP	K	ERA	WHIP	OBA	vL	vR	BF/G	H%	S%	xERA	G	L	F	Ctl	Dom	Cmd	hr/f	hr/9	RAR	BPV	R$
RH	Starter	03	MON	10	12	0	199	118	4.16	1.40	293	311	279	25.3	32%	73%	4.38	45	19	36	2.0	5.3	2.6	10%	1.1	2.9	51	$11
Age	32	04	MON	3	7	0	84	38	3.42	1.40	292	278	298	24.3	30%	80%	4.95	42	17	41	2.1	4.1	1.9	9%	1.2	8.7	26	$4
Peak		05	2NL	11	9	0	180	98	4.05	1.35	271	258	277	24.1	29%	73%	4.66	42	22	37	2.7	4.9	1.8	10%	1.1	4.4	35	$11
Type	Con	06	MIL	4	5	0	97	50	4.82	1.37	264	265	266	23.1	28%	67%	5.02	39	21	40	3.2	4.6	1.4	9%	1.1	-4.0	27	$4
Reliability	21	07	TOR *	2	10	0	97	33	8.47	1.97	360	376	348	27.9	36%	58%	5.95	44	20	36	3.5	3.1	0.9	14%	1.8	-47.4	-34	($11)
ERA Potl	55%	1st Half		2	7	0	74	27	6.32	1.66	319			26.1	32%	64%	5.43	44	20	36	3.0	3.3	1.1	12%	1.5	-16.5	-10	($2)
LIMA Plan	F	2nd Half		0	3	0	23	6	15.44	2.98	464			33.8	45%	48%					4.8	2.3	0.5		2.9	-30.9	*****	($9)
+/- Score	69	08	Proj	1	4	0	44	20	5.59	1.68	313			25.0	32%	70%	5.44	42	20	38	3.5	4.1	1.2	12%	1.4	-5.1	-2	($1)

2-5, 5.79 ERA in 56 IP at TOR. Five-year trend of declining Cmd tells the story here. Dom level now microscopic. Even when hit and strand rates regress to normal levels, he's still not rosterable.

Ohman,Will

Ohman,Will		Yr	Tm	W	L	Sv	IP	K	ERA	WHIP	OBA	vL	vR	BF/G	H%	S%	xERA	G	L	F	Ctl	Dom	Cmd	hr/f	hr/9	RAR	BPV	R$
LH	Reliever	03		0	0	0	0	0	0.00	0.00											0.0	0.0						
Age	30	04	aaa	3	3	0	52	64	4.73	1.70	286			5.3	39%	74%	5.47				5.1	11.0	2.2		1.1	-2.5	76	$2
Peak		05	CHC *	3	2	1	51	55	3.21	1.22	201	175	231	2.8	24%	81%	3.36	53	15	33	4.6	9.7	2.1	20%	1.4	6.5	74	$6
Type	Pwr FB	06	CHC	1	1	0	65	74	4.15	1.31	217	158	243	3.5	29%	70%	3.95	34	23	44	4.7	10.2	2.2	9%	0.8	2.7	94	$5
Reliability	11	07	CHC *	2	4	1	43	39	5.14	1.80	308	236	325	3.1	38%	71%	4.97	41	18	42	4.9	8.2	1.7	5%	0.6	-3.8	58	$0
ERA Potl	60%	1st Half		0	4	1	23	27	4.30	1.43	262			2.9	37%	69%	3.79	41	16	44	3.9	10.6	2.7	4%	0.4	0.3	111	$1
LIMA Plan	B+	2nd Half		2	0	0	20	12	6.13	2.23	356			3.2	40%	73%	6.54	41	20	39	6.1	5.4	0.9	7%	0.9	-4.1	7	($1)
+/- Score	13	08	Proj	3	3	0	54	53	4.50	1.50	258			3.2	32%	72%	4.36	40	19	41	4.7	8.8	1.9	10%	1.0	0.3	66	$3

2-4, 4.95 ERA in 36 IP at CHC. Wheels came off in 2nd half, but complained of shoulder trouble, so that's the likely cause. Nice LIMA option if he recaptures 1st half skills, but durability and Ctl issues raise the risk level.

Okajima,Hideki

Okajima,Hideki		Yr	Tm	W	L	Sv	IP	K	ERA	WHIP	OBA	vL	vR	BF/G	H%	S%	xERA	G	L	F	Ctl	Dom	Cmd	hr/f	hr/9	RAR	BPV	R$
LH	Reliever	03	JPN	2	3	0	39	28	6.31	1.88	305			4.6	32%	72%	7.36				5.7	6.3	1.1		2.3	-9.2	-13	($2)
Age	32	04	JPN	4	3	5	47	50	3.81	1.28	211			3.7	25%	78%	3.90				4.8	9.6	2.0		1.6	3.1	66	$7
Peak		05	JPN	1	0	0	53	53	6.54	1.56	283			5.7	31%	67%	6.68				4.0	9.0	2.3		2.8	-14.6	15	($1)
Type	Pwr FB	06	JPN	2	2	4	55	60	2.85	1.21	241			4.1	30%	84%	3.83				2.8	9.8	3.4		1.4	11.4	97	$8
Reliability	14	07	BOS	3	2	5	69	63	2.22	0.97	204	236	182	4.1	25%	82%	3.41	45	15	41	2.2	8.2	3.7	8%	0.8	19.5	118	$13
ERA Potl	40%	1st Half		2	0	4	38	34	0.95	0.84	170			4.1	22%	90%	3.17	51	13	36	2.4	8.1	3.4	3%	0.2	16.7	134	$10
LIMA Plan	B	2nd Half		1	2	1	31	29	3.77	1.13	243			4.0	28%	73%	3.67	38	16	46	2.0	8.4	4.1	13%	1.5	2.8	100	$4
+/- Score	-28	08	Proj	3	3	3	73	70	3.48	1.26	247			4.3	30%	77%	3.78	43	15	42	3.0	8.7	2.9	11%	1.1	6.4	86	$9

Great skills + great luck = great year. xERA tells the true story, FB% suggests that 2nd half HR issues may linger into 2008. Solid LIMA option, just don't pay for ERA repeat or double-digit saves.

Oliver,Darren

Oliver,Darren		Yr	Tm	W	L	Sv	IP	K	ERA	WHIP	OBA	vL	vR	BF/G	H%	S%	xERA	G	L	F	Ctl	Dom	Cmd	hr/f	hr/9	RAR	BPV	R$
LH	Reliever	03	COL	13	11	0	180	88	5.05	1.46	284	256	292	23.9	30%	67%	4.83	48	16	35	3.1	4.4	1.4	10%	1.1	-17.1	23	$7
Age	37	04	2NL	3	3	0	72	46	5.98	1.48	297	321	300	11.8	31%	63%	4.73	39	19	42	2.6	5.7	2.2	14%	1.7	-15.3	24	$0
Decline		05	aaa	1	3	0	31	15	10.93	2.50	441			24.1	46%	56%	11.11				2.4	4.4	1.8		1.5	-25.5	-24	($7)
Type		06	NYM	4	1	0	81	60	3.44	1.12	235	208	244	7.3	25%	77%	3.70	48	17	35	2.3	6.7	2.9	16%	1.4	10.4	65	$9
Reliability	0	07	LAA	3	1	0	64	51	3.78	1.26	242	289	209	4.4	29%	71%	4.10	48	12	40	3.2	7.1	2.2	7%	0.7	5.8	75	$6
ERA Potl	45%	1st Half		0	0	0	22	17	6.55	1.82	303			3.7	35%	65%	5.20	45	18	38	5.3	7.0	1.3	11%	1.2	-5.5	27	($1)
LIMA Plan	C	2nd Half		3	1	0	42	34	2.34	0.97	206			5.0	25%	77%	3.58	50	9	41	2.1	7.2	3.4	4%	0.4	11.3	116	$8
+/- Score	-26	08	Proj	2	3	0	58	41	4.81	1.41	272			6.3	31%	68%	4.44	46	15	38	3.3	6.4	2.0	10%	1.1	0.4	47	$3

PRO: Defied the odds, repeating 2006's unlikely skill surge. Even took it up a notch in 2nd half. CON: Didn't fool LH batters, LD was unsustainably low. Don't bet on this late-career revival extending into a 3rd year.

Olsen,Scott

Olsen,Scott		Yr	Tm	W	L	Sv	IP	K	ERA	WHIP	OBA	vL	vR	BF/G	H%	S%	xERA	G	L	F	Ctl	Dom	Cmd	hr/f	hr/9	RAR	BPV	R$
LH	Starter	03		0	0	0	0	0	0.00	0.00																		
Age	24	04		0	0	0	0	0	0.00	0.00																		
Growth		05	FLA *	7	5	0	100	106	4.68	1.47	277	333	238	23.1	35%	70%	3.99	41	14	45	3.5	9.5	2.7	9%	1.1	-5.3	82	$6
Type	Pwr	06	FLA	12	10	0	180	166	4.05	1.30	239	182	255	24.6	29%	73%	3.89	45	18	37	3.7	8.3	2.2	12%	1.1	9.8	69	$17
Reliability	41	07	FLA	10	15	0	177	133	5.81	1.76	312	331	311	25.1	35%	70%	5.07	38	24	39	4.3	6.8	1.6	13%	1.5	-30.1	22	($1)
ERA Potl	55%	1st Half		5	6	0	91	67	4.75	1.58	284			25.6	33%	72%	4.85	40	23	38	4.2	6.6	1.6	9%	1.0	-3.6	42	$3
LIMA Plan	D	2nd Half		5	9	0	86	66	6.93	1.95	339			24.5	37%	68%	5.30	36	25	40	4.5	6.9	1.5	16%	2.0	-26.5	1	($4)
+/- Score	32	08	Proj	11	12	0	174	145	4.60	1.52	276			24.2	32%	73%	4.51	40	22	38	4.0	7.5	1.9	11%	1.2	-2.4	48	$9

Sophomore slump driven by both declining skills and bad luck. Off-field issues suggest that both problems may be rooted in his head. Could rebound, but that would require getting inside his head. Pass the crowbar.

Ortiz,Ramon

Ortiz,Ramon		Yr	Tm	W	L	Sv	IP	K	ERA	WHIP	OBA	vL	vR	BF/G	H%	S%	xERA	G	L	F	Ctl	Dom	Cmd	hr/f	hr/9	RAR	BPV	R$
RH	Reliever	03	ANA	16	13	0	180	94	5.20	1.51	292	291	282	24.9	30%	69%	5.28	39	17	44	3.2	4.7	1.5	10%	1.4	-15.0	14	$9
Age	34	04	ANA	5	7	0	128	82	4.43	1.38	278	305	253	16.2	30%	72%	4.72	38	18	44	2.7	5.8	2.2	10%	1.3	0.0	41	$6
Past Peak		05	CIN	9	11	0	171	96	5.37	1.50	299	288	315	25.2	31%	70%	4.73	45	17	38	2.7	5.0	1.9	15%	1.8	-23.6	11	$3
Type	Con	06	WAS	11	16	0	190	104	5.58	1.55	300	316	278	25.7	32%	67%	5.03	41	20	39	3.0	4.9	1.6	12%	1.5	-25.7	15	$3
Reliability	56	07	2TM	5	4	0	104	51	5.45	1.43	302	313	287	11.9	31%	65%	4.66	43	20	37	1.9	4.4	2.3	12%	1.5	-12.7	28	$3
ERA Potl	50%	1st Half		3	4	0	72	30	5.50	1.42	307			19.5	32%	63%	4.67	44	20	35	1.5	3.8	2.5	11%	1.3	-9.2	31	$1
LIMA Plan	C	2nd Half		2	0	0	32	21	5.34	1.47	291			6.4	31%	68%	4.65	39	21	40	2.8	5.9	2.1	14%	1.7	-3.5	26	$1
+/- Score	-7	08	Proj	2	2	0	44	24	5.38	1.49	298			9.6	31%	67%	4.85	42	20	39	2.7	5.0	1.8	12%	1.4	-2.2	21	$1

Turned some heads with 3 wins and 2.57 ERA in April, then turned back into a pumpkin. Made a minor gain in Cmd, but gets hit so hard whenever they get the bat on the ball that it doesn't really matter.

Ortiz,Russ

Ortiz,Russ		Yr	Tm	W	L	Sv	IP	K	ERA	WHIP	OBA	vL	vR	BF/G	H%	S%	xERA	G	L	F	Ctl	Dom	Cmd	hr/f	hr/9	RAR	BPV	R$
RH	Reliever	03	ATL	21	7	0	212	149	3.82	1.32	228	265	187	26.4	26%	72%	4.70	43	17	40	4.3	6.3	1.5	7%	0.7	12.0	56	$21
Age	33	04	ATL	15	9	0	204	143	4.14	1.51	255	257	262	26.6	29%	75%	5.00	42	21	37	4.9	6.3	1.3	10%	1.0	3.0	38	$12
Past Peak		05	ARI	5	11	0	115	46	6.89	1.84	312	329	296	24.9	32%	64%	6.30	37	26	37	5.1	3.6	0.7	11%	1.4	-37.5	-13	($8)
Type		06	2TM *	1	8	0	83	53	6.96	1.89	324	378	299	13.4	34%	67%	5.66	37	24	39	4.9	5.7	1.2	17%	2.1	-25.1	-13	($6)
Reliability	0	07	SF *	3	4	0	65	36	5.28	1.54	298	346	259	17.1	33%	65%	4.93	42	22	35	3.1	4.9	1.6	7%	0.7	-6.9	37	$1
ERA Potl		1st Half		3	2	0	40	25	4.93	1.44	293			17.5	34%	64%	4.23	47	24	29	2.5	5.6	2.3	5%	0.4	-2.5	64	$2
LIMA Plan		2nd Half		0	2	0	25	11	5.84	1.70	307			16.5	32%	67%	6.40	30	20	50	4.1	3.8	0.9	7%	1.1	-4.4	1	($1)
+/- Score	-26	08	Proj	0	0	0	0	0	0.00	0.00																		

2-3, 5.51 ERA in 49 IP at SF. 1st half performance was better than anything we've seen in years, but he'll miss all of '08 after September TJ surgery. And there was much joy and merrymaking.

Oswalt,Roy

Oswalt,Roy		Yr	Tm	W	L	Sv	IP	K	ERA	WHIP	OBA	vL	vR	BF/G	H%	S%	xERA	G	L	F	Ctl	Dom	Cmd	hr/f	hr/9	RAR	BPV	R$
RH	Starter	03	HOU	10	5	0	127	108	2.98	1.14	245	263	234	24.6	29%	79%	3.44	46	21	34	2.1	7.7	3.7	12%	1.1	20.4	98	$17
Age	30	04	HOU	20	10	0	237	206	3.49	1.24	259	257	264	27.4	32%	73%	3.69	43	23	35	2.4	7.8	3.3	7%	0.6	22.5	101	$26
Peak		05	HOU	20	12	0	241	184	2.95	1.21	263	279	247	28.4	31%	78%	3.49	49	22	29	1.8	6.9	3.8	8%	0.7	38.6	104	$29
Type	GB	06	HOU	15	8	0	220	166	2.98	1.17	262	264	262	27.3	31%	77%	3.50	49	20	31	1.6	6.8	4.4	9%	0.7	40.8	113	$27
Reliability	97	07	HOU	14	7	0	212	154	3.18	1.33	270	272	259	27.3	32%	77%	3.83	53	16	31	2.5	6.5	2.6	7%	0.6	32.5	76	$21
ERA Potl	50%	1st Half		7	5	0	114	79	3.55	1.38	265			28.8	31%	76%	4.00	55	15	30	3.2	6.2	1.9	8%	0.7	12.3	59	$9
LIMA Plan	C	2nd Half		7	2	0	98	75	2.76	1.27	275			25.6	33%	79%	3.64	51	17	33	1.7	6.9	3.9	5%	0.5	20.2	110	$12
+/- Score	3	08	Proj	15	7	0	207	157	3.26	1.25	265			27.0	31%	76%	3.63	50	18	31	2.0	6.8	3.3	9%	0.8	19.7	90	$23

Cmd briefly deserted him in 1st half, but 2nd half recovery matched historical levels. LD% will likely rise, so any further Ctl/Dom slip will be felt in ERA. But this skill set is just about as stable as they come.

RAY MURPHY

Otsuka,Akinori

	Yr	Tm	W	L	Sv	IP	K	ERA	WHIP	OBA	vL	vR	BF/G	H%	S%	xERA	G	L	F	Ctl	Dom	Cmd	hr/f	hr/9	RAR	BPV	R$
RH Reliever	03	JPN	1	3	17	43	59	2.60	0.92	215			3.2	30%	82%	2.80				1.3	12.4	9.5		1.4	9.5	244	$13
Age 36	04	SD	7	2	2	77	87	1.75	1.06	205	214	183	4.2	28%	88%	2.93	51	16	33	3.0	10.2	3.3	10%	0.7	23.9	124	$15
Decline	05	SD	2	8	1	62	60	3.62	1.43	239	207	263	4.1	31%	74%	3.87	47	26	27	4.9	8.7	1.8	7%	0.4	4.8	83	$4
Type GB	06	TEX	2	4	32	59	47	2.13	1.08	241	287	190	3.8	29%	82%	3.22	52	19	28	1.7	7.1	4.3	6%	0.5	17.7	126	$19
Reliability 11	07	TEX	2	1	4	32	23	2.51	1.08	222	172	262	3.8	28%	74%	3.42	55	20	25	2.5	6.4	2.6	0%	0.0	8.0	103	$6
ERA Potl 55%	1st Half		2	1	4	31	23	2.61	1.03	208			3.8	26%	72%	3.26	56	21	23	2.6	6.7	2.6	0%	0.0	7.2	107	$6
LIMA Plan B+	2nd Half		0	0	0	1	0	0.00	2.31	450			3.4	45%	100%	7.32	50	0	50	0.0	0.0		0%	0.0	0.7	-35	($0)
+/- Score -40	08	Proj	2	3	15	44	35	3.31	1.20	237			3.9	29%	73%	3.49	51	22	27	2.9	7.2	2.5	9%	0.6	5.4	85	$10

Dom trend has been down, down, down... and that's before a sore elbow ended his season. There's enough uncertainty, both with his arm and in the TEX pen to peg his value at much closer to $10 than $20.

Owens,Henry

	Yr	Tm	W	L	Sv	IP	K	ERA	WHIP	OBA	vL	vR	BF/G	H%	S%	xERA	G	L	F	Ctl	Dom	Cmd	hr/f	hr/9	RAR	BPV	R$
RH Reliever	03		0	0	0	0	0	0.00	0.00																		
Age 29	04		0	0	0	0	0	0.00	0.00																		
Pre-Peak	05		0	0	0	0	0	0.00	0.00																		
Type Pwr xFB	06	aa	2	2	20	40	52	2.71	0.99	197			4.2	30%	72%	1.70				2.7	11.8	4.3		0.3	8.9	169	$14
Reliability 0	07	FLA	2	0	4	23	16	1.96	1.26	227	262	174	4.4	25%	92%	4.80	36	18	46	3.9	6.3	1.6	10%	1.2	7.0	46	$5
ERA Potl 25%	1st Half		2	0	4	23	16	1.96	1.26	227			4.4	25%	92%	4.80	36	18	46	3.9	6.3	1.6	10%	1.2	7.0	46	$5
LIMA Plan A	2nd Half		0	0	0	0	0	0.00	0.00																		
+/- Score -118	08	Proj	1	0	0	15	14	3.72	1.24	227			4.3	29%	71%	4.12	36	18	46	3.7	8.7	2.3	6%	0.6	0.5	92	$2

Briefly showed signs that he could be a closer, but got hurt and ended up having rotator-cuff surgery. Unlikely to make it back in '08, and even if he does, he'll be back to square one in the bullpen hierarchy.

Owings,Micah

	Yr	Tm	W	L	Sv	IP	K	ERA	WHIP	OBA	vL	vR	BF/G	H%	S%	xERA	G	L	F	Ctl	Dom	Cmd	hr/f	hr/9	RAR	BPV	R$
RH Starter	03		0	0	0	0	0	0.00	0.00																		
Age 25	04		0	0	0	0	0	0.00	0.00																		
Growth	05		0	0	0	0	0	0.00	0.00																		
Type FB	06	a/a	16	2	0	162	112	4.41	1.54	301			26.8	35%	71%	4.80				2.9	6.2	2.1		0.6	2.2	59	$12
Reliability 0	07	ARI	8	8	0	153	106	4.30	1.28	253	265	240	22.1	28%	70%	4.49	37	20	42	2.9	6.2	2.1	10%	1.2	2.3	51	$11
ERA Potl 50%	1st Half		5	2	0	70	47	3.86	1.40	270			23.3	31%	73%	4.57	40	24	36	3.2	6.0	1.9	6%	0.6	4.9	57	$5
LIMA Plan D+	2nd Half		3	6	0	83	59	4.68	1.18	238			21.2	25%	66%	4.43	35	17	47	2.7	6.4	2.4	13%	1.6	-2.6	46	$6
+/- Score 3	08	Proj	11	9	0	189	131	4.34	1.38	272			23.8	30%	72%	4.62	37	20	43	2.9	6.3	2.1	10%	1.2	-5.2	47	$12

July meltdown (9.55 ERA) masked some improvement. Had 3.5 Cmd in Aug/Sept. Doesn't have great stuff, and hr/f can be a problem, but there's enough here to make him a serviceable starter.

Padilla,Vicente

	Yr	Tm	W	L	Sv	IP	K	ERA	WHIP	OBA	vL	vR	BF/G	H%	S%	xERA	G	L	F	Ctl	Dom	Cmd	hr/f	hr/9	RAR	BPV	R$
RH Starter	03	PHI	14	12	0	208	133	3.63	1.24	250	267	239	27.0	28%	74%	4.16	48	17	35	2.7	5.8	2.1	10%	1.0	16.5	56	$19
Age 30	04	PHI	7	7	0	115	82	4.54	1.35	268	289	241	24.6	30%	70%	4.26	44	18	38	2.8	6.4	2.3	12%	1.3	-3.9	50	$7
Peak	05	PHI	9	12	0	147	103	4.71	1.50	260	297	222	24.0	28%	72%	4.61	46	22	32	4.5	6.3	1.4	15%	1.3	-8.5	30	$6
Type	06	TEX	15	10	0	200	156	4.50	1.38	268	305	228	26.1	31%	69%	4.12	44	22	34	3.2	7.0	2.2	10%	0.9	1.4	62	$17
Reliability 48	07	TEX	6	10	0	120	71	5.76	1.63	301	329	271	23.8	33%	66%	4.91	46	21	34	3.7	5.3	1.4	11%	1.2	-18.6	21	$1
ERA Potl 50%	1st Half		3	8	0	81	47	6.67	1.80	327			25.5	35%	64%	5.06	46	23	31	3.9	5.2	1.3	13%	1.3	-21.6	9	($3)
LIMA Plan C+	2nd Half		3	2	0	39	24	3.89	1.27	240			20.6	26%	72%	4.60	46	15	39	3.4	5.5	1.6	8%	0.9	3.0	46	$4
+/- Score 8	08	Proj	10	10	0	160	106	4.74	1.44	271			24.0	30%	69%	4.54	45	20	35	3.6	6.0	1.7	11%	1.1	-0.8	40	$9

Triceps injury cost him time, but he didn't pitch well until September. Shaky skill set which produces poor ERAs and WHIPs year after year. If you can afford that hit, he could give you a dozen wins.

Papelbon,Jonathan

	Yr	Tm	W	L	Sv	IP	K	ERA	WHIP	OBA	vL	vR	BF/G	H%	S%	xERA	G	L	F	Ctl	Dom	Cmd	hr/f	hr/9	RAR	BPV	R$
RH Reliever	03		0	0	0	0	0	0.00	0.00											0.0	0.0						
Age 27	04		0	0	0	0	0	0.00	0.00											0.0	0.0						
Growth	05	BOS *	9	5	1	148	125	3.11	1.14	233	190	319	15.9	27%	77%	3.90	35	25	40	2.6	7.6	2.9	10%	1.0	23.0	86	$19
Type Pwr xFB	06	BOS	4	2	35	68	75	0.93	0.78	172	203	128	4.3	24%	92%	2.96	37	17	46	1.7	9.9	5.8	4%	0.4	30.5	189	$28
Reliability 46	07	BOS	1	3	37	58	84	1.85	0.77	154	104	200	3.6	24%	83%	2.61	29	18	53	2.3	13.0	5.6	8%	0.8	19.1	196	$25
ERA Potl 40%	1st Half		0	1	18	29	40	1.55	0.86	155			3.9	24%	87%	2.79	33	17	49	3.1	12.4	4.0	7%	0.6	10.6	164	$12
LIMA Plan C+	2nd Half		1	2	19	29	44	2.15	0.68	154			3.4	24%	76%	2.44	24	14	62	1.5	13.5	8.8	9%	0.9	8.5	263	$13
+/- Score -22	08	Proj	3	3	45	63	78	2.29	0.95	188			4.5	26%	81%	3.16	32	16	51	2.7	11.1	4.1	8%	0.9	10.4	145	$27

Is there even any room for improvement here? OPS against him was a miniscule .463, and he got stronger as the season progressed. He is entering Vintage Eck territory.

Paronto,Chad

	Yr	Tm	W	L	Sv	IP	K	ERA	WHIP	OBA	vL	vR	BF/G	H%	S%	xERA	G	L	F	Ctl	Dom	Cmd	hr/f	hr/9	RAR	BPV	R$
RH Reliever	03	aaa	3	5	18	56	38	6.22	1.94	344			5.6	40%	66%	6.49				4.1	6.1	1.5		0.5	-12.6	38	$4
Age 32	04	aaa	5	3	4	55	30	2.34	1.44	258			5.1	29%	86%	3.96				4.1	4.9	1.2		0.5	13.6	42	$7
Peak	05	aaa	6	2	4	79	51	4.68	1.87	323			7.3	37%	76%	6.18				4.7	5.8	1.2		0.8	-3.6	29	$2
Type Con	06	ATL *	3	4	4	73	53	2.84	1.33	266	288	234	4.0	31%	81%	4.05	43	25	32	2.7	6.5	2.4	8%	0.7	14.9	69	$8
Reliability 3	07	ATL *	3	1	3	57	23	4.06	1.63	303	333	287	4.9	33%	74%	5.40	51	15	34	3.7	3.6	1.0	3%	0.3	2.6	27	$2
ERA Potl 40%	1st Half		3	1	1	29	10	4.66	1.66	300			4.3	32%	70%	5.81	49	13	37	4.0	3.1	0.8	3%	0.3	-0.8	21	$1
LIMA Plan C	2nd Half		0	0	2	28	13	3.43	1.61	305			5.9	34%	78%	4.77	54	20	27	3.3	4.1	1.2	4%	0.3	3.4	34	$1
+/- Score -48	08	Proj	3	2	0	54	26	4.50	1.57	293			5.1	31%	73%	5.06	48	20	33	3.7	4.3	1.2	8%	0.8	-4.4	22	$1

3-1, 3.57 ERA in 40 IP at ATL. Gave back '06 gains, as Cmd collapsed and Dom sunk by almost three strikeouts per game. In truth, his BPIs scream journeyman reliever.

Parra,Manny

	Yr	Tm	W	L	Sv	IP	K	ERA	WHIP	OBA	vL	vR	BF/G	H%	S%	xERA	G	L	F	Ctl	Dom	Cmd	hr/f	hr/9	RAR	BPV	R$
LH Starter	03		0	0	0	0	0	0.00	0.00																		
Age 25	04		0	0	0	0	0	0.00	0.00																		
Growth	05	aa	5	6	0	91	75	4.55	1.58	324			25.6	40%	70%	5.12				2.1	7.4	3.6		0.4	-2.7	98	$4
Type Pwr FB	06	aa	3	0	0	31	25	4.18	1.36	273			22.2	35%	66%	3.38				2.7	7.3	2.7		0.0	1.3	101	$3
Reliability 0	07	MIL *	10	5	0	133	119	3.34	1.32	254	174	280	21.6	33%	74%	4.30	33	23	44	3.3	8.1	2.5	2%	0.3	17.8	96	$14
ERA Potl 60%	1st Half		9	4	0	101	92	3.02	1.25	244			26.3	32%	75%					3.0	8.2	2.7		0.3	17.5	104	$13
LIMA Plan B	2nd Half		1	1	0	31	27	4.35	1.57	284			14.1	36%	71%	4.83	33	23	44	4.0	7.8	1.9	3%	0.3	0.3	76	$1
+/- Score -1	08	Proj	7	4	0	123	108	3.97	1.36	264			23.8	33%	71%	4.32	33	23	44	3.1	7.9	2.6	5%	0.6	1.2	86	$10

0-1, 3.76 ERA in 26 IP at MIL. Promising debut pitching out of the pen. Dom went up; Ctl was manageable. Has a history of arm problems, so don't go overboard, but he could earn $10+ if he's in the rotation.

Parrish,John

	Yr	Tm	W	L	Sv	IP	K	ERA	WHIP	OBA	vL	vR	BF/G	H%	S%	xERA	G	L	F	Ctl	Dom	Cmd	hr/f	hr/9	RAR	BPV	R$
LH Reliever	03	BAL *	3	4	6	99	82	2.77	1.42	253			6.8	30%	84%	4.15				4.1	7.4	1.8		0.9	21.5	60	$11
Age 30	04	BAL	6	3	1	78	71	3.46	1.58	236			6.3	30%	78%	4.00				6.3	8.2	1.3		0.5	9.3	70	$7
Peak	05	BAL *	1	0	0	26	38	3.12	1.88	262			6.6	40%	85%	3.87	47	26	28	8.0	13.2	1.7	12%	0.7	4.0	95	$2
Type Pwr GB	06		0	0	0	0	0	0.00	0.00																		
Reliability 0	07	2AL	2	2	0	52	41	5.71	1.92	301	293	298	4.8	37%	68%	5.10	54	16	29	6.4	7.1	1.1	4%	0.3	-7.7	50	($1)
ERA Potl 60%	1st Half		2	0	0	30	27	5.40	1.70	242			4.3	30%	67%	5.16	47	17	36	7.2	8.1	1.1	7%	0.6	-3.3	61	$1
LIMA Plan D+	2nd Half		0	2	0	22	14	6.14	2.23	367			5.4	43%	69%	4.98	62	16	22	5.3	5.7	1.1	0%	0.0	-4.4	39	($2)
+/- Score 12	08	Proj	1	1	0	29	24	4.66	1.69	268			5.3	33%	72%	4.53	54	19	27	5.9	7.4	1.3	8%	0.6	-0.1	54	$1

Has a live arm, and keeps the ball down, but simply walks far too many hitters to be successful. Showed tiny gains after move to SEA, but at this rate, he won't be rosterable until at least 2012.

Patterson,John

	Yr	Tm	W	L	Sv	IP	K	ERA	WHIP	OBA	vL	vR	BF/G	H%	S%	xERA	G	L	F	Ctl	Dom	Cmd	hr/f	hr/9	RAR	BPV	R$
RH Starter	03	ARI *	11	9	1	164	107	4.12	1.50	275	281	281	21.3	31%	74%	5.22	34	22	44	3.9	5.9	1.5	6%	0.8	3.3	44	$9
Age 30	04	MON	4	7	0	98	99	5.05	1.49	266	228	283	22.8	32%	71%	4.41	32	21	47	4.2	9.1	2.2	14%	1.7	-9.5	52	$4
Peak	05	WAS	9	7	0	198	185	3.13	1.20	235	229	237	26.3	29%	77%	4.06	30	23	46	3.0	8.4	2.8	8%	0.9	27.1	92	$21
Type Pwr xFB	06	WAS	1	2	0	40	42	4.48	1.12	241	299	188	20.3	31%	61%	3.75	30	16	54	2.0	9.4	4.7	7%	0.9	0.0	134	$4
Reliability 0	07	WAS	1	5	0	31	15	7.48	1.95	306	328	294	21.8	32%	63%	6.91	36	19	46	6.3	4.3	0.7	10%	1.4	-11.8	-9	($3)
ERA Potl 55%	1st Half		1	5	0	31	15	7.55	1.97	308			21.6	32%	63%	6.94	36	19	46	6.4	4.4	0.7	10%	1.5	-11.9	-10	($3)
LIMA Plan D	2nd Half		0	0	0	0	0	0.00	0.00																		
+/- Score 9	08	Proj	5	10	0	116	93	4.89	1.49	268			22.2	31%	71%	4.95	33	20	48	4.1	7.2	1.8	10%	1.3	-7.8	42	$4

Had surgery in Sept 2007 to correct a nerve problem in his elbow. But, he had similar "successful" surgery in 2006, and look where that got him. Due for his next successful surgery in late 2008.

TOM TODARO

Patton,Troy

Patton,Troy		Yr	Tm	W	L	Sv	IP	K	ERA	WHIP	OBA	vL	vR	BF/G	H%	S%	xERA	G	L	F	Ctl	Dom	Cmd	hr/f	hr/9	RAR	BPV	R$
RH Starter		03		0	0	0	0	0	0.00	0.00																		
Age	22	04		0	0	0	0	0	0.00	0.00																		
Growth		05		0	0	0	0	0	0.00	0.00																		
Type	Con xFB	06	aa	2	5	0	45	31	5.39	1.51	302			25.0	33%	67%	5.50				2.6	6.2	2.4		1.4	-4.8	40	$1
Reliability	0	07	HOU *	10	10	0	164	88	4.12	1.32	268	100	243	25.8	28%	72%	5.29	28	21	51	2.6	4.8	1.8	7%	1.1	6.2	36	$11
ERA Potl	40%	1st Half		5	6	0	95	52	3.40	1.33	265			27.0	29%	78%					2.8	4.9	1.7		0.9	12.0	39	$8
LIMA Plan	C	2nd Half		5	4	0	69	36	5.12	1.31	271			24.2	28%	64%	5.23	28	21	51	2.4	4.7	2.0	8%	1.3	-5.8	32	$4
+/- Score	-33	08	Proj	8	12	0	145	86	4.78	1.39	283			25.0	30%	71%	5.17	28	21	51	2.5	5.3	2.1	10%	1.6	-13.9	28	$7

0-2, 3.55 ERA in 13 IP at HOU. Rotation hopeful shut down with tendinitis in early Sept. Has decent upside and room for growth, but a rookie LH FBer with marginal Dom in HOU is a risky play.

Pavano,Carl

Pavano,Carl		Yr	Tm	W	L	Sv	IP	K	ERA	WHIP	OBA	vL	vR	BF/G	H%	S%	xERA	G	L	F	Ctl	Dom	Cmd	hr/f	hr/9	RAR	BPV	R$
RH Starter		03	FLA	12	13	0	201	133	4.30	1.26	265	267	263	25.5	30%	67%	4.33	41	18	41	2.2	6.0	2.7	7%	0.9	-0.5	69	$15
Age	32	04	FLA	18	8	0	222	139	3.00	1.18	253	267	240	29.3	29%	76%	3.91	48	19	32	2.0	5.6	2.8	7%	0.6	34.6	78	$26
Peak		05	NYY	4	6	0	100	56	4.77	1.47	314	335	294	25.8	33%	72%	4.16	50	19	31	1.6	5.0	3.1	15%	1.5	-4.9	42	$3
Type	Con	06	a/a	2	0	0	17	15	1.59	1.12	250			17.2	33%	84%	2.45				1.6	7.9	5.0		0.0	6.1	158	$3
Reliability	0	07	NYY	1	0	0	11	4	4.78	1.24	274	208	350	23.5	28%	62%	4.67	46	18	36	1.6	3.2	2.0	7%	0.8	-0.4	38	$1
ERA Potl	60%	1st Half		1	0	0	11	4	4.91	1.27	279			23.1	29%	62%	4.69	46	18	36	1.6	3.3	2.0	7%	0.8	-0.5	36	$1
LIMA Plan	B	2nd Half		0	0	0	0	0	0.00	0.00																		
+/- Score	-6	08	Proj	2	3	0	44	24	4.34	1.31	281			23.0	30%	69%	4.25	47	19	34	1.9	5.0	2.7	10%	1.0	1.3	54	$3

TJ surgery ended his season in June. Still flashes exquisite Ctl, but has now effectively missed 2 1/2 seasons. Might pitch sometime after the All-Star break, but we've been saying that for three years.

Peavy,Jake

Peavy,Jake		Yr	Tm	W	L	Sv	IP	K	ERA	WHIP	OBA	vL	vR	BF/G	H%	S%	xERA	G	L	F	Ctl	Dom	Cmd	hr/f	hr/9	RAR	BPV	R$
RH Starter		03	SD	12	11	0	194	156	4.13	1.31	240	246	230	25.7	26%	75%	4.36	40	19	41	3.8	7.2	1.9	14%	1.5	3.6	44	$15
Age	26	04	SD	15	6	0	166	173	2.28	1.20	238	235	238	25.3	31%	84%	3.40	43	20	37	2.9	9.4	3.3	8%	0.7	40.7	111	$25
Growth		05	SD	13	7	0	203	216	2.88	1.04	221	223	212	26.8	29%	76%	3.04	44	20	35	2.2	9.6	4.3	10%	0.8	34.2	135	$29
Type	Pwr	06	SD	11	14	0	202	215	4.10	1.23	247	242	243	26.2	32%	69%	3.60	38	18	44	2.8	9.6	3.5	10%	1.0	9.7	105	$20
Reliability	73	07	SD	19	6	0	223	240	2.54	1.06	212	242	174	26.1	29%	78%	3.23	44	17	39	2.7	9.7	3.5	6%	0.5	52.0	129	$37
ERA Potl	55%	1st Half		9	2	0	105	113	2.14	1.07	217			26.2	31%	78%	3.08	47	18	35	2.6	9.7	3.8	1%	0.1	29.6	146	$19
LIMA Plan	C	2nd Half		10	4	0	118	127	2.89	1.06	207			26.1	27%	77%	3.35	41	17	42	2.9	9.7	3.3	10%	0.9	22.4	114	$19
+/- Score	3	08	Proj	16	9	0	218	229	3.06	1.14	230			26.0	30%	77%	3.38	42	18	40	2.7	9.5	3.5	10%	0.9	27.3	111	$30

Bottom line improvement came from H%, S% regressions and a crazy-lucky 1st half hr/f. Expect him to give up some more HR in 2008, but how bad can it get in Petco? One of best / stable SP skill sets going.

Pelfrey,Mike

Pelfrey,Mike		Yr	Tm	W	L	Sv	IP	K	ERA	WHIP	OBA	vL	vR	BF/G	H%	S%	xERA	G	L	F	Ctl	Dom	Cmd	hr/f	hr/9	RAR	BPV	R$
RH Starter		03		0	0	0	0	0	0.00	0.00																		
Age	24	04		0	0	0	0	0	0.00	0.00																		
Growth		05		0	0	0	0	0	0.00	0.00																		
Type	Pwr	06	NYM *	7	3	0	95	84	4.16	1.57	279	278	326	23.7	35%	73%	4.07	49	23	29	4.3	7.9	1.9	6%	0.5	3.9	72	$6
Reliability	0	07	NYM *	6	14	0	147	92	5.16	1.60	292	321	279	22.9	33%	68%	4.64	48	23	28	4.0	5.6	1.4	9%	0.7	-13.4	38	$2
ERA Potl	50%	1st Half		2	7	0	66	38	5.17	1.62	295			23.1	33%	68%	4.87	48	22	30	3.9	5.2	1.3	7%	0.7	-6.0	34	($0)
LIMA Plan	C+	2nd Half		4	7	0	81	54	5.16	1.59	290			22.7	33%	68%	4.45	49	24	27	4.0	6.0	1.5	10%	0.8	-7.3	40	$1
+/- Score	17	08	Proj	6	7	0	102	71	4.61	1.52	278			22.5	32%	70%	4.34	48	23	28	3.9	6.3	1.6	10%	0.8	0.7	47	$4

3-8, 5.57 ERA in 73 IP at NYM. Dominance improved in 2nd half MLB tour, but Ctl remains a problem area. Room for growth here, but for growing pains as well. Could be worth an extra dollar, but not more.

Pena,Tony

Pena,Tony		Yr	Tm	W	L	Sv	IP	K	ERA	WHIP	OBA	vL	vR	BF/G	H%	S%	xERA	G	L	F	Ctl	Dom	Cmd	hr/f	hr/9	RAR	BPV	R$
RH Reliever		03		0	0	0	0	0	0.00	0.00																		
Age	26	04		0	0	0	0	0	0.00	0.00																		
Growth		05	aa	7	13	0	148	83	5.58	1.59	318			26.7	34%	67%	5.88				2.5	5.1	2.0		1.3	-23.2	27	$0
Type	FB	06	ARI *	8	5	14	76	53	3.33	1.22	266			4.8	30%	75%	4.11	39	22	39	1.8	6.2	3.5	7%	0.8	10.9	87	$15
Reliability	11	07	ARI	5	4	2	85	63	3.27	1.10	208	245	176	4.6	24%	73%	4.06	48	12	40	3.3	6.6	2.0	8%	0.8	12.2	71	$11
ERA Potl	45%	1st Half		2	1	1	42	28	2.14	0.83	157			4.5	17%	78%	3.66	52	12	36	2.8	6.0	2.2	7%	0.6	11.8	86	$7
LIMA Plan	C	2nd Half		3	3	1	43	35	4.36	1.36	251			4.6	29%	70%	4.44	45	12	44	3.7	7.3	1.9	9%	1.0	0.3	58	$4
+/- Score	-14	08	Proj	5	6	3	83	58	3.90	1.30	262			5.5	30%	73%	4.30	46	14	40	2.7	6.3	2.3	9%	1.0	1.0	60	$8

Clearly tired down the stretch. Most of the 1st half magic - GB, Ctl, H%, S% - disappeared in 2nd half, adding 2+ runs to his ERA. Dom holding its own, but other skills have yet to stabilize. Bid cautiously.

Penny,Brad

Penny,Brad		Yr	Tm	W	L	Sv	IP	K	ERA	WHIP	OBA	vL	vR	BF/G	H%	S%	xERA	G	L	F	Ctl	Dom	Cmd	hr/f	hr/9	RAR	BPV	R$
RH Starter		03	FLA	14	10	0	196	138	4.13	1.28	261	269	258	25.7	30%	70%	4.12	45	18	36	2.6	6.3	2.5	9%	1.0	3.5	64	$16
Age	29	04	2NL	9	10	0	143	111	3.15	1.22	244	242	243	24.7	29%	77%	4.06	43	19	38	2.8	7.0	2.5	7%	0.8	19.7	77	$15
Peak		05	LA	7	9	0	175	122	3.91	1.29	273	263	276	25.4	31%	72%	3.94	47	20	34	2.1	6.3	3.0	9%	0.9	7.3	74	$12
Type		06	LA	16	9	0	189	148	4.33	1.38	279	275	283	23.9	33%	70%	4.07	44	20	36	2.6	7.0	2.7	9%	0.9	3.6	72	$16
Reliability	90	07	LA	16	4	0	208	135	3.03	1.31	253	229	286	26.6	30%	77%	4.20	49	20	31	3.2	5.8	1.8	4%	0.4	35.8	67	$22
ERA Potl	45%	1st Half		10	1	0	106	70	2.04	1.12	233			26.8	28%	81%	3.67	53	20	28	2.4	5.9	2.5	2%	0.2	31.2	91	$17
LIMA Plan	D	2nd Half		6	3	0	102	65	4.06	1.50	273			26.5	31%	73%	4.77	45	21	34	4.0	5.7	1.4	6%	0.6	4.6	47	$6
+/- Score	-25	08	Proj	14	7	0	203	137	3.90	1.36	265			25.6	30%	73%	4.28	46	20	34	3.1	6.1	2.0	9%	0.9	3.1	53	$16

Kept ball down in 1st half with stellar results. Ctl issues and S%, hr/f regressions led to 2nd half drop-off. Stable skill set now dogged by troubling Cmd trend. Pay only for a level supported by xERA history.

Penn,Hayden

Penn,Hayden		Yr	Tm	W	L	Sv	IP	K	ERA	WHIP	OBA	vL	vR	BF/G	H%	S%	xERA	G	L	F	Ctl	Dom	Cmd	hr/f	hr/9	RAR	BPV	R$
RH Starter		03		0	0	0	0	0	0.00	0.00											0.0	0.0						
Age	23	04	aa	3	0	0	20	19	5.85	1.70	299			23.1	38%	64%	5.09				4.5	8.6	1.9		0.5	-3.7	73	$1
Growth		05	BAL *	10	8	0	148	128	5.40	1.49	282	289	301	23.4	33%	66%	3.92	49	20	32	3.5	7.8	2.2	14%	1.2	-18.8	55	$7
Type	Pwr	06	BAL *	7	8	0	108	89	5.43	1.53	290	327	467	23.0	33%	67%	4.51	38	21	40	3.5	7.4	2.1	11%	1.3	-11.6	47	$5
Reliability	0	07	aaa	2	1	0	21	18	6.94	1.68	340			24.1	40%	59%	6.43				2.0	7.7	3.7		1.2	-6.4	75	$0
ERA Potl	0%	1st Half		0	0	0	5	5	5.40	0.80	124			18.6	18%	25%					3.6	9.0	2.5		0.0	-0.6	137	$1
LIMA Plan	B	2nd Half		2	1	0	16	13	7.42	1.95	387			26.0	44%	64%					1.6	7.2	4.7		1.6	-5.8	70	($0)
+/- Score	56	08	Proj	4	6	0	73	60	4.84	1.43	276			22.6	32%	69%	4.16	43	21	37	3.2	7.4	2.3	12%	1.2	2.6	56	$4

Lost season due to May surgery to remove bone spur from right elbow. 5.3 Ctl, 2.6 HR/9 in 58 career MLB IP, but projects better. If healthy, a possible sleeper, but after AFL debacle, growing pains are more likely.

Peralta,Joel

Peralta,Joel		Yr	Tm	W	L	Sv	IP	K	ERA	WHIP	OBA	vL	vR	BF/G	H%	S%	xERA	G	L	F	Ctl	Dom	Cmd	hr/f	hr/9	RAR	BPV	R$
RH Reliever		03	a/a	5	4	20	52	36	2.98	1.26	256			4.5	30%	78%	3.50				2.6	6.2	2.4		0.6	9.1	73	$13
Age	32	04	aaa	4	2	1	56	54	5.18	1.56	307			6.4	38%	67%	5.24				2.8	8.7	3.1		0.9	-5.8	86	$3
Peak		05	ANA *	5	1	10	54	47	3.82	1.16	216	273	178	4.7	25%	70%	4.22	34	20	46	3.5	7.8	2.2	9%	1.0	3.7	76	$10
Type	FB	06	KC	1	3	1	73	57	4.43	1.24	264	338	234	4.8	30%	68%	4.27	32	22	46	2.1	7.0	3.4	10%	1.2	1.2	78	$6
Reliability	36	07	KC	1	3	1	88	66	3.80	1.28	273	248	290	5.9	32%	73%	4.17	36	22	42	1.9	6.8	3.5	8%	0.9	7.7	86	$7
ERA Potl	55%	1st Half		1	2	0	51	45	3.71	1.16	250			6.1	30%	70%	3.71	36	23	40	1.9	7.9	4.1	8%	0.9	5.0	112	$5
LIMA Plan	B	2nd Half		0	1	1	37	21	3.92	1.44	303			5.7	33%	76%	4.85	36	21	43	2.0	5.1	2.6	7%	1.0	2.6	51	$2
+/- Score	2	08	Proj	3	3	0	87	66	3.93	1.26	268			5.3	30%	73%	4.23	34	22	44	2.1	6.8	3.3	10%	1.2	2.8	74	$7

Solid 1st half, career high IP contributed to Dom fizzling down the stretch with minimal bottom line impact. FBer with stable skill set allowed one HR at home. LIMA worthy, bid on a near repeat.

Percival,Troy

Percival,Troy		Yr	Tm	W	L	Sv	IP	K	ERA	WHIP	OBA	vL	vR	BF/G	H%	S%	xERA	G	L	F	Ctl	Dom	Cmd	hr/f	hr/9	RAR	BPV	R$
RH Reliever		03	ANA	0	5	33	49	48	3.49	1.14	193	165	205	3.8	22%	76%	4.49	22	19	59	4.2	8.8	2.1	10%	1.3	6.3	75	$17
Age	38	04	ANA	2	3	33	49	33	2.93	1.26	237	218	244	4.0	25%	84%	4.98	32	16	52	3.5	6.0	1.7	9%	1.3	9.1	42	$16
Decline		05	DET	1	3	8	25	20	5.76	1.20	212	173	250	4.0	19%	61%	4.81	27	14	59	4.0	7.2	1.8	17%	2.5	-4.3	18	$4
Type	Pwr xFB	06		0	0	0	0	0	0.00	0.00																		
Reliability	0	07	STL *	3	0	0	46	43	1.79	0.97	181	220	136	4.5	23%	85%	4.04	33	12	55	3.1	8.3	2.7	5%	0.6	15.0	108	$8
ERA Potl	25%	1st Half		0	0	0	6	8	1.45	1.45	186			4.5	30%	89%					7.3	11.6	1.6		0.0	2.3	121	$1
LIMA Plan	C+	2nd Half		3	0	0	40	35	1.84	0.89	180			4.5	22%	84%	3.96	33	12	55	2.4	7.8	3.2	5%	0.7	12.8	113	$8
+/- Score	-51	08	Proj	2	2	0	44	35	3.72	1.33	251			4.3	28%	78%	4.85	30	15	55	3.5	7.2	2.1	10%	1.4	-2.4	48	$4

3-0, 1.80 ERA in 40 IP at STL. Back for 2nd half after missing two years due to elbow injuries. Surprising Cmd, minimal FB damage, but Rel is instructive. A tough encore in the face of aches, pains and Father Time.

ROD TRUESDELL

Perez,Chris		Yr	Tm	W	L	Sv	IP	K	ERA	WHIP	OBA	vL	vR	BF/G	H%	S%	xERA	G	L	F	Ctl	Dom	Cmd	hr/f	hr/9	RAR	BPV	R$
RH	Reliever	03		0	0	0	0	0	0.00	0.00																		
Age	22	04		0	0	0	0	0	0.00	0.00																		
Growth		05		0	0	0	0	0	0.00	0.00																		
Type	Pwr	06		0	0	0	0	0	0.00	0.00																		
Reliability	0	07	aa	2	1	36	54	68	3.33	1.19	141			4.1	19%	75%	2.16				6.5	11.3	**1.7**		0.8	7.5	106	$19
ERA Potl	50%	1st Half		2	0	21	32	46	3.09	1.25	166			4.4	25%	78%					6.2	12.9	**2.1**		0.8	5.4	118	$12
LIMA Plan	C	2nd Half		0	1	15	22	22	3.68	1.09	101			3.7	11%	68%					7.0	9.0	**1.3**		0.8	2.1	91	$7
+/- Score	-2	08	Proj	**1**	**1**	**0**	**44**	**51**	**4.76**	**1.49**	**212**			**4.3**	**28%**	**70%**	**3.90**				**6.6**	**10.6**	**1.6**		**1.0**	**2.9**	**78**	**$2**

Prospect with power arm, closer upside, Ctl issues and no MLB experience. Struggled in initial AAA exposure (14 IP, 15 BB) after dominating AA. Risky LIMA potential in rookie year, growing pains possible.

Perez,Odalis		Yr	Tm	W	L	Sv	IP	K	ERA	WHIP	OBA	vL	vR	BF/G	H%	S%	xERA	G	L	F	Ctl	Dom	Cmd	hr/f	hr/9	RAR	BPV	R$
LH	Starter	03	LA	12	12	0	185	141	4.52	1.28	268	201	284	25.9	30%	69%	3.45	53	20	27	2.2	6.9	**3.1**	18%	1.4	-5.6	66	$14
Age	30	04	LA	7	6	0	196	128	3.26	1.14	246	270	241	25.7	27%	77%	3.69	52	16	32	2.0	5.9	**2.9**	14%	1.2	24.3	66	$18
Peak		05	LA	7	8	0	108	74	4.57	1.27	263	256	264	23.8	29%	66%	4.07	44	20	36	2.3	6.2	**2.6**	11%	1.1	-4.4	62	$8
Type	Con	06	2TM	6	8	0	126	81	6.21	1.59	322	336	316	17.8	35%	62%	4.42	44	23	34	2.2	5.8	**2.6**	12%	1.3	-26.3	42	$0
Reliability	30	07	KC	8	11	0	137	64	5.57	1.66	315	301	323	24.2	34%	67%	5.22	45	20	35	3.3	4.2	**1.3**	8%	0.9	-18.1	17	$1
ERA Potl	50%	1st Half		4	7	0	84	41	5.89	1.65	317			24.0	34%	65%	5.16	45	19	36	3.1	4.4	**1.4**	9%	1.1	-14.4	15	($1)
LIMA Plan	C+	2nd Half		4	4	0	53	23	5.07	1.67	311			24.5	33%	69%	5.33	46	21	33	3.5	3.9	**1.1**	6%	0.7	-3.7	19	$1
+/- Score	-9	08	Proj	**7**	**12**	**0**	**145**	**81**	**4.97**	**1.54**	**303**			**22.3**	**33%**	**69%**	**4.69**	**46**	**21**	**34**	**2.8**	**5.0**	**1.8**	**10%**	**1.1**	**-3.5**	**31**	**$4**

No longer a GB machine, now Dom plunge and Ctl spike make him unrosterable. Only 0.6 hr/9 at Kauffman checked his slide. Could rebound some, but he needs to stop accumulating DL days faster than games played.

Perez,Oliver		Yr	Tm	W	L	Sv	IP	K	ERA	WHIP	OBA	vL	vR	BF/G	H%	S%	xERA	G	L	F	Ctl	Dom	Cmd	hr/f	hr/9	RAR	BPV	R$
LH	Starter	03	2NL *	7	13	0	173	183	4.84	1.51	263	292	258	23.9	33%	72%	4.22	33	26	41	4.5	9.5	**2.1**	14%	1.4	-11.9	62	$8
Age	26	04	PIT	12	10	0	196	239	2.98	1.15	208	220	204	26.6	28%	79%	3.47	37	15	48	3.7	11.0	**3.0**	10%	1.0	30.9	111	$26
Growth		05	PIT	7	5	0	103	97	5.85	1.67	260	313	255	23.6	29%	70%	5.23	34	17	49	6.1	8.5	**1.4**	16%	2.0	-20.4	23	$1
Type	Pwr xFB	06	2NL *	5	18	0	163	152	7.08	1.71	288	260	300	23.6	33%	61%	5.05	30	23	47	5.1	8.4	**1.7**	14%	1.8	-52.2	29	($5)
Reliability	27	07	NYM	15	10	0	177	174	3.56	1.31	235	206	235	25.8	29%	77%	4.34	33	17	50	4.0	8.8	**2.2**	9%	1.1	18.9	74	$20
ERA Potl	50%	1st Half		7	6	0	95	85	3.13	1.16	214			25.8	25%	78%	4.28	31	18	50	3.5	8.1	**2.3**	9%	1.0	15.2	77	$13
LIMA Plan	D+	2nd Half		8	4	0	82	89	4.06	1.49	257			25.8	33%	77%	4.40	34	15	51	4.6	9.8	**2.1**	10%	1.2	3.7	70	$8
+/- Score	-9	08	Proj	**13**	**13**	**0**	**193**	**191**	**4.16**	**1.43**	**255**			**24.7**	**31%**	**75%**	**4.46**	**33**	**18**	**49**	**4.2**	**8.9**	**2.1**	**10%**	**1.2**	**-1.5**	**66**	**$15**

PRO: Stable Dom, three-year Ctl trend, hr/9 friendly Shea.
CON: 2nd half Ctl slide, growing fly ball tendency.
BPI growth still possible, but 2007 result is his upside here. Pay for less in 2008.

Perez,Rafael		Yr	Tm	W	L	Sv	IP	K	ERA	WHIP	OBA	vL	vR	BF/G	H%	S%	xERA	G	L	F	Ctl	Dom	Cmd	hr/f	hr/9	RAR	BPV	R$
LH	Reliever	03		0	0	0	0	0	0.00	0.00																		
Age	26	04		0	0	0	0	0	0.00	0.00																		
Growth		05	aa	4	3	1	66	39	2.10	1.12	249			17.8	28%	85%	3.15				1.7	5.3	**3.1**		0.7	18.0	82	$9
Type	GB	06	CLE *	4	8	0	106	90	3.65	1.28	246			10.4	31%	71%	3.66	58	9	33	3.2	7.6	**2.4**	5%	0.4	11.9	88	$11
Reliability	6	07	CLE *	4	5	1	107	90	2.97	1.19	252	145	213	8.5	31%	77%	3.37	53	17	30	2.2	7.6	**3.4**	9%	0.7	20.3	102	$13
ERA Potl	55%	1st Half		3	3	0	67	53	3.35	1.32	278			15.8	33%	76%	3.53	54	17	29	2.1	7.1	**3.3**	8%	0.7	9.6	91	$7
LIMA Plan	B+	2nd Half		1	2	1	40	37	2.32	0.98	204			4.5	25%	80%	3.03	52	17	31	2.3	8.3	**3.6**	9%	0.7	10.7	120	$7
+/- Score	20	08	Proj	**2**	**3**	**5**	**58**	**47**	**3.26**	**1.17**	**241**			**4.9**	**29%**	**75%**	**3.47**	**53**	**16**	**31**	**2.5**	**7.3**	**2.9**	**10%**	**0.8**	**7.4**	**89**	**$8**

1-2, 1.78 ERA in 61 IP at CLE. Stellar across-the-board BPIs for rookie RP. Aided by fortunate H% and S% in 2nd half, but Ctl, Dom and GB% were real enough. Will come back to earth, but still solid LIMA pick.

Perkins,Glen		Yr	Tm	W	L	Sv	IP	K	ERA	WHIP	OBA	vL	vR	BF/G	H%	S%	xERA	G	L	F	Ctl	Dom	Cmd	hr/f	hr/9	RAR	BPV	R$
LH	Reliever	03		0	0	0	0	0	0.00	0.00																		
Age	25	04		0	0	0	0	0	0.00	0.00																		
Growth		05	aa	4	4	0	79	58	6.04	1.62	292			25.6	35%	60%	4.78				4.1	6.6	**1.6**		0.5	-16.9	56	($0)
Type	Pwr FB	06	a/a	4	12	0	121	113	5.50	1.64	294			23.0	36%	68%	5.36				4.2	8.4	**2.0**		1.0	-14.6	57	$2
Reliability	0	07	MIN *	0	2	0	42	27	5.04	1.43	246	250	222	7.9	25%	70%	5.15	39	18	44	4.6	5.8	**1.3**	14%	1.8	-2.7	14	$1
ERA Potl	40%	1st Half		0	0	0	30	18	3.30	1.20	214			9.5	23%	76%	4.77	41	18	41	3.9	5.4	**1.4**	8%	0.9	4.5	47	$2
LIMA Plan	C+	2nd Half		0	2	0	12	9	9.46	2.01	317			5.8	30%	61%	6.44	29	14	57	6.3	6.7	**1.1**	23%	4.0	-7.2	-65	($2)
+/- Score	-7	08	Proj	**2**	**4**	**0**	**83**	**64**	**4.45**	**1.46**	**266**			**15.8**	**31%**	**72%**	**4.64**	**41**	**18**	**41**	**3.9**	**6.9**	**1.8**	**10%**	**1.1**	**-1.4**	**48**	**$4**

0-0, 3.14 ERA in 29 IP at MIN. Missed four months with shoulder strain, pitching well out of pen before and after. Health risk, LIMA candidate, but minors record also suggests rotation as a possibility.

Petit,Yusmeiro		Yr	Tm	W	L	Sv	IP	K	ERA	WHIP	OBA	vL	vR	BF/G	H%	S%	xERA	G	L	F	Ctl	Dom	Cmd	hr/f	hr/9	RAR	BPV	R$
RH	Starter	03		0	0	0	0	0	0.00	0.00											0.0	0.0						
Age	23	04	aa	1	1	0	12	15	5.25	1.50	262			26.5	37%	65%	4.31				4.5	11.3	**2.5**		0.8	-1.3	100	$1
Growth		05	a/a	9	6	0	132	133	3.65	1.03	234			21.7	28%	70%	3.24				1.5	9.1	**6.1**		1.3	10.6	152	$18
Type	xFB	06	FLA *	5	7	0	122	88	5.27	1.39	293	381	400	16.5	33%	65%	4.59	29	24	46	2.0	6.5	**3.2**	10%	1.4	-11.8	62	$5
Reliability	0	07	ARI *	11	8	0	150	93	4.91	1.40	268	274	250	21.0	28%	70%	5.27	33	15	52	3.4	5.6	**1.7**	10%	1.6	-9.0	23	$8
ERA Potl	50%	1st Half		7	5	0	90	53	4.99	1.42	266			24.5	28%	68%	5.71	26	16	58	3.6	5.3	**1.5**	8%	1.3	-6.3	26	($5)
LIMA Plan	C	2nd Half		4	3	0	60	40	4.80	1.38	271			17.2	28%	73%	4.98	33	15	52	3.0	6.0	**2.0**	13%	1.9	-2.8	20	$4
+/- Score	-6	08	Proj	**6**	**7**	**0**	**116**	**84**	**4.81**	**1.38**	**273**			**18.5**	**30%**	**70%**	**4.82**	**32**	**17**	**51**	**2.9**	**6.5**	**2.3**	**11%**	**1.6**	**-6.0**	**41**	**$6**

3-4, 4.58 ERA in 57 IP at ARI. Once-elite prospect, failing dominance has left him well-traveled. Dom, Ctl improved in 2nd half, but ARI is no place for an extreme FBer. Merely watch-list material for now.

Pettitte,Andy		Yr	Tm	W	L	Sv	IP	K	ERA	WHIP	OBA	vL	vR	BF/G	H%	S%	xERA	G	L	F	Ctl	Dom	Cmd	hr/f	hr/9	RAR	BPV	R$
LH	Starter	03	NYY	21	8	0	208	180	4.02	1.33	279	321	254	26.8	34%	72%	3.43	50	22	29	2.2	7.8	**3.6**	11%	0.9	12.8	94	$24
Age	35	04	HOU	6	4	0	83	79	3.90	1.23	233	290	208	23.0	29%	70%	3.21	53	21	26	3.4	8.6	**2.5**	14%	0.9	3.7	87	$9
Decline		05	HOU	17	9	0	222	171	2.39	1.03	231	200	239	26.6	27%	80%	3.18	50	23	27	1.7	6.9	**4.2**	10%	0.7	50.8	117	$33
Type		06	HOU	14	13	0	214	178	4.20	1.44	283	259	290	25.9	33%	74%	3.72	50	22	29	2.9	7.5	**2.5**	14%	1.1	7.5	63	$15
Reliability	73	07	NYY	15	9	0	215	141	4.05	1.43	282	298	282	26.0	32%	72%	4.32	48	19	33	2.9	5.9	**2.0**	7%	0.7	12.0	57	$16
ERA Potl	50%	1st Half		4	5	0	106	56	3.23	1.33	265			25.0	30%	76%	4.47	50	17	33	2.8	4.8	**1.7**	5%	0.5	16.7	51	$9
LIMA Plan	D+	2nd Half		11	4	0	109	85	4.86	1.52	297			27.0	35%	69%	4.18	45	22	33	3.0	7.0	**2.4**	9%	0.8	-4.8	63	$8
+/- Score	-13	08	Proj	**13**	**11**	**0**	**203**	**143**	**4.12**	**1.40**	**274**			**26.6**	**31%**	**72%**	**4.09**	**49**	**21**	**30**	**3.0**	**6.3**	**2.1**	**10%**	**0.8**	**10.2**	**57**	**$16**

Recent xERA trend is first hint of decline. H% is to blame for 2nd half ERA, and Dom rebound allays fears of faster slide. Always a health risk, but this skill profile remains viable.

Pineiro,Joel		Yr	Tm	W	L	Sv	IP	K	ERA	WHIP	OBA	vL	vR	BF/G	H%	S%	xERA	G	L	F	Ctl	Dom	Cmd	hr/f	hr/9	RAR	BPV	R$
RH	Reliever	03	SEA	16	11	0	211	151	3.80	1.27	244	234	251	27.6	28%	72%	4.26	45	17	37	3.2	6.4	**2.0**	8%	0.8	19.0	62	$22
Age	29	04	SEA	6	11	0	140	111	4.69	1.33	267	209	316	28.4	30%	69%	4.09	43	17	39	2.8	7.1	**2.6**	13%	1.3	-4.4	58	$8
Peak		05	SEA	7	11	0	189	107	5.62	1.48	296	295	305	27.7	32%	63%	4.54	45	22	33	2.7	5.1	**1.9**	11%	1.1	-29.1	34	$3
Type	Con	06	SEA	8	13	1	165	87	6.37	1.65	310	287	332	18.9	33%	62%	4.82	47	23	29	3.5	4.7	**1.4**	13%	1.3	-37.0	12	($1)
Reliability	51	07	2TM	7	5	0	98	60	4.33	1.39	285	250	308	10.0	31%	73%	4.25	49	17	34	2.4	5.5	**2.3**	13%	1.3	1.6	41	$7
ERA Potl	45%	1st Half		1	1	0	30	16	5.10	1.63	299			5.1	32%	70%	4.70	56	15	29	3.9	4.8	**1.2**	10%	0.9	-2.4	23	$0
LIMA Plan	C	2nd Half		6	4	0	68	44	3.99	1.29	279			19.0	30%	75%	4.06	45	18	37	1.7	5.8	**3.4**	13%	1.5	4.0	61	$7
+/- Score	-4	08	Proj	**8**	**9**	**0**	**145**	**87**	**4.47**	**1.41**	**285**			**25.1**	**31%**	**71%**	**4.31**	**48**	**19**	**33**	**2.5**	**5.4**	**2.1**	**11%**	**1.1**	**2.5**	**43**	**$8**

Newest poster boy for SP scarcity. Rode 4.10 ERA as SP in Aug-Sept to two-year, $13m deal with STL. 2nd half Dom spike and unprecedented 2nd half Ctl minimized gopheritis. It will be a tough trick to repeat.

Pinto,Renyel		Yr	Tm	W	L	Sv	IP	K	ERA	WHIP	OBA	vL	vR	BF/G	H%	S%	xERA	G	L	F	Ctl	Dom	Cmd	hr/f	hr/9	RAR	BPV	R$
LH	Reliever	03		0	0	0	0	0	0.00	0.00																		
Age	25	04	a/a	12	9	0	151	169	3.58	1.38	230			24.0	31%	76%	3.55				4.8	10.1	**2.1**		0.7	14.3	92	$16
Growth		05	a/a	11	5	0	152	129	4.50	1.53	258			24.2	32%	69%	4.02				5.0	7.6	**1.5**		0.4	-3.6	69	$9
Type	Pwr FB	06	FLA *	8	2	1	124	123	3.40	1.46	234			12.1	30%	78%	4.33	45	16	39	5.4	8.9	**1.7**	8%	0.7	16.6	75	$12
Reliability	4	07	FLA	2	4	1	59	56	3.68	1.31	214	210	227	4.4	26%	76%	4.36	37	19	44	4.9	8.6	**1.8**	10%	1.1	5.4	68	$5
ERA Potl	45%	1st Half		0	3	1	34	33	4.50	1.50	256			4.7	30%	76%	4.56	35	19	46	4.8	8.7	**1.8**	14%	1.6	-0.3	47	$1
LIMA Plan	C+	2nd Half		2	1	0	25	23	2.55	1.05	147			3.9	19%	76%	4.06	42	19	40	5.1	8.4	**1.6**	4%	0.4	5.7	99	$4
+/- Score	-1	08	Proj	**3**	**2**	**0**	**54**	**52**	**4.17**	**1.48**	**247**			**4.9**	**30%**	**74%**	**4.49**	**39**	**19**	**42**	**5.0**	**8.7**	**1.7**	**9%**	**1.0**	**-0.6**	**64**	**$4**

Ctl-deficient arm with brutal hr/9 splits: 0.3 home / 2.1 away; 0.0 vs LHB / 1.6 vs RHB. 1st half driven by hr/f, 2nd half aided by h%. Career .218 BAA vs. RH shows upside, but too many walks to expect a repeat.

JOCK THOMPSON

Prior,Mark		Yr	Tm	W	L	Sv	IP	K	ERA	WHIP	OBA	vL	vR	BF/G	H%	S%	xERA	G	L	F	Ctl	Dom	Cmd	hr/f	hr/9	RAR	BPV	R$
RH	Reliever	03	CHC	18	6	0	211	245	2.43	1.10	235	240	223	27.4	32%	81%	3.01	37	26	37	2.1	10.5	4.9	8%	0.6	48.1	154	$34
Age	27	04	CHC	6	4	0	118	139	4.04	1.35	252	258	245	24.1	34%	73%	3.67	37	19	44	3.7	10.6	2.9	10%	1.1	3.3	97	$10
Pre-Peak		05	CHC	11	7	0	166	188	3.68	1.22	234	216	236	25.5	30%	76%	3.43	37	21	41	3.2	10.2	3.2	14%	1.4	11.5	96	$19
Type	Pwr FB	06	CHC	1	6	0	43	38	7.29	1.71	274	321	226	22.2	31%	60%	5.15	37	21	43	5.8	7.9	1.4	16%	1.9	-14.9	20	($2)
Reliability	0	07	CHC	0	0	0	0	0	0.00	0.00																		
ERA Potl		1st Half		0	0	0	0	0	0.00	0.00																		
LIMA Plan		2nd Half		0	0	0	0	0	0.00	0.00																		
+/- Score		08	Proj	4	6	0	87	84	4.45	1.39	253			23.4	31%	71%	4.18	37	21	42	3.9	8.7	2.2	11%	1.1	2.3	69	$6

Lost season to shoulder surgery. Still young enough that we can't rule out a return to some level of productivity, but too injury-prone to consider him a building block for future success.

Proctor,Scott		Yr	Tm	W	L	Sv	IP	K	ERA	WHIP	OBA	vL	vR	BF/G	H%	S%	xERA	G	L	F	Ctl	Dom	Cmd	hr/f	hr/9	RAR	BPV	R$
RH	Reliever	03	a/a	7	4	1	85	66	3.29	1.36	270			7.1	32%	77%	3.93				2.8	6.9	2.5		0.6	11.6	77	$9
Age	31	04	aaa	2	3	4	44	33	3.66	1.44	263			5.5	31%	77%	4.30				3.9	6.8	1.8		0.9	3.7	54	$4
Peak		05	NYY *	6	1	14	85	77	5.65	1.53	297	300	217	6.0	34%	69%	4.66	30	17	53	3.0	8.1	2.7	13%	2.0	-13.5	41	$8
Type	Pwr xFB	06	NYY	6	4	1	102	89	3.53	1.19	236	204	250	5.1	28%	75%	4.23	33	18	49	2.9	7.8	2.7	8%	1.1	13.0	80	$13
Reliability	28	07	2TM	5	5	0	86	64	3.65	1.41	243	250	237	4.5	27%	79%	5.40	28	16	55	4.6	6.7	1.5	8%	1.3	8.7	40	$7
ERA Potl	35%	1st Half		1	5	0	41	27	3.51	1.41	237			4.6	27%	78%	5.73	29	15	56	4.8	5.9	1.2	6%	0.9	4.8	43	$3
LIMA Plan	C	2nd Half		4	0	0	45	37	3.77	1.41	247			4.5	27%	80%	5.12	27	18	55	4.4	7.4	1.7	11%	1.6	3.8	37	$4
+/- Score	-45	08	Proj	3	5	0	73	56	4.32	1.48	267			5.1	30%	75%	5.20	30	17	53	4.1	6.9	1.7	9%	1.4	-6.8	38	$4

Another solid ERA season, but warning signs abound:
- Falling Dom, Ctl struggles
- H% due for correction
- Rising FB%
- 2 years, 166 games played

DN: 4.75 ERA, or worse

Putz,J.J.		Yr	Tm	W	L	Sv	IP	K	ERA	WHIP	OBA	vL	vR	BF/G	H%	S%	xERA	G	L	F	Ctl	Dom	Cmd	hr/f	hr/9	RAR	BPV	R$
RH	Reliever	03	aaa	0	3	11	86	52	3.24	1.37	253			9.0	29%	76%	3.58				3.8	5.4	1.4		0.4	12.2	55	$8
Age	31	04	SEA	0	3	9	63	47	4.71	1.43	271	234	308	5.1	30%	71%	4.06	52	15	32	3.4	6.7	2.0	16%	1.4	-2.2	39	$5
Peak		05	SEA	6	5	1	60	45	3.60	1.35	255	321	197	4.0	29%	78%	3.78	55	17	28	3.5	6.8	2.0	16%	1.2	5.7	50	$7
Type	Pwr	06	SEA	4	1	36	78	104	2.30	0.92	211	211	204	4.2	32%	76%	2.22	51	16	33	1.5	12.0	8.0	7%	0.5	21.7	239	$27
Reliability	51	07	SEA	6	1	40	72	82	1.38	0.70	155	148	158	3.8	21%	89%	2.60	42	17	41	1.6	10.3	6.3	9%	0.8	27.6	196	$32
ERA Potl	40%	1st Half		0	0	22	36	40	1.00	0.58	129			3.7	16%	94%	2.43	48	13	39	1.5	10.0	6.7	10%	0.8	15.6	207	$16
LIMA Plan	C	2nd Half		6	1	18	36	42	1.76	0.81	179			3.9	24%	85%	2.77	37	21	43	1.8	10.6	6.0	9%	0.8	12.1	186	$16
+/- Score	-64	08	Proj	6	2	48	73	79	2.61	1.01	215			4.2	28%	78%	2.90	47	17	36	2.1	9.8	4.6	9%	0.7	14.2	146	$29

To post a 1.38 ERA, you have to be both lucky and good. ERA will rise as both H% and S% normalize. But don't be deterred by that... He clearly belongs in the top tier of closers.

Qualls,Chad		Yr	Tm	W	L	Sv	IP	K	ERA	WHIP	OBA	vL	vR	BF/G	H%	S%	xERA	G	L	F	Ctl	Dom	Cmd	hr/f	hr/9	RAR	BPV	R$
RH	Reliever	03	aa	8	11	0	175	101	5.24	1.66	310			28.6	34%	69%	5.52				3.5	5.2	1.5		0.8	-18.3	31	$1
Age	29	04	HOU *	7	6	2	139	82	5.95	1.64	326	264	267	11.1	36%	63%	4.15	58	15	27	2.5	5.3	2.2	9%	0.8	-29.0	44	($1)
Peak		05	HOU	6	4	0	79	60	3.30	1.21	246	218	275	4.3	29%	75%	3.17	58	21	20	2.6	6.8	2.6	15%	0.8	9.3	78	$9
Type	Pwr xGB	06	HOU	7	3	0	88	56	3.78	1.18	234	229	251	4.5	26%	71%	3.59	60	14	26	2.9	5.7	2.0	14%	1.0	7.7	54	$10
Reliability	37	07	HOU	6	5	5	83	78	3.05	1.32	265	248	289	4.4	32%	82%	3.24	57	14	29	2.7	8.5	3.1	14%	1.1	14.1	86	$11
ERA Potl	40%	1st Half		5	3	2	40	41	4.05	1.38	267			4.4	33%	76%	3.18	57	13	29	3.2	9.2	2.9	18%	1.4	1.9	78	$6
LIMA Plan	B	2nd Half		1	2	3	43	37	2.11	1.26	263			4.5	32%	88%	3.29	56	15	29	2.3	7.8	3.4	11%	0.8	12.2	95	$6
+/- Score	17	08	Proj	5	4	8	73	63	3.48	1.26	252			4.7	30%	75%	3.24	58	15	27	2.7	7.8	2.9	12%	0.9	10.3	86	$10

Nice growth season with strong 2nd half. Extreme GB pitcher added dominance to arsenal. Only struggles vs RHP holding him back. Sleeper saves source although HOU says "no."
UP: 20 saves (We say "yes.")

Ramirez,Horacio		Yr	Tm	W	L	Sv	IP	K	ERA	WHIP	OBA	vL	vR	BF/G	H%	S%	xERA	G	L	F	Ctl	Dom	Cmd	hr/f	hr/9	RAR	BPV	R$
LH	Starter	03	ATL	12	4	0	182	100	4.01	1.39	261	206	278	27.0	28%	74%	4.49	53	16	31	3.6	4.9	1.4	11%	1.0	6.1	31	$12
Age	28	04	ATL	2	4	0	60	31	2.40	1.35	231	220	227	25.6	24%	88%	4.53	54	20	26	4.5	4.6	1.0	14%	1.0	13.8	27	$5
Pre-Peak		05	ATL	11	9	0	202	80	4.63	1.39	273	267	286	26.4	27%	71%	4.69	48	23	29	3.0	3.6	1.2	15%	1.4	-9.6	5	$8
Type	Con GB	06	ATL	5	5	0	76	37	4.49	1.52	284	286	288	24.2	31%	71%	4.60	54	20	26	3.7	4.4	1.2	9%	0.7	-0.1	28	$3
Reliability	13	07	SEA	8	7	0	98	40	7.16	1.85	335	330	340	23.4	35%	61%	5.48	48	21	31	3.9	3.7	1.0	11%	1.2	-32.1	-6	($4)
ERA Potl	50%	1st Half		4	2	0	40	14	6.53	1.90	340			24.1	36%	64%	5.87	47	22	31	4.1	3.2	0.8	6%	0.7	-10.0	2	($1)
LIMA Plan	F	2nd Half		4	5	0	58	26	7.60	1.81	331			22.9	34%	59%	5.22	50	20	30	3.7	4.0	1.1	15%	1.6	-22.2	-11	($3)
+/- Score	40	08	Proj	3	9	0	91	40	5.74	1.65	306			24.5	32%	66%	5.04	50	21	29	3.7	4.0	1.1	10%	1.0	-6.1	11	($1)

To post a 7.16 ERA, you have to be both unlucky and bad. He was bad in ATL. Bringing him to the AL where he'd have to face 9 legitimate hitters, did they think he would become "good?" Proves it's possible to be worse.

Ramirez,Ramon		Yr	Tm	W	L	Sv	IP	K	ERA	WHIP	OBA	vL	vR	BF/G	H%	S%	xERA	G	L	F	Ctl	Dom	Cmd	hr/f	hr/9	RAR	BPV	R$
RH	Reliever	03	a/a	1	2	0	27	22	2.66	1.29	254			19.0	28%	90%	4.55				3.0	7.3	2.4		1.7	5.8	50	$3
Age	26	04	a/a	4	9	0	133	121	6.02	1.49	296			26.7	36%	60%	5.06				2.7	8.2	3.0		1.0	-27.6	78	$2
Growth		05	a/a	9	9	0	141	107	4.73	1.43	274			20.5	31%	71%	4.91				3.3	6.8	2.1		1.4	-7.5	43	$8
Type	Pwr xFB	06	COL	4	3	0	67	61	3.48	1.26	234	274	194	4.6	29%	74%	4.19	41	14	45	3.6	8.2	2.3	6%	0.7	8.3	85	$7
Reliability	9	07	COL *	12	3	1	91	83	4.83	1.49	264	240	357	5.9	32%	69%	4.87	31	17	52	4.3	8.2	1.9	7%	1.0	-4.5	63	$9
ERA Potl	55%	1st Half		5	1	1	33	37	5.96	1.48	261			4.6	34%	60%	4.41	33	13	55	4.3	10.0	2.3	8%	1.1	-6.3	79	$3
LIMA Plan	B	2nd Half		7	2	0	57	46	4.17	1.50	266			7.0	31%	74%	4.95	29	29	43	4.3	7.2	1.7	8%	0.9	1.8	54	$5
+/- Score	5	08	Proj	4	3	0	50	45	4.14	1.42	262			6.6	31%	74%	4.54	38	13	49	3.8	8.1	2.1	8%	1.1	-0.9	64	$4

2-2, 8.36 ERA in 17 IP at COL. More here than meets the eye. Allowed no runs in 17 of 22 appearances. Sore elbow clouds his immediate future, but with health and consistency these are LIMA-worthy skills.

Rasner,Darrell		Yr	Tm	W	L	Sv	IP	K	ERA	WHIP	OBA	vL	vR	BF/G	H%	S%	xERA	G	L	F	Ctl	Dom	Cmd	hr/f	hr/9	RAR	BPV	R$
RH	Reliever	03		0	0	0	0	0	0.00	0.00																		
Age	27	04		0	0	0	0	0	0.00	0.00																		
Growth		05	aa	6	7	0	150	79	4.17	1.34	288			23.7	32%	69%	4.20				1.8	4.7	2.7		0.6	2.6	63	$8
Type	Con FB	06	NYY *	7	1	0	78	50	3.82	1.35	287			20.9	32%	73%	4.50	40	18	42	2.0	5.7	2.9	7%	0.8	7.1	68	$8
Reliability	0	07	NYY *	2	3	0	33	14	3.03	1.38	276	375	212	17.6	28%	83%	5.15	40	20	40	2.8	3.8	1.4	9%	1.1	6.0	19	$3
ERA Potl	25%	1st Half		2	3	0	33	14	3.03	1.38	276			17.6	28%	83%	5.15	40	20	40	2.8	3.8	1.4	9%	1.1	6.0	19	$3
LIMA Plan	C+	2nd Half		0	0	0	0	0	0.00	0.00																		
+/- Score	-70	08	Proj	3	2	0	44	23	4.14	1.40	285			20.9	31%	73%	4.86	40	20	40	2.5	4.8	1.9	8%	1.0	-2.0	36	$3

1-3, 4.01 ERA in 24 IP at NYY. Fractured right index finger in May led to lost season. Weak Dom and xERA say he's not this good, and at 27, there's little time to prove himself before he turns back into a pumpkin.

Rauch,Jon		Yr	Tm	W	L	Sv	IP	K	ERA	WHIP	OBA	vL	vR	BF/G	H%	S%	xERA	G	L	F	Ctl	Dom	Cmd	hr/f	hr/9	RAR	BPV	R$
RH	Reliever	03	aaa	7	1	0	124	84	5.43	1.45	291			22.6	31%	66%	5.42				2.6	6.1	2.3		1.6	-16.0	34	$4
Age	29	04	2TM *	11	5	0	122	82	3.91	1.29	257	321	203	18.4	28%	74%	4.62	43	11	47	2.9	6.0	2.1	10%	1.3	6.6	46	$12
Peak		05	WAS *	3	5	0	51	43	3.53	1.16	234	255	186	9.5	27%	74%	4.33	26	23	51	2.6	7.6	2.9	8%	1.1	4.5	82	$6
Type	Pwr xFB	06	WAS	4	5	2	91	86	3.36	1.25	233	254	216	4.5	28%	79%	4.24	30	21	49	3.6	8.5	2.4	11%	1.3	12.7	71	$10
Reliability	18	07	WAS	8	4	4	87	71	3.61	1.10	234	208	249	4.0	28%	69%	4.25	33	13	53	2.2	7.3	3.4	5%	0.7	8.8	102	$13
ERA Potl	60%	1st Half		3	1	3	41	34	4.17	1.10	232			3.9	28%	62%	4.20	36	11	53	2.2	7.5	3.4	5%	0.7	1.3	105	$6
LIMA Plan	C+	2nd Half		5	3	1	46	37	3.11	1.10	235			4.0	28%	74%	4.29	31	16	53	2.1	7.2	3.4	6%	0.8	7.5	99	$8
+/- Score	-8	08	Proj	4	5	3	73	61	3.85	1.23	250			5.0	28%	74%	4.33	32	17	51	2.6	7.6	2.9	10%	1.4	0.6	71	$8

Has found a home in the bullpen with excellent Cmd and consistent sub-4.00 ERA's. But higher xERA's are warning signs. If h% rises just a couple of points...
DN: 4.25 ERA

Ray,Chris		Yr	Tm	W	L	Sv	IP	K	ERA	WHIP	OBA	vL	vR	BF/G	H%	S%	xERA	G	L	F	Ctl	Dom	Cmd	hr/f	hr/9	RAR	BPV	R$
RH	Reliever	03		0	0	0	0	0	0.00	0.00											0.0	0.0						
Age	26	04		0	0	0	0	0	0.00	0.00											0.0	0.0						
Growth		05	BAL *	2	5	18	77	77	2.12	1.05	203	284	174	4.3	25%	87%	3.54	35	23	41	2.9	9.0	3.1	11%	1.1	21.5	100	$18
Type	Pwr	06	BAL	4	4	33	66	51	2.73	1.09	195	184	202	4.3	21%	84%	4.41	35	16	48	3.7	7.0	1.9	11%	1.4	14.9	57	$20
Reliability	13	07	BAL	5	6	16	43	44	4.43	1.24	225	233	212	4.1	28%	67%	3.62	45	18	38	3.8	9.3	2.4	12%	1.1	0.4	85	$11
ERA Potl	65%	1st Half		4	5	13	35	32	4.63	1.29	233			4.2	28%	66%	4.08	40	19	40	3.9	8.2	2.1	10%	1.0	-0.5	72	$9
LIMA Plan	B	2nd Half		1	1	3	8	12	3.51	1.04	187			3.8	29%	71%	1.54	73	7	20	3.5	14.0	4.0	34%	1.2	0.9	151	$3
+/- Score	34	08	Proj	1	1	0	9	8	4.00	1.22	240			4.1	29%	70%	3.78	46	15	39	3.0	8.0	2.7	10%	1.0	0.8	81	$1

Could miss all of 2008 recovering from TJ surgery. Has shown nice growth in GB rate, which bodes well for an eventual return to closing effectively. Just don't expect that until 2009.

HAROLD NICHOLS

Redding,Tim

Redding,Tim				W	L	Sv	IP	K	ERA	WHIP	OBA	vL	vR	BF/G	H%	S%	xERA	G	L	F	Ctl	Dom	Cmd	hr/f	hr/9	RAR	BPV	R$
RH Starter		03	HOU	10	14	0	176	116	3.68	1.39	265	297	229	23.0	30%	75%	4.60	44	18	38	3.3	5.9	**1.8**	7%	0.8	13.0	51	$12
Age	30	04	HOU	* 6	11	0	128	77	6.11	1.70	308	345	283	18.5	34%	65%	5.21	42	21	37	4.0	5.4	**1.4**	10%	1.2	-29.2	18	($3)
Peak		05	2TM	* 3	9	0	92	61	7.02	1.70	323			19.4	36%	58%	6.08				3.2	5.9	**1.9**		1.1	-30.8	32	($4)
Type		06	aaa	12	10	0	187	118	4.91	1.50	292			28.5	31%	72%	5.48				3.1	5.7	**1.9**		1.6	-9.0	23	$9
Reliability	22	07	WAS	* 12	11	0	173	95	5.54	1.68	315	245	282	24.9	34%	68%	5.34	38	22	39	3.4	4.9	**1.5**	8%	1.0	-23.7	21	$2
ERA Potl	50%	1st Half		9	5	0	89	53	6.66	1.72	337			24.3	37%	60%					2.5	5.3	**2.1**		0.9	-24.6	37	($0)
LIMA Plan	C+	2nd Half		3	6	0	84	42	4.34	1.63	290			25.5	31%	77%	5.63	38	22	39	4.3	4.5	**1.0**	9%	1.2	0.9	11	$1
+/- Score	-8	08	Proj	**3**	**6**	**0**	**70**	**41**	**5.14**	**1.56**	**293**			**24.1**	**32%**	**69%**	**5.03**	**41**	**20**	**38**	**3.5**	**5.3**	**1.5**	**10%**	**1.2**	**-5.5**	**25**	**$1**

3-6, 3.64 ERA in 84 IP at WAS MLB ERA was all smoke and mirrors. xERA hasn't been below 5.00 since 2003 and Dom hit a 5-year low. Hope that someone else drafts him so you can enjoy watching the devastation.

Reyes,Al

Reyes,Al				W	L	Sv	IP	K	ERA	WHIP	OBA	vL	vR	BF/G	H%	S%	xERA	G	L	F	Ctl	Dom	Cmd	hr/f	hr/9	RAR	BPV	R$
RH Reliever		03	NYY	* 1	1	2	34	26	3.71	1.35	250			5.2	30%	73%	3.62				3.7	6.9	**1.9**		0.5	3.4	69	$3
Age	38	04	STL	* 4	3	37	74	68	2.92	1.20	240			4.4	29%	80%	3.36				2.8	8.3	**3.0**		0.9	12.3	92	$20
Decline		05	STL	4	2	3	62	67	2.17	0.93	178	174	172	3.7	23%	81%	3.48	34	15	50	2.9	9.7	**3.4**	7%	0.7	15.9	126	$12
Type	Pwr xFB	06		0	0	0	0	0	0.00	0.00																		
Reliability	0	07	TAM	2	4	26	61	70	4.89	1.15	223	240	187	4.1	26%	65%	3.88	20	19	61	3.1	10.4	**3.3**	14%	1.9	-2.9	85	$15
ERA Potl	65%	1st Half		1	1	17	32	38	3.09	0.94	174			3.7	21%	76%	3.59	22	16	62	3.1	10.7	**3.5**	11%	1.4	5.6	115	$11
LIMA Plan	B	2nd Half		1	3	9	29	32	6.90	1.39	270			4.4	31%	56%	4.21	19	22	59	3.1	10.0	**3.2**	17%	2.5	-8.5	53	$4
+/- Score	10	08	Proj	**3**	**3**	**13**	**58**	**61**	**4.34**	**1.24**	**241**			**4.2**	**30%**	**70%**	**4.14**	**25**	**18**	**57**	**3.1**	**9.5**	**3.1**	**10%**	**1.4**	**2.6**	**86**	**$10**

Two reasons why he's a poor choice for a closer:
1. Extreme flyball pitcher. You don't want closers yielding HRs.
2. Poor strand rate. A closer has nobody to blame but himself for a low S%.

Reyes,Anthony

Reyes,Anthony				W	L	Sv	IP	K	ERA	WHIP	OBA	vL	vR	BF/G	H%	S%	xERA	G	L	F	Ctl	Dom	Cmd	hr/f	hr/9	RAR	BPV	R$
RH Starter		03		0	0	0	0	0	0.00	0.00											0.0	0.0						
Age	26	04	aa	6	2	0	74	90	3.28	1.09	246			24.8	35%	69%	2.70				1.6	10.9	**6.9**		0.4	9.7	206	$11
Growth		05	STL	* 8	7	0	141	132	3.82	1.10	230	125	148	21.0	28%	67%	3.91	35	13	52	2.3	8.4	**3.7**	7%	0.9	7.4	110	$16
Type	Pwr xFB	06	STL	* 11	9	0	169	143	4.20	1.25	259	278	249	23.5	30%	72%	4.11	35	20	46	2.4	7.6	**3.2**	12%	1.4	5.9	72	$16
Reliability	17	07	STL	* 3	15	0	144	99	5.49	1.37	259	290	234	22.0	28%	62%	4.80	35	21	44	3.5	6.2	**1.8**	10%	1.3	-18.9	40	$3
ERA Potl	65%	1st Half		1	11	0	85	59	5.40	1.29	257			23.9	29%	58%	4.49	40	18	43	2.9	6.2	**2.2**	8%	1.0	-10.2	58	$2
LIMA Plan	C+	2nd Half		2	4	0	59	40	5.62	1.48	261			19.8	27%	67%	5.27	28	25	47	4.3	6.2	**1.4**	13%	1.8	-8.6	17	$1
+/- Score	22	08	Proj	**7**	**10**	**0**	**145**	**119**	**4.72**	**1.29**	**254**			**21.8**	**29%**	**66%**	**4.34**	**34**	**21**	**45**	**3.0**	**7.4**	**2.5**	**10%**	**1.2**	**1.0**	**63**	**$10**

2-14, 6.04 ERA, 107 IP in STL Third consecutive season of Cmd erosion, continuing in 2nd half, raises gigantic red flag. xERA says he could rebound some, but caution is warranted.

Reyes,Dennys

Reyes,Dennys				W	L	Sv	IP	K	ERA	WHIP	OBA	vL	vR	BF/G	H%	S%	xERA	G	L	F	Ctl	Dom	Cmd	hr/f	hr/9	RAR	BPV	R$
LH Reliever		03	PIT	* 2	1	2	41	36	5.27	1.68	247	118	394	4.2	32%	66%	4.06				6.8	7.9	**1.2**		0.2	-5.0	71	$1
Age	31	04	KC	4	8	0	108	91	4.75	1.52	272	316	254	12.0	32%	70%	4.12	51	17	32	4.2	7.6	**1.8**	11%	1.0	-4.2	54	$4
Peak		05	SD	3	2	0	43	35	5.21	2.06	319	208	359	6.0	38%	74%	4.41	65	17	18	6.7	7.3	**1.1**	11%	0.6	-5.1	39	($1)
Type	Pwr xGB	06	MIN	* 6	0	0	68	59	0.80	1.01	208	148	244	3.8	26%	95%	2.58	69	11	20	2.4	7.8	**3.2**	8%	0.4	31.6	116	$15
Reliability	1	07	MIN	2	1	0	29	21	3.99	1.88	292	273	364	2.8	35%	78%	4.70	64	13	22	6.5	6.5	**1.0**	5%	0.3	1.9	47	$1
ERA Potl	45%	1st Half		1	1	0	17	12	4.76	1.88	315			2.9	37%	74%	3.93	70	13	17	5.3	6.4	**1.2**	10%	0.5	-0.5	40	$0
LIMA Plan	B	2nd Half		1	0	0	12	9	2.93	1.87	257			2.7	32%	83%	5.80	54	14	31	8.0	6.6	**0.8**	0%	0.0	2.4	60	$1
+/- Score	-18	08	Proj	**3**	**3**	**0**	**58**	**46**	**4.50**	**1.60**	**268**			**4.2**	**32%**	**72%**	**4.02**	**62**	**14**	**24**	**5.1**	**7.1**	**1.4**	**9%**	**0.6**	**3.4**	**55**	**$3**

After tantalizing 2006, reverted to previous form. 60%+ GB rate will hide a lot of ills, but as long as he can't find the plate, he's high risk. There are much better LIMA choices.

Reyes,Jo-jo

Reyes,Jo-jo				W	L	Sv	IP	K	ERA	WHIP	OBA	vL	vR	BF/G	H%	S%	xERA	G	L	F	Ctl	Dom	Cmd	hr/f	hr/9	RAR	BPV	R$
LH Starter		03		0	0	0	0	0	0.00	0.00																		
Age	23	04		0	0	0	0	0	0.00	0.00																		
Growth		05		0	0	0	0	0	0.00	0.00																		
Type	Pwr	06		0	0	0	0	0	0.00	0.00																		
Reliability	0	07	ATL	* 14	3	0	160	121	4.34	1.48	260	129	317	23.5	30%	73%	4.74	45	15	40	4.4	6.8	**1.5**	9%	1.0	1.8	47	$11
ERA Potl	45%	1st Half		9	1	0	91	76	4.15	1.51	266			25.3	32%	74%					4.4	7.5	**1.7**		0.8	3.1	59	$7
LIMA Plan	C+	2nd Half		5	2	0	69	45	4.59	1.44	251			21.4	27%	71%	4.93	45	15	40	4.5	5.9	**1.3**	11%	1.2	-1.3	33	$4
+/- Score	-12	08	Proj	**3**	**3**	**0**	**58**	**42**	**5.12**	**1.57**	**275**			**23.7**	**31%**	**69%**	**4.92**	**45**	**15**	**40**	**4.5**	**6.5**	**1.4**	**10%**	**1.1**	**-3.7**	**37**	**$1**

2-2, 6.22 ERA in 51 IP at ATL Rushed to the majors because of injuries in ATL rotation, and clearly wasn't ready. First challenge is to improve his control. From there, everything else potentially falls into place.

Rhodes,Arthur

Rhodes,Arthur				W	L	Sv	IP	K	ERA	WHIP	OBA	vL	vR	BF/G	H%	S%	xERA	G	L	F	Ctl	Dom	Cmd	hr/f	hr/9	RAR	BPV	R$
LH Reliever		03	SEA	3	3	3	54	48	4.17	1.31	258	269	243	3.4	32%	69%	3.85	43	22	35	3.0	8.0	**2.7**	7%	0.7	2.4	87	$6
Age	38	04	OAK	3	3	9	38	34	5.18	1.75	299	314	283	4.8	33%	78%	4.89	40	17	43	4.9	8.0	**1.6**	18%	2.1	-3.5	14	$4
Decline		05	CLE	3	1	0	43	43	2.09	1.04	214	286	155	3.6	28%	81%	3.32	41	23	36	2.5	9.0	**3.6**	5%	0.4	12.1	129	$8
Type	Pwr FB	06	PHI	0	5	4	45	48	5.38	1.70	269	290	246	3.8	36%	67%	4.78	36	22	41	6.0	9.6	**1.6**	4%	0.4	-5.0	80	$1
Reliability	0	07	SEA	0	0	0	0	0	0.00	0.00																		
ERA Potl		1st Half		0	0	0	0	0	0.00	0.00																		
LIMA Plan		2nd Half		0	0	0	0	0	0.00	0.00																		
+/- Score		08	Proj	**1**	**2**	**0**	**29**	**27**	**4.74**	**1.51**	**265**			**3.9**	**32%**	**72%**	**4.35**	**40**	**20**	**40**	**4.4**	**8.5**	**1.9**	**12%**	**1.3**	**0.5**	**56**	**$1**

Should return from TJ surgery in early 2008, but at his age, full recovery could take longer. Control is the key to future success. High risk, low reward at this point, which means don't bother drafting him.

Rincon,Juan

Rincon,Juan				W	L	Sv	IP	K	ERA	WHIP	OBA	vL	vR	BF/G	H%	S%	xERA	G	L	F	Ctl	Dom	Cmd	hr/f	hr/9	RAR	BPV	R$
RH Reliever		03	MIN	5	6	0	85	63	3.71	1.32	236	222	239	6.2	28%	72%	4.63	42	17	41	4.0	6.7	**1.7**	5%	0.5	8.6	67	$8
Age	29	04	MIN	11	6	2	82	106	2.63	1.02	184	148	206	4.2	27%	76%	2.86	45	16	39	3.5	11.6	**3.3**	7%	0.5	18.2	141	$18
Pre-Peak		05	MIN	6	6	0	77	84	2.45	1.21	225	218	228	4.2	31%	79%	3.26	48	20	32	3.5	9.8	**2.8**	3%	0.2	18.2	121	$12
Type	Pwr	06	MIN	3	1	1	74	65	2.91	1.35	267	222	303	4.2	34%	78%	3.54	51	22	28	2.9	7.9	**2.7**	3%	0.2	15.0	99	$8
Reliability	24	07	MIN	3	3	0	60	49	5.13	1.56	279	313	236	4.2	32%	70%	4.38	49	16	36	4.2	7.4	**1.8**	14%	1.4	-4.6	40	$2
ERA Potl	55%	1st Half		3	1	0	28	23	4.18	1.61	288			4.2	33%	80%	4.48	46	18	37	4.2	7.4	**1.8**	16%	1.6	1.1	31	$2
LIMA Plan	B+	2nd Half		0	2	0	32	26	5.96	1.51	270			4.3	31%	61%	4.28	52	13	35	4.3	7.4	**1.7**	12%	1.1	-5.7	48	($0)
+/- Score	19	08	Proj	**3**	**3**	**0**	**58**	**52**	**3.88**	**1.41**	**262**			**4.3**	**32%**	**74%**	**3.91**	**49**	**18**	**34**	**3.7**	**8.1**	**2.2**	**9%**	**0.8**	**4.2**	**73**	**$5**

Seven bad pitches. That's the difference between his 3% hr/f in '05-'06 and his 14% hr/f this year. Call it a correction, call it a debacle, but with eroding Ctl and Dom, call it concerning. Will rebound, but not all the way.

Riske,David

Riske,David				W	L	Sv	IP	K	ERA	WHIP	OBA	vL	vR	BF/G	H%	S%	xERA	G	L	F	Ctl	Dom	Cmd	hr/f	hr/9	RAR	BPV	R$
RH Reliever		03	CLE	2	2	8	74	82	2.31	0.97	199	145	241	4.2	25%	84%	3.11	37	22	41	2.4	10.0	**4.1**	12%	1.1	20.2	128	$15
Age	31	04	CLE	7	3	5	77	78	3.74	1.43	241	224	255	4.7	29%	79%	4.37	36	18	45	4.8	9.1	**1.9**	12%	1.3	6.6	63	$10
Peak		05	CLE	3	4	1	72	48	3.12	0.97	213	210	204	4.8	22%	76%	3.78	42	20	38	1.9	6.0	**3.2**	14%	1.4	11.2	74	$10
Type	FB	06	2AL	1	2	0	44	28	3.89	1.30	244	280	224	4.5	26%	75%	4.77	36	22	42	3.5	5.7	**1.6**	11%	1.2	3.6	38	$3
Reliability	20	07	KC	1	4	4	70	52	2.45	1.26	237	202	265	4.5	27%	86%	4.39	41	17	41	3.5	6.7	**1.9**	9%	1.0	17.6	57	$9
ERA Potl	30%	1st Half		1	2	3	36	29	2.50	1.39	251			4.3	29%	87%	4.42	42	20	39	4.0	7.3	**1.8**	10%	1.0	8.9	56	$5
LIMA Plan	C+	2nd Half		0	2	1	34	23	2.40	1.13	221			4.7	24%	85%	4.36	41	14	44	2.9	6.1	**2.1**	9%	1.1	8.7	59	$4
+/- Score	-77	08	Proj	**2**	**4**	**5**	**73**	**53**	**4.10**	**1.35**	**260**			**4.7**	**29%**	**73%**	**4.50**	**40**	**19**	**41**	**3.2**	**6.6**	**2.0**	**10%**	**1.1**	**-0.0**	**52**	**$7**

Why a sub-3.00 ERA is history:
- Strand rate likely to regress.
- Borderline command
- Rising FB rate in 2nd half

Has been outperforming his xERA for years; eventually his luck will run out. Why not 2008?

Rivera,Mariano

Rivera,Mariano				W	L	Sv	IP	K	ERA	WHIP	OBA	vL	vR	BF/G	H%	S%	xERA	G	L	F	Ctl	Dom	Cmd	hr/f	hr/9	RAR	BPV	R$
RH Reliever		03	NYY	5	2	40	70	63	1.67	1.01	236	197	283	4.3	30%	85%	2.80	54	20	26	1.3	8.1	**6.3**	6%	0.4	24.6	177	$27
Age	38	04	NYY	4	2	53	78	66	1.96	1.09	228	234	215	4.2	29%	83%	3.13	60	11	29	2.3	7.6	**3.3**	5%	0.3	23.9	114	$30
Decline		05	NYY	7	4	43	78	80	1.38	0.87	185	177	176	4.2	25%	85%	2.62	57	14	29	2.1	9.2	**4.4**	4%	0.2	28.8	160	$31
Type	GB	06	NYY	5	5	34	75	55	1.80	0.96	224	194	248	4.6	27%	83%	3.21	54	16	30	1.3	6.6	**5.0**	5%	0.4	25.5	144	$25
Reliability	49	07	NYY	3	4	30	71	74	3.16	1.12	253	255	241	4.3	33%	72%	2.76	53	19	29	1.5	9.3	**6.2**	7%	0.5	11.9	175	$20
ERA Potl	60%	1st Half		2	3	9	29	27	4.03	1.14	255			4.2	31%	67%	3.09	51	17	32	1.6	8.4	**5.4**	11%	0.9	1.7	140	$7
LIMA Plan	B	2nd Half		1	1	21	42	47	2.55	1.11	251			4.4	35%	76%	2.54	54	20	26	1.5	10.0	**6.7**	3%	0.2	10.2	199	$13
+/- Score	14	08	Proj	**4**	**4**	**38**	**73**	**68**	**2.61**	**1.05**	**236**			**4.4**	**30%**	**77%**	**2.88**	**54**	**17**	**29**	**1.6**	**8.4**	**5.2**	**9%**	**0.6**	**14.5**	**150**	**$24**

Others think rising ERA is the beginning of the end. You see high h%, strong 2nd half, and best BPV since 2003. Age and minor injuries advise caution, but he's still among the elite. Bid with confidence.

HAROLD NICHOLS

Rivera,Saul			W	L	Sv	IP	K	ERA	WHIP	OBA	vL	vR	BF/G	H%	S%	xERA	G	L	F	Ctl	Dom	Cmd	hr/f	hr/9	RAR	BPV	R$
RH Reliever		03	0	0	0	0	0	0.00	0.00																		
Age	30	04 aa	2	3	4	54	30	7.08	2.23	358			6.3	39%	69%	8.10				5.9	4.9	0.8		1.1	-18.2	-4	($5)
Peak		05 aa	3	3	9	76	50	3.27	1.53	304			8.5	35%	79%	4.72				2.7	5.9	2.2		0.4	9.7	62	$7
Type	Pwr	06 WAS *	4	1	2	88	61	3.01	1.52	264	194	290	5.9	31%	81%	4.83	46	19	35	4.6	6.2	1.3	5%	0.5	16.1	52	$7
Reliability	32	07 WAS	4	6	3	93	64	3.68	1.40	251	271	244	4.7	30%	71%	4.46	50	18	32	4.1	6.2	1.5	1%	0.1	8.6	71	$7
ERA Potl	50%	1st Half	2	2	3	44	29	3.68	1.16	230			4.5	27%	66%	4.23	47	15	38	2.9	5.9	2.1	2%	0.2	4.0	82	$5
LIMA Plan	C	2nd Half	2	4	0	49	35	3.67	1.61	270			4.9	33%	75%	4.64	52	21	27	5.1	6.4	1.3	0%	0.0	4.5	66	$2
+/- Score	-28	08 Proj	3	3	0	73	49	4.10	1.50	268			5.5	31%	73%	4.62	49	19	33	4.2	6.1	1.4	7%	0.6	-2.0	49	$3

Managed to post an acceptable ERA despite control issues because of his growing GB tendency. Allowed just 1 HR all season... THAT won't happen again. A sub-4.00 ERA is a huge risk as well.

Robertson,Nate			W	L	Sv	IP	K	ERA	WHIP	OBA	vL	vR	BF/G	H%	S%	xERA	G	L	F	Ctl	Dom	Cmd	hr/f	hr/9	RAR	BPV	R$
LH Starter		03 DET *	10	9	0	199	119	4.48	1.51	292	300	307	27.6	32%	72%	4.60	46	21	32	3.2	5.4	1.7	9%	0.9	1.2	38	$9
Age	30	04 DET	12	10	1	196	155	4.91	1.41	275	252	279	25.0	31%	69%	3.90	50	17	33	3.0	7.1	2.3	15%	1.4	-11.5	51	$12
Peak		05 DET	7	16	0	196	122	4.50	1.36	267	244	272	26.2	29%	71%	4.17	49	20	30	3.0	5.6	1.9	15%	1.3	-3.0	36	$10
Type		06 DET	13	13	0	208	137	3.85	1.31	260	181	284	27.5	28%	75%	4.17	47	20	33	2.9	5.9	2.0	13%	1.3	18.2	44	$19
Reliability	91	07 DET	9	13	0	178	119	4.76	1.47	284	296	278	26.0	32%	70%	4.58	45	18	37	3.2	6.0	1.9	10%	1.1	-5.6	41	$9
ERA Potl	50%	1st Half	4	6	0	71	38	4.82	1.62	308			24.8	33%	73%	4.81	50	18	33	3.3	4.8	1.5	11%	1.1	-2.7	19	$2
LIMA Plan	C	2nd Half	5	7	0	107	81	4.72	1.38	268			27.0	31%	68%	4.41	41	18	41	3.1	6.8	2.2	10%	1.1	-2.9	56	$7
+/- Score	-3	08 Proj	10	13	0	189	125	4.49	1.41	275			26.3	30%	71%	4.38	46	19	35	3.1	6.0	2.0	11%	1.1	2.8	42	$12

Extremely reliable, just not very good. 2006 now looks like an outlier thanks to 75% strand rate. Should continue at pre-2006 levels, but increasing FB rate says things could get worse first.

Rodney,Fernando			W	L	Sv	IP	K	ERA	WHIP	OBA	vL	vR	BF/G	H%	S%	xERA	G	L	F	Ctl	Dom	Cmd	hr/f	hr/9	RAR	BPV	R$
RH Reliever		03 aaa	1	1	23	40	49	1.85	1.00	191			4.1	30%	79%	1.44				3.0	11.1	3.7		0.0	12.6	161	$15
Age	31	04 DET	0	0	0	0	0	0.00	0.00											0.0	0.0						
Peak		05 DET	2	3	9	44	42	2.86	1.27	239	265	219	4.7	29%	82%	3.64	40	28	31	3.5	8.6	2.5	13%	1.0	8.2	80	$8
Type	Pwr	06 DET	7	4	7	71	65	3.54	1.19	203	202	192	4.6	25%	72%	3.57	57	12	31	4.3	8.2	1.9	10%	0.8	8.9	81	$13
Reliability	0	07 DET	2	6	1	51	54	4.26	1.32	243	247	231	4.5	32%	69%	3.55	45	19	35	3.7	9.6	2.6	11%	0.9	1.5	91	$5
ERA Potl	65%	1st Half	1	5	1	28	25	5.46	1.46	275			4.5	32%	67%	4.00	44	21	35	3.5	8.0	2.3	17%	1.6	-3.3	48	$1
LIMA Plan	A+	2nd Half	1	1	0	23	29	2.78	1.15	200			4.4	31%	73%	3.00	48	17	35	4.0	11.5	2.9	0%	0.0	4.8	145	$4
+/- Score	34	08 Proj	4	6	5	73	77	3.45	1.23	223			4.5	30%	73%	3.41	49	18	33	3.8	9.5	2.5	8%	0.6	9.8	101	$11

Blame shoulder tendinitis and a touch of acute gopheritis for his poor 1st half. Overall numbers obscure outstanding 2nd half. History of strong Cmd and xERA say big rebound coming if health allows.

Rodriguez,Francisco			W	L	Sv	IP	K	ERA	WHIP	OBA	vL	vR	BF/G	H%	S%	xERA	G	L	F	Ctl	Dom	Cmd	hr/f	hr/9	RAR	BPV	R$
RH Reliever		03 ANA	8	3	2	86	95	3.03	0.99	171	186	156	5.7	20%	77%	3.12	43	22	35	3.7	9.9	2.7	17%	1.3	15.8	100	$17
Age	26	04 ANA	4	1	12	84	123	1.82	1.00	177	213	127	4.8	30%	82%	2.52	44	19	37	3.5	13.2	3.7	3%	0.2	27.0	170	$20
Growth		05 ANA	2	5	45	67	91	2.68	1.15	192	213	153	4.1	28%	81%	2.92	46	17	38	4.3	12.2	2.8	13%	0.9	14.0	121	$25
Type	Pwr FB	06 LAA	2	3	47	73	98	1.73	1.10	202	215	179	4.2	30%	89%	3.07	39	14	47	3.5	12.1	3.5	8%	0.7	25.5	138	$28
Reliability	70	07 LAA	5	2	40	67	90	2.81	1.25	209	187	217	4.4	32%	78%	3.22	43	17	40	4.5	12.0	2.6	5%	0.4	14.1	129	$24
ERA Potl	55%	1st Half	1	2	22	33	49	2.45	1.18	212			4.1	34%	81%	2.36	52	19	29	3.8	13.4	3.5	10%	0.5	8.3	150	$13
LIMA Plan	C+	2nd Half	4	0	18	34	41	3.15	1.31	205			4.7	30%	75%	4.09	36	14	50	5.2	10.8	2.1	2%	0.3	5.7	114	$12
+/- Score	16	08 Proj	4	3	40	73	96	2.98	1.24	215			4.5	31%	80%	3.22	42	16	42	4.2	11.9	2.8	10%	0.9	11.4	117	$24

Looks vintage, but there were 2nd half warning signs: Rising FB rate, Ctl struggles, xERA. 4-year trend of BA vs. RH also a concern. Maybe an abberation, but worth monitoring in case it's not.

Rodriguez,Wandy			W	L	Sv	IP	K	ERA	WHIP	OBA	vL	vR	BF/G	H%	S%	xERA	G	L	F	Ctl	Dom	Cmd	hr/f	hr/9	RAR	BPV	R$
LH Starter		03	0	0	0	0	0	0.00	0.00											0.0	0.0						
Age	29	04 aa	11	6	0	142	86	5.98	1.85	334			26.1	37%	69%	6.77				3.9	5.5	1.4		1.2	-28.7	14	($2)
Pre-Peak		05 HOU *	14	12	0	177	118	5.42	1.50	279	275	273	23.1	30%	67%	4.46	46	23	31	3.7	6.0	1.6	16%	1.4	-25.6	26	$6
Type	Pwr	06 HOU *	11	12	0	161	110	5.97	1.65	294	262	298	21.0	33%	65%	4.82	45	22	33	4.3	6.1	1.4	11%	1.1	-29.6	30	$1
Reliability	47	07 HOU	9	13	0	183	158	4.58	1.32	258	252	254	25.0	31%	68%	4.04	41	19	40	3.1	7.8	2.5	10%	1.1	-3.5	71	$13
ERA Potl	55%	1st Half	4	7	0	89	78	4.55	1.28	266			24.9	31%	68%	3.78	43	18	39	2.3	7.9	3.4	12%	1.2	-1.4	84	$7
LIMA Plan	C	2nd Half	5	6	0	94	80	4.61	1.36	250			25.0	30%	68%	4.30	40	19	41	3.7	7.7	2.1	9%	1.1	-2.1	65	$6
+/- Score	15	08 Proj	11	13	0	185	151	4.49	1.40	267			23.5	31%	70%	4.17	43	20	36	3.4	7.4	2.2	11%	1.0	5.1	59	$12

Primed for a breakout?
PRO: Home ERA of 2.94, Dom and Ctl growth. PQS DOM/DIS of 48/13, improving xERA
CON: Road ERA of 6.37. Ctl rose above 4.0 in Aug/Sept.
UP: Sub-4.00 ERA

Rogers,Kenny			W	L	Sv	IP	K	ERA	WHIP	OBA	vL	vR	BF/G	H%	S%	xERA	G	L	F	Ctl	Dom	Cmd	hr/f	hr/9	RAR	BPV	R$
LH Starter		03 MIN	13	8	0	195	116	4.57	1.42	292	251	307	25.6	32%	70%	4.61	43	18	39	2.3	5.4	2.3	9%	1.0	-1.1	47	$12
Age	43	04 TEX	18	9	0	213	127	5.07	1.52	300	292	292	27.0	33%	69%	4.67	43	21	35	2.8	5.4	1.9	10%	1.1	-16.7	33	$10
Decline		05 TEX	14	8	0	195	87	3.46	1.32	271	201	291	27.6	29%	75%	4.62	47	20	33	2.4	4.0	1.6	7%	0.7	21.9	39	$16
Type	Con	06 DET	17	8	0	204	99	3.84	1.26	253	200	268	25.1	27%	73%	4.38	50	18	32	2.7	4.4	1.6	11%	1.0	18.1	34	$21
Reliability	20	07 DET	3	4	0	63	36	4.43	1.43	268	197	289	24.9	29%	72%	4.49	48	23	29	3.6	5.1	1.4	13%	1.1	0.6	28	$3
ERA Potl	40%	1st Half	1	0	0	6	5	0.00	0.33	106			19.5	14%	100%	1.96	57	21	21	0.0	7.5		0%	0.0	3.3	79	$2
LIMA Plan	C	2nd Half	2	4	0	57	31	4.89	1.54	282			25.4	30%	71%	4.79	47	23	30	3.9	4.9	1.2	14%	1.3	-2.7	16	$1
+/- Score	-44	08 Proj	9	10	0	164	85	4.57	1.47	277			26.6	30%	71%	4.68	49	21	30	3.5	4.7	1.3	11%	1.0	-3.7	24	$8

Shoulder surgery derailed first half, then came back to earth upon his return. Age, declining Cmd, xERA all say he'll stay grounded. Really, xERA tells you all you need to know.

Romero,J.C.			W	L	Sv	IP	K	ERA	WHIP	OBA	vL	vR	BF/G	H%	S%	xERA	G	L	F	Ctl	Dom	Cmd	hr/f	hr/9	RAR	BPV	R$
LH Reliever		03 MIN	2	0	0	63	50	5.00	1.71	271	214	314	4.0	32%	72%	4.82	51	19	30	6.0	7.1	1.2	12%	1.0	-3.7	39	$1
Age	31	04 MIN	7	4	1	74	69	3.52	1.34	226	261	199	4.3	29%	74%	3.70	56	15	29	4.6	8.4	1.8	7%	0.5	8.3	84	$9
Peak		05 MIN	4	3	0	57	48	3.47	1.56	237	198	268	3.8	28%	81%	4.51	55	14	31	6.2	7.6	1.2	12%	0.9	6.3	50	$4
Type	Pwr xGB	06 LAA	1	2	0	48	31	6.74	1.77	296	202	382	3.5	34%	60%	4.82	57	16	27	5.2	5.8	1.1	7%	0.6	-12.9	37	($2)
Reliability	25	07 2TM	2	2	1	56	42	1.92	1.40	197	208	198	3.3	24%	88%	4.53	60	11	29	6.4	6.7	1.1	7%	0.5	17.7	64	$6
ERA Potl	20%	1st Half	1	0	1	20	11	3.15	1.95	299			4.2	33%	86%	6.02	55	10	34	6.8	5.0	0.7	8%	0.9	3.2	13	$1
LIMA Plan	C	2nd Half	1	2	0	36	31	1.24	1.10	128			2.9	16%	90%	3.73	64	11	25	6.2	7.7	1.2	5%	0.2	14.4	94	$6
+/- Score	******	08 Proj	2	4	0	73	54	4.22	1.61	252			3.5	30%	75%	4.66	58	13	29	6.0	6.7	1.1	9%	0.7	-1.9	46	$2

Unsustainable 2nd half H% and S% produced this miracle. xERA and poor Ctl say that he'll go right back to familiar territory. These "luck" gauges are all pct. plays, but I'd lay odds on a major ERA spike at about 99%.

Ryan,B.J.			W	L	Sv	IP	K	ERA	WHIP	OBA	vL	vR	BF/G	H%	S%	xERA	G	L	F	Ctl	Dom	Cmd	hr/f	hr/9	RAR	BPV	R$
LH Reliever		03 BAL	4	1	0	50	63	3.42	1.38	230	186	273	2.8	34%	74%	3.26	45	27	28	4.9	11.3	2.3	3%	0.2	6.8	121	$7
Age	32	04 BAL	4	6	3	87	122	2.28	1.14	207	94	252	4.6	33%	81%	2.81	41	22	38	3.6	12.6	3.5	6%	0.4	23.1	150	$15
Peak		05 BAL	1	4	36	70	100	2.44	1.14	215	211	206	4.1	34%	80%	2.58	45	21	34	3.3	12.8	3.8	8%	0.5	16.7	154	$22
Type	Pwr	06 TOR	2	2	38	72	86	1.37	0.86	171	120	182	4.2	25%	86%	2.93	37	20	43	2.5	10.7	4.3	4%	0.4	28.3	164	$27
Reliability	2	07 TOR	0	2	3	4	3	12.56	2.56	366	333	333	4.7	40%	50%	7.68	24	35	41	8.4	6.3	0.8	15%	2.1	-4.3	-28	($0)
ERA Potl	85%	1st Half	0	2	3	4	3	13.50	2.75	383			4.5	42%	50%	7.98	24	35	41	9.0	6.8	0.8	16%	2.3	-4.4	-33	($0)
LIMA Plan	B	2nd Half	0	0	0	0	0	0.00	0.00																		
+/- Score	169	08 Proj	2	2	13	44	43	3.10	1.24	232			4.1	30%	76%	3.73	41	22	37	3.5	8.9	2.5	7%	0.6	4.1	97	$10

Will probably miss first two months recovering from TJ surgery. Watch Dom when he returns. If it's back to pre-injury levels, he could be golden in second half. More likely doesn't return to vintage form until '09.

Sabathia,C.C.			W	L	Sv	IP	K	ERA	WHIP	OBA	vL	vR	BF/G	H%	S%	xERA	G	L	F	Ctl	Dom	Cmd	hr/f	hr/9	RAR	BPV	R$
LH Starter		03 CLE	13	9	0	197	141	3.61	1.30	255	275	248	27.7	29%	75%	4.33	43	19	39	3.0	6.4	2.1	8%	0.9	22.2	62	$20
Age	27	04 CLE	11	10	0	188	139	4.12	1.32	249	265	248	26.6	29%	71%	4.50	39	20	41	3.4	6.7	1.9	9%	1.0	7.3	57	$15
Pre-Peak		05 CLE	15	10	0	196	161	4.04	1.26	251	248	248	26.4	30%	70%	3.64	49	20	31	2.8	7.4	2.6	11%	0.9	8.1	78	$20
Type		06 CLE	12	11	0	192	172	3.23	1.18	251	271	242	28.1	31%	75%	3.48	45	19	36	2.1	8.1	3.9	9%	0.8	31.5	111	$25
Reliability	77	07 CLE	19	7	0	241	209	3.21	1.14	259	203	275	28.8	32%	74%	3.42	45	18	37	1.4	7.8	5.6	8%	0.7	38.5	146	$33
ERA Potl	60%	1st Half	11	2	0	122	108	3.25	1.14	262			29.1	32%	75%	3.40	45	17	38	1.3	8.0	6.4	9%	0.9	19.0	157	$18
LIMA Plan	C	2nd Half	8	5	0	119	101	3.18	1.14	257			28.4	32%	73%	3.45	45	20	35	1.5	7.6	5.1	7%	0.6	19.5	137	$16
+/- Score	20	08 Proj	16	9	0	218	185	3.56	1.19	255			27.9	31%	73%	3.56	45	19	36	2.0	7.7	3.9	10%	0.9	25.1	104	$27

Superb Cmd and pinpoint Ctl fed great season. Deserves his place among the elite. Burnout is a concern with IP spike, history of high BF/G and post-season struggles. Expect some regression.

HAROLD NICHOLS

Saito,Takashi

		Yr	Tm	W	L	Sv	IP	K	ERA	WHIP	OBA	vL	vR	BF/G	H%	S%	xERA	G	L	F	Ctl	Dom	Cmd	hr/f	hr/9	RAR	BPV	R$
RH	Reliever	03	JPN	6	7	0	103	76	5.21	1.34	276			25.8	28%	70%	5.59				2.4	6.6	2.8		2.3	-10.4	29	$6
Age	38	04	JPN	2	5	0	44	39	9.65	1.93	356			13.3	36%	58%	10.02				3.3	8.0	2.4		4.1	-28.8	-40	($5)
Decline		05	JPN	3	4	0	106	98	4.75	1.46	285			22.1	33%	73%	5.41				3.1	8.3	2.7		1.7	-5.8	54	$4
Type	Pwr FB	06	LA	6	2	24	78	107	2.07	0.91	179	229	129	4.2	28%	78%	2.79	36	16	49	2.7	12.3	4.7	4%	0.3	23.2	181	$24
Reliability	22	07	LA	2	1	39	64	78	1.40	0.72	154	186	114	3.7	21%	88%	2.49	46	13	41	1.8	10.9	6.0	9%	0.7	24.0	195	$27
ERA Potl	40%	1st Half		1	0	21	32	41	1.41	0.75	189			3.8	26%	95%	2.23	48	11	41	0.8	11.5	13.7	14%	1.1	11.9	340	$14
LIMA Plan	C+	2nd Half		1	1	18	32	37	1.39	0.68	116			3.6	17%	81%	2.77	44	15	41	2.8	10.3	3.7	4%	0.3	12.1	163	$13
+/- Score	-78	08	Proj	3	2	30	58	67	2.79	1.03	212			5.1	28%	78%	3.12	42	14	44	2.5	10.4	4.2	10%	0.9	9.1	135	$19

Proved 2006 was no fluke by improving Cmd, GB rate and xERA. Expect regression as low H%, high S% return to normal. Shoulder tightness, age and viable alternatives in pen will increase risk. Be cautious.

Sampson,Chris

		Yr	Tm	W	L	Sv	IP	K	ERA	WHIP	OBA	vL	vR	BF/G	H%	S%	xERA	G	L	F	Ctl	Dom	Cmd	hr/f	hr/9	RAR	BPV	R$
RH	Starter	03		0	0	0	0	0	0.00	0.00																		
Age	29	04		0	0	0	0	0	0.00	0.00																		
Peak		05	aa	4	12	4	150	63	5.28	1.61	339			21.2	36%	68%	6.04				1.4	3.8	2.6		1.0	-18.0	35	($0)
Type	Con	06	aaa	12	3	4	125	54	3.17	1.19	274			19.0	29%	78%	3.94				1.1	3.9	3.6		1.0	20.9	69	$17
Reliability	17	07	HOU	7	8	0	122	51	4.59	1.38	287	291	292	21.8	29%	72%	4.73	47	17	36	2.2	3.8	1.7	13%	1.5	-2.4	12	$6
ERA Potl	40%	1st Half		6	5	0	90	36	3.70	1.26	266			25.1	27%	74%	4.69	47	16	37	2.1	3.6	1.7	9%	1.0	8.1	29	$8
LIMA Plan	D+	2nd Half		1	3	0	32	15	7.10	1.73	340			16.4	33%	67%	4.83	48	19	33	2.6	4.3	1.7	25%	2.8	-10.4	-38	($2)
+/- Score	-8	08	Proj	5	7	0	102	44	4.79	1.47	304			19.4	31%	70%	4.74	48	18	35	2.1	3.9	1.8	11%	1.2	-4.3	19	$3

The good news: Unlucky hr/f ruined 2nd half, so he'll get better. The bad news: As an extreme soft-tosser, he needs pinpoint Ctl to have any chance at success. But he's 29 and we can't wait around forever.

Sanchez,Anibal

		Yr	Tm	W	L	Sv	IP	K	ERA	WHIP	OBA	vL	vR	BF/G	H%	S%	xERA	G	L	F	Ctl	Dom	Cmd	hr/f	hr/9	RAR	BPV	R$
RH	Starter	03		0	0	0	0	0	0.00	0.00																		
Age	24	04		0	0	0	0	0	0.00	0.00																		
Growth		05	aa	3	5	0	57	54	4.41	1.38	281			22.3	35%	70%	4.46				2.5	8.5	3.4		0.9	-0.8	92	$4
Type	Pwr FB	06	FLA	* 13	9	0	199	155	3.48	1.33	252	229	202	25.7	30%	76%	4.36	45	14	41	3.5	7.0	2.0	7%	0.8	24.8	66	$19
Reliability	0	07	FLA	2	1	0	30	14	4.80	2.07	337	329	357	24.9	36%	78%	6.56	45	15	40	5.7	4.2	0.7	7%	0.9	-1.4	1	($1)
ERA Potl	45%	1st Half		2	1	0	30	14	4.80	2.07	337			24.9	36%	78%	6.56	45	15	40	5.7	4.2	0.7	7%	0.9	-1.4	1	($1)
LIMA Plan	D+	2nd Half		0	0	0	0	0	0.00	0.00																		
+/- Score	-24	08	Proj	5	5	0	87	67	3.83	1.47	275			23.9	32%	77%	4.51	45	15	40	3.6	6.9	1.9	9%	1.0	-1.2	51	$6

Had surgery for torn labrum on June 21, and we can only hope that everything that happened from April 1 to June 21 was a result of him pitching hurt. 2008 remains a bit of a question mark.

Sanchez,Jonathan

		Yr	Tm	W	L	Sv	IP	K	ERA	WHIP	OBA	vL	vR	BF/G	H%	S%	xERA	G	L	F	Ctl	Dom	Cmd	hr/f	hr/9	RAR	BPV	R$
LH	Reliever	03		0	0	0	0	0	0.00	0.00																		
Age	25	04		0	0	0	0	0	0.00	0.00																		
Growth		05		0	0	0	0	0	0.00	0.00																		
Type	Pwr FB	06	SF	* 7	4	2	95	96	3.79	1.22	210	256	248	8.6	28%	67%	4.10	36	20	45	4.3	9.1	2.1	3%	0.3	8.2	104	$12
Reliability	0	07	SF	* 1	5	0	72	84	5.03	1.54	269	197	321	8.3	36%	69%	3.90	39	22	39	4.5	10.5	2.3	11%	1.0	-5.3	82	$2
ERA Potl	70%	1st Half		1	1	0	31	38	3.19	1.32	194			5.3	26%	81%	3.96	33	24	44	5.8	11.0	1.9	13%	1.2	4.7	88	$3
LIMA Plan	B+	2nd Half		0	4	0	41	46	6.40	1.71	317			13.6	41%	62%	3.86	43	20	36	3.6	10.0	2.8	9%	0.9	-10.1	84	($1)
+/- Score	54	08	Proj	3	5	0	81	88	4.36	1.33	238			8.3	31%	69%	3.79	38	21	41	4.0	9.8	2.4	11%	1.0	6.0	88	$6

1-5, 5.88 ERA in 52 IP at SF
Much better than surface stats. Unlucky H%, low S% in 2nd half ruined his ERA but Ctl gain was a plus. That's the one thing standing in the way of him leveraging that great 80+ BPV.

Santana,Ervin

		Yr	Tm	W	L	Sv	IP	K	ERA	WHIP	OBA	vL	vR	BF/G	H%	S%	xERA	G	L	F	Ctl	Dom	Cmd	hr/f	hr/9	RAR	BPV	R$
RH	Starter	03	aa	1	1	0	29	21	4.70	1.27	238			20.4	25%	68%	4.11				3.5	6.5	1.8		1.5	-1.1	41	$2
Age	25	04	aa	2	1	0	43	41	3.75	1.44	270			23.5	34%	75%	4.16				3.5	8.5	2.4		0.6	3.2	84	$3
Growth		05	ANA	* 18	9	0	191	140	4.14	1.34	264	261	271	24.7	30%	72%	4.58	37	19	44	3.0	6.6	2.2	8%	1.0	5.5	59	$18
Type	Pwr FB	06	LAA	16	8	0	204	141	4.28	1.23	239	254	229	25.7	27%	67%	4.54	38	17	44	3.1	6.2	2.0	8%	0.9	7.0	59	$21
Reliability	36	07	LAA	* 9	15	0	182	152	5.94	1.60	302	284	292	24.9	35%	65%	4.73	36	19	46	3.4	7.5	2.2	11%	1.5	-32.3	41	$4
ERA Potl	60%	1st Half		5	8	0	96	70	5.25	1.48	285			26.4	31%	70%	4.82	35	18	47	3.2	6.6	2.1	13%	1.8	-8.8	27	$4
LIMA Plan	C	2nd Half		4	7	0	86	82	6.71	1.73	320			23.6	39%	62%	4.59	37	19	44	3.6	8.5	2.4	9%	1.2	-23.4	57	($1)
+/- Score	40	08	Proj	12	12	0	199	160	4.67	1.40	267			26.0	31%	70%	4.51	37	18	45	3.3	7.3	2.2	10%	1.3	-0.4	53	$14

7-14, 5.76 ERA, 150 IP at LAA
How bad were home/road splits?

	HOME	ROAD
Record	6-4	1-10
PQS Avg	3.9	2.0
DOM%	75%	29%
DIS%	8%	43%

Santana,Johan

		Yr	Tm	W	L	Sv	IP	K	ERA	WHIP	OBA	vL	vR	BF/G	H%	S%	xERA	G	L	F	Ctl	Dom	Cmd	hr/f	hr/9	RAR	BPV	R$
LH	Starter	03	MIN	12	3	0	158	169	3.08	1.10	222	191	227	14.1	28%	76%	3.68	28	23	49	2.7	9.6	3.6	9%	1.0	28.2	115	$25
Age	29	04	MIN	20	6	0	228	265	2.61	0.92	195	192	191	25.8	26%	77%	2.92	41	16	43	2.1	10.5	4.9	10%	0.9	51.4	153	$42
Pre-Peak		05	MIN	16	7	0	231	238	2.88	0.97	216	256	200	27.3	28%	74%	3.21	40	17	43	1.8	9.3	5.3	9%	0.9	42.5	153	$38
Type	Pwr FB	06	MIN	19	6	0	233	245	2.78	1.00	220	254	206	26.9	28%	77%	3.09	41	20	40	1.8	9.5	5.2	10%	0.9	51.2	149	$41
Reliability	92	07	MIN	15	13	0	219	235	3.33	1.07	229	197	234	26.5	28%	76%	3.28	38	18	44	2.1	9.7	4.5	13%	1.4	31.8	121	$33
ERA Potl	55%	1st Half		8	6	0	108	114	2.83	1.05	220			26.8	27%	81%	3.42	35	18	47	2.3	9.5	4.2	12%	1.3	22.3	119	$18
LIMA Plan	C	2nd Half		7	7	0	111	121	3.81	1.10	237			26.2	29%	72%	3.14	41	19	41	2.0	9.8	4.8	15%	1.5	9.5	124	$15
+/- Score	28	08	Proj	16	9	0	218	232	3.06	1.03	224			25.3	29%	75%	3.22	39	19	42	2.0	9.6	4.8	10%	1.0	34.3	141	$35

There were minor ticks in the BPIs -- FB rate and hr/f, Ctl, S% in 1st half -- that pushed around his '07 numbers. But there is nothing that screams WARNING. It's mostly just normal statistical fluctuation. Buy, buy, buy.

Santos,Victor

		Yr	Tm	W	L	Sv	IP	K	ERA	WHIP	OBA	vL	vR	BF/G	H%	S%	xERA	G	L	F	Ctl	Dom	Cmd	hr/f	hr/9	RAR	BPV	R$
RH	Reliever	03	aaa	5	4	1	108	54	4.83	1.67	318			24.8	35%	71%	5.52				3.2	4.5	1.4		0.7	-5.8	28	$1
Age	31	04	MIL	11	12	0	154	115	4.97	1.47	280	244	303	21.8	32%	68%	4.61	41	17	42	3.3	6.7	2.0	9%	1.1	-13.4	50	$7
Peak		05	MIL	4	13	0	141	89	4.59	1.51	278	259	277	21.6	30%	73%	4.82	42	23	36	3.8	5.7	1.5	12%	1.3	-6.0	26	$3
Type		06	PIT	5	9	0	115	81	5.71	1.67	316	264	361	21.1	35%	68%	4.64	44	22	35	3.3	6.3	1.9	12%	1.3	-17.3	33	($0)
Reliability	35	07	2TM	* 2	7	0	87	60	4.66	1.59	290	280	307	9.0	31%	76%	4.70	43	23	35	3.9	6.2	1.6	16%	1.7	-2.1	18	$2
ERA Potl	35%	1st Half		1	2	0	37	29	4.86	1.43	257			6.4	28%	70%	4.12	48	22	30	4.1	7.1	1.7	18%	1.5	-1.8	38	$1
LIMA Plan	C+	2nd Half		1	5	0	50	31	4.50	1.70	312			12.3	33%	80%	5.26	37	23	40	3.8	5.6	1.5	14%	1.8	-0.2	3	$0
+/- Score	-6	08	Proj	3	7	0	91	62	4.95	1.52	282			9.6	31%	70%	4.66	43	22	36	3.7	6.1	1.7	12%	1.3	-2.4	32	$0

1-6, 5.83 ERA in 63 IP at BAL/CIN.
Hard to believe he opened MLB career with 0.00 ERA in first 27 IP. That was in 2001. Now RHBs hit .300+ against him, he has chronic gopheritis and poor Cmd. Not rosterable.

Saunders,Joe

		Yr	Tm	W	L	Sv	IP	K	ERA	WHIP	OBA	vL	vR	BF/G	H%	S%	xERA	G	L	F	Ctl	Dom	Cmd	hr/f	hr/9	RAR	BPV	R$
LH	Starter	03		0	0	0	0	0	0.00	0.00																		
Age	26	04	aa	4	3	0	39	20	6.66	1.85	344			23.3	37%	65%	6.94				3.3	4.7	1.4		1.2	-11.2	8	($1)
Growth		05	a/a	10	7	0	160	88	4.00	1.47	290			26.0	32%	73%	4.55				2.8	5.0	1.7		0.6	6.1	44	$9
Type		06	LAA	* 17	7	0	205	132	3.48	1.27	254	220	274	25.3	29%	75%	4.12	48	20	32	2.8	5.8	2.1	8%	0.8	27.2	60	$23
Reliability	22	07	LAA	* 12	12	0	193	131	5.78	1.58	313	274	304	27.2	35%	64%	4.43	45	21	34	2.7	6.1	2.3	10%	1.1	-30.5	44	$5
ERA Potl	60%	1st Half		7	5	0	96	66	5.34	1.50	296			26.5	34%	64%	4.32	46	22	33	2.8	6.2	2.2	9%	0.8	-9.9	54	$4
LIMA Plan	C	2nd Half		5	7	0	97	65	6.22	1.66	329			27.9	36%	64%	4.51	45	20	34	2.5	6.0	2.4	12%	1.4	-20.6	35	($0)
+/- Score	39	08	Proj	9	7	0	131	86	4.41	1.44	287			25.9	32%	72%	4.32	46	20	34	2.8	5.9	2.2	10%	1.0	2.9	47	$9

8-5, 4.44 ERA in 107 IP at LAA
Excellent growth trend in Dom and Cmd could foreshadow a possible breakout. Chronically high H% is a concern, but with a little more luck...
UP: Sub-4.00 ERA

Schilling,Curt

		Yr	Tm	W	L	Sv	IP	K	ERA	WHIP	OBA	vL	vR	BF/G	H%	S%	xERA	G	L	F	Ctl	Dom	Cmd	hr/f	hr/9	RAR	BPV	R$
RH	Starter	03	ARI	8	9	0	168	194	2.95	1.05	233	255	210	27.8	31%	76%	2.85	39	25	36	1.7	10.4	6.1	11%	0.9	27.6	171	$24
Age	41	04	BOS	21	6	0	226	203	3.26	1.07	244	238	241	28.2	30%	73%	3.36	42	20	38	1.4	8.1	5.8	9%	0.9	32.6	149	$33
Decline		05	BOS	* 8	9	9	104	95	5.92	1.57	323	290	343	13.7	39%	63%	4.21	34	23	43	2.0	8.2	4.1	10%	1.2	-19.9	89	$7
Type	Con FB	06	BOS	15	7	0	204	183	3.97	1.22	277	277	275	27.2	33%	72%	3.56	40	20	40	1.2	8.1	6.5	11%	1.2	14.8	148	$24
Reliability	15	07	BOS	9	8	0	151	101	3.87	1.25	279	274	277	26.2	31%	74%	4.25	37	19	44	1.4	6.0	4.4	10%	1.3	11.8	90	$15
ERA Potl	55%	1st Half		6	4	0	94	71	4.21	1.36	291			26.8	33%	72%	4.20	40	18	42	1.8	6.8	3.7	9%	1.1	3.4	82	$8
LIMA Plan	C+	2nd Half		3	4	0	57	30	3.32	1.05	258			25.2	26%	76%	4.30	33	21	46	0.6	4.7	7.5	10%	1.4	8.4	147	$7
+/- Score	-5	08	Proj	10	9	0	160	111	4.01	1.29	278			23.2	31%	73%	4.31	37	20	43	1.9	6.3	3.4	10%	1.2	3.7	70	$15

Dom trend charts the erosion of his skills, but pinpoint control maintains his value. Rising FB rate is worrisome in Fenway, and there are the health issues. Still, you have to go $15 for the guts and the grit.

HAROLD NICHOLS

Schmidt,Jason

			W	L	Sv	IP	K	ERA	WHIP	OBA	vL	vR	BF/G	H%	S%	xERA	G	L	F	Ctl	Dom	Cmd	hr/f	hr/9	RAR	BPV	R$
RH	Starter	03 SF	17	5	0	207	208	2.35	0.96	207	197	204	27.7	27%	78%	3.34	36	20	44	2.0	9.0	**4.5**	6%	0.6	49.3	145	$36
Age	35	04 SF	18	7	0	225	251	3.20	1.08	206	191	212	28.1	28%	72%	3.17	46	15	39	3.1	10.0	**3.3**	9%	0.7	29.5	121	$32
Past Peak		05 SF	12	7	0	172	165	4.40	1.42	248	264	223	25.8	31%	70%	4.30	38	21	40	4.4	8.6	**1.9**	8%	0.8	-3.2	73	$12
Type	Pwr xFB	06 SF	11	9	0	213	180	3.59	1.26	239	262	215	27.9	29%	74%	4.26	37	19	43	3.4	7.6	**2.3**	8%	0.9	23.6	73	$20
Reliability	12	07 LA	1	4	0	26	22	6.23	1.77	304	250	333	20.3	35%	67%	5.30	34	19	47	4.8	7.6	**1.6**	10%	1.4	-5.8	31	($1)
ERA Potl	60%	1st Half	1	4	0	26	22	6.23	1.77	304			20.3	35%	67%	5.30	34	19	47	4.8	7.6	**1.6**	10%	1.4	-5.8	31	($1)
LIMA Plan	D+	2nd Half	0	0	0	0	0	0.00	0.00																		
+/- Score	8	08 Proj	**9**	**10**	**0**	**145**	**125**	**4.41**	**1.41**	**255**			**24.2**	**30%**	**72%**	**4.60**	**35**	**19**	**46**	**4.0**	**7.8**	**1.9**	**10%**	**1.2**	**-3.6**	**56**	**$10**

Shoulder surgery ended his season in June and will likely limit him in early '08. Negative trends -- declining Dom and BPV, rising FB rate and xERA -- make him high risk even when he's back to full strength.

Schoeneweis,Scott

			W	L	Sv	IP	K	ERA	WHIP	OBA	vL	vR	BF/G	H%	S%	xERA	G	L	F	Ctl	Dom	Cmd	hr/f	hr/9	RAR	BPV	R$
LH	Reliever	03 2AL	3	2	0	64	56	4.22	1.30	262	227	275	4.6	33%	66%	3.53	49	21	29	2.7	7.9	**2.9**	5%	0.4	2.4	99	$6
Age	34	04 CHW	6	9	0	112	69	5.61	1.59	290	244	303	25.3	31%	67%	4.95	44	19	36	3.9	5.5	**1.4**	12%	1.4	-16.4	19	$1
Past Peak		05 TOR	3	4	1	57	43	3.32	1.39	251	188	306	3.1	31%	75%	3.76	59	17	24	3.9	6.8	**1.7**	5%	0.3	7.4	72	$5
Type	Pwr GB	06 2TM	4	2	4	51	29	4.92	1.41	250	236	257	3.1	28%	65%	4.36	58	16	26	4.2	5.1	**1.2**	9%	0.7	-2.5	40	$4
Reliability	23	07 NYM	0	2	2	59	41	5.03	1.53	271	204	316	3.7	30%	70%	4.41	51	19	30	4.3	6.3	**1.5**	14%	1.2	-4.4	32	$1
ERA Potl	50%	1st Half	0	2	0	28	13	5.79	1.79	275			3.9	27%	71%	5.69	52	22	27	6.4	4.2	**0.7**	19%	1.6	-4.7	-10	($2)
LIMA Plan	C+	2nd Half	0	0	2	31	28	4.35	1.29	268			3.6	33%	68%	3.45	51	16	33	2.3	8.1	**3.5**	10%	0.9	0.3	98	$2
+/- Score	-6	08 Proj	**2**	**2**	**3**	**58**	**40**	**4.50**	**1.45**	**262**			**3.6**	**30%**	**70%**	**4.39**	**51**	**18**	**31**	**4.0**	**6.2**	**1.5**	**9%**	**0.8**	**0.0**	**49**	**$3**

2nd half rebound looks good, but two scary three-year trends here -- eroding Ctl and falling GB/rising FB rate. Not good for GB specialist who already gives up too many hits. There are safer LIMA choices.

Seanez,Rudy

			W	L	Sv	IP	K	ERA	WHIP	OBA	vL	vR	BF/G	H%	S%	xERA	G	L	F	Ctl	Dom	Cmd	hr/f	hr/9	RAR	BPV	R$
RH	Reliever	03 aaa	3	5	5	38	37	5.68	1.74	277			5.1	33%	70%	5.75				5.9	8.8	**1.5**		1.4	-6.1	41	$2
Age	39	04 2TM *	5	3	3	80	79	2.81	1.17	218	256	202	5.2	28%	79%	3.53	48	16	37	3.5	8.9	**2.5**	9%	0.8	15.2	95	$12
Decline		05 SD	7	1	0	60	84	2.70	1.18	224	231	212	4.3	34%	79%	2.87	37	23	39	3.3	12.6	**3.8**	8%	0.6	11.5	148	$11
Type	Pwr FB	06 2TM	3	3	0	53	54	4.92	1.70	280	266	273	5.0	34%	74%	4.87	31	24	45	5.4	9.2	**1.7**	12%	1.4	-2.6	49	$2
Reliability	0	07 LA	6	3	1	76	73	3.79	1.38	267	269	264	4.5	32%	77%	4.10	36	20	44	3.2	8.6	**2.7**	10%	1.2	6.0	75	$8
ERA Potl	45%	1st Half	4	1	0	37	37	3.41	1.41	282			4.7	36%	78%	3.83	36	24	39	2.7	9.0	**3.4**	7%	0.7	4.7	101	$4
LIMA Plan	C+	2nd Half	2	2	1	39	36	4.15	1.36	252			4.3	29%	76%	4.35	36	16	48	3.7	8.3	**2.3**	13%	1.6	1.3	53	$3
+/- Score	-9	08 Proj	**3**	**2**	**0**	**44**	**40**	**4.34**	**1.45**	**260**			**4.6**	**31%**	**72%**	**4.47**	**35**	**21**	**44**	**4.1**	**8.3**	**2.0**	**9%**	**1.0**	**-0.4**	**64**	**$3**

Another pitcher who gives up a lot of hits, but in this case, improved Ctl led to a rebound season. At his age, this may be the last hurrah. Odds of a repeat are slim.

Seay,Bobby

			W	L	Sv	IP	K	ERA	WHIP	OBA	vL	vR	BF/G	H%	S%	xERA	G	L	F	Ctl	Dom	Cmd	hr/f	hr/9	RAR	BPV	R$
LH	Reliever	03 TAM *	3	0	0	39	30	2.79	1.45	238			4.6	29%	80%	3.42				5.1	6.9	**1.3**		0.2	8.3	70	$4
Age	29	04 TAM *	2	1	1	58	47	2.20	1.13	240			4.7	28%	85%	3.24				2.2	7.3	**3.3**		0.8	16.1	96	$8
Peak		05 COL *	1	0	0	38	36	4.97	1.82	314			4.7	38%	75%	4.35	47	21	32	4.7	8.5	**1.8**	13%	1.2	-3.4	46	($1)
Type	Pwr FB	06 DET *	1	2	0	39	24	6.23	1.51	281			4.5	31%	59%	4.89	37	28	35	3.7	5.5	**1.5**	11%	1.2	-8.0	29	$0
Reliability	12	07 DET	3	0	1	46	38	2.33	1.14	225	209	250	3.2	29%	79%	4.16	38	18	44	2.9	7.4	**2.5**	2%	0.2	12.4	102	$7
ERA Potl	45%	1st Half	0	0	1	20	13	4.05	1.10	232			3.2	27%	62%	4.54	30	23	47	2.3	5.9	**2.6**	4%	0.5	1.1	85	$2
LIMA Plan	C+	2nd Half	3	0	0	26	25	1.03	1.18	221			3.3	30%	90%	3.82	45	14	41	3.4	8.6	**2.5**	0%	0.0	11.3	115	$5
+/- Score	-40	08 Proj	**1**	**2**	**0**	**44**	**34**	**4.14**	**1.36**	**255**			**3.9**	**29%**	**72%**	**4.44**	**39**	**20**	**41**	**3.5**	**7.0**	**2.0**	**9%**	**1.0**	**0.3**	**57**	**$3**

Reasons he won't see another sub-3.00 ERA:
- Unsustainable hr/f rate
- Rising FB trend
- xERA remained elevated

BPV says that he has skills, but xERA says a 4.00 ERA pitcher.

Sele,Aaron

			W	L	Sv	IP	K	ERA	WHIP	OBA	vL	vR	BF/G	H%	S%	xERA	G	L	F	Ctl	Dom	Cmd	hr/f	hr/9	RAR	BPV	R$
RH	Reliever	03 ANA	7	11	0	121	53	5.80	1.60	283	252	322	21.9	29%	65%	5.83	41	16	43	4.3	3.9	**0.9**	9%	1.3	-19.1	3	$1
Age	37	04 ANA	9	4	0	132	51	5.05	1.62	305	296	324	21.4	31%	71%	5.72	44	15	42	3.5	3.5	**1.0**	8%	1.1	-10.0	3	$2
Decline		05 SEA	6	12	0	116	53	5.66	1.62	310	325	302	25.1	32%	68%	5.40	40	20	39	3.2	4.1	**1.3**	11%	1.4	-18.5	3	($0)
Type	Con	06 LA *	11	6	0	132	80	4.11	1.38	283	280	298	17.2	32%	72%	4.52	46	15	39	2.4	5.4	**2.3**	7%	0.8	6.2	54	$11
Reliability	10	07 NYM	3	2	0	54	29	5.36	1.84	340	420	321	7.5	37%	71%	5.23	44	23	32	3.5	4.9	**1.4**	8%	0.8	-6.2	20	($1)
ERA Potl	40%	1st Half	1	0	0	26	17	5.19	1.88	335			7.8	38%	72%	5.31	40	26	34	4.2	5.9	**1.4**	6%	0.7	-2.5	32	($1)
LIMA Plan	F	2nd Half	2	2	0	28	12	5.52	1.80	344			7.3	36%	70%	5.15	48	22	30	2.9	3.9	**1.3**	9%	1.0	-3.7	8	($0)
+/- Score	-17	08 Proj	**2**	**4**	**0**	**50**	**26**	**5.09**	**1.66**	**318**			**7.3**	**34%**	**71%**	**5.06**	**44**	**20**	**36**	**3.1**	**4.7**	**1.5**	**9%**	**1.1**	**-4.1**	**19**	**($0)**

Obviously, teams have found value in this skill set. What is it? Now, how many teams will continue to employ him in quest of 2006's 4.50 ERA? NYM tried to no avail. Who's next?

Seo,Jae

			W	L	Sv	IP	K	ERA	WHIP	OBA	vL	vR	BF/G	H%	S%	xERA	G	L	F	Ctl	Dom	Cmd	hr/f	hr/9	RAR	BPV	R$
RH	Starter	03 NYM	9	12	0	188	110	3.83	1.27	267	223	291	24.6	29%	72%	4.74	37	17	46	2.2	5.3	**2.4**	6%	0.9	10.4	58	$14
Age	30	04 NYM *	5	12	0	139	70	4.66	1.57	288	273	322	22.3	30%	73%	5.51	38	21	41	3.9	4.5	**1.2**	9%	1.2	-6.8	14	$1
Peak		05 NYM *	15	6	0	211	145	4.22	1.35	284	233	272	27.3	32%	71%	4.34	38	23	40	2.1	6.2	**3.0**	9%	1.0	0.6	68	$15
Type	Con FB	06 2TM	3	12	0	157	88	5.33	1.61	308	310	313	19.8	32%	72%	5.32	35	21	44	3.2	5.0	**1.6**	13%	1.8	-15.7	3	($0)
Reliability	35	07 TAM *	12	8	0	149	78	6.52	1.67	339	375	368	24.4	36%	62%	5.14	37	21	41	2.0	4.7	**2.4**	10%	1.3	-37.1	26	$0
ERA Potl	55%	1st Half	4	5	0	71	36	8.22	1.80	348			22.4	36%	56%	5.43	37	21	41	2.7	4.6	**1.7**	14%	2.0	-32.6	-12	($5)
LIMA Plan	C+	2nd Half	8	3	0	78	42	4.97	1.55	332			26.8	37%	68%					1.3	4.9	**3.6**		0.7	-4.5	73	$4
+/- Score	30	08 Proj	**3**	**4**	**0**	**58**	**33**	**4.81**	**1.48**	**303**			**23.2**	**32%**	**71%**	**4.91**	**37**	**21**	**42**	**2.3**	**5.1**	**2.2**	**11%**	**1.4**	**-2.9**	**29**	**$2**

3-4, 8.13 ERA in 52 IP at TAM

Finesse pitcher who allows too many hits and too many home runs. Needs pinpoint control to succeed, and a supportive, nurturing defense. He has none of that.

Sheets,Ben

			W	L	Sv	IP	K	ERA	WHIP	OBA	vL	vR	BF/G	H%	S%	xERA	G	L	F	Ctl	Dom	Cmd	hr/f	hr/9	RAR	BPV	R$
RH	Starter	03 MIL	11	13	0	220	157	4.46	1.25	272	247	286	27.0	30%	67%	4.01	42	19	39	1.8	6.4	**3.7**	11%	1.2	-4.9	80	$15
Age	29	04 MIL	12	14	0	237	264	2.70	0.98	231	232	220	27.2	30%	78%	2.85	43	17	40	1.2	10.0	**8.3**	10%	0.9	45.8	214	$35
Peak		05 MIL	10	9	0	156	141	3.34	1.07	244	234	241	28.3	29%	74%	3.51	37	21	42	1.4	8.1	**5.6**	10%	1.1	17.4	141	$20
Type	FB	06 MIL	6	7	0	106	116	3.82	1.09	260	248	266	25.0	34%	66%	3.01	40	19	40	0.9	9.8	**10.5**	8%	0.8	8.7	261	$13
Reliability	11	07 MIL	12	5	0	141	106	3.82	1.24	257	200	300	24.5	29%	73%	4.28	37	19	45	2.4	6.8	**2.9**	9%	1.1	10.5	72	$15
ERA Potl	55%	1st Half	9	3	0	102	70	3.09	1.18	252			26.1	28%	79%	4.25	37	19	43	2.0	6.2	**3.0**	9%	1.1	16.8	74	$13
LIMA Plan	C+	2nd Half	3	2	0	39	36	5.73	1.40	270			21.2	32%	60%	4.37	34	18	48	3.2	8.2	**2.6**	9%	1.1	-6.3	70	$2
+/- Score	-2	08 Proj	**12**	**9**	**0**	**174**	**149**	**3.88**	**1.23**	**258**			**24.9**	**31%**	**72%**	**3.96**	**37**	**19**	**43**	**2.2**	**7.7**	**3.5**	**9%**	**1.1**	**9.4**	**90**	**$18**

Had first healthy half season in three years, then injuries struck. Again. Note, though, that BPIs were down from his vintage years so his claim on "elite" status is fading. It may be time to start discounting.

Sherrill,George

			W	L	Sv	IP	K	ERA	WHIP	OBA	vL	vR	BF/G	H%	S%	xERA	G	L	F	Ctl	Dom	Cmd	hr/f	hr/9	RAR	BPV	R$
LH	Reliever	03 aa	3	0	0	27	24	0.38	1.44	249			7.4	32%	100%	3.64				4.6	8.1	**1.8**		0.4	13.4	79	$5
Age	31	04 SEA *	6	3	13	74	70	3.00	1.23	257			5.4	32%	79%	3.78				2.2	8.5	**3.8**		0.9	13.0	108	$14
Peak		05 SEA *	5	6	7	43	54	3.98	1.14	219	116	273	3.4	31%	67%	3.08	42	16	42	3.1	11.3	**3.6**	9%	0.8	2.1	130	$9
Type	Pwr xFB	06 SEA	2	4	1	40	42	4.28	1.43	210	143	297	2.4	30%	67%	4.88	30	19	51	6.1	9.5	**1.6**	0%	0.0	1.4	102	$4
Reliability	9	07 SEA	2	0	3	46	56	2.36	0.98	178	156	212	2.4	25%	80%	3.47	25	21	55	3.3	11.0	**3.3**	7%	0.8	12.1	131	$9
ERA Potl	40%	1st Half	2	0	0	24	26	1.50	0.67	161			2.5	22%	80%	3.02	26	21	53	1.1	9.8	**8.7**	3%	0.4	8.9	252	$6
LIMA Plan	B+	2nd Half	0	0	3	22	30	3.32	1.34	197			2.4	28%	81%	4.00	22	20	58	5.8	12.4	**2.1**	11%	1.2	3.2	98	$3
+/- Score	-24	08 Proj	**2**	**2**	**3**	**44**	**48**	**3.31**	**1.29**	**227**			**2.8**	**29%**	**78%**	**4.16**	**28**	**20**	**53**	**4.1**	**9.9**	**2.4**	**9%**	**1.0**	**1.8**	**89**	**$6**

Low H% fed this career year. xERA says to expect some regression. Growing FB rate is a concern, but this lefty specialist is still a high Dom pitcher with elite skills. Great LIMA pick.

Shields,James

			W	L	Sv	IP	K	ERA	WHIP	OBA	vL	vR	BF/G	H%	S%	xERA	G	L	F	Ctl	Dom	Cmd	hr/f	hr/9	RAR	BPV	R$
RH	Starter	03	0	0	0	0	0	0.00	0.00																		
Age	26	04 aa	0	3	0	18	13	8.50	1.94	339			21.9	36%	60%	8.30				4.5	6.5	**1.4**		2.5	-9.2	-18	($2)
Growth		05 a/a	8	5	0	115	94	3.13	1.23	253			26.5	31%	74%	3.19				2.5	7.4	**2.9**		0.4	16.7	98	$13
Type		06 TAM *	9	10	0	185	159	4.37	1.38	289	266	309	25.7	34%	71%	3.75	43	23	34	2.1	7.7	**3.6**	11%	1.0	4.3	89	$15
Reliability	46	07 TAM	12	8	0	215	184	3.85	1.11	250	243	250	27.9	29%	70%	3.53	43	16	40	1.5	7.7	**5.1**	11%	1.2	17.3	123	$26
ERA Potl	60%	1st Half	6	3	0	116	100	3.80	1.03	236			28.7	27%	70%	3.50	43	14	43	1.5	7.8	**5.3**	13%	1.4	10.1	123	$15
LIMA Plan	C+	2nd Half	6	5	0	99	84	3.91	1.19	266			27.1	32%	69%	3.56	44	19	37	1.5	7.6	**4.9**	9%	0.9	7.3	124	$11
+/- Score	36	08 Proj	**12**	**10**	**0**	**218**	**185**	**3.72**	**1.21**	**262**			**27.2**	**31%**	**72%**	**3.65**	**43**	**19**	**38**	**1.9**	**7.7**	**4.1**	**10%**	**1.0**	**22.7**	**105**	**$24**

Breakout season, but hidden in TAM so you still might be able to grab him at a discount. Growing Cmd trend and xERA say he could get better, especially if TAM's pen improves. If so...

UP: 3.25 ERA

HAROLD NICHOLS

Shields,Scot		Yr	Tm	W	L	Sv	IP	K	ERA	WHIP	OBA	vL	vR	BF/G	H%	S%	xERA	G	L	F	Ctl	Dom	Cmd	hr/f	hr/9	RAR	BPV	R$
RH Reliever		03	ANA	5	6	1	148	111	2.86	1.19	248	229	264	13.8	29%	79%	3.68	49	19	32	2.3	6.8	**2.9**	8%	0.7	30.4	85	$17
Age	32	04	ANA	8	2	4	105	109	3.34	1.30	247	235	242	7.4	33%	75%	3.23	56	14	30	3.4	9.3	**2.7**	7%	0.5	14.2	103	$14
Peak		05	ANA	10	11	7	91	98	2.76	1.13	204	202	203	4.7	28%	77%	3.03	54	17	28	3.7	9.7	**2.6**	8%	0.5	18.1	113	$18
Type	Pwr	06	LAA	7	7	2	87	84	2.89	1.08	222	207	227	4.7	28%	77%	3.15	52	15	33	2.5	8.7	**3.5**	10%	0.8	17.9	111	$15
Reliability	40	07	LAA	4	5	2	77	77	3.86	1.23	222	214	226	4.5	28%	70%	3.67	45	19	36	3.9	9.0	**2.3**	10%	0.8	6.2	89	$9
ERA Potl	60%	1st Half		1	2	2	43	41	1.88	0.88	159			4.5	19%	85%	3.22	47	18	35	3.1	8.6	**2.7**	11%	0.8	13.9	107	$8
LIMA Plan	B+	2nd Half		3	3	0	34	36	6.35	1.68	289			4.5	38%	61%	4.25	42	20	37	4.8	9.5	**2.0**	8%	0.8	-7.7	73	$1
+/- Score	13	08	Proj	**5**	**6**	**3**	**73**	**72**	**3.72**	**1.26**	**236**			**4.9**	**30%**	**73%**	**3.51**	**48**	**18**	**34**	**3.5**	**8.9**	**2.6**	**11%**	**0.9**	**8.8**	**89**	**$10**

Ctl struggles and a high H% derailed 2nd half. History says he'll solve the Ctl issue and rebound some. xERA says he was never really a sub-3.00 ERA guy. BPV says he's on the wrong side of the bell curve.

Shouse,Brian		Yr	Tm	W	L	Sv	IP	K	ERA	WHIP	OBA	vL	vR	BF/G	H%	S%	xERA	G	L	F	Ctl	Dom	Cmd	hr/f	hr/9	RAR	BPV	R$
LH Reliever		03	TEX	0	1	1	61	40	3.10	1.25	265	195	364	4.1	32%	73%	3.32	61	17	21	2.1	5.9	**2.9**	2%	0.1	10.7	93	$5
Age	39	04	TEX	2	0	0	45	34	2.59	1.31	239	188	277	3.6	28%	84%	3.56	58	20	22	3.8	6.8	**1.8**	14%	0.8	10.2	61	$5
Decline		05	TEX	3	2	0	53	35	5.25	1.37	269	209	337	3.6	29%	64%	3.82	54	21	25	3.1	5.9	**1.9**	17%	1.2	-5.8	42	$2
Type	GB	06	2TM	1	3	2	38	23	4.02	1.52	271	238	309	2.6	30%	76%	4.61	51	20	29	4.3	5.4	**1.3**	11%	0.9	2.4	32	$2
Reliability	0	07	MIL	1	1	1	48	32	3.02	1.26	255	214	295	2.7	31%	73%	3.64	55	21	24	2.6	6.0	**2.3**	0%	0.0	8.3	88	$4
ERA Potl	50%	1st Half		1	1	1	19	8	3.32	1.32	251			2.5	28%	72%	3.94	63	19	18	3.3	3.8	**1.1**	0%	0.0	2.6	51	$2
LIMA Plan	B	2nd Half		0	0	0	29	24	2.82	1.22	257			2.9	33%	74%	3.42	50	22	28	2.2	7.5	**3.4**	0%	0.0	5.7	121	$3
+/- Score	-47	08	Proj	**1**	**2**	**0**	**44**	**29**	**3.52**	**1.36**	**264**			**2.9**	**30%**	**76%**	**3.84**	**55**	**21**	**25**	**3.1**	**6.0**	**1.9**	**12%**	**0.8**	**3.0**	**54**	**$3**

Lefty GB specialist solved last season's Ctl struggles, pumped up his Dom in the 2nd half, and soared to levels he hadn't seen since 2003. ERA likely to rise a bit, but a good end game LIMA choice.

Silva,Carlos		Yr	Tm	W	L	Sv	IP	K	ERA	WHIP	OBA	vL	vR	BF/G	H%	S%	xERA	G	L	F	Ctl	Dom	Cmd	hr/f	hr/9	RAR	BPV	R$
RH Starter		03	PHI	3	1	1	87	48	4.45	1.48	273	300	266	6.2	30%	70%	4.51	55	17	28	3.8	5.0	**1.3**	9%	0.7	-1.8	36	$3
Age	29	04	MIN	14	8	0	203	76	4.21	1.43	308	328	289	26.8	32%	73%	4.56	51	17	32	1.6	3.4	**2.2**	10%	1.0	5.5	29	$10
Pre-Peak		05	MIN	9	8	0	188	71	3.44	1.17	286	302	277	28.5	29%	76%	4.04	49	20	31	0.4	3.4	**7.9**	12%	1.2	21.5	148	$16
Type	Con	06	MIN	11	15	0	180	70	5.95	1.54	326	329	320	22.3	32%	66%	4.82	44	22	34	1.6	3.5	**2.2**	16%	1.9	-30.9	-0	$2
Reliability	69	07	MIN	13	14	0	202	89	4.19	1.31	287	294	280	25.9	30%	70%	4.44	48	19	34	1.6	4.0	**2.5**	8%	0.9	7.9	47	$15
ERA Potl	50%	1st Half		5	8	0	93	38	3.97	1.35	288			26.5	31%	71%	4.65	47	20	33	1.9	3.7	**1.9**	5%	0.6	6.2	42	$6
LIMA Plan	D+	2nd Half		8	6	0	109	51	4.38	1.28	286			25.4	30%	69%	4.25	48	18	34	1.3	4.2	**3.2**	11%	1.2	1.7	55	$9
+/- Score	-16	08	Proj	**11**	**12**	**0**	**189**	**80**	**4.54**	**1.37**	**297**			**25.3**	**31%**	**70%**	**4.49**	**47**	**20**	**33**	**1.6**	**3.8**	**2.4**	**11%**	**1.2**	**0.1**	**34**	**$11**

Was positioned in the free agent market as "The Innings-Eater Your Rotation Needs!" He's the ultimate "pitches to contact" arm. He is workable with a good defense but deadly with a porous defense.

Simontacchi,Jason		Yr	Tm	W	L	Sv	IP	K	ERA	WHIP	OBA	vL	vR	BF/G	H%	S%	xERA	G	L	F	Ctl	Dom	Cmd	hr/f	hr/9	RAR	BPV	R$
RH Starter		03	STL	9	5	1	126	74	5.57	1.54	301	307	294	12.2	32%	67%	4.93	53	0	47	2.9	5.3	**1.8**	10%	1.5	-20.0	19	$3
Age	34	04	STL *	7	4	2	96	46	4.97	1.61	334			9.5	35%	72%	6.14				1.8	4.3	**2.4**		1.2	-8.4	28	$2
Past Peak		05		0	0	0	0	0	0.00	0.00																		
Type	Con FB	06	ind	1	0	2	10	10	0.90	0.60	175			3.5	22%	100%	1.08				0.0	9.0			0.9	4.5	47	$3
Reliability	0	07	WAS *	6	8	0	81	45	6.62	1.73	337	311	346	25.1	36%	63%	5.44	34	22	44	2.7	5.0	**1.9**	10%	1.4	-21.9	13	($2)
ERA Potl	55%	1st Half		5	6	0	67	36	6.16	1.62	324			25.4	35%	62%	5.39	34	21	45	2.4	4.8	**2.0**	6%	0.9	-14.4	33	$0
LIMA Plan	C	2nd Half		1	2	0	14	9	8.85	2.27	393			23.7	39%	70%	5.71	35	25	39	4.0	5.8	**1.5**	28%	3.9	-7.5	-76	($2)
+/- Score	14	08	Proj	**4**	**3**	**0**	**50**	**27**	**5.04**	**1.50**	**302**			**13.8**	**32%**	**70%**	**5.01**	**41**	**16**	**43**	**2.5**	**4.9**	**1.9**	**11%**	**1.4**	**-3.8**	**21**	**$2**

6-7, 6.37 ERA in 70 IP at WAS
Made first MLB appearance since 2004 shoulder surgery. Returned to old ways, yielding OBA above .300. Sore elbow ended season early. Unrosterable even if healthy.

Slaten,Doug		Yr	Tm	W	L	Sv	IP	K	ERA	WHIP	OBA	vL	vR	BF/G	H%	S%	xERA	G	L	F	Ctl	Dom	Cmd	hr/f	hr/9	RAR	BPV	R$
LH Reliever		03		0	0	0	0	0	0.00	0.00																		
Age	28	04		0	0	0	0	0	0.00	0.00																		
Pre-Peak		05	aa	2	2	1	61	59	5.73	1.75	311			4.9	40%	65%	5.24				4.3	8.6	**2.0**		0.3	-10.7	77	($0)
Type	Pwr FB	06	a/a	4	4	10	63	63	2.06	1.23	231			4.5	31%	83%	2.63				3.5	9.0	**2.6**		0.2	19.1	112	$13
Reliability	0	07	ARI	3	2	0	36	28	2.73	1.52	286	268	284	2.6	33%	86%	4.50	44	17	39	3.5	6.9	**2.0**	9%	1.0	7.6	52	$4
ERA Potl	35%	1st Half		3	1	0	19	14	3.32	1.53	291			2.7	32%	85%	4.11	50	20	30	3.3	6.6	**2.0**	16%	1.4	2.6	36	$2
LIMA Plan	B+	2nd Half		0	1	0	17	14	2.08	1.50	280			2.6	34%	88%	4.90	37	14	49	3.6	7.3	**2.0**	4%	0.5	5.0	69	$1
+/- Score	-40	08	Proj	**3**	**2**	**0**	**44**	**38**	**3.93**	**1.38**	**260**			**3.3**	**31%**	**75%**	**4.21**	**42**	**17**	**41**	**3.5**	**7.9**	**2.2**	**9%**	**1.0**	**1.0**	**66**	**$4**

Sub-3.00 ERA in his rookie season looks pretty good until you see his xERA. May have LIMA-worthy skills, but MLB sample size is too small to tell. Worth monitoring.

Slowey,Kevin		Yr	Tm	W	L	Sv	IP	K	ERA	WHIP	OBA	vL	vR	BF/G	H%	S%	xERA	G	L	F	Ctl	Dom	Cmd	hr/f	hr/9	RAR	BPV	R$
RH Starter		03		0	0	0	0	0	0.00	0.00																		
Age	24	04		0	0	0	0	0	0.00	0.00																		
Growth		05		0	0	0	0	0	0.00	0.00																		
Type	Con xFB	06	aa	4	3	0	59	44	4.42	1.29	268			27.6	30%	69%	4.28				2.3	6.7	**2.9**		1.2	0.8	67	$5
Reliability	0	07	MIN *	14	6	0	200	134	3.42	1.26	281	267	309	25.3	32%	76%	4.60	29	21	50	1.4	6.0	**4.2**	6%	0.9	26.7	95	$22
ERA Potl	45%	1st Half		8	2	0	91	61	3.06	1.17	270			26.6	30%	81%	4.37	29	23	49	1.2	6.0	**5.1**	9%	1.3	16.2	105	$12
LIMA Plan	C+	2nd Half		6	4	0	109	73	3.72	1.33	289			24.4	33%	73%	4.80	29	19	51	1.7	6.0	**3.7**	4%	0.7	10.5	90	$10
+/- Score	6	08	Proj	**9**	**6**	**0**	**141**	**99**	**4.15**	**1.28**	**277**			**25.7**	**30%**	**72%**	**4.58**	**29**	**21**	**50**	**1.8**	**6.3**	**3.5**	**9%**	**1.3**	**-1.5**	**72**	**$13**

4-1, 4.73 ERA in 66 IP at MIN
Breakout coming?
PRO: 4.3 Cmd, 1.5 Ctl in MLB
CON: High xERA, 2.2 hr/9 in MLB
May still be a year away, but should be a good one. Could be your last chance to buy cheap.

Smith,Joe		Yr	Tm	W	L	Sv	IP	K	ERA	WHIP	OBA	vL	vR	BF/G	H%	S%	xERA	G	L	F	Ctl	Dom	Cmd	hr/f	hr/9	RAR	BPV	R$
RH Reliever		03		0	0	0	0	0	0.00	0.00																		
Age	24	04		0	0	0	0	0	0.00	0.00																		
Growth		05		0	0	0	0	0	0.00	0.00																		
Type	Pwr xGB	06		0	0	0	0	0	0.00	0.00																		
Reliability	0	07	NYM *	3	2	2	53	50	3.38	1.50	268	298	266	3.8	34%	78%	3.31	62	17	21	4.2	8.4	**2.0**	9%	0.5	6.9	79	$5
ERA Potl	50%	1st Half		2	0	0	31	33	2.90	1.39	243			3.7	33%	79%	2.76	69	13	18	4.4	9.6	**2.2**	7%	0.3	5.8	101	$4
LIMA Plan	B+	2nd Half		1	2	2	22	17	4.04	1.66	300			3.9	35%	77%	4.21	51	23	26	4.0	6.9	**1.7**	11%	0.8	1.1	48	$1
+/- Score	31	08	Proj	**2**	**2**	**0**	**44**	**39**	**3.93**	**1.43**	**255**			**3.7**	**32%**	**73%**	**3.43**	**59**	**19**	**22**	**4.1**	**8.1**	**2.0**	**11%**	**0.6**	**5.2**	**75**	**$3**

3-2, 3.45 ERA in 44 IP at NYM
Had a 100+ BPV in three of five months. Struggled in the other two. Dom of 9.1 in majors says he has the makings of an elite reliever as he becomes consistent. Tuck him away.

Smoltz,John		Yr	Tm	W	L	Sv	IP	K	ERA	WHIP	OBA	vL	vR	BF/G	H%	S%	xERA	G	L	F	Ctl	Dom	Cmd	hr/f	hr/9	RAR	BPV	R$
RH Starter		03	ATL	0	2	45	64	73	1.13	0.88	210	189	218	3.9	30%	89%	2.60	42	23	35	1.1	10.3	**9.1**	4%	0.3	24.9	258	$26
Age	41	04	ATL	0	1	44	81	85	2.77	1.08	247	255	236	4.5	32%	79%	2.89	48	18	34	1.4	9.4	**6.5**	11%	0.9	14.9	173	$22
Decline		05	ATL	14	7	0	229	169	3.06	1.15	245	252	233	28.3	29%	76%	3.59	48	22	30	2.1	6.6	**3.2**	9%	0.7	33.4	92	$26
Type	Pwr	06	ATL	16	9	0	232	211	3.49	1.19	253	278	226	27.2	31%	74%	3.39	46	20	33	2.1	8.2	**3.8**	10%	0.9	28.5	107	$27
Reliability	77	07	ATL	14	8	0	206	197	3.11	1.18	253	262	237	26.4	32%	76%	3.36	45	20	35	2.1	8.6	**4.2**	9%	0.8	33.5	121	$26
ERA Potl	55%	1st Half		9	4	0	100	90	2.97	1.22	264			25.9	33%	78%	3.52	44	20	36	1.9	8.1	**4.3**	8%	0.7	18.0	119	$14
LIMA Plan	C+	2nd Half		5	4	0	106	107	3.24	1.14	242			26.9	31%	75%	3.21	45	20	35	2.2	9.1	**4.1**	10%	0.9	15.5	122	$13
+/- Score	-2	08	Proj	**12**	**7**	**0**	**199**	**180**	**3.48**	**1.18**	**248**			**26.3**	**30%**	**73%**	**3.42**	**46**	**20**	**34**	**2.2**	**8.1**	**3.7**	**10%**	**0.9**	**24.0**	**104**	**$22**

Second consecutive year that he's improved. His senior citizen discount is bound to kick in one day, but there are no signs of it yet.

Snell,Ian		Yr	Tm	W	L	Sv	IP	K	ERA	WHIP	OBA	vL	vR	BF/G	H%	S%	xERA	G	L	F	Ctl	Dom	Cmd	hr/f	hr/9	RAR	BPV	R$
RH Starter		03		0	0	0	0	0	0.00	0.00											0.0	0.0						
Age	26	04	aa	11	7	0	151	120	3.75	1.34	280			24.8	33%	75%	4.47				2.2	7.2	**3.2**		1.0	10.9	80	$13
Growth		05	PIT *	12	5	0	154	122	4.32	1.21	245	304	239	19.3	28%	67%	4.13	37	21	42	2.6	7.1	**2.7**	9%	1.1	-1.5	74	$15
Type	Pwr	06	PIT	14	11	0	186	169	4.74	1.46	274	305	251	25.5	32%	72%	4.04	43	21	36	3.6	8.2	**2.3**	15%	1.4	-5.8	55	$13
Reliability	74	07	PIT	9	12	0	208	177	3.76	1.33	263	284	245	27.6	31%	75%	3.94	46	17	37	2.9	7.7	**2.6**	9%	1.0	17.0	75	$17
ERA Potl	55%	1st Half		6	5	0	102	83	2.91	1.20	238			28.0	29%	77%	3.92	45	16	39	2.8	7.3	**2.6**	6%	0.6	19.1	87	$12
LIMA Plan	C	2nd Half		3	7	0	106	94	4.58	1.46	285			27.3	34%	72%	3.95	47	17	36	3.1	8.0	**2.6**	13%	1.3	-2.1	63	$5
+/- Score	13	08	Proj	**13**	**12**	**0**	**218**	**193**	**3.60**	**1.29**	**258**			**24.7**	**31%**	**76%**	**3.77**	**44**	**19**	**37**	**2.8**	**8.0**	**2.9**	**12%**	**1.1**	**16.8**	**78**	**$21**

ERA has bounced around but xERA says this is for real. Two encouraging signs: improved OBA vs lefties and Cmd growth. If growth continues... UP: 3.25 ERA.

HAROLD NICHOLS

Snyder,Kyle

Snyder,Kyle		W	L	Sv	IP	K	ERA	WHIP	OBA	vL	vR	BF/G	H%	S%	xERA	G	L	F	Ctl	Dom	Cmd	hr/f	hr/9	RAR	BPV	R$
RH Reliever	03 KC *	4	6	0	119	52	4.69	1.36	285	273	297	24.3	30%	68%	4.73				2.1	3.9	1.9		1.1	-2.4	27	$5
Age 30	04	0	0	0	0	0	0.00	0.00																		
Peak	05 KC *	4	6	0	107	56	5.24	1.60	311			16.7	34%	66%	5.08				2.9	4.7	1.6		0.5	-11.5	38	$0
Type FB	06 2AL *	5	10	1	140	97	5.99	1.66	337	349	314	21.4	38%	65%	4.43	40	26	34	2.1	6.2	3.0	11%	1.2	-24.9	53	$0
Reliability 21	07 BOS	2	3	0	54	41	3.81	1.42	227	195	242	5.1	25%	77%	5.21	37	15	48	5.3	6.8	1.3	9%	1.2	4.6	42	$4
ERA Potl 35%	1st Half	1	1	0	27	20	2.67	1.37	232			4.8	27%	83%	5.15	33	19	48	4.7	6.7	1.4	5%	0.7	6.1	59	$3
LIMA Plan C+	2nd Half	1	2	0	27	21	4.94	1.47	222			5.4	23%	71%	5.27	41	12	47	5.9	6.9	1.2	14%	1.6	-1.5	27	$1
+/- Score -42	08 Proj	2	4	0	58	39	4.81	1.52	275			6.3	30%	71%	5.12	38	17	44	4.0	6.1	1.5	10%	1.2	-4.5	31	$2

Despite lower ERA, took an overall step backward.
PRO: Growing Dom, BA vs LH.
CON: Control struggles, rising FB rate, xERA.
Expect major ERA regression.
DN: 5.30 ERA

Sonnanstine,Andrew

Sonnanstine,Andrew		W	L	Sv	IP	K	ERA	WHIP	OBA	vL	vR	BF/G	H%	S%	xERA	G	L	F	Ctl	Dom	Cmd	hr/f	hr/9	RAR	BPV	R$
RH Starter	03	0	0	0	0	0	0.00	0.00																		
Age 25	04	0	0	0	0	0	0.00	0.00																		
Growth	05	0	0	0	0	0	0.00	0.00																		
Type FB	06 aa	15	8	0	185	127	4.11	1.27	274			27.7	31%	70%	4.08				1.9	6.2	3.2		1.0	9.4	77	$18
Reliability 0	07 TAM *	12	14	0	202	155	5.09	1.31	283	318	266	25.8	32%	64%	4.13	39	18	43	1.8	6.9	3.9	10%	1.2	-14.5	84	$14
ERA Potl 60%	1st Half	7	6	0	103	85	4.37	1.23	275			26.7	31%	70%	3.92	34	22	44	1.5	7.4	5.0	12%	1.5	1.7	105	$10
LIMA Plan C	2nd Half	5	8	0	99	70	5.84	1.39	291			25.0	33%	58%	4.41	41	17	43	2.1	6.4	3.0	8%	1.0	-16.2	69	$4
+/- Score 51	08 Proj	12	10	0	174	127	4.24	1.28	275			26.1	31%	70%	4.19	39	18	43	1.9	6.6	3.5	10%	1.2	6.6	78	$16

6-10, 5.85 ERA, 130 IP at TAM
Tough debut season, but a lot to like. Excellent Cmd, just needs to solve LHed hitters. Low strand rate could be helped by an improved TAM pen. A worthy investment.

Soriano,Rafael

Soriano,Rafael		W	L	Sv	IP	K	ERA	WHIP	OBA	vL	vR	BF/G	H%	S%	xERA	G	L	F	Ctl	Dom	Cmd	hr/f	hr/9	RAR	BPV	R$
RH Reliever	03 SEA *	7	3	1	115	125	2.82	0.90	198	191	132	8.6	28%	68%	1.61				1.9	9.8	5.2		0.3	24.2	174	$21
Age 28	04 SEA *	1	3	0	15	17	4.80	1.47	274			6.0	36%	70%	4.91				3.6	10.2	2.8		1.2	-0.7	85	$1
Pre-Peak	05 SEA	0	0	0	7	9	2.54	0.99	231	571	100	4.0	35%	71%	3.04	32	16	53	1.3	11.4	9.0	0%	0.0	1.6	266	$1
Type Pwr xFB	06 SEA	1	2	2	60	65	2.25	1.08	206	244	179	4.5	27%	85%	3.84	27	19	54	3.2	9.8	3.1	7%	0.9	17.1	110	$10
Reliability 0	07 ATL	3	3	9	72	70	3.00	0.86	188	164	197	3.8	21%	76%	3.41	33	16	51	1.9	8.8	4.7	13%	1.5	12.7	123	$14
ERA Potl 45%	1st Half	2	0	5	34	31	2.91	0.79	165			3.7	19%	70%	3.58	31	17	52	2.1	8.2	3.9	9%	1.1	6.4	121	$8
LIMA Plan B+	2nd Half	1	3	4	38	39	3.08	0.92	207			3.9	23%	81%	3.27	35	16	50	1.7	9.2	5.6	17%	1.9	6.3	129	$7
+/- Score 4	08 Proj	3	3	28	73	72	3.35	1.05	227			4.6	28%	73%	3.70	31	17	52	2.0	8.9	4.5	9%	1.1	6.3	124	$18

Has long had the skills to close, and finally got opportunity. Has the makings of an elite closer if health allows. 2007 was DL-free but he racked up over 300 DL days in the three prior years. Caution still warranted.

Soria,Joakim

Soria,Joakim		W	L	Sv	IP	K	ERA	WHIP	OBA	vL	vR	BF/G	H%	S%	xERA	G	L	F	Ctl	Dom	Cmd	hr/f	hr/9	RAR	BPV	R$
RH Reliever	03	0	0	0	0	0	0.00	0.00																		
Age 23	04	0	0	0	0	0	0.00	0.00																		
Growth	05	0	0	0	0	0	0.00	0.00																		
Type Pwr	06	0	0	0	0	0	0.00	0.00																		
Reliability 13	07 KC	2	3	17	69	75	2.48	0.94	191	167	200	4.3	26%	74%	3.14	39	20	40	2.5	9.8	3.9	4%	0.4	17.3	147	$17
ERA Potl 60%	1st Half	1	2	10	33	36	2.45	1.06	191			4.4	28%	74%	3.59	36	20	44	3.5	9.8	2.8	0%	0.0	8.3	134	$9
LIMA Plan B	2nd Half	1	1	7	36	39	2.50	0.83	191			4.2	25%	74%	2.75	42	21	37	1.5	9.7	6.5	9%	0.7	8.9	189	$9
+/- Score -4	08 Proj	2	3	25	73	76	3.23	1.13	221			4.5	29%	74%	3.46	40	21	40	3.0	9.4	3.2	8%	0.7	9.2	112	$18

Spectacular debut with 2nd half growth. Low H%, low hr/f, xERA say he could regress a bit. Youth and inexperience at upper levels increase risk, but elite skills make him worth owning.

Sosa,Jorge

Sosa,Jorge		W	L	Sv	IP	K	ERA	WHIP	OBA	vL	vR	BF/G	H%	S%	xERA	G	L	F	Ctl	Dom	Cmd	hr/f	hr/9	RAR	BPV	R$
RH Reliever	03 TAM *	6	13	0	152	87	5.09	1.61	291	315	241	20.9	32%	70%	5.58	38	17	45	4.1	5.2	1.3	7%	1.0	-10.6	24	$2
Age 31	04 TAM *	5	9	1	112	112	5.30	1.49	263	286	236	10.7	32%	67%	4.40	38	16	47	4.3	9.0	2.1	11%	1.4	-12.0	59	$5
Peak	05 ATL	13	3	0	134	85	2.55	1.39	244	247	235	13.1	27%	85%	5.10	35	24	41	4.3	5.7	1.3	7%	0.8	28.0	44	$15
Type FB	06 2NL	3	11	4	118	75	5.42	1.51	293	326	270	11.6	30%	72%	4.92	35	21	44	3.1	5.7	1.9	17%	2.3	-13.5	1	$2
Reliability 44	07 NYM *	13	8	0	145	87	3.93	1.39	275	326	202	13.3	31%	73%	4.94	38	19	43	2.9	5.4	1.9	6%	0.7	8.9	50	$12
ERA Potl 45%	1st Half	10	3	0	91	59	2.97	1.18	244			24.8	28%	76%	4.36	40	19	41	2.4	5.8	2.5	5%	0.6	16.4	75	$13
LIMA Plan C+	2nd Half	3	5	0	54	28	5.55	1.76	321			7.9	35%	69%	5.93	35	20	45	3.8	4.6	1.2	6%	0.9	-7.5	17	($1)
+/- Score -47	08 Proj	6	7	0	98	60	4.80	1.50	284			11.3	31%	71%	5.12	36	20	44	3.4	5.5	1.6	9%	1.2	-8.7	30	$4

9-8, 4.47 ERA in 112 IP at NYM
2nd half collapse mirrors '06 collapse after '05. xERA shows a realistic level of expectation, so don't get too comfortable if he surges. He's a living, breathing Plexiglass Principle.

Sowers,Jeremy

Sowers,Jeremy		W	L	Sv	IP	K	ERA	WHIP	OBA	vL	vR	BF/G	H%	S%	xERA	G	L	F	Ctl	Dom	Cmd	hr/f	hr/9	RAR	BPV	R$
LH Starter	03	0	0	0	0	0	0.00	0.00																		
Age 25	04	0	0	0	0	0	0.00	0.00																		
Growth	05 a/a	6	1	0	88	65	2.25	1.11	262			25.4	31%	84%	3.31				1.0	6.6	6.5		0.7	22.3	158	$13
Type Con FB	06 CLE *	16	5	0	185	83	2.62	1.23	253	225	259	26.5	27%	80%	4.39	48	21	30	2.4	4.0	1.7	6%	0.5	44.2	47	$24
Reliability 0	07 CLE *	5	11	0	164	79	5.56	1.57	315	206	338	26.2	34%	65%	5.33	40	16	44	2.5	4.3	1.8	6%	0.9	-21.3	29	$0
ERA Potl 55%	1st Half	1	8	0	81	25	6.56	1.64	323			24.6	32%	62%	5.86	40	16	44	2.7	2.8	1.0	10%	1.4	-20.5	-14	($4)
LIMA Plan C	2nd Half	4	3	0	83	54	4.58	1.50	307			28.1	36%	68%	5.02	31	23	46	2.3	5.9	2.6	2%	0.3	-0.8	73	$4
+/- Score -6	08 Proj	5	4	0	87	46	4.24	1.38	285			26.7	30%	72%	4.74	42	17	40	2.3	4.8	2.1	9%	1.1	-2.6	36	$6

1-6, 6.42 ERA in 67 IP at CLE
Took a large step backwards. H% and S% over-correction was most of his undoing. Dom of only 3.2 in majors and jump in FB rate made things worse. Not much upside here.

Speier,Justin

Speier,Justin		W	L	Sv	IP	K	ERA	WHIP	OBA	vL	vR	BF/G	H%	S%	xERA	G	L	F	Ctl	Dom	Cmd	hr/f	hr/9	RAR	BPV	R$
RH Reliever	03 COL	3	1	9	73	66	4.07	1.32	262	273	245	4.3	31%	74%	4.18	32	22	46	2.8	8.1	2.9	11%	1.4	1.9	71	$8
Age 34	04 TOR	3	8	7	69	52	3.91	1.25	239	258	220	4.6	27%	72%	4.63	34	17	49	3.3	6.8	2.1	8%	1.0	4.4	60	$8
Past Peak	05 TOR	3	2	0	66	56	2.58	0.95	205	167	219	3.9	23%	83%	3.79	35	16	49	2.0	7.6	3.7	11%	1.4	14.6	97	$10
Type Pwr xFB	06 TOR	2	0	0	51	55	2.99	1.33	246	183	264	3.7	32%	81%	4.13	30	20	50	3.7	9.7	2.6	7%	0.9	9.9	93	$6
Reliability 0	07 LAA	2	3	0	50	47	2.88	0.96	203	222	186	3.8	24%	76%	3.64	37	12	50	2.2	8.5	3.9	9%	1.1	10.0	115	$8
ERA Potl 45%	1st Half	0	0	0	16	17	1.69	0.75	134			3.9	15%	90%	3.19	33	19	47	2.8	9.6	3.4	12%	1.1	5.6	123	$3
LIMA Plan B+	2nd Half	2	3	0	34	30	3.44	1.06	232			3.8	28%	72%	3.85	39	9	52	1.9	7.9	4.3	8%	1.1	4.5	114	$5
+/- Score -17	08 Proj	2	2	0	58	55	3.41	1.24	252			4.0	30%	78%	4.04	34	16	50	2.6	8.5	3.2	10%	1.2	3.3	87	$6

Consistently outperforms his xERA, which I suppose is better than the alternative. Just don't pay for a sub-3.00 ERA. But do invest. BPVs over 100 don't grow on trees. Or on vines. Or in petri dishes.

Springer,Russ

Springer,Russ		W	L	Sv	IP	K	ERA	WHIP	OBA	vL	vR	BF/G	H%	S%	xERA	G	L	F	Ctl	Dom	Cmd	hr/f	hr/9	RAR	BPV	R$
RH Reliever	03 STL *	1	1	0	23	16	6.65	1.35	245			4.1	20%	64%	6.30				3.9	6.3	1.6		3.5	-6.7	-28	$0
Age 39	04 HOU *	1	3	6	45	36	3.80	1.62	291			5.2	35%	78%	5.04				4.2	7.2	1.7		0.8	2.6	52	$3
Decline	05 HOU	4	4	0	59	54	4.73	1.19	228	209	231	3.9	26%	64%	3.92	40	16	44	3.2	8.2	2.6	13%	1.4	-3.5	72	$5
Type Pwr xFB	06 HOU	1	1	0	59	46	3.50	1.05	216	253	187	3.3	23%	75%	4.43	27	15	58	2.4	7.0	2.9	10%	1.5	7.2	69	$6
Reliability 7	07 STL	8	1	0	66	66	2.18	0.91	181	235	158	3.3	24%	77%	3.65	30	20	51	2.6	9.0	3.5	4%	0.4	18.3	134	$14
ERA Potl 40%	1st Half	3	1	0	28	35	3.21	1.14	210			3.1	30%	73%	3.76	16	26	57	3.5	11.3	3.2	5%	0.6	4.2	128	$5
LIMA Plan C	2nd Half	5	0	0	38	31	1.42	0.74	157			3.6	20%	81%	3.53	40	15	46	1.9	7.3	3.9	2%	0.2	14.1	142	$9
+/- Score -58	08 Proj	4	2	0	58	48	3.88	1.26	245			3.7	28%	74%	4.54	31	17	52	3.1	7.4	2.4	9%	1.2	-1.0	64	$6

This is what you do with a guy like this... Nothing. You might have tucked him on reserve last year and enjoyed the ride but the odds of a repeat at age 39 are virtually nil. Best case, just tuck him on reserve again.

Stanton,Mike

Stanton,Mike		W	L	Sv	IP	K	ERA	WHIP	OBA	vL	vR	BF/G	H%	S%	xERA	G	L	F	Ctl	Dom	Cmd	hr/f	hr/9	RAR	BPV	R$
LH Reliever	03 NYM	2	7	5	45	34	4.60	1.24	226	206	226	3.7	25%	66%	4.71	34	17	49	3.8	6.8	1.8	9%	1.2	-1.8	52	$5
Age 40	04 NYM	2	6	0	77	58	3.16	1.34	244	269	219	3.9	29%	78%	4.40	44	18	38	3.9	6.8	1.8	7%	0.7	10.5	63	$6
Decline	05 2TM	3	3	0	42	27	4.69	1.52	292	235	358	3.2	33%	69%	4.59	41	27	32	3.2	5.8	1.8	7%	0.6	-2.0	50	$2
Type	06 2NL	7	7	8	67	48	4.02	1.44	270	271	276	3.6	32%	71%	4.70	42	19	39	3.6	6.4	1.8	2%	0.3	3.9	69	$9
Reliability 8	07 CIN	1	3	0	58	40	5.93	1.61	316	306	321	3.8	36%	63%	4.85	36	24	40	2.8	6.2	2.2	8%	0.9	-10.7	48	($1)
ERA Potl 60%	1st Half	1	2	0	26	19	4.50	1.65	323			3.4	38%	71%	4.65	38	27	36	2.8	6.6	2.4	3%	0.3	-0.2	69	$0
LIMA Plan D	2nd Half	0	1	0	32	21	7.10	1.58	309			4.2	34%	56%	5.01	34	21	44	2.8	6.0	2.1	10%	1.4	-10.4	30	($2)
+/- Score 11	08 Proj	2	3	0	44	29	4.97	1.52	285			3.6	32%	69%	4.87	38	22	39	3.5	6.0	1.7	9%	1.0	-2.5	39	$1

Another demonstration of the longevity of right-brain dominance. Hasn't even gotten LHBs out for two years -- really, his sole purpose for being -- and he'd still gainfully employed. Bid a lot. Bid it all. Not.

HAROLD NICHOLS

Stokes,Brian

Stokes,Brian		W	L	Sv	IP	K	ERA	WHIP	OBA	vL	vR	BF/G	H%	S%	xERA	G	L	F	Ctl	Dom	Cmd	hr/f	hr/9	RAR	BPV	R$
RH Reliever	03 aa	2	5	0	50	27	4.53	1.70	333			23.2	37%	72%	5.57				2.6	4.8	**1.8**		0.4	-0.8	44	$0
Age 28	04	0	0	0	0	0	0.00	0.00																		
Pre-Peak	05 aa	4	5	0	85	50	4.86	1.54	297			25.3	33%	69%	5.02				3.2	5.2	**1.7**		0.9	-5.9	36	$2
Type	06 TAM *	8	7	0	157	99	5.51	1.66	308			21.2	35%	66%	5.37	40	15	45	3.6	5.6	**1.5**	5%	0.7	-18.4	40	$2
Reliability 24	07 TAM	2	7	0	62	35	7.08	1.85	339	346	341	5.0	36%	63%	5.17	48	17	35	3.6	5.1	**1.4**	14%	1.6	-19.8	-1	($4)
ERA Potl 55%	1st Half	2	6	0	32	21	6.47	1.88	370			4.3	40%	69%	4.58	48	17	34	2.0	5.9	**3.0**	14%	1.7	-7.7	29	($1)
LIMA Plan F	2nd Half	0	1	0	30	14	7.72	1.82	302			6.2	31%	58%	5.88	48	16	36	5.3	4.2	**0.8**	13%	1.5	-12.0	-9	($3)
+/- Score 45	08 Proj	**2**	**4**	**0**	**58**	**33**	**5.43**	**1.66**	**306**			**6.3**	**33%**	**69%**	**5.04**	**47**	**16**	**36**	**3.7**	**5.1**	**1.4**	**11%**	**1.2**	**-3.9**	**16**	**($0)**

How it normally works: Player shows skill in minors and merits promotion. How it works in TAM: Life form with pulse is pushed up through system, repeatedly fails as starter so is moved to pen where he fails some more.

Street,Huston

Street,Huston		W	L	Sv	IP	K	ERA	WHIP	OBA	vL	vR	BF/G	H%	S%	xERA	G	L	F	Ctl	Dom	Cmd	hr/f	hr/9	RAR	BPV	R$
RH Reliever	03	0	0	0	0	0	0.00	0.00											0.0	0.0						
Age 24	04 a/a	1	0	4	15	13	2.40	1.33	262			5.3	32%	84%	3.78				3.0	7.8	**2.6**		0.6	3.6	86	$3
Growth	05 OAK	5	1	23	78	72	1.73	1.01	194	224	172	4.6	25%	84%	3.54	45	17	38	3.0	8.3	**2.8**	4%	0.3	25.5	114	$21
Type Pwr FB	06 OAK	4	4	37	70	67	3.33	1.10	244	274	211	4.1	31%	70%	3.51	37	21	42	1.7	8.6	**5.2**	5%	0.5	10.6	151	$22
Reliability 26	07 OAK	5	2	16	50	63	2.88	0.94	199	224	162	4.0	28%	74%	2.81	40	15	45	2.2	11.3	**5.3**	10%	0.9	10.0	167	$16
ERA Potl 60%	1st Half	2	1	9	18	20	2.50	0.89	151			3.8	21%	73%	3.47	37	12	51	3.5	10.0	**2.9**	5%	0.5	4.5	130	$7
LIMA Plan B	2nd Half	3	1	7	32	43	3.09	0.97	224			4.1	32%	74%	2.48	42	16	42	1.4	12.1	**8.6**	13%	1.1	5.6	230	$9
+/- Score 25	08 Proj	**5**	**2**	**35**	**58**	**65**	**3.26**	**1.09**	**231**			**4.2**	**30%**	**74%**	**3.20**	**39**	**18**	**43**	**2.2**	**10.1**	**4.6**	**9%**	**0.9**	**9.3**	**139**	**$21**

Missed more than two months due to elbow nerve irritation. 2nd half BPIs marked by huge Cmd spike suggest that health is the only risk here. Pay up depending on your tolerance.

Suppan,Jeff

Suppan,Jeff		W	L	Sv	IP	K	ERA	WHIP	OBA	vL	vR	BF/G	H%	S%	xERA	G	L	F	Ctl	Dom	Cmd	hr/f	hr/9	RAR	BPV	R$
RH Starter	03 2TM	13	11	0	204	110	4.19	1.31	274	310	239	27.0	29%	71%	4.34	49	16	35	2.3	4.9	**2.2**	10%	1.0	5.1	44	$15
Age 33	04 STL	16	9	0	188	110	4.16	1.37	266	272	260	26.0	28%	73%	4.44	48	18	34	3.1	5.3	**1.7**	12%	1.2	2.2	33	$14
Peak	05 STL	16	10	0	194	114	3.57	1.39	273	271	279	26.1	30%	78%	4.41	46	21	32	2.9	5.3	**1.8**	12%	1.1	16.2	37	$16
Type Con	06 STL	12	7	0	190	104	4.12	1.45	279	302	257	26.0	30%	74%	4.59	47	23	31	3.3	4.9	**1.5**	11%	1.0	8.6	31	$11
Reliability 99	07 MIL	12	12	0	207	114	4.62	1.50	294	334	271	26.9	32%	70%	4.77	45	20	35	3.0	5.0	**1.7**	7%	0.8	-4.8	38	$8
ERA Potl 50%	1st Half	8	7	0	107	55	4.88	1.48	291			27.7	31%	68%	4.79	45	21	34	2.9	4.6	**1.6**	9%	1.0	-6.0	28	$5
LIMA Plan C	2nd Half	4	5	0	100	59	4.33	1.53	297			26.1	34%	71%	4.76	46	19	35	3.1	5.3	**1.7**	5%	0.5	1.1	48	$3
+/- Score -25	08 Proj	**11**	**10**	**0**	**189**	**106**	**4.25**	**1.46**	**285**			**26.6**	**31%**	**73%**	**4.62**	**46**	**20**	**33**	**3.0**	**5.1**	**1.7**	**10%**	**1.0**	**-5.0**	**34**	**$10**

BPIs remain extremely stable and unspectacular. 3rd straight season with 2nd half spike, but poor H% capped turnaround. Still, 3.88 ERA in Aug-Sept suggests that he remains a reasonable mid-season buy.

Tallet,Brian

Tallet,Brian		W	L	Sv	IP	K	ERA	WHIP	OBA	vL	vR	BF/G	H%	S%	xERA	G	L	F	Ctl	Dom	Cmd	hr/f	hr/9	RAR	BPV	R$
LH Reliever	03 aaa	4	4	0	84	55	7.07	1.74	316			26.1	35%	60%	6.39				4.0	5.9	**1.5**		1.4	-27.7	16	($3)
Age 30	04 a/a	1	1	1	32	23	6.45	1.86	314			8.1	38%	62%	5.33				5.2	6.6	**1.3**		0.0	-8.3	59	($1)
Peak	05 aaa	6	5	0	97	49	4.48	1.40	288			19.1	30%	73%	5.07				2.4	4.6	**1.9**		1.4	-2.1	23	$5
Type Pwr FB	06 TOR *	4	2	3	79	53	5.36	1.65	282	220	246	5.7	31%	70%	5.34	41	18	41	4.9	6.1	**1.2**	10%	1.2	-7.8	25	$2
Reliability 18	07 TOR	2	4	0	62	54	3.47	1.24	218	247	194	5.4	28%	70%	4.25	40	19	40	4.0	7.8	**1.9**	1%	0.1	8.0	94	$6
ERA Potl 55%	1st Half	2	2	0	33	30	2.73	1.15	205			5.8	28%	74%	4.08	40	17	42	3.8	8.2	**2.1**	0%	0.0	7.2	108	$5
LIMA Plan C+	2nd Half	0	2	0	29	24	4.30	1.33	232			5.0	29%	66%	4.45	40	21	38	4.3	7.4	**1.7**	3%	0.3	0.7	80	$2
+/- Score -31	08 Proj	**2**	**3**	**0**	**58**	**43**	**4.50**	**1.43**	**258**			**5.7**	**30%**	**70%**	**4.70**	**40**	**19**	**40**	**4.0**	**6.7**	**1.7**	**8%**	**0.9**	**-1.5**	**50**	**$3**

At face value, it's Bull Durham Prospect Makes Good. But the skill set is soft... Middling control. Allowed only 1 HR in '07, a feat he won't repeat. xERA is still the best indicator. And at 30, peak may already have been in '07.

Tankersley,Taylor

Tankersley,Taylor		W	L	Sv	IP	K	ERA	WHIP	OBA	vL	vR	BF/G	H%	S%	xERA	G	L	F	Ctl	Dom	Cmd	hr/f	hr/9	RAR	BPV	R$
LH Reliever	03	0	0	0	0	0	0.00	0.00																		
Age 25	04	0	0	0	0	0	0.00	0.00																		
Growth	05	0	0	0	0	0	0.00	0.00																		
Type Pwr FB	06 FLA *	6	2	9	69	81	2.23	1.29	192	236	222	4.1	27%	85%	3.80	44	16	40	5.5	10.5	**1.9**	6%	0.5	19.2	104	$14
Reliability 0	07 FLA *	6	2	1	53	54	4.14	1.45	234	179	301	3.1	30%	73%	4.49	37	19	44	5.3	9.2	**1.7**	8%	0.9	1.8	74	$6
ERA Potl 55%	1st Half	4	2	0	23	16	6.26	1.65	262			3.4	28%	65%	5.59	38	20	42	5.9	6.3	**1.1**	13%	1.6	-5.2	16	$1
LIMA Plan B	2nd Half	2	0	1	30	38	2.49	1.30	210			2.9	32%	81%	3.72	36	18	46	4.9	11.5	**2.3**	3%	0.3	7.0	122	$5
+/- Score 8	08 Proj	**4**	**4**	**3**	**58**	**63**	**4.34**	**1.47**	**234**			**3.5**	**30%**	**72%**	**4.30**	**39**	**18**	**43**	**5.4**	**9.8**	**1.8**	**9%**	**0.9**	**0.7**	**77**	**$5**

6-1, 3.99 ERA in 47 IP at FLA. Zero HR, 2.55 ERA in 24 IP at home. Walked 7 RH batters per 9 IP for 2nd straight year. Dom, age and Dolphins Stadium make him a speculative LIMA option. But he's gotta find the plate.

Taschner,Jack

Taschner,Jack		W	L	Sv	IP	K	ERA	WHIP	OBA	vL	vR	BF/G	H%	S%	xERA	G	L	F	Ctl	Dom	Cmd	hr/f	hr/9	RAR	BPV	R$
LH Reliever	03 aa	0	6	0	75	35	6.91	1.86	306			10.6	33%	61%	5.83				5.6	4.2	**0.8**		0.7	-23.4	15	($6)
Age 30	04 a/a	7	8	0	111	76	7.02	1.74	314			16.2	35%	61%	6.38				4.1	6.1	**1.5**		1.4	-36.7	18	($3)
Peak	05 SF *	5	0	10	71	68	1.70	1.15	188			4.3	25%	86%	4.35	35	13	52	4.4	8.6	**1.9**	2%	0.3	22.4	102	$15
Type Pwr xFB	06 SF *	6	8	14	68	69	5.50	1.65	314			4.5	39%	69%	4.39	27	29	44	3.2	9.1	**2.8**	10%	1.2	-8.5	69	$8
Reliability 18	07 SF	3	1	0	50	51	5.40	1.46	238	316	176	3.5	31%	62%	4.67	33	18	49	5.2	9.2	**1.8**	6%	0.7	-6.0	78	$2
ERA Potl 0%	1st Half	1	0	0	23	21	5.48	1.35	198			3.2	24%	59%	5.04	30	19	51	5.9	8.2	**1.4**	7%	0.8	-3.0	71	$1
LIMA Plan B+	2nd Half	2	1	0	27	30	5.33	1.56	269			3.8	36%	65%	4.37	35	18	47	4.7	10.0	**2.1**	6%	0.7	-3.0	86	$1
+/- Score 21	08 Proj	**4**	**3**	**0**	**58**	**56**	**4.66**	**1.41**	**245**			**4.1**	**30%**	**69%**	**4.55**	**32**	**20**	**48**	**4.5**	**8.7**	**1.9**	**9%**	**1.1**	**-1.1**	**66**	**$4**

Another FB pitcher with good Dom but Ctl issues. A LIMA platoon candidate?

	Ctl	hr/9	ERA
Home	2.7	0.3	2.73
Away	8.0	1.1	8.37

AT&T Park limits the long ball.

Tavarez,Julian

Tavarez,Julian		W	L	Sv	IP	K	ERA	WHIP	OBA	vL	vR	BF/G	H%	S%	xERA	G	L	F	Ctl	Dom	Cmd	hr/f	hr/9	RAR	BPV	R$
RH Reliever	03 PIT	3	3	11	83	39	3.69	1.23	243	292	215	5.4	28%	67%	3.67	67	13	20	2.9	4.2	**1.4**	2%	0.1	6.1	59	$9
Age 34	04 STL	7	4	4	64	48	2.39	1.19	240	253	231	3.4	30%	79%	3.69	50	21	29	2.7	6.7	**2.5**	2%	0.1	14.8	96	$11
Past Peak	05 STL	2	3	4	65	47	3.45	1.33	270	294	271	3.7	31%	77%	3.80	51	21	28	2.6	6.5	**2.5**	10%	0.8	6.4	67	$6
Type GB	06 BOS	5	4	1	98	56	4.49	1.57	284	248	327	7.6	31%	73%	4.43	57	17	26	4.0	5.1	**1.3**	12%	0.9	0.8	28	$4
Reliability 46	07 BOS	7	11	0	135	77	5.14	1.50	284	260	300	17.5	31%	66%	4.47	54	16	30	3.4	5.1	**1.5**	10%	0.9	-10.6	33	$5
ERA Potl 50%	1st Half	5	5	0	78	47	4.62	1.38	264			24.0	29%	67%	4.20	56	14	30	3.3	5.4	**1.6**	9%	0.8	-1.1	44	$5
LIMA Plan C+	2nd Half	2	6	0	57	30	5.87	1.66	310			13.0	33%	66%	4.84	51	18	31	3.5	4.8	**1.4**	11%	1.1	-9.6	17	($1)
+/- Score -12	08 Proj	**4**	**6**	**0**	**87**	**48**	**4.66**	**1.49**	**283**			**13.2**	**31%**	**70%**	**4.45**	**54**	**18**	**28**	**3.4**	**5.0**	**1.5**	**10%**	**0.8**	**0.5**	**34**	**$3**

Consistent GBer victimized by S%, poor skills trending in the wrong direction. Ongoing struggles vs. RH hitters limit hopes for big rebound. 2006 may represent his remaining upside.

Tejeda,Robinson

Tejeda,Robinson		W	L	Sv	IP	K	ERA	WHIP	OBA	vL	vR	BF/G	H%	S%	xERA	G	L	F	Ctl	Dom	Cmd	hr/f	hr/9	RAR	BPV	R$
RH Starter	03	0	0	0	0	0	0.00	0.00											0.0	0.0						
Age 26	04 aa	8	14	0	150	117	5.52	1.46	273			24.3	30%	66%	5.22				3.6	7.0	**2.0**		1.6	-21.7	35	$5
Growth	05 PHI *	6	3	0	113	96	3.34	1.36	220	210	226	15.6	28%	75%	4.80	36	21	43	5.1	7.6	**1.5**	4%	0.4	12.7	76	$10
Type Pwr xFB	06 TEX *	11	7	0	153	108	4.52	1.56	271	331	250	23.7	30%	74%	5.27	37	18	45	4.6	6.3	**1.4**	10%	1.2	0.6	31	$9
Reliability 4	07 TEX *	6	12	0	114	84	7.49	1.96	313	317	264	23.1	35%	62%	6.25	35	14	51	6.1	6.7	**1.1**	9%	1.3	-41.8	15	($7)
ERA Potl 60%	1st Half	5	7	0	77	55	6.55	1.69	293			23.7	32%	64%	5.64	34	15	52	4.7	6.4	**1.4**	11%	1.8	-19.4	11	($0)
LIMA Plan C+	2nd Half	1	5	0	37	29	9.48	2.53	351			22.1	42%	60%	7.54	41	14	46	9.0	7.2	**0.8**	3%	0.5	-22.4	30	($7)
+/- Score 28	08 Proj	**5**	**8**	**0**	**90**	**68**	**5.33**	**1.74**	**278**			**23.2**	**32%**	**72%**	**5.76**	**37**	**16**	**47**	**5.9**	**6.8**	**1.2**	**9%**	**1.2**	**-13.9**	**29**	**$1**

5-9, 6.61 ERA in 95 IP at TEX. Teased again early with great stuff. But poor Ctl and lack of consistent put-away pitch from an extreme flyball pitcher in TEX is a flammable combination. Avoid until further notice.

Thompson,Brad

Thompson,Brad		W	L	Sv	IP	K	ERA	WHIP	OBA	vL	vR	BF/G	H%	S%	xERA	G	L	F	Ctl	Dom	Cmd	hr/f	hr/9	RAR	BPV	R$
RH Reliever	03	0	0	0	0	0	0.00	0.00											0.0	0.0						
Age 26	04 a/a	9	2	0	87	59	3.31	1.13	253			22.0	28%	75%	3.56				1.6	6.1	**3.9**		1.0	11.1	93	$12
Growth	05 STL *	6	1	1	68	39	3.04	1.19	235	224	228	5.7	26%	77%	3.77	58	17	25	2.9	5.1	**1.8**	11%	0.8	10.2	52	$8
Type Con GB	06 STL *	3	2	0	98	61	3.11	1.28	265	284	256	7.3	30%	77%	3.67	55	21	24	2.4	5.6	**2.3**	9%	0.6	16.7	66	$8
Reliability 20	07 STL	8	6	0	129	53	4.73	1.52	301	343	267	13.1	30%	74%	4.91	49	17	34	2.8	3.7	**1.3**	15%	1.6	-4.9	-3	$4
ERA Potl 40%	1st Half	6	3	0	70	27	5.01	1.50	299			12.4	31%	69%	4.81	51	18	31	2.7	3.5	**1.3**	12%	1.2	-5.1	8	$3
LIMA Plan C+	2nd Half	2	3	0	59	26	4.40	1.55	304			14.0	29%	81%	5.02	47	15	37	2.9	3.9	**1.4**	18%	2.1	0.2	-17	$1
+/- Score -3	08 Proj	**3**	**2**	**0**	**58**	**29**	**4.03**	**1.40**	**281**			**10.0**	**30%**	**74%**	**4.41**	**52**	**18**	**31**	**2.6**	**4.5**	**1.7**	**11%**	**1.1**	**-0.1**	**29**	**$3**

Solid Ctl and GB rates get our attention. Recent trends in the latter and sub-par Dom are troubling, but reversible at his age. A small rebound with expected hr/f regression could yield LIMA material.

JOCK THOMPSON

Thornton,Matt			W	L	Sv	IP	K	ERA	WHIP	OBA	vL	vR	BF/G	H%	S%	xERA	G	L	F	Ctl	Dom	Cmd	hr/f	hr/9	RAR	BPV	R$
LH Reliever	03	a/a	3	2	0	34	18	3.43	1.26	232			23.8	26%	73%	3.14				3.7	4.8	1.3		0.5	4.0	48	$4
Age 31	04	SEA *	8	7	0	115	93	5.63	1.93	286	300	225	16.0	35%	69%	5.97	40	20	40	7.2	7.3	1.0	4%	0.5	-17.0	49	($1)
Peak	05	SEA	0	4	0	57	57	5.21	1.68	251	262	235	4.8	28%	76%	4.84	43	15	42	6.6	9.0	1.4	20%	2.1	-5.9	26	($0)
Type Pwr	06	CHW	5	3	2	54	49	3.33	1.24	232	211	240	3.6	28%	76%	3.61	49	19	32	3.5	8.2	2.3	10%	0.8	8.2	82	$8
Reliability 21	07	CHW	4	4	2	56	55	4.80	1.51	271	283	260	3.7	35%	68%	3.98	47	19	34	4.2	8.8	2.1	7%	0.6	-2.0	79	$5
ERA Potl 60%	1st Half		2	3	1	24	20	5.63	1.63	293			3.3	34%	67%	4.31	47	21	32	4.1	7.5	1.8	12%	1.1	-3.3	46	$1
LIMA Plan B+	2nd Half		2	1	1	32	35	4.18	1.42	254			4.0	35%	69%	3.75	47	17	36	4.2	9.8	2.3	3%	0.3	1.3	103	$3
+/- Score 28	08	Proj	4	4	3	58	54	4.34	1.45	252			4.1	31%	72%	4.10	47	18	35	4.5	8.4	1.9	10%	0.9	2.8	66	$6

Hit rate and strand rate over-correction caused his ERA to spike, but his true level remains with xERA. 31-year-old hard thrower with periodic control issues, he's not likely going to see 2006 numbers again.

Timlin,Mike			W	L	Sv	IP	K	ERA	WHIP	OBA	vL	vR	BF/G	H%	S%	xERA	G	L	F	Ctl	Dom	Cmd	hr/f	hr/9	RAR	BPV	R$
RH Reliever	03	BOS	6	4	2	83	65	3.58	1.04	248	287	198	4.6	28%	71%	3.11	51	18	31	1.0	7.0	7.2	15%	1.2	9.7	164	$12
Age 42	04	BOS	5	4	1	76	56	4.14	1.24	259	269	247	4.2	30%	69%	3.63	50	21	29	2.2	6.6	2.9	12%	0.9	2.7	76	$7
Decline	05	BOS	7	3	13	80	59	2.25	1.32	276	296	257	4.2	33%	83%	3.84	45	27	29	2.2	6.6	3.0	3%	0.2	21.0	95	$15
Type Con	06	BOS	6	6	9	64	30	4.36	1.47	302	306	303	4.1	32%	72%	5.01	40	21	39	2.3	4.2	1.9	8%	1.0	1.6	30	$7
Reliability 0	07	BOS *	2	1	1	64	34	3.72	1.18	243	173	274	4.5	26%	72%	4.75	39	16	45	2.4	4.8	2.0	8%	1.0	6.1	47	$6
ERA Potl 35%	1st Half		1	0	1	25	12	6.07	1.67	324			4.6	33%	68%	5.48	36	21	43	2.9	4.3	1.5	13%	1.8	-4.9	-6	($0)
LIMA Plan C	2nd Half		1	1	0	38	22	2.18	0.85	179			4.4	20%	76%	4.27	40	13	47	2.2	5.1	2.4	4%	0.5	11.0	86	$6
+/- Score -70	08	Proj	2	3	0	58	27	4.81	1.52	297			4.6	31%	71%	5.19	41	20	39	2.9	4.2	1.4	10%	1.2	-5.0	13	$1

2-1, 3.42 ERA in 55 IP at BOS. The last hurrah? Low hr/f and lucky h% combined with Cmd spike in 2nd half to fashion solid season. The FB trend, age and balky shoulder say repeat isn't in the offing. Oh, and he's 42.

Tomko,Brett			W	L	Sv	IP	K	ERA	WHIP	OBA	vL	vR	BF/G	H%	S%	xERA	G	L	F	Ctl	Dom	Cmd	hr/f	hr/9	RAR	BPV	R$
RH Reliever	03	STL	13	9	0	202	114	5.30	1.53	307	325	292	27.2	32%	69%	4.57	47	18	35	2.5	5.1	2.0	14%	1.6	-25.5	19	$5
Age 35	04	SF	11	7	0	194	108	4.04	1.34	264	294	233	25.8	29%	72%	4.69	42	21	37	3.0	5.0	1.7	8%	0.9	5.4	41	$12
Past Peak	05	SF	8	15	1	190	114	4.50	1.38	277	282	264	24.8	30%	69%	4.64	40	22	38	2.7	5.4	2.0	8%	0.9	-5.9	46	$9
Type	06	LA	8	7	0	112	76	4.74	1.36	280	300	258	10.9	31%	69%	4.56	37	18	45	2.3	6.1	2.6	10%	1.4	-3.4	50	$8
Reliability 57	07	2NL	4	12	0	131	105	5.55	1.50	287	276	291	14.5	33%	65%	4.40	41	20	39	3.3	7.2	2.2	11%	1.2	-18.2	50	$2
ERA Potl 55%	1st Half		1	5	0	61	53	5.61	1.48	289			12.8	34%	64%	4.17	38	23	39	3.0	7.8	2.7	12%	1.3	-8.9	60	$1
LIMA Plan C+	2nd Half		3	7	0	70	52	5.50	1.52	285			16.4	32%	65%	4.60	44	18	39	3.6	6.7	1.9	10%	1.2	-9.4	42	$1
+/- Score 13	08	Proj	5	9	0	116	82	4.81	1.41	275			14.8	31%	69%	4.53	40	20	40	3.1	6.4	2.1	11%	1.2	-1.9	44	$5

Start or relieve? You decide: As SP: 6.4 Dom / 1.8 Cmd. As RP: 10.0 Dom / 4.7 Cmd. Another 5.00+ ERA in 101 IP as a starter suggests that his only value depends on removal from SP and swingman roles.

Torres,Salomon			W	L	Sv	IP	K	ERA	WHIP	OBA	vL	vR	BF/G	H%	S%	xERA	G	L	F	Ctl	Dom	Cmd	hr/f	hr/9	RAR	BPV	R$
RH Reliever	03	PIT	7	5	2	121	84	4.76	1.40	273	307	252	12.8	30%	70%	3.89	53	19	27	3.1	6.2	2.0	18%	1.4	-7.2	38	$7
Age 36	04	PIT	7	7	0	92	62	2.64	1.18	251	254	257	4.5	29%	80%	3.43	59	15	26	2.2	6.1	2.8	8%	0.6	18.4	83	$11
Decline	05	PIT	5	5	3	94	55	2.77	1.19	222	272	189	5.0	25%	79%	4.33	51	16	34	3.4	5.3	1.5	7%	0.7	17.1	54	$11
Type GB	06	PIT	3	6	12	93	72	3.29	1.46	272	281	269	4.3	33%	78%	3.87	55	19	26	3.7	7.0	1.9	8%	0.6	13.8	65	$10
Reliability 27	07	PIT	2	4	12	53	45	5.46	1.40	277	275	278	4.1	33%	63%	3.82	48	19	34	2.9	7.7	2.6	13%	1.2	-6.8	65	$6
ERA Potl 60%	1st Half		0	3	12	28	25	5.14	1.36	262			4.0	31%	65%	3.76	49	17	35	3.2	8.0	2.5	14%	1.3	-2.5	65	$5
LIMA Plan C+	2nd Half		2	1	0	25	20	5.83	1.46	294			4.2	34%	61%	3.90	47	21	32	2.6	7.3	2.9	12%	1.1	-4.3	67	$1
+/- Score 47	08	Proj	3	5	3	74	57	3.92	1.37	268			4.4	31%	74%	3.88	51	18	31	3.1	7.0	2.3	11%	1.0	4.7	62	$6

Irony is a lightly-skilled closer losing job as his Dom and Cmd spike. Gopheritis and S% crash are part reversion, part misfortune and partly due to GB drop. Will rebound a tad, but closing days are over.

Towers,Josh			W	L	Sv	IP	K	ERA	WHIP	OBA	vL	vR	BF/G	H%	S%	xERA	G	L	F	Ctl	Dom	Cmd	hr/f	hr/9	RAR	BPV	R$
RH Starter	03	TOR *	13	8	1	196	106	4.50	1.31	293	281	250	23.7	31%	69%	4.49	40	18	41	1.3	4.9	3.8	10%	1.2	0.6	68	$15
Age 31	04	TOR *	12	10	0	152	72	4.73	1.46	306	312	308	24.7	32%	71%	4.57	47	19	34	2.0	4.3	2.2	12%	1.3	-5.7	26	$7
Peak	05	TOR	13	12	0	208	112	3.72	1.28	288	274	297	26.5	31%	74%	4.25	45	19	37	1.3	4.8	3.9	9%	1.0	16.8	77	$17
Type Con	06	TOR *	7	15	0	163	95	6.96	1.75	356	325	357	25.4	38%	63%	4.91	39	21	40	1.7	5.2	3.1	14%	1.9	-48.3	24	($5)
Reliability 40	07	TOR	5	10	0	107	76	5.38	1.41	299	305	290	18.5	33%	65%	4.06	44	20	36	1.9	6.4	3.5	14%	1.5	-11.6	61	$5
ERA Potl 50%	1st Half		3	5	0	58	46	5.59	1.41	309			18.0	35%	65%	3.80	43	21	36	1.4	7.1	5.1	16%	1.7	-7.7	92	$3
LIMA Plan C+	2nd Half		2	5	0	49	30	5.14	1.41	288			19.3	31%	66%	4.39	45	20	36	2.4	5.5	2.3	12%	1.3	-3.9	40	$2
+/- Score 35	08	Proj	4	7	0	87	53	4.86	1.41	298			20.9	32%	69%	4.36	44	20	37	2.0	5.5	2.8	12%	1.3	1.5	47	$4

1st half Dom and Cmd spiked to join Ctl at elite levels, but he remained a HR magnet. xERA says he deserves better but until hr/f and S% show some regression, stay away.

Trachsel,Steve			W	L	Sv	IP	K	ERA	WHIP	OBA	vL	vR	BF/G	H%	S%	xERA	G	L	F	Ctl	Dom	Cmd	hr/f	hr/9	RAR	BPV	R$
RH Starter	03	NYM	16	10	0	204	111	3.79	1.32	262	199	312	26.2	28%	75%	4.90	40	16	43	2.9	4.9	1.7	9%	1.1	12.2	33	$17
Age 37	04	NYM	12	13	0	202	117	4.01	1.41	263	245	279	26.6	28%	76%	4.91	43	18	39	3.7	5.2	1.4	10%	1.1	6.4	30	$12
Decline	05	NYM	1	4	0	37	24	4.14	1.32	262	288	243	26.2	28%	74%	4.37	41	23	36	2.9	5.8	2.0	14%	1.5	0.5	36	$2
Type Con	06	NYM	15	8	0	164	79	4.99	1.60	285	267	306	24.7	30%	72%	5.60	42	18	40	4.3	4.3	1.0	10%	1.3	-10.1	7	$6
Reliability 11	07	2TM	7	11	0	158	56	4.90	1.59	283	250	319	24.6	29%	71%	5.97	41	19	40	4.3	3.2	0.7	8%	1.1	-8.5	1	$2
ERA Potl 40%	1st Half		5	6	0	91	31	4.55	1.44	251			24.8	25%	71%	5.92	41	17	42	4.5	3.1	0.7	8%	1.1	-1.0	5	$4
LIMA Plan C	2nd Half		2	5	0	67	25	5.37	1.81	323			24.4	33%	72%	6.04	41	21	37	4.2	3.4	0.8	8%	1.1	-7.5	-5	($2)
+/- Score -68	08	Proj	4	5	0	73	30	5.09	1.63	296			25.4	30%	71%	5.70	41	20	39	4.0	3.7	0.9	10%	1.2	-11.3	1	$1

Never a BPI poster boy, but in the past two years he's done more with less than just about anyone. There's nothing commendable in these levels or trends and this is no time to start taking flyers.

Tsao,Chin-hui			W	L	Sv	IP	K	ERA	WHIP	OBA	vL	vR	BF/G	H%	S%	xERA	G	L	F	Ctl	Dom	Cmd	hr/f	hr/9	RAR	BPV	R$
RH Reliever	03	aa	11	4	0	113	109	3.58	1.20	256			25.9	32%	73%	3.68				2.1	8.7	4.2		1.0	11.3	115	$15
Age 26	04	COL *	2	2	1	34	30	6.07	1.67	333	286	143	9.8	37%	71%	3.64	48	24	28	2.4	7.9	3.3	28%	2.4	-7.6	35	$0
Growth	05	COL	1	0	3	11	4	6.55	1.91	340	462	182	5.3	32%	72%	6.92	26	21	53	4.1	3.3	0.8	13%	2.5	-3.1	-50	$0
Type xFB	06	COL	0	0	0	0	0	0.00	0.00																		
Reliability 0	07	LA *	0	2	2	30	23	4.20	1.07	214	195	213	4.6	25%	62%	4.17	39	14	47	2.7	6.9	2.6	8%	0.9	0.8	80	$3
ERA Potl 55%	1st Half		0	2	2	23	23	3.13	1.00	198			4.5	28%	65%	3.58	38	18	44	2.7	9.0	3.3	0%	0.0	3.7	138	$3
LIMA Plan B	2nd Half		0	0	0	7	0	7.71	1.29	262			4.9	17%	50%	6.26	40	8	52	2.6	0.0	0.0	22%	3.9	-2.8	-113	($0)
+/- Score 13	08	Proj	2	2	0	29	21	4.74	1.33	265			4.7	30%	68%	4.74	33	16	51	2.8	6.6	2.3	9%	1.3	-1.2	53	$2

0-1, 4.38 ERA in 25 IP at LA. Once COL's closer-in-waiting. MLB return after surgery for a torn labrum in May 2005. Pitched well before shoulder woes again ended season in May. Murky future.

Turnbow,Derrick			W	L	Sv	IP	K	ERA	WHIP	OBA	vL	vR	BF/G	H%	S%	xERA	G	L	F	Ctl	Dom	Cmd	hr/f	hr/9	RAR	BPV	R$
RH Reliever	03	ANA *	4	2	5	84	82	4.82	1.49	282			7.0	36%	67%	4.52				3.4	8.8	2.6		0.7	-3.1	85	$7
Age 30	04	aaa	2	6	6	74	46	5.13	1.60	275			7.3	31%	68%	4.79				4.8	5.5	1.2		0.8	-7.2	35	$2
Peak	05	MIL	7	1	39	67	64	1.74	1.09	206	233	167	3.9	26%	88%	3.20	50	22	28	3.2	8.6	2.7	10%	0.7	20.7	101	$25
Type Pwr	06	MIL	4	9	24	56	69	6.90	1.69	261	245	263	4.0	35%	60%	4.02	42	25	33	6.3	11.1	1.8	17%	1.3	-16.7	68	$9
Reliability 39	07	MIL	4	5	1	68	84	4.63	1.32	187	172	189	3.7	27%	64%	3.76	47	14	40	6.1	11.1	1.8	7%	0.5	-1.7	107	$6
ERA Potl 0%	1st Half		1	3	1	36	46	3.75	1.11	191			3.7	28%	66%	3.05	45	16	38	4.0	11.5	2.9	7%	0.5	3.0	131	$5
LIMA Plan B+	2nd Half		3	2	0	32	38	5.62	1.56	181			3.8	26%	63%	4.71	48	11	41	8.4	10.7	1.3	7%	0.6	-4.7	93	$2
+/- Score 22	08	Proj	4	5	0	58	66	4.50	1.43	220			4.1	30%	69%	3.91	46	19	36	5.7	10.2	1.8	10%	0.8	3.5	87	$5

PRO: 1H; sustained Dom; GB rebound, hr/f reversion returned hr/9 and BPV to Elite levels. CON: 2H; poor Ctl, imploding into 9.9 debacle in Aug-Sept. Unpredictable at best without more strike zone consistency.

Uehara,Koji			W	L	Sv	IP	K	ERA	WHIP	OBA	vL	vR	BF/G	H%	S%	xERA	G	L	F	Ctl	Dom	Cmd	hr/f	hr/9	RAR	BPV	R$
RH Reliever	03	JPN	16	5	0	207	184	3.94	1.12	259			31.0	28%	76%	4.52				1.2	8.0	6.4		2.0	11.5	126	$25
Age 33	04	JPN	13	5	0	163	145	3.22	1.06	240			29.5	25%	86%	4.30				1.6	8.0	5.1		2.2	22.5	96	$23
Peak	05	JPN	9	12	0	187	138	4.12	1.09	250			27.8	26%	72%	4.21				1.3	6.6	5.0		1.9	4.2	93	$18
Type Pwr	06	JPN	8	9	0	168	143	3.99	1.16	262			28.5	28%	78%	4.72				1.4	7.7	5.5		2.1	10.9	100	$18
Reliability 38	07	JPN	4	3	32	62	63	2.16	0.89	224			4.3	28%	83%	2.49				0.7	9.1	12.6		1.0	17.6	301	$23
ERA Potl 40%	1st Half		0	0	0	0	0	0.00	0.00																		
LIMA Plan D	2nd Half		4	3	32	62	63	2.16	0.89	224			4.3	28%	83%					0.7	9.1	12.6		1.0	17.6	301	$23
+/- Score -30	08	Proj	4	4	0	73	62	3.97	1.28	263			5.0	29%	77%	4.71				2.5	7.7	3.1		1.7	-2.4	62	$7

Former SP turned closer with apparent success. Eliminated severe gopheritis and raised Cmd to ridiculous levels, his ERA dropping by almost two full runs. It won't be this easy in MLB parks. ETA now 2009.

JOCK THOMPSON

Valverde,Jose				W	L	Sv	IP	K	ERA	WHIP	OBA	vL	vR	BF/G	H%	S%	xERA	G	L	F	Ctl	Dom	Cmd	hr/f	hr/9	RAR	BPV	R$
RH	Reliever	03	ARI *	3	2	15	79	94	2.73	1.16	192	169	112	4.2	27%	78%	3.73	28	26	46	4.4	10.7	2.4	6%	0.6	15.0	114	$15
Age	28	04	ARI	1	2	8	29	38	4.32	1.37	218	152	258	4.3	27%	79%	3.49	36	25	39	5.2	11.7	2.2	27%	2.2	-0.2	64	$5
Pre-Peak		05	ARI	3	4	15	66	75	2.45	1.07	215	168	241	4.3	29%	80%	3.28	38	19	43	2.7	10.2	3.8	7%	0.7	14.6	132	$15
Type	Pwr FB	06	ARI	2	3	18	49	69	5.87	1.47	265	323	192	4.9	39%	61%	3.28	35	24	41	4.0	12.6	3.1	12%	1.1	-8.3	111	$8
Reliability	59	07	ARI	1	4	47	64	78	2.66	1.12	202	202	189	4.0	27%	82%	3.42	36	17	47	3.6	10.9	3.0	10%	1.0	14.0	114	$24
ERA Potl	50%	1st Half		0	2	25	32	37	2.81	1.13	210			3.8	27%	81%	3.63	31	18	51	3.4	10.4	3.1	10%	1.1	6.4	106	$12
LIMA Plan	C+	2nd Half		1	2	22	32	41	2.51	1.11	195			4.2	28%	82%	3.18	42	15	43	3.9	11.4	2.9	10%	0.8	7.6	121	$12
+/- Score	-2	08	Proj	2	4	43	68	82	3.31	1.21	220			4.3	30%	76%	3.46	36	19	44	3.7	10.9	2.9	10%	0.9	7.9	110	$22

All he needed was a healthy season. While his ERAs had been fluctuating, xERA says his skills have been perfectly stable. That's curse of the short reliever, whose numbers can be skewed with just one bad outing.

Vanden Hurk,Rick				W	L	Sv	IP	K	ERA	WHIP	OBA	vL	vR	BF/G	H%	S%	xERA	G	L	F	Ctl	Dom	Cmd	hr/f	hr/9	RAR	BPV	R$
RH	Starter	03		0	0	0	0	0	0.00	0.00																		
Age	22	04		0	0	0	0	0	0.00	0.00																		
Growth		05		0	0	0	0	0	0.00	0.00																		
Type	Pwr xFB	06		0	0	0	0	0	0.00	0.00																		
Reliability	0	07	FLA *	8	8	0	147	151	5.51	1.50	263	289	298	22.4	32%	66%	4.54	27	25	48	4.5	9.3	2.1	12%	1.4	-19.7	59	$6
ERA Potl	60%	1st Half		4	4	0	82	88	5.58	1.44	257			22.4	33%	62%	4.30	26	26	48	4.2	9.6	2.3	9%	1.1	-11.7	77	$4
LIMA Plan	B	2nd Half		4	4	0	65	63	5.42	1.59	272			22.5	32%	71%	4.84	28	24	49	4.9	8.8	1.8	14%	1.8	-8.0	37	$2
+/- Score	42	08	Proj	5	5	0	91	92	4.95	1.47	255			22.2	31%	70%	4.56	27	24	48	4.5	9.1	2.0	11%	1.4	-1.8	59	$5

4-6, 6.83 ERA in 81 IP at FLA. Rushed to the majors with only 65 IP of aa/aaa experience. Live arm, but has yet to post a walk rate lower than 4.5 at any level of pro ball. xFB means it could get worse outside of FLA.

Vargas,Claudio				W	L	Sv	IP	K	ERA	WHIP	OBA	vL	vR	BF/G	H%	S%	xERA	G	L	F	Ctl	Dom	Cmd	hr/f	hr/9	RAR	BPV	R$
RH	Starter	03	MON *	7	8	0	135	82	3.93	1.30	249	270	242	21.1	27%	73%	5.10	34	16	50	3.3	5.5	1.7	8%	1.1	5.7	39	$10
Age	29	04	MON	5	5	0	118	89	5.26	1.56	265	301	239	11.8	28%	73%	5.19	33	22	45	4.9	6.8	1.4	16%	2.0	-14.5	12	$2
Peak		05	2NL *	11	11	0	160	124	5.10	1.44	276	268	288	23.3	31%	69%	4.54	35	23	41	3.3	6.9	2.1	14%	1.6	-16.8	38	$7
Type	FB	06	ARI	12	10	0	167	123	4.84	1.42	282	275	272	23.4	31%	70%	4.46	40	18	42	2.8	6.6	2.4	12%	1.5	-7.4	44	$10
Reliability	49	07	MIL	11	6	1	134	107	5.09	1.54	288	320	255	20.7	32%	71%	4.77	34	22	44	3.6	7.2	2.0	12%	1.5	-11.1	36	$7
ERA Potl	50%	1st Half		6	1	1	78	69	4.27	1.50	276			21.5	31%	78%	4.58	32	22	45	3.8	8.0	2.1	14%	1.7	1.5	39	$6
LIMA Plan	C	2nd Half		5	5	0	56	38	6.23	1.60	303			19.6	34%	62%	5.05	36	22	43	3.4	6.1	1.8	10%	1.3	-12.6	30	$1
+/- Score	4	08	Proj	11	9	0	152	114	4.57	1.45	277			22.8	31%	73%	4.67	36	21	43	3.3	6.8	2.0	12%	1.4	-5.0	40	$9

We had higher hopes for him this year. Aside from the back spasms that "officially" sidelined him for only 15 days, he had more control problems and struggled keeping the ball down. There's talent here; wait for it.

Vargas,Jason				W	L	Sv	IP	K	ERA	WHIP	OBA	vL	vR	BF/G	H%	S%	xERA	G	L	F	Ctl	Dom	Cmd	hr/f	hr/9	RAR	BPV	R$
LH	Starter	03		0	0	0	0	0	0.00	0.00											0.0	0.0						
Age	25	04		0	0	0	0	0	0.00	0.00											0.0	0.0						
Growth		05	FLA *	6	5	0	92	79	3.90	1.36	249	192	269	19.7	30%	73%	4.63	31	21	47	3.8	7.7	2.0	6%	0.8	3.9	71	$8
Type	Pwr xFB	06	FLA *	4	8	0	112	71	7.55	1.89	328	262	302	21.6	36%	61%	6.17	32	17	51	4.7	5.7	1.2	9%	1.5	-42.4	4	($8)
Reliability	0	07	NYM *	9	8	0	135	92	6.67	1.70	325		370	24.1	36%	61%	5.82	27	13	60	3.1	6.1	2.0	7%	1.2	-37.5	31	($2)
ERA Potl	55%	1st Half		6	4	0	79	50	5.46	1.44	292			24.6	32%	63%	5.94	23	4	73	2.5	5.7	2.3	5%	1.0	-10.1	48	$3
LIMA Plan	F	2nd Half		3	4	0	56	42	8.38	2.07	366			23.4	41%	60%	5.59	32	26	42	4.6	6.8	1.7	11%	1.6	-27.4	11	($6)
+/- Score	32	08	Proj	3	4	0	65	46	5.86	1.61	297			20.9	33%	67%	5.35	31	18	50	3.8	6.4	1.7	10%	1.5	-7.5	24	($0)

0-1, 12.19 ERA in 10 IP at NYM. Extreme flyball pitcher, which means plenty of homers even with an average HR rate (as his 2nd half debacle shows). Yikes! Imagine if he pitched for TEX, or CIN, or PHI.

Vazquez,Javier				W	L	Sv	IP	K	ERA	WHIP	OBA	vL	vR	BF/G	H%	S%	xERA	G	L	F	Ctl	Dom	Cmd	hr/f	hr/9	RAR	BPV	R$
RH	Starter	03	MON	13	12	0	230	241	3.25	1.11	234	233	225	27.3	29%	76%	3.42	34	23	43	2.2	9.4	4.2	11%	1.1	29.2	121	$29
Age	31	04	NYY	14	10	0	198	150	4.91	1.29	259	253	256	26.0	28%	66%	4.29	39	18	43	2.7	6.8	2.5	13%	1.5	-11.6	52	$15
Peak		05	ARI	11	15	0	215	192	4.43	1.25	269	244	285	27.2	31%	70%	3.46	43	23	34	1.9	8.0	4.2	16%	1.5	-5.0	93	$17
Type	Pwr FB	06	CHW	11	12	0	202	184	4.85	1.30	265	256	261	25.8	32%	64%	3.86	40	20	41	2.5	8.2	3.3	10%	1.0	-7.3	89	$17
Reliability	90	07	CHW	15	8	0	217	213	3.74	1.14	244	230	253	27.5	30%	72%	3.52	40	17	43	2.1	8.8	4.3	11%	1.2	20.5	113	$28
ERA Potl	60%	1st Half		3	5	0	91	83	4.15	1.12	235			26.3	28%	67%	3.79	37	17	46	2.3	8.2	3.6	11%	1.3	3.9	94	$10
LIMA Plan	C+	2nd Half		12	3	0	126	130	3.44	1.15	250			28.4	31%	75%	3.32	42	17	41	1.9	9.3	4.8	11%	1.1	16.6	128	$19
+/- Score	25	08	Proj	14	9	0	203	192	3.72	1.17	248			26.8	30%	73%	3.58	40	19	41	2.2	8.5	3.9	12%	1.2	22.9	103	$25

Nothing like a good strand rate to help one's ERA. High FB rate leads to potential HR troubles, but great command limits the damage. xERA says that there still might be a bit more upside, but don't pay for it.

Verlander,Justin				W	L	Sv	IP	K	ERA	WHIP	OBA	vL	vR	BF/G	H%	S%	xERA	G	L	F	Ctl	Dom	Cmd	hr/f	hr/9	RAR	BPV	R$
RH	Starter	03		0	0	0	0	0	0.00	0.00																		
Age	25	04		0	0	0	0	0	0.00	0.00																		
Growth		05	DET *	2	2	0	43	35	2.08	0.88	181			18.2	22%	78%	1.40				2.3	7.3	3.2		0.4	12.2	117	$8
Type	Pwr	06	DET	17	9	0	186	124	3.63	1.33	263	279	253	26.3	29%	76%	4.33	42	23	35	2.9	6.0	2.1	10%	1.0	21.3	51	$21
Reliability	16	07	DET	18	6	0	202	183	3.66	1.23	241	232	234	26.2	29%	73%	3.85	41	19	40	3.0	8.2	2.7	9%	0.9	21.1	86	$26
ERA Potl	55%	1st Half		9	2	0	97	85	2.78	1.13	217			26.2	27%	78%	3.76	45	17	38	3.2	7.9	2.5	8%	0.7	20.6	89	$16
LIMA Plan	C	2nd Half		9	4	0	105	98	4.47	1.32	262			26.1	32%	68%	3.92	38	21	41	2.8	8.4	3.0	10%	1.0	0.5	84	$11
+/- Score	17	08	Proj	19	7	0	209	184	3.28	1.24	246			26.3	30%	77%	3.83	41	21	38	2.8	7.9	2.8	10%	0.9	17.2	83	$28

Good command, great PQS DOM/DIS (72/9)... and this year's 2nd half decline was due to H%/S% bad luck, not from wearing down as in 2006. Poised for another step up.

Villanueva,Carlos				W	L	Sv	IP	K	ERA	WHIP	OBA	vL	vR	BF/G	H%	S%	xERA	G	L	F	Ctl	Dom	Cmd	hr/f	hr/9	RAR	BPV	R$
RH	Reliever	03		0	0	0	0	0	0.00	0.00																		
Age	24	04		0	0	0	0	0	0.00	0.00																		
Growth		05	aa	1	3	0	21	13	8.14	1.57	280			23.6	29%	48%	5.66				4.3	5.6	1.3		1.7	-9.9	8	($1)
Type	Pwr xFB	06	MIL *	13	8	0	181	146	4.22	1.22	246	226	204	23.5	28%	69%	4.01	43	16	41	2.7	7.2	2.7	11%	1.1	6.0	71	$18
Reliability	0	07	MIL	8	5	1	114	99	3.94	1.35	239	250	227	8.3	28%	75%	4.56	36	17	47	4.2	7.8	1.9	11%	1.3	6.9	55	$11
ERA Potl	45%	1st Half		5	0	0	54	48	2.67	1.15	208			6.9	26%	79%	4.18	38	16	47	3.7	8.0	2.2	6%	0.7	11.7	87	$8
LIMA Plan	C	2nd Half		3	5	1	60	51	5.07	1.53	264			9.9	29%	73%	4.90	35	17	47	4.6	7.6	1.6	14%	1.8	-4.8	29	$2
+/- Score	3	08	Proj	5	3	0	73	61	4.10	1.38	258			8.4	30%	74%	4.50	37	17	46	3.6	7.6	2.1	10%	1.2	-0.9	56	$6

Pitched in 59 games, just 6 as a starter, but interesting BPIs: 2.06 ERA, 1.5 Cmd, 6.4 Dom PQS scores: 4,5,3,3,4,3. Hit rate 24%, strand rate 96%. So... his long-term outlook for that role is still a question.

Villarreal,Oscar				W	L	Sv	IP	K	ERA	WHIP	OBA	vL	vR	BF/G	H%	S%	xERA	G	L	F	Ctl	Dom	Cmd	hr/f	hr/9	RAR	BPV	R$
RH	Reliever	03	ARI	10	7	0	98	80	2.57	1.29	224	252	204	4.8	27%	82%	4.26	38	28	34	4.2	7.3	1.7	6%	0.6	20.6	74	$13
Age	26	04	ARI *	0	4	0	29	28	9.93	2.03	365	250	400	6.2	43%	51%	4.68	29	35	35	3.7	8.7	2.3	17%	1.9	-20.3	27	($5)
Growth		05	ARI *	2	3	0	31	12	5.52	1.35	262	207	278	5.8	27%	59%	5.36	33	29	38	3.2	3.5	1.1	7%	0.9	-4.9	20	$1
Type		06	ATL	9	1	0	92	55	3.62	1.30	264	264	259	6.7	28%	78%	4.27	47	19	34	2.6	5.4	2.0	13%	1.3	9.9	39	$10
Reliability	16	07	ATL	2	2	1	76	58	4.25	1.40	258	315	220	6.5	31%	70%	4.29	44	23	33	3.8	6.8	1.8	8%	0.7	1.7	61	$4
ERA Potl	50%	1st Half		1	0	0	40	35	3.38	1.28	237			6.2	30%	73%	3.79	46	22	31	3.6	7.9	2.2	6%	0.5	5.2	87	$4
LIMA Plan	C+	2nd Half		1	2	1	36	23	5.21	1.54	281			6.7	31%	67%	4.86	42	23	34	4.0	5.7	1.4	10%	1.0	-3.5	33	$1
+/- Score	-1	08	Proj	4	3	0	73	47	4.22	1.41	266			6.3	30%	72%	4.53	43	23	34	3.5	5.8	1.7	10%	1.0	-1.1	42	$4

Wasn't quite so lucky with the vulture wins this time, even though xERA says '06 and '07 were identical seasons. BPIs are borderline in any case, so his vulture potential can be measured with a microscope.

Vizcaino,Luis				W	L	Sv	IP	K	ERA	WHIP	OBA	vL	vR	BF/G	H%	S%	xERA	G	L	F	Ctl	Dom	Cmd	hr/f	hr/9	RAR	BPV	R$
RH	Reliever	03	MIL	4	3	0	62	61	6.39	1.44	268	253	269	3.6	30%	62%	4.17	32	24	45	3.6	8.9	2.4	20%	2.3	-16.1	36	$2
Age	33	04	MIL	4	4	1	72	63	3.75	1.18	231	163	290	4.0	26%	75%	4.14	35	17	48	3.0	7.9	2.6	12%	1.5	4.5	66	$8
Past Peak		05	CHW	6	5	0	70	43	3.73	1.47	273	330	242	4.7	30%	78%	4.82	43	21	36	3.7	5.5	1.5	10%	1.0	5.6	34	$5
Type	Pwr FB	06	ARI	4	6	0	65	72	3.59	1.23	217	163	256	3.9	28%	75%	3.42	45	19	36	4.0	10.0	2.5	14%	1.1	7.2	90	$8
Reliability	16	07	NYY	8	2	0	75	62	4.30	1.45	237	265	213	4.3	29%	71%	5.02	36	19	45	5.1	7.4	1.4	6%	0.7	1.9	61	$7
ERA Potl	55%	1st Half		4	1	0	37	22	5.35	1.54	223			4.6	25%	65%	6.30	33	19	49	6.6	5.4	0.8	5%	0.7	-3.9	38	$2
LIMA Plan	B	2nd Half		4	1	0	38	40	3.29	1.36	250			4.0	33%	78%	3.94	39	19	42	3.8	9.4	2.5	7%	0.7	5.7	93	$5
+/- Score	-25	08	Proj	6	4	0	73	72	3.85	1.32	241			4.1	30%	75%	3.98	39	19	42	3.8	8.9	2.3	11%	1.1	4.6	76	$9

1st half debacle, caused by wildness and inflated strand rate, obscured the fact that he had a pretty decent 2nd half. Fly ball tendency will always be problematic but there is decent end-game rosterability here.

TOM TODARO

Volquez,Edinson

			W	L	Sv	IP	K	ERA	WHIP	OBA	vL	vR	BF/G	H%	S%	xERA	G	L	F	Ctl	Dom	Cmd	hr/f	hr/9	RAR	BPV	R$
RH Starter	03		0	0	0	0	0	0.00	0.00																		
Age 24	04		0	0	0	0	0	0.00	0.00																		
Growth	05	TEX *	1	9	0	72	53	6.88	1.68	316			20.7	36%	60%	6.13				3.4	6.6	2.0		1.4	-22.2	31	($3)
Type Pwr FB	06	TEX *	7	12	0	153	127	5.40	1.68	273			24.3	32%	70%	5.23				5.6	7.5	1.3		1.2	-16.0	36	$3
Reliability 0	07	TEX *	16	3	0	143	133	3.72	1.25	233	222	299	23.9	28%	73%	3.99	38	22	40	3.6	8.3	2.3	10%	1.0	13.9	78	$20
ERA Potl 45%	1st Half		6	0	0	40	32	4.71	1.37	252			21.5	27%	72%					3.8	7.2	1.9		1.8	-1.0	33	$5
LIMA Plan D+	2nd Half		10	3	0	103	101	3.33	1.21	225			25.0	29%	74%	3.84	38	22	40	3.5	8.8	2.5	7%	0.7	14.9	95	$15
+/- Score 5	08	Proj	11	11	0	164	139	4.84	1.48	262			24.8	31%	70%	4.56	38	22	40	4.3	7.7	1.8	11%	1.2	-1.2	50	$10

2-1, 4.50 ERA in 34 IP at TEX. Progression through minors marked by improved Dom but spotty control. However, the scariest indicator is the fact that he's a fly ball pitcher... in TEX! TEX FB ERAs start at 5.00.

Wagner,Billy

			W	L	Sv	IP	K	ERA	WHIP	OBA	vL	vR	BF/G	H%	S%	xERA	G	L	F	Ctl	Dom	Cmd	hr/f	hr/9	RAR	BPV	R$
LH Reliever	03	HOU	1	4	44	86	105	1.78	0.87	177	216	154	4.2	24%	87%	2.70	39	24	37	2.4	11.0	4.6	11%	0.8	26.5	156	$29
Age 36	04	PHI	4	0	21	48	59	2.43	0.77	186	103	197	3.9	25%	75%	2.41	45	14	41	1.1	11.0	9.8	11%	0.9	10.9	262	$16
Decline	05	PHI	4	3	38	77	87	1.52	0.84	171	128	173	3.9	23%	88%	2.72	46	19	35	2.3	10.1	4.4	10%	0.7	26.0	152	$28
Type Pwr	06	NYM	3	2	40	72	94	2.25	1.11	225	161	234	4.2	32%	85%	2.48	53	16	31	2.6	11.7	4.5	13%	0.9	19.9	148	$25
Reliability 54	07	NYM	2	2	34	68	80	2.64	1.13	222	241	209	4.2	30%	80%	3.34	37	18	45	2.9	10.5	3.6	8%	0.8	15.1	126	$20
ERA Potl 50%	1st Half		1	0	15	34	44	1.85	0.91	193			4.1	27%	89%	2.82	33	20	48	2.1	11.6	5.5	11%	1.1	10.8	170	$11
LIMA Plan C+	2nd Half		1	2	19	34	36	3.41	1.34	249			4.3	33%	75%	3.89	40	17	43	3.7	9.4	2.6	5%	0.5	4.3	100	$9
+/- Score -8	08	Proj	3	2	35	73	81	2.98	1.16	230			4.2	30%	78%	3.26	43	18	39	2.9	10.1	3.5	10%	0.9	10.2	117	$21

For the first time in years, he had an ordinary second half. Admitted to a "tired arm", and wasn't his usual dominant self. And he still had a BPV of 100. I hate people like that. All of them.

Wagner,Ryan

			W	L	Sv	IP	K	ERA	WHIP	OBA	vL	vR	BF/G	H%	S%	xERA	G	L	F	Ctl	Dom	Cmd	hr/f	hr/9	RAR	BPV	R$
RH Reliever	03	CIN *	3	1	0	31	34	2.03	1.13	194	240	140	4.8	26%	85%	2.32				4.1	9.9	2.4		0.6	8.6	109	$6
Age 25	04	CIN *	4	3	1	67	52	4.42	1.68	284	224	307	4.8	33%	75%	4.49	50	24	26	5.1	7.0	1.4	12%	0.9	-1.3	41	$2
Growth	05	CIN	3	2	0	45	39	6.17	1.62	305	311	297	4.9	37%	61%	3.15	61	23	15	3.4	7.8	2.3	18%	0.8	-10.7	65	$0
Type Pwr xGB	06	WAS *	4	6	1	77	48	6.64	1.85	337	197	387	5.5	38%	63%	4.14	62	18	20	3.7	5.6	1.5	12%	0.8	-20.5	28	($3)
Reliability 0	07	WAS	0	2	0	16	9	5.73	1.78	311	269	342	5.3	34%	69%	5.12	51	18	31	4.6	5.2	1.1	12%	1.1	-2.5	13	($1)
ERA Potl 55%	1st Half		0	2	0	16	9	5.63	1.75	307			5.3	33%	69%	5.09	51	18	31	4.5	5.1	1.1	12%	1.1	-2.4	14	($1)
LIMA Plan D	2nd Half		0	0	0	-0	0	0.00	0.00																		
+/- Score 3	08	Proj	1	2	0	29	21	4.97	1.59	288			5.0	33%	70%	4.01	56	21	23	4.0	6.5	1.6	14%	0.9	1.4	43	$0

BPIs continue to move in the wrong direction, thanks to a sore shoulder that turned into a torn labrum. Odds are against a positive contribution in 2008... and we can remove the "future closer" label.

Wainwright,Adam

			W	L	Sv	IP	K	ERA	WHIP	OBA	vL	vR	BF/G	H%	S%	xERA	G	L	F	Ctl	Dom	Cmd	hr/f	hr/9	RAR	BPV	R$
RH Starter	03	aa	10	8	0	149	108	4.58	1.33	277			23.5	32%	65%	4.04				2.3	6.5	2.8		0.7	-3.5	79	$11
Age 26	04	aaa	4	4	0	63	56	5.55	1.55	288			23.5	33%	68%	5.60				3.7	8.0	2.2		1.6	-9.4	44	$2
Growth	05	aaa	9	10	0	176	123	4.86	1.48	301			27.7	35%	68%	4.91				2.4	6.3	2.6		0.8	-12.0	63	$7
Type	06	STL	2	1	3	75	72	3.12	1.15	232	301	182	5.0	29%	75%	3.38	48	17	35	2.6	8.6	3.3	8%	0.7	12.7	108	$10
Reliability 9	07	STL	14	12	0	202	136	3.70	1.40	271	249	283	27.2	31%	74%	4.34	48	18	34	3.1	6.1	1.9	6%	0.6	18.1	61	$16
ERA Potl 55%	1st Half		6	6	0	90	52	4.60	1.56	297			26.9	33%	71%	4.82	48	16	36	3.3	5.2	1.6	7%	0.8	-1.9	36	$3
LIMA Plan C	2nd Half		8	6	0	112	84	2.97	1.27	249			27.6	30%	77%	3.97	48	19	33	3.0	6.7	2.3	4%	0.4	20.1	81	$13
+/- Score -2	08	Proj	14	7	0	203	155	3.59	1.32	262			26.9	30%	75%	3.99	48	17	35	2.9	6.9	2.4	9%	0.9	10.2	67	$19

These half-season splits don't do justice to his turnaround:

	DOM	DIS
1st half	19%	13%
2nd half	56%	6%

The skills are there. It only gets better from here...

Wakefield,Tim

			W	L	Sv	IP	K	ERA	WHIP	OBA	vL	vR	BF/G	H%	S%	xERA	G	L	F	Ctl	Dom	Cmd	hr/f	hr/9	RAR	BPV	R$
RH Starter	03	BOS	11	7	1	202	169	4.10	1.31	253	266	228	24.4	30%	71%	4.13	40	20	40	3.2	7.5	2.4	10%	1.0	10.6	69	$19
Age 41	04	BOS	12	10	0	188	116	4.88	1.38	271	230	298	25.3	29%	68%	4.58	47	14	40	3.0	5.6	1.8	12%	1.4	-10.4	31	$10
Decline	05	BOS	16	12	0	225	151	4.16	1.24	249	202	278	28.3	27%	72%	4.35	41	17	42	2.7	6.0	2.2	12%	1.4	5.9	46	$21
Type FB	06	BOS	7	11	0	140	90	4.63	1.33	255	221	265	25.9	28%	68%	4.78	39	16	44	3.3	5.8	1.8	10%	1.2	-1.2	39	$10
Reliability 51	07	BOS	17	12	0	189	110	4.76	1.35	264	247	276	26.0	29%	67%	4.88	39	19	42	3.0	5.2	1.7	8%	1.0	-6.0	38	$15
ERA Potl 45%	1st Half		7	8	0	94	56	4.50	1.30	245			26.4	26%	68%	4.77	38	23	39	3.4	5.4	1.6	10%	1.1	0.1	36	$8
LIMA Plan D+	2nd Half		10	4	0	95	54	5.02	1.40	282			25.7	31%	65%	4.98	40	15	45	2.7	5.1	1.9	7%	0.9	-6.0	41	$7
+/- Score -45	08	Proj	12	10	0	160	94	4.91	1.46	279			25.9	30%	69%	5.04	40	17	43	3.3	5.3	1.6	9%	1.2	-10.7	29	$9

Pick your tenet: Knuckleballers don't follow any of the rules, live forever, etc. A 17-win season with a near-5.00 ERA seems to support all of them. Late-season injuries raise a red flag. As if we needed a reason to be cautious.

Walker,Jamie

			W	L	Sv	IP	K	ERA	WHIP	OBA	vL	vR	BF/G	H%	S%	xERA	G	L	F	Ctl	Dom	Cmd	hr/f	hr/9	RAR	BPV	R$
LH Reliever	03	DET	4	3	3	65	45	3.32	1.20	250	212	276	3.4	27%	78%	4.48	35	17	48	2.4	6.2	2.6	9%	1.2	9.6	61	$9
Age 36	04	DET	3	4	1	64	53	3.22	1.26	276	200	313	3.8	32%	79%	4.02	36	20	44	1.7	7.4	4.4	9%	1.1	9.6	103	$7
Decline	05	DET	4	3	0	48	30	3.73	1.29	265	245	271	3.1	29%	74%	4.46	41	19	40	2.4	5.6	2.3	8%	0.9	3.8	56	$5
Type xFB	06	DET	0	1	0	48	37	2.81	1.15	258	238	262	3.5	28%	85%	4.13	31	20	49	1.5	6.9	4.6	11%	1.5	10.3	97	$5
Reliability 18	07	BAL	3	2	7	61	41	3.23	1.21	248	216	268	3.1	28%	76%	4.56	34	21	46	2.5	6.0	2.4	7%	0.9	9.6	66	$9
ERA Potl 45%	1st Half		1	1	0	30	21	3.30	1.23	262			3.1	31%	72%	4.41	36	20	44	2.1	6.3	3.0	2%	0.3	4.5	94	$3
LIMA Plan C+	2nd Half		2	1	7	31	20	3.16	1.18	234			3.1	24%	81%	4.71	31	22	47	2.9	5.8	2.0	11%	1.4	5.2	42	$6
+/- Score -36	08	Proj	3	2	18	58	40	3.88	1.28	268			3.3	30%	74%	4.49	34	20	46	2.2	6.2	2.9	10%	1.2	0.0	61	$11

Did an acceptable job when pressed into closer duty, but BPIs for that role are borderline. High FB rate in Camden Yards means immediate HR issues; RHBs hit him well; Dom is "eh." Don't play with fire. It's their fire.

Walker,Tyler

			W	L	Sv	IP	K	ERA	WHIP	OBA	vL	vR	BF/G	H%	S%	xERA	G	L	F	Ctl	Dom	Cmd	hr/f	hr/9	RAR	BPV	R$
RH Reliever	03	aaa	2	9	0	131	97	6.04	1.69	319			23.2	37%	64%	5.84				3.3	6.7	2.0		1.0	-26.6	45	($3)
Age 32	04	SF *	6	2	1	78	60	3.79	1.44	282	287	288	5.6	33%	77%	4.33	42	20	38	3.0	6.9	2.3	10%	1.0	4.6	57	$6
Peak	05	SF	6	4	23	61	54	4.26	1.55	283	284	278	4.1	33%	77%	4.44	42	18	41	4.0	7.9	2.0	12%	1.3	-0.1	48	$12
Type Pwr FB	06	2TM	1	4	10	25	19	7.17	1.55	276	333	226	4.3	33%	50%	4.91	35	28	37	4.3	6.8	1.6	3%	0.4	-8.2	63	$3
Reliability 0	07	SF *	3	2	7	37	26	4.46	1.63	299	182	308	4.8	33%	77%	5.28	35	18	48	3.8	6.3	1.6	10%	1.4	-0.1	25	$4
ERA Potl 40%	1st Half		0	0	0	0	0	0.00	0.00																		
LIMA Plan C+	2nd Half		3	2	7	37	26	4.46	1.63	299			4.8	33%	77%	5.28	35	18	48	3.8	6.3	1.6	10%	1.4	-0.1	25	$4
+/- Score -28	08	Proj	3	4	3	58	44	4.66	1.52	284			4.9	32%	73%	4.66	39	21	40	3.6	6.8	1.9	11%	1.2	-1.8	42	$3

2-0, 1.26 ERA in 14 IP at SF. There's a very small group of pitchers who succeed despite low command ratios. He's in the very large group that doesn't.

Wang,Chien-Ming

			W	L	Sv	IP	K	ERA	WHIP	OBA	vL	vR	BF/G	H%	S%	xERA	G	L	F	Ctl	Dom	Cmd	hr/f	hr/9	RAR	BPV	R$
RH Starter	03	aa	7	6	0	122	71	5.63	1.63	325			26.4	37%	64%	5.50				2.4	5.2	2.1		0.6	-18.6	48	$1
Age 28	04	a/a	11	6	0	149	102	4.23	1.34	282			26.5	33%	68%	4.12				2.1	6.1	2.9		0.6	2.0	78	$11
Pre-Peak	05	NYY *	10	6	0	150	65	4.21	1.30	271	258	254	26.4	29%	69%	3.81	64	14	22	2.3	3.9	1.7	11%	0.8	3.0	36	$10
Type Con xGB	06	NYY	19	6	1	218	76	3.63	1.31	275	275	279	27.1	29%	72%	3.93	63	17	20	2.1	3.1	1.5	8%	0.5	24.9	35	$21
Reliability 61	07	NYY	19	7	0	199	104	3.70	1.29	261	286	242	28.0	29%	71%	3.89	58	18	23	2.7	4.7	1.8	6%	0.4	19.7	56	$21
ERA Potl 50%	1st Half		7	4	0	85	41	3.49	1.15	250			28.9	27%	70%	3.69	59	17	24	1.9	4.3	2.3	7%	0.5	10.6	63	$10
LIMA Plan D	2nd Half		12	3	0	114	63	3.86	1.40	270			27.4	31%	71%	4.03	58	19	23	3.2	5.0	1.5	5%	0.3	9.1	54	$11
+/- Score -13	08	Proj	17	8	0	203	102	3.81	1.33	271			27.8	30%	71%	3.80	61	17	22	2.5	4.5	1.8	8%	0.5	17.3	50	$18

#5 in the majors in ground outs. Gave up four+ runs in only three of his wins, so he didn't need a lot of run support. Rise in Dom gives him a little boost in 5x5, but overall, dollar value for this skill set is peaking.

Washburn,Jarrod

			W	L	Sv	IP	K	ERA	WHIP	OBA	vL	vR	BF/G	H%	S%	xERA	G	L	F	Ctl	Dom	Cmd	hr/f	hr/9	RAR	BPV	R$
LH Starter	03	ANA	10	15	0	207	118	4.43	1.25	260	230	264	27.0	27%	70%	4.96	32	17	51	2.3	5.1	2.2	10%	1.5	2.3	35	$15
Age 33	04	ANA	11	8	0	149	86	4.65	1.33	274	225	283	25.4	29%	68%	4.69	38	20	41	2.4	5.2	2.2	10%	1.2	-4.0	40	$10
Past Peak	05	ANA	8	8	0	177	94	3.20	1.33	269	266	276	25.9	29%	80%	4.79	39	21	40	2.6	4.8	1.8	8%	1.0	25.6	40	$14
Type Con FB	06	SEA	8	14	0	187	103	4.67	1.35	273	317	257	25.8	29%	68%	4.84	40	18	42	2.6	5.0	1.9	10%	1.2	-2.6	33	$11
Reliability 89	07	SEA	10	15	0	194	114	4.32	1.38	269	213	288	26.1	29%	71%	5.04	37	18	45	3.1	5.3	1.7	8%	1.1	4.4	37	$12
ERA Potl 40%	1st Half		6	6	0	92	49	4.11	1.37	268			26.3	29%	71%	4.86	45	16	39	3.0	4.8	1.6	6%	0.7	4.5	43	$7
LIMA Plan D+	2nd Half		4	9	0	102	65	4.51	1.40	270			25.8	29%	72%	5.18	29	20	51	3.2	5.8	1.8	10%	1.4	-0.1	31	$6
+/- Score -41	08	Proj	9	13	0	178	102	4.55	1.40	278			26.5	29%	71%	4.97	37	19	44	2.8	5.2	1.8	10%	1.3	-10.4	29	$10

For all intents and purposes, two virtually identical seasons in SEA. And not too dissimilar from the previous seasons in ANA. You pay for consistency here. Not for skill, or much to help your team. Just consistency.

TOM TODARO

Weathers,David

Weathers,David		Yr	Tm	W	L	Sv	IP	K	ERA	WHIP	OBA	vL	vR	BF/G	H%	S%	xERA	G	L	F	Ctl	Dom	Cmd	hr/f	hr/9	RAR	BPV	R$
RH	Reliever	03	NYM	1	6	7	87	75	3.10	1.46	262	239	276	4.9	32%	80%	4.09	47	22	31	4.1	7.8	1.9	7%	0.6	12.6	70	$7
Age	38	04	2NL	7	7	0	82	61	4.17	1.46	269	241	294	5.5	30%	76%	4.28	49	18	33	3.8	6.7	1.7	14%	1.3	1.0	39	$6
Decline		05	CIN	7	4	15	77	61	3.96	1.30	246	265	226	4.5	29%	71%	3.77	50	21	28	3.4	7.1	2.1	11%	0.8	2.7	68	$12
Type		06	CIN	4	4	12	73	50	3.57	1.30	228	219	230	4.6	24%	80%	4.55	45	17	38	4.2	6.1	1.5	14%	1.5	8.3	33	$11
Reliability	43	07	CIN	2	6	33	78	48	3.59	1.21	234	254	218	4.6	27%	70%	4.76	36	21	43	3.1	5.6	1.8	4%	0.5	8.0	65	$17
ERA Potl	45%	1st Half		1	3	15	38	32	3.32	1.00	201			4.7	25%	67%	3.98	33	20	47	2.6	7.6	2.9	4%	0.5	5.2	107	$10
LIMA Plan	D	2nd Half		1	3	18	40	16	3.85	1.41	263			4.5	28%	72%	5.57	38	22	41	3.6	3.6	1.0	4%	0.5	2.8	32	$8
+/- Score	-57	08	Proj	3	5	20	73	43	4.34	1.41	263			4.8	28%	72%	4.87	41	20	39	3.6	5.3	1.5	10%	1.1	-4.2	32	$10

Having a rising flyball tendency in Cincy is living on the edge to begin with. Managing to get through the year allowing just 4 HRs in 78 IP is dumb luck. It won't happen again, and his ERA will soar.

Weaver,Jeff

Weaver,Jeff		Yr	Tm	W	L	Sv	IP	K	ERA	WHIP	OBA	vL	vR	BF/G	H%	S%	xERA	G	L	F	Ctl	Dom	Cmd	hr/f	hr/9	RAR	BPV	R$
RH	Starter	03	NYY	7	9	0	159	93	6.00	1.62	320	342	290	22.6	35%	63%	4.97	41	20	39	2.7	5.3	2.0	7%	0.9	-28.9	37	($0)
Age	31	04	LA	13	13	0	220	153	4.01	1.30	261	291	231	27.3	30%	70%	4.38	40	21	39	2.7	6.3	2.3	7%	0.8	6.9	65	$16
Peak		05	LA	14	11	0	224	157	4.22	1.17	258	297	208	27.0	28%	69%	3.93	41	21	38	1.7	6.3	3.7	13%	1.4	0.7	76	$20
Type	Con FB	06	2TM	8	14	0	172	107	5.76	1.51	305	340	267	24.6	32%	66%	4.64	39	23	38	2.5	5.6	2.3	15%	1.8	-26.2	22	$3
Reliability	63	07	SEA	7	13	0	147	80	6.20	1.53	315	324	306	24.2	33%	61%	5.17	36	17	47	2.1	4.9	2.3	9%	1.4	-30.6	27	$1
ERA Potl	55%	1st Half		2	6	0	47	25	7.66	1.79	352			22.1	39%	55%	5.41	38	20	42	2.3	4.8	2.1	5%	0.8	-18.3	34	($3)
LIMA Plan	C+	2nd Half		5	7	0	100	55	5.51	1.41	296			25.4	30%	66%	5.06	35	16	49	2.1	5.0	2.4	11%	1.7	-12.3	24	$3
+/- Score	19	08	Proj	9	12	0	160	90	4.91	1.42	294			24.7	31%	69%	4.81	38	20	43	2.2	5.1	2.3	11%	1.4	-6.1	33	$8

Doesn't walk many, but why would hitters care when they're busy hitting .300 against him? Dom is fading, flyballs are increasing, and despite BPIs that aren't horrible, there is a black cloud following him.

Weaver,Jered

Weaver,Jered		Yr	Tm	W	L	Sv	IP	K	ERA	WHIP	OBA	vL	vR	BF/G	H%	S%	xERA	G	L	F	Ctl	Dom	Cmd	hr/f	hr/9	RAR	BPV	R$
RH	Starter	03		0	0	0	0	0	0.00	0.00																		
Age	25	04		0	0	0	0	0	0.00	0.00																		
Growth		05	aa	3	3	0	43	39	4.19	1.49	275			23.7	33%	75%	4.73				3.8	8.2	2.2		1.0	0.6	63	$3
Type	xFB	06	LAA *	17	3	0	200	184	2.43	1.02	222	250	174	25.4	27%	82%	3.83	30	18	52	1.9	8.3	4.4	8%	1.0	52.5	123	$36
Reliability	21	07	LAA	13	7	0	161	115	3.91	1.39	282	291	269	24.8	32%	74%	4.68	36	17	47	2.5	6.4	2.6	7%	1.0	11.8	62	$15
ERA Potl	50%	1st Half		6	4	0	71	57	3.55	1.45	273			23.9	32%	78%	4.75	35	19	47	3.5	7.2	2.0	7%	0.9	8.4	60	$7
LIMA Plan	C	2nd Half		7	3	0	90	58	4.20	1.33	289			25.5	32%	71%	4.63	36	16	47	1.7	5.8	3.4	7%	1.0	3.4	74	$8
+/- Score	5	08	Proj	12	8	0	174	131	4.03	1.32	266			25.5	30%	74%	4.58	34	17	48	2.7	6.8	2.5	9%	1.2	-1.7	58	$16

Heavy workload in '06 may have caught up with him. Began the spring with a sore shoulder; velocity faded in second half. More questions than answers right now, so a cautious bid is in order. Think #3 starter, not ace.

Webb,Brandon

Webb,Brandon		Yr	Tm	W	L	Sv	IP	K	ERA	WHIP	OBA	vL	vR	BF/G	H%	S%	xERA	G	L	F	Ctl	Dom	Cmd	hr/f	hr/9	RAR	BPV	R$
RH	Starter	03	ARI *	11	10	0	198	187	3.23	1.20	223	257	167	25.5	28%	74%	2.88	61	20	19	3.5	8.5	2.4	12%	0.5	25.7	96	$22
Age	29	04	ARI	7	16	0	208	164	3.59	1.50	249	268	223	26.3	30%	78%	3.66	64	17	19	5.1	7.1	1.4	15%	0.7	17.2	55	$10
Pre-Peak		05	ARI	14	12	0	229	172	3.54	1.26	262	298	228	29.0	31%	74%	2.85	65	19	16	2.3	6.8	2.9	18%	0.8	20.0	80	$21
Type	xGB	06	ARI	16	8	0	235	178	3.10	1.13	246	261	231	28.9	29%	74%	2.66	66	17	16	1.9	6.8	3.6	13%	0.6	40.2	104	$29
Reliability	82	07	ARI	18	10	0	236	194	3.01	1.19	239	272	199	28.6	29%	75%	3.00	62	18	20	2.7	7.4	2.7	9%	0.5	41.3	94	$29
ERA Potl	55%	1st Half		8	5	0	118	100	3.05	1.27	245			29.1	30%	77%	3.16	61	18	21	3.2	7.6	2.4	11%	0.6	20.0	83	$14
LIMA Plan	C+	2nd Half		10	5	0	118	94	2.97	1.11	232			28.0	29%	72%	2.84	63	19	19	2.3	7.2	3.1	6%	0.3	21.3	108	$17
+/- Score	16	08	Proj	18	8	0	233	185	3.02	1.17	243			28.0	30%	75%	2.86	64	18	18	2.4	7.2	3.0	11%	0.5	44.3	96	$29

He's the model for extreme groundball pitchers. Used off-speed pitches as effective complement to sinker. Piling up the innings, but hasn't shown any ill effects so far. 20 wins can come at any time.

Wellemeyer,Todd

Wellemeyer,Todd		Yr	Tm	W	L	Sv	IP	K	ERA	WHIP	OBA	vL	vR	BF/G	H%	S%	xERA	G	L	F	Ctl	Dom	Cmd	hr/f	hr/9	RAR	BPV	R$
RH	Reliever	03	CHC *	7	7	1	114	105	6.69	1.71	286	219	257	16.5	35%	61%	5.48				5.2	8.3	1.6		1.1	-34.0	48	($1)
Age	29	04	CHC *	3	2	0	46	50	5.48	1.85	286	302	275	6.6	38%	70%	5.24	25	30	45	6.5	9.8	1.5	7%	0.8	-6.9	65	$0
Peak		05	CHC *	5	3	1	85	72	4.55	1.56	264	234	284	11.2	31%	73%	4.63	47	15	38	5.0	7.6	1.5	9%	1.0	-3.2	52	$4
Type	Pwr FB	06	2TM	1	4	1	78	54	4.15	1.51	236	208	265	7.5	27%	73%	5.10	49	14	37	5.8	6.2	1.1	7%	0.7	3.6	47	$3
Reliability	22	07	2TM	3	3	0	79	60	4.54	1.48	256	311	200	10.9	29%	73%	4.85	40	18	41	4.5	6.8	1.5	11%	1.2	-0.8	39	$4
ERA Potl	45%	1st Half		2	1	0	51	39	6.00	1.73	301			10.8	34%	68%	5.07	40	21	40	4.6	6.9	1.5	12%	1.4	-9.7	25	($1)
LIMA Plan	C+	2nd Half		1	2	0	28	21	1.91	1.02	158			11.2	17%	88%	4.44	41	13	45	4.5	6.7	1.5	9%	1.0	8.9	66	$4
+/- Score	-22	08	Proj	2	3	0	58	42	4.81	1.52	255			9.9	29%	70%	5.04	42	17	41	5.0	6.5	1.3	10%	1.1	-4.3	38	$2

Wild swings in H%/S% rocked the halves of his season back and forth, but came to rest at about where we'd expect. There are minor gains in control, but at 29, he should be much further along, and he's not even close.

Wells,David

Wells,David		Yr	Tm	W	L	Sv	IP	K	ERA	WHIP	OBA	vL	vR	BF/G	H%	S%	xERA	G	L	F	Ctl	Dom	Cmd	hr/f	hr/9	RAR	BPV	R$
LH	Starter	03	NYY	15	7	0	213	101	4.14	1.23	287	274	290	28.5	30%	69%	4.31	45	16	38	0.8	4.3	5.1	8%	1.0	10.1	99	$18
Age	45	04	SD	12	8	0	195	101	3.73	1.14	269	275	263	25.6	29%	71%	3.94	49	17	35	0.9	4.7	5.1	10%	1.1	12.7	103	$18
Decline		05	BOS	15	7	0	184	107	4.45	1.31	298	343	282	25.9	33%	68%	3.85	48	22	30	1.0	5.2	5.1	11%	1.0	-1.8	103	$15
Type	Con	06	2TM	3	5	0	75	38	4.43	1.45	314	303	317	25.3	33%	73%	4.34	49	18	33	1.4	4.6	3.2	12%	1.3	0.8	46	$3
Reliability	12	07	2NL	9	9	0	157	82	5.44	1.54	312	288	323	24.2	33%	67%	4.87	44	19	38	2.4	4.7	2.0	10%	1.3	-19.6	24	$3
ERA Potl	50%	1st Half		3	5	0	86	48	4.50	1.48	304			25.2	33%	71%	4.78	40	22	39	2.2	5.0	2.3	8%	0.9	-0.8	44	$3
LIMA Plan	C	2nd Half		6	4	0	71	34	6.56	1.63	321			23.2	33%	62%	4.98	48	15	37	2.7	4.3	1.6	13%	1.6	-18.8	1	($0)
+/- Score	-27	08	Proj	6	9	0	131	63	5.03	1.49	302			24.0	32%	69%	4.75	47	18	35	2.4	4.3	1.8	11%	1.2	-5.7	21	$3

On the Steve Carlton Path To Retirement. The pinpoint control is slowly fading, and with it his command. As his age slowly approaches his waist size, it's time to let go.

Wells,Kip

Wells,Kip		Yr	Tm	W	L	Sv	IP	K	ERA	WHIP	OBA	vL	vR	BF/G	H%	S%	xERA	G	L	F	Ctl	Dom	Cmd	hr/f	hr/9	RAR	BPV	R$
RH	Starter	03	PIT	10	9	0	197	147	3.29	1.25	235	252	219	26.5	26%	78%	3.87	52	18	31	3.5	6.7	1.9	14%	1.1	24.0	56	$18
Age	31	04	PIT	5	7	0	138	116	4.56	1.53	271	300	244	25.6	32%	72%	4.27	46	22	32	4.3	7.6	1.8	11%	0.9	-5.1	56	$5
Peak		05	PIT	8	18	0	182	132	5.09	1.57	266	288	249	24.7	30%	69%	4.75	47	20	33	4.9	6.5	1.3	12%	1.1	-19.0	35	$3
Type	Pwr	06	2TM	2	5	0	44	20	6.53	1.86	329	353	323	23.4	36%	63%	5.41	51	20	29	4.3	4.1	1.0	6%	0.6	-10.9	15	($2)
Reliability	28	07	STL	7	17	0	163	122	5.70	1.62	288	287	287	21.7	33%	66%	4.56	48	19	33	4.3	6.7	1.6	11%	1.1	-25.5	39	$1
ERA Potl	50%	1st Half		3	11	0	84	63	6.43	1.58	271			23.6	30%	60%	4.69	47	18	34	4.8	6.8	1.4	13%	1.3	-20.7	32	($1)
LIMA Plan	C+	2nd Half		4	6	0	79	59	4.92	1.66	306			20.0	36%	71%	4.43	49	20	31	3.8	6.7	1.8	9%	0.8	-4.8	48	$1
+/- Score	13	08	Proj	5	11	0	116	78	5.20	1.57	280			22.6	32%	68%	4.64	49	20	31	4.3	6.1	1.4	10%	0.9	-3.5	37	$2

Used to have an advantage vs. righties, but now everyone hits him... and that's on top of all the walks. It's been five years since he resembled a big-league pitcher.

Westbrook,Jake

Westbrook,Jake		Yr	Tm	W	L	Sv	IP	K	ERA	WHIP	OBA	vL	vR	BF/G	H%	S%	xERA	G	L	F	Ctl	Dom	Cmd	hr/f	hr/9	RAR	BPV	R$
RH	Starter	03	CLE	7	10	0	133	58	4.33	1.49	275	276	287	17.2	30%	71%	4.31	63	15	22	3.8	3.9	1.0	9%	0.6	3.2	27	$6
Age	30	04	CLE	14	9	0	215	116	3.39	1.25	255	255	247	27.2	28%	75%	3.67	63	14	23	2.6	4.9	1.9	12%	0.8	27.7	49	$20
Peak		05	CLE	15	15	0	210	119	4.50	1.30	269	275	255	26.1	30%	66%	3.43	62	19	19	2.4	5.1	2.1	15%	0.8	-3.2	52	$15
Type	Con xGB	06	CLE	15	10	0	211	109	4.18	1.43	293	290	300	28.7	32%	71%	3.83	61	17	22	2.3	4.6	2.0	9%	0.6	9.9	47	$15
Reliability	72	07	CLE	6	9	0	152	93	4.32	1.41	271	288	263	26.3	30%	70%	4.13	54	20	27	3.3	5.5	1.7	10%	0.8	3.4	46	$9
ERA Potl	50%	1st Half		1	3	0	34	20	7.15	1.56	289			21.8	30%	55%	4.39	53	21	27	3.7	5.3	1.4	19%	1.6	-11.1	11	($1)
LIMA Plan	C	2nd Half		5	6	0	118	73	3.51	1.36	265			28.1	30%	75%	4.06	54	20	27	3.1	5.6	1.8	7%	0.5	14.5	57	$9
+/- Score	-4	08	Proj	13	9	0	189	107	4.11	1.36	272			25.2	30%	71%	3.87	58	19	24	2.7	5.1	1.9	11%	0.8	14.6	46	$15

Sidelined by oblique strain, but it didn't take long for him to get back in stride. BPIs are just OK for a groundball pitcher, so ERA will remain north of 4.00, but if he gets back to 200 IP, no reason he can't win 15.

Wheeler,Dan

Wheeler,Dan		Yr	Tm	W	L	Sv	IP	K	ERA	WHIP	OBA	vL	vR	BF/G	H%	S%	xERA	G	L	F	Ctl	Dom	Cmd	hr/f	hr/9	RAR	BPV	R$
RH	Reliever	03	NYM *	5	5	6	96	72	4.31	1.45	279	208	279	7.4	32%	72%	4.50	41	18	40	3.2	6.8	2.1	8%	0.9	-0.4	56	$7
Age	30	04	2NL	3	1	0	65	55	4.29	1.48	293	380	226	6.2	34%	76%	4.22	38	22	40	2.8	7.6	2.8	12%	1.4	-0.2	58	$3
Peak		05	HOU	2	3	3	73	69	2.22	0.98	205	206	204	4.0	25%	83%	3.53	38	18	44	2.3	8.5	3.6	8%	0.9	18.3	115	$12
Type	Pwr FB	06	HOU	3	5	9	71	68	2.53	1.15	224	273	183	3.9	29%	81%	3.85	37	20	44	3.0	8.6	2.8	6%	0.6	17.2	102	$13
Reliability	41	07	2TM	1	9	11	75	82	5.30	1.30	260	260	253	4.5	33%	62%	3.64	37	18	45	2.8	9.9	3.6	12%	1.3	-7.7	97	$8
ERA Potl	0%	1st Half		1	4	11	36	42	6.25	1.22	256			4.4	31%	53%	3.33	36	16	47	2.3	10.5	4.7	18%	2.0	-7.9	105	$6
LIMA Plan	A	2nd Half		0	5	0	39	40	4.42	1.37	263			4.6	34%	68%	3.93	37	20	43	3.3	9.3	2.9	6%	0.7	0.2	97	$2
+/- Score	74	08	Proj	4	4	13	73	73	3.35	1.17	233			4.4	29%	76%	3.69	37	19	44	2.9	9.1	3.2	11%	1.1	6.8	96	$13

Good skills, bad results. Had some HR problems, and poor hit/strand rates really hurt. Ignore the ERA, look at his command ratio, invest... then wait for opportunity to knock.

TOM TODARO

Wickman,Bob

Wickman,Bob		Yr	Tm	W	L	Sv	IP	K	ERA	WHIP	OBA	vL	vR	BF/G	H%	S%	xERA	G	L	F	Ctl	Dom	Cmd	hr/f	hr/9	RAR	BPV	R$
RH Reliever		03	aa	0	0	0	1	2	37.50	5.00	596			4.8	78%	17%	20.77				7.5	15.0	**2.0**		0.0	-4.9	68	($1)
Age	39	04	CLE	* 0	2	13	33	29	5.95	1.59	283	354	192	4.3	34%	63%	3.88	57	15	27	4.3	7.8	**1.8**	14%	1.1	-6.2	51	$4
Decline		05	CLE	0	4	45	62	41	2.47	1.26	246	243	250	4.0	26%	88%	3.96	50	20	30	3.0	6.0	**2.0**	16%	1.3	14.6	43	$20
Type		06	2TM	1	6	33	54	42	2.67	1.22	258	267	236	3.9	32%	78%	3.84	42	24	34	2.2	7.0	**3.2**	4%	0.3	12.3	103	$17
Reliability	37	07	2NL	3	4	20	50	37	3.58	1.49	276	277	252	3.9	32%	77%	4.64	44	17	39	3.8	6.6	**1.8**	7%	0.7	5.3	55	$10
ERA Potl		1st Half		1	2	14	26	20	3.12	1.42	254			3.9	31%	78%	4.64	41	21	38	4.2	6.9	**1.7**	3%	0.3	4.2	70	$7
LIMA Plan		2nd Half		2	2	6	24	17	4.07	1.56	297			3.9	34%	77%	4.64	47	14	39	3.3	6.3	**1.9**	10%	1.1	1.1	40	$3
+/- Score		08	Proj	**0**	**0**	**0**	**0**	**0**	**0.00**	**0.00**																		

In a career full of highs and lows, and disconnects, it is interesting to look at these numbers and see his greatest year as a closer in 2005 but one of his greatest skills seasons in 2006.

Williams,Woody

Williams,Woody		Yr	Tm	W	L	Sv	IP	K	ERA	WHIP	OBA	vL	vR	BF/G	H%	S%	xERA	G	L	F	Ctl	Dom	Cmd	hr/f	hr/9	RAR	BPV	R$
RH Starter		03	STL	18	9	0	220	153	3.89	1.25	262	268	246	27.0	30%	71%	4.37	39	18	43	2.3	6.3	**2.8**	7%	0.8	10.6	74	$21
Age	41	04	STL	11	8	0	189	131	4.19	1.33	266	223	296	25.9	30%	71%	4.52	38	20	42	2.8	6.2	**2.3**	8%	1.0	1.8	58	$13
Decline		05	SD	9	12	0	159	106	4.86	1.41	279	259	288	24.6	30%	69%	4.72	35	22	42	2.9	6.0	**2.1**	11%	1.4	-12.1	38	$7
Type	Con FB	06	SD	12	5	0	145	72	3.66	1.29	271	245	287	24.4	28%	77%	4.87	36	21	43	2.2	4.5	**2.1**	10%	1.3	14.8	32	$14
Reliability	48	07	HOU	8	15	0	188	101	5.27	1.43	289	279	292	24.8	30%	68%	5.00	39	16	45	2.5	4.8	**1.9**	12%	1.7	-19.5	16	$5
ERA Potl	45%	1st Half		3	10	0	98	51	5.60	1.53	299			25.7	31%	67%	5.33	35	20	45	2.9	4.7	**1.6**	11%	1.6	-14.2	10	($0)
LIMA Plan	C	2nd Half		5	5	0	90	50	4.90	1.32	279			23.9	28%	69%	4.63	44	12	44	2.1	5.0	**2.4**	13%	1.8	-5.3	25	$5
+/- Score	-33	08	Proj	**6**	**10**	**0**	**131**	**64**	**5.10**	**1.44**	**294**			**24.7**	**30%**	**68%**	**5.10**	**38**	**18**	**44**	**2.4**	**4.4**	**1.8**	**11%**	**1.4**	**-11.3**	**18**	**$3**

His luck-induced ERA in 2006 bought him another year of employment, but smoke-and-mirrors can last for just so long. Read the BPV trend and close the book. (Unfortunately, HOU can't; he's signed for 2008.)

Willis,Dontrelle

Willis,Dontrelle		Yr	Tm	W	L	Sv	IP	K	ERA	WHIP	OBA	vL	vR	BF/G	H%	S%	xERA	G	L	F	Ctl	Dom	Cmd	hr/f	hr/9	RAR	BPV	R$
LH Starter		03	FLA	* 18	6	0	196	171	3.03	1.23	240	216	250	24.7	30%	78%	3.94	40	21	39	3.1	7.9	**2.6**	7%	0.7	30.2	87	$25
Age	26	04	FLA	10	11	0	197	139	4.02	1.38	274	203	287	26.4	31%	73%	4.26	45	19	36	2.8	6.4	**2.3**	9%	0.9	5.9	59	$12
Growth		05	FLA	22	10	0	236	170	2.63	1.14	242	222	247	28.2	29%	77%	3.73	45	24	32	2.1	6.5	**3.1**	5%	0.4	47.0	98	$33
Type		06	FLA	12	12	0	223	160	3.87	1.42	271	231	281	28.5	31%	75%	4.25	48	20	33	3.3	6.5	**1.9**	9%	0.8	16.9	55	$15
Reliability	64	07	FLA	10	15	0	205	146	5.17	1.60	294	123	320	26.5	33%	70%	4.52	46	21	32	3.8	6.4	**1.7**	13%	1.3	-18.9	32	$4
ERA Potl	50%	1st Half		7	7	0	104	73	4.85	1.57	285			27.5	32%	72%	4.40	50	19	30	4.0	6.3	**1.6**	14%	1.2	-5.4	33	$4
LIMA Plan	B	2nd Half		3	8	0	101	73	5.51	1.63	303			25.6	34%	69%	4.63	42	23	34	3.6	6.5	**1.8**	13%	1.3	-13.5	31	($0)
+/- Score	12	08	Proj	**11**	**12**	**0**	**198**	**143**	**4.33**	**1.43**	**274**			**26.9**	**31%**	**72%**	**4.26**	**46**	**21**	**33**	**3.3**	**6.5**	**2.0**	**11%**	**1.0**	**3.3**	**50**	**$11**

2007 looks like a huge drop-off, but it's clear that the pieces for this were in place a year ago. Excessive workload could be to blame, but to be honest, xERA has never been all that impressed anyway.

Wilson,Brian

Wilson,Brian		Yr	Tm	W	L	Sv	IP	K	ERA	WHIP	OBA	vL	vR	BF/G	H%	S%	xERA	G	L	F	Ctl	Dom	Cmd	hr/f	hr/9	RAR	BPV	R$
RH Reliever		03		0	0	0	0	0	0.00	0.00																		
Age	26	04		0	0	0	0	0	0.00	0.00																		
Growth		05	a/a	1	1	8	27	35	2.00	1.00	155			4.4	25%	78%	1.02				4.3	11.7	**2.7**		0.0	7.7	150	$7
Type	Pwr GB	06	SF	* 3	6	8	58	50	4.50	1.60	252			4.8	31%	72%	4.63	45	26	29	5.9	7.8	**1.3**	8%	0.6	-0.1	60	$5
Reliability	0	07	SF	* 2	4	17	58	47	2.66	1.38	220	304	145	4.5	28%	80%	4.17	56	15	29	5.2	7.3	**1.4**	2%	0.2	12.6	79	$11
ERA Potl	50%	1st Half		0	1	3	16	16	3.91	1.86	236			5.1	32%	77%					8.9	8.9	**1.0**		0.0	1.0	83	$1
LIMA Plan	C+	2nd Half		2	3	14	42	31	2.18	1.19	214			4.3	26%	81%	3.82	56	15	29	3.8	6.6	**1.7**	3%	0.2	11.5	82	$10
+/- Score	-37	08	Proj	**2**	**5**	**23**	**58**	**49**	**3.88**	**1.43**	**241**			**4.6**	**30%**	**73%**	**4.10**	**51**	**20**	**29**	**4.8**	**7.6**	**1.6**	**8%**	**0.6**	**2.2**	**67**	**$11**

6 SV, 2.28 ERA in 23 IP at SF. Showed some small signs of control in the 2nd half, but H% and S% made it look better than it really was. BPIs are intriguing; the missing pieces are Ctl and BA vs LHers, but that's a lot.

Wilson,C.J.

Wilson,C.J.		Yr	Tm	W	L	Sv	IP	K	ERA	WHIP	OBA	vL	vR	BF/G	H%	S%	xERA	G	L	F	Ctl	Dom	Cmd	hr/f	hr/9	RAR	BPV	R$
LH Reliever		03	aa	6	9	0	123	78	6.73	1.63	318			25.5	35%	59%	5.85				2.9	5.7	**2.0**		1.1	-35.5	35	($2)
Age	27	04	TEX	0	0	0	0	0	0.00	0.00											0.0	0.0						
Growth		05	TEX	* 1	11	1	92	65	6.49	1.72	327	290	339	11.9	36%	64%	3.72	60	20	20	3.2	6.4	**2.0**	23%	1.4	-24.1	27	($3)
Type	Pwr	06	TEX	2	4	1	44	43	4.08	1.29	239	155	292	4.2	28%	74%	3.43	49	21	30	3.7	8.8	**2.4**	20%	1.4	2.6	67	$5
Reliability	24	07	TEX	2	1	12	68	63	3.03	1.22	206	112	275	4.3	26%	76%	3.60	49	24	27	4.3	8.3	**1.9**	8%	0.5	12.4	88	$12
ERA Potl	50%	1st Half		0	1	0	36	33	2.75	1.22	198			4.7	24%	80%	3.48	54	22	23	4.8	8.3	**1.7**	14%	0.8	7.8	79	$4
LIMA Plan	B	2nd Half		2	0	12	32	30	3.34	1.21	215			3.9	28%	71%	3.72	44	25	31	3.9	8.4	**2.1**	4%	0.3	4.6	99	$8
+/- Score	-15	08	Proj	**2**	**3**	**10**	**58**	**54**	**3.72**	**1.33**	**245**			**4.7**	**30%**	**74%**	**3.55**	**50**	**23**	**28**	**3.7**	**8.4**	**2.3**	**11%**	**0.8**	**6.7**	**80**	**$9**

Very tough on lefties -- because that's his job -- and has good stuff, but must improve control to get more consistent results. Don't look at the 3.03 ERA and think he's already arrived. He hasn't. Yet. But soon.

Wise,Matt

Wise,Matt		Yr	Tm	W	L	Sv	IP	K	ERA	WHIP	OBA	vL	vR	BF/G	H%	S%	xERA	G	L	F	Ctl	Dom	Cmd	hr/f	hr/9	RAR	BPV	R$
RH Reliever		03		0	0	0	0	0	0.00	0.00											0.0	0.0						
Age	32	04	MIL	* 2	3	0	72	46	3.86	1.18	242	244	259	8.0	27%	69%	4.11	47	16	36	2.5	5.7	**2.3**	9%	0.9	3.5	63	$5
Peak		05	MIL	4	4	1	64	62	3.37	0.97	170	130	187	5.1	21%	68%	3.71	41	12	47	3.5	8.7	**2.5**	8%	0.8	6.9	100	$10
Type	xFB	06	MIL	5	6	0	44	27	3.88	1.34	266	206	310	4.7	29%	75%	4.45	45	18	37	2.9	5.5	**1.9**	11%	1.2	3.3	39	$5
Reliability	11	07	MIL	3	2	1	54	43	4.19	1.45	287	264	296	4.2	34%	73%	4.69	35	16	49	2.8	7.2	**2.5**	6%	0.8	1.6	69	$4
ERA Potl	55%	1st Half		2	1	0	33	24	3.00	1.00	218			3.9	25%	73%	4.01	41	12	47	1.9	6.5	**3.4**	7%	0.8	5.8	98	$5
LIMA Plan	B	2nd Half		1	1	1	21	19	6.09	2.17	375			4.6	46%	72%	5.78	27	22	51	4.3	8.3	**1.9**	5%	0.9	-4.2	43	($1)
+/- Score	-13	08	Proj	**5**	**5**	**3**	**73**	**56**	**3.97**	**1.32**	**263**			**4.6**	**30%**	**74%**	**4.42**	**38**	**17**	**45**	**2.9**	**7.0**	**2.4**	**10%**	**1.2**	**-0.2**	**58**	**$7**

Was rolling along until hitting Pedro Lopez in the face on July 25. Wasn't the same after that, and MIL cut him down to just 9 IP in Aug/Sep. Such fragile psyches play this game. Has the skills, though.

Wolf,Randy

Wolf,Randy		Yr	Tm	W	L	Sv	IP	K	ERA	WHIP	OBA	vL	vR	BF/G	H%	S%	xERA	G	L	F	Ctl	Dom	Cmd	hr/f	hr/9	RAR	BPV	R$
LH Starter		03	PHI	16	10	0	200	177	4.23	1.27	238	232	234	25.4	28%	70%	4.03	40	20	40	3.5	8.0	**2.3**	12%	1.2	1.2	66	$19
Age	31	04	PHI	5	8	0	136	89	4.30	1.33	274	254	276	25.2	30%	72%	4.59	35	21	43	2.4	5.9	**2.5**	10%	1.3	-0.6	48	$7
Peak		05	PHI	6	4	0	80	61	4.39	1.41	278	238	293	26.7	31%	75%	4.47	35	23	42	2.9	6.9	**2.3**	13%	1.6	-1.4	43	$5
Type	Pwr FB	06	PHI	4	0	0	56	44	5.60	1.71	284	86	323	21.7	30%	73%	5.29	37	19	44	5.3	7.0	**1.3**	17%	2.1	-7.7	6	$1
Reliability	2	07	LA	9	6	0	103	94	4.73	1.45	275	250	278	24.9	34%	68%	4.16	41	19	40	3.4	8.2	**2.4**	8%	0.9	-3.9	74	$8
ERA Potl	55%	1st Half		8	6	0	94	89	4.31	1.38	276			25.3	34%	70%	3.88	41	20	39	2.8	8.5	**3.1**	8%	0.9	1.4	90	$9
LIMA Plan	C+	2nd Half		1	0	0	9	5	9.31	2.18	268			22.2	29%	56%	8.27	43	10	47	10.3	5.2	**0.5**	8%	1.1	-5.2	12	($1)
+/- Score	10	08	Proj	**7**	**5**	**0**	**102**	**83**	**4.52**	**1.40**	**267**			**24.4**	**30%**	**72%**	**4.42**	**40**	**17**	**44**	**3.4**	**7.4**	**2.2**	**11%**	**1.3**	**-0.3**	**52**	**$7**

Was looking like the steal of the year for LA, but alas, he got hurt again. Shoulder surgery showed no structural damage. You can speculate, but it's been a long time since he's been able to stay healthy.

Wood,Kerry

Wood,Kerry		Yr	Tm	W	L	Sv	IP	K	ERA	WHIP	OBA	vL	vR	BF/G	H%	S%	xERA	G	L	F	Ctl	Dom	Cmd	hr/f	hr/9	RAR	BPV	R$
RH Reliever		03	CHC	14	11	0	211	266	3.20	1.19	203	198	206	27.1	28%	78%	3.18	39	26	35	4.3	11.3	**2.7**	14%	1.0	28.1	108	$28
Age	30	04	CHC	8	9	0	140	144	3.73	1.27	243	262	227	26.7	31%	74%	3.47	46	19	35	3.3	9.3	**2.8**	12%	1.0	9.3	90	$14
Peak		05	CHC	3	4	0	66	77	4.23	1.18	218	220	211	12.9	26%	73%	3.40	34	24	42	3.5	10.5	**3.0**	21%	1.9	0.1	79	$7
Type	Pwr FB	06	CHC	1	2	0	19	13	4.22	1.41	260	206	293	20.8	25%	82%	5.00	39	10	51	3.8	6.1	**1.6**	16%	2.3	0.6	3	$1
Reliability	0	07	CHC	1	1	0	24	24	3.33	1.28	208	148	233	4.6	29%	71%	4.48	34	18	48	4.8	8.9	**1.8**	0%	0.0	3.3	105	$2
ERA Potl	60%	1st Half		0	0	0	0	0	0.00	0.00																		
LIMA Plan	B+	2nd Half		1	1	0	24	24	3.33	1.28	208			4.6	29%	71%	4.48	34	18	48	4.8	8.9	**1.8**	0%	0.0	3.3	106	$2
+/- Score	-45	08	Proj	**2**	**2**	**0**	**44**	**42**	**3.93**	**1.31**	**237**			**4.8**	**29%**	**73%**	**4.15**	**37**	**18**	**44**	**3.9**	**8.7**	**2.2**	**9%**	**1.0**	**1.3**	**75**	**$4**

Has accumulated 446 DL days over the past four years. During that time, his BPIs have held up reasonably well, but you can see the problem areas. Can he find rebirth in the pen? Can he stay healthy enough to find out?

Wood,Mike

Wood,Mike		Yr	Tm	W	L	Sv	IP	K	ERA	WHIP	OBA	vL	vR	BF/G	H%	S%	xERA	G	L	F	Ctl	Dom	Cmd	hr/f	hr/9	RAR	BPV	R$
RH Reliever		03	aaa	9	3	0	91	50	3.36	1.27	268			23.9	30%	74%	3.62				2.2	4.9	**2.3**		0.5	11.6	64	$10
Age	28	04	KC	* 14	11	0	190	110	4.50	1.32	272	323	234	25.2	29%	69%	4.12	52	16	32	2.4	5.2	**2.2**	12%	1.1	-1.6	43	$13
Pre-Peak		05	KC	5	8	2	115	60	4.46	1.57	285	295	279	11.0	30%	76%	4.82	53	17	31	4.1	4.7	**1.2**	15%	1.4	-1.3	8	$4
Type	Con GB	06	KC	3	3	0	64	29	5.75	1.70	322	320	309	12.9	33%	69%	4.98	52	16	32	3.2	4.1	**1.3**	13%	1.4	-9.4	-1	($1)
Reliability	12	07	TEX	* 12	5	0	148	76	5.12	1.53	309	342	296	17.8	33%	69%	4.49	51	19	31	2.5	4.7	**1.9**	12%	1.2	-11.3	25	$6
ERA Potl	45%	1st Half		8	2	0	88	61	3.68	1.19	255			22.6	29%	73%	3.39	56	19	25	2.0	6.2	**3.1**	14%	1.0	9.0	75	$11
LIMA Plan	C	2nd Half		4	3	0	60	15	7.26	2.03	375			14.1	37%	66%	6.09	47	18	35	3.1	2.3	**0.8**	11%	1.5	-20.3	-34	($5)
+/- Score	5	08	Proj	**3**	**2**	**0**	**44**	**20**	**4.97**	**1.63**	**317**			**15.2**	**33%**	**72%**	**4.85**	**51**	**17**	**32**	**2.9**	**4.1**	**1.4**	**12%**	**1.2**	**-1.9**	**9**	**$1**

3-2, 5.33 ERA in 50 IP at TEX. Soft-tosser gives up a bunch of hits, and despite being a GB pitcher, gets taken deep with regularity. There's little light at the end of this BPI tunnel.

TOM TODARO

Wright,Jamey	Yr	Tm	W	L	Sv	IP	K	ERA	WHIP	OBA	vL	vR	BF/G	H%	S%	xERA	G	L	F	Ctl	Dom	Cmd	hr/f	hr/9	RAR	BPV	R$
RH Starter	03	KC *	7	11	0	163	113	6.13	1.79	311	296	175	24.8	34%	68%	4.85	51	18	31	4.7	6.2	1.3	14%	1.4	-32.3	17	($3)
Age 33	04	COL *	10	9	0	182	96	5.28	1.69	307	253	281	26.3	32%	72%	4.88	50	22	28	4.0	4.7	1.2	15%	1.3	-22.9	7	($0)
Peak	05	COL	8	16	0	171	101	5.47	1.65	294	314	279	23.0	32%	68%	4.65	53	20	27	4.3	5.3	1.2	14%	1.2	-25.9	20	($1)
Type GB	06	SF	6	10	0	156	79	5.19	1.48	275	261	300	20.2	29%	66%	4.30	58	18	23	3.7	4.6	1.2	13%	0.9	-13.6	26	$3
Reliability 32	07	TEX *	6	6	0	97	48	4.29	1.59	286	268	253	18.2	31%	75%	4.80	55	17	28	4.1	4.5	1.1	10%	0.9	2.6	21	$4
ERA Potl 40%	1st Half		3	2	0	33	18	6.53	1.87	344			22.7	36%	69%	5.19	41	27	32	3.5	4.9	1.4	18%	1.9	-8.2	-13	($1)
LIMA Plan C	2nd Half		3	4	0	64	30	3.14	1.44	252			16.4	28%	78%	4.73	58	15	27	4.4	4.3	1.0	4%	0.4	10.8	40	$5
+/- Score -28	08	Proj	6	8	0	116	61	4.58	1.55	281			21.6	30%	72%	4.60	55	19	26	4.0	4.7	1.2	11%	0.9	-1.5	24	$4

4-5, 3.62 ERA in 77 IP at TEX, which was the best ERA in his 12 year major league career. His lifetime ERA is 5.06. Now..... 12 years in the bigs. Lifetime ERA of 5.06 and Cmd of 1.1. What am I missing here?

Wright,Jaret	Yr	Tm	W	L	Sv	IP	K	ERA	WHIP	OBA	vL	vR	BF/G	H%	S%	xERA	G	L	F	Ctl	Dom	Cmd	hr/f	hr/9	RAR	BPV	R$
RH Reliever	03	2NL *	4	6	2	75	66	5.88	1.76	308	365	313	5.7	37%	67%	4.44	45	25	31	4.6	7.9	1.7	12%	1.1	-14.8	45	($0)
Age 32	04	ATL	15	8	0	186	159	3.29	1.28	242	261	225	24.4	30%	75%	3.92	46	19	35	3.4	7.7	2.3	6%	0.5	22.3	84	$20
Peak	05	NYY	5	5	0	63	34	6.12	1.79	312	273	358	22.9	34%	67%	5.36	45	23	32	4.6	4.8	1.1	11%	1.1	-13.7	10	($1)
Type	06	NYY	11	7	0	140	84	4.50	1.53	284	314	255	20.8	32%	71%	5.08	38	24	38	3.7	5.4	1.5	6%	0.6	1.1	42	$9
Reliability 0	07	BAL	0	3	0	10	7	6.99	2.04	292	300	316	17.0	33%	65%	6.85	38	19	44	7.9	6.1	0.8	7%	0.9	-3.2	23	($1)
ERA Potl 55%	1st Half		0	3	0	10	7	7.20	2.10	299			16.7	34%	65%	6.94	38	19	44	8.1	6.3	0.8	7%	0.9	-3.3	22	($1)
LIMA Plan D	2nd Half		0	0	0	0	0	0.00	0.00																		
+/- Score -17	08	Proj	4	5	0	73	48	4.59	1.52	279			20.1	31%	72%	4.84	41	21	37	3.8	6.0	1.5	9%	1.0	-3.1	38	$3

Injuries have taken a toll on his velocity and control. Simply not the same pitcher he was in '04, and even that was just a 1-year trip to wonderland in an 11 year career of mediocrity. $3 million, 10 IP, 6.99 ERA. Thrifty!

Wuertz,Mike	Yr	Tm	W	L	Sv	IP	K	ERA	WHIP	OBA	vL	vR	BF/G	H%	S%	xERA	G	L	F	Ctl	Dom	Cmd	hr/f	hr/9	RAR	BPV	R$
RH Reliever	03	aaa	3	9	1	124	81	5.23	1.53	307			12.8	34%	68%	5.54				2.5	5.9	2.3		1.2	-12.7	40	$2
Age 29	04	CHC *	2	1	20	73	82	3.20	1.17	207	212	221	4.4	27%	77%	3.99	29	16	55	3.9	10.1	2.6	8%	1.0	9.6	98	$14
Pre-Peak	05	CHC	6	2	0	75	89	3.83	1.33	221	260	197	4.3	30%	72%	3.67	43	17	40	4.8	10.7	2.2	8%	0.7	3.9	100	$8
Type Pwr	06	CHC *	9	1	10	81	98	2.61	1.22	241	184	245	4.7	33%	83%	2.76	54	16	30	2.9	10.8	3.7	13%	0.9	18.9	122	$17
Reliability 17	07	CHC	2	3	0	72	79	3.49	1.37	239	238	233	4.2	31%	78%	3.82	44	15	41	4.4	9.8	2.3	10%	1.0	8.4	84	$6
ERA Potl 55%	1st Half		1	2	0	35	30	3.09	1.31	227			4.0	27%	81%	4.28	45	14	40	4.4	7.7	1.8	10%	1.0	5.8	62	$3
LIMA Plan A	2nd Half		1	1	0	37	49	3.86	1.42	250			4.5	36%	76%	3.41	42	16	41	4.3	11.8	2.7	11%	1.0	2.6	104	$3
+/- Score 18	08	Proj	4	2	0	78	88	3.35	1.31	236			4.5	31%	78%	3.56	44	16	40	3.9	10.2	2.6	10%	0.9	8.0	95	$8

Walks are the one thing holding him back. There are others ahead of him on the bullpen depth chart, but he's still a fine LIMA pick... and a turnaround in control could lead to better things.

Yates,Tyler	Yr	Tm	W	L	Sv	IP	K	ERA	WHIP	OBA	vL	vR	BF/G	H%	S%	xERA	G	L	F	Ctl	Dom	Cmd	hr/f	hr/9	RAR	BPV	R$
RH Reliever	03	a/a	2	4	0	59	39	5.48	1.66	293			22.5	33%	67%	5.33				4.4	5.9	1.3		0.9	-7.9	33	($0)
Age 30	04	NYM *	8	6	4	85	69	5.48	1.70	285	330	296	7.7	34%	68%	4.28	55	21	25	5.2	7.3	1.4	12%	0.8	-12.8	46	$3
Peak	05	NYM	0	0	0	0	0	0.00	0.00																		
Type Pwr	06	ATL	2	5	1	50	46	3.96	1.46	230	217	235	3.9	27%	76%	4.52	41	22	37	5.6	8.3	1.5	12%	1.1	3.3	58	$4
Reliability 0	07	ATL	2	3	2	66	69	5.18	1.44	256	310	213	3.8	33%	64%	3.84	46	17	37	4.2	9.4	2.2	9%	0.8	-6.2	82	$3
ERA Potl 0%	1st Half		2	0	0	33	34	3.27	1.12	191			3.8	25%	71%	3.84	38	17	44	4.1	9.3	2.3	6%	0.5	4.7	104	$4
LIMA Plan B+	2nd Half		0	3	2	33	35	7.09	1.76	311			3.9	40%	59%	3.79	54	16	30	4.4	9.5	2.2	13%	1.1	-10.8	63	($1)
+/- Score 36	08	Proj	2	4	0	58	58	4.03	1.41	248			4.5	31%	74%	3.87	46	19	35	4.3	9.0	2.1	11%	0.9	3.8	75	$4

Has really improved his Dom since missing '05 season, but walks remain a problem. Chalk up 2H ERA to brutal H%/S%. BPV looking better, but without further improvement in control, he'll stall at this level.

Youman,Shane	Yr	Tm	W	L	Sv	IP	K	ERA	WHIP	OBA	vL	vR	BF/G	H%	S%	xERA	G	L	F	Ctl	Dom	Cmd	hr/f	hr/9	RAR	BPV	R$
LH Starter	03		0	0	0	0	0	0.00	0.00																		
Age 28	04		0	0	0	0	0	0.00	0.00																		
Pre-Peak	05	aa	7	6	2	93	57	5.16	1.83	316			10.3	35%	73%	6.16				4.7	5.5	1.2		1.0	-9.8	20	$0
Type Con FB	06	PIT *	11	4	1	158	66	3.53	1.37	277			18.9	30%	74%	4.62	58	8	34	2.6	3.7	1.4	5%	0.5	18.7	37	$12
Reliability 13	07	PIT *	7	11	0	139	71	6.50	1.86	330	306	297	21.5	37%	63%	6.01	38	20	42	4.2	4.6	1.1	4%	0.6	-35.6	23	($6)
ERA Potl 55%	1st Half		4	6	0	82	51	5.70	1.73	316			25.4	37%	65%					3.8	5.6	1.5		0.3	-12.9	46	($1)
LIMA Plan C	2nd Half		3	5	0	57	20	7.64	2.04	350			17.8	37%	61%	6.82	38	20	42	4.7	3.2	0.7	6%	0.9	-22.7	-8	($6)
+/- Score 7	08	Proj	3	3	0	44	22	4.76	1.59	294			16.3	31%	72%	5.47	40	19	41	3.7	4.6	1.2	8%	1.0	-5.7	18	$1

3-5, 5.97 ERA in 57 IP at PIT. H% and S% destroyed his ERA but there isn't much skill behind it anyway.Lefties sometimes blossom late, but there's nothing here to germinate... He'll still probably be pitching at 40, right?

Young,Chris	Yr	Tm	W	L	Sv	IP	K	ERA	WHIP	OBA	vL	vR	BF/G	H%	S%	xERA	G	L	F	Ctl	Dom	Cmd	hr/f	hr/9	RAR	BPV	R$
RH Starter	03	aa	4	4	0	83	50	4.91	1.45	295			24.2	32%	68%	5.05				2.4	5.5	2.3		1.1	-5.3	42	$3
Age 28	04	a/a	9	6	0	118	89	5.05	1.57	299			23.1	34%	70%	5.48				3.3	6.8	2.1		1.2	-10.3	43	$5
Pre-Peak	05	TEX	12	7	0	164	137	4.28	1.26	259	281	220	22.1	30%	69%	4.32	33	18	49	2.5	7.5	3.0	8%	1.0	2.0	81	$16
Type Pwr xFB	06	SD	11	5	0	179	164	3.47	1.13	210	175	234	23.4	24%	77%	4.38	25	18	56	3.5	8.2	2.4	10%	1.4	22.5	70	$22
Reliability 80	07	SD	9	8	0	173	167	3.12	1.10	195	231	155	23.2	25%	72%	4.26	29	16	54	3.7	8.7	2.3	4%	0.5	27.8	101	$22
ERA Potl 55%	1st Half		7	3	0	91	81	2.08	1.07	195			24.2	25%	81%	4.24	33	16	51	3.5	8.0	2.3	2%	0.3	26.4	104	$15
LIMA Plan D+	2nd Half		2	5	0	82	86	4.28	1.13	195			22.2	25%	63%	4.28	25	17	59	4.1	9.4	2.3	6%	0.8	1.5	98	$8
+/- Score -27	08	Proj	10	8	0	174	159	3.93	1.26	238			23.5	28%	73%	4.49	28	17	55	3.4	8.2	2.4	9%	1.2	-1.9	70	$16

BPV shows skills improvement. xERA has a more stable view and more moderate skills. As a flyball pitcher, there is always risk, although pitching in Petco helps. Unless he improves his control, this is peak value.

Zambrano,Carlos	Yr	Tm	W	L	Sv	IP	K	ERA	WHIP	OBA	vL	vR	BF/G	H%	S%	xERA	G	L	F	Ctl	Dom	Cmd	hr/f	hr/9	RAR	BPV	R$
RH Starter	03	CHC	13	11	0	214	168	3.11	1.32	238	245	235	28.3	29%	76%	3.75	56	18	26	4.0	7.1	1.8	6%	0.4	30.8	76	$21
Age 26	04	CHC	16	8	0	209	188	2.75	1.22	228	232	218	27.9	28%	79%	3.58	51	18	31	3.5	8.1	2.3	8%	0.6	38.9	89	$26
Growth	05	CHC	14	6	0	223	202	3.27	1.15	213	212	212	27.5	26%	74%	3.43	50	20	30	3.5	8.1	2.3	12%	0.8	26.9	85	$26
Type Pwr	06	CHC	16	7	0	214	210	3.41	1.29	212	247	174	27.3	27%	76%	3.92	47	17	36	4.8	8.8	1.8	10%	0.8	28.5	79	$24
Reliability 71	07	CHC	18	13	0	216	177	3.95	1.33	235	268	200	27.0	27%	73%	4.22	47	17	37	4.2	7.4	1.8	10%	1.0	12.6	60	$21
ERA Potl 50%	1st Half		9	6	0	111	94	4.22	1.33	244			27.8	28%	73%	4.13	45	16	39	3.8	7.6	2.0	13%	1.3	2.9	55	$10
LIMA Plan D+	2nd Half		9	7	0	105	83	3.68	1.33	225			26.3	27%	73%	4.32	48	17	34	4.6	7.1	1.5	7%	0.6	9.8	67	$11
+/- Score -0	08	Proj	15	12	0	218	184	4.01	1.35	237			27.3	28%	72%	4.11	48	18	34	4.3	7.6	1.8	9%	0.8	7.7	66	$19

We're not just crying wolf; all those IP really are taking a toll. Dom fell, Ctl is poor, rising FB rate means more HRs. xERA trend can't be ignored. DN: 4.50+ ERA, for real

Zito,Barry	Yr	Tm	W	L	Sv	IP	K	ERA	WHIP	OBA	vL	vR	BF/G	H%	S%	xERA	G	L	F	Ctl	Dom	Cmd	hr/f	hr/9	RAR	BPV	R$
LH Starter	03	OAK	14	12	0	231	146	3.31	1.19	222	223	218	27.1	25%	74%	4.72	40	15	45	3.4	5.7	1.7	6%	0.7	34.6	57	$25
Age 30	04	OAK	11	11	0	213	163	4.48	1.39	264	263	248	27.0	30%	71%	4.62	37	19	44	3.4	6.9	2.0	10%	1.2	-1.2	50	$13
Peak	05	OAK	14	13	0	228	171	3.87	1.20	223	215	223	26.9	25%	71%	4.19	42	21	37	3.5	6.7	1.9	11%	1.0	14.2	60	$23
Type FB	06	OAK	16	10	0	221	151	3.83	1.40	253	260	257	28.1	28%	76%	5.00	38	17	45	4.0	6.1	1.5	9%	1.1	19.9	40	$20
Reliability 75	07	SF	11	13	0	197	131	4.53	1.35	247	242	244	24.7	27%	69%	4.76	39	20	41	3.8	6.0	1.6	10%	1.1	-2.5	42	$12
ERA Potl 50%	1st Half		6	8	0	96	58	4.59	1.38	250			25.8	27%	69%	4.86	41	21	38	3.9	5.4	1.4	10%	1.0	-2.0	36	$6
LIMA Plan D+	2nd Half		5	5	0	101	73	4.47	1.32	245			23.7	27%	69%	4.67	37	19	44	3.7	6.5	1.8	10%	1.2	-0.5	48	$7
+/- Score -16	08	Proj	12	13	0	218	150	4.39	1.40	258			26.1	28%	72%	4.79	39	19	42	3.8	6.2	1.6	10%	1.2	-10.5	39	$13

xERA has been ringing the warning bell for nearly forever. Yes, he'll have the occasional up year, but for the most part, these are not Cy Young-caliber skills and any bid that even approaches $20 is just silly.

Zumaya,Joel	Yr	Tm	W	L	Sv	IP	K	ERA	WHIP	OBA	vL	vR	BF/G	H%	S%	xERA	G	L	F	Ctl	Dom	Cmd	hr/f	hr/9	RAR	BPV	R$
RH Reliever	03		0	0	0	0	0	0.00	0.00																		
Age 23	04	aa	2	2	0	20	25	7.20	1.65	271			22.9	31%	65%	7.07				5.4	11.3	2.1		3.2	-7.0	17	$0
Growth	05	a/a	9	5	0	151	181	3.46	1.25	212			24.2	30%	73%	2.88				4.4	10.8	2.4		0.6	15.7	110	$18
Type Pwr xFB	06	DET	6	3	1	83	97	1.95	1.18	193	183	188	5.5	27%	87%	3.74	34	21	45	4.5	10.5	2.3	7%	0.6	26.7	108	$15
Reliability 0	07	DET	2	3	1	34	27	4.27	1.19	195	271	135	4.9	23%	65%	4.67	36	16	48	4.5	7.2	1.6	7%	0.8	1.0	69	$4
ERA Potl 60%	1st Half		1	1	1	17	17	3.71	1.41	213			5.7	26%	77%	5.00	28	17	55	5.8	9.0	1.5	8%	1.1	1.7	67	$2
LIMA Plan B+	2nd Half		1	2	0	17	10	4.85	0.96	175			4.3	20%	47%	4.31	45	14	41	3.2	5.4	1.7	5%	0.5	-0.7	71	$2
+/- Score -12	08	Proj	2	2	0	33	32	4.09	1.30	205			5.4	26%	70%	4.47	37	17	46	5.2	8.7	1.7	8%	0.8	0.1	77	$3

2007: Needed surgery to repair a ruptured tendon in his right middle finger.
2008: Will miss half the season after surgery to repair the AC joint in his throwing shoulder. No 100 mph heaters for awhile.

TOM TODARO

PQS Pitching Logs

We've always approached performance measures on an aggregate basis. Each individual event that our statistics chronicle gets dumped into a huge pool of data. We then use our formulas to try to sort and slice and manipulate the data into more usable information.

Pure Quality Starts (PQS) take a different approach. *(See Glossary for complete definition)*. It says that the smallest unit of measure should not be the "event" but instead be the "game." Within that game, we can accumulate all the strikeouts, hits and walks, and evaluate that outing as a whole. After all, when a pitcher takes the mound, he is either "on" or "off" his game; he is either dominant or struggling, or somewhere in between.

PQS captures the array of events and slaps an evaluative label on that outing, on a scale of 0 to 5. It doesn't matter if a few extra balls got through the infield, or the pitcher was given the hook in the fourth or sixth inning, or the bullpen was able to strand their inherited baserunners. When we look at performance in the aggregate, *those events do matter,* and will affect a pitcher's BPIs and ERA. But with PQS, the minutia is less relevant than the overall performance.

In the end, a dominating performance is a dominating performance, whether Jake Peavy is hurling a 1-hit shutout or giving up 3 runs while striking out 7 in 6 IP. And a disaster is still a disaster, whether Casey Fossum gets a first inning hook after giving up 5 runs, or "takes one for the team" getting shelled for 9 runs in 5 IP.

With Gene McCaffrey's Domination and Disaster percentages, we can sort out the PQS scores even more.

Domination Per Cent (DOM%) measures the portion of a pitcher's starts that scored a 4 or 5 on the PQS scale.

Disaster Per Cent (DIS%) measures the portion of a pitcher's starts that scored a 0 or 1 on the PQS scale.

DOM/DIS percentages open up a new perspective, providing us with two separate scales of performance. In tandem, they measure something completely different — *consistency.* For instance, a pitcher with a 50/20% DOM/DIS split was dominating in half of his starts but was rocked one every five outings. Compare him to a pitcher with a 50/5% split — also dominating half of the time but saw an early shower only once every 20 times out.

This is important because a pitcher might possess incredible skill but be unable to sustain it on a start-by-start basis. For instance, a pitcher who posts PQS scores of 5,0,5,0,5 might have an ERA that is identical to one who posts scores of 3,3,3,3,3 — less skill, but more consistent. ERAs, WHIPs, and even BPIs don't capture that subtle difference. DOM/DIS *does* capture that difference, and in doing so, helps us identify pitchers who might be better or worse than their stats — and sabermetrics — indicate.

The final step is to convert a pitcher's DOM/DIS split back to an equivalent ERA. By creating a grid of individual DOM and DIS levels, we can determine the average ERA at each cross point. The result is an ERA based purely on PQS, and so we can call it the PQS ERA, or *qERA.*

Some important comparisons:

ERA: The pitcher's actual season earned run average.

xERA: The pitcher's ERA based on the component elements of his skill, essentially stripping away the effects of bullpen and defense.

qERA: The pitcher's ERA based on a comparison of his dominating versus disastrous starts.

Is qERA predictive? We looked at all pitchers with at least 15 starts in the three year period of 2001-2003, then isolated those with a qERA to ERA variance of at least half a run. How often did those variances predict an ERA swing for the following year?

Year	IMPROVEMENT			DECLINE		
	Hit	Miss	%	Hit	Miss	%
2001-2002	11	3	79%	14	9	61%
2002-2003	11	2	85%	32	7	82%

The following pitching logs include:

- Up to three years of data for all pitchers who had at least five starts in 2007.
- Number of starts in that year. (No.)
- Start-by-start listing of PQS scores, separated by half season. These are not time-phased, so any gaps do not necessarily represent gaps of time.
- Average pitch counts for all starts (PC)
- Domination and Disaster percentages (DOM, DIS)
- Earned Run Average (ERA)
- Expected Earned Run Average (xERA)
- PQS Earned Run Average (qERA)

There is much insight that can be gleaned from these charts. A casual scan uncovers a few random tidbits:

Jeremy Bonderman apparently crashed in 2007, but a glance at his xERA and qERA shows a skill set even stronger than before.

Daniel Cabrera's ERA trend says he's regressing. His 50/15 DOM/DIS in 2007 says he made some gains.

Jose Contrera's performance drop-off doesn't look as severe when viewed through the qERA lens. The exact opposite goes for **Roy Halladay**.

Livan Hernandez's workload and performance have been a source of constant intrigue. Dipping back into some history, look at his DOM, ERA and pitch count trends. It appears that the branch breaks each time his PC peaks:

Year	DOM	DIS	PC	ERA	qERA
1999	39%	10%	113	4.64	4.32
2000	48%	6%	116	3.75	3.98
2001	32%	18%	109	5.25	4.60
2002	36%	18%	105	4.38	4.52
2003	64%	9%	108	3.21	3.50
2004	57%	6%	112	3.60	3.68
2005	32%	18%	114	3.99	4.60
2006	26%	9%	103	4.83	4.48
2007	21%	27%	102	4.93	4.98

C.C. Sabathia's ERAs have been flat the past two years but DOM/DIS and qERA show a pitcher who is soaring.

How do you spell consistency? **Johan Santana**.

PQS PITCHING LOGS

Pitcher	Year	No.	FIRST HALF	SECOND HALF	PC	DOM	DIS	ERA	xERA	qERA
Albers,Matt	2007	18	3 4 0 4 0 0 3	4 0 2 1 5 3 0 3 0 2 3	88	22%	39%	5.86	4.89	5.36
Armas Jr.,Tony	2005	19	2 3 2 2 3 3 4 1 0 3 4	0 4 3 3 4 3 0 0	94	21%	26%	4.99	4.88	4.98
	2006	30	4 4 2 5 4 0 5 5 1 3 5 5 5 3 0 0	4 4 0 0 4 5 1 0 0 3 2 0 3 5 3	92	43%	33%	5.03	4.13	4.92
	2007	15	0 0 2 4 2 0 0	5 4 0 0 3 5 5 4	86	40%	40%	6.03	4.81	5.21
Arroyo,Bronson	2005	32	5 1 3 3 5 5 3 4 4 0 4 0 5 4 2 4 3	0 4 2 3 0 4 3 4 1 3 4 3 3 3 0	101	41%	22%	4.52	4.40	4.56
	2006	34	4 4 1 5 5 3 2 5 4 5 4 4 4 4 4 5 4 5 0	4 4 3 4 0 3 3 2 3 3 5 5 5 1 5	110	65%	12%	3.29	3.37	3.61
	2007	34	4 4 2 4 4 4 3 4 0 0 2 3 2 4 3 5 3	2 5 2 4 0 5 3 3 1 5 4 4 5 2 3 2	101	47%	12%	4.23	4.53	4.28
Backe,Brandon	2005	25	3 4 5 3 5 1 3 4 3 4 2 4 0 3 4 0 2 4	4 3 0 0 5 5 0	91	44%	24%	4.77	4.33	4.56
	2006	8	4 0	0 2 3 3 2 3	84	13%	25%	3.77	4.60	5.08
	2007	5		1 2 2 3 5	91	20%	20%	3.77	5.51	4.75
Bacsik,Mike	2007	20	3 3 3 0 1 0 2 1 4 1	2 3 2 4 2 0 4 1 0 0	85	15%	45%	5.11	5.22	6.25
Baek,Cha Seung	2006	6		4 2 4 4 0 5	96	67%	17%	3.67	3.65	3.73
	2007	12	0 5 0 4 4 4 5 3 3 3 0	3	96	42%	25%	5.15	4.48	4.74
Bailey,Homer	2007	9	3 2 3 0 0 4	3 4 2	90	22%	22%	5.76	5.32	4.75
Baker,Scott	2005	9	4	5 5 4 0 3 4 2 3	90	56%	11%	3.38	3.89	3.97
	2006	16	0 4 1 5 1 3 0 2 0	3 3 0 3 1 3 0	90	13%	50%	6.37	3.87	7.08
	2007	23	3 2 0 2 0 3 5 4 3	4 3 5 5 4 2 4 2 2 5 3 3 3 0	90	35%	13%	4.26	4.31	4.41
Bannister,Brian	2006	6	4 4 2 3 1	4	100	50%	17%	4.26	4.86	4.37
	2007	27	0 3 0 3 4 2 5 4 5 2 3 4 3	3 4 5 3 3 0 4 3 4 4 0 3 0 0	96	37%	22%	3.87	4.75	4.64
Barone,Daniel	2007	6		0 0 1 0 0 0	81	0%	100%	5.71	5.72	15.00
Batista,Miguel	2006	33	5 2 3 2 0 2 4 2 3 2 4 4 0 4 1 3 4 0	3 3 5 3 0 2 2 4 3 4 3 5 3 3 0	99	30%	18%	4.58	3.97	4.60
	2007	32	0 4 2 4 3 2 0 3 4 2 5 5 2 2 4 3 2	5 4 4 4 3 2 4 0 3 5 2 4 4 2 4	101	47%	9%	4.29	4.85	3.98
Beckett,Josh	2005	29	5 5 4 5 4 0 5 4 4 5 4 4 4 1 5 0	5 5 5 2 5 5 0 4 3 5 3 4 5	97	76%	14%	3.38	3.20	3.41
	2006	33	5 3 5 2 0 2 5 5 2 5 0 0 4 4 5 4 4 3	0 5 5 4 2 5 4 1 3 3 3 3 4 4 5	98	52%	15%	5.01	3.49	4.37
	2007	30	3 5 5 4 4 5 5 0 5 3 5 0 3 5 3 4	5 5 5 4 5 5 2 4 5 4 5 5 3	103	73%	7%	3.27	3.28	3.25
Bedard,Erik	2005	24	5 2 0 5 5 5 5 2 5	5 4 3 0 3 3 5 3 4 0 3 2 4 5 0	103	50%	17%	4.02	3.65	4.37
	2006	33	1 5 4 4 1 2 0 2 3 0 0 0 3 4 5 5 5 5 5	5 5 4 3 4 5 2 4 4 5 5 5 0 2	100	58%	21%	3.76	3.13	4.23
	2007	28	0 5 5 3 0 5 5 5 5 5 5 4 4 3 5 5 5 2 5	5 5 5 4 3 5 5 5 3	105	75%	7%	3.16	2.86	3.13
Belisle,Matt	2005	5	4 0 3 5 1		73	40%	40%	4.44	3.65	5.21
	2007	30	5 4 1 3 4 4 5 2 0 3 5 3 3 2 3 2 0	4 0 0 3 3 2 3 3 0 4 5 1 4	93	33%	23%	5.32	4.25	4.71
Benson,Kris	2005	28	0 2 5 3 5 4 4 4 1 3 3 3 5	5 4 4 2 1 4 3 0 1 3 1 0 3 2 4	98	39%	25%	4.14	4.04	4.82
	2006	30	3 5 1 2 3 3 3 0 5 3 0 1 1 5 4 4 3 0 2 0	3 2 1 0 4 0 3 2 5 3 0	95	23%	37%	4.82	4.15	5.36
Bergmann,Jason	2006	6		4 3 2 4 0 0	87	33%	33%	6.68	4.01	5.08
	2007	21	0 5 5 5 5 4 3 5 0 0 2	0 3 0 3 5 5 1 5 1 0	90	43%	38%	4.45	4.63	5.07
Billingsley,Chad	2006	16	1 2 1 3 1	2 4 0 4 5 3 5 3 2 0 2	95	25%	31%	3.80	4.48	5.13
	2007	20	0 0 5 2	3 2 4 0 5 2 2 3 5 4 5 5 4 4 3 0	95	45%	20%	3.31	3.98	4.53
Blanton,Joe	2005	33	2 3 3 4 0 3 0 0 0 0 3 4 4 4 4 4 2	2 1 4 4 5 3 4 4 5 5 3 2 3 3 4 5	93	45%	18%	3.54	4.02	4.40
	2006	31	5 4 0 3 2 2 2 4 0 3 4 1 4 3 3 0 3 2	4 2 4 2 3 3 3 4 2 3 0 2 2	101	26%	16%	4.82	4.06	4.62
	2007	34	5 2 4 4 3 4 4 5 5 3 2 4 3 3 4 5 4 4 3	3 2 3 4 2 0 5 5 3 5 4 2 5 1 2	102	53%	6%	3.95	3.96	3.85
Bonderman,Jeremy	2005	29	5 3 4 3 4 3 5 5 3 4 3 4 2 3 5 0 4 4	4 4 5 2 4 5 3 0 0 5 0	98	55%	14%	4.57	3.58	3.97
	2006	34	5 4 0 3 5 5 2 5 0 3 3 5 5 5 5 5 5 3 4	1 4 3 5 3 4 5 0 4 2 0 3 3 3 4 0	97	50%	18%	4.08	2.93	4.37
	2007	28	3 4 4 5 4 3 4 4 5 5 4 3 4 5 5 5	4 4 2 0 2 3 5 3 1 4 0 0	97	61%	14%	5.01	3.83	3.71
Bonser,Boof	2006	18	5 3 4 1 0 4 0	0 3 3 3 5 5 4 5 5 2	87	44%	22%	4.22	3.33	4.56
	2007	30	5 0 2 2 3 3 4 3 5 3 4 1 3 5 4 2 3 4	5 4 0 3 3 1 0 3 4 0 3 1	92	33%	23%	5.10	4.43	4.71
Bowie,Micah	2007	8	0 2 2 3 3 5 0 0		87	13%	38%	4.55	4.69	5.54
Braden,Dallas	2007	14	5 0 0 1	4 3 0 2 3 0 0 0 0 0	85	14%	64%	6.72	4.88	8.46
Buchholz,Clay	2007	3		3 5 0	91	33%	33%	1.59	3.53	5.08
Buchholz,Taylor	2006	19	3 4 3 4 0 0 4 0 2 1 5 5 5 5 4	2 2 0 0	87	42%	32%	5.89	3.57	4.92
	2007	8	3 0 3 0 4 5 3	0	79	25%	38%	4.23	4.24	5.27
Buckner,William	2007	5		0 3 4 1 4	87	40%	40%	5.29	5.24	5.21
Buehrle,Mark	2005	33	4 3 5 4 2 3 3 4 3 4 3 4 5 4 5 4 2 3	5 2 2 3 4 1 3 5 2 4 3 2 3 4 4	105	48%	3%	3.12	2.63	3.68
	2006	32	0 3 4 5 4 1 3 2 3 3 3 2 3 4 3 4 2 3	0 3 1 4 1 4 2 1 4 3 0 3 2 0	97	25%	25%	4.99	3.99	4.93
	2007	30	0 3 5 4 3 2 4 4 3 4 3 4 3 3 3 4 3 3	2 3 4 5 3 0 3 3 3 4 4 1 2	103	37%	10%	3.63	4.38	4.41
Burnett,A.J.	2005	32	4 4 3 5 3 5 3 5 3 5 5 3 4 5 0 5	1 5 4 5 2 3 5 5 4 2 3 0 4 5 5	103	63%	9%	3.44	2.95	3.50
	2006	21	3 0 5 5 0 3	5 5 0 0 4 5 3 2 2 4 5 5 4 5 5	103	57%	19%	3.98	2.97	4.10
	2007	25	0 4 3 3 4 1 4 5 5 5 5 5 5 0 0	3 5 5 3 5 5 5 4 4 3	106	64%	16%	3.75	3.18	3.83
Burres,Brian	2007	17	0 2 3 4 3 1 4 0 3 0	4 5 0 3 5 0 0	93	29%	41%	5.95	5.10	5.40
Bush,David	2005	24	1 4 0 4 3 4 0 3 0 0	3 4 0 0 4 0 5 5 5 3 0 0 5 3	88	38%	42%	4.50	3.84	5.25
	2006	32	5 2 4 5 3 5 3 0 3 4 0 5 4 4 4	3 0 4 5 1 4 3 4 3 5 0 3 4	93	56%	16%	4.41	2.96	4.10
	2007	31	4 4 3 5 3 4 2 4 3 2 5 3 0 4 4 5 5	3 5 2 1 3 3 5 4 4 0 0 4 3 3	95	48%	13%	5.12	4.19	4.28
Byrd,Paul	2005	31	3 2 3 0 3 3 3 4 3 3 4 3 4 4 4 3	3 4 0 3 4 3 3 1 4 4 4 4 0 3	94	39%	13%	3.75	3.98	4.41
	2006	31	3 0 4 0 4 4 2 4 4 5 3 3 5 3 4 4 0	1 3 0 0 3 2 4 0 3 3 1 2 0 2	92	32%	29%	4.88	4.07	4.90
	2007	31	5 3 3 4 3 3 0 3 3 4 3 3 4 4	3 2 2 1 3 0 4 2 3 3 0 2 2 0 2	91	23%	16%	4.59	4.40	4.63
Cabrera,Daniel	2005	29	0 2 2 3 5 5 4 0 5 1 4 0 4 4 3 5 3	5 3 3 0 4 0 0 5 3 4 3 3	99	41%	24%	4.53	3.53	4.56
	2006	26	0 3 5 3 5 5 3 0 3 4 5 2 0 3 3	1 5 0 5 5 1 3 3 0 5 4	103	38%	27%	4.74	3.69	4.82
	2007	34	5 4 3 4 4 3 4 2 4 0 4 3 4 0 3 5 3 4 4	3 2 3 4 4 3 4 2 5 4 0 0 2 4 0	105	50%	15%	5.55	4.52	4.37
Cain,Matt	2005	7		2 4 5 3 5 4 3	102	57%	0%	2.34	4.15	3.38
	2006	31	3 4 1 4 5 0 1 3 3 3 0 4 5 0 5 0	4 4 3 5 0 3 0 5 5 5 4 5 2 4 3	106	52%	23%	4.15	3.56	4.50
	2007	32	4 3 5 3 3 0 3 5 5 4 4 2 5 4 1 5 3	1 0 0 5 5 4 5 4 3 5 0 3 5 4 4	105	56%	19%	3.65	4.34	4.10
Capuano,Chris	2005	35	4 2 2 2 3 5 4 5 4 4 3 5 0 3 3 3 2 3 2	4 3 4 3 1 0 5 5 2 5 3 4 3 3 3 0	104	37%	11%	3.99	3.95	4.41
	2006	34	5 4 5 5 3 4 3 5 3 4 3 4 4 5 5 4 0 4	0 3 2 3 4 4 5 3 4 5 3 2 2 1 0	99	59%	12%	4.03	3.29	3.97
	2007	25	4 4 4 4 3 0 5 0 1 0 5 5 0 0 1	0 5 5 4 3 2 0 3 3	91	40%	36%	5.10	4.18	5.07
Carlyle,Buddy	2007	20	0 4 2 3 0 5 0 5	4 3 3 3 1 0 2 3 3 0 0 0	82	20%	40%	5.21	4.67	5.50
Carmona,Fausto	2006	7	5 0 3	0 2 3 5	87	29%	29%	5.42	3.46	4.93
	2007	32	0 4 3 3 4 4 4 2 2 4 5 5 5 2 0 5 2	3 5 5 4 4 3 5 3 3 3 3 3 5 4 3	98	50%	6%	3.06	3.51	3.85
Carpenter,Chris	2005	33	4 0 4 4 3 4 4 4 4 5 4 4 5 5 5 5 5	5 3 5 4 4 5 2 4 4 5 5 3 0 2 3	103	76%	6%	2.84	2.76	3.13
	2006	32	2 5 5 5 3 3 5 4 5 4 3 5 4 3 4 3 5	5 5 3 0 3 4 4 5 4 5 3 4 5 2 4	102	66%	3%	3.09	2.69	3.14
	2007	1	3		101	0%	0%	7.50	3.56	4.50
Chacin,Gustavo	2005	34	4 4 3 5 3 3 3 0 3 2 2 5 4 0 2 2 3 4	1 4 4 4 2 2 4 3 1 3 5 5 3 0 0 4	95	38%	18%	3.72	4.17	4.52
	2006	17	4 2 1 3 5 2 0 2 0 0	0 3 3 3 4 1 0	86	18%	41%	5.05	4.45	5.60
	2007	5	3 4 4 0 1		84	40%	40%	5.60	5.08	5.21

PQS PITCHING LOGS

Pitcher	Year	No.	FIRST HALF	SECOND HALF	PC	DOM	DIS	ERA	xERA	qERA
Chacon,Shawn	2005	24	5 5 1 3 2 2 4 0 1 2	5 4 4 4 3 3 3 3 4 2 3 0 3 4 3	102	38%	17%	3.45	4.50	4.52
	2006	20	0 4 3 3 4 0 0 0 0 2 0	3 0 2 0 3 3 3 3 3	86	10%	40%	6.36	5.11	5.70
	2007	4	0 5 1 0		94	25%	75%	3.94	4.56	9.46
Chico,Matthew	2007	31	0 0 2 0 2 0 4 0 3 1 0 3 4 3 0 3 3 4	2 1 0 2 0 3 0 4 3 5 2 1 4	91	19%	42%	4.63	5.56	5.60
Claussen,Brandon	2005	29	3 2 0 0 0 3 3 3 4 2 2 5 5 3	0 0 5 4 3 5 4 3 2 5 3 5 5 2 2	98	34%	17%	4.22	4.12	4.60
	2006	14	4 3 5 0 1 4 2 5 3 4 1 3 5 0		95	43%	29%	6.19	4.00	4.74
Clemens,Roger	2005	32	5 5 5 4 4 4 5 5 3 4 5 3 4 5 4 5 4 3	3 5 4 5 4 5 5 5 5 2 0 4 3 4	100	78%	3%	1.88	2.97	2.84
	2006	19	3 3 3 4	3 5 4 5 4 5 3 5 4 5 4 3 5 4 5	96	68%	0%	2.30	2.78	3.14
	2007	17	5 4 0 2 4 4	2 3 4 4 0 5 4 2 3 0 4	92	53%	18%	4.18	4.16	4.37
Clement,Matt	2005	32	0 4 5 5 0 4 5 4 1 5 4 4 0 5 5 4 3 3	0 4 0 3 5 5 4 3 4 3 5 0 4 1	99	59%	25%	4.57	3.71	4.39
	2006	12	4 0 4 3 4 3 3 4 0 0 5 0		97	42%	33%	6.61	4.44	4.92
Clippard,Tyler	2007	6	5 0 2 3 0 0		88	17%	50%	6.33	6.05	6.90
Colon,Bartolo	2005	33	4 4 5 5 0 5 4 2 3 4 4 4 3 4 5 3 4 2	2 2 5 4 4 4 4 4 4 4 2 4 2 3	98	67%	3%	3.48	3.52	3.14
	2006	10	3 0 3 3 2 3 4	4 3 0	85	20%	20%	5.11	3.85	4.75
	2007	18	4 5 3 4 5 2 0 2 0 3 1 3 4 0	3 0 0 4	88	33%	33%	6.34	4.52	5.08
Contreras,Jose	2005	32	5 3 0 0 5 5 3 2 4 5 4 5 2 4 2 0 2	5 3 2 3 3 5 4 3 5 4 3 4 3 5 5	99	50%	9%	3.61	3.68	3.85
	2006	30	3 4 5 3 4 3 3 4 2 3 5 4 1 3 4 4	3 3 4 2 4 4 3 1 0 3 5 5 2 0	101	43%	13%	4.27	3.56	4.32
	2007	30	0 4 3 3 2 5 4 5 4 2 2 4 0 2 3 2 3	1 2 0 0 4 4 4 4 1 3 4 4 3	97	40%	20%	5.57	4.76	4.56
Cook,Aaron	2005	13		0 3 4 3 3 1 3 3 3 2 3 0 1	91	8%	31%	3.68	3.94	5.45
	2006	32	4 3 4 2 5 2 3 5 1 4 3 3 2 4 4 3 2 3	3 0 3 3 1 2 2 2 4 1 3 4 4 3	97	31%	13%	4.23	3.66	4.49
	2007	25	3 4 2 4 3 3 2 3 4 3 3 3 2 4 1 0 4 4 3	5 5 4 4 2 3	96	40%	8%	4.12	4.36	4.11
Cormier,Lance	2006	9	0 1	0 4 3 4 0 4 0	84	33%	56%	4.89	4.28	6.91
	2007	9	0 0	0 1 3 4 4 4 0	86	33%	56%	7.09	4.99	6.91
Correia,Kevin	2005	11	1 2	0 4 5 4 1 3 5 0 0	82	36%	45%	4.65	4.42	5.75
	2007	8		0 4 4 5 2 3 5 5	88	63%	13%	3.45	4.30	3.71
Danks,John	2007	26	5 2 0 4 3 3 3 4 2 0 3 2 0 0 3 5 3	2 3 5 0 5 0 2 0 3 0	93	23%	31%	5.50	4.81	5.21
Davies,Kyle	2005	14	4 4 2 3 3 0 0 1 2 3 2	5 4 3	98	29%	21%	4.95	4.77	4.73
	2006	14	3 0 4 5 3 2 0 0	0 2 0 4 0 0	89	21%	50%	8.38	4.34	6.74
	2007	28	4 1 0 0 5 3 0 3 0 4 3 0 1 5 0 5	0 0 5 3 2 0 4 3 3 0 1 0	88	25%	50%	6.09	5.16	6.56
Davis,Doug	2005	35	5 4 0 3 0 5 1 3 4 4 4 5 4 1 0 5 5 3 4	5 0 5 0 4 5 5 3 5 5 3 4 4 5 3	106	60%	20%	3.85	3.45	3.95
	2006	34	4 3 5 0 3 3 3 3 3 3 0 5 3 3 5 0 3 2	3 3 2 3 1 4 4 4 0 3 5 4 5 3 4	103	32%	15%	4.91	3.81	4.60
	2007	33	2 4 2 4 4 5 4 0 0 3 4 5 0 2 0 2 2 4	3 3 5 5 4 3 2 0 5 5 4 0 0 0 3	102	42%	24%	4.25	4.66	4.56
de la Rosa,Jorge	2006	13	0 1 0	3 0 5 3 0 2 3 3 2 0	84	8%	46%	6.49	4.30	6.53
	2007	23	4 2 3 4 2 4 0 3 4 0 1 5 0 0 2 2 2 4	0 0 3 2 0	91	26%	35%	5.82	5.10	5.27
DeSalvo,Matthew	2007	6	3 2 0 0 0	0	80	0%	67%	6.18	7.02	9.80
Dessens,Elmer	2005	7	2 0 5 0 1	0 0	70	14%	71%	3.59	3.82	9.84
	2007	5		0 0 3 0 0	62	0%	80%	7.15	4.70	12.14
Dinardo,Lenny	2006	6	1 0 0 3 0	0	73	0%	83%	7.85	4.55	12.14
	2007	20	2 3 5 0 1 3 0	1 4 4 0 3 3 1 4 0 1 1 0 0	80	20%	55%	4.11	4.57	7.36
Duke,Zach	2005	14	5 5	4 3 0 4 4 0 5 0 0 3 5 3	91	50%	29%	1.82	3.35	4.61
	2006	34	4 0 5 3 2 4 3 4 4 4 3 3 3 1 1 2 3 3 1	1 4 0 3 2 5 3 3 3 2 4 5 5 3 3	96	32%	18%	4.47	3.76	4.60
	2007	19	2 5 0 0 3 3 1 2 2 0 1 2 2 2 3 1 0	0 3	88	5%	42%	5.53	4.96	5.80
Dumatrait,Phillip	2007	6		0 2 0 0 0 0	67	0%	83%	15.00	7.69	12.14
Durbin,Chad	2007	19	0 0 1 5 0 4 2 3 2 3 0 3 0 5	0 0 0 2 0	86	16%	53%	4.72	5.09	6.90
Durbin,J.D.	2007	10	0	3 3 2 3 2 5 0 0 0	82	10%	40%	6.06	5.42	5.70
Eaton,Adam	2005	22	0 4 2 2 5 4 3 4 4 3 5 3 5 0	2 3 5 4 2 2 0 5	100	45%	14%	4.28	3.81	4.28
	2006	13		0 4 0 3 5 1 0 4 3 4 3 2 2	87	31%	31%	5.12	4.03	5.08
	2007	30	0 4 5 3 0 2 3 4 3 3 0 5 4 3 1 2 4 2	0 3 3 1 0 0 2 4 2 0 2 0	92	23%	33%	6.29	5.29	5.21
Elarton,Scott	2005	31	2 0 0 3 4 3 1 3 4 3 4 3 3 2 4 3	2 3 4 4 2 0 5 0 0 5 3 4 4 0 0	92	32%	26%	4.62	4.30	4.90
	2006	20	0 4 3 0 3 0 4 3 3 2 3 3 3 1 0 5 3 2 2 0	2	95	15%	30%	5.34	5.04	5.29
	2007	9	0 1 0 2 1 2 0 0	0	76	0%	78%	10.46	7.27	11.36
Escobar,Kelvim	2005	7	5 3 4 3 4 5 0		91	57%	14%	3.04	2.99	3.97
	2006	30	4 0 4 3 4 5 3 4 4 3 2 3 5 4 0 4 2	2 5 4 5 2 5 4 5 5 4 0 5 0	97	60%	13%	3.61	3.28	3.71
	2007	30	3 4 4 4 4 5 0 4 5 2 3 5 4 4 0 5	5 2 2 5 3 4 5 5 5 4 0 3 0 0 5	101	60%	17%	3.40	4.03	3.83
Feierabend,Ryan	2007	9	2 3 0 3 0 0	2 0 0	83	0%	56%	8.03	6.03	8.24
Floyd,Gavin	2006	11	0 5 2 0 3 1 2 2 1 0 0		91	9%	55%	7.29	4.77	7.99
	2007	10	0	0 4 0 4 5 4 4 3 4	96	60%	30%	5.27	4.52	4.39
Fogg,Josh	2005	28	5 4 2 0 3 4 3 3 1 3 0 4 3 4 4 4	0 2 1 2 2 4 2 3 2 1 3	93	32%	21%	5.06	4.45	4.71
	2006	31	4 3 3 3 0 2 4 3 3 3 2 0 4 1 2 3 3	5 2 0 4 0 2 2 0 0 3 1 0 4 4	89	23%	29%	5.49	4.18	4.98
	2007	29	4 2 0 4 4 1 4 3 3 3 4 3 4 3 0 3	5 3 1 3 3 3 0 3 4 1 3 2 4 0	91	28%	24%	4.94	5.05	4.73
Fossum,Casey	2005	25	3 3 4 0 0 4 4 4 3 2	4 0 4 4 2 0 4 1 2 3 4 5 3 4 0	98	44%	24%	4.94	3.90	4.56
	2006	25	0 3 3 0 3 3 3 2 0 0 2 1 4 2 4 5	2 3 0 5 5 0 4 4 0	88	28%	32%	5.33	3.98	5.13
	2007	10	0 4 4 1 1 4 1 2 2 0		85	30%	50%	7.70	4.72	6.37
Francis,Jeff	2005	33	0 2 3 3 3 4 3 1 4 2 3 4 5 5 3 0	2 3 4 5 0 0 2 0 3 4 0 0 4 4 1	95	33%	27%	5.70	4.26	4.90
	2006	32	0 3 5 4 3 5 4 3 1 4 4 3 3 1 3 2	4 4 5 2 3 3 4 2 2 2 2 0 4 1 3	99	34%	16%	4.16	3.79	4.60
	2007	34	4 5 0 4 2 3 3 4 5 4 4 5 5 3 5 3 3 3	2 5 3 4 5 3 0 5 3 4 3 3 0 5 5 4	103	53%	9%	4.22	4.13	3.85
Gabbard,Kason	2006	4		1 0 5 0	88	25%	75%	3.51	4.14	9.46
	2007	15	3 0 3 3	5 3 0 3 4 0 3 3 0 3 0	90	13%	33%	4.65	4.35	5.37
Gallardo,Yovani	2007	17	3 5 5	5 3 4 5 0 2 5 0 5 5 5 3 5 4	96	65%	12%	3.67	3.87	3.61
Garcia,Freddy	2005	33	5 4 1 4 4 3 3 3 4 5 1 5 3 3 5 5 3 2	3 1 4 2 3 4 3 3 0 5 2 1 1 3 4	103	39%	18%	3.87	3.60	4.52
	2006	33	0 5 3 3 4 4 5 3 4 2 4 3 0 4 4 1 2 3	2 4 4 2 4 4 3 2 5 3 5 4 4 3 4	101	52%	9%	4.53	3.68	3.85
	2007	11	0 4 0 1 4 4 2 3 5 2 0		95	36%	36%	5.90	4.31	5.13
Garland,Jon	2005	32	3 3 4 4 4 2 4 3 3 3 4 3 4 4 3 2	2 3 4 3 3 3 3 4 0 5 1 5 2 3 5	104	41%	6%	3.50	3.74	4.11
	2006	32	3 1 4 3 3 0 4 3 4 3 3 2 4 1 4 4	5 4 2 3 3 5 4 4 3 4 5 1 3 2 4	104	44%	13%	4.51	3.80	4.32
	2007	32	2 3 3 4 3 2 4 3 3 3 3 3 4 5 3 4 0	2 2 0 3 0 5 0 0 4 2 4 4 4 4 3	103	34%	16%	4.23	4.83	4.60
Garza,Matt	2006	9		0 4 3 5 0 0 3 1 0	89	22%	56%	5.76	4.20	7.36
	2007	15	5	4 1 5 0 5 2 0 2 3 0 2 5 1 3	95	33%	33%	3.69	4.35	5.08
Gaudin,Chad	2007	34	3 4 4 5 0 1 5 0 2 4 3 1 3 0 3 4 3 2	0 3 0 4 1 3 5 2 5 4 1 0 4 0 0 5	97	35%	35%	4.42	4.40	5.13
Germano,Justin	2007	23	4 4 3 4 4 2 5 5 5 5 1 0	3 1 0 3 2 3 3 2 3 3 0 1	88	30%	26%	4.46	4.31	4.90
Glavine,Tom	2005	33	0 5 3 5 0 0 2 4 2 2 4 3 5 2 0 2 1 1	3 4 3 4 2 3 3 4 4 4 3 3 3 5 5	99	36%	18%	3.54	4.03	4.52
	2006	32	4 5 5 4 3 3 5 2 3 3 5 3 0 0 4 3 2 3 3	3 2 1 0 3 4 3 3 5 5 3 4 4	102	38%	13%	3.82	3.52	4.41
	2007	34	4 2 3 3 4 4 4 5 3 2 3 3 3 0 0 4 3 2 3	4 0 2 3 3 4 4 1 3 3 4 3 3 2 0	98	29%	15%	4.45	5.02	4.62

PQS PITCHING LOGS

Pitcher	Year	No.	FIRST HALF	SECOND HALF	PC	DOM	DIS	ERA	xERA	qERA
Gonzalez,Edgar	2006	5	4 4	4 4 3	94	80%	0%	4.17	3.54	2.69
	2007	12	3 3 3 5 2 4 2 0	3 1 0 0	79	17%	33%	5.03	4.55	5.29
Gorzelanny,Tom	2006	11	3 0	0 4 5 5 4 5 0 2 3	92	45%	27%	3.79	3.83	4.67
	2007	32	3 5 3 5 4 3 5 5 2 1 3 2 4 3 4 3 5 5	5 4 0 5 4 2 4 2 0 3 3 2 3 2	104	44%	9%	3.88	4.58	4.11
Greinke,Zack	2005	33	0 4 2 5 0 4 3 4 3 2 2 0 0 3 3 3 1 1	2 4 0 2 5 0 4 2 0 1 3 3 4 5 0	94	27%	33%	5.80	4.22	5.13
	2007	14	4 5 0 2 3 2 0	0 0 4 0 2 5 2	86	29%	36%	3.69	4.16	5.27
Guthrie,Jeremy	2007	26	4 4 3 5 2 4 4 5 5 5 5 4 4 3	0 3 5 4 0 0 0 5 1 3 3 3 3	96	50%	19%	3.70	4.12	4.37
Halladay,Roy	2005	19	4 3 5 2 3 5 2 4 5 3 5 5 5 4 4 5 5 5 0		101	68%	5%	2.42	2.64	3.38
	2006	32	3 3 2 2 2 4 4 4 5 3 4 3 4 4 3 4 4 5	2 3 4 3 4 3 4 4 4 4 5 0 4 0	95	56%	6%	3.19	2.88	3.68
	2007	31	5 5 5 4 3 5 5 5 1 2 5 0 3 5 4 3 3 2	1 5 4 4 4 4 4 3 3 3 3 3 4 3	107	48%	10%	3.71	3.84	4.28
Hamels,Cole	2006	23	3 4 2 3 0 5 1 0 3	2 2 5 5 5 5 4 0 3 4 0 5 5 4	95	48%	22%	4.08	2.98	4.53
	2007	28	5 5 3 5 2 3 4 4 5 5 4 4 4 3 4 3 0 2 4	2 4 5 5 5 3 5 0 4 5	100	64%	7%	3.39	3.41	3.50
Hammel,Jason	2006	9	0 3	2 1 4 0 0 0 3	89	11%	56%	7.77	4.30	7.77
	2007	14		0 4 0 0 0 2 0 3 4 3 5 2 2 3	89	21%	36%	6.14	5.03	5.36
Hanrahan,Joel	2007	11		5 2 1 4 1 0 4 0 0 0 0	90	27%	64%	6.00	5.89	7.72
Harang,Aaron	2005	32	4 2 5 4 3 4 5 3 5 5 3 5 5 0 3 4 3 5	5 3 2 4 2 3 2 4 5 3 4 4 3 2 3	107	50%	3%	3.84	3.56	3.47
	2006	34	2 4 4 0 4 5 5 3 0 5 4 5 2 3 4 4 4 2 4	5 0 5 4 3 3 3 5 2 2 4 4 3 3 2 4	106	56%	9%	3.76	3.06	3.68
	2007	34	5 3 0 5 4 4 3 3 4 3 3 5 4 5 2 5 2 4 5	4 4 5 0 5 4 3 3 5 2 5 5 5 4 3	106	62%	6%	3.73	3.57	3.50
Harden,Rich	2005	19	4 5 5 3 5 4 0 4 4 4 3	5 5 3 5 4 5 5	99	74%	5%	2.53	3.01	3.25
	2006	9	2 5 4 3 0 0	0 4 0	89	33%	44%	4.24	3.05	5.29
	2007	4	5 4 5 0		89	75%	25%	2.45	3.63	3.87
Haren,Dan	2005	34	5 3 4 0 5 0 0 1 2 4 4 4 5 3 3 4 2	4 1 3 3 5 4 2 3 3 4 0 5 5 3 5	99	50%	18%	3.73	3.35	4.37
	2006	34	3 3 4 3 4 2 5 4 3 5 4 5 3 4 5 1 3 5 3	3 4 4 5 5 4 2 5 3 2 5 0 3 3	103	53%	6%	4.12	3.12	3.85
	2007	34	4 3 3 4 5 5 5 5 5 5 4 3 4 5 5 4 2 3 3	2 4 5 4 4 2 4 4 4 4 0 4 4 4 5	107	74%	3%	3.07	3.72	2.99
Hendrickson,Mark	2005	31	3 2 3 3 2 2 2 1 2 0 2 2 2 0 3 0	1 0 0 4 2 1 2 5 4 5 3 2 2 4 3	91	16%	26%	5.91	4.25	5.03
	2006	25	4 5 2 3 4 2 2 1 3 5 2 4 1 3	4 1 3 3 5 2 0 5 0 0	98	32%	24%	4.21	3.93	4.71
	2007	15	3 4 5 0 1 2 2 0 3 4	0 3 4 3 0	83	27%	33%	5.21	3.97	5.13
Hensley,Clay	2006	29	0 2 3 3 1 4 3 4 2 0 3 1 0 4 4 2	3 3 4 4 3 3 5 1 4 5 2 4 5	94	38%	21%	3.71	3.57	4.64
	2007	9	0 0 0 2 4 0	0 1 0	83	11%	78%	6.84	5.74	10.53
Hernandez,Felix	2005	12		4 5 5 5 4 3 5 4 0 5 4 4	102	83%	8%	2.68	2.54	3.00
	2006	31	3 0 2 5 1 3 5 0 3 5 4 5 5 3 3 4 5	2 5 4 3 4 3 4 0 4 3 3 3 4 5	99	48%	13%	4.52	2.80	4.28
	2007	30	5 4 0 0 3 3 3 3 3 4 5 3 4 3	4 3 2 5 5 5 3 5 3 5 2 4 2 5 2 3 5	100	43%	7%	3.92	3.26	4.11
Hernandez,Livan	2005	34	0 4 3 1 2 3 3 3 5 4 5 3 3 4 2 3 3 1 2	4 4 4 3 1 3 3 0 3 2 4 2 1 4 5	114	32%	18%	3.99	3.22	4.60
	2006	34	4 4 2 3 3 2 2 2 2 3 5 2 3 2 3 0 3 3 0	3 3 5 4 5 3 2 4 3 1 3 3	103	26%	9%	4.83	4.24	4.48
	2007	33	4 3 4 1 3 4 3 0 3 4 3 2 3 0 3 0 2 2	2 1 5 0 5 2 1 2 4 3 1 2 2 2 0	102	21%	27%	4.93	5.53	4.98
Hernandez,Orlando	2005	22	5 1 3 3 4 3 3 0 4 4 0	3 3 3 5 4 5 4 2 5 0 0	100	41%	23%	5.13	4.14	4.56
	2006	29	3 0 3 4 5 0 1 0 5 4 3 3 0 4 0 4 5	0 4 5 4 4 0 5 3 5 5 5 3	98	52%	28%	4.66	3.32	4.61
	2007	24	3 4 1 5 5 5 4 3 2 0 5 4 0	5 4 2 5 5 5 4 3 0 0 0	100	58%	21%	3.72	4.35	4.23
Hill,Rich	2006	16	0 3 3 0	0 5 5 0 4 4 5 5 3 5 3 5	101	50%	25%	4.17	3.58	4.61
	2007	32	5 4 5 3 5 5 5 3 3 4 3 5 5 3 0 3 0 3	3 4 3 0 5 3 5 5 5 2 3 5 0 4 5	96	50%	13%	3.92	3.85	4.23
Hill,Shawn	2006	6	3 2 3 2 1 2		96	0%	17%	4.66	4.08	4.69
	2007	16	4 3 4 5 3 4 3 4	5 3 5 3 4 5 2 0	90	56%	6%	3.42	3.68	3.68
Hirsh,Jason	2006	9		0 3 0 3 5 4 5 0 0	86	33%	44%	6.04	4.68	5.29
	2007	19	5 2 4 5 3 3 0 3 3 3 0 5 4 0 0 3 4	2 3	93	32%	21%	4.81	5.16	4.71
Howell,J.P.	2005	15	4 3 1 0 2 0	0 4 3 5 4 0 0 4 5	86	40%	40%	6.23	3.93	5.21
	2006	8		0 0 5 3 0 1 3 3	89	13%	50%	5.10	3.42	7.08
	2007	10	5 3 3 2 3 0 0	2 5 0	95	20%	30%	7.59	4.13	5.21
Hudson,Luke	2005	16	2 3 2 0 0 0	0 4 3 5 2 0 4 4 0 0	82	25%	44%	6.41	4.84	5.40
	2006	15	2	3 4 4 3 2 0 3 2 5 4 3 2 4 4	95	40%	7%	5.12	3.65	4.11
	2007	1	0		50	0%	100%	18.00	15.17	15.00
Hudson,Tim	2005	29	1 5 5 3 2 4 0 4 1 3 3 3 0 0	4 3 5 3 4 5 3 4 3 3 3 2 3 3 5	100	34%	17%	3.52	3.58	4.60
	2006	35	0 0 2 4 3 3 2 5 4 3 3 5 2 3 5 3 0 0 4	0 2 2 1 5 5 2 3 4 2 3 5 1 5 2 3	98	31%	20%	4.86	3.46	4.71
	2007	34	4 5 3 3 4 3 4 4 4 0 2 4 3 0 4 1 5 5 0	4 4 3 5 5 3 4 3 1 3 3 3 4 3 4	93	50%	15%	3.33	3.57	4.37
Hughes,Philip	2007	13	0 5	0 5 3 3 4 0 5 3 1 3 5	95	38%	31%	4.46	4.46	5.00
Igawa,Kei	2007	12	0 2 5 0 0 0 2 2	1 2 3 2	93	8%	42%	6.25	5.51	5.80
Jackson,Edwin	2005	6		0 3 2 0 2 2	88	0%	33%	6.38	4.15	5.53
	2007	31	3 0 4 4 0 4 4 0 4 0 5 0 0 3 5 3	5 4 0 5 2 5 3 3 2 0 3 4 0 3 4	95	42%	29%	5.76	4.94	4.74
James,Chuck	2006	18	5 3 1	3 4 0 2 5 4 4 3 5 3 5 5 0 1 5	99	50%	22%	3.78	3.95	4.50
	2007	30	3 4 3 0 3 3 0 3 3 0 5 4 3 0 2 4 4 3	4 4 4 3 0 5 0 2 3 0 5 0	89	33%	27%	4.24	4.85	4.90
Jennings,Jason	2005	20	0 4 3 3 4 2 0 3 0 3 3 2 2 4 5 5 3 3	5 4	99	35%	15%	5.02	4.31	4.52
	2006	32	5 3 2 2 2 3 5 2 2 4 5 2 2 5 4 4 5 5	4 2 4 4 5 4 3 4 2 3 5 1 1 1	103	50%	9%	3.78	3.81	3.85
	2007	18	5 4 3 2 5 0 3 4 5 3	3 1 5 0 2 1 2 0	87	33%	28%	6.45	4.86	4.90
Jimenez,Ubaldo	2007	15		3 5 3 0 0 5 4 4 5 0 3 0 3 0 5	90	40%	33%	4.28	4.18	4.92
Johnson,Jason	2005	33	4 0 4 3 3 3 4 3 5 3 5 3 0 2 1 4 0 3	3 0 2 3 4 2 3 1 1 3 3 3 3 3 5	91	24%	21%	4.54	4.02	4.75
	2006	20	4 3 4 3 2 0 3 3 0 4 3 3 0 1 0 0	1 4 3 0	87	20%	40%	6.10	3.89	5.50
Johnson,Josh	2006	24	3 5 3 4 5 5 4 4 2 4 3 3	2 5 4 5 0 5 3 5 4 5 0 4	99	63%	8%	3.10	3.37	3.50
	2007	4	0 0 0 4		80	25%	75%	7.47	5.48	9.46
Johnson,Randy	2005	34	5 4 4 4 5 5 2 4 2 4 3 5 5 0 5 1 5 4	3 5 5 4 0 5 3 5 4 5 0 5 4 4	101	74%	12%	3.80	3.05	3.51
	2006	33	4 5 4 0 4 1 3 0 3 1 2 4 5 0 5 5 5 5 4	5 5 4 0 3 5 4 3 3 4 5 4 3 3	99	58%	18%	5.00	3.34	4.10
	2007	10	1 4 3 5 5 3 5 4 5 0		91	60%	20%	3.81	2.86	3.95
Jurrjens,Jair	2007	7		3 3 0 2 4 0 0	68	14%	43%	4.70	5.10	5.70
Kazmir,Scott	2005	32	2 0 2 4 4 4 4 0 2 4 3 4 0 0 4 4 5 0	4 5 5 4 3 5 5 0 1 5 5 4 1 4	103	59%	25%	3.77	3.87	4.39
	2006	24	0 3 4 4 1 5 3 5 5 5 3 0 4 3 2 5 2 5 3	4 5 4 4 5	101	58%	13%	3.24	2.84	3.97
	2007	34	2 4 5 0 5 2 5 4 0 3 4 4 2 4 3 3 2 5 2	4 5 4 5 5 5 5 3 5 1 3 5 5 4 5	106	62%	9%	3.48	3.61	3.50
Kendrick,Kyle	2007	20	5 3 2 3 3	4 1 2 4 3 3 1 1 5 4 2 0 2 5 3	88	30%	20%	3.87	4.49	4.71
Kennedy,Joe	2005	24	1 0 2 2 3 2 1 4 2 2 1 1 2 5 2 2	4 2 5 2 4 0 0 4	95	25%	29%	6.03	4.37	4.93
	2007	16	3 3 3 1 3 4 1 0 3 5 1 1 0 3 0		88	13%	44%	4.80	5.40	5.70
Kim,Byung-Hyun	2005	22	3 1 5 5 0 3 3 5	2 5 3 4 3 1 0 4 5 5 4 0 2 0	97	41%	27%	4.86	4.19	4.74
	2006	27	5 5 0 4 3 2 1 3 0 4 5 0 0	5 0 5 4 1 4 0 3 0 2 4 4 4 0	94	44%	37%	5.57	3.57	5.07
	2007	22	0 1 3 4 3 0 4 2 3 5	2 5 3 3 0 0 2 4 2 0 4 2	91	27%	27%	6.08	4.83	4.93
Kuo,Hong-Chih	2006	5		5 4 3 5 3	92	60%	0%	4.22	2.98	3.29
	2007	6	0 5 4 0 4 0		88	50%	50%	7.42	4.94	5.81

PQS PITCHING LOGS

Pitcher	Year	No.	FIRST HALF	SECOND HALF	PC	DOM	DIS	ERA	xERA	qERA
Lackey,John	2005	33	0 3 3 3 2 5 3 2 5 5 2 4 2 5 5 3 3 4	5 4 5 4 5 4 3 4 4 3 4 3 2 5 4	106	55%	3%	3.44	3.26	3.38
	2006	33	0 5 4 3 4 3 4 4 3 4 5 3 0 5 3 4 5 5	5 0 5 4 0 4 2 0 4 3 4 5 0 5 5	106	61%	18%	3.56	3.25	3.83
	2007	33	3 5 3 3 4 4 5 5 5 5 3 4 4 3 5 0 5 3 5	4 3 3 3 4 3 0 2 4 4 5 4 5 5 4	103	61%	6%	3.01	3.75	3.50
Laffey,Aaron	2007	9		1 3 4 3 0 2 2 2 3	80	11%	22%	4.56	3.77	4.79
Lannan,John	2007	6		0 2 2 3 2 2	94	0%	17%	4.15	5.74	4.69
Lawrence,Brian	2005	33	5 0 4 0 5 2 3 3 2 4 0 4 4 4 5 3 4 3	3 4 5 1 3 0 2 4 4 0 4 0 0 0 4	89	45%	27%	4.84	4.01	4.67
	2007	6		3 4 3 1 0 0	87	17%	50%	6.83	5.58	6.90
Lee,Cliff	2005	32	0 4 5 5 1 1 5 3 4 4 3 5 4 2 4 2 1 5	4 3 4 2 4 5 5 5 4 4 4 3 4	97	66%	13%	3.79	3.84	3.61
	2006	33	2 5 5 3 4 3 2 3 4 1 0 4 4 3 3 4 3 2	3 2 0 4 3 4 3 5 1 4 3 0 1 4 4	102	39%	18%	4.40	4.13	4.52
	2007	16	4 3 2 3 0 3 0 2 2 5 2 5 0	2 4 0	97	25%	25%	6.29	5.15	4.93
Leicester,Jon	2007	5		2 2 0 4 0	86	20%	40%	7.59	5.56	5.50
Lester,Jon	2006	15	0 4 5 3 2 3	3 3 3 3 3 2 2 0 1	101	13%	20%	4.76	4.15	4.79
	2007	11		5 3 3 0 4 2 3 4 0 4 0	97	36%	27%	4.57	4.96	4.82
Lieber,Jon	2005	35	2 3 4 3 2 5 5 1 0 4 3 3 4 3 3 2 0 0 4	3 5 4 0 5 5 5 3 5 5 4 4 3 5 4 5	89	51%	14%	4.21	3.43	4.23
	2006	27	0 3 3 5 3 4 2 4 2 1 0 4	1 2 3 0 5 4 4 4 1 4 2 2 0 5 2	92	37%	26%	4.93	3.48	4.82
	2007	12	4 5 3 2 3 4 2 4 1 5 3 1		95	42%	17%	4.73	4.13	4.44
Lilly,Ted	2005	25	3 3 0 3 3 0 0 5 3 0 3 1 5 5 0 2 5	5 1 0 0 2 5 0 3	86	24%	40%	5.57	4.31	5.50
	2006	32	0 5 2 2 4 5 2 0 0 3 0 4 4 5 5 5 5 3	3 5 3 1 3 2 0 3 4 4 5 4 4 4	100	50%	19%	4.31	3.68	4.37
	2007	34	5 5 5 5 4 3 4 5 5 5 0 4 1 0 4 4 4 4 4	5 1 3 1 4 4 2 2 5 3 4 4 5 4 3 0	95	65%	18%	3.83	4.08	3.73
Lincecum,Tim	2007	24	0 5 5 4 5 3 0 0 0 5 5 4	4 5 5 4 4 3 4 5 4 0 3 4	99	67%	21%	4.00	3.70	3.85
Liriano,Francisco	2006	16	3 4 4 2 5 5 5 4 5 5	3 5 4 5 0 0	89	69%	13%	2.16	2.03	3.61
Litsch,Jesse	2007	20	3 0 0 0 4	3 0 4 3 2 3 5 3 4 0 2 0 3 4 3	89	25%	30%	3.81	4.80	5.13
Livingston,Bobby	2007	10	1 2	3 3 3 0 3 3 3 0	90	0%	30%	5.27	4.64	5.53
Loaiza,Esteban	2005	34	3 4 4 2 5 5 2 3 4 3 3 5 3 0 5 4 5 4	4 3 4 3 3 3 2 4 4 0 5 4 5 5 5 4	98	59%	6%	3.77	3.43	3.68
	2006	26	0 0 4 0 5 3 0 4 3 1	2 3 0 1 3 3 4 5 5 4 4 3 5 4 2 0	92	38%	31%	4.89	3.76	5.00
	2007	7		4 3 3 0 0 0 0	90	14%	57%	5.79	5.98	7.77
Loewen,Adam	2006	19	2 2 2 0 3	3 2 4 4 0 3 5 1 3 5 1 3 4 3	97	26%	21%	5.37	3.60	4.73
	2007	6	2 3 0 3 4 3		95	17%	17%	3.56	5.60	4.65
Loe,Kameron	2005	8		4 4 3 2 1 0 3 1	91	25%	38%	3.42	3.81	5.27
	2006	15	3 3 4 0 2 4 2 4 1 3 1 3 0 3 0		86	20%	33%	5.86	4.14	5.21
	2007	23	4 2 0 5 2 1 1 3 1 0 5 3 3 3 3	0 3 4 1 2 3 5 0	91	22%	35%	5.36	4.57	5.36
Lohse,Kyle	2005	30	1 4 2 0 4 2 3 4 2 2 4 0 3 5 2	2 2 0 1 3 5 1 3 1 4 0 3 2 4 2	95	27%	27%	4.19	4.18	4.93
	2006	19	0 3 0 4 1 0 4 0	4 5 5 3 2 3 5 0 3 0 4	89	37%	37%	5.83	3.68	5.13
	2007	32	3 3 5 4 3 3 0 0 0 4 3 4 4 0 2 5 4	0 3 3 0 2 3 5 4 0 4 4 2 0 5	94	38%	25%	4.62	4.64	4.82
Looper,Braden	2007	30	3 3 3 5 4 3 3 5 0 3 1 3 2 0 3 2	4 0 3 0 4 4 4 5 4 4 0 5 1 0	93	37%	27%	4.94	4.74	4.82
Lopez,Rodrigo	2005	35	3 5 3 5 0 2 0 3 2 4 4 0 2 5 2 4 3 0 5	2 4 4 0 4 1 3 0 5 0 3 3 1 4 0 3	94	34%	29%	4.91	4.15	4.90
	2006	29	3 1 4 0 4 2 3 3 0 1 4 2 2 5 0 5 3 0 3	3 0 3 4 3 4 3 4 3 4	97	31%	24%	5.90	3.70	4.71
	2007	14	5 3 0 4 0 4 3 2 0 0 3	5 4 5	84	43%	29%	4.42	4.57	4.74
Lowe,Derek	2005	35	4 0 4 3 4 4 2 3 5 4 4 2 4 3 2 3 3 0 2	0 5 4 2 5 2 3 0 4 5 5 4 4 0 4 3	95	49%	14%	3.61	3.22	4.28
	2006	34	1 3 4 5 4 3 5 3 3 5 4 3 3 1 3 3 1 1 0	4 0 4 3 5 4 3 5 0 1 3 2 5 3 4	96	38%	24%	3.63	3.06	4.64
	2007	32	0 3 5 0 2 2 5 4 1 4 4 5 4 4 5 5 3 3 3	4 0 0 4 4 4 4 3 0 4 5 0 5	94	56%	22%	3.88	3.29	4.23
Lowry,Noah	2005	33	3 2 4 3 0 4 4 0 4 5 0 3 3 1 4 4 4 4	5 5 4 4 5 5 5 4 5 3 3 2 3 2 5	107	58%	12%	3.79	3.69	3.97
	2006	27	0 3 1 3 2 5 2 3 0 4 3 2	0 4 4 1 4 4 3 4 3 0 0 0 3 4	97	30%	30%	4.74	4.30	5.08
	2007	26	4 3 4 2 2 5 3 3 3 0 3 2 4 0 2 5 4	1 4 4 2 0 2 2 3 0	98	31%	19%	3.92	5.32	4.60
Maddux,Greg	2005	35	2 0 4 4 3 3 5 2 3 3 4 4 4 0 2 4 2 4 4	5 2 3 0 5 3 5 2 4 4 3 4 3 4 3 2	89	46%	9%	4.24	3.35	3.98
	2006	34	3 5 5 4 4 3 0 4 1 4 2 1 2 3 4 4 2 4	4 4 4 5 3 3 4 5 1 3 1 3 3 3 3 4	82	47%	15%	4.20	3.28	4.40
	2007	34	4 5 1 4 4 4 4 4 0 2 3 3 3 3 2 4 4 0	0 4 4 3 3 5 4 4 4 5 4 0 1 0 3	80	50%	21%	4.14	3.91	4.50
Maholm,Paul	2005	6		3 3 4 5 1 4	102	50%	17%	2.19	3.62	4.37
	2006	30	3 1 4 0 4 2 1 5 4 2 3 3 3 2 0 4 2 0	3 5 4 4 4 2 3 2 2 3 5 3	97	33%	17%	4.76	3.78	4.60
	2007	29	0 2 3 4 0 0 3 2 1 4 4 3 1 5 3 4 4 4	3 4 4 3 2 4 2 5 3 0 0	91	38%	24%	5.02	4.19	4.64
Maine,John	2005	8		3 0 3 3 2 0 0 0	79	0%	50%	6.30	4.77	7.46
	2006	15	3 0 3	4 5 4 3 4 2 3 3 1 5 3 3	100	33%	13%	3.60	3.56	4.49
	2007	32	5 0 4 4 5 5 4 2 1 5 5 4 0 4 5 5 5	0 3 5 4 0 1 3 2 3 5 0 4 0 3 5	102	56%	25%	3.91	4.09	4.39
Marcum,Shaun	2006	14		4 3 0 0 3 1 0 4 3 3 0 0 5 0	88	21%	50%	5.06	4.12	6.74
	2007	25	5 5 2 5 0 3 4 3 4 3 0	4 3 2 5 4 4 5 0 2 1 2 0 4 0	91	44%	24%	4.13	4.18	4.56
Maroth,Mike	2005	34	0 3 4 4 4 3 4 1 1 0 2 3 4 1 3 2 4 3	2 3 0 3 1 3 4 0 5 5 3 1 3 3 3	96	29%	26%	4.74	3.98	4.93
	2006	9	1 5 3 2 4 2 3 4 0		85	33%	22%	4.19	4.34	4.71
	2007	20	3 2 1 0 3 0 3 3 2 1 1 2 3 4 0 2	2 0 0 0	92	5%	45%	6.89	5.81	6.53
Marquis,Jason	2005	32	4 5 4 3 3 3 3 3 0 2 4 2 3 1 0 3 5 5	3 0 3 2 1 2 2 0 4 4 4 3 3 3	100	28%	19%	4.13	4.10	4.62
	2006	33	3 4 4 1 1 1 3 2 4 3 2 3 3 2 3 4 4	4 2 4 0 2 0 0 4 3 1 4 3 0 1 0	93	27%	30%	6.02	4.40	5.13
	2007	33	3 3 4 5 3 4 4 2 4 4 2 1 0 4 2 3 5 0	0 4 1 3 1 5 2 4 0 5 4 2 4 0 3	91	42%	24%	4.60	4.65	4.56
Marshall,Sean	2006	24	0 3 3 5 4 5 0 4 0 2 3 4 0 0 0 4 3	2 0 1 0 0 0 3	86	25%	46%	5.59	4.14	5.98
	2007	19	5 5 5 5 4 0 4 0 2	3 5 4 0 2 1 1 5 0 0	84	47%	37%	3.92	4.41	4.98
Martinez,Pedro	2005	31	5 5 5 5 5 5 4 4 5 5 5 5 3 4 3 5 4 5	5 3 5 4 2 4 5 4 3 3 5 5 1	98	77%	3%	2.82	3.02	2.84
	2006	23	4 4 5 5 5 5 4 5 5 5 5 2 4 4 4 0	3 5 2 0 0 4 0	92	70%	17%	4.48	2.92	3.63
	2007	5		3 3 4 3 5	92	40%	0%	2.57	3.69	3.89
Matsuzaka,Daisuke	2007	32	5 3 5 4 4 2 5 4 4 2 3 5 5 5 4 5 5 2	1 3 4 4 4 4 3 5 2 2 0 3 5 5	109	63%	6%	4.40	4.01	3.50
McCarthy,Brandon	2005	10	4 1 0 5 0	4 5 4 2 3	95	50%	30%	4.03	3.72	4.71
	2007	22	2 5 0 0 0 3 2 5 3 0 4 0 3	5 2 3 3 5 0 0 0 0	84	23%	41%	4.87	5.59	5.53
McGowan,Dustin	2005	7		4 2 3 0 0 2 0	89	14%	43%	6.39	3.92	5.70
	2006	3		0 0 0	62	0%	100%	7.24	5.18	15.00
	2007	27	2 2 0 2 5 4 4 3 0 5 2 4	2 3 3 4 5 4 5 3 5 4 5 4 5 0 4	100	56%	11%	4.08	3.65	3.97
Meche,Gil	2005	26	0 0 4 2 4 4 3 2 4 3 0 2 4 3 2 0 0 5	3 3 0 0 2 0 3 0	98	23%	35%	5.09	4.79	5.36
	2006	32	4 0 2 5 2 3 5 2 5 5 1 5 2 5 4 4 3 5	4 5 0 2 1 0 1 5 5 2 4 2 0 4	103	50%	22%	4.48	3.63	4.50
	2007	34	5 2 4 5 3 4 5 4 5 2 0 3 4 4 4 0 4 3 3	3 5 1 5 0 3 3 3 4 3 2 5 5 4 4	105	53%	12%	3.67	4.07	4.23
Miller,Andrew	2007	13	3 3 3 3 3 4	3 3 0 3 0 0 0	94	8%	31%	5.63	4.65	5.45
Millwood,Kevin	2005	30	3 4 3 3 5 3 5 0 5 0 4 3 5 0 4 3 3	5 2 4 3 4 4 3 5 4 2 2 3 4 3 5	99	47%	7%	2.86	3.43	3.98
	2006	33	3 4 5 3 4 3 0 5 5 2 4 5 4 4 3 4 0	3 5 2 1 4 3 4 5 5 5 5 5 4 0 4	97	59%	12%	4.52	3.33	3.97
	2007	31	4 2 2 2 4 3 0 2 0 0 4 3 4 4 4	5 4 2 0 0 4 5 3 3 5 3 0 0 2 5 2	95	39%	23%	5.16	4.56	4.64
Milton,Eric	2005	34	1 0 5 2 1 5 2 0 1 4 0 1 2 1 2 3 5 4 5	3 0 4 5 0 4 2 5 5 0 0 3 0 4 5	93	38%	38%	6.48	4.43	5.13
	2006	26	4 5 0 1 5 4 4 5 2 0 0 5 3	5 2 4 3 4 3 3 0 2 0 4 3 0	91	42%	27%	5.19	4.20	4.74
	2007	6	3 4 4 0 1 3		83	33%	33%	5.17	5.40	5.08

PQS PITCHING LOGS

Pitcher	Year	No.	FIRST HALF	SECOND HALF	PC	DOM	DIS	ERA	xERA	qERA
Mitre,Sergio	2005	7	5 0 0 5 4 1 0		97	43%	57%	5.39	3.72	6.59
	2006	7	5 1 4 3 5 0 0		81	43%	43%	5.71	3.67	5.21
	2007	27	3 2 0 4 3 3 3 4 4 0 4 2 2 2 2 3 3	4 4 0 3 4 5 3 0 2 0 0 0	83	30%	26%	4.65	4.09	4.90
Morales,Franklin	2007	8		4 0 1 0 4 5 4 4	74	63%	38%	3.43	3.87	4.53
Morris,Matt	2005	31	5 4 5 5 1 5 3 5 2 3 4 5 0 4 5 4	3 3 3 2 4 1 5 3 3 0 2 2 4 4 0	93	48%	16%	4.12	3.55	4.40
	2006	33	3 4 2 0 1 4 1 2 3 2 5 4 5 4 3 5 5 2	5 3 0 3 5 1 4 4 4 4 3 2 2 0 4	99	45%	18%	4.98	3.76	4.40
	2007	32	3 1 4 3 2 2 2 3 2 5 3 3 5 4 0 2 2 3	0 0 4 4 3 2 4 2 3 2 2 2 0 0 5	95	25%	19%	4.89	4.68	4.62
Moseley,Dustin	2007	8	5 3	0 2 0 2 3 0	82	13%	38%	4.40	4.47	5.54
Moyer,Jamie	2005	32	4 2 3 4 4 0 0 0 1 3 3 4 4 3 3 0 4 2	3 2 4 3 2 5 1 4 1 4 2 5 2 4	102	38%	22%	4.28	4.36	4.64
	2006	33	3 3 4 2 5 2 4 4 3 3 3 2 4 1 4 4 3 3 3	2 0 3 3 0 1 2 5 4 2 4 3 4 1 3	99	33%	15%	4.30	3.93	4.60
	2007	33	2 4 3 4 4 4 3 1 0 4 2 2 0 3 4 5 2 1	2 4 4 3 4 3 0 0 4 3 2 3 2 2 4	95	36%	18%	5.01	4.64	4.52
Mulder,Mark	2005	32	3 3 3 4 2 4 5 2 1 4 3 0 3 2 0 3 1 3	3 3 1 2 3 0 4 3 5 3 3 2 0 0	94	19%	25%	3.64	3.72	5.03
	2006	17	4 4 2 4 3 3 3 5 4 3 0 1 0 2 0	0 0	87	29%	35%	7.14	3.90	5.27
	2007	3		0 0 0	65	0%	100%	12.27	8.25	15.00
Mussina,Mike	2005	30	2 2 2 3 2 3 3 5 3 5 0 1 5 4 5 4 4 4	4 5 3 3 0 4 4 5 0 0 5 0	99	47%	20%	4.42	3.59	4.53
	2006	32	4 5 5 5 5 4 5 3 5 4 5 4 4 5 3 1 5 0 4	4 5 5 5 3 4 5 0 3 5 4 0 5	95	75%	13%	3.51	2.97	3.41
	2007	27	0 0 4 4 1 2 5 0 5 4 3 4 5	2 0 3 5 3 4 1 0 0 2 5 5 2	86	30%	30%	5.15	4.50	4.92
Myers,Brett	2005	34	4 4 4 4 5 5 4 5 4 3 2 3 5 3 0 0 5 3	3 2 5 5 3 3 4 4 0 5 5 0 4 3 5 5	102	59%	12%	3.72	3.04	3.97
	2006	31	1 3 4 4 4 5 5 5 3 4 5 2 0 0 4 2	4 5 5 4 2 2 0 5 4 5 4 2 5 5 5	104	65%	13%	3.91	3.02	3.61
	2007	3	4 0 0		94	33%	67%	4.33	3.19	7.99
Nolasco,Ricky	2006	22	0 3 0 5 5 5 3 3 0 0	4 5 3 0 3 3 2 0 0 4 0 3	87	27%	36%	4.82	3.71	5.27
	2007	4	3 4 0 2		81	25%	25%	5.48	5.62	4.93
Nunez,Leo	2007	6		0 3 4 0 0 3	84	17%	50%	3.92	4.16	6.90
Obermueller,Wes	2005	8	0 0 4 3 0 0	0 0	80	13%	75%	5.26	4.94	10.53
	2007	7	4 4 1 3 0 5 2		95	43%	29%	6.56	5.88	4.74
Ohka,Tomo	2005	29	3 3 1 0 4 3 0 4 2 2 1 4	5 2 3 0 5 3 3 2 3 5 0 5 2 3 2	94	28%	24%	4.05	4.16	4.73
	2006	18	4 0 5 0 4 4	3 5 3 2 0 2 4 1 2 3 0 0	86	33%	33%	4.82	4.15	5.08
	2007	10	0 3 3 2 3 1 0 1 2 0		89	0%	50%	5.79	5.53	7.46
Olsen,Scott	2006	31	3 2 2 0 0 5 0 2 4 4 5 5 4 4 4 3	2 5 5 5 4 2 0 4 4 5 3 3 5 0 4	93	55%	16%	4.04	3.25	4.10
	2007	33	2 3 0 4 4 3 2 3 4 3 1 0 5 3 2 4 2 0	1 4 2 2 5 2 5 2 0 0 1 0 1 3	93	24%	30%	5.81	5.09	5.21
Olson,Garrett	2007	7	0	1 3 0 4 2 0	92	14%	57%	7.79	6.51	7.77
Ortiz,Ramon	2005	30	4 0 2 1 4 2 3 5 0 2 2 4 0 3 2	3 5 3 0 3 3 3 5 4 4 4 1 2 2	88	33%	20%	5.37	4.28	4.71
	2006	33	2 2 1 4 2 1 2 2 5 4 5 5 4 0 3 4 2	1 4 3 1 2 4 0 0 3 3 3 2 1 0 4 0	95	30%	30%	5.57	4.23	5.08
	2007	10	4 4 1 4 3 0 3 0 0 3		87	30%	40%	5.45	4.73	5.29
Ortiz,Russ	2005	22	3 1 5 3 3 0 0 3 1 2 0 3 3 1	2 0 0 1 4 0 1 0	94	9%	55%	6.89	5.59	7.99
	2006	11	3 0 0 0 3 0 0 0	0 0 0	74	0%	82%	8.14	4.84	12.14
	2007	8	2 4 2 2 0	2 3 0	87	13%	25%	5.51	5.06	5.08
Oswalt,Roy	2005	35	2 3 5 5 5 1 3 4 5 4 3 4 4 4 4 3 5 4 4	4 5 5 3 2 3 4 0 0 4 5 4 3 4 4 4	103	66%	6%	2.95	3.19	3.38
	2006	32	5 2 3 3 5 3 3 0 3 2 5 4 3 4 5 3 4	4 2 2 5 4 5 4 5 5 5 3 4 3 5	101	56%	3%	2.98	2.95	3.38
	2007	32	4 4 2 5 3 4 4 4 4 5 3 2 4 2 5 3 2 3 4 5	3 4 5 5 4 3 0 5 1 3 5 3	103	56%	6%	3.18	3.88	3.68
Owings,Micah	2007	27	4 4 0 4 2 0 5 2 4 3 3 4 0 0	2 0 0 5 4 5 4 3 5 0 0 4 4	90	48%	30%	4.30	4.49	4.82
Padilla,Vicente	2005	27	0 0 2 0 3 3 3 4 2 0 0 0 3	5 4 5 3 5 4 5 4 0 3 1 5 0 3	95	33%	33%	4.71	4.19	5.08
	2006	33	5 2 2 5 1 5 0 4 5 2 0 4 4 5 3 3 4 5	3 4 5 0 5 0 3 5 2 3 3 3 2 2	100	45%	15%	4.50	3.45	4.40
	2007	23	0 3 3 3 0 2 4 3 0 4 3 0 0 2 0	4 0 4 2 5 5 0 2	89	26%	35%	5.76	4.98	5.27
Patterson,John	2005	31	5 5 5 4 4 0 2 3 4 5 3 2 3 5 5	4 5 5 5 5 0 3 4 4 0 5 0 4 3 3 1	103	58%	16%	3.13	3.52	4.10
	2006	8	0 4 5 5 4 0 4 0		82	63%	38%	4.43	3.10	4.53
	2007	7	0 2 2 0 1 3 0		81	0%	57%	7.47	6.87	8.24
Pavano,Carl	2005	17	4 0 0 4 3 2 2 0 5 3 0 1 3 4 2 4 2		91	29%	29%	4.77	3.85	4.93
	2007	2	0 4		76	50%	50%	4.76	4.65	5.81
Peavy,Jake	2005	30	5 5 5 5 5 5 3 5 5 4 0 3 5 5 2 5 3	5 2 5 5 5 5 5 4 3 3 4 3 4	105	70%	3%	2.88	2.74	2.99
	2006	32	5 0 5 5 2 4 3 5 2 5 2 0 3 4 5 4 5	2 0 5 4 3 5 5 5 0 5 2 4 2 5 4	105	59%	13%	4.09	2.96	3.97
	2007	34	5 3 3 3 5 5 4 5 5 4 5 4 2 5 5 3 5 5	5 4 5 5 4 5 5 5 0 5 5 5 3 2	106	76%	3%	2.54	3.22	2.84
Pelfrey,Mike	2006	4	3	2 0 3	95	0%	25%	5.48	4.29	5.18
	2007	13	1 2 0 3 2 2 3 4	4 5 1 2 2	94	23%	23%	5.57	5.03	4.75
Penny,Brad	2005	29	3 5 4 0 1 4 4 4 2 3 4 5 3 5 3	0 4 3 1 4 4 4 0 2 5 5 3 0	96	52%	21%	3.91	3.57	4.50
	2006	33	4 5 5 4 3 2 2 3 5 4 0 4 4 4 5 2 3 5 5	3 3 3 4 3 2 0 3 2 2 5 3 3 0	98	42%	9%	4.33	3.39	4.11
	2007	33	2 3 3 3 3 4 5 4 1 4 4 3 5 5 5 4 5 0	5 5 3 3 5 5 4 3 3 1 3 2 3 2 1	98	45%	12%	3.03	4.18	4.28
Perez,Odalis	2005	19	1 5 3 1 5 3 3 4 2 3	2 5 3 3 4 5 0 0 0	86	32%	26%	4.57	3.65	4.90
	2006	20	0 1 3 5 0 0 0 0	0 1 5 4 4 0 4 5 3 4 2 0	87	35%	50%	6.20	3.74	6.25
	2007	26	2 0 2 2 3 4 2 4 5 4 1 3 1 0 3 2 3 4	0 1 2 4 1 0 3 2	90	23%	31%	5.57	5.23	5.21
Perez,Oliver	2005	20	4 0 2 0 5 0 0 4 3 3 5 5 2 4 1	0 0 0 4 3	94	35%	40%	5.85	4.59	5.25
	2006	22	4 0 0 3 3 0 0 4 4 5 0 0 4 4 0	3 0 4 4 4 1 0	96	41%	45%	6.55	4.30	5.67
	2007	29	5 0 4 4 4 0 4 4 5 4 4 2 5 2 5	5 5 5 5 2 2 1 4 4 2 5 0 5 0	104	66%	17%	3.56	4.34	3.73
Petit,Yusmeiro	2007	10	4 2 3	1 5 2 0 0 0 4	79	30%	40%	4.58	4.88	5.29
Pettitte,Andy	2005	33	4 3 2 5 3 4 4 5 3 5 5 5 4 4 4 4	3 5 5 5 4 4 5 5 4 4 4 3 5 5	97	82%	0%	2.39	2.93	2.69
	2006	35	0 1 2 5 4 3 2 2 5 3 0 3 2 4 5 4 0 2 2 5	5 1 3 5 4 5 5 3 3 5 3 0 2 2 5	100	40%	17%	4.20	3.18	4.44
	2007	34	0 4 4 2 0 4 4 3 4 3 4 0 2 4 3 2 0 3	3 5 4 3 5 2 4 4 5 4 3 3 0 4 3 0	99	44%	18%	4.05	4.32	4.44
Pineiro,Joel	2005	30	1 2 3 4 3 0 2 0 5 3 4 4 2 1 3	3 3 1 1 2 4 4 2 2 5 4 3 1 4 0	98	30%	27%	5.62	4.10	4.90
	2006	25	2 4 5 2 0 4 5 0 2 0 2 4 1 0 3 4 0 2	4 3 3 0 2 0 0	96	28%	36%	6.36	4.12	5.27
	2007	11		1 4 3 2 0 4 1 0 4 2 5	90	36%	36%	4.33	4.32	5.13
Ponson,Sidney	2005	23	3 0 4 4 2 5 3 0 3 2 2 4 2 4 1 1 0 1	1 3 0 0 0	90	22%	43%	6.23	4.37	5.50
	2006	16	2 4 1 4 2 0 3 3 2 0 3 0 4	4 0 0	82	25%	38%	6.25	4.14	5.27
	2007	7	0 3 0 1 5 2 0		90	14%	57%	6.93	4.97	7.77
Prior,Mark	2005	27	5 5 5 2 5 5 4 4 0 4 3 0	5 4 2 5 0 3 3 5 4 3 5 5 3 5 2	105	59%	11%	3.68	3.07	3.97
	2006	9	0 3 3 4	0 2 1 3 0	93	11%	44%	7.21	4.29	5.70
Ramirez,Horacio	2005	32	0 1 3 1 3 4 0 2 0 2 3 2 1 3 3 0 4	2 3 2 4 1 3 3 5 3 4 2 0 3 2 4	93	19%	28%	4.63	4.29	5.03
	2006	14	0 4 3 4 0 3 4 4 0	2 4 0 3 0	87	36%	36%	4.48	3.99	5.13
	2007	20	2 0 3 0 1 3 3 0	4 0 4 0 3 1 3 2 1 1 0 0	84	10%	55%	7.16	5.56	7.77
Rasner,Darrell	2006	3		4 3 0	86	33%	33%	4.43	3.75	5.08
	2007	6	0 3 0 4 1 0		67	17%	67%	4.01	5.30	8.85
Redding,Tim	2005	7	2 2 0 0 5 0	0	71	14%	57%	10.73	5.33	7.77
	2007	15	2 3	2 3 5 4 2 5 3 0 2 0 0 4 2	93	27%	20%	3.64	5.16	4.73

Pitcher	Year	No.	FIRST HALF	SECOND HALF	PC	DOM	DIS	ERA	xERA	qERA
Redman,Mark	2005	30	4 5 3 4 2 2 3 4 5 0 5 4 3 3 3 0 3 4	0 2 4 2 0 3 3 2 3 2 0 4	91	33%	17%	4.90	3.91	4.60
	2006	29	1 5 0 2 5 3 0 1 3 3 1 3 2 3	2 5 2 0 2 0 0 3 2 4 4 0 3 0 3	95	17%	34%	5.71	4.36	5.29
	2007	8	2 0 3 0 0	1 0 3	78	0%	63%	7.62	5.53	9.02
Reyes,Anthony	2006	17	2 5 5 3 1 3	3 1 3 4 4 0 5 0 4 4 0	85	41%	29%	5.06	3.71	4.74
	2007	20	4 1 4 4 5 5 3 2 2 2 2 0 3	5 3 4 4 5 3 0 0	88	45%	20%	6.04	4.90	4.53
Reyes,Jo-jo	2007	10	0	2 2 0 0 0 4 4 2 2	82	20%	40%	6.22	5.74	5.50
Rheinecker,John	2006	13	0 4 4 1 0 1 0 4 3	0 0 0 0	82	23%	69%	5.86	3.98	8.60
	2007	7	0	4 0 1 5 3 1	90	29%	57%	5.36	4.54	7.14
Robertson,Nate	2005	32	4 2 0 3 2 4 0 4 3 3 3 2 4 4 5 4 0	3 4 3 2 2 3 3 5 2 3 3 0 3 4 3	92	31%	13%	4.50	3.86	4.49
	2006	32	3 5 0 4 5 5 0 1 4 3 4 3 3 3 4 3 3 3	3 3 3 4 3 5 3 3 3 3 5 4 4 0	97	38%	13%	3.84	3.55	4.41
	2007	30	3 4 5 3 3 2 0 3 2 0 0 0 4 3 2	5 4 3 3 4 3 4 4 0 5 0 4 4 4 3	96	40%	20%	4.76	4.61	4.56
Rodriguez,Wandy	2005	22	2 4 0 3 2 3 2 3 0	4 4 3 1 0 2 2 4 5 3 3 0 3	92	23%	23%	5.55	4.12	4.75
	2006	24	1 4 5 5 5 2 4 0 4 2 0 3 2 4 3 3 1 1	0 3 0 4 2	92	33%	29%	5.64	3.90	4.90
	2007	31	5 4 3 5 5 3 3 5 3 3 4 2 5 4 2 4 5	0 3 5 0 5 3 3 2 3 4 0 0 4 5	98	48%	13%	4.58	4.06	4.28
Rogers,Kenny	2005	30	3 2 3 3 3 4 3 4 2 3 5 3 4 2 0 4 3	3 4 2 3 5 2 4 3 1 4 3 3 2	100	30%	7%	3.46	4.17	4.48
	2006	33	5 3 3 3 3 4 1 3 4 1 0 5 5 5 3 1 0 2	0 3 0 2 2 4 2 4 3 3 2 2 2 3 4 0	93	27%	24%	3.84	3.76	4.73
	2007	11	5 4 1	2 3 0 4 3 3 4 2	92	36%	18%	4.43	4.61	4.52
Sabathia,C.C.	2005	31	4 5 4 0 3 2 4 3 3 4 5 0 0 3 4 0	3 3 0 3 4 4 4 4 5 5 5 4 5 2 5	102	55%	16%	4.04	3.34	4.10
	2006	28	0 2 4 5 5 5 4 1 5 4 0 4 3 5	4 0 2 4 5 5 5 4 4 4 5 3 2 5	105	68%	14%	3.22	2.93	3.61
	2007	34	2 4 5 5 4 4 4 3 4 3 5 3 5 4 4 5 5 5 0	4 3 5 5 2 5 5 5 4 5 2 5 4 5 5 3	105	74%	3%	3.21	3.41	2.99
Sampson,Chris	2006	3	3	0 0	65	0%	67%	2.12	3.01	9.80
	2007	19	4 2 0 5 0 1 3 3 3 3 3 3 2 4 1 2	3 1 0	86	16%	32%	4.59	4.79	5.29
Sanchez,Anibal	2006	17	2 1	4 4 4 0 5 3 3 3 4 5 3 4 4 5 1	99	53%	18%	2.83	3.83	4.37
	2007	6	2 2 3 3 2 0		95	0%	17%	4.80	6.54	4.69
Santana,Ervin	2005	23	0 5 4 0 4 0 3 0	5 0 5 5 5 3 4 0 4 0 2 5 3 4 4	98	52%	30%	4.66	4.11	4.71
	2006	33	2 3 2 5 3 0 5 4 0 3 3 5 4 5 2 4 4 4	5 0 4 3 3 0 1 4 3 0 3 5 1 3 3	97	39%	21%	4.28	3.75	4.64
	2007	26	5 0 0 5 1 4 5 3 4 0 4 5 4 4 4 0 2 0	3 5 4 0 3 3 5 2	97	50%	27%	5.76	4.68	4.61
Santana,Johan	2005	33	4 5 4 5 5 4 5 4 2 5 5 4 5 5 3 2 4 2	4 3 5 5 3 5 5 5 5 5 1 5 4 5 5	101	79%	3%	2.88	2.85	2.84
	2006	34	2 3 3 5 5 5 5 5 5 4 4 3 5 5 5 5 3 4	5 4 4 1 5 5 5 3 5 5 5 5 2 4	102	76%	3%	2.77	2.57	2.84
	2007	33	4 5 5 5 3 3 5 4 5 4 4 5 5 4 5 5	5 5 2 5 5 4 4 5 3 2 3 5 5 3 0	101	76%	3%	3.33	3.30	2.84
Santos,Victor	2005	24	3 4 4 0 5 4 0 4 5 3 4 4 2 2 1 2 0	0 2 3 1 0 3 0	94	33%	33%	4.59	4.35	5.08
	2006	19	0 4 0 4 2 5 3 3 2 4 5 3 4 0	2 2 3 3 0	95	32%	21%	5.70	3.88	4.71
	2007	3		0 0 2	80	0%	67%	5.83	4.81	9.80
Saunders,Joe	2006	13		4 3 5 5 0 2 0 4 4 0 5 4 0	89	54%	31%	4.71	3.61	4.71
	2007	18	2 4 2 3 3	5 3 3 2 3 5 1 3 3 3 4 2 2	99	22%	6%	4.44	4.54	4.49
Schilling,Curt	2005	11	2 3 4	3 4 2 5 2 5 4 3	105	45%	0%	5.70	3.66	3.68
	2006	31	5 4 5 5 4 5 4 2 1 5 4 4 3 4 4 4 5 3 5	5 4 4 2 2 4 3 5 4 2 3 5	105	71%	3%	3.97	2.96	2.99
	2007	24	0 5 4 3 4 4 3 3 2 5 1 4 3 0	4 3 2 4 3 3 5 3 5	95	42%	13%	3.87	4.25	4.32
Schmidt,Jason	2005	29	5 5 2 5 2 2 0 4 0 0 3 4 5 4 0 3	4 5 5 5 3 4 0 3 3 5 0 3 0	105	45%	24%	4.40	3.79	4.53
	2006	32	3 5 4 3 5 5 4 3 4 5 4 5 4 5 4 3 4 5 3 3	3 4 5 5 2 5 3 2 0 4 3 0 2 5	108	56%	6%	3.59	3.50	3.68
	2007	6	3 0 0 4 0 0		79	17%	67%	6.31	5.32	8.85
Seo,Jae	2005	14	5 2 5	4 5 4 4 2 5 4 3 3 1 5	98	64%	7%	2.60	3.56	3.50
	2006	26	2 4 0 4 4 0 3 4 0 0 1 4	2 0 1 0 3 5 3 0 3 0 2 3 0 2	87	23%	42%	5.33	4.43	5.50
	2007	10	3 0 3 2 0 3 0 5 0 1		85	10%	50%	8.13	5.55	7.08
Shearn,Thomas	2007	6		3 0 3 4 2 0	83	17%	33%	4.96	5.36	5.29
Sheets,Ben	2005	22	4 4 5 3 2 4 4 4 3 3 5 5 3	3 4 5 5 5 5 4 5 5	104	73%	0%	3.34	3.12	2.99
	2006	17	3 5 5 0	5 5 0 5 5 4 4 5 4 5 4	92	76%	12%	3.82	2.49	3.41
	2007	24	4 3 0 4 0 4 4 5 5 5 3 4 5 3 4 4 4 5 3	0 4 4 5 0 0	94	63%	21%	3.82	4.27	3.95
Shields,James	2006	21	2 4 5 5 4 3 3 2	2 0 4 3 4 5 5 4 3 5 0 3 3	95	48%	10%	4.84	3.31	4.28
	2007	31	3 4 3 5 5 4 4 4 5 2 4 3 5 3 2 3 5 5	2 4 0 3 5 5 5 5 4 4 5 5 4	102	68%	3%	3.85	3.54	3.14
Silva,Carlos	2005	27	3 5 3 3 3 4 4 1 4 2 3 4 2 2 4	4 3 4 4 4 4 4 4 2 3 0	85	48%	7%	3.44	3.70	3.98
	2006	31	2 2 2 1 0 3 2 0 3 3 3 5 4 0 0	5 0 3 4 2 2 4 0 1 0 4 3 4 1 0 2	84	23%	35%	5.94	4.15	5.36
	2007	33	2 3 3 3 4 3 3 2 0 4 4 0 4 2 5 5 2 1	4 2 1 3 5 4 5 3 0 4 3 0 3 4 3	93	36%	18%	4.19	4.47	4.52
Simontacchi,Jason	2007	13	4 3 4 3 3 0 4 2 0 5 0 3	0	86	31%	31%	6.37	5.27	5.08
Slowey,Kevin	2007	11	3 2 2 1 2 2 0	4 5 5 2	94	27%	18%	4.73	4.72	4.62
Smoltz,John	2005	33	0 4 3 5 2 2 3 4 0 3 3 3 4 4 5 5 3	5 5 4 4 4 4 5 4 4 2 4 4 5 4	100	64%	6%	3.06	3.26	3.50
	2006	35	2 4 4 2 4 5 5 5 5 5 2 3 5 5 4 0 5 4 5	5 4 3 5 5 5 3 5 5 1 4 0 5 4 5 4	101	74%	9%	3.49	2.86	3.25
	2007	32	4 3 4 4 1 4 5 4 5 5 5 0 4 4 4 4	5 4 5 3 3 4 5 5 5 3 5 5 5 0	96	78%	9%	3.11	3.37	3.13
Snell,Ian	2005	5		3 0 0 3 3	80	0%	40%	4.32	3.75	5.90
	2006	32	2 0 1 5 5 3 5 0 3 2 3 5 4 1 1 2 5	2 5 5 3 4 5 4 3 3 2 2 5 5 2	95	44%	16%	4.74	3.36	4.44
	2007	32	5 4 4 3 4 3 4 5 3 2 5 5 5 5 3 5 3	2 4 0 5 1 5 4 3 5 2 3 4 4 5 3	98	59%	6%	3.76	3.94	3.68
Sonnanstine,Andrew	2007	22	4 4 2 2 5 2 5	2 4 3 3 0 0 3 3 4 4 4 0 5 1 3	95	41%	18%	5.85	4.21	4.44
Sosa,Jorge	2005	20	4 0 2 3 3 2	4 3 3 2 5 1 3 2 3 4 1 4 1 0	85	25%	25%	2.55	4.45	4.93
	2006	13	0 0 0 4 3 2 5 3 4 3 0 2 2		91	23%	31%	5.42	4.15	5.21
	2007	14	3 2 4 0 3 4 4 1 0 5 3	5 0 1	93	36%	36%	4.47	4.86	5.13
Sowers,Jeremy	2006	14	3 4 0	2 4 4 4 2 4 3 5 1 4 1	91	50%	21%	3.57	3.72	4.50
	2007	13	3 4 0 3 3 0 2 1 3 0 0 0	4	82	15%	46%	6.42	5.68	6.25
Speigner,Levale	2007	6	0 0 0 0 4 0		73	17%	83%	8.77	6.06	10.80
Stults,Eric	2007	5		4 5 0 0 0	87	40%	60%	5.82	4.90	7.05
Suppan,Jeff	2005	32	0 3 2 3 4 2 4 0 2 3 0 3 3 2 4 0 3 2	4 3 0 4 3 5 4 3 4 3 1 5 3 5	95	31%	19%	3.57	3.99	4.60
	2006	32	1 3 0 4 3 3 3 3 2 1 2 2 0 3 1 1 0	5 3 3 1 5 2 0 3 4 4 1 4 4 0 3	96	22%	34%	4.12	3.89	5.21
	2007	34	3 4 5 4 4 4 3 2 3 3 3 2 1 2 0 3 4 3 2	4 2 1 3 3 3 3 5 3 5 2 4 2 2	98	29%	9%	4.62	4.77	4.48
Tavarez,Julian	2006	6		0 5 4 1 3 1	84	33%	50%	4.47	3.87	6.37
	2007	23	0 2 0 2 5 2 3 2 3 1 5 3 4 0 1 0	0 0 1 3 5 0 0	90	17%	48%	5.15	4.58	6.25
Tejeda,Robinson	2005	13	4 2 5 0 4 0	4 3 5 4 5 0 3	88	54%	23%	3.59	4.25	4.50
	2006	14	2 0 3 0 0	4 3 0 2 5 4 1 3 1	90	21%	43%	4.28	4.60	5.50
	2007	19	3 2 3 4 3 5 0 3 0 0 2 3 0 1 0 0 2	0 3	94	11%	42%	6.61	5.94	5.70
Thompson,Brad	2007	17	2 2 2 2 3 2 0 4 4 2	2 3 0 0 0 4 3	82	18%	24%	4.73	5.01	4.77
Thomson,John	2005	17	4 3 3 5 4 4 0 0	4 0 0 2 4 2 5 4 1	92	47%	29%	4.49	3.82	4.67
	2006	15	3 5 3 4 1 3 2 1 3 0 0 0 3 0 0		82	13%	47%	4.82	4.15	6.39
	2007	2	3 0		84	0%	50%	3.37	5.16	7.46

PQS PITCHING LOGS

Pitcher	Year	No.	FIRST HALF	SECOND HALF	PC	DOM	DIS	ERA	xERA	qERA
Tomko,Brett	2005	30	3 0 2 2 5 3 5 4 3 4 3 4 4 0 3 0 3	5 2 5 3 3 2 0 4 5 4 3 0 4	100	40%	17%	4.50	4.12	4.44
	2006	15	3 2 3 4 4 5 3 4 4 0 0 0 0 1 3		95	33%	33%	4.73	3.82	5.08
	2007	19	5 1 4 4 0 5 0 2	3 4 2 2 4 2 0 5 5 3 0	90	42%	26%	5.55	4.42	4.74
Towers,Josh	2005	33	5 5 0 3 5 4 4 2 0 3 0 2 2 2 4 5 0 4	0 4 4 4 4 4 2 4 3 4 4 3 1 4 4	90	55%	18%	3.72	3.82	4.10
	2006	12	0 3 0 1 0 1 0 4 1 0 3 0		73	8%	75%	8.42	4.36	10.91
	2007	15	3 4 2 0 0 4 0 3 4 4	1 4 3 2 1	89	33%	33%	5.38	4.13	5.08
Trachsel,Steve	2005	6		5 2 1 3 5 0	94	33%	33%	4.14	3.93	5.08
	2006	30	5 3 3 3 0 4 0 3 1 3 4 0 2 3 0 2 2	3 0 0 0 2 4 5 0 4 0 0 0 4 1	94	23%	40%	4.97	4.67	5.50
	2007	29	3 3 0 2 2 1 4 0 2 3 3 3 0 4 3 0 0 0	1 0 3 1 2 2 3 3 3 0 1 0	91	7%	45%	4.90	5.95	6.53
Van Benschoten,Joh	2007	9	3 1 0 5 0	0 0 2 0	80	11%	67%	10.15	6.29	9.15
Vanden Hurk,Rick	2007	17	0 0 0 5 3 4	4 2 0 0 0 3 2 4 4 3 0	87	29%	41%	6.83	4.99	5.40
Vargas,Claudio	2005	23	4 0 0 0 2 2 5 2 5	2 5 5 5 3 5 5 3 1 2 4 4 2 2	96	43%	17%	5.25	4.15	4.44
	2006	30	5 0 0 4 3 5 0 5 1 2 3 3 5 5 4 0	0 5 5 0 5 5 5 0 2 5 4 3 3 5	95	50%	17%	4.83	3.76	4.61
	2007	23	4 5 0 3 4 5 3 0 2 5 3 4 3 3 4	2 5 4 0 2 3 2 0	94	39%	17%	5.09	4.80	4.52
Vazquez,Javier	2005	33	0 4 4 2 4 5 5 5 5 5 3 0 2 4 3 4 4 5	4 0 4 4 3 2 0 5 5 2 3 4 5 5 3	101	61%	12%	4.43	3.14	3.71
	2006	32	5 4 5 3 5 5 2 2 3 4 4 3 3 2 1 4 3	4 3 1 5 2 1 4 3 2 5 5 5 5 5 0	103	50%	13%	4.84	3.22	4.23
	2007	32	4 3 5 4 4 5 2 4 3 4 4 4 4 5 5 5 5	2 4 4 3 5 2 3 3 4 4 4 5 5 5	108	75%	0%	3.74	3.53	2.84
Verlander,Justin	2006	30	5 0 4 3 4 2 2 4 5 5 2 3 3 2 3 5 4	5 4 5 3 2 3 3 0 4 4 0 0 2	99	43%	13%	3.63	3.61	4.32
	2007	32	4 4 5 4 0 4 3 5 4 4 2 5 5 4 5 3 5	4 3 4 2 4 4 2 0 5 5 4 5 1 5 5	105	72%	9%	3.66	3.88	3.25
Villanueva,Carlos	2006	6	5 1 3	5 3 3	98	33%	17%	3.69	3.19	4.60
	2007	6	4	5 3 3 4 3	87	50%	0%	3.94	4.55	3.47
Volquez,Edinson	2006	8		4 3 0 0 0 2 0 0	81	13%	63%	7.29	5.14	8.46
	2007	6		3 4 2 5 3 1	99	33%	17%	4.50	4.45	4.60
Wainwright,Adam	2007	32	3 2 3 2 0 2 4 0 3 5 4 2 3 2 2 3 3	5 5 3 3 4 4 5 4 5 1 3 3 4 3 4	99	38%	9%	3.70	4.36	4.29
Wakefield,Tim	2005	33	3 5 4 2 4 4 2 2 2 3 0 1 4 4 5 2 4 2	2 1 3 4 5 3 0 1 3 5 5 4 5 5 1	103	45%	18%	4.16	3.92	4.40
	2006	23	0 5 4 3 2 3 2 5 4 3 4 4 5 4 5 4 2	0 1 0 2 3	98	48%	17%	4.63	4.02	4.40
	2007	31	5 3 3 4 2 3 5 2 0 4 0 4 4 1 2 2 2	2 3 3 5 5 0 5 5 5 5 0 0 1 2 3	93	35%	23%	4.76	4.86	4.64
Wang,Chien-Ming	2005	17	3 2 3 4 4 3 0 4 1 3 4 2	1 3 4 4 3	90	35%	18%	4.03	3.79	4.52
	2006	33	0 2 5 1 3 1 3 3 4 2 4 0 2 4 3 3 4 1 3	3 2 3 3 1 1 2 5 3 2 3 3 4 4	92	24%	21%	3.63	3.58	4.75
	2007	30	3 2 4 3 4 3 4 1 4 4 5 3 2 3 3	4 4 2 2 4 0 3 4 5 4 3 3 1 4 4	95	47%	10%	3.70	4.00	4.28
Washburn,Jarrod	2005	29	4 0 5 3 3 3 0 1 3 1 2 4 3 2 4 4 4 1	3 4 4 3 3 3 5 3 2 3 0	93	31%	21%	3.20	4.21	4.71
	2006	31	5 0 4 4 4 4 3 1 3 0 5 0 5 1 4 4 3 2	2 3 5 2 4 0 2 5 3 3 5 0 0	99	42%	26%	4.67	4.06	4.74
	2007	32	3 4 4 3 3 1 5 2 3 4 0 0 4 0 3 2 4	4 4 1 2 3 3 5 5 5 0 4 1 0 4 3	102	41%	25%	4.32	5.01	4.74
Weaver,Jeff	2005	34	4 0 5 0 3 4 4 5 1 0 4 5 5 4 5 4 3 5 4	4 3 2 3 4 5 2 4 5 4 4 3	99	65%	14%	4.22	3.53	3.61
	2006	31	2 3 4 5 0 4 1 0 0 5 3 2 3 4 5 0	0 1 1 0 5 1 4 3 2 4 3 1 5 4 2	93	35%	35%	5.76	3.92	5.13
	2007	27	0 3 0 0 1 1 0 3 4 1 4 4	2 4 2 0 3 5 3 3 0 0 1 0 4 1 3	89	22%	48%	6.20	5.16	6.12
Weaver,Jered	2006	19	5 5 4 5 5 5	3 3 3 1 5 5 5 0 5 3 5 3 3	102	58%	11%	2.56	3.36	3.97
	2007	28	5 0 3 4 4 5 5 2 0 4 0 2 5 1	5 3 1 2 5 4 0 5 4 3 3 5 2 4	98	50%	21%	3.91	4.63	4.50
Webb,Brandon	2005	33	2 4 5 4 2 4 3 4 5 3 5 3 4 5 4 2 4 2	2 0 3 4 5 5 2 3 4 4 4 4 5 4	102	64%	3%	3.54	2.94	3.29
	2006	33	3 4 2 4 4 4 4 3 5 4 5 5 5 3 4 5 5	5 4 3 3 3 2 3 3 5 4 5 4 5 0	101	64%	3%	3.10	2.54	3.29
	2007	34	2 5 2 5 5 3 3 3 5 2 3 5 5 4 4 4 3 3 3 5	3 4 5 5 4 5 4 5 2 5 4 4 4 4 2	101	65%	0%	3.01	3.15	3.14
Wellemeyer,Todd	2007	11	2 0 3 0 4 4 0 2	0 4 5	77	36%	36%	4.54	4.87	5.13
Wells,David	2005	30	0 2 4 4 0 0 3 3 3 4 5 3 2 4 3	5 4 4 4 4 0 4 4 4 1 3 0 3 5	93	50%	20%	4.45	3.53	4.50
	2006	13	0 0	0 4 3 2 4 3 4 2 2 4 4	85	38%	23%	4.42	3.72	4.64
	2007	29	4 0 4 2 2 1 1 4 5 3 3 4 3 2 3 5 0	3 0 0 2 0 1 3 4 3 1 0 3	82	24%	34%	5.43	4.88	5.21
Wells,Kip	2005	33	1 2 4 3 4 4 4 4 5 5 0 5 4 0 0 3 0 5 1	0 5 3 0 3 5 0 4 1 0 2 0 2 3	94	39%	36%	5.09	4.31	5.13
	2006	9	0 1 0 3	4 1 3 1 0	86	11%	67%	6.50	4.59	9.15
	2007	26	4 5 4 5 0 3 0 3 2 4 2 0 2 0 4	0 4 2 3 4 4 4 0 1 0 0	94	38%	35%	5.70	4.63	5.13
Westbrook,Jake	2005	34	4 0 3 4 0 3 0 0 5 3 3 3 4 4 4 3 4 4	3 4 4 1 5 0 2 2 3 4 3 3 2 5 3	94	38%	18%	4.50	3.43	4.52
	2006	32	4 4 3 0 1 5 4 2 4 1 4 2 4 5 4 5 3 4	0 3 3 2 5 3 3 2 5 3 3 3 1 5	102	44%	16%	4.17	3.45	4.44
	2007	25	1 4 0 3 5 0 4 5 2	3 2 2 3 5 1 4 3 3 3 3 3 5 4	99	36%	16%	4.32	4.21	4.52
Williams,Woody	2005	28	0 5 2 3 4 2 3 4 4 4 3 3	1 3 2 2 0 5 3 4 3 5 3 2 0 1 4	96	32%	18%	4.86	4.19	4.60
	2006	24	3 5 3 2 3 4 0 4 1	3 2 1 2 3 3 4 0 1 4 5 3 1 3	95	29%	25%	3.65	4.07	4.93
	2007	31	0 4 1 1 3 3 3 3 3 0 3 3 2 5 3 0 5 2 4	4 4 4 1 4 3 4 5 0 3 3 1	100	32%	26%	5.27	5.02	4.90
Willis,Dontrelle	2005	34	4 5 5 5 5 4 4 4 4 2 4 5 3 5 3 5 0	2 0 5 3 3 5 4 2 5 4 3 4 5 5 0 4	105	68%	6%	2.63	3.33	3.38
	2006	33	3 4 1 4 5 4 0 0 2 3 3 3 3 2 5 5 3	5 3 4 0 3 2 4 3 4 5 4 3 5 4 3 1 0	106	38%	18%	3.87	3.57	4.52
	2007	35	3 4 4 3 2 4 4 3 4 4 2 3 2 3 4 0 5 0 4	0 0 3 3 5 1 3 2 2 1 3 0 2 5 5 0	100	34%	23%	5.17	4.59	4.71
Wolf,Randy	2005	13	4 3 3 0 2 3 4 5 4 3 4 3 2		100	38%	8%	4.39	3.94	4.29
	2006	12		0 0 4 2 2 3 3 4 0 3 3 0	88	17%	33%	5.56	4.40	5.29
	2007	18	3 3 5 5 4 2 3 5 3 3 5 2 3 3 1 3 4 0		99	33%	11%	4.73	4.15	4.49
Wood,Mike	2005	10		3 1 4 1 2 3 0 3 1 0	88	10%	50%	4.46	4.48	7.08
	2006	7	0 2 0 3 1 0 0		83	0%	71%	5.71	4.33	10.58
	2007	4	4 0 0 3		95	25%	50%	5.33	4.81	6.56
Wright,Jamey	2005	27	3 0 4 2 4 1 3 3 0 3 4 4 4 2 2 4 1	3 4 0 3 3 2 3 3 4 3	95	30%	19%	5.47	4.33	4.60
	2006	21	3 4 3 2 1 3 4 5 4 0 3 0 3 2 2 2 4	4 1 2 2	98	29%	19%	5.19	3.81	4.62
	2007	9	0 0 3 2 3	3 0 2 2	88	0%	33%	3.62	4.91	5.53
Wright,Jaret	2005	13	0 1 2 1	4 4 3 2 2 3 0 0 0	86	15%	46%	6.12	4.85	6.25
	2006	27	0 1 3 3 4 3 2 3 1 2 3 5 0 5	1 0 3 4 3 2 0 0 5 3 2 4 3	84	22%	30%	4.49	4.17	5.21
	2007	3	3 4 0		67	33%	67%	6.97	6.70	7.99
Youman,Shane	2006	3		2 0 3	85	0%	33%	2.91	4.51	5.53
	2007	8	3 3	2 3 0 3 3 0	88	0%	25%	5.97	5.33	5.18
Young,Chris	2005	31	0 0 3 4 4 1 4 2 4 4 5 4 5 3 3 0 0	3 0 0 0 4 0 5 4 5 3 0 4 2	92	42%	32%	4.28	3.80	4.92
	2006	31	3 5 4 0 5 3 2 3 4 0 5 4 5 3 4 4 5 4	0 3 1 0 3 5 0 5 2 4 4 4 5	98	55%	19%	3.46	3.58	4.10
	2007	30	2 5 0 5 0 5 5 1 5 5 5 4 3 0 5 4 5	5 5 0 4 5 4 0 0 3 5 5 2 4	96	63%	23%	3.12	4.17	3.95
Zambrano,Carlos	2005	33	0 5 4 4 0 5 3 0 5 4 5 4 3 2 0 5 5 4	3 5 2 4 0 5 5 5 5 5 5 4 2 2 5	108	64%	15%	3.27	3.15	3.83
	2006	33	0 4 4 3 5 0 5 4 5 4 4 5 5 3 5 3 5 3 5	4 5 3 4 4 0 3 5 5 5 0 4 5 5	110	70%	12%	3.41	3.28	3.51
	2007	34	0 4 0 2 4 4 4 4 4 1 5 5 3 5 5 5 4	5 3 4 5 3 2 2 2 4 0 4 3 1 5 4	109	59%	12%	3.95	4.24	4.10
Zambrano,Victor	2005	27	3 3 2 2 0 2 4 3 3 3 3 3 4 4 3 4	4 0 4 0 3 4 4 3 3 0 3	100	30%	15%	4.17	4.07	4.60
	2006	5	2 2 0 5 0		73	20%	40%	6.75	4.46	5.50
	2007	4	0 0	4 0	59	25%	75%	10.17	6.55	9.46
Zito,Barry	2005	35	3 0 5 4 3 4 4 4 4 5 3 5 3 3 3 5	4 5 1 5 4 5 4 5 5 0 5 2 5 4 1	109	66%	11%	3.87	3.75	3.61
	2006	34	0 5 5 3 4 4 4 2 4 4 5 4 3 3 5 3 2 3 3	2 4 2 3 1 2 5 3 4 0 1 3 5 4	108	41%	12%	3.83	4.09	4.32
	2007	33	2 3 4 3 3 3 4 2 0 3 5 4 0 3 0 3 3 0	5 2 0 3 0 4 5 4 5 4 4 0 0 1 4	103	39%	24%	4.53	4.77	4.64

Bullpen Indicators

2007 Volatility Report

Closer value and volatility stabilized in 2007. While the cost of saves dropped to another all-time low of $17.67, that level was just pennies off of last year's $17.80 mark. The upside, however, is this continuing risk aversion on draft day netted quite a few large-scale profits:

Drafted closers that returned at least 30% profit were Jason Isringhausen ($21 return on $12 average draft price), Jose Valverde ($26 on $16), Takashi Saito ($30 on $19), Bobby Jenks ($25 on $16, the second year in a row he realized a 30%-plus profit), J.J. Putz ($32 on $21), Joe Borowski ($19 on $13, another repeat member of this list) and Ryan Dempster ($13 on $9). Jonathan Papelbon was also technically on this list, however, his draft price ($15) was deflated due to the expectation that he'd be in the starting rotation. He earned $25.

Of the pitchers drafted for saves in March, 10 failed to return at least 50% of their draft value, about the same failure rate as 2006. Of these 2007 failures, seven were due to injury, only one to ineffectiveness and two to trades. Of the 11 new sources, perhaps six can be considered front-line closer candidates for 2008. Al Reyes and Dan Wheeler are both on this list, yet only one will likely anchor the Ray's bullpen.

Since many of the new closers look like they could be fixtures in their respective teams' bullpens, this potentially leaves fewer unsettled pen situations going into 2008 than there have been in a long while. As of this writing, the only teams that do not have a firm "go-to guy" are Baltimore and Texas in the American League, and Atlanta, Chicago, Houston and San Francisco in the National League (with a few free agents possibly impacting these lists).

The fallout from all this? With more settled pens, I'd expect the average closer price to rise in 2008. Be prepared to pay more for saves.

However, I would not make wholesale changes in draft strategy based on the events of one year. We continue to advise that you should not invest heavily in closers at the draft table. Instead, work the free agent pool for saves during the season (particularly in 5x5 leagues).

The Closer Volatility Chart summarizes all this.

A bit of explanation... CLOSERS DRAFTED refers to the number of saves sources purchased in both AL and NL LABR Leagues each year. These only include relievers drafted for at least $10 specifically for saves. AVG $ refers to the average purchase price of these pitchers. FAILED is the number (and percentage) of CLOSERS DRAFTED that did not return at least 50% of their value that year. The Failures include those that lost their value due to ineffectiveness, injury or managerial decision. NEW SOURCES are arms that were drafted for less than $10 (if they were drafted at all) but finished with at least double-digit saves and/or double-digit value. The body of the chart lists the pitchers who make up the study.

Tools for Speculation

The structured analysis provided in the following Bullpen Indicator Charts (which are compiled by HQ analyst Matt Dodge) can offer some insight for the speculating process.

To aid in this process, these charts help focus on many of the statistical and situational factors that might go into a manager's decision to grant any individual pitcher a save opportunity. It's not all-encompassing, but it's a good start. In the following pages, we provide a three-year scan of indicators for all pitchers who posted at least 1 save and/or three holds in 2006.

Some of the tidbits worthy of analysis...

Saves Percentage: What it says is simple... "Who is getting it done?" Intuitively, this percentage should be a major factor in determining which closers might be in danger of losing their jobs. However, Doug Dennis' study showed little correlation between saves success rate alone and future opportunity. Better to prospect for pitchers who have *both* a high saves percentage (80% or better) *and* high skills, as measured by base performance value.

Base Performance Value: The components of BPV are evaluated in many ways. Big league managers tend to look for a pitcher who can strike out eight or nine batters per 9 IP, sometimes even if he's also walking that many. In using BPV, we set a benchmark of 75 as the minimum necessary for success. BPV's over 100 are much better, however.

Situational Performance: is the last piece of the puzzle. Our chart includes the opposition batting averages for each pitcher versus RH and LH hitters, with runners on base, in his first 15 pitches, etc. which are all good indicators. We'll set a benchmark of a .250 BA; anything over and the risk level increases.

There are other variables that come into play as well. Left-handed relievers rarely move into a closer's role unless the team's bullpen has sufficient southpaw depth. Some managers do see the value of having a high-skills arm available for the middle innings, so those pitchers don't get promoted into a closer's role either.

The tools are here. Whether or not a major league manager will make a decision reflective of this information remains to be seen. But I do think the data can help us increase our odds of uncovering those elusive saves and minimizing at least some of the risk.

Closer Volatility Analysis

FAILURES

2001	2002	2003	2004	2005	2006	2007
Jones,T	Alfonseca	Alfonseca	Biddle	Adams	Benitez	Benitez
Kohlmeier	Anderson,M	Anderson,M	Borowski	Affeldt	Dempster	Dotel
Leskanic	Foulke	Benitez	Guardado	Benitez	Foulke	Fuentes
Lowe	Fox	Dejean	Koch	Dotel	Gagne	Gagne
Mantei	Gordon	Embree	Lopez,Aq	Foulke	Guardado	Gonzalez,M
Rocker	Strickland	Escobar	MacDougal	Gagne	MacDougal	Gordon
Veres	Wickman	Hoffman	Mantei	Graves	Orvella	Ray
	Zimmerman	Isringhausen	Nen	Kolb	Reitsma	Ryan
		Jimenez	Rhodes	Mota	Turnbow	Torres
		Koch	Riske	Percival	Valverde	Wickman
		Mesa	Wagner	Speier		
		Nen		Takatsu		
		Sasaki				
		Stewart				
		Urbina				
		Williams,M				
		Williamson				

NEW SOURCES

2001	2002	2003	2004	2005	2006	2007
Fassero	Acevedo	Beck	Affeldt	Brazoban	Burgos	Accardo
Gordon	Baez	Biddle	Aquino	Bruney	Duchscherer	Capps
Kim	Cordero	Borowski	Chacon	Dempster	Julio,J	Corpas
Mesa	DeJean	Carter,L	Cordero	Farnsworth	Nelson,J	Embree
Prinz	Gagne	Cordero,F	Frasor	Fuentes	Otsuka	Gregg
Yan	Irabu	Gordon	Herges	Hermanson	Papelbon	Hennessy
Zimmerman	Julio	Hasegawa	Hermanson	Jones,T	Putz	Myers,B
	Looper	Kolb,D	Hawkins	Lyon	Saito,T	Reyes,A
	Marte	Lopez,Aq	Lidge	MacDougal	Timlin	Soria
	Nunez,V	MacDougal	Putz	Reitsma	Torres,S	Wheeler
	Osuna	Marte	Rodriguez,Fr	Rodney	Walker,T	Wilson,CJ
	Williamson	Politte	Takatsu	Street	Wheeler	
		Tavarez	Wickman	Turnbow		
		Worrell	Worrell	Walker,T		
			Yan	Weathers		

SUMMARY

NUMBER OF CLOSERS

YEAR	Drafted	Avg R$	Failed	Failure %	New Sources
1996	24	$30	3	13%	2
1997	26	$30	5	19%	8
1998	25	$32	11	44%	9
1999	23	$25	5	22%	7
2000	27	$25	10	37%	9
2001	25	$26	7	28%	7
2002	28	$22	8	29%	12
2003	29	$21.97	17	59%	14
2004	29	$19.78	11	38%	15
2005	28	$20.79	12	43%	15
2006	30	$17.80	10	33%	12
2007	28	$17.67	10	36%	11

Bullpen Indicators

				BPIs			Results		Runners		Pitch Ct		Platoon	
Pitcher			**Tm**	**IP/g**	**bpv**	**S%**	**Sv%**	**Eff%**	**Emp**	**On**	**1-15**	**16-30**	**vLH**	**vRH**
Aardsma,David	R	06	CHC	1.2	41	75%	0%	100%	189	247	219	197	190	225
		07	CHW	1.3	66	63%	0%	56%	262	338	274	356	283	310
Abreu,Winston	R	07	WAS	1.2	54	67%	0%	60%	273	328	364	194	222	351
Accardo,Jeremy	R	05	SF	1.0	48	67%	0%	45%	239	222	203	313	182	265
		06	TOR	1.1	72	62%	38%	62%	226	364	286	276	241	307
		07	TOR	1.1	85	83%	86%	80%	201	211	181	290	161	250
Acosta,Manuel	R	07	ATL	1.1	87	84%	0%	83%	159	171	190	105	250	93
Affeldt,Jeremy	L	05	KC	1.0	55	68%	0%	86%	300	259	293	268	263	283
		06	COL	1.8	9	62%	33%	58%	165	315	260	180	213	240
		07	COL	0.8	58	74%	0%	65%	240	213	241	129	250	211
Alfonseca,Antoni	R	07	PHI	0.8	8	70%	62%	80%	337	294	322	278	370	278
Atchison,Scott	R	07	SF	1.4	64	76%	0%	83%	311	232	250	292	278	272
Ayala,Luis	R	05	WAS	1.0	64	83%	33%	78%	308	261	275	328	352	229
		07	WAS	1.0	52	80%	50%	75%	256	282	302	138	243	286
Baez,Danys	R	05	TAM	1.1	48	82%	84%	79%	256	234	234	280	268	215
		06	ATL	1.1	70	65%	53%	65%	252	287	249	327	295	244
		07	BAL	0.9	27	61%	60%	68%	214	305	258	257	346	200
Bayliss,Jonah	R	07	PIT	1.0	12	56%	0%	67%	306	342	294	390	333	319
Beimel,Joe	L	06	LA	1.1	26	79%	100%	93%	258	267	286	185	232	279
		07	LA	0.8	42	67%	100%	91%	250	256	256	235	188	294
Bell,Heath	R	07	SD	1.2	134	79%	33%	84%	162	214	182	206	216	157
Benitez,Armando	R	05	SF	1.0	27	72%	83%	75%	269	167	233	182	212	246
		06	SF	0.9	32	83%	68%	69%	301	222	268	290	270	265
		07	FLA	0.9	71	69%	56%	59%	230	286	283	173	273	243
Benoit,Joaquin	R	05	TEX	2.7	64	72%	0%	69%	143	133	172	106	119	156
		06	TEX	1.4	88	62%	0%	73%	240	210	231	178	191	245
		07	TEX	1.2	104	78%	46%	74%	250	192	218	216	172	268
Betancourt,Raf	R	05	CLE	1.2	129	77%	33%	75%	215	238	233	200	264	204
		06	CLE	1.1	104	71%	50%	65%	214	278	248	236	221	254
		07	CLE	1.2	223	84%	50%	91%	190	173	191	157	239	148
Bootcheck,Chris	R	07	LAA	1.5	58	65%	0%	64%	275	273	257	317	302	253
Borkowski,Dave	R	07	HOU	1.1	56	68%	25%	70%	277	270	253	342	300	256
Borowski,Joe	R	05	TAM	1.1	32	64%	0%	70%	159	328	240	184	198	244
		06	FLA	1.0	63	75%	84%	80%	237	233	239	230	167	291
		07	CLE	1.0	77	67%	85%	79%	284	296	303	254	293	286
Bradford,Chad	R	05	BOS	0.8	64	72%	0%	83%	308	315	297	389	409	282
		06	NYM	0.9	108	73%	67%	84%	284	224	238	333	262	251
		07	BAL	0.8	36	75%	29%	68%	273	312	291	310	321	282
Bray,Bill	L	06	CIN	1.1	63	74%	67%	73%	302	267	259	283	329	254
		07	CIN	0.8	78	55%	100%	70%	269	290	313	111	158	342
Brocail,Doug	R	07	SD	1.1	42	78%	0%	94%	192	283	217	221	182	268
Brown,Andrew	R	07	OAK	1.3	85	63%	0%	55%	215	276	283	192	242	247
Broxton,Jonathan	R	06	LA	1.1	106	83%	43%	79%	253	172	234	192	244	196
		07	LA	1.0	137	77%	25%	79%	228	220	245	152	200	247
Bruney,Brian	R	05	ARI	1.0	55	62%	75%	71%	227	364	277	339	280	314
		06	NYY	1.1	87	96%	0%	83%	195	182	184	200	115	229
		07	NYY	0.9	31	72%	0%	69%	256	232	262	204	303	209
Bukvich,Ryan	R	07	CHW	0.8	4	73%	0%	83%	242	270	290	182	209	278
Burton,Jared	R	07	CIN	0.9	68	79%	0%	75%	195	176	179	222	130	219
Byrdak,Tim	L	05	BAL	0.6	85	77%	100%	92%	250	260	247	261	214	300
		06	BAL	0.4	-56	60%	0%	100%	412	467	444	400	381	545
		07	DET	1.2	80	79%	50%	92%	231	230	193	290	176	268
Cabrera,Fernando	R	06	CLE	1.2	56	68%	0%	56%	225	270	275	172	235	248
		07	BAL	1.3	52	64%	100%	60%	273	307	323	246	319	267
Calero,Kiko	R	05	OAK	1.0	82	75%	50%	89%	205	233	204	271	319	162
		06	OAK	0.8	102	74%	40%	85%	213	258	230	238	278	208
		07	OAK	0.9	29	64%	25%	58%	293	293	308	239	245	315
Camp,Shawn	R	06	TAM	1.0	64	71%	67%	79%	316	310	300	365	370	284
		07	TAM	0.8	54	66%	0%	69%	382	362	397	212	370	368
Capps,Matt	R	06	PIT	1.0	95	72%	10%	70%	265	268	266	288	250	275
		07	PIT	1.0	99	80%	86%	79%	228	207	197	364	281	181
Casilla,Santiago	R	07	OAK	1.1	73	68%	40%	81%	216	233	208	266	212	230
Chacon,Shawn	R	07	PIT	1.5	51	75%	12%	62%	298	214	311	138	267	255
Chamberlain,Joba	R	07	NYY	1.3	198	100%	100%	100%	179	74	158	125	132	156
Chulk,Vinnie	R	05	TOR	1.2	27	74%	0%	87%	276	230	245	273	283	231
		06	SF	1.0	60	66%	0%	58%	217	295	303	157	206	282
		07	SF	0.9	67	72%	0%	70%	286	243	282	209	290	250
Coffey,Todd	R	05	CIN	1.0	51	73%	50%	80%	413	289	322	433	337	348
		06	CIN	1.0	64	77%	67%	72%	269	280	278	288	344	243
		07	CIN	0.9	58	73%	0%	69%	323	323	359	255	343	313
Colome,Jesus	R	07	WAS	1.1	33	74%	25%	82%	274	239	287	186	311	218
Condrey,Clay	R	07	PHI	1.3	32	67%	100%	100%	290	309	322	206	299	302
Cordero,Chad	R	05	WAS	1.0	87	90%	87%	82%	194	204	242	74	192	205
		06	WAS	1.1	69	81%	88%	82%	236	183	239	113	219	212
		07	WAS	1.0	57	79%	80%	77%	247	276	275	224	221	295
Cordero,Francisco	R	05	TEX	1.0	98	76%	82%	82%	231	236	249	194	250	214
		06	MIL	1.0	90	74%	67%	75%	229	266	260	231	286	219
		07	MIL	1.0	156	74%	86%	80%	187	260	191	340	225	212
Cormier,Rheal	L	05	PHI	0.8	32	65%	0%	84%	303	288	300	308	260	321
		06	CIN	0.8	17	87%	0%	70%	298	240	268	261	286	250
		07	ATL	0.5	3	50%	0%	100%	333	375	400	0	200	500
Corpas,Manuel	R	06	COL	0.9	91	76%	0%	67%	282	291	311	150	281	290
		07	COL	1.0	90	84%	86%	89%	211	245	213	300	234	214

Bullpen Indicators

				BPIs			Results		Runners		Pitch Ct		Platoon	
Pitcher			**Tm**	**IP/g**	**bpv**	**S%**	**Sv%**	**Eff%**	**Emp**	**On**	**1-15**	**16-30**	**vLH**	**vRH**
Correia,Kevin	R	06	SF	1.5	79	73%	0%	92%	215	273	266	241	275	218
		07	SF	1.7	57	76%	0%	62%	244	280	276	246	219	278
Coutlangus,Jon	L	07	CIN	0.6	59	73%	0%	72%	234	267	256	222	231	264
Crain,Jesse	R	05	MIN	1.1	15	79%	25%	75%	218	219	228	185	209	225
		06	MIN	1.1	91	74%	25%	65%	243	289	250	256	259	263
		07	MIN	0.9	47	68%	0%	78%	200	440	224	500	269	308
Cruz,Juan	R	07	ARI	1.2	120	80%	0%	91%	198	211	219	208	269	143
Davis,Jason	R	06	CLE	1.4	87	72%	33%	71%	288	317	281	342	316	294
Davis,Kane	R	07	PHI	1.0	12	78%	0%	75%	333	345	367	313	316	355
Delcarmen,Mann	R	06	BOS	1.1	91	66%	0%	80%	273	345	283	371	319	302
		07	BOS	1.0	93	85%	50%	92%	193	169	195	143	164	196
Dempster,Ryan	R	05	CHC	1.5	79	78%	94%	88%	204	233	196	313	245	197
		06	CHC	1.0	69	68%	73%	60%	269	254	268	265	307	228
		07	CHC	1.0	65	67%	90%	75%	236	245	228	291	259	224
Dohmann,Scott	R	05	COL	1.0	47	67%	0%	69%	250	279	321	86	328	212
		06	KC	1.0	27	67%	33%	60%	330	295	287	415	357	293
		07	TAM	1.1	53	80%	0%	100%	298	214	265	222	241	271
Donnelly,Brendar	R	05	ANA	1.0	65	74%	0%	76%	258	228	260	194	213	274
		06	ANA	1.0	51	74%	0%	94%	234	246	256	194	290	204
		07	BOS	0.8	66	71%	0%	91%	235	234	225	300	212	250
Dotel,Octavio	R	05	OAK	1.0	52	79%	64%	57%	143	212	175	273	269	107
		07	ATL	0.9	117	73%	73%	74%	322	164	278	133	265	225
Downs,Scott	L	06	TOR	1.3	54	72%	25%	72%	246	134	199	203	177	208
		07	TOR	0.7	97	84%	25%	85%	198	250	233	184	209	238
Duchscherer,Justin	R	05	OAK	1.3	126	82%	71%	79%	179	273	211	235	230	203
		06	OAK	1.1	149	75%	82%	90%	276	190	265	182	248	241
		07	OAK	1.0	44	74%	0%	62%	353	200	321	91	400	176
Embree,Alan	L	05	NYY	0.8	45	48%	33%	65%	268	330	303	265	317	278
		06	SD	0.7	108	75%	0%	87%	212	289	256	208	240	258
		07	OAK	1.0	62	69%	81%	85%	252	264	228	344	205	278
Eyre,Scott	L	05	SF	0.8	92	76%	0%	89%	233	167	188	239	182	213
		06	CHC	0.8	67	85%	0%	76%	280	248	298	179	281	255
		07	CHC	1.0	41	77%	0%	58%	258	321	271	339	253	317
Farnsworth,Kyle	R	05	ATL	1.0	116	82%	89%	92%	180	181	168	200	197	165
		06	NYY	0.9	85	70%	60%	73%	209	294	234	292	215	264
		07	NYY	0.9	40	71%	0%	81%	282	227	257	255	273	242
Feliciano,Pedro	L	06	NYM	0.9	87	86%	0%	77%	255	242	270	173	231	266
		07	NYM	0.8	87	75%	67%	88%	233	165	199	208	168	221
Flores,Randy	L	05	STL	0.8	93	76%	33%	83%	280	194	228	310	176	300
		06	STL	0.6	58	68%	0%	90%	286	293	306	182	258	329
		07	STL	0.8	72	71%	50%	95%	261	360	307	333	326	299
Francisco,Frank	R	07	TEX	1.0	42	71%	0%	96%	309	220	245	284	221	286
Franklin,Ryan	R	07	STL	1.2	92	74%	17%	77%	227	244	256	172	238	231
Frasor,Jason	R	05	TOR	1.1	63	78%	33%	73%	248	246	250	244	236	257
		06	TOR	1.0	75	71%	0%	83%	207	293	248	235	211	262
		07	TOR	1.1	93	61%	50%	50%	217	222	213	224	245	200
Fuentes,Brian	L	05	COL	1.0	101	79%	91%	83%	261	171	235	182	164	237
		06	COL	1.0	86	75%	83%	77%	240	173	216	184	183	218
		07	COL	1.0	82	76%	74%	72%	167	271	190	275	204	207
Fultz,Aaron	L	05	PHI	1.3	85	81%	0%	0%	148	267	192	182	286	171
		06	PHI	1.1	67	71%	0%	80%	304	265	262	342	263	291
		07	CLE	0.8	48	79%	0%	79%	208	254	209	308	191	265
Gagne,Eric	R	05	LA	0.9	203	82%	100%	100%	200	200	238	0	217	185
		06	LA	1.0	144	0%	100%	0%	0	0	0	0	0	0
		07	BOS	1.0	79	72%	80%	80%	243	247	247	229	224	265
Gallagher,Sean	R	07	CHC	1.8	-27	61%	100%	0%	185	424	227	389	294	346
Gardner,Lee	R	07	FLA	1.2	69	84%	100%	78%	259	248	209	375	308	208
Geary,Geoff	R	05	PHI	1.5	58	73%	0%	71%	222	277	212	313	192	294
		06	PHI	1.1	81	79%	25%	85%	337	234	303	253	348	249
		07	PHI	1.2	35	72%	0%	71%	318	259	290	263	248	309
Glover,Gary	R	07	TAM	1.2	31	71%	50%	73%	311	262	315	225	286	290
Gobble,Jimmy	L	05	KC	1.9	19	71%	0%	83%	219	371	277	174	304	287
		06	KC	1.4	71	68%	50%	68%	285	243	273	233	289	250
		07	KC	0.7	62	84%	33%	88%	284	270	282	270	241	319
Gonzalez,Mike	L	05	PIT	1.0	91	80%	100%	86%	225	169	207	173	152	223
		06	PIT	1.0	102	83%	100%	88%	168	267	223	184	163	227
		07	ATL	0.9	51	87%	100%	100%	290	200	235	300	333	189
Gordon,Tom	R	05	NYY	1.0	70	81%	22%	78%	210	194	227	103	187	217
		06	PHI	1.0	86	80%	87%	80%	218	250	247	200	185	277
		07	PHI	0.9	69	70%	55%	77%	258	270	276	167	310	222
Grabow,John	L	05	PIT	0.8	48	66%	0%	80%	217	257	242	237	219	250
		06	PIT	1.0	70	73%	0%	79%	223	307	259	214	275	251
		07	PIT	0.8	63	71%	50%	80%	263	291	293	231	238	303
Green,Sean	R	06	SEA	1.3	33	69%	0%	75%	273	286	250	294	190	325
		07	SEA	1.1	57	75%	0%	78%	300	297	292	324	329	286
Gregg,Kevin	R	07	FLA	1.1	76	73%	89%	81%	194	220	166	276	162	247
Grilli,Jason	R	06	DET	1.2	27	71%	0%	79%	239	290	223	319	292	249
		07	DET	1.4	52	66%	0%	76%	245	280	305	226	237	275
Guardado,Eddie	L	05	SEA	1.0	80	83%	88%	83%	234	244	240	239	231	242
		06	CIN	0.9	47	87%	72%	67%	303	288	308	250	234	327
Guerrier,Matt	R	06	MIN	1.8	31	81%	100%	100%	304	273	276	318	337	258
		07	MIN	1.2	92	83%	25%	71%	218	224	232	195	264	187
Gwyn,Marcus	R	07	LAA	1.8	-43	64%	100%	0%	400	333	444	222	300	400

Bullpen Indicators

				BPIs			Results		Runners		Pitch Ct		Platoon	
Pitcher			Tm	IP/g	bpv	S%	Sv%	Eff%	Emp	On	1-15	16-30	vLH	vRH
Hampson,Justin	L	07	SD	1.4	55	76%	0%	67%	234	253	288	217	213	255
Hawkins,LaTroy	R	05	SF	0.9	45	77%	40%	58%	203	370	236	345	228	297
		06	BAL	1.0	44	69%	0%	76%	313	287	314	278	323	285
		07	COL	0.9	53	76%	0%	67%	262	237	222	433	237	266
Heilman,Aaron	R	05	NYM	2.0	98	73%	83%	79%	198	216	207	213	185	225
		06	NYM	1.2	85	69%	0%	76%	205	267	228	239	231	231
		07	NYM	1.1	87	75%	17%	71%	197	261	211	237	234	218
Hennessey,Brad	R	06	SF	2.9	11	71%	100%	57%	192	232	159	255	132	258
		07	SF	1.0	43	77%	79%	78%	298	207	252	280	245	265
Herges,Matt	R	05	ARI	1.0	-23	59%	0%	80%	317	288	346	154	256	333
		06	FLA	1.1	35	75%	0%	61%	318	323	296	386	300	340
		07	COL	1.4	61	73%	0%	73%	170	250	223	164	216	184
Hernandez,Rob	R	05	NYM	1.0	74	81%	40%	71%	211	244	225	258	244	213
		06	NYM	0.9	51	81%	40%	70%	287	205	258	219	293	218
		07	LA	0.9	24	65%	0%	67%	275	347	326	283	259	356
Hoey,James	R	06	BAL	0.8	31	44%	0%	67%	316	400	321	375	375	348
		07	BAL	1.1	26	56%	0%	50%	269	275	210	409	351	218
Hoffman,Trevor	R	05	SD	1.0	131	74%	93%	83%	240	230	235	235	298	179
		06	SD	1.0	98	84%	90%	87%	257	122	212	133	194	214
		07	SD	0.9	70	73%	86%	79%	215	247	230	211	299	169
Howry,Bob	R	05	CLE	0.9	84	74%	60%	87%	181	212	201	148	180	198
		06	CHC	0.9	110	76%	56%	77%	240	250	253	224	247	244
		07	CHC	1.0	95	75%	67%	77%	196	317	269	162	192	283
Huber,Jon	R	06	SEA	1.0	74	88%	0%	89%	143	217	133	308	67	209
		07	SEA	1.3	56	69%	0%	100%	368	250	286	286	400	250
Isringhausen,Jas	R	05	STL	0.9	68	85%	91%	87%	200	205	208	175	168	229
		06	STL	1.0	31	83%	77%	67%	239	202	237	204	270	187
		07	STL	1.0	75	79%	94%	95%	185	170	183	180	196	167
Janssen,Casey	R	07	TOR	1.0	47	82%	55%	80%	240	254	248	254	257	241
Jenks,Bobby	R	05	CHW	1.2	118	80%	75%	77%	224	227	221	268	105	298
		06	CHW	1.0	97	72%	91%	85%	241	266	254	261	227	268
		07	CHW	1.0	131	68%	87%	80%	149	269	202	176	237	169
Johnson,Tyler	L	06	STL	0.7	52	71%	0%	68%	167	296	237	235	221	276
		07	STL	0.7	36	70%	0%	75%	191	240	220	188	224	211
Jones,Todd	R	05	FLA	1.1	131	79%	89%	81%	236	222	220	280	231	229
		06	DET	1.0	60	69%	86%	76%	236	340	249	409	264	284
		07	DET	1.0	31	69%	86%	80%	248	291	261	263	265	269
Julio,Jorge	R	05	BAL	1.1	42	62%	0%	68%	274	261	240	354	281	257
		06	ARI	1.1	84	73%	80%	70%	223	195	190	259	185	234
		07	COL	0.9	61	69%	0%	59%	286	281	306	230	227	322
King,Ray	L	05	STL	0.5	34	81%	0%	67%	236	341	282	400	244	352
		06	COL	0.7	16	77%	50%	77%	364	298	325	350	299	351
		07	MIL	0.6	32	72%	0%	92%	247	250	252	214	187	311
Kline,Steve	L	05	BAL	0.9	8	77%	0%	61%	270	241	281	160	317	209
		06	SF	0.7	45	76%	100%	88%	295	255	258	367	269	280
		07	SF	0.7	-1	70%	50%	75%	330	275	309	241	318	287
Ledezma,Wil	L	07	SD	1.3	30	70%	0%	58%	292	283	294	321	297	283
Lewis,Colby	R	07	OAK	1.5	22	61%	0%	50%	186	322	185	359	273	240
Lewis,Jensen	R	07	CLE	1.1	107	83%	0%	86%	222	246	274	188	244	229
Lidge,Brad	R	05	HOU	1.0	154	83%	91%	85%	239	205	235	186	244	202
		06	HOU	1.0	100	64%	84%	78%	224	256	242	236	286	201
		07	HOU	1.0	116	79%	70%	74%	223	212	213	234	184	243
Lindstrom,Matt	R	07	FLA	0.9	87	75%	0%	79%	230	289	247	280	263	255
Linebrink,Scott	R	05	SD	1.0	101	85%	17%	85%	227	186	208	200	197	221
		06	SD	1.0	81	75%	18%	78%	258	224	248	230	204	294
		07	MIL	1.0	54	79%	12%	68%	268	232	251	258	215	284
Littleton,Wes	R	06	TEX	1.1	38	85%	100%	91%	205	163	176	250	256	157
		07	TEX	1.4	37	71%	67%	70%	221	316	273	236	236	279
Logan,Boone	L	06	CHW	0.8	37	59%	50%	75%	194	378	302	176	357	244
		07	CHW	0.7	40	71%	0%	81%	301	295	248	465	221	357
Lopez,Aquilino	R	07	DET	1.7	7	64%	100%	100%	242	303	233	321	258	286
Lopez,Javier	L	05	ARI	0.5	30	49%	50%	75%	231	417	354	333	278	421
		06	BOS	0.6	45	81%	100%	100%	222	237	204	1000	250	208
		07	BOS	0.7	50	77%	0%	83%	208	274	233	300	293	176
Lyon,Brandon	R	05	ARI	0.9	12	69%	93%	83%	382	311	356	320	317	364
		06	ARI	1.0	52	72%	0%	69%	290	226	294	143	244	270
		07	ARI	1.0	39	78%	40%	86%	294	210	278	146	233	267
Macdougal,Mike	R	05	KC	1.0	95	77%	84%	72%	231	281	266	238	240	270
		06	CHW	1.0	103	85%	50%	87%	180	244	195	250	281	171
		07	CHW	0.8	49	64%	0%	72%	261	311	302	267	298	288
Madson,Ryan	R	05	PHI	1.1	81	70%	0%	76%	247	273	304	160	292	233
		06	PHI	2.7	41	68%	50%	63%	344	256	342	235	296	311
		07	PHI	1.5	64	79%	50%	77%	198	280	222	200	170	275
Mahay,Ron	L	05	TEX	1.2	24	65%	100%	78%	314	313	326	370	302	322
		06	TEX	0.9	62	76%	0%	71%	248	252	245	254	240	258
		07	ATL	1.2	62	82%	50%	92%	227	210	210	203	189	242
Majewski,Gary	R	05	WAS	1.1	54	77%	20%	78%	275	221	223	298	236	259
		06	CIN	1.1	45	70%	0%	52%	303	265	316	203	287	281
		07	CIN	0.7	34	58%	0%	46%	451	351	404	308	333	420
Marmol,Carlos	R	07	CHC	1.2	123	89%	50%	92%	183	154	150	208	209	146
Marshall,Jay	L	07	BOS	0.8	13	61%	0%	71%	269	322	321	256	296	299

Bullpen Indicators

				BPIs			Results		Runners		Pitch Ct		Platoon	
Pitcher			Tm	IP/g	bpv	S%	Sv%	Eff%	Emp	On	1-15	16-30	vLH	vRH
Marte,Damaso	L	05	CHW	0.7	69	81%	50%	78%	222	291	269	222	267	244
		06	PIT	0.8	78	75%	0%	56%	257	230	238	206	225	258
		07	PIT	0.7	107	79%	0%	100%	202	197	211	160	94	271
Mastny,Tom	R	06	CLE	1.1	67	62%	67%	57%	300	258	349	63	273	282
		07	CLE	1.1	49	73%	0%	88%	296	269	246	347	282	283
McBeth,Marcus	R	07	CIN	0.9	44	59%	0%	60%	267	313	328	77	273	295
Mcbride,Macay	L	05	ATL	0.6	151	64%	100%	100%	474	225	209	500	172	433
		06	ATL	0.8	64	75%	50%	88%	269	226	225	359	187	308
		07	DET	0.9	45	74%	0%	83%	232	288	222	355	263	254
Meredith,Cla	R	06	SD	1.1	153	91%	0%	88%	216	114	161	200	281	107
		07	SD	1.0	97	76%	0%	58%	267	327	295	262	286	303
Mesa,Jose	R	05	PIT	1.0	32	71%	79%	67%	317	257	291	229	309	265
		06	COL	0.9	18	78%	12%	64%	254	289	274	262	270	271
		07	PHI	0.9	20	55%	100%	77%	235	313	247	381	263	280
Messenger,Rand	R	06	FLA	1.0	44	66%	0%	58%	299	293	265	338	333	267
		07	SF	1.1	17	75%	20%	64%	314	343	357	292	342	320
Miller,Justin	R	07	FLA	1.0	108	72%	0%	88%	242	213	252	148	324	184
Miller,Trever	L	05	TAM	0.7	44	77%	0%	72%	239	308	282	257	267	289
		06	HOU	0.7	113	79%	33%	75%	271	176	234	161	221	228
		07	HOU	0.6	61	69%	33%	87%	205	290	242	333	209	289
Miner,Zach	R	07	DET	1.6	44	80%	0%	67%	326	222	318	210	219	312
Moehler,Brian	R	07	HOU	1.4	46	75%	100%	43%	282	280	252	273	303	268
Morrow,Brandon	R	07	SEA	1.1	58	75%	0%	78%	222	265	277	187	278	221
Mota,Guillermo	R	05	FLA	1.2	68	67%	50%	82%	231	279	283	211	243	262
		06	NYM	1.1	32	75%	0%	81%	261	253	237	300	252	261
		07	NYM	1.1	65	59%	0%	62%	225	317	264	215	235	284
Moylan,Peter	R	07	ATL	1.1	76	87%	50%	78%	215	199	223	171	242	184
Munoz,Arnie	L	07	WAS	0.4	2	82%	0%	80%	300	250	286	0	286	267
Myers,Brett	R	07	PHI	1.3	113	70%	88%	74%	224	237	226	211	165	282
Myers,Mike	L	05	BOS	0.6	43	75%	0%	86%	266	186	226	200	158	385
		06	NYY	0.5	59	78%	0%	86%	176	294	267	67	254	229
		07	CHW	0.8	25	70%	0%	77%	255	296	271	262	292	262
Nathan,Joe	R	05	MIN	1.0	143	75%	90%	85%	165	215	171	224	158	206
		06	MIN	1.1	188	82%	95%	96%	168	141	176	63	193	130
		07	MIN	1.1	129	84%	90%	87%	174	262	209	207	221	199
Neshek,Pat	R	06	MIN	1.2	219	87%	0%	78%	202	128	157	225	244	140
		07	MIN	1.0	99	75%	0%	81%	171	197	167	255	181	185
O Flaherty,Eric	L	07	SEA	0.9	53	61%	0%	85%	218	247	228	267	183	277
Ohman,Will	L	05	CHC	0.6	58	84%	0%	75%	202	200	194	286	173	231
		06	CHC	0.8	82	70%	0%	91%	190	227	215	224	157	245
		07	CHC	0.6	54	69%	100%	79%	296	269	298	136	236	325
Okajima,Hideki	L	07	BOS	1.0	112	82%	71%	90%	230	168	219	155	236	182
Oliver,Darren	L	06	NYM	1.8	57	77%	0%	88%	215	259	259	161	208	244
		07	LAA	1.1	63	71%	0%	92%	222	263	219	221	289	209
Osoria,Franquelis	R	07	PIT	1.1	28	68%	0%	67%	278	300	307	241	353	263
Otsuka,Akinori	R	05	SD	0.9	76	74%	14%	64%	277	190	230	220	207	263
		06	TEX	1.0	119	82%	89%	84%	250	229	242	233	287	190
		07	TEX	1.0	83	74%	57%	81%	197	250	212	250	172	262
Owens,Henry	R	07	FLA	1.0	42	92%	80%	92%	207	233	213	261	262	174
Papelbon,Jon	R	05	BOS	2.0	64	87%	0%	78%	262	259	262	292	200	308
		06	BOS	1.2	169	92%	85%	83%	199	112	180	132	203	128
		07	BOS	1.0	189	82%	92%	87%	123	187	161	83	104	200
Paronto,Chad	R	06	ATL	0.9	61	78%	0%	67%	245	259	273	147	288	234
		07	ATL	1.0	-1	77%	50%	75%	284	326	288	302	333	287
Parrish,John	L	07	SEA	1.0	35	68%	0%	75%	198	362	328	200	293	298
Peguero,Jailen	R	07	ARI	0.8	4	54%	0%	100%	208	387	279	400	240	367
Pena,Tony	R	06	ARI	1.2	39	66%	100%	60%	253	356	309	289	382	179
		07	ARI	1.1	65	73%	40%	84%	209	205	211	205	245	176
Peralta,Joel	R	06	KC	1.2	76	68%	33%	79%	276	250	271	259	338	234
		07	KC	1.4	79	73%	20%	56%	289	260	286	266	248	290
Percival,Troy	R	07	STL	1.2	106	84%	0%	100%	161	186	218	30	214	138
Perez,Rafael	L	07	CLE	1.4	137	86%	50%	82%	185	191	147	254	145	213
Perkins,Glen	L	07	MIN	1.5	50	76%	0%	100%	233	232	286	200	250	222
Pinto,Renyel	L	06	FLA	1.1	66	84%	100%	100%	156	217	207	222	150	215
		07	FLA	1.0	71	76%	17%	68%	271	167	228	200	210	227
Proctor,Scott	R	06	NYY	1.2	71	75%	12%	74%	216	251	236	210	204	250
		07	LA	1.0	32	79%	0%	68%	274	204	253	202	250	237
Putz,J.J.	R	05	SEA	0.9	46	78%	25%	78%	236	276	225	364	321	197
		06	SEA	1.1	226	76%	84%	85%	176	257	200	229	211	204
		07	SEA	1.1	194	89%	95%	94%	180	109	173	26	148	158
Qualls,Chad	R	05	HOU	1.0	72	75%	0%	88%	263	234	251	242	218	275
		06	HOU	1.1	46	71%	0%	77%	242	242	258	181	227	253
		07	HOU	1.0	96	82%	50%	76%	292	252	264	333	248	289
Ramirez,Edwar	R	07	NYY	1.0	84	59%	33%	62%	225	341	241	400	342	239
Ramirez,Ramon	R	06	COL	1.1	76	74%	0%	74%	241	218	265	141	274	194
		07	COL	0.8	51	44%	0%	71%	321	308	316	300	240	357
Rauch,Jon	R	06	WAS	1.1	63	79%	40%	75%	215	252	257	180	254	216
		07	WAS	1.0	81	69%	40%	82%	200	278	230	232	208	249
Ray,Chris	R	05	BAL	1.0	74	85%	0%	56%	208	237	218	261	284	174
		06	BAL	1.1	41	84%	87%	80%	188	202	221	119	184	202
		07	BAL	1.0	90	67%	80%	68%	190	276	218	216	233	212
Reyes,Al	R	07	TAM	1.0	100	65%	87%	78%	176	279	185	281	240	187

Bullpen Indicators

Pitcher			Tm	BPIs IP/g	bpv	S%	Results Sv%	Eff%	Runners Emp	On	Pitch Ct 1-15	16-30	Platoon vLH	vRH
Reyes,Dennys	L	05	SD	1.4	39	74%	0%	100%	192	237	219	190	136	262
		06	MIN	0.8	105	96%	0%	95%	229	151	205	143	148	244
		07	MIN	0.6	38	78%	0%	91%	302	319	293	455	273	364
Rhodes,Arthur	L	05	CLE	0.9	117	81%	0%	83%	220	188	200	235	286	155
		06	PHI	0.8	79	67%	57%	77%	224	305	243	333	286	248
Rincon,Juan	R	05	MIN	1.0	111	79%	0%	74%	229	219	207	278	218	228
		06	MIN	1.0	97	77%	33%	91%	273	266	260	313	222	303
		07	MIN	0.9	50	70%	0%	77%	270	277	272	292	313	236
Riske,David	R	05	CLE	1.2	62	76%	100%	50%	201	220	212	187	213	204
		06	CHW	1.1	38	75%	0%	50%	236	247	254	233	280	224
		07	KC	1.1	56	86%	50%	72%	281	193	267	175	202	265
Rivera,Mariano	R	05	NYY	1.1	142	85%	91%	86%	166	194	166	179	177	176
		06	NYY	1.2	132	83%	92%	83%	258	174	237	194	192	250
		07	NYY	1.1	168	72%	88%	80%	245	252	257	208	255	241
Rivera,Saul	R	06	WAS	1.1	46	78%	33%	87%	232	263	275	209	194	290
		07	WAS	1.1	48	71%	60%	76%	298	215	275	231	271	244
Rodney,Fernandc	R	05	DET	1.1	73	82%	60%	61%	273	207	283	130	265	219
		06	DET	1.1	67	72%	64%	80%	185	208	176	214	202	192
		07	DET	1.1	92	69%	33%	65%	200	276	262	207	247	231
Rodriguez,Francs	R	05	ANA	1.0	105	81%	90%	82%	190	173	184	154	213	153
		06	ANA	1.1	124	89%	92%	88%	201	191	202	176	215	179
		07	LAA	1.1	116	78%	87%	85%	205	204	230	138	187	217
Romero,J.C.	L	05	MIN	0.8	43	81%	0%	79%	248	223	244	214	198	268
		06	ANA	0.7	41	60%	0%	73%	225	363	300	333	202	382
		07	PHI	0.8	57	88%	50%	90%	250	158	209	176	208	198
Rosario,Francisc	R	07	PHI	1.1	46	70%	100%	40%	315	327	305	351	340	304
Rowland-Smith,R	L	07	SEA	1.5	86	74%	0%	100%	301	236	311	289	275	266
Ryan,B.J.	L	05	BAL	1.0	142	80%	88%	80%	229	181	193	246	211	206
		06	TOR	1.1	150	86%	90%	87%	190	142	196	85	120	182
		07	TOR	0.9	-8	50%	60%	43%	250	444	231	667	333	333
Saarloos,Kirk	R	06	OAK	3.5	1	75%	67%	0%	266	278	259	371	347	217
		07	CIN	1.3	29	60%	0%	45%	293	263	270	367	233	303
Saito,Takashi	R	06	LA	1.1	161	78%	92%	90%	159	206	170	164	227	129
		07	LA	1.0	192	88%	91%	89%	143	169	155	135	186	114
Sarfate,Dennis	R	07	HOU	1.2	392	83%	0%	100%	105	300	211	125	182	167
Schoeneweis,S	L	05	TOR	0.7	67	75%	25%	78%	238	252	246	240	188	306
		06	CIN	0.7	35	65%	67%	87%	200	310	233	364	236	257
		07	NYM	0.8	43	70%	67%	81%	319	221	243	373	204	316
Seanez,Rudy	R	05	SD	1.1	138	79%	0%	86%	220	223	255	138	231	212
		06	SD	1.1	50	74%	0%	55%	263	277	259	250	266	273
		07	LA	1.0	76	77%	33%	69%	261	273	306	165	269	264
Seay,Bobby	L	07	DET	0.8	74	79%	50%	93%	284	165	209	333	209	250
Sherrill,George	L	05	SEA	0.7	98	53%	0%	81%	188	200	204	182	156	273
		06	SEA	0.6	89	67%	100%	83%	194	232	217	158	143	297
		07	SEA	0.6	122	80%	43%	87%	222	143	174	208	156	212
Shields,Scot	R	05	ANA	1.2	99	77%	54%	75%	186	220	205	202	199	203
		06	ANA	1.2	101	77%	25%	75%	217	218	232	174	207	227
		07	LAA	1.1	88	70%	25%	77%	199	243	242	170	214	226
Shouse,Brian	L	05	TEX	0.8	41	64%	0%	78%	200	340	247	342	209	337
		06	MIL	0.6	31	76%	40%	75%	200	333	244	429	238	309
		07	MIL	0.7	68	73%	25%	85%	260	255	275	167	214	295
Shuey,Paul	R	07	BAL	1.0	31	51%	100%	88%	304	328	286	267	355	301
Sisco,Andy	L	05	KC	1.1	71	81%	0%	62%	273	217	301	175	216	255
		06	KC	0.9	38	61%	20%	50%	286	292	297	262	318	271
		07	CHW	0.7	23	61%	0%	80%	364	275	295	333	250	367
Slaten,Doug	L	07	ARI	0.6	47	86%	0%	77%	305	239	273	294	268	284
Smith,Joe	R	07	NYM	0.8	83	79%	0%	87%	203	327	274	257	298	266
Smith,Matt	L	06	PHI	0.8	92	89%	0%	86%	105	111	82	231	167	85
		07	PHI	0.4	5	67%	0%	100%	222	286	231	333	400	182
Soriano,Rafael	R	06	SEA	1.1	97	85%	33%	78%	214	192	232	121	244	179
		07	ATL	1.0	132	76%	75%	84%	165	221	190	154	164	197
Soria,Joakim	R	07	KC	1.1	131	74%	81%	80%	173	211	168	246	167	200
Speier,Justin	R	05	TOR	1.0	83	83%	0%	70%	191	211	210	137	167	219
		06	TOR	0.9	87	81%	0%	90%	235	235	254	143	183	264
		07	LAA	1.0	112	76%	0%	87%	220	179	193	257	222	186
Springer,Russ	R	05	HOU	1.0	62	64%	0%	67%	205	247	206	286	209	231
		06	HOU	0.8	57	75%	0%	91%	220	198	221	156	253	187
		07	STL	0.9	112	77%	0%	86%	191	167	178	175	235	158
Stanton,Mike	L	05	BOS	0.7	53	69%	0%	75%	307	286	318	250	235	358
		06	SF	0.8	68	70%	57%	70%	289	261	272	298	271	276
		07	CIN	0.8	39	63%	0%	65%	281	350	316	328	306	321
Stokes,Brian	R	07	TAM	1.1	12	63%	0%	53%	354	333	341	344	346	341
Street,Huston	R	05	OAK	1.2	98	84%	85%	85%	192	197	194	195	224	172
		06	OAK	1.0	144	70%	77%	74%	205	276	238	242	274	211
		07	OAK	1.0	164	74%	76%	79%	179	213	184	222	224	162
Switzer,Jon	L	06	TAM	0.8	9	77%	0%	58%	328	243	274	320	220	321
		07	TAM	0.9	17	53%	0%	60%	342	333	365	304	242	404
Tankersley,Taylo	L	06	FLA	0.8	71	84%	43%	84%	246	214	231	182	232	225
		07	FLA	0.7	68	75%	33%	88%	286	213	243	250	179	301

Bullpen Indicators

Pitcher			Tm	BPIs IP/g	bpv	S%	Results Sv%	Eff%	Runners Emp	On	Pitch Ct 1-15	16-30	Platoon vLH	vRH
Taschner,Jack	L	05	SF	0.9	77	86%	0%	83%	238	128	193	182	265	128
		06	SF	0.8	31	59%	0%	60%	316	365	359	318	275	400
		07	SF	0.8	63	62%	0%	84%	236	235	250	214	316	176
Thornton,Matt	L	05	SEA	1.0	21	76%	0%	50%	292	213	262	167	262	235
		06	CHW	0.9	73	76%	40%	81%	223	235	213	316	211	240
		07	CHW	0.8	71	68%	29%	72%	245	289	303	146	283	260
Timlin,Mike	R	05	BOS	1.0	95	83%	65%	81%	281	271	275	299	299	257
		06	BOS	0.9	35	72%	53%	72%	306	303	301	328	306	303
		07	BOS	1.1	49	74%	100%	92%	233	232	205	333	173	274
Torres,Salomon	R	05	PIT	1.2	44	79%	100%	76%	233	208	212	221	272	189
		06	PIT	1.0	64	78%	80%	80%	294	255	265	298	281	269
		07	PIT	0.9	74	63%	67%	66%	193	391	255	364	275	278
Tsao,Chin-hui	R	05	COL	1.1	-37	72%	75%	80%	455	231	389	167	462	182
		07	LA	1.2	55	61%	0%	60%	220	184	164	316	195	213
Turnbow,Derrick	R	05	MIL	1.0	87	88%	91%	91%	226	165	205	150	235	165
		06	MIL	0.9	65	60%	75%	65%	239	270	240	313	245	263
		07	MIL	0.9	98	64%	25%	83%	132	241	160	277	172	189
Valverde,Jose	R	05	ARI	1.1	120	80%	88%	81%	222	200	236	172	168	241
		06	ARI	1.1	109	61%	82%	75%	245	268	270	246	323	192
		07	ARI	1.0	112	82%	87%	81%	197	194	203	173	202	189
Veras,Jose	R	07	NYY	1.0	48	54%	100%	100%	250	111	130	125	154	190
Villanueva,Carlos	R	07	MIL	1.9	57	75%	33%	78%	209	278	229	219	230	243
Villarreal,Oscar	R	07	ATL	1.5	55	70%	50%	62%	222	304	263	253	315	220
Villone,Ron	L	05	FLA	0.8	84	72%	11%	68%	181	298	263	170	222	258
		06	NYY	1.1	47	70%	0%	67%	239	259	237	240	185	286
		07	NYY	1.1	34	69%	0%	80%	184	299	247	150	239	230
Vizcaino,Luis	R	05	CHW	1.1	33	78%	0%	65%	282	268	276	257	321	242
		06	ARI	0.9	79	75%	0%	78%	229	194	216	196	163	256
		07	NYY	1.0	46	71%	0%	81%	200	270	221	271	265	213
Wagner,Billy	L	05	PHI	1.0	131	88%	93%	88%	176	147	174	143	128	173
		06	NYM	1.0	138	85%	89%	86%	248	171	250	136	161	234
		07	NYM	1.0	119	80%	87%	84%	229	198	223	150	241	209
Wagner,Ryan	R	05	CIN	1.1	71	61%	0%	83%	294	313	285	360	311	297
		06	WAS	1.2	37	73%	0%	55%	273	309	299	229	197	387
Walker,Jamie	L	05	DET	0.7	54	74%	0%	78%	250	264	268	185	245	271
		06	DET	0.9	94	85%	0%	92%	252	250	257	225	238	262
		07	BAL	0.8	53	76%	54%	79%	246	241	248	217	216	268
Walker,Tyler	R	05	SF	0.9	50	77%	82%	78%	231	343	292	241	287	276
		06	TAM	1.0	63	50%	71%	60%	350	224	253	364	333	226
		07	SF	1.0	55	88%	0%	90%	182	308	238	500	182	308
Wassermann,E	R	07	CHW	0.7	67	74%	0%	83%	243	234	250	143	533	174
Weathers,David	R	05	CIN	1.1	62	71%	79%	79%	229	258	244	222	265	226
		06	CIN	1.1	24	80%	63%	69%	234	216	230	239	219	230
		07	CIN	1.1	42	70%	85%	74%	222	248	247	188	254	218
Wheeler,Dan	R	05	HOU	1.0	101	83%	60%	81%	205	202	225	145	204	204
		06	HOU	1.0	92	81%	75%	82%	204	245	232	200	273	183
		07	TAM	1.1	103	62%	61%	65%	179	371	239	284	260	253
White,Rick	R	05	PIT	1.1	47	76%	67%	69%	286	329	273	375	314	305
		06	PHI	1.0	42	65%	50%	86%	261	330	283	340	299	290
		07	SEA	1.2	10	57%	0%	71%	278	386	365	333	298	347
White,William	L	07	TEX	1.0	64	71%	0%	100%	333	190	294	250	286	211
Wickman,Bob	R	05	CLE	1.0	38	88%	90%	83%	306	149	279	98	243	250
		06	ATL	1.0	100	78%	89%	77%	274	223	267	158	267	236
		07	ARI	0.9	42	77%	77%	71%	270	257	253	310	277	252
Wilson,Brian	R	06	SF	1.0	55	67%	50%	64%	404	177	280	294	348	235
		07	SF	1.0	90	77%	86%	84%	218	133	178	182	304	145
Wilson,C.J.	L	05	TEX	2.0	41	58%	100%	46%	140	270	213	286	178	204
		06	TEX	1.0	60	74%	50%	67%	218	247	241	238	155	292
		07	TEX	1.0	84	76%	86%	91%	171	248	209	243	112	275
Wise,Matt	R	05	MIL	1.3	79	68%	33%	71%	153	170	125	193	130	187
		06	MIL	1.1	37	75%	0%	66%	275	258	283	217	206	310
		07	MIL	1.0	52	73%	50%	85%	284	286	294	269	264	296
Wolfe,Brian	R	07	TOR	1.2	62	75%	0%	75%	231	214	228	190	348	130
Wuertz,Mike	R	05	CHC	1.0	89	72%	0%	83%	208	232	218	231	260	197
		06	CHC	1.0	78	85%	0%	82%	200	253	207	231	184	245
		07	CHC	1.0	84	78%	0%	77%	255	210	246	203	241	232
Yates,Tyler	R	06	ATL	0.9	48	76%	17%	60%	196	268	240	188	217	235
		07	ATL	0.9	79	64%	67%	81%	222	283	257	220	310	213
Zagurski,Mike	L	07	PHI	0.9	58	67%	0%	75%	231	333	300	235	216	340
Zumaya,Joel	R	06	DET	1.3	92	87%	17%	82%	162	207	174	228	183	188
		07	DET	1.2	56	65%	20%	61%	141	241	200	156	271	135

Injuries

The bane of our existence

The impact of injuries has always infected our player values. But the rampant increase in health woes — and our inability to manage the fallout — has put us all at a severe disadvantage. Here is the problem in a nutshell...

Players get hurt. No news here. However, for whatever reason, players are getting hurt more often and for longer periods these days. This is counterintuitive given the constant progress in medical research, but nobody seems to be bothered by that little tidbit.

Hurt players can potentially lose a lot, given the high salaries and the lack of stability of major league jobs. Therefore...

There is an incentive for players to hide injuries, and

There is an incentive for teams to hide injuries, since nobody wants to show their hand to the competition.

For those injuries we do know about, **HIPAA laws restrict the dissemination of information**, which you all should know if you've been to a doctor in the past few years and had to sign those forms.

All team doctors and trainers were informed during the 2006 winter meetings that they were no longer permitted to speak with the media, leaving all media contact to the obviously-more-medically-trained GMs and field managers.

So, when it comes to even marginally accurate info on players' health status, we're all pretty much in the dark.

How do we deal with this?

For the extreme risk-averse, you can simply avoid all hurt players. That means you can choose to ignore nearly a third of the player pool. Of course, even that will not prevent you from rostering the next emergency appendectomy.

You can become more educated about injuries. Injury analysis has to be a vital element of our draft prep and roster management. We need to know which types of injuries are now in vogue and which teams are best at managing their players' health. These days, ADPs are not enough. We also need to know ADTs (average DL times).

We can also become smarter when it comes to injuries:

At the draft table

1. Make sure your projected values are appropriately discounted for injury risk. That might be via some reduction in expected playing time, or a manual adjustment to the dollar value. Don't go into your draft and expect to adjust on the fly. Either you'll forget, or you end up following the marketplace (which may be wrong).

How much to discount? This is not an exact science, but you can do some "back-of-the-envelope" calculations. If you think it is reasonable to expect a player to miss a month of action, then discount by 17% (one month out of six). For a player like Chris Carpenter, who is expected back sometime in August, perhaps a 75% reduction in his $25 potential (and a maximum bid of $6). But all players with injury concerns, or an injury history, need to be discounted, even just a little. Hedging your bets = good tactical management.

2. It is a viable strategy to incorporate an injury risk budget into your draft plan. As long as you have a grasp of fair value for all players, designate some roster slots for risky picks with upside. I'd suggest no more than three slots, unless you are playing for 2009, in which case you should grab as many discounted players as you can.

3. Don't wimp out when it comes to injured players. Decide who you are going to take a chance on and who you will let pass. Don't be sitting in the middle of the draft with a $9 Brian Giles on the board thinking, "should I or shouldn't I?" Know what you are going to, and stick to it.

During the season

One of the reasons my Tout Wars team failed in 2006 was that I spent most of the first two months with nearly all of my high-priced batters on the DL. However, my attitude was one of acceptance; there was still a long season ahead and I'd have all these players back in time to help my team.

The error in my thinking was that these players would come back at their expected productivity levels. The reality was that some remained hobbled all year, and some just underperformed (though they may not have been completely healed either). Perhaps it is possible that the reduced availability of PEDs might be preventing players from rebounding to form as quickly as they had in the past.

So in the future, it might be advisable to view all injured players as sell-high candidates. Consider this scenario:

You draft Ben Sheets for $18. By mid-May, he's perhaps 4-2 with a 3.25 ERA but then hits the DL again. The prognosis is a short stay. Normally, you'd find a cheap, short-term replacement and ride out the DL stint.

What I am suggesting now is that as soon as Sheets hits the DL (or shortly before, if your league prohibits trading DLed players), you aggressively work the trade wires and try to get something for him. Optimally, look to get at least 50 cents on the dollar (in this case, at least $9 of value).

What this buys you... For starters, at least $9 of more stable value. There is no guarantee that Sheets will be fully productive upon his return or that he won't get hurt again. Realistically, those $9 could even represent profit over what Sheets might do the rest of the season.

The second thing this tactic does is shifts risk away from your team and onto someone else's roster. Of course, if Sheets returns to full productivity, you lose, but the underlying percentage play on this is that a full return is not likely. In fact, Sheets' $18 value may even be inflated since he is already missing time, and his future value is also depressed, so the drop in return value from $18 to $9 is really not as steep as it seems.

And finding a trading partner who will deal you $9 of value for $18 of potential may not be that difficult. If you had a $9 Tim Wakefield or Heath Bell, wouldn't you take a chance on Ben Sheets, even up? And as a Sheets owner, wouldn't you rather have one of those arms and sleep easier at night?

Perhaps, when it comes down to it, the goal of injury management is to allow you to sleep easier.

Hidden injuries: 2008 Speculations

by Ray Murphy

Along the continuing theme of "evaluating players based on unreliable information", we are not always aware of a player's health condition. Often, the truth will eventually come out: a player reports to spring training and says "my knee/shoulder/back really hampered me last year. But I'm 100% now!" Rather than wait for such an admission, we can speculate on some 2007 disappointments that may be rooted in unreported or under-reported injuries.

In a season riddled with underperforming power hitters, **Travis Hafner's** (DH, CLE) case was particularly mystifying. His skills were all trending upward entering 2007, a monster year seemed on the way. What happened? Remnants of 2006 may be relevant here: specifically, the broken hand that ended his 2006 season. Lingering effects of that injury could be responsible for Hafner's disappointing 2007. His season-high 152 PX in September offers hope for a 2008 rebound.

The infuriating thing about **Richie Sexson's** (1B, SEA) season was that his BPIs stayed largely intact while his production plunged. His H% was down substantially, which we can attribute to luck. Or can we? Sexson's PX also plummeted. When we see BPIs intact and raw power down (for a once-prolific power hitter), injury is a clear possibility. So many types of injuries can sap power. Sexson has a history of shoulder issues. Or was he having leg problems all year, before the hamstring injury that shut him down in September? Such an injury could impact his power, feeding the hit rate decline.

J.D. Drew (OF, BOS) was a monumental disappointment in 2007, although a hot September softened the blow. He missed short bursts of time for a variety of reasons, among them a bad back and a family medical issue. Also recall that his contract with BOS was delayed due to concerns about his shoulder. There may not be a single root cause for his lost season. An accumulation of seemingly minor issues, both physical and mental, could have been contributing factors. A 2008 rebound may be on the way.

Jason Bay (OF, PIT) hit our hidden injury radar very early in the season, due to his lack of SB attempts. The SB outage proved to be a leading indicator, as Bay's overall production fell well short of expectations. Without a diagnosis, projecting 2008 is a speculative exercise at best. But someone on the "good" side of 30 should not see his skills evaporate in this way. A leg injury that sapped both speed and power remains a plausible explanation.

Cliff Lee (SP, CLE) has never been the most durable of pitchers. After a terrible summer that left him in Triple-A, we can look back at his history and see that he was not the same pitcher as in prior seasons. After 600 IP of 2.0+ Cmd from 2004-2006, his Cmd dipped to 1.7 this year. Perhaps he was just never quite right after missing April due to injury, or he was negatively impacted by not having a proper spring training, or had a mechanical issue. But since Lee owns the better skills from his past, we should anticipate some improvement in 2008.

Bronson Arroyo (SP, CIN) was among the league leaders in pitches thrown in 2006. During 2007, workload seemed to be an ongoing issue. He went through a three-start stretch of high pitch counts in May (120-117-129) that triggered a month of struggles. Our research suggests that some pitchers may react adversely to high pitch counts; the evidence says that Arroyo is one such case. In July, he followed a 123-pitch PQS-5 outing with a 58-pitch PQS-0, then came back strong with another PQS-5. Between May 6 and September 2, Arroyo could not manage consecutive PQS-DOM starts. More considerate handling may be what he needs to once again be a strong SP option.

Dontrelle Willis (SP, FLA) is another pitcher who seems to be feeling some obvious and adverse effects of his workload. There is no "smoking gun" sequence of starts as with Arroyo. However, it is worth noting a sequence of starts from June, where he alternated PQS-DOM and PQS-0 outings for a solid month. Following that stretch, things got worse. Willis only managed one more PQS-DOM outing until late September. Willis' future career path may resemble that of Javier Vazquez, another pitcher who suffered from high workloads, and then struggled to find consistency for several years thereafter.

Justin Morneau (1B, MIN) hit 28 HR thru July, then managed only three more for the rest of the season. This power outage does not correlate well to the bruised lung he suffered in a June collision. But could that collision be a root cause anyway? Between the reported bruised lung from that collision, some allusions to related back trouble, and a foot problem suffered in August, Morneau may have simply been "beat up" by the end of the season.

Eric Gagne (RP, BOS) struggled upon arrival in BOS in August, and missed some time in September with a sore arm. Usage patterns from his final days before the July trade suggest the problem dates back to TEX: he had his busiest stretch of the season (67 pitches in 4 days) from July 21-24, then was shut down from July 25 thru the trade deadline. It is possible that Gagne felt something after that three-games-in-four-days stretch, and TEX shut him down to hide the situation from potential trade partners. If Gagne's 2008 team is willing to coddle him a bit more, he may yet re-emerge as a capable closer option.

Scott Olsen (SP, FLA) had some well-documented off-field problems in 2007. Were they the root cause for his sophomore slump? Perhaps not: Olsen's workload had jumped by 80 IP from 2005 to 2006. Perhaps that should have been a warning sign for this 23-year old. His 2007 performance could best be described as "erratic". In particular his Ctl bounced up and down from month to month. FLA wisely eased his workload in the 2nd half (80 IP, only three 100-plus pitch outings). That discipline could yield rewards in 2008.

Andruw Jones (OF, ATL) had the worst year of his career in 2007, in terms of both BA and power. Jones has occasionally missed time due to back problems in recent years. He remains remarkably durable, consistently playing 150-plus games a year at a demanding defensive position. As Jones enters his 30s, is it possible that his legs and back can no longer handle that workload? If Jones' new team tries limiting him to six games per week, his overall production may increase despite the lost ABs.

Off-Season Injury Report
By Rick Wilton

Erik Bedard (LHP, BAL): The Orioles shut him down in early September due to a strained oblique injury. He'll be 100% in spring training.

Danys Baez (RHP, BAL) underwent Tommy John surgery in the fall and will miss the 2008 season.

Rocco Baldelli (OF, TAM) was shut down with hamstring injuries late in the year even though the Devil Rays admitted he did not have a serious injury. He is a huge injury risk until he can prove he can stay healthy.

Kris Benson (RHP, BAL) needed surgery to repair a torn labrum and rotator cuff back in March 2007. He is a long shot to return to form at this point in his career.

Chris Capuano (LHP, MIL): The good news is the labrum surgery was on his non-pitching shoulder. The rehab process should have him ready for spring training and should not cost him time in 2008.

Chris Carpenter (RHP, STL) underwent Tommy John surgery July 24 and the Cardinals expect him back for the last two months of 2008.

Jesse Crain (RHP, MIN): Surgery was needed in May 2007 to repair a torn rotator cuff and labrum. While the Twins are optimistic for 2008, this extensive type of surgery has ended more than one career.

Joe Crede (3B, CHW) finally underwent back surgery (microdiscectomy) in September to end an extended period of back woes. If the disc surgery is successful, the White Sox believe he will be pain-free in 2008.

Bobby Crosby (SS, OAK) just can't stay healthy. A fractured left hand cost him playing time late in the year. He has yet to play in more than 97 games the last three seasons. Enough said.

Justin Duchscherer (RHP, OAK) needed surgery in July to help alleviate the pain caused by a an arthritic right hip. The A's expect him back and healthy by spring training.

Shelley Duncan (OF, NYY) underwent hernia surgery in late October and the Yanks believe he will be ready to play by February.

Adam Dunn (OF, CIN) had surgery on his right knee to repair some damage to the meniscus. He should be very close to 100% by the start of spring training.

Ryan Freel (OF, CIN): August surgery on his right knee repaired damage to the cartilage and he also had a lesion on the bone removed. Barring a setback, he should be ready to go with little or no restrictions coming Opening Day.

Freddy Garcia's (RHP, PHI) surgery in August repaired a frayed rotator cuff and labrum. He's a free agent but of little value until he can demonstrate he's healthy again.

Nomar Garciaparra (SS, LA) posted another injury-marred season though he did manage 431 at-bats. The strained left calf muscle that plagued him late in the season was still preventing him from running as of early November. That being said, it should be cleared up by the start of spring training.

Brian Giles (OF, SD) underwent micro-fracture surgery on his right knee in October. This is tricky surgery as each player reacts differently to it. He could start the 2008 season on the DL if he is slow to heal over the winter.

Troy Glaus (3B, TOR): A plantar fasciitis issue, inflamed tendon and aches and pains with his feet bugged him most of the season. He underwent surgery to repair nerve damage (nerve decompression) to his left foot in September. Glaus plays through injuries but his durability becomes an issue if he gets hurt again in 2008. Don't forget about a chronically sore left shoulder too.

Rich Harden (RHP, OAK): The irritated shoulder capsule in his pitching shoulder did not respond to treatment fast enough to allow him to return at the end of the season. The elbow and shoulder maladies that plagued him in 2007 make him a huge injury risk in 2008. Don't get fooled by a great spring.

Trevor Hoffman (RHP, SD): The surgery he underwent just after the end of the season removed bone chips from his pitching elbow. The surgery was considered minor and he should take his regular throwing turn once spring training starts.

Luke Hudson (RHP, KC) had surgery on his pitching shoulder in June and missed the rest of the season. The Royals have not officially released what the surgery repaired.

Josh Johnson (RHP, FLA) underwent Tommy John surgery in early August. He isn't expected back in 2008.

Randy Johnson (LHP, ARI) now has endured a herniation to the same lumbar disc twice in the last year. Combine this fact with his age (44) and he is a risky investment at best in 2008.

Mark Kotsay (OF, OAK) had back surgery on March 8 to repair damage from a herniated disc in his lumbar spine. While he managed 200+ at-bats in 2007, he was still dealing with back issues at season's end.

Francisco Liriano (LHP, MIN) underwent Tommy John surgery in November 2006. He was throwing off a pitching mound by October and the Twins believe he will be ready to join the rotation in spring training.

Mark Lowe (RHP, SEA) needed surgery in spring training to remove scar tissue that was causing pain in his pitching elbow. The Mariners believe he'll be ready by spring training.

Dustin Moseley (RHP, LAA) needed surgery in October to relieve irritation of the ulna nerve in his pitching elbow. He is expected to be close to 100% by the start of spring training.

Mark Mulder (LHP, STL): The torn labrum that was surgically repaired in 2006 healed, but rotator cuff issues required another round of surgery in late September. The medical staff believes he'll be ready to take his regular turn in spring training. Still, he remains a question mark.

Pat Neshek (RHP, MIN): The Twins believe they caught the source of his elbow troubles late in the season – a weak pitching shoulder. He'll rehab over the winter and should be OK by the start of spring training.

Ricky Nolasco (RHP, FLA) spent part of the fall in the Arizona Fall League trying to test his troublesome pitching elbow. His velocity returned but that's not the big question. Can he avoid another season of elbow issues in 2008? Time will tell.

Akinori Otsuka (RHP, TEX): The Rangers shut him down late in the year due to arm fatigue and tightness in his pitching forearm. He bypassed surgery and hopes a rehab program will get his pitching arm ready by the start of spring training. Avoiding surgery now does not guarantee success in the future. He is somewhat risky in 2008.

Carl Pavano (RHP, NYY) will go down as one of the biggest free agent busts in history. There isn't any reason to believe he can get healthy and stay healthy in 2008.

Hayden Penn (RHP, BAL) was sent to the Arizona Fall League to test his surgically repaired pitching elbow. He struggled early on and has a long ways to go to be ready to battle for a major league job in 2008.

Mark Prior (RHP, CHC) underwent surgery in April to repair a significant tear to the labrum in his pitching shoulder. Prior says he'll be ready for Opening Day 2008. Recent DL history numbers state he could struggle next spring and into the 2008 season.

Hanley Ramirez (SS, FLA): The Marlins do not believe Ramirez will be close to 100% in spring training. He underwent surgery after the season to repair damage to his non-throwing shoulder. It was discovered he had a torn labrum during the surgery that could land him on the DL at the start of the 2008 season.

Chris Reitsma (RHP, FA) underwent surgery in July to help repair some of the damage to his arthritic pitching elbow. The terms "arthritis" and "pitching elbow" don't mix very well. His future is cloudy at best.

Scott Rolen (3B, STL): Surgery was completed on his troublesome left shoulder in mid-September. It is expected the surgery repaired scar tissue and 'loosened' up his frozen shoulder. If the surgery is successful, the Cardinals medical staff believes he will regain range of movement with the shoulder and most, if not all, of his power.

Anibel Sanchez's (RHP, FLA) June surgery repaired a torn labrum in his pitching shoulder. His status for the early part of 2008 is in question as he recovers from this serious surgery.

Jason Schmidt (RHP, LA): When the surgeon opened up his shoulder he found a torn labrum, frayed biceps tendon and scarring of the bursa sac in his pitching shoulder. This is significant damage that puts a huge cloud over his 2008 season, and career.

Ben Sheets (RHP, MIL): It's official, Sheets is injury prone. The good news is he didn't have any issues with his pitching shoulder. The bad news, a blister problem, strained groin injury and strained ligament involving a finger in his pitching hand cost him a chunk of time. Look for more of the same in 2008.

Gary Sheffield (OF, DET) needed surgery on his right shoulder to remove several bone chips from the A/C joint. He also had a torn labrum repaired and this news may indicate he will be brought along slowly in the spring. A stint on the DL at the start of 2008 isn't out of the question.

Chad Tracy's (3B, ARI) season ended when he needed surgery to repair damage to a troublesome right knee. The Diamondbacks have not revealed the damage, though baseball sources indicate it was cartilage. If he does not have a bone-on-bone situation, he should be fairly close to 100% by March.

Randy Wolf (LHP, LA) worked his way back from Tommy John surgery in 2007 only to develop shoulder problems late in the year. Exploratory surgery ruled out any serious damage and he's expected to rebound in 2008.

Ryan Zimmerman (3B, WAS) suffered a fractured hamate bone in his left hand while taking batting practice. At press time, there was talk he needed surgery to remove the fractured portion of the bone. Players with wrist injuries similar to his lose a noticeable amount of their power for up to a year.

Joel Zumaya (RHP, DET) suffered a freak injury to the A/C joint of his pitching shoulder while helping his family evacuate from the southern California fires in October. The surgery repaired the damage and he is expected to miss at least the first half of the 2008 season. Because this was not a pitching injury, it is difficult to make an accurate prediction when he will return.

5-Year Injury Log

The following chart details the disabled list stints for all players during the past five years. For each injury, the number of days the player missed during the season is listed. Note that a few DL stints are for fewer than 15 days; these are cases when a player was placed on the DL prior to Opening Day (only in-season time lost is listed).

There are a few abbreviations used in this table:

Lt = left
Rt = right
R/C = rotator cuff
Surg = surgery
x 2 = two occurrences of the same injury
x 3 = three occurrences of the same injury

All data provided by Baseball-Injury-Report.com

BATTERS	Yr	Days	Injury
Alou,Moises	05	31	Right hamstring strain & calf
	06	49	Lumbar strain; sprained rt ankle
	07	75	Strained left quad
Anderson,Garret	04	49	Arthritic upper back
	07	96	Hip flexor x 2; rt. elbow
Ankiel,Rick	04	150	Recovery from left elbow surgery
	06	182	Torn patella tendon
Atkins,Garrett	05	22	Strained right hamstring
Aurilia,Rich	03	15	Appendectomy
	05	18	Strained left hamstring
	06	15	Strained right groin
	07	25	Strained right hamstring; neck
Aybar,Erick	07	49	Strained left hamstring; bruised hand
Baker,Jeff	07	21	Concussion
Bako,Paul	05	128	Left knee surgery
	06	31	Partially torn right oblique
Baldelli,Rocco	04	18	Strained right quadriceps
	05	182	Recovery from left knee surgery
	06	65	Left hamstring strain
	07	138	Strained left hamstring
Barajas,Rod	03	39	Strained left hamstring ; Lt wrist
	07	29	Strained right groin
Bard,Josh	04	92	Strained left groin
	07	15	Strained left groin
Barmes,Clint	05	119	Fractured left clavicle
Barrett,Michael	03	45	Strained right hip flexor
	06	29	Intrascrotal hematoma
	07	21	Concussion
Bautista,José	07	17	Puncture wound-left hand
Bay,Jason	03	93	Fractured right wrist
	04	33	Recovery from right shoulder surgery
Belliard,Ronnie	03	21	Sprained right ankle
Bellorin,Edwin	07	26	Strained right hamstring
Beltran,Carlos	03	19	Strained right oblique
	07	16	Strained abdominal muscle
Berkman,Lance	05	31	Right knee soreness
Blake,Casey	06	48	Sprained right ankle; oblique
Blalock,Hank	07	107	Thoracic Outlet Syndrome
Blanco,Henry	07	82	Herniated disc - neck
Bloomquist,Willie	04	19	Strained lower back
Blum,Geoff	05	18	Left chest contusion
Bonds,Barry	05	160	Recovery from right knee surgery
Boone,Aaron	04	100	Torn left ACL
	07	98	Sprained MCL - left knee
Bourn,Michael	07	41	Sprained right ankle
Bowen,Rob	06	16	Left thumb sprain
Bradley,Milton	03	64	Lower lumbar bruise; Rt hamstring
	05	94	Ligament tear right finger; patella tendon
	06	79	Sprained right knee; Lt shoulder
	07	66	Calf, hamstring, wrist, oblique
Branyan,Russell	03	75	Post shoulder surgery; Rt ankle
	05	32	Fractured left middle finger
Broussard,Ben	03	7	Strained right oblique
Buck,Travis	07	44	Strained left hamstring
	07	15	Sprained right thumb
Budde,Ryan	07	22	Strained left abdominal muscle
Burke,Chris	06	15	Dislocated left shoulder
Burrell,Pat	04	30	Left wrist surgery
Buscher,Brian	07	16	Infection-right leg
Bynum,Freddie	06	57	Right shoulder inflammation
	07	44	Strained left hamstring
Byrd,Marlon	03	15	Lacerated left knee
	05	29	Broken right ring finger
Cabrera,Orlando	05	15	Inflammation of the right elbow
Cairo,Miguel	03	40	Fractured left hand
	05	17	Strained left hamstring
	06	36	Strained left hamstring
Cameron,Mike	05	83	Multiple facial fractures; Lt wrist
	06	20	Strained left oblique
Cano,Robinson	06	43	Strained left hamstring
Cantu,Jorge	06	43	Broken bone, left foot
Casey,Sean	04	16	Strained right calf
	06	44	Fractured vertebrae
Castillo,Jose	05	69	Torn MCL - left knee; oblique
Castro,Juan	03	15	Sore knee
	04	21	Strained left ribcage
	05	22	Strained left knee
	07	84	Tendinitis right elbow x 2

BATTERS	Yr	Days	Injury
Castro,Ramon	04	124	Right toe inflammation
	05	18	Strained right quadriceps
	06	62	Strained left oblique
	07	49	Arthritis - lower back
Catalanotto,Frank	04	95	Groin injury x 3
	07	22	Acute strain - right biceps muscle
Chavez,Endy	07	82	Strained left hamstring
Chavez,Eric	04	37	Broken bone, right hand
	07	66	Lower back spasms
Church,Ryan	05	35	Right rib cage sprain; fractured toe
Cirillo,Jeff	03	26	Subluxated right shoulder
	04	37	Broken right index finger
	05	68	Left hand fracture
	07	23	Torn meniscus Lt knee
Clark,Brady	03	16	Hamstring pull
	05	15	Ribcage contusion
Clark,Tony	06	39	Right shoulder strain
Costa,Shane	06	20	Strained left hamstring
Coste,Chris	07	7	Strained hamstring
Cota,Humberto	04	66	Strained left oblique
	05	23	Strained oblique
	07	27	Strained left shoulder
Counsell,Craig	03	61	Dislocated right thumb
	06	38	Right rib fracture
Crede,Joe	05	15	Stress fracture - right index finger
	07	118	Inflammation - lower back
Crisp,Coco	05	15	Sprained right thumb
	06	49	Fractured left finger
Crosby,Bobby	05	77	Fractured rib; Lt ankle
	06	59	Lower back strain x 2
	07	68	Fractured left hand
Cruz Jr.,Jose	05	29	Lower back strain
Cuddyer,Michael	05	17	Bone bruise in right hand
	07	15	Torn ligament-left thumb
DaVanon,Jeff	04	17	Back spasms
	06	56	Left ankle surgery
	07	107	Post ankle shoulder surgery
De Aza,Alejandro	07	114	Sprained right ankle
DeJesus,David	06	40	Strained left hamstring
Delgado,Carlos	04	37	Strained rib cage
	05	16	Sore left elbow
Dellucci,David	03	45	Sprained left ankle; concussion
	07	79	Severely strained left hamstring
Denorfia,Chris	07	183	Pending surgery - right elbow
DeRosa,Mark	06	15	Sprained left foot
Diaz,Matt	05	37	Strained oblique
Doumit,Ryan	06	100	Strained left hamstring x 2
	07	46	High ankle sprain; Lt wrist sprain
Drew,J.D.	03	23	Strained right oblique muscle
	03	21	Recovery from knee surgery
	05	91	Broken left wrist
Duffy,Chris	05	38	Strained left hamstring
	07	93	Sprained left ankle
Dunn,Adam	03	44	Sprained ligament, left thumb
Durham,Ray	03	40	Strained right hamstring; ankle
	04	38	Strained left hamstring; knee
	06	15	Left hamstring strain
Dye,Jermaine	03	122	Torn cartilage in Rt knee; Rt shoulder
Easley,Damion	07	43	Sprained left ankle
Eckstein,David	03	22	Inflamed nerve, left leg
	06	27	Torn oblique muscle
	07	28	Lower back spasms
Edmonds,Jim	07	33	Pinched nerve in lower back
Ellis,Mark	04	183	Torn right labrum
	06	30	Broken right thumb
Encarnacion,Edwin	06	29	Sprained left ankle
Encarnacion,Juan	04	15	Left shoulder tendinitis
	07	43	Scar tissue left wrist; facial fracture
Ensberg,Morgan	06	22	Right shoulder contusion
Erstad,Darin	03	102	Strained right hamstring x 2
	04	36	Strained right hamstring
	06	75	Right ankle irritation x 2
	07	59	Sprained left ankle x 2
Escobar,Alex	04	48	Navicular fracture, right foot
	05	181	Strained right quadriceps
	06	82	Separated right shoulder; left hamstring
	07	183	Post labrum surgery
Estrada,Johnny	05	16	Lumbar and cervical strain

BATTERS	Yr	Days	Injury
Everett,Adam	04	53	Broken bone in left wrist
	07	94	Fractured left fibula
Fick,Robert	03	16	Strained right shoulder
	06	64	Minor surgery - right elbow; rib
Figgins,Chone	07	29	Fractured two fingers rt hand
Finley,Steve	05	23	Strained right shoulder
Floyd,Cliff	03	41	Right Achilles tendon surgery
	04	31	Strained right quadriceps
	06	47	Left Achilles; Lt ankle
Ford,Lew	03	50	Cracked bone in arm
	06	28	Strained right external oblique
	07	40	Postsurgery rt knee surgery
Frandsen,Kevin	06	15	Broken jaw
Freel,Ryan	03	36	Torn left hamstring
	05	51	Left foot inflammation; Rt knee
	07	94	Torn cartilage Rt knee; neck bruise
Furcal,Rafael	07	12	Sprained left ankle
Garciaparra,Nomar	04	67	Right Achilles tendinitis
	05	106	Torn left groin muscle
	06	34	Right knee sprain; ribcage
	07	21	Strained left calf
German,Esteban	04	27	Left oblique strain
Giambi,Jason	04	70	Benign tumor
	05	15	Sprained right ankle
	07	68	Torn Plantar fascia tendon - Lt foot
Gibbons,Jay	04	61	Left hip flexor strain; back
	06	61	Sprained right knee; Lt groin
	07	49	Torn labrum-left shoulder
Giles,Brian	03	26	Sprained right MCL
	07	39	Bone bruise right knee
Giles,Marcus	04	60	Broken collarbone
	07	15	Sprained left knee
Gimenez,Hector	07	183	Torn labrum + surgery
Glaus,Troy	03	20	Torn rotator cuff
	04	109	Right shoulder surgery
	07	32	Left foot surgery; heel
Gload,Ross	05	83	Left shoulder inflammation
	07	47	Torn right quad muscle
Gomes,Jonny	06	41	Right shoulder surgery
Gomez,Carlos	07	64	Fractured hamate bone - left hand
Gomez,Chris	03	28	Right knee ligament
	06	61	Broken hand
Gonzalez,Alex	06	15	Oblique strain
Gonzalez,Luis	04	63	Right elbow surgery
Graffanino,Tony	04	91	Ligament tear, left knee; surgery
	07	53	Torn ACL-right knee
Greene,Khalil	05	37	Fractured right finger; left toe
	06	16	Torn left middle finger ligament
Green,Shawn	07	16	Fractured first metatarsal - right foot
Griffey Jr.,Ken	03	110	Ruptured ankle tendon; Rt shoulder
	04	76	Torn right hamstring x 2
	06	28	Strained biceps tendon in right knee
Grudzielanek,Mark	03	30	Broken bone, right hand
	04	70	Partial tear in right Achilles tendon
	07	23	Torn meniscus - left knee
Guerrero,Vladimir	03	46	Herniated disc in back
	05	20	Partial dislocation of left shoulder
Guillen,Carlos	03	25	Pelvis inflammation
	05	68	Sore right knee; Lt hamstring
Guillen,Jose	06	90	Left hamstring strain;Rt elbow
Gutierrez,Franklin	07	12	Strained left hamstring
Guzman,Christian	06	182	Right shoulder surgery
	07	122	Strained left hamstring; left thumb
Guzman,Freddy	05	182	Right elbow surgery
Hafner,Travis	03	16	Hairline fracture, right toe
	05	18	Post-concussion syndrome
Hairston Jr.,Jerry	03	106	Right foot fracture
	04	85	Fractured left ankle; finger
	05	15	Left elbow ligament injury
	07	73	Lower back soreness; neck
Hairston,Scott	05	31	Torn labrum
	06	39	Left biceps strain
	07	29	Strained left oblique muscle
Hall,Bill	07	19	Sprained right ankle
Hall,Toby	07	46	Torn labrum - throwing shoulder
Hamilton,Josh	07	51	Sprained rt wrist; stomach ailment
Hardy,J.J.	06	138	Right ankle surgery

5-Year Injury Log

BATTERS	Yr	Days	Injury
Harris,Willie	03	25	Mild separated right shoulder
Hawpe,Brad	05	52	Strained left hamstring
Helms,Wes	03	16	Strained right hamstring
	04	40	Torn meniscus, right knee
Helton,Todd	05	15	Left calf strain
	06	15	Stomach ailment
Hermida,Jeremy	06	40	Sore right hip flexor, groin strain
	07	43	Bruised right patellar
Hernandez,Ramon	04	35	Strained left knee
	05	58	Sprained Left wrist; surgery
	07	33	Groin contusion; oblique
Hillenbrand,Shea	03	20	Left oblique strain
Hill,Koyie	04	47	Fractured right ankle
Hinske,Eric	03	30	Broken bone, right hand
Holliday,Matt	05	40	Fractured right pinkie finger
Hopper,Norris	07	17	Bruised heel
House,J.R.	05	182	Right shoulder surgery
Howard,Ryan	07	15	Strained left quad muscle
Hudson,Orlando	04	23	Strained left hamstring
Huff,Aubrey	06	23	Left knee sprain
Hunter,Torii	04	18	Strained right hamstring
	05	65	Fractured left ankle
	06	15	Stress fracture, left foot
Ibanez,Raul	04	37	Strained right hamstring
Ingett,Joe	07	17	Strained left hamstring
Inge,Brandon	04	19	Broken finger
Iwamura,Akinori	07	34	Strained right oblique
Izturis,Cesar	05	15	Strained right hamstring
	05	56	Lower back sprain; hamstring
	06	93	Post elbow surgery; hamstring
Izturis,Maicer	05	53	Sprained MCL, left knee
	06	46	Strained left hamstring
	07	63	Strained right hamstring x 2
Jacobs,Mike	07	40	Fractured right thumb
Jenkins,Geoff	03	41	Fractured left thumb; wrist
Jeter,Derek	03	42	Dislocated left shoulder
Johnson,Ben	06	27	Left shoulder strain
	07	27	Fractured right ankle
Johnson,Dan	07	24	Torn cartilage - left hip
Johnson,Kelly	06	182	Right elbow surgery
Johnson,Nick	03	70	Fractured right hand
	04	53	Strained lower back
	05	29	Right heel contusion
	07	183	Fractured right femur + surgery x 2
Johnson,Reed	07	85	Herniated disc lower back
Jones,Chipper	04	19	Strained right hamstring
	05	42	Ligament strain, left foot
	06	44	Right ankle; oblique x 2
	07	20	Bone bruise right wrist/hand
Jones,Jacque	03	16	Strained left groin
Kata,Matt	04	127	Torn left labrum
Kearns,Austin	03	82	Rotator cuff surgery
	04	105	Rt thumb surgery; fractured left forearm
Kemp,Matt	07	17	Separated right shoulder
Kendrick,Howie	07	78	Fractured index finger lt hand x 2
Kennedy,Adam	03	15	Strained right hamstring
	05	27	Recovery from right knee surgery
	07	50	Torn cartilage-right knee
Kent,Jeff	03	27	Left wrist tendinitis
	06	36	Abdominal strain; sprained lt wrist
Keppinger,Jeff	05	23	Left knee (tibia plate) fracture
	07	21	Fractured right index finger
Kielty,Bobby	07	70	Strained left calf muscle
Kinsler,Ian	06	43	Dislocated left thumb
	07	29	Stress fracture left foot
Klesko,Ryan	03	28	Strained shoulder joint
	04	20	Strained right oblique
	06	170	Left shoulder surgery
Koskie,Corey	03	23	Strained back
	04	15	Strained sternum
	05	67	Fractured right thumb
	06	88	Post-concussion syndrome
	07	183	Post concussion syndrome
Kotchman,Casey	06	146	Mononucleosis
Kotsay,Mark	03	17	Herniated disc, lower back
	07	108	Lower back spasms; surgery
Kubel,Jason	05	182	Left knee surgery

BATTERS	Yr	Days	Injury
Laird,Gerald	04	63	Torn ligament, left thumb
LaRoche,Adam	04	34	Separated left shoulder
LaRue,Jason	04	15	Fractured right index finger
	06	15	Right knee surgery
	07	15	Contusion left shoulder
LeCroy,Matthew	04	33	Pulled right rib cage muscle
Ledee,Ricky	04	15	Hemorrhoidal surgery
	05	33	Strained left hamstring
	06	73	Strained left groin
Lee,Derrek	06	101	Inflammation, fractured rt wrist
Lewis,Fred	07	20	Strained right oblique
Lieberthal,Mike	06	61	Right knee contusion; hip
Lo Duca,Paul	07	15	Strained right hamstring
Lofton,Kenny	04	30	Left hamstring strain; quad
	05	20	Acute tendinitis, right hamstring
	06	11	Left calf muscle
Logan,Nook	07	34	Sprained left foot
Lopez,Pedro	07	45	Fractured left cheek bone
Loretta,Mark	05	60	Torn ligament in left thumb
Lowell,Mike	03	28	Broken left thumb
Ludwick,Ryan	03	19	Right knee contusion
	04	92	Right knee surgery
Lugo,Julio	06	31	Strained abdominal muscle
Marte,Andy	07	26	Strained left hamstring
Martinez,Ramon	05	20	Sprained left thumb
	07	34	Lower back strain
Martinez,Victor	03	24	Bruised bone in right ankle
Matos,Luis	04	74	Fractured right shin
	05	39	Broken right index finger
	06	18	Right shoulder inflammation
Matsui,Hideki	06	123	Broken left wrist
	07	15	Strained left hamstring
Matsui,Kaz	04	46	Lower back strain
	05	52	Bruised left knee
	06	17	Sprained MCL, right knee
	07	36	Strained lower back
Matthews Jr.,Gary	05	24	Strained left hamstring
	06	9	Ribcage strain
Mauer,Joe	04	136	Sprained left knee x 2
	07	34	Strained left quad muscle
McCann,Brian	06	16	Sprained right ankle
McDonald,John	03	45	Lower back strain x 2
	06	15	Groin injury
McLouth,Nate	06	51	Left ankle sprain
McPherson,Dallas	05	87	Left hip surgery
	06	71	Lower back spasms
	07	183	Back surgery
Mechardo,Alejandro	07	183	Torn labrum right shoulder
Mench,Kevin	03	100	Broken left wrist x 2
	04	19	Strained left oblique
Metcalf,Travis	07	15	Strained left hamstring
Michaels,Jason	03	15	Strained oblique
	06	18	Sprained right ankle
Mientkiewicz,Doug	04	16	Left wrist soreness
	05	49	Bruised lower back; hamstring
	06	68	Lower back strain
	07	91	Fractured right wrist
Miles,Aaron	05	33	Right intercostal strain
Mirabelli,Doug	05	24	Left wrist injury
	07	15	Strained right calf
Mohr,Dustan	05	23	Left calf strain
Molina,Bengie	03	24	Broken left wrist
	04	31	Fractured rt index finger; calf
	05	25	Strained right quadriceps
Molina,Yadier	05	40	Hairline fracture, left pinkie finger
	07	29	Fractured left wrist
Monroe,Craig	04	17	Strained left hamstring
Morales,Jose	07	22	Sprained left ankle
Mora,Melvin	03	32	Right hand contusion
	04	15	Strained right hamstring
	07	23	Sprained left foot
Morneau,Justin	05	15	Concussion
Munson,Eric	03	47	Fractured left thumb
	05	34	Bruised ribs
Murphy,Donnie	05	15	Fractured finger - right hand
	07	15	Strained oblique
Nady,Xavier	06	19	Appendectomy
Napoli,Mike	07	51	Strained right hamstring; ankle

5-Year Injury Log

BATTERS	Yr	Days	Injury
Navarro,Dioner	06	41	Bruised right wrist
Newhan,David	06	133	Fractured right fibula
Niekro,Lance	04	6	Right ankle sprain
	06	31	Right groin strain; shoulder
Nixon,Trot	04	118	Strained lt quad; back
	05	27	Left oblique strain
	06	34	Strained right biceps
Nix,Laynce	04	26	Sprained right shoulder
	05	80	Left shoulder surgery
	06	23	Turf toe
	07	183	Strained right oblique
Norton,Greg	04	37	Left knee inflammation
	07	46	Torn meniscus - Rt. Knee - surgery
Nunez,Abraham	03	85	Strained left hamstring
Olivo,Miguel	04	15	Kidney stones
Ordonez,Magglio	04	117	Bone marrow edema; strain
	05	79	Hernia surgery
Overbay,Lyle	07	38	Fractured right hand
Owens,Jerry	06	15	Sprained right ankle
Ozuna,Pablo	03	67	Right knee strain
	07	126	Fractured right fibula, torn ligament
Pagan,Angel	06	75	Torn left hamstring
	07	54	Colitis
Patterson,Corey	03	84	Torn left ACL
Paul,Josh	05	24	Sprained right thumb
	07	68	Strained left elbow
Payton,Jay	07	19	Strained right hamstring
Pena,Brayan	07	15	Concussion
Pena,Carlos	03	25	Strained right hamstring
Pena,Wily Mo	03	25	Strained right hamstring
	05	35	Strained left quadriceps muscle
	06	52	Left wrist surgery
Pence,Hunter	07	29	Chip fracture-right wrist
Perez,Timo	03	15	Right calf strain
Phelps,Josh	03	18	Lower back spasms
Phillips,Andy	06	15	Strained left rib cage muscle
	07	26	Fractured right wrist
Piazza,Mike	03	88	Right groin tear
	04	23	Fluid in left knee
	05	24	Hairline fracture in left hand
	07	78	Sprained A/C joint - right shoulder
Podsednik,Scott	05	16	Strained left adductor muscle
	07	89	Strained lt rib cage muscle; adductor
Polanco,Placido	03	15	Fractured finger
	04	30	Strained left quadriceps
	05	15	Strained left hamstring
	06	37	Separated left shoulder
Pujols,Albert	06	18	Strained right oblique
Punto,Nick	04	121	Fractured right clavicle; oblique
	05	30	Pulled right hamstring
Quentin,Carlos	07	45	Strained hamstring; torn labrum
Quinlan,Robb	04	49	Left oblique strain
	05	53	Bulging disc in neck
Quintanilla,Omar	06	19	Right shin contusion
Rabe,Josh	07	144	Inflammation - right shoulder
Ramirez,Aramis	05	39	Strained left quadriceps
	07	15	Tendinitis - left patellar
Reed,Jeremy	06	91	Fractured right thumb
Renteria,Edgar	07	34	Sprained Rt ankle x 2
Resop,Chris	07	84	Surgery right elbow - bone spurs
Riggans,Shawn	07	119	Tendinitis - throwing elbow
Rios,Alex	06	30	Staph infection in lower left leg
Rivera,Juan	06	21	Rib cage tightness
	07	154	Fractured left leg + Surgery
Roberts,Brian	06	24	Strained groin
Roberts,Dave	03	39	Strained Rt hamstring x 2
	04	23	Strained right hamstring
	05	14	Groin strain
	06	17	Right knee contusion
	07	29	Bone spurs and chip in left elbow
Robles,Oscar	07	15	Torn tendon -- left wrist
Rolen,Scott	05	111	Sprained Lt shoulder; tendinitis
	07	33	Sore left shoulder
Ross,Cody	06	24	Bruised left pinky finger
	07	74	Strained left hamstring
Ross,Dave	06	18	Lower abdominal strain
	07	15	Concussion
Rowand,Aaron	06	56	Fractured Lt ankle; fractured nose

BATTERS	Yr	Days	Injury
Sanchez,Angel	07	183	Strained elbow
Sanchez,Freddy	04	96	Recovery from right ankle surgery
	07	6	Sprained MCL right knee
Sanders,Reggie	05	58	Hairline fracture, right fibula
	06	53	Groin injury; patellar tendon
	07	133	Torn Lt hamstring x 2
Schneider,Brian	06	15	Strained left hamstring
Sexson,Richie	04	156	Lt shoulder surgery; labrum
Shealy,Ryan	06	39	Right elbow strain
	07	60	Strained Lt hamstring x 2
Sheffield,Gary	06	129	Lt wrist contusion; surgery
	07	15	Sore right shoulder
Sledge,Terrmel	05	153	Right hamstring surgery
	07	20	Sprained right thumb
Smith,Jason	07	53	Appendicitis
Snelling,Chris	03	188	Recovery from ACL surgery
	04	182	Broken right wrist
	05	62	Sprained Lt knee; meniscus
	06	69	Post surgery - Lt shoulder strain
	07	143	Contusion - left knee
Snyder,Brad	07	31	Fractured right thumb
Soriano,Alfonso	07	22	Strained right quad muscle
Sosa,Sammy	03	20	Toe infection
	04	33	Strained ligaments, lower back
	05	57	Infection Lt foot
Spiezio,Scott	04	12	Lower back strain
	05	73	Strained left oblique
	07	15	Infected index finger-left hand
Stairs,Matt	03	22	Torn ligament, right ring finger
	04	15	Strained left oblique
Stewart,Shannon	03	25	Right hamstring
	04	58	Plantar fasciitis, right heel
	06	119	Torn plantaar fascia x 2
Sweeney,Mark	07	11	Bruised right foot
Sweeney,Mike	03	48	Upper back tightness
	04	43	Herniated disc
	05	15	Sprained left wrist and elbow
	06	98	Bulging disc in upper back
	07	74	Cartilage damage right knee
Swisher,Nick	05	23	Sprained right shoulder
Taveras,Willy	07	47	Strained right quad muscle
Teahen,Mark	05	21	Lower back strain
	07	15	Strained left forearm
Teixeira,Mark	04	16	Strained left oblique muscle
	07	34	Strained left quad muscle
Tejada,Miguel	07	35	Fractured radius left wrist
Terrero,Luis	05	22	Left groin strain
	07	39	Strained left groin
Thames,Marcus	07	21	Strained left hamstring
Thomas,Frank	04	89	Fracture, left foot
	05	130	Fractured left foot; surgery
	06	15	Strained right quadriceps
Thome,Jim	05	114	Back strain; Rt elbow surgery
	07	22	Strained right ribcage
Torrealba,Yorvit	06	82	Right shoulder strain x 2
Tracy,Chad	07	57	Strained Rt knee; ribcage
Treanor,Matt	06	15	Left shoulder
Upton,B.J.	07	34	Strained left quad
Uribe,Juan	03	64	Stress fracture, right foot
Utley,Chase	07	31	Fractured right hand
Valentin,Jose	04	18	Pulled left hamstring
	05	88	Torn ligaments - right knee
	07	111	Strained Lt knee; fractured fibula
Varitek,Jason	06	33	Cartilage damage, left knee
Vazquez,Ramon	03	36	Abdominal strain
	04	31	Strained right oblique
Victorino,Shane	07	22	Strained right calf
Vidro,Jose	04	39	Right knee surgery
	05	61	High left ankle sprain
	06	31	Left hamstring strain
Vizquel,Omar	03	86	Torn miniscus, right knee
Ward,Daryle	03	19	Tendinitis in right wrist
	04	50	Right thumb ligament sprain
	07	40	Strained Rt calf; Lt hip
Watkins,Tommy	07	39	lower abdominal strain
Weeks,Rickie	06	69	Right wrist surgery
	07	19	Tendinitis right wrist
Wells,Vernon	04	30	Strained right calf
	07	10	Left shoulder surgery (labrum & cyst)

BATTERS	Yr	Days	Injury
Werth,Jayson	03	14	Wrist strain
	04	59	Strained oblique muscle
	05	65	Lt wrist fractured; bursitis
	06	182	Left wrist surgery
	07	33	Sprained last wrist
White,Rondell	05	49	Left shoulder surgery
	06	41	Sore Lt shoulder; hamstring
	07	109	Strained right calf muscle
Wigginton,Ty	04	16	Ulcer
	06	33	Broken bone in left hand
Wilkerson,Brad	06	53	Right shoulder surgery
	07	24	Strained right hamstring
Willingham,Josh	05	95	Stress fracture, left forearm
	06	15	Strained ligament - left hand
Wilson,Craig	05	105	Fractured finger Lt hand; surgery
Wilson,Josh	06	65	Broken left big toe
Wilson,Preston	04	110	Sore Lt knee; meniscus
	07	148	Arthritis right knee
Wilson,Vance	04	41	Lt wrist surgery; hamstring
	07	183	Strained throwing elbow
Woodward,Chris	04	27	Tightness in right hamstring
Youkilis,Kevin	04	16	Bruised right ankle
Young,Dmitri	04	54	Broken right leg
	06	80	Strained Rt quad x 2
Zaun,Gregg	05	15	Concussion
	06	5	Muscle pull, right calf
	07	44	Fractured right thumb
Zobrist,Ben	07	43	Strained left oblique muscle

PITCHERS	Yr	Days	Injury
Acevedo,Jose	03	53	Left ankle surgery
	05	49	Strained right groin
	07	183	Injuries from motorcycle accident
Affeldt,Jeremy	03	16	Blister on left middle finger
	04	55	Strained right rib cage
	05	67	Left groin strain x 2
Alfonseca,Antonio	03	36	Strained right hamstring
	05	95	Stress fracture, right elbow
	06	27	Sore right elbow
Aquino,Greg	05	68	Ulnar nerve irritation
	06	24	Sore right forearm
	07	34	Tightness in pitching forearm
Arias,Joanquin	07	183	Infection right thumb
Armas,Tony	03	161	Slight tear, right labrum
	04	56	Recovery from rotator cuff surgery
	05	35	Right groin strain
	06	27	Strained right forearm
Ayala,Luis	03	29	Inflammation of right shoulder
	06	182	Right elbow surgery
	07	80	Tommy John surgery 3/06
Backe,Brandon	05	40	Left intercostal strain
	06	143	Right elbow sprain; elbow surgery
	07	153	Tommy John surgery 9/06
Baek,Cha Seung	06	7	Right triceps tendinitis
	07	92	Inflammation right shoulder
Baez,Danys	06	40	Appendectomy
	07	27	Tendinitis pitching forearm
Bale,John	07	103	Strained left biceps +_ shoulder
Bannister,Brian	06	120	Strained right hamstring
Bautista,Denny	05	144	Right shoulder tendinitis
	06	24	Sore right pectoral muscle
Beckett,Josh	03	54	Mild sprain, right elbow
	04	58	Finger injury x 2; lower back
	05	32	Strained left oblique; finger
	07	15	Avulsion of skin - right index finger
Bedard,Erik	03	155	Left elbow surgery
	05	57	Strained left MCL
	07	22	Strained right oblique
Belisle,Matt	06	71	Lower back strain x 2
Bell,Rob	05	56	Personal reasons
Benitez,Armando	04	20	Right elbow inflammation
	05	110	Torn right hamstring
	06	17	Left knee bursitis
	06	18	Right knee inflammation
Benoit,Joaquin	03	21	Tendinitis in right shoulder
	04	15	Sore right rotator cuff
	05	27	Sore right shoulder
	05	19	Right elbow tendinitis

5-Year Injury Log

PITCHERS	Yr	Days	Injury
Benson,Kris	03	73	Right shoulder irritation
	05	31	Strained right pectoral
	06	17	Right elbow tendinitis
	07	183	Torn rotator cuff
Bergmann,Jason	07	72	Tight left hamstring; sore elbow
Betancourt,Rafael	04	15	Right biceps tendinitis
	05	18	Right shoulder inflammation
	06	26	Right upper back strain
Bonderman,Jermy	07	15	Blister right middle finger
Bootcheck,Chris	06	19	Strained left hamstring
Borowski,Joe	04	121	Slight tear, right rotator cuff
	05	46	Fractured right ulnar bone
Bowie,Micah	03	101	Strained left elbow
	06	53	Left latissimus dorsi strain
	07	154	Hernia; hip x 2
Bradford,Chad	04	15	Lower back sprain
	05	100	Lower back surgery
Bray,Bill	07	110	Sprained left index finger
Brazoban,Yhency	06	172	Right elbow surgery
	07	157	Recov from Tommy John surg; torn labrum
Brocail,Doug	04	44	Left hamstring; Appendicitis
	06	113	Coronary angioplasty; hamstring
	07	16	Strained left gluteus muscle
Bruney,Brian	04	40	Inflamed right elbow
Burnett,A.J.	03	166	Right elbow surgery; sore elbow
	04	59	Recovery from right elbow surgery
	06	73	Right elbow soreness x 2
	07	59	Sore pitching shoulder x 2
Burton,Jared	07	57	Lower back spasms; Lt hamstring
Byrdak,Tim	06	102	Bone spurs in left elbow
	07	26	Strained flexor tendon - pitching arm
Byrd,Paul	03	183	Right elbow surgery
	04	75	Recovery from right elbow surgery
Cabrera,Daniel	05	20	Lower back strain
	06	21	Tightness in right shoulder
Cabrera,Fernando	06	16	Bruised right heel
Calero,Kiko	03	92	Ruptured right patella tendon
	04	28	Right rotator cuff tendinitis
	05	27	Right elbow tendinitis
	07	17	Inflammation right shoulder
Campusano,Edward	07	183	Strained pitching elbow
Capellan,Jose	06	15	Right shoulder strain
Capuano,Chris	04	93	Sore left elbow; Lt arm; Lt quad
	07	22	Strained left groin
Carpenter,Chris	03	183	Right shoulder surgery
	06	15	Right shoulder bursitis
	07	182	Bone chips right elbow
Cassidy,Scott	07	59	Surgery right knee
Chacin,Gustavo	06	93	Left forearm strain & elbow sprain
	07	89	Strained pitching shoulder
Chacon,Shawn	03	62	Right elbow inflammation x 2
	05	33	Strained left hamstring
	06	25	Left leg hematoma
Cherry,Rocky	07	17	Strained right lat muscle
Chulk,Vinnie	07	35	Blood clot - right hand
Clarke,Darren	07	46	Right shoulder inflamation
Claussen,Brandon	06	107	Rotator cuff surgery
Clement,Matt	06	109	Right shoulder surgery
	07	183	Torn R/C & labrum Rt shoulder
Cocoran,Tim	07	60	Strained pitching elbow
Colome,Jesus	04	20	Right shoulder tendinitis
	05	67	Right shoulder inflammation x 2
	07	56	Soft tissue infection
Colon,Bartolo	06	130	Inflammation & Rt R/C tear
	07	67	Sore pitching elbow; R/C
Colon,Roman	06	49	Neck spasms
	07	183	Post cervical spine surgery (neck)
Condrey,Clay	03	55	Left oblique strain
Contreras,Jose	03	78	Right shoulder strain
	06	16	Pinched nerve in right hip
Cook,Aaron	04	57	Blood clots in both lungs
	05	117	Pulmonary embolism
	07	46	Strained right oblique
Cormier,Lance	06	15	Strained left oblique
	07	84	Tired pitching arm; triceps
Crain,Jesse	07	138	Torn R/C and Labrum
Cruz,Juan	06	29	Sore right shoulder
	07	18	Strained muscle - right shoulder

5-Year Injury Log

PITCHERS	Yr	Days	Injury
Davies,Kyle	06	108	Strained right groin
Day,Dewon	07	20	Strained lower back
De La Rosa,Jorge	06	45	Blisters on left hand
	07	41	Strained pitching elbow
Dempster,Ryan	03	77	Right elbow surg, inflamed nerve in neck
	04	119	Recovery from right elbow surgery
	07	27	Strained left oblique muscle
Dessens,Elmer	05	56	Bone spur, right shoulder
	06	15	Sprained left ankle
	07	74	Strained pitching shoulder
Dinardo,Lenny	04	89	Blister left index finger; shoulder
	06	101	Neck strain
Dingman,Craig	06	182	Arterial bypass surgery
Dohmann,Scott	06	15	Viral infection
Donnelly,Brendan	04	73	Nasal fractures
	07	112	Strained pitching forearm
Dotel,Octavio	05	137	Right elbow surgery
	06	135	Recovery from right elbow surgery
	07	94	Strained left oblique; shoulder
Duchscherer,Justin	06	47	Right elbow tendinitis
	07	139	Strained right hip
Duckworth,Brandon	03	21	Right elbow tendinitis
	06	63	Right elbow strain
	07	79	Torn left oblique
Duke,Zach	05	23	Sprained left ankle
	07	75	Tightness in pitching elbow
Eaton,Adam	03	15	Strained right groin
	05	46	Strained right middle finger x 2
	06	113	Right finger surgery
	07	16	Strained pitching shoulder
Elarton,Scott	03	30	Recovery from shoulder surgery
	06	77	Right shoulder surgery
	07	75	Strained right foot; labrum surgery
Embree,Alan	03	20	Left shoulder tendinitis
	06	15	Strained left groin
Escobar,Kelvim	05	89	Right elbow strain x 3
	06	15	Right elbow irritation
	07	15	Irritation right shoulder
Estes,Shawn	05	65	Stress fracture, left navicular bone
	06	179	Left elbow surgery
	07	183	Tommy John surgery 6/06
Eyre,Scott	04	18	Lower back strain
	06	16	Strained right hamstring
Eyre,Willy	07	45	Stiffness - pitching elbow
Farnsworth,Kyle	04	15	Right knee contusion
Flores,Randy	05	15	Avulsed callus pad on left foot
Fogg,Josh	03	35	Strained abdominal muscle
	07	15	Strained left groin
Fossum,Casey	03	39	Left shoulder inflammation
	04	39	Left shoulder strain
	06	15	Groin strain
Francisco,Frank	05	181	Right elbow surgery
	06	77	Recovery from right elbow surgery
Fuentes,Brian	04	69	Back strain
	07	41	Strained left lat muscle
Fultz,Aaron	03	18	Bruised joint in left shoulder
	07	35	strained rib cage muscle
Gagne,Eric	05	151	Right elbow sprain & surgery
	06	174	Back surgery & elbow surgery
	07	27	Strained right hip, back.elbow
Garcia,Freddy	07	127	Tendinitis right biceps; R/C; labrum
Garcia,Jose	07	183	Inflammation - pitching elbow
Geary,Geoff	05	15	Right eye contusion
Gonzalez,Mike	05	54	Sprained MCL - left knee
	06	38	Left arm fatigue
	07	138	Torn UCL
Gordon,Tom	06	21	Strained right shoulder
	07	74	Inflammed R/C Rt shoulder
Gorzelanny,Tom	06	29	Left elbow soreness
Grabow,John	07	23	Inflamed pitching elbow
Green,Sean	06	50	Back spasms; strained side
Greinke,Zack	06	79	Personal reasons
Guardado,Eddie	04	64	Left rotator tear
	06	43	Left elbow surgery
	07	128	Tommy John surgery 9/06
Guerrier,Matt	06	53	Fractured right thumb
Guzman,Angel	07	121	Strained right elbow

PITCHERS	Yr	Days	Injury
Halladay,Roy	04	81	Right shoulder fatigue x 2
	05	86	Fractured left tibia
	07	20	Appendectomy
Hamels,Cole	06	18	Left shoulder strain
	07	32	Strained pitching elbow
Harang,Aaron	04	24	Sprained ligament, right elbow
Harden,Rich	05	38	Strained left oblique
	06	146	Sprain Rt elbow; back strain
	07	151	Strained pitching shoulder x 2
Hawkins,LaTroy	05	24	Right ulnar neuritis
	07	31	Inflammation in pitching elbow
Hendrickson,Mark	05	16	Left shoulder stiffness
	06	18	Left shoulder tightness
Hensley,Clay	07	34	Strained groin; Labrum surgery
Hernandez,Felix	07	26	Strained flexor muscle - right forearm
Hernandez,Orlando	03	183	Right shoulder surgery
	04	103	Recovery from right shoulder surgery
	05	50	Strained right shoulder x 2
	07	30	Bursitis in pitching shoulder
Hernandez,Roberto	03	35	Strained left hamstring; strained ab
	04	15	Right calf strain
Hernandez,Yoel	07	42	Strained pitching shoulder
Hill,Shawn	06	95	Right elbow soreness
	07	94	Strained left (non-throwing) shoulder
Hirsh,Jason	07	84	Fractured right fibula; ankle
Hoffman,Trevor	03	156	Right shoulder surgery (modified Mumford)
Howry,Bob	03	37	Right elbow surgery
Huber,Jon	07	97	Strained pitching forearm
Hudson,Luke	05	66	Right shoulder strain
	07	182	Tendinitis right triceps x 2
Hudson,Tim	04	45	Left oblique strain
	05	32	Strained left oblique
Hughes,Philip	07	94	Strained left hamstring
Isringhausen,Jason	03	72	Sore right shoulder
	05	16	Strained right abdominal muscle
Jackson,Edwin	04	60	Strained right forearm
James,Chuck	06	32	Strained right hamstring
	07	15	Sore pitching shoulder
Jennings,Jason	05	74	Fractured right finger
	07	91	Torn flexor tendon; elbow
Jimenez,Cesar	07	183	Stress fractured pitching elbow
Johnson,Josh	07	166	Tight pitching elbow; nueritis
Johnson,Randy	03	98	Knee sprain; surgery
	07	134	Lower back pain x 3
Johnson,Tyler	07	48	Tendinitis - left triceps
Jones,Todd	06	18	Pulled hamstring
Julio,Jorge	07	17	Strained right calf
Jurrjens,Jair	07	16	Sore pitching shoulder
Karstens,Jeff	07	104	Fractured right fibula; elbow
Kazmir,Scott	06	55	Lt shoulder sorenes x 2
Kennedy,Joe	03	38	Left shoulder tendinitis
	04	38	Left shoulder inflammation
	06	95	Sore left shoulder
Kensing,Logan	05	130	Sore right elbow
	06	56	Right wrist flexor strain
	07	129	Tommy John surgery 8/06
Ketchner,Ryan	07	31	Tendintis left rotator cuff
Kim,Byung-Hyun	03	27	Right ankle contusion
	04	26	Right shoulder strain
	06	27	Strained right hamstring
	07	27	Bruised Rt thumb
King,Ray	07	17	Tendinitis left shoulder
Kinney,Josh	07	184	Tommy John surgery 3/07
Kline,Steve	04	32	Strained left groin
Kuo,Hong-Chih	07	126	Irritation - left elbow x 2
Lawrence,Brian	06	182	Labrum -rotator cuff surgery
	07	183	Labrum and R/C surgery 2/06
League,Brandon	07	105	Strained lat/weak shoulder
	07	30	Strained oblique muscle
Lee,Cliff	03	61	Lower abdominal strain
	07	32	Strained upper abdominal muscle
Leicester,Jon	07	66	Strained pitching shoulder
Lerew,Andrew	07	134	Ulnar nerve neuritis
Lester,Jon	06	39	Lymphoma
	07	71	Recovery from lymphoma
Lewis,Colby	04	169	Right shoulder surgery
	05	182	Right rotator cuff soreness
Lidge,Brad	07	23	Stained left oblique

5-Year Injury Log

PITCHERS	Yr	Days	Injury
Lieber,Jon	03	182	Right elbow surgery
	04	32	Groin strain
	06	38	Strained left groin
	07	110	Ruptured tendon Lt foot; oblique
Lilly,Ted	05	49	Left biceps tendinitis x 2
Liriano,Francisco	06	34	Sore left elbow & forearm
	07	183	Torn UCL - pitching elbow + surgery
Livingston,Bobby	07	40	Torn labrum - pitching shoulder
Loaiza,Esteban	06	40	Left shoulder and back strain
	07	143	Tightness in upper back; meniscus
Loewen,Adam	07	152	Stress fracture - right elbow
Loe,Kameron	06	45	Right elbow bone bruise
	07	14	Strained lower back
Looper,Braden	07	16	Strained pitching shoulder
Lopez,Rodrigo	04	44	Strained ribcage muscle
	07	106	Torn flexor tendon-pitching arm x 2
Lowe,Mark	06	43	Right elbow tendinitis
	07	148	Sore right elbow; surgery
Lowry,Noah	06	31	Right oblique strain
Lugo,Ruddy	06	23	Mid-back strain
Lyon,Brandon	03	39	Right elbow pain
	04	182	Right elbow surgery
	05	92	Right elbow tendinitis
MacDougal,Mike	04	20	Stomach virus
	06	101	Right shoulder strain
	07	28	Inflamed pitching shoulder
Madson,Ryan	04	39	Sprained right finger
	07	81	Strained pitching shoulder; oblique
Mahay,Ron	05	16	Groin strain
	07	34	Strained ribcage muscle
Maine,John	06	40	Inflammation in right middle finger
Marmol,Carlos	06	16	Right shoulder fatigue
Maroth,Mike	06	103	Bone chips, left elbow
	07	26	Tendinitis-pitching elbow
Marshall,Sean	06	40	Strained left oblique muscle
Marte,Damaso	05	17	Inflamed left trapezius
Martinez,Carlos	06	147	Right elbow strain; surgery
	07	183	Tommy John surgery 7/06
Martinez,Pedro	03	26	Strained muscle high on right side
	06	30	Right hip inflammation; calf
	07	156	Rotator cuff surgery
Martin,Tom	07	23	Strained left groin
Mateo,Juan	07	62	Impingement right shoulder
Mateo,Julio	04	50	Right elbow tendinitis
	06	56	Broken left hand; shoulder
Mathieson,Scott	06	29	Right elbow surgery
	07	183	Tommy John surgery 9/06
McCarthy,Brandon	07	31	Stress fractured - Rt shoulder blade
	07	22	Blister right middle finger
McClellan,Zach	07	140	Inflammation - pitching shoulder
McClung,Seth	03	128	Right elbow surgery
	04	126	Recovery from right elbow surgery
Meche,Gil	05	27	Right knee patellar tendinitis
Mesa,Jose	07	16	Strained right groin
Messenger,Randy	07	28	Fractured metatarsal-left hand
Miller,Andrew	07	20	Strained left hamstring
Miller,Matt	05	79	Right forearm tightness
	06	138	Right elbow strain
	07	38	Strained right forearm
Miller,Trever	05	15	Right hamstring strain
	06	23	Left elbow sprain
Miller,Wade	04	100	Frayed right rotator cuff
	05	90	Right shoulder soreness x 2
	06	151	Recovery from right shoulder surgery
	07	161	Back spasms
Millwood,Kevin	04	37	Sprained ligament/tendon, Rt elbow
	05	21	Strained right groin
	07	50	Strained left hamstring x 2
Milton,Eric	03	168	Knee surgery
	06	31	Left knee surgery
	07	67	Sprained left elbow; back
Miner,Zach	07	23	Tendinitis pitching elbow
Mitre,Sergio	06	88	Right shoulder inflammation
	07	17	Torn callus on pitching hand
Moehler,Brian	03	165	Right elbow surgery
	06	28	Sprained right ankle
Morris,Matt	03	32	Fractured index finger
	05	16	Recovering from Rt shoulder surgery

PITCHERS	Yr	Days	Injury
Mota,Guillermo	05	26	Right elbow inflammation
Mulder,Mark	03	39	Stress fracture, right femur
	06	99	Lt shoulder soreness; surgery
	07	158	Recovery from shoulder surgery
Mussina,Mike	04	42	Right elbow injury
	06	15	Groin strain
	07	22	Strained left hamstring
Myers,Brett	07	64	Soreness in pitching shoulder
Nelson,Joe	07	183	Shoulder surgery
Nolasco,Ricky	07	119	Inflamed rt elbow x 2
Novoa,Roberto	07	183	Fractured right humerus
Nunez,Leo	07	183	Hairline fractured - Rt wrist
O'Connor,Mike	07	78	Elbow surgery
Ohka,Tomo	04	95	Fractured right forearm
	06	77	Partial right rotator cuff tear
Ohman,Will	03	183	Left elbow surgery
Oliver,Darren	04	31	Tight left shoulder
Ortiz,Ramon	05	22	Strained right groin
Ortiz,Russ	05	58	Strained right rib cage
	06	43	Right calf injury
	07	120	Torn flexor tendon; neuritis
Oswalt,Roy	03	80	Right groin strain x 3
	06	15	Strained middle back
Otsuka,Akinori	07	74	Tightness pitching forearm
Owens,Henry	07	132	Inflamed pitching shoulder x 2
Owings,Micah	07	15	Strained right hamstring
Padilla,Juan	06	182	Right elbow surgery
	07	184	Surgery torn flexor tendon
Padilla,Vicente	04	72	Right triceps tendinitis
	05	15	Right triceps tendinitis
	07	54	Strained right triceps
Park,Chan Ho	03	152	Lower back strain x 2
	04	98	Strained lower back
	06	49	Abdomonal pain; intestinal bleeding
Paronto,Chad	07	16	Strained right groin
Parra,Manny	07	21	Displaced chip fracture - left thumb
Parrish,John	05	27	Right elbow strain
	06	182	Recovery from left elbow surgery
Patterson,John	04	78	Right groin strain
	05	15	Lower back spasms
	06	146	Right forearm strain; surgery
	07	148	Strained right biceps
Pauley,David	06	34	Strained right forearm
Pavano,Carl	05	97	Right shoulder tendinitis
	06	182	Back strain, bone chips in right elbow
	07	174	Torn ulnar collateral ligament
Peavy,Jake	04	43	Strained tendon, right forearm
Penny,Brad	04	44	Strained right biceps
	05	19	Nerve irritation - right arm
Penn,Hayden	06	58	Appendicitis
Percival,Troy	03	15	Strained right hip
	04	25	Right elbow inflammation
	05	113	Torn forearm muscle x 2
	06	182	Partial tear, right flexor pronator
Perez,Odalis	04	20	Inflamed left rotator cuff
	05	88	Lt shoulder soreness; oblique
	07	43	Strained left knee
Perez,Oliver	05	68	Fractured left big toe
	07	18	Lower back stiffness
Perkins,Glen	07	112	Strained teres major muscle
Pettitte,Andy	04	102	Strained elbow x 2; surgery
Pineiro,Joel	04	70	Right elbow strain
	05	11	Sore right shoulder
	07	15	Sprained right ankle
Pinto,Renyel	07	42	Strained left shoulder
Politte,Cliff	03	26	Strained right shoulder
	06	24	Right shoulder inflammation
	07	183	Shoulder surgery
Ponson,Sidney	05	24	Strained right calf
	06	19	Slight flexor strain - right elbow
Prior,Mark	03	23	Right shoulder contusion
	04	61	Inflamed right Achilles
	05	38	Fractured right elbow; inflamed
	06	122	Rt shoulder tendinitis, strain x 2
	07	183	Right shoulder surgery
Rakers,Aaron	06	182	Right labrum surgery
Ramirez,Elizardo	06	28	Right shoulder tendinitis
	07	72	Soreness right shoulder

5-Year Injury Log

PITCHERS	Yr	Days	Injury
Ramirez,Horacio	04	122	Left shoulder tendinitis
	06	105	Sprained finger; left hamstring strain
	07	51	Tendinitis pitching shoulder
Ramirez,Ramon	07	48	Inflammation right elbow x 2
Randolph,Stephen	03	26	Strained left oblique muscle
	07	45	Strained right knee
Rasner,Darrell	06	83	Right shoulder tendinitis
	07	11	Fractured right index finger
Rauch,Jon	04	31	Left oblique strain
	05	103	Torn right labrum
Ray,Chris	07	72	Bone spur pitching elbow
Redding,Tim	05	44	Strained right shoulder
Redman,Mark	03	30	Non-displaced fracture of left thumb
	06	13	Torn left knee cartilage
	07	16	Toe infection
Reitsma,Chris	06	110	Right elbow surgery; neuritis
	07	103	Inflamed pitching elbow x 3
Reyes,Al	07	15	Strained rotator cuff
Reyes,Dennys	07	64	Inflamed elbow; shoulder
Rheinecker,John	07	65	Back spasms
Rhodes,Arthur	04	51	Strained back
	05	21	Right knee inflammation
	07	183	Tommy John surgery
Riske,David	06	47	Lower back strain
Rivera,Mariano	03	30	Groin strain
Rleal,Sendy	07	183	Strained right elbow
Robertson,Connor	07	132	Fractured right thumb
Robertson,Nate	07	20	Tired pitching arm
Rodney,Fernando	04	183	Right elbow sprain
	05	66	Right shoulder inflammation
	07	56	Tendinitis Rt shoulder; biceps
Rodriguez,Francisco	05	17	Strained right forearm
Rogers,Kenny	07	123	Tendinitis Lt elbow; blood clot
Romero,Davis	07	183	Torn labrum
Rosario,Francisco	07	107	Strained pitching shoulder
Rupe,Josh	06	87	Left elbow inflammation
	07	107	Sore pitching elbow
Ryan,BJ	07	169	Strained pitching elbow
Saarloos,Kirk	04	66	Bone spur in right elbow
Sabathia,C.C.	05	13	Strained right oblique
	06	30	Strained right oblique muscle
Sampson,Chris	07	29	Sprained ulnar collateral ligament
Sanchez,Duaner	06	64	Separated right shoulder
	07	184	Shoulder surgery x 2
Sanchez,Humberto	07	183	Ligament replacement surgery - throwing arm
Sanchez,Jonathan	07	23	Strained rib cage muscle
Santos,Victor	06	25	Right rotator cuff strain
Schilling,Curt	03	57	Fractured Rt hand; appendectomy
	05	90	Bruise Rt ankle; ankle pain
	07	48	Sore pitching shoulder
Schmidt,Jason	04	12	Right shoulder stiffness
	05	16	Strained right shoulder
	07	157	R/C surgery; bursitis
Schoeneweis,Scott	04	71	Inflammed Lt elbow; surgery
Seanez,Rudy	05	35	Right shoulder strain
Seay,Bobby	03	40	Left shoulder tendinitis
	05	49	Strained left pectoral muscle
Sele,Aaron	03	41	Recovery from right shoulder surgery
	04	15	Right shoulder fatigue
Seo,Jae	06	15	Left groin strain
Sheets,Ben	05	74	Torn back muscle; virus
	06	96	Rt shoulder strain; tendinitis
	07	45	Sprained index finger right hand
Sherrill,George	04	17	Fatigue
Shouse,Brian	04	39	Inflamed left rotator cuff
	06	16	Strained right calf
Silva,Carlos	05	15	Torn meniscus in right knee
Simontacchi,Jason	07	77	Tendinitis-pitching elbow
Smoltz,John	03	27	Right elbow tendinitis
	07	15	Inflamed pitching shoulder
Snyder,Kyle	03	20	Right shoulder muscle strain
	03	53	Right shoulder stiffness
	04	183	Right shoulder surgery
	05	64	Strained right shoulder
Soriano,Rafael	04	147	Right elbow surgery
	05	154	Recovery from right elbow surgery
	06	15	Right shoulder fatigue
Soria,Joakim	07	15	Inflammation right shoulder

5-Year Injury Log

PITCHERS	Yr	Days	Injury
Sosa,Jorge	07	14	Strained left hamstring
Speier,Justin	04	28	Right elbow soreness
	06	32	Right forearm tightness
	07	74	Intestinal virus
Springer,Russ	03	121	Right elbow surgery
Stanton,Mike	03	47	Sore Lt knee; surgery
	07	18	Strained left hamstring
Street,Huston	06	20	Strained right groin
	07	71	Irritated pitching elbow
Sturtze,Tanyon	05	18	Strained left oblique
	06	141	Right shoulder tendinitis
	07	142	R/C surgery 5/06
Switzer,Jon	07	62	Tendinitis Lt shoulder
Tallet,Brian	04	113	Recovery from left elbow surgery
Tankersley,Taylor	07	10	Shoulder tendinitis
Thomson,John	05	88	Strained tendon, right middle finger
	06	97	Inflamed Rt shoulder; blister
	07	77	Lower back spasms
	07	80	Pitching shoulder soreness
Thornton,Matt	03	44	Left elbow surgery
Timlin,Mike	06	18	Strained right shoulder
	07	45	Tendinitis Rt shoulder; oblique
Tomko,Brett	04	16	Right elbow inflammation
	06	33	Strained left oblique
Torres,Salomon	03	23	Strained right hamstring
	07	56	Inflammed Rt elbow x 2
Traber,Billy	04	183	Recovery from left elbow surgery
Trachsel,Steve	05	141	Herniated disc, lower back
	07	21	Strain gluteus muscle
Tsao,Chin-hui	03	23	Strained left hamstring
	05	152	Inflammed Rt elbow; shoulder
	06	182	Recovery from right shoulder surgery
	07	118	Strained Rt shoulder x 2
Valdez,Merkin	07	183	Tommy John surgery 10/06
Valverde,Jose	04	112	Right shoulder tendinitis
	05	28	Right biceps tendinitis
Van Benschoten,John	05	185	Torn right labrum
	06	135	Recovery from right shoulder surgery
Vargas,Claudio	03	40	Right rotator cuff tendinitis
	05	37	Right elbow sprain
	07	15	Lower back spasms
Vargas,Jason	07	9	Bone spur Rt elbow
Veras,Jose	07	136	Inflammation right arm
Villarreal,Oscar	04	147	Right flexor strain
	05	144	Right rotator cuff strain
Villone,Ron	07	14	Strained lower back
Wagner,Billy	04	75	Strained Lr R/C; groin
Wagner,Ryan	05	87	Right shoulder inflammation
	07	147	Torn Labrum
Wakefield,Tim	06	57	Stress fracture in rib cage
Walker,Tyler	05	18	Right shoulder inflammation
	06	111	Right elbow surgery
	07	183	Tommy John surgery 7/06
Wang,Chien-Ming	05	59	Right shoulder inflammation
	07	23	Strained right hamstring

5-Year Injury Log

PITCHERS	Yr	Days	Injury
Washburn,Jarrod	04	43	Inflammation of chest ligament
	05	18	Left forearm strain
Weaver,Jeff	07	29	Inflammation in his pitching shoulder
Weaver,Jered	07	16	Tendinitis right biceps
Webb,Brandon	03	15	Tendinitis - pitching elbow
Wellemeyer,Todd	04	55	Right shoulder strain
	07	81	Sore pitching elbow
Wells,David	04	21	Hand lacerations
	06	117	Rt knee ailments x 3
Wells,Kip	04	22	Right elbow inflammation
	06	127	Sprained Rt foot; blood clot
Westbrook,Jake	07	52	Strained left internal oblique muscle
White,Rick	07	32	Pinched nerve in neck; oblique
White,Sean	07	121	Tendinitis right biceps
Wickman,Bob	03	182	Recovery from elbow surgery
	04	93	Sprained right elbow
	07	15	Tendinitis upper right back
Williams,Dave	03	65	Recovery from left shoulder surgery
	04	18	Strained rib cage
	07	99	Herniated disc-neck
Williams,Jerome	04	47	Right elbow surgery
	07	87	Strained Rt shoulder; ankle
Williams,Woody	05	34	Strained left oblique
	06	49	Muscle tear, left calf
Wilson,Brian	06	26	Muscle strain - left side
Wilson,C.J.	06	11	Right hamstring strain
Wise,Matt	03	183	Elbow surgery
	05	23	Strained left intercostal
	06	49	Right elbow surgery
Witasick,Jay	03	71	Strained tendon, right elbow
	04	33	Strained left oblique muscle
	06	102	Sprained Lt ankle; tendinitis
	07	41	Strained left oblique muscle
Wolf,Randy	04	59	Lt elbow tendinitis x 2
	05	113	Left elbow surgery
	06	118	Recovery from left elbow surgery
	07	89	Soreness -pitching shoulder
Wood,Kerry	04	52	Tendinitis, lower right triceps
	05	108	Strained Rt shoulder; surgery
	06	162	Post surgical; R/C tear
	07	124	Shoulder stiffness
Wood,Mike	06	64	Back inflammation
Wright,Jamey	07	66	Inflamed right shoulder
Wright,Jaret	05	113	Right shoulder inflammation
	07	172	Sore Rt shoulder x 2
Yates,Tyler	03	7	Recovery from elbow surgery
	05	182	Torn rotator cuff
Young,Chris	07	15	Strained left oblique
Zagurski,Mike	07	43	Pulled left hamstring
Zambrano,Victor	04	47	Right elbow inflammation
	06	148	Torn right elbow tendon
	07	60	Strained pitching forearm
Zumaya,Joel	07	107	Ruptured tendon right middle finger

IV.
PROSPECTS

Prospects in perspective

Winning this game is all about playing the percentages. We've spent an inordinate amount of effort trying to find courses of action that yield the best percentage plays. One of the "foundation" approaches is simply targeting players with a track record. The longer the track record, the better the percentage play.

So it is incredibly frustrating when I see a chat question that asks, "I have a chance to win this year. Should I trade Roy Oswalt for Tim Lincecum?"

Now, there is nothing wrong with Tim Lincecum. He is a fine talent and, by all accounts, should one day develop into one of the best pitchers in the game. The thing is, Roy Oswalt is *already* one of the best pitchers in the game. There's no waiting. No speculating. No risk.

The fascination with rising minor league players often reaches heights of absurdity. This chatter is essentially questioning whether the value of owning a possible future star trumps winning a championship now. Have our priorities shifted so much? I thought our goal was to win now. Given the long odds in pulling off that feat, *you never, ever pass up a chance to win now.*

The way I see it, you can pat yourself on the back if you had Joe Mauer on your farm team before anyone had ever heard of him. But if your fantasy team is still finishing in the second division, there's something intrinsically wrong.

Not only are fantasy leaguers obsessed with minor leaguers, they are also incredibly impatient. I am constantly asked, "When is so-and-so going to get called up?" with the expectation of a time frame measured in days. But the asker never stops to consider the context. Some 2007 examples:

"When is Cameron Maybin going to get the call?" Detroit has three fine outfielders so they are in no hurry to promote Maybin. Who is still only 21, incidentally.

"When is Evan Longoria going to get the call?" Tampa Bay is not going to contend this year so they have no incentive to start Longoria's arbitration time clock sooner than they need to.

The Major League Baseball First Year Player Draft brings out an additional level of fascination. This past June, everyone was focused on #1 pick David Price, and the rest of the first-rounders. These are baseball's future superstars, right? Here is some information to keep things in perspective...

Yr	#1 pick	First round picks who became MLB stars
96	Kris Benson	Eric Chavez
97	Matt Anderson	JD Drew, T.Glaus, V.Wells, L.Berkman
98	Pat Burrell	JD Drew, M.Mulder, B.Lidge
99	Josh Hamilton	J.Beckett, B.Zito, B.Sheets, B.Myers
00	Adr. Gonzalez	C.Utley
01	Joe Mauer	M.Teixeira, M.Prior, J.Bonderman
02	Br. Bullington	P.Fielder, N.Swisher, S.Kazmir, C.Hamels
03	Delmon Young	None
04	Matt Bush	J.Verlander
05	Justin Upton	R.Zimmerman
06	Luke Hochevar	

For those keeping score, that's about two dozen major league stars out of 296 first round picks (omitting 2006 since it's too soon to see the fruits of that draft), a hit rate of 8%. On #1 picks alone, the best we can say is that most of them became at least serviceable major league players. No fantasy leaguers have been breaking the bank for Kris Benson lately. This does not seem to be a percentage play we should be obsessing over.

That's not to say that minor league prospecting is not an important exercise. The issue is one of keeping it in perspective. Here are my top 10 reminders and guidelines...

1. Some prospects are going to hit the ground running (Ryan Braun) and some are going to immediately struggle (Alex Gordon), no matter what level of hype follows them.

2. Some prospects are going to start fast (since the league is unfamiliar with them) and then fade (as the league figures them out). Others will start slow (since they are unfamiliar with the opposition) and then improve (as they adjust to the competition). So if you make your free agent and roster decisions based on small early samples sizes, you are just as likely to be a genius as an idiot. But don't worry — it will all change tomorrow.

3. How any individual player will perform relative to his talent is largely unknown because there is a psychological element that is vastly unexplored. Some make the transition to the majors seamlessly, some not, completely regardless of how talented they are. Never forget Rick Ankiel.

4. Still, talent is the best predictor of future success, so major league equivalent base performance indicators still have a valuable role in the process. As do scouting reports, carefully filtered. And Deric's integrated approach.

5. Follow the player's path to the majors. Did he have to repeat certain levels? Was he allowed to stay at a level long enough to learn how to adjust to the level of competition? A player with only two great months at Double-A is a good bet to struggle if promoted directly to the majors because he was never fully tested at Double-A, let alone Triple-A.

6. Younger players holding their own against older competition is a good thing. Older players reaching their physical peak, regardless of their current address, can be a good thing too. The Ryan Freels and Casey Blakes can have some very profitable years.

7. Always consider team context. A prospect with superior potential is not going to unseat a steady but unspectacular incumbent, especially one with a large contract.

8. Don't try to anticipate how a team is going to manage their talent, both at the major and minor league level. You might think it's time to move Kenji Johjima and let Jeff Clement get his turn. You are not running the Mariners.

9. Those who play in shallow, one-year leagues should have little cause to be looking at minor leaguers at all. The risk versus reward is so skewed against you, and there is so much talent available with a track record, that taking a chance on a call-up makes no sense. That means, no, you don't jettison Ryan Zimmerman for Evan Longoria in a 10-team mixed league.

10. Decide where your priorities really are. If your goal is to win, prospect analysis is just a *part* of the process, not the entire process. Congratulations, you drafted Jay Bruce. Now, what place is your team in?

Bull Durham prospects

In Deric McKamey's 2007 *Minor League Baseball Analyst,* the following players were among those on his "Top 50 Fantasy Prospects" list that received the most hype and put up the most playing time in 2007:

BATTERS	R$
Braun, Ryan	31
Tulowitzki, Troy	23
Pence, Hunter	21
Young, Chris	19
Pedroia, Dustin	18
Young, Delmon	18
Loney, James	14
Iwamura, Akinori	14
Gordon, Alex	11
Kouzmanoff, Kevin	11
Fields, Josh	9
Butler, Billy	8
Lind, Adam	4
Montero, Miguel	1
Aybar, Erick	1
Jones, Adam	1
Pie, Felix	0
Baker, Jeff	-2
Iannetta, Chris	-2
MEAN	**$10.52**

PITCHERS	R$
Soria, Joakim	17
Matsuzaka, Daisuke	13
Bannister, Brian	11
Lincecum, Timothy	10
Gallardo, Yovani	9
Owings, Micah	7
Hughes, Philip	3
Sampson, Chris	0
Hirsh, Jason	0
Danks, John	-2
Igawa, Kei	-5
Bailey, Homer	-5
Albers, Matt	-9
MEAN	**$3.77**

Thirty-two players and between them not even enough Rotisserie value to stock a standard $260 23-man roster. Should we have expected any better? Probably not, although we were spoiled by 2006's pitching successes. But the amount of draft dollars and FAAB dollars spent to get these names onto our rosters likely surpassed the $249 they earned this year.

The average age of the batters on this list is 23.5. The average age of the pitchers is 24.1 (23.5 if we filter out the two Japanese imports.) It would be a fair conclusion to state that most of these young players — the group as a whole, even — underperformed expectations. But that's okay. These are long-term investments, right? Intuitively, we know this, but that is not typically how we viewed these commodities when we drafted them.

Here is another group of players who share some similar characteristics. Prior to 2007, none of these players ever spent a full season in the majors. For all but one, 2007 represented the most major league playing time they ever

saw. Few, if any, of these players were likely rostered on draft day, which means that most of them were in-season pick-ups from the free agent pool.

BATTERS	R$
Theriot, Ryan	15
Diaz, Matt	15
Byrd, Marlon	15
Harris, Brendan	13
Cust, Jack	12
Hopper, Norris	12
Spilborghs, Ryan	10
Harris, Willie	9
Dobbs, Greg	7
Tyner, Jason	7
Ruiz, Carlos	6
Fontenot, Mike	4
MEAN	**$10.41**

PITCHERS	R$
Moylan, Peter	14
Guthrie, Jeremy	12
Seay, Bobby	5
Dinardo, Lenny	4
Lindstrom, Matt	4
Durbin, Chad	2
Cameron, Kevin	0
Carlyle, Buddy	0
Bacsik, Mike	-4
MEAN	**$4.11**

The average age of all these players, both batters and pitchers, is 28.1. None of them is under the age of 27. None of them appear on any top prospects list. Many of these players have *never* appeared on a top prospects list.

I'll admit that there is some selection bias here, as only the success stories got enough playing time to make the list. Nevertheless, the *caliber* of these success stories, as compared to all those well-hyped younger players, is notable. More important, nearly all 21 of these players returned a profit on their respective fantasy investments, which in most cases was no more than a free agent pick.

This is not the first time that there have been success stories among what we call "Bull Durham" prospects. History is chock full of older rookies who are overlooked during their formative years. Geronimo Berroa is a favorite case study. He bounced around several organizations before backing into 340 ABs with Oakland in 1994 at age 29. The 13 HRs and .306 BA he posted that year earned him a full-time job, and the next two seasons he averaged nearly 30 HRs and 100 RBIs.

Other older debuts who had productive years included Rick Reed, Brian Daubach, Tony Womack and Billy Taylor. More recently, Dave Roberts, Ryan Freel, Casey Blake, Emil Brown and Marcus Thames all fit the profile.

The reason these types of players may have untapped value is because, at age 27 and older, they are entering into their physical peak years. Even if they have already been categorized as minor league journeymen, a physical peak is still a player's opportunity to post elevated numbers. The question is whether he will post them in the minors, or whether a major league club will see fit to reap the benefits of those peak numbers in the bigs.

Most of these players will have short baseball life spans, which is one of the reasons why major league teams are less interested in investing in them. But for fantasy purposes, we're not looking for players who are going to provide double-digit years worth of productivity. Even in most keeper leagues, the longest we can hold onto any player is perhaps 3-5 years anyway. And that is just about the average lifespan of these Bull Durham commodities.

Finding older minor leaguers who have the *potential* to be productive in the majors is not that difficult. I could take the time to develop a formal statistical profile, but the process is the same as uncovering any talent. We just need to look at players with solid underlying skills.

The bigger challenge is figuring out which ones will get a call to the majors. Openings are often created when you are 23; not so much when you are 29. Analyzing each team's depth chart to uncover possible opportunities is helpful, but in the end, it is usually an injury that opens up a spot. Jack Cust may have never gotten a chance if Mike Piazza hadn't gotten hurt. Marlon Byrd may have never gotten a chance if Brad Wilkerson hadn't gotten hurt. Jeremy Guthrie may have never gotten a chance if Adam Loewen hadn't gotten hurt. We cannot predict these. We have to resign ourselves to being reactive instead of proactive.

So whenever an older player gets a call to the majors, we should probably take notice. Evaluate his BPIs. See if he has even a moderately clear path to some playing time. And then speculate. Remember that these are players who may have a greater motivation to succeed because they know that this may be their last chance. And based on this year's results, these Bull Durham prospects could return greater profit than all those hot young things we salivate over each spring.

The value of minor leaguers

by Craig Neuman

Those in keeper leagues know a good farm system can be important in both a team's short term and long term success. But, how much are minor leaguers *actually* worth?

The player pool for this study was comprised of Deric McKamey's Top 50 minor leaguers from 1999-2003. There were 167 players who appeared on these lists. For each player, we compiled their 5x5 values for the first three years after their MLB debut though, some players did not appear in the majors for three years. In looking at the data, the most telling fact is that 91 (55%) of players returned an average value of $5 or less while only 13 (8%) returned an average value of $20 or greater. Let's see if we can drill deeper into the data to learn anything more.

Pos	# of Players	$21+	$16-$20	$11-15	$6-10	$0-5	<$0	Never Played
OF	42	5	5	9	2	10	10	1
CI	24	3	4	4	4	5	1	3
MI	23	2	5	1	4	5	5	1
C	8	0	1	1	0	3	2	1
P	70	3	5	9	9	13	19	12
Total	167	13	20	24	19	36	37	18

Pitchers are particularly unpredictable as 45 of them (64%) returned an average value of $5 or less with a whopping 31 (44%) returning negative value or never yet appearing in an MLB game. Outfielders and cornermen were the most profitable on offense as 30 of them (45%) returned an average value of $11 or more with 8 of the 13 studs ($21+) playing one of those three positions.

Let's analyze the players based on their ranking within the list. Note that some of the players will be over-

Rank	$21+	$16-$20	$11-$15	$6-$10	$0-$5	<$0	Never Played
1-10	6	8	17	5	5	5	4
11-20	5	5	10	6	9	11	4
21-30	6	3	9	8	11	11	2
31-40	2	6	5	4	16	11	6
41-50	3	3	4	5	11	16	8

represented in this data as they appeared in the top 50 more than once.

Top 20 players produced a value of $11 or greater 52 times compared to 41 times for everyone else. At the same time, players ranked 31-50 produced a value of $5 or less (or never played) 68 times compared to 62 times for everyone else.

Finally, let's look at the average value earned by decile. If a player never appeared in the majors, we'll assign a value of zero:

Rank	Avg. Value
-10	$10.85
11-20	$7.74
21-30	$8.03
31-40	$5.25
41-50	$4.39

Clearly, McKamey has a good eye for talent. The players ranked higher on his lists ultimately perform better than those ranked lower.

The slight uptick in the value of 21-30 ranked players was skewed by two players (Albert Pujols, ranked #24 in 2001 and Alfonso Soriano, ranked #27 in 1999 and #22 in 2000). Without them, the average dips to $6.35.

Top Prospects for 2008

by Deric McKamey

Matt Antonelli (2B, SD) established himself as the top 2B in the minors after hitting .307/.404/.491 with 21 HR and 28 SB. In addition to his secondary skills of power and speed, he draws walks and has excellent plate discipline (0.88 Eye). He may lack range, but his soft hands and arm strength give him defensive value.

Homer Bailey (RHP, CIN) was slated to spend 2007 in the Reds' rotation, but a strained groin and lack of command/efficiency (1.8 Cmd) put him back in Triple-A where he went 6-3 with a 3.07 ERA, 7.9 K/9, and a .204 oppBA. His 89-96 MPH fastball and curveball remain plus pitches and he did pitch well in his final two starts.

Wladimir Balentien (RF, SEA) tightened up his strike zone and shortened swing, which cut down on his strikeouts and improved his performance. At Triple-A, he hit .291/ 362/.509 with 24 HR, 15 SB, and a 0.51 Eye. His power can be game changing and adds the elements of above average speed and defense, but will need to find a place to play.

Daric Barton (1B, OAK) has as much BA ability as any minor league hitter with good contact and plate discipline (1.13 Eye). He hit .393 with a .389 OBP in Triple-A, but his power is more of the doubles variety (nine HR/.438 SLG). His speed is below average and lacks defensive ability, but can be the on-base machine that Oakland craves.

Jay Bruce (CF, CIN) produces BA and power from his strong frame and bat speed. He runs well for his size, and has the range and arm strength to play a solid CF. At three levels, he hit .319/.375/.587 with 26 HR, 46 doubles, and a 0.35 Eye. The Reds' OF is crowded, but they'll find room.

Clay Buchholz (RHP, BOS) opened up eyes with the no-hitter he threw, and he has the ability to succeed in the Sox' rotation. His fastball hits 95 MPH and he has three complementary pitches that he can go to with confidence. Between Triple and Double-A, he went 8-5 with a 2.44 ERA, a 4.9 Cmd, 12.3 K/9, and a .193 oppBA.

Joba Chamberlain (RHP, NYY) was dominant as the Yankees' setup reliever (0.38 ERA), but will return to the starting rotation in 2008. Fans were witness to his overpowering 88-97 MPH fastball and slider, but his curveball can be a solid pitch as well. He went 9-2 with a 2.45 ERA, a 5.0 Cmd, 13.9 K/9, and a .198 oppBA.

Jeff Clement (C, SEA) has the bat to star in the Majors with plus bat speed, power (20 HR/.497 SLG), and plate discipline (0.69 Eye). His improved approach should allow him to hit for BA, as he did in Triple-A (.275 BA). With his questionable defense and Johjima entrenched behind the plate, he might find ABs as a DH/1B/backup catcher.

Johnny Cueto (RHP, CIN) alleviated concerns about his short stature and stamina by decimating three levels with a three-pitch mix that features plus movement and command (5.0 Cmd). He went 12-9 with a 3.07 ERA, 9.5 K/9, and a .239 oppBA.

Ross Detwiler (LHP, WAS), the Nationals' #1 pick in 2007 could make little work of the minors with his stuff and pitchability. His 88-94 MPH fastball and curveball are legitimate strikeout pitches and he commands the plate. He posted a 3.51 ERA in 33 IP at two levels and should have a rotation spot locked up by mid-season.

Joey Devine (RHP, ATL) put things together in 2007, improving his command (4.1 Cmd) and unleashing his deadly fastball/slider combination on opposing batters. Between Triple and Double-A, he saved 20 games with a 1.89 ERA, 12.3 K/9, and a .202 oppBA. He rode the Majors-to-minors train all season and could hold down a role of prominence in the Braves bullpen.

Shelley Duncan (LF/1B, NYY) possesses raw power with plus bat speed and natural strength. His swing does tend to get long and he struggles to make contact, but he hit .295/.380/.577 with 25 HR and a 0.55 Eye in Triple-A. A natural first baseman, he has been forced to play LF where his range and arm strength are lacking. His ability to torch LH pitching could slot him into a platoon role.

Chase Headley (3B, SD) was the MVP of the Texas League, leading the circuit in all three percentage categories (.330/.437/.580). The switch-hitter added 20 HR, but is more of a doubles hitter who hits well from both sides. He is a below average runner and lacks the arm strength and range to be any more than average defensively.

Wade Davis (RHP, TAM) dominated two levels, going 10-3 with a 2.50 ERA, a 3.3 Cmd, 9.6 K/9, and a .223 oppBA. He generates downward plane to all three pitches, which helps in that his fastball packs velocity (87-94 MPH), but not movement. He was very stingy with the long ball (0.5 HR/9) and has the stamina to hold his velocity.

Jacoby Ellsbury (CF, BOS) electrified fans with his plus speed (41 SB) and aggressive style of play. He uses the whole field with his line-drive stroke, hitting .323, and judges the strike zone (0.70 Eye) giving him a solid .387 OBP between Triple and Double-A. His defense in CF is outstanding and will open 2008 as the Sox' leadoff hitter.

Gio Gonzalez (LHP, CHW) possesses outstanding movement, especially to his plus curveball and fastball, and a high leg kick provides deception. He led the minors with 185 strikeouts and went 9-7 with a 3.18 ERA, a 3.2 Cmd, 11.1 K/9, and a .216 oppBA in Double-A. His small, athletic frame hasn't caused any stamina issues.

Luke Hochevar (RHP, KC) is a prototype pitcher in a lot of ways with his tall, athletic frame, arm action, and velocity (88-95 MPH). He was supposed to be a fixture in the Royals' rotation, but his lukewarm performance (10-10 with a 4.86 ERA, a 2.9 Cmd, 8.2 K/9, and a .271 oppBA) kept him in the minors. His 2.13 ERA for Kansas City bodes well for 2008.

James Hoey (RHP, BAL) missed bats with regularity (12.6 K/9 and a .177 oppBA) as one of the more dominant closers in the minors. His 90-97 MPH fastball and power slider possess excellent movement and helped him save 16 games with a microscopic 0.79 ERA between Triple and Double-A. He should be the Orioles' primary setup reliever.

Eric Hurley (RHP, TEX) may be the best pitcher Texas has developed recently and figures to earn a rotation spot. He went 11-9 with a 4.00 ERA, a 2.5 Cmd, 7.5 K/9, and a .227 oppBA between Triple and Double-A, torturing hitters with excellent pitch movement, velocity (88-94 MPH), and two complementary pitches (slider, change-up).

Brandon Jones (LF, ATL) seems a natural fit in LF with his LH bat and platoon advantage. He hit .295/.367/.490 with 19 HR and 17 SB between Triple and Double-A, which makes him solid in the middle half of the batting order. He has power is to all fields and is an instinctive runner, but his defense, especially route taking, needs work.

Jair Jurrjens (RHP, ATL) jumped from Double-A, where he went 7-5 with a 3.20 ERA, to a starting role in Detroit where he held his own (4.70 ERA). He changes speeds effectively, sports good command (3.0 Cmd) and gets good fastball movement and velocity (88-94 MPH), but did struggle to miss bats (7.5 K/9 and a .257 oppBA).

Ian Kennedy (RHP, NYY) went 12-3 with a 1.91 ERA, a 3.4 Cmd, 10.0 K/9, and a .182 oppBA between three levels with his knack for changing speeds and disrupting hitters' timing. He keeps the ball low in the strike zone, but can get K's with his curveball and deceptively quick fastball. The #5 rotation spot is his with a strong spring training.

Aaron Laffey (LHP, CLE) gave the Indians a shot in the arm with nine late-season starts (4.56 ERA) and will vie for a spot in 2008. Not blessed with much velocity (85-90 MPH) and he doesn't repeat his delivery, but keeps the ball low and has excellent command (3.3 Cmd). At two levels, he went 13-4 with a 2.88 ERA, 6.8 K/9, and a .238 oppBA.

John Lannan (LHP, WAS) presents an odd combination in that he pitches to contact and has marginal velocity (87-91 MPH), but doesn't have good command (1.8 Cmd). He mixes his pitches well and keeps the ball down. At two levels, he went 12-3 with a 2.31 ERA, 5.3 K/9, and a .206 oppBA and posted a 4.15 ERA for the Nationals.

Andy LaRoche (3B/LF, LA) possesses pure hitting ability both in BA (.302) and power (16 HR/.565 SLG) by having good bat speed and plate discipline (0.95 Eye). He can get pull conscious, but is making progress in going the other way. His defense is improving and he will go into spring training as the favorite to start at 3B.

Radhames Liz (RHP, BAL) overpowered hitters with his 89-98 MPH fastball and power slider, notching 10.6 K/9 and holding hitters to a .204 oppBA. His quick arm action provides movement and allowed him to go 11-4 with a 3.22 ERA in Double-A. His command could improve, but he still might nail down the Orioles' #4 starter slot.

Evan Longoria (3B, TAM) has done nothing but hit since turning pro and was named Southern League MVP. At Triple and Double-A, he hit .299/.402/.520 with 26 HR and a 0.66 Eye. He makes solid contact and drives the ball hard to all fields. He is a solid defender at 3B and could open there in 2008 while being a strong ROY contender.

Chris Lubanski (LF, KC) has been the model of inconsistency, but could play his way into a platoon situation. He drives the ball well to all fields and has above average speed, but his BA will always lag behind and he doesn't hit LH pitching that well. Between Triple and Double-A, he hit .259/.325/.438 with 15 HR and a 0.46 Eye.

Cameron Maybin (CF, DET) has one of the better power/speed combinations in the minors and hit .316/.409/.523 with 14 HR, 25 SB, and a 0.55 Eye at three levels while missing time with a dislocated shoulder. He has groundball tendencies which could suppress power. Defensively, he has a strong arm and good range in CF.

Andrew McCutchen (CF, PIT) struggled for much of the season after he was promoted, but hit better in Triple-A (.313 BA). Highly athletic with plus speed and power potential, he hit .265/.329/.388 with 11 HR, 21 SB, and a 0.53 Eye between Triple and Double-A. His CF defense is stellar and could be in the Majors by mid-season.

Jacob McGee (LHP, TAM) is a tall, projectable pitcher with a heavy fastball that induces groundball outs and strikeouts (11.3 K/9). Between Double and high Class-A, he went 8-6 with a 3.15 ERA, and repeats his high ¾ delivery well, giving him plus command (3.4 Cmd) and ability to disguise his change-up.

Jon Meloan (RHP, LA) has been the minors' most dominant reliever the past two seasons and could thrive immediately in a role of responsibility. He saved 20 games with a 2.03 ERA, a 3.4 Cmd, 12.3 K/9, and a .156 oppBA between Triple and Double-A with an 88-94 MPH fastball and two solid breaking pitches (slider and knuckle-curve).

Adam Miller (RHP, CLE) might have helped Cleveland late if not for a sore elbow which plagued him in the second half. His 89-98 MPH fastball and hard slider from a quick arm action are plus pitches and helped him notch 9.4 K/9 and a 4.82 ERA in Triple-A. His command (3.2 Cmd) was much improved and he can succeed in a variety of roles.

Franklin Morales (LHP, COL) was a fixture in the post-season after his impressive final six weeks (3.43 ERA in eight starts). His electric, 89-96 MPH fastball and two solid comps, along with a repeatable delivery are tough to beat. At two stops, he had a 3.51 ERA, 7.4 K/9, and .241 oppBA.

Brandon Moss (RF, BOS) resurrected his career by improving his approach at the plate, hitting .284/.366/.474 with 16 HR and a 0.42 Eye in Triple-A. His strong, muscular build generates good bat speed, but he struggles vs. LH pitching, which could put him in a platoon role. He shows good arm strength in both corner outfield positions.

Garrett Olson (LHP, BAL) keeps hitters off balance by mixing pitches and repeating his high ¾ delivery. At Triple-A, he went 9-7 with a 3.16 ERA, a 3.0 Cmd, 8.4 K/9, and a .208 oppBA. He relies on the groundball out and did well with balls in play. He does lose his velocity (87-92 MPH) easily and may work out initially as a fifth starter.

Manny Parra (LHP, MIL) has always been able to dominate, but has had a tough time staying healthy. Armed with a plus curveball and above average velocity, he went 10-4 with a 2.45 ERA, a 3.2 Cmd, 8.9 K/9, and a .220 oppBA between Triple and Double-A. He pitched well for Milwaukee (3.76 ERA) and could gain a rotation spot.

Troy Patton (LHP, HOU) gets hitters out with a deceptively quick delivery and excellent pitch movement. He focused on pitching to contact, which lowered his K rate, but he fared well at two levels, going 10-8 with a 3.51 ERA, a 2.2 Cmd, 5.6 K/9, and a .247 oppBA. He was victimized by HRs, so will need to keep the ball down.

Steven Pearce (RF/1B, PIT) was one of the more prolific power hitters in the minors, hitting 31 HR and 40 doubles, with a .622 SLG between three levels. A better approach and plate discipline (0.52 Eye), coupled with strong wrists, allowed him to hit .333. A natural first baseman, the Pirates gave him action in RF to expedite his ascent to the Majors.

Chris Perez (RHP, STL) was drafted to provide a quick return and he will do just that. He pitches aggressively and overpowers hitters with his 90-95 MPH fastball and power slider, but his command (1.9 Cmd) can be spotty. Between Triple and Double-A, he saved 35 games with a 2.96 ERA, 12.7 K/9, and an impressive .130 oppBA.

David Price (LHP, TAM), the #1 pick in the 2007 Draft, didn't pitch in the minors after signing late, but has the ability to be fast-tracked into the D-Rays' rotation. Quick arm action provides movement to his 89-95 MPH four-seam fastball and has three complementary pitches to choose from. His command and dominance are obvious strengths.

Colby Rasmus (CF, STL) led the Texas League with 29 HR with his fluid swing and bat speed. The aggressive promotion didn't faze him as he hit .275/.381/.551 and utilized his speed to swipe 18 bases. His arm strength and range are solid in CF.

Nate Schierholtz (RF, SF), with his incredible raw power and bat speed, could take over in either corner outfield spot. He made better contact in 2007, which allowed him to hit for BA in Triple-A (.333) and for the Giants (.304), but his swing can get lengthy. His power is his calling card, hitting 16 HR with a .560 SLG. He is an average defender.

Ian Stewart (3B/2B, COL) produces above average power with plus bat speed, and hit .304/.379/.478 with 15 HR in Triple-A. His plate discipline (0.53 Eye) is improving, but he can still be tied up by good pitching. He has turned into a solid defender with a strong arm, but unless a trade happens, he may have to move to 2B or RF.

Ryan Sweeney (CF, CHW) didn't get an opportunity with Chicago after a disappointing Triple-A season that saw him hit .270/.348/.398 with 10 HR and a 0.68 Eye. A lean athlete with good bat speed, his mediocre power hasn't matched projections. He does square up well to the ball for a solid BA and should make the White Sox' roster.

Geovany Soto (C/1B, CHC) led the minors in SLG and was named PCL MVP in a breakthrough offensive performance. In Triple-A, he hit .350/.422/.645 with 25 HR and a 0.56 Eye. The power was quite a surprise, but he has always made good contact. He doesn't have a lot of agility, but has good arm strength and could be the Cubs' starter.

Justin Towles (C, HOU) could begin 2008 as the starting catcher with his strong September (.375 BA) and improved defense. His athleticism, arm strength and quick release are strengths, but he needs better receiving skills and accuracy. Hit .287/.393/.447 with 11 HR, 15 SB and a 0.68 Eye at three levels.

Joey Votto (1B, CIN), the top 1B prospect in the minors, hit .294/.381/.478 with 22 HR in Triple-A and hit .321 in 84 AB for Cincinnati, which should give him the starting nod in 2008. Not a big HR threat, but can hit for BA and produce doubles. Steals bases (17 SB) despite below average speed and his defense is much improved.

Neil Walker (3B, PIT) made a smooth defensive transition to 3B, which gave him better focus offensively. With his smooth, LH stroke, he hit .277/.349/.434 with 13 HR, 33 doubles, and a 0.64 Eye between Triple and Double-A. Offensively, he's ready for the Majors, but Pittsburgh may want him to clean up his footwork at 3B.

Brandon Wood (3B, LAA) possesses the bat speed and loft power to be solid run producer and hit .272/.338/.497 with 23 HR and 10 SB at Triple-A. He racks-up tons of strikeouts due to his aggressive nature which suppresses his BA. The defensive transition to 3B went well, showing good arm strength, and will be given first shot this spring.

The Top Ranked Prospects for 2008

Evan Longoria (3B, TAM)
Clay Buchholz (RHP, BOS)
Joba Chamberlain (RHP, NYY)
Jacoby Ellsbury (CF, BOS)
Franklin Morales (LHP, COL)
Geovany Soto (C/1B, CHC)
Homer Bailey (RHP, CIN)
Ian Kennedy (RHP, NYY)
Brandon Wood (3B, LAA)
Joey Votto (1B, CIN)

Steven Pearce (RF/1B, PIT)
Andy LaRoche (3B/LF, LAD)
Daric Barton (1B, OAK)
Aaron Laffey (LHP, CLE)
Jay Bruce (CF, CIN)
Jon Meloan RHP, LAD)
Brandon Jones (LF, ATL)
Gio Gonzalez (LHP, CHW)
Luke Hochevar (RHP, KC)
Matt Antonelli (2B, SD)

Justin Towles (C, HOU)
Ian Stewart (3B/2B, COL)
Colby Rasmus (CF, STL)
Cameron Maybin (CF, DET)
Nate Schierholtz (RF, SF)
Adam Miller (RHP, CLE)
Manny Parra (LHP, MIL)
Jair Jurrjens (RHP, ATL)
Neil Walker (3B, PIT)
Shelley Duncan (LF/1B, NYY)

Eric Hurley (RHP, TEX)
Chris Perez (RHP, STL)
Joey Devine (RHP, ATL)
Garrett Olson (LHP, BAL)
John Lannan (LHP, WAS)
Radhames Liz (RHP, BAL)
James Hoey (RHP, BAL)
Andrew McCutchen (CF, PIT)
Jacob McGee (LHP, TAM)
Wade Davis (RHP, TAM)

Johnny Cueto (RHP, CIN)
Troy Patton (LHP, HOU)
Wladimir Balentien (RF, SEA)
Chase Headley (3B, SD)
David Price (LHP, TAM)
Ross Detwiler (LHP, WAS)
Jeff Clement (C, SEA)
Ryan Sweeney (CF, CHW)
Chris Lubanski (LF, KC)

Top Japanese Prospects

by Tom Mulhall

Aoki, Norichika (OF, Yakult Swallows) could be the best player on this list, but has just three years of service time. Think "Ichiro-lite" – high BA and plenty of speed. Aoki has expressed an interest in coming over "Down the road." His team will post, but it would be very surprising if Aoki was posted soon. If you can afford to stash him on reserve for a few years, it may be worth the wait. *Possible ETA: 2009 at the earliest with 2010 more likely.*

Darvish, Yu (RHP, Nippon Ham Fighters) is a hugely talented young pitcher who followed a sterling first full season (12 wins, 2.89 ERA) with an even more impressive year (15 wins, 1.82 ERA) to unanimously win the Sawamura Award (Japan's equivalent of the Cy Young Award). Half Iranian, some journalists wonder if he would feel comfortable playing in the U.S. With only two full years of service time, he could be years away from the Majors. *Possible ETA: 2010 at the earliest.*

Fujikawa, Kyuji (RHP, Hanshin Tigers) is a very capable closer whose team previously posted Kei Igawa. He has the talent to succeed in the Majors but it would be surprising if he is posted any time soon since he only has a few years service time. *Possible ETA: 2010 at the earliest.*

Fukudome, Kosuke (OF, Chunichi Dragons, and pronounced "Fookoo-Doh-Meh") is the best all-around hitter coming over from Japan. Described as a "Bobby Abreu type," he should have moderate across-the-board success. Good defensive player as well, although some question if he can handle CF in the Majors. Coming off elbow surgery so don't let the hype make you go overboard. *Probable ETA: 2008*

Fukumori, Kazuo (RHP, Rakuten Golden Eagles) is a good closer on a bad team – just 59 saves in the past four years. He was average in 2005, very good in '06, and then slid a little in '07. Still, 9.0 K/9 the past two years may mean he's worth a gamble even if he starts off as a middle reliever in the ML. He has announced he will only return to Rakuten or sign with a ML team. Probable ETA: 2008.

Ishii, Hirotoshi (LHP, Yakult Swallows) wants to join MLB badly. His team agreed to post him after the 2006 season, but an injury derailed those plans and caused him to miss all of 2007. He needs to rebound this year and prove he is healthy. Since time on the DL does not count towards free agency, he again may have to rely on the kindness of his strange owner. *Probable ETA: 2009.*

Iwase, Hitoki (LHP, Chunichi Dragons) is coming off four straight successful years as a closer and was the highest paid native born pitcher in Japan last year. Just signed a one-year extension rather than an offered four-year deal, so *probable ETA: 2008 or 2009.*

Kawakami, Kenshin (RHP, Chunichi Dragons) has impressive credentials for someone with less hype than other pitchers: 1998 Rookie of the Year; 2004 Central League MVP, Sawamura winner and multiple All-Star selections. He is the highest paid starting pitcher in Japan and will be a free agent after 2008. *Possible ETA: 2009.*

Kobayashi, Mashahide (RHP, Chiba Lotte Marines) is an experienced closer with a 2.72 lifetime ERA. A free agent, but there is not much to indicate he may be willing to cross over. If he does, he could be a decent but not dominant closer. *Possible ETA: 2008 or never.*

Kroon, Marc (RHP, Yokohama BayStars) is a former major leaguer who turned himself into one of Japan's best closers over the past three seasons. Negotiations with his team have hit a snag and he may now be coming home. Might be worth a gamble, but he'll be 35 and never had much MLB success. *Possible ETA: 2008 or never.*

Kuroda, Hiroki (RHP, Hiroshima Toyo Carp) had two solid years, then fell off in 2007. Good control, a mid-90's fastball and several off pitches including a "shootball", supposedly a combination fastball, slider and sinker. Played in a bandbox, so could be helped by a larger MLB park. Could make a decent #3 or #4 starter. *Probable ETA: 2008.*

Lee, Seung-yeop (1B, Yomiuri Giants) has three years remaining on a four year contract, but could have opted out and signed with an MLB team if the Giants had won the championship. They didn't. He is having off-season surgery on his thumb, which could have some nerve damage, and he'll be 33 when he can first make a move, so he may not be worth following. *Possible ETA: 2009 at the earliest.*

Maeda, Yukinaga (LHP, Yomiuri Giants) was productive from 1998 through 2004, but since then has had ERA's of 4.65, 7.23 and 5.06. Released by his team and is now almost 38 years old. Avoid. *Possible ETA: 2008*

Nioka, Tomohiro (SS/3B, Yomiuri Giants) has decent power for a middle infielder. His batting eye is a little questionable and he may struggle at first. If he comes over, he might be worth a gamble. *Possible ETA: 2008.*

Saito, Kazumi (RHP, Softbank Hawks) is possibly Japan's best starting pitcher, even better than Matsuzaka. He led the Pacific League in ERA, wins, winning percentage and strikeouts in 2006. Had a solid season in '07 despite missing time with a recurring shoulder problem. His team doesn't post so he won't come over until 2009. Risky due to his shoulder, but big upside. *Probable ETA: 2009.*

Saito, Yuki (RHP, Waseda University) is a sensational starting pitcher who elected to attend college rather than sign with a Japanese team and is therefore not bound by the posting system. He has the potential to be the best pitcher on this list, but is years away. *Possible ETA: 2010.*

Shimoyangi, Tsuyoshi (LHP, Hanshin Tigers) was used in middle relief unsuccessfully after two decent years as a starter. He is 39 years old. Pass. *Possible ETA: 2008.*

Uehara, Koji (RHP, Yomiuri Giants) was once considered the best starter pitcher in Japan after Matsuzaka, but has fallen in some estimations. A control pitcher, he was used as a closer against his wishes in 2007 after coming off an injury. He did very well and his team plans to use him there again in '08. He's been yanked around by the Giants, both with his usage and free agency, so odds are he will leave at the first opportunity. The question is whether it's for another Japanese team or MLB. *Probable ETA: 2009.*

Yabuta, Yasuhiko (RHP, Chiba Lotte Marines) is the set-up man for Mashahide Kobayashi. He has expressed some interest in coming over to the Majors. Four very solid years in a row with almost a strikeout an inning. Only a middle reliever, but could be a good one. *Probable ETA: 2008.*

Major League Equivalents

In his 1985 *Baseball Abstract*, Bill James introduced the concept of major league equivalencies. His assertion was that, with the proper adjustments, a minor leaguer's statistics could be converted to an equivalent major league level performance with a great deal of accuracy.

Because of wide variations in the level of play among different minor leagues, it is difficult to get a true reading on a player's potential. For instance, a .300 AVG achieved in the high-offense Pacific Coast League is not nearly as much of an accomplishment as a similar level in the Eastern League. MLEs normalize these type of variances, for all statistical categories.

The actual MLEs are not projections. They represent how a player's previous performance might look at the major league level. However, that MLE stat line can be used in forecasting future performance in just the same way as a major league stat line would.

The model we use contains a few variations to James' version and updates all of the minor league and ballpark factors. In addition, we designed a module to convert pitching statistics, which is something James did not do.

Another of the enhancements we made is to include an adjustment for each player's age and relative level reached at that age. This serves to truly separate the prospects from the suspects. In other words, it might seem that John Lindsey's 30 HR, .317 season looks worthy of a shot in the majors, but a 31-year-old facing young Double-A pitching is bound to put up good numbers. His MLE of 18 HRs, .202 shows the appropriate — albeit radical — adjustment facing potential big league pitchers, and diffuses any thought of him being able to help a major league club.

Do MLEs really work?

Used correctly, MLEs are excellent indicators of potential. But, just like we cannot take traditional major league statistics at face value, the same goes for MLEs. The underlying measures of base skill — batting eye ratios, pitching command ratios, etc. — are far more accurate in evaluating future talent than raw home runs, batting averages or ERAs.

The charts we present here also provide the unique perspective of looking at two year's worth of data. These are only short-term trends, for sure. But even here we can find small indications of players improving their skills, or struggling, as they rise through more difficult levels of competition. Since players — especially those with any modicum of talent — are promoted rapidly through major league systems, a two-year scan is often all we get to spot any trends. Five-year trends do appear in the *Minor League Baseball Analyst*.

Here are some things to look for as you scan these charts:
Target players who...
- spent a full season in Double-A and then a full season at Triple-A
- had consistent playing time from one year to the next
- maintained or improved their base skills levels as they were promoted.

Raise the warning flag for players who...
- were stuck at the same level both years, or regressed
- displayed marked changes in playing time from one year to the next.
- showed large drops in BPIs from one year to the next.

Players are listed on the charts if they spent at least part of 2006 or 2007 in Triple-A or Double-A and had at least 100 at bats or 30 innings pitched within those two levels. Each is listed with the organization they finished the season with.

Only statistics accumulated in Triple-A and Double-A ball are included (players who split a season are indicated as a/a); major league and Single-A stats are excluded.

Each player's actual AB and IP totals are used as the base for the conversion. However, it is more useful to compare performances using common levels, so rely on the ratios and sabermetric gauges. Complete explanations of these formulas appear in the glossary.

Batters who have a BPV of at least 50, and pitchers who have a BPV of at least 90, and are under 26 years of age (the "unofficial" break point between prospect and suspect) are indicated with an "a" after their age. This should provide a pool of the best rising prospects.

However, also be sure to keep an eye on players over 26, but under 30, with similarly high BPVs. These are your "Bull Durham" prospects, indicated with a "b" after their age. Keep these players on your end-game or reserve list radar as there could be hidden short-term value here too.

Major League Equivalent Statistics

BATTER	Yr	Age	Pos	Lev	Org	ab	r	h	d	t	hr	rbi	bb	k	sb	cs	ba	ob	slg	ops	bb%	ct%	eye	px	sx	rc/g	bpv
Abad,Andy	06	34	8	aaa	CIN	266	32	62	11	0	8	28	22	32	0	1	233	291	365	656	8%	88%	0.67	83	33	3.69	25
	07	35	3	aaa	MIL	269	39	71	11	0	10	47	20	36	5	2	264	315	415	730	7%	87%	0.56	93	70	4.69	37
Abercrombie,Reg	07	27	8	aa	FLA	353	51	86	17	6	12	39	8	104	29	6	245	262	426	687	2%	71%	0.08	109	214	3.85	28
Abernathy,Brent	06	29	4	aaa	MIL	439	52	107	15	0	5	35	34	59	15	10	245	298	309	607	7%	86%	0.57	45	79	3.14	12
	07	30	543	aaa	WAS	357	32	78	14	1	2	30	28	38	13	6	219	276	280	556	7%	89%	0.74	46	85	2.64	7
Abreu,Michel	06	27	3	aa	NYM	398	52	111	23	1	13	59	37	95	0	0	280	342	439	781	9%	76%	0.39	103	36	5.61	44
Abreu,Tony	06	22	4	aa	LA	457	64	123	22	2	6	53	31	69	8	4	269	316	365	681	6%	85%	0.45	67	93	4.16	26
	07	23 ε	4	aa	LA	234	41	75	20	3	2	15	12	29	4	0	321	354	457	811	5%	88%	0.41	100	133	6.36	56
Aceves,Jonathan	06	29	2	a/a	FLA	255	27	47	16	0	4	23	17	69	0	1	183	234	297	531	6%	73%	0.24	82	44	2.26	-0
Acuna,Ron	06	27	8	aa	MIL	400	37	85	15	2	1	41	22	94	2	5	212	253	264	517	5%	77%	0.24	40	66	2.17	-8
Adams,Russ	06	26	6	aaa	TOR	161	18	48	9	2	0	14	15	22	3	2	295	354	374	727	8%	87%	0.67	59	100	4.95	36
	07	27	4	aaa	TOR	431	50	100	21	2	10	44	32	52	3	3	231	285	355	640	7%	88%	0.63	81	68	3.47	23
Aguila,Chris	06	28	8	aaa	FLA	302	40	80	12	2	8	46	21	48	6	4	264	312	393	705	6%	84%	0.43	81	93	4.31	30
	07	29	8	aa	PIT	172	16	32	4	1	2	15	6	43	2	2	186	212	260	472	3%	75%	0.13	46	84	1.72	-16
Airoso,Kurt	06	32	8	aa	DET	430	43	68	11	1	11	42	54	163	1	1	158	252	260	512	11%	62%	0.33	62	43	2.21	-15
Aldridge,Cory	06	27	8	a/a	NYM	376	29	79	17	2	3	29	24	120	8	5	211	259	285	543	6%	68%	0.20	54	84	2.43	-4
	07	28	8	aa	CHW	421	44	83	25	2	8	43	54	136	4	2	198	288	325	613	11%	68%	0.39	87	80	3.24	9
Alexander,Manny	06	36	6	aaa	SD	430	54	86	16	0	5	25	24	52	10	5	201	244	270	514	5%	88%	0.47	50	95	2.18	-3
	07	37	6	a/a	WAS	293	23	48	10	2	2	16	12	60	2	2	164	197	229	426	4%	80%	0.20	45	95	1.39	-23
Alfaro,Jason	06	29	5	aaa	PIT	374	33	86	22	1	9	47	20	48	2	4	229	269	368	637	5%	87%	0.42	94	46	3.26	23
	07	30	6	aa	NYM	312	26	59	11	0	8	32	10	48	1	1	190	214	296	510	3%	85%	0.20	67	42	2.03	-5
Alfonzo,Edgardo	06	33	4	aaa	NYM	141	9	30	5	0	3	16	14	16	0	1	211	280	306	586	9%	89%	0.87	64	16	2.91	14
Alfonzo,Eliezer	06	28	2	a/a	SF	139	10	26	3	1	2	10	8	33	1	0	188	231	257	488	5%	76%	0.23	42	66	1.99	-16
Allegra,Matthew	06	25	8	aa	OAK	355	40	77	23	1	11	47	29	107	3	3	215	274	378	652	8%	70%	0.27	108	63	3.47	22
	07	26	8	aa	MIN	373	41	70	23	1	9	41	22	92	2	2	187	231	324	556	6%	75%	0.24	94	69	2.42	6
Allen,Chad	06	32	8	aaa	KC	417	32	111	23	3	10	63	26	58	1	4	265	309	406	714	6%	86%	0.45	92	42	4.36	36
Allen,Luke	06	28	8	aaa	SD	305	28	68	14	1	7	42	25	68	1	1	223	282	338	620	8%	78%	0.37	76	47	3.29	13
	07	29	8	aa	LA	106	9	17	3	0	1	5	8	19	2	2	156	217	205	422	7%	82%	0.44	36	63	1.35	-24
Almonte,Erick	07	30	6	a/a	DET	297	30	66	13	1	3	34	42	67	5	3	224	319	306	626	12%	77%	0.62	59	65	3.53	11
Alomar Jr.,Sandy	07	41	2	aa	NYM	160	9	28	5	1	2	18	5	30	1	0	175	200	254	453	3%	81%	0.16	51	53	1.63	-17
Alvarez,Gerardo	06	27	4	aa	BAL	326	34	57	10	0	3	25	21	74	8	5	176	226	238	463	6%	77%	0.28	43	84	1.71	-18
Alvarez,Nick	06	30	8	a/a	LA	202	23	39	6	1	2	12	9	39	3	2	195	229	268	497	4%	81%	0.23	48	97	2.00	-11
Alvarez,Rafael	06	30	8	aa	PIT	244	21	44	5	2	3	18	16	85	0	0	178	228	252	480	6%	65%	0.18	44	76	1.90	-19
Alvarez,Tony	06	28	8	a/a	BAL	334	34	72	12	1	6	31	18	73	12	9	216	256	310	567	5%	78%	0.24	61	91	2.47	2
Amador,Christoph	06	24	6	aa	CHW	231	24	47	9	1	2	15	13	71	12	3	202	243	273	516	5%	69%	0.18	50	123	2.28	-9
Ambres,Chip	06	27	8	aaa	KC	187	16	34	8	1	2	13	19	36	2	4	182	258	265	523	9%	81%	0.54	57	68	2.16	-5
	07	28	8	aa	NYM	427	56	87	17	0	13	49	49	106	5	0	204	286	338	624	10%	75%	0.46	84	73	3.43	12
Anderson,Brian	07	26	1	aaa	CHW	200	26	49	7	1	9	28	18	43	3	2	243	305	421	725	8%	78%	0.41	104	78	4.43	32
Anderson,Bryan	07	21	2	aa	STL	389	44	107	14	1	5	45	28	59	0	1	275	325	356	681	7%	85%	0.48	54	39	4.24	24
Anderson,Drew	06	25	4	aa	CIN	148	16	35	8	2	2	13	12	26	2	2	237	293	353	646	7%	83%	0.46	78	102	3.52	20
	07	26	48	a/a	CIN	518	64	116	28	4	10	48	42	108	10	7	225	282	350	633	7%	79%	0.39	84	105	3.33	17
Anderson,Drew	06	25	8	a/a	MIL	465	67	124	28	4	7	46	37	93	18	10	268	322	386	708	7%	80%	0.40	82	123	4.38	31
	07	26	48	a/a	MIL	420	54	101	31	4	4	37	23	100	14	8	240	280	356	636	5%	76%	0.23	85	129	3.32	20
Anderson,Josh	06	24	8	aa	HOU	561	67	152	22	4	3	41	22	65	35	14	271	298	339	637	4%	88%	0.33	48	128	3.53	17
	07	25	8	aa	HOU	513	48	114	14	5	2	32	23	70	30	8	223	257	277	534	4%	86%	0.33	36	135	2.48	-4
Andino,Robert	06	22	6	aaa	FLA	498	57	116	16	5	6	38	28	79	11	14	232	273	323	596	5%	84%	0.36	57	109	2.76	8
	07	23	6	aa	FLA	598	70	146	22	10	11	42	35	121	17	15	245	287	368	655	6%	80%	0.29	75	143	3.44	18
Andrus,Erold	07	23	8	aa	TAM	206	22	43	13	0	2	12	10	37	2	1	207	243	297	539	4%	82%	0.26	69	68	2.39	3
Ankiel,Rick	07	28	8	aa	STL	387	41	73	10	2	20	58	17	90	2	3	188	222	378	600	4%	77%	0.19	107	68	2.61	11
Antonelli,Matthew	07	22	4	aa	SD	187	31	50	9	1	6	22	27	34	9	3	267	360	422	782	13%	82%	0.79	97	108	5.71	45
Appert,Luke	07	27	8	aa	OAK	275	25	58	13	1	3	32	33	48	1	1	211	296	302	598	11%	82%	0.69	64	45	3.17	11
Ardoin,Danny	07	33	2	aa	STL	197	13	25	8	0	1	6	15	60	1	0	124	188	185	373	7%	70%	0.26	46	45	1.13	-35
Arhart,Josh	07	28	2	aa	TAM	167	12	26	7	0	2	11	12	36	0	0	153	210	225	435	7%	78%	0.33	53	26	1.54	-20
Arias,Joaquin	06	22	6	aaa	TEX	493	56	139	15	12	4	48	19	56	26	11	281	308	383	691	4%	89%	0.34	60	178	4.17	25
Arlis,Patrick	06	26	2	aa	FLA	205	18	41	12	0	2	12	32	54	2	1	202	311	285	596	14%	73%	0.60	64	40	3.23	6
Arnold,Eric	06	26	5	aa	TOR	141	11	31	9	0	4	22	8	53	0	3	222	263	376	639	5%	63%	0.15	102	26	3.07	19
Arteaga,Josh	06	27	6	aa	ATL	328	24	61	10	0	6	23	23	75	2	0	186	240	271	511	7%	77%	0.31	55	42	2.19	-9
Asadoorian,Rick	06	26	8	aa	CIN	300	30	66	10	2	3	23	15	82	4	5	220	257	302	559	5%	73%	0.18	54	88	2.48	-1
Asanovich,Robert	07	25	4	aa	TAM	401	36	83	16	1	4	28	32	64	6	6	206	265	280	545	7%	84%	0.50	52	65	2.45	0
Ashby,Chris	06	32	2	aaa	FLA	198	19	48	9	0	3	27	12	27	2	1	241	283	327	611	6%	87%	0.44	61	50	3.24	14
	07	33	2	aa	FLA	152	11	22	4	0	3	14	15	39	0	1	143	222	221	443	9%	75%	0.40	49	28	1.59	-24
Ash,Jonathan	06	24	4	aa	HOU	392	32	108	19	5	1	23	20	33	4	9	276	311	356	668	5%	92%	0.61	57	80	3.72	28
	07	25	4	aa	HOU	280	25	69	13	2	3	25	19	16	2	3	248	295	334	629	6%	94%	1.22	60	62	3.40	32
Aspito,Jason	06	28	8	a/a	LAA	386	36	74	10	1	11	37	20	71	3	8	192	231	311	542	5%	82%	0.28	71	53	2.14	-1
Athas,Jamie	06	27	6	aa	FLA	159	14	28	3	1	3	9	12	39	3	0	175	234	257	491	7%	75%	0.31	50	87	2.06	-15
Aubrey,Michael	07	25	30	aa	CLE	207	17	42	10	0	5	27	9	34	0	0	204	238	330	568	4%	83%	0.26	83	22	2.60	7
Aviles,Mike	06	26	6	aaa	KC	469	46	115	21	3	6	42	25	41	12	5	245	283	340	623	5%	91%	0.60	64	97	3.33	20
	07	27	654	aa	KC	538	58	129	23	4	11	57	23	56	3	5	239	270	362	632	4%	90%	0.40	78	79	3.25	20
Avlas,Phil	06	24	2	aa	ARI	278	39	70	17	0	7	26	42	46	3	5	251	349	387	736	13%	83%	0.90	93	47	4.80	40
	07	25	8	aa	ARI	228	22	41	3	1	1	12	22	38	3	1	179	251	213	463	9%	83%	0.58	21	78	1.86	-20
Aybar,Erick	06	23	6	aaa	LAA	339	51	88	19	2	5	37	17	27	26	23	260	295	375	670	5%	92%	0.63	79	135	3.11	32
Aybar,Willy	06	24 ε	5	aaa	ATL	207	25	57	11	1	7	32	19	21	1	4	275	336	440	776	8%	90%	0.90	104	52	5.09	53
Bacani,David	06	27	4	aa	BOS	406	45	76	17	1	3	33	39	70	8	4	186	257	258	515	9%	83%	0.56	52	86	2.25	-5
Bacon,Dwaine	06	28	8	aa	LAA	339	26	51	11	2	3	17	22	71	22	12	152	204	223	427	6%	79%	0.32	48	122	1.36	-23
Badeaux,Brooks	06	30	4	a/a	BAL	272	22	47	7	0	5	24	16	57	1	3	172	219	253	472	6%	79%	0.29	52	39	1.70	-16
	07	31	84	aa	TAM	396	32	69	13	1	1	29	21	63	1	4	175	217	219	436	5%	84%	0.33	34	54	1.49	-21
Bailey,Jeff	06	28	3	aaa	BOS	458	57	118	23	4	19	72	67	111	1	2	257	351	448	799	13%	76%	0.60	116	63	5.78	45
	07	29	3	aaa	BOS	404	54	89	23	1	12	50	49	96	7	6	221	306	373	679	11%	76%	0.52	99	76	3.91	25
Baisley,Jeffrey	07	25	5	aa	OAK	404	48	90	20	2	9	37	23	72	3	1	223	265	346	611	5%	82%	0.32	81	83	3.13	14
Baker,Jeff	06	25	8	aaa	COL	482	52	137	28	3	17	80	34	78	5	1	283	330	458	788	7%	84%	0.43	110	78	5.61	49
Baker,John	06	26	2	aaa	OAK	293	39	70	18	1	3	30	31	61	5	0	240	312	338	650	9%	79%	0.51	73	91	3.91	20
	07	27	2	aa	FLA	270	26	61	12	0	6	30	22	61	2	0	226	283	338	622	7%	77%	0.36	75	46	3.38	13

BATTER	Yr	Age	Pos	Lev	Org	ab	r	h	d	t	hr	rbi	bb	k	sb	cs	ba	ob	slg	ops	bb%	ct%	eye	px	sx	rc/g	bpv
Baker,Steve	06	26	8	aa	SD	128	12	24	4	1	1	10	13	48	1	0	190	265	258	524	9%	62%	0.27	47	82	2.41	-12
Baldiris,Aarom	06	24	4	a/a	TEX	352	30	81	17	1	4	30	13	47	3	5	230	258	318	576	4%	87%	0.28	63	58	2.63	8
	07	25	5	aa	NYY	286	33	65	8	1	8	32	26	49	1	0	226	290	339	628	8%	83%	0.52	68	57	3.47	14
Balentien,Wladimii	06	22	8	aa	SEA	444	72	96	22	1	21	77	69	139	13	7	216	322	412	734	13%	69%	0.50	119	91	4.60	31
	07	23	8	aa	SEA	477	65	122	22	2	19	71	48	100	13	5	256	324	433	757	9%	79%	0.48	108	93	5.03	39
Ball,Jarred	07	24	8	aa	ARI	270	31	66	21	2	2	29	17	40	9	5	243	288	355	643	6%	85%	0.43	86	110	3.47	25
Bankston,Wes	06	23	3	a/a	TAM	362	41	98	19	1	9	47	21	77	4	2	271	311	403	714	5%	79%	0.27	87	67	4.50	32
	07	24	30	aaa	TAM	390	44	88	22	1	15	56	24	85	2	0	226	271	403	673	6%	78%	0.28	112	63	3.75	27
Bannon,Jeff	06	27	6	a/a	CIN	350	26	73	20	1	6	37	12	68	4	3	209	235	323	559	3%	81%	0.18	80	66	2.47	6
	07	28	8	aaa	CIN	313	27	65	11	1	4	33	18	58	3	0	208	250	285	536	5%	81%	0.30	53	70	2.45	-3
Barden,Brian	06	26	5	aaa	ARI	494	61	134	34	2	13	73	35	71	1	4	271	318	425	743	7%	86%	0.49	104	49	4.77	43
	07	27	56	aa	STL	352	30	71	9	1	3	26	26	63	2	3	203	258	255	512	7%	82%	0.41	36	50	2.17	-10
Barker,Kevin	06	31	3	aaa	TOR	473	59	114	36	2	15	62	66	122	5	3	242	334	422	757	12%	74%	0.54	121	67	5.09	41
	07	32	3	aaa	TOR	470	52	103	19	1	15	58	56	113	3	0	218	301	360	661	11%	76%	0.49	88	57	3.87	19
Barker,Sean	06	26	8	aaa	COL	330	39	90	13	8	11	40	21	74	13	8	273	317	456	773	6%	78%	0.29	105	174	4.94	40
	07	27	8	aa	COL	261	36	69	18	2	4	32	10	61	9	5	264	291	394	685	4%	76%	0.16	92	121	3.89	29
Barmes,Clint	07	29	6	aa	COL	428	45	98	15	4	8	29	15	50	6	6	230	256	340	597	3%	88%	0.30	69	98	2.83	11
Barnes,Larry	07	33	38	aa	LA	178	12	26	3	1	5	14	6	37	1	1	146	172	260	431	3%	79%	0.15	64	74	1.34	-22
Barnwell,Chris	06	28	6	aaa	MIL	383	39	103	17	2	4	31	33	59	13	7	268	326	352	679	8%	85%	0.56	59	90	4.15	25
	07	29	6	aaa	MIL	456	58	105	21	2	7	32	29	70	10	4	230	276	328	605	6%	85%	0.41	67	102	3.14	13
Bartlett,Jason	06	27	6	aaa	MIN	235	41	69	22	3	1	19	10	30	6	3	293	321	425	746	4%	87%	0.32	101	141	4.92	46
Barton,Brian	06	24	8	aa	CLE	151	29	47	5	0	5	23	11	26	13	5	308	357	434	791	7%	83%	0.43	77	112	5.77	43
	07	25	8	a/a	CLE	476	54	126	20	1	8	55	42	111	18	10	265	325	359	684	8%	77%	0.38	64	84	4.12	22
Barton,Daric	06	21	3	aaa	OAK	147	22	36	7	2	2	19	28	18	1	0	247	366	367	732	16%	88%	1.51	76	103	5.19	44
	07	22	3	aaa	OAK	516	71	139	37	3	7	59	65	56	3	5	269	351	393	745	11%	89%	1.16	90	65	5.06	50
Basak,Chris	06	28	6	aaa	NYM	371	49	91	21	2	7	33	36	77	16	3	246	313	366	679	9%	79%	0.47	82	118	4.24	25
	07	29	5	aaa	MIN	341	46	77	19	1	7	38	19	71	13	3	226	266	344	610	5%	79%	0.26	80	117	3.19	14
Bass,Bryan	06	24	5	aa	BAL	212	29	41	10	2	3	22	37	80	9	3	193	313	296	609	15%	62%	0.46	68	129	3.39	2
	07	25	5	aa	BAL	339	39	63	14	0	8	27	26	103	12	5	186	244	300	544	7%	70%	0.25	75	93	2.41	-2
Batista,Tony	07	34	5	aaa	WAS	107	12	25	5	1	5	18	6	17	1	0	236	278	429	707	6%	84%	0.38	117	78	4.16	34
Batista,Wilson	06	26	6	aa	NYM	468	55	98	17	1	9	36	36	88	5	7	210	266	308	574	7%	81%	0.41	64	68	2.66	4
	07	27	4	aa	NYM	301	23	55	13	1	4	18	6	55	5	3	182	198	275	473	2%	82%	0.11	63	87	1.69	-11
Bautista,Jose	06	26 ε	5	aaa	PIT	101	12	28	9	0	2	9	13	18	2	1	274	356	421	778	11%	82%	0.71	108	52	5.61	50
Bautista,Rayner	06	28	6	aa	BAL	424	35	85	19	1	6	30	5	131	3	2	200	209	289	498	1%	69%	0.04	62	71	1.90	-7
Bear,Ryan	06	26	3	aa	FLA	477	32	100	18	1	6	52	56	104	4	5	209	292	291	583	10%	78%	0.53	56	39	2.94	3
	07	27	8	aa	FLA	357	35	71	14	0	7	37	27	85	3	1	200	256	297	553	7%	76%	0.32	65	54	2.59	-0
Beattie,Andrew	06	29	4	aaa	OAK	276	36	64	11	1	7	42	33	57	6	3	233	316	361	676	11%	79%	0.59	81	80	4.05	22
	07	30	4	a/a	FLA	269	26	50	6	1	9	33	29	72	4	4	186	264	314	578	10%	73%	0.40	74	64	2.69	0
Bellhorn,Mark	07	33	40	aaa	CIN	326	31	70	20	0	11	45	50	91	0	0	215	319	375	694	13%	72%	0.54	105	13	4.30	26
Bellorin,Edwin	06	25	2	aaa	LA	321	24	63	11	0	6	37	10	46	1	2	196	221	287	507	3%	86%	0.22	59	38	2.00	-6
	07	26 ε	2	aa	COL	221	29	62	15	0	7	33	13	23	1	0	281	320	448	768	5%	89%	0.54	112	46	5.27	51
Bell,Bubba Wayne	07	25	8	aa	BOS	147	18	34	5	1	3	17	11	15	4	0	233	288	336	624	7%	90%	0.77	64	101	3.54	20
Bell,Rick	06	28	5	aaa	KC	364	24	68	11	2	3	27	14	60	2	1	188	219	253	472	4%	84%	0.24	44	64	1.80	-14
Benjamin,Casey	06	26	6	aa	TEX	329	35	77	17	2	6	34	25	53	3	3	233	287	352	639	7%	84%	0.48	80	70	3.46	20
	07	27	6	aa	TEX	469	51	89	20	3	7	38	50	71	6	1	189	267	294	561	10%	85%	0.70	69	98	2.73	5
Bergeron,Peter	06	29	8	a/a	PHI	446	51	93	19	3	8	35	42	91	9	9	208	275	313	588	9%	80%	0.46	69	89	2.79	7
	07	30	8	aa	PIT	104	8	17	3	1	0	6	5	20	2	0	166	206	209	415	5%	81%	0.26	32	90	1.45	-26
Bergolla,William	06	24	4	aaa	CIN	416	44	112	21	1	2	32	21	45	14	8	269	304	339	643	5%	89%	0.47	54	87	3.59	21
	07	25	4	aa	SF	356	49	95	20	1	5	29	24	41	10	3	267	313	368	681	6%	88%	0.58	73	97	4.19	30
Bernadina,Rogear	07	23	8	a/a	WAS	413	56	96	16	2	5	33	40	81	35	16	232	300	317	617	9%	80%	0.49	57	129	3.24	11
Bernier,Douglas	06	26	6	aa	COL	246	30	57	13	3	1	18	20	38	3	1	230	288	315	603	8%	85%	0.53	62	105	3.20	13
	07	27	5	aa	COL	216	18	53	12	0	2	18	22	48	2	2	246	314	323	637	9%	78%	0.45	60	44	3.65	15
Berroa,Angel	07	30	6	aa	KC	307	30	64	13	0	5	26	17	49	2	2	208	248	293	541	5%	84%	0.33	59	50	2.41	0
Bibbs,Kennard	06	27	8	a/a	MIL	164	23	50	8	1	1	17	27	44	14	5	302	401	379	779	14%	73%	0.61	57	114	6.19	36
Bigbie,Larry	07	30	8	a/a	ATL	312	36	71	18	2	3	28	27	68	4	0	226	288	326	614	8%	78%	0.40	72	93	3.37	13
Bixler,Brian	06	24	6	aa	PIT	226	32	64	13	1	3	16	14	53	6	2	283	324	386	710	6%	77%	0.26	73	99	4.61	30
	07	25	6	aa	PIT	475	62	116	22	7	4	41	42	115	23	5	244	305	342	647	8%	76%	0.36	65	161	3.84	16
Blakely,Darren	06	30	8	a/a	CHW	321	24	48	10	1	5	17	12	82	3	2	151	182	232	415	4%	75%	0.15	53	77	1.31	-25
Blalock,Jake	06	23	8	aa	TEX	376	30	91	17	0	7	34	33	72	7	3	243	304	343	647	8%	81%	0.46	69	53	3.71	18
	07	24	8	aa	KC	158	6	22	5	1	1	13	10	26	2	0	138	187	198	386	6%	83%	0.36	41	65	1.22	-30
Blanco,Andres	06	22	6	aaa	KC	283	28	66	9	3	2	19	20	33	5	4	234	284	312	596	7%	88%	0.60	51	102	3.00	11
Blanco,Gregor	06	23	8	a/a	ATL	520	84	146	27	3	0	27	93	107	30	16	281	390	344	734	15%	79%	0.87	51	110	5.20	32
	07	24	8	aaa	ATL	464	73	124	17	4	3	31	56	78	21	20	267	346	341	687	11%	83%	0.72	50	116	4.00	24
Blanco,Tony	07	26	80	aa	WAS	253	23	48	10	1	7	33	11	57	4	0	189	222	320	542	4%	78%	0.19	82	85	2.36	0
Blasi,Nicholas	07	26	8	aa	OAK	341	43	88	11	1	3	32	21	85	8	4	258	301	319	619	6%	75%	0.25	43	88	3.38	9
Blue,Vincent	06	24	8	aa	DET	409	43	88	13	1	0	19	46	102	22	15	216	294	251	546	10%	75%	0.45	29	94	2.52	-7
Bocachica,Hiram	06	31	8	aaa	OAK	291	44	77	13	2	14	43	31	48	13	4	263	333	458	791	10%	84%	0.64	116	112	5.56	48
	07	32	8	aa	SD	169	19	30	7	1	6	22	24	36	6	2	178	280	327	607	12%	79%	0.67	92	92	3.15	10
Boeve,Adam	06	26	8	a/a	PIT	454	50	115	25	2	7	52	39	119	23	6	254	312	365	677	8%	74%	0.33	77	108	4.16	23
	07	27	8	aa	PIT	413	48	86	12	2	14	42	44	124	17	7	209	285	350	635	10%	70%	0.35	83	101	3.37	11
Boggs,Brandon	07	25	8	aa	TEX	354	55	85	19	3	16	45	56	89	9	4	239	343	445	788	14%	75%	0.63	125	107	5.50	44
Bohn,T.J.	06	27	8	aaa	SEA	378	44	93	17	1	8	36	28	75	13	3	246	299	359	658	7%	80%	0.37	75	95	3.86	21
	07	28	8	a/a	ATL	230	27	44	10	0	2	16	27	67	9	3	193	278	257	535	10%	71%	0.40	49	86	2.52	-8
Bolivar,Luis	06	26	4	aa	CIN	318	38	75	12	1	4	24	18	54	10	4	235	276	311	587	5%	83%	0.33	53	99	2.98	7
	07	27	845	a/a	CIN	392	43	95	19	5	4	39	22	80	13	5	243	283	342	625	5%	80%	0.27	67	131	3.33	14
Bonifacio,Emilio	07	22	46	aa	ARI	551	70	147	20	4	2	34	32	86	34	15	267	307	328	636	5%	84%	0.37	44	129	3.54	15
Bonifay,Josh	06	28	4	aa	HOU	394	42	75	18	2	14	51	25	103	3	4	191	239	347	586	6%	74%	0.24	97	73	2.62	8
Bonvechio,Brett	06	24	3	aa	SD	263	28	56	13	3	6	31	40	92	0	1	214	317	350	668	13%	65%	0.43	86	79	3.95	16
	07	25 ε	0	aa	SD	128	20	29	8	0	8	23	19	27	0	0	230	330	468	797	13%	79%	0.69	144	28	5.53	50
Borowiak,Zach	06	25	6	aa	BOS	306	29	58	13	0	3	26	12	57	4	3	188	218	256	474	4%	81%	0.21	50	71	1.77	-12
	07	26	45	a/a	BOS	271	32	52	7	0	2	25	19	49	3	0	193	245	239	484	7%	82%	0.39	34	75	2.03	-14

BATTER	Yr	Age	Pos	Lev	Org	ab	r	h	d	t	hr	rbi	bb	k	sb	cs	ba	ob	slg	ops	bb%	ct%	eye	px	sx	rc/g	bpv
Boscan,Jean	06	27	2	a/a	MIL	132	5	22	7	0	0	13	9	43	0	1	164	217	218	435	6%	67%	0.21	48	22	1.50	-21
	07	28	2	a/a	CIN	107	5	18	1	0	1	8	22	25	1	0	171	311	203	514	17%	76%	0.86	20	21	2.49	-18
Botts,Jason	06	26 b	8	a/a	TEX	236	37	61	17	1	12	32	27	62	5	0	259	335	488	823	10%	74%	0.43	144	91	6.09	55
	07	27	80	aa	TEX	369	49	93	29	2	10	55	56	101	0	1	252	351	425	776	13%	73%	0.56	117	57	5.52	44
Boucher,Sebastier	06	25	8	aa	SEA	416	54	91	9	4	1	26	61	96	24	10	219	319	265	584	13%	77%	0.63	30	130	3.15	-2
	07	26	8	a/a	BAL	395	57	83	13	1	3	29	50	80	16	12	209	299	269	568	11%	80%	0.63	43	98	2.72	0
Bourgeois,Jason	06	25	4	aa	SEA	411	59	102	20	5	4	34	35	69	21	7	247	307	347	653	8%	83%	0.51	67	148	3.83	20
	07	26	84	a/a	CHW	500	67	139	25	4	10	48	41	66	33	10	277	332	399	731	8%	87%	0.62	80	130	4.92	38
Bourn,Michael	06	24	8	a/a	PHI	470	91	129	10	12	5	39	51	91	42	5	274	345	379	724	10%	81%	0.56	58	232	5.28	27
Bowers,Jason	06	29	6	aaa	BAL	174	15	36	7	1	0	7	14	30	5	1	208	267	257	524	7%	83%	0.46	38	91	2.44	-6
	07	30	4	aa	PIT	426	36	81	20	2	5	32	32	69	11	5	190	246	280	526	7%	84%	0.45	63	94	2.27	-2
Bowker,John	07	24	8	aa	SF	522	63	139	31	5	16	71	32	89	2	8	266	308	437	745	6%	83%	0.36	109	71	4.56	41
Boyd,Shaun	06	25	8	a/a	STL	320	40	69	13	1	2	23	29	44	10	4	217	283	282	565	8%	86%	0.67	49	98	2.80	6
Bozied,Tagg	06	27	3	aaa	NYM	160	17	38	11	0	7	21	19	44	0	1	238	318	433	752	11%	72%	0.43	127	22	4.82	40
	07	28	3	aa	STL	449	45	83	18	1	15	54	35	96	2	0	185	245	331	576	7%	79%	0.37	90	54	2.71	6
Brantley,Michael	07	20	8	aa	MIL	187	25	45	6	1	0	19	27	22	15	3	241	338	286	624	13%	88%	1.25	35	119	3.88	20
Braun,Ryan	06	23 a	5	aa	MIL	231	40	68	19	1	15	38	21	45	11	0	294	353	580	933	8%	81%	0.47	177	118	8.02	81
	07	24 a	5	aaa	MIL	117	25	37	12	0	9	19	14	10	4	3	316	389	650	1039	11%	91%	1.40	210	80	9.20	120
Brazell,Craig	06	26	3	aa	LA	421	47	85	21	1	18	76	16	107	1	0	203	231	386	618	4%	75%	0.15	113	58	2.94	17
	07	27	3	aa	KC	542	60	131	32	0	25	65	22	102	0	1	242	272	438	710	4%	81%	0.22	123	26	4.08	36
Breen,Patrick	07	25	80	aa	TAM	279	26	44	9	4	5	29	28	100	3	6	158	235	274	509	9%	64%	0.28	70	116	1.93	-13
Brewer,Jace	06	27	6	a/a	TEX	213	11	44	8	2	2	14	10	40	2	4	208	245	286	531	5%	81%	0.26	52	65	2.15	-4
	07	28	6	aa	KC	220	20	42	10	1	2	12	8	40	2	2	189	218	265	483	4%	82%	0.20	56	81	1.80	-10
Brignac,Reid	06	21 a	6	aa	TAM	110	20	35	6	2	3	18	7	31	3	0	315	358	496	854	6%	71%	0.23	112	172	7.04	56
	07	22	6	aa	TAM	527	77	124	27	4	15	69	48	82	13	6	235	299	387	686	8%	84%	0.59	96	115	4.02	30
Brinkley,Dante	07	26	8	aa	FLA	311	35	63	15	1	8	24	23	118	11	7	201	257	330	588	7%	62%	0.20	84	100	2.71	6
Brito,Javier	07	25 a	3	aa	ARI	440	57	129	27	2	10	58	64	78	1	0	294	383	428	810	13%	82%	0.82	91	52	6.44	52
Brito,Juan	06	27	2	aaa	ARI	247	26	65	14	0	7	32	18	42	0	1	263	314	401	715	7%	83%	0.44	91	26	4.49	34
	07	28	2	aaa	WAS	196	11	41	12	0	3	21	12	46	0	0	208	255	315	570	6%	76%	0.27	78	12	2.73	7
Broadway,Larry	06	26	3	aaa	WAS	444	53	114	23	2	13	69	40	109	4	1	256	317	404	721	8%	75%	0.36	94	76	4.65	32
	07	27	3	aaa	WAS	338	40	74	19	2	11	44	51	81	1	0	218	321	382	703	13%	76%	0.63	105	61	4.43	29
Brown,Adrian	06	33	8	aaa	TEX	122	13	32	4	1	1	9	14	19	9	1	266	343	332	675	11%	85%	0.76	44	113	4.64	22
Brown,Dee	06	29	8	a/a	KC	437	42	97	19	0	10	57	20	71	2	0	222	256	335	591	4%	84%	0.29	74	48	2.93	10
	07	30	8	aa	OAK	377	46	77	15	0	10	50	23	83	2	1	203	249	320	570	6%	78%	0.28	75	64	2.68	4
Brown,Dee	07	25	8	aa	WAS	174	16	36	6	0	3	12	7	38	2	0	207	237	289	526	4%	78%	0.18	54	61	2.32	-5
Brown,Dustin	06	24	2	aa	BOS	295	28	62	17	0	4	34	21	59	2	1	209	262	306	568	7%	80%	0.35	71	50	2.72	6
	07	25	2	a/a	BOS	281	36	67	19	1	7	38	25	67	0	0	237	298	382	680	8%	76%	0.37	99	48	4.04	27
Brown,Hunter	06	27	5	aaa	SEA	385	52	87	26	1	6	40	48	82	10	6	227	312	345	657	11%	79%	0.58	86	87	3.77	23
Brown,Jeremy	06	27	2	aaa	OAK	275	31	60	13	0	10	31	17	48	0	0	219	265	370	636	6%	82%	0.36	95	30	3.35	19
	07	28	2	aa	OAK	339	32	71	17	1	10	41	32	70	0	0	211	279	355	634	9%	79%	0.46	93	30	3.43	18
Brown,Jordan Cas	07	24 a	30	aa	CLE	483	73	145	35	1	9	65	57	53	10	2	299	373	430	803	11%	89%	1.09	94	84	6.30	60
Brown,Matthew	06	24	5	aa	LAA	515	54	124	34	2	13	56	32	84	5	8	240	285	391	676	6%	84%	0.38	102	62	3.67	30
	07	25	58	aa	LAA	391	57	90	25	1	15	49	36	107	5	9	230	295	417	712	8%	73%	0.34	120	70	3.94	33
Brown,Tim	07	25	3	aa	SD	351	48	83	13	0	11	43	34	64	0	0	235	303	371	674	9%	82%	0.53	84	33	4.01	24
Bruce,Jay	07	20 a	8	a/a	CIN	253	36	81	20	2	15	39	22	54	3	3	322	376	600	976	8%	79%	0.41	171	83	8.45	86
Bruntlett,Eric	07	30	8	aa	HOU	227	20	43	6	3	1	14	19	40	8	4	188	250	251	501	8%	82%	0.47	40	130	2.11	-11
Buck,Travis	06	23	8	aa	OAK	212	27	58	21	1	3	19	18	32	8	1	274	330	425	755	8%	85%	0.56	114	105	5.30	49
Budde,Ryan	06	27	2	aaa	LAA	215	24	42	12	0	6	25	16	45	1	1	194	251	331	582	7%	79%	0.36	92	51	2.74	10
	07	28	2	aa	LAA	156	15	34	9	0	2	20	13	30	2	2	221	280	323	603	8%	81%	0.43	74	50	3.05	12
Burgamy,Brian	07	26	8	aa	PHI	183	14	28	6	0	3	8	18	44	3	2	152	229	228	457	9%	76%	0.42	52	54	1.72	-20
Burke,Jamie	06	35	2	aaa	TEX	370	39	93	19	1	9	41	19	42	0	0	251	287	379	666	5%	89%	0.45	85	35	3.83	28
Burnham,Gary	06	32	3	a/a	PHI	336	46	92	19	0	14	51	24	44	2	1	274	322	460	782	7%	87%	0.55	117	47	5.38	50
	07	33	3	aaa	PHI	493	45	122	31	0	10	65	53	71	0	1	246	320	369	688	10%	86%	0.75	86	18	4.26	33
Burroughs,Sean	06	26	5	aaa	TAM	131	7	25	2	0	1	10	8	28	1	3	193	238	230	467	6%	79%	0.28	25	32	1.66	-20
Burrus,Josh	06	23	8	aa	ATL	291	33	58	12	0	3	26	13	69	5	4	200	233	270	503	4%	76%	0.18	51	81	2.00	-9
	07	24	80	aa	ATL	239	25	45	10	0	5	27	27	77	7	3	187	268	286	554	10%	68%	0.35	66	73	2.62	-4
Buscher,Brian	06	25	5	aa	SF	467	40	109	21	3	6	45	36	83	5	4	233	288	330	618	7%	82%	0.43	65	69	3.28	13
	07	26	50	a/a	MIN	379	47	98	23	1	11	48	33	42	3	2	259	319	408	727	8%	89%	0.79	99	58	4.67	43
Butera,Andrew	07	24	2	aa	MIN	167	8	29	4	1	1	6	5	24	0	0	176	199	228	427	3%	86%	0.20	34	36	1.45	-23
Butler,Billy	06	20 a	8	aa	KC	477	67	147	33	1	11	79	34	48	1	0	308	354	447	801	7%	90%	0.71	96	54	6.08	57
	07	21 a	83	aa	KC	203	34	54	10	1	10	40	38	27	1	0	266	382	473	855	16%	87%	1.41	124	61	6.95	68
Butler,Brent	06	29	4	aaa	TAM	439	33	103	22	3	2	33	20	46	3	5	235	268	311	579	4%	89%	0.42	57	63	2.76	10
	07	30	3	aaa	TAM	284	24	66	16	0	4	23	13	45	1	1	231	264	327	591	4%	84%	0.28	71	38	2.93	12
Buttler,Vic	06	26	8	a/a	PIT	490	55	127	22	11	5	48	34	63	23	6	259	307	375	682	7%	87%	0.54	73	175	4.17	27
	07	27	8	aa	PIT	263	27	56	6	2	2	17	22	27	16	8	211	271	271	543	8%	90%	0.81	38	125	2.44	2
Bynum,Seth	06	26	6	aa	WAS	203	15	38	8	0	0	9	23	48	4	2	186	270	226	496	10%	76%	0.49	35	55	2.16	-14
	07	27	6	aa	WAS	212	16	37	3	1	4	25	14	44	3	2	176	227	263	490	6%	79%	0.32	50	66	1.93	-14
Byrd,Marlon	06	29	8	aaa	WAS	155	16	35	7	0	5	24	13	32	3	1	223	282	376	658	8%	79%	0.40	96	57	3.66	22
	07	30	8	aa	TEX	176	18	42	10	1	4	19	8	36	2	1	239	271	370	640	4%	80%	0.22	87	89	3.38	20
Cabrera,Asdrubal	06	21	6	aaa	SEA	393	58	106	25	1	5	39	37	78	13	12	269	332	375	706	9%	80%	0.47	78	90	4.25	31
	07	22 a	6	a/a	CLE	406	78	122	27	2	6	53	45	43	23	8	300	370	424	794	10%	89%	1.05	88	124	6.00	57
Cabrera,Jolbert	07	35	58	aa	COL	200	12	36	9	1	3	12	5	31	0	1	179	198	273	471	2%	84%	0.16	65	42	1.65	-11
Cabrera,Melky	06	22 a	8	aaa	NYY	122	18	46	5	1	4	23	9	8	3	1	379	423	542	966	7%	94%	1.24	99	87	9.68	92
Caligiuri,Jay	06	27	5	aa	NYM	410	43	79	14	1	14	54	49	98	1	1	193	279	333	612	11%	76%	0.50	84	42	3.19	9
Callaspo,Alberto	06	23 a	4	aaa	ARI	490	72	152	24	10	6	53	44	21	6	6	310	367	437	804	8%	96%	2.10	80	126	6.03	78
	07	24 a	64	aa	ARI	226	38	69	14	2	5	24	23	15	1	2	307	370	450	820	9%	93%	1.55	96	78	6.30	73
Calloway,Ron	06	30	8	aaa	BOS	406	41	104	27	2	4	41	34	77	7	5	257	315	359	674	8%	81%	0.45	76	76	3.98	26
Calzado,Napoleon	06	30	8	aaa	BAL	246	27	63	14	1	3	25	5	31	5	0	255	271	351	623	2%	87%	0.18	70	94	3.41	17
Campusano,Jose	06	23	8	aa	FLA	337	41	92	13	1	1	15	16	82	37	12	273	306	326	632	5%	76%	0.20	41	130	3.60	12
	07	24	8	aa	FLA	108	13	24	3	2	1	2	3	24	8	2	225	245	314	559	3%	78%	0.12	54	188	2.62	-1
Cancel,Robinson	07	31	2	aa	NYM	236	13	39	11	1	4	18	8	54	2	1	163	192	258	450	3%	77%	0.15	65	60	1.53	-16

Major League Equivalent Statistics

BATTER	Yr	Age	Pos	Lev	Org	ab	r	h	d	t	hr	rbi	bb	k	sb	cs	ba	ob	slg	ops	bb%	ct%	eye	px	sx	rc/g	bpv
Canizares,Barbarc	06	27	8	aa	ATL	279	28	70	15	1	3	28	24	49	0	0	253	313	349	662	8%	82%	0.49	69	36	3.97	23
	07	28 b	3	aaa	ATL	163	21	50	12	1	3	29	10	27	0	0	309	351	449	799	6%	83%	0.38	99	52	6.02	52
Cannizaro,Andy	06	28	6	aaa	NYY	416	60	102	28	1	3	28	42	58	5	5	244	313	336	649	9%	86%	0.72	71	74	3.70	25
	07	29	46	a/a	NYY	198	26	46	10	0	2	18	18	38	0	1	232	295	309	604	8%	81%	0.47	59	45	3.20	11
Cannon,Chip	06	25	3	aa	TOR	475	70	111	25	1	26	62	46	160	0	2	234	301	452	753	9%	66%	0.29	131	44	4.70	38
	07	26	3	aa	TOR	394	42	79	20	1	14	40	40	143	1	0	201	274	359	633	9%	64%	0.28	100	50	3.37	14
Cantu,Jorge	07	26	3	aaa	CIN	185	21	48	13	1	3	20	11	32	0	0	257	298	385	683	6%	83%	0.34	91	51	4.10	30
Caraballo,Francisc	07	24	8	aa	HOU	390	37	88	23	1	11	47	21	96	4	2	226	266	373	640	5%	75%	0.22	97	65	3.36	20
Carlin,Luke	06	26	2	aaa	SD	249	21	54	12	1	3	22	38	44	0	0	219	321	310	631	13%	82%	0.85	64	31	3.66	16
	07	27	2	aa	SD	300	27	50	15	2	0	13	37	83	0	3	168	260	229	490	11%	72%	0.45	49	56	2.00	-15
Carp,Christopher	07	21	3	aa	NYM	359	46	80	15	0	8	40	32	62	2	1	223	286	331	618	8%	83%	0.52	71	56	3.32	14
Carroll,Brett	06	24	8	aa	FLA	251	28	52	13	3	8	29	18	68	4	1	208	261	375	636	7%	73%	0.26	104	119	3.32	17
	07	25 a	8	aa	FLA	417	56	110	29	5	17	67	26	84	0	7	264	307	481	788	6%	80%	0.30	136	78	4.92	50
Carson,Matt	07	26	8	aa	NYY	471	63	100	20	2	15	66	28	128	8	0	212	256	356	613	6%	73%	0.22	89	111	3.16	12
Carter,Chris	06	24 a	3	aaa	ARI	509	67	140	29	2	16	75	62	52	8	5	275	354	434	788	11%	90%	1.19	103	72	5.68	58
Carter,William	07	25 a	38	a/a	BOS	548	65	158	42	2	14	72	44	68	1	0	288	340	449	789	7%	88%	0.64	111	49	5.74	54
Casanova,Raul	07	35	2	aaa	TAM	141	12	35	8	0	5	18	11	34	0	0	249	302	402	704	7%	76%	0.31	100	12	4.33	31
Cash,Kevin	06	29	2	aaa	TAM	240	15	38	8	1	2	18	20	75	1	2	159	225	225	450	8%	69%	0.27	46	51	1.63	-23
	07	30	2	aaa	BOS	176	18	27	7	0	5	20	18	55	0	0	155	234	290	524	9%	69%	0.33	85	30	2.24	-7
Casilla,Alexi	06	22	4	aa	MIN	170	26	48	10	1	1	12	17	20	18	4	282	348	371	718	9%	88%	0.85	66	136	5.07	38
	07	23	46	aaa	MIN	320	52	84	13	1	3	20	31	51	24	12	263	328	338	665	9%	84%	0.61	53	120	3.88	22
Castellano,John	06	29	8	a/a	PHI	188	12	46	7	0	3	21	5	27	0	0	244	264	331	595	3%	86%	0.18	58	14	3.01	9
Castillo,Alberto	06	37	2	aaa	WAS	254	26	55	14	0	0	24	28	43	1	2	216	294	273	567	10%	83%	0.64	50	41	2.81	6
	07	38	2	aaa	BAL	203	21	48	5	0	3	21	29	36	0	0	235	330	301	632	12%	82%	0.81	44	21	3.72	13
Castillo,Wilkin	07	23	2	aa	ARI	410	41	113	28	3	6	38	15	53	15	16	277	302	402	704	3%	87%	0.28	89	97	3.82	35
Casto,Kory	06	25	5	aa	WAS	489	72	114	21	5	16	68	67	102	5	6	233	326	394	720	12%	79%	0.66	98	94	4.50	31
	07	26	58	aaa	WAS	408	50	91	18	2	9	50	48	98	4	4	223	304	342	646	10%	76%	0.48	77	74	3.62	16
Castro,Bernie	06	27	4	aaa	WAS	268	30	65	5	2	2	21	15	34	19	2	241	282	294	576	5%	87%	0.45	33	136	3.17	3
	07	28	4	aaa	WAS	428	53	102	17	5	1	27	31	63	29	8	239	290	306	596	7%	85%	0.48	48	150	3.20	9
Castro,Ismael	06	23	4	a/a	SEA	287	33	73	21	2	5	27	9	41	6	3	254	277	394	671	3%	86%	0.22	98	104	3.72	30
Castro,Ofilio	07	24	5	aa	WAS	197	19	42	7	1	0	18	19	39	1	3	212	281	256	537	9%	80%	0.49	34	61	2.41	-5
Cates Jr.,Gary	06	25	4	aa	CHC	237	33	58	11	1	2	24	25	38	7	3	243	316	319	635	10%	84%	0.67	55	98	3.67	17
	07	26	46	aa	CHC	343	21	72	9	1	2	20	13	43	11	7	211	239	256	496	4%	88%	0.31	33	77	1.96	-10
Cedeno,Ronny	07	25 a	6	aa	CHC	287	42	91	13	2	9	29	24	41	5	5	318	370	467	837	8%	86%	0.58	93	82	6.43	56
Cepicky,Matt	06	29	8	aaa	FLA	320	28	68	15	2	5	25	33	59	2	1	212	287	314	601	9%	82%	0.57	69	63	3.15	10
	07	30	80	a/a	BAL	395	36	71	18	2	12	43	33	124	1	2	181	243	332	576	8%	69%	0.26	94	63	2.63	4
Cervenak,Mike	06	30	5	aaa	SF	269	25	60	14	1	5	37	9	31	0	0	224	249	341	591	3%	88%	0.29	78	41	2.87	13
	07	31	35	aaa	BAL	554	60	137	22	3	14	68	20	83	2	0	247	273	369	642	3%	85%	0.24	77	70	3.51	19
Chang,Ray Bo-shu	07	24	6	aa	SD	267	21	60	14	0	3	29	14	58	1	2	224	263	310	573	5%	78%	0.25	64	35	2.72	6
Chaves,Brandon	06	27	6	aa	PIT	377	32	69	12	2	3	40	37	82	7	1	183	256	251	507	9%	78%	0.46	47	87	2.26	-11
	07	28	6	aa	PIT	336	28	66	14	1	0	27	26	83	13	6	198	254	243	497	7%	75%	0.31	38	92	2.10	-12
Chavez,Angel	06	25	5	a/a	PHI	464	55	114	30	2	10	54	26	85	13	3	246	285	387	672	5%	82%	0.30	96	106	3.90	28
	07	26	546	aaa	NYY	430	55	114	23	1	10	58	23	76	5	3	266	304	393	696	5%	82%	0.31	85	74	4.22	30
Chavez,Ozzie	06	23	6	a/a	MIL	398	35	95	16	4	2	36	34	61	6	5	239	299	314	613	8%	85%	0.56	52	90	3.25	12
	07	24	64	aaa	MIL	306	31	73	12	2	4	28	35	48	4	9	239	317	330	647	10%	84%	0.73	61	67	3.43	19
Chavez,Raul	06	34	2	aa	BAL	196	12	34	7	0	1	14	8	26	0	0	171	203	229	431	4%	87%	0.30	43	23	1.49	-19
	07	35	2	aaa	NYY	290	23	54	12	0	4	25	9	40	1	0	186	211	264	474	3%	86%	0.23	55	48	1.81	-11
Chen,Yung Chi	06	23	4	aa	SEA	149	20	40	9	1	3	20	17	24	5	3	267	344	397	741	10%	84%	0.74	88	95	4.91	40
Chiaffredo,Paul	06	30	2	aaa	PIT	129	7	14	5	0	1	7	5	48	1	1	112	147	174	322	4%	63%	0.11	48	60	0.76	-41
Chiaravalloti,Vito	06	26	3	aa	TOR	137	14	23	3	0	5	15	12	48	0	0	171	236	309	545	8%	65%	0.24	78	28	2.40	-6
Chirinos,Robinson	07	23	6	aa	CHC	127	9	25	4	2	2	13	11	27	1	1	199	261	306	566	8%	79%	0.40	64	97	2.65	1
Choi,Hee Seop	06	28	3	aaa	BOS	227	31	44	10	1	7	24	42	54	0	0	193	318	331	649	16%	76%	0.78	86	47	3.80	15
Choo,Shin-Soo	06	24	8	aaa	SEA	375	61	109	19	2	11	41	40	66	22	5	291	359	440	799	10%	82%	0.61	95	122	6.10	48
	07	25	8	aaa	CLE	208	29	49	11	1	2	23	19	35	9	3	233	297	324	620	8%	83%	0.53	65	114	3.42	15
Choy Foo,Rodney	07	26	50	aa	CLE	367	36	76	14	2	9	36	56	80	11	4	206	311	326	637	13%	78%	0.70	75	86	3.65	13
Christianson,Ryan	06	25	2	aa	TAM	328	36	57	8	0	13	36	29	130	8	1	173	240	313	552	8%	60%	0.22	81	84	2.54	-4
	07	26	2	aa	STL	114	12	18	3	0	3	10	8	32	0	1	160	214	282	497	6%	72%	0.24	74	49	1.87	-11
Christian,Justin	06	26	8	aa	NYY	467	64	108	16	6	5	37	35	84	57	11	231	284	324	608	7%	82%	0.41	59	186	3.43	9
	07	27	8	a/a	NYY	424	48	96	13	4	3	40	21	69	30	5	226	262	302	564	5%	84%	0.30	49	156	2.85	2
Church,Ryan	06	28	8	a/a	WAS	194	25	37	5	0	7	25	22	49	4	1	188	270	323	593	10%	75%	0.44	79	76	3.02	4
Ciofrone,Peter	07	24	8	aa	SD	497	65	109	18	2	9	47	36	72	1	7	220	273	315	588	7%	86%	0.50	62	58	2.80	9
Ciriaco,Juan	06	23	6	aa	SD	442	44	88	18	3	2	29	31	102	9	3	200	252	268	520	7%	77%	0.30	50	107	2.30	-7
	07	24	6	aa	SD	131	11	18	3	0	1	5	5	24	4	1	138	168	181	349	3%	82%	0.20	30	101	0.97	-38
Clark,Doug	06	31	8	aaa	OAK	494	67	113	18	1	11	48	41	90	18	9	230	288	335	623	8%	82%	0.45	68	98	3.29	13
	07	32	8	aaa	ATL	451	60	105	20	3	12	56	48	92	16	5	233	307	367	674	10%	80%	0.52	84	114	4.04	23
Clark,Howie	06	33	8	aaa	BAL	308	37	71	14	1	3	24	33	30	2	2	231	306	310	616	10%	90%	1.11	58	60	3.37	23
Clark,Jermaine	06	30	4	aaa	MIL	375	46	74	12	2	5	30	40	73	27	6	197	274	274	547	10%	80%	0.54	50	131	2.72	-3
Clement,Jeff	06	23	2	aaa	SEA	304	26	72	15	1	5	36	20	55	0	2	237	284	342	626	6%	82%	0.36	72	36	3.31	16
	07	24	20	aaa	SEA	455	62	107	31	2	16	66	52	85	0	0	236	315	420	734	10%	81%	0.61	120	47	4.72	40
Cleveland,Brian	06	25	4	aa	FLA	134	15	27	4	1	1	7	8	31	1	0	199	242	262	504	5%	77%	0.25	42	93	2.16	-11
Clevlen,Brent	06	23	8	aa	DET	395	44	86	15	0	10	43	44	128	6	2	218	296	332	628	10%	68%	0.34	73	63	3.48	9
	07	24	8	aaa	DET	322	30	67	13	5	6	33	36	100	4	4	208	288	335	623	10%	69%	0.36	78	120	3.25	9
Closser,JD	06	27	2	aaa	COL	225	23	61	14	1	7	22	22	28	6	2	272	337	431	768	9%	88%	0.80	104	75	5.36	49
	07	28	20	a/a	OAK	334	39	60	15	1	9	37	42	70	2	3	180	271	307	578	11%	79%	0.60	82	58	2.78	6
Coats,Buck	06	24	8	aaa	CHC	450	55	120	20	0	7	47	36	81	16	4	267	321	358	679	7%	82%	0.44	63	86	4.27	24
	07	25	8	a/a	CIN	471	67	128	21	2	10	52	37	73	16	2	272	325	391	717	7%	85%	0.51	77	112	4.81	33
Colamarino,Brant	06	26	3	aa	OAK	495	52	115	30	5	13	69	45	100	2	2	233	297	387	684	8%	80%	0.45	101	76	4.01	28
	07	27	3	aa	OAK	361	30	69	18	0	6	32	23	72	1	1	190	240	292	531	6%	80%	0.32	71	37	2.31	-1
Colangelo,Mike	06	30	8	aaa	FLA	176	23	45	13	0	4	15	15	33	0	2	253	314	388	701	8%	81%	0.47	96	38	4.21	33
Coleman,Michael	06	31	8	aa	TAM	435	37	71	18	2	12	45	29	141	4	0	164	217	296	513	6%	67%	0.21	82	84	2.10	-7
Coles,Corey	07	26	8	aa	NYM	304	31	70	9	1	1	17	20	43	7	5	231	278	275	553	6%	86%	0.46	33	82	2.62	-0

Major League Equivalent Statistics

BATTER	Yr	Age	Pos	Lev	Org	ab	r	h	d	t	hr	rbi	bb	k	sb	cs	ba	ob	slg	ops	bb%	ct%	eye	px	sx	rc/g	bpv
Colina,Alvin	06	25	2	aa	COL	323	33	73	12	1	10	33	16	58	2	2	226	263	359	622	5%	82%	0.28	82	59	3.16	15
	07	26	2	aa	COL	272	16	45	16	0	4	26	13	59	0	0	165	202	265	467	4%	78%	0.21	73	20	1.71	-10
Colina,Javier	06	28	6	aa	CIN	358	32	61	19	1	6	32	24	90	4	2	172	224	278	502	6%	75%	0.27	74	77	2.03	-7
Collaro,Thomas	06	24	8	aa	CHW	389	34	80	16	2	13	48	18	129	1	4	204	240	352	592	5%	67%	0.14	90	56	2.67	8
	07	24	8	a/a	CHW	539	56	133	30	1	24	71	31	148	6	4	247	288	441	728	5%	72%	0.21	121	59	4.34	36
Collier,Lou	07	34	8	aaa	PHI	168	17	43	7	1	2	17	7	34	2	1	257	288	343	631	4%	79%	0.21	59	76	3.46	14
Collins,Michael	07	23	3	aa	LAA	429	38	94	16	2	4	40	11	65	5	4	219	238	294	532	2%	85%	0.16	52	80	2.27	-2
Colonel,Christian	06	25	8	aa	COL	387	34	94	22	0	9	31	26	48	8	6	243	290	366	656	6%	87%	0.53	84	56	3.59	26
	07	26	58	aa	COL	527	59	140	41	0	14	63	35	69	5	5	266	312	420	732	6%	87%	0.51	108	49	4.62	43
Colvin,Tyler	07	22	8	aa	CHC	247	29	67	10	2	8	26	4	46	6	1	271	283	425	708	2%	81%	0.09	93	112	4.29	31
Concepcion,Albert	06	25	2	a/a	BOS	268	25	55	14	0	4	25	26	72	1	2	206	275	301	576	9%	73%	0.36	69	37	2.80	4
	07	26	23	aa	LA	289	33	54	11	1	9	44	17	66	0	2	187	231	322	553	5%	77%	0.25	84	57	2.36	2
Concepcion,Ambic	06	25	8	aa	NYM	218	22	52	10	1	3	27	7	57	10	2	240	262	336	598	3%	74%	0.12	67	116	3.10	10
Conrad,Brooks	06	27	4	aaa	HOU	532	81	126	34	13	19	76	43	114	12	7	237	294	458	751	7%	78%	0.37	134	185	4.54	42
	07	28	4	aa	HOU	533	58	87	27	2	16	48	42	146	8	2	164	225	308	533	7%	73%	0.29	93	97	2.26	-1
Conti,Jason	06	32	8	aaa	STL	171	17	38	7	0	2	10	13	37	2	1	221	275	295	569	7%	79%	0.34	54	55	2.80	3
Conway,Dan	06	27	2	aaa	COL	128	9	25	6	0	2	7	7	22	0	1	197	237	288	525	5%	83%	0.31	64	28	2.19	-2
	07	28	2	a/a	NYY	118	9	17	3	0	2	9	7	39	0	1	140	188	206	394	6%	67%	0.18	42	41	1.18	-32
Coon,Bradley	07	25	8	aa	LAA	226	32	61	7	3	1	14	19	35	22	12	269	326	336	662	8%	85%	0.55	44	154	3.65	19
Cooper,Jason	06	26	8	aaa	CLE	412	52	87	23	3	11	57	40	123	5	2	211	281	360	641	9%	70%	0.32	96	103	3.48	17
	07	27	80	aaa	CLE	339	50	78	25	5	8	43	45	74	8	3	229	319	401	719	12%	78%	0.60	114	139	4.54	35
Cordido,Julio	07	27	4	aa	SF	153	12	27	8	0	2	15	12	25	2	1	174	232	260	492	7%	83%	0.46	65	55	1.99	-6
Cornejo,Eduardo	06	25	6	aa	OAK	157	13	29	6	0	0	7	12	12	0	0	182	241	218	459	7%	93%	1.07	32	31	1.79	-5
	07	26	4	aa	OAK	224	19	53	10	0	2	23	14	27	3	2	237	283	305	588	6%	88%	0.54	52	50	2.99	11
Coronado,Jose	07	21	6	aa	NYM	307	26	58	6	1	1	12	26	69	6	3	189	252	225	477	8%	78%	0.38	25	79	1.94	-19
Corona,Reegie	07	21	6	aa	NYY	140	20	32	6	0	0	6	19	29	7	2	225	317	270	587	12%	80%	0.66	40	93	3.26	5
Corporan,Carlos	07	24	2	aa	MIL	179	15	32	13	0	2	20	7	44	1	0	179	209	282	491	4%	75%	0.15	79	54	1.91	-5
Corsaletti,Jeffrey A	07	25	8	aa	BOS	462	73	109	22	2	5	46	65	76	16	8	236	330	323	653	12%	84%	0.85	61	105	3.89	21
Cortes,Jorge	06	26	8	aa	HOU	457	45	111	25	3	6	40	38	60	3	7	242	300	351	651	8%	87%	0.63	75	58	3.53	24
	07	27	8	aa	CHC	355	45	84	17	2	2	29	42	55	5	2	235	316	309	625	11%	84%	0.76	55	87	3.58	16
Cortez,Fernando	06	25	4	aaa	TAM	461	45	99	15	3	0	18	20	62	12	10	215	247	260	507	4%	87%	0.32	34	102	2.04	-8
	07	26	45	aa	KC	304	30	71	13	1	3	18	19	40	9	1	235	280	309	589	6%	87%	0.48	54	93	3.13	10
Cosby,Rob	06	26	3	aaa	TOR	453	49	110	25	1	17	59	19	91	1	3	243	273	413	686	4%	80%	0.21	108	44	3.78	29
	07	27	53	aa	TOR	437	36	103	28	1	12	50	17	76	0	1	235	264	386	650	4%	83%	0.23	101	28	3.46	25
Cosme,Caonabo	06	28	6	a/a	NYY	211	23	37	8	0	5	17	14	66	1	2	177	228	289	517	6%	69%	0.21	71	56	2.08	-7
	07	29	36	aa	CIN	293	28	60	14	1	9	36	7	89	3	0	205	224	349	573	2%	70%	0.08	92	82	2.60	8
Costanzo,Michael	07	24	5	aa	PHI	508	70	120	26	1	23	66	57	136	2	0	236	313	425	737	10%	73%	0.42	116	58	4.75	35
Costa,Shane	06	25 a	8	a/a	KC	207	28	63	12	3	7	24	11	22	3	0	305	339	487	826	5%	90%	0.49	113	115	6.31	58
	07	26 a	8	aa	KC	233	35	64	18	2	4	11	21	19	6	2	274	333	413	747	8%	92%	1.10	99	110	5.11	54
Coste,Chris	06	34	3	aaa	PHI	147	11	23	7	0	2	13	8	30	1	1	159	203	245	448	5%	80%	0.27	62	50	1.56	-16
	07	35	23	a/a	PHI	198	14	38	7	0	4	27	10	29	0	0	194	231	291	522	5%	85%	0.33	63	20	2.22	-2
Cota,Carlo	06	26	4	aa	TOR	202	25	34	9	1	1	10	28	74	3	0	168	269	233	501	12%	64%	0.38	49	99	2.28	-16
Cota,Jesus	06	25	3	aa	ARI	446	42	97	19	0	14	48	27	73	2	1	217	261	356	617	6%	84%	0.37	87	41	3.15	16
Cotto,Pedro	07	25	8	aa	DET	202	23	44	5	2	0	14	12	27	2	2	218	261	263	524	5%	87%	0.44	32	97	2.30	-5
Crabbe,Callix	06	24	4	aa	MIL	472	54	117	17	2	5	43	68	63	30	14	249	343	325	668	13%	87%	1.08	52	99	4.11	26
	07	25	48	aaa	MIL	457	74	122	22	7	8	33	62	64	15	16	267	355	398	753	12%	86%	0.97	83	131	4.84	43
Craig,Matthew	07	26	53	aa	CHC	386	42	97	23	2	11	50	36	85	1	0	252	316	408	724	8%	78%	0.42	101	53	4.66	34
Creek,Greg	07	25	3	aa	ATL	232	23	48	13	0	1	14	21	58	2	5	206	271	272	542	8%	75%	0.36	54	49	2.32	-2
Crespo,Cesar	06	27	4	aaa	ATL	423	47	92	13	2	5	26	50	85	13	6	218	301	292	593	11%	80%	0.59	49	94	3.14	5
	07	28	846	aaa	BAL	340	29	74	12	1	3	32	34	70	10	7	219	291	284	575	9%	79%	0.49	47	75	2.84	2
Cresse,Brad	06	28	2	aa	LA	162	14	32	6	0	6	22	18	58	0	0	198	276	336	612	10%	65%	0.31	84	15	3.19	7
Crew,Ryan	07	24	8	aa	MIL	137	16	30	6	0	0	11	13	21	3	0	222	291	264	554	9%	85%	0.63	37	73	2.85	2
Crowe,Trevor	06	23	8	aa	CLE	154	18	33	7	1	1	12	19	22	15	6	214	301	292	593	11%	86%	0.86	56	127	3.08	12
	07	24	8	aa	CLE	518	74	119	25	2	4	43	55	66	24	10	230	305	309	614	10%	87%	0.84	58	113	3.36	17
Crozier,Eric	07	29	3	aa	BOS	220	23	37	9	1	5	27	22	89	1	0	167	242	286	528	9%	59%	0.24	76	66	2.32	-8
Cruz,Enrique	06	25	6	a/a	TEX	350	35	90	21	1	4	39	23	101	10	8	258	304	358	662	6%	71%	0.23	74	79	3.68	21
	07	26	5	aa	CIN	484	46	106	24	1	6	47	31	109	9	5	219	266	312	578	6%	78%	0.28	66	77	2.81	6
Cruz,Jacob	06	34	8	aaa	NYM	157	16	40	14	0	1	17	19	34	0	0	252	333	361	694	11%	78%	0.55	90	24	4.45	32
Cruz,Jose	07	23	4	aa	NYM	264	19	48	13	2	3	22	28	56	4	3	180	259	276	535	10%	79%	0.51	66	80	2.38	-3
Cruz,Luis	06	23	6	aa	SD	499	63	121	33	3	10	63	29	63	8	4	242	284	381	665	5%	87%	0.46	95	99	3.72	29
	07	24	6	aa	SD	394	34	75	16	1	8	31	19	42	3	0	190	228	295	523	5%	89%	0.46	70	69	2.23	1
Cruz,Nelson	06	26 b	8	aaa	MIL	371	60	104	21	1	19	65	39	94	15	7	280	348	494	842	9%	75%	0.41	130	97	6.19	55
	07	27 b	8	aa	TEX	162	22	45	7	1	12	32	15	34	1	2	277	338	548	886	8%	79%	0.44	156	56	6.56	66
Cuevas,Aneudi	06	25	5	aa	TAM	111	9	23	5	0	1	7	6	53	1	0	203	246	276	521	5%	52%	0.12	56	47	2.31	-7
Cumberland,Shau	07	23	8	aa	CIN	467	36	108	20	1	7	42	29	79	3	10	231	276	322	598	6%	83%	0.37	63	38	2.82	10
Cunningham,Aaro	07	21 a	8	aa	ARI	118	21	32	8	3	5	17	10	22	1	3	271	328	517	845	8%	81%	0.45	148	169	5.60	61
Curtis,Colin	07	23	8	aa	NYY	240	32	57	11	1	3	15	17	48	1	1	238	288	329	617	7%	80%	0.35	64	73	3.30	12
Cust,Jack	06	28	8	aaa	SD	441	71	103	19	0	19	57	108	106	0	4	233	384	405	789	20%	76%	1.02	105	20	5.81	41
Czarniecki,Jordan	06	26	8	aa	COL	408	41	92	23	3	8	38	30	71	13	4	226	280	356	636	7%	83%	0.43	86	114	3.44	19
	07	27	8	aa	COL	427	53	100	26	0	10	42	41	67	13	4	234	301	363	664	9%	84%	0.61	89	84	3.87	27
D'Antona,James	06	24 a	5	aa	ARI	461	64	134	29	0	16	59	48	84	2	1	291	358	460	818	10%	82%	0.58	111	43	6.24	54
	07	25	532	aa	ARI	483	59	127	37	4	11	65	31	52	3	2	263	307	421	728	6%	89%	0.59	109	80	4.60	44
Daigle,Leo	06	27	3	aa	BAL	421	42	78	14	1	12	51	38	137	2	4	185	253	311	565	8%	67%	0.28	77	48	2.54	-1
Danielson,Sean P.	07	25	8	aa	STL	320	41	74	13	1	3	25	29	37	11	5	231	294	301	595	8%	89%	0.79	50	95	3.09	13
Daubach,Brian	06	35	3	aaa	STL	226	23	53	11	0	8	31	30	48	0	1	235	324	390	714	12%	79%	0.62	98	20	4.51	31
Davenport,Ron	06	25	8	aa	TOR	138	8	24	4	0	3	13	8	25	0	1	172	215	262	477	5%	82%	0.30	56	20	1.76	-13
Davidson,Kevin	06	26	2	aa	HOU	172	17	28	2	1	3	10	23	32	2	1	162	259	228	487	12%	81%	0.70	37	72	2.06	-17
Davis,Ben	06	30	2	aaa	NYY	162	8	31	5	0	4	16	5	37	1	1	191	217	286	504	3%	77%	0.15	60	27	1.98	-9
	07	31	2	aa	LA	110	8	15	3	0	1	6	6	29	0	1	134	176	178	354	5%	74%	0.20	32	46	0.95	-38
Davis,Blake	07	24	6	aa	BAL	115	10	21	6	0	0	8	8	21	1	1	186	237	236	473	6%	82%	0.38	45	54	1.83	-12
Davis,Bradley	07	25	1	aa	FLA	152	10	38	15	1	3	17	16	37	0	1	250	322	419	741	10%	76%	0.44	123	42	4.76	43
Davis,Christopher	07	22 a	5	aa	TEX	109	18	30	7	0	11	21	11	22	0	0	275	342	642	984	9%	80%	0.50	213	20	8.04	90

BATTER	Yr	Age	Pos	Lev	Org	ab	r	h	d	t	hr	rbi	bb	k	sb	cs	ba	ob	slg	ops	bb%	ct%	eye	px	sx	rc/g	bpv
Davis,Rajai	06	26	8	aaa	PIT	385	50	107	18	1	2	20	26	57	44	13	278	323	345	668	6%	85%	0.46	51	128	4.14	23
	07	27	8	aa	PIT	211	23	55	10	3	3	23	15	24	21	9	260	308	371	679	7%	89%	0.61	74	147	3.88	29
Dawkins,Gookie	06	27	6	aaa	PIT	203	20	50	14	1	5	24	11	55	3	6	248	288	398	686	5%	73%	0.21	102	71	3.59	29
	07	28	46	a/a	PHI	421	34	84	15	1	4	27	21	86	9	5	200	238	271	509	5%	80%	0.25	50	77	2.09	-8
Day,Devin	06	26	5	aa	LAA	173	13	21	6	0	1	9	6	44	1	3	121	151	171	322	3%	75%	0.14	39	73	0.68	-41
De Aza,Alejandro	06	22	8	aa	FLA	230	40	61	11	2	2	16	22	49	27	10	265	329	357	686	9%	79%	0.45	63	162	4.20	24
de Caster,Yurende	06	27	5	aaa	PIT	421	44	107	22	2	10	48	31	100	7	7	255	307	384	690	7%	76%	0.31	85	73	4.02	26
	07	28	38	aa	PIT	407	38	86	20	1	6	37	38	99	9	7	210	278	305	583	9%	76%	0.39	67	70	2.82	5
de la Rosa,Tomas	07	30	54	aa	SF	459	40	90	20	2	6	44	21	71	13	6	196	231	284	516	4%	85%	0.30	61	95	2.12	-4
	06	29	6	aaa	SF	300	31	73	18	1	6	31	16	37	6	6	242	280	363	642	5%	88%	0.43	84	74	3.32	24
De Renne,Keoni	06	27	6	a/a	BOS	283	27	53	6	0	1	17	20	29	3	1	188	241	218	459	7%	90%	0.70	24	63	1.80	-14
Deardorff,Jeff	06	28	3	aaa	CHC	320	34	67	19	1	10	36	28	84	7	1	209	273	369	642	8%	74%	0.33	104	86	3.49	19
Deeds,Doug	06	24	8	aa	MIN	440	64	113	32	3	12	65	62	112	4	3	257	348	428	776	12%	75%	0.55	114	81	5.46	44
	07	26	8	aaa	MIN	235	27	53	7	2	8	18	18	81	2	1	227	283	371	655	7%	65%	0.23	84	93	3.63	15
Del Chiaro,Brent	06	27	2	aa	LAA	180	10	20	2	0	3	11	7	65	1	0	111	142	180	322	4%	64%	0.10	41	46	0.78	-44
Delaney,Jason	07	25	38	aa	PIT	223	20	52	10	0	6	29	29	45	0	0	234	324	354	677	12%	80%	0.65	77	14	4.18	23
Delgado,Mario	06	27	3	aa	BAL	208	14	43	8	1	4	14	10	42	0	0	208	244	315	559	5%	80%	0.24	70	32	2.57	3
Delucchi,Dustin	06	29	8	a/a	SD	197	14	35	5	0	0	9	21	38	3	2	177	257	203	460	10%	81%	0.56	23	50	1.82	-20
Dement,Dan	06	28	4	a/a	WAS	476	52	81	14	2	14	47	38	148	4	9	170	231	296	528	7%	69%	0.26	75	73	2.08	-7
	07	29	458	aa	WAS	407	43	76	20	2	6	43	28	115	2	0	186	238	286	524	6%	72%	0.24	68	74	2.28	-5
Denorfia,Chris	06	26 b	8	aaa	CIN	312	43	103	18	1	7	42	31	40	14	1	330	390	460	850	9%	87%	0.77	89	97	7.46	62
Desmond,Ian	06	21	6	aa	WAS	121	7	20	4	1	0	3	4	32	4	1	165	192	215	407	3%	74%	0.13	37	114	1.34	-27
Dewitt,Blake	06	21	5	aa	LA	104	6	18	1	0	1	6	7	21	0	1	173	225	212	437	6%	80%	0.33	23	26	1.51	-26
	07	22	5	aa	LA	178	17	45	12	1	5	17	6	22	0	1	253	277	416	693	3%	88%	0.27	108	51	3.91	34
Diaz,Einar	06	34	2	aaa	LA	227	18	42	13	0	3	25	12	26	0	1	186	226	278	504	5%	89%	0.46	68	34	2.02	-1
	07	35	2	aa	PIT	118	9	20	6	0	1	8	5	10	3	1	166	199	249	449	4%	92%	0.49	60	76	1.60	-10
Diaz,Frank	06	23	8	aa	WAS	402	39	90	16	1	8	44	16	57	4	6	224	255	326	581	4%	86%	0.29	66	61	2.66	8
	07	24	8	aa	WAS	416	46	91	17	2	11	47	21	61	8	3	219	257	347	605	5%	85%	0.35	81	95	3.01	13
Diaz,Robinzon	07	24	2	a/a	TOR	366	30	106	18	1	4	32	10	20	4	0	289	307	376	684	3%	95%	0.50	63	64	4.28	32
Diaz,Victor	06	25	8	aaa	TEX	392	31	92	16	0	9	40	26	103	5	5	235	282	344	627	6%	74%	0.25	72	43	3.26	13
	07	26	80	aa	TEX	271	30	74	13	2	12	50	16	74	3	0	272	313	462	775	6%	73%	0.22	114	80	5.30	42
Dickerson,Christop	06	25	8	aa	CIN	389	58	85	20	4	11	43	56	126	19	6	217	316	376	692	13%	68%	0.44	99	144	4.26	22
	07	25	8	a/a	CIN	468	57	108	13	4	12	46	48	147	25	8	231	304	355	659	9%	69%	0.33	73	131	3.84	14
DiFelice,Mike	06	37	2	a/a	NYM	114	8	24	6	0	1	14	12	29	0	0	211	286	281	566	10%	75%	0.42	54	16	2.84	1
	07	38	2	aa	NYM	248	22	44	6	0	4	22	12	71	0	1	178	215	243	458	5%	71%	0.17	42	39	1.68	-20
Dillon,Joe	07	32	5	aaa	MIL	319	55	85	24	2	16	58	41	34	5	1	265	350	505	855	11%	89%	1.20	151	91	6.55	75
Dobbs,Greg	06	28	5	aaa	SEA	379	47	100	16	2	7	44	31	56	11	6	263	318	373	691	7%	85%	0.55	72	95	4.22	28
Dobson,Patrick	07	27	83	aa	SF	305	27	54	17	1	3	19	23	71	6	3	177	236	274	510	7%	77%	0.33	71	85	2.12	-5
Donachie,Adam	07	24	2	aa	KC	271	28	49	12	0	7	29	26	65	0	0	183	255	301	555	9%	76%	0.40	77	29	2.59	1
Donovan,Todd	06	28	8	a/a	BAL	334	35	69	8	2	3	18	26	56	29	11	206	264	262	526	7%	83%	0.47	37	128	2.36	-7
Dopirak,Brian	06	23	3	aa	CHC	179	17	47	12	0	1	25	18	45	0	0	263	330	346	676	9%	75%	0.40	68	22	4.25	24
Dorta,Melvin	06	25	6	a/a	WAS	434	52	102	15	2	5	29	26	35	31	13	235	278	311	589	6%	92%	0.75	51	124	2.93	14
	07	26	6	a/a	WAS	356	35	72	15	3	1	24	21	45	10	11	203	247	270	517	6%	87%	0.46	49	108	2.00	-3
Dowdy,Brett	06	25	4	a/a	SD	262	31	57	9	2	1	15	26	43	9	6	218	289	278	567	9%	83%	0.60	42	108	2.74	2
	07	26	48	aa	SD	312	36	65	11	2	4	23	28	60	10	4	208	273	288	561	8%	81%	0.47	54	109	2.73	1
Dragicevich,Jeffrey	07	25	4	aa	COL	117	9	24	6	0	4	14	8	33	0	1	208	259	354	613	6%	72%	0.24	95	23	2.98	13
Drew,Stephen	06	24	6	aaa	ARI	342	42	88	16	2	11	39	26	38	2	4	257	310	412	722	7%	89%	0.68	96	64	4.40	39
Dubois,Jason	06	28	8	aaa	CLE	455	59	111	29	1	17	79	42	135	4	1	244	308	426	734	8%	70%	0.31	117	69	4.68	36
	07	29	80	aaa	BAL	378	36	86	20	0	12	38	26	97	0	0	226	276	376	653	6%	74%	0.27	97	21	3.59	21
Duenas,Tomas	07	26	2	aa	COL	218	14	38	7	0	4	23	7	49	1	0	176	201	267	468	3%	77%	0.14	59	37	1.73	-14
Duffy,Chris	06	26 b	8	aaa	PIT	106	17	36	7	2	2	17	10	12	13	3	339	394	494	888	8%	88%	0.78	101	175	7.92	70
Duff,Timothy Micha	07	26	2	aa	LAA	195	11	32	5	0	3	16	11	59	3	3	165	211	232	443	5%	70%	0.19	44	47	1.51	-23
Dukes,Elijah	06	22 a	8	aaa	TAM	283	57	82	15	4	9	49	43	43	8	4	289	383	471	854	13%	85%	1.00	111	139	6.85	62
Duncan,Chris	06	25	8	aaa	STL	181	21	46	11	0	6	28	23	47	1	2	252	335	410	745	11%	74%	0.48	104	34	4.87	36
Duncan,Eric	06	22	5	a/a	NYY	316	39	74	18	2	11	35	39	57	0	1	233	317	402	719	11%	82%	0.68	107	54	4.50	35
	07	23	30	aaa	NYY	411	44	98	25	1	11	59	45	71	2	2	238	313	381	694	10%	83%	0.63	96	49	4.22	31
Duncan,Jeff	06	28	8	aaa	LA	278	39	67	8	1	5	19	23	46	15	9	243	300	328	628	8%	83%	0.49	54	109	3.32	13
	07	29	8	aaa	TOR	141	18	26	1	0	0	5	17	30	5	2	185	271	191	462	11%	79%	0.56	6	84	1.91	-25
Duncan,Shelly	06	27	8	a/a	NYY	394	39	81	20	0	17	53	30	97	3	1	205	262	382	644	7%	75%	0.32	110	46	3.38	20
	07	28 b	8	aaa	NYY	336	49	87	16	1	22	67	37	82	2	2	260	334	512	846	10%	76%	0.46	147	53	6.12	56
Dunlap,Cory	07	23	30	aa	LA	399	37	79	16	0	6	49	55	66	0	0	197	295	282	577	12%	83%	0.84	59	21	2.98	7
Duran,Carlos	06	24	8	a/a	ATL	123	15	33	4	0	2	10	6	26	4	4	268	302	350	652	5%	79%	0.23	54	73	3.43	16
Duran,German	07	23 a	4	aa	TEX	480	67	132	30	4	19	69	28	65	9	2	275	315	475	790	6%	86%	0.43	125	109	5.44	52
Durazo,Erubiel	06	32	0	aaa	MIN	192	19	48	12	0	5	22	27	42	0	0	248	341	380	721	12%	78%	0.64	90	16	4.82	33
Durbin,Chris	06	25	8	aa	BOS	341	42	75	27	1	4	27	32	62	3	5	219	285	335	620	8%	82%	0.51	89	67	3.19	20
Durrington,Trent	06	31	5	aaa	BOS	391	41	81	14	2	3	25	28	88	27	6	207	260	272	532	7%	78%	0.32	45	129	2.52	-6
	07	32	40	aaa	CLE	195	23	36	5	1	1	15	22	40	12	5	185	266	231	497	10%	79%	0.54	32	118	2.12	-15
Edwards,Mike	06	30	5	aaa	PIT	325	35	76	20	2	3	25	24	51	5	4	232	284	330	615	7%	84%	0.47	72	84	3.20	17
	07	31	8	a/a	CIN	167	18	31	9	0	2	14	10	28	3	0	187	231	268	499	5%	84%	0.35	61	82	2.12	-5
Ehlers,Cody	07	25	30	aa	NYY	385	35	86	27	0	7	48	52	83	0	1	222	315	348	663	12%	78%	0.63	91	19	3.92	24
Eldred,Brad	07	27	38	aa	PIT	311	26	50	8	1	10	32	13	90	7	2	160	195	288	483	4%	71%	0.15	76	89	1.74	-13
Eldridge,Rashad	06	25	8	a/a	TEX	329	30	80	14	3	4	33	27	90	4	7	242	300	336	636	8%	73%	0.30	63	82	3.34	12
	07	26	8	aa	MIN	361	49	86	17	3	5	31	23	63	5	5	237	282	337	618	6%	82%	0.36	68	102	3.16	14
Ellison,Jason	06	29 b	8	aaa	SF	192	30	66	16	2	1	13	10	16	5	5	344	377	460	837	5%	92%	0.63	89	104	6.46	64
Ellis,Andrew	07	26	2	aa	LA	357	43	75	17	1	6	41	44	60	1	4	210	297	314	611	11%	83%	0.74	72	46	3.16	14
Ellis,A.J.	06	26	2	aa	LA	252	30	53	7	1	0	18	45	59	2	0	211	330	246	577	15%	77%	0.76	28	65	3.16	-3
Ellsbury,Jacoby	06	23	8	aa	BOS	198	25	57	11	2	3	16	21	23	14	9	289	358	407	765	10%	89%	0.94	79	119	5.06	48
	07	24	8	a/a	BOS	436	69	131	25	5	2	35	32	48	35	8	300	348	394	742	7%	89%	0.66	68	156	5.36	41
Emmerick,Joshua	06	26	2	aa	WAS	143	5	20	4	0	1	6	9	46	0	0	138	189	183	372	6%	68%	0.20	32	11	1.12	-37
Erickson,Matt	06	31	4	aaa	ARI	293	29	64	11	0	2	17	20	40	3	2	218	268	273	541	6%	86%	0.50	42	56	2.51	-0
	07	32	46	aa	ARI	231	22	46	9	1	1	20	13	39	2	1	197	241	258	498	5%	83%	0.34	45	86	2.09	-9
Escalona,Felix	06	28	6	a/a	NYY	357	35	70	18	0	10	44	16	74	1	0	197	231	329	560	4%	79%	0.21	87	47	2.51	6

Major League Equivalent Statistics

BATTER	Yr	Age	Pos	Lev	Org	ab	r	h	d	t	hr	rbi	bb	k	sb	cs	ba	ob	slg	ops	bb%	ct%	eye	px	sx	rc/g	bpv
Escobar,Alcides	07	21	6	aa	MIL	226	24	62	5	3	1	25	11	31	3	3	274	306	339	646	4%	86%	0.33	40	108	3.62	15
Escobar,Alex	06	28	8	aa	WAS	122	15	27	8	0	3	19	14	28	2	2	223	305	367	672	11%	77%	0.52	99	55	3.83	25
Escobar,Yunel	06	24	6	aa	ATL	428	51	107	19	3	2	43	56	77	7	9	249	337	322	658	12%	82%	0.73	53	79	3.84	20
	07	25	6	aaa	ATL	180	18	57	10	2	2	26	13	25	6	3	317	363	428	790	7%	86%	0.52	76	103	5.87	47
Espinosa,David	06	25	8	aaa	DET	293	46	76	12	8	8	25	40	63	11	6	259	348	437	785	12%	78%	0.63	103	194	5.44	42
	07	26	80	aaa	DET	372	39	70	15	5	4	45	31	84	11	2	189	251	287	538	8%	77%	0.37	64	146	2.49	-3
Espino,Damaso	06	23	2	aa	KC	182	14	38	2	0	0	14	16	12	0	2	208	270	219	489	8%	93%	1.25	9	27	1.99	-2
	07	24	2	aa	KC	231	13	53	10	0	2	17	18	25	1	2	230	286	300	586	7%	89%	0.71	53	24	2.95	13
Esposito,Brian	06	28	2	aaa	STL	175	11	37	9	0	2	10	3	31	0	1	212	224	293	517	2%	83%	0.09	60	29	2.09	-3
	07	29	2	aa	STL	242	7	30	4	0	2	10	7	51	0	2	122	148	169	316	3%	79%	0.14	30	16	0.72	-44
Espy,Nathan	06	28	3	aaa	OAK	357	33	81	21	0	7	35	37	68	2	0	227	300	349	649	9%	81%	0.55	85	41	3.74	22
Esquivel,Matt	06	24	8	aa	ATL	253	24	61	16	1	5	36	17	72	4	5	242	291	368	659	6%	71%	0.24	87	69	3.52	21
	07	25	8	aa	ATL	372	55	82	14	1	15	58	38	92	12	2	220	292	386	678	9%	75%	0.41	99	107	4.01	23
Estrada,Kevin	06	26	6	a/a	STL	242	27	45	6	1	2	13	23	46	9	3	186	258	242	499	9%	81%	0.51	38	105	2.19	-12
Eure,Jeffrey	06	26	5	aa	MIL	332	37	70	16	1	10	45	18	99	3	3	212	253	359	612	5%	70%	0.18	93	72	2.95	13
	07	27	5	aa	KC	163	10	25	5	2	2	12	8	53	2	1	153	194	234	428	5%	67%	0.16	52	100	1.43	-25
Evans,Terry	06	25	8	aa	STL	263	42	66	11	1	11	29	14	58	10	9	249	288	430	718	5%	78%	0.25	109	112	3.89	33
	07	26	8	aa	LAA	475	58	126	34	3	12	61	21	120	20	9	265	296	423	718	4%	75%	0.17	107	117	4.28	36
Eylward,Mike	06	27	3	a/a	LAA	509	49	126	26	1	9	58	32	64	2	9	248	293	354	646	6%	87%	0.50	73	35	3.41	23
	07	28	30	aa	LAA	479	52	110	23	0	8	58	33	73	1	4	229	278	327	606	6%	85%	0.45	69	35	3.06	14
Ezi,Travis	06	25	8	aa	MIL	168	23	32	4	2	2	15	17	61	7	4	193	267	268	535	9%	64%	0.28	45	151	2.42	-12
Fagan,John	06	27	8	aa	HOU	127	7	23	6	1	2	12	10	35	2	2	183	242	301	543	7%	72%	0.29	77	75	2.26	-2
Fahey,Brandon	07	27	6	aaa	BAL	343	35	76	8	6	2	26	29	44	12	5	221	282	294	576	8%	87%	0.66	44	142	2.88	5
Faison,Vince	06	26	8	aa	NYY	408	60	92	19	5	13	58	42	101	1	5	225	298	390	688	9%	75%	0.42	101	102	3.91	25
	07	27	8	aa	OAK	348	26	63	15	5	3	34	17	77	8	3	180	217	283	500	5%	78%	0.21	66	139	1.98	-8
Falu,Irving	07	24	64	aa	KC	476	37	102	11	5	1	23	29	38	12	10	214	258	263	521	6%	92%	0.75	33	101	2.21	-0
Fasano,James	06	23	3	aa	TEX	365	39	81	25	0	7	45	25	79	2	0	223	273	348	622	6%	78%	0.32	90	54	3.31	18
	07	24	30	aa	TEX	236	22	60	12	1	8	31	14	33	0	0	254	296	411	707	6%	86%	0.44	100	32	4.31	34
Fasano,Sal	07	36	2	aaa	TOR	145	14	32	4	0	6	11	5	31	1	0	223	247	379	625	3%	79%	0.14	89	39	3.16	14
Feiner,Korey	07	26	2	a/a	MIN	168	12	28	5	0	1	13	14	49	0	0	166	228	214	442	7%	71%	0.28	37	24	1.64	-24
Feliciano,Jesus	06	27	8	aa	WAS	178	11	31	2	0	1	10	7	17	2	5	173	206	201	406	4%	91%	0.44	20	52	1.17	-26
	07	28	8	aa	NYM	235	23	54	8	0	2	18	14	25	3	2	228	273	293	565	6%	89%	0.58	46	60	2.75	6
Fernandez,Alexan	07	26	8	aa	PIT	215	17	38	10	0	2	17	9	29	1	0	178	210	247	457	4%	87%	0.30	52	49	1.69	-13
Fernando,Osvaldo	06	26	3	aa	HOU	180	14	32	5	0	0	5	6	27	6	5	175	203	200	403	3%	85%	0.24	22	84	1.18	-28
	07	27	6	aa	HOU	105	7	20	3	0	0	3	1	13	4	2	191	197	224	421	1%	88%	0.07	29	16	1.38	-23
Ferris,Michael	07	25	30	aa	STL	227	22	42	9	0	4	19	25	57	2	2	184	264	272	536	10%	75%	0.43	59	48	2.42	-5
Fields,Josh	06	24 a	5	aaa	CHW	462	78	137	30	3	20	64	49	125	26	5	297	364	504	868	10%	73%	0.39	130	132	7.10	60
	07	25 a	5	a/a	CHW	205	25	54	13	0	11	33	36	57	7	5	265	374	483	857	15%	72%	0.63	135	53	6.50	57
Figueroa,Francisc	07	25	4	aa	BAL	350	48	86	16	1	1	15	35	44	12	12	244	313	304	617	9%	87%	0.80	47	90	3.16	17
Figueroa,Luis	06	30	6	aaa	TOR	377	32	92	21	2	5	32	20	35	9	9	244	282	352	634	5%	91%	0.57	76	77	3.21	24
	07	34	6	aa	SF	443	39	86	15	2	2	31	16	40	4	7	194	223	251	474	4%	91%	0.40	41	76	1.71	-10
Fiorentino,Jeff	06	23	8	aa	BAL	385	59	99	13	0	13	58	51	56	9	3	257	345	388	733	12%	86%	0.92	80	74	4.99	37
	07	24	8	aa	BAL	436	54	106	15	2	12	52	36	76	7	5	244	302	373	674	8%	83%	0.48	79	80	3.90	23
Fleming,Ryan	06	31	8	aaa	PHI	232	24	49	10	3	1	18	17	40	4	5	209	264	287	551	7%	83%	0.43	54	109	2.43	1
Flores,Jose	06	33	6	aaa	SF	183	20	40	8	0	2	21	20	23	1	1	216	293	290	583	10%	87%	0.85	54	45	2.99	12
Flores,Joshua	07	22	8	aa	HOU	192	24	38	7	2	2	10	15	34	12	0	198	256	286	542	7%	82%	0.44	58	159	2.76	-1
Fontenot,Mike	06	26	4	aaa	CHC	362	49	98	26	2	8	32	43	61	5	4	271	348	418	766	11%	83%	0.70	102	77	5.31	46
	07	27	6	aa	CHC	211	32	55	13	2	5	24	11	33	2	1	260	296	417	713	5%	85%	0.33	103	121	4.36	36
Ford,Joshua M	07	25	2	aa	ARI	257	24	61	12	0	3	23	25	51	0	1	237	304	318	621	9%	80%	0.49	60	25	3.42	13
Ford,Lew	07	31	8	aaa	MIN	122	13	28	11	0	2	15	14	34	2	1	229	310	361	672	11%	72%	0.42	101	52	3.97	26
Foster,Quincy	06	32	8	aa	SF	148	17	29	2	1	1	6	9	34	5	1	194	241	241	482	6%	77%	0.27	28	132	2.04	-18
Fox,Adam	07	26	53	aa	TEX	352	37	82	14	3	6	32	18	58	4	4	233	270	343	613	5%	84%	0.31	71	86	3.08	13
Fox,Jacob	06	24	2	aa	CHC	193	21	50	16	0	6	26	10	51	0	0	261	296	433	729	5%	74%	0.19	120	25	4.55	40
	07	25	83	aa	CHC	458	59	109	25	1	20	59	16	90	6	2	238	264	426	690	3%	80%	0.18	117	87	3.83	31
Francia,Juan	06	25	4	aa	DET	190	19	29	4	2	0	8	7	26	10	4	150	179	190	369	3%	86%	0.25	27	161	1.05	-34
	07	26	4	a/a	NYY	227	29	54	5	1	0	19	14	28	10	10	239	284	268	551	6%	87%	0.50	22	106	2.34	-1
Francisco,Ben	06	25	8	aaa	CLE	515	76	134	32	3	14	56	44	70	24	5	260	318	416	734	8%	86%	0.63	102	125	4.86	41
	07	26 a	8	aaa	CLE	377	51	109	27	1	10	44	33	60	19	9	289	346	444	789	8%	84%	0.55	106	97	5.53	51
Franco,Iker	06	25	2	aa	STL	340	34	64	14	1	7	33	18	71	0	1	188	229	296	525	5%	79%	0.25	70	50	2.20	-3
	07	26	2	aaa	ATL	177	14	36	8	0	2	23	17	31	0	2	203	274	279	554	9%	83%	0.56	56	24	2.55	2
Frandsen,Kevin	06	24	4	aaa	SF	293	35	79	23	2	2	23	9	23	5	5	270	291	382	674	3%	92%	0.39	86	95	3.74	33
Frazier,Alex	06	26	8	aa	ARI	313	30	65	15	0	8	36	14	86	1	2	207	240	334	573	4%	73%	0.16	83	42	2.59	7
Frazier,Jeffrey	07	25	8	aa	SEA	302	23	60	10	1	3	23	17	56	0	2	200	243	265	508	5%	82%	0.31	45	38	2.10	-9
Freeman,Choo	07	28	8	aa	LA	400	36	81	12	2	7	33	36	94	2	1	201	267	288	555	8%	77%	0.38	55	64	2.65	-3
Freire,Alejandro	06	32	3	aaa	BAL	177	19	35	6	0	3	12	14	44	0	2	198	259	280	538	8%	75%	0.32	55	40	2.35	-5
Frey,Christopher	07	24	8	aa	COL	474	51	128	28	5	1	27	29	49	10	8	271	313	355	668	6%	90%	0.60	63	104	3.90	28
Frostad,Emerson	07	25	3	aa	TEX	307	31	66	11	1	11	35	27	72	3	1	214	276	368	644	8%	77%	0.37	93	63	3.49	17
Frost,Jeremy	07	28	23	aa	CHW	238	22	46	4	1	6	16	12	71	2	1	192	232	289	521	5%	70%	0.18	56	73	2.22	-9
Fuld,Samuel	07	26	8	aa	CHC	387	52	92	23	2	3	22	37	41	10	3	237	304	328	632	9%	89%	0.90	68	104	3.60	25
Fuller,Cody	07	25	8	aa	LAA	330	30	61	8	2	2	23	24	89	15	8	185	241	237	479	7%	73%	0.27	35	113	1.86	-18
Fulse,Sheldon	07	26	8	aa	WAS	178	31	41	7	1	3	13	26	51	11	3	228	326	324	650	13%	71%	0.51	64	127	3.99	12
Furmaniak,J.J.	06	27	6	aaa	PIT	371	40	74	11	2	6	25	23	85	14	5	200	246	287	533	6%	77%	0.27	56	117	2.37	-5
	07	28	645	aa	OAK	424	47	90	14	1	10	34	33	106	14	7	213	270	317	587	7%	75%	0.31	65	91	2.86	4
Gaetti,Joe	06	25	8	aa	COL	392	49	105	21	4	13	46	28	75	4	2	267	315	441	756	7%	81%	0.37	108	96	4.98	41
	07	26	8	aa	COL	421	48	93	22	4	15	45	33	121	4	5	220	277	398	675	7%	71%	0.27	109	88	3.61	24
Gaffney,Michael	07	26	4	aa	KC	218	15	44	9	0	2	13	14	30	2	0	202	249	268	517	6%	86%	0.45	49	46	2.30	-3
Gall,John	06	29	8	aaa	STL	289	26	73	12	1	5	29	23	34	3	4	251	307	348	654	7%	88%	0.68	65	52	3.69	24
	07	30	83	aa	FLA	413	48	85	20	2	8	38	26	59	7	4	205	253	320	572	6%	86%	0.45	76	91	2.67	9
Garabito,Eddy	06	30	4	aaa	BAL	474	50	108	21	1	5	42	45	57	17	7	228	295	305	600	9%	88%	0.78	56	88	3.17	15
Garciaparra,Micha	06	24	4	a/a	SEA	241	35	69	8	1	2	23	28	45	4	4	286	361	353	713	10%	81%	0.62	46	75	4.73	27
	07	25	6	a/a	PHI	284	26	59	4	1	3	21	30	51	5	2	208	284	260	544	10%	82%	0.60	31	72	2.63	-6
Garcia,Danny	06	26	4	aaa	NYY	392	41	85	22	1	3	34	29	64	18	8	218	272	302	574	7%	84%	0.46	64	103	2.78	8

BATTER	Yr	Age	Pos	Lev	Org	ab	r	h	d	t	hr	rbi	bb	k	sb	cs	ba	ob	slg	ops	bb%	ct%	eye	px	sx	rc/g	bpv
Garcia,Jesse	06	33	6	aaa	HOU	255	24	54	11	1	5	20	5	43	4	1	212	228	314	542	2%	83%	0.12	68	87	2.37	1
	07	34	6	aa	HOU	270	20	45	9	0	5	19	6	53	1	4	166	183	254	437	2%	80%	0.11	58	51	1.34	-19
Garcia,Sergio	06	27	4	a/a	LA	385	56	89	20	0	6	40	32	48	5	2	231	291	332	623	8%	88%	0.68	71	80	3.42	20
	07	28	46	aa	LA	250	31	55	12	0	6	22	17	40	4	1	219	270	335	605	7%	84%	0.44	77	76	3.14	14
Garcia,Yunir	06	24	2	a/a	NYM	156	16	18	5	0	1	6	23	71	0	0	118	233	168	401	13%	54%	0.33	37	35	1.39	-39
Gardner,Brett	06	23	8	aa	NYY	217	39	55	4	2	0	13	24	40	26	5	255	330	291	620	10%	81%	0.60	24	166	3.93	7
	07	24	8	a/a	NYY	384	75	100	16	6	1	24	49	75	36	7	260	343	341	684	11%	80%	0.64	55	189	4.66	22
Garko,Ryan	06	26	3	aaa	CLE	364	41	83	18	0	13	55	44	66	4	5	228	311	383	694	11%	82%	0.66	98	43	4.08	30
Garrabrants,Steve	06	25	8	aa	ARI	241	25	49	8	0	3	23	27	56	4	4	205	284	272	556	10%	77%	0.48	46	56	2.62	-3
Garrett,Shawn	06	28	8	aaa	STL	385	38	79	20	5	6	48	19	98	2	1	205	242	326	568	5%	75%	0.19	80	108	2.62	5
	07	29	30	aa	CHW	451	44	100	25	2	9	45	31	131	5	3	222	272	346	618	6%	71%	0.24	84	80	3.18	13
Garthwaite,Jay	07	27	80	aa	CIN	253	18	48	13	0	8	27	14	82	1	1	189	231	334	565	5%	68%	0.17	94	31	2.50	5
Gates,David	06	26	8	aa	LAA	121	10	18	4	1	3	10	9	39	1	0	151	208	288	496	7%	68%	0.22	83	84	1.94	-11
Gathright,Joey	07	26	8	aa	KC	223	33	62	9	3	0	18	33	23	18	8	277	370	339	710	13%	90%	1.44	45	136	4.81	40
Gautreau,Jake	06	27	4	aaa	CLE	248	25	45	12	0	6	26	23	63	1	1	180	250	297	548	9%	75%	0.37	78	45	2.47	-1
	07	28	4	aa	NYM	226	12	37	10	0	4	21	3	35	0	0	165	177	264	442	1%	85%	0.10	67	19	1.45	-15
Geiger,Kyle	06	24	2	aa	MIN	102	5	12	1	0	2	5	6	34	1	0	121	168	186	354	5%	67%	0.17	37	37	1.00	-41
	07	25	2	aa	MIN	276	27	56	14	1	3	26	12	41	0	0	202	235	287	522	4%	85%	0.28	61	49	2.23	-2
Gemoll,Brandon	06	26	3	aa	PHI	283	17	56	18	2	3	21	15	60	1	2	197	237	301	538	5%	79%	0.25	77	55	2.30	2
Getz,Christopher	06	23	4	aa	CHW	508	63	124	15	5	2	34	49	47	17	6	244	310	304	614	9%	91%	1.02	40	121	3.45	18
	07	24	4	aa	CHW	278	35	75	9	1	3	26	32	29	11	7	270	346	338	684	10%	89%	1.10	46	87	4.28	31
Giarratano,Tony	06	24	6	aa	DET	269	32	72	16	6	0	17	20	43	15	4	267	318	371	690	7%	84%	0.47	73	177	4.36	29
Gil,Jerry	06	24	6	a/a	ARI	493	64	120	28	5	24	74	15	103	6	7	243	266	467	732	3%	79%	0.15	135	109	4.01	40
Gimenez,Chris	07	25	5	aa	CLE	113	17	22	6	0	5	10	8	29	1	0	193	244	370	614	6%	74%	0.26	110	76	3.02	15
Gimenez,Hector	06	24	2	aaa	HOU	275	26	68	7	0	7	31	20	35	2	3	247	298	349	647	7%	87%	0.57	62	37	3.58	19
Ginter,Keith	06	30	4	aaa	OAK	422	50	90	24	0	9	49	41	64	2	0	213	284	335	618	9%	85%	0.64	84	54	3.33	19
	07	31	503	aaa	CLE	369	39	75	14	1	11	49	51	67	3	3	202	300	332	631	12%	82%	0.77	80	50	3.45	16
Godwin,Tyrell	06	27	8	aaa	WAS	411	50	86	19	5	6	38	27	66	16	7	210	258	321	580	6%	84%	0.40	73	145	2.76	8
	07	28	8	a/a	WAS	390	37	72	17	1	5	31	32	79	8	9	185	248	272	520	8%	80%	0.41	61	73	2.11	-5
Gold,Nate	06	26	3	aa	TEX	452	54	110	23	1	28	76	40	80	3	3	243	304	481	785	8%	82%	0.50	141	43	5.02	49
	07	27	3	aa	TEX	469	52	107	20	1	20	73	28	104	0	0	228	272	402	674	6%	78%	0.27	105	33	3.75	25
Goleski,Ryan	06	25	8	aaa	CLE	324	42	85	23	0	13	55	32	86	4	2	261	328	454	782	9%	73%	0.37	126	54	5.37	46
	07	26	8	aa	CLE	471	40	100	16	2	6	58	42	101	7	9	212	277	294	571	8%	79%	0.42	55	64	2.67	2
Golson,Gregory	07	22	8	aa	PHI	153	16	33	5	1	3	13	2	40	4	0	216	226	320	546	1%	74%	0.05	65	118	2.48	-0
Gomez,Alexis	06	28	8	aaa	DET	226	32	58	15	4	9	32	16	47	7	4	255	304	477	781	7%	79%	0.33	137	149	4.93	48
	07	29	8	aa	COL	322	25	68	15	3	5	23	11	80	3	2	210	235	324	558	3%	75%	0.13	75	92	2.46	3
Gomez,Carlos	06	21	8	aa	NYM	430	54	122	25	5	6	48	27	88	42	9	283	326	410	736	6%	80%	0.31	85	163	5.03	36
	07	22	8	aa	NYM	140	20	36	7	1	2	11	13	19	14	5	257	320	364	685	8%	86%	0.68	73	137	4.15	29
Gonzalez,Alberto	06	23	6	a/a	ARI	449	58	122	20	3	5	43	33	35	4	1	272	322	363	685	7%	92%	0.94	63	87	4.31	35
	07	24	6	a/a	NYY	493	58	120	28	8	1	48	31	63	12	6	244	289	338	627	6%	87%	0.49	67	139	3.38	19
Gonzalez,Andy	06	25	4	aaa	CHW	402	44	105	25	0	6	47	42	71	15	9	261	331	368	699	9%	82%	0.59	78	72	4.32	31
	07	26	4	aaa	CHW	124	14	29	7	1	3	15	21	35	5	1	232	342	375	717	14%	71%	0.59	94	102	4.84	28
Gonzalez,Carlos	07	22	8	aa	ARI	500	60	136	37	3	16	71	32	89	8	6	272	316	454	770	6%	82%	0.36	120	85	5.03	47
Gonzalez,Edgar	06	24 a	4	a/a	FLA	353	42	108	18	3	9	54	41	65	9	7	306	378	450	829	10%	82%	0.63	92	89	6.36	53
	07	29	45	aa	STL	459	40	94	23	2	5	33	32	75	9	4	204	255	289	545	6%	84%	0.42	61	83	2.49	2
Gonzalez,Juan	07	26	46	aa	LA	349	45	81	16	1	7	39	29	59	6	3	232	291	346	636	8%	83%	0.49	75	85	3.51	18
Gonzalez,Raul	06	33	8	aaa	PIT	399	43	94	22	2	6	49	46	62	4	5	235	314	345	659	10%	84%	0.74	76	62	3.78	24
Gonzalez,Wiki	07	33	2	aaa	CHW	235	21	53	6	0	10	33	13	19	1	1	226	265	379	644	5%	92%	0.67	89	30	3.39	25
Gordon,Alex	06	23 a	5	aa	KC	486	87	139	37	1	20	79	57	85	17	4	286	361	490	851	10%	83%	0.67	133	103	6.72	64
Gordon,Brian	06	28	8	aaa	HOU	303	37	61	17	3	13	46	21	97	1	3	203	255	405	660	7%	68%	0.22	124	92	3.31	23
Gorecki,Reid	06	26	8	a/a	STL	401	51	82	23	1	13	48	42	91	16	12	204	279	365	644	9%	77%	0.46	104	96	3.20	20
Gorneault,Nick	07	28	8	aa	LAA	471	59	92	18	1	13	42	41	123	12	7	195	259	318	577	8%	74%	0.33	77	92	2.70	3
	06	27	8	aaa	LAA	407	49	96	21	5	10	58	28	87	5	5	236	284	387	672	6%	79%	0.32	96	109	3.69	24
Gotay,Ruben	06	24	4	aaa	NYM	491	55	119	27	2	10	55	31	81	9	7	242	287	367	654	6%	84%	0.38	84	83	3.55	23
Gradoville,Tim	06	27	2	a/a	PHI	119	10	26	6	0	1	11	5	38	0	0	219	253	295	548	4%	68%	0.14	59	27	2.54	0
	07	28	2	a/a	PHI	149	10	19	3	0	0	3	10	46	3	1	128	181	152	333	6%	69%	0.21	21	69	0.91	-44
Grayson,Luke	06	24	8	aa	TEX	176	19	37	10	0	4	16	11	37	6	4	211	259	329	588	6%	79%	0.31	81	80	2.72	10
Greenberg,Adam	06	26	8	a/a	LA	320	44	60	10	2	1	17	56	111	11	6	187	308	238	546	15%	65%	0.51	36	111	2.71	-13
	07	27	8	aa	KC	467	54	101	25	7	5	32	56	102	17	8	216	300	333	633	11%	78%	0.54	78	144	3.48	15
Greene,Tyler T	07	24	6	aa	STL	221	31	45	14	1	6	19	12	53	8	2	202	244	352	597	5%	76%	0.23	101	129	2.87	14
Green,Nick	07	29	648	aa	SEA	387	40	83	15	3	14	43	16	117	3	5	213	244	372	616	4%	70%	0.13	95	88	2.87	13
Gregorio,Tom	06	29	2	a/a	TEX	118	6	21	2	0	2	11	7	28	0	0	174	222	229	452	6%	76%	0.26	34	10	1.69	-23
Griffin,John-Ford	06	27	8	aaa	TOR	227	26	49	18	0	6	19	16	56	2	0	214	267	372	639	7%	75%	0.30	112	61	3.42	23
	07	28	80	aaa	TOR	484	55	109	26	3	23	67	47	129	3	0	226	294	432	725	9%	73%	0.36	125	76	4.45	34
Griffin,Michael J	07	24	8	aa	CIN	165	15	47	9	2	3	17	8	23	4	0	282	314	409	723	4%	86%	0.33	83	105	4.82	35
Groves,Brett	06	28	6	aa	KC	166	11	24	2	0	0	11	16	26	1	2	145	220	159	379	9%	84%	0.61	13	41	1.16	-34
Guarno,Rick	07	25	2	aa	COL	248	21	55	13	0	5	28	13	58	3	0	221	259	327	586	5%	77%	0.22	73	55	2.93	8
Guerrero,Cristian	06	26	8	aa	WAS	140	11	28	3	3	3	16	8	48	3	3	199	241	336	577	5%	66%	0.16	77	154	2.53	1
	07	27	8	a/a	WAS	139	16	27	4	2	5	19	17	52	3	1	194	280	363	643	11%	63%	0.32	97	125	3.47	11
Guiel,Aaron	06	34	8	aaa	NYY	227	34	48	13	1	11	32	33	57	0	0	210	311	416	727	13%	75%	0.59	126	50	4.57	34
Gutierrez,Franklin	06	24	8	aaa	CLE	349	60	92	27	0	8	36	48	82	12	8	264	353	410	762	12%	77%	0.59	104	83	5.17	42
	07	25	8	aaa	CLE	129	25	41	7	0	3	14	7	18	6	3	318	353	442	795	5%	86%	0.39	84	100	5.74	48
Gutierrez,Jesse	06	28	3	aaa	CIN	397	41	101	25	1	9	55	43	76	0	0	255	328	394	721	10%	81%	0.56	94	29	4.73	35
	07	29	30	a/a	CIN	308	25	66	16	1	7	28	15	56	0	1	216	252	335	587	5%	82%	0.26	80	35	2.81	10
Gutierrez,Tonys	07	24	3	aa	CIN	135	10	33	6	0	2	13	19	32	4	1	246	339	331	670	12%	77%	0.60	59	48	4.27	19
Guzman,Freddy	06	26	8	aaa	TEX	376	47	96	15	4	3	22	39	42	33	14	255	325	340	664	9%	89%	0.91	56	139	3.91	27
	07	27	8	aa	TEX	535	68	117	18	6	3	25	45	83	42	14	220	280	296	576	8%	85%	0.55	50	158	2.91	5
Guzman,Garrett	06	24	8	aa	MIN	222	31	56	15	1	7	23	16	28	4	3	253	305	419	725	7%	87%	0.59	109	86	4.40	41
	07	25	8	aa	MIN	475	57	127	20	1	10	69	27	46	5	7	268	307	380	687	5%	90%	0.57	73	59	4.01	31
Guzman,Javier	06	22	6	aa	PIT	485	52	125	23	4	6	37	23	58	11	9	258	291	359	650	5%	88%	0.40	68	99	3.51	22
	07	23	6	aa	PIT	171	16	49	13	0	2	20	4	18	6	0	284	300	391	691	2%	90%	0.22	83	78	4.42	33
Guzman,Jesus	06	22	5	aa	SEA	408	54	98	17	2	9	52	45	74	7	3	240	316	358	674	10%	82%	0.61	75	89	4.06	23

Major League Equivalent Statistics

BATTER	Yr	Age	Pos	Lev	Org	ab	r	h	d	t	hr	rbi	bb	k	sb	cs	ba	ob	slg	ops	bb%	ct%	eye	px	sx	rc/g	bpv
Guzman,Joel	06	22	5	aaa	TAM	405	44	107	20	2	12	56	26	70	8	7	263	309	413	721	6%	83%	0.38	94	79	4.37	34
	07	23	50	aaa	TAM	414	44	100	17	2	16	64	23	108	9	2	241	281	406	687	5%	74%	0.21	99	96	3.98	26
Gwynn,Tony	06	24	8	aaa	MIL	447	66	125	20	4	4	38	39	78	27	12	280	337	369	707	8%	83%	0.50	61	134	4.52	29
	07	25	8	aaa	MIL	126	17	33	3	2	0	11	8	13	4	3	262	306	317	623	6%	90%	0.62	35	136	3.33	14
Haad,Yamid	06	29	2	aaa	SF	115	9	16	5	0	2	7	2	16	0	0	142	156	237	393	2%	86%	0.11	67	46	1.12	-23
	07	30	2	aaa	CLE	113	11	28	4	0	2	11	7	22	2	0	247	292	327	619	6%	80%	0.32	53	53	3.47	11
Haerther,Cody	06	23	8	aa	STL	412	45	100	25	2	9	42	29	49	2	5	243	292	377	669	7%	88%	0.59	91	57	3.71	30
	07	24	8	aa	STL	142	17	34	10	0	4	22	12	26	0	0	241	302	395	696	8%	81%	0.47	107	29	4.23	34
Hairston,Scott	06	26 b	8	aaa	ARI	381	62	110	21	1	20	61	40	61	2	0	288	355	509	864	9%	84%	0.65	135	63	6.85	64
Haley,Adam	06	26	4	aa	DET	290	22	51	9	2	2	15	29	70	3	3	177	251	237	488	9%	76%	0.41	41	75	2.00	-16
Hall,Noah	06	29	8	aa	BAL	431	49	86	18	3	9	42	38	80	13	6	198	264	317	580	8%	81%	0.48	75	111	2.79	7
	07	30	80	aa	NYY	271	27	54	13	1	6	35	23	60	1	3	199	262	320	582	8%	78%	0.39	79	53	2.74	7
Hamilton,Mark	07	23	3	aa	STL	248	25	52	13	0	5	32	19	45	1	1	211	268	321	589	7%	82%	0.43	75	43	2.92	10
Hammock,Robby	06	29	2	aaa	ARI	369	40	89	18	1	15	46	17	49	2	2	242	276	414	690	4%	87%	0.35	107	53	3.88	32
	07	30	2	aa	ARI	246	20	53	11	1	3	20	26	40	2	1	213	288	299	587	10%	84%	0.65	60	53	3.01	9
Hammond,Joey	06	29	4	aa	PHI	469	41	96	11	2	6	39	39	76	2	3	205	266	280	546	8%	84%	0.51	47	59	2.51	-2
	07	30	846	a/a	PHI	408	47	92	10	1	5	39	33	57	2	2	225	283	289	572	7%	86%	0.57	42	60	2.84	4
Hanigan,Ryan	06	26	2	a/a	CIN	139	16	29	2	0	0	13	21	27	0	0	207	310	220	530	13%	81%	0.78	11	31	2.58	-11
	07	27	2	a/a	CIN	324	35	73	16	1	3	27	41	45	0	2	226	312	311	624	11%	86%	0.91	62	37	3.46	19
Hannahan,Jack	06	27	5	aaa	DET	415	53	107	23	0	8	56	55	108	8	6	257	344	369	714	12%	74%	0.51	79	60	4.63	28
	07	28	405	aaa	DET	336	49	88	17	1	10	55	67	87	5	5	263	385	413	798	17%	74%	0.76	96	60	5.97	42
Hansen,Jed	06	34	4	aaa	SF	365	32	71	14	1	6	30	22	60	7	4	195	240	288	528	6%	84%	0.36	62	80	2.27	-2
Hanson,Travis	06	26	5	a/a	STL	475	34	92	21	1	2	30	29	84	1	1	194	241	254	495	6%	82%	0.35	47	43	2.05	-9
	07	27	5	aa	STL	254	11	42	3	1	3	10	6	53	1	1	164	184	212	396	2%	79%	0.12	28	44	1.21	-31
Harper,Brandon	06	30	2	aaa	WAS	120	14	28	8	0	2	9	12	22	3	1	233	301	345	646	9%	81%	0.53	83	68	3.69	22
	07	31	2	aaa	WAS	276	23	41	11	0	2	22	20	51	2	0	150	207	209	416	7%	81%	0.39	45	61	1.43	-24
Harper,Brett	07	26	38	aa	NYM	476	50	110	20	0	17	64	24	114	2	0	232	270	378	648	5%	76%	0.21	91	47	3.52	19
Harrison,Ben	06	25	8	aa	TEX	163	21	40	7	1	6	21	7	29	5	1	243	275	414	689	4%	82%	0.25	104	104	3.97	29
Harrison,Vince	07	28	5	aa	NYM	218	21	43	7	0	3	22	15	36	1	4	198	249	278	527	6%	83%	0.41	54	42	2.14	-4
Harris,Brendan	06	26	4	aaa	CIN	367	50	100	26	1	10	51	33	76	4	2	272	332	428	760	8%	79%	0.43	106	71	5.21	43
Harris,Gary	06	27	8	aa	SEA	224	17	40	9	1	0	18	10	51	7	2	178	213	226	439	4%	77%	0.20	39	100	1.57	-21
Harris,Willie	06	28	8	aaa	BOS	218	28	44	7	1	7	15	25	55	9	3	201	283	328	612	10%	75%	0.46	76	107	3.25	8
Hart,Bo	06	30	4	aaa	COL	261	26	50	11	2	3	11	17	43	4	1	193	243	279	522	6%	83%	0.39	59	97	2.29	-4
	07	31	4	a/a	BAL	118	6	18	4	1	0	4	4	26	2	0	149	177	197	374	3%	78%	0.15	36	87	1.13	-32
Hart,Corey	06	31	8	aaa	MIL	100	15	27	9	1	4	17	10	26	9	2	270	336	486	822	9%	74%	0.39	143	147	6.08	57
Hart,Jason	06	29	3	aaa	TEX	387	46	89	21	1	18	47	25	93	1	2	230	278	430	708	6%	76%	0.27	123	47	4.04	33
Hassey,Brad	06	27	6	aa	TOR	331	27	56	14	0	2	18	16	49	1	2	168	206	226	432	5%	85%	0.32	45	49	1.47	-19
Hattig,John	06	27	5	aaa	TOR	373	43	97	30	1	4	32	31	103	0	0	260	317	377	694	8%	72%	0.30	90	41	4.35	30
	07	28	5	aaa	TOR	347	30	83	16	1	10	42	31	97	0	2	238	301	372	674	8%	72%	0.32	86	29	3.90	21
Hayes,Brett G	07	24	2	aa	FLA	273	18	56	15	0	2	25	16	47	2	0	206	249	281	529	5%	83%	0.33	58	46	2.39	-1
Haynes,Nathan	06	27	8	a/a	LAA	264	30	53	11	3	2	20	17	56	14	13	201	248	283	532	6%	79%	0.29	57	139	1.98	-4
	07	28	8	aa	LAA	171	24	50	7	3	3	23	16	41	10	6	290	351	426	777	9%	76%	0.39	83	165	5.20	39
Headley,Chase J	07	23 a	5	aa	SD	433	72	126	32	4	17	69	66	112	1	0	291	385	504	889	13%	74%	0.59	136	82	7.54	65
Heether,Adam	06	25	5	aa	MIL	244	19	48	6	0	1	16	25	53	1	1	195	269	230	498	9%	78%	0.47	27	36	2.16	-15
	07	26	5	aa	MIL	432	47	107	23	4	7	49	42	89	2	6	248	315	369	684	9%	79%	0.48	81	67	3.98	26
Heintz,Chris	06	32	2	aaa	MIN	374	41	95	20	0	3	35	21	73	0	4	253	292	327	619	5%	80%	0.28	58	33	3.25	14
	07	33	2	aaa	MIN	167	16	41	7	0	1	14	9	37	0	0	243	281	302	583	5%	78%	0.25	46	30	2.99	5
Hermansen,Chad	07	30	8	aa	NYM	392	33	69	13	1	6	34	22	133	6	2	177	221	264	486	5%	66%	0.17	56	89	1.91	-14
Hernandez,Anders	06	24	6	aaa	NYM	414	43	100	11	3	0	22	20	67	15	5	242	276	283	559	5%	84%	0.30	30	117	2.75	-1
	07	25	64	aa	NYM	554	67	143	25	3	4	33	25	72	12	10	259	291	334	625	4%	87%	0.35	55	96	3.30	16
Hernandez,Diory	07	23	64	aa	ATL	433	43	121	23	1	6	50	24	63	18	22	280	318	379	697	5%	85%	0.39	70	76	3.70	30
Hernandez,Jose	07	38	50	aa	PIT	322	24	50	11	1	7	33	20	94	1	1	157	205	261	466	6%	71%	0.21	66	47	1.70	-16
Hernandez,Luis	06	22	6	a/a	ATL	453	40	112	15	3	2	33	20	52	4	5	247	279	307	586	4%	89%	0.38	42	72	2.89	7
	07	23	6	a/a	BAL	397	42	90	14	4	0	36	16	48	5	5	227	257	282	539	4%	88%	0.33	40	104	2.37	-1
Hernandez,Michel	06	28	2	aaa	STL	285	20	69	9	1	2	23	22	28	3	1	241	297	300	597	7%	90%	0.80	42	54	3.20	14
	07	29	2	aaa	TAM	170	19	41	4	0	4	16	15	14	0	1	241	301	327	627	8%	92%	1.02	52	33	3.44	22
Herrera,Javi	06	26	2	aa	CLE	150	13	26	6	0	2	9	7	34	3	0	174	212	252	464	5%	77%	0.21	56	73	1.79	-15
Herrera,Javier	07	26	8	aa	WAS	167	14	31	4	0	3	18	19	24	1	2	183	266	253	520	10%	85%	0.77	44	37	2.26	-5
Herrera,Jonathan	07	23	6	aa	COL	509	54	126	23	3	3	33	31	53	15	13	248	291	322	613	6%	90%	0.58	54	94	3.09	17
Herr,Aaron	06	26	5	a/a	CIN	389	49	103	26	0	12	52	27	101	4	5	264	311	425	736	6%	74%	0.26	108	53	4.57	38
	07	27	54	aaa	CIN	507	65	126	28	3	18	72	33	132	8	4	249	295	425	719	6%	74%	0.25	110	95	4.34	33
Hessman,Mike	06	29	3	aaa	DET	345	39	49	9	0	20	42	39	126	3	1	143	230	340	570	10%	64%	0.31	112	55	2.52	-0
	07	30	5	aaa	DET	422	60	90	20	2	25	85	54	151	5	11	213	302	444	746	11%	64%	0.36	136	73	4.24	34
Hietpas,Joe	06	27	2	a/a	NYM	237	14	34	5	0	3	14	10	69	0	1	143	179	198	378	4%	71%	0.15	37	30	1.09	-34
Hill,Bobby	06	29	5	aaa	SD	309	40	68	19	0	3	24	35	58	0	1	220	300	307	607	10%	81%	0.61	67	39	3.26	13
Hill,Jamar	07	25	8	aa	NYM	170	17	41	7	0	5	17	5	40	3	3	244	267	365	632	3%	76%	0.14	78	59	3.17	16
Hill,Jason	06	30	2	a/a	SD	241	14	41	8	0	2	24	16	44	0	0	170	223	225	448	6%	82%	0.37	41	18	1.66	-19
	07	31	23	aa	PHI	434	32	84	22	0	6	38	19	73	1	1	194	227	282	509	4%	83%	0.26	64	34	2.08	-4
Hill,Koyie	07	29	2	aa	CHC	149	15	36	12	0	2	16	7	25	1	1	242	277	354	631	5%	83%	0.29	88	49	3.35	23
Hoffpauir,Jarrett	06	23	4	aa	STL	393	44	85	18	1	5	36	43	34	7	7	217	294	306	600	10%	91%	1.25	63	69	3.04	23
	07	24 a	4	aa	STL	393	39	106	22	0	9	45	44	34	4	5	271	344	392	735	10%	91%	1.30	83	37	4.87	50
Hoffpauir,Micah	06	27	3	a/a	CHC	393	55	94	18	2	21	71	48	98	1	2	238	321	451	772	11%	75%	0.49	126	55	5.10	41
	07	28	3	aa	CHC	310	39	76	19	0	12	51	17	35	2	1	246	285	428	713	5%	89%	0.48	117	52	4.23	40
Hollimon,Michael	07	25	46	a/a	DET	490	84	124	30	9	11	70	58	120	14	6	252	331	419	750	11%	76%	0.48	106	167	5.00	38
Holm,Stephen	07	28	2	aa	SF	254	24	51	11	0	6	19	28	39	2	1	203	282	314	596	10%	85%	0.73	73	42	3.08	12
Holt,John	07	25	4	a/a	ATL	433	49	122	19	4	0	21	38	79	19	10	282	340	345	685	8%	82%	0.48	48	115	4.30	23
Hooper,Kevin	06	30	4	aaa	DET	504	56	121	12	5	1	25	19	71	20	12	240	268	287	555	4%	86%	0.27	32	125	2.54	-2
	07	31	4	aaa	DET	246	38	63	9	0	1	16	14	24	9	4	256	295	304	598	5%	90%	0.55	38	101	3.18	12
Hoover,Paul	06	30	2	aaa	FLA	302	27	66	16	1	4	29	24	67	2	2	218	276	313	589	7%	78%	0.36	69	55	2.95	8
Hopper,Norris	06	28	8	a/a	CIN	429	45	122	11	2	0	30	21	31	23	6	284	317	318	636	5%	93%	0.67	27	107	3.81	19
Horwitz,Brian	06	24	8	a/a	SF	285	21	74	10	1	2	26	29	32	3	3	260	328	323	651	9%	89%	0.91	45	48	3.84	23
	07	25	8	aa	SF	400	39	111	24	2	2	25	27	27	3	1	278	323	361	684	6%	93%	0.97	64	65	4.31	39

Major League Equivalent Statistics

BATTER	Yr	Age	Pos	Lev	Org	ab	r	h	d	t	hr	rbi	bb	k	sb	cs	ba	ob	slg	ops	bb%	ct%	eye	px	sx	rc/g	bpv
House,J.R.	06	27	2	a/a	HOU	493	64	140	31	2	12	81	31	56	2	2	285	327	425	752	6%	89%	0.55	95	59	5.08	45
	07	28	203	aaa	BAL	419	48	115	29	1	10	62	41	58	1	5	274	339	424	763	9%	86%	0.71	103	36	5.12	48
Howard,Josh Way	07	24	8	aa	SD	205	25	37	3	0	0	11	29	58	8	4	181	284	195	478	13%	72%	0.51	12	82	2.05	-25
Howard,Kevin	06	25	4	aa	NYY	376	39	83	16	3	7	37	22	74	1	5	220	263	335	598	5%	80%	0.29	74	66	2.81	10
	07	26	4	aa	LA	243	25	56	9	1	5	20	17	25	6	2	229	281	337	617	7%	90%	0.69	68	85	3.31	18
Hubbard,Thomas	06	24	3	aa	SEA	242	27	63	13	1	5	29	29	61	0	2	259	337	381	718	11%	75%	0.47	82	41	4.63	30
	07	25	3	aa	SEA	488	57	106	26	3	12	60	52	138	1	1	218	293	354	647	10%	72%	0.38	89	64	3.63	17
Hubele,Ryan	06	26	2	aa	BAL	312	34	64	13	1	8	29	17	82	3	3	206	248	329	577	5%	74%	0.21	78	76	2.67	5
	07	27	2	a/a	BAL	258	30	48	10	1	5	21	13	54	3	1	185	225	293	518	5%	79%	0.24	70	89	2.15	-4
Huber,Justin	06	24	3	aaa	KC	352	42	91	22	2	12	39	36	81	2	2	259	327	435	762	9%	77%	0.44	113	65	5.10	42
	07	25	83	aa	KC	286	30	65	12	1	13	52	16	44	1	0	227	268	406	674	5%	84%	0.36	107	49	3.73	27
Huckaby,Ken	06	36	2	aaa	BOS	288	15	56	10	0	2	19	7	72	4	0	194	213	247	460	2%	75%	0.10	40	56	1.75	-17
	07	37	2	aa	LA	237	8	41	4	0	1	17	6	63	0	0	174	193	198	391	2%	73%	0.09	18	11	1.22	-33
Huffman,Chad Dai	07	22	8	aa	SD	167	25	41	3	1	6	25	20	41	0	0	246	326	383	709	11%	75%	0.49	77	60	4.57	23
Huffman,Royce	06	30	3	aaa	HOU	351	47	86	20	2	8	45	37	66	3	2	246	319	384	702	10%	81%	0.57	91	76	4.38	31
	07	31	538	aa	SD	478	34	79	19	1	4	39	46	103	4	1	165	239	230	469	9%	78%	0.45	48	55	1.86	-16
Hughes,Luke	07	23	48	aa	MIN	315	45	78	16	1	7	34	25	60	3	1	246	302	366	669	7%	81%	0.42	80	79	3.96	23
Hulett,Timothy	06	24	4	aa	TEX	185	29	52	8	4	0	13	25	31	8	2	283	369	367	736	12%	83%	0.82	56	165	5.35	34
	07	25	4	aa	TEX	517	77	125	28	2	10	54	51	99	16	6	243	311	358	669	9%	81%	0.52	79	107	4.00	24
Hundley,Nicholas	07	24	2	aa	SD	373	47	79	18	1	17	61	36	75	0	2	211	281	402	683	9%	80%	0.48	116	40	3.80	28
Hunt,Kelly	06	25	3	aa	DET	382	32	74	13	1	18	44	8	127	0	1	193	210	372	582	2%	67%	0.06	104	35	2.47	9
Hu,Chin-lung	06	23	6	aa	LA	488	68	116	19	1	5	33	46	62	11	5	238	303	311	615	9%	87%	0.74	52	90	3.37	16
	07	24	6	aa	LA	517	73	147	35	3	12	50	26	45	13	9	285	320	432	751	5%	91%	0.58	100	99	4.84	48
Hyzdu,Adam	06	35	8	aaa	TEX	439	54	107	23	4	18	68	63	104	6	4	244	339	435	773	13%	76%	0.60	116	88	5.31	41
Iannetta,Chris	06	24 a	2	a/a	COL	307	47	98	20	3	12	37	36	39	1	0	319	391	521	912	10%	87%	0.92	127	77	8.10	77
Inglett,Joe	06	28	4	a/a	CLE	221	33	65	14	1	3	18	20	32	8	4	292	350	396	746	8%	86%	0.62	76	95	5.09	41
	07	29	48	aaa	CLE	392	35	82	14	5	3	45	33	60	5	13	209	270	293	562	8%	85%	0.54	54	101	2.39	3
Iribarren,Hernan	07	23	4	aa	MIL	479	61	132	21	10	4	44	39	102	16	17	275	330	385	714	7%	79%	0.38	70	153	4.19	28
Isenia,Chairon	06	28	2	aa	TAM	288	22	56	11	0	2	22	15	64	2	0	193	233	256	489	5%	78%	0.23	47	49	2.01	-12
Ishikawa,Travis	06	23	3	aa	SF	298	33	67	13	4	10	42	35	91	0	0	225	306	391	697	10%	70%	0.38	99	83	4.24	24
	07	24	3	aa	SF	173	13	31	3	1	2	13	13	41	1	0	181	240	242	481	7%	76%	0.32	36	65	1.97	-18
Jackson,Nic	06	27	8	aa	CHC	256	31	64	15	3	4	35	26	66	14	4	250	318	383	701	9%	74%	0.39	88	147	4.41	27
Jacobs,Gregory	07	31	8	aa	PHI	462	43	92	26	1	13	47	24	76	1	4	200	239	345	585	5%	84%	0.31	96	43	2.62	12
Janish,Paul	07	25	6	a/a	CIN	523	55	110	26	2	4	33	53	75	10	3	210	283	289	572	9%	86%	0.71	59	88	2.90	8
Jaramillo,Jason	06	24	2	a/a	PHI	328	32	77	23	1	6	37	28	53	0	1	234	294	364	658	8%	84%	0.54	93	38	3.73	27
	07	25	2	aaa	PHI	435	44	110	14	2	6	48	42	69	0	1	253	319	336	654	9%	84%	0.61	54	41	3.89	19
Jaso,John	07	24 a	20	aa	TAM	380	50	104	21	2	10	58	49	45	2	2	273	356	413	769	12%	88%	1.09	92	59	5.50	51
Jay,Jonathan	07	23	8	aa	STL	102	14	21	3	1	2	9	9	15	3	1	206	270	314	584	8%	85%	0.60	65	122	2.92	7
Jennings,Jeffery	07	26	2	aa	SF	250	13	38	8	0	1	14	10	51	2	5	151	184	194	378	4%	80%	0.19	34	44	1.02	-32
Jennings,Robin	07	35	3	a/a	WAS	182	16	34	10	0	5	15	10	31	1	0	189	230	321	551	5%	83%	0.31	88	44	2.43	5
Jennings,Todd	06	25	2	aa	SF	138	9	31	4	0	1	16	4	24	1	0	227	248	275	523	3%	82%	0.16	35	38	2.34	-7
Jimenez,D'Angelo	06	29 b	6	aaa	OAK	125	22	32	7	1	3	17	18	12	2	5	253	345	387	732	12%	91%	1.49	87	91	4.39	50
	07	30 b	6	aaa	WAS	171	24	53	11	2	5	21	25	20	2	2	309	398	490	888	13%	88%	1.29	115	81	7.54	76
Jimenez,Luis Anto	06	24	3	aa	BOS	395	63	101	23	1	14	60	49	82	8	2	255	338	426	763	11%	79%	0.60	109	87	5.31	42
	07	25	30	a/a	BAL	401	52	105	17	0	20	75	44	84	2	1	261	333	452	786	10%	79%	0.52	115	40	5.50	45
Jimerson,Charlton	06	27	8	aaa	HOU	470	44	100	23	5	14	35	18	158	22	9	212	241	372	613	4%	66%	0.11	99	145	2.88	14
	07	28	8	aa	SEA	387	42	79	17	2	17	56	25	160	24	9	205	253	387	639	6%	59%	0.16	109	125	3.14	16
Johnson,Ben	06	25	8	aaa	SD	198	27	44	9	1	5	17	18	44	5	1	220	284	350	634	8%	78%	0.40	83	104	3.51	16
	07	26	8	aa	LAA	204	23	45	10	0	3	12	20	40	3	1	222	291	307	598	9%	80%	0.50	61	59	3.18	9
Johnson,Brent	07	25	80	aa	SEA	453	53	108	25	1	5	39	44	57	6	7	238	306	334	640	9%	87%	0.78	69	65	3.50	24
Johnson,Dan	06	27 b	3	aaa	OAK	172	26	46	11	1	5	33	24	22	0	1	265	354	425	780	12%	87%	1.07	106	56	5.55	54
Johnson,Elliot	06	23	4	aa	TAM	494	72	138	21	10	15	52	40	130	21	18	279	333	453	787	7%	74%	0.31	103	172	5.01	42
	07	24	4	aaa	TAM	463	53	91	16	5	11	43	41	134	15	6	197	262	324	586	8%	71%	0.31	77	137	2.84	3
Johnson,Gabe	06	27	2	a/a	STL	212	22	31	9	1	6	25	17	67	0	1	148	212	283	496	8%	69%	0.26	84	63	1.89	-11
Johnson,Jay Justi	07	25	80	aa	BOS	411	37	98	28	3	4	50	34	68	4	3	238	297	347	643	8%	83%	0.50	80	75	3.59	22
Johnson,Mark	06	31	2	aaa	MIL	143	12	24	6	0	2	8	12	32	1	0	170	233	252	484	8%	77%	0.36	58	46	1.98	-12
	07	32	2	aa	ARI	242	21	50	7	0	2	18	32	24	0	1	208	299	263	563	12%	90%	1.30	39	23	2.80	11
Johnson,Michael	06	26	3	aa	SD	183	18	34	7	0	7	32	26	57	0	0	185	287	338	625	12%	69%	0.45	93	17	3.37	9
	07	27	30	aa	HOU	341	37	61	12	2	13	41	43	117	0	1	180	272	343	615	11%	66%	0.37	97	50	3.15	7
Johnson,Michael	07	26	30	aa	LAA	128	19	30	6	1	3	17	6	26	1	2	232	268	359	627	5%	80%	0.25	82	100	3.11	16
Johnson,Rob	06	23	2	aaa	SEA	337	24	69	8	2	3	28	11	66	12	8	205	230	267	497	3%	80%	0.17	40	99	1.89	-12
	07	24	20	aa	SEA	422	47	97	23	0	5	32	33	60	6	8	230	286	317	603	7%	86%	0.55	65	58	3.00	15
Johnson,Russ	06	34	5	aaa	NYY	375	48	86	14	1	12	32	51	54	2	3	230	323	367	690	12%	85%	0.94	84	48	4.21	30
	07	35	5	aa	PIT	360	26	62	14	1	5	29	27	44	3	3	171	228	255	483	7%	88%	0.60	57	52	1.87	-7
Johnson,Tripper	06	24	5	aa	BAL	131	10	24	4	0	2	6	7	23	1	1	181	221	254	475	5%	82%	0.29	48	45	1.79	-14
Jones,Adam	06	21	8	aaa	SEA	380	65	108	19	2	15	58	28	64	12	6	284	332	466	798	7%	83%	0.43	111	113	5.57	49
	07	22 a	8	aa	SEA	420	65	120	25	4	21	73	32	98	7	8	286	336	514	851	7%	77%	0.33	139	104	6.01	59
Jones,Brandon	06	23	8	aa	ATL	176	17	46	9	3	7	24	15	37	4	2	261	319	466	785	8%	79%	0.41	122	123	5.25	46
	07	24	8	a/a	ATL	535	75	149	32	5	17	89	54	109	15	8	279	345	452	797	9%	80%	0.50	110	113	5.65	48
Jones,Garrett	06	25	3	aaa	MIN	525	71	121	32	3	21	91	48	128	3	4	230	294	421	714	8%	76%	0.37	120	76	4.21	33
	07	26	83	aaa	MIN	400	54	105	30	3	12	67	29	88	2	2	262	312	439	751	7%	78%	0.33	118	82	4.86	43
Jones,Kennard	06	25	8	a/a	SD	332	33	63	7	2	0	19	46	78	7	7	189	287	220	507	12%	77%	0.59	23	83	2.20	-16
Jones,Mitch	06	29	8	aaa	NYY	441	47	89	22	1	18	66	41	145	4	3	202	270	377	648	8%	67%	0.28	109	60	3.40	18
	07	30	83	aa	LA	185	26	38	10	1	13	38	19	68	2	0	207	280	474	754	9%	63%	0.28	157	76	4.54	39
Jorgensen,Ryan	06	27	2	aaa	CIN	230	23	46	9	0	8	28	28	57	1	0	198	284	335	619	11%	75%	0.48	84	35	3.32	10
	07	28	2	aaa	CIN	249	24	51	14	0	2	21	17	49	1	0	205	255	284	539	6%	80%	0.34	61	49	2.49	0
Joseph,Onil	06	25	8	aa	ATL	338	30	83	10	3	3	29	12	93	7	7	245	271	315	586	4%	73%	0.13	45	98	2.78	3
	07	26	8	aa	KC	347	30	74	11	3	2	23	15	67	8	12	213	246	275	521	4%	81%	0.23	42	96	1.98	-7
Jova,Maikel	06	26	8	a/a	TOR	150	10	28	9	0	0	12	3	27	0	0	184	199	241	440	2%	82%	0.10	50	33	1.53	-16
Joyce,Matthew	07	23	8	aa	DET	456	57	108	29	3	15	66	48	123	4	6	236	308	408	717	9%	73%	0.39	112	76	4.29	32
Jurich,Mark	07	27	38	aa	ATL	373	35	82	27	2	5	48	27	63	1	2	219	272	343	615	7%	83%	0.43	90	55	3.15	19
Jurries,J.J.	06	27	3	aaa	ATL	307	27	57	11	0	7	25	31	106	2	0	186	261	288	549	9%	65%	0.29	66	45	2.60	-5

Major League Equivalent Statistics

BATTER	Yr	Age	Pos	Lev	Org	ab	r	h	d	t	hr	rbi	bb	k	sb	cs	ba	ob	slg	ops	bb%	ct%	eye	px	sx	rc/g	bpv
Kaaihue,Kala Kala	07	23	3	aa	ATL	118	12	14	5	1	0	7	9	45	0	0	119	181	178	359	7%	62%	0.20	45	98	1.04	-38
Kaaihue,Kila	06	23	3	aa	KC	327	31	56	14	0	4	35	38	54	0	1	171	258	251	508	10%	83%	0.70	57	31	2.19	-5
	07	24	30	aa	KC	244	31	53	13	0	9	33	35	34	0	0	219	316	378	694	13%	86%	1.03	101	25	4.28	35
Kata,Matt	06	29	4	aaa	CIN	331	40	78	19	2	8	31	16	49	4	4	236	271	379	650	5%	85%	0.32	94	86	3.40	24
Katin,Brendan	07	25	8	aa	MIL	450	59	102	22	0	20	77	35	155	3	2	226	282	407	689	7%	66%	0.23	112	55	3.93	26
Kazmar,Sean	07	23	4	aa	SD	269	26	49	9	2	5	28	21	44	5	1	180	241	281	522	7%	84%	0.48	63	101	2.29	-4
Keim,Adam	06	26	4	aa	KC	228	14	43	8	1	1	21	5	20	2	4	189	208	245	453	2%	91%	0.27	41	59	1.52	-15
Kelly,Christopher	07	26	5	aa	CHW	459	30	91	16	0	5	37	15	99	0	0	198	224	263	487	3%	78%	0.15	46	21	1.93	-12
Kelly,Don	06	27	6	a/a	DET	444	45	95	20	5	0	36	43	56	20	10	215	284	280	564	9%	87%	0.78	48	123	2.74	7
	07	28	8	aa	PIT	150	14	29	4	1	0	7	12	17	4	3	194	255	232	488	8%	89%	0.74	29	91	1.94	-9
Kelly,Kenny	06	28	8	aaa	WAS	351	40	74	11	2	1	29	36	74	16	9	211	285	263	547	9%	79%	0.49	38	110	2.58	-4
	07	29	8	aaa	CHW	246	33	57	7	0	9	23	26	59	10	3	231	304	370	675	10%	76%	0.44	82	85	4.03	19
Kelton,Dave	06	27	8	aaa	ATL	153	12	31	6	1	1	9	14	53	2	0	203	268	273	540	8%	66%	0.26	49	80	2.59	-7
Kemp,Matt	06	22 a	8	a/a	LA	381	63	118	26	4	9	61	31	57	22	6	310	362	470	831	8%	85%	0.54	106	143	6.53	58
	07	23 a	8	aa	LA	161	26	47	15	2	4	16	9	23	8	2	289	326	476	802	5%	86%	0.38	128	149	5.71	57
Kendrick,Howie	06	23 a	4	aaa	LAA	290	45	95	23	3	10	49	9	38	9	4	328	348	531	879	3%	87%	0.24	133	124	6.90	69
Keppinger,Jeff	06	26	4	aaa	KC	450	56	136	19	1	4	42	40	30	0	4	302	358	375	734	8%	93%	1.33	53	32	5.03	49
	07	27 b	54	aaa	CIN	228	27	75	13	1	2	15	19	14	1	1	329	381	421	802	8%	94%	1.39	68	51	6.33	66
Keylor,Cory	06	27	8	aa	BAL	446	46	105	16	1	8	55	40	104	5	4	234	297	329	627	8%	77%	0.38	62	60	3.41	11
	07	28	8	a/a	BOS	414	40	82	22	3	6	37	30	118	5	3	199	253	312	565	7%	72%	0.25	77	101	2.63	3
Kiger,Mark	06	26	6	a/a	OAK	427	57	95	17	2	6	25	44	93	8	4	223	296	316	612	9%	78%	0.47	62	94	3.31	10
	07	27	543	aa	NYM	424	56	94	22	2	7	36	57	107	11	7	221	314	333	647	12%	75%	0.53	76	90	3.67	16
King,Brennan	06	26	5	aaa	PHI	364	40	95	25	2	13	48	19	67	5	0	261	297	446	743	5%	82%	0.28	120	87	4.79	42
	07	27	5	aaa	PHI	465	45	116	16	1	10	49	32	67	1	0	250	299	350	649	6%	86%	0.48	64	43	3.75	19
Kinkade,Mike	06	33	5	aaa	FLA	381	42	98	20	2	3	35	22	52	5	5	257	297	340	637	5%	86%	0.41	61	74	3.45	19
	07	34	58	a/a	NYY	223	35	55	10	1	7	34	12	36	3	0	248	286	395	681	5%	84%	0.33	91	99	4.03	27
Kirkland,Kody	06	23	5	a/a	DET	445	58	91	24	6	20	62	24	153	8	11	204	245	420	665	5%	66%	0.16	129	147	3.06	25
	07	24	5	aa	DET	411	52	75	19	3	12	47	38	125	9	6	183	252	333	585	8%	70%	0.30	94	114	2.70	6
Klassen,Danny	07	32	65	aa	HOU	379	31	71	13	1	5	25	18	126	2	2	187	222	268	490	4%	67%	0.14	54	67	1.91	-13
Klink,Simon	07	26	5	aa	SF	408	30	87	15	2	7	33	27	100	1	1	214	263	313	576	6%	75%	0.27	64	47	2.80	3
Klosterman,Ryan	06	24	6	aa	TOR	137	20	32	5	0	4	14	15	38	7	3	236	312	354	666	10%	72%	0.40	74	87	3.89	17
	07	25	54	aa	TOR	341	32	59	14	1	3	22	27	62	16	5	172	232	243	475	7%	82%	0.43	52	110	1.92	-13
Knoedler,Justin	06	26	2	a/a	SF	304	31	62	16	3	4	27	20	78	4	1	204	253	311	564	6%	74%	0.25	73	106	2.67	3
	07	27	2	aa	SF	302	30	66	23	2	4	29	17	77	5	1	217	260	346	606	5%	74%	0.23	94	98	3.09	16
Knott,Jon	06	28	8	aaa	SD	479	58	104	25	5	20	82	38	90	2	4	217	275	412	687	7%	81%	0.42	118	82	3.76	30
	07	29	8	aaa	BAL	288	37	64	13	1	12	30	43	82	4	2	221	322	395	717	13%	71%	0.52	106	68	4.52	28
Knox,Ryan	06	29	8	a/a	TAM	190	12	25	8	0	2	9	11	68	4	2	129	179	211	391	6%	64%	0.17	58	74	1.18	-29
Koonce,Graham	06	31	3	aaa	MIL	297	35	64	14	1	16	42	42	81	2	1	215	313	430	743	12%	73%	0.52	127	51	4.73	35
	07	32	30	a/a	ATL	253	22	43	11	1	10	40	27	85	0	1	171	251	335	586	10%	66%	0.32	101	37	2.76	5
Koshansky,Josepł	06	24	3	aa	COL	500	62	127	26	0	26	80	47	101	2	2	255	318	460	778	9%	80%	0.46	125	36	5.20	46
	07	25	3	aa	COL	498	59	127	26	2	16	74	51	111	3	3	255	324	412	736	9%	78%	0.46	100	56	4.79	35
Kottaras,George	06	23	2	a/a	SD	376	46	84	26	2	7	43	54	88	0	1	223	321	359	680	13%	77%	0.61	95	51	4.13	26
	07	24	2	aaa	BOS	294	29	70	24	0	8	35	28	64	1	1	238	304	401	706	9%	78%	0.44	114	34	4.29	35
Kouzmanoff,Kevin	06	25 a	5	a/a	CLE	346	61	117	27	1	17	67	30	46	4	4	338	391	568	960	8%	87%	0.66	147	66	8.62	86
Kratz,Erik	06	26	2	a/a	TOR	298	39	60	11	0	6	28	17	61	1	0	202	246	302	548	5%	79%	0.28	65	63	2.50	-0
	07	27	2	a/a	TOR	272	23	52	14	1	10	36	14	59	0	1	192	231	365	596	5%	78%	0.24	108	39	2.71	13
Kroeger,Josh	06	24	8	aaa	PHI	441	41	103	26	4	10	41	22	100	6	3	234	270	379	649	5%	77%	0.22	95	98	3.46	22
	07	25	8	aa	CHC	400	51	111	18	2	17	62	35	69	6	5	277	335	459	794	8%	83%	0.51	110	73	5.52	48
Krynzel,Dave	06	25	8	aaa	MIL	359	44	77	16	3	6	36	39	99	21	4	214	291	326	617	10%	72%	0.39	73	140	3.46	9
Kubel,Jason	06	24 a	8	aaa	MIN	120	18	33	7	2	4	22	12	24	2	0	275	341	467	808	9%	80%	0.50	118	132	6.01	50
Labandeira,Josh	06	28	6	aaa	WAS	395	42	93	15	2	3	37	30	51	10	14	236	290	305	596	7%	87%	0.60	49	80	2.77	11
	07	29	4	aa	FLA	292	22	64	14	1	2	24	20	61	1	4	219	269	288	557	6%	79%	0.33	52	41	2.53	1
LaForest,Pete	07	30	25	aa	SD	296	35	47	4	0	20	48	37	115	2	0	157	250	367	618	11%	61%	0.32	113	43	3.05	5
Lahair,Bryan	06	24	3	a/a	SEA	424	52	121	21	0	15	67	44	95	3	0	285	353	441	794	9%	78%	0.46	99	49	5.93	45
	07	25	3	aa	SEA	552	65	131	41	1	10	67	42	122	0	1	238	291	367	658	7%	78%	0.34	94	41	3.73	25
Laker,Tim	06	37	2	aaa	CLE	188	21	33	13	0	0	10	12	53	0	0	177	225	244	469	6%	72%	0.22	59	48	1.82	-12
Lambin,Chase	06	27	6	a/a	NYM	403	48	80	19	2	7	43	47	99	4	3	199	282	307	589	10%	75%	0.48	73	78	2.96	6
	07	28	64	aa	FLA	434	44	90	22	4	10	40	33	126	2	6	206	262	343	605	7%	71%	0.26	88	85	2.89	10
Lane,Jason	07	31	8	aa	HOU	185	22	38	9	0	6	24	13	31	1	1	204	258	344	602	7%	83%	0.42	90	57	2.97	14
Lane,Richard	06	27	3	aa	WAS	228	14	36	9	2	2	21	9	53	1	1	156	187	233	420	4%	77%	0.16	52	75	1.35	-23
Larish,Jeffrey	07	25	3	aa	DET	454	66	109	22	2	25	93	80	107	5	2	241	354	460	815	15%	76%	0.74	131	69	5.99	49
Larkin,Shaun	06	27	4	aa	CLE	391	30	76	19	0	4	36	26	53	1	3	195	245	276	521	6%	86%	0.49	60	31	2.19	-1
Laroche,Andy	06	23 a	5	a/a	LA	432	66	122	24	1	17	69	55	57	8	6	282	363	461	824	11%	87%	0.96	112	70	6.16	60
	07	24 a	5	aa	LA	265	44	71	15	1	15	38	31	38	2	2	269	346	505	852	11%	86%	0.83	143	64	6.34	65
Larson,Brandon	06	30	5	aaa	WAS	380	47	82	14	1	15	61	30	104	4	3	216	272	379	651	7%	73%	0.28	98	69	3.46	18
	07	31	5	aa	WAS	189	18	28	6	0	4	11	8	47	1	1	148	181	244	426	4%	75%	0.16	61	72	1.37	-22
Lauderdale,Matt	06	25	2	aa	SD	116	11	23	6	1	2	14	17	29	0	0	194	298	310	608	13%	75%	0.59	79	53	3.28	9
Leahy,Ryan	07	26	4	aa	LAA	173	10	30	3	0	0	5	10	24	0	3	171	218	191	409	6%	86%	0.43	18	30	1.27	-27
Leandro,Franciscc	06	26	8	aa	TAM	218	18	41	10	0	1	13	23	47	3	1	188	267	247	514	10%	78%	0.50	49	54	2.31	-7
LeCroy,Matthew	07	32	2	aaa	MIN	247	11	41	11	0	3	23	22	54	0	0	168	235	244	479	8%	78%	0.40	56	7	1.92	-13
Ledee,Ricky	07	34	8	aa	NYM	290	22	48	7	1	6	37	18	74	0	0	164	212	258	470	6%	74%	0.24	57	34	1.77	-17
Lee,Taber	06	26	4	a/a	PIT	226	23	46	9	2	3	14	9	51	8	1	202	231	294	525	4%	78%	0.17	60	131	2.32	-4
	07	27	46	aa	PIT	196	22	37	7	0	0	12	22	30	8	1	191	272	226	498	10%	85%	0.73	31	92	2.32	-9
Leone,Justin	06	30	5	aaa	SD	453	46	89	15	0	12	51	44	95	3	5	197	267	309	577	9%	79%	0.46	71	42	2.73	4
	07	31	85	aa	SF	428	48	73	20	2	11	35	45	127	15	1	170	249	299	548	9%	70%	0.35	83	125	2.62	-2
Leon,Carlos	06	27	4	a/a	PHI	372	53	93	12	2	3	35	37	48	7	5	250	319	313	632	9%	87%	0.77	44	89	3.57	17
	07	28	6	a/a	PHI	222	20	37	7	0	0	9	14	35	0	5	165	213	195	408	6%	84%	0.39	27	48	1.20	-26
Leslie,Myron	07	25	8	aa	OAK	386	41	92	24	1	4	36	49	68	1	1	238	323	333	656	11%	82%	0.72	72	44	3.93	23
Lewis,Fred	06	26	8	aaa	SF	439	64	106	18	8	9	43	50	79	14	10	241	320	379	698	10%	82%	0.64	83	151	4.15	28
	07	27	8	aa	SF	171	23	40	7	4	5	23	14	34	6	1	234	292	417	709	8%	80%	0.40	106	192	4.34	30
Lewis,Richard	06	26	4	aa	CHC	345	39	77	16	2	2	28	28	80	16	4	222	280	293	573	7%	77%	0.35	52	117	2.92	3
	07	27	45	aa	KC	342	31	62	11	1	3	27	16	67	2	2	182	218	248	466	4%	80%	0.23	45	70	1.74	-16

BATTER	Yr	Age	Pos	Lev	Org	ab	r	h	d	t	hr	rbi	bb	k	sb	cs	ba	ob	slg	ops	bb%	ct%	eye	px	sx	rc/g	bpv
Lillibridge,Brent	07	24	6	a/a	ATL	525	67	135	20	4	11	50	34	111	36	13	257	302	371	673	6%	79%	0.30	72	135	3.94	22
Linden,Todd	06	26	8	aaa	SF	187	23	45	10	2	4	17	21	34	4	0	239	317	373	690	10%	82%	0.63	87	110	4.39	28
Lindsey,John	07	31	30	aa	LA	454	46	92	20	1	18	71	21	114	0	0	202	237	370	607	4%	75%	0.18	103	34	2.90	13
Lind,Adam	06	23 a	8	a/a	TOR	457	58	149	32	0	24	83	44	99	3	1	326	385	554	939	9%	78%	0.44	143	39	8.41	77
	07	24	8	aaa	TOR	174	17	49	8	2	6	24	12	36	0	0	282	328	454	782	6%	79%	0.33	104	63	5.49	44
Little,Mark	06	34	8	aaa	FLA	251	28	57	13	2	2	22	23	66	5	6	226	292	312	604	9%	74%	0.36	62	95	2.98	8
Loadenthal,Carl	07	26	8	aa	ATL	476	57	121	14	4	0	24	49	80	32	18	253	323	299	621	9%	83%	0.61	33	120	3.37	10
Logan,Nook	06	27	8	a/a	DET	142	19	27	4	2	0	5	17	41	10	5	190	277	241	518	11%	71%	0.42	34	161	2.33	-14
Lomasney,Steve	06	29	2	a/a	MIN	151	7	24	4	0	2	12	6	63	0	2	157	188	234	422	4%	58%	0.09	49	25	1.25	-25
Lombard,George	06	31	8	aaa	WAS	189	28	46	8	1	7	20	18	51	14	2	243	309	410	718	9%	73%	0.35	101	131	4.73	30
	07	32	8	aaa	WAS	127	11	25	5	0	3	9	13	43	8	3	198	271	305	575	9%	66%	0.29	71	82	2.83	1
Loney,James	06	22 a	3	aaa	LA	366	53	127	30	1	6	56	26	26	7	6	347	391	488	879	7%	93%	1.02	103	71	7.37	79
	07	23	38	aa	LA	233	22	56	16	1	1	26	20	42	2	1	241	302	333	635	8%	82%	0.48	73	65	3.60	20
Longoria,Evan	06	21	6	aa	TAM	105	15	27	5	0	6	20	1	21	2	1	257	264	476	740	1%	80%	0.05	131	79	4.22	41
	07	22 a	5	a/a	TAM	485	91	142	28	0	25	90	70	96	4	0	292	382	507	889	13%	80%	0.73	132	68	7.55	67
Long,Terrence	06	31	8	aaa	NYY	308	28	73	14	1	9	40	18	72	0	0	237	279	374	653	6%	77%	0.25	87	32	3.63	20
Lopez,Gabe	06	27	4	aa	NYY	479	57	105	19	2	3	40	58	69	2	1	220	304	289	593	11%	86%	0.85	50	61	3.18	11
	07	28	4	aa	NYY	409	32	83	17	1	1	39	30	65	2	2	203	257	254	511	7%	84%	0.46	41	52	2.20	-6
Lopez,Pedro	06	22	6	a/a	CHW	466	58	137	26	2	11	55	25	57	7	6	294	330	429	759	5%	88%	0.44	90	75	5.08	44
	07	23	6	aaa	CIN	285	36	76	12	1	3	25	25	34	4	3	267	326	347	673	8%	88%	0.74	57	73	4.09	27
Lowrie,Jed	07	23 a	6	a/a	BOS	497	71	143	51	5	10	60	66	78	4	4	288	371	471	842	12%	84%	0.85	131	88	6.57	67
Lubanski,Chris	06	22	8	aa	KC	524	72	131	32	8	10	54	56	84	9	8	250	322	399	721	10%	84%	0.67	97	125	4.48	37
	07	23	8	aa	KC	409	45	98	20	3	12	48	38	75	3	8	240	304	391	695	9%	82%	0.51	95	67	3.92	29
Lucas,Edward	07	25	5	aa	KC	125	14	29	5	1	2	14	7	21	2	1	230	272	331	604	5%	83%	0.34	67	93	3.08	11
Lucena,Juan	07	24	45	aa	STL	303	28	66	11	1	2	26	14	16	1	1	218	251	279	530	4%	95%	0.82	44	57	2.35	7
Lucy,Donald	07	25	2	a/a	CHW	365	41	85	18	0	7	26	29	81	12	1	232	289	336	625	7%	78%	0.36	72	91	3.55	14
Ludwick,Ryan	06	28	8	aaa	DET	508	71	118	29	2	23	70	42	165	2	6	233	291	434	725	8%	68%	0.25	124	62	4.20	34
	07	29	8	aa	STL	106	17	24	5	0	5	23	6	21	1	1	226	268	403	671	5%	80%	0.28	110	70	3.60	26
Luna,Hector	07	28	6	aaa	TOR	390	44	92	23	1	7	35	24	56	3	4	236	280	351	631	6%	86%	0.43	80	62	3.31	20
Lydon,Wayne	06	25	8	aaa	TOR	513	72	130	16	10	9	42	48	112	24	11	253	316	374	691	8%	78%	0.42	71	173	4.16	22
	07	26	8	a/a	TOR	524	64	113	19	4	5	35	41	102	22	9	215	271	295	566	7%	80%	0.40	54	125	2.73	2
Machado,Alejandr	06	24	6	aaa	BOS	373	43	96	13	3	4	30	49	46	20	6	257	344	340	684	12%	88%	1.07	55	113	4.46	30
Machado,Andy	06	26	6	aa	CIN	396	41	81	18	1	6	33	43	108	5	5	205	283	302	585	10%	73%	0.40	67	61	2.87	4
	07	27	6	aaa	CIN	278	39	55	7	2	4	21	46	67	10	3	199	312	279	591	14%	76%	0.68	49	114	3.23	0
Macias,Drew	06	24	8	aa	SD	430	41	100	18	3	6	44	43	99	4	13	232	302	329	631	9%	77%	0.43	65	64	3.17	13
	07	25	8	aa	SD	441	48	98	17	5	9	52	62	78	7	10	222	317	340	658	12%	82%	0.79	74	89	3.66	20
Macias,Jose	07	36	8	aaa	MIL	285	20	58	10	2	2	25	9	48	4	2	202	227	268	495	3%	83%	0.19	46	82	1.98	-10
Macri,Matthew	06	24	5	aa	COL	288	26	60	10	2	7	26	16	49	2	5	208	250	327	576	5%	83%	0.33	74	68	2.55	6
	07	25	54	a/a	MIN	331	45	86	24	0	12	37	18	69	4	4	261	299	445	744	5%	79%	0.26	121	62	4.56	42
Mahar,Kevin	06	25	8	aa	TEX	505	62	115	32	2	17	62	25	101	10	7	228	265	401	666	5%	80%	0.25	112	92	3.46	27
	07	26	8	aa	TEX	482	50	106	20	3	7	37	18	115	5	1	220	249	316	565	4%	76%	0.16	64	96	2.67	3
Mahoney,Mike	06	34	2	aaa	TOR	225	14	39	7	0	1	14	10	54	0	2	172	207	216	423	4%	76%	0.18	35	30	1.38	-25
Maier,Mitch	06	24	8	aa	KC	543	70	140	31	5	10	68	30	76	10	14	257	297	385	681	5%	86%	0.40	86	99	3.68	29
	07	25	8	aa	KC	544	58	127	26	4	10	48	26	82	5	2	233	268	349	617	5%	85%	0.32	76	91	3.22	16
Majewski,Dustin	06	25	8	aa	TOR	236	37	50	7	1	12	28	43	60	1	1	210	332	397	729	15%	75%	0.72	107	59	4.71	29
	07	26	8	aa	TOR	466	44	91	24	2	11	43	53	103	1	4	196	278	329	607	10%	78%	0.51	87	41	3.04	12
Majewski,Val	06	25	8	aaa	BAL	323	44	80	15	4	4	39	39	71	7	8	248	329	356	684	11%	78%	0.55	71	114	4.01	23
	07	26	8	a/a	BAL	456	53	104	24	3	5	43	40	92	11	5	229	291	324	614	8%	80%	0.43	68	103	3.30	13
Maldonado,Carlos	06	28	2	a/a	PIT	354	31	85	18	0	4	38	29	78	2	0	241	298	329	627	8%	78%	0.37	65	42	3.53	14
	07	29	2	aa	PIT	143	10	22	3	0	1	13	13	29	0	0	157	226	196	422	8%	80%	0.45	28	22	1.50	-27
Malek,Bobby	06	25	8	a/a	NYM	277	30	58	10	2	5	28	19	53	3	3	209	260	312	572	6%	81%	0.36	66	87	2.67	4
Maniscalco,Matthe	06	26	6	a/a	TAM	387	29	81	10	4	0	30	41	82	9	6	209	284	253	537	10%	79%	0.50	30	96	2.50	-8
Manriquez,Salomc	06	24	2	aa	WAS	339	33	74	16	0	8	38	27	84	0	0	219	275	333	609	7%	75%	0.32	77	25	3.18	11
	07	25	20	aa	TEX	247	26	58	11	0	14	41	19	51	0	1	233	288	441	729	7%	79%	0.37	123	20	4.34	36
Manzella,Thomas	07	24	6	aa	HOU	228	28	57	10	2	1	12	15	36	8	2	250	297	325	622	6%	84%	0.42	54	118	3.50	14
Maples,Chris	06	27	5	a/a	DET	376	47	87	23	1	18	65	22	103	4	4	232	274	440	714	5%	73%	0.21	129	68	4.00	35
	07	28	80	aaa	DET	181	15	30	6	1	0	13	15	63	3	1	168	232	210	442	8%	65%	0.24	33	91	1.66	-26
Marsters,Brandon	06	32	2	aaa	BAL	190	17	36	4	0	7	24	6	70	0	0	189	215	322	538	3%	63%	0.09	75	26	2.24	-4
Marte,Andy	06	23	5	aaa	CLE	357	49	91	24	0	14	46	35	75	1	0	256	322	438	760	9%	79%	0.46	119	45	5.13	44
	07	24	5	aaa	CLE	352	41	86	17	1	13	52	19	57	0	0	244	283	409	692	5%	84%	0.33	102	39	4.04	30
Martinez-Esteve,E	07	24	8	aa	SF	134	8	28	2	1	1	8	10	28	1	1	206	258	255	513	7%	79%	0.33	30	60	2.22	-12
Martinez,Fernandc	07	19	8	aa	NYM	236	31	66	12	1	3	20	20	37	2	6	278	333	380	713	8%	85%	0.54	70	68	4.31	32
Martinez,Gabriel	06	23	3	aa	TAM	425	60	108	24	1	10	47	65	139	5	1	253	352	383	736	13%	67%	0.47	88	73	5.12	30
	07	24	30	aa	TAM	386	35	90	13	1	12	67	26	92	0	1	234	282	369	651	6%	76%	0.28	82	31	3.58	17
Martinez,Jose Gre	07	22	6	aa	STL	250	30	66	11	0	8	38	12	19	0	0	264	298	404	702	5%	92%	0.63	88	30	4.30	37
Martinez,Sandy	06	36	2	aaa	NYM	272	27	53	9	0	9	34	24	69	1	0	195	261	328	589	8%	75%	0.35	81	39	2.92	5
Martin,Brian	06	26	8	a/a	STL	284	24	61	14	0	5	30	20	78	0	1	215	267	323	590	7%	73%	0.25	74	25	2.91	8
Marti,Amaury	06	32	8	aa	STL	132	10	19	3	0	4	8	8	47	1	1	143	190	244	434	6%	64%	0.16	60	44	1.44	-24
	07	25	8	aa	STL	107	19	28	4	0	5	15	8	20	1	0	257	307	426	733	7%	81%	0.38	100	69	4.73	35
Mateo,Henry	06	30	4	aaa	WAS	433	45	90	17	5	2	28	30	79	26	11	208	259	282	541	6%	82%	0.38	51	144	2.44	-2
	07	31	48	aaa	DET	311	36	68	13	2	3	16	28	54	20	10	217	281	295	577	8%	82%	0.51	54	121	2.78	5
Mather,Joe	07	25	83	aa	STL	487	59	104	21	1	22	57	39	74	7	0	213	270	392	662	7%	85%	0.52	108	84	3.68	26
Mathews,Aaron	07	25	8	aa	TOR	471	48	115	29	3	6	36	20	73	4	2	245	275	357	632	4%	84%	0.27	80	79	3.39	20
Mathis,Jeff	06	24	2	aaa	LAA	384	48	98	30	2	4	35	20	59	2	1	255	292	375	667	5%	85%	0.34	90	79	3.87	29
	07	25	2	aa	LAA	250	33	54	12	1	4	22	14	43	3	1	217	259	319	578	5%	83%	0.33	71	93	2.81	8
Matienzo,Daniel	06	26	3	aa	MIN	472	47	99	20	1	14	62	20	132	2	2	210	242	345	587	4%	72%	0.15	85	55	2.74	8
Matos,Julius	06	32	4	a/a	SD	104	7	21	1	0	0	4	7	28	0	0	200	252	208	459	6%	74%	0.26	7	23	1.81	-25
Matos,Luis	07	29	8	aa	NYM	392	33	70	19	1	2	22	16	66	6	7	180	212	251	463	4%	83%	0.24	55	79	1.59	-13
Matos,Pascual	06	32	2	aaa	CHW	177	13	27	9	0	2	15	3	37	2	0	153	165	234	399	2%	79%	0.07	61	72	1.21	-23
Matranga,Dave	06	30	4	aaa	SD	302	27	49	8	0	6	22	15	70	3	1	163	204	253	457	5%	77%	0.22	57	66	1.65	-18
	07	31	6	aa	TEX	248	22	43	6	1	6	18	18	73	6	1	175	231	288	519	7%	71%	0.25	67	99	2.25	-9
Matsui,Kazuo	06	31	4	aaa	COL	127	24	33	5	0	3	14	7	21	3	1	262	302	369	670	5%	83%	0.34	71	97	3.98	23

Major League Equivalent Statistics

BATTER	Yr	Age	Pos	Lev	Org	ab	r	h	d	t	hr	rbi	bb	k	sb	cs	ba	ob	slg	ops	bb%	ct%	eye	px	sx	rc/g	bpv
Mayberry,John	07	24	8	aa	TEX	245	29	53	10	0	13	31	16	53	6	1	218	267	412	679	6%	79%	0.31	115	74	3.77	26
Mayorson,Manuel	06	24	6	aa	TOR	477	44	126	19	1	2	50	19	43	11	11	264	293	321	614	4%	91%	0.45	44	69	3.14	15
	07	25	45	aa	TOR	452	43	108	23	2	1	23	31	32	6	8	240	289	305	594	6%	93%	0.99	52	67	2.95	21
Maysonet,Edwin	07	26	64	aa	HOU	341	26	76	11	2	4	30	13	61	4	2	222	249	296	545	4%	82%	0.21	49	74	2.47	-2
Maza,Luis	06	26	4	aaa	MIN	305	28	60	10	5	3	34	15	62	2	2	197	234	289	523	5%	80%	0.24	57	119	2.19	-6
	07	27	458	aa	LA	324	32	73	18	1	4	29	22	54	2	2	225	274	325	599	6%	83%	0.40	72	62	3.05	13
McAnulty,Paul	06	26	3	aaa	SD	478	58	124	29	4	12	60	49	66	1	3	259	327	410	737	9%	86%	0.74	99	64	4.80	42
	07	27	8	aa	SD	233	19	48	9	1	3	24	23	51	0	2	205	276	295	571	9%	78%	0.45	59	39	2.74	2
McCarthy,Bill	06	27	8	aaa	ATL	345	28	76	16	1	6	29	20	69	2	0	219	263	321	583	6%	80%	0.29	68	56	2.91	7
	07	28	8	a/a	KC	270	23	53	9	2	7	23	14	61	3	2	197	236	319	555	5%	77%	0.23	74	85	2.45	1
McClain,Scott	06	34	3	aaa	OAK	547	59	110	28	0	20	77	34	101	5	5	201	248	360	608	6%	82%	0.34	101	60	2.89	15
	07	35	3	aa	SF	468	40	78	16	0	16	58	34	116	1	1	168	223	305	528	7%	75%	0.29	84	31	2.18	-4
McCoy,Mike	06	26	4	aa	STL	474	47	95	12	1	2	27	46	88	22	9	201	272	241	513	9%	81%	0.52	29	96	2.30	-10
	07	27	68	aa	STL	306	25	57	8	1	2	18	43	52	10	7	185	284	233	518	12%	83%	0.82	34	73	2.30	-8
McCracken,Quinto	06	36	8	aaa	MIN	109	9	27	4	0	1	10	8	20	2	1	248	300	306	605	7%	82%	0.41	42	48	3.26	8
McCutchen,Andre	07	21	8	aa	PIT	513	68	133	25	2	9	47	42	74	19	5	260	316	373	688	8%	86%	0.57	76	107	4.30	29
McDonald,Darnell	06	28	8	aaa	TAM	538	71	140	29	1	12	50	41	115	27	12	260	312	387	699	7%	79%	0.36	86	101	4.19	29
	07	29	8	aaa	MIN	491	65	132	26	5	7	67	43	110	31	7	269	328	381	708	8%	78%	0.39	76	143	4.71	29
McDougall,Marsha	07	29	5	aa	LA	515	48	106	26	1	15	62	22	94	2	2	205	237	346	583	4%	82%	0.23	91	49	2.68	11
McEwing,Joe	06	34	4	aaa	HOU	422	49	109	17	1	8	34	17	60	12	7	258	287	360	647	4%	86%	0.29	67	86	3.50	20
	07	35	45	aaa	BOS	477	41	112	23	1	6	41	23	104	5	9	234	268	326	595	5%	78%	0.22	66	51	2.80	9
McGehee,Casey	06	24	5	aaa	CHC	497	51	132	27	1	11	62	38	65	0	3	266	318	390	708	7%	87%	0.58	84	27	4.41	35
	07	25	52	aa	CHC	436	45	100	26	2	9	48	33	75	1	3	229	283	355	639	7%	83%	0.44	86	51	3.42	21
McIntyre,Nick	07	27	65	aa	DET	278	28	49	7	1	2	15	11	77	4	0	175	207	225	433	4%	72%	0.15	35	103	1.57	-24
McMains,Derin	06	27	4	a/a	SF	372	35	69	11	2	2	17	38	37	14	6	186	261	240	501	9%	90%	1.03	37	100	2.16	-2
McPherson,Dallas	06	26	5	aaa	LAA	208	26	44	10	3	13	34	11	70	2	1	210	248	466	715	5%	66%	0.15	148	133	3.79	34
Meadows,Tydus	06	29	8	a/a	LA	249	30	55	7	1	8	31	44	67	1	2	221	338	356	694	15%	73%	0.66	80	45	4.36	20
Melian,Jackson	06	27	8	a/a	DET	377	45	84	19	5	13	50	21	79	4	1	222	263	396	659	5%	79%	0.26	107	117	3.53	23
	07	28	8	aa	DET	320	38	79	12	2	11	51	24	76	6	5	246	299	394	693	7%	76%	0.32	89	83	3.99	25
Melillo,Kevin	06	24	4	aa	OAK	500	59	121	29	2	10	59	54	85	11	8	241	315	363	678	10%	83%	0.64	83	82	4.01	27
	07	25	4	aa	OAK	382	48	82	23	4	7	41	41	90	6	7	214	290	351	641	10%	76%	0.45	92	104	3.35	18
Melo,Juan	06	30	5	aaa	SF	384	30	80	10	1	5	34	16	58	2	2	209	241	281	522	4%	85%	0.28	47	50	2.23	-6
	07	31	5	aa	WAS	188	8	28	5	0	2	14	9	34	1	4	149	188	209	397	5%	82%	0.27	40	27	1.11	-28
Mendez,Carlos	06	32	2	aaa	ATL	366	24	92	12	0	5	46	5	38	1	2	251	260	320	580	1%	90%	0.12	47	28	2.80	6
	07	33	30	aaa	ATL	263	23	62	16	0	5	28	6	38	0	2	236	254	349	603	2%	86%	0.17	81	32	2.91	15
Mendez,Victor	06	26	8	a/a	DET	101	14	20	4	0	3	7	8	27	0	0	196	256	312	568	7%	74%	0.30	73	48	2.70	2
Mendoza,Carlos	07	28	5	aa	NYY	268	22	46	11	0	0	14	32	67	3	1	170	260	211	470	11%	75%	0.48	36	58	1.96	-19
Menechino,Frank	07	37	4	aa	SD	128	16	31	10	1	2	13	9	26	1	0	241	291	377	668	7%	80%	0.35	98	84	3.92	28
Mercedes,Victor	07	28	64	aa	CHW	341	36	72	16	1	6	23	18	68	5	6	211	252	312	564	5%	80%	0.27	69	74	2.49	4
Merchan,Jesus	06	26	6	aa	PHI	317	35	76	13	4	1	31	10	16	5	4	238	262	309	571	3%	95%	0.64	50	114	2.70	13
	07	27	64	a/a	SEA	378	51	95	17	2	7	40	22	28	9	5	250	291	362	652	5%	93%	0.78	74	101	3.64	29
Merloni,Lou	06	36	5	aaa	CLE	330	28	80	20	0	5	32	25	53	0	2	243	296	352	648	7%	84%	0.47	78	20	3.62	23
	07	36	5	aa	OAK	393	28	64	14	1	1	23	23	59	1	4	162	209	212	421	6%	85%	0.39	39	43	1.38	-22
Merrill,Ronnie	06	28	6	aa	OAK	446	32	82	23	1	3	32	27	94	7	12	184	231	262	494	6%	79%	0.29	59	61	1.79	-8
	07	29	65	aa	ARI	377	40	73	13	3	10	38	30	84	10	4	193	253	320	574	7%	78%	0.36	77	114	2.69	3
Metcalf,Travis	06	24	5	aa	TEX	425	41	85	14	2	7	29	36	97	8	8	199	262	288	550	8%	77%	0.37	58	79	2.44	-2
	07	25	5	aa	TEX	261	31	55	18	0	5	31	21	56	2	1	210	268	341	610	7%	79%	0.37	93	58	3.12	16
Meyer,Drew	06	25	6	aaa	TEX	364	35	82	14	4	2	26	25	85	8	11	226	275	302	577	6%	77%	0.29	52	107	2.59	2
	07	26	6	aa	TEX	225	21	39	10	0	1	7	20	41	2	3	174	241	228	470	8%	82%	0.48	44	54	1.79	-14
Milledge,Lastings	06	22 a	8	aaa	NYM	307	56	90	23	3	7	39	46	58	14	11	294	386	455	841	13%	81%	0.79	109	127	6.33	59
Miller,Corky	06	31	2	aaa	SEA	204	25	45	9	0	12	31	21	49	0	0	221	292	437	729	9%	76%	0.42	128	22	4.43	35
	07	32	2	aaa	ATL	181	10	32	7	0	4	20	20	27	4	0	179	260	278	538	10%	85%	0.74	66	47	2.56	2
Miller,Jai	07	23	8	aa	FLA	406	46	96	24	2	12	49	50	115	10	6	236	320	394	714	11%	72%	0.43	102	86	4.41	30
Miller,Matthew	06	24	8	a/a	COL	107	12	25	1	1	1	8	11	13	1	2	234	305	290	595	9%	88%	0.85	31	82	3.01	8
	07	25	8	aa	COL	446	47	106	20	2	10	48	34	57	1	4	239	293	356	649	7%	87%	0.60	76	47	3.55	23
Miller,Tony	06	26	8	a/a	COL	208	22	40	7	0	0	7	35	70	5	5	190	307	225	532	14%	66%	0.50	31	61	2.50	-14
Minaker,Christoph	07	24	6	aa	SEA	353	32	70	9	1	3	22	22	62	2	8	198	246	253	498	6%	82%	0.36	37	53	1.89	-12
Minges,Tyler	06	27	8	a/a	BOS	439	49	108	33	1	5	45	25	87	5	2	246	287	357	644	5%	80%	0.29	85	73	3.59	23
Minicozzi,Mark	07	25	645	aa	SF	275	24	51	10	2	1	13	14	39	2	1	187	227	249	475	5%	86%	0.37	45	83	1.85	-12
Miranda,Juan Migu	07	24	30	aa	NYY	196	28	48	15	1	7	44	21	49	0	1	247	320	436	756	10%	75%	0.42	125	58	4.92	43
Mitchell,Lee	06	24	5	aa	FLA	462	52	105	33	1	10	52	46	155	2	6	228	298	366	664	9%	67%	0.29	97	48	3.67	22
	07	25	5	aa	FLA	451	56	103	23	2	15	56	59	154	2	1	227	316	389	705	11%	66%	0.38	102	62	4.40	25
Moeller,Chad	06	32	2	aaa	MIL	132	8	24	5	0	2	14	13	29	0	2	184	255	266	521	9%	78%	0.44	57	22	2.17	-6
Mohr,Dustan	06	30	8	aaa	DET	252	26	52	11	5	5	26	36	94	1	4	207	306	350	656	13%	63%	0.38	87	124	3.61	13
	07	31	8	aaa	TAM	201	22	40	13	0	8	21	15	84	1	1	197	254	381	634	7%	58%	0.18	118	44	3.18	18
Molina,Angel	06	25	8	aa	FLA	189	14	40	10	0	3	20	24	48	3	2	211	299	312	611	11%	74%	0.49	72	43	3.26	10
Molina,Felix	06	23	4	aa	MIN	385	36	96	15	3	9	46	25	66	8	10	249	296	370	666	6%	83%	0.38	75	82	3.56	22
	07	24	4	aa	MIN	426	40	99	17	2	6	35	26	63	7	7	232	276	321	597	6%	85%	0.41	60	74	2.93	10
Molina,Gustavo	06	25	2	a/a	CHW	374	23	79	13	0	8	31	23	68	5	6	210	256	306	562	6%	82%	0.34	62	38	2.52	2
	07	26	2	a/a	BAL	216	15	50	7	0	2	13	10	33	0	2	233	268	290	559	5%	85%	0.32	41	23	2.59	1
Montanez,Luis	06	25	8	a/a	CHC	386	46	102	22	0	11	53	31	72	5	4	264	319	405	723	7%	81%	0.43	94	54	4.57	35
	07	26	8	a/a	BAL	333	44	86	11	0	9	32	28	46	4	5	257	314	368	682	8%	86%	0.59	70	55	4.00	26
Montero,Miguel	06	23	2	a/a	ARI	423	38	114	23	0	15	63	45	54	1	5	270	340	430	770	10%	87%	0.83	103	14	5.19	49
Montz,Luke	07	24	2	aa	WAS	146	18	29	4	1	4	15	7	45	0	0	195	230	312	543	4%	69%	0.15	69	78	2.37	-3
Monzon,Erick	06	25	6	a/a	SEA	274	29	59	16	1	3	26	23	49	8	0	216	277	312	589	8%	82%	0.47	70	100	3.14	10
	07	26	6	aa	SEA	230	15	41	9	1	5	23	21	53	3	3	180	248	286	533	8%	77%	0.39	68	57	2.29	-4
Moore,Frank	06	28	4	aa	FLA	157	11	26	4	1	2	10	12	45	3	2	163	222	229	452	7%	71%	0.27	43	83	1.62	-23
	07	29	8	aa	FLA	235	19	41	9	2	2	19	15	71	2	2	172	222	252	474	6%	70%	0.21	54	85	1.81	-16
Moore,Scott	06	23 a	5	a/a	CHC	467	52	127	28	0	23	74	56	127	12	7	272	350	480	830	11%	73%	0.44	129	55	6.05	53
	07	24	5	aa	CHC	321	49	77	17	3	16	56	38	88	3	3	239	319	465	784	11%	73%	0.43	136	97	5.15	44
Morales,Jose	06	24	2	a/a	MIN	258	22	52	14	1	3	25	18	57	2	1	202	254	298	552	7%	78%	0.32	69	66	2.55	2
	07	25	2	aaa	MIN	376	41	114	24	1	2	37	28	45	1	4	303	351	388	740	7%	88%	0.62	67	40	5.04	41

Major League Equivalent Statistics

BATTER	Yr	Age	Pos	Lev	Org	ab	r	h	d	t	hr	rbi	bb	k	sb	cs	ba	ob	slg	ops	bb%	ct%	eye	px	sx	rc/g	bpv
Morales,Kendry	06	23	3	aaa	LAA	256	32	73	12	1	9	41	11	31	0	4	285	315	445	760	4%	88%	0.35	99	46	4.77	43
	07	24	30	aa	LAA	255	36	78	18	1	4	32	12	28	0	2	305	338	428	766	5%	89%	0.43	89	53	5.29	47
Moran,Javon	06	24	8	aa	CIN	250	30	72	10	2	1	10	10	25	14	7	289	315	357	672	4%	90%	0.38	50	121	3.97	24
	07	25	8	a/a	PHI	425	62	102	17	3	2	17	35	72	23	15	239	297	306	604	8%	83%	0.49	48	127	3.01	10
Morgan,Matthew	07	26	24	aa	ARI	216	11	37	5	0	0	11	16	36	1	0	173	229	197	426	7%	84%	0.44	21	33	1.54	-25
Morgan,Nyjer	06	26	8	aa	PIT	219	31	56	5	3	1	8	12	29	17	10	254	294	322	615	5%	87%	0.42	41	168	3.00	10
	07	27	8	aa	PIT	164	22	39	3	1	0	7	10	28	18	7	238	282	268	550	6%	83%	0.36	22	142	2.64	-4
Morrissey,Adam	06	25	4	a/a	TEX	352	29	91	20	2	6	37	30	78	4	5	259	318	375	693	8%	78%	0.39	80	61	4.16	27
	07	26	4	aa	LAA	486	67	104	22	1	7	39	71	136	10	7	213	314	304	618	13%	72%	0.53	63	78	3.38	8
Morris,Jed	06	27	2	aa	OAK	170	20	41	5	0	4	12	16	24	1	1	241	305	348	653	8%	86%	0.65	67	43	3.75	21
Morse,Mike	06	25	5	aaa	SEA	206	20	46	14	1	4	29	12	41	0	1	223	266	359	625	6%	80%	0.29	94	53	3.19	19
	07	26	56	aa	SEA	291	38	74	22	0	5	31	21	49	4	3	254	303	374	677	7%	83%	0.42	90	65	3.97	30
Mortimer,Steve	07	26	38	aa	WAS	228	23	41	10	1	6	24	25	93	1	2	179	261	313	574	10%	59%	0.27	85	62	2.69	0
Morton,Colt	06	25	2	aa	SD	139	14	32	9	0	5	20	10	47	0	0	232	286	396	682	7%	66%	0.22	107	22	3.95	26
Moses,Matt	06	22	6	aa	MIN	474	44	113	15	2	14	68	32	111	2	2	238	287	367	654	6%	77%	0.29	77	53	3.64	17
	07	23	5	a/a	MIN	436	40	100	30	0	5	55	18	87	11	3	229	260	333	592	4%	80%	0.21	79	82	2.96	13
Moss,Brandon	06	23	8	aa	BOS	508	66	138	38	2	11	72	49	97	7	5	271	336	416	752	9%	81%	0.51	102	75	5.07	43
	07	24 a	8	aaa	BOS	493	59	136	46	1	13	70	54	133	3	5	276	347	452	800	10%	73%	0.41	125	47	5.68	52
Moss,Steve	06	23	8	aa	MIL	484	65	112	27	1	7	41	70	134	7	13	231	329	335	663	13%	72%	0.52	74	61	3.71	18
	07	24	8	aa	MIL	443	47	91	19	4	10	48	61	114	10	6	206	302	333	635	12%	74%	0.53	80	100	3.49	12
Moss,Timothy	06	25	4	aa	PHI	206	19	34	5	5	7	19	13	74	5	2	166	217	332	549	6%	64%	0.18	91	193	2.27	-4
Mottola,Chad	06	35	8	aaa	TOR	431	40	100	25	2	14	53	24	106	6	0	232	273	399	672	5%	76%	0.23	107	84	3.81	26
	07	36	80	aaa	TOR	405	54	91	21	3	14	42	25	74	5	1	224	270	396	665	6%	82%	0.34	106	102	3.67	25
Mulhern,Ryan	06	26	3	aa	CLE	452	54	101	23	2	11	58	34	129	1	0	223	278	354	632	7%	71%	0.27	86	65	3.42	15
	07	27	30	aaa	CLE	476	56	123	34	1	13	64	35	122	1	3	259	309	414	723	7%	74%	0.29	106	44	4.50	36
Munhall,Brian	06	26	2	aa	SF	140	9	30	4	1	2	11	8	34	2	0	218	259	298	557	5%	75%	0.23	52	69	2.69	-1
Muniz,J.C.	06	31	8	aa	FLA	206	20	34	10	1	6	19	15	84	1	1	163	221	309	531	7%	59%	0.18	92	64	2.19	-4
Munson,Eric	07	30	2	aa	HOU	173	17	33	12	0	5	17	15	39	1	1	191	255	338	593	8%	78%	0.39	102	44	2.86	13
Murillo,Agustin	06	24	5	aa	ARI	362	39	79	9	0	8	33	32	56	3	1	218	282	304	586	8%	85%	0.58	53	54	3.01	6
Murphy,David	06	25	8	a/a	BOS	490	59	127	43	4	10	61	49	74	6	5	259	327	422	749	9%	85%	0.67	115	86	4.91	47
	07	26	8	a/a	TEX	407	39	101	18	4	8	37	31	59	7	2	247	301	366	668	7%	86%	0.53	76	97	3.95	25
Murphy,Donnie	06	24	4	aa	KC	366	43	77	22	1	9	34	15	49	5	4	209	240	347	587	4%	86%	0.29	93	86	2.66	14
	07	25	6	aa	OAK	175	25	50	17	1	2	18	13	38	3	2	288	338	429	767	7%	78%	0.35	108	89	5.29	48
Murphy,Steven Ma	07	23	8	aa	TEX	488	57	123	31	3	10	54	23	88	4	4	252	286	388	674	5%	82%	0.27	92	80	3.80	28
Murphy,Tommy	06	27	8	aaa	LAA	285	32	72	13	2	5	27	14	51	5	15	253	289	363	652	5%	82%	0.28	73	83	2.92	20
	07	28	8	aa	LAA	307	26	62	14	3	2	23	16	76	11	9	201	240	289	529	5%	75%	0.21	61	126	2.11	-4
Murton,Matt	07	26 a	8	aa	CHC	151	23	41	14	1	5	21	14	17	1	0	274	334	483	817	8%	89%	0.81	140	73	5.97	65
Myers,Casey	07	28	0	aa	OAK	122	15	28	2	1	2	9	11	18	0	0	231	294	306	600	8%	85%	0.60	45	60	3.21	8
Myers,Corey	06	26	2	aaa	LAA	156	17	35	4	0	2	9	14	24	1	1	224	286	286	572	8%	85%	0.57	41	49	2.85	3
	07	27	20	aa	LAA	174	13	34	5	0	2	22	17	29	2	2	196	266	267	533	9%	83%	0.57	47	46	2.36	-4
Myers,Michael	06	27	6	aa	CHW	414	45	93	19	2	4	19	43	89	17	9	225	297	311	608	9%	79%	0.48	61	98	3.19	10
	07	28	34	aa	CHW	278	22	40	7	1	2	24	25	67	5	6	143	214	203	417	8%	76%	0.37	40	75	1.33	-28
Myrow,Brian	07	31	3	aa	SD	347	39	78	19	2	8	47	36	101	1	0	226	299	365	665	9%	71%	0.36	91	66	3.88	20
Nanita,Ricardo	06	25	8	aa	CHW	364	42	93	13	2	8	37	44	61	10	5	255	335	366	701	11%	83%	0.72	69	84	4.45	28
	07	26	8	aa	CHW	427	37	92	17	0	4	34	27	56	8	8	216	263	287	550	6%	87%	0.48	52	59	2.44	3
Natale,Jeff Paul	07	25	34	aa	BOS	404	50	93	27	1	4	48	65	33	4	3	229	336	327	663	14%	92%	1.94	75	58	4.05	46
Navarrete,Ray	06	28	5	a/a	NYM	165	18	27	6	0	3	12	8	27	1	1	165	202	263	465	4%	84%	0.28	64	68	1.66	-13
Navarro,Oswaldo	06	22	6	a/a	SEA	449	38	106	21	1	3	40	54	85	7	9	236	318	307	625	11%	81%	0.64	54	52	3.39	14
	07	23	64	aa	SEA	446	44	100	20	0	3	39	29	79	3	3	224	272	289	561	6%	82%	0.37	50	51	2.68	3
Negron,Miguel	06	24	8	aa	TOR	395	38	105	26	4	4	38	36	81	11	9	267	328	380	708	8%	79%	0.45	81	101	4.37	31
	07	25	8	aa	NYM	506	44	104	21	1	4	54	38	87	15	9	205	260	270	530	7%	83%	0.44	49	82	2.33	-3
Nelson,Brad	06	24	3	a/a	MIL	395	64	93	24	1	9	52	77	93	9	6	235	360	370	730	16%	76%	0.83	91	79	4.91	33
	07	25	38	aaa	MIL	411	47	100	22	1	18	57	29	90	8	7	243	293	433	726	7%	78%	0.32	117	70	4.22	36
Nelson,John	06	28	6	aaa	STL	423	48	81	15	1	17	41	36	144	10	2	191	255	353	607	8%	66%	0.25	96	94	3.04	8
	07	29	53	aa	CHC	263	25	42	7	0	11	30	18	91	0	1	158	211	313	524	6%	65%	0.19	90	31	2.08	-6
Nelson,Jon	06	27	8	a/a	SEA	434	53	96	21	3	15	51	15	143	5	4	222	248	388	636	3%	67%	0.11	102	101	3.14	18
	07	28	8	aa	SEA	191	17	31	11	2	3	17	4	71	2	1	161	179	287	465	2%	63%	0.06	85	131	1.58	-10
Nettles,Jeff	07	29	5	aa	KC	221	16	41	11	0	5	26	11	57	1	0	187	224	295	519	5%	74%	0.18	74	36	2.17	-4
Newhan,David	07	34	4	aa	NYM	173	16	38	8	1	4	18	12	33	4	4	218	269	340	609	6%	81%	0.36	78	95	2.94	12
Nicholson,David	07	25	48	aa	LA	182	22	31	5	1	2	16	18	40	2	3	172	247	240	487	9%	78%	0.45	44	87	1.91	-15
Nicholson,Derek	06	30	8	a/a	HOU	162	10	28	8	1	3	16	17	34	1	0	173	251	291	542	9%	79%	0.50	79	49	2.48	0
Nickeas,Mike	07	25	2	aa	NYM	212	20	39	9	0	1	11	14	32	2	3	184	235	238	473	6%	85%	0.45	43	58	1.78	-12
	06	24	2	aa	TEX	125	16	29	7	0	2	17	21	26	1	1	233	345	334	678	15%	79%	0.83	72	42	4.25	24
Nicolas,Cesar	07	25	53	aa	ARI	310	40	63	15	0	7	39	36	71	2	7	203	286	322	608	10%	77%	0.51	80	46	2.93	11
Niekro,Lance	06	28 b	3	aaa	SF	144	20	39	6	0	10	25	5	18	0	0	270	294	508	802	3%	88%	0.27	137	29	5.30	52
	07	29	3	aa	SF	143	14	31	6	2	3	14	8	33	0	1	218	260	352	612	5%	77%	0.25	84	81	3.02	12
Nieves,Wil	06	29	2	aaa	NYY	321	24	71	11	0	5	28	15	30	2	1	221	255	298	553	4%	91%	0.49	52	41	2.57	5
Niles,Drew	06	30	6	aaa	FLA	152	5	28	4	1	1	8	13	35	1	2	186	249	239	488	8%	77%	0.36	36	46	1.94	-16
Nix,Jayson	06	24	4	aaa	COL	358	29	84	13	1	2	19	24	43	11	4	235	283	293	576	6%	88%	0.56	43	82	2.92	7
	07	25	4	aa	COL	439	59	111	29	2	9	43	23	68	18	8	252	290	387	677	5%	85%	0.35	93	114	3.83	29
Nix,Laynce	06	26	8	aaa	MIL	354	50	99	19	2	16	62	21	91	4	1	280	320	478	798	6%	74%	0.23	121	90	5.58	48
	07	27	8	a/a	MIL	358	49	81	18	1	20	63	26	107	4	0	226	279	447	726	7%	70%	0.24	132	80	4.33	35
Norris,Dax	06	35	2	a/a	ATL	233	14	42	7	0	2	22	6	43	0	1	182	201	244	445	2%	82%	0.13	43	29	1.54	-19
Nowak,Christophe	07	25	3	aa	TAM	368	44	97	18	3	6	45	45	67	14	3	263	343	374	717	11%	82%	0.66	74	112	4.90	32
Nunez,Abraham	06	30	8	aaa	SF	283	31	64	15	2	8	40	28	54	4	4	225	295	379	675	9%	81%	0.52	99	77	3.78	26
	07	31	8	aaa	WAS	414	38	95	21	0	13	56	26	113	3	5	228	274	370	644	6%	73%	0.23	91	37	3.35	18
Nye,Rodney	06	30	5	aaa	TAM	298	25	62	15	1	4	26	25	74	1	0	208	270	302	572	8%	75%	0.35	68	49	2.83	4
O'Riordan,Christop	06	27	4	aa	SD	113	8	16	3	0	1	9	15	28	0	1	139	238	192	431	12%	76%	0.54	39	28	1.54	-27
Ochoa,Ivan	06	24	6	a/a	CLE	374	53	86	12	2	1	28	39	65	22	4	230	303	281	583	9%	83%	0.60	37	131	3.24	4
	07	25	6	aa	SF	179	17	46	10	2	2	16	8	26	7	2	255	285	361	646	4%	85%	0.29	73	119	3.63	21
Oeltjen,Trent	06	24	8	aa	MIN	401	55	112	16	8	3	40	32	59	21	12	278	332	377	709	7%	85%	0.54	63	164	4.41	29
	07	25	8	aaa	MIN	244	32	56	9	4	2	23	9	45	14	7	230	257	324	581	4%	82%	0.20	60	177	2.66	5

Major League Equivalent Statistics

BATTER	Yr	Age	Pos	Lev	Org	ab	r	h	d	t	hr	rbi	bb	k	sb	cs	ba	ob	slg	ops	bb%	ct%	eye	px	sx	rc/g	bpv
Offerman,Jose	06	38	4	aaa	NYM	344	37	71	11	1	6	38	47	63	8	0	207	302	298	600	12%	82%	0.74	58	86	3.35	8
Ojeda,Augie	06	32	6	aaa	CHC	306	33	65	9	1	3	21	39	39	4	1	212	300	274	574	11%	87%	1.00	42	69	3.00	8
Oliveros,Luis	06	23	2	aa	SEA	153	8	24	3	0	0	5	2	19	0	0	158	169	178	347	1%	88%	0.10	17	27	0.93	-38
	07	24	2	aa	SEA	175	16	43	10	0	3	15	10	25	0	0	244	287	353	640	6%	86%	0.41	78	23	3.57	22
Olmedo,Ray	06	25	6	aaa	CIN	383	45	103	20	2	3	28	32	69	16	6	269	325	354	679	8%	82%	0.46	62	104	4.21	25
	07	26	6	aaa	TOR	328	26	85	11	1	1	21	23	47	6	6	260	309	308	617	7%	86%	0.49	36	60	3.30	11
Olson,Tim	06	28	6	a/a	TEX	207	16	42	9	0	5	15	14	55	5	2	201	250	320	571	6%	73%	0.25	78	63	2.69	4
Ordaz,Luis	07	32	4	aa	PIT	351	23	70	15	1	1	22	11	63	6	4	199	224	257	481	3%	82%	0.18	45	68	1.83	-11
Orr,Pete	07	28	8	aaa	ATL	154	21	33	6	3	1	7	11	39	6	3	211	265	302	567	7%	75%	0.29	57	175	2.66	-0
Ortmeier,Dan	06	25	8	a/a	SF	429	45	94	21	3	7	36	27	71	12	10	219	265	328	593	6%	84%	0.38	73	102	2.75	11
	07	26	8	aa	SF	305	28	63	16	1	7	39	19	60	11	2	205	252	331	583	6%	80%	0.32	83	99	2.88	9
Osborn,Pat	06	26	5	aa	CLE	408	39	86	13	1	1	31	28	66	12	10	210	260	251	512	6%	84%	0.43	33	82	2.11	-8
	07	27	5	aa	CLE	183	12	34	6	0	1	15	15	24	4	2	185	246	233	479	7%	87%	0.61	37	60	1.96	-11
Otness,John J.	07	26	2	aa	BOS	251	12	46	10	1	0	17	6	30	1	1	184	203	229	432	2%	88%	0.20	37	48	1.47	-20
Owens,Jeremy	06	30	8	aa	TAM	414	47	73	11	3	11	32	25	201	19	5	176	222	293	516	6%	51%	0.12	70	159	2.15	-10
	07	31	8	aaa	TAM	341	36	77	14	5	6	27	16	132	13	2	224	260	346	605	5%	61%	0.12	75	166	3.14	8
Owens,Jerry	06	26	8	aaa	CHW	439	68	109	14	4	4	44	41	57	37	13	248	312	325	636	8%	87%	0.72	50	150	3.65	18
	07	27	8	aaa	CHW	232	35	61	9	0	3	18	26	35	20	9	263	338	339	677	10%	85%	0.75	53	104	4.15	24
Padgett,Matt	06	29	8	a/a	CHC	196	21	41	10	2	4	21	21	66	0	0	209	284	339	623	9%	66%	0.31	84	67	3.35	11
	07	30	83	a/a	PHI	454	29	83	22	1	9	36	22	98	1	0	183	222	294	516	5%	79%	0.23	75	37	2.13	-3
Padilla,Jorge	06	27	8	aa	NYM	482	53	115	22	1	7	43	33	99	7	4	238	287	332	619	6%	80%	0.34	65	71	3.29	13
	07	28	8	aa	KC	443	54	104	18	2	10	47	32	69	13	6	235	286	347	633	7%	84%	0.47	72	97	3.42	17
Pagan,Angel	07	26	8	aa	CHC	116	13	23	3	2	3	7	7	20	4	1	203	248	330	578	6%	83%	0.36	75	147	2.78	5
Pagnozzi,Matt	07	25	2	aa	STL	182	11	33	8	0	2	10	7	40	1	0	183	212	256	467	4%	78%	0.17	53	41	1.77	-14
Pali,Matthew	06	26	3	aa	LAA	345	26	61	10	0	5	30	13	57	5	4	177	206	253	459	4%	84%	0.22	50	62	1.62	-16
	07	27	803	aa	LAA	322	22	64	8	1	5	28	17	64	4	6	197	238	276	514	5%	80%	0.27	49	56	2.03	-9
Palmisano,Lou	06	24	2	aa	MIL	332	35	73	16	1	4	33	45	67	2	0	220	313	309	622	12%	80%	0.66	63	58	3.55	13
	07	25	2	aa	MIL	351	38	75	19	1	9	50	47	80	6	2	213	305	349	654	12%	77%	0.59	90	73	3.80	20
Panther,Nathan	06	25	8	aa	CLE	221	25	42	7	3	0	19	18	49	3	4	191	252	248	501	8%	78%	0.37	40	117	2.02	-12
Parrish,Dave	06	27	2	a/a	NYY	252	26	64	13	1	3	30	25	48	0	0	252	320	352	672	9%	81%	0.52	70	37	4.13	23
	07	28	2	aa	PIT	250	15	38	10	0	3	18	12	56	1	1	150	189	227	417	5%	78%	0.21	54	39	1.34	-23
Pascucci,Val	07	29	3	aa	FLA	447	64	92	20	1	22	67	49	140	6	1	206	284	404	688	10%	69%	0.35	119	86	3.98	25
Patchett,Gary	07	29	6	aa	LAA	221	23	40	2	0	0	12	11	59	1	1	180	220	187	406	5%	73%	0.19	6	59	1.35	-34
Patterson,Eric	06	24	4	a/a	CHC	508	79	137	23	8	11	59	53	98	46	12	270	339	411	750	9%	81%	0.54	88	178	5.21	37
	07	24	48	aa	CHC	516	75	135	26	5	12	52	42	76	19	10	261	317	401	718	7%	85%	0.55	89	125	4.46	35
Patterson,Ryan	06	23	8	aa	TOR	187	17	47	15	1	6	18	12	49	2	0	249	293	431	724	6%	74%	0.24	122	70	4.50	38
	07	24	8	aa	TOR	446	42	105	24	0	15	53	18	89	1	5	234	264	390	654	4%	80%	0.20	100	28	3.35	23
Paul,Xavier	07	23	8	aa	LA	422	53	111	19	1	10	42	41	95	15	10	263	328	384	712	9%	77%	0.43	79	84	4.40	29
Pavkovich,Adam	06	25	6	aaa	LAA	317	31	68	14	1	8	36	27	51	5	7	215	276	341	617	8%	84%	0.53	81	64	3.00	15
	07	26	48	aa	LAA	281	35	63	21	1	2	26	23	58	3	7	224	284	323	607	8%	79%	0.41	78	71	2.90	15
Pearce,Steven	07	24 a	3	aa	PIT	412	61	121	34	2	15	72	30	51	10	2	293	341	496	837	7%	88%	0.60	135	99	6.36	65
Pedroia,Dustin	06	23 a	4	aaa	BOS	423	51	128	33	2	5	46	45	24	1	4	303	370	426	795	10%	94%	1.88	92	45	5.92	76
Peel,Aaron	06	24	8	aa	LAA	495	49	117	31	2	12	48	19	80	10	14	237	266	378	644	4%	84%	0.24	95	77	3.08	23
	07	25	8	aa	LAA	310	29	69	18	1	6	32	5	41	2	0	224	235	343	579	2%	87%	0.12	83	71	2.71	11
Pena,Brayan	06	25	2	aaa	ATL	325	30	94	17	1	1	31	20	27	6	6	289	330	357	687	6%	92%	0.74	54	63	4.19	33
	07	26	23	aaa	ATL	345	38	98	19	1	5	43	17	35	5	8	284	317	387	705	5%	90%	0.48	73	62	4.16	34
Pena,Carlos	06	28	3	aaa	NYY	418	63	103	17	0	20	65	58	98	4	0	247	338	434	772	12%	77%	0.59	111	61	5.43	40
Pena,Ramiro	07	22	6	aa	NYY	203	23	50	7	1	0	10	21	33	7	3	246	317	291	608	9%	84%	0.64	35	94	3.38	9
Pena,Tony	06	25	6	aaa	ATL	298	36	81	12	3	1	22	12	54	11	3	272	300	342	642	4%	82%	0.22	50	131	3.73	16
Pence,Hunter	06	23	8	aa	HOU	523	81	133	27	7	24	79	49	95	15	5	254	317	471	788	8%	82%	0.51	129	140	5.32	48
Pennington,Clifton	07	23	6	aa	OAK	271	34	60	12	1	2	17	31	29	7	2	222	302	294	595	10%	89%	1.08	52	91	3.23	17
Peralta,Juan	07	24	4	aa	TOR	272	23	67	8	1	3	22	20	51	2	1	248	299	314	614	7%	81%	0.39	44	54	3.37	9
Perez,Fernando	07	24	8	aa	TAM	393	68	105	21	8	7	27	63	96	26	20	268	369	411	780	14%	76%	0.65	90	173	5.15	40
Perez,Kenny	06	25	6	aaa	ARI	284	27	64	9	2	2	22	20	31	5	4	227	277	293	570	7%	89%	0.63	45	85	2.74	7
	07	26	40	a/a	CHW	324	27	75	12	3	7	35	17	48	2	3	231	269	350	619	5%	85%	0.36	74	68	3.14	14
Perez,Miguel	06	23	2	aa	CIN	394	30	88	16	0	3	30	16	85	5	1	224	255	286	541	4%	79%	0.20	46	61	2.51	-2
Perez,Timo	06	32	8	aaa	STL	268	34	67	14	1	10	33	17	27	4	2	249	294	420	713	6%	90%	0.64	108	76	4.28	40
	07	32	80	aaa	DET	489	63	127	32	1	10	58	29	47	11	6	260	301	388	689	6%	90%	0.62	90	85	4.05	36
Perez,Tomas	07	34	6	a/a	CHW	476	45	92	18	0	6	41	23	90	3	1	193	231	266	496	5%	81%	0.26	51	63	2.04	-9
Perez,Yohannis	07	25	6	aa	MIL	190	15	32	4	2	0	13	13	52	2	3	170	224	210	434	7%	73%	0.26	27	98	1.48	-27
Perry,Jason	06	26	8	a/a	OAK	425	47	99	20	2	9	47	25	96	4	4	233	276	352	627	6%	78%	0.26	78	72	3.27	15
	07	27	8	a/a	DET	411	70	85	21	1	19	64	50	132	3	0	207	293	402	695	11%	68%	0.38	119	88	4.13	26
Peterson,Brian	06	28	2	a/a	DET	193	18	45	7	2	5	15	9	46	2	2	234	267	370	637	4%	76%	0.19	82	86	3.29	16
	07	29	2	aa	PIT	251	20	51	11	1	2	20	18	40	0	2	204	256	274	530	7%	84%	0.44	52	41	2.32	-2
Peterson,Brock	07	24	30	aa	MIN	389	53	97	19	2	12	51	33	79	1	0	249	308	399	707	8%	80%	0.42	95	69	4.42	31
Petit,Gregorio	07	23	6	aa	OAK	503	45	135	25	0	5	50	34	75	8	6	268	315	348	663	6%	85%	0.45	59	53	3.89	23
Phelps,Josh	06	28	3	aaa	DET	464	52	126	21	4	20	78	33	123	6	1	273	322	467	789	7%	74%	0.27	116	93	5.50	44
Phillips,Andy	07	30	4	aaa	NYY	249	31	64	9	1	9	30	25	44	2	1	257	325	408	733	9%	82%	0.57	91	59	4.82	34
Phillips,Jason	06	33	2	aaa	TOR	249	25	59	10	0	6	32	18	44	1	1	239	290	354	644	7%	82%	0.41	74	37	3.58	18
Phillips,Paul	06	29	2	aaa	KC	345	35	71	10	1	6	32	18	35	0	0	206	246	295	541	5%	90%	0.52	57	42	2.44	2
	07	30	2	aa	KC	202	13	31	5	0	1	8	11	30	0	0	152	194	198	392	5%	85%	0.35	32	25	1.23	-29
Piedra,Jorge	06	27	8	aaa	COL	138	10	29	7	0	5	12	10	23	0	2	213	269	365	634	7%	83%	0.45	96	20	3.14	20
	07	28	8	aa	OAK	265	29	66	18	1	6	38	22	38	0	1	248	306	386	693	8%	86%	0.60	97	40	4.18	34
Pie,Felix	06	22 a	8	aaa	CHC	559	78	165	34	7	17	57	47	106	18	13	295	350	468	818	8%	81%	0.44	110	120	5.82	53
	07	23 a	8	aa	CHC	229	43	77	9	4	8	37	16	34	8	7	336	380	515	895	7%	85%	0.47	104	148	7.11	65
Pilittere,Peter	07	26	2	aa	NYY	348	39	80	14	1	2	31	23	48	0	1	230	277	290	567	6%	86%	0.47	45	48	2.78	5
Pinckney,Andrew	07	25	5	aa	BOS	458	54	103	27	3	10	48	31	92	3	7	224	273	360	632	6%	80%	0.33	91	73	3.16	19
Pinckney,Brandon	07	25	6	aa	CLE	278	32	62	12	1	2	29	16	34	0	2	223	266	291	558	6%	88%	0.47	50	55	2.60	5
Plouffe,Trevor	07	21	6	aa	MIN	497	62	122	34	1	7	41	29	76	10	8	245	287	360	647	6%	85%	0.38	84	84	3.47	24
Plumley,Grant	06	25	6	aa	NYY	105	11	26	7	0	2	14	7	20	0	0	244	289	362	651	6%	81%	0.33	84	29	3.69	23
Pond,Simon	06	30	3	aa	PIT	461	44	83	24	2	8	54	40	145	2	2	181	246	293	538	8%	68%	0.27	77	64	2.37	-3
Pope,Van	07	24	5	aa	ATL	421	41	85	21	3	5	37	30	71	9	6	203	256	302	558	7%	83%	0.42	69	98	2.53	4

BATTER	Yr	Age	Pos	Lev	Org	ab	r	h	d	t	hr	rbi	bb	k	sb	cs	ba	ob	slg	ops	bb%	ct%	eye	px	sx	rc/g	bpv
Porter,Gregory	06	26	3	aa	LAA	440	47	98	22	0	13	46	17	89	3	3	223	252	362	613	4%	80%	0.19	90	52	2.97	15
	07	27	80	aa	LAA	472	51	116	21	2	8	59	25	106	12	6	246	284	350	634	5%	78%	0.23	69	93	3.42	15
Powell,Landon	07	26	2	aa	OAK	236	38	57	8	1	11	32	27	40	1	0	240	318	419	738	10%	83%	0.68	105	67	4.82	37
Prado,Martin	06	23	4	a/a	ATL	417	45	113	17	2	3	36	25	61	4	4	271	312	343	655	6%	85%	0.41	51	70	3.80	20
	07	24	4	aaa	ATL	395	55	119	22	2	4	37	30	38	5	4	301	351	397	748	7%	90%	0.79	69	79	5.20	45
Pressley,Josh	06	27	3	a/a	FLA	177	11	32	5	1	2	16	28	36	1	0	178	290	244	534	14%	80%	0.78	43	46	2.59	-7
Prettyman,Ronald	07	26	5	aa	SEA	291	25	60	12	1	5	28	16	64	3	2	206	247	308	555	5%	78%	0.24	67	64	2.51	1
Price,Jared	06	25	2	aaa	KC	139	11	20	6	0	3	11	8	43	1	0	144	190	252	442	5%	69%	0.19	72	54	1.53	-19
Pride,Curtis	06	38	8	aaa	LAA	273	38	68	14	0	5	31	37	66	14	6	247	337	359	696	12%	76%	0.56	77	87	4.39	26
	07	39	80	aa	LAA	215	17	32	9	1	2	17	18	84	6	3	147	211	225	435	8%	61%	0.21	55	94	1.52	-24
Pridie,Jason	06	23	8	aa	TAM	460	40	102	11	4	5	35	31	102	16	5	221	271	293	564	6%	78%	0.30	44	116	2.77	-2
	07	24	8	a/a	TAM	525	80	149	30	10	13	59	33	85	23	11	284	326	453	779	6%	84%	0.39	106	170	5.22	46
Prieto,Alex	06	30	6	aaa	KC	221	19	42	7	0	2	14	18	41	2	2	191	252	248	501	8%	81%	0.44	41	48	2.09	-10
	07	31	6	aaa	BOS	182	18	39	11	1	3	17	15	32	2	3	213	274	326	600	8%	82%	0.47	80	70	2.92	13
Pritz,Bryan A.	07	25	8	a/a	BOS	372	41	98	23	2	6	40	33	53	4	1	263	324	381	704	8%	86%	0.63	82	75	4.53	34
Psomas,Grant	07	25	3	aa	FLA	442	50	86	23	3	14	43	43	119	7	6	193	265	348	613	9%	73%	0.36	98	92	2.99	12
Putnam,Danny	06	24	8	aa	OAK	225	27	48	11	1	7	29	18	32	2	1	211	270	359	629	7%	86%	0.57	94	73	3.28	21
	07	25	8	aa	OAK	223	17	44	15	1	2	24	16	40	3	5	198	252	299	551	7%	82%	0.41	77	65	2.34	6
Quentin,Carlos	06	24 a	8	aaa	ARI	318	51	85	29	2	7	40	35	35	4	0	267	340	437	777	10%	89%	1.00	120	98	5.59	59
	07	25 a	8	aa	ARI	115	23	34	11	1	4	21	7	13	0	1	297	339	501	840	6%	88%	0.54	138	90	6.15	67
Quinn,Mark	06	32	8	a/a	CHW	243	21	49	11	0	10	30	18	50	1	1	201	255	365	620	7%	79%	0.35	102	30	3.09	16
Quintanilla,Omar	06	25	6	aaa	COL	308	36	79	22	2	3	22	21	38	3	1	256	304	370	674	6%	88%	0.55	84	85	4.04	31
	07	26	64	aa	COL	348	41	96	26	3	3	32	23	57	2	1	277	322	391	713	6%	84%	0.41	85	79	4.62	36
Quintero,Humberto	06	27	2	aaa	HOU	292	31	75	18	2	3	29	15	42	3	0	257	294	361	655	5%	86%	0.36	76	86	3.83	24
	07	28	2	aa	HOU	177	15	43	9	1	3	15	2	23	0	2	244	254	357	611	1%	87%	0.11	76	50	2.95	15
Quiroz,Guillermo	06	25	2	a/a	SEA	202	17	49	10	0	5	32	13	42	0	0	240	285	360	645	6%	79%	0.30	80	18	3.60	19
	07	26	2	aa	TEX	259	17	59	14	0	5	25	12	48	1	0	226	259	330	589	4%	82%	0.24	73	30	2.94	10
Rabelo,Mike	06	27	2	a/a	DET	350	42	82	21	1	7	42	25	73	3	2	234	285	360	645	7%	79%	0.34	86	69	3.55	21
Rabe,Josh	06	28	8	aaa	MIN	355	48	99	19	1	6	45	32	41	7	4	278	338	385	724	8%	88%	0.79	75	78	4.79	39
Raburn,John	06	28	6	a/a	TAM	394	45	91	14	4	0	28	49	70	23	9	232	316	289	606	11%	82%	0.69	41	133	3.36	8
	07	29	84	aa	FLA	372	39	66	10	3	2	20	36	74	15	6	178	251	234	485	9%	80%	0.49	37	128	2.03	-15
Raburn,Ryan	06	25	4	aaa	DET	451	62	116	26	5	18	73	48	111	15	4	257	328	454	782	10%	75%	0.43	121	132	5.41	44
	07	26 b	8	aaa	DET	315	53	83	18	3	15	57	46	67	11	4	265	358	480	838	13%	79%	0.68	131	120	6.34	56
Raglani,John	06	24	8	aa	LA	336	46	75	22	0	9	37	40	90	6	2	222	305	367	671	11%	73%	0.44	99	73	3.96	24
	07	24	8	aa	LA	456	60	96	21	3	17	53	68	123	7	8	210	313	381	695	13%	73%	0.56	104	82	4.04	24
Ragsdale,Corey	06	24	6	aa	NYM	437	44	82	18	2	9	35	37	177	12	9	189	252	300	551	8%	59%	0.21	72	99	2.40	-3
Rahl,Christopher	07	24	8	aa	ARI	423	49	98	24	4	7	41	13	73	13	6	232	254	355	609	3%	83%	0.17	84	131	2.97	15
Raines Jr.,Tim	06	27	8	a/a	WAS	306	37	66	12	0	5	22	20	72	23	5	216	264	307	571	6%	76%	0.28	62	118	2.88	3
	07	28	8	aa	HOU	367	39	84	11	2	9	38	14	69	17	4	229	258	344	602	4%	81%	0.21	70	124	3.05	9
Ramirez,Julio	06	29	8	aaa	NYM	154	14	25	5	0	2	14	8	56	4	3	165	208	230	438	5%	64%	0.15	44	78	1.46	-24
Ramirez,Wilkin	07	22	8	aa	DET	121	14	25	3	1	2	13	8	35	6	2	207	256	298	553	6%	71%	0.23	55	132	2.58	-4
Ramirez,Yordany	07	23	8	aa	SD	127	16	35	3	0	4	16	5	21	5	6	275	302	390	691	4%	84%	0.24	68	73	3.57	24
Ramos,Peeter	06	25	4	a/a	PHI	238	35	61	9	2	4	25	16	34	4	6	257	305	359	664	6%	86%	0.48	65	100	3.61	22
	07	26	4	aa	PHI	282	30	71	7	0	6	27	23	36	4	5	252	309	345	654	8%	87%	0.66	57	46	3.62	21
Randel,Kevin	06	25	6	aa	FLA	325	48	78	22	2	10	50	44	102	3	3	241	332	410	741	12%	69%	0.43	111	79	4.84	35
	07	26	4	aa	FLA	125	10	18	6	0	2	5	21	44	3	1	146	268	237	505	14%	65%	0.48	65	51	2.26	-15
Ransom,Cody	06	31	6	aaa	HOU	380	48	77	18	1	16	46	40	93	2	1	201	277	381	658	9%	75%	0.42	110	60	3.59	21
	07	32	563	aa	HOU	503	44	93	22	0	18	53	29	157	13	4	185	230	332	562	6%	69%	0.19	92	77	2.48	3
Rasmus,Colby	07	21	8	aa	STL	472	76	113	32	2	22	59	58	87	15	4	239	323	456	778	11%	82%	0.67	136	108	5.27	49
Recker,Anthony Vi	07	24	2	aa	OAK	201	12	35	10	0	3	16	13	54	0	1	175	226	269	495	6%	73%	0.25	68	23	1.95	-9
Redman,Prentice	06	27	8	a/a	STL	353	35	80	21	1	9	40	31	76	7	8	227	290	365	655	8%	79%	0.41	93	66	3.44	22
	07	28	80	aa	SEA	412	41	76	16	2	10	38	38	106	2	4	184	254	307	561	9%	74%	0.36	77	61	2.53	0
Redman,Tike	06	30	8	a/a	DET	403	36	84	13	2	2	15	22	46	12	5	210	251	262	513	5%	89%	0.48	39	97	2.22	-5
	07	31	8	aaa	BAL	296	47	78	13	4	2	23	29	26	23	7	265	330	350	679	9%	91%	1.13	58	154	4.28	35
Reed,Eric	06	26	8	aaa	FLA	390	52	102	17	7	4	31	20	80	16	11	261	297	371	668	5%	80%	0.25	70	164	3.65	21
	07	27	8	aa	FLA	303	40	69	8	9	0	15	13	61	23	3	227	259	310	569	4%	80%	0.21	48	245	2.94	-0
Reed,Jeremy	07	26	8	aa	SEA	563	70	132	30	3	10	47	37	78	10	9	235	282	349	631	6%	86%	0.47	78	91	3.28	20
Reed,Keith	06	28	8	aaa	BAL	426	53	108	32	1	9	61	19	66	13	10	253	284	397	682	4%	85%	0.28	101	93	3.67	32
Reese,Kevin	06	29	8	aaa	NYY	212	25	52	7	1	5	18	12	38	4	7	246	286	351	637	5%	82%	0.32	65	78	3.13	15
	07	30	8	aaa	NYY	433	48	93	12	2	8	49	44	75	7	7	214	286	307	593	9%	83%	0.58	57	76	2.94	7
Reimold,Nolan	07	24 a	8	aa	BAL	186	24	50	14	0	10	28	15	39	2	3	271	324	501	825	7%	79%	0.37	145	46	5.58	58
Relaford,Desi	07	34	5	aa	TEX	316	27	55	11	1	4	31	24	63	4	0	175	233	253	485	7%	80%	0.38	52	82	2.00	-12
Requena,Alexande	07	27	8	aa	SF	117	9	20	5	1	0	8	10	28	9	5	170	235	227	462	8%	76%	0.36	44	127	1.66	-18
Restovich,Mike	06	28 b	8	aaa	CHC	443	66	118	26	3	25	74	47	118	2	1	266	336	504	840	10%	73%	0.39	143	75	6.17	56
	07	29	80	aaa	WAS	356	35	81	17	2	16	49	27	108	3	2	227	282	418	700	7%	70%	0.25	115	67	4.01	28
Reyes,Argenis	07	25	4	aa	CLE	467	52	108	19	2	2	25	19	56	22	8	231	261	291	552	4%	88%	0.34	45	117	2.58	3
Reyes,Jose	06	23	2	a/a	CHC	252	25	59	9	0	0	22	23	36	0	2	234	298	270	568	8%	86%	0.64	32	31	2.81	4
	07	25	2	aa	NYM	126	10	23	5	0	2	16	10	22	2	0	181	244	264	508	8%	82%	0.47	57	52	2.23	-7
Reyes,Milver	06	24	2	aa	PIT	166	8	29	4	0	0	10	5	18	0	0	177	200	200	401	3%	89%	0.27	20	18	1.29	-27
	07	25	2	aa	PIT	105	4	20	5	0	0	7	7	24	0	0	189	241	231	472	6%	77%	0.29	38	7	1.88	-16
Reynolds,Kyle C	07	24	5	aa	CHC	139	19	34	9	0	8	28	7	26	2	2	246	280	472	752	5%	81%	0.25	139	64	4.36	44
Reynolds,Mark	06	23 a	6	aa	ARI	114	20	30	7	0	8	18	10	34	0	1	264	322	528	849	8%	70%	0.29	158	48	5.90	59
	07	24 a	5	aa	ARI	134	22	37	9	2	6	17	16	27	3	1	276	354	496	851	11%	80%	0.59	135	126	6.54	60
Rhymes,William D	07	25	4	aa	DET	155	19	37	6	0	1	19	6	20	5	1	239	266	294	560	4%	87%	0.29	42	91	2.76	3
Richardson,Juan	06	28	5	aa	STL	444	48	104	25	1	11	53	32	112	0	7	234	284	366	651	7%	75%	0.28	89	34	3.40	20
	07	29	50	aa	STL	430	42	88	15	1	11	51	31	120	0	2	205	258	322	580	7%	72%	0.26	73	36	2.77	4
Richardson,Kevin	06	26	2	aa	TEX	303	39	68	10	3	14	34	24	90	3	1	224	282	411	692	7%	70%	0.27	107	99	3.98	24
	07	27	2	aa	TEX	320	30	56	7	0	11	32	17	84	0	2	174	216	296	512	5%	74%	0.21	71	33	2.01	-9
Richard,Chris	06	32	3	aaa	PIT	337	47	72	15	3	14	59	50	86	5	5	214	314	403	718	13%	75%	0.58	113	94	4.34	30
	07	33	83	aaa	TAM	342	54	83	21	2	13	49	36	92	8	3	242	314	424	738	10%	73%	0.39	115	108	4.74	36
Richar,Danny	06	23	4	aa	ARI	480	71	134	25	5	8	38	48	72	14	5	279	344	400	744	9%	85%	0.66	80	122	5.14	39
	07	24 a	4	a/a	CHW	398	53	113	22	6	14	54	34	67	6	5	283	339	470	809	8%	83%	0.51	115	115	5.73	52

Major League Equivalent Statistics

BATTER	Yr	Age	Pos	Lev	Org	ab	r	h	d	t	hr	rbi	bb	k	sb	cs	ba	ob	slg	ops	bb%	ct%	eye	px	sx	rc/g	bpv
Richie,Anthony	06	25	2	aa	CHC	222	13	49	14	0	0	11	6	52	1	0	223	242	287	529	3%	77%	0.11	57	38	2.35	-0
	07	26	2	aa	CHC	220	16	44	6	0	7	21	9	32	2	1	200	232	327	559	4%	85%	0.28	76	40	2.47	4
Rifkin,Aaron	07	29	3	aa	COL	453	40	94	28	0	10	50	26	115	2	1	208	251	339	590	5%	75%	0.22	90	42	2.85	11
Riggans,Shawn	06	26	2	aaa	TAM	417	39	111	23	2	10	49	24	87	2	2	265	306	400	706	5%	79%	0.28	90	55	4.34	31
	07	27	2	aaa	TAM	121	10	30	9	1	4	14	4	31	0	3	251	274	432	706	3%	75%	0.12	118	62	3.65	35
Riggs,Eric	06	30	6	aaa	LA	303	23	70	11	1	6	32	20	52	2	0	232	279	336	614	6%	83%	0.38	66	49	3.29	12
	07	31	4	aa	FLA	297	32	55	16	3	6	30	21	57	2	2	186	240	323	563	7%	81%	0.37	89	97	2.50	6
Rios,Kevin	06	25	5	aa	NYM	139	10	27	6	0	1	17	5	38	1	0	194	220	259	479	3%	73%	0.12	50	47	1.88	-12
Rivas,Luis	06	27	4	aaa	TAM	229	18	45	7	1	2	21	9	34	2	1	195	224	257	481	4%	85%	0.25	42	70	1.88	-13
	07	28	64	aaa	CLE	410	47	91	16	2	8	34	35	66	10	7	222	284	331	615	8%	84%	0.54	70	89	3.14	14
Rivera,Carlos	06	28	3	aaa	COL	421	38	119	22	1	7	49	12	39	2	2	283	303	393	696	3%	91%	0.31	76	45	4.25	32
Rivera,Mike	06	30	2	aaa	MIL	213	24	53	10	0	8	37	11	41	3	3	249	286	410	695	5%	81%	0.26	100	54	3.92	30
	07	31	2	aaa	MIL	349	29	62	13	0	15	48	20	72	4	5	178	222	346	568	5%	79%	0.27	100	43	2.31	6
Rivera,Rene	07	24	2	aa	SEA	323	24	59	14	0	4	31	20	83	1	2	182	230	262	492	6%	74%	0.24	57	36	1.94	-11
Rivera,Ruben	06	33	8	aaa	CHW	331	42	69	15	1	15	34	26	92	4	1	209	267	400	667	7%	72%	0.28	115	79	3.62	23
Roberson,Chris	06	27	8	aaa	PHI	284	42	79	13	2	1	16	21	58	24	9	278	327	348	675	7%	80%	0.36	53	138	4.16	21
	07	28	8	aaa	PHI	463	51	106	19	2	4	38	24	54	15	9	229	267	301	569	5%	88%	0.45	52	100	2.65	7
Roberts,Brandon	07	23	8	aa	MIN	369	41	98	12	3	2	32	25	48	12	8	266	312	331	643	6%	87%	0.52	44	104	3.59	17
Roberts,Ryan	06	26	4	aaa	TOR	362	39	94	28	1	10	43	26	82	5	3	260	310	423	733	7%	77%	0.32	113	67	4.63	39
	07	27	54	aaa	TOR	337	37	74	14	1	10	38	44	77	1	2	220	309	361	670	11%	77%	0.57	88	43	3.91	21
Robinson,Christop	07	23	2	aa	CHC	289	23	68	16	0	1	22	16	61	3	0	235	276	302	578	5%	79%	0.27	56	55	2.97	7
Robinson,Kerry	06	33	8	aaa	KC	396	55	104	22	3	2	32	27	34	14	14	264	311	345	656	6%	91%	0.78	61	107	3.51	29
Robinson,Wade	06	26	6	a/a	HOU	169	9	42	2	1	1	11	6	26	0	5	247	272	287	559	3%	84%	0.22	24	38	2.36	-3
	07	27	4	aa	WAS	110	7	17	3	0	0	4	9	17	3	1	158	220	190	410	7%	84%	0.50	28	62	1.42	-26
Robles,Oscar	06	31	4	aaa	LA	275	20	60	7	0	0	20	24	18	0	1	219	283	245	528	8%	94%	1.37	23	22	2.44	10
	07	31	6	aa	SD	102	6	18	3	1	0	7	5	13	0	1	178	216	233	449	5%	87%	0.38	36	80	1.59	-18
Robnett,Richie	07	24	8	aa	OAK	523	64	118	35	1	14	60	30	124	3	3	225	268	378	646	5%	76%	0.24	103	65	3.40	23
Rodland,Eric	06	27	4	aa	LAA	397	42	90	17	1	5	33	37	46	1	5	226	291	311	602	8%	88%	0.79	59	40	3.04	16
Rodriguez,Guilder	06	23	6	aa	MIL	160	19	32	3	1	0	7	21	31	2	1	200	294	230	525	12%	81%	0.69	21	84	2.48	-11
	07	24	6	aa	MIL	175	23	46	1	0	0	13	20	26	7	6	261	336	266	602	10%	85%	0.76	5	72	3.20	4
Rodriguez,Guillern	06	28	2	aaa	SF	127	14	22	7	1	6	11	8	20	0	1	176	227	373	600	6%	84%	0.41	120	72	2.63	16
	07	29	2	aa	SF	103	9	17	5	0	1	10	7	9	1	0	167	219	233	452	6%	91%	0.72	50	55	1.70	-9
Rodriguez,John	07	30	0	aa	STL	157	21	27	8	1	4	16	14	37	1	0	172	241	301	542	8%	76%	0.38	83	85	2.43	-1
Rodriguez,Mike	06	26	8	aaa	HOU	439	57	109	14	6	5	32	41	45	23	7	248	312	341	652	8%	90%	0.89	57	146	3.87	24
	07	27	8	aa	HOU	241	24	52	10	2	2	17	14	34	7	4	217	259	296	555	5%	86%	0.40	56	106	2.51	3
Rodriguez,Sean	07	22	6	aa	LAA	508	76	120	29	1	15	66	48	119	14	9	236	302	386	688	9%	77%	0.40	98	93	3.96	27
Rogers,Eddie	06	28	6	aaa	BAL	339	37	92	17	1	5	28	13	55	11	7	272	299	368	666	4%	84%	0.24	67	89	3.77	23
	07	29	654	aaa	BOS	405	34	89	16	0	5	28	16	65	7	5	220	251	294	545	4%	84%	0.25	53	65	2.43	0
Rogowski,Casey	06	25	3	aaa	CHW	459	62	120	30	2	14	68	48	90	24	10	261	330	425	755	9%	80%	0.53	108	108	4.99	42
	07	26	38	aaa	CHW	453	54	103	25	0	15	48	55	102	15	5	227	311	379	690	11%	77%	0.54	99	78	4.19	27
Rohan,Jimmy	06	22	6	aa	LA	182	13	42	8	0	0	19	20	21	0	3	231	307	275	582	10%	88%	0.95	39	21	2.88	12
	07	23	3	aa	LA	164	13	34	6	1	0	17	14	25	0	0	207	268	254	522	8%	85%	0.55	37	45	2.37	-5
Rojas,Carlos	06	23	6	aa	CHC	353	29	73	8	0	0	17	31	59	3	0	207	271	229	500	8%	83%	0.53	20	55	2.24	-12
	07	24	64	aa	CHC	319	25	69	13	1	0	21	21	43	3	0	216	265	262	527	6%	86%	0.49	38	67	2.44	-3
Romero,Alexandei	06	23	8	a/a	MIN	403	47	102	19	3	5	41	39	42	20	9	253	319	352	671	9%	90%	0.93	68	112	3.99	31
	07	24	8	aa	ARI	533	66	148	29	5	5	52	30	45	10	10	278	317	378	695	5%	92%	0.67	71	98	4.13	35
Roneberg,Brett	06	28	8	aa	PIT	400	48	97	16	1	7	56	38	63	7	1	243	309	342	651	9%	84%	0.61	66	80	3.87	20
	07	29	83	aa	PIT	238	26	44	8	2	5	24	21	40	6	0	185	250	292	543	8%	83%	0.52	67	109	2.56	-0
Rosales,Adam	07	24	3	aa	CIN	255	41	62	16	3	11	25	29	59	3	5	242	321	462	783	10%	77%	0.50	135	107	4.97	46
Rosamond Jr.,Micl	06	28	8	aa	ATL	338	37	63	14	2	11	37	16	144	4	2	187	224	343	567	5%	57%	0.11	95	115	2.47	4
Rosa,Wally	06	25	2	a/a	CHW	129	8	19	1	0	0	4	12	28	1	0	150	221	158	379	8%	78%	0.42	7	41	1.23	-39
Rose,Mike	06	30	2	aaa	TAM	338	36	66	17	0	14	35	38	111	2	1	194	275	365	640	10%	67%	0.34	107	42	3.42	16
	07	31	2	aaa	CLE	290	29	63	16	1	5	28	28	70	1	4	217	286	335	621	9%	76%	0.40	81	47	3.19	14
Rottino,Vinny	06	27	5	aaa	MIL	398	49	113	23	2	7	37	36	71	11	8	285	344	405	749	8%	82%	0.50	82	85	5.01	39
	07	27	28	aaa	MIL	377	49	96	15	2	10	45	32	56	12	10	255	313	388	701	8%	85%	0.58	83	94	4.10	31
Rouse,Mike	06	26	6	aaa	OAK	345	46	77	18	1	5	36	32	54	3	1	222	288	323	611	8%	84%	0.60	72	77	3.28	15
Rowlett,Casey	07	25	48	aa	STL	246	28	49	10	2	2	15	15	34	5	0	201	247	278	525	6%	86%	0.45	53	115	2.40	-2
Rozema,Mike	06	25	6	aa	ATL	271	23	55	8	2	0	18	14	59	4	3	203	243	246	489	5%	78%	0.24	32	87	1.96	-14
	07	26	5	a/a	ATL	202	23	44	6	1	4	23	13	46	5	2	218	264	312	576	6%	77%	0.28	59	93	2.80	3
Ruan,Wilkin	06	28	8	a/a	LA	340	32	69	14	1	1	15	11	34	10	4	203	228	258	485	3%	90%	0.32	44	101	1.91	-8
	07	29	8	aa	LA	369	32	71	9	2	2	25	8	45	7	2	191	207	240	447	2%	88%	0.17	33	109	1.62	-19
Ruchti,Justin	06	26	2	aa	SEA	144	11	27	5	0	3	14	5	37	0	0	188	217	275	492	4%	75%	0.15	57	24	1.94	-11
Ruggiano,Justin	06	24	8	aa	TAM	400	72	103	30	6	11	68	61	111	13	9	257	355	447	801	13%	72%	0.55	124	149	5.64	48
	07	25 a	8	aaa	TAM	482	73	141	27	2	19	69	51	148	25	12	292	360	472	832	10%	69%	0.35	113	106	6.19	51
Ruiz,Carlos	06	28 b	2	aaa	PHI	368	53	108	24	0	17	66	39	57	4	3	294	362	498	860	10%	85%	0.69	129	50	6.74	65
Ruiz,Randy	06	29	3	aa	NYY	491	46	98	25	1	18	56	28	140	2	0	199	242	360	602	5%	71%	0.20	102	52	2.90	12
	07	30	38	a/a	SF	474	48	103	22	2	13	53	30	115	1	1	216	262	356	619	6%	76%	0.26	89	60	3.16	14
Rundgren,Rex	06	26	6	a/a	FLA	397	28	78	10	0	0	25	29	83	1	4	196	252	220	472	7%	79%	0.35	21	29	1.83	-19
	07	27	6	aa	FLA	250	17	41	3	1	2	16	12	49	1	3	164	202	205	408	5%	80%	0.25	26	54	1.27	-30
Rushford,Jim	06	33	8	a/a	PHI	444	35	94	18	0	4	40	34	49	3	1	211	268	277	545	7%	89%	0.71	49	49	2.58	5
	07	34	83	aaa	PHI	413	21	92	21	0	2	36	23	30	2	0	222	262	285	548	5%	93%	0.75	51	33	2.60	10
Ryal,Rusty Allen	07	25	45	aa	ARI	178	17	40	6	2	6	17	7	36	3	3	224	252	374	626	4%	80%	0.19	87	102	2.98	14
Ryan,Brendan	07	26	6	aa	STL	321	41	68	6	3	1	11	19	34	13	6	213	257	258	515	6%	89%	0.55	29	130	2.21	-6
Ryan,Mike	06	29	8	aaa	ATL	363	30	76	15	1	5	34	26	79	2	3	211	264	303	567	7%	78%	0.33	63	48	2.67	3
	07	30	8	aa	PIT	379	32	64	15	3	9	31	17	106	0	2	168	203	294	497	4%	72%	0.16	78	68	1.84	-9
Saccomanno,Mark	06	26	5	aa	HOU	298	31	58	11	3	16	47	17	82	2	1	196	238	409	647	5%	73%	0.20	123	88	3.16	20
	07	27	3	aa	HOU	470	44	99	17	3	16	59	22	116	1	2	210	246	360	606	5%	75%	0.19	89	64	2.91	11
Sadler,Donnie	06	31	4	aaa	ARI	190	25	44	12	3	1	9	18	33	5	2	232	299	336	635	9%	82%	0.54	74	134	3.55	19
	07	32	6	aa	ARI	112	11	16	1	3	1	10	13	30	3	0	144	235	238	472	11%	73%	0.44	47	183	1.97	-24
Sadler,Ray	06	26	8	a/a	PIT	400	42	77	12	4	14	44	40	131	8	5	191	264	340	604	9%	67%	0.30	86	109	2.94	5
	07	27	8	aa	HOU	491	50	94	17	2	17	64	36	122	9	8	191	246	340	586	7%	75%	0.29	89	79	2.62	6
Sain,Greg	06	27	3	aa	MIL	129	14	18	3	0	7	21	13	55	3	0	142	220	324	544	9%	57%	0.24	101	66	2.36	-6

Major League Equivalent Statistics BATTERS

BATTER	Yr	Age	Pos	Lev	Org	ab	r	h	d	t	hr	rbi	bb	k	sb	cs	ba	ob	slg	ops	bb%	ct%	eye	px	sx	rc/g	bpv
Salas,Issmael	07	25	384	aa	CHC	344	35	70	16	0	6	41	20	34	2	2	204	247	306	553	5%	90%	0.57	70	52	2.50	8
Salazar,Jeff	06	26	8	aaa	COL	328	46	81	13	6	7	29	34	45	9	6	248	318	386	704	9%	86%	0.74	83	143	4.26	32
	07	27	8	aa	ARI	400	55	98	26	7	8	49	42	53	12	5	246	317	405	722	9%	87%	0.79	103	148	4.54	40
Salazar,Oscar	07	29	540	aa	BAL	532	47	105	26	1	14	61	17	84	2	2	197	222	330	551	3%	84%	0.20	86	53	2.34	5
Saltalamacchia,Ja	06	21	2	aa	ATL	313	29	69	17	1	8	38	54	69	0	1	220	335	358	693	15%	78%	0.78	90	28	4.36	26
Sammons,Clint	07	24	2	aa	ATL	296	23	64	10	0	4	30	22	67	1	1	215	269	286	555	7%	77%	0.32	48	33	2.64	-2
Sanchez,Alex	06	30	8	a/a	CIN	203	13	39	2	1	2	11	5	29	5	2	193	212	236	448	2%	86%	0.17	26	82	1.63	-22
	07	31	8	aaa	CHW	103	10	32	4	1	3	5	3	11	3	3	315	332	446	778	3%	89%	0.24	79	84	5.12	42
Sanchez,Angel	06	23	6	aa	KC	542	80	131	21	1	3	43	34	48	6	11	242	286	301	587	6%	91%	0.70	45	75	2.83	13
Sanchez,Danilo	06	26	2	aa	DET	237	16	37	5	0	5	21	21	49	1	0	156	224	247	470	8%	79%	0.42	55	33	1.83	-17
Sandberg,Jared	06	29	5	aa	HOU	265	23	40	17	0	5	25	17	86	3	1	151	202	269	470	6%	67%	0.19	84	72	1.73	-11
Sandoval,Danny	06	28	6	a/a	PHI	376	26	83	15	1	2	34	12	56	3	1	220	244	278	522	3%	85%	0.22	44	57	2.29	-4
	07	28	6	aaa	PHI	365	22	77	9	1	3	19	7	32	5	3	211	225	265	490	2%	91%	0.20	37	63	1.93	-10
Sandoval,Freddy	07	25	5	aa	LAA	472	68	122	27	4	9	59	54	79	17	11	257	334	387	721	10%	83%	0.68	87	111	4.54	35
Sansoe,Mike	07	25	8	aa	SD	301	32	61	9	2	1	14	26	66	9	6	202	265	252	517	8%	78%	0.39	36	104	2.23	-10
Santangelo,Louis	07	25	2	aa	HOU	206	24	43	8	2	4	13	18	51	2	0	208	271	318	590	8%	75%	0.36	69	100	3.02	5
Santiago,Ramon	07	28	6	aaa	DET	365	34	85	16	4	3	26	14	58	7	9	232	260	318	579	4%	84%	0.24	59	101	2.56	7
Santos,Chad	06	25	3	aaa	SF	353	30	80	16	1	10	52	18	65	0	0	227	264	362	626	5%	82%	0.28	86	30	3.27	17
	07	26	3	aa	SF	103	16	20	6	0	3	10	11	29	0	1	194	274	329	603	10%	72%	0.39	92	56	2.99	10
Santos,Omir	06	25	2	aa	NYY	324	27	76	15	0	4	33	16	72	1	0	233	270	314	584	5%	78%	0.22	59	38	2.95	7
	07	26	2	a/a	NYY	205	14	41	8	0	3	16	9	46	1	1	198	231	277	508	4%	78%	0.20	55	38	2.08	-7
Santos,Sergio	06	23	6	aaa	TOR	481	44	100	25	1	5	34	22	89	1	3	208	243	295	538	4%	81%	0.25	64	49	2.33	1
	07	24	6	a/a	TOR	479	54	106	33	2	17	53	35	93	3	0	221	274	407	681	7%	81%	0.38	121	74	3.84	31
Sardinha,Bronson	06	24	8	a/a	NYY	519	69	131	18	4	15	63	51	110	3	4	252	319	389	709	9%	79%	0.46	82	78	4.40	27
	07	24	8	a/a	NYY	444	57	102	22	4	15	69	48	87	12	3	229	304	395	699	10%	80%	0.55	103	117	4.27	30
Sardinha,Dane	06	28	2	aaa	CIN	229	17	37	7	0	2	10	13	64	0	0	162	208	216	424	5%	72%	0.21	39	30	1.46	-26
	07	28	2	aaa	DET	381	33	67	12	1	8	40	21	94	2	0	176	220	278	498	5%	75%	0.23	64	62	2.01	-10
Sardinha,Duke	07	27	3	aa	COL	222	23	49	10	1	8	24	14	46	1	3	219	266	380	646	6%	79%	0.30	100	55	3.26	20
Sasser,Rob	06	32	5	aa	CHW	120	7	20	4	0	2	11	13	44	1	0	163	247	245	492	10%	63%	0.30	53	27	2.08	-18
Scales,Bobby	06	29	5	aaa	PHI	357	42	96	20	6	7	40	39	105	3	3	268	340	421	761	10%	70%	0.37	97	126	5.20	37
	07	30	843	aaa	BOS	432	53	113	28	5	8	46	41	93	12	3	261	325	409	734	9%	78%	0.44	98	132	4.89	36
Schierholtz,Nate	06	23	8	aa	SF	470	56	127	26	7	14	55	27	81	8	3	270	310	445	755	5%	83%	0.33	108	127	4.93	41
	07	24 a	8	aa	SF	411	54	122	28	6	12	55	14	49	8	5	297	320	479	799	3%	88%	0.27	117	124	5.48	53
Schneider,John	07	28	2	a/a	TOR	193	16	26	7	0	4	15	21	57	0	0	135	220	239	459	10%	70%	0.36	67	24	1.73	-20
Schnurstein,Micah	06	22	5	aa	CHW	480	47	104	24	2	10	45	23	98	8	6	217	252	338	590	5%	80%	0.23	80	84	2.76	10
Schrager,Tony	06	29	4	a/a	FLA	109	15	25	7	2	1	8	10	27	0	2	233	297	346	643	8%	75%	0.37	78	114	3.41	17
Schuerholz,Jonath	06	26	4	aaa	ATL	375	30	64	11	2	2	23	30	93	5	2	171	232	225	457	7%	75%	0.32	38	85	1.76	-21
	07	27	4	a/a	ATL	152	17	26	6	0	3	15	12	33	6	1	172	233	263	496	7%	78%	0.37	62	96	2.12	-10
Schumaker,Skip	06	27	8	aaa	STL	369	42	104	13	2	3	23	20	44	10	4	281	319	350	668	5%	88%	0.46	47	94	4.08	22
	07	28	8	aa	STL	232	23	52	12	0	4	21	19	36	2	3	225	284	329	613	8%	84%	0.53	72	43	3.10	15
Scott,Luke	06	28	8	aaa	HOU	318	48	81	12	1	16	48	39	58	5	1	254	336	447	783	11%	82%	0.67	113	77	5.53	45
Seabol,Scott	06	31	5	aaa	FLA	242	28	59	14	1	12	32	22	51	0	4	245	307	454	761	8%	79%	0.42	128	39	4.64	43
	07	32	5	aa	FLA	503	60	96	19	4	19	63	36	123	4	1	191	244	358	602	7%	76%	0.29	99	101	2.88	10
Sears,Todd	06	31	3	aaa	FLA	181	18	38	7	1	4	19	11	38	2	0	209	253	318	572	6%	79%	0.29	70	78	2.77	4
Self,Todd	07	29	3	aa	HOU	428	48	92	17	1	10	46	46	101	2	2	215	292	325	617	10%	76%	0.46	71	55	3.32	10
Sellers,Patrick	07	25	53	aa	HOU	358	37	83	19	1	5	32	14	58	0	2	231	261	334	595	4%	84%	0.25	72	45	2.91	12
Sellier,Brian	06	29	8	aa	PHI	125	12	27	6	1	5	10	10	15	0	0	218	273	397	670	7%	88%	0.64	110	42	3.71	31
Serrano,Ray	06	26	2	aa	ATL	227	20	48	13	0	3	19	3	39	1	1	210	219	301	521	1%	83%	0.07	68	53	2.12	-1
	07	27	2	a/a	ATL	126	17	32	11	1	3	12	7	20	2	0	250	291	414	705	5%	84%	0.36	115	99	4.31	38
Sevilla,Walter	06	25	4	aa	KC	163	13	25	3	3	1	10	13	32	2	0	155	215	221	436	7%	80%	0.39	38	124	1.60	-25
Shabala,Adam	06	29	8	aaa	SF	289	32	66	17	1	4	29	33	54	5	4	228	309	331	640	10%	81%	0.62	74	70	3.57	19
	07	30	8	aa	CHW	331	35	51	7	1	3	14	38	105	8	5	154	240	206	446	10%	68%	0.36	34	88	1.67	-27
Shanks,James	06	28	8	aaa	FLA	231	23	57	12	2	4	22	11	45	7	7	247	282	366	648	5%	80%	0.25	80	101	3.27	20
Shealy,Ryan	06	27 b	3	aaa	COL	222	27	56	14	1	12	39	14	25	0	0	252	298	492	790	6%	89%	0.56	147	37	5.16	56
	07	28	0	aa	KC	122	10	23	6	0	4	17	10	29	0	0	190	254	334	588	8%	76%	0.36	91	14	2.85	8
Shelton,Chris	06	26	3	aaa	DET	109	18	27	5	2	3	13	16	35	1	0	249	348	409	757	13%	68%	0.47	96	142	5.36	32
	07	27	3	aaa	DET	498	66	119	27	1	11	57	73	133	4	2	238	336	364	700	13%	73%	0.55	84	61	4.51	25
Shier,Pete	06	26	5	aa	BAL	224	22	55	14	1	0	21	11	41	3	7	245	280	317	597	5%	82%	0.26	60	69	2.71	12
Shorey,Mark	07	23	8	aa	STL	190	19	43	10	0	8	26	12	37	0	0	225	269	398	668	6%	80%	0.31	108	22	3.67	26
Simokaitis,Joseph	07	25	6	aa	CHC	340	33	72	14	1	4	20	28	68	1	5	212	271	293	565	7%	80%	0.40	57	47	2.60	2
Singleton,Justin	06	28	8	a/a	TOR	231	23	40	10	1	5	17	20	97	2	0	173	239	290	529	8%	58%	0.21	75	79	2.33	-7
Sing,Brandon	06	26	3	a/a	CHC	337	34	62	12	0	12	47	59	115	1	1	183	305	330	635	15%	66%	0.51	89	27	3.54	8
	07	27	3	aa	BAL	214	12	31	8	0	2	10	10	53	3	1	146	183	207	390	4%	75%	0.18	45	58	1.20	-29
Sinisi,Vince	06	25	8	a/a	TEX	497	56	125	37	2	7	54	52	80	8	4	252	323	375	698	10%	84%	0.65	90	77	4.37	34
	07	26	8	aa	SD	303	36	77	16	1	7	30	16	43	5	3	252	290	383	674	5%	86%	0.37	87	77	3.85	27
Sisk,Aaron	06	28	5	aa	SF	237	23	38	7	0	8	23	18	78	6	1	159	219	290	510	7%	67%	0.24	79	80	2.11	-10
Slack,Jonathan	06	25	8	aa	NYM	157	12	25	4	1	0	9	10	41	5	3	157	210	194	404	6%	74%	0.25	27	106	1.30	-31
Sledge,Termel	06	30	8	aaa	SD	367	49	87	14	4	15	52	43	67	4	4	238	318	414	732	10%	82%	0.64	103	91	4.58	35
Smitherman,Steph	06	28	8	aa	SD	287	29	50	14	0	13	46	26	124	0	0	173	243	354	597	8%	57%	0.21	111	22	2.83	8
Smith,Bobby	06	32	5	aaa	CHW	193	16	43	14	0	5	21	11	61	3	0	224	265	382	647	5%	68%	0.18	109	54	3.52	23
Smith,Casey	06	28	6	a/a	LAA	425	43	88	22	2	3	38	16	52	4	9	207	235	291	526	4%	88%	0.30	62	77	2.06	0
	07	29	46	aa	LAA	393	35	86	18	2	2	38	20	61	10	2	218	256	287	543	5%	84%	0.33	51	104	2.53	0
Smith,Coby Lee	07	27	8	aa	LAA	243	32	51	9	1	2	16	26	34	19	7	208	284	273	557	10%	86%	0.76	47	123	2.72	4
Smith,Corey	06	24	5	aa	CHW	425	43	95	17	2	13	48	56	116	5	1	224	314	367	681	12%	73%	0.48	88	71	4.16	20
Smith,David	06	26	8	aa	TOR	483	57	109	31	1	17	63	34	126	6	4	225	277	399	675	7%	74%	0.27	113	73	3.73	27
	07	27	80	aa	TOR	458	60	103	29	1	19	50	37	99	3	5	224	283	416	699	8%	78%	0.38	122	57	3.88	33
Smith,Jason	06	29	4	aaa	COL	141	17	35	7	4	3	15	10	32	2	1	252	301	413	714	7%	77%	0.31	99	167	4.37	31
Smith,Ryan	07	28	2	aaa	CHW	103	3	12	1	0	1	3	3	31	0	0	117	141	153	294	3%	70%	0.09	22	7	0.65	-50
Smith,Sean	07	25	8	aa	CHW	269	22	50	4	0	1	12	15	64	11	6	187	231	211	442	5%	76%	0.24	17	82	1.57	-26
Smith,Seth	06	24 a	8	aa	COL	524	61	146	44	4	13	55	39	53	3	5	279	329	452	781	7%	90%	0.74	119	68	5.29	57
	07	25	8	aa	COL	451	50	124	28	5	14	61	30	63	5	3	275	320	447	767	6%	86%	0.47	110	93	5.16	47
Smith,Will	06	25	8	aaa	TEX	132	13	37	7	0	3	14	14	24	0	0	280	349	402	751	10%	82%	0.58	82	16	5.31	39

Major League Equivalent Statistics

BATTER	Yr	Age	Pos	Lev	Org	ab	r	h	d	t	hr	rbi	bb	k	sb	cs	ba	ob	slg	ops	bb%	ct%	eye	px	sx	rc/g	bpv
Snead,Esix	06	30	8	aaa	BAL	127	10	24	3	0	1	13	18	21	14	4	191	292	234	526	12%	83%	0.85	30	91	2.65	-7
Snelling,Chris	06	25	8	aaa	SEA	241	30	46	12	1	4	33	27	53	3	2	191	272	299	571	10%	78%	0.51	73	83	2.76	4
Snyder,Brad	06	24	8	aa	CLE	523	75	124	27	3	14	63	56	157	17	2	236	310	380	690	10%	70%	0.36	92	123	4.33	24
	07	25	8	aaa	CLE	259	36	61	12	2	8	30	33	82	10	0	237	322	390	712	11%	68%	0.40	95	127	4.77	26
Snyder,Brian	06	25	5	aa	OAK	151	19	27	6	1	4	20	30	39	1	1	176	314	302	616	17%	74%	0.78	78	69	3.39	6
	07	26	4	aa	OAK	370	48	77	27	1	6	36	56	90	1	1	209	313	338	651	13%	76%	0.62	93	53	3.78	21
Snyder,Earl	06	30	3	aaa	CIN	463	50	104	23	1	16	67	36	104	1	0	225	281	383	664	7%	77%	0.34	99	46	3.74	23
	07	31	56	aaa	CHW	404	43	75	17	0	13	43	31	96	0	1	185	242	321	563	7%	76%	0.32	86	35	2.55	3
Solano,Danny	06	31	6	a/a	TOR	134	8	20	6	0	1	6	10	43	1	0	149	206	209	415	7%	68%	0.23	46	41	1.43	-27
Sollmann,Steven	07	26	3	aa	MIL	445	61	104	23	2	3	40	50	63	17	6	235	312	313	626	10%	86%	0.80	60	107	3.56	19
Sorensen,Zach	06	30	4	aaa	MIL	202	17	45	6	1	2	18	22	45	4	4	221	297	288	585	10%	78%	0.48	46	68	2.92	2
Sosa,Carlos	07	26	8	aa	SF	376	41	83	20	2	6	40	34	82	3	5	220	285	333	618	8%	78%	0.42	77	66	3.18	13
Sosa,Juan	06	31	6	a/a	PHI	149	10	22	4	0	0	7	8	33	1	1	150	194	177	371	5%	78%	0.25	24	49	1.09	-35
Soto,Geovany	06	24	2	aaa	CHC	342	31	88	20	0	6	35	38	68	0	1	257	332	368	700	10%	80%	0.56	79	18	4.47	29
	07	25 a	23	aa	CHC	385	61	122	29	2	23	87	42	84	0	0	316	383	577	960	10%	78%	0.50	162	45	8.64	82
Spann,Chad	06	23 a	5	aa	BOS	360	47	104	30	2	9	45	26	74	3	3	289	337	458	795	7%	79%	0.35	117	74	5.61	52
	07	24	5	a/a	BOS	347	30	76	19	0	6	37	27	94	1	4	219	275	326	601	7%	73%	0.29	75	30	2.96	10
Spanos,Vasili	06	26	5	aa	OAK	439	53	111	25	1	6	51	40	67	0	1	252	314	357	671	8%	85%	0.59	75	40	4.04	27
	07	27	35	aa	OAK	392	37	86	21	2	7	38	12	64	3	2	220	243	335	578	3%	84%	0.19	79	74	2.69	9
Span,Denard	06	23	8	aa	MIN	536	75	146	16	5	2	42	37	77	23	12	272	319	332	651	6%	86%	0.48	40	127	3.78	17
	07	24	8	aaa	MIN	487	58	127	20	6	3	54	37	92	25	14	261	313	345	658	7%	81%	0.40	57	137	3.72	18
Spearman,Jemel	07	27	84	aa	CHC	355	39	74	13	4	5	30	21	53	6	2	208	252	314	566	6%	85%	0.39	66	125	2.68	5
Spears,Nathaniel	07	22	4	aa	CHC	114	19	32	2	2	4	9	11	16	2	0	281	344	439	783	9%	86%	0.69	85	135	5.77	43
Spidale,Michael	07	26	8	aa	PHI	264	32	68	5	4	2	15	14	18	8	4	256	292	320	612	5%	93%	0.76	38	130	3.28	16
Spilborghs,Ryan	06	27	8	aaa	COL	269	36	81	18	1	4	25	21	36	6	2	300	351	417	767	7%	87%	0.58	84	83	5.56	47
	07	28	8	aa	COL	124	17	30	6	1	3	11	12	19	2	2	245	312	381	692	9%	85%	0.64	86	88	4.03	30
Spivey,Junior	06	32	4	aaa	STL	285	30	48	11	1	7	23	47	64	11	5	167	285	287	572	14%	77%	0.73	75	87	2.85	1
Stansberry,Craig	06	25	4	a/a	PIT	457	70	105	28	4	12	50	59	93	16	6	229	318	384	702	11%	80%	0.64	101	127	4.35	31
	07	26	465	aa	SD	466	68	103	25	2	12	61	58	100	8	10	220	306	357	663	11%	79%	0.58	90	82	3.64	22
Stavinoha,Nick	06	24	8	aa	STL	417	43	106	24	2	9	57	22	69	2	1	255	292	383	675	5%	83%	0.31	86	63	3.95	27
	07	25	8	aa	STL	499	37	103	14	0	9	36	23	72	5	1	206	241	287	528	4%	86%	0.32	52	58	2.34	-4
Stavisky,Brian	06	26	8	a/a	OAK	438	56	105	23	1	5	42	59	68	2	1	240	330	335	665	12%	85%	0.86	68	55	4.08	26
Stern,Adam	06	27	8	aaa	BOS	392	53	97	22	2	7	31	21	72	20	7	247	286	366	653	5%	82%	0.30	82	127	3.64	22
	07	28	8	aaa	BAL	289	37	71	10	4	1	22	23	64	16	6	247	302	319	620	7%	78%	0.36	49	153	3.44	9
Stewart,Caleb	07	25	8	aa	NYM	433	47	87	12	1	11	51	27	93	3	7	202	248	308	556	6%	78%	0.29	64	57	2.38	-0
Stewart,Chris	06	25	2	aaa	CHW	272	37	69	16	2	4	26	14	32	3	0	254	290	371	662	5%	88%	0.44	81	102	3.87	27
	07	26	2	aa	TEX	153	14	32	7	0	2	16	9	18	0	2	206	250	288	538	6%	88%	0.51	60	36	2.29	3
Stewart,Ian	06	22	5	aa	COL	462	58	118	39	6	9	55	38	74	2	9	255	312	424	736	8%	84%	0.51	116	90	4.39	43
	07	22 a	5	aa	COL	414	60	121	22	2	13	54	42	72	9	2	292	357	449	807	9%	83%	0.58	100	93	6.15	50
Stinnett,Kelly	07	38	2	aa	STL	103	6	13	1	0	1	6	5	26	0	0	122	162	177	339	5%	75%	0.19	33	23	0.89	-42
Stocker,Mel	07	27	8	aa	MIL	267	40	52	7	7	0	17	20	54	24	6	196	252	270	522	7%	80%	0.37	44	238	2.41	-9
Stodolka,Michael	07	26	3	aa	KC	381	51	90	23	1	8	44	56	87	3	0	235	333	363	696	13%	77%	0.64	88	66	4.49	28
Stokes,Jason	06	25	3	aaa	FLA	237	30	53	11	2	5	27	29	71	2	1	224	308	350	658	11%	70%	0.41	81	92	3.84	16
Stotts,JT	06	27	6	a/a	NYY	321	33	63	5	0	0	21	35	63	8	3	196	275	210	486	10%	80%	0.55	12	77	2.12	-18
Strait,William	07	24	8	aa	CIN	217	25	41	13	0	6	22	13	56	9	2	188	235	328	563	6%	74%	0.24	95	102	2.57	7
Stratton,Robert	06	29	8	aaa	NYY	207	21	45	7	0	12	34	13	85	0	1	215	261	422	683	6%	59%	0.15	120	21	3.63	24
Strong,Jamal	06	28	8	aaa	CHC	357	38	76	12	2	1	23	38	72	15	2	214	289	266	555	10%	80%	0.53	39	114	2.89	-2
	07	29	8	a/a	NYY	292	38	57	5	2	0	16	40	52	11	2	194	291	222	513	12%	82%	0.77	20	115	2.47	-12
St. Pierre,Max	06	26	2	aaa	DET	247	22	46	13	1	3	28	15	34	0	0	185	230	279	509	6%	86%	0.43	67	47	2.12	-2
Suarez,Ignacio	07	26	64	aa	BOS	352	38	73	16	1	3	23	25	85	5	1	208	261	279	540	7%	76%	0.30	53	87	2.53	-3
Sullivan,Cory	07	28	8	aa	COL	206	19	42	7	2	1	14	12	43	2	2	202	246	264	510	6%	79%	0.28	44	91	2.11	-9
Suomi,Richard	07	27	2	a/a	WAS	129	11	23	5	2	2	12	7	22	0	0	174	218	286	504	5%	83%	0.32	71	84	2.02	-6
Sutton,Stephen	07	24	54	aa	HOU	480	65	111	24	1	8	42	45	77	19	6	232	297	333	629	9%	84%	0.58	70	104	3.53	18
Suzuki,Kurt	06	23	2	aa	OAK	376	52	94	24	1	6	45	47	42	4	3	250	333	366	699	11%	89%	1.10	83	68	4.43	40
	07	24	2	aa	OAK	211	26	52	9	0	2	22	17	34	0	0	248	306	317	623	8%	84%	0.51	51	35	3.51	14
Swann,Pedro	06	36	8	a/a	PHI	213	30	54	12	1	5	30	15	53	7	1	252	301	383	685	7%	75%	0.29	88	108	4.24	26
	07	37	8	a/a	PHI	308	23	57	14	1	5	23	17	75	2	5	184	227	281	507	5%	76%	0.22	66	56	1.94	-7
Sweeney,Ryan	06	22 a	8	aaa	CHW	449	64	142	26	2	15	70	35	61	7	8	316	366	488	853	7%	86%	0.58	109	72	6.56	62
	07	23	8	aaa	CHW	397	47	107	17	1	12	45	47	62	7	5	270	347	405	752	11%	84%	0.76	85	64	5.13	40
Tatis,Fernando	06	32	5	aaa	BAL	326	40	86	14	1	6	33	33	60	7	2	262	331	367	698	9%	82%	0.56	69	81	4.53	27
	07	33	5	aa	NYM	497	53	85	20	2	11	39	36	121	5	5	172	227	289	516	7%	76%	0.29	75	83	2.07	-6
Tatum,Craig	07	25	2	aa	CIN	173	17	34	9	1	2	18	13	43	0	1	198	255	291	546	7%	75%	0.31	66	62	2.45	-1
Taylor,JR	06	24	6	aa	MIN	203	18	39	10	0	1	12	31	37	5	4	191	298	253	552	13%	82%	0.84	50	57	2.65	1
Teagarden,Taylor	07	24	0	aa	TEX	102	16	27	3	0	6	14	8	33	0	0	266	318	466	784	7%	68%	0.24	114	32	5.37	40
Tejeda,Juan	06	25	3	aaa	NYM	152	10	32	3	1	2	16	10	33	0	1	211	259	283	542	6%	78%	0.30	44	49	2.43	-6
	07	26	30	aa	PHI	314	25	64	20	2	8	44	19	36	1	0	204	249	355	604	6%	89%	0.53	101	56	2.97	20
Terrero,Luis	06	26 b	8	aaa	BAL	302	50	91	19	1	16	43	16	61	17	9	302	338	527	865	5%	80%	0.27	139	113	6.22	64
Theriot,Ryan	06	27	4	aaa	CHC	280	37	78	10	4	0	19	24	33	13	3	277	335	340	674	8%	88%	0.74	43	141	4.36	25
Thigpen,Curtis	06	23	2	a/a	TOR	362	48	92	29	4	6	42	50	66	5	2	254	345	406	751	12%	82%	0.76	106	105	5.18	44
	07	24	2	aaa	TOR	179	17	48	10	0	3	17	14	20	1	0	268	321	374	696	7%	89%	0.70	75	37	4.45	34
Thigpen,Jud	06	26	8	aa	COL	310	24	59	13	1	3	23	10	49	4	2	191	215	272	487	3%	84%	0.19	57	79	1.89	-9
Thissen,Greg	06	25	4	a/a	WAS	132	10	23	5	0	2	10	15	20	2	2	173	258	252	510	10%	85%	0.76	54	47	2.15	-5
Thomas,Charles	06	28	8	aaa	OAK	383	44	87	7	1	7	32	29	63	6	10	228	282	303	584	7%	84%	0.45	44	65	2.70	3
	07	29	8	a/a	MIL	264	24	48	9	0	3	19	19	62	6	1	180	235	245	479	7%	76%	0.30	46	79	1.97	-15
Thomas,Clete	07	24	8	aa	DET	528	91	138	27	6	7	49	55	106	16	11	261	331	373	704	9%	80%	0.52	75	135	4.37	28
Thompson,Kevin	06	27	8	aaa	NYY	362	60	85	19	3	8	38	36	62	14	8	234	303	365	668	9%	83%	0.58	86	130	3.78	25
	07	28	8	aaa	NYY	267	33	65	16	2	5	32	34	56	20	8	244	330	369	699	11%	79%	0.62	86	123	4.33	29
Thompson,Rich	06	27	8	a/a	PIT	282	44	70	13	4	2	23	31	53	14	10	247	322	342	665	10%	81%	0.59	64	155	3.75	21
	07	28	8	aa	ARI	324	40	73	14	4	2	27	19	50	10	2	225	268	314	582	6%	85%	0.38	60	146	2.98	7
Thorman,Scott	06	25 a	3	aaa	ATL	309	36	88	15	2	14	46	30	46	4	2	285	348	482	830	9%	85%	0.65	119	72	6.22	57
Thurston,Joe	06	27	4	aaa	PHI	479	70	129	28	9	10	52	40	65	19	10	270	326	422	748	8%	86%	0.61	97	158	4.86	42
	07	28	48	a/a	PHI	509	51	120	26	4	4	43	32	56	12	14	235	281	327	608	6%	89%	0.57	65	95	2.91	17

BATTER	Yr	Age	Pos	Lev	Org	ab	r	h	d	t	hr	rbi	bb	k	sb	cs	ba	ob	slg	ops	bb%	ct%	eye	px	sx	rc/g	bpv
Tiffee,Terry	06	27	5	aaa	MIN	308	35	78	19	0	4	36	19	55	1	0	253	296	352	648	6%	82%	0.35	74	47	3.73	22
	07	28	5	aaa	BAL	475	41	116	23	1	9	50	22	54	0	1	245	279	356	635	4%	89%	0.42	75	30	3.44	21
Timmons,Wes	06	27 b	6	aaa	ATL	250	26	64	13	0	6	24	35	19	5	4	255	346	376	723	12%	92%	1.86	82	48	4.72	56
	07	28	5	aaa	ATL	355	39	80	16	0	4	44	20	29	7	5	225	268	301	569	5%	92%	0.70	56	72	2.69	12
Timpner,Clay	06	23	8	a/a	SF	499	51	118	18	4	5	28	20	53	14	14	236	266	319	585	4%	89%	0.38	55	104	2.64	9
	07	24	8	aa	SF	392	40	103	10	3	5	30	29	59	7	12	262	312	337	649	7%	85%	0.48	47	76	3.41	16
Tolbert,Christophe	07	25	4	aaa	MIN	417	63	118	23	6	6	51	34	58	11	3	283	336	408	744	7%	86%	0.58	83	141	5.14	40
Tolbert,Matt	06	24	6	aa	MIN	248	29	58	14	1	3	31	27	44	5	1	234	308	333	641	10%	82%	0.60	72	85	3.74	20
Tomlin,James	07	25	8	aa	LA	289	31	59	16	0	0	20	14	49	11	2	206	241	262	503	4%	83%	0.28	50	104	2.19	-6
Torbert,Wallace	07	24	8	aa	HOU	300	23	65	13	1	1	25	24	71	3	8	215	273	276	548	7%	76%	0.34	47	52	2.36	-2
Torcato,Tony	06	27	8	aaa	CHW	225	19	52	10	1	2	19	15	33	1	1	233	279	310	590	6%	85%	0.44	55	55	3.00	9
Toregas,Wyatt	06	24	2	aa	CLE	163	18	38	10	0	3	26	13	32	1	3	232	287	345	632	7%	80%	0.39	80	48	3.24	18
	07	25	2	aa	CLE	284	30	62	15	0	5	32	24	42	3	1	217	278	321	599	8%	85%	0.56	73	59	3.10	14
Torrealba,Steve	07	30	2	aa	DET	298	28	50	7	0	7	32	18	79	1	0	166	214	257	470	6%	74%	0.23	55	48	1.79	-17
Torres,Andres	06	29	8	aaa	MIN	348	43	74	16	7	2	28	45	98	18	7	214	303	318	621	11%	72%	0.46	67	187	3.43	8
	07	30	8	a/a	DET	473	58	110	16	16	7	40	38	116	17	9	232	289	381	670	7%	76%	0.33	84	235	3.70	19
Torres,Eider	06	24	6	a/a	CLE	472	51	118	12	1	2	41	33	55	41	14	250	299	292	591	7%	88%	0.60	31	113	3.16	8
	07	25	46	aaa	BAL	393	37	102	15	0	4	40	24	52	21	11	260	302	328	630	6%	87%	0.46	50	82	3.40	16
Tousa,Scott	06	27	4	aa	DET	114	3	17	2	0	0	6	9	29	1	1	146	209	160	369	7%	75%	0.32	13	27	1.11	-40
Towles,Justin	07	24	2	aa	HOU	259	43	73	11	2	10	42	21	37	9	9	281	336	449	785	8%	86%	0.57	101	108	5.04	47
Tracy,Andy	06	33	3	aaa	BAL	455	58	95	25	1	18	66	65	116	6	5	208	306	386	692	12%	75%	0.56	112	64	4.04	27
	07	34	3	aa	NYM	472	51	80	15	1	13	51	52	130	1	2	169	251	285	536	10%	72%	0.40	72	50	2.38	-6
Truby,Chris	06	33	5	aaa	LA	333	29	62	16	1	6	39	27	97	7	2	186	248	297	545	8%	71%	0.28	75	84	2.49	-1
Trzesniak,Nick	06	26	2	aaa	TEX	210	22	50	9	1	4	21	18	30	3	2	240	300	349	649	8%	86%	0.59	71	71	3.65	21
	07	27	2	aa	DET	123	15	30	5	0	3	14	11	22	0	1	248	311	354	665	8%	82%	0.52	70	36	3.86	22
Tucker,Michael	06	35	8	aaa	NYM	275	39	64	16	1	5	29	42	48	9	3	232	335	347	682	13%	83%	0.89	80	93	4.32	28
	07	36	0	aaa	BOS	235	22	46	16	0	5	21	38	62	1	2	195	307	322	629	14%	74%	0.61	91	29	3.44	15
Tuiasosopo,Matt	06	20	6	aa	SEA	216	16	39	4	0	1	9	21	60	2	1	180	253	214	466	9%	72%	0.35	25	46	1.87	-23
	07	21	5	aa	SEA	446	64	105	25	3	8	49	68	104	3	9	235	337	359	695	13%	77%	0.65	83	71	4.17	26
Tulowitzki,Troy	06	22 a	6	aa	COL	423	58	116	32	2	11	47	35	51	5	6	274	330	437	767	8%	88%	0.69	111	74	5.07	51
Tupman,Matt	06	27	2	a/a	KC	293	33	70	7	1	1	26	42	29	1	1	240	336	280	615	13%	90%	1.46	29	48	3.54	21
	07	28	2	aa	KC	299	15	65	13	0	1	22	26	34	2	2	217	279	269	548	8%	89%	0.76	44	27	2.60	5
Turner,Lloyd	06	27	4	aa	OAK	318	27	51	4	3	6	30	22	66	9	5	161	215	254	470	6%	79%	0.33	51	121	1.71	-18
Tyner,Jason	06	29	8	aaa	MIN	316	47	93	13	4	0	20	22	45	7	2	294	339	357	696	6%	86%	0.48	46	127	4.63	27
Upton,B.J.	06	22	6	aaa	TAM	398	70	105	18	4	7	40	63	80	45	19	264	364	385	750	14%	80%	0.79	78	155	5.11	36
Upton,Justin	07	20 a	8	aa	ARI	259	42	80	17	4	13	46	34	40	8	8	308	388	551	939	11%	85%	0.84	147	128	7.60	80
Ust,Brant	06	28	5	aa	PIT	166	10	26	2	0	3	13	10	43	0	1	154	200	227	427	5%	74%	0.23	43	26	1.42	-26
	07	29	4	aa	SEA	151	7	25	6	0	2	11	7	45	0	0	164	200	248	448	4%	70%	0.15	58	10	1.58	-18
Valbuena,Luis	07	22	4	aa	SEA	444	47	95	21	2	9	38	43	76	9	7	214	283	331	614	9%	83%	0.57	77	82	3.14	14
Valdez,Wilson	06	28	6	aaa	LA	528	67	125	19	0	5	38	39	44	19	20	236	289	298	586	7%	92%	0.89	45	82	2.71	15
	07	29	6	aa	LA	361	51	85	13	1	3	18	28	39	9	5	235	289	299	589	7%	89%	0.72	46	94	3.00	12
Valentin,Geraldo	07	25	48	aa	KC	437	37	106	17	2	2	41	20	42	4	11	243	276	303	579	4%	90%	0.47	45	54	2.62	9
Valido,Robert	06	21	6	aa	CHW	168	15	34	9	2	1	11	13	24	8	3	202	260	298	557	7%	86%	0.54	67	130	2.60	6
	07	22	6	aa	CHW	266	21	44	7	1	0	16	9	39	9	6	165	193	199	392	3%	85%	0.23	27	107	1.15	-29
Van Der Bosch,Ma	06	24	8	a/a	BOS	168	22	31	3	1	4	16	19	32	12	2	185	269	283	552	10%	81%	0.61	56	131	2.79	-3
Van Every,Jonatha	06	27	8	a/a	CLE	387	49	84	23	5	11	48	37	139	8	3	216	285	381	666	9%	64%	0.27	105	138	3.74	21
	07	28	8	a/a	CLE	309	34	76	17	3	9	44	34	108	4	8	245	320	405	725	10%	65%	0.31	101	101	4.28	30
Varner,Noochie	06	26	8	aa	CIN	460	53	113	30	1	9	62	27	93	2	0	247	288	374	662	6%	80%	0.29	89	61	3.81	25
	07	27	80	aa	HOU	352	24	80	17	2	4	37	22	56	3	1	227	272	321	594	6%	84%	0.39	65	60	3.03	10
Vazquez,Ramon	07	31	6	aa	TEX	132	16	22	7	1	1	8	14	31	2	1	170	249	276	525	10%	76%	0.45	73	119	2.33	-5
Velandia,Jorge	06	32	6	aaa	CHW	475	57	120	22	1	10	46	23	87	13	2	252	286	364	650	5%	82%	0.26	74	98	3.73	20
	07	33	6	aaa	TAM	433	38	93	21	4	5	27	24	102	5	5	214	256	310	566	5%	76%	0.24	66	91	2.58	3
Velazquez,Gilbert	06	27	6	a/a	MIN	180	23	41	5	1	1	17	12	40	2	2	225	272	280	552	6%	78%	0.29	39	88	2.58	-3
	07	28	56	a/a	MIN	228	25	45	9	3	2	23	17	52	3	0	198	253	282	535	7%	77%	0.32	56	124	2.48	-4
Velez,Eugenio	07	25	84	aa	SF	394	45	97	14	6	1	19	21	62	41	18	247	284	322	606	5%	84%	0.33	50	176	2.99	10
Venable,William	07	25	8	aa	SD	515	56	123	15	2	7	58	33	83	18	2	238	284	314	598	6%	84%	0.40	49	109	3.26	8
Vento,Mike	06	28	8	aaa	WAS	217	29	62	12	0	6	28	17	35	3	5	287	338	420	758	7%	84%	0.47	89	52	4.94	42
	07	29	80	aaa	TOR	295	29	66	18	0	6	32	19	63	0	0	222	269	349	618	6%	79%	0.31	88	27	3.23	16
Von Schell,Tyler	06	27	3	aa	SF	369	29	70	20	1	7	30	20	123	0	1	189	230	308	539	5%	67%	0.16	81	38	2.31	-0
	07	28	3	aa	SF	243	22	42	8	0	9	28	14	66	0	0	171	215	313	528	5%	73%	0.21	85	27	2.17	-4
Votto,Joey	06	23 a	3	aa	CIN	508	78	152	45	1	21	71	69	105	22	7	300	383	517	901	12%	79%	0.65	144	92	7.64	73
	07	24	38	aaa	CIN	496	66	138	20	1	22	82	62	98	15	11	278	358	456	814	11%	80%	0.63	106	70	5.85	49
Wald,Jake	06	26	6	aa	SF	435	39	79	17	3	4	28	32	124	6	6	182	237	259	496	7%	71%	0.25	53	91	1.95	-12
	07	27	6	aa	SF	361	32	69	17	3	4	27	22	89	8	3	190	236	289	526	6%	75%	0.25	68	109	2.27	-4
Walker,Christophe	06	26	8	aa	CHC	513	66	132	19	9	2	33	38	128	47	19	258	309	339	648	7%	75%	0.30	53	183	3.65	14
	07	27	8	aa	CHC	267	16	46	5	0	2	17	8	57	8	6	174	199	221	420	3%	79%	0.15	31	72	1.31	-26
Walker,Neil	07	22	5	aa	PIT	495	71	128	33	2	10	56	45	72	8	6	259	320	394	714	8%	85%	0.63	94	85	4.46	37
Wallace,David	06	27	2	aa	CLE	155	20	29	7	0	4	17	14	36	3	1	185	252	314	567	8%	77%	0.39	83	76	2.66	4
	07	28	2	a/a	CLE	179	17	23	3	0	5	13	18	62	0	1	126	207	228	436	9%	65%	0.29	58	37	1.50	-28
Walter,Randy	06	25	8	aa	SF	251	23	47	12	3	5	21	14	72	10	5	186	228	308	536	5%	71%	0.19	79	139	2.22	-2
Washington,Rico	06	28	6	a/a	STL	451	56	100	27	3	13	55	56	86	6	3	222	308	379	687	11%	81%	0.65	102	85	4.13	29
	07	29	53	aa	STL	262	23	51	11	1	7	26	15	37	2	0	195	238	318	556	5%	86%	0.40	78	57	2.53	5
Wathan,Derek	06	30	4	aaa	STL	258	22	58	15	5	4	16	8	42	7	3	226	250	360	609	3%	84%	0.20	87	145	2.98	15
	07	31	5	aa	KC	189	13	30	6	1	1	12	9	30	1	1	159	198	219	416	5%	84%	0.30	41	65	1.35	-24
Wathan,Dusty	06	33	2	aaa	PHI	238	23	51	9	0	5	24	18	50	1	0	216	271	321	592	7%	79%	0.36	69	39	3.02	7
	07	34	32	a/a	PHI	248	17	50	10	1	0	15	12	41	2	1	200	237	248	485	5%	83%	0.29	40	58	1.96	-11
Watkins,Tommy	06	26	5	a/a	MIN	275	30	61	11	1	4	27	24	58	9	3	223	286	308	593	8%	79%	0.42	58	94	3.11	6
	07	27	685	aaa	MIN	349	49	87	21	0	7	46	34	68	11	7	250	317	367	685	9%	80%	0.50	82	83	4.08	28
Watson,Brandon	06	25	8	aaa	CIN	219	24	56	6	1	0	19	12	19	7	3	258	296	294	590	5%	91%	0.62	28	94	3.10	10
	07	26	8	aaa	WAS	399	42	113	10	5	2	26	18	48	16	9	282	314	345	659	4%	88%	0.38	40	122	3.81	18
Watson,Matt	06	28 b	8	aaa	OAK	126	16	33	7	1	4	20	14	13	0	1	266	339	421	760	10%	90%	1.08	98	58	5.14	51
Webb,Trey	07	26	486	aa	SF	322	32	64	12	3	2	18	5	71	7	3	198	209	268	478	1%	78%	0.06	48	129	1.80	-13

BATTER	Yr	Age	Pos	Lev	Org	ab	r	h	d	t	hr	rbi	bb	k	sb	cs	ba	ob	slg	ops	bb%	ct%	eye	px	sx	rc/g	bpv
Weber,Jon	06	29	8	aaa	LA	428	47	97	29	0	6	43	30	54	7	5	226	276	332	609	7%	87%	0.55	80	71	3.11	19
	07	30	8	aaa	TAM	136	17	31	5	2	3	18	18	25	0	0	228	319	348	667	12%	81%	0.72	73	82	4.03	20
Webster,Anthony	06	24	8	a/a	TEX	458	60	129	24	6	8	34	28	53	17	10	282	323	413	736	6%	88%	0.53	85	131	4.67	40
	07	24	80	aa	TEX	411	53	102	23	3	7	31	17	47	24	11	247	277	365	643	4%	88%	0.36	80	133	3.33	23
Wesson,Barry	07	30	8	aa	HOU	222	12	34	5	1	2	10	16	66	6	1	155	212	211	423	7%	70%	0.25	37	77	1.50	-28
West,Jeremy	06	25	3	aa	BOS	450	54	113	33	1	10	56	35	58	1	3	251	305	399	704	7%	87%	0.61	103	45	4.25	38
	07	26	30	aa	CHW	190	16	45	3	0	0	15	13	29	1	1	237	284	251	535	6%	85%	0.44	13	40	2.52	-7
West,Kevin	06	27	8	aaa	MIN	256	33	60	9	1	11	40	19	74	0	2	235	289	402	690	7%	71%	0.26	98	52	3.92	24
	07	28	803	aa	TEX	371	32	80	16	0	11	37	24	89	0	1	215	263	345	607	6%	76%	0.27	83	22	3.05	11
Whiteman,Tommy	06	27	6	aaa	COL	147	8	21	3	1	2	7	5	39	1	1	142	169	213	382	3%	74%	0.12	43	72	1.08	-32
Whitesell,Josh	06	24	3	aa	WAS	402	40	90	10	0	15	48	45	123	2	7	225	302	362	664	10%	69%	0.36	79	25	3.63	15
	07	25	30	aa	WAS	387	60	88	19	1	15	58	66	103	5	2	228	340	400	740	15%	73%	0.64	106	71	4.97	33
Whiteside,Eli	06	27	2	aaa	BAL	315	36	73	17	1	11	46	10	73	1	3	231	254	394	648	3%	77%	0.13	104	60	3.24	23
	07	28	2	a/a	BAL	202	18	42	6	3	5	29	7	44	1	3	207	233	340	573	3%	78%	0.16	78	98	2.39	4
Whitrock,Scott	06	26	8	aa	MIN	222	26	40	11	2	3	14	15	87	13	1	178	231	280	511	6%	61%	0.18	50	89	2.30	-9
Williams,Glenn	06	29	5	aaa	MIN	370	34	85	18	4	6	33	32	97	3	1	229	290	349	639	8%	74%	0.33	79	89	3.56	15
	07	30	3	aaa	MIN	405	38	83	17	2	7	50	24	107	1	2	204	249	309	558	6%	74%	0.23	69	58	2.55	1
Williams,Marland	07	26	8	aa	CIN	322	28	55	5	3	9	30	24	139	13	2	170	229	284	512	7%	57%	0.18	63	137	2.21	-14
Willits,Reggie	06	25	8	aaa	LAA	352	62	101	16	2	2	31	58	59	24	18	287	388	360	748	14%	89%	1.48	54	113	5.05	47
Wilson,Andy	06	31	2	aa	NYM	319	21	49	12	0	4	19	21	117	0	1	154	206	224	430	6%	63%	0.18	50	24	1.46	-25
Wilson,Bobby	06	24	2	aa	LAA	374	32	89	22	0	7	38	23	36	1	8	239	283	353	636	6%	90%	0.65	81	26	3.18	26
Wilson,Enrique	06	33	4	aaa	BOS	203	14	41	9	1	3	15	20	16	3	3	200	271	293	563	9%	92%	1.27	64	56	2.63	18
Wilson,Josh	06	26 a	6	aaa	COL	335	46	96	17	3	8	34	28	29	11	5	287	341	426	767	8%	91%	0.95	89	109	5.32	51
Wilson,Michael	06	23	8	aa	SEA	249	29	55	11	1	12	40	27	87	1	1	222	299	413	711	10%	65%	0.31	114	56	4.27	27
	07	24	8	aa	SEA	208	25	33	6	1	8	23	14	85	3	0	160	214	306	520	6%	59%	0.17	85	107	2.15	-8
Wilson,Robert	07	24	2	aa	LAA	313	33	78	20	1	8	42	26	42	5	3	249	306	392	697	8%	87%	0.61	97	68	4.20	35
Wilson,Tom	06	36	2	aaa	FLA	278	35	65	18	0	7	32	23	86	1	2	233	293	376	668	8%	77%	0.37	97	46	3.77	25
Wimberly,Corey	07	24	4	aa	COL	365	50	91	14	1	3	26	16	41	29	10	250	280	316	597	4%	89%	0.38	48	131	3.09	10
Winfree,David	07	22	350	aa	MIN	460	47	110	24	3	9	42	20	91	0	0	239	271	363	634	4%	80%	0.22	82	56	3.40	18
Wise,Dewayne	06	29	8	a/a	CIN	204	31	51	14	2	6	23	13	42	6	2	250	294	425	719	6%	79%	0.30	115	127	4.39	37
	07	30	8	aaa	CIN	207	24	44	9	4	6	16	6	55	6	2	211	235	382	617	3%	73%	0.12	102	184	2.94	15
Witt,Kevin	06	31	3	aaa	TAM	485	69	119	24	1	29	83	41	140	0	0	245	304	477	781	8%	71%	0.30	138	38	5.13	44
Wood,Brandon	06	22	6	aa	LAA	453	55	107	37	2	18	61	39	110	14	4	236	297	446	743	8%	76%	0.35	138	103	4.61	43
	07	23	56	aa	LAA	437	66	111	25	1	20	70	40	109	9	1	254	317	453	770	8%	75%	0.37	124	94	5.23	43
Wood,Jason	06	37	5	aaa	FLA	441	45	99	17	2	7	54	32	86	1	1	224	280	320	597	7%	81%	0.37	63	56	3.06	8
Wooten,Shawn	06	34	2	aaa	MIN	352	22	78	18	0	5	37	20	90	1	0	222	264	320	583	5%	74%	0.22	69	27	2.90	7
	07	35	2	aa	NYM	146	6	22	3	0	0	8	7	21	0	0	149	188	168	355	5%	85%	0.33	17	18	1.01	-37
Yan,Ruddy	06	25	8	a/a	TEX	252	36	59	8	2	0	16	22	26	13	5	235	297	281	578	8%	90%	0.87	34	128	3.00	10
	07	26	8	a/a	LAA	420	48	93	12	2	3	19	31	38	13	10	222	276	280	556	7%	91%	0.83	41	97	2.54	7
Yepez,Marcos	07	26	64	a/a	WAS	224	29	56	7	1	1	17	17	49	4	2	250	303	301	605	7%	78%	0.35	37	89	3.28	5
Youngbauer,Scott	06	28	4	a/a	SEA	361	39	71	14	3	9	31	25	89	3	5	198	250	323	573	7%	75%	0.29	78	88	2.56	4
Young,Chris	06	27	8	aaa	ARI	402	57	97	29	3	16	56	39	56	12	6	241	308	449	757	9%	86%	0.70	133	111	4.77	49
Young,Delmon	06	21 a	8	aaa	TAM	342	52	112	23	4	8	61	15	56	23	4	328	357	489	846	4%	84%	0.27	106	157	6.88	59
Young,Delwyn	06	24	8	aaa	LA	532	58	124	35	0	14	75	32	82	2	5	233	277	378	654	6%	85%	0.30	99	40	3.48	26
	07	25	8	aa	LA	490	81	134	44	3	14	74	30	100	3	4	274	315	457	773	6%	80%	0.30	127	87	5.10	50
Young,Ernie	06	37	3	aaa	CHW	350	42	92	23	0	13	56	45	87	2	2	262	346	435	781	11%	75%	0.52	113	36	5.52	44
	07	38	0	aaa	CHW	374	36	69	10	0	13	34	32	99	0	0	185	249	313	561	8%	74%	0.32	76	24	2.60	-1
Young,Walter	06	27	3	a/a	SD	381	28	81	14	0	8	50	12	49	3	6	213	236	312	548	3%	87%	0.24	64	38	2.26	2
Yount,Dustin	06	24	3	aa	BAL	167	19	36	5	0	5	18	24	51	0	2	215	314	331	646	13%	70%	0.48	71	28	3.59	10
Zapp,A.J.	06	28	3	aa	LA	269	22	45	12	0	6	26	31	123	0	1	167	253	283	536	10%	54%	0.25	76	23	2.39	-8
Zeringue,Jon	06	24	8	aa	ARI	203	14	42	5	1	4	17	17	40	1	2	205	268	296	565	8%	80%	0.43	55	46	2.64	-0
Zinter,Alan	06	38	3	aaa	HOU	212	31	45	9	2	9	32	25	58	1	0	212	296	399	695	11%	73%	0.44	111	89	4.14	25
Zobrist,Ben	06	25	6	a/a	TAM	384	58	109	25	6	3	30	54	53	10	7	285	373	401	774	12%	86%	1.03	82	126	5.62	49
	07	26 b	6	aaa	TAM	222	39	57	13	2	7	20	41	38	8	3	258	373	424	797	16%	83%	1.07	105	113	5.98	51

					Actual				Major League Equivalents																
PITCHER	Yr	Age	Lev	Org	w	l	g	sv	ip	h	er	hr	bb	k	era	WHIP	bf/g	oob	ctl	dom	cmd	hr/9	h%	s%	bpv
Aardsma,David	06	25	aaa	CHC	2	3	29	8	36	38	18	1	16	32	4.49	1.50	5.5	265	4.0	8.0	2.0	0.2	35%	68%	84
	07	26	aaa	CHW	3	2	28	15	35	32	23	10	12	40	5.96	1.27	5.2	240	3.1	10.2	3.3	2.6	27%	62%	59
Abraham,Paul	06	27	aa	SD	3	4	43	1	65	80	33	6	39	42	4.62	1.84	7.2	298	5.4	5.8	1.1	0.8	35%	76%	29
	07	28	aa	SD	1	3	47	8	52	53	20	2	25	38	3.53	1.50	4.9	258	4.4	6.6	1.5	0.4	32%	76%	62
Abreu,Winston	06	29 b	aaa	BAL	9	4	46	1	65	72	28	5	23	65	3.87	1.45	6.2	275	3.1	9.0	2.9	0.7	36%	75%	92
	07	30	aaa	WAS	3	0	37	5	52	31	10	2	23	62	1.73	1.04	5.6	170	4.0	10.7	2.7	0.4	25%	85%	130
Acevedo,Jose	06	29	aaa	COL	6	8	15	0	87	135	73	14	19	42	7.56	1.78	27.3	348	2.0	4.3	2.2	1.4	37%	58%	13
Acosta,Manny	06	25	a/a	ATL	1	6	51	21	60	58	33	6	54	48	4.89	1.86	5.6	248	8.1	7.1	0.9	0.9	30%	75%	38
	07	26	aaa	ATL	9	3	40	12	59	56	19	0	38	47	2.82	1.58	6.7	244	5.8	7.1	1.2	0.0	32%	80%	74
Adams,Mike	06	28	aaa	SD	1	3	48	2	60	76	32	3	25	39	4.84	1.68	5.8	304	3.7	5.9	1.6	0.5	36%	70%	48
Adams,Terry	06	34	aaa	PIT	5	3	48	1	63	85	44	9	24	34	6.31	1.73	6.1	316	3.5	4.9	1.4	1.4	35%	65%	10
Adenhart,Nicholas	07	21	aa	LAA	10	8	26	0	153	184	78	8	66	98	4.59	1.63	26.8	292	3.9	5.8	1.5	0.5	35%	71%	48
Adkins,Jon	07	30	aa	NYM	2	4	48	5	65	111	46	11	23	27	6.32	2.06	6.8	370	3.2	3.7	1.2	1.6	39%	72%	-20
Aguilar,Ray	06	27	aa	OAK	12	7	28	0	158	245	107	15	46	75	6.08	1.84	26.9	346	2.6	4.3	1.6	0.9	38%	67%	20
Aguilar,Salvador	07	26	aa	NYM	7	9	28	0	119	203	99	4	44	50	7.47	2.08	21.3	369	3.4	3.7	1.1	0.3	41%	61%	17
Akin,Brian	06	25	aa	LA	2	1	20	6	36	32	17	2	25	37	4.19	1.57	8.1	230	6.3	9.2	1.5	0.5	31%	73%	79
	07	26	aa	LA	2	4	44	2	82	98	52	4	56	87	5.72	1.87	8.9	290	6.1	9.6	1.6	0.5	39%	68%	73
Albaladejo,Jonathan	06	24	aa	PIT	1	2	18	1	36	51	22	5	5	22	5.41	1.55	8.9	325	1.3	5.6	4.3	1.3	36%	67%	76
	07	25	a/a	WAS	7	3	36	2	60	52	25	5	23	46	3.70	1.23	6.9	227	3.4	6.8	2.0	0.8	27%	72%	70
Albers,Matt	06	24	a/a	HOU	12	3	23	0	141	136	46	7	56	102	2.94	1.36	26.2	248	3.6	6.5	1.8	0.4	30%	79%	69
	07	25	aa	HOU	2	3	9	0	53	60	27	7	23	34	4.65	1.57	26.4	279	3.9	5.8	1.5	1.3	31%	74%	27
Alexander,Mark	06	26 a	a/a	LA	5	3	52	27	61	43	12	2	24	68	1.71	1.10	4.7	195	3.6	10.1	2.8	0.3	28%	85%	127
	07	27	aa	LA	5	1	48	5	79	91	69	15	62	73	7.85	1.93	8.0	282	7.1	8.3	1.2	1.7	34%	61%	22
Alvarado,Carlos	06	29	a/a	CIN	5	2	33	0	51	58	31	4	31	42	5.38	1.72	7.2	278	5.4	7.3	1.4	0.6	35%	68%	53
Alvarez,Abe	06	24	aaa	BOS	6	9	22	0	118	168	105	28	42	62	8.01	1.78	25.2	328	3.2	4.7	1.5	2.1	34%	58%	-15
	07	25	aaa	BOS	5	8	25	0	100	123	72	10	48	59	6.48	1.71	18.5	296	4.3	5.3	1.2	0.9	34%	61%	26
Alvarez,Carlos	06	22	aa	LA	4	1	33	1	55	58	23	9	15	47	3.76	1.32	7.1	265	2.5	7.7	3.1	1.5	31%	78%	70
Alvarez,Oscar	06	26	aa	WAS	8	8	30	0	133	193	108	18	45	65	7.30	1.79	20.9	332	3.0	4.4	1.5	1.2	36%	59%	8
	07	27	aa	BAL	11	7	25	0	135	180	112	22	65	48	7.47	1.81	25.6	313	4.3	3.2	0.7	1.4	32%	59%	-16
Anderson,Brian	07	24	aa	SF	1	5	47	29	50	65	27	4	21	37	4.92	1.72	4.9	308	3.8	6.7	1.8	0.8	37%	72%	48
Anderson,Craig	06	26	a/a	BAL	3	4	17	0	90	126	59	9	17	50	5.89	1.59	23.9	325	1.7	5.0	3.0	0.9	36%	63%	55
	07	27	a/a	BAL	12	4	28	0	166	223	104	24	41	75	5.66	1.59	26.8	315	2.2	4.0	1.8	1.3	34%	67%	15
Anderson,Jason	06	27	aaa	SD	5	2	60	4	79	79	29	6	28	52	3.35	1.36	5.6	255	3.2	5.9	1.8	0.7	30%	77%	57
	07	28	a/a	PHI	4	3	37	1	64	94	47	11	18	37	6.60	1.74	8.1	334	2.5	5.2	2.1	1.5	37%	64%	20
Anderson,Jimmy	06	31	aaa	FLA	2	3	22	0	43	68	32	7	21	29	6.71	2.06	9.8	350	4.4	6.0	1.4	1.4	40%	69%	8
Anderson,Matt	06	30	aaa	SF	1	2	26	0	34	58	42	8	30	25	11.14	2.57	7.2	367	7.9	6.7	0.8	2.1	41%	57%	-22
Andrade,Steve	06	29	aaa	SD	3	2	38	0	67	63	29	4	32	55	3.89	1.42	7.7	244	4.3	7.3	1.7	0.6	31%	73%	69
	07	30	aaa	TAM	3	2	38	0	59	70	45	5	37	40	6.86	1.82	7.4	290	5.7	6.1	1.1	0.8	34%	61%	31
Appier,Kevin	06	39	aaa	SEA	1	2	10	0	35	46	22	0	26	22	5.65	2.06	17.5	311	6.7	5.6	0.8	0.0	37%	70%	44
Aquino,Greg	07	30	aaa	MIL	3	2	35	7	38	33	14	2	22	37	3.37	1.44	4.8	228	5.2	8.8	1.7	0.5	30%	77%	82
Ardoin,Kevin	07	25	aa	DET	3	5	34	0	47	70	32	9	29	14	6.17	2.10	6.9	338	5.5	2.8	0.5	1.7	34%	74%	-37
Arias,Alberto	06	23	aa	COL	8	6	49	0	111	121	70	20	43	71	5.67	1.47	10.0	271	3.5	5.7	1.7	1.6	29%	65%	21
Arredondo,Jose	06	23	aa	LAA	2	3	11	0	60	83	44	7	20	41	6.58	1.71	25.3	321	3.0	6.1	2.1	1.0	37%	61%	39
	07	24	aa	LAA	0	1	25	10	28	22	10	2	14	24	3.31	1.29	4.7	209	4.6	7.8	1.7	0.7	26%	76%	75
Asadoorian,Eric	07	27	aa	CIN	1	1	37	0	52	55	31	7	34	34	5.40	1.71	6.5	267	5.8	5.9	1.0	1.2	30%	71%	21
Asahina,Jonathan	06	26	a/a	COL	4	10	29	0	147	239	136	32	44	54	8.31	1.92	24.6	357	2.7	3.3	1.2	1.9	37%	59%	-29
	07	27	aa	COL	3	5	10	0	49	80	44	13	29	11	7.99	2.22	25.3	359	5.3	2.1	0.4	2.3	35%	68%	-66
Ascanio,Jose	06	21	aa	ATL	4	2	24	0	38	46	25	2	19	33	5.92	1.71	7.3	293	4.5	7.8	1.7	0.5	37%	63%	66
	07	22 a	aa	ATL	2	2	44	10	78	77	28	1	19	61	3.23	1.23	7.4	253	2.2	7.0	3.2	0.1	32%	72%	111
Asencio,Miguel	06	26	aaa	COL	8	7	38	1	111	153	80	18	40	59	6.52	1.74	13.6	320	3.3	4.8	1.5	1.4	35%	64%	8
	07	27	aa	HOU	2	6	38	3	84	151	81	17	40	32	8.65	2.27	11.5	380	4.3	3.4	0.8	1.8	39%	63%	-38
Asher,David	07	25	aa	SEA	0	0	23	2	19	27	16	1	9	12	7.48	1.94	4.0	330	4.5	5.9	1.3	0.5	39%	59%	36
Astacio,Ezequiel	06	27	aaa	HOU	8	4	21	0	92	110	60	16	43	62	5.84	1.67	20.1	291	4.2	6.1	1.4	1.6	32%	68%	15
	07	28	aa	TEX	3	5	31	2	52	69	51	13	30	40	8.74	1.90	8.1	311	5.2	6.9	1.3	2.3	34%	56%	-7
Atchison,Scott	06	31	aaa	SEA	4	0	30	1	50	61	17	2	17	32	3.00	1.56	7.5	295	3.0	5.7	1.9	0.4	35%	81%	58
	07	32	aa	SF	3	2	38	4	53	59	16	1	9	37	2.79	1.28	5.9	275	1.6	6.3	4.0	0.2	34%	77%	116
Atencio,Greg	07	26	aa	KC	4	7	36	0	113	167	94	15	52	68	7.50	1.93	15.2	335	4.1	5.4	1.3	1.2	38%	61%	12
Atlee,Thomas	06	27	a/a	CHC	3	6	56	6	83	98	48	10	51	44	5.23	1.79	7.0	287	5.5	4.8	0.9	1.1	32%	73%	11
Avery,James	07	23	aa	CIN	11	10	27	0	146	193	108	21	62	80	6.66	1.74	25.2	311	3.8	4.9	1.3	1.3	34%	63%	11
Avery,Matt	07	24	aa	CHC	2	2	31	0	49	61	31	11	20	29	5.61	1.65	7.2	299	3.7	5.2	1.4	1.9	32%	72%	-1
Babula,Shaun	07	30	aaa	CHW	3	3	37	0	61	82	49	10	36	36	7.20	1.93	8.0	315	5.2	5.3	1.0	1.5	35%	64%	1
Backe,Brandon	07	29	aa	HOU	4	2	6	0	30	48	24	8	17	19	7.20	2.18	25.5	354	5.2	5.6	1.1	2.4	38%	72%	-31
Bacsik,Mike	06	29	aaa	ARI	11	0	28	0	87	98	33	10	19	47	3.45	1.35	13.3	278	2.0	4.8	2.4	1.0	31%	78%	49
	07	30	aaa	WAS	1	3	9	0	36	51	22	7	7	21	5.49	1.59	18.0	325	1.6	5.2	3.2	1.6	35%	70%	39
Baek,Cha Seung	06	26	aaa	SEA	12	4	24	0	147	154	59	19	39	90	3.60	1.31	25.9	264	2.4	5.5	2.3	1.1	29%	77%	50
	07	27	aa	SEA	1	1	6	0	31	45	16	1	13	13	4.55	1.87	24.7	330	3.8	3.9	1.0	0.3	37%	74%	23
Baerlocher,Ryan	06	29	aaa	KC	5	4	20	1	80	100	49	10	32	46	5.56	1.65	18.3	300	3.6	5.2	1.5	1.1	33%	68%	24
	07	30	a/a	ATL	4	5	17	0	98	163	69	10	28	43	6.31	1.94	28.0	362	2.5	4.0	1.6	0.9	40%	67%	12
Baez,Federico	06	25	a/a	CHC	2	5	34	1	88	103	47	17	36	54	4.84	1.58	11.6	286	3.7	5.5	1.5	1.7	31%	75%	11
Bailey,Cory	07	37	aa	CHC	5	3	44	5	91	136	42	9	19	43	4.18	1.70	9.6	339	1.9	4.3	2.3	0.9	37%	77%	33
Bailey,Homer	06	20 a	aa	CIN	7	1	13	0	68	57	15	1	28	68	2.02	1.25	21.8	223	3.7	9.0	2.5	0.1	31%	83%	113
	07	21	aaa	CIN	6	3	12	0	67	53	27	5	30	55	3.66	1.23	23.2	212	4.0	7.4	1.8	0.6	26%	71%	77
Bajenaru,Jeff	06	29	aaa	ARI	4	3	52	7	80	95	51	8	41	59	5.69	1.69	7.1	288	4.6	6.6	1.4	0.8	34%	66%	42
Baker,Brad	06	26	a/a	BOS	3	4	41	3	63	102	56	9	22	42	7.96	1.97	7.5	357	3.2	6.0	1.9	1.4	40%	60%	19
	07	27	a/a	MIN	2	7	29	0	94	142	87	18	37	56	8.29	1.90	15.6	341	3.5	5.3	1.5	1.7	37%	57%	-0
Baker,Chris	06	29	aaa	TEX	9	4	27	1	86	103	37	7	33	32	3.91	1.58	14.3	291	3.5	3.3	1.0	0.7	31%	76%	16
	07	30	aa	TEX	4	6	18	0	74	164	97	26	36	25	11.78	2.70	23.1	431	4.3	3.0	0.7	3.1	43%	59%	-93
Baker,Scott	06	25	aaa	MIN	5	4	12	0	84	98	37	5	29	57	4.00	1.51	31.1	285	3.1	6.1	2.0	0.5	34%	74%	60
	07	26 b	aaa	MIN	3	2	7	1	42	44	23	4	5	32	4.84	1.17	24.7	265	1.1	6.8	6.2	0.9	32%	59%	147
Baldwin,Andrew	07	25 a	aa	SEA	5	12	27	0	166	227	96	14	21	98	5.19	1.50	27.2	319	1.1	5.3	4.6	0.7	37%	65%	98

Major League Equivalent Statistics

PITCHERS

PITCHER	Yr	Age	Lev	Org	Actual				Major League Equivalents																	
					w	l	g	sv	ip	h	er	hr	bb	k	era	WHIP	bf/g	oob	ctl	dom	cmd	hr/9	h%	s%	bpv
Balester,Collin	07	21	a/a	WAS	4	10	27	0	150	165	74	11	46	103	4.45	1.40	24.0	273	2.7	6.2	2.3	0.7	32%	68%	64
Balfour,Grant	07	30 b	a/a	MIL	1	1	32	7	43	35	13	2	20	51	2.80	1.27	5.6	219	4.1	10.6	2.6	0.5	32%	79%	114
Ballouli,Khalid	06	27	aa	MIL	2	4	23	1	56	84	43	6	25	40	6.82	1.95	11.9	339	4.1	6.4	1.6	0.9	40%	64%	31
Banks,Josh	06	24	aaa	TOR	10	11	29	0	170	224	135	47	30	109	7.14	1.49	25.9	311	1.6	5.8	3.6	2.5	32%	57%	29
	07	25	aaa	TOR	12	10	27	0	169	227	112	28	25	85	5.97	1.49	27.6	315	1.3	4.5	3.4	1.5	34%	63%	45
Bannister,Brian	06	26	aaa	NYM	3	3	6	0	30	42	18	5	5	21	5.44	1.58	22.6	326	1.5	6.2	4.1	1.5	37%	69%	68
Barnes,John	07	31	a/a	BOS	2	3	7	0	36	28	14	1	38	20	3.60	1.82	24.4	209	9.4	4.9	0.5	0.3	25%	79%	46
Barone,Daniel	07	24	aa	FLA	8	3	23	0	136	151	73	14	35	79	4.80	1.36	25.3	275	2.3	5.2	2.3	0.9	31%	66%	52
Barratt,Jonathan	07	23	aa	TAM	4	10	20	0	90	107	66	10	60	42	6.59	1.85	21.5	289	6.0	4.2	0.7	1.0	31%	64%	7
Barrett,Ricky	06	26	aaa	MIN	5	1	27	1	47	39	26	0	30	41	5.02	1.48	7.7	223	5.8	7.8	1.3	0.0	30%	62%	85
	07	27	aaa	MIN	2	1	22	1	30	39	21	4	16	27	6.14	1.84	6.5	308	4.9	8.1	1.6	1.2	38%	68%	40
Barry,Kevin	06	28	aaa	ATL	4	5	18	0	95	114	52	6	42	60	4.88	1.64	24.1	291	4.0	5.6	1.4	0.6	34%	70%	42
	07	29	aaa	ATL	5	7	24	0	112	154	76	16	47	65	6.08	1.79	22.0	320	3.8	5.2	1.4	1.3	35%	68%	11
Barthmaier,James	07	24	aa	HOU	2	9	24	0	90	135	76	13	45	60	7.63	2.00	18.5	339	4.5	6.0	1.3	1.3	39%	62%	11
Barzilla,Phil	06	28	aaa	HOU	8	5	25	1	112	135	59	5	49	65	4.73	1.64	20.5	292	4.0	5.2	1.3	0.4	34%	70%	43
	07	29	aa	HOU	9	7	31	1	135	236	103	9	59	51	6.83	2.18	22.2	375	3.9	3.4	0.9	0.6	41%	67%	1
Basner,Ryan	06	25	a/a	ATL	4	5	41	1	82	111	53	11	32	60	5.76	1.73	9.3	315	3.5	6.6	1.9	1.2	37%	68%	36
	07	26	a/a	ATL	4	5	36	1	91	123	54	14	34	61	5.38	1.73	11.8	317	3.4	6.0	1.8	1.4	36%	72%	22
Bass,Adam	06	25	a/a	ARI	11	7	29	0	170	226	120	22	60	92	6.35	1.68	27.0	313	3.2	4.9	1.5	1.2	34%	63%	19
	07	26	aa	ARI	3	1	19	0	50	57	17	5	18	27	3.10	1.52	11.7	282	3.3	4.9	1.5	0.8	32%	82%	34
Bass,Brian	06	25	a/a	KC	5	6	13	0	59	90	46	8	20	24	7.08	1.85	21.7	342	3.0	3.7	1.2	1.3	36%	62%	-3
	07	26	aaa	MIN	7	3	37	1	103	121	59	10	27	64	5.11	1.44	12.1	287	2.4	5.6	2.4	0.9	33%	65%	54
Bateman,Joe	06	26	aa	SF	4	6	53	10	72	95	53	5	29	57	6.61	1.72	6.3	312	3.6	7.2	2.0	0.6	38%	60%	60
	07	27	aa	SF	4	1	29	0	56	71	25	6	25	33	4.06	1.72	9.0	303	4.1	5.3	1.3	1.0	34%	79%	25
Bauer,Rick	07	31	a/a	LA	2	6	41	2	68	115	53	15	55	45	6.95	2.50	9.0	367	7.3	5.9	0.8	2.0	40%	76%	-25
Baugh,Kenneth	07	29	aa	FLA	7	9	21	0	96	188	128	18	78	43	11.93	2.75	26.0	400	7.3	4.0	0.6	1.6	43%	56%	-38
Bausher,Tim	06	27	aaa	CIN	4	4	39	0	73	105	59	7	42	33	7.27	2.02	9.2	331	5.2	4.1	0.8	0.9	36%	63%	3
Bautista,Denny	06	26	aaa	COL	3	9	16	0	80	126	80	6	51	52	9.05	2.20	25.6	350	5.7	5.9	1.0	0.7	41%	56%	21
	07	27	aa	COL	3	2	51	0	64	80	35	1	37	46	4.90	1.82	6.0	298	5.2	6.5	1.2	0.2	37%	71%	56
Bayliss,Jonah	06	26	aaa	PIT	3	3	46	23	58	47	21	5	31	55	3.20	1.35	5.4	219	4.8	8.6	1.8	0.8	28%	79%	76
Bay,Ronald	06	23	a/a	CLE	8	8	28	0	138	147	80	24	56	107	5.22	1.47	21.6	267	3.7	7.0	1.9	1.6	30%	69%	37
Bazardo,Yorman	06	22	aa	SEA	6	5	25	0	138	171	73	12	49	72	4.76	1.59	24.9	298	3.2	4.7	1.5	0.8	33%	71%	31
	07	23	aaa	DET	10	6	23	0	136	159	74	9	43	60	4.89	1.48	26.1	286	2.8	4.0	1.4	0.6	32%	66%	33
Beam,Randy	06	24	aa	BOS	3	3	35	1	51	61	37	13	13	34	6.49	1.44	6.4	290	2.2	6.0	2.7	2.2	31%	60%	23
Beam,T.J.	06	26	a/a	NYY	6	0	37	4	73	56	14	2	30	53	1.78	1.17	8.1	206	3.7	6.5	1.8	0.3	26%	85%	82
	07	27	aaa	NYY	4	3	29	3	47	63	26	7	11	36	5.03	1.56	7.3	315	2.0	6.9	3.4	1.4	37%	71%	63
Bean,Colter	06	30	aaa	NYY	9	2	47	0	88	78	36	2	62	87	3.70	1.58	8.4	233	6.3	8.9	1.4	0.2	32%	75%	85
	07	31	aaa	NYY	2	0	28	0	59	87	56	4	36	42	8.47	2.07	10.5	335	5.4	6.5	1.2	0.7	40%	57%	31
Beckstead,Jentry	06	26	a/a	COL	6	3	48	0	72	83	31	11	27	52	3.88	1.53	6.7	284	3.3	6.5	2.0	1.4	32%	80%	37
	07	27	aa	COL	3	1	45	1	71	113	66	13	39	37	8.38	2.13	8.0	353	4.9	4.7	1.0	1.7	38%	62%	-17
Begg,Chris	06	27	aa	SF	13	10	26	0	174	246	122	12	41	69	6.29	1.65	30.6	326	2.1	3.6	1.7	0.6	36%	60%	28
	07	28	aa	SF	14	5	27	0	166	283	110	24	33	57	5.96	1.90	29.6	368	1.8	3.1	1.7	1.3	39%	70%	-2
Bell,Heath	06	29 b	aaa	NYM	3	3	30	12	35	36	8	1	9	44	1.98	1.29	4.9	262	2.3	11.2	5.0	0.3	39%	85%	166
Bell,Rob	06	30	aaa	CLE	9	10	30	1	142	187	95	22	41	79	5.99	1.60	21.4	311	2.6	5.0	1.9	1.4	34%	65%	22
	07	31	aaa	BAL	4	3	10	0	66	83	34	8	20	46	4.68	1.56	29.7	301	2.7	6.2	2.3	1.1	35%	72%	49
Beltran,Francis	07	28	aaa	BAL	2	9	47	8	59	95	46	3	17	39	7.05	1.89	6.0	354	2.6	5.9	2.3	0.5	42%	60%	54
Benes,Alan	06	35	aaa	STL	5	6	30	0	66	83	47	18	25	37	6.45	1.64	10.0	301	3.4	5.0	1.5	2.4	30%	67%	-17
Bennett,Jeff	07	27	a/a	ATL	3	5	42	1	95	123	53	7	48	38	5.01	1.80	10.7	307	4.6	3.6	0.8	0.7	34%	72%	12
Bentz,Chad	06	26	a/a	CHW	6	4	39	0	50	56	49	22	42	24	8.78	1.95	6.3	275	7.6	4.4	0.6	4.0	22%	65%	-82
Bergmann,Jason	06	25	aaa	WAS	8	2	26	4	60	62	26	5	21	51	3.93	1.38	9.9	260	3.2	7.7	2.4	0.8	32%	73%	78
Bergman,Dusty	06	29	aaa	SF	0	5	49	1	46	83	42	2	24	28	8.17	2.30	4.9	380	4.6	5.4	1.2	0.4	44%	62%	24
Berg,Christopher	07	23	aa	CHC	7	7	27	0	140	189	98	5	73	56	6.30	1.87	24.8	316	4.7	3.6	0.8	0.3	35%	64%	20
Bernero,Adam	06	30	aaa	KC	6	4	21	1	104	105	49	12	32	51	4.28	1.32	21.0	258	2.8	4.4	1.6	1.0	28%	70%	32
Bierd,Randor	07	24 a	aa	DET	3	2	27	1	45	39	24	1	10	44	4.72	1.09	6.7	229	2.1	8.7	4.2	0.2	31%	53%	144
Billingsley,Chad	06	22 a	aaa	LA	6	3	13	0	70	56	30	7	29	69	3.79	1.21	22.3	215	3.7	8.9	2.4	0.9	28%	71%	91
Birkins,Kurt	07	27	aaa	BAL	8	4	20	0	105	133	54	8	41	81	4.59	1.65	24.0	302	3.5	6.9	2.0	0.7	37%	73%	56
Bisenius,Joseph	07	25	aaa	PHI	3	4	35	0	46	62	35	6	32	35	6.92	2.04	6.5	314	6.3	6.8	1.1	1.2	37%	67%	20
Bittner,Tim	06	26	aa	LAA	3	2	35	0	43	86	47	7	38	18	9.86	2.89	7.1	407	7.9	3.8	0.5	1.4	44%	66%	-37
	07	27	aa	CHW	2	4	48	0	66	136	55	13	39	22	7.55	2.64	7.7	414	5.2	3.1	0.6	1.8	43%	74%	-51
Blackburn,Nick	06	25	aa	MIN	7	8	30	0	132	181	94	15	43	66	6.38	1.70	20.3	319	2.9	4.5	1.5	1.0	35%	62%	20
	07	26	a/a	MIN	10	4	25	0	148	164	54	9	22	58	3.26	1.26	24.8	275	1.3	3.5	2.6	0.6	30%	75%	59
Blackley,Travis	06	24	a/a	SEA	9	12	27	0	155	172	86	23	53	94	4.99	1.45	25.1	275	3.1	5.5	1.8	1.3	30%	69%	30
	07	25	aa	SF	10	8	28	0	162	186	105	22	71	98	5.84	1.58	26.1	282	3.9	5.4	1.4	1.2	31%	65%	23
Bland,Nate	06	32	aaa	LAA	7	6	33	0	108	151	74	14	26	66	6.13	1.64	14.9	323	2.2	5.5	2.5	1.1	36%	63%	41
Blank,Matt	06	31	aaa	SD	4	3	28	0	80	124	63	14	49	34	7.01	2.15	14.5	346	5.5	3.9	0.7	1.5	36%	69%	-22
Blevins,Jerry	07	24 a	aa	OAK	4	5	41	4	54	51	17	3	13	57	2.81	1.17	5.4	243	2.1	9.5	4.5	0.5	33%	77%	142
Boehringer,Brian	06	37	aaa	KC	5	5	18	0	71	108	40	7	13	27	5.07	1.70	18.2	343	1.6	3.4	2.1	0.9	37%	71%	23
Boggs,Mitch	07	24	aa	STL	11	7	26	0	152	190	75	15	61	100	4.45	1.65	26.7	299	3.6	5.9	1.6	0.9	35%	75%	38
Bohorquez,Carlos	07	26	aa	CIN	3	2	22	0	30	36	19	1	21	18	5.65	1.88	6.6	288	6.3	5.4	0.9	0.3	34%	68%	38
Bonilla,Henry	06	28	aaa	MIN	3	7	35	1	95	120	71	9	40	49	6.72	1.69	12.5	303	3.8	4.7	1.2	0.8	34%	59%	24
	07	29	aa	LAA	12	8	29	0	165	316	179	32	68	57	9.75	2.33	29.9	396	3.7	3.1	0.8	1.7	41%	58%	-40
Bonine,Eddie	07	26	a/a	DET	15	5	26	0	162	221	102	17	29	60	5.67	1.54	27.8	318	1.6	3.3	2.1	0.9	34%	63%	28
Bonser,Boof	06	25	aaa	MIN	6	4	14	0	86	86	40	5	41	70	4.18	1.48	27.0	255	4.3	7.3	1.7	0.5	32%	71%	68
Booker,Chris	06	30	a/a	WAS	2	2	29	0	32	39	18	4	23	33	5.14	1.94	5.4	295	6.5	9.2	1.4	1.0	38%	75%	50
	07	31	aaa	WAS	2	5	55	30	58	48	27	4	44	63	4.14	1.59	4.8	220	6.9	9.8	1.4	0.7	30%	75%	79
Bootcheck,Chris	06	28	aaa	LAA	4	3	40	1	65	94	54	9	34	34	7.41	1.95	7.9	330	4.6	4.7	1.0	1.3	36%	63%	-1
Borrell,Danny	06	28	aa	NYY	3	5	15	0	81	111	67	16	33	48	7.49	1.77	25.3	319	3.6	5.3	1.5	1.7	35%	59%	2
	07	29	aa	OAK	3	3	19	0	64	61	30	11	33	50	4.21	1.46	14.8	247	4.6	7.0	1.5	1.6	28%	77%	32
Bostick II,Adam	06	24	a/a	FLA	9	9	27	0	142	157	70	11	85	126	4.44	1.70	24.3	275	5.4	8.0	1.5	0.7	35%	74%	58
	07	25	aa	NYM	6	7	21	0	97	125	75	21	46	75	6.93	1.77	21.7	307	4.3	7.0	1.6	2.0	34%	64%	11

Major League Equivalent Statistics

PITCHER	Yr	Age	Lev	Org	w	l	g	sv	ip	h	er	hr	bb	k	era	WHIP	bf/g	oob	ctl	dom	cmd	hr/9	h%	s%	bpv
					Actual				Major League Equivalents																
Bouknight,Kip	06	28	a/a	WAS	9	8	27	0	157	205	110	17	62	84	6.32	1.70	26.9	308	3.6	4.8	1.4	1.0	34%	63%	21
	07	29	aa	PIT	12	7	27	0	156	220	105	20	54	64	6.05	1.75	27.0	325	3.1	3.7	1.2	1.2	35%	67%	2
Bowden,Michael M	07	21	aa	BOS	8	6	19	0	96	121	57	9	33	69	5.33	1.60	22.9	301	3.1	6.5	2.1	0.8	36%	67%	52
Bowie,Micah	06	32	aaa	WAS	2	0	31	1	42	39	22	0	26	46	4.73	1.55	6.1	241	5.6	9.7	1.7	0.0	35%	66%	102
Bowles,Brian	06	30	aaa	BAL	10	10	30	0	156	216	89	18	62	63	5.13	1.78	24.4	321	3.6	3.6	1.0	1.0	34%	73%	3
Boyer,Blaine	07	26	aaa	ATL	4	3	21	2	73	93	46	1	55	51	5.71	2.02	17.2	303	6.7	6.3	0.9	0.1	37%	69%	48
Braden,Dallas	07	24 a	aa	OAK	3	3	13	0	76	67	31	6	21	70	3.61	1.16	23.9	233	2.5	8.3	3.3	0.7	30%	71%	106
Bradley,David	06	29	aa	OAK	6	11	31	0	131	232	123	15	75	52	8.42	2.34	22.2	377	5.1	3.6	0.7	1.0	41%	63%	-15
Brandenburg,Adam	06	25	aa	FLA	1	2	21	0	34	62	41	4	24	16	10.82	2.53	8.9	384	6.4	4.3	0.7	1.2	42%	55%	-17
Braun,Ryan	06	23 a	a/a	KC	1	8	43	13	65	59	19	2	27	70	2.62	1.32	6.4	237	3.7	9.7	2.6	0.3	33%	80%	112
	07	27	aa	KC	2	2	23	9	33	27	6	1	14	27	1.64	1.24	6.0	216	3.9	7.2	1.8	0.3	28%	88%	84
Bray,Bill	06	23 a	aaa	WAS	4	1	21	5	31	29	17	5	9	38	4.90	1.22	6.1	241	2.6	11.0	4.2	1.4	32%	64%	118
Bray,Steve	06	26 a	a/a	MIL	7	4	50	1	85	86	32	9	13	64	3.34	1.16	6.9	258	1.3	6.7	5.0	1.0	30%	75%	120
	07	27	aaa	MIL	5	2	42	1	77	71	19	5	29	64	2.16	1.30	7.7	240	3.4	7.5	2.2	0.6	30%	86%	80
Brazelton,Dewon	06	26	aaa	SD	5	7	17	0	91	105	45	11	24	46	4.48	1.41	23.2	283	2.3	4.5	1.9	1.1	31%	71%	32
	07	27	aa	PIT	5	9	19	0	105	154	71	10	30	46	6.08	1.75	25.9	334	2.6	3.9	1.5	0.8	37%	65%	19
Breslow,Craig	06	26 b	aaa	BOS	7	1	39	7	67	63	29	4	26	65	3.88	1.32	7.3	243	3.5	8.7	2.5	0.6	32%	71%	95
	07	27	aaa	BOS	2	3	49	1	68	89	44	7	27	59	5.84	1.72	6.4	310	3.6	7.8	2.2	1.0	38%	66%	56
Bright,Adam	07	23	aa	COL	1	3	52	0	46	55	28	4	27	35	5.45	1.77	4.1	289	5.2	6.8	1.3	0.8	35%	69%	41
Brito,Eude	06	28	aaa	PHI	10	8	26	1	147	161	87	18	65	80	5.33	1.53	25.2	273	3.9	4.9	1.2	1.1	30%	67%	22
	07	29	aaa	PHI	1	6	20	0	58	95	56	13	38	25	8.68	2.29	15.1	358	6.0	3.8	0.6	2.0	37%	64%	-42
Britton,Chris	07	25 a	aaa	NYY	4	2	37	8	57	60	21	4	15	49	3.31	1.31	6.5	265	2.4	7.7	3.3	0.6	33%	76%	98
Broadway,Lance	06	23	a/a	CHW	8	8	26	0	160	202	68	15	44	100	3.82	1.54	27.4	302	2.5	5.6	2.3	0.8	35%	77%	51
	07	24	aaa	CHW	8	9	27	0	155	189	110	25	83	96	6.39	1.75	26.8	295	4.8	5.6	1.2	1.5	32%	66%	10
Brooks,Frank	06	28	a/a	KC	2	8	34	0	104	141	76	24	53	69	6.61	1.86	14.6	317	4.6	6.0	1.3	2.0	34%	69%	-6
	07	29	aa	SD	3	1	25	1	31	27	9	3	13	20	2.70	1.29	5.2	227	3.9	5.9	1.5	0.8	26%	82%	54
Broshuis,Garrett	06	25	aa	SF	7	10	27	0	152	216	135	17	47	85	7.98	1.73	26.2	327	2.8	5.0	1.8	1.0	37%	52%	27
	07	26	aa	SF	3	17	26	0	153	208	88	13	39	57	5.16	1.61	26.7	317	2.3	3.3	1.5	0.8	34%	68%	19
Brower,Jim	06	34	aaa	SD	5	3	39	1	52	62	28	7	21	34	4.90	1.59	6.0	289	3.6	5.9	1.6	1.3	33%	72%	28
	07	35	a/a	NYY	5	2	44	22	55	71	22	3	18	37	3.64	1.62	5.7	307	2.9	6.0	2.1	0.5	36%	78%	57
Brownlie,Robert	06	26	a/a	CHC	3	14	41	0	86	178	101	18	50	52	10.56	2.64	11.7	414	5.2	5.5	1.0	1.9	46%	60%	-29
	07	27	aa	CLE	1	2	9	0	48	55	24	6	16	30	4.52	1.48	23.5	282	3.0	5.5	1.8	1.1	32%	72%	38
Brown,Andrew	06	26	aaa	CLE	5	4	39	5	62	62	23	5	38	47	3.37	1.61	7.2	254	5.6	6.7	1.2	0.7	31%	81%	48
	07	27	aa	OAK	2	3	37	4	40	43	18	5	16	37	4.12	1.46	4.8	266	3.6	8.2	2.3	1.0	33%	74%	68
Brown,Brooks	07	22	aa	ARI	4	4	12	0	66	88	41	4	42	41	5.61	1.98	27.0	314	5.8	5.6	1.0	0.5	37%	70%	31
Bruback,Matt	06	28	aa	BAL	1	4	18	0	43	77	39	5	11	32	8.07	2.05	11.9	380	2.3	6.8	3.0	1.0	45%	59%	52
Buchholz,Clay	07	23 a	a/a	BOS	8	5	24	0	125	103	44	10	36	146	3.17	1.11	21.0	220	2.6	10.5	4.1	0.7	31%	74%	138
Buchholz,Taylor	06	25	aaa	HOU	1	3	7	0	44	53	28	2	17	31	5.73	1.59	28.4	292	3.5	6.3	1.8	0.4	35%	62%	61
Buckner,Billy	06	23	aa	KC	5	3	13	0	75	87	43	6	36	53	5.18	1.63	26.3	283	4.3	6.4	1.5	0.7	34%	68%	46
	07	24	aa	KC	10	10	31	0	124	156	71	16	33	81	5.12	1.52	17.8	301	2.4	5.9	2.5	1.1	34%	68%	48
Bueno,Francisley	06	26	aa	ATL	1	7	17	0	80	106	50	13	23	67	5.62	1.61	21.3	311	2.6	7.5	2.9	1.5	37%	68%	53
	07	27	a/a	ATL	5	6	25	0	132	198	74	14	33	74	5.08	1.75	24.7	339	2.3	5.0	2.2	1.0	38%	72%	34
Bukvich,Ryan	06	28	aaa	TEX	3	2	31	0	35	60	39	13	26	30	9.93	2.45	6.1	370	6.6	7.6	1.2	3.3	41%	65%	-48
	07	29	aaa	CHW	1	3	23	9	28	32	13	3	11	25	4.24	1.53	5.4	280	3.5	8.2	2.3	1.1	35%	75%	65
Bulger,Jason	06	28 b	aaa	LAA	2	2	27	4	34	34	20	0	15	35	5.28	1.42	5.5	253	3.9	9.3	2.4	0.0	36%	59%	110
	07	29	aa	LAA	5	2	49	10	52	75	35	5	31	55	6.03	2.04	5.3	330	5.4	9.5	1.8	0.9	43%	70%	57
Bullard,Jim	06	27	aa	TOR	3	2	42	2	39	59	24	6	24	33	5.54	2.11	4.7	339	5.5	7.6	1.4	1.3	41%	76%	22
Bullington,Bryan	07	27	aa	PIT	11	9	26	0	150	201	98	12	70	62	5.85	1.80	27.3	314	4.2	3.7	0.9	0.7	34%	67%	12
Bumatay,Mike	06	27	a/a	BOS	2	4	53	3	56	87	54	7	44	38	8.67	2.34	5.6	348	7.0	6.1	0.9	1.1	40%	62%	7
	07	28	a/a	OAK	4	2	55	3	52	74	44	6	38	46	7.56	2.14	4.8	326	6.6	8.0	1.2	1.0	40%	64%	33
Bumstead,Michael	06	29	a/a	TEX	1	2	34	5	56	60	20	0	26	39	3.12	1.52	7.3	267	4.1	6.3	1.5	0.0	33%	77%	72
	07	30	aa	TEX	1	2	20	1	31	81	69	11	30	15	19.91	3.59	10.1	474	8.7	4.5	0.5	3.3	49%	43%	-102
Bumstead,Nathan	06	24	aa	DET	7	14	27	0	158	216	120	17	85	105	6.84	1.91	28.2	319	4.9	6.0	1.2	1.0	37%	64%	24
Burch,Jason	06	24	aa	COL	3	4	45	0	63	75	46	7	28	43	6.61	1.63	6.4	290	4.0	6.1	1.5	1.0	33%	59%	35
Burke,Erick	06	29	aaa	SD	3	3	49	0	80	88	40	8	46	64	4.44	1.67	7.5	273	5.2	7.2	1.4	0.9	33%	75%	46
Burnett,Sean	06	24	aaa	PIT	8	11	25	0	120	168	97	16	49	39	7.27	1.81	22.7	324	3.7	2.9	0.8	1.2	34%	60%	-11
	07	25	aa	PIT	4	5	15	0	70	106	47	4	42	23	5.99	2.11	23.5	340	5.4	3.0	0.6	0.6	37%	71%	-1
Burnside,Adrian	06	30	aaa	TOR	3	0	33	0	33	35	20	5	15	25	5.36	1.52	4.5	266	4.2	6.9	1.7	1.5	30%	68%	33
	07	31	aa	SD	0	0	35	0	45	74	39	4	29	19	7.68	2.28	6.7	360	5.7	3.8	0.7	0.9	39%	65%	-6
Burns,Mike	06	28	aaa	CIN	6	1	40	0	56	61	16	4	14	41	2.58	1.34	6.0	272	2.2	6.6	2.9	0.7	33%	83%	81
	07	29	aaa	BOS	4	9	35	3	112	166	87	19	34	62	6.98	1.79	15.1	337	2.7	5.0	1.8	1.5	37%	62%	11
Burres,Brian	06	26	aaa	BAL	10	6	26	0	139	167	84	19	61	98	5.43	1.64	24.4	291	3.9	6.3	1.6	1.2	33%	69%	32
Burton,Jared	06	25	aa	OAK	6	5	53	1	74	88	43	8	29	50	5.27	1.58	6.3	289	3.5	6.1	1.7	0.9	34%	67%	42
Burton,TJ	07	24	aa	CLE	2	2	29	0	37	57	21	2	23	26	5.11	2.16	6.5	344	5.6	6.2	1.1	0.5	41%	76%	31
Bush,Paul	06	27	a/a	ATL	5	9	37	0	98	129	77	16	48	74	7.06	1.80	12.5	310	4.4	6.8	1.5	1.5	36%	62%	22
Butto,Francisco	06	26	a/a	NYY	3	2	32	0	78	98	39	6	36	47	4.48	1.71	11.3	300	4.1	5.4	1.3	0.6	35%	74%	36
Buzachero,Edward	06	25	aa	CLE	8	3	49	4	79	94	32	2	29	57	3.67	1.56	7.2	290	3.3	6.5	2.0	0.3	36%	75%	69
	07	26	a/a	CLE	6	8	52	3	77	113	62	9	23	41	7.26	1.77	7.0	335	2.7	4.8	1.8	1.0	37%	58%	23
Cali,Carmen	06	28	a/a	STL	1	6	50	1	66	103	41	6	39	41	5.63	2.16	6.7	349	5.3	5.6	1.0	0.8	40%	74%	17
	07	29	aaa	MIN	5	1	31	1	47	57	20	1	17	21	3.90	1.57	6.8	293	3.3	4.1	1.2	0.2	33%	74%	41
Camacho,Eddie	06	24	aa	NYM	3	4	53	1	79	92	46	7	27	49	5.27	1.50	6.6	284	3.1	5.6	1.8	0.8	33%	65%	45
	07	25	aa	NYM	2	1	37	3	58	76	30	7	18	41	4.65	1.61	7.1	308	2.8	6.3	2.3	1.0	36%	73%	48
Cameron,Kevin	06	27	aaa	MIN	6	4	40	9	66	69	33	3	31	53	4.49	1.51	7.3	264	4.2	7.3	1.7	0.4	33%	69%	69
Cameron,Ryan	06	29	aaa	PHI	6	2	45	7	59	68	36	7	37	35	5.52	1.79	6.2	283	5.7	5.3	0.9	1.0	32%	70%	19
	07	30	a/a	PHI	0	1	45	1	68	123	66	13	58	49	8.77	2.65	8.4	382	7.6	6.5	0.8	1.7	43%	68%	-14
Campbell,Brett	06	25	a/a	WAS	0	4	28	8	35	35	18	1	24	32	4.51	1.68	5.7	255	6.1	8.2	1.3	0.3	34%	71%	74
	07	26	aa	WAS	3	5	48	9	58	68	41	6	38	45	6.36	1.81	5.7	285	5.8	7.0	1.2	0.9	34%	64%	39
Campillo,Jorge	07	29	aa	SEA	9	6	24	0	149	225	79	15	55	67	4.75	1.88	29.8	341	3.3	4.0	1.2	0.9	37%	76%	10
Capellan,Jose	07	27	aaa	DET	3	3	26	4	37	42	24	4	15	22	5.75	1.56	6.4	281	3.8	5.4	1.4	1.0	32%	63%	32

					Actual				Major League Equivalents																
PITCHER	Yr	Age	Lev	Org	w	l	g	sv	ip	h	er	hr	bb	k	era	WHIP	bf/g	oob	ctl	dom	cmd	hr/9	h%	s%	bpv
Carlson,Jesse	06	26	a/a	TEX	6	5	53	3	69	93	44	11	24	41	5.77	1.69	6.0	315	3.2	5.3	1.7	1.4	35%	68%	18
	07	27	aa	TOR	8	2	58	6	70	102	54	6	21	60	6.94	1.75	5.6	333	2.7	7.7	2.9	0.7	41%	59%	73
Carlyle,Buddy	07	30 b	aaa	ATL	5	2	9	0	48	52	20	7	11	44	3.69	1.30	22.6	268	2.1	8.2	4.0	1.2	33%	76%	97
Carrara,Giovanni	06	39	aaa	PIT	3	2	30	4	40	35	20	4	17	27	4.49	1.29	5.6	229	3.8	6.0	1.6	0.9	26%	67%	50
Carrasco,Carlos	07	21	aa	PHI	6	4	14	0	70	70	43	10	44	44	5.50	1.63	22.8	256	5.6	5.7	1.0	1.3	28%	69%	19
Carrasco,D.J.	07	30	aa	ARI	5	14	34	0	137	309	184	29	86	64	12.10	2.88	23.4	435	5.6	4.2	0.7	1.9	46%	57%	-48
Carrillo,Cesar	06	22	a/a	SD	1	3	10	0	53	51	21	4	18	39	3.56	1.30	22.4	248	3.1	6.6	2.2	0.7	30%	74%	70
Carter,Lance	06	32	aaa	LA	2	4	45	13	57	63	26	7	16	41	4.15	1.38	5.5	275	2.5	6.4	2.6	1.2	32%	74%	58
Carvajal,Marcos	06	22	aa	TAM	2	2	39	0	72	84	46	9	44	59	5.74	1.78	8.7	285	5.5	7.4	1.3	1.1	34%	69%	37
	07	23	aa	NYM	5	10	28	0	119	138	82	13	63	77	6.24	1.69	19.6	284	4.8	5.8	1.2	1.0	33%	63%	28
Casadiego,Gerardo	06	26	aa	NYY	2	3	22	1	34	33	12	1	17	24	3.24	1.47	6.8	251	4.4	6.4	1.5	0.3	31%	77%	65
	07	27	aa	COL	4	3	41	9	50	70	33	13	26	43	5.98	1.92	5.9	324	4.7	7.6	1.6	2.3	37%	75%	2
Casilla,Santiago	06	24 a	aaa	OAK	2	0	25	4	33	27	13	2	9	27	3.55	1.09	5.3	219	2.5	7.4	3.0	0.5	27%	68%	102
	07	27	aa	OAK	2	1	22	3	24	22	14	1	16	21	5.42	1.56	4.9	236	5.9	7.8	1.3	0.5	30%	63%	69
Cassel,Jack	06	26	a/a	SD	9	8	30	0	155	196	91	14	51	95	5.29	1.59	23.3	302	3.0	5.5	1.8	0.8	35%	67%	41
	07	27	aa	SD	7	14	27	0	156	277	98	17	53	85	5.62	2.11	29.1	378	3.1	4.9	1.6	1.0	42%	74%	13
Cassidy,Scott	07	32	aa	SD	4	4	40	10	40	74	41	6	18	37	9.26	2.29	5.2	388	4.0	8.2	2.1	1.3	47%	59%	30
Castellanos,Hugo	07	27	aa	STL	4	3	46	0	67	81	34	8	43	32	4.52	1.85	7.0	291	5.8	4.3	0.7	1.1	32%	78%	5
Castellanos,Jonathan	06	25	a/a	ARI	3	1	25	0	38	42	25	6	15	20	5.98	1.50	6.7	275	3.5	4.7	1.4	1.5	29%	63%	12
	07	26	aa	ARI	5	6	13	0	68	109	43	7	22	29	5.62	1.92	25.4	354	2.9	3.8	1.3	0.9	39%	71%	7
Castillo,Osbek	07	27	aa	ARI	1	3	29	1	67	74	62	9	60	45	8.31	1.98	11.4	273	8.0	6.1	0.8	1.2	31%	57%	16
Castro,Fabio	07	23	a/a	PHI	7	5	32	2	75	75	38	9	40	61	4.56	1.53	10.4	255	4.8	7.3	1.5	1.1	30%	73%	48
Cate,Troy	07	27	aa	STL	2	5	33	0	71	111	70	16	33	46	8.88	2.04	10.7	349	4.2	5.8	1.4	2.0	38%	58%	-12
Cavazos,Andy	06	26 a	aaa	STL	1	5	44	4	56	56	28	2	16	48	4.54	1.28	5.4	253	2.6	7.6	2.9	0.3	33%	62%	102
	07	27	aa	STL	2	5	44	0	47	51	22	6	29	37	4.16	1.68	4.9	268	5.5	7.0	1.3	1.1	32%	78%	37
Cave,Kevin	06	26	aa	FLA	3	2	43	5	51	77	38	8	45	34	6.68	2.38	6.3	340	7.9	6.0	0.8	1.4	38%	74%	-4
Cedeno,Juan	06	23	aa	KC	2	9	37	2	90	102	64	7	72	55	6.38	1.93	11.8	280	7.2	5.5	0.8	0.7	32%	66%	27
	07	24	aa	KC	3	2	35	0	69	108	64	11	28	39	8.35	1.98	9.7	349	3.7	5.1	1.4	1.4	39%	58%	3
Cerda,Jaime	06	28	aaa	COL	3	3	36	1	45	59	39	11	26	33	7.76	1.89	6.0	309	5.2	6.6	1.3	2.1	34%	62%	-3
Chamberlain,Joba	07	22 a	a/a	NYY	5	2	11	0	48	45	20	5	17	70	3.74	1.29	18.4	243	3.2	13.1	4.1	0.9	38%	74%	143
Chavez,Jesse	06	23	a/a	PIT	4	6	51	4	78	86	47	6	37	74	5.42	1.58	6.9	274	4.3	8.5	2.0	0.7	35%	65%	73
	07	24	aa	PIT	3	3	46	2	80	113	44	4	19	51	4.97	1.64	7.9	325	2.1	5.8	2.7	0.5	38%	69%	67
Chavez,Wilton	06	28	aaa	CHC	3	3	13	0	31	42	31	5	15	14	9.05	1.84	11.3	317	4.4	4.1	0.9	1.6	33%	50%	-11
	06	28	aaa	MIL	6	4	40	0	85	108	62	14	45	53	6.60	1.79	10.0	302	4.8	5.6	1.2	1.5	33%	65%	9
Chenard,Kenneth	07	29	aa	TEX	3	8	34	2	68	123	85	17	59	58	11.26	2.66	11.2	381	7.7	7.6	1.0	2.3	44%	59%	-23
Cherry,Rocky	06	27	a/a	CHC	5	1	33	2	51	67	25	5	20	40	4.45	1.69	7.1	309	3.4	7.0	2.0	0.8	37%	75%	54
	07	28	aa	CHC	2	0	43	7	51	73	41	8	24	38	7.28	1.89	5.7	327	4.2	6.6	1.6	1.3	38%	62%	23
Chiasson,Scott	06	29	aaa	CIN	3	2	60	29	61	54	20	4	34	37	2.91	1.44	4.4	232	5.0	5.5	1.1	0.6	27%	82%	45
Chiavacci,Ron	06	29	a/a	PIT	5	7	27	0	99	144	72	16	38	57	6.53	1.83	17.5	332	3.4	5.2	1.5	1.4	37%	66%	9
	07	30	aaa	DET	12	6	26	0	151	194	82	18	48	98	4.90	1.60	26.3	306	2.8	5.8	2.1	1.1	35%	71%	40
Chick,Travis	06	22	aa	CIN	8	7	27	0	151	161	87	18	75	101	5.18	1.56	25.1	267	4.5	6.0	1.3	1.1	31%	68%	34
	07	23	aa	SEA	6	7	20	0	91	107	65	13	43	64	6.42	1.65	20.8	287	4.3	6.3	1.5	1.3	33%	62%	27
Chico,Matt	06	23	aa	WAS	9	2	17	0	103	108	37	11	32	62	3.24	1.36	25.9	265	2.8	5.4	1.9	1.0	30%	80%	46
Childers,Jason	06	32	aaa	TAM	2	3	39	2	52	73	40	9	24	31	6.91	1.86	6.4	323	4.2	5.4	1.3	1.6	35%	65%	1
	07	33	aaa	CHW	3	2	46	0	53	67	34	9	23	32	5.72	1.71	5.3	303	3.9	5.5	1.4	1.6	33%	70%	8
Childers,Matt	06	28	a/a	NYY	4	7	36	0	111	162	90	20	37	57	7.26	1.79	14.5	333	3.0	4.6	1.5	1.6	36%	61%	1
	07	29	aaa	PHI	7	4	19	0	102	173	81	15	29	58	7.10	1.98	26.3	367	2.6	5.1	2.0	1.3	41%	65%	14
Choate,Randy	06	31	aaa	ARI	6	0	43	8	45	46	14	0	11	37	2.72	1.26	4.4	260	2.1	7.4	3.5	0.0	34%	76%	121
	07	32	aa	ARI	3	1	54	3	62	92	32	5	19	45	4.60	1.78	5.4	336	2.7	6.5	2.4	0.7	40%	74%	57
Choi,Hyang-Nam	06	36	aaa	CLE	8	5	34	0	106	117	38	5	39	87	3.21	1.47	13.7	274	3.3	7.4	2.2	0.4	35%	78%	78
Christensen,Daniel	07	24	aa	KC	3	15	27	0	140	211	126	24	58	83	8.11	1.91	25.1	340	3.7	5.3	1.4	1.6	37%	58%	2
Chulk,Vinnie	06	28	aaa	TOR	3	2	19	1	32	25	12	5	16	35	3.26	1.28	7.1	213	4.4	9.9	2.2	1.5	27%	82%	74
Clippard,Tyler	06	22	aa	NYY	12	10	28	0	166	144	85	18	60	145	4.61	1.23	24.6	229	3.3	7.9	2.4	1.0	28%	64%	78
	07	23	a/a	NYY	6	5	20	0	96	126	65	15	50	70	6.09	1.83	22.8	310	4.7	6.6	1.4	1.4	36%	69%	20
Clontz,Brad	06	35	aaa	FLA	6	5	57	23	58	64	25	4	27	47	3.92	1.58	4.6	275	4.2	7.2	1.7	0.7	34%	76%	59
Collazo,Willie	06	27	a/a	NYM	10	9	25	0	160	203	98	14	34	81	5.50	1.49	28.2	303	1.9	4.6	2.4	0.8	34%	63%	47
	07	28	aa	NYM	6	5	53	4	98	123	37	6	22	50	3.42	1.47	8.1	300	2.0	4.6	2.3	0.6	34%	77%	54
Colome,Jesus	06	29	a/a	NYY	3	1	28	0	38	52	24	6	22	19	5.57	1.95	6.6	318	5.3	4.4	0.8	1.4	34%	74%	-6
Colyer,Steve	06	28	a/a	COL	2	3	54	1	63	83	62	14	56	42	8.85	2.20	6.0	310	8.0	6.0	0.7	2.0	34%	61%	-15
Condrey,Clay	06	31	aaa	PHI	4	2	39	6	51	59	19	2	18	21	3.33	1.50	5.8	283	3.1	3.6	1.2	0.4	31%	78%	33
Connolly,Jonathan	06	23	a/a	DET	3	4	11	0	63	97	57	7	17	33	8.12	1.80	27.1	345	2.4	4.7	1.9	1.0	38%	53%	25
	07	24	a/a	DET	8	8	25	1	135	179	93	24	35	70	6.19	1.59	24.3	313	2.3	4.7	2.0	1.6	33%	64%	15
Connolly,Michael	06	24	a/a	PIT	8	10	29	0	136	171	109	24	63	81	7.22	1.72	21.8	301	4.2	5.3	1.3	1.6	33%	59%	7
	07	25	aa	KC	4	7	29	1	110	167	88	14	37	57	7.18	1.85	18.1	341	3.0	4.6	1.5	1.2	37%	61%	12
Cooper,Brian	06	32	aaa	SF	4	9	27	0	123	164	76	22	41	58	5.54	1.67	20.9	314	3.0	4.2	1.4	1.6	33%	71%	-1
Cooper,Mike D.	07	24	aa	STL	1	2	21	0	28	41	28	6	20	17	8.95	2.17	6.8	335	6.3	5.6	0.9	2.0	36%	60%	-19
Corcoran,Roy	06	26 b	a/a	WAS	2	6	49	27	59	46	13	1	40	59	2.03	1.45	5.3	209	6.1	8.9	1.5	0.2	29%	86%	92
	07	27	aa	FLA	4	4	53	15	61	84	34	1	41	40	4.98	2.05	5.7	321	6.0	5.9	1.0	0.2	39%	74%	41
Corcoran,Tim	06	28	aaa	TAM	5	1	19	1	37	38	11	2	11	25	2.60	1.30	8.3	257	2.6	6.1	2.3	0.5	31%	81%	73
	07	29	a/a	TAM	3	2	24	3	32	35	17	2	20	24	4.77	1.70	6.2	273	5.5	6.6	1.2	0.7	33%	72%	45
Corey,Bryan	06	33	a/a	BOS	1	0	28	15	37	41	13	3	11	31	3.23	1.41	5.7	275	2.7	7.4	2.8	0.8	34%	80%	78
	07	34	aaa	BOS	6	8	58	3	68	73	40	7	22	54	5.28	1.39	5.1	267	2.9	7.1	2.4	1.0	32%	63%	67
Corey,Mark	06	32	aaa	NYY	7	4	53	8	81	97	53	5	31	53	5.85	1.57	6.9	291	3.4	5.9	1.7	0.6	34%	61%	51
	07	33	aa	PIT	1	1	23	0	32	48	21	1	29	16	5.92	2.41	7.5	339	8.2	4.5	0.5	0.3	39%	74%	16
Cormier,Lance	06	26	aaa	ATL	4	3	9	0	54	81	34	5	15	23	5.65	1.79	28.4	340	2.6	3.9	1.5	0.9	37%	69%	16
	07	27	a/a	ATL	5	3	12	0	60	86	36	7	18	28	5.34	1.74	23.3	330	2.8	4.2	1.5	1.0	36%	71%	15
Corpas,Manuel	06	24 a	a/a	COL	2	1	42	19	45	32	6	1	6	36	1.20	0.84	4.0	195	1.2	7.2	6.0	0.2	25%	86%	179
Cortez,Renee	06	24	aaa	SEA	5	3	31	5	51	68	28	3	29	45	4.92	1.89	8.0	313	5.1	7.9	1.6	0.5	40%	73%	57
Cotts,Neal	07	28	aa	CHC	2	2	24	0	50	60	41	6	37	33	7.36	1.95	10.2	292	6.7	6.0	0.9	1.1	33%	62%	19
Coutlangus,Jon	06	26	a/a	CIN	1	3	51	9	65	54	28	0	37	47	3.92	1.39	5.5	220	5.1	6.4	1.3	0.0	28%	69%	76

Major League Equivalent Statistics

					Actual				Major League Equivalents																
PITCHER	Yr	Age	Lev	Org	w	l	g	sv	ip	h	er	hr	bb	k	era	WHIP	bf/g	oob	ctl	dom	cmd	hr/9	h%	s%	bpv
Cox,Benjamin	07	26	aa	SF	0	8	17	0	54	75	37	5	32	28	6.13	1.98	15.6	321	5.4	4.6	0.9	0.8	36%	69%	14
Cox,J.B.	06	22	aa	NYY	6	2	41	3	77	66	21	3	26	50	2.45	1.19	7.7	227	3.0	5.8	1.9	0.4	27%	80%	75
Cramer,Bob	07	28	aa	OAK	5	1	12	0	52	61	16	4	12	36	2.71	1.41	18.8	288	2.1	6.2	3.0	0.6	34%	83%	78
Crawford,Tristan	06	24	aa	MIN	6	5	46	2	98	114	58	11	39	78	5.31	1.56	9.5	284	3.6	7.1	2.0	1.0	34%	67%	54
	07	25	a/a	MIN	8	6	30	0	84	129	69	16	35	51	7.43	1.95	13.7	345	3.7	5.5	1.5	1.7	38%	64%	-1
Cromer,Jason	06	26	a/a	TAM	4	6	32	0	106	132	51	6	52	64	4.29	1.73	15.4	298	4.4	5.4	1.2	0.5	35%	75%	38
	07	27	aa	KC	3	8	36	1	85	138	71	6	32	44	7.53	2.00	11.6	357	3.4	4.6	1.4	0.6	40%	60%	21
Crowder,Justin	06	27	aa	OAK	1	2	41	2	47	67	35	8	22	31	6.69	1.90	5.5	330	4.2	5.9	1.4	1.6	37%	67%	6
Crowell,Jim	06	32	aaa	PHI	2	3	40	2	73	112	49	8	25	34	6.08	1.87	8.8	343	3.1	4.2	1.4	1.0	37%	68%	9
	07	33	aaa	TOR	1	4	28	0	56	93	62	4	29	19	9.98	2.18	10.2	362	4.7	3.1	0.6	0.7	39%	51%	-6
Cruceta,Francisco	06	25	aaa	SEA	13	9	28	0	160	170	91	27	79	164	5.11	1.55	25.6	266	4.4	9.2	2.1	1.5	33%	71%	55
	07	26	aaa	TEX	3	0	25	1	65	52	33	3	46	52	4.60	1.50	11.5	214	6.3	7.2	1.1	0.5	27%	68%	65
Cueto,Johnny	07	22 a	a/a	CIN	8	4	14	0	83	83	31	10	12	88	3.41	1.15	24.1	255	1.3	9.6	7.1	1.0	33%	74%	180
Cullen,Ryan	06	27	a/a	NYM	5	4	39	1	68	74	39	7	21	45	5.15	1.41	7.5	273	2.8	6.0	2.1	0.9	32%	64%	54
	07	28	aa	NYM	2	5	48	0	80	116	41	13	19	45	4.61	1.69	7.7	331	2.2	5.0	2.3	1.5	36%	77%	23
Cummings,Jeremy	06	30	aaa	PHI	8	6	25	0	138	169	104	31	58	77	6.80	1.65	25.2	296	3.8	5.0	1.3	2.0	31%	63%	-6
	07	31	aaa	TOR	6	8	29	0	120	160	78	18	40	77	5.83	1.67	19.0	313	3.0	5.7	1.9	1.3	35%	67%	27
Curtis,Dan	06	27	a/a	ATL	5	10	28	0	153	218	119	13	80	83	6.99	1.94	26.6	328	4.7	4.9	1.0	0.8	37%	63%	17
Cyr,Eric	07	29	aa	LA	9	9	28	0	145	224	95	21	51	74	5.89	1.89	25.0	345	3.2	4.6	1.4	1.3	38%	71%	4
Daigle,Casey	06	26	aaa	ARI	3	5	42	4	48	68	29	7	16	36	5.49	1.75	5.3	326	3.0	6.7	2.2	1.3	38%	71%	37
	07	26	aa	ARI	9	5	41	0	107	208	116	26	36	73	9.76	2.28	13.6	399	3.0	6.1	2.1	2.2	44%	59%	-12
Daley,Matt	07	25	aa	COL	2	6	43	0	95	112	57	18	24	68	5.36	1.44	9.6	288	2.3	6.4	2.8	1.7	32%	67%	43
Daniels,Adam	07	25	aa	STL	5	7	15	0	72	103	60	6	36	34	7.48	1.92	23.3	329	4.4	4.3	1.0	0.7	37%	59%	14
Danks,John	06	21	a/a	TEX	9	9	27	0	140	166	89	30	56	140	5.69	1.59	23.4	288	3.6	9.0	2.5	1.9	35%	69%	46
Darensbourg,Vic	06	36	aaa	CLE	1	5	33	0	41	51	24	2	17	33	5.30	1.64	5.7	296	3.7	7.3	2.0	0.5	37%	66%	67
	07	37	aaa	DET	6	2	50	0	52	54	14	0	18	34	2.36	1.37	4.5	261	3.1	5.9	1.9	0.0	32%	81%	78
Davidson,Daniel	06	26	a/a	LAA	3	10	33	0	136	197	93	16	47	64	6.12	1.79	19.5	331	3.1	4.2	1.3	1.0	36%	66%	11
	07	27	aa	LAA	2	4	7	0	43	46	15	5	9	18	3.11	1.28	25.9	267	1.9	3.8	2.0	1.0	29%	80%	37
Davidson,David	07	23	aa	PIT	4	1	45	2	67	60	37	3	33	52	4.98	1.38	6.4	234	4.4	7.0	1.6	0.4	29%	62%	71
Davis,Allen	06	31	a/a	PHI	8	8	26	0	140	214	118	39	48	65	7.57	1.87	25.8	344	3.1	4.2	1.4	2.5	35%	65%	-35
	07	32	aa	PHI	3	2	31	1	47	84	35	6	21	28	6.76	2.23	7.8	378	4.1	5.4	1.3	1.1	43%	70%	6
Davis,Kane	07	32	aaa	PHI	3	3	41	4	53	57	24	3	28	48	4.11	1.61	5.9	269	4.8	8.2	1.7	0.5	35%	74%	70
Davis,Lance	06	30	a/a	DET	3	3	30	1	69	115	54	10	16	26	7.00	1.90	11.1	363	2.1	3.3	1.6	1.3	38%	64%	-4
Davis,Wade	07	22	aa	TAM	7	3	14	0	80	84	34	3	31	71	3.83	1.44	24.9	264	3.5	8.0	2.3	0.3	34%	72%	88
Day,Dewon	07	27	a/a	CHW	2	5	34	2	39	51	32	1	39	49	7.41	2.29	6.0	307	9.0	11.2	1.2	0.3	45%	65%	79
Day,Zach	07	29	aa	KC	1	1	11	0	36	52	27	3	35	8	6.63	2.39	17.5	330	8.6	1.9	0.2	0.7	34%	71%	-15
De Jong,Jordan	06	28	a/a	TOR	6	0	45	0	76	91	39	8	34	53	4.62	1.64	7.7	290	4.1	6.3	1.5	1.0	34%	74%	38
	07	28	a/a	TOR	6	5	38	2	66	75	35	6	32	58	4.80	1.62	7.9	280	4.3	7.9	1.8	0.8	35%	71%	60
De La Cruz,Eulogio	07	24	a/a	DET	7	5	33	0	104	114	54	6	38	71	4.67	1.46	13.8	273	3.3	6.1	1.9	0.5	33%	67%	61
De La Cruz,Jose	07	24	aa	SEA	1	2	42	5	61	74	38	4	36	40	5.58	1.79	6.9	292	5.3	5.9	1.1	0.6	34%	68%	37
De La Cruz,Julio	07	27	aa	PHI	1	4	48	6	64	85	48	6	37	44	6.77	1.90	6.4	312	5.2	6.1	1.2	0.8	37%	63%	30
De La Cruz,Sandy	06	19	a/a	DET	5	6	39	2	107	110	50	4	42	90	4.17	1.42	11.9	261	3.5	7.5	2.1	0.4	33%	69%	82
De La Rosa,Jorge	06	26 a	aa	MIL	3	1	6	0	30	42	12	1	3	18	3.67	1.52	22.2	325	1.0	5.4	5.4	0.3	38%	75%	126
De Los Santos,Richa	07	23	a/a	TAM	6	5	46	0	87	102	43	7	19	38	4.45	1.39	8.2	286	2.0	3.9	2.0	0.7	31%	68%	42
De Los Santos,Valeri	06	34	aaa	CHW	1	1	19	0	56	59	26	9	26	38	4.21	1.52	13.1	264	4.2	6.1	1.4	1.5	29%	78%	23
De Paula,Jorge	06	28	a/a	NYY	4	14	24	0	132	215	100	24	39	57	6.82	1.92	26.6	358	2.7	3.9	1.4	1.6	38%	67%	-12
Deago,Roger	06	29	a/a	SD	10	8	28	0	124	159	83	16	65	61	6.01	1.80	20.9	304	4.7	4.4	0.9	1.1	33%	68%	6
	07	30	aa	SD	6	8	34	0	132	220	124	21	74	75	8.47	2.23	20.0	363	5.1	5.1	1.0	1.5	40%	62%	-10
Deaton,Kevin	07	26	aa	OAK	0	4	6	0	34	55	36	7	14	17	9.40	2.02	28.1	357	3.6	4.4	1.2	1.8	38%	54%	-20
Debarr,Nick	07	24	aa	TAM	3	4	53	4	83	94	41	6	36	44	4.45	1.56	7.0	279	3.9	4.7	1.2	0.7	31%	72%	33
Deduno,Samuel	07	24	aa	COL	5	8	21	0	124	154	106	18	69	104	7.72	1.80	27.9	298	5.0	7.5	1.5	1.3	36%	57%	33
DeHoyos,Gabe	06	26	aa	KC	2	1	22	7	33	24	7	1	20	21	1.88	1.32	6.4	200	5.3	5.7	1.1	0.3	24%	86%	62
	07	27	aa	KC	6	1	38	4	69	81	29	5	29	39	3.76	1.58	8.2	285	3.8	5.1	1.3	0.6	33%	77%	38
DeJean,Mike	07	37	aa	COL	0	3	20	0	30	62	42	15	11	18	12.62	2.42	8.1	414	3.2	5.3	1.7	4.6	41%	53%	-97
Delcarmen,Manny	07	26 a	aaa	BOS	3	2	20	0	29	34	15	1	15	32	4.69	1.70	6.7	288	4.7	9.8	2.1	0.3	40%	71%	91
Delgado,Jesus	07	23	aa	FLA	5	7	31	1	93	111	60	6	48	67	5.77	1.71	13.9	290	4.7	6.5	1.4	0.6	35%	65%	47
Demaria,Chris	06	26	aaa	MIL	4	0	38	1	51	59	23	5	19	43	3.99	1.51	6.0	282	3.3	7.5	2.3	0.9	35%	76%	65
Denham,Dan	06	24	a/a	CLE	7	4	32	0	91	124	74	6	52	48	7.31	1.93	13.8	318	5.1	4.7	0.9	0.6	36%	60%	21
DePaula,Jorge	07	29	aa	COL	9	6	20	0	104	204	125	26	59	39	10.81	2.52	28.3	401	5.1	3.4	0.7	2.3	41%	58%	-59
Depaula,Julio	07	25	aaa	MIN	12	5	49	2	83	83	39	10	31	51	4.22	1.37	7.3	255	3.4	5.5	1.6	1.1	28%	72%	39
	06	24	aa	MIN	2	2	43	7	66	73	27	1	31	35	3.64	1.57	6.9	275	4.2	4.7	1.1	0.1	32%	75%	48
DePriest,Derrick	06	30	aa	KC	0	4	24	1	34	63	39	4	21	15	10.18	2.46	7.7	386	5.6	3.9	0.7	1.1	42%	55%	-15
Desalvo,Matt	07	27	aaa	NYY	9	5	20	0	113	115	46	5	61	81	3.69	1.55	25.3	258	4.9	6.4	1.3	0.4	31%	76%	57
	06	26	a/a	NYY	6	10	27	0	116	168	121	14	111	61	9.38	2.40	22.9	331	8.6	4.7	0.6	1.1	37%	60%	-5
Deschenes,Marc	06	34	aaa	BOS	8	5	29	0	117	149	88	11	41	61	6.80	1.63	18.4	304	3.2	4.7	1.5	0.8	34%	57%	29
Devaney,Michael	06	24	aa	NYM	4	2	11	0	53	51	26	6	39	35	4.47	1.69	22.2	246	6.6	6.0	0.9	1.1	28%	76%	28
	07	25	aa	NYM	6	9	22	0	104	130	72	12	47	55	6.25	1.70	21.8	300	4.0	4.8	1.2	1.1	33%	64%	17
Devine,Joey	07	24 a	a/a	ATL	5	4	50	20	57	49	15	2	21	65	2.44	1.23	4.7	229	3.3	10.3	3.2	0.3	33%	80%	127
Deza,Fredy	07	25	aa	BAL	7	8	36	0	124	157	77	25	43	84	5.58	1.61	15.6	302	3.1	6.1	1.9	1.8	33%	70%	17
Diamond,Thomas	06	24	aa	TEX	12	5	27	0	129	128	84	20	82	121	5.82	1.63	21.8	253	5.7	8.5	1.5	1.4	31%	66%	45
Diaz,Amalio	07	21	aa	LAA	0	2	6	0	37	50	24	3	7	13	5.82	1.54	27.6	316	1.7	3.2	1.9	0.7	34%	61%	28
Diaz,Felix	07	27	a/a	BOS	9	8	30	0	129	192	120	26	52	77	8.33	1.89	20.7	337	3.6	5.3	1.5	1.8	37%	57%	-5
Diaz,Jose	06	23	a/a	KC	4	3	49	4	82	68	36	6	56	79	3.95	1.51	7.4	221	6.1	8.7	1.4	0.7	29%	75%	73
Dickey,R.A.	06	32	aaa	TEX	9	8	22	1	131	180	115	27	53	50	7.87	1.77	28.0	320	3.6	3.5	1.0	1.9	32%	57%	-24
	07	33	aaa	MIL	13	6	31	0	169	196	94	22	67	103	4.99	1.56	24.4	284	3.6	5.5	1.5	1.2	32%	70%	28
Difelice,Mark	07	31	a/a	MIL	10	3	36	0	124	123	44	11	18	101	3.22	1.14	14.0	254	1.3	7.3	5.7	0.8	31%	74%	143
Dillard,Tim	06	23	aa	MIL	10	7	29	0	163	212	84	13	41	93	4.61	1.56	25.2	309	2.3	5.1	2.3	0.7	35%	71%	49
	07	24	aaa	MIL	8	4	34	0	133	196	91	15	39	56	6.16	1.77	18.3	335	2.6	3.8	1.4	1.0	36%	65%	10
Dittler,Jake	06	24	aaa	CLE	5	12	25	0	130	178	87	6	52	48	6.02	1.77	24.4	319	3.6	3.3	0.9	0.4	35%	64%	18
	07	25	a/a	CLE	9	2	27	0	92	121	58	5	33	43	5.64	1.67	15.7	309	3.2	4.2	1.3	0.5	35%	65%	30

					Actual				Major League Equivalents																
PITCHER	Yr	Age	Lev	Org	w	l	g	sv	ip	h	er	hr	bb	k	era	WHIP	bf/g	oob	ctl	dom	cmd	hr/9	h%	s%	bpv
Dobies,Andrew	06	23	aa	BOS	1	2	6	0	34	47	21	7	7	14	5.44	1.60	25.7	323	1.9	3.6	1.9	1.9	33%	72%	-6
	07	24	aa	BOS	4	3	34	0	75	109	58	11	29	57	6.93	1.85	10.5	333	3.5	6.8	1.9	1.3	39%	63%	32
Dohmann,Scott	07	30	aaa	TAM	4	1	37	5	48	49	16	3	15	38	3.08	1.35	5.6	260	2.9	7.1	2.5	0.6	32%	79%	80
Dominguez,Juan	06	26	aaa	OAK	5	10	17	0	87	116	64	10	37	40	6.60	1.76	24.0	314	3.8	4.1	1.1	1.1	34%	63%	7
Done,Juan	07	27	aa	SEA	4	11	32	1	107	149	76	10	55	42	6.37	1.91	16.2	323	4.6	3.5	0.8	0.9	35%	66%	1
Dorman,Rich	06	28	aaa	SEA	7	7	31	1	118	122	75	15	74	95	5.73	1.66	17.4	260	5.6	7.2	1.3	1.1	31%	67%	39
Douglass,Chance	06	23	aa	HOU	7	8	28	0	161	165	76	15	56	86	4.25	1.37	24.7	260	3.1	4.8	1.5	0.8	29%	70%	39
	07	24	aa	HOU	6	9	27	0	145	176	88	18	61	82	5.43	1.63	24.5	294	3.8	5.1	1.4	1.1	33%	68%	23
Doyne,Cory	06	25	a/a	STL	1	7	56	6	71	61	32	1	47	67	4.00	1.52	5.6	227	6.0	8.4	1.4	0.1	31%	72%	86
Doyne,Michael	07	26 b	aaa	BAL	0	1	42	29	44	29	15	0	18	42	3.16	1.05	4.2	183	3.6	8.5	2.4	0.0	26%	67%	119
Driskill,Travis	06	35	aaa	HOU	4	8	52	15	64	67	28	9	14	47	3.98	1.26	5.2	264	1.9	6.5	3.4	1.3	30%	74%	73
	07	36	aa	HOU	4	3	44	9	65	80	38	9	19	45	5.20	1.52	6.6	296	2.6	6.2	2.4	1.3	34%	68%	44
DuBose,Eric	06	30	a/a	BAL	10	5	28	0	123	175	93	16	74	70	6.77	2.02	21.7	328	5.4	5.1	0.9	1.2	36%	67%	4
	07	31	a/a	CLE	5	8	22	0	100	158	91	13	52	65	8.20	2.10	22.8	351	4.7	5.8	1.2	1.2	40%	60%	10
Duckworth,Brandon	06	31	aaa	PIT	8	3	12	0	74	92	31	6	27	43	3.78	1.60	27.9	299	3.2	5.2	1.6	0.7	34%	77%	40
Duensing,Brian	06	24	aa	MIN	1	2	10	0	49	64	28	8	21	24	5.10	1.72	22.8	308	3.8	4.4	1.2	1.5	33%	74%	-1
	07	25	a/a	MIN	15	6	28	0	167	198	76	18	41	98	4.11	1.43	26.0	289	2.2	5.3	2.4	0.9	33%	73%	51
Dumatrait,Phil	06	25	a/a	CIN	8	11	26	0	137	183	95	20	64	82	6.22	1.80	24.9	314	4.2	5.4	1.3	1.3	35%	67%	12
	07	26	aaa	CIN	10	6	22	0	125	139	66	13	53	63	4.75	1.53	25.3	276	3.8	4.5	1.2	1.0	30%	71%	23
Dunn,Scott	06	28	aaa	TAM	4	2	38	0	66	72	28	2	32	56	3.81	1.58	7.8	272	4.4	7.6	1.7	0.3	35%	75%	74
Durbin,Chad	06	29	aaa	DET	11	8	28	0	185	215	89	20	51	120	4.34	1.44	28.8	285	2.5	5.8	2.4	1.0	33%	72%	53
Durbin,J.D.	06	25	aaa	MIN	4	3	16	0	89	84	34	4	58	69	3.44	1.60	25.1	244	5.9	7.0	1.2	0.4	31%	78%	61
	07	26	aaa	PHI	2	4	10	0	59	79	38	12	22	38	5.85	1.71	27.4	313	3.4	5.7	1.7	1.8	34%	70%	7
Echols,Justin	06	26	a/a	WAS	6	8	25	0	124	148	81	16	93	92	5.88	1.94	24.2	290	6.8	6.7	1.0	1.1	34%	71%	24
Eckert,Harold	06	29	aaa	LA	5	10	29	1	119	186	109	26	69	67	8.23	2.14	20.8	348	5.2	5.1	1.0	2.0	37%	64%	-24
Edens,Kyle	06	27	aa	LAA	3	3	25	1	47	82	39	6	31	23	7.47	2.39	10.0	372	5.9	4.5	0.8	1.1	41%	69%	-10
Edwards,Bill	06	26	aa	LAA	8	7	52	4	80	108	57	4	39	34	6.37	1.83	7.3	315	4.4	3.8	0.9	0.5	35%	63%	18
	07	27	aa	LAA	4	4	54	4	68	94	52	8	43	36	6.84	2.01	6.2	322	5.6	4.7	0.8	1.1	36%	66%	5
Edwards,Bryan	06	27	aa	NYM	4	8	21	0	87	125	77	10	46	38	7.96	1.96	20.3	330	4.7	3.9	0.8	1.0	36%	58%	0
Egbert,John	07	24 a	aa	CHW	12	8	28	0	161	178	81	5	49	140	4.53	1.41	24.9	274	2.8	7.8	2.8	0.3	35%	66%	97
Ekstrom,Michael	06	23	aa	SD	3	7	14	0	84	104	46	2	21	42	4.96	1.48	26.5	298	2.2	4.5	2.0	0.2	34%	64%	58
	07	24	aa	SD	7	10	27	0	143	218	95	6	52	81	5.95	1.88	25.5	343	3.2	5.1	1.6	0.4	40%	66%	38
Elarton,Scott	07	32	a/a	CLE	4	4	19	0	71	98	56	17	28	31	7.04	1.77	17.5	320	3.5	3.9	1.1	2.1	32%	64%	-26
Elbert,Scott	06	21	aa	LA	6	4	11	0	62	47	33	13	47	64	4.78	1.51	25.0	206	6.8	9.3	1.4	1.9	23%	75%	42
Elder,Dave	06	31	aaa	KC	1	0	20	1	38	53	15	1	19	23	3.49	1.88	9.1	322	4.5	5.4	1.2	0.2	38%	81%	41
Elliott,Matthew	07	23	aa	ARI	1	6	46	5	63	72	39	8	34	59	5.60	1.69	6.3	282	4.9	8.5	1.7	1.2	35%	68%	51
Ellis,Jonathan	07	25	aa	SD	3	4	55	2	51	57	34	8	35	33	5.93	1.79	4.4	276	6.1	5.9	1.0	1.5	30%	70%	11
Emanuel,Brandon	06	31	aaa	CHC	1	2	54	1	75	107	46	14	31	50	5.45	1.83	6.6	327	3.7	5.9	1.6	1.7	36%	75%	7
Embry,Byron	07	31	aa	SEA	0	6	25	4	36	51	32	5	38	31	7.92	2.44	7.7	324	9.4	7.8	0.8	1.2	39%	68%	20
Ennis,John	06	27	a/a	DET	2	4	46	13	63	76	28	3	28	44	3.97	1.64	6.2	291	4.0	6.3	1.6	0.5	35%	76%	54
	07	28	aaa	PHI	4	4	37	1	88	111	44	9	35	67	4.52	1.65	10.9	301	3.6	6.9	1.9	1.0	36%	74%	48
Espineli,Eugene	06	24	aa	SF	8	7	35	2	107	158	79	8	34	53	6.63	1.79	14.4	335	2.8	4.5	1.6	0.7	38%	61%	27
	07	25	aa	SF	8	10	29	0	140	179	71	9	40	81	4.56	1.56	21.7	304	2.6	5.2	2.0	0.6	35%	70%	51
Esposito,Mike	06	25	aaa	COL	6	13	27	0	140	220	132	25	43	77	8.50	1.88	24.9	350	2.8	5.0	1.8	1.6	38%	55%	3
	07	26	aa	COL	5	6	28	1	109	197	110	24	47	40	9.09	2.23	20.1	381	3.9	3.3	0.8	2.0	39%	61%	-43
Estrada,Paul	06	24 a	aa	HOU	8	5	56	15	88	74	38	12	39	107	3.87	1.28	6.6	222	4.0	11.0	2.8	1.2	31%	74%	99
	07	25	aa	HOU	1	8	53	8	70	91	53	8	47	52	6.85	1.97	6.5	308	6.0	6.7	1.1	1.0	36%	65%	27
Etherton,Seth	06	30	aaa	SD	3	6	19	0	84	109	59	19	30	63	6.36	1.65	20.2	307	3.2	6.7	2.1	2.0	34%	66%	18
Evangelista,Nicholas	06	25	aa	PHI	3	0	22	1	43	43	20	4	11	18	4.19	1.25	8.1	256	2.2	3.8	1.7	0.9	27%	68%	36
Eveland,Dana	06	23 a	aaa	MIL	6	5	20	0	105	81	40	5	42	103	3.43	1.17	21.5	209	3.6	8.8	2.5	0.4	28%	70%	105
Evert,Brett	06	26	a/a	BOS	1	6	37	0	54	72	45	15	34	40	7.53	1.95	7.1	312	5.6	6.6	1.2	2.5	34%	66%	-16
Fahrner,Evan	06	29	aa	TOR	1	4	36	3	51	69	38	5	39	38	6.62	2.11	7.1	316	6.8	6.8	1.0	0.9	38%	68%	27
Falkenborg,Brian	06	29	aaa	STL	4	5	47	16	51	65	33	8	16	43	5.86	1.58	4.9	301	2.8	7.5	2.7	1.3	36%	65%	56
	07	30	aa	STL	3	4	51	23	52	80	28	3	21	38	4.83	1.94	5.0	344	3.7	6.6	1.8	0.5	42%	74%	50
Farnsworth,Jeff	06	31	aaa	CHW	7	3	48	14	49	72	37	12	11	32	6.74	1.67	4.7	333	1.9	5.9	3.1	2.1	36%	64%	25
Feierabend,Ryan	06	21	aa	SEA	9	12	28	0	153	185	96	19	60	114	5.64	1.60	24.7	293	3.5	6.7	1.9	1.1	34%	66%	43
	07	22	aa	SEA	6	4	19	0	108	147	56	9	35	63	4.66	1.68	26.2	318	2.9	5.2	1.8	0.7	36%	73%	38
Feldkamp,Derek	07	24	aa	TAM	2	7	22	0	77	118	71	19	29	44	8.23	1.91	16.9	344	3.4	5.1	1.5	2.2	36%	60%	-18
Feldman,Scott	07	25	aa	TEX	1	1	21	2	30	35	20	1	13	20	6.00	1.58	6.4	284	3.8	6.0	1.6	0.3	34%	59%	58
Fernandez,Jared	06	35	aaa	MIL	6	4	24	3	129	177	65	12	26	65	4.55	1.57	24.2	319	1.8	4.5	2.5	0.8	36%	72%	45
Field,Nate	06	31	aaa	COL	3	3	49	25	49	82	37	10	10	42	6.72	1.88	4.8	364	1.8	7.8	4.2	1.8	43%	68%	62
	07	32	aa	FLA	6	6	44	11	46	48	25	7	21	35	4.82	1.51	4.6	264	4.1	6.8	1.6	1.4	30%	72%	36
Figueroa,Nelson	06	32	aaa	WAS	3	5	16	0	76	91	46	13	23	35	5.48	1.50	21.0	290	2.7	4.2	1.5	1.5	30%	67%	9
Fillinger,Chad	06	24	aa	SEA	7	1	32	0	68	77	35	7	26	48	4.64	1.52	9.4	280	3.4	6.3	1.8	1.0	33%	71%	47
	07	25	aa	SEA	1	2	20	1	33	41	23	3	15	28	6.30	1.69	7.6	298	4.0	7.5	1.9	0.9	37%	62%	54
Finch,Brian	06	25	aa	BAL	6	12	27	0	145	198	90	26	79	68	5.58	1.91	26.0	318	4.9	4.2	0.9	1.6	33%	74%	-13
Fisher,Charles	07	25	aa	CIN	5	9	21	0	113	162	74	16	47	72	5.92	1.85	25.7	329	3.7	5.7	1.5	1.2	37%	70%	19
Fister,Douglas	07	24	aa	SEA	7	8	24	0	131	180	80	15	35	74	5.52	1.64	24.9	320	2.4	5.1	2.1	1.1	36%	68%	34
Flanagan,Jeremy	06	25	aa	TAM	6	1	32	1	56	72	38	3	27	30	6.05	1.76	8.2	306	4.3	4.8	1.1	0.5	35%	64%	30
	07	26	aa	TAM	5	3	40	1	76	114	61	10	41	30	7.21	2.04	9.4	339	4.9	3.6	0.7	1.2	36%	65%	-12
Flannery,Mike	06	27	a/a	SEA	0	7	36	1	60	89	49	3	48	35	7.39	2.27	8.7	335	7.2	5.2	0.7	0.5	39%	66%	19
	07	28	aa	OAK	0	2	30	1	35	53	39	4	33	22	9.96	2.43	6.2	339	8.4	5.8	0.7	1.0	39%	57%	7
Flinn,Chris	06	26	a/a	TAM	1	6	24	0	74	127	67	9	38	40	8.11	2.22	15.9	370	4.6	4.8	1.0	1.1	41%	63%	-0
Flores,Ron	07	28	aa	OAK	1	2	40	1	36	54	16	5	20	18	4.05	2.04	4.5	338	5.0	4.4	0.9	1.2	37%	84%	-5
Floyd,Gavin	06	24	aaa	PHI	7	4	17	0	115	151	84	14	41	71	6.57	1.67	31.0	310	3.2	5.6	1.7	1.1	35%	61%	30
	07	25	aaa	CHW	7	3	17	0	106	113	51	13	36	85	4.32	1.40	27.0	267	3.1	7.2	2.4	1.1	32%	72%	61
Floyd,Jesse	06	26	aa	SF	4	14	25	0	135	178	101	13	47	77	6.74	1.66	24.7	311	3.1	5.2	1.7	0.9	35%	58%	32
	07	27	aa	MIN	7	9	27	0	130	179	99	20	61	70	6.84	1.85	23.0	321	4.2	4.9	1.2	1.4	35%	64%	4
Foley,Travis	06	24	a/a	CLE	4	5	43	3	85	99	45	7	33	78	4.75	1.55	8.9	285	3.5	8.2	2.4	0.7	36%	70%	75
	07	25	aa	OAK	5	4	46	4	54	63	36	3	23	46	5.96	1.60	5.3	286	3.9	7.6	2.0	0.5	36%	61%	69

					Actual				Major League Equivalents																
PITCHER	Yr	Age	Lev	Org	w	l	g	sv	ip	h	er	hr	bb	k	era	WHIP	bf/g	oob	ctl	dom	cmd	hr/9	h%	s%	bpv
Foli,Daniel	06	26	a/a	WAS	5	1	24	3	47	60	32	2	27	39	6.05	1.86	9.4	304	5.2	7.5	1.4	0.4	38%	65%	57
	07	27	a/a	WAS	0	2	24	1	45	69	40	4	34	35	8.00	2.30	9.8	344	6.9	7.0	1.0	0.9	41%	64%	23
Ford,Matt	06	26	aaa	MIN	1	2	33	0	58	78	43	9	29	28	6.74	1.85	8.4	315	4.5	4.3	0.9	1.4	34%	65%	-5
Forystek,Brian	06	28	aa	BAL	6	3	43	2	70	77	46	12	40	47	5.87	1.66	7.5	273	5.1	6.1	1.2	1.5	30%	68%	15
	07	29	aa	MIN	1	1	16	1	40	56	31	3	28	26	7.03	2.09	12.5	325	6.2	5.8	0.9	0.6	38%	65%	27
Fowler,Eric	07	25	aa	TOR	4	4	9	0	40	77	41	9	19	17	9.21	2.39	23.7	396	4.3	3.8	0.9	2.1	41%	63%	-46
Franklin,Wayne	06	33	aaa	ATL	2	3	35	4	53	51	20	2	19	44	3.39	1.31	6.4	246	3.2	7.4	2.3	0.4	31%	73%	88
Fritz,Benjamin	06	26	a/a	OAK	7	10	29	0	168	201	105	20	65	88	5.64	1.58	26.1	291	3.5	4.7	1.4	1.1	32%	65%	22
	07	27	aa	OAK	11	11	28	0	149	226	130	10	75	65	7.85	2.02	26.3	342	4.5	3.9	0.9	0.6	38%	59%	10
Fruto,Emiliano	06	22 a	aaa	SEA	1	3	28	10	45	35	18	1	21	51	3.61	1.25	6.7	211	4.2	10.3	2.5	0.2	31%	69%	120
	07	23	a/a	ARI	3	10	24	0	98	96	63	7	66	72	5.78	1.65	18.7	251	6.1	6.6	1.1	0.6	30%	64%	48
Fulchino,Jeff	06	27	aaa	FLA	6	10	25	0	140	158	75	11	58	96	4.84	1.54	25.0	278	3.7	6.2	1.7	0.7	33%	69%	49
	07	28	aa	FLA	6	2	16	0	88	146	80	16	48	42	8.13	2.20	28.2	362	4.9	4.2	0.9	1.6	39%	64%	-22
Fussell,Christopher	07	31	aa	LA	4	1	24	2	38	54	36	7	27	25	8.64	2.14	8.0	328	6.4	5.8	0.9	1.7	36%	60%	-7
Gabbard,Kason	06	25	a/a	BOS	10	9	22	0	125	129	73	15	55	98	5.27	1.47	24.9	261	3.9	7.0	1.8	1.1	31%	66%	49
	07	25	aaa	BOS	7	2	14	0	75	81	37	11	26	54	4.48	1.43	23.3	270	3.2	6.5	2.1	1.3	31%	73%	44
Galarraga,Armando	06	25	aa	TEX	1	6	9	0	41	71	35	7	14	31	7.63	2.05	22.7	371	3.0	6.9	2.3	1.6	43%	64%	22
	07	26	aa	TEX	11	8	27	0	152	191	101	21	64	104	5.98	1.68	25.9	301	3.8	6.1	1.6	1.2	34%	66%	28
Gallagher,Sean	06	21	aa	CHC	7	5	15	0	86	94	41	6	62	84	4.28	1.81	27.2	273	6.5	8.8	1.4	0.6	36%	77%	64
	07	22	aa	CHC	10	3	19	0	101	101	44	5	38	76	3.91	1.37	22.9	255	3.4	6.8	2.0	0.4	31%	71%	73
Gallardo,Yovani	06	21 a	aa	MIL	5	2	13	0	77	59	19	3	30	80	2.22	1.15	24.1	208	3.4	9.3	2.7	0.3	29%	81%	116
	07	22 a	aaa	MIL	8	3	13	0	77	56	29	5	27	110	3.39	1.08	23.8	200	3.2	12.8	4.0	0.5	32%	69%	161
Gallo,Mike	06	30	aaa	HOU	2	0	33	0	40	57	32	4	18	19	7.17	1.87	5.8	329	4.0	4.3	1.1	1.0	36%	61%	8
	07	31	aa	COL	2	6	56	6	60	111	67	13	41	27	10.07	2.55	5.9	389	6.2	4.1	0.7	1.9	41%	61%	-42
Garcia,Anderson	06	26	a/a	BAL	4	6	40	1	67	86	44	5	25	39	5.93	1.66	7.7	306	3.4	5.2	1.5	0.7	35%	63%	36
	07	27	a/a	PHI	1	7	51	11	77	101	54	11	24	47	6.36	1.63	6.9	310	2.9	5.5	1.9	1.3	35%	62%	27
Garcia,Harvey	07	24	aa	FLA	6	3	60	1	72	92	53	12	41	62	6.56	1.84	5.7	304	5.1	7.7	1.5	1.5	36%	67%	26
Garcia,Jaime	07	21	aa	STL	5	9	18	0	103	103	48	14	43	85	4.19	1.42	24.8	255	3.8	7.4	2.0	1.2	30%	74%	53
Garcia,James	06	27	a/a	SF	8	11	27	0	140	173	103	17	76	86	6.63	1.78	24.4	297	4.9	5.5	1.1	1.1	34%	63%	21
Garcia,Jose	06	22 a	a/a	FLA	6	8	15	0	88	90	42	10	30	87	4.28	1.35	25.1	258	3.0	8.9	3.0	1.0	33%	70%	90
	07	26	aa	STL	2	2	18	0	36	61	30	9	13	17	7.47	2.04	9.9	367	3.2	4.1	1.3	2.3	38%	68%	-35
Garcia,Rosman	07	29	aa	BAL	3	5	33	1	86	153	85	9	45	40	8.90	2.30	13.6	378	4.7	4.2	0.9	0.9	42%	60%	-4
Gardner,Lee	06	32	aaa	DET	5	5	58	30	61	58	27	3	18	37	4.02	1.24	4.4	245	2.6	5.4	2.1	0.5	29%	67%	68
Gardner,Michael	07	26	aa	NYY	3	5	44	2	81	105	45	1	38	47	4.97	1.76	8.6	306	4.2	5.2	1.2	0.1	36%	69%	47
Gardner,Richard	07	26	a/a	CIN	6	6	19	0	99	135	64	15	31	60	5.83	1.67	23.9	318	2.8	5.4	2.0	1.3	35%	67%	25
Garza,Justin	06	24	aa	STL	2	3	25	0	39	42	16	1	25	22	3.63	1.72	7.3	269	5.8	5.0	0.9	0.2	32%	78%	42
Garza,Matt	06	23 a	a/a	MIN	9	3	15	0	91	74	33	4	24	85	3.26	1.08	24.3	218	2.4	8.4	3.5	0.4	29%	69%	124
	07	24	aaa	MIN	4	6	16	0	92	116	54	6	35	77	5.28	1.64	26.2	302	3.4	7.5	2.2	0.6	38%	67%	68
Gassner,Dave	07	29	aaa	MIN	6	12	26	0	149	214	128	23	52	63	7.73	1.78	26.9	330	3.1	3.8	1.2	1.4	35%	57%	-3
Geer,Joshua B	07	24	aa	SD	17	6	27	0	177	202	79	11	31	89	4.01	1.31	27.8	281	1.6	4.5	2.9	0.5	32%	69%	71
George,Chris	06	27	aaa	FLA	5	6	22	0	107	147	74	5	55	69	6.19	1.89	23.4	320	4.6	5.8	1.3	0.4	38%	65%	39
	07	28	aa	FLA	7	11	26	0	139	219	124	26	88	70	8.01	2.20	27.4	350	5.7	4.5	0.8	1.7	37%	65%	-22
Germano,Justin	06	24	aaa	PHI	10	6	25	0	155	207	88	19	25	77	5.11	1.50	27.4	314	1.5	4.5	3.1	1.1	34%	68%	51
	07	25 a	aa	SD	4	0	5	0	32	29	8	0	3	15	2.19	1.01	25.1	236	0.9	4.3	4.6	0.0	28%	76%	130
German,Franklyn	07	28	aa	TEX	2	2	47	7	59	63	36	7	55	51	5.50	2.00	6.2	266	8.4	7.8	0.9	1.1	32%	74%	35
Giese,Dan	06	29	a/a	PHI	3	4	48	1	72	111	39	15	23	41	4.88	1.86	7.2	345	2.9	5.1	1.8	1.8	37%	80%	-1
	07	30	aa	SF	3	1	47	2	73	106	39	3	14	46	4.75	1.64	7.1	331	1.8	5.6	3.2	0.4	39%	70%	79
Gil,David	06	28	a/a	WAS	3	4	20	0	71	101	45	9	20	36	5.67	1.71	16.4	328	2.5	4.5	1.8	1.2	36%	68%	18
Ginter,Matt	06	29	aaa	BOS	5	14	24	1	141	204	113	22	30	69	7.20	1.66	26.9	331	1.9	4.4	2.3	1.4	36%	57%	22
	07	30	a/a	MIL	2	6	32	2	69	126	52	7	13	32	6.83	2.01	10.6	384	1.7	4.2	2.4	1.0	42%	66%	25
Giron,Roberto	06	31	aaa	HOU	2	5	47	13	86	116	60	13	34	50	6.26	1.74	8.5	315	3.6	5.3	1.5	1.4	35%	66%	13
	07	32	aa	KC	2	5	39	6	85	80	51	16	34	69	5.36	1.34	9.3	244	3.6	7.3	2.0	1.7	27%	65%	40
Glant,Dustin	06	25	aa	ARI	4	6	51	1	62	96	52	11	26	39	7.58	1.95	5.9	345	3.7	5.6	1.5	1.6	38%	63%	3
	07	26	aa	ARI	5	3	47	5	79	124	59	10	30	45	6.68	1.95	8.2	350	3.4	5.2	1.5	1.2	39%	66%	12
Gomez,Mariano	07	25	aa	CLE	3	3	48	2	66	69	41	7	28	43	5.59	1.46	6.0	263	3.8	5.9	1.6	0.9	30%	62%	43
Gonzalez,Edgar	06	24	aaa	ARI	3	8	24	0	138	159	70	12	26	94	4.56	1.34	24.5	283	1.7	6.1	3.6	0.8	33%	66%	88
Gonzalez,Enrique	06	24	aaa	ARI	4	3	10	0	60	68	17	2	13	31	2.55	1.35	25.6	279	1.9	4.6	2.4	0.3	32%	81%	68
	07	25	aa	ARI	8	10	27	0	153	241	124	16	68	94	7.31	2.02	28.0	350	4.0	5.5	1.4	0.9	40%	63%	20
Gonzalez,Gio	06	21	aa	PHI	7	12	27	0	154	170	109	33	83	139	6.36	1.64	26.0	274	4.8	8.1	1.7	1.9	32%	65%	26
	07	22 a	aa	CHW	9	7	27	0	150	142	74	15	61	165	4.44	1.35	23.7	245	3.7	9.9	2.7	0.9	33%	69%	95
Gonzalez,Jeremi	06	32	aaa	NYM	1	2	6	0	35	40	18	1	9	25	4.58	1.41	25.4	280	2.4	6.3	2.6	0.3	34%	65%	84
Gonzalez,Luis	06	39	aaa	LA	2	4	35	1	44	52	28	4	40	31	5.81	2.08	6.3	286	8.2	6.4	0.8	0.9	34%	72%	27
	07	25	aa	LA	3	4	33	3	42	31	24	2	54	41	5.19	2.01	6.3	199	11.5	8.8	0.8	0.5	27%	73%	70
Gonzalez,Miguel	06	22	aa	LAA	0	2	31	4	53	42	23	7	15	32	3.90	1.07	6.8	213	2.5	5.4	2.1	1.2	23%	68%	54
	07	23	aa	LAA	8	4	30	1	130	154	64	14	44	67	4.42	1.52	19.3	288	3.1	4.6	1.5	1.0	32%	73%	27
Goocher,Clint	06	24	aa	ARI	7	7	42	0	85	115	49	12	34	44	5.24	1.75	9.4	316	3.6	4.6	1.3	1.2	34%	72%	10
	07	25	aa	ARI	5	4	52	6	76	91	41	10	26	52	4.86	1.53	6.5	291	3.0	6.2	2.0	1.2	33%	71%	41
Good,Andy	06	27	aaa	WAS	9	9	28	0	147	209	99	23	38	75	6.05	1.68	24.2	328	2.3	4.6	2.0	1.4	35%	66%	16
Gordon,Brian	07	29	aa	HOU	6	2	39	1	61	88	35	7	27	32	5.11	1.88	7.5	330	3.9	4.8	1.2	1.0	37%	74%	13
Gorzelanny,Tom	06	24 a	aaa	PIT	6	5	16	0	99	83	37	5	29	80	3.36	1.13	25.1	223	2.6	7.3	2.8	0.5	28%	70%	98
Gosling,Mike	06	26	aaa	CIN	6	8	23	0	118	148	86	16	58	81	6.53	1.75	23.9	301	4.4	6.2	1.4	1.3	34%	64%	24
	07	27	aaa	CIN	5	3	13	0	78	88	36	9	25	53	4.13	1.46	26.3	280	2.9	6.1	2.1	1.1	32%	75%	47
Gothreaux,Jared	06	27	aaa	HOU	9	9	29	0	143	190	84	22	40	73	5.26	1.61	22.3	312	2.5	4.6	1.8	1.4	34%	70%	17
	07	28	aa	HOU	5	8	36	1	133	213	105	28	47	52	7.08	1.95	18.0	354	3.2	3.5	1.1	1.9	36%	67%	-27
Gracesqui,Franklyn	06	27	aaa	BAL	0	2	29	0	36	45	28	1	22	29	7.11	1.87	5.9	301	5.5	7.4	1.3	0.3	38%	59%	59
Graves,Danny	06	33	aaa	CLE	1	1	33	1	51	68	31	5	15	23	5.37	1.62	7.1	314	2.6	4.0	1.5	0.9	34%	68%	21
Gray,Jeffrey	07	26	aa	OAK	4	4	54	15	67	82	33	2	26	44	4.47	1.61	5.6	296	3.4	5.9	1.7	0.3	36%	71%	59
Green,Matthew	07	26	aa	ARI	12	6	28	0	148	197	91	21	61	102	5.54	1.74	24.6	313	3.7	6.2	1.7	1.3	36%	70%	26
Green,Nick	06	22	aa	LAA	8	5	17	0	112	149	69	25	24	52	5.52	1.54	29.4	312	1.9	4.2	2.2	2.0	32%	70%	3
	07	23	aa	LAA	10	8	28	0	178	197	95	20	34	88	4.79	1.30	26.8	275	1.7	4.5	2.6	1.0	30%	64%	52

					Actual				Major League Equivalents																
PITCHER	Yr	Age	Lev	Org	w	l	g	sv	ip	h	er	hr	bb	k	era	WHIP	bf/g	oob	ctl	dom	cmd	hr/9	h%	s%	bpv
Green,Steve	06	29	aaa	DET	5	5	32	2	54	67	31	2	32	28	5.18	1.83	8.0	296	5.4	4.6	0.9	0.4	34%	70%	31
	07	30	aaa	BAL	2	4	52	3	67	98	56	9	42	55	7.52	2.08	6.5	333	5.6	7.3	1.3	1.2	40%	64%	24
Greinke,Zack	06	23 a	aa	KC	8	3	18	0	105	103	55	10	24	82	4.71	1.21	24.1	251	2.1	7.0	3.4	0.9	30%	62%	93
Gronkiewicz,Lee	06	28	aaa	TOR	2	3	41	17	44	61	24	5	10	27	4.84	1.61	4.9	323	2.0	5.5	2.8	1.1	37%	72%	49
	07	29 b	a/a	TOR	6	3	47	13	74	98	30	11	12	58	3.70	1.48	6.9	310	1.5	7.1	4.8	1.3	36%	80%	96
Grube,Jarrett	07	26	aa	COL	7	3	52	0	67	78	29	6	23	49	3.87	1.50	5.7	284	3.1	6.5	2.1	0.7	34%	76%	59
Gryboski,Kevin	06	33	aaa	WAS	4	6	52	7	60	80	32	3	28	34	4.72	1.80	5.5	313	4.2	5.1	1.2	0.5	36%	73%	34
Guevara,Carlos	06	25	aa	CIN	2	3	49	1	77	94	45	8	29	71	5.28	1.60	7.1	294	3.4	8.3	2.4	1.0	37%	68%	67
	07	26 a	aa	CIN	1	2	51	16	62	66	22	6	26	67	3.23	1.47	5.3	266	3.7	9.7	2.6	0.8	36%	81%	90
Gulin,Lindsay	07	31	a/a	MIL	12	6	24	0	129	163	78	24	63	88	5.40	1.74	25.1	301	4.4	6.1	1.4	1.7	33%	73%	11
Guthrie,Jeremy	06	28	aaa	CLE	9	5	21	0	123	128	58	6	53	74	4.23	1.47	25.7	263	3.8	5.4	1.4	0.5	31%	70%	51
Gutierrez,Juan	06	23	aa	HOU	8	4	20	0	103	111	43	11	35	87	3.78	1.42	22.4	270	3.1	7.6	2.5	1.0	33%	76%	69
	07	24	aa	HOU	5	10	26	0	156	184	91	21	66	86	5.22	1.61	27.2	288	3.8	5.0	1.3	1.2	32%	70%	18
Guzman,Angel	06	25	aaa	CHC	4	4	15	0	75	87	46	7	26	68	5.51	1.50	22.2	284	3.1	8.1	2.6	0.8	36%	63%	77
Gwyn,Marcus	06	29	a/a	LAA	3	1	51	7	67	82	33	6	33	41	4.41	1.72	6.1	296	4.4	5.5	1.2	0.8	34%	75%	31
	07	30	aa	LAA	2	1	47	15	57	105	39	8	23	35	6.11	2.25	6.3	388	3.6	5.4	1.5	1.3	44%	74%	4
Haberer,Eric	06	24	aa	STL	3	3	11	0	61	76	45	11	35	30	6.67	1.81	26.3	298	5.1	4.5	0.9	1.6	32%	65%	-6
	07	25	aa	STL	13	8	28	0	152	199	91	13	77	57	5.39	1.81	25.7	309	4.5	3.4	0.7	0.8	33%	70%	5
Hackman,Luther	07	33	a/a	TEX	1	3	45	18	46	47	24	6	28	30	4.77	1.61	4.6	257	5.4	5.8	1.1	1.1	29%	73%	28
Haeger,Charlie	06	23	aaa	CHW	14	6	26	0	170	172	78	13	83	111	4.13	1.50	28.9	257	4.4	5.9	1.3	0.7	30%	73%	46
	07	24	aaa	CHW	5	16	24	0	147	168	92	24	71	112	5.63	1.62	27.9	281	4.3	6.8	1.6	1.5	32%	68%	29
Haehnel,David	07	25	aa	BAL	2	1	40	0	69	88	61	10	50	45	7.97	2.00	8.5	303	6.5	5.9	0.9	1.3	34%	60%	9
Haigwood,Daniel	06	23	aa	TEX	3	7	27	0	146	174	86	16	93	123	5.30	1.83	25.7	290	5.7	7.6	1.3	1.0	35%	72%	41
	07	24	aa	BOS	3	5	17	0	69	80	56	12	51	60	7.26	1.90	19.6	285	6.6	7.8	1.2	1.6	34%	63%	22
Haines,Talley	06	30	a/a	PHI	5	3	38	0	67	93	46	9	23	33	6.22	1.73	8.2	321	3.1	4.4	1.4	1.1	35%	65%	13
Hale,Beau	06	28	aa	BAL	4	6	19	0	95	124	57	12	25	48	5.36	1.57	22.5	309	2.4	4.6	1.9	1.1	34%	68%	26
	07	29	aa	BAL	6	5	15	0	71	130	61	10	34	30	7.74	2.30	24.8	385	4.3	3.8	0.9	1.3	41%	67%	-18
Hall,Bo	07	27	aa	MIL	5	2	34	1	54	58	31	8	46	42	5.20	1.91	7.7	268	7.6	7.0	0.9	1.4	31%	76%	21
Hall,Josh	06	26	a/a	CIN	10	9	26	0	151	209	86	20	54	72	5.14	1.74	27.1	322	3.2	4.3	1.3	1.2	35%	73%	9
	07	27	a/a	WAS	3	4	31	1	67	79	44	3	38	36	5.97	1.74	10.1	287	5.1	4.8	1.0	0.4	33%	64%	33
Hamman,Corey	06	27	aaa	DET	2	8	37	0	103	126	62	18	28	47	5.40	1.49	12.3	295	2.4	4.1	1.7	1.5	31%	67%	10
	07	27	a/a	DET	1	9	35	1	83	149	69	18	34	36	7.46	2.21	12.2	381	3.7	3.9	1.0	2.0	40%	69%	-36
Hammel,Jason	06	24	aaa	TAM	5	9	24	0	127	157	78	12	38	100	5.52	1.53	23.6	297	2.7	7.1	2.6	0.8	36%	64%	68
	07	25	aaa	TAM	4	5	13	0	76	75	40	4	30	65	4.78	1.38	25.2	252	3.6	7.7	2.2	0.5	32%	64%	82
Hammes,Zachary	07	23	aa	LA	5	8	26	0	94	127	66	12	31	65	6.30	1.67	16.6	316	3.0	6.2	2.1	1.2	36%	63%	38
Hammond,Steve	06	24	aa	MIL	5	6	13	0	73	82	36	9	29	49	4.40	1.52	25.0	278	3.6	6.1	1.7	1.2	32%	74%	36
	07	25	aa	MIL	7	9	29	1	142	211	103	24	51	89	6.55	1.85	23.3	337	3.2	5.6	1.7	1.5	37%	67%	12
Hampson,Justin	06	26	aaa	COL	8	4	31	0	121	145	59	13	38	79	4.36	1.51	17.3	291	2.8	5.8	2.1	1.0	33%	73%	45
Hamulack,Tim	06	30	aaa	LA	0	1	28	3	38	34	7	1	26	34	1.56	1.59	6.1	235	6.2	8.0	1.3	0.3	31%	91%	75
Hanrahan,Joel	06	25	a/a	LA	11	5	26	0	140	139	67	13	81	91	4.32	1.57	24.2	253	5.2	5.9	1.1	0.8	29%	74%	39
	07	26	aaa	WAS	5	4	15	0	75	77	39	11	37	58	4.72	1.52	22.2	259	4.5	7.0	1.6	1.3	30%	73%	38
Hansack,Devern	06	29	aa	BOS	8	7	31	1	132	184	81	21	46	86	5.54	1.74	19.9	323	3.2	5.9	1.9	1.4	36%	71%	22
	07	30	aaa	BOS	10	7	25	0	139	167	84	20	46	102	5.40	1.53	24.8	291	3.0	6.6	2.2	1.3	34%	67%	44
Hansen,Craig	06	23	a/a	BOS	2	2	19	0	47	43	17	0	24	33	3.26	1.43	10.7	239	4.6	6.3	1.4	0.0	30%	75%	74
	07	24	aaa	BOS	3	1	40	3	51	70	30	2	34	41	5.28	2.04	6.3	319	6.0	7.2	1.2	0.4	40%	73%	49
Happ,James	06	24	a/a	PHI	7	2	13	0	80	76	33	4	32	71	3.70	1.35	26.3	245	3.6	8.0	2.2	0.4	32%	72%	87
	07	25	aaa	PHI	4	6	24	0	118	138	84	15	65	100	6.40	1.72	22.8	286	5.0	7.6	1.5	1.1	35%	63%	42
Harben,Adam	06	23	aa	MIN	4	9	29	1	122	148	76	6	77	61	5.62	1.85	20.1	294	5.7	4.5	0.8	0.5	33%	68%	26
Harikkala,Tim	07	36	aa	COL	3	1	8	0	32	55	25	4	13	9	6.91	2.12	20.3	370	3.6	2.4	0.7	1.0	39%	67%	-21
Harrison,Matt	06	21	aa	ATL	3	4	13	0	77	102	44	7	19	48	5.14	1.57	26.6	312	2.2	5.6	2.5	0.8	36%	68%	55
	07	22	aa	ATL	5	7	20	0	116	138	56	7	35	67	4.34	1.49	25.6	289	2.7	5.2	1.9	0.5	33%	70%	52
Harris,Jeff	06	32	aaa	SEA	0	3	15	0	31	51	23	6	7	11	6.72	1.87	9.9	358	2.1	3.3	1.5	1.8	37%	67%	-19
	07	33	aaa	CLE	6	9	27	0	138	174	92	25	39	71	5.97	1.54	22.8	301	2.5	4.6	1.8	1.6	32%	65%	12
Hart,Kevin	07	25	aa	CHC	12	6	27	0	158	192	93	25	54	105	5.28	1.55	26.2	293	3.1	6.0	1.9	1.4	33%	69%	30
Harville,Chad	07	31	aa	ARI	6	4	46	24	52	60	32	7	25	32	5.50	1.63	5.1	283	4.3	5.6	1.3	1.2	32%	68%	23
Hawksworth,Blake	06	24	aa	STL	4	2	13	0	79	82	35	8	31	55	3.98	1.43	26.5	263	3.5	6.3	1.8	0.9	31%	75%	50
	07	25	aa	STL	4	13	25	0	129	174	91	24	41	74	6.31	1.66	23.7	315	2.9	5.2	1.8	1.7	34%	65%	10
Hayhurst,Dirk	06	26	a/a	SD	4	7	16	0	72	99	49	8	28	51	6.18	1.77	21.1	320	3.5	6.4	1.8	1.1	37%	65%	36
	07	27	aa	SD	4	1	34	2	62	82	38	10	10	43	5.51	1.48	8.0	311	1.5	6.2	4.1	1.5	35%	66%	71
Heaverlo,Jeff	06	29	a/a	LAA	2	5	25	0	60	86	51	9	41	29	7.58	2.11	12.1	329	6.2	4.3	0.7	1.4	35%	65%	-12
Hedrick,Justin	07	25	aa	SF	4	6	41	1	71	69	22	4	40	56	2.81	1.53	7.7	249	5.1	7.1	1.4	0.6	31%	83%	60
Henderson,Brian	06	24	aa	TAM	2	2	41	5	50	62	19	3	13	23	3.41	1.49	5.4	298	2.3	4.1	1.8	0.6	33%	78%	41
	07	25	aa	TAM	6	3	59	1	66	79	29	7	28	36	3.93	1.61	5.1	290	3.8	4.9	1.3	0.9	32%	78%	26
Henderson,Jim	07	25	aa	CHC	7	3	50	10	71	81	26	12	34	44	3.34	1.62	6.4	281	4.3	5.5	1.3	1.5	31%	86%	15
Hendrickson,Ben	06	26	aaa	MIL	9	8	23	0	139	145	69	11	49	85	4.44	1.40	26.1	264	3.2	5.5	1.7	0.7	30%	69%	50
	07	27	aa	KC	11	5	27	0	135	180	89	11	61	50	5.90	1.79	23.6	314	4.1	3.4	0.8	0.8	34%	67%	7
Henn,Sean	06	25	aaa	NYY	3	1	18	0	42	52	24	1	21	27	5.17	1.72	10.9	295	4.5	5.7	1.3	0.2	35%	68%	50
	07	26	aaa	NYY	1	2	15	0	31	32	13	1	9	23	3.88	1.33	8.8	260	2.7	6.7	2.5	0.3	32%	69%	87
Hensley,Clay	07	28	aa	SD	1	7	13	0	71	145	79	14	44	35	9.98	2.66	30.5	412	5.5	4.5	0.8	1.7	44%	63%	-36
Hensley,Matt	06	28	aaa	LAA	2	1	20	2	33	47	23	3	11	21	6.14	1.75	7.7	329	2.9	5.8	2.0	0.9	38%	65%	40
Herges,Matt	07	38	aa	COL	2	1	32	1	35	34	8	4	12	25	2.11	1.31	4.6	250	3.0	6.3	2.1	0.9	29%	89%	60
Hernandez,Buddy	07	29	aaa	ATL	9	3	47	3	74	97	37	9	20	57	4.43	1.58	7.1	309	2.5	6.9	2.8	1.0	37%	74%	62
Hernandez,Chris	06	26	aa	PIT	5	3	42	2	66	79	41	3	25	52	5.63	1.58	7.1	291	3.4	7.1	2.1	0.5	36%	63%	69
	07	27	aa	PIT	6	4	52	7	69	88	37	7	29	45	4.86	1.69	6.1	303	3.8	5.8	1.6	0.9	35%	73%	34
Hernandez,Fernando	07	23	aa	CHW	1	3	60	9	85	92	41	6	26	73	4.36	1.38	6.1	270	2.7	7.7	2.8	0.7	34%	69%	87
Hernandez,Gabriel	07	21	aa	FLA	9	11	28	0	153	162	85	14	58	103	4.99	1.44	23.8	266	3.4	6.1	1.8	0.8	31%	66%	51
Hernandez,Moises	07	24	a/a	ATL	2	3	11	0	54	74	47	9	33	19	7.80	1.97	24.1	319	5.5	3.2	0.6	1.5	33%	61%	-23
Hernandez,Runelvys	06	28	aaa	KC	5	6	12	0	64	82	44	6	28	35	6.18	1.71	24.8	304	3.9	5.0	1.3	0.9	34%	64%	23
	07	29	a/a	PIT	1	7	17	0	82	138	60	18	35	35	6.54	2.11	24.3	365	3.9	3.9	1.0	2.0	38%	73%	-34
Hernandez,Yoel	07	27	aaa	PHI	1	3	22	5	29	41	17	0	16	13	5.19	1.95	6.5	325	4.9	4.1	0.8	0.0	37%	70%	32

Major League Equivalent Statistics

					Actual				Major League Equivalents																
PITCHER	Yr	Age	Lev	Org	w	l	g	sv	ip	h	er	hr	bb	k	era	WHIP	bf/g	oob	ctl	dom	cmd	hr/9	h%	s%	bpv
Herndon,Junior	06	28	aa	KC	12	6	27	0	160	265	126	23	43	61	7.10	1.92	28.7	362	2.4	3.4	1.4	1.3	38%	64%	-5
Herrera,Daniel R.	07	23 a	aa	TEX	5	2	34	0	52	51	29	4	20	55	5.01	1.36	6.6	251	3.5	9.5	2.8	0.7	34%	63%	99
Herrera,Yoslan	07	26	aa	PIT	6	9	25	0	128	199	93	13	43	51	6.54	1.88	24.6	347	3.0	3.6	1.2	0.9	38%	65%	6
Hertzler,Barry	06	26	a/a	BOS	4	2	50	7	77	97	37	1	54	38	4.30	1.95	7.5	301	6.3	4.4	0.7	0.1	35%	76%	33
	07	27	a/a	BOS	4	3	40	1	70	117	68	4	30	22	8.70	2.09	8.8	363	3.9	2.8	0.7	0.6	39%	55%	-3
Hill,Danny	06	25	aa	TOR	3	7	44	0	74	118	69	15	35	51	8.43	2.06	8.4	352	4.2	6.2	1.5	1.8	40%	60%	-1
Hill,Joshua	07	25	aa	MIN	3	2	16	0	53	67	33	2	29	35	5.52	1.82	15.8	302	5.0	5.9	1.2	0.4	36%	68%	45
Hill,Rich	06	27 b	aaa	CHC	7	1	15	0	100	77	28	4	24	115	2.51	1.01	26.2	209	2.1	10.4	4.9	0.4	31%	76%	167
Hill,Shawn	06	25 a	a/a	WAS	3	3	11	0	55	62	21	2	7	28	3.44	1.26	20.9	279	1.2	4.5	3.7	0.3	32%	72%	95
Hinckley,Michael	07	25	aa	WAS	9	10	25	0	117	172	94	16	61	56	7.20	1.99	23.0	334	4.7	4.3	0.9	1.2	36%	64%	-3
Hines,Carlos	06	32	aaa	TAM	3	6	52	2	65	88	38	7	28	41	5.24	1.79	5.9	317	3.9	5.6	1.4	1.0	36%	72%	25
	07	27	aa	SF	1	1	29	2	40	61	28	2	27	17	6.22	2.19	7.1	344	5.9	3.9	0.7	0.5	38%	70%	7
Hinshaw,Alex	07	25 a	aa	SF	3	1	17	0	41	26	12	2	20	41	2.54	1.13	9.8	180	4.4	8.9	2.0	0.5	24%	79%	102
Hinton,Robert	07	23	aa	MIL	2	3	39	2	53	60	45	5	30	39	7.70	1.69	6.3	279	5.1	6.6	1.3	0.9	33%	52%	40
Hirsh,Jason	06	25	aaa	HOU	13	2	23	0	137	106	37	5	50	100	2.43	1.14	24.2	209	3.3	6.6	2.0	0.3	26%	79%	85
Hochevar,Luke	07	24	aa	KC	4	9	27	0	152	198	107	25	48	116	6.36	1.62	25.6	308	2.9	6.9	2.4	1.5	36%	63%	40
Hodges,Trey	07	29	aaa	ATL	6	6	30	1	122	163	91	13	74	63	6.73	1.94	19.8	313	5.4	4.6	0.9	1.0	35%	65%	9
Hoelscher,Nate	06	27	aa	KC	0	5	44	3	46	56	34	6	15	31	6.72	1.54	4.7	295	2.9	6.1	2.1	1.1	34%	56%	43
	07	28	aa	KC	5	3	35	3	80	122	69	12	25	32	7.73	1.84	10.9	343	2.8	3.5	1.2	1.4	36%	58%	-7
Hoey,James	07	25 a	a/a	BAL	3	0	40	16	45	34	5	1	14	58	1.03	1.07	4.5	205	2.9	11.6	4.0	0.2	32%	91%	162
Holcomb,James	06	26	aa	LAA	0	7	13	0	62	87	42	6	20	32	6.11	1.71	22.2	323	2.9	4.7	1.6	0.8	36%	64%	28
Holdzkom,Lincoln	06	25	aa	CHC	2	3	18	0	32	35	13	0	13	23	3.54	1.48	7.8	270	3.5	6.4	1.8	0.0	34%	73%	77
	07	26	a/a	BOS	5	1	42	1	63	67	28	5	47	44	4.05	1.82	7.1	267	6.7	6.2	0.9	0.7	32%	79%	36
Holliman,Mark	07	24	aa	CHC	10	11	27	0	161	193	84	20	62	86	4.70	1.58	26.9	291	3.5	4.8	1.4	1.1	32%	73%	21
Homer,Chris	06	26	aa	DET	1	4	42	13	48	80	58	13	16	32	10.81	1.99	5.6	363	2.9	6.1	2.1	2.5	39%	46%	-12
Honel,Kristopher	07	25	aa	CHW	2	2	17	0	60	73	57	9	59	37	8.50	2.19	18.1	292	8.8	5.5	0.6	1.4	32%	61%	0
Hoorelbeke,Casey	06	27	aa	LA	2	2	52	7	72	57	31	6	37	44	3.88	1.31	5.9	215	4.6	5.5	1.2	0.7	25%	71%	49
	07	27	aa	LA	4	4	63	2	94	153	81	11	37	36	7.73	2.03	7.4	358	3.6	3.4	1.0	1.0	38%	61%	-7
Horgan,Joe	06	29	aaa	FLA	5	6	45	3	43	42	22	5	19	26	4.60	1.41	4.1	250	3.9	5.5	1.4	1.2	28%	70%	33
Horne,Alan	07	25	aa	NYY	12	4	27	0	153	196	80	15	66	131	4.70	1.71	26.3	305	3.9	7.7	2.0	0.9	38%	74%	56
Hottovy,Thomas	06	25	aa	BOS	2	4	7	0	41	38	29	1	17	24	6.34	1.33	24.9	240	3.7	5.3	1.5	0.2	29%	48%	62
	07	26	aa	BOS	4	10	24	0	120	191	106	21	56	51	7.92	2.06	24.9	352	4.2	3.8	0.9	1.6	37%	62%	-20
Houlton,D.J.	06	27	aaa	LA	9	11	29	0	162	197	106	25	59	106	5.90	1.58	25.1	294	3.3	5.9	1.8	1.4	33%	65%	28
	07	28	aa	LA	6	4	23	0	106	148	63	16	49	65	5.31	1.85	22.0	323	4.1	5.5	1.3	1.4	36%	74%	10
Houser Jr.,James	07	23	aa	TAM	5	4	20	0	103	100	51	11	40	80	4.45	1.36	22.1	249	3.5	7.0	2.0	1.0	30%	69%	60
Housman,Jeff	06	25	aa	MIL	1	4	12	0	56	77	37	1	23	35	5.88	1.78	22.0	319	3.7	5.6	1.5	0.2	38%	64%	51
	07	26	aa	MIL	3	2	32	0	40	64	34	3	36	22	7.74	2.49	6.8	355	8.0	4.9	0.6	0.8	40%	68%	3
Houston,Ryan	06	27	a/a	TOR	3	4	51	2	72	105	47	5	51	59	5.87	2.15	7.2	332	6.3	7.4	1.2	0.6	41%	72%	40
	07	28	aaa	TOR	2	2	50	5	60	69	42	9	32	49	6.27	1.68	5.5	281	4.8	7.4	1.5	1.3	33%	64%	36
Howard,Ben	06	28	aaa	TOR	3	2	45	11	57	77	51	8	24	24	7.98	1.77	5.9	316	3.8	3.8	1.0	1.3	33%	55%	-5
	07	29	aa	CHC	6	10	55	2	82	123	61	20	31	46	6.72	1.88	7.1	338	3.4	5.0	1.5	2.2	36%	69%	-18
Howell,J.P.	06	23	aaa	TAM	8	5	18	0	91	107	44	5	30	70	4.35	1.51	22.4	287	3.0	6.9	2.3	0.5	35%	70%	73
	07	24	aaa	TAM	7	8	21	0	128	133	65	20	37	128	4.57	1.33	25.9	262	2.6	9.0	3.5	1.4	33%	70%	87
Hrynio,Michael	07	25	aa	SEA	3	1	21	2	35	35	18	0	21	25	4.58	1.58	7.6	253	5.4	6.3	1.2	0.0	32%	68%	67
Huber,Jon	06	25	a/a	SEA	3	4	50	23	65	93	33	3	16	48	4.51	1.67	6.0	328	2.2	6.7	3.1	0.4	40%	72%	81
	07	26	aa	SEA	1	4	24	5	33	55	38	6	10	22	10.28	1.97	6.8	363	2.8	5.9	2.1	1.6	41%	46%	15
Hudgins,John	06	25	a/a	TEX	6	5	18	0	76	89	45	6	26	64	5.35	1.52	18.8	287	3.1	7.5	2.4	0.7	35%	64%	71
Hudson,Luke	06	29	aaa	KC	2	0	13	1	35	38	15	0	8	16	3.94	1.31	11.4	273	2.0	4.2	2.1	0.0	32%	67%	70
Hughes,Dustin	07	25	aa	KC	6	2	25	1	108	126	51	6	49	61	4.26	1.62	19.6	285	4.1	5.1	1.3	0.5	33%	73%	41
Hughes,Philip	06	20 a	a/a	NYY	10	3	21	0	116	85	38	6	33	120	2.96	1.02	21.8	200	2.6	9.3	3.6	0.4	28%	71%	133
	07	21 a	a/a	NYY	4	1	7	0	35	24	10	0	10	35	2.68	0.97	19.6	188	2.7	8.9	3.3	0.0	27%	69%	140
Hughes,Travis	06	28	aaa	WAS	2	6	51	4	73	61	25	3	45	69	3.04	1.45	6.3	223	5.6	8.5	1.5	0.4	30%	79%	81
	07	29	aaa	BOS	7	6	57	24	75	81	31	3	34	56	3.69	1.54	5.9	271	4.1	6.8	1.7	0.4	33%	75%	64
Huisman,Justin	06	27	aaa	SEA	2	0	22	0	40	61	46	8	22	28	10.42	2.08	9.1	343	5.0	6.2	1.2	1.9	38%	49%	-7
Hull,Eric	06	27	aaa	LA	2	4	44	2	73	58	35	6	41	64	4.32	1.36	7.1	213	5.1	7.9	1.6	0.8	27%	69%	69
	07	28	aa	LA	4	3	49	11	65	80	28	4	31	59	3.83	1.70	6.1	295	4.3	8.1	1.9	0.5	38%	78%	69
Humber,Philip	06	24	aa	NYM	2	2	6	0	34	32	15	5	10	30	4.08	1.24	23.6	243	2.7	7.9	2.9	1.4	29%	72%	74
	07	25	aaa	NYM	11	9	25	0	139	152	81	22	45	99	5.25	1.42	24.1	272	2.9	6.4	2.2	1.4	31%	66%	42
Hunter,Christopher	06	26	aa	LAA	4	14	25	0	125	193	114	21	69	37	8.23	2.09	25.1	346	5.0	2.7	0.5	1.5	35%	61%	-33
	07	27	aa	LAA	3	4	22	1	38	77	56	10	28	17	13.34	2.75	9.8	410	6.5	3.9	0.6	2.5	42%	51%	-64
Hurley,Eric	06	21	aa	TEX	3	1	6	0	37	25	11	5	11	27	2.68	0.97	24.0	188	2.7	6.6	2.5	1.2	21%	81%	72
	07	22	aa	TEX	11	9	28	0	162	161	93	33	55	115	5.17	1.33	24.6	254	3.1	6.4	2.1	1.8	27%	67%	31
Igawa,Kei	07	28	aaa	NYY	5	4	11	0	68	86	39	13	17	55	5.12	1.52	27.5	302	2.3	7.3	3.2	1.7	35%	71%	54
Ingram,Jesse	07	25	aa	TEX	3	1	56	26	62	57	42	14	31	54	6.13	1.42	4.8	238	4.5	7.8	1.7	2.1	26%	62%	28
Inman,William	07	21	aa	SD	4	8	15	0	80	76	49	13	34	76	5.45	1.38	23.0	245	3.8	8.5	2.2	1.5	29%	64%	58
Iriki,Yusaku	06	34	aaa	NYM	4	8	19	0	76	119	59	9	36	50	6.96	2.03	19.9	348	4.2	5.9	1.4	1.1	40%	66%	17
	07	35	a/a	TOR	3	6	19	0	88	127	66	12	42	47	6.70	1.92	22.4	330	4.3	4.8	1.1	1.2	36%	66%	4
Isenberg,Kurt	06	25	aa	TOR	3	9	20	0	87	159	83	7	25	46	8.59	2.11	21.9	385	2.6	4.7	1.8	0.8	43%	57%	21
	07	26	aa	TOR	4	11	23	0	123	209	104	11	44	69	7.63	2.06	26.7	367	3.2	5.1	1.6	0.8	42%	61%	20
Jackson,Edwin	06	23	aaa	TAM	3	7	22	5	73	99	58	8	37	56	7.15	1.86	15.9	317	4.6	6.9	1.5	1.0	38%	61%	35
Jackson,Kyle	06	24	aa	BOS	3	1	22	1	36	40	14	2	27	30	3.59	1.85	7.9	276	6.7	7.5	1.1	0.5	35%	81%	53
	07	24	aa	BOS	4	9	42	1	70	84	61	9	51	67	7.83	1.92	8.1	291	6.5	8.6	1.3	1.2	36%	59%	40
Jackson,Steven	06	25	aa	ARI	8	11	24	0	149	172	66	8	51	105	4.00	1.49	27.4	283	3.0	6.3	2.1	0.5	34%	73%	65
	07	26	a/a	NYY	4	9	28	1	90	144	78	16	43	52	7.79	2.08	16.1	354	4.3	5.2	1.2	1.6	39%	64%	-6
Jackson,Zach	06	23	aaa	MIL	4	6	18	0	107	126	65	14	47	52	5.47	1.62	27.0	287	4.0	4.4	1.1	1.2	31%	68%	12
	07	24	aaa	MIL	11	10	29	0	169	216	107	15	68	112	5.69	1.68	26.8	304	3.6	6.0	1.6	0.8	36%	66%	41
Jacobsen,Landon	06	27	a/a	PIT	14	10	28	0	164	223	105	13	70	61	5.74	1.79	27.6	318	3.8	3.3	0.9	0.7	34%	67%	9
	07	28	a/a	PHI	8	12	29	0	163	247	122	16	80	60	6.76	2.01	27.7	342	4.4	3.3	0.8	0.9	37%	66%	-5
Jakubauskas,Chris	07	29	aa	SEA	0	4	16	0	51	74	41	4	28	28	7.28	1.99	15.6	331	4.9	4.9	1.0	0.7	38%	62%	20
James,Brad	07	23	aa	HOU	1	5	9	0	47	62	33	2	21	18	6.32	1.75	24.4	311	3.9	3.5	0.9	0.4	34%	62%	21

					Actual				Major League Equivalents																
PITCHER	Yr	Age	Lev	Org	w	l	g	sv	ip	h	er	hr	bb	k	era	WHIP	bf/g	oob	ctl	dom	cmd	hr/9	h%	s%	bpv
James,Chuck	06	25	aaa	ATL	1	0	7	0	33	37	14	4	6	22	3.80	1.30	20.0	276	1.6	6.0	3.7	1.1	32%	74%	80
James,Craig	06	24	aa	SEA	4	3	43	1	62	66	25	4	37	49	3.59	1.66	6.6	267	5.4	7.0	1.3	0.6	33%	79%	53
	07	25	aa	SEA	5	4	44	10	58	84	49	5	28	39	7.65	1.94	6.4	331	4.4	6.0	1.4	0.8	39%	59%	29
James,Justin	06	25	aa	TOR	2	0	24	0	41	58	18	3	12	30	3.88	1.70	7.9	324	2.7	6.5	2.4	0.7	39%	78%	58
	07	26	a/a	TOR	3	5	43	2	88	111	53	10	30	45	5.45	1.60	9.3	302	3.1	4.6	1.5	1.0	33%	67%	23
James,Michael	07	26	aa	BOS	2	3	55	22	57	75	34	9	43	44	5.44	2.05	5.2	309	6.7	7.0	1.0	1.4	36%	77%	14
Jamison,Neil	07	24	aa	SD	3	5	53	12	58	78	35	8	28	37	5.38	1.83	5.2	315	4.4	5.7	1.3	1.3	35%	73%	15
Janssen,Casey	06	25	aaa	TOR	1	5	9	0	42	58	32	4	9	28	6.89	1.58	21.1	318	1.9	5.9	3.0	0.9	37%	55%	65
Jan,Carlos	06	27	aa	CHC	1	2	31	1	53	61	38	7	44	46	6.44	1.97	8.4	282	7.4	7.8	1.1	1.2	34%	68%	33
Jarvis,Kevin	06	37	aaa	ARI	3	6	15	0	83	89	39	8	22	48	4.21	1.34	23.6	269	2.4	5.2	2.2	0.9	30%	70%	51
Jensen,Ryan	06	31	aa	TEX	2	4	11	0	50	87	52	9	15	27	9.32	2.05	22.6	374	2.8	4.9	1.8	1.7	41%	54%	-4
Jimenez,Cesar	06	22	a/a	SEA	5	12	27	3	123	129	67	9	60	71	4.87	1.53	20.3	263	4.4	5.2	1.2	0.6	30%	68%	40
Jimenez,Kelvin	06	26	aaa	TEX	4	2	26	1	38	52	33	6	26	35	7.89	2.05	7.3	317	6.2	8.2	1.3	1.4	39%	62%	25
	07	27	aa	STL	2	3	30	1	39	59	16	2	13	26	3.69	1.82	6.2	339	2.9	6.0	2.1	0.5	40%	80%	51
Jimenez,Ubaldo	06	23	a/a	COL	14	4	26	0	151	145	82	12	79	128	4.88	1.48	25.6	247	4.7	7.6	1.6	0.7	31%	67%	64
	07	24	aa	COL	8	5	19	0	103	138	95	12	64	77	8.29	1.96	26.5	315	5.6	6.7	1.2	1.1	37%	57%	25
Johnson,David	07	25	aa	MIL	1	1	26	4	41	46	31	7	21	38	6.80	1.62	7.2	275	4.6	8.3	1.8	1.5	33%	59%	44
Johnson,Grant	07	24	aa	CHC	1	1	28	3	48	44	31	6	22	34	5.71	1.38	7.4	239	4.1	6.4	1.5	1.2	27%	60%	43
Johnson,James	06	23	aa	BAL	13	6	27	0	156	207	109	18	61	108	6.30	1.72	26.8	313	3.5	6.2	1.8	1.0	36%	63%	37
Johnson,Jeremy	06	24	aa	DET	2	4	8	0	38	72	38	7	12	20	8.98	2.19	24.3	392	2.7	4.7	1.7	1.7	42%	60%	-11
	07	25	a/a	DET	5	3	41	2	73	83	39	5	27	40	4.80	1.51	7.9	280	3.4	4.9	1.5	0.6	32%	68%	40
Johnson,Jim	07	24	aaa	BAL	6	12	26	0	148	202	94	20	50	95	5.72	1.70	26.3	319	3.0	5.8	1.9	1.2	36%	68%	29
Johnson,Jonathan	06	32	aaa	ATL	2	3	23	0	51	58	29	2	19	39	5.18	1.50	9.8	279	3.3	6.8	2.1	0.4	35%	63%	72
	07	33	aaa	ATL	1	4	10	0	44	71	44	8	23	21	9.00	2.12	22.3	353	4.7	4.3	0.9	1.7	37%	58%	-23
Johnston,Mike	06	28	aaa	PIT	1	3	28	0	42	63	40	7	22	29	8.55	2.03	7.4	339	4.7	6.1	1.3	1.6	38%	58%	3
Jones,Bobby	06	35	aa	DET	3	4	28	0	80	114	54	15	49	50	6.08	2.04	14.2	328	5.6	5.6	1.0	1.7	36%	74%	-7
Jones,David H	07	24	aa	BOS	2	1	23	2	42	41	19	3	16	36	3.97	1.37	7.9	251	3.5	7.7	2.2	0.7	32%	72%	77
Jones,Geoffrey	06	27	aa	SD	1	1	53	1	61	92	43	4	31	44	6.39	2.01	5.7	339	4.6	6.5	1.4	0.5	41%	67%	40
	07	28	aa	CHC	4	4	50	9	59	83	24	0	26	47	3.61	1.84	5.6	323	4.0	7.2	1.8	0.0	41%	78%	71
Jones,Greg	06	30	aaa	LAA	5	6	47	17	55	60	30	8	20	35	4.86	1.46	5.1	273	3.2	5.7	1.7	1.3	30%	70%	33
	07	31	aa	LAA	4	2	36	3	53	113	54	11	20	23	9.18	2.50	8.0	421	3.4	3.9	1.2	1.9	44%	65%	-39
Jones,Jason	06	30	aa	NYY	4	3	10	0	50	105	49	19	27	17	8.86	2.63	27.8	419	4.8	3.1	0.6	3.4	41%	73%	-97
	07	25	aa	NYY	8	11	28	0	131	171	80	16	36	62	5.49	1.57	21.1	308	2.5	4.2	1.7	1.1	33%	66%	23
Juarez,William	06	25	aaa	LA	4	5	11	0	57	53	26	7	36	24	4.14	1.56	23.2	240	5.7	3.7	0.7	1.1	25%	77%	10
	07	26	aa	LA	10	8	29	0	142	221	113	23	71	87	7.14	2.06	24.4	347	4.5	5.5	1.2	1.5	39%	67%	1
Julianel,Ben	06	27	aa	FLA	1	3	7	0	34	35	14	0	11	17	3.83	1.35	20.7	260	2.9	4.4	1.5	0.0	31%	68%	61
	07	28	aa	FLA	2	2	36	0	53	84	48	8	36	38	8.04	2.26	7.6	350	6.1	6.4	1.0	1.3	40%	64%	7
Junge,Eric	06	30	aaa	SD	4	5	21	0	71	97	44	5	26	49	5.56	1.73	15.8	317	3.3	6.2	1.9	0.7	38%	67%	47
	07	31	aaa	NYY	3	1	8	0	29	34	24	4	17	14	7.53	1.75	17.0	288	5.1	4.4	0.9	1.4	31%	57%	1
Jurrjens,Jair	06	21	aa	DET	4	3	12	0	67	81	31	8	21	48	4.22	1.52	24.8	293	2.8	6.5	2.3	1.0	34%	75%	53
	07	22	aa	DET	7	5	19	0	112	136	55	8	32	81	4.41	1.50	26.1	293	2.6	6.5	2.5	0.6	35%	71%	69
Kahn,Stephen	06	23	aa	SEA	1	3	31	0	39	59	35	4	34	30	8.08	2.38	6.7	341	7.8	6.9	0.9	0.9	41%	65%	19
Kaiser,Marc	06	24	aa	COL	10	10	25	0	164	217	104	21	41	59	5.71	1.57	29.5	311	2.3	3.2	1.4	1.2	33%	65%	8
	07	25	aa	COL	6	8	27	0	131	227	132	20	88	39	9.08	2.40	25.8	372	6.0	2.7	0.4	1.4	38%	62%	-35
Karnuth,Jason	06	30	aaa	OAK	2	7	62	17	71	92	49	8	28	32	6.19	1.69	5.3	308	3.5	4.0	1.1	1.0	33%	63%	12
	07	31	aaa	DET	2	2	30	6	37	45	19	6	7	22	4.61	1.42	5.4	295	1.8	5.3	3.0	1.5	32%	73%	44
Karstens,Jeff	06	24	a/a	NYY	11	5	25	0	147	165	73	16	48	92	4.48	1.45	25.7	277	3.0	5.6	1.9	1.0	31%	71%	43
	07	25	a/a	NYY	4	0	7	0	36	37	11	3	13	26	2.63	1.37	22.1	260	3.2	6.4	2.0	0.8	31%	84%	61
Keisler,Randy	06	31	aaa	OAK	9	5	25	0	103	129	53	2	49	63	4.66	1.72	19.2	300	4.3	5.5	1.3	0.2	36%	71%	49
	07	32	aaa	STL	8	11	25	0	156	231	111	21	58	77	6.38	1.85	29.8	336	3.3	4.4	1.3	1.2	37%	67%	5
Kelly,Steven	06	27	a/a	CIN	13	11	27	0	151	218	78	17	64	79	4.66	1.87	26.8	331	3.8	4.7	1.2	1.0	37%	77%	12
	07	28	a/a	CIN	1	9	27	0	78	154	87	13	41	33	10.02	2.50	15.7	403	4.7	3.8	0.8	1.5	43%	59%	-30
Kemp,Bo	06	26	aaa	MIN	7	4	49	3	89	117	34	3	30	30	3.47	1.66	8.3	311	3.1	3.0	1.0	0.3	34%	78%	22
Kendrick,Kyle	07	23	aa	PHI	4	7	12	0	81	96	35	4	19	42	3.89	1.41	29.3	288	2.1	4.6	2.2	0.5	33%	72%	59
Kennard,Jeff	06	25	aa	NYY	3	6	27	1	54	69	30	7	26	43	4.98	1.74	9.4	303	4.2	7.2	1.7	1.1	36%	73%	40
	07	26	aa	LAA	3	4	47	6	72	91	39	5	36	43	4.89	1.76	7.2	302	4.5	5.3	1.2	0.6	35%	72%	35
Kennedy,Ian	07	23 a	a/a	NYY	6	2	15	0	83	63	30	5	30	76	3.25	1.12	22.4	206	3.2	8.2	2.5	0.5	27%	72%	100
Kent,Steve	06	28	a/a	HOU	1	0	38	2	41	60	27	7	36	15	5.94	2.35	5.7	334	8.0	3.4	0.4	1.5	35%	78%	-29
Keppel,Bob	06	24	aaa	KC	6	7	25	1	98	147	78	12	27	38	7.16	1.77	18.4	339	2.5	3.5	1.4	1.1	36%	59%	5
	07	25	aa	COL	8	10	26	0	138	219	128	20	67	51	8.33	2.07	26.5	352	4.3	3.3	0.8	1.3	37%	59%	-18
Kershner,Jason	06	30	aaa	MIL	3	2	23	2	33	54	19	1	11	20	5.06	1.95	7.0	357	3.0	5.4	1.8	0.3	42%	72%	45
	07	31	aaa	CIN	5	4	39	1	63	76	41	10	22	32	5.87	1.55	7.2	291	3.2	4.6	1.5	1.4	31%	65%	12
Kester,Tim	06	35	a/a	BAL	8	5	19	0	107	172	74	14	19	39	6.26	1.79	26.5	355	1.6	3.3	2.0	1.2	37%	66%	10
	07	36	aaa	BAL	9	9	28	0	127	184	101	14	32	57	7.16	1.70	21.0	332	2.2	4.0	1.8	1.0	36%	57%	22
Ketchner,Ryan	07	25	aa	SD	1	11	19	0	99	139	82	20	43	67	7.47	1.84	24.8	324	3.9	6.0	1.5	1.8	36%	62%	4
Key,Chris	06	29	aa	PHI	3	2	37	20	49	91	24	4	16	14	4.35	2.19	6.8	389	3.0	2.5	0.8	0.7	41%	81%	-11
	07	30	aa	PHI	5	2	58	18	74	115	35	7	16	18	4.20	1.76	6.0	346	1.9	2.2	1.1	0.8	36%	77%	-2
Kilby,Brad	07	25	aa	OAK	3	3	47	0	65	76	26	6	22	56	3.63	1.50	6.1	285	3.1	7.7	2.5	0.9	35%	78%	72
Kim,Sun-Woo	06	29	aaa	COL	8	6	21	0	124	191	97	20	37	56	7.01	1.84	28.2	345	2.7	4.0	1.5	1.4	37%	63%	-2
	07	30	aa	SF	8	8	25	0	118	213	109	16	49	53	8.27	2.21	24.3	382	3.7	4.0	1.1	1.2	41%	62%	-11
Kinney,Josh	06	28 b	aaa	STL	2	2	51	3	71	57	16	2	32	63	2.00	1.25	5.8	215	4.0	7.9	2.0	0.3	28%	84%	93
Kinney,Matt	06	30	aaa	SF	8	7	28	0	153	188	98	23	54	99	5.75	1.58	24.6	296	3.2	5.8	1.8	1.4	33%	66%	29
	07	31	aa	SF	12	10	27	0	156	266	119	36	50	85	6.83	2.02	28.6	368	2.9	4.9	1.7	2.1	39%	70%	-16
Kinsey,Chris	06	24	a/a	ARI	2	2	48	3	58	66	35	9	28	39	5.43	1.62	5.5	280	4.3	6.1	1.4	1.4	31%	69%	23
	07	25	aa	ARI	4	7	28	0	121	167	81	14	63	70	6.02	1.90	20.9	321	4.7	5.2	1.1	1.0	36%	69%	15
Knight,Brandon	06	31	aa	PIT	2	7	51	27	64	72	25	8	24	62	3.47	1.49	5.5	277	3.3	8.7	2.6	1.2	35%	81%	72
Knotts,Gary	07	31	a/a	PHI	2	4	6	0	39	48	21	6	21	18	4.89	1.76	30.5	294	4.9	4.2	0.9	1.4	31%	76%	-3
Knox,Brad	06	24	aa	OAK	12	5	27	0	161	181	81	11	62	82	4.53	1.51	26.4	278	3.5	4.6	1.3	0.6	31%	70%	37
	07	25	aa	OAK	10	7	27	0	163	214	108	18	52	61	5.94	1.63	27.5	310	2.9	3.4	1.2	1.0	33%	64%	8
Koehler,Kurt	07	23	aa	FLA	1	1	21	5	25	33	21	0	11	9	7.42	1.77	5.6	311	4.1	3.1	0.8	0.0	35%	53%	28

Major League Equivalent Statistics

					Actual				Major League Equivalents																
PITCHER	Yr	Age	Lev	Org	w	l	g	sv	ip	h	er	hr	bb	k	era	WHIP	bf/g	oob	ctl	dom	cmd	hr/9	h%	s%	bpv
Kohn,Shawn	06	27	a/a	OAK	3	2	52	4	68	63	32	7	18	52	4.26	1.19	5.4	242	2.3	6.9	2.9	0.9	29%	66%	83
	07	28	aa	OAK	1	6	50	1	86	117	71	20	41	66	7.43	1.83	8.2	317	4.3	6.9	1.6	2.1	35%	63%	3
Kolb,Dan	06	26	aa	WAS	4	2	40	8	78	78	44	7	39	60	5.03	1.50	8.6	255	4.5	6.9	1.5	0.8	31%	67%	54
	07	27	a/a	WAS	2	2	31	2	55	63	45	8	46	32	7.32	1.98	8.7	282	7.5	5.3	0.7	1.3	31%	64%	5
Kometani,Paul	06	24	aa	TEX	8	5	17	0	88	116	63	5	35	65	6.42	1.72	24.0	312	3.6	6.6	1.9	0.5	38%	61%	56
	07	25	aa	TEX	3	4	39	8	78	102	51	4	31	57	5.83	1.70	9.2	310	3.5	6.6	1.9	0.5	38%	64%	57
Komine,Shane	06	26	aaa	OAK	11	8	24	0	140	159	69	13	35	98	4.42	1.39	25.1	280	2.3	6.3	2.8	0.8	33%	69%	70
	07	27	aa	OAK	5	12	23	0	133	187	100	25	51	74	6.77	1.79	27.2	325	3.4	5.0	1.5	1.7	35%	65%	-1
Koplove,Mike	06	30	aaa	ARI	5	0	48	0	65	79	33	6	26	39	4.62	1.61	6.1	294	3.5	5.4	1.5	0.8	34%	72%	37
	07	31	aaa	CLE	4	2	51	14	54	59	19	3	23	38	3.16	1.52	4.7	272	3.9	6.3	1.6	0.5	33%	80%	57
Korecky,Robert	06	27	a/a	MIN	6	5	50	13	76	116	46	8	38	31	5.44	2.02	7.5	343	4.5	3.7	0.8	1.0	37%	74%	-3
	07	28	aaa	MIN	5	6	66	35	85	108	55	6	42	54	5.81	1.76	6.0	302	4.4	5.7	1.3	0.7	35%	66%	35
Koronka,John	07	27	a/a	CLE	9	7	23	0	132	198	84	13	63	64	5.72	1.98	28.1	339	4.3	4.4	1.0	0.9	38%	71%	9
Kown,Andrew	07	25	aa	DET	6	8	27	1	120	163	80	12	39	70	6.00	1.68	20.5	318	2.9	5.3	1.8	0.9	36%	64%	35
Kozlowski,Ben	06	26	a/a	LA	3	6	41	1	97	138	59	14	48	59	5.46	1.91	11.4	327	4.4	5.5	1.2	1.3	37%	74%	9
	07	27	aaa	NYY	5	7	42	1	81	88	37	11	34	64	4.09	1.51	8.5	272	3.7	7.1	1.9	1.2	32%	76%	48
Kranawetter,Josh	06	26	aa	TAM	2	0	28	3	31	44	32	7	17	15	9.31	1.96	5.4	325	5.0	4.3	0.9	2.0	34%	53%	-26
Kuo,Hong-Chih	06	25	aaa	LA	4	3	23	1	53	55	18	5	21	52	3.09	1.43	10.0	261	3.6	8.9	2.5	0.9	34%	81%	83
Laffey,Aaron	06	21	aa	CLE	8	3	19	0	112	139	54	9	34	54	4.34	1.54	26.3	298	2.7	4.3	1.6	0.7	33%	73%	33
	07	22	a/a	CLE	13	4	22	0	131	135	51	7	31	90	3.50	1.27	24.9	261	2.1	6.2	2.9	0.5	31%	72%	86
Lahey,Timothy	07	26	a/a	MIN	8	4	52	14	81	102	45	9	40	46	5.02	1.75	7.3	301	4.4	5.1	1.1	1.1	34%	73%	18
Lambert,Chris	06	24	a/a	STL	10	10	24	0	124	150	90	21	63	99	6.52	1.71	24.0	293	4.6	7.2	1.6	1.5	34%	64%	27
	07	25	a/a	DET	1	6	34	0	90	123	80	18	41	65	8.04	1.82	12.6	318	4.1	6.5	1.6	1.8	36%	57%	11
Lamura,BJ	06	26	aa	LA	6	1	48	4	76	61	21	8	56	70	2.50	1.53	7.1	216	6.6	8.3	1.3	0.9	27%	88%	61
	07	27	aa	LA	2	7	36	0	68	78	48	9	63	52	6.39	2.08	9.4	282	8.4	6.9	0.8	1.2	33%	70%	21
Lannan,John	07	23	a/a	WAS	6	3	13	0	74	70	24	3	27	33	2.92	1.31	24.1	245	3.3	4.0	1.2	0.4	28%	78%	45
Lara,Juan	06	26	a/a	CLE	5	3	53	8	61	60	25	3	26	53	3.72	1.41	5.0	251	3.9	7.8	2.0	0.5	32%	73%	80
	07	27	a/a	CLE	4	3	54	2	59	69	33	3	31	42	5.08	1.69	5.0	285	4.7	6.4	1.4	0.5	35%	69%	50
Larrison,Preston	07	27	aaa	DET	2	2	45	1	58	66	34	2	30	31	5.26	1.65	5.9	280	4.6	4.8	1.0	0.3	32%	66%	40
Lavigne,Tim	06	28	aaa	NYM	3	2	45	4	82	97	37	9	28	39	4.01	1.52	8.1	288	3.1	4.3	1.4	0.9	31%	76%	24
	07	29	a/a	HOU	1	4	35	7	58	89	45	9	21	33	6.98	1.89	8.0	344	3.2	5.1	1.6	1.3	38%	64%	10
Lawrence,Brian	07	31	aa	NYM	8	5	16	0	104	158	75	11	16	49	6.50	1.67	29.9	341	1.4	4.3	3.0	0.9	38%	60%	48
League,Brandon	06	24	aaa	TOR	3	2	31	8	54	69	18	0	16	37	2.99	1.57	7.8	304	2.7	6.1	2.3	0.0	37%	79%	80
Leblanc,Wade	07	23	aa	SD	7	3	12	0	57	56	27	9	21	47	4.22	1.34	20.3	250	3.2	7.3	2.3	1.5	29%	74%	53
Lecure,Samuel R	07	23	aa	CIN	7	5	21	0	110	141	65	15	47	86	5.31	1.72	24.3	305	3.9	7.1	1.8	1.3	36%	71%	37
Ledezma,Wil	06	26	aaa	DET	4	3	12	0	71	72	26	7	23	56	3.32	1.34	25.2	257	2.9	7.1	2.4	0.9	31%	78%	71
Leek,Randy	06	29	aaa	STL	3	7	17	0	101	164	74	22	26	40	6.55	1.88	28.6	357	2.3	3.6	1.5	2.0	37%	69%	-22
Lee,Cliff	07	29	a/a	CLE	2	3	9	0	46	48	23	1	33	43	4.53	1.75	23.9	261	6.4	8.3	1.3	0.2	35%	72%	73
Lee,David	06	34	aaa	BOS	1	2	36	1	50	58	29	6	32	43	5.29	1.79	6.5	284	5.7	7.7	1.4	1.1	34%	72%	39
Lee,Derek	06	32	aaa	TEX	6	12	29	0	143	209	108	24	61	75	6.81	1.89	23.7	334	3.8	4.7	1.2	1.5	36%	66%	-3
	07	33	aa	TEX	1	3	8	0	30	54	25	4	14	14	7.36	2.26	19.6	380	4.2	4.1	1.0	1.1	41%	67%	-8
Lee,Seung Hak	06	27	aaa	PHI	8	9	31	2	93	121	74	17	38	49	7.13	1.71	13.9	308	3.7	4.8	1.3	1.6	33%	60%	0
Lehr,Justin	06	29	aaa	MIL	4	7	19	0	112	157	71	21	36	73	5.74	1.73	27.4	325	2.9	5.9	2.0	1.7	36%	71%	17
	07	30	aa	SEA	7	1	27	1	119	211	89	11	61	39	6.69	2.29	23.0	378	4.6	2.9	0.6	0.9	40%	70%	-16
Leicester,Jon	07	29	aaa	BAL	3	3	13	0	65	63	25	8	25	44	3.42	1.36	21.4	251	3.4	6.1	1.8	1.0	29%	79%	47
Lerew,Anthony	06	24	a/a	ATL	7	7	25	0	119	166	98	16	53	93	7.40	1.84	22.7	323	4.0	7.0	1.8	1.2	38%	60%	33
Lester,Jon	06	23	aaa	BOS	3	4	11	0	46	50	19	6	25	40	3.71	1.63	19.1	272	4.8	7.8	1.6	1.1	33%	81%	48
	07	24	a/a	BOS	5	5	15	0	77	85	41	4	36	47	4.78	1.57	23.1	274	4.2	5.5	1.3	0.5	32%	68%	47
Lewis Jr.,Rommie	07	25	aa	BAL	5	5	47	1	69	101	54	12	31	50	7.10	1.92	7.1	334	4.1	6.6	1.6	1.6	38%	65%	14
Lewis,Colby	06	27	aaa	DET	6	7	24	0	147	193	89	16	39	86	5.47	1.57	27.6	309	2.4	5.2	2.2	1.0	35%	66%	42
	07	28	aa	OAK	8	3	15	0	95	100	30	11	28	66	2.84	1.34	27.0	265	2.6	6.3	2.4	1.1	31%	84%	59
Lewis,Jensen	06	22 a	aa	CLE	1	2	7	0	39	47	21	4	12	39	4.83	1.51	24.7	292	2.8	9.0	3.3	0.9	38%	69%	91
	07	23 a	a/a	CLE	3	0	34	2	52	37	12	3	17	55	2.08	1.04	6.1	196	2.9	9.5	3.2	0.5	27%	82%	125
Lewis,Scott	07	24	aa	CLE	7	9	27	0	134	163	71	14	37	105	4.73	1.49	21.9	294	2.5	7.0	2.8	0.9	35%	69%	70
Ligtenberg,Kerry	06	35	aaa	CHC	4	4	53	18	58	82	33	12	6	37	5.06	1.52	4.9	327	1.0	5.7	5.9	1.8	36%	73%	93
Lima,Jose	06	34	aaa	NYM	7	8	25	0	140	181	91	19	22	71	5.82	1.45	24.5	307	1.4	4.6	3.2	1.2	33%	61%	52
Lincecum,Timothy	07	23 a	aa	SF	4	0	5	0	31	14	1	0	11	38	0.30	0.83	23.3	138	3.3	11.0	3.3	0.0	23%	96%	163
Lindstrom,Matt	06	27	aa	NYM	2	4	35	11	40	59	28	2	17	40	6.18	1.89	5.5	333	3.9	9.0	2.3	0.5	43%	66%	75
Liotta,Ray	06	24	aa	CHW	3	8	18	0	96	140	78	5	53	43	7.33	2.00	26.3	333	4.9	4.0	0.8	0.5	37%	61%	15
Liriano,Pedro	06	26	aaa	SF	1	6	24	0	67	92	43	5	27	32	5.83	1.78	13.1	320	3.7	4.3	1.2	0.7	36%	66%	21
	07	27	aa	LAA	4	12	28	0	130	226	117	24	53	50	8.11	2.15	23.5	373	3.7	3.4	0.9	1.7	39%	64%	-30
Litsch,Jesse	06	22	aa	TOR	3	4	12	0	69	106	56	8	14	47	7.29	1.74	26.8	344	1.8	6.1	3.4	1.0	40%	57%	62
	07	23	a/a	TOR	8	2	12	0	76	73	24	6	17	48	2.84	1.18	26.0	247	2.0	5.7	2.8	0.7	29%	79%	78
Littleton,Wes	06	24	a/a	TEX	7	1	30	5	44	34	8	6	13	34	1.69	1.08	5.9	209	2.7	6.9	2.5	1.3	24%	95%	70
	07	25	aa	TEX	0	1	23	2	32	41	26	7	9	16	7.17	1.56	6.2	305	2.5	4.5	1.8	1.9	32%	56%	3
Livingston,Bobby	06	24	aaa	SEA	8	11	23	0	135	184	80	19	37	62	5.33	1.64	26.8	318	2.5	4.1	1.7	1.3	34%	70%	13
	07	25	aaa	CIN	3	4	17	0	104	147	58	9	18	53	4.98	1.59	27.6	327	1.6	4.6	2.9	0.8	37%	69%	56
Liz,Radhames	06	23	aa	BAL	3	1	10	0	50	69	42	12	33	48	7.59	2.04	24.8	321	5.9	8.5	1.4	2.2	38%	67%	6
	07	24	aa	BAL	11	4	25	0	137	121	61	15	71	133	4.01	1.40	23.7	232	4.6	8.7	1.9	1.0	30%	74%	72
Lockwood,Luke	07	26	aa	CIN	1	7	14	0	70	120	61	11	25	38	7.83	2.07	24.9	369	3.3	4.9	1.5	1.5	40%	63%	-2
Loewen,Adam	06	23 a	a/a	BAL	6	2	12	0	71	69	25	4	30	68	3.17	1.39	25.5	250	3.8	8.6	2.3	0.5	33%	78%	89
Lofgren,Charles	07	22	a/a	CLE	12	8	27	0	151	174	89	14	69	124	5.28	1.61	25.3	283	4.1	7.4	1.8	0.9	35%	68%	55
Logan,Boone	06	22 a	aaa	CHW	3	1	38	11	42	40	20	1	12	51	4.27	1.24	4.6	245	2.6	11.0	4.2	0.2	37%	63%	153
Looper,Aaron	06	30	aaa	SEA	0	2	41	0	64	110	56	11	26	29	7.79	2.11	7.9	370	3.6	4.0	1.1	1.6	39%	64%	-18
Lopez,Aquilino	06	31	aaa	SD	3	4	41	2	62	71	39	13	24	60	5.65	1.53	6.7	280	3.5	8.7	2.5	1.8	33%	68%	48
	07	32	aaa	DET	3	5	48	26	53	58	19	6	12	48	3.21	1.31	4.7	272	2.0	8.0	4.1	1.1	33%	80%	103
Lopez,Javier	06	29	aaa	BOS	2	1	39	16	49	64	16	3	15	30	3.02	1.61	5.7	307	2.8	5.5	2.0	0.6	36%	83%	49
Lopez,Javier Arturo	07	25	aa	SD	2	2	30	0	35	41	22	3	20	23	5.65	1.73	5.5	285	5.1	5.8	1.1	0.8	33%	67%	33
Loux,Shane	06	27	aaa	KC	2	5	31	2	54	91	52	2	16	19	8.58	1.97	8.5	364	2.6	3.2	1.2	0.4	40%	53%	16
Lowery,Devon	06	24	aa	KC	5	1	24	4	33	32	23	4	18	26	6.17	1.50	6.1	248	4.8	7.1	1.5	1.1	29%	59%	46

					Actual				Major League Equivalents																
PITCHER	Yr	Age	Lev	Org	w	l	g	sv	ip	h	er	hr	bb	k	era	WHIP	bf/g	oob	ctl	dom	cmd	hr/9	h%	s%	bpv
Lo,Ching	07	22	aa	COL	8	8	26	0	139	197	119	26	66	77	7.69	1.89	25.7	326	4.3	5.0	1.2	1.7	35%	61%	-6
Lugo,Ruddy	07	27	a/a	OAK	5	1	28	10	34	22	6	0	21	22	1.51	1.24	5.1	179	5.4	5.7	1.1	0.0	23%	86%	76
Lumsden,Tyler	06	23	aa	CHW	11	5	27	0	159	168	56	10	60	80	3.15	1.43	25.6	266	3.4	4.5	1.3	0.6	30%	79%	39
	07	24	aa	KC	9	6	25	0	119	172	102	12	61	62	7.72	1.95	23.2	330	4.6	4.7	1.0	0.9	37%	59%	12
Lundberg,Spike	06	29	a/a	LA	15	6	28	0	172	218	76	7	57	86	3.96	1.60	27.8	303	3.0	4.5	1.5	0.4	35%	75%	41
	07	30	aa	LA	7	7	33	0	120	281	154	34	51	49	11.55	2.77	20.7	445	3.9	3.7	1.0	2.6	46%	60%	-69
Mabeus,Chris	06	28	a/a	OAK	2	3	36	0	48	61	45	5	41	30	8.39	2.13	6.7	303	7.7	5.7	0.7	0.9	35%	59%	18
Macdonald,Michael	07	26	a/a	TOR	9	9	28	0	163	235	106	15	46	76	5.87	1.72	27.0	330	2.6	4.2	1.6	0.8	36%	66%	24
	06	25	aa	TOR	13	9	28	0	171	236	114	14	43	85	5.98	1.63	27.8	321	2.3	4.4	2.0	0.7	36%	62%	37
Machi,Jean	06	24	aa	TAM	6	1	49	16	71	89	32	3	43	56	4.04	1.85	6.9	299	5.5	7.1	1.3	0.4	37%	78%	53
	07	25	aa	TOR	2	4	48	2	81	82	41	11	25	46	4.55	1.32	7.2	257	2.8	5.1	1.8	1.2	28%	68%	37
Mackintosh,Jason	06	26	aa	SEA	4	5	36	0	98	132	55	11	43	46	5.06	1.78	12.8	316	3.9	4.2	1.1	1.1	34%	73%	8
	07	27	aa	SEA	2	2	30	1	53	92	42	11	20	33	7.13	2.11	8.9	371	3.5	5.6	1.6	1.8	41%	69%	-6
Maclane,Evan	07	25	aa	ARI	7	7	32	0	115	234	132	28	39	45	10.28	2.37	19.0	410	3.0	3.5	1.1	2.2	42%	58%	-49
	06	24	a/a	ARI	13	9	28	0	162	228	108	20	41	85	6.00	1.66	26.5	325	2.3	4.7	2.1	1.1	36%	65%	28
Madsen,Michael	07	25	aa	OAK	10	3	21	0	123	126	67	12	57	88	4.92	1.49	25.9	260	4.2	6.5	1.6	0.8	31%	67%	49
Maduro,Calvin	06	32	aa	BAL	1	5	24	0	38	46	31	1	20	36	7.24	1.73	7.4	293	4.7	8.5	1.8	0.3	38%	55%	76
Magrane,Jim	06	28	a/a	TAM	12	12	28	0	172	233	114	15	66	88	5.97	1.74	28.6	317	3.4	4.6	1.3	0.8	35%	65%	23
	07	29	a/a	WAS	7	10	30	0	148	228	98	13	50	64	5.93	1.88	23.7	345	3.0	3.9	1.3	0.8	38%	68%	12
Mahomes,Pat	06	36	aaa	KC	1	1	7	0	35	45	29	3	16	23	7.56	1.74	23.4	306	4.0	5.8	1.4	0.8	36%	55%	35
Maine,John	06	25	aaa	NYM	3	5	10	0	56	69	31	2	21	41	5.01	1.60	25.4	295	3.4	6.5	1.9	0.3	36%	67%	65
Majewski,Gary	07	28	aaa	CIN	1	1	38	4	38	41	23	3	17	25	5.46	1.52	4.5	269	4.0	5.8	1.5	0.7	31%	63%	45
Maldonado,Ivan	06	26	aa	NYM	2	3	48	3	61	87	28	8	32	43	4.07	1.96	6.2	329	4.7	6.3	1.3	1.2	38%	82%	19
	07	27	aa	NYM	2	1	39	9	42	54	25	5	19	32	5.40	1.74	5.0	306	4.1	6.9	1.7	1.0	36%	70%	40
Mallett,Justin	07	26	a/a	CIN	4	6	45	1	96	106	64	9	51	76	6.01	1.63	9.7	275	4.7	7.1	1.5	0.9	33%	63%	48
Maloney,Matthew	07	24	a/a	CIN	13	10	28	0	170	168	88	24	55	151	4.65	1.31	25.7	253	2.9	8.0	2.7	1.3	30%	68%	72
Malone,Corwin	06	26	aa	CHW	9	11	27	0	154	201	125	23	118	90	7.32	2.07	28.5	309	6.9	5.2	0.8	1.3	34%	66%	0
	07	27	a/a	CHW	2	7	43	1	77	138	79	8	53	61	9.27	2.48	9.7	380	6.2	7.1	1.2	0.9	45%	61%	18
Manning,Charlie	06	28	a/a	NYY	8	3	49	1	84	86	38	7	34	59	4.06	1.44	7.5	260	3.7	6.3	1.7	0.7	31%	73%	55
	07	29	a/a	NYY	4	2	41	3	61	65	40	4	33	48	5.89	1.60	6.7	266	4.9	7.1	1.5	0.5	33%	61%	60
Manon,Julio	06	33	aaa	BAL	0	2	47	30	50	45	18	5	22	52	3.21	1.34	4.6	236	4.0	9.4	2.4	0.9	31%	80%	85
	07	34	a/a	OAK	2	1	20	1	21	13	9	3	11	25	3.79	1.16	4.3	178	4.7	10.7	2.3	1.4	23%	74%	89
Mansfield,Monte	06	26	aa	HOU	2	1	30	0	52	68	30	3	37	37	5.17	2.00	8.6	308	6.3	6.4	1.0	0.6	37%	74%	36
Marcum,Shaun	06	25 a	aaa	TOR	4	0	18	0	52	58	27	8	10	52	4.66	1.30	12.2	276	1.7	9.0	5.2	1.4	34%	68%	121
Markray,Thad	06	27	aa	KC	5	0	35	1	64	76	25	10	27	32	3.55	1.60	8.3	288	3.7	4.5	1.2	1.4	31%	83%	10
	07	28	aa	KC	8	7	37	2	87	139	70	13	30	44	7.22	1.94	11.4	353	3.1	4.5	1.5	1.3	38%	63%	4
Marmol,Carlos	06	24 a	a/a	CHC	3	2	13	0	61	60	28	1	30	58	4.11	1.47	20.6	251	4.4	8.6	1.9	0.2	34%	70%	93
	07	25	aa	CHC	4	1	8	0	41	37	24	5	13	38	5.31	1.21	21.1	235	2.8	8.3	3.0	1.2	29%	57%	87
Marquez,Jeffrey	07	23	aa	NYY	15	9	27	0	155	213	94	15	51	77	5.44	1.70	26.5	320	2.9	4.4	1.5	0.9	35%	68%	23
Martinez,Anastacio	06	28	a/a	WAS	7	11	26	0	141	171	94	16	72	93	6.02	1.73	25.2	294	4.6	5.9	1.3	1.0	34%	66%	28
	07	29	a/a	DET	6	9	29	0	96	132	78	8	69	57	7.26	2.09	16.6	319	6.5	5.3	0.8	0.8	37%	64%	17
Martinez,Carlos	07	25	aa	FLA	2	1	23	0	23	30	11	2	7	17	4.31	1.58	4.5	307	2.6	6.6	2.6	0.9	37%	74%	61
Martinez,Edgar	06	25	aa	BOS	5	3	49	12	69	65	28	12	19	48	3.71	1.22	5.8	245	2.5	6.3	2.6	1.5	27%	77%	52
	07	26	aaa	BOS	2	6	42	1	68	84	54	13	30	50	7.09	1.68	7.4	297	4.0	6.6	1.6	1.7	33%	60%	17
Martinez,Jonathan	07	25	a/a	MIN	3	6	35	2	56	68	40	3	40	39	6.41	1.93	7.8	294	6.4	6.2	1.0	0.5	35%	65%	39
Martinez,Ronnie	06	23	aa	HOU	3	1	10	0	49	66	37	7	19	37	6.82	1.73	22.8	316	3.4	6.8	2.0	1.3	37%	61%	34
Martin,J.D.	07	25	a/a	CLE	2	3	9	0	42	51	25	4	17	20	5.40	1.60	21.1	291	3.6	4.3	1.2	0.9	32%	67%	20
Mason,Christopher	07	23	aa	TAM	15	4	28	0	161	172	57	8	46	116	3.17	1.36	24.6	268	2.6	6.5	2.5	0.5	33%	77%	79
Masset,Nick	06	24	a/a	TEX	6	7	32	3	115	148	68	6	53	88	5.32	1.75	16.8	306	4.1	6.9	1.7	0.5	38%	68%	56
	07	25	aaa	CHW	0	4	11	0	45	63	32	9	10	29	6.45	1.61	18.6	322	2.0	5.7	2.8	1.8	35%	63%	30
Masterson,Justin	07	22	aa	BOS	4	3	10	0	58	66	40	5	21	43	6.21	1.50	25.6	280	3.3	6.6	2.0	0.7	34%	57%	59
Mastny,Tom	06	26 a	a/a	CLE	2	2	36	1	62	48	19	0	26	65	2.74	1.20	7.1	210	3.8	9.3	2.5	0.0	30%	75%	121
Mata,Frank	07	24	aa	MIN	0	4	32	3	48	76	34	4	24	22	6.35	2.07	7.5	352	4.4	4.2	0.9	0.8	39%	69%	6
Mateo,Juan	06	24	aa	CHC	7	4	18	0	92	107	49	10	32	60	4.83	1.51	22.7	285	3.1	5.9	1.9	1.0	33%	70%	43
	07	25	aa	CHC	2	3	8	0	40	61	24	11	12	23	5.45	1.82	23.7	343	2.6	5.1	2.0	2.4	36%	78%	-13
Mateo,Julio	07	30	aa	PHI	4	1	35	15	50	63	14	9	4	26	2.56	1.34	6.1	300	0.8	4.6	6.0	1.5	32%	90%	104
Mateo,Nathaniel	06	26	aa	SEA	3	7	26	0	68	103	64	13	37	49	8.52	2.06	13.0	342	4.8	6.4	1.3	1.8	39%	60%	0
Mathes,JR	06	25	aa	CHC	10	8	27	0	159	232	101	17	39	95	5.71	1.70	27.2	333	2.2	5.4	2.4	1.0	38%	67%	43
	07	26	aa	CHC	10	8	27	0	151	263	131	28	42	65	7.80	2.02	27.7	374	2.5	3.9	1.5	1.7	39%	63%	-14
Mathieson,Scott	06	23	a/a	PHI	10	3	19	0	127	124	70	15	41	113	4.96	1.30	28.2	251	2.9	8.0	2.8	1.1	31%	63%	79
Mathis,Douglas	07	24	aa	TEX	11	10	25	0	144	201	96	12	48	82	5.98	1.73	26.8	323	3.0	5.1	1.7	0.7	37%	65%	35
Matos,Osiris	07	23	aa	SF	5	0	35	4	56	59	22	3	22	36	3.48	1.44	7.0	264	3.5	5.8	1.7	0.5	31%	76%	57
Mattheus,Ryan	07	24	aa	COL	9	11	26	0	158	228	138	18	57	88	7.86	1.80	28.7	330	3.2	5.0	1.6	1.0	37%	55%	22
Mattioni,Nick	06	28	a/a	PHI	5	5	40	5	71	95	47	17	21	39	5.97	1.63	8.1	315	2.6	5.0	1.9	2.2	33%	70%	-4
Mattox Jr,David	07	27	aa	KC	0	4	8	0	38	53	45	7	24	19	10.53	2.02	23.5	323	5.7	4.5	0.8	1.7	34%	47%	-17
Matumoto,Jo	07	37	aa	TOR	3	4	45	1	86	100	49	6	52	56	5.16	1.76	9.0	285	5.4	5.9	1.1	0.6	34%	70%	38
Maust,David	06	28	aa	WAS	6	10	23	0	121	171	94	19	47	44	6.98	1.80	24.9	326	3.5	3.3	0.9	1.4	34%	62%	-14
Mays,Joe	06	31	aaa	CIN	6	3	10	0	67	92	36	6	16	31	4.77	1.61	30.4	320	2.1	4.1	2.0	0.7	35%	71%	35
	07	32	aa	LA	1	2	8	0	45	71	35	5	12	22	7.04	1.83	26.8	349	2.3	4.4	1.9	0.9	39%	61%	23
May,Darrell	06	34	aaa	CIN	3	3	8	0	46	53	29	8	15	29	5.74	1.46	25.3	281	2.9	5.7	2.0	1.6	30%	64%	26
Mazone,Brian	06	30	a/a	PHI	14	6	26	0	166	219	71	16	56	74	3.86	1.66	29.2	311	3.0	4.0	1.3	0.9	34%	79%	18
	07	31	aaa	PHI	3	2	6	0	36	37	12	5	8	16	2.88	1.25	25.2	258	2.1	4.0	1.9	1.3	27%	84%	28
McBeth,Marcus	06	26	a/a	OAK	3	3	51	25	61	61	30	8	28	56	4.41	1.45	5.2	255	4.1	8.2	2.0	1.1	31%	73%	61
	07	27	a/a	CIN	2	1	38	17	41	54	16	6	11	26	3.52	1.59	4.9	310	2.5	5.7	2.3	1.3	35%	83%	37
McBride,Macay	07	25	aaa	DET	2	2	12	0	31	41	13	4	12	26	3.77	1.71	12.0	312	3.5	7.5	2.2	1.2	38%	82%	49
McClaskey,Tim	06	31	aa	PHI	4	8	32	0	128	241	139	23	30	48	9.73	2.12	20.2	392	2.1	3.3	1.6	1.6	41%	53%	-18
	07	32	aa	PHI	4	4	13	0	57	74	35	12	14	23	5.57	1.55	19.6	308	2.2	3.6	1.6	1.9	31%	69%	-6
McClellan,Kyle	07	23 a	aa	STL	2	0	24	0	30	27	9	2	6	25	2.77	1.09	5.0	233	1.8	7.5	4.1	0.6	29%	77%	121
McClellan,Zach	06	28	aaa	COL	4	3	54	3	64	95	40	4	29	40	5.61	1.93	5.8	336	4.1	5.6	1.4	0.6	39%	70%	32
McClung,Seth	07	27	aaa	MIL	3	5	45	5	77	63	21	6	53	81	2.40	1.50	7.6	218	6.1	9.5	1.5	0.7	29%	87%	79

					Actual				Major League Equivalents																
PITCHER	Yr	Age	Lev	Org	w	l	g	sv	ip	h	er	hr	bb	k	era	WHIP	bf/g	oob	ctl	dom	cmd	hr/9	h%	s%	bpv
McCrory,Robert	07	25	aa	BAL	1	2	22	13	23	29	13	0	17	17	5.22	1.98	5.1	301	6.5	6.7	1.0	0.0	38%	71%	57
McCurdy,Nick	06	27	a/a	BAL	5	2	52	3	79	121	40	8	24	49	4.56	1.84	7.2	344	2.8	5.5	2.0	0.9	39%	77%	35
	07	28	a/a	BAL	3	6	45	3	76	95	40	11	25	50	4.76	1.59	7.6	301	3.0	5.9	2.0	1.4	34%	74%	30
McCutchen,Daniel	07	25	aa	NYY	3	2	7	0	41	41	18	3	14	27	3.90	1.36	25.0	256	3.2	5.9	1.9	0.7	30%	72%	57
McDonald,James	07	23 a	aa	LA	7	2	10	0	52	46	10	6	16	56	1.72	1.19	21.4	232	2.8	9.7	3.5	1.0	30%	93%	109
McGinley,Blake	06	28	aaa	NYM	2	2	22	1	58	78	29	8	16	29	4.51	1.63	12.0	317	2.5	4.5	1.8	1.2	35%	75%	21
	07	29	aa	FLA	6	9	43	1	81	119	65	15	41	45	7.26	1.98	9.2	334	4.6	5.0	1.1	1.6	36%	65%	-8
McGowan,Dustin	06	25	aaa	TOR	4	5	23	1	84	94	56	9	42	74	6.00	1.62	16.6	277	4.5	7.9	1.8	1.0	34%	63%	55
McKae,Dave	07	26	aa	SF	6	4	17	0	104	120	64	10	19	50	5.58	1.34	26.0	283	1.6	4.4	2.7	0.9	31%	58%	55
McLeary,Marty	06	32	aaa	PIT	3	4	35	2	104	124	46	7	37	92	4.01	1.55	13.3	290	3.2	8.0	2.5	0.6	37%	75%	78
	07	33	aa	PIT	5	8	24	0	122	171	89	15	61	68	6.59	1.90	24.5	323	4.5	5.0	1.1	1.1	36%	66%	10
McLemore,Mark	06	26	aaa	HOU	2	3	21	0	57	56	22	5	38	43	3.41	1.64	12.4	250	6.0	6.7	1.1	0.8	30%	81%	44
	07	27	aa	HOU	0	1	21	0	52	45	22	2	40	38	3.78	1.64	11.3	228	7.0	6.6	1.0	0.4	28%	76%	57
McNab,Timothy	06	26 b	a/a	NYM	3	2	16	1	42	71	28	4	2	20	5.95	1.75	12.2	367	0.5	4.2	8.9	1.0	40%	66%	166
	07	27	aa	NYM	8	6	46	2	91	124	43	5	27	37	4.28	1.65	9.1	318	2.6	3.6	1.4	0.5	35%	74%	28
McNiven,Brooks	07	26	aa	SF	7	6	30	0	116	160	63	11	32	30	4.90	1.65	17.7	320	2.5	2.4	0.9	0.9	33%	71%	-2
Meacham,Cory	07	23	aa	STL	11	8	28	0	144	168	88	15	53	68	5.47	1.53	22.9	285	3.3	4.2	1.3	1.0	31%	65%	22
Meaux,Ryan	06	28	a/a	SD	3	4	48	1	86	135	66	9	40	51	6.89	2.04	8.9	350	4.2	5.3	1.3	1.0	40%	66%	14
	07	29	aa	OAK	0	4	36	0	42	78	43	5	15	27	9.06	2.19	6.0	386	3.2	5.8	1.8	1.1	44%	57%	19
Medders,Brandon	07	28	aa	ARI	5	3	35	5	48	77	39	5	29	27	7.23	2.21	7.0	355	5.4	5.1	0.9	0.9	40%	67%	8
Medlock,Calvin	06	24	aa	CIN	7	2	42	2	63	67	29	5	30	57	4.11	1.53	6.7	266	4.3	8.1	1.9	0.7	34%	74%	69
	07	25	a/a	TAM	6	3	51	2	79	74	39	6	30	72	4.46	1.32	6.6	243	3.4	8.2	2.4	0.7	31%	66%	85
Meek,Evan	07	24	aa	TAM	2	1	44	1	67	88	41	2	37	58	5.51	1.87	7.3	311	4.9	7.8	1.6	0.3	40%	68%	64
Megrew,Michael	07	24	aa	LA	6	6	21	0	93	111	66	8	47	77	6.38	1.71	20.5	291	4.6	7.4	1.6	0.8	36%	62%	51
Melendez,German	07	27	aa	HOU	6	5	44	4	79	92	53	18	40	48	6.02	1.66	8.2	284	4.5	5.5	1.2	2.1	30%	69%	-5
Meloan,Jonathan	07	23 a	aa	LA	7	2	49	20	66	41	18	6	28	78	2.38	1.04	5.4	176	3.8	10.5	2.8	0.8	24%	82%	116
Mendez,Adalberto	07	26	aa	CHC	3	4	40	1	59	68	44	14	38	38	6.76	1.78	7.0	282	5.7	5.7	1.0	2.2	29%	67%	-12
Mendoza,Luis	06	23	aa	TEX	3	9	16	0	86	158	95	8	27	43	9.93	2.15	27.3	386	2.8	4.5	1.6	0.8	43%	51%	13
	07	24	aa	TEX	15	4	26	0	148	177	87	14	49	78	5.26	1.53	25.4	291	3.0	4.7	1.6	0.9	32%	66%	32
Mendoza,Ramiro	06	34	aaa	NYY	2	5	24	0	63	109	65	14	16	29	9.31	1.99	12.9	373	2.3	4.2	1.9	2.0	39%	54%	-14
Mercado,Hector	06	32	aaa	DET	3	2	26	1	32	45	19	1	19	21	5.33	2.01	6.1	326	5.3	5.9	1.1	0.3	39%	72%	39
Meredith,Cla	06	23 a	aaa	SD	3	0	32	2	46	47	15	3	9	33	2.93	1.22	5.9	259	1.8	6.5	3.7	0.6	31%	77%	101
Meyers,Mike	06	29	a/a	MIL	5	6	32	0	72	89	48	7	35	54	6.02	1.73	10.5	298	4.4	6.7	1.5	0.9	35%	65%	41
Meyer,Dan	06	25	aaa	OAK	3	3	10	0	49	69	30	10	19	25	5.54	1.79	23.2	323	3.5	4.5	1.3	1.8	34%	74%	-11
	07	26	aa	OAK	8	2	22	0	119	141	62	17	61	79	4.69	1.70	25.0	289	4.6	6.0	1.3	1.3	33%	76%	21
Miadich,Bart	06	31	aaa	TAM	3	8	61	10	67	48	36	6	58	66	4.78	1.58	4.9	196	7.8	8.8	1.1	0.7	26%	70%	70
Michalak,Chris	06	36	aaa	CIN	9	5	23	0	132	183	64	24	32	48	4.37	1.63	26.1	322	2.2	3.3	1.5	1.6	33%	79%	-7
	07	37	aaa	WAS	5	8	20	0	100	121	48	12	28	37	4.36	1.49	22.1	293	2.6	3.3	1.3	1.0	31%	73%	13
Mickolio,Kameron	07	23	aa	SEA	6	4	32	3	53	49	20	3	24	48	3.31	1.38	7.1	242	4.0	8.0	2.0	0.5	31%	76%	81
Middleton,Kyle	06	26	a/a	KC	5	11	29	1	159	252	107	20	56	77	6.04	1.94	26.6	352	3.1	4.3	1.4	1.1	38%	70%	6
	07	27	aa	HOU	3	2	44	23	51	63	28	6	22	31	4.89	1.65	5.3	296	3.8	5.4	1.4	1.1	33%	72%	26
Mijares,Jose	07	23	a/a	MIN	5	4	51	9	69	58	39	11	57	66	5.07	1.66	6.2	223	7.4	8.6	1.2	1.4	27%	73%	43
Mildren,Paul	06	22	aa	FLA	10	10	28	0	167	195	105	22	61	136	5.66	1.53	26.6	286	3.3	7.3	2.2	1.2	34%	65%	53
	07	23	aa	KC	6	8	24	0	119	161	106	19	61	65	8.03	1.86	23.7	316	4.6	4.9	1.1	1.4	34%	57%	2
Miller,Adam	06	22 a	a/a	CLE	15	6	27	0	158	147	60	9	46	150	3.42	1.22	24.2	241	2.6	8.5	3.3	0.5	32%	72%	112
	07	23 a	aaa	CLE	5	4	19	0	65	73	40	4	20	65	5.53	1.43	14.9	278	2.8	9.0	3.3	0.5	37%	60%	106
Miller,Andrew	07	22 a	a/a	DET	2	0	6	0	36	34	12	2	10	29	2.98	1.22	25.0	243	2.5	7.2	2.9	0.5	30%	76%	96
Miller,Derek	07	26	aa	MIL	6	2	11	0	68	74	33	13	19	53	4.41	1.37	26.5	273	2.5	7.0	2.8	1.8	31%	75%	49
Miller,Greg	06	22	a/a	LA	4	0	44	1	59	48	22	1	44	49	3.33	1.54	6.0	216	6.7	7.5	1.1	0.1	28%	77%	76
	07	23	aa	LA	2	3	34	1	76	73	58	3	89	85	6.85	2.13	11.3	247	10.5	10.0	1.0	0.4	35%	65%	75
Miller,Jason	06	24	aaa	MIN	3	8	32	1	99	127	62	14	42	74	5.63	1.71	14.3	305	3.8	6.7	1.8	1.3	35%	69%	33
	07	25	aaa	MIN	1	5	31	0	75	106	48	13	27	30	5.81	1.78	11.4	326	3.3	3.6	1.1	1.6	34%	71%	-13
Miller,Jim	06	24	aa	COL	0	3	45	12	44	62	26	14	14	33	5.37	1.72	4.5	325	2.8	6.8	2.4	2.8	35%	80%	-2
	07	25	a/a	BAL	3	5	52	7	66	63	34	4	43	66	4.59	1.61	5.8	247	5.9	8.9	1.5	0.6	33%	71%	74
Miller,Joshua	06	28	aa	HOU	11	10	33	0	152	224	102	19	49	72	6.06	1.80	21.7	336	2.9	4.3	1.5	1.1	36%	67%	10
	07	29	aa	HOU	6	6	35	3	137	205	83	23	31	54	5.41	1.72	18.2	338	2.0	3.6	1.7	1.5	35%	72%	1
Miller,Matt	07	36	aaa	CLE	0	1	38	1	37	29	15	4	22	31	3.57	1.39	4.2	214	5.4	7.6	1.4	1.0	26%	78%	57
Mills,Alan	07	41	aa	DET	1	1	29	23	29	31	14	1	13	16	4.38	1.50	4.4	265	4.0	5.0	1.2	0.4	31%	69%	47
Miner,Zach	06	25	aaa	DET	6	0	9	0	51	51	21	2	21	35	3.71	1.41	24.5	255	3.7	6.2	1.7	0.4	31%	73%	65
	07	26	a/a	DET	1	4	13	0	53	59	41	5	24	29	6.94	1.56	18.3	275	4.1	4.8	1.2	0.9	31%	54%	27
Minix,Travis	06	29	aaa	PHI	1	3	40	3	48	63	22	7	14	21	4.10	1.60	5.4	308	2.7	3.9	1.5	1.2	33%	78%	11
Misch,Patrick	06	25	a/a	SF	9	6	28	0	168	208	74	16	37	110	3.94	1.46	26.3	298	2.0	5.9	3.0	0.8	35%	75%	68
	07	26	aa	SF	2	5	34	1	66	70	30	5	22	55	4.06	1.39	8.4	266	3.0	7.5	2.5	0.6	33%	71%	80
Mitchell,Andy	06	28	aaa	BAL	1	1	50	0	67	96	26	4	30	41	3.46	1.87	6.4	328	4.0	5.5	1.4	0.6	38%	82%	34
	07	29	aaa	BAL	8	8	39	0	116	167	79	9	45	56	6.14	1.83	14.1	330	3.5	4.3	1.2	0.7	37%	65%	20
Mobley,Chris	06	23	aa	FLA	1	4	52	4	58	72	36	6	35	45	5.58	1.84	5.3	298	5.4	6.9	1.3	1.0	36%	70%	35
	07	24	aa	FLA	7	2	39	11	41	58	24	3	14	25	5.29	1.74	4.9	325	3.0	5.4	1.8	0.7	37%	69%	40
Mock,Garrett	06	23	aa	WAS	4	12	27	0	147	209	120	21	61	104	7.31	1.83	25.9	327	3.7	6.3	1.7	1.3	38%	60%	26
	07	24	aa	WAS	1	5	11	0	51	78	40	5	29	32	7.05	2.10	23.3	343	5.2	5.7	1.1	0.9	39%	66%	16
Molldrem,Craig	07	26	aa	FLA	5	4	53	0	70	90	48	8	46	43	6.20	1.93	6.4	305	5.9	5.5	0.9	1.0	34%	68%	15
Montero,Agustin	06	29	aaa	CHW	2	3	39	1	59	71	47	12	23	43	7.20	1.60	6.8	293	3.5	6.5	1.9	1.8	32%	57%	19
Montero,Oscar	06	28	aa	SF	2	1	32	1	46	73	43	6	28	43	8.32	2.17	7.3	351	5.4	8.5	1.6	1.2	43%	61%	32
Moorhead,Brandon	06	27	aa	SEA	2	3	9	0	40	70	40	5	22	19	9.03	2.29	23.2	375	4.9	4.3	0.9	1.0	41%	59%	-7
Morales,Alexis	07	25	a/a	WAS	4	3	28	2	38	32	24	2	44	42	5.62	2.01	6.7	224	10.5	9.9	0.9	0.5	31%	71%	75
Morales,Franklin	07	22	aa	COL	5	4	20	0	112	118	60	12	58	83	4.81	1.57	25.2	265	4.7	6.7	1.4	1.0	31%	71%	43
Morales,Ricardo	07	24	aa	NYM	3	2	13	0	44	53	31	7	11	22	6.31	1.45	14.8	290	2.3	4.6	2.0	1.5	31%	58%	21
Moreno,Victor	06	27	aaa	OAK	5	4	34	4	100	134	68	7	40	55	6.15	1.74	13.7	314	3.6	5.0	1.4	0.7	36%	63%	31
	07	28	aaa	BAL	2	5	39	3	64	91	55	5	35	42	7.71	1.98	8.0	328	5.0	5.9	1.2	0.8	38%	59%	27
Morillo,Juan	06	23	aa	COL	12	8	27	0	140	151	93	17	77	113	5.97	1.63	23.6	270	4.9	7.3	1.5	1.1	32%	64%	43
	07	24	aa	COL	6	5	53	0	67	64	27	3	32	61	3.60	1.43	5.5	246	4.3	8.2	1.9	0.4	32%	74%	83

					Actual				Major League Equivalents																
PITCHER	Yr	Age	Lev	Org	w	l	g	sv	ip	h	er	hr	bb	k	era	WHIP	bf/g	oob	ctl	dom	cmd	hr/9	h%	s%	bpv
Morris,Cory	06	27	a/a	BAL	2	9	18	0	78	107	57	9	72	56	6.61	2.29	22.6	319	8.3	6.4	0.8	1.1	37%	72%	14
Morton,Charlie	07	24	aa	ATL	4	6	41	0	79	96	49	3	40	55	5.62	1.72	9.0	293	4.6	6.3	1.4	0.4	36%	65%	52
Moseley,Dustin	06	25	aaa	LAA	13	8	26	0	149	175	82	17	48	96	4.95	1.49	25.3	287	2.9	5.8	2.0	1.0	33%	68%	44
Motte,Jason	07	25	aa	STL	3	3	45	8	49	44	13	3	23	50	2.45	1.38	4.7	237	4.3	9.1	2.1	0.6	32%	84%	88
Moylan,Peter	06	28	aaa	ATL	1	7	35	1	56	78	58	5	43	46	9.27	2.15	8.1	322	6.9	7.3	1.1	0.8	39%	55%	31
Muecke,Joshua	06	25	aa	HOU	0	7	25	0	62	111	65	9	28	34	9.47	2.24	12.8	379	4.1	5.0	1.2	1.4	42%	57%	-7
	07	26	aa	HOU	9	5	32	0	131	168	76	23	50	59	5.19	1.66	18.8	305	3.4	4.1	1.2	1.6	32%	73%	-5
Muegge,Danny	06	26	aa	LA	9	9	25	0	141	190	88	26	44	64	5.59	1.66	25.9	315	2.8	4.1	1.4	1.6	33%	70%	-2
Mujica,Edward	06	22 a	a/a	CLE	4	1	34	13	51	49	11	1	15	41	1.93	1.25	6.3	247	2.6	7.2	2.7	0.2	32%	84%	101
	07	23 a	aaa	CLE	2	1	34	14	37	40	25	4	9	40	6.05	1.32	4.6	269	2.2	9.7	4.4	1.0	36%	53%	124
Mullins,Ryan	07	24	a/a	MIN	4	6	18	0	101	136	73	8	30	64	6.50	1.64	25.6	316	2.7	5.7	2.1	0.7	37%	59%	50
Mulvey,Kevin	07	22	aa	NYM	12	10	27	0	157	164	65	4	42	98	3.72	1.31	24.6	263	2.4	5.6	2.3	0.2	32%	70%	78
Muniz,Carlos	07	27 b	aa	NYM	2	4	47	23	64	61	22	2	20	50	3.07	1.26	5.7	246	2.7	7.0	2.5	0.3	31%	75%	91
Munoz,Arnie	06	24	a/a	CHW	2	5	33	2	52	61	41	7	24	44	7.12	1.62	7.2	286	4.1	7.5	1.8	1.2	34%	56%	44
	07	25	aaa	WAS	3	1	54	0	52	54	19	5	18	39	3.31	1.37	4.2	260	3.1	6.7	2.1	0.9	31%	79%	61
Munoz,Luis	07	26	aa	PIT	14	6	28	0	153	193	82	14	39	79	4.83	1.52	24.3	302	2.3	4.7	2.0	0.8	34%	69%	40
Munro,Pete	06	31	aaa	MIN	8	12	30	0	162	249	121	20	57	78	6.72	1.89	26.0	345	3.2	4.3	1.4	1.1	38%	65%	7
Munter,Scott	06	27	aa	SF	1	4	28	1	40	67	37	1	20	17	8.28	2.16	7.3	363	4.4	3.7	0.8	0.3	40%	58%	15
	07	28	aa	SF	1	6	48	1	58	84	39	4	29	10	5.97	1.95	5.9	332	4.5	1.5	0.3	0.6	34%	68%	-12
Murphy,Bill	06	25	a/a	ARI	5	5	42	0	101	134	85	9	49	82	7.58	1.81	11.4	311	4.4	7.3	1.7	0.8	38%	56%	46
	07	26	aa	ARI	3	3	54	1	100	125	60	15	49	78	5.37	1.75	8.6	300	4.4	7.0	1.6	1.3	35%	72%	30
Murray,Arlington	07	26	aa	TEX	3	3	41	5	52	56	26	3	28	40	4.41	1.60	5.8	267	4.8	6.8	1.4	0.6	33%	72%	55
Musser,Neal	06	26	a/a	ARI	8	6	28	2	129	166	93	19	81	72	6.50	1.91	22.3	305	5.7	5.0	0.9	1.3	33%	67%	3
	07	27 b	aa	KC	4	1	32	8	55	45	5	1	13	34	0.79	1.05	6.8	217	2.2	5.6	2.6	0.2	26%	94%	93
Nageotte,Clint	06	26	aaa	SEA	7	7	19	0	89	115	67	6	55	46	6.73	1.90	22.6	307	5.5	4.6	0.8	0.6	35%	63%	20
Nall,Brandon M	07	26	aa	NYM	2	0	34	0	43	62	29	0	18	29	6.03	1.86	6.1	331	3.7	6.0	1.6	0.0	40%	64%	59
Nall,T.J.	06	26 a	a/a	LA	10	7	31	2	143	144	56	12	33	125	3.51	1.23	19.2	256	2.1	7.9	3.8	0.7	32%	73%	110
	07	27	a/a	BOS	3	12	18	0	88	158	82	21	42	46	8.41	2.27	25.4	380	4.3	4.7	1.1	2.2	40%	66%	-35
Nannini,Micke	06	26	a/a	DET	1	2	39	2	61	77	43	19	31	43	6.39	1.77	7.3	301	4.6	6.4	1.4	2.8	31%	73%	-21
	07	27	aa	CHC	1	2	28	1	53	73	41	11	31	35	6.96	1.98	9.3	322	5.3	5.9	1.1	1.8	35%	68%	-6
Narron,Sam	07	26	aa	MIL	7	9	27	0	151	236	102	15	32	75	6.09	1.77	26.3	348	1.9	4.5	2.3	0.9	39%	65%	34
Narveson,Chris	06	25	aaa	STL	8	5	15	0	80	83	32	10	34	50	3.60	1.46	23.4	262	3.8	5.6	1.5	1.1	29%	79%	33
	07	26	aa	STL	3	2	9	0	45	50	37	7	22	28	7.30	1.60	22.7	275	4.4	5.6	1.3	1.3	30%	54%	20
Neal,Blaine	06	29	aa	PIT	2	0	29	2	40	51	15	3	13	31	3.36	1.59	6.2	304	2.8	7.0	2.5	0.6	37%	80%	72
	07	29	aaa	TOR	5	7	47	11	56	74	36	11	31	39	5.82	1.86	5.7	310	4.9	6.3	1.3	1.8	34%	73%	4
Nelson,Brad	07	26	a/a	ATL	6	2	32	0	87	97	47	6	28	47	4.90	1.44	11.9	276	2.9	4.8	1.6	0.7	31%	65%	43
Nelson,Bubba	06	25	aa	SD	5	7	52	2	83	87	49	8	52	65	5.30	1.67	7.3	263	5.7	7.0	1.2	0.8	32%	69%	45
	07	26	a/a	PHI	5	8	36	1	112	117	66	17	49	65	5.26	1.48	13.7	263	3.9	5.2	1.3	1.3	28%	67%	21
Nelson,Joe	06	32	aaa	KC	2	2	24	7	32	23	9	4	13	32	2.66	1.12	5.4	199	3.6	9.1	2.6	1.2	25%	83%	88
Neshek,Patrick	06	26 b	aaa	MIN	6	2	33	14	60	54	20	9	16	72	2.94	1.17	7.4	234	2.5	10.8	4.4	1.4	31%	83%	122
Ness,Joe	07	24	aa	CLE	4	3	26	0	71	94	62	7	46	53	7.83	1.97	13.4	311	5.9	6.8	1.1	0.9	37%	59%	30
Nestor,Scott	07	23	aa	FLA	2	4	58	1	75	75	44	5	43	77	5.32	1.58	5.8	256	5.2	9.2	1.8	0.6	34%	65%	78
Newman,Joshua	06	24	aa	COL	9	5	62	2	77	69	37	11	24	63	4.31	1.22	5.1	236	2.8	7.3	2.6	1.2	28%	68%	69
	07	25	aa	COL	3	2	55	0	62	99	42	4	33	40	6.13	2.13	5.7	353	4.8	5.7	1.2	0.6	41%	70%	24
Newsom,Randy	07	25	aa	CLE	4	1	47	18	49	67	23	3	19	18	4.29	1.75	4.9	318	3.5	3.3	1.0	0.6	35%	76%	13
Niemann,Jeff	06	24	aa	TAM	5	5	14	0	77	73	35	8	34	70	4.09	1.39	23.7	245	4.0	8.2	2.1	1.0	31%	73%	69
	07	25	aaa	TAM	12	6	25	0	131	175	79	16	50	108	5.43	1.72	24.3	314	3.4	7.4	2.2	1.1	38%	70%	49
Nin,Sandy	06	26	aaa	COL	1	3	6	0	31	38	21	4	8	21	5.95	1.49	22.9	295	2.4	6.2	2.6	1.2	34%	61%	52
Nippert,Dustin	06	25	aaa	ARI	13	8	25	0	140	182	89	12	51	114	5.71	1.66	25.7	308	3.2	7.3	2.3	0.8	38%	65%	61
	07	26	aa	ARI	0	3	10	0	36	31	28	5	26	36	6.90	1.60	16.3	228	6.6	8.9	1.3	1.1	29%	57%	57
Nitkowski,C.J.	06	34	aaa	PIT	5	1	58	4	60	74	29	5	32	46	4.41	1.75	4.8	295	4.7	6.8	1.4	0.8	36%	76%	44
Nix,Michael Ward	07	24	aa	ATL	4	6	44	0	69	71	24	2	33	59	3.15	1.49	6.9	259	4.2	7.7	1.8	0.3	33%	78%	79
Norderum,Jason	06	25	a/a	WAS	1	0	19	0	48	58	27	3	29	20	5.02	1.80	11.9	291	5.4	3.8	0.7	0.6	32%	72%	17
Norrito,Giuseppe	07	25	aa	LA	8	5	24	0	117	166	71	20	29	45	5.46	1.66	22.4	326	2.2	3.5	1.6	1.5	34%	71%	-3
Nottingham,Shawn	07	23	aa	CLE	9	12	27	0	149	180	97	11	60	87	5.86	1.61	25.0	293	3.6	5.3	1.5	0.7	34%	62%	39
Nunez,Franklin	06	30	aaa	ATL	1	6	30	2	44	74	45	5	31	28	9.19	2.37	7.8	364	6.3	5.8	0.9	1.1	41%	60%	2
Nunez,Leo	06	23	a/a	KC	3	4	38	8	59	61	22	7	23	48	3.36	1.42	6.7	261	3.5	7.3	2.1	1.1	31%	81%	58
	07	24	aa	KC	2	2	11	0	43	32	12	4	11	27	2.41	0.97	15.3	200	2.2	5.5	2.5	0.9	22%	81%	75
Nunez,Vladimir	07	33	aaa	CHW	4	10	29	1	111	144	97	23	52	66	7.84	1.76	17.9	308	4.2	5.3	1.3	1.9	33%	57%	-4
O'Connor,Brian	06	29	aaa	ATL	8	10	28	0	148	214	104	11	87	62	6.34	2.03	26.2	331	5.3	3.8	0.7	0.7	36%	68%	6
O'Connor,Mike	07	27	aa	WAS	3	7	15	0	71	116	78	25	23	32	9.91	1.95	23.1	358	2.9	4.1	1.4	3.2	35%	53%	-58
O'Day,Darren	07	25	aa	LAA	3	4	29	10	29	34	17	3	15	18	5.21	1.66	4.6	284	4.6	5.6	1.2	1.0	32%	70%	28
O'Flaherty,Eric	06	22 a	a/a	SEA	3	2	27	7	43	52	6	0	16	38	1.20	1.59	7.2	294	3.4	7.9	2.3	0.0	39%	92%	93
O'Malley,Ryan	06	27	aaa	CHC	7	7	26	0	123	169	78	12	33	61	5.72	1.64	21.6	320	2.4	4.5	1.9	0.9	35%	65%	30
	07	27	aa	CHC	5	9	29	0	122	240	142	37	48	51	10.47	2.36	22.2	402	3.5	3.7	1.1	2.8	41%	58%	-63
Obermueller,Wes	07	31	aa	FLA	4	1	11	0	63	107	53	9	40	29	7.54	2.33	30.1	368	5.7	4.1	0.7	1.2	40%	68%	-16
Ohka,Tomo	07	32	aa	SEA	0	5	7	0	41	86	55	9	15	12	12.14	2.47	31.6	418	3.4	2.6	0.8	2.1	42%	50%	-59
Ohlendorf,Ross	06	24	a/a	ARI	10	8	28	0	182	226	88	16	30	111	4.33	1.40	28.1	298	1.5	5.5	3.7	0.8	34%	70%	81
	07	25	aaa	NYY	3	4	22	0	68	106	51	9	25	41	6.67	1.93	15.0	348	3.3	5.4	1.6	1.2	39%	66%	15
Ojeda,Alvis	06	23	aa	LA	7	3	30	1	85	100	37	6	39	51	3.93	1.64	12.9	287	4.1	5.4	1.3	0.7	33%	77%	38
	07	24	aa	LA	4	7	26	0	106	160	82	14	60	57	6.96	2.07	20.4	340	5.1	4.8	1.0	1.2	38%	67%	1
Olenberger,Kasey	06	29	aaa	LAA	7	5	25	0	121	149	78	16	48	57	5.83	1.63	22.1	297	3.6	4.2	1.2	1.2	32%	66%	10
	07	30	aaa	LAA	10	7	29	0	180	319	177	52	63	74	8.87	2.12	31.3	377	3.1	3.7	1.2	2.6	38%	62%	-52
Olivera,Manuel	06	29	aa	FLA	5	9	25	0	108	181	81	6	55	47	6.76	2.19	22.1	365	4.6	3.9	0.9	0.5	40%	67%	8
Olsen,Kevin	06	30	aa	OAK	6	1	13	0	84	123	56	10	27	29	5.96	1.78	30.5	333	2.9	3.1	1.1	1.1	35%	67%	-2
Olson,Garrett	06	23	aa	BAL	6	5	14	0	84	95	44	6	32	76	4.71	1.51	26.6	279	3.4	8.1	2.4	0.6	36%	69%	79
	07	24	aaa	BAL	9	7	22	0	128	117	63	17	40	105	4.43	1.23	24.1	238	2.8	7.4	2.6	1.2	28%	67%	71
Olson,Justin	06	27	aa	MIN	7	7	32	1	88	134	79	15	52	75	8.10	2.11	13.9	343	5.3	7.6	1.4	1.5	41%	62%	17
Ool,Kevin	06	26	aa	STL	3	3	45	0	83	104	49	11	21	33	5.29	1.51	8.2	301	2.3	3.6	1.6	1.2	32%	67%	13
	07	27	aa	STL	4	2	21	0	56	101	41	5	18	27	6.63	2.13	13.5	381	2.9	4.3	1.5	0.7	42%	68%	13

Major League Equivalent Statistics

PITCHER	Yr	Age	Lev	Org	Actual w	l	g	sv	Major League Equivalents ip	h	er	hr	bb	k	era	WHIP	bf/g	oob	ctl	dom	cmd	hr/9	h%	s%	bpv
Orenduff,Justin	06	23	aa	LA	4	2	10	0	50	48	26	5	21	45	4.63	1.38	21.5	249	3.7	8.0	2.2	0.9	31%	68%	71
	07	24	aa	LA	8	5	27	0	109	132	62	19	47	95	5.13	1.64	18.4	292	3.9	7.8	2.0	1.6	35%	73%	39
Ormond,Rodney	06	29	a/a	TOR	6	6	55	6	79	90	41	17	24	41	4.72	1.45	6.3	281	2.8	4.7	1.7	1.9	29%	75%	4
Orvella,Chad	06	26 b	aaa	TAM	4	0	27	1	38	38	10	2	10	46	2.43	1.27	5.9	255	2.4	10.7	4.4	0.5	37%	82%	147
	07	27	aaa	TAM	3	3	42	20	52	49	26	8	22	45	4.55	1.38	5.3	246	3.8	7.7	2.0	1.5	29%	72%	51
Osborne,Donovan	06	37	aaa	KC	0	6	17	0	52	105	52	9	15	25	8.89	2.30	16.0	408	2.5	4.3	1.7	1.6	44%	62%	-15
Osoria,Franquelis	06	25	aaa	LA	2	2	44	2	51	85	25	2	20	24	4.44	2.05	5.8	362	3.6	4.2	1.2	0.4	41%	77%	22
	07	26	aa	PIT	2	5	39	11	54	67	22	3	22	24	3.63	1.63	6.3	296	3.6	4.0	1.1	0.6	33%	78%	26
Ostlund,Ian	06	28	aa	DET	9	5	53	0	65	96	52	8	30	50	7.17	1.95	6.0	337	4.2	6.9	1.7	1.2	40%	63%	29
	07	29	a/a	DET	2	1	29	1	38	52	22	7	8	30	5.27	1.57	5.9	317	1.9	7.0	3.6	1.7	36%	71%	60
Outman,Joshua	07	23	aa	PHI	2	3	7	0	42	44	26	6	24	28	5.52	1.62	27.2	265	5.1	6.0	1.2	1.3	30%	68%	23
Overbey,Seth	07	23	aa	TOR	2	4	30	2	50	65	31	4	15	26	5.54	1.60	7.6	307	2.8	4.7	1.7	0.7	35%	65%	35
Overholt,Patrick	07	23	aa	PHI	6	9	15	0	79	122	73	14	51	39	8.30	2.19	26.9	346	5.8	4.4	0.8	1.6	37%	63%	-20
Owens,Henry	06	27 b	aa	NYM	2	2	37	20	40	28	12	1	12	52	2.71	0.99	4.2	192	2.7	11.8	4.3	0.3	30%	72%	170
Owings,Micah	06	24	a/a	ARI	16	2	27	0	162	197	79	10	53	112	4.41	1.54	26.8	294	2.9	6.2	2.1	0.6	35%	71%	61
Oxspring,Chris	07	30	aaa	MIL	7	5	18	0	96	118	53	12	51	86	5.00	1.76	25.0	296	4.8	8.1	1.7	1.1	36%	74%	46
Oyervidez,Jose	06	25	aa	SD	6	12	28	0	149	179	86	12	84	109	5.21	1.76	24.9	291	5.1	6.6	1.3	0.7	35%	70%	43
	07	26	aa	SD	0	1	7	0	30	46	28	2	13	16	8.33	1.96	20.9	342	4.0	4.9	1.2	0.7	39%	55%	21
Palmer,Jonathan	07	29	aa	SF	11	8	30	0	155	231	116	24	65	69	6.75	1.91	25.0	338	3.8	4.0	1.1	1.4	36%	66%	-8
Palmer,Matt	06	28	a/a	SF	11	7	30	0	153	190	72	14	46	85	4.26	1.54	22.8	298	2.7	5.0	1.9	0.8	34%	74%	40
Pals,Jordan	06	26	aa	STL	8	7	27	0	160	249	112	27	43	69	6.31	1.83	28.1	347	2.4	3.9	1.6	1.5	37%	68%	-2
Parisi,Mike	06	23	aa	STL	9	8	27	0	150	193	91	13	63	89	5.44	1.70	25.7	305	3.8	5.3	1.4	0.8	35%	68%	32
	07	24	aa	STL	8	13	28	0	165	223	106	21	65	93	5.80	1.75	27.5	317	3.6	5.1	1.4	1.1	35%	68%	18
Parker,Zack	06	25	a/a	COL	4	8	25	0	86	125	101	17	73	52	10.58	2.30	18.0	333	7.6	5.5	0.7	1.8	36%	53%	-17
	07	26	aa	COL	2	1	16	0	33	49	38	6	29	15	10.34	2.37	10.9	339	7.8	4.0	0.5	1.6	36%	56%	-25
Park,Chan Ho	07	34	aa	HOU	6	14	24	0	135	219	126	36	47	86	8.38	1.97	27.5	357	3.1	5.7	1.8	2.4	38%	61%	-17
Parnell,Robert	07	23	aa	NYM	5	5	17	0	88	113	56	9	38	62	5.68	1.72	24.1	306	3.9	6.3	1.6	0.9	36%	67%	38
Parque,Jim	07	32	aa	SEA	1	3	11	0	45	96	53	7	24	19	10.59	2.67	22.9	423	4.7	3.7	0.8	1.4	45%	59%	-33
Parra,Manuel	06	24 a	aa	MIL	3	0	6	0	31	33	14	0	9	25	4.18	1.36	22.2	266	2.7	7.3	2.7	0.0	35%	66%	103
	07	25 a	a/a	MIL	10	4	17	0	106	102	38	3	36	93	3.23	1.30	26.4	248	3.1	7.9	2.6	0.3	32%	74%	99
Parr,James	07	22	aa	ATL	4	5	18	0	98	130	63	9	26	64	5.79	1.59	24.6	312	2.4	5.9	2.5	0.8	36%	63%	55
Patterson,Scott	06	27	aa	NYY	0	1	26	1	38	39	17	10	11	30	3.97	1.29	6.2	257	2.6	7.0	2.8	2.3	27%	82%	36
	07	28 b	a/a	NYY	4	2	44	2	77	65	14	1	19	65	1.65	1.08	7.0	223	2.2	7.6	3.5	0.1	29%	84%	125
Patton,Troy	06	21	aa	HOU	2	5	8	0	45	55	27	7	13	31	5.39	1.51	25.0	295	2.6	6.2	2.4	1.4	33%	67%	41
	07	22	aa	HOU	10	8	24	0	151	159	70	17	44	80	4.17	1.34	26.8	265	2.6	4.8	1.8	1.0	29%	72%	38
Pauley,David	06	23	a/a	BOS	3	6	19	0	110	139	65	20	36	63	5.31	1.59	26.1	302	2.9	5.1	1.8	1.6	32%	71%	13
	07	24	aaa	BOS	6	6	27	0	153	198	100	21	52	94	5.87	1.63	25.8	307	3.1	5.5	1.8	1.2	34%	66%	28
Paulino,Felipe	07	24	aa	HOU	4	5	22	0	112	121	56	7	51	90	4.47	1.53	22.6	269	4.1	7.2	1.8	0.6	33%	70%	65
Paulk,Robert	06	26	a/a	NYM	6	2	28	0	56	67	23	1	19	26	3.72	1.54	8.9	292	3.0	4.1	1.4	0.2	33%	74%	45
	07	27	aa	NYM	2	5	36	2	82	133	52	11	32	42	5.68	2.02	11.2	358	3.5	4.6	1.3	1.3	39%	74%	0
Pavlik,Isaac	06	26	aa	CHC	2	1	9	0	40	66	29	6	20	27	6.47	2.13	22.4	359	4.4	6.1	1.4	1.3	41%	71%	10
Pearson,Jason	06	31	aa	BAL	3	6	50	2	65	96	43	11	21	39	5.92	1.80	6.2	335	3.0	5.3	1.8	1.6	37%	70%	10
Peguero,Jailen	06	24 a	a/a	HOU	3	2	48	15	75	59	20	3	33	66	2.40	1.23	6.5	212	4.0	7.9	2.0	0.4	28%	81%	91
	07	27	aa	ARI	6	2	53	4	66	63	21	7	30	52	2.81	1.41	5.4	246	4.1	7.1	1.7	0.9	30%	84%	57
Peguero,Tony	06	26	aa	TAM	10	12	31	1	151	186	82	14	49	72	4.89	1.55	21.8	296	2.9	4.3	1.5	0.9	33%	69%	27
	07	27	a/a	TAM	3	5	29	0	93	148	96	26	64	41	9.23	2.28	16.7	352	6.2	4.0	0.6	2.5	36%	63%	-52
Pelfrey,Mike	06	23	a/a	NYM	5	2	14	0	74	79	31	4	33	71	3.77	1.51	23.5	267	4.0	8.6	2.2	0.5	35%	75%	84
	07	24	a/a	NYM	3	6	14	0	74	86	39	6	26	47	4.76	1.50	23.4	284	3.1	5.7	1.8	0.8	33%	69%	48
Pelland,Tyler	06	23	aa	CIN	9	5	28	0	142	179	88	15	96	87	5.55	1.94	24.6	302	6.1	5.5	0.9	1.0	34%	72%	18
	07	24	a/a	CIN	6	5	54	2	89	94	47	9	40	84	4.74	1.50	7.3	265	4.0	8.5	2.1	0.9	34%	70%	70
Pena,Luismar	07	25 a	a/a	MIL	0	4	35	12	46	44	20	1	16	36	3.90	1.30	5.6	247	3.1	7.0	2.3	0.2	31%	68%	90
Pena,Tony	06	25 a	a/a	ARI	5	1	41	13	46	42	9	1	7	32	1.81	1.07	4.5	239	1.4	6.2	4.4	0.2	30%	83%	132
Penn,Hayden	06	22 a	a/a	BAL	7	4	15	0	89	87	32	8	29	81	3.27	1.29	25.0	250	2.9	8.2	2.8	0.8	32%	77%	90
Pereira,Nick	06	24	aaa	SF	4	3	15	0	79	94	57	9	45	51	6.49	1.76	24.6	290	5.1	5.8	1.1	1.0	33%	63%	25
	07	25	aa	SF	9	9	26	0	143	157	71	17	71	95	4.47	1.59	24.8	273	4.5	5.9	1.3	1.0	31%	74%	33
Perez,Beltran	06	25	aa	WAS	8	6	31	1	121	152	53	8	43	86	3.91	1.61	17.7	300	3.2	6.4	2.0	0.6	36%	76%	57
	07	26	a/a	WAS	7	7	24	0	124	172	80	19	39	56	5.81	1.70	23.9	322	2.8	4.1	1.4	1.4	34%	68%	4
Perez,Christopher	07	22 a	aa	STL	2	1	54	36	54	25	20	5	39	68	3.32	1.18	4.1	136	6.5	11.3	1.7	0.8	19%	75%	107
Perez,Franklin	06	28	a/a	PIT	2	5	33	3	49	59	32	7	22	26	5.81	1.65	6.8	291	4.1	4.8	1.2	1.3	32%	67%	12
Perez,Juan	06	28	aaa	PIT	0	1	47	0	70	90	30	5	42	48	3.87	1.89	7.2	306	5.4	6.2	1.2	0.7	36%	81%	34
	07	29	aa	PIT	3	2	40	2	55	79	47	7	33	40	7.61	2.03	6.8	328	5.4	6.5	1.2	1.1	38%	62%	21
Perez,Marcelo	07	27	aa	NYM	1	5	47	0	70	109	57	7	37	52	7.39	2.09	7.5	348	4.7	6.7	1.4	0.9	41%	64%	29
Perez,Miguel	06	23	aa	NYM	6	9	24	0	130	177	95	13	56	76	6.58	1.79	25.5	318	3.9	5.3	1.4	0.9	36%	63%	24
Perez,Oliver	06	25	aaa	NYM	2	5	10	0	51	58	46	12	24	50	8.18	1.60	23.1	278	4.3	8.9	2.1	2.1	33%	51%	32
Perez,Oneli	07	24 a	aa	CHW	6	2	59	16	77	80	26	8	22	75	3.08	1.33	5.5	262	2.6	8.8	3.4	1.0	33%	81%	97
Perez,Rafael	06	25 a	a/a	CLE	4	8	25	0	94	88	37	3	32	75	3.55	1.27	15.8	242	3.1	7.1	2.3	0.3	31%	71%	90
	07	26	aaa	CLE	3	3	8	0	46	61	23	3	11	28	4.53	1.55	25.8	310	2.2	5.4	2.5	0.6	36%	71%	60
Perisho,Matt	06	31	aaa	STL	2	4	47	1	46	66	37	4	23	39	7.21	1.95	4.8	331	4.5	7.6	1.7	0.8	41%	62%	45
Perkins,Glen	06	24	a/a	MIN	4	12	24	0	121	142	74	14	57	113	5.50	1.64	23.0	286	4.2	8.4	2.0	1.0	36%	68%	59
Perrin,Devin	06	25	a/a	WAS	3	4	37	3	58	72	39	6	49	39	6.02	2.08	7.9	296	7.7	6.0	0.8	1.0	34%	72%	19
Pesco,Nick	06	23	aa	CLE	6	8	18	0	88	119	72	13	42	55	7.37	1.83	23.2	315	4.3	5.6	1.3	1.4	35%	60%	12
Petersen,Jeff	06	25	a/a	SF	3	6	35	0	63	95	64	5	33	25	9.13	2.03	8.9	340	4.7	3.6	0.8	0.7	37%	52%	3
Peterson,John	07	26	aa	OAK	3	6	13	0	75	101	51	7	34	30	6.13	1.81	27.3	316	4.1	3.6	0.9	0.8	34%	66%	7
Peterson,Matt	06	25	aa	PIT	6	6	31	0	112	144	87	13	51	67	7.01	1.74	16.9	306	4.1	5.3	1.3	1.0	34%	59%	23
	07	26	aa	PIT	4	2	54	29	68	68	20	4	33	44	2.65	1.49	5.5	254	4.4	5.8	1.3	0.6	30%	84%	49
Petit,Yusmeiro	06	22	aaa	FLA	4	6	17	0	96	97	44	12	18	68	4.08	1.20	23.3	257	1.7	6.4	3.8	1.1	30%	69%	87
	07	23	aa	ARI	8	4	17	0	93	97	53	14	38	53	5.12	1.45	23.9	263	3.7	5.1	1.4	1.4	28%	68%	22
Petrick,William	07	23	aa	CHC	2	2	27	2	42	46	20	8	10	33	4.18	1.34	6.7	274	2.2	7.0	3.2	1.8	31%	77%	57
Pettyjohn,Adam	06	29	a/a	OAK	5	6	28	2	115	161	67	13	40	62	5.24	1.75	19.2	324	3.1	4.8	1.5	1.0	36%	71%	20
	07	30	a/a	MIL	16	6	28	0	161	234	115	35	45	99	6.42	1.73	26.8	332	2.5	5.5	2.2	2.0	36%	67%	9

					Actual				Major League Equivalents																
PITCHER	Yr	Age	Lev	Org	w	l	g	sv	ip	h	er	hr	bb	k	era	WHIP	bf/g	oob	ctl	dom	cmd	hr/9	h%	s%	bpv
Phelps,Tommy	06	33	aaa	NYY	7	4	17	0	95	137	62	13	33	47	5.88	1.78	26.3	330	3.1	4.4	1.4	1.2	36%	68%	9
Phelps,Travis	06	29	aa	MIL	5	8	31	5	86	124	64	12	60	53	6.69	2.14	14.0	330	6.3	5.5	0.9	1.3	37%	70%	3
Phillips,Heath	06	25	aaa	CHW	13	5	25	0	155	183	68	17	41	87	3.95	1.45	27.1	288	2.4	5.1	2.1	1.0	32%	75%	43
	07	26	aaa	CHW	13	7	28	0	173	243	115	34	61	95	5.98	1.76	28.9	325	3.1	4.9	1.6	1.8	35%	70%	-1
Piersoll,Chris	06	29	aaa	BAL	6	2	42	0	67	89	45	9	31	46	6.05	1.79	7.5	313	4.1	6.2	1.5	1.2	36%	67%	26
Pignatiello,Carmen	06	24 a	a/a	CHC	3	1	46	0	67	77	31	4	25	67	4.15	1.52	6.5	283	3.3	9.0	2.7	0.6	37%	73%	92
	07	25	aa	CHC	2	0	50	4	55	54	21	7	21	38	3.44	1.37	4.7	252	3.4	6.2	1.8	1.1	29%	79%	46
Pinango,Miguel	06	24	aa	NYM	10	7	28	0	152	201	107	24	44	66	6.35	1.61	24.6	312	2.6	3.9	1.5	1.4	33%	62%	5
	07	25	aa	LA	10	7	23	0	126	168	71	22	40	77	5.03	1.65	25.1	314	2.9	5.5	1.9	1.6	34%	74%	18
Pino,Johan	07	24	aa	MIN	2	4	9	0	47	66	33	6	9	31	6.30	1.60	23.6	324	1.8	5.9	3.3	1.2	37%	61%	61
Pinto,Renyel	06	24	aaa	FLA	8	2	18	0	95	87	37	7	47	87	3.50	1.41	22.9	239	4.4	8.2	1.9	0.7	31%	76%	76
Plexico,Gerald	06	27	aa	WAS	4	3	34	3	65	85	40	6	29	35	5.56	1.75	8.9	309	4.0	4.8	1.2	0.8	35%	68%	24
	07	28	aa	WAS	2	5	43	1	66	88	42	13	40	26	5.74	1.93	7.5	313	5.4	3.5	0.6	1.8	32%	75%	-27
Plummer,Jarod	07	24 a	aa	KC	5	6	46	11	82	84	41	15	19	78	4.53	1.24	7.4	259	2.0	8.5	4.2	1.7	31%	70%	91
Pollok,Dwayne	06	26	aa	CHW	4	5	54	3	82	121	47	13	24	41	5.11	1.77	7.1	335	2.7	4.5	1.7	1.5	36%	75%	7
	07	27	a/a	LA	2	3	46	2	82	133	53	8	21	25	5.84	1.88	8.6	357	2.3	2.8	1.2	0.9	38%	69%	-0
Pomeranz,Stuart	06	22	aa	STL	7	4	18	0	98	119	55	13	29	55	5.05	1.51	24.1	293	2.7	5.0	1.9	1.2	32%	69%	31
Pope,Justin	06	27	a/a	NYY	2	3	46	23	63	79	36	7	32	41	5.07	1.76	6.4	300	4.6	5.9	1.3	1.0	35%	72%	29
	07	28	a/a	NYY	4	3	42	6	62	72	46	14	21	34	6.67	1.50	6.5	286	3.0	4.9	1.6	2.0	29%	59%	2
Pote,Lou	06	35	aa	TEX	3	2	17	0	30	46	26	5	18	18	7.74	2.11	8.9	343	5.3	5.3	1.0	1.4	38%	64%	-3
Powers,Daniel	07	25	aa	MIN	2	5	34	1	59	96	46	4	27	32	6.93	2.06	8.7	356	4.1	4.8	1.2	0.7	40%	65%	17
Prinz,Bret	07	30	a/a	PIT	1	2	37	7	44	55	16	4	28	31	3.32	1.88	5.7	300	5.6	6.4	1.1	0.8	36%	84%	34
Prochaska,Mike	06	26	a/a	TAM	5	7	24	0	104	140	83	14	53	48	7.20	1.86	20.7	315	4.6	4.1	0.9	1.2	34%	61%	-2
	07	27	a/a	TAM	8	8	26	0	138	164	83	23	57	70	5.40	1.61	24.0	290	3.7	4.5	1.2	1.5	31%	70%	5
Puffer,Brandon	06	31	aaa	OAK	5	1	50	4	69	80	45	12	20	42	5.90	1.45	6.0	284	2.6	5.4	2.1	1.5	31%	62%	30
	07	32	aa	TEX	3	3	51	1	64	85	35	9	25	35	4.95	1.70	5.8	311	3.5	4.9	1.4	1.3	34%	74%	12
Pullin,Aaron	06	26	aa	LAA	2	0	28	1	46	53	27	4	27	22	5.22	1.74	7.7	284	5.2	4.2	0.8	0.9	31%	71%	14
	07	27	aa	LAA	5	5	51	0	61	77	43	7	33	31	6.27	1.81	5.7	302	4.9	4.6	0.9	1.0	33%	66%	12
Purcey,David	06	24	a/a	TOR	6	12	28	0	140	191	125	23	93	106	8.02	2.03	24.7	318	6.0	6.8	1.1	1.5	37%	61%	12
	07	25	aa	TOR	3	5	11	0	62	86	51	6	18	42	7.42	1.67	25.9	321	2.6	6.1	2.4	0.8	38%	53%	53
Rakers,Aaron	07	31	aa	SD	4	5	61	0	79	163	86	26	30	36	9.76	2.44	6.9	414	3.4	4.1	1.2	2.9	42%	64%	-66
Ramirez,Edwar	07	27 b	a/a	NYY	4	0	34	7	56	36	8	1	27	77	1.25	1.11	6.7	178	4.3	12.3	2.9	0.2	30%	89%	148
Ramirez,Elizardo	07	25	aaa	CIN	4	3	12	0	65	84	35	5	20	38	4.85	1.60	24.5	307	2.8	5.3	1.9	0.7	35%	70%	44
Ramirez,Erasmo	06	30	aaa	TEX	6	3	54	9	67	98	46	9	9	37	6.10	1.59	5.6	333	1.2	4.9	4.2	1.2	37%	63%	70
	07	31	aa	FLA	5	1	41	3	43	61	18	4	7	16	3.69	1.59	4.7	328	1.5	3.4	2.3	0.7	35%	78%	36
Ramirez,Ismael	06	26	a/a	TOR	9	5	23	0	126	131	51	19	40	68	3.61	1.35	23.4	262	2.9	4.9	1.7	1.4	28%	79%	27
	07	27	a/a	TOR	2	5	20	0	72	141	66	12	24	33	8.17	2.29	18.8	401	3.0	4.2	1.4	1.5	43%	65%	-17
Ramirez,Luis	07	25	aa	OAK	4	6	14	0	70	96	53	7	26	41	6.84	1.73	23.3	318	3.3	5.3	1.6	0.9	36%	59%	32
Ramirez,Ramon	07	25	a/a	CIN	6	1	21	1	46	45	21	4	19	41	4.12	1.40	9.5	252	3.7	8.0	2.2	0.8	32%	72%	73
	07	26	aa	COL	4	0	25	0	27	25	11	3	18	27	3.80	1.61	4.9	241	6.1	8.9	1.5	1.1	31%	80%	57
Ramos,Cesar	07	23	aa	SD	13	9	27	0	163	178	76	16	46	77	4.21	1.38	26.0	272	2.6	4.2	1.7	0.9	30%	71%	33
Ramos,Mario	06	29	a/a	SD	0	3	15	0	35	59	36	6	19	20	9.32	2.21	12.0	364	4.8	5.0	1.0	1.5	40%	57%	-11
	07	30	aa	OAK	2	3	17	1	54	107	53	7	27	27	8.86	2.46	17.2	403	4.4	4.5	1.0	1.1	44%	63%	-11
Ramos,Victor	06	25	aa	BOS	3	1	29	1	35	49	34	10	14	23	8.86	1.81	5.7	324	3.7	6.0	1.6	2.6	34%	54%	-17
Randolph,Stephen	06	32	aaa	CHW	9	9	28	0	154	164	88	28	127	117	5.16	1.89	26.5	267	7.4	6.8	0.9	1.7	30%	77%	12
	07	33	aa	HOU	10	2	31	4	52	31	15	7	26	56	2.65	1.09	6.7	168	4.5	9.7	2.2	1.2	21%	83%	89
Rapada,Clay	06	26	a/a	CHC	6	4	61	21	67	76	19	1	29	55	2.54	1.57	4.9	279	4.0	7.4	1.9	0.1	36%	83%	79
	07	27	a/a	DET	7	2	57	17	57	80	37	6	30	41	5.77	1.92	4.9	324	4.7	6.5	1.4	0.9	38%	70%	32
Rasner,Darrell	06	26	aaa	NYY	4	0	10	0	58	71	23	5	12	39	3.59	1.42	25.3	294	1.9	6.0	3.2	0.8	34%	77%	76
Rawson,Anthony	06	26	aa	OAK	1	2	31	0	35	59	31	2	29	24	7.96	2.49	6.1	364	7.4	6.2	0.8	0.6	43%	66%	20
Ray,Ken	07	33	a/a	MIL	3	4	37	3	63	83	39	10	38	50	5.56	1.92	8.2	312	5.4	7.1	1.3	1.4	36%	74%	20
Reames,Britt	06	33	aaa	PIT	4	2	14	0	64	80	29	4	16	34	4.14	1.49	20.2	299	2.2	4.8	2.2	0.6	34%	72%	52
Redding,Tim	06	29	aaa	CHW	12	10	29	0	187	217	102	32	63	118	4.91	1.50	28.5	284	3.1	5.7	1.9	1.6	31%	72%	25
	07	30	aaa	WAS	9	5	17	0	89	141	73	10	27	48	7.32	1.88	25.2	351	2.8	4.9	1.8	1.0	39%	60%	21
Redman,Mark	07	34	a/a	COL	3	6	17	0	98	160	74	12	43	45	6.84	2.07	28.8	359	4.0	4.1	1.0	1.1	39%	67%	-4
Register,Steven	06	23	aa	COL	4	10	27	0	155	231	129	34	53	64	7.48	1.83	27.3	338	3.1	3.7	1.2	2.0	35%	62%	-24
	07	24	aa	COL	1	3	61	37	58	81	38	4	17	41	5.88	1.69	4.4	324	2.6	6.3	2.4	0.7	39%	64%	60
Reid,Justin	06	29	aaa	LA	2	7	43	3	107	134	71	15	48	67	6.00	1.70	11.5	300	4.1	5.7	1.4	1.3	34%	66%	19
Reineke,Chad	06	25	aa	HOU	1	3	15	0	44	40	19	3	27	36	3.87	1.53	13.1	237	5.6	7.4	1.3	0.6	29%	75%	60
	07	25	aa	HOU	5	5	32	0	100	124	69	9	58	72	6.20	1.82	14.8	299	5.2	6.5	1.2	0.8	35%	65%	36
Reinhard,Gregory	07	24	aa	CHC	1	1	20	0	28	35	19	6	17	21	6.05	1.83	6.7	297	5.4	6.7	1.2	2.0	33%	72%	1
Resop,Chris	06	24	aaa	FLA	4	0	40	2	49	52	22	4	15	39	4.02	1.36	5.3	266	2.7	7.1	2.6	0.7	32%	71%	77
	07	25	aa	LAA	1	3	27	0	45	61	31	4	17	31	6.09	1.73	7.8	317	3.4	6.3	1.9	0.8	37%	64%	43
Reyes,Anthony	06	25 a	aaa	STL	6	1	13	0	84	83	31	10	11	71	3.32	1.12	26.1	253	1.2	7.6	6.5	1.1	31%	75%	153
	07	26	aa	STL	1	1	6	0	36	33	16	4	12	25	3.87	1.26	25.2	240	3.0	6.3	2.1	1.1	27%	73%	55
Reyes,Jo-jo	07	23	a/a	ATL	12	1	19	0	109	103	42	8	49	94	3.46	1.39	24.8	244	4.0	7.8	1.9	0.7	31%	76%	73
Reynolds,Gregory	07	22 a	aa	COL	4	1	8	0	50	39	11	3	9	31	1.97	0.96	24.3	210	1.6	5.6	3.4	0.5	25%	82%	103
Reynoso,Paulino	06	26	aaa	CHW	3	3	47	0	59	60	40	4	49	49	6.11	1.85	6.0	257	7.5	7.4	1.0	0.6	32%	66%	50
	07	27	aaa	CHW	3	0	21	0	22	34	15	1	22	15	6.03	2.54	5.7	344	9.0	6.2	0.7	0.4	41%	75%	25
Rheinecker,John	06	27	aaa	TEX	4	5	15	0	93	125	41	8	27	56	3.97	1.64	28.3	316	2.6	5.4	2.0	0.8	36%	77%	43
	07	28	aa	TEX	4	2	9	0	58	88	38	6	15	21	5.82	1.77	30.2	341	2.3	3.2	1.4	1.0	36%	68%	6
Rice,Scott	06	25	aaa	BAL	3	4	52	1	65	82	40	5	30	34	5.59	1.72	5.8	301	4.2	4.7	1.1	0.7	34%	67%	25
Ridgway,Jeff	06	26	a/a	TAM	2	4	50	2	58	61	28	6	24	51	4.31	1.48	5.1	265	3.8	8.0	2.1	0.9	33%	72%	68
	07	27	aaa	TAM	2	3	54	4	64	69	32	11	34	56	4.43	1.61	5.4	270	4.7	7.9	1.7	1.5	32%	77%	39
Righter,Matthew	07	26	aa	DET	3	4	19	0	54	89	46	13	20	27	7.65	2.00	14.0	359	3.3	4.5	1.4	2.1	38%	65%	-24
Riley,Matt	07	28	aa	LA	5	5	45	4	69	90	58	11	61	58	7.49	2.19	7.8	308	8.0	7.6	1.0	1.5	37%	67%	15
Ring,Royce	06	26	aaa	NYM	2	2	36	11	39	37	18	2	16	34	4.19	1.37	4.7	247	3.7	7.7	2.1	0.5	32%	69%	82
	07	27	a/a	ATL	5	2	42	2	44	51	21	2	21	45	4.31	1.64	4.8	284	4.3	9.2	2.1	0.5	38%	73%	84
Rivera,Mumba	07	27	aa	SEA	4	7	42	6	56	70	44	16	46	56	7.01	2.07	6.7	300	7.4	8.9	1.2	2.6	35%	72%	-3
Rleal,Sendy	07	27	aa	BAL	5	3	29	1	45	47	24	7	22	26	4.82	1.53	6.9	263	4.3	5.1	1.2	1.4	28%	73%	15

PITCHER	Yr	Age	Lev	Org	Actual w	l	g	sv	Major League Equivalents ip	h	er	hr	bb	k	era	WHIP	bf/g	oob	ctl	dom	cmd	hr/9	h%	s%	bpv
Roach,Jason	06	30	a/a	PIT	8	9	27	0	149	238	103	25	51	49	6.18	1.94	26.8	353	3.1	2.9	1.0	1.5	36%	71%	-23
	07	31	aa	PIT	4	3	33	1	63	102	49	5	32	28	7.06	2.13	9.6	357	4.5	4.0	0.9	0.7	39%	65%	6
Robbins,Jake	06	30	aaa	CIN	2	3	51	4	53	73	28	6	38	40	4.70	2.09	5.2	321	6.4	6.7	1.0	0.9	38%	79%	25
	07	31	aaa	CHW	0	0	20	0	24	40	20	0	18	10	7.44	2.39	6.4	361	6.7	3.9	0.6	0.0	41%	65%	18
Robertson,Connor	06	25 a	aa	OAK	7	2	55	6	83	91	33	1	23	75	3.61	1.38	6.5	273	2.5	8.1	3.2	0.1	36%	72%	113
	07	26	aa	OAK	4	1	31	2	39	56	26	3	23	30	6.09	2.03	6.2	330	5.3	6.8	1.3	0.8	40%	70%	33
Robertson,Jeriome	06	30	aaa	NYM	1	6	11	0	38	78	51	8	21	16	11.91	2.59	19.1	412	4.9	3.9	0.8	1.8	44%	53%	-42
Rodriguez,Eddy	06	25 a	aaa	BAL	3	1	42	12	47	41	13	0	19	49	2.51	1.29	4.7	231	3.7	9.3	2.5	0.0	33%	78%	117
Rodriguez,Fernando	07	23	aa	LAA	8	4	21	0	117	159	79	15	45	48	6.10	1.74	26.0	317	3.5	3.6	1.0	1.2	34%	66%	-0
Rodriguez,Jose	06	25	a/a	TAM	4	2	54	2	80	93	33	6	34	56	3.70	1.58	6.7	284	3.8	6.3	1.7	0.7	34%	78%	50
	07	26	aa	HOU	4	4	52	4	72	97	53	12	37	43	6.67	1.85	6.6	315	4.6	5.4	1.2	1.5	35%	66%	3
Rodriguez,Nerio	06	36	a/a	PIT	1	4	12	0	61	80	54	12	20	41	8.01	1.63	23.2	309	2.9	6.1	2.1	1.8	34%	52%	19
Rodriguez,Rafael	06	22	aa	LAA	5	10	24	0	133	181	97	25	50	70	6.56	1.74	25.8	318	3.4	4.7	1.4	1.7	34%	65%	-2
	07	23	aa	LAA	0	6	46	0	71	95	43	7	32	35	5.48	1.78	7.3	314	4.0	4.4	1.1	0.9	35%	70%	14
Rodriguez,Ricardo	06	28	aaa	STL	8	12	27	0	162	252	141	31	57	67	7.83	1.90	28.9	347	3.2	3.7	1.2	1.7	36%	60%	-19
	07	29	aa	PIT	2	6	16	0	61	140	76	9	21	21	11.18	2.64	21.3	439	3.1	3.1	1.0	1.4	46%	56%	-35
Rodriguez,Ryan	06	22	aa	CHW	4	10	21	0	116	178	102	6	56	53	7.91	2.02	27.3	344	4.3	4.1	0.9	0.5	39%	58%	17
Rogers,Brian	06	24 a	a/a	PIT	4	3	46	3	76	64	24	9	18	67	2.80	1.07	6.6	223	2.1	7.9	3.8	1.1	27%	80%	105
	07	25	aa	PIT	2	1	48	2	65	63	30	1	34	49	4.15	1.50	6.0	250	4.8	6.7	1.4	0.2	32%	70%	70
Rohlicek,Russ	06	27	aa	MIL	0	2	24	0	34	46	28	5	21	25	7.30	1.96	6.9	317	5.5	6.7	1.2	1.2	37%	63%	21
Rohrbaugh,Robert	06	23	aa	SEA	5	5	14	0	85	103	47	11	29	57	4.96	1.55	27.2	293	3.1	6.0	2.0	1.2	33%	70%	39
	07	24	aa	SEA	13	8	28	0	170	194	71	16	51	97	3.76	1.44	26.5	281	2.7	5.1	1.9	0.9	32%	76%	44
Rojas,Chris	07	31	aa	PHI	7	4	19	0	78	114	63	20	71	32	7.24	2.38	21.8	334	8.2	3.7	0.5	2.3	33%	74%	-49
Rollandini,David	06	28	aa	HOU	4	4	47	2	76	96	55	14	34	35	6.56	1.71	7.5	303	4.0	4.1	1.0	1.7	31%	65%	-10
Roman,Orlando	06	28	a/a	NYM	4	3	39	2	68	92	46	6	41	40	6.09	1.96	8.5	317	5.5	5.3	1.0	0.8	36%	68%	21
Romero,Davis	06	24 a	a/a	TOR	10	9	30	1	118	127	60	8	29	92	4.57	1.32	16.7	269	2.2	7.0	3.2	0.6	33%	65%	92
Romero,Felix	07	27	aa	BAL	2	7	46	0	80	105	53	11	49	70	5.95	1.92	8.4	309	5.5	7.8	1.4	1.2	38%	71%	33
Romero,Ricardo	06	22	aa	TOR	2	7	12	0	67	81	55	10	29	35	7.38	1.64	25.5	292	3.9	4.7	1.2	1.3	32%	55%	10
Romero,Ricky	07	23	aa	TOR	3	6	18	0	88	113	59	11	52	68	6.03	1.87	23.5	305	5.3	6.9	1.3	1.1	36%	69%	29
Roney,Matt	06	27 b	aaa	OAK	4	3	47	6	58	65	22	4	19	54	3.36	1.44	5.4	277	2.9	8.4	2.9	0.6	36%	78%	92
	07	28	a/a	TOR	4	3	29	4	45	71	34	2	18	37	6.87	1.98	7.6	351	3.7	7.4	2.0	0.5	43%	63%	59
Roquet,Rocky	07	25	aa	CHC	4	0	28	7	39	39	21	5	20	33	4.83	1.50	6.2	254	4.6	7.6	1.7	1.2	30%	71%	49
Rosales,Leonel	06	25	aa	SD	5	6	53	0	61	69	31	7	21	43	4.58	1.47	5.1	278	3.1	6.4	2.0	1.0	32%	71%	51
	07	26	aa	SD	1	1	24	14	24	30	13	3	11	21	4.70	1.71	4.7	297	4.3	7.8	1.8	1.3	36%	76%	42
Rosario,Francisco	06	26 b	aaa	TOR	0	3	14	1	42	36	19	3	14	42	3.98	1.20	12.4	227	3.1	8.9	2.9	0.7	30%	67%	104
Rosa,Carlos	07	23	aa	KC	6	6	21	1	97	121	60	8	43	60	5.55	1.69	21.3	299	4.0	5.6	1.4	0.8	34%	67%	35
Rosen,Mark	07	23	aa	ARI	4	4	50	7	66	97	30	8	23	67	4.07	1.81	6.3	334	3.1	9.1	3.0	1.1	43%	81%	71
Rouwenhorst,Jonathc	06	27	aaa	LAA	6	7	50	1	89	107	47	12	37	52	4.78	1.62	8.1	292	3.7	5.3	1.4	1.2	32%	73%	23
	07	28	aa	LAA	10	10	33	0	158	288	138	23	56	56	7.83	2.18	24.4	384	3.2	3.2	1.0	1.3	40%	64%	-20
Rowe,Steven	06	26	aa	TEX	5	5	45	0	83	130	77	22	39	50	8.35	2.04	9.1	349	4.2	5.5	1.3	2.4	37%	63%	-26
	07	27	aa	TEX	6	4	39	0	82	134	89	19	34	37	9.79	2.04	10.4	358	3.7	4.0	1.1	2.1	37%	53%	-33
Rowland-Smith,Ryan	06	24	aa	SEA	1	3	23	4	41	46	18	2	21	42	3.84	1.63	8.1	279	4.5	9.1	2.0	0.5	37%	76%	83
	07	25	aa	SEA	3	4	25	1	41	41	21	2	24	43	4.60	1.58	7.4	254	5.3	9.3	1.8	0.5	35%	70%	83
Rueckel,Danny	06	27	a/a	WAS	7	5	41	1	66	86	40	7	28	41	5.48	1.72	7.5	309	3.8	5.6	1.5	0.9	35%	69%	30
Rundles,Rich	06	25	aa	STL	6	9	27	0	129	208	102	17	60	54	7.13	2.07	23.9	355	4.2	3.8	0.9	1.2	38%	66%	-9
	07	26	a/a	CLE	5	4	40	2	61	70	20	1	30	40	2.95	1.64	7.0	282	4.4	5.8	1.3	0.2	34%	81%	56
Rupe,Josh	07	25	aa	TEX	2	2	7	0	37	51	28	6	16	15	6.76	1.80	25.0	321	3.8	3.7	1.0	1.4	34%	64%	-7
Rusch,Matt	07	24	aa	DET	6	1	40	3	53	54	29	5	20	46	5.00	1.39	5.7	258	3.4	7.7	2.3	0.9	32%	65%	71
Russell,Adam	06	23	aa	CHW	3	3	10	0	55	75	43	8	22	39	7.09	1.76	25.8	319	3.5	6.3	1.8	1.3	37%	60%	26
	07	24	aa	CHW	9	11	38	1	138	204	107	13	65	81	6.99	1.95	17.7	336	4.3	5.3	1.2	0.8	38%	63%	21
Russ,Chris	06	28	aa	STL	4	4	55	0	73	104	47	4	29	36	5.79	1.81	6.3	327	3.6	4.4	1.2	0.4	37%	66%	29
Russ,James	06	26	aa	FLA	6	10	28	0	156	208	100	21	79	102	5.77	1.84	26.5	313	4.5	5.9	1.3	1.2	36%	70%	18
	07	27	aa	FLA	1	6	21	1	89	99	51	9	37	48	5.11	1.52	18.8	275	3.7	4.8	1.3	0.9	31%	67%	28
Ryu,Jae Kuk	06	23	aaa	CHC	8	8	24	0	139	149	68	16	55	100	4.40	1.47	25.4	268	3.6	6.5	1.8	1.0	31%	72%	47
	07	24	aaa	TAM	5	4	14	0	71	81	44	6	23	59	5.57	1.46	22.3	281	2.9	7.5	2.6	0.8	35%	61%	75
Saarloos,Kirk	07	28	aaa	CIN	0	2	18	0	41	60	26	4	10	22	5.66	1.70	10.5	335	2.1	4.9	2.3	0.9	37%	67%	38
Sack,Darren	07	25	aa	SF	2	5	9	0	39	70	49	8	24	19	11.22	2.41	23.2	379	5.6	4.3	0.8	1.8	40%	53%	-32
Sadler,Billy	06	25 a	a/a	SF	6	3	51	21	55	35	20	2	33	65	3.26	1.22	4.5	177	5.3	10.5	2.0	0.3	26%	73%	114
	07	26	aa	SF	3	2	49	7	54	51	40	7	46	57	6.68	1.78	5.2	242	7.6	9.5	1.2	1.1	31%	63%	56
Sadowski,Ryan	07	25	aa	SF	4	3	35	1	68	66	28	3	28	41	3.76	1.39	8.4	250	3.8	5.4	1.4	0.4	30%	72%	55
Saenz,Chris	07	26	aa	LAA	1	7	19	0	46	83	62	3	37	17	12.14	2.60	13.4	381	7.2	3.4	0.5	0.7	41%	50%	-11
Salas,Juan	06	28 b	a/a	TAM	4	1	50	17	63	39	8	5	31	64	1.15	1.11	5.1	175	4.4	9.1	2.0	0.7	23%	95%	98
Salas,Marino	06	26	aa	BAL	2	6	44	19	49	52	24	4	19	37	4.48	1.45	4.9	267	3.5	6.8	2.0	0.8	32%	70%	59
	07	27	a/a	MIL	0	1	51	17	61	68	27	11	26	44	3.92	1.53	5.3	275	3.8	6.5	1.7	1.6	31%	81%	26
Salmon,Brad	06	27	a/a	CIN	7	2	55	5	81	73	33	4	50	72	3.70	1.52	6.5	237	5.6	8.0	1.4	0.5	31%	76%	71
	07	28	aaa	CIN	2	2	37	4	43	52	25	4	19	32	5.29	1.64	5.3	291	4.0	6.8	1.7	0.9	35%	68%	47
Samardzija,Jeffrey Al	07	23	aa	CHC	3	3	6	0	34	38	16	10	9	17	4.22	1.38	24.4	276	2.4	4.5	1.9	2.6	26%	84%	-13
Sampson,Chris	06	28	aaa	HOU	12	3	27	4	125	133	44	14	15	54	3.17	1.19	19.0	267	1.1	3.9	3.6	1.0	29%	78%	70
Sanches,Brian	06	28 b	aaa	PHI	3	2	36	19	43	33	15	3	15	41	3.14	1.12	4.8	209	3.1	8.5	2.7	0.7	27%	74%	101
	07	29 b	aaa	PHI	2	3	36	16	47	71	35	7	9	40	6.72	1.70	6.0	342	1.7	7.7	4.6	1.3	41%	61%	90
Sanchez,Anibal	06	23	aa	FLA	3	6	15	0	85	99	41	8	31	83	4.33	1.53	25.3	285	3.3	8.8	2.7	0.8	37%	73%	82
Sanchez,Humberto	06	23 a	a/a	DET	10	6	20	0	123	116	47	5	48	111	3.44	1.33	26.2	244	3.5	8.1	2.3	0.4	32%	74%	92
Sanchez,Jonathan	06	24 a	a/a	SF	4	3	19	2	55	32	18	1	22	63	2.95	0.98	11.3	166	3.6	10.3	2.9	0.2	25%	68%	139
Sanchez,Jose	07	23	aa	NYM	4	9	27	0	145	189	88	14	58	82	5.44	1.70	24.8	308	3.6	5.1	1.4	0.9	35%	68%	27
Sanchez,Romulo	07	23	aa	PIT	6	3	40	1	57	51	23	8	18	43	3.57	1.19	5.9	232	2.8	6.7	2.4	1.3	26%	76%	61
Sandoval,Juan	07	27	aa	SEA	2	6	40	3	67	108	57	11	29	27	7.71	2.04	8.3	355	3.9	3.6	0.9	1.5	37%	63%	-21
Santana,Ervin	07	25	aa	LAA	2	1	5	0	32	48	24	4	11	26	6.79	1.84	30.5	341	3.0	7.2	2.4	1.2	41%	63%	46
Santiago,Jose	07	33	aa	NYM	7	8	32	0	119	204	101	16	45	38	7.64	2.08	18.6	369	3.4	2.9	0.9	1.2	39%	63%	-21
Santos,Alex	06	29	a/a	OAK	1	2	23	4	32	51	22	5	13	16	6.17	2.02	6.9	354	3.8	4.4	1.2	1.4	38%	71%	-6

Major League Equivalent Statistics

PITCHER	Yr	Age	Lev	Org	Actual				Major League Equivalents																
					w	l	g	sv	ip	h	er	hr	bb	k	era	WHIP	bf/g	oob	ctl	dom	cmd	hr/9	h%	s%	bpv
Santos,Arthur	06	25	aa	ATL	2	3	26	3	40	39	12	4	9	22	2.60	1.21	6.4	250	2.1	4.9	2.3	0.9	28%	83%	55
	07	26	aa	KC	1	2	19	2	33	72	33	7	20	13	9.04	2.78	10.0	427	5.4	3.4	0.6	1.8	45%	69%	-51
Santos,Jarrett	07	26	aa	FLA	3	1	22	0	43	63	21	5	24	21	4.32	2.03	9.7	334	5.0	4.4	0.9	1.0	37%	81%	4
Santos,Reid	07	25	aa	CLE	8	3	39	2	96	102	39	11	34	69	3.65	1.42	10.7	267	3.2	6.5	2.0	1.0	31%	78%	52
Sarfate,Dennis	06	26	aaa	MIL	10	7	34	0	125	151	68	9	85	103	4.87	1.88	17.7	292	6.1	7.4	1.2	0.7	36%	74%	47
	07	26	aaa	MIL	2	7	45	4	61	74	41	7	52	60	6.06	2.06	6.8	293	7.6	8.8	1.2	1.1	37%	71%	42
Sauerbeck,Scott	07	36	a/a	TOR	2	1	41	1	42	67	27	1	23	38	5.71	2.14	5.2	352	5.0	8.1	1.6	0.2	45%	71%	60
Saunders,Joe	06	25	aaa	LAA	10	4	21	0	135	126	42	11	35	81	2.83	1.20	26.5	243	2.4	5.4	2.3	0.7	28%	79%	65
	07	26	aa	LAA	4	7	14	0	86	120	71	13	23	62	7.45	1.66	28.1	322	2.4	6.5	2.7	1.3	37%	55%	46
Savickas,Russell	07	24	aa	TOR	3	3	8	0	33	63	39	9	24	10	10.59	2.64	23.0	395	6.6	2.8	0.4	2.6	39%	62%	-75
Sawatski,Jay	06	24	aa	MIN	4	2	44	0	75	88	35	4	26	55	4.16	1.53	7.6	287	3.2	6.6	2.1	0.5	35%	72%	66
	07	25	a/a	MIN	4	3	42	0	70	100	49	6	28	43	6.35	1.83	7.9	328	3.6	5.5	1.5	0.8	38%	65%	30
Scalamandre,Rich	06	26	a/a	STL	8	0	55	2	63	81	46	7	29	45	6.49	1.74	5.4	305	4.1	6.4	1.6	0.9	36%	62%	37
	07	27	a/a	ATL	3	6	38	3	55	86	48	9	29	22	7.89	2.09	7.3	349	4.7	3.6	0.8	1.5	37%	63%	-23
Schappert,Paul	06	25	aa	CHC	5	0	24	0	46	64	32	6	25	17	6.15	1.94	9.3	322	4.9	3.3	0.7	1.2	34%	70%	-12
	07	26	aa	CHC	3	7	27	0	82	134	91	28	36	24	10.00	2.07	15.2	360	3.9	2.7	0.7	3.0	34%	55%	-78
Scherer,Matthew	07	25	aa	STL	4	3	55	1	70	81	34	6	24	58	4.33	1.50	5.6	284	3.1	7.5	2.4	0.8	35%	72%	69
Scherzer,Max	07	23	aa	ARI	4	4	14	0	73	77	42	4	41	65	5.20	1.62	23.7	266	5.1	8.0	1.6	0.5	34%	67%	68
Schlact,Michael	07	22	aa	TEX	3	3	6	0	33	43	25	8	8	20	6.78	1.54	24.7	307	2.2	5.4	2.5	2.2	32%	60%	14
Schmitt,Eric	06	28	a/a	ATL	0	4	33	1	63	124	80	20	20	28	11.39	2.27	9.9	401	2.8	4.0	1.4	2.8	41%	51%	-57
Schmoll,Steve	06	27	aaa	NYM	5	4	42	0	55	71	42	5	21	35	6.89	1.66	6.0	306	3.4	5.7	1.7	0.8	35%	57%	38
	07	28	aa	NYM	2	3	54	4	76	113	45	6	20	34	5.27	1.76	6.6	337	2.4	4.0	1.7	0.7	37%	70%	25
Schreiber,Zach	06	24	aa	ATL	1	2	35	21	39	34	17	4	33	38	3.87	1.69	5.2	227	7.5	8.7	1.2	1.0	29%	80%	57
	07	25	a/a	ATL	4	6	58	6	78	63	27	5	37	62	3.16	1.28	5.7	217	4.3	7.1	1.7	0.6	27%	77%	71
Schroder,Chris	06	28	a/a	WAS	4	1	37	2	61	58	22	5	27	53	3.29	1.38	7.1	244	4.0	7.8	1.9	0.7	31%	78%	73
	07	29 b	aaa	WAS	2	2	26	1	33	30	9	0	19	35	2.40	1.47	5.6	235	5.1	9.4	1.9	0.0	34%	82%	103
Schultz,Mike	06	27	a/a	ARI	3	4	58	7	65	81	33	1	26	38	4.61	1.64	5.1	299	3.5	5.2	1.5	0.2	35%	69%	53
	07	28	aa	ARI	4	5	54	4	77	118	52	6	42	37	6.06	2.08	7.1	344	4.9	4.3	0.9	0.7	38%	70%	9
Scobie,Jason	06	27	a/a	NYM	4	18	29	1	139	251	145	28	54	64	9.36	2.19	24.5	381	3.5	4.1	1.2	1.8	40%	58%	-25
Searles,Jonathan	06	26	aa	BOS	7	4	53	1	77	97	54	10	43	44	6.36	1.82	6.9	300	5.1	5.1	1.0	1.2	33%	66%	12
	07	27	aa	SD	4	3	37	0	68	71	34	6	43	38	4.56	1.67	8.4	264	5.6	5.1	0.9	0.8	30%	73%	29
Seddon,Chris	06	23	aaa	TAM	9	9	28	0	154	190	100	22	47	97	5.84	1.53	24.5	296	2.7	5.6	2.1	1.3	33%	64%	35
	07	24	aa	FLA	6	10	26	0	139	157	86	13	52	87	5.53	1.50	23.6	278	3.3	5.6	1.7	0.9	32%	63%	43
Segovia,Zach	06	24	aa	PHI	11	5	17	0	107	112	52	11	25	61	4.34	1.28	26.4	265	2.1	5.1	2.5	1.0	30%	68%	56
	07	24	a/a	PHI	6	12	23	0	135	195	105	15	53	43	7.01	1.83	27.9	331	3.5	2.8	0.8	1.0	35%	61%	-8
Seibel,Phil	06	28	a/a	BOS	4	3	18	0	60	43	13	8	18	49	1.90	1.02	13.1	195	2.8	7.3	2.6	1.2	22%	91%	79
Seo,Jae	07	30	aaa	TAM	9	4	17	0	97	132	61	11	17	50	5.66	1.53	25.5	318	1.5	4.7	3.0	1.0	35%	64%	52
Serfass,Joseph	07	26	aa	NYM	3	3	32	0	46	69	40	9	10	23	7.85	1.72	6.7	339	2.0	4.6	2.3	1.8	36%	56%	9
Serrano,Alex	07	27	aa	LAA	3	5	47	4	69	125	56	10	11	34	7.33	1.98	7.2	383	1.5	4.4	3.0	1.3	42%	64%	27
Serrano,Jimmy	06	30	aaa	BOS	4	5	13	0	72	99	31	3	30	48	3.89	1.79	26.1	320	3.8	6.0	1.6	0.4	38%	78%	48
	07	31	aa	FLA	5	3	24	0	71	100	51	9	26	37	6.40	1.77	13.9	325	3.3	4.6	1.4	1.2	36%	65%	12
Shackelford,Brian	07	31	aaa	TAM	0	5	52	1	44	58	32	4	19	17	6.44	1.74	4.0	310	3.9	3.5	0.9	0.9	33%	62%	7
Shafer,David	06	25	aa	CIN	1	2	44	26	49	47	19	3	18	42	3.47	1.33	4.7	248	3.3	7.6	2.3	0.6	31%	75%	83
	07	26	aa	OAK	1	1	51	8	58	71	48	11	34	34	7.40	1.82	5.4	295	5.3	5.3	1.0	1.7	32%	61%	-3
Shappi,Austin	07	25	aa	ARI	1	7	40	2	76	94	41	8	18	48	4.86	1.47	8.3	297	2.1	5.6	2.7	1.0	34%	68%	55
Sharpe,Steven	07	26	aa	OAK	3	1	26	8	28	37	13	3	7	10	4.06	1.56	4.8	310	2.2	3.4	1.5	1.1	33%	77%	12
Sharpless,Josh	06	26	a/a	PIT	3	1	37	9	54	52	16	1	26	48	2.63	1.44	6.4	246	4.4	8.1	1.8	0.2	33%	81%	88
	07	27	aa	PIT	1	5	43	3	64	80	44	11	44	50	6.13	1.94	7.2	301	6.1	7.1	1.2	1.6	35%	71%	13
Shaver,Chris	06	25	aa	CHC	7	10	26	0	150	217	91	12	73	95	5.46	1.93	28.0	331	4.4	5.7	1.3	0.7	38%	72%	28
Shearn,Tom	06	29	a/a	CIN	9	4	33	0	98	129	49	16	55	57	4.47	1.88	14.3	311	5.0	5.3	1.0	1.5	34%	80%	3
	07	30	aaa	CIN	7	10	26	0	143	202	98	13	59	84	6.15	1.82	26.1	326	3.7	5.3	1.4	0.8	37%	66%	26
Shell,Steven	06	24	a/a	LAA	6	11	27	0	140	185	94	15	33	78	6.03	1.55	23.2	311	2.1	5.0	2.4	1.0	35%	61%	44
	07	25	aa	LAA	7	3	36	0	83	115	51	19	21	57	5.47	1.63	10.5	321	2.3	6.2	2.7	2.0	35%	73%	23
Shields,Jamie	06	25 a	aaa	TAM	3	2	10	0	61	71	23	3	6	55	3.39	1.26	25.5	285	0.9	8.1	9.2	0.4	37%	73%	226
Shiell,Jason	06	30	aaa	ATL	2	4	9	0	52	68	40	4	19	27	6.85	1.67	26.5	310	3.2	4.7	1.5	0.8	35%	57%	29
	07	31	aa	KC	2	4	29	3	85	157	74	17	39	28	7.86	2.30	15.3	387	4.1	3.0	0.7	1.8	40%	68%	-44
Shipman,Andy	06	25	a/a	CHC	3	4	57	2	72	99	41	1	34	48	5.15	1.85	6.0	320	4.3	5.9	1.4	0.1	39%	70%	52
	07	26	aa	OAK	4	7	28	0	117	182	102	13	50	69	7.85	1.98	20.5	347	3.8	5.3	1.4	1.0	39%	59%	16
Shoemaker,Scott	07	26	aa	TEX	6	3	29	0	96	129	76	22	40	43	7.10	1.76	15.5	314	3.8	4.0	1.1	2.0	32%	63%	-23
Shortslef,Josh	06	25	aa	PIT	6	2	12	0	60	78	42	5	14	40	6.29	1.52	22.3	307	2.0	6.0	2.9	0.8	36%	57%	67
	07	26	aa	PIT	5	13	27	0	149	216	98	13	64	64	5.90	1.88	26.5	331	3.9	3.9	1.0	0.8	36%	68%	9
Shuey,Paul	07	37	a/a	BAL	0	0	22	1	24	39	16	2	10	19	5.83	2.04	5.4	357	3.8	7.1	1.9	0.8	43%	71%	41
Sierra,Eduardo	06	24	a/a	COL	2	1	31	0	50	68	49	3	39	39	8.91	2.14	8.2	318	7.1	7.0	1.0	0.6	39%	55%	37
	07	25	a/a	CHW	2	7	47	2	62	76	45	4	42	51	6.55	1.90	6.4	294	6.1	7.4	1.2	0.6	37%	64%	48
Silva,Jesus	07	25	aa	FLA	1	5	10	0	43	71	40	8	12	17	8.37	1.91	20.8	360	2.4	3.6	1.5	1.8	37%	57%	-17
Simard,Michel	06	25	aa	LAA	0	1	16	0	33	53	27	4	17	18	7.23	2.11	10.4	355	4.5	4.9	1.1	1.2	39%	66%	-0
Simmons,James	07	21	aa	OAK	0	0	13	0	29	41	16	2	8	20	4.93	1.68	10.3	325	2.5	6.2	2.5	0.6	38%	70%	61
Simmons,Justin	06	25	a/a	LA	1	3	31	1	53	55	34	12	34	28	5.72	1.67	7.8	261	5.7	4.7	0.8	2.0	26%	71%	-11
Simonitsch,Errol	06	24	aa	MIN	8	14	27	0	148	238	107	25	46	71	6.52	1.92	26.6	355	2.8	4.3	1.5	1.5	38%	68%	-4
Simon,Alfredo	06	25	aaa	SF	0	6	10	0	52	83	42	7	18	30	7.34	1.94	25.3	353	3.1	5.1	1.6	1.2	39%	62%	13
	07	26	aa	TEX	5	10	22	0	119	207	126	28	53	54	9.56	2.18	27.6	373	4.0	4.1	1.0	2.1	39%	57%	-36
Simpson,Allan	06	29	aaa	MIL	2	4	42	10	56	59	31	10	32	43	4.93	1.62	6.1	266	5.1	6.8	1.3	1.6	30%	74%	24
Simpson,Gerrit	06	27	aa	MIL	3	3	51	0	76	89	36	10	31	45	4.22	1.57	6.7	285	3.7	5.4	1.5	1.2	32%	77%	24
Sipp,Tony	06	23 a	aa	CLE	4	2	29	3	60	53	27	2	23	69	4.01	1.25	8.6	231	3.4	10.3	3.0	0.3	33%	66%	125
Sisco,Andy	07	25	aaa	CHW	3	6	23	0	78	92	52	15	47	68	5.98	1.78	16.0	287	5.4	7.8	1.4	1.7	34%	70%	23
Skaggs,Jon	06	29	aa	HOU	0	0	14	1	30	43	30	6	26	19	8.97	2.28	11.2	326	7.8	5.7	0.7	1.9	36%	62%	-16
Slaten,Doug	06	27 b	a/a	ARI	4	4	58	10	63	53	14	1	24	63	2.06	1.23	4.5	225	3.5	9.0	2.6	0.2	31%	83%	113
Slocum,Brian	06	26	aaa	CLE	6	3	27	1	94	93	45	5	39	80	4.35	1.41	15.1	253	3.8	7.7	2.0	0.5	32%	68%	79
Slowey,Kevin	06	22	aa	MIN	4	3	9	0	59	61	29	8	15	44	4.42	1.29	27.6	261	2.3	6.7	2.9	1.2	30%	69%	68
	07	23 a	aaa	MIN	10	5	20	0	133	138	41	5	21	87	2.77	1.19	27.4	262	1.4	5.9	4.1	0.3	32%	77%	115

					Actual				Major League Equivalents																
PITCHER	Yr	Age	Lev	Org	w	l	g	sv	ip	h	er	hr	bb	k	era	WHIP	bf/g	oob	ctl	dom	cmd	hr/9	h%	s%	bpv
Small,Aaron	06	35	aaa	NYY	2	4	11	0	41	79	35	5	14	13	7.59	2.25	19.4	396	3.0	2.9	1.0	1.1	42%	66%	-21
Smith,Brett	07	24	aa	NYY	7	4	17	0	91	80	45	11	55	64	4.48	1.48	23.6	231	5.4	6.3	1.2	1.0	26%	72%	40
Smith,Chris	06	26	a/a	BOS	10	7	27	0	149	189	94	15	41	84	5.65	1.55	24.7	303	2.5	5.0	2.0	0.9	34%	63%	41
	07	26	a/a	BOS	6	9	32	1	109	181	74	13	48	63	6.15	2.10	17.1	363	3.9	5.2	1.3	1.1	41%	72%	8
Smith,Cody	06	24	aa	KC	9	0	46	4	86	99	29	4	22	48	3.08	1.41	8.1	282	2.3	5.1	2.2	0.4	33%	78%	62
Smith,Dan	06	31	aa	ATL	3	6	28	0	60	60	35	5	41	65	5.29	1.68	9.9	255	6.2	9.7	1.6	0.7	35%	68%	74
	07	24	a/a	ATL	7	7	23	0	109	115	61	8	64	66	5.02	1.65	21.6	266	5.3	5.4	1.0	0.7	31%	69%	36
Smith,Gregory	06	23	aa	ARI	5	4	11	0	60	81	37	6	25	33	5.55	1.77	25.6	316	3.8	5.0	1.3	0.9	36%	69%	22
	07	24	aa	ARI	9	5	22	0	122	151	63	14	33	82	4.64	1.50	24.5	297	2.4	6.1	2.5	1.1	34%	71%	53
Smith,Jesse	06	26	a/a	LAA	8	13	29	0	167	237	106	24	66	76	5.69	1.81	27.2	327	3.5	4.1	1.2	1.3	35%	71%	-1
Smith,Matt	06	27	a/a	MIL	1	7	20	1	43	84	51	6	22	17	10.54	2.45	11.6	399	4.5	3.6	0.8	1.2	43%	55%	-22
	06	27	aaa	PHI	0	1	33	4	35	40	11	5	15	22	2.71	1.56	4.8	281	3.8	5.6	1.5	1.4	31%	89%	23
Smith,Mike	06	29	aaa	MIN	11	5	28	0	150	210	105	18	73	85	6.32	1.88	25.8	324	4.3	5.1	1.2	1.1	36%	67%	14
	07	30	aa	STL	11	13	31	0	159	287	149	23	69	78	8.40	2.23	26.5	382	3.9	4.4	1.1	1.3	42%	62%	-10
Smith,Sean	06	23	aa	CLE	10	5	25	0	144	161	76	10	46	84	4.75	1.44	25.1	277	2.9	5.3	1.8	0.6	32%	66%	51
	07	24	aaa	CLE	9	7	24	0	133	148	76	16	59	82	5.14	1.56	24.8	276	4.0	5.5	1.4	1.1	31%	69%	30
Smith,Travis	06	34	aaa	STL	8	7	23	0	135	192	102	14	46	76	6.80	1.76	27.5	327	3.1	5.1	1.6	0.9	37%	61%	27
Snare,Ryan	06	28	aa	KC	2	2	7	0	35	63	34	4	22	19	8.65	2.40	26.7	379	5.6	4.9	0.9	0.9	42%	63%	-1
Snyder,Kyle	06	29	aaa	KC	1	5	13	1	80	114	49	7	12	40	5.55	1.58	27.7	328	1.4	4.5	3.3	0.7	37%	64%	64
Soler,Alay	07	28	aa	PIT	1	1	14	1	39	66	37	4	23	17	8.62	2.29	14.5	368	5.3	3.8	0.7	0.8	40%	61%	-5
Songster,Judd	06	27	aa	COL	2	1	47	2	65	62	34	14	32	54	4.77	1.45	6.0	246	4.5	7.5	1.7	1.9	27%	74%	28
	07	28	aa	COL	5	5	42	2	67	104	53	11	37	41	7.12	2.10	8.0	346	5.0	5.5	1.1	1.5	38%	68%	-2
Song,Seung	06	26	aa	KC	5	10	27	0	130	170	97	16	72	75	6.67	1.86	23.1	309	5.0	5.2	1.0	1.1	35%	64%	13
Sonnanstine,Andrew	06	24	aa	TAM	15	8	28	0	185	197	85	20	39	127	4.11	1.27	27.7	267	1.9	6.2	3.2	1.0	31%	70%	78
	07	25 a	aaa	TAM	6	4	11	0	71	73	29	10	14	58	3.68	1.23	26.8	260	1.8	7.4	4.1	1.3	31%	75%	96
Sosa,Jorge	07	30	aa	NYM	4	0	5	0	32	46	7	1	6	18	2.01	1.61	29.0	329	1.6	4.9	3.1	0.4	38%	89%	71
Sosa,Oswaldo	07	22	aa	MIN	1	4	9	0	48	51	28	4	23	28	5.25	1.54	23.8	267	4.3	5.3	1.2	0.8	30%	66%	36
Sowers,Jeremy	06	23	aaa	CLE	9	1	15	0	97	92	19	1	30	48	1.76	1.26	27.0	245	2.8	4.4	1.6	0.1	29%	85%	64
	07	24	aaa	CLE	4	5	15	0	96	128	53	6	24	55	4.96	1.58	28.9	313	2.2	5.1	2.3	0.6	36%	68%	55
Speier,Ryan	07	28	aa	COL	1	4	50	33	49	71	41	5	29	29	7.56	2.04	4.9	332	5.3	5.3	1.0	0.9	38%	62%	14
Speigner,Levale	06	26	a/a	MIN	4	3	49	14	70	106	44	9	24	34	5.70	1.85	6.8	340	3.1	4.4	1.4	1.1	37%	71%	9
	07	27	aaa	WAS	3	4	17	0	49	77	36	1	22	27	6.57	2.02	14.2	349	4.1	4.9	1.2	0.2	40%	65%	34
Spiehs,RD	06	27	aa	SF	4	1	41	2	64	114	47	3	26	20	6.61	2.18	8.0	378	3.7	2.8	0.8	0.5	41%	68%	-2
Spurling,Chris	06	29	aaa	DET	1	4	49	5	66	79	22	5	11	26	3.00	1.37	5.8	291	1.5	3.6	2.4	0.7	32%	81%	46
Stahl,Richard	06	26	a/a	CIN	3	10	28	0	80	119	84	9	72	48	9.46	2.38	15.2	337	8.0	5.4	0.7	1.1	38%	59%	3
Standridge,Jason	06	28	aaa	CIN	2	2	37	0	46	52	22	3	17	34	4.32	1.49	5.5	277	3.3	6.7	2.0	0.6	34%	71%	64
Stanford,Jason	06	30	aaa	CLE	6	6	22	0	112	132	70	12	44	66	5.65	1.57	22.9	287	3.5	5.3	1.5	1.0	32%	64%	31
	07	31	aaa	CLE	5	1	18	0	87	107	53	9	39	49	5.50	1.67	22.2	295	4.0	5.0	1.2	0.9	33%	67%	25
Starling,Wardell	06	24	aa	PIT	6	5	15	0	86	100	37	7	29	35	3.87	1.49	25.4	284	3.0	3.6	1.2	0.8	31%	75%	23
	07	25	aa	PIT	3	8	32	1	84	116	78	5	33	41	8.33	1.76	12.3	320	3.5	4.4	1.3	0.6	36%	49%	27
Startup,Will	06	22 a	a/a	ATL	8	2	46	4	67	77	25	4	18	59	3.36	1.42	6.3	282	2.4	7.9	3.3	0.5	36%	77%	99
	07	23	a/a	SD	3	2	57	1	68	57	24	5	29	57	3.17	1.26	5.0	223	3.8	7.5	2.0	0.7	28%	77%	77
Stauffer,Tim	06	24	aaa	SD	7	12	28	0	153	203	91	15	49	78	5.35	1.65	25.0	312	2.9	4.6	1.6	0.9	35%	68%	27
	07	25	aa	SD	8	5	25	0	130	186	83	14	41	76	5.76	1.74	24.3	328	2.8	5.2	1.8	1.0	37%	68%	29
Stephens,John	06	27	a/a	BAL	2	7	20	0	86	132	79	10	41	48	8.25	2.01	21.2	345	4.3	5.0	1.2	1.0	39%	58%	9
Stertzbach,Von Davic	07	26	aa	LAA	1	2	21	0	25	39	26	5	16	17	9.48	2.20	6.1	348	5.8	6.2	1.1	1.6	39%	57%	-4
Stetter,Mitch	06	26	aaa	MIL	2	5	51	0	38	45	25	4	17	32	5.97	1.64	3.4	290	4.1	7.5	1.8	1.0	35%	64%	52
	07	27 b	a/a	MIL	1	0	26	1	15	10	10	1	6	17	5.92	1.02	2.3	184	3.3	10.1	3.1	0.7	26%	38%	124
Stevens,Jeffrey	07	24 a	aa	CLE	3	1	34	2	48	48	22	4	17	56	4.14	1.36	6.1	256	3.2	10.5	3.3	0.8	36%	71%	113
Stewart,Josh	06	28	aaa	FLA	1	3	13	0	35	46	27	5	16	18	7.02	1.77	12.7	311	4.0	4.6	1.1	1.3	34%	61%	4
Stidfole,Sean	07	24	aa	TOR	1	0	30	0	52	54	19	4	31	32	3.21	1.63	7.9	261	5.4	5.5	1.0	0.7	30%	82%	36
Stockman,Phil	06	27 b	a/a	ATL	0	0	21	2	40	19	4	0	14	42	1.00	0.83	7.2	139	3.2	9.5	2.9	0.0	21%	87%	146
	07	28	a/a	ATL	2	0	21	3	31	21	6	1	16	23	1.67	1.19	6.1	186	4.7	6.8	1.5	0.3	23%	87%	79
Stokes,Brian	06	27	aaa	TAM	7	7	29	0	133	166	83	9	55	84	5.62	1.66	21.0	300	3.7	5.6	1.5	0.6	35%	65%	42
Stone,Ricky	07	33	aaa	CIN	5	6	59	16	62	62	18	5	12	31	2.59	1.18	4.3	255	1.7	4.5	2.7	0.8	28%	82%	65
Strickland,Scott	06	30	aaa	PIT	5	2	53	5	73	87	27	6	18	53	3.28	1.43	6.0	289	2.2	6.5	3.0	0.7	35%	79%	79
Stults,Eric	06	27	aaa	LA	10	11	26	0	153	164	74	9	66	105	4.36	1.50	26.0	268	3.9	6.2	1.6	0.5	32%	71%	55
	07	28	aa	LA	5	7	21	0	89	181	105	16	43	59	10.59	2.52	23.1	410	4.4	6.0	1.4	1.6	46%	57%	-10
Stutes,Kyle	07	26	aa	SD	0	1	27	2	31	47	27	6	17	19	7.69	2.03	5.7	339	4.8	5.5	1.1	1.6	37%	63%	-4
Swarzak,Anthony	07	22	aa	MIN	5	4	15	0	86	88	37	6	24	62	3.87	1.30	24.2	259	2.5	6.5	2.6	0.6	31%	71%	77
Sweeney,Brian	06	32	aaa	SD	2	1	7	0	30	36	16	2	7	18	4.71	1.43	18.8	289	2.2	5.4	2.4	0.6	33%	67%	62
Switzer,Jon	06	27	aaa	TAM	3	0	26	3	31	27	4	1	15	24	1.22	1.36	5.1	232	4.3	6.9	1.6	0.3	29%	92%	75
	07	28	aaa	TAM	0	0	23	1	33	34	4	0	10	19	1.17	1.34	6.1	263	2.6	5.1	1.9	0.0	32%	90%	73
Tadano,Kazuhito	06	26	aaa	OAK	2	4	34	3	56	76	36	9	19	49	5.78	1.69	7.6	317	3.0	7.9	2.7	1.5	38%	69%	50
	07	27	aa	OAK	8	7	29	0	129	195	101	27	42	95	7.05	1.84	21.2	341	2.9	6.6	2.2	1.8	38%	65%	18
Talbot,Mitch	06	23 a	aa	TAM	10	7	28	1	156	168	59	7	48	133	3.40	1.38	24.0	269	2.8	7.7	2.8	0.4	34%	75%	93
	07	24	aaa	TAM	13	9	29	0	161	205	110	16	64	109	6.15	1.67	25.5	304	3.6	6.1	1.7	0.9	35%	63%	40
Tankersley,Dennis	06	28	aaa	STL	4	15	29	0	167	215	109	23	64	101	5.89	1.67	26.5	305	3.5	5.4	1.6	1.2	34%	66%	22
	07	29	aaa	DET	10	7	24	0	138	213	96	15	55	64	6.23	1.94	28.0	345	3.6	4.2	1.2	1.0	38%	68%	6
Taschner,Jack	06	28 b	aaa	SF	6	7	45	14	49	57	24	5	17	54	4.34	1.51	4.8	284	3.2	9.9	3.1	1.0	38%	73%	94
Tata,Jordan	06	25	aaa	DET	10	6	21	0	122	140	69	13	51	73	5.07	1.56	26.1	283	3.7	5.4	1.5	1.0	32%	69%	32
	07	26	aaa	DET	4	5	14	0	82	81	37	9	29	42	4.06	1.34	25.0	253	3.2	4.6	1.4	1.0	28%	72%	32
Taubenheim,Ty	06	24	aaa	TOR	2	4	18	0	75	91	33	12	20	41	3.95	1.48	18.4	293	2.4	4.9	2.1	1.4	32%	79%	26
	07	25	a/a	TOR	6	8	24	0	120	154	91	18	46	84	6.80	1.67	22.9	305	3.5	6.3	1.8	1.3	35%	60%	31
Tejeda,Rob	06	25	aaa	TEX	6	2	15	0	80	78	42	11	46	68	4.73	1.55	23.8	250	5.2	7.7	1.5	1.2	30%	73%	45
Tejera,Michael	06	30	aaa	SF	8	5	35	0	111	134	56	12	43	63	4.54	1.59	14.3	292	3.5	5.1	1.5	1.0	33%	73%	28
	07	31	aa	PIT	8	5	27	0	127	187	96	20	60	41	6.78	1.95	22.9	335	4.3	2.9	0.7	1.4	35%	67%	-23
Thatcher,Joe	07	26 a	a/a	SD	4	1	46	1	46	46	8	0	11	53	1.64	1.23	4.2	256	2.1	10.4	5.1	0.0	38%	85%	172
Thayer,Dale	06	26	a/a	SD	7	4	59	27	68	69	22	3	24	51	2.92	1.38	5.0	259	3.2	6.8	2.1	0.4	32%	79%	76
	07	27	a/a	TAM	9	0	55	21	69	59	26	6	27	50	3.33	1.24	5.2	226	3.5	6.4	1.9	0.7	27%	75%	66

					Actual				Major League Equivalents																
PITCHER	Yr	Age	Lev	Org	w	l	g	sv	ip	h	er	hr	bb	k	era	WHIP	bf/g	oob	ctl	dom	cmd	hr/9	h%	s%	bpv
Thomas,Brad	07	30	aa	SEA	8	6	34	2	116	207	97	11	59	68	7.55	2.29	17.8	379	4.5	5.2	1.2	0.8	43%	66%	10
Thomas,Justin	07	24	aa	SEA	4	9	24	0	119	170	88	11	66	87	6.62	1.98	24.3	328	5.0	6.6	1.3	0.9	39%	66%	31
Thompson,Brad	06	25 a	aaa	STL	2	0	14	0	42	42	13	3	6	29	2.77	1.14	12.2	254	1.3	6.2	4.8	0.6	30%	78%	124
Thompson,Justin	06	34	aaa	MIL	2	3	8	0	35	55	34	9	8	19	8.64	1.80	20.7	348	2.2	4.9	2.3	2.4	36%	55%	-11
Thompson,Lavon	07	25	aa	HOU	4	3	38	3	54	66	30	17	10	41	4.99	1.40	6.1	293	1.7	6.7	4.1	2.8	30%	77%	39
Thompson,Mike	06	26	aaa	SD	6	1	13	0	69	71	28	3	19	36	3.68	1.30	22.4	259	2.5	4.6	1.9	0.4	30%	71%	58
	07	27	aa	SD	4	11	23	0	132	223	126	23	48	54	8.61	2.05	28.6	366	3.3	3.7	1.1	1.6	39%	58%	-20
Thompson,Richard	06	22	a/a	LAA	3	5	46	11	71	64	45	13	28	53	5.70	1.30	6.5	236	3.5	6.7	1.9	1.6	26%	59%	38
	07	23 a	aa	LAA	5	3	37	1	74	62	22	8	21	67	2.63	1.11	8.1	223	2.5	8.1	3.2	1.0	27%	82%	97
Thompson,Sean	06	24	aa	SD	6	10	27	0	154	177	86	18	51	114	5.00	1.48	25.1	283	3.0	6.7	2.3	1.0	33%	68%	55
	07	25	aa	COL	9	8	27	0	133	161	79	16	61	68	5.33	1.67	22.6	293	4.1	4.6	1.1	1.1	32%	69%	16
Thomson,John	07	34	a/a	KC	2	7	10	0	47	76	49	9	19	29	9.32	2.00	23.2	354	3.6	5.5	1.5	1.7	39%	53%	-2
Thorpe,Tracy	06	26	aa	TOR	3	1	54	18	55	46	29	7	36	49	4.71	1.47	4.5	220	5.8	7.9	1.4	1.1	27%	70%	55
	07	27	aa	TOR	5	4	46	10	56	61	41	7	34	41	6.63	1.70	5.6	271	5.5	6.5	1.2	1.1	31%	61%	32
Thorp,Paul	07	27	aa	NYY	0	1	15	1	30	39	14	5	25	15	4.34	2.13	10.1	306	7.6	4.5	0.6	1.4	33%	84%	-10
Threets,Erick	06	25	aaa	SF	2	1	49	0	62	55	22	4	41	44	3.18	1.54	5.7	232	5.9	6.4	1.1	0.6	28%	80%	52
	07	26	aa	SF	3	1	40	1	54	58	28	4	38	31	4.61	1.76	6.3	267	6.3	5.1	0.8	0.7	30%	74%	27
Thurman,Corey	06	28	a/a	MIL	6	10	26	0	148	201	91	15	56	102	5.52	1.74	26.5	318	3.4	6.2	1.8	0.9	37%	69%	39
	07	29	aa	MIL	5	8	30	0	95	118	74	26	39	65	6.99	1.64	14.5	298	3.7	6.1	1.7	2.5	31%	63%	-7
Till,Brock	06	26	aa	CIN	6	1	40	6	62	69	23	1	36	30	3.33	1.68	7.1	276	5.2	4.3	0.8	0.2	32%	79%	38
	07	27	a/a	CIN	4	1	42	1	47	71	29	1	18	23	5.49	1.90	5.4	341	3.5	4.3	1.2	0.2	39%	69%	32
Tomey,Anthony	07	26	a/a	DET	4	0	37	2	51	52	21	2	32	39	3.71	1.65	6.3	259	5.7	6.8	1.2	0.4	32%	77%	58
Torres,Carlos	07	25	aa	CHW	2	2	36	1	56	74	34	5	25	49	5.41	1.77	7.3	311	4.1	7.9	2.0	0.8	39%	70%	56
Totten,Heath	06	28	aa	LA	8	5	21	0	126	183	75	13	36	55	5.36	1.74	27.9	332	2.6	3.9	1.5	0.9	36%	70%	18
	07	29	a/a	PHI	3	10	20	0	89	154	71	7	27	30	7.15	2.03	22.0	372	2.7	3.0	1.1	0.7	40%	63%	-0
Touchet,Danny	06	25	aa	TEX	3	4	34	2	65	98	52	8	19	37	7.12	1.79	9.0	340	2.6	5.1	2.0	1.2	38%	60%	24
Traber,Billy	06	27	aaa	WAS	7	7	21	0	124	171	71	8	28	82	5.11	1.60	26.7	320	2.1	5.9	2.9	0.6	38%	67%	69
	07	28	aaa	WAS	2	3	14	0	40	49	17	2	8	22	3.86	1.42	12.4	297	1.7	5.0	3.0	0.5	34%	73%	73
Tracey,Sean	06	26	aaa	CHW	8	9	29	0	129	134	84	24	82	86	5.84	1.67	20.5	263	5.7	6.0	1.1	1.7	28%	69%	10
Trahern,Dallas	07	22	a/a	DET	13	6	27	0	169	207	90	13	52	85	4.82	1.53	27.9	295	2.8	4.5	1.6	0.7	33%	69%	36
Trolia,Aaron	07	26	aa	SEA	3	2	21	1	43	68	44	6	22	30	9.14	2.09	10.2	351	4.6	6.4	1.4	1.2	41%	55%	16
Troncoso,Ramon	07	25	aa	LA	7	3	35	7	52	61	22	3	19	32	3.83	1.54	6.6	287	3.3	5.6	1.7	0.5	34%	75%	51
Tucker,Glenn	06	26	aa	ATL	2	4	50	0	66	98	44	8	21	30	6.04	1.80	6.2	336	2.9	4.0	1.4	1.1	36%	67%	10
Tucker,Rusty	06	26	aa	CHW	1	4	45	2	58	91	59	6	54	33	9.10	2.50	7.0	349	8.4	5.1	0.6	0.9	39%	62%	2
Tyler,Scott	06	24	aa	FLA	1	2	48	3	61	72	36	6	53	45	5.27	2.03	6.3	286	7.8	6.6	0.8	0.9	34%	75%	27
	07	25	aa	FLA	0	2	28	1	30	32	39	2	51	27	11.59	2.76	6.1	268	15.2	8.0	0.5	0.7	34%	55%	41
Ungs,Nick	06	27	aaa	FLA	9	9	26	0	144	184	71	14	47	69	4.40	1.61	25.1	304	3.0	4.3	1.5	0.9	34%	74%	25
	07	28	aa	FLA	5	5	29	1	112	170	90	21	59	48	7.23	2.04	19.2	342	4.7	3.9	0.8	1.7	36%	67%	-24
Urdaneta,Lino	07	28	aa	NYM	2	1	26	9	35	51	28	5	12	10	7.13	1.79	6.3	331	3.1	2.6	0.8	1.2	34%	60%	-16
Vaclavik,Justin	07	23	aa	PIT	2	6	24	0	34	59	40	3	23	22	10.61	2.39	7.5	371	6.0	5.9	1.0	0.8	43%	53%	12
Valdez,Edward	06	27	aa	CIN	7	10	29	0	136	186	92	14	46	81	6.08	1.70	21.7	319	3.0	5.3	1.8	0.9	36%	64%	33
	07	28	a/a	WAS	2	5	46	3	84	132	59	9	46	47	6.27	2.12	9.2	350	4.9	5.0	1.0	1.0	39%	71%	7
Valdez,Merkin	06	25	aaa	SF	0	4	46	5	49	56	35	6	36	41	6.40	1.87	5.1	280	6.6	7.5	1.1	1.1	34%	66%	35
Valdez,Raul	07	30	aa	NYM	0	1	20	1	29	52	19	4	12	17	5.77	2.20	7.4	380	3.7	5.3	1.4	1.2	43%	76%	4
Valentine,Joe	06	27	a/a	MIL	3	2	42	13	61	77	36	7	33	32	5.25	1.80	6.9	301	4.9	4.8	1.0	1.0	33%	72%	14
Van Benschoten,Johr	07	27	aa	PIT	10	7	19	0	109	135	46	10	60	55	3.78	1.79	27.0	298	5.0	4.5	0.9	0.8	33%	81%	18
Van Buren,Jermaine	06	26	aaa	BOS	4	0	33	16	45	47	22	3	20	39	4.32	1.49	6.0	265	3.9	7.7	2.0	0.6	33%	71%	72
	07	27	a/a	OAK	1	3	47	3	64	72	36	10	34	44	5.01	1.67	6.3	279	4.8	6.1	1.3	1.5	31%	74%	19
Van Hekken,Andy	06	27	aaa	KC	3	5	9	0	53	74	35	7	12	28	5.88	1.60	26.7	322	2.0	4.7	2.4	1.2	35%	65%	31
Vanden Hurk,Rick	07	22 a	aa	FLA	4	2	11	0	65	54	28	8	25	69	3.87	1.21	24.5	221	3.5	9.5	2.8	1.1	29%	72%	93
Vaquedano,Jose	06	25	aa	BOS	9	8	24	0	105	176	114	12	78	68	9.79	2.41	23.4	364	6.7	5.8	0.9	1.0	42%	58%	4
	07	26	aa	BOS	2	1	22	0	38	49	24	6	21	17	5.69	1.84	8.3	307	4.9	4.1	0.8	1.4	33%	71%	-5
Vargas,Jason	06	24	aaa	FLA	3	6	13	0	69	104	59	10	28	46	7.70	1.91	25.7	340	3.7	6.0	1.6	1.3	39%	60%	18
	07	25	aa	NYM	9	7	24	0	125	166	86	15	45	88	6.21	1.69	24.0	313	3.3	6.4	2.0	1.1	36%	64%	40
Vasquez,Carlos	06	24	aa	CHC	3	5	36	3	50	57	34	3	39	51	6.10	1.91	6.7	279	7.0	9.2	1.3	0.6	37%	67%	65
	07	25	a/a	CHW	4	3	52	4	76	73	33	3	39	49	3.90	1.47	6.4	248	4.6	5.8	1.3	0.4	30%	73%	56
Vasquez,Esmerling	07	24	aa	ARI	10	6	29	0	165	151	72	14	62	129	3.93	1.29	23.9	238	3.4	7.0	2.1	0.8	29%	71%	70
Vasquez,Jorge	06	28	aa	PIT	3	3	47	5	65	68	26	3	36	59	3.63	1.60	6.2	262	5.0	8.2	1.6	0.3	34%	77%	76
	07	29	aa	TEX	2	3	34	0	52	63	40	11	53	44	6.90	2.22	7.9	291	9.2	7.6	0.8	1.8	34%	72%	5
Vasquez,Virgil	06	24	aa	DET	7	12	27	0	173	219	101	25	54	105	5.25	1.57	28.8	302	2.8	5.5	2.0	1.3	34%	69%	29
	07	25	aaa	DET	12	5	25	0	155	167	79	20	33	109	4.57	1.29	26.1	269	1.9	6.3	3.3	1.2	31%	67%	73
Vaughan,Beau	07	26	aa	BOS	1	3	42	6	59	69	31	2	36	48	4.73	1.77	6.6	286	5.4	7.3	1.3	0.4	36%	72%	59
Vazquez,Camilo	06	23	aa	CIN	3	5	11	0	60	82	40	8	27	46	6.02	1.82	25.9	320	4.0	6.8	1.7	1.2	37%	68%	31
	07	24	aa	CIN	4	8	21	0	112	158	81	11	43	71	6.54	1.79	25.1	325	3.5	5.7	1.6	0.9	37%	63%	31
Veal II,Donald T	07	23	aa	CHC	8	10	28	0	130	152	93	14	77	107	6.42	1.76	21.7	285	5.3	7.4	1.4	1.0	35%	63%	41
Venafro,Mike	06	33	aaa	COL	3	1	56	2	38	41	17	2	15	23	3.98	1.46	3.0	270	3.5	5.4	1.5	0.5	32%	73%	51
	07	34	a/a	STL	1	2	51	2	50	74	33	2	21	23	5.99	1.91	4.7	337	3.8	4.0	1.1	0.4	38%	67%	22
Ventura,Ronnie	07	24	aa	HOU	4	9	20	0	87	113	69	8	31	47	7.18	1.64	19.9	307	3.2	4.8	1.5	0.9	34%	55%	28
Veras,Jose	06	26 a	aaa	NYY	5	3	50	21	59	58	20	4	20	55	3.07	1.31	5.0	250	3.1	8.4	2.7	0.6	32%	78%	95
Vermilyea,James	06	25	a/a	TOR	6	7	30	2	131	182	75	12	32	59	5.17	1.64	19.9	323	2.2	4.1	1.9	0.8	35%	69%	28
	07	26	aaa	TOR	2	2	25	1	43	47	25	5	21	27	5.27	1.59	7.8	274	4.4	5.6	1.3	1.1	31%	68%	29
Villa,Kelvin	07	22	aa	ATL	8	12	28	0	143	197	109	16	69	103	6.85	1.86	24.4	320	4.3	6.5	1.5	1.0	38%	63%	31
Vogelsong,Ryan	06	29	aaa	PIT	4	5	11	0	67	74	31	7	14	33	4.12	1.31	25.8	273	1.9	4.4	2.3	0.9	30%	70%	48
Volquez,Edinson	06	23	aaa	TEX	6	6	21	0	120	110	65	14	79	112	4.87	1.57	25.7	239	5.9	8.4	1.4	1.0	30%	71%	56
	07	24	aa	TEX	14	2	19	0	109	88	42	12	42	104	3.47	1.20	23.6	217	3.5	8.5	2.5	1.0	27%	74%	86
Volstad,Christopher	07	21	aa	FLA	4	2	7	0	42	46	17	4	10	23	3.63	1.33	25.6	272	2.1	4.9	2.3	0.9	30%	75%	53
Waddell,Jason	06	25	aa	SF	1	3	38	1	48	91	33	6	19	38	6.22	2.28	6.6	393	3.5	7.1	2.0	1.0	47%	73%	30
Wade,Cory	07	24	aa	LA	0	1	14	0	33	29	7	2	13	25	1.93	1.28	9.9	234	3.5	6.7	1.9	0.6	28%	88%	69
Wagner,Ryan	06	24	aaa	WAS	1	3	41	1	47	75	41	4	17	28	7.83	1.95	5.6	353	3.2	5.4	1.6	0.8	40%	58%	28
Waldrop,Steven	07	22	aa	MIN	3	6	11	0	59	83	41	7	20	27	6.25	1.75	25.0	325	3.1	4.1	1.4	1.1	35%	65%	11

					Actual				Major League Equivalents																
PITCHER	Yr	Age	Lev	Org	w	l	g	sv	ip	h	er	hr	bb	k	era	WHIP	bf/g	oob	ctl	dom	cmd	hr/9	h%	s%	bpv
Walker,Andy	06	23	aa	TEX	4	4	20	0	93	146	81	29	23	44	7.88	1.82	22.0	350	2.2	4.2	1.9	2.8	35%	63%	-33
Walker,Kevin	06	30	aaa	TEX	6	5	46	2	68	109	59	9	39	46	7.79	2.17	7.5	354	5.1	6.1	1.2	1.2	41%	64%	10
	07	31	aa	COL	4	6	15	0	79	138	75	9	24	30	8.56	2.04	26.2	373	2.7	3.4	1.3	1.1	40%	57%	-5
Walker,Tyler	07	31	aa	SF	1	2	20	7	23	33	16	6	12	17	6.45	1.94	5.6	329	4.6	6.7	1.4	2.3	36%	73%	-10
Walrond,Les	06	30	aaa	CHC	10	5	31	0	133	178	88	16	69	84	5.94	1.86	20.5	314	4.7	5.7	1.2	1.1	36%	69%	18
	07	31	aa	CHC	11	5	27	0	137	277	131	23	70	55	8.62	2.53	27.7	409	4.6	3.6	0.8	1.5	43%	67%	-34
Walters,Phillip	07	23	aa	STL	3	4	8	0	49	46	15	4	14	33	2.75	1.22	25.4	243	2.6	6.0	2.4	0.7	28%	80%	70
Warden,Jim Ed	06	27	aa	CLE	5	2	55	11	59	48	28	4	36	35	4.23	1.43	4.7	219	5.5	5.3	1.0	0.6	25%	70%	47
	07	28	a/a	CLE	5	5	56	6	74	119	49	7	34	53	5.99	2.06	6.6	354	4.1	6.4	1.5	0.9	42%	71%	29
Wassermann,Ehren	06	26	aa	CHW	4	8	61	22	63	83	29	6	30	36	4.12	1.80	4.9	311	4.3	5.1	1.2	0.8	35%	78%	25
	07	27	aaa	CHW	2	4	38	5	42	42	14	0	20	28	3.08	1.47	4.9	255	4.2	6.0	1.4	0.0	32%	77%	70
Waters,Chris	06	26	aa	ATL	8	14	27	0	155	216	134	34	99	90	7.81	2.03	28.4	323	5.7	5.2	0.9	2.0	34%	64%	-19
	07	27	a/a	BAL	8	9	28	0	158	208	116	23	101	91	6.61	1.96	27.5	311	5.8	5.2	0.9	1.3	34%	67%	4
Watkins,Steve	06	28	aaa	WAS	7	7	21	0	112	128	61	11	45	61	4.92	1.54	23.8	281	3.6	4.9	1.4	0.9	32%	69%	31
	07	29	aa	SD	2	5	34	0	78	133	72	19	60	37	8.30	2.48	12.4	369	6.9	4.2	0.6	2.2	38%	69%	-45
Wayne,Brett	07	27	aa	TAM	2	0	29	0	47	77	36	8	41	26	6.92	2.51	8.8	360	7.8	4.9	0.6	1.6	39%	75%	-23
Weatherby III,Charles	07	29	a/a	PHI	2	2	17	0	45	69	42	8	24	19	8.47	2.07	13.2	346	4.7	3.7	0.8	1.6	36%	60%	-24
Webber,Nick	07	23	aa	STL	1	3	33	0	50	70	28	4	22	25	4.99	1.83	7.2	324	3.9	4.5	1.2	0.7	36%	73%	20
Webb,John	06	27	aaa	STL	6	11	29	0	176	249	112	15	59	92	5.70	1.75	28.4	327	3.0	4.7	1.6	0.8	37%	67%	28
	07	28	aa	CHC	4	6	31	1	80	143	73	8	49	35	8.16	2.39	13.7	379	5.5	4.0	0.7	0.8	41%	65%	-7
Wells,Jared	06	25	a/a	SD	6	12	27	0	134	157	87	10	75	89	5.81	1.73	23.1	286	5.1	6.0	1.2	0.7	34%	66%	38
	07	26	aa	SD	4	7	47	8	92	134	71	11	56	68	6.94	2.06	9.8	333	5.4	6.7	1.2	1.1	39%	66%	22
Wells,Randy	06	24	a/a	CHC	9	7	25	0	131	172	75	13	41	97	5.17	1.63	23.8	310	2.8	6.7	2.4	0.9	37%	69%	55
	07	25	aa	CHC	5	6	40	2	95	129	67	16	47	77	6.30	1.84	11.3	317	4.4	7.2	1.6	1.5	37%	68%	25
Whelan,Kevin	07	24	aa	NYY	4	2	31	4	54	43	27	3	47	55	4.46	1.68	8.0	215	7.9	9.2	1.2	0.5	29%	73%	76
Whisler,Wesley	06	24	aa	CHW	2	3	7	0	44	64	33	8	16	23	6.72	1.82	29.9	331	3.4	4.7	1.4	1.7	35%	66%	-4
	07	24	aa	CHW	6	13	28	0	156	252	127	16	47	63	7.34	1.91	27.0	355	2.7	3.6	1.3	0.9	38%	61%	6
White,Bill	06	28	aa	ARI	0	1	54	12	63	88	43	10	42	56	6.18	2.06	5.8	323	6.0	7.9	1.3	1.4	39%	72%	24
	07	29	aa	TEX	2	0	44	2	50	74	39	6	35	45	6.96	2.17	5.8	335	6.3	8.0	1.3	1.1	41%	68%	29
White,Matt	06	29	aaa	PHI	7	9	38	1	110	158	75	13	43	53	6.10	1.82	13.8	330	3.5	4.3	1.2	1.1	36%	67%	8
	07	30	aa	LA	2	4	40	2	51	81	36	10	24	27	6.28	2.06	6.4	353	4.3	4.8	1.1	1.8	38%	73%	-16
White,Sean	06	25	aa	ATL	5	6	21	1	102	170	79	4	52	58	6.95	2.18	24.8	363	4.6	5.1	1.1	0.4	42%	66%	24
White,Steven	06	25	a/a	NYY	8	10	28	0	175	191	100	11	79	105	5.14	1.54	27.9	271	4.1	5.4	1.3	0.5	32%	65%	44
	07	26	aaa	NYY	6	4	16	1	91	103	45	4	34	45	4.48	1.50	25.2	279	3.4	4.4	1.3	0.4	32%	69%	41
Wigdahl,Jeffrey	07	25	aa	HOU	2	2	22	0	37	56	30	7	24	31	7.28	2.16	8.6	339	5.9	7.4	1.3	1.6	40%	68%	10
Wilhite,Matt	06	25	aaa	LAA	7	2	54	1	80	85	33	7	20	30	3.75	1.31	6.3	266	2.3	3.3	1.5	0.8	28%	73%	29
	07	26	aa	LAA	3	4	49	3	74	120	61	10	23	30	7.39	1.92	7.3	356	2.8	3.6	1.3	1.3	38%	62%	-5
Wilkerson,Wes	06	30	aaa	FLA	0	0	38	0	40	46	23	2	19	28	5.24	1.61	4.8	280	4.2	6.3	1.5	0.5	34%	66%	53
	07	31	a/a	ATL	3	4	44	1	63	98	56	8	32	32	7.91	2.06	7.1	346	4.6	4.6	1.0	1.1	38%	61%	1
Williams,Dave	06	28	aaa	NYM	2	2	7	0	36	43	22	4	12	14	5.50	1.51	22.9	290	2.9	3.5	1.2	1.0	31%	65%	13
	07	29	aa	NYM	3	4	10	0	61	81	39	14	16	26	5.71	1.60	27.6	313	2.4	3.9	1.6	2.0	32%	70%	-11
Williams,Jerome	06	25	aaa	CHC	5	7	29	0	111	176	80	23	38	46	6.47	1.92	18.6	352	3.1	3.7	1.2	1.9	36%	70%	-23
	07	26	a/a	MIN	0	4	23	1	52	94	66	11	28	29	11.43	2.34	11.9	381	4.9	4.9	1.0	1.8	41%	50%	-25
Williams,Randy	06	31	aaa	COL	1	2	47	0	59	87	56	8	29	37	8.51	1.98	6.2	336	4.5	5.7	1.3	1.3	38%	56%	9
	07	32	aa	TEX	3	2	50	1	64	100	58	16	24	37	8.08	1.92	6.2	348	3.3	5.2	1.6	2.3	37%	62%	-19
Wilson,Brian	07	26	aa	SF	1	2	31	11	34	30	11	0	27	29	2.93	1.66	5.0	232	7.0	7.6	1.1	0.0	31%	80%	77
Windsor,Jason	06	24 a	a/a	OAK	17	2	26	0	151	175	70	9	41	131	4.18	1.43	25.3	284	2.5	7.8	3.2	0.6	36%	71%	95
	07	25	aa	OAK	5	3	10	0	56	84	46	3	27	32	7.30	1.98	27.5	340	4.3	5.0	1.2	0.5	39%	61%	26
Wing,Ryan	07	26	aa	CHW	6	6	35	0	114	121	63	13	54	75	5.00	1.54	14.5	267	4.3	5.9	1.4	1.1	30%	69%	34
Winkelsas,Joe	07	34	a/a	ATL	2	2	19	0	36	42	17	0	17	22	4.17	1.64	8.6	287	4.2	5.4	1.3	0.0	35%	72%	57
Woerman,Joseph	07	25	aa	SEA	7	7	27	0	144	140	74	8	75	105	4.60	1.49	23.5	250	4.7	6.6	1.4	0.5	30%	68%	58
Wolf,Ross	06	24	aa	FLA	5	3	60	0	66	87	35	1	18	37	4.76	1.59	5.0	310	2.4	5.0	2.1	0.1	36%	67%	62
	07	25	aa	FLA	4	3	46	2	47	63	22	5	19	20	4.22	1.74	4.8	315	3.6	3.8	1.1	1.0	34%	78%	7
Woods,Jake	07	26	aa	SEA	5	7	25	1	114	194	118	21	51	62	9.33	2.14	23.1	368	4.0	4.9	1.2	1.6	40%	56%	-13
Woody,Abraham	07	25	aa	ARI	8	6	48	5	72	108	49	9	26	40	6.18	1.87	7.2	340	3.3	5.0	1.5	1.2	38%	68%	13
Wood,Mike	07	27	aa	TEX	9	3	16	0	97	118	54	11	25	51	5.02	1.48	26.7	294	2.3	4.8	2.0	1.0	33%	67%	37
Worrell,Mark	06	24	aa	STL	3	7	57	27	61	60	37	10	20	63	5.46	1.30	4.5	251	2.9	9.3	3.2	1.5	31%	61%	83
	07	25	aa	STL	3	2	49	4	67	67	27	6	25	55	3.68	1.38	5.9	256	3.4	7.4	2.2	0.8	31%	76%	69
Wright,Chase	07	25	a/a	NYY	13	5	25	1	145	168	88	20	70	66	5.44	1.64	26.5	284	4.4	4.1	0.9	1.2	30%	69%	6
Wright,Matt	06	25	a/a	ATL	10	8	25	0	137	166	76	11	64	101	5.01	1.68	25.2	293	4.2	6.6	1.6	0.7	35%	70%	47
	07	26	aa	KC	10	5	28	0	137	182	86	23	42	77	5.62	1.64	22.3	313	2.8	5.1	1.8	1.5	34%	69%	15
Wright,Wesley	07	23	aa	LA	7	4	44	2	78	82	39	9	49	75	4.50	1.68	8.2	265	5.7	8.7	1.5	1.0	33%	75%	55
Wylie,Mitch	06	25 a	aaa	NYM	2	4	27	1	48	59	22	0	12	45	4.15	1.47	7.8	294	2.3	8.3	3.7	0.0	39%	69%	123
Yates,Kyle	06	24	aa	TOR	6	9	28	1	127	152	78	14	43	85	5.55	1.53	20.2	290	3.1	6.0	2.0	1.0	33%	65%	44
	07	25	aa	TOR	9	9	27	0	151	223	99	28	46	80	5.90	1.78	26.3	336	2.8	4.8	1.7	1.7	36%	71%	2
Youman,Shane	06	27	a/a	PIT	11	2	31	1	137	156	55	8	36	61	3.62	1.40	19.1	281	2.3	4.0	1.7	0.5	31%	74%	43
	07	28	a/a	PIT	4	6	15	0	82	129	63	4	42	42	6.87	2.08	27.4	350	4.6	4.6	1.0	0.4	40%	65%	22
Young,Christopher	06	25	a/a	FLA	5	4	49	12	76	85	34	2	25	54	3.98	1.45	6.8	277	3.0	6.4	2.1	0.2	34%	71%	76
	07	26	aa	FLA	0	3	42	1	45	86	38	8	18	15	7.55	2.31	5.6	395	3.7	2.9	0.8	1.6	41%	69%	-38
Yourkin,Matt	06	25	a/a	FLA	1	4	56	3	66	80	34	5	32	58	4.58	1.69	5.4	293	4.3	7.9	1.8	0.7	37%	73%	61
	07	26	aa	FLA	1	1	52	0	57	76	36	3	29	38	5.63	1.84	5.2	313	4.5	6.0	1.3	0.5	37%	68%	40
Zarate,Mauro	07	25	aa	FLA	2	1	42	1	59	51	16	4	23	48	2.40	1.24	5.9	226	3.5	7.2	2.1	0.6	28%	83%	77
Zell,Danny	07	26 a	aa	DET	2	5	47	2	48	63	29	7	9	41	5.42	1.50	4.5	311	1.7	7.8	4.7	1.3	38%	66%	100
Ziegler,Brad	06	27	a/a	OAK	9	7	27	0	162	231	86	23	46	74	4.78	1.71	27.8	328	2.6	4.1	1.6	1.3	35%	75%	10
	07	28	aa	OAK	12	3	50	2	78	89	30	0	20	44	3.47	1.40	6.8	281	2.4	5.1	2.1	0.0	34%	73%	74
Zinicola,Zechry	07	23	aa	WAS	0	4	42	6	57	59	41	3	36	38	6.45	1.66	6.2	261	5.7	6.0	1.1	0.5	31%	59%	47
Zink,Charlie	06	27	a/a	BOS	10	4	25	0	116	149	79	11	77	50	6.14	1.95	22.6	306	6.0	3.8	0.6	0.9	33%	68%	4
	07	28	a/a	BOS	11	6	24	0	140	199	109	18	86	57	7.03	2.03	28.9	327	5.5	3.7	0.7	1.1	35%	66%	-9
Zuercher,Zachary	07	23	aa	STL	3	0	37	1	43	42	15	3	22	24	3.22	1.48	5.1	251	4.5	5.1	1.1	0.6	29%	80%	39
Zumwalt,Alec	06	26	a/a	MIL	1	3	50	20	54	65	31	11	23	49	5.08	1.63	4.9	292	3.9	8.2	2.1	1.8	35%	74%	38
	07	27	a/a	MIL	0	5	34	1	52	78	49	11	31	40	8.43	2.09	7.7	338	5.4	6.8	1.3	1.9	38%	61%	-2

VI.
RATINGS,
RANKINGS,
CHEAT
SHEETS

Ratings, Rankings, Cheat Sheets

Here is what you will find in this section:

Skills Rankings

We start by looking at some important component skills. For batters, we've ranked the top players in terms of pure power, speed, and batting average skill, breaking each down in a number of different ways to provide more insight. For pitchers, we rank some of the key base skills, differentiating between starters and relievers, and provide a few interesting cuts that might uncover some late round sleepers.

These are clearly not exhaustive lists of sorts and filters. If there is another cut you'd like to see, drop me a note and I'll consider it for next year's book. Also note that the database at Baseball HQ allows you to construct your own custom sorts and filters. Finally, remember that these are just tools. Some players will appear on multiple lists — even mutually exclusive lists — so you have to assess what makes most sense and make decisions for your specific application.

POWER

Top PX, 400+ AB: Top power skills from among projected full-time players.

Top PX, -300 AB: Top power skills from among projected part-time players. You might find some end-game options here.

Position Scarcity: A quick scan to see which positions have deeper power options than others.

Top PX, Ct% over 85%: Top power skills from among the top contact hitters. Best pure power options here.

Top PX, Ct% under 75%: Top power skills from among the worst contact hitters. These are free-swingers who might be prone to streakiness or lower batting averages.

Top PX, FB% over 40%: Top power skills from among the most extreme fly ball hitters. Most likely to convert their power into home runs.

Top PX, FB% under 35%: Top power skills from among those with lesser fly ball tendencies. There may be more downside to their home run potential.

SPEED

Top SX, 400+ AB: Top speed skills from among projected full-time players.

Top SX, -300 AB: Top speed skills from among projected part-time players. You might find some end-game options here.

Position Scarcity: A quick scan to see which positions have deeper speed options than others.

Top SX, OB% over .350: Top speed skills from among those who get on base most often. Best opportunities for stolen bases here.

Top SX, OB% under .310: Top speed skills from among those who have trouble getting on base. While "you can't steal 1B," these names may bear watching if they can improve their on base ability.

Top SX, SBO% over 20%: Top speed skills from among those who get the green light most often. Most likely to convert their speed into stolen bases.

Top SX, SBO% under 15%: Top speed skills from among those who are currently not getting the green light. There may be sleeper SB's here if given more opportunities to run.

BATTING AVERAGE

Top Ct%, 400+ AB: Top contact skills from among projected full-time players. Contact does not necessarily convert directly to higher batting averages, but BA and Ct% are still strongly correlated.

Top Ct%, -300 AB: Top contact skills from among projected part-time players. You might find some end-game options here.

Low Ct%, 400+ AB: The poorest contact skills from among projected full-time players. These are potential batting average killers.

Top Ct%, bb% over 10%: Top contact skills from among the most patient hitters. Best pure batting eye and batting average upside here.

Top Ct%, bb% under 6%: Top contact skills from among the least patient hitters. These are free-swingers who might be prone to streakiness or lower batting averages.

Top Ct%, GB% over 50%: Top contact skills from among the most extreme ground ball hitters. A ground ball has a higher chance of becoming a hit than a non-HR fly ball so there may be some batting average upside here.

Top Ct%, GB% under 40%: Top contact skills from among those with lesser ground ball tendencies. These players are making contact but hitting more fly balls, which tend to convert to hits at a lower rate than GB.

PITCHING SKILLS

Top Command: Leaders in projected K/BB rates.

Top Control: Leaders in fewest projected walks allowed.

Top Dominance: Leaders in projected strikeout rate.

Top Ground Ball Rate: GB pitchers tend to have lower ERA's (and higher WHIP) than fly ball pitchers.

Top Fly Ball Rate: FB pitchers tend to have higher ERA's (and lower WHIP) than ground ball pitchers.

High GB, Low Dom: GB pitchers tend to have lower K rates, but these are the most extreme examples.

High GB, High Dom: The best at dominating hitters and keeping the ball down. These are the pitchers who keep runners off the bases and batted balls in the park, a skills combination that is probably the most valuable a pitcher can own.

Lowest xERA: Leaders in projected skills-based ERA.

Top BPV: Two lists of top skilled pitchers here. For starters, those projected to be rotation regulars (180+ IP) and fringe starters with skill (-150 IP). For relievers, those projected to be frontline closers (15+ saves) and high-skilled bullpen fillers (5– saves).

+/- Scores

These lists rank those players with the highest and lowest +/- scores. The scores measure potential 2008 performance as compared to 2007. As such, the highest "+" scores represent both players who have the potential to break out as well as those who we expect to rebound. Note that, typically productive players who had awful 2007 seasons, even due to injury, might be ranked high on this list just by virtue of the fact that 2008 has to be considerably better (e.g. B.J. Ryan, Chris Carpenter, etc.)

The flipside is similar. The lowest "-" scores represent players who are likely to collapse as well as those who are due for a correction. For instance, a pitcher like Takashi Saito sits high on this list because the odds of him maintaining a sub-2.00 ERA are slim.

A more detailed description of how these scores work appears in the glossary.

Risk Management

Our focus on integrating skills analysis with risk presents us with a few important lists to consider. On these pages are the players who've accumulated the most days on the disabled list over the past three years, and the most reliable batters and pitchers, broken out by position and skill. As a reminder, a high reliability score has nothing to do with skill; it is a gauge of which players manage to accumulate playing time and post consistent output from year to year.

Portfolio3 Plan

Here, the players are sorted and ranked based on how they fit into the three draft tiers of the Portfolio3 Plan. A full description of how this plan works appears in the Gaming section.

Position Scarcity Chart

There has been much discussion about position scarcity, its importance and how to leverage it in your draft. This chart provides a visual representation of the depth of talent for the top 45 players at each position and shows you why, in a straight draft league, it might make sense to draft a Kaz Matsui before you draft a Nick Markakis.

Rotisserie Auction Draft

This list is presented with both AL and NL players, mostly because we don't know who is going to end up on what team yet. The values are mostly representative of standard 75%-plus depth leagues. However, remember that these values are for player-to-player comparative purposes only, and allow us to provide rankings. You should not use these as actual in-draft bid values (see the Consumer Advisory earlier in the book for a full explanation).

The free projections update in March will provide better estimates of playing time, and as such, better information for drafting purposes. The custom draft guides on Baseball HQ are available to those who wish to produce accurate valuations for their particular league configuration.

But in the interim, you can still use the information here to plan out the core of your draft. For those who subscribe to Baseball HQ, full projections begin appearing online in mid-December.

Rotisserie Snake Draft

This ranking takes the previous auction list, re-sets it into rounds and adjusts the rankings based on position scarcity. Given the growing popularity of 15-team mixed leagues, like the National Fantasy Baseball Championship, we've set this list up for that type of format.

In the first eight rounds, your target players should be those that are shaded (though your first round pick may depend upon your seed). These are the position scarcity picks. Also pay attention to the bolded players; these are categorical scarcity picks (primarily steals and saves).

If you reach a point where there are still undrafted players from earlier rounds, you can judiciously target those. To build the best foundation, you should come out of the first 10 rounds with all your middle infielders, all your corner infielders, one outfielder, at least one catcher and two pitchers (at least one closer).

The reason we target scarce positions first is that there will be plenty of solid outfielders and starting pitchers later on. The Position Scarcity Chart shows you why. The 24th best catcher on the list is Miguel Olivo; the 24th best starting pitcher is Roy Halladay. Which one would you rather have on your team?

Simulation League Draft

Using Runs Above Replacement creates a more real-world ranking of player value, which serves simulation gamers well. Batters and pitchers are integrated, and value break-points are delineated.

The Missing Piece of Information

For all these lists, equally important to how the players are ranked is how the other owners in your league perceive each player's positioning. For instance, if you see Brandon Phillips as a first round pick but you know the other owners see him as a third-rounder, you can probably wait to pick him up in round 2.

The Universal Disclaimer

This section is intended solely as a preliminary look based on current factors. Do not treat this guide as the Draft Day gospel. Use the ratings and rankings as a rough guide to get a general sense of where a player falls. For Draft Day, you will need to make your own adjustments based upon about 7,341 different criteria that can impact the world between now and then. Updates will appear next spring online at BaseballHQ.com. And don't forget the free projections update at http://www.baseballhq.com/books/freeupdate/index.shtml.

BATTER SKILLS RANKINGS - POWER

TOP PX, 400+ AB

NAME	POS	PX
Howard,Ryan	3	219
Dunn,Adam	7	190
Ortiz,David	0	186
Thome,Jim	0	185
Fielder,Prince	3	177
Braun,Ryan	5	177
Rodriguez,Alex	5	176
Pena,Carlos	3	173
Teixeira,Mark	3	169
Dye,Jermaine	9	168
Wilkerson,Brad	37	167
Cabrera,Miguel	5	166
Soriano,Alfonso	7	164
Holliday,Matt	7	163
Duncan,Chris	7	159
Hawpe,Brad	9	159
Hafner,Travis	0	158
Burrell,Pat	7	158
Hamilton,Josh	8	157
Gomes,Jonny	097	156
Pujols,Albert	3	155
Beltran,Carlos	8	155
Jones,Chipper	5	153
Scott,Luke	9	153
Berkman,Lance	39	153
Cust,Jack	90	152
Wright,David	5	152
LaRoche,Adam	3	152
Utley,Chase	4	152
Ramirez,Manny	7	150
Fields,Josh	57	149
Glaus,Troy	5	145
Young,Chris	8	144
Pena,Wily Mo	79	144
Hart,Corey	98	144
Swisher,Nick	893	144
Delgado,Carlos	3	144
Hall,Bill	8	143

TOP PX, -300 AB

NAME	POS	PX
Branyan,Russell	5	187
Maybin,Cameron	7	187
Betemit,Wilson	5	172
Shoppach,Kelly	2	172
Thames,Marcus	73	168
Clark,Tony	3	158
Ross,Cody	8	158
Castro,Ramon	2	154
Bonds,Barry	7	148
Ross,Dave	2	146
Stairs,Matt	37	145
Bruce,Jay	8	144
Moore,Scott	5	144
Reynolds,Mark	5	142
Giambi,Jason	0	141
Buck,John	2	140
Napoli,Mike	2	138
Duncan,Shelley	0	138
Johnson,Nick	3	138
Phelps,Josh	3	137
Headley,Chase	5	136
Longoria,Evan	5	136
Sosa,Sammy	0	135
Hinske,Eric	37	135
Dellucci,David	7	134

POSITIONAL SCARCITY

NAME	POS	PX
Ortiz,David	DH	186
Thome,Jim	2	185
Hafner,Travis	3	158
Gomes,Jonny	4	156
Giambi,Jason	5	141
Duncan,Shelley	6	138
Shoppach,Kelly	CA	172
Castro,Ramon	2	154
Ross,Dave	3	146
Buck,John	4	140
Napoli,Mike	5	138
Posada,Jorge	6	129
Snyder,Chris	7	126
Soto,Geovany	8	120
Howard,Ryan	1B	219
Fielder,Prince	2	177
Pena,Carlos	3	173
Teixeira,Mark	4	169
Wilkerson,Brad	5	167
Clark,Tony	6	158
Pujols,Albert	7	155
Berkman,Lance	8	153
LaRoche,Adam	9	152
Stairs,Matt	10	145
Utley,Chase	2B	152
Uggla,Dan	2	139
Weeks,Rickie	3	134
Johnson,Kelly	4	116
Valentin,Jose	5	114
Kent,Jeff	6	113
Cano,Robinson	7	112
Phillips,Brandon	8	110
Branyan,Russell	3B	187
Braun,Ryan	2	177
Rodriguez,Alex	3	176
Betemit,Wilson	4	172
Cabrera,Miguel	5	166
Jones,Chipper	6	153
Wright,David	7	152
Fields,Josh	8	149
Glaus,Troy	9	145
Moore,Scott	10	144
Ramirez,Hanley	SS	132
Greene,Khalil	2	126
Guillen,Carlos	3	126
Tulowitzki,Troy	4	125
Murphy,Donnie	5	119
Rollins,Jimmy	6	118
Smith,Jason	7	116
Uribe,Juan	8	111
Dunn,Adam	OF	190
Maybin,Cameron	2	187
Thames,Marcus	3	168
Dye,Jermaine	4	168
Soriano,Alfonso	5	164
Holliday,Matt	6	163
Duncan,Chris	7	159
Hawpe,Brad	8	159
Ross,Cody	9	158
Burrell,Pat	10	158
Hamilton,Josh	11	157
Beltran,Carlos	12	155
Scott,Luke	13	153
Cust,Jack	14	152
Ramirez,Manny	15	150
Bonds,Barry	16	148

TOP PX, Ct% over 85%

NAME	Ct%	PX
Pujols,Albert	90	155
Bonds,Barry	86	148
Ramirez,Aramis	88	141
Guerrero,Vladimir	89	128
Lee,Carlos	89	128
Wells,Vernon	85	125
Ordonez,Magglio	87	122
McCann,Brian	86	120
Rollins,Jimmy	88	118
Pearce,Steven	87	117
Alou,Moises	90	116
Matsui,Hideki	87	115
Rolen,Scott	86	114
Kent,Jeff	86	113
Helton,Todd	87	112
Murton,Matt	86	112
Cano,Robinson	88	112
Atkins,Garrett	86	112
Martinez,Victor	86	111
Martin,Russell	85	111
Hill,Aaron	86	110
Lowell,Mike	88	108
Anderson,Garret	85	108
Mientkiewicz,Doug	86	108
Kotchman,Casey	91	107
Barrett,Michael	86	105
Rivera,Juan	88	104
Huff,Aubrey	85	104
House,J.R.	85	104
Jackson,Conor	88	103
Barton,Daric	88	103
Sanchez,Freddy	89	101
Mench,Kevin	90	101
Ruiz,Carlos	87	101
Butler,Billy	87	100
Schierholtz,Nathan	85	100
Kendrick,Howie	85	100
Catalanotto,Frank	89	100

TOP PX, Ct% under 75%

NAME	Ct%	PX
Howard,Ryan	66	219
Dunn,Adam	68	190
Branyan,Russell	59	187
Maybin,Cameron	57	187
Thome,Jim	69	185
Pena,Carlos	72	173
Betemit,Wilson	70	172
Shoppach,Kelly	67	172
Thames,Marcus	74	168
Wilkerson,Brad	68	167
Duncan,Chris	72	159
Clark,Tony	72	158
Burrell,Pat	73	158
Gomes,Jonny	67	156
Castro,Ramon	73	154
Cust,Jack	66	152
Fields,Josh	71	149
Ross,Dave	72	146
Glaus,Troy	74	145
Pena,Wily Mo	67	144
Moore,Scott	71	144
Hall,Bill	72	143
Reynolds,Mark	68	142
Giambi,Jason	74	141
Jenkins,Geoff	73	139

TOP PX, FB% over 40%

NAME	FB%	PX
Howard,Ryan	40	219
Dunn,Adam	47	190
Branyan,Russell	51	187
Maybin,Cameron	43	187
Ortiz,David	46	186
Thome,Jim	40	185
Fielder,Prince	43	177
Braun,Ryan	45	177
Rodriguez,Alex	41	176
Pena,Carlos	44	173
Teixeira,Mark	40	169
Thames,Marcus	51	168
Dye,Jermaine	44	168
Wilkerson,Brad	46	167
Soriano,Alfonso	49	164
Duncan,Chris	40	159
Burrell,Pat	49	158
Gomes,Jonny	53	156
Pujols,Albert	40	155
Beltran,Carlos	43	155
Castro,Ramon	45	154
Scott,Luke	41	153
LaRoche,Adam	41	152
Utley,Chase	42	152
Ramirez,Manny	41	150
Fields,Josh	43	149
Bonds,Barry	46	148
Ross,Dave	49	146
Stairs,Matt	41	145
Glaus,Troy	46	145
Young,Chris	47	144
Hart,Corey	44	144
Swisher,Nick	46	144
Delgado,Carlos	41	144
Hall,Bill	42	143
Konerko,Paul	43	142
Reynolds,Mark	44	142
Ramirez,Aramis	44	141

TOP PX, FB% under 35%

NAME	FB%	PX
Hamilton,Josh	33	157
Pena,Wily Mo	34	144
Johnson,Nick	33	138
Markakis,Nick	34	129
Pence,Hunter	31	128
Diaz,Victor	32	126
Kubel,Jason	34	126
Young,Dmitri	34	121
Abreu,Bobby	32	119
Pearce,Steven	32	117
Jones,Brandon	25	113
Murton,Matt	30	112
Overbay,Lyle	31	112
Cano,Robinson	30	112
Milledge,Lastings	29	111
Martin,Russell	33	111
Wilson,Preston	31	109
Matthews Jr.,Gary	33	109
Pie,Felix	33	109
Kotchman,Casey	32	107
Peralta,Jhonny	34	107
Crawford,Carl	31	105
Jones,Jacque	24	102
Teahen,Mark	30	101
Diaz,Matt	31	101

BATTER SKILLS RANKINGS - SPEED

TOP SX, 400+ AB

NAME	POS	SX
Reyes,Jose	6	174
Crawford,Carl	7	173
Rollins,Jimmy	6	167
Roberts,Dave	87	164
Victorino,Shane	9	159
Figgins,Chone	5	158
Pierre,Juan	8	156
Matsui,Kaz	4	154
Weeks,Rickie	4	153
Patterson,Corey	8	150
Granderson,Curtis	8	148
Ramirez,Hanley	6	147
Taveras,Willy	8	142
Lofton,Kenny	87	142
Kemp,Matt	9	142
Byrnes,Eric	798	142
Ellsbury,Jacoby	7	140
Bartlett,Jason	6	138
Furcal,Rafael	6	138
Duffy,Chris	8	137
Suzuki,Ichiro	8	136
McLouth,Nate	87	132
Crisp,Coco	8	132
Roberts,Brian	4	131
Sizemore,Grady	8	128
Pie,Felix	8	127
Hart,Corey	98	127
Cameron,Mike	8	125
Rios,Alex	98	124
Theriot,Ryan	64	124
Casilla,Alexi	4	124
Braun,Ryan	5	124
Soriano,Alfonso	7	122
Teahen,Mark	9	122
Damon,Johnny	807	122
Phillips,Brandon	4	121
Fukudome,Kosuke	9	121
Iwamura,Akinori	5	121

TOP SX, -300 AB

NAME	POS	SX
Bourn,Michael	7	189
Bynum,Freddie	7	152
Harris,Willie	78	146
Maybin,Cameron	7	144
Logan,Nook	8	140
Gomez,Carlos	79	139
Lewis,Fred	97	135
Morgan,Nyjer	8	135
Cairo,Miguel	35	131
Podsednik,Scott	7	126
De Aza,Alejandro	8	123
Guzman,Cristian	6	122
Raburn,Ryan	9	120
Salazar,Jeff	9	119
Gwynn,Tony	8	118
Aybar,Erick	46	118
Pagan,Angel	89	114
Chavez,Endy	79	114
Baldelli,Rocco	8	113
DaVanon,Jeff	8	113
Cora,Alex	46	113
Ryan,Brendan	65	109
Smith,Jason	6	108
Ozuna,Pablo	5	107
Hopper,Norris	87	107

POSITIONAL SCARCITY

NAME	POS	SX
Gomes,Jonny	DH	92
Sheffield,Gary	2	75
White,Rondell	3	64
Hillenbrand,Shea	4	59
Huff,Aubrey	5	57
Ortiz,David	6	56
Laird,Gerald	CA	100
Martin,Russell	2	94
Mauer,Joe	3	88
Towles,J.R.	4	87
Olivo,Miguel	5	79
Napoli,Mike	6	78
Ruiz,Carlos	7	78
Mathis,Jeff	8	74
Cairo,Miguel	1B	131
Ortmeier,Dan	2	102
Hinske,Eric	3	97
Gload,Ross	4	87
Votto,Joey	5	81
Barton,Daric	6	80
Baker,Jeff	7	75
Wilkerson,Brad	8	75
Klesko,Ryan	9	72
Phillips,Andy	10	71
Matsui,Kaz	2B	154
Weeks,Rickie	2	153
Roberts,Brian	3	131
German,Esteban	4	125
Casilla,Alexi	5	124
Phillips,Brandon	6	121
Burke,Chris	7	118
Aybar,Erick	8	118
Figgins,Chone	3B	158
Braun,Ryan	2	124
Iwamura,Akinori	3	121
Punto,Nick	4	114
Wright,David	5	109
Ozuna,Pablo	6	107
Izturis,Maicer	7	106
Gordon,Alex	8	103
Rodriguez,Alex	9	103
Counsell,Craig	10	99
Reyes,Jose	SS	174
Rollins,Jimmy	2	167
Ramirez,Hanley	3	147
Bartlett,Jason	4	138
Furcal,Rafael	5	138
Theriot,Ryan	6	124
Guzman,Cristian	7	122
Lopez,Felipe	8	120
Bourn,Michael	OF	189
Crawford,Carl	2	173
Roberts,Dave	3	164
Victorino,Shane	4	159
Pierre,Juan	5	156
Bynum,Freddie	6	152
Patterson,Corey	7	150
Granderson,Curtis	8	148
Harris,Willie	9	146
Maybin,Cameron	10	144
Taveras,Willy	11	142
Lofton,Kenny	12	142
Kemp,Matt	13	142
Byrnes,Eric	14	142
Ellsbury,Jacoby	15	140
Logan,Nook	16	140

TOP SX, OB% over .350

NAME	OB%	SX
Figgins,Chone	357	158
Weeks,Rickie	354	153
Ramirez,Hanley	360	147
Suzuki,Ichiro	363	136
Roberts,Brian	367	131
Sizemore,Grady	357	128
German,Esteban	357	125
Rios,Alex	351	124
Braun,Ryan	355	124
Utley,Chase	368	117
Hudson,Orlando	357	116
Castillo,Luis	368	116
Werth,Jayson	361	113
DeJesus,David	355	113
Guillen,Carlos	370	113
Beltran,Carlos	368	111
Abreu,Bobby	397	110
Johnson,Kelly	357	110
Wright,David	401	109
Buck,Travis	354	107
Holliday,Matt	378	105
Rodriguez,Alex	400	103
Willits,Reggie	371	102
Antonelli,Matt	374	99
Pedroia,Dustin	360	98
Markakis,Nick	360	98
Renteria,Edgar	358	97
Upton,B.J.	361	97
Jeter,Derek	369	96
Martin,Russell	368	94
Bay,Jason	367	92
Gross,Gabe	359	92
Hamilton,Josh	359	91
Drew,J.D.	389	90
Mauer,Joe	391	88
Scott,Luke	352	88
Young,Michael	353	87
Blalock,Hank	351	86

TOP SX, OB% under .310

NAME	OB%	SX
Bynum,Freddie	293	152
Patterson,Corey	293	150
Logan,Nook	297	140
Cairo,Miguel	292	131
Anderson,Joshua	284	124
De Aza,Alejandro	279	123
Burke,Chris	299	118
Aybar,Erick	288	118
Barfield,Josh	292	115
Pagan,Angel	299	114
Punto,Nick	309	114
Baldelli,Rocco	304	113
Cora,Alex	283	113
Ryan,Brendan	301	109
Smith,Jason	250	108
Ozuna,Pablo	303	107
Wilson,Josh	285	107
Terrero,Luis	291	107
Schierholtz,Nathan	301	107
Sullivan,Cory	296	104
Ortmeier,Dan	294	102
Laird,Gerald	293	100
Pena,Tony	286	100
Gutierrez,Franklin	309	98
Linden,Todd	308	96

TOP SX, SBO% over 20%

NAME	SBO	SX
Bourn,Michael	40%	189
Reyes,Jose	47%	174
Crawford,Carl	43%	173
Rollins,Jimmy	26%	167
Roberts,Dave	32%	164
Victorino,Shane	32%	159
Figgins,Chone	35%	158
Pierre,Juan	40%	156
Matsui,Kaz	23%	154
Weeks,Rickie	21%	153
Bynum,Freddie	36%	152
Patterson,Corey	41%	150
Ramirez,Hanley	38%	147
Harris,Willie	31%	146
Maybin,Cameron	36%	144
Taveras,Willy	35%	142
Kemp,Matt	23%	142
Byrnes,Eric	27%	142
Ellsbury,Jacoby	33%	140
Logan,Nook	32%	140
Gomez,Carlos	45%	139
Furcal,Rafael	22%	138
Duffy,Chris	28%	137
Lewis,Fred	22%	135
Morgan,Nyjer	32%	135
McLouth,Nate	21%	132
Crisp,Coco	21%	132
Cairo,Miguel	25%	131
Roberts,Brian	26%	131
Davis,Rajai	43%	129
Sizemore,Grady	20%	128
Pie,Felix	24%	127
Freel,Ryan	31%	127
Hart,Corey	25%	127
Redman,Tike	23%	127
Podsednik,Scott	31%	126
Owens,Jerry	37%	125
Theriot,Ryan	25%	124

TOP SX, SBO% under 15%

NAME	SBO	SX
Cameron,Mike	14%	125
Rios,Alex	14%	124
Guzman,Cristian	9%	122
Teahen,Mark	9%	122
Fukudome,Kosuke	9%	121
Iwamura,Akinori	11%	121
Raburn,Ryan	12%	120
Pence,Hunter	13%	118
Utley,Chase	9%	117
Hudson,Orlando	8%	116
Castillo,Luis	14%	116
Werth,Jayson	11%	113
DeJesus,David	9%	113
Guillen,Carlos	13%	113
Cora,Alex	9%	113
Iguchi,Tadahito	12%	112
Beltran,Carlos	13%	111
Johnson,Kelly	9%	110
Giles,Marcus	11%	109
Smith,Jason	11%	108
Richar,Danny	11%	108
Buck,Travis	11%	107
Cabrera,Melky	11%	107
Schierholtz,Nathan	14%	107
Matthews Jr.,Gary	13%	107

BATTER SKILLS RANKINGS - BATTING AVERAGE

TOP Ct%, 400+ AB

NAME	Ct%	BA
Polanco,Placido	94	315
Pierre,Juan	94	294
Eckstein,David	93	291
Pedroia,Dustin	93	298
Lo Duca,Paul	93	295
Johjima,Kenji	92	280
Kendall,Jason	92	269
Castillo,Luis	91	300
Vizquel,Omar	91	254
Loretta,Mark	91	282
Betancourt,Yuniesk	91	284
Kotchman,Casey	91	300
Casey,Sean	90	285
Cabrera,Orlando	90	279
Pujols,Albert	90	332
Estrada,Johnny	90	279
Lofton,Kenny	90	277
Theriot,Ryan	90	267
Molina,Bengie	90	281
Vidro,Jose	90	279
Izturis,Maicer	90	281
Wilson,Jack	89	280
Suzuki,Ichiro	89	319
Guerrero,Vladimir	89	315
Catalanotto,Frank	89	290
Molina,Yadier	89	260
Sanchez,Freddy	89	293
Stewart,Shannon	89	278
Lee,Carlos	89	300
Tejada,Miguel	89	294
Ellsbury,Jacoby	88	293
Giles,Brian	88	270
Rollins,Jimmy	88	293
Barton,Daric	88	268
Mauer,Joe	88	308
Reyes,Jose	88	283
Lowell,Mike	88	285
Jackson,Conor	88	288

TOP Ct%, -300 AB

NAME	Ct%	BA
Callaspo,Alberto	94	279
Izturis,Cesar	93	255
Redmond,Mike	91	281
Hopper,Norris	90	276
Tyner,Jason	90	284
Hatteberg,Scott	90	298
Gomez,Chris	90	288
Mench,Kevin	90	276
Kotsay,Mark	90	255
Ryan,Brendan	90	252
Hall,Toby	90	254
Ozuna,Pablo	89	278
Aybar,Erick	89	256
Chavez,Endy	89	277
Costa,Shane	89	267
Lieberthal,Mike	89	275
Cora,Alex	89	247
Cirillo,Jeff	89	270
Rodriguez,Luis	88	233
Martinez,Ramon	88	233
Hernandez,Luis	88	254
Ojeda,Augie	88	232
Schumaker,Skip	87	273
Taguchi,So	87	278
Abreu,Tony	87	288

LOW Ct%, 400+ AB

NAME	Ct%	BA
Howard,Ryan	66	274
Cust,Jack	66	238
Pena,Wily Mo	67	264
Gomes,Jonny	67	243
Dunn,Adam	68	251
Wilkerson,Brad	68	259
Thome,Jim	69	269
Fields,Josh	71	258
Duncan,Chris	72	255
Hall,Bill	72	259
Pena,Carlos	72	266
Cameron,Mike	72	250
Olivo,Miguel	73	239
Burrell,Pat	73	265
Jenkins,Geoff	73	266
Weeks,Rickie	73	261
Varitek,Jason	73	246
Bay,Jason	74	282
Glaus,Troy	74	256
Inge,Brandon	74	245
Upton,B.J.	74	275
Hawpe,Brad	75	284
Sexson,Richie	75	264
Peralta,Jhonny	75	267
Cruz,Nelson	75	254
Swisher,Nick	75	251
Church,Ryan	76	276
Granderson,Curtis	76	281
Hermida,Jeremy	76	290
Iwamura,Akinori	77	277
Scott,Luke	77	271
LaRoche,Adam	77	279
Hafner,Travis	77	292
Saltalamacchia,Jarr	77	258
Sizemore,Grady	77	273
Soriano,Alfonso	77	278
Jones,Andruw	77	254
Delgado,Carlos	77	264
Willingham,Josh	78	265
Uggla,Dan	78	251
Jacobs,Mike	78	269
Gordon,Alex	78	263
Teahen,Mark	78	278
Kearns,Austin	78	272
McLouth,Nate	78	263
Rodriguez,Alex	78	305
Ankiel,Rick	78	259
Blake,Casey	78	268
Johnson,Kelly	78	269
Teixeira,Mark	79	303
Bautista,Jose	79	247
Abreu,Bobby	79	291
Drew,J.D.	79	280
Hamilton,Josh	79	301
Cuddyer,Michael	79	274
Nady,Xavier	79	274
Chavez,Eric	79	255
Dye,Jermaine	79	281
Young,Chris	79	258
Greene,Khalil	79	260
Lee,Derrek	79	296
Cabrera,Miguel	79	331
Braun,Ryan	79	302
Ramirez,Manny	79	300
Wigginton,Ty	79	272
Fielder,Prince	80	292

TOP Ct%, bb% over 10%

NAME	bb%	Ct%
Castillo,Luis	10	91
Hatteberg,Scott	12	90
Pujols,Albert	14	90
Vidro,Jose	10	90
Guerrero,Vladimir	10	89
Giles,Brian	14	88
Barton,Daric	13	88
Mauer,Joe	12	88
Jackson,Conor	11	88
Gonzalez,Luis	11	87
Butler,Billy	10	87
Helton,Todd	16	87
Matsui,Hideki	12	87
Sheffield,Gary	12	87
Martinez,Victor	10	86
Damon,Johnny	10	86
Scutaro,Marco	10	86
Atkins,Garrett	10	86
Mientkiewicz,Doug	10	86
Kent,Jeff	11	86
Davis,Rajai	10	86
Bonds,Barry	28	86
Carroll,Jamey	10	86
Durham,Ray	10	86
Roberts,Brian	11	85
Schneider,Brian	11	85
Counsell,Craig	11	85
Roberts,Dave	10	85
Suzuki,Kurt	10	85
Bard,Josh	10	85
Martin,Russell	11	85
Salazar,Jeff	10	85
Kinsler,Ian	10	84
Jimenez,D'Angelo	14	84
Hudson,Orlando	10	84
German,Esteban	10	84
Jones,Chipper	14	84
Zaun,Gregg	13	84

TOP Ct%, bb% under 6%

NAME	bb%	Ct%
Polanco,Placido	5	94
Pierre,Juan	5	94
Lo Duca,Paul	5	93
Johjima,Kenji	4	92
Frandsen,Kevin	5	91
Redmond,Mike	5	91
Betancourt,Yuniesk	3	91
Hopper,Norris	5	90
Estrada,Johnny	4	90
Hall,Toby	4	90
Payton,Jay	5	90
Molina,Bengie	4	90
Ozuna,Pablo	3	89
Aybar,Erick	4	89
Sanchez,Freddy	5	89
Cora,Alex	5	89
Gload,Ross	5	88
Hernandez,Luis	4	88
Cano,Robinson	5	88
Lopez,Jose	4	88
Abreu,Tony	5	87
Anderson,Joshua	4	87
Burke,Jamie	5	87
Morales,Kendry	5	87
Bellorin,Edwin	4	87

TOP Ct%, GB% over 50%

NAME	GB%	Ct%
Pierre,Juan	54	94
Frandsen,Kevin	52	91
Castillo,Luis	64	91
Kotchman,Casey	51	91
Hopper,Norris	57	90
Tyner,Jason	59	90
Gomez,Chris	51	90
Miles,Aaron	54	90
Redman,Tike	50	90
Ozuna,Pablo	57	89
Aybar,Erick	55	89
Suzuki,Ichiro	55	89
Chavez,Endy	58	89
Tejada,Miguel	51	89
Ellsbury,Jacoby	52	88
Rodriguez,Luis	51	88
Mauer,Joe	52	88
Gload,Ross	50	88
Hernandez,Luis	51	88
Cano,Robinson	52	88
Cabrera,Melky	51	88
Schumaker,Skip	54	87
Abreu,Tony	50	87
Anderson,Joshua	64	87
Guzman,Cristian	57	87
Grudzielanek,Mark	50	87
Winn,Randy	50	86
Casilla,Alexi	62	86
Murton,Matt	53	86
Owens,Jerry	62	85
Roberts,Dave	50	85
Taveras,Willy	53	85
Quinlan,Robb	50	85
Kendrick,Howie	54	85
Quintanilla,Omar	56	85
Green,Shawn	53	85
Bard,Josh	52	85
Gwynn,Tony	52	85

TOP Ct%, GB% under 40%

NAME	GB%	Ct%
Loretta,Mark	39	91
Estrada,Johnny	39	90
Molina,Bengie	39	90
Sanchez,Freddy	39	89
Lee,Carlos	38	89
Lieberthal,Mike	36	89
Giles,Brian	39	88
Barton,Daric	32	88
Lowell,Mike	35	88
Jackson,Conor	38	88
Ramirez,Aramis	37	88
Burke,Jamie	37	87
Valentin,Javier	36	87
Towles,J.R.	34	87
Helton,Todd	37	87
Barmes,Clint	35	86
McCann,Brian	37	86
Aurilia,Rich	39	86
Atkins,Garrett	36	86
Crede,Joe	34	86
Kent,Jeff	36	86
Rolen,Scott	35	86
Sweeney,Mike	35	86
Bonds,Barry	35	86
Roberts,Brian	38	85

PITCHER SKILLS RANKINGS - Starting Pitchers

Top Command (k/bb)		Top Control (bb/9)		Top Dominance (k/9)		Top Ground Ball Rate		Top Fly Ball Rate	
NAME	**Cmd**	**NAME**	**Ctl**	**NAME**	**Dom**	**NAME**	**GB**	**NAME**	**FB**
Santana,Johan	4.8	Maddux,Greg	1.4	Kazmir,Scott	10.2	Lowe,Derek	65	Young,Chris	55
Shields,James	4.1	Silva,Carlos	1.6	Gallardo,Yovani	9.9	Webb,Brandon	64	Liz,Radhames	52
Vazquez,Javier	3.9	Byrd,Paul	1.8	Bedard,Erik	9.8	Hochevar,Luke	63	Patton,Troy	51
Sabathia,C.C.	3.9	Slowey,Kevin	1.8	Chamberlain,Joba	9.8	Carmona,Fausto	63	Kennedy,Ian	51
Harang,Aaron	3.8	Pavano,Carl	1.9	Liriano,Francisco	9.8	Wang,Chien-Ming	61	Hirsh,Jason	51
Hamels,Cole	3.8	Sonnanstine,A	1.9	Santana,Johan	9.6	Hudson,Tim	60	James,Chuck	51
Haren,Dan	3.7	Schilling,Curt	1.9	Peavy,Jake	9.5	Hernandez,Felix	60	Igawa,Kei	51
Smoltz,John	3.7	Shields,James	1.9	Morrow,Brandon	9.4	Cook,Aaron	59	Petit,Yusmeiro	51
Slowey,Kevin	3.5	Baker,Scott	2.0	Matsuzaka,Daisuke	9.4	Dinardo,Lenny	59	Slowey,Kevin	50
Beckett,Josh	3.5	Towers,Josh	2.0	Gonzalez,Gio	9.2	Mitre,Sergio	58	Vargas,Jason	50
Sonnanstine,A	3.5	Santana,Johan	2.0	Hill,Rich	9.2	Westbrook,Jake	58	Milton,Eric	50
Peavy,Jake	3.5	Sabathia,C.C.	2.0	Hamels,Cole	9.2	Miller,Andrew	57	Perez,Oliver	49
Sheets,Ben	3.5	Lieber,Jon	2.0	Lincecum,Tim	9.2	Gabbard,Kason	56	Bergmann,Jason	49
Martinez,Pedro	3.5	Bush,David	2.0	Vanden Hurk,Rick	9.1	Loe,Kameron	55	Vanden Hurk,Rick	48
Maddux,Greg	3.4	Livingston,Bobby	2.0	Martinez,Pedro	9.0	Wright,Jamey	55	Weaver,Jered	48
Schilling,Curt	3.4	Oswalt,Roy	2.0	Perez,Oliver	8.9	Liriano,Francisco	55	Patterson,John	48
Oswalt,Roy	3.3	Blanton,Joe	2.1	Burnett,A.J.	8.8	Morales,Franklin	55	Lee,Cliff	48
Hernandez,Felix	3.3	Bacsik,Mike	2.1	Myers,Brett	8.8	Carpenter,Chris	55	Hernandez,Orlando	47
Baker,Scott	3.3	Buehrle,Mark	2.1	Beckett,Josh	8.8	Halladay,Roy	54	Morrow,Brandon	47
Bush,David	3.2	Hill,Shawn	2.1	Prior,Mark	8.7	Burnett,A.J.	54	Tejeda,Robinson	47
Hill,Rich	3.2	Haren,Dan	2.1	Liz,Radhames	8.7	Hill,Shawn	53	Chico,Matt	47
Bonderman,Jeremy	3.1	Harang,Aaron	2.1	Howell,J.P.	8.6	Maholm,Paul	53	Humber,Philip	46
Howell,J.P.	3.1	Sampson,Chris	2.1	Harden,Rich	8.6	Hensley,Clay	52	McCarthy,Brandon	46
Gallardo,Yovani	3.1	Kendrick,Kyle	2.2	Buchholz,Clay	8.5	Maddux,Greg	52	Lilly,Ted	46
Greinke,Zack	3.1	Germano,Justin	2.2	Vazquez,Javier	8.5	Loewen,Adam	51	Cain,Matt	46
Matsuzaka,Daisuke	3.1	Vazquez,Javier	2.2	Hernandez,Felix	8.5	Lannan,John	51	Carlyle,Buddy	46
Bedard,Erik	3.1	Weaver,Jeff	2.2	Billingsley,Chad	8.3	McGowan,Dustin	51	Schmidt,Jason	46
Webb,Brandon	3.0	Duke,Zach	2.2	Miller,Adam	8.3	Oswalt,Roy	50	Danks,John	45
Lackey,John	3.0	Smoltz,John	2.2	Davis,Wade	8.3	Ramirez,Horacio	50	Reyes,Anthony	45
Lieber,Jon	2.9	Cook,Aaron	2.2	Young,Chris	8.2	Clement,Matt	49	Hill,Rich	45
Miller,Adam	2.9			Maine,John	8.2	Duke,Zach	49.2	Braden,Dallas	44.8

High GB, Low Dom			High GB, High Dom			Lowest xERA		Top BPV, 180+ IP		Top BPV, -150 IP	
NAME	**GB**	**Dom**	**NAME**	**GB**	**Dom**	**NAME**	**xERA**	**NAME**	**BPV**	**NAME**	**BPV**
Wang,Chien-M	61	4.5	Lowe,Derek	65	5.9	Santana,Johan	2.78	Santana,Johan	141	Howell,J.P.	90
Hudson,Tim	60	5.5	Webb,B	64	7.2	Gallardo,Yovani	3.07	Peavy,Jake	111	Parra,Manny	86
Cook,Aaron	59	3.5	Hochevar,L	63	6.2	Webb,Brandon	3.09	Bedard,Erik	106	Miller,Adam	85
Dinardo,Lenny	59	4.7	Carmona,F	63	6.3	Peavy,Jake	3.16	Shields,James	105	Bailey,Homer	82
Westbrook,J	58	5.1	Hernandez,F	60	8.5	Bailey,Homer	3.25	Smoltz,John	104	Buchholz,Clay	82
Loe,Kameron	55	5.0	Mitre,Sergio	58	5.6	Burnett,A.J.	3.25	Sabathia,C.C.	104	Clemens,Roger	77
Wright,Jamey	55	4.7	Miller,Andrew	57	8.0	Bedard,Erik	3.29	Kazmir,Scott	103	Miller,Andrew	76
Hill,Shawn	53	5.2	Gabbard,K	56	6.1	Hamels,Cole	3.33	Beckett,Josh	103	Harden,Rich	76
Hensley,Clay	52	5.3	Liriano,F	55	9.8	Lincecum,Tim	3.37	Vazquez,Javier	103	Braden,Dallas	74
Maddux,Greg	52	4.7	Morales,F	55	6.4	Kazmir,Scott	3.44	Hernandez,Felix	99	Kennedy,Ian	72
Lannan,John	51	3.7	Carpenter,C	55	6.8	Smoltz,John	3.48	Harang,Aaron	98	Johnson,Josh	72
Ramirez,H	50	4.0	Halladay,Roy	54	5.6	Harden,Rich	3.51	Haren,Dan	97	Slowey,Kevin	72
Duke,Zach	49	4.9	Burnett,A.J.	54	8.8	Escobar,Kelvim	3.54	Webb,Brandon	96	Carpenter,Chris	71
Rogers,Kenny	49	4.7	Maholm,Paul	53	5.7	Sabathia,C.C.	3.55	Matsuzaka,Daisuke	95	Prior,Mark	69
Germano,J	49	5.3	Loewen,Adam	51	7.2	Beckett,Josh	3.56	Hill,Rich	93	Gonzalez,Gio	68
Mulder,Mark	49	5.3	McGowan,D	51	7.9	Martinez,Pedro	3.56	Oswalt,Roy	90	Morrow,Brandon	67
Marquis,J	48	4.9	Oswalt,Roy	50	6.8	Liriano,Francisco	3.56	Lackey,John	88	Davis,Wade	66
Litsch,Jesse	48	5.2	Clement,Matt	49	7.6	Clemens,Roger	3.57	Myers,Brett	86	Reyes,Anthony	63
Morris,Matt	48	4.9	Wells,Kip	49	6.1	Verlander,Justin	3.59	Verlander,Justin	83	Hill,Shawn	63
Pineiro,Joel	48	5.4	Pettitte,Andy	49	6.3	Matsuzaka,Daisuke	3.59	Escobar,Kelvim	82	Loewen,Adam	62
Bazardo,Y	48	4.6	Pelfrey,Mike	48	6.3	McGowan,Dustin	3.60	Snell,Ian	78	Colon,Bartolo	60
Sampson,C	48	3.9	Howell,J.P.	48	8.6	Billingsley,Chad	3.63	Greinke,Zack	78	Vanden Hurk,Rick	59
Silva,Carlos	47	3.8	Bonderman,J	48	7.8	Lackey,John	3.65	McGowan,Dustin	77	Mussina,Mike	59
Kendrick,Kyle	47	4.0	Zambrano,C	48	7.6	Hernandez,Felix	3.66	Billingsley,Chad	76	Clement,Matt	58
Pavano,Carl	47	5.0	Albers,Matt	48	6.1	Vazquez,Javier	3.68	Cain,Matt	73	Johnson,Randy	56
Wells,David	47	4.3	Wainwright,A	48	6.9	Cain,Matt	3.69	Garza,Matt	71	Penn,Hayden	56
Looper,B	46	4.8	Clemens,R	48	6.9	Chamberlain,Joba	3.71	Bush,David	70	Schmidt,Jason	56
Suppan,Jeff	46	5.1	Marshall,S	48	5.6	Zambrano,Carlos	3.72	Halladay,Roy	69	Nolasco,Ricky	54
Perez,Odalis	46	5.0	Cabrera,D	47	7.9	Hill,Rich	3.74	Maine,John	69	Hochevar,Luke	54
Blanton,Joe	45	5.3	Lincecum,Tim	47	9.2	Shields,James	3.78	Carmona,Fausto	68	Hammel,Jason	54
Obermuellr,W	44	5.0	Batista,M	47	5.9	Hughes,Philip	3.79	Wainwright,Adam	67	Pavano,Carl	54

PITCHER SKILLS RANKINGS - Relief Pitchers

Top Command (k/bb)

NAME	Cmd
Rivera,Mariano	5.2
Betancourt,Rafael	5.1
Putz,J.J.	4.6
Street,Huston	4.6
Capps,Matt	4.6
Soriano,Rafael	4.5
Saito,Takashi	4.2
Papelbon,Jonathan	4.1
Duchscherer,Justin	3.9
Nathan,Joe	3.9
Howry,Bob	3.8
Broxton,Jonathan	3.8
Cordero,Francisco	3.8
Meredith,Cla	3.6
Wagner,Billy	3.5
Corpas,Manuel	3.5
Bell,Heath	3.5
Peralta,Joel	3.3
Speier,Justin	3.2
Dotel,Octavio	3.2
Wheeler,Dan	3.2
Soria,Joakim	3.2
Bray,Bill	3.2
Ayala,Luis	3.1
Uehara,Koji	3.1
Reyes,Al	3.1
Lidge,Brad	3.0
Jenks,Bobby	3.0
Perez,Rafael	2.9
Valverde,Jose	2.9
Okajima,Hideki	2.9

Top Control (bb/9)

NAME	Ctl
Rivera,Mariano	1.6
Capps,Matt	1.6
Betancourt,Rafael	1.7
Meredith,Cla	1.8
Soriano,Rafael	2.0
Ayala,Luis	2.0
Corpas,Manuel	2.0
Howry,Bob	2.0
Peralta,Joel	2.1
Duchscherer,Justin	2.1
Putz,J.J.	2.1
Street,Huston	2.2
Walker,Jamie	2.2
Guerrier,Matt	2.2
Janssen,Casey	2.2
Gardner,Lee	2.3
Franklin,Ryan	2.4
Buchholz,Taylor	2.4
Embree,Alan	2.4
Nathan,Joe	2.5
Hawkins,LaTroy	2.5
Perez,Rafael	2.5
Coffey,Todd	2.5
Saito,Takashi	2.5
Uehara,Koji	2.5
Hendrickson,Mark	2.5
Bradford,Chad	2.5
Simontacchi,Jason	2.5
Geary,Geoff	2.5
Heilman,Aaron	2.6
Rauch,Jon	2.6

Top Dominance (k/9)

NAME	Dom
Lidge,Brad	12.0
Rodriguez,Francisco	11.9
Dotel,Octavio	11.4
Cordero,Francisco	11.3
Cruz,Juan	11.2
Papelbon,Jonathan	11.1
Kuo,Hong-Chih	11.0
Valverde,Jose	10.9
Broxton,Jonathan	10.8
Perez,Chris	10.6
Saito,Takashi	10.4
Turnbow,Derrick	10.2
Wuertz,Mike	10.2
Street,Huston	10.1
Wagner,Billy	10.1
Marmol,Carlos	10.0
Marte,Damaso	9.9
Sherrill,George	9.9
Meloan,Jonathan	9.9
Sanchez,Jonathan	9.8
Putz,J.J.	9.8
Bray,Bill	9.8
Tankersley,Taylor	9.8
Hoey,James	9.7
Nathan,Joe	9.6
Rodney,Fernando	9.5
Cabrera,Fernando	9.5
Reyes,Al	9.5
Fuentes,Brian	9.4
Soria,Joakim	9.4
Bell,Heath	9.4

Top Ground Ball Rate

NAME	GB
Meredith,Cla	72
Bradford,Chad	62
Reyes,Dennys	62
Moylan,Peter	62
Green,Sean	60
Smith,Joe	59
Littleton,Wes	59
Qualls,Chad	58
MacDougal,Mike	58
Romero,J.C.	58
Downs,Scott	57
Marshall,Jay	56
Wagner,Ryan	56
Jenks,Bobby	56
Lopez,Javier	55
Shouse,Brian	55
Corpas,Manuel	54
Parrish,John	54
Rivera,Mariano	54
Tavarez,Julian	54
Miner,Zach	54
Coffey,Todd	54
Bell,Heath	54
Alfonseca,Antonio	54
Cali,Carmen	53
Feliciano,Pedro	53
Hawkins,LaTroy	53
Perez,Rafael	53
Devine,Joey	52
Myers,Mike	52
Affeldt,Jeremy	51.6

Top Fly Ball Rate

NAME	FB
Reyes,Al	57
Percival,Troy	55
Proctor,Scott	53
Sherrill,George	53
Marmol,Carlos	53
Neshek,Pat	52
Springer,Russ	52
Soriano,Rafael	52
Rauch,Jon	51
Papelbon,Jonathan	51
Betancourt,Rafael	51
Britton,Chris	51
Tsao,Chin-hui	51
Casilla,Santiago	50
Speier,Justin	50
Guardado,Eddie	50
Ramirez,Ramon	49
Benitez,Armando	48
Hoffman,Trevor	48
Taschner,Jack	48
Gregg,Kevin	48
Meloan,Jonathan	48
Bruney,Brian	48
Cordero,Chad	47
Farnsworth,Kyle	47
Dotel,Octavio	46
Donnelly,Brendan	46
Zumaya,Joel	46
Villanueva,Carlos	46
Owens,Henry	46
Walker,Jamie	45.8

High GB, Low Dom

NAME	GB	Dom
Bradford,Chad	62	5.1
Littleton,Wes	59	5.3
Marshall,Jay	56	4.2
Tavarez,Julian	54	5.0
Miner,Zach	54	5.5
Alfonseca,Anto	54	4.6
Hawkins,LaTroy	53	5.0
Myers,Mike	52	5.0
Thompson,Bra	52	4.5
Wood,Mike	51	4.1
Janssen,Case	51	5.0
Kline,Steve	49	4.5
Jones,Todd	49	4.5
Beimel,Joe	49	5.0
Moehler,Brian	48	4.8
Condrey,Clay	48	4.3
Geary,Geoff	48	5.3
Paronto,Chad	48	4.3
Stokes,Brian	47	5.1
Moseley,Dusti	47	5.0
Franklin,Ryan	46	5.0
Mesa,Jose	46	5.1
Herges,Matt	45	5.4
Hennessey,Br	45	4.7
Eyre,Willie	45	5.4
Duckworth,Bra	45	4.8

High GB, High Dom

NAME	GB	Dom
Meredith,Cla	72	6.6
Reyes,Dennys	62	7.1
Moylan,Peter	62	6.8
Green,Sean	60	5.6
Smith,Joe	59	8.1
Qualls,Chad	58	7.8
MacDougal,Mi	58	8.1
Romero,J.C.	58	6.7
Downs,Scott	57	7.4
Wagner,Ryan	56	6.5
Jenks,Bobby	56	8.2
Lopez,Javier	55	5.8
Shouse,Brian	55	6.0
Corpas,Manue	54	7.0
Parrish,John	54	7.4
Rivera,Marian	54	8.4
Coffey,Todd	54	6.6
Bell,Heath	54	9.4
Cali,Carmen	53	5.6
Feliciano,Pedr	53	8.4
Perez,Rafael	53	7.3
Devine,Joey	52	8.5
Affeldt,Jeremy	52	7.0
Wilson,Brian	51	7.6
Otsuka,Akinor	51	7.2
Torres,Salomo	51	7.0
Schoeneweis,	51	6.2
Logan,Boone	50	7.9
Wilson,C.J.	50	8.4
Gordon,Tom	50	7.0
Crain,Jesse	49	6.4

Lowest xERA

NAME	xERA
Papelbon,Jonathan	2.04
Putz,J.J.	2.40
Nathan,Joe	2.50
Betancourt,Rafael	2.52
Rivera,Mariano	2.66
Saito,Takashi	2.68
Broxton,Jonathan	2.75
Soria,Joakim	2.79
Rodney,Fernando	2.95
Street,Huston	2.97
Corpas,Manuel	2.99
Otsuka,Akinori	3.06
Fuentes,Brian	3.08
Soriano,Rafael	3.08
Rodriguez,Francisco	3.09
Ryan,B.J.	3.10
Jenks,Bobby	3.10
Owens,Henry	3.11
Zumaya,Joel	3.11
Heilman,Aaron	3.14
Dotel,Octavio	3.14
Benoit,Joaquin	3.15
Wagner,Billy	3.15
Bell,Heath	3.16
Feliciano,Pedro	3.17
Capps,Matt	3.19
Valverde,Jose	3.19
Perez,Rafael	3.21
Cordero,Francisco	3.27
Cruz,Juan	3.28
Lidge,Brad	3.28

Top BPV, 10+ Saves

NAME	BPV
Rivera,Mariano	150
Putz,J.J.	146
Papelbon,Jonathan	145
Street,Huston	139
Broxton,Jonathan	137
Saito,Takashi	135
Cordero,Francisco	132
Nathan,Joe	132
Soriano,Rafael	124
Capps,Matt	122
Lidge,Brad	118
Wagner,Billy	117
Rodriguez,Francisco	117
Soria,Joakim	112
Valverde,Jose	110
Corpas,Manuel	103
Jenks,Bobby	99
Ryan,B.J.	97
Wheeler,Dan	96
Gagne,Eric	90
Marmol,Carlos	88
Reyes,Al	86
Otsuka,Akinori	85
Gregg,Kevin	84
Wilson,C.J.	80
Accardo,Jeremy	79
Cordero,Chad	72
Borowski,Joe	70
Hoffman,Trevor	69
Wilson,Brian	67
Isringhausen,Jason	66

Top BPV, 9- Saves

NAME	BPV
Betancourt,Rafael	149
Bell,Heath	120
Dotel,Octavio	117
Duchscherer,Justin	109
Cruz,Juan	107
Howry,Bob	105
Kuo,Hong-Chih	105
Meredith,Cla	102
Rodney,Fernando	101
Bray,Bill	101
Benoit,Joaquin	96
Hoey,James	95
Wuertz,Mike	95
Fuentes,Brian	94
Marte,Damaso	93
Owens,Henry	92
Frasor,Jason	91
Shields,Scot	89
Perez,Rafael	89
Sherrill,George	89
Feliciano,Pedro	88
Sanchez,Jonathan	88
Delcarmen,Manny	87
Heilman,Aaron	87
Turnbow,Derrick	87
Speier,Justin	87
Chulk,Vinnie	86
Miller,Justin	86
Qualls,Chad	86
Okajima,Hideki	86
Meloan,Jonathan	84

+/- SCORES

BREAKOUTS and REBOUNDS

BATTERS	Pos	+
Dukes,Elijah	8	49
Hinske,Eric	37	47
Wood,Brandon	5	45
Blalock,Hank	5	44
Navarro,Dioner	2	44
Weeks,Rickie	4	43
Sexson,Richie	3	43
Kubel,Jason	70	42
Fielder,Prince	3	42
Rodriguez,Luis	54	41
Overbay,Lyle	3	41
LaRue,Jason	2	41
Hairston,Scott	7	39
Martinez,Ramon	4	34
Mench,Kevin	79	34
Woodward,Chris	5	33
LaRoche,Andy	5	33
Crosby,Bobby	6	33
Kotchman,Casey	3	33
Carroll,Jamey	45	32
Butler,Billy	0	32
Hernandez,Luis	6	32
Zimmerman,Ryan	5	31
Beltre,Adrian	5	31
Adams,Russ	5	31
Costa,Shane	7	31
Rivera,Juan	9	30
Montero,Miguel	2	30
Kotsay,Mark	8	29
Catalanotto,Frank	7	29
Mauer,Joe	2	29
Anderson,Joshua	8	28
Jones,Andruw	8	28
Maybin,Cameron	7	27
Lugo,Julio	6	27
Chavez,Eric	5	26
Vazquez,Ramon	5	26
Cirillo,Jeff	50	25
Langerhans,Ryan	78	25
Hairston,Jerry	87	25
Buck,John	2	25
Salazar,Jeff	9	25
White,Rondell	0	25
Zobrist,Ben	6	24
Moore,Scott	5	24
Lopez,Felipe	64	24
Lane,Jason	8	24
Wells,Vernon	8	23
Kinsler,Ian	4	23
Murton,Matt	97	23
Metcalf,Travis	5	23
Pagan,Angel	89	23
Howard,Ryan	3	22
Uggla,Dan	4	22
Branyan,Russell	5	22
Milledge,Lastings	9	22
Crisp,Coco	8	22
Johnson,Dan	3	22
Cabrera,Melky	8	21
DeJesus,David	8	21
Burke,Chris	48	21
Gross,Gabe	9	21
Konerko,Paul	3	21
Thorman,Scott	3	21
Cantu,Jorge	3	21
Pena,Carlos	3	21
Richar,Danny	4	21
Castillo,Jose	54	20
Ortmeier,Dan	37	20
Morneau,Justin	3	20

PITCHERS	+
Nolasco,Ricky	173
Ryan,B.J.	169
Carpenter,Chris	148
Mulder,Mark	116
Bray,Bill	100
Fossum,Casey	94
Miller,Adam	77
Guardado,Eddie	76
Howell,J.P.	75
Wheeler,Dan	74
Kuo,Hong-Chih	71
Hochevar,Luke	70
Nippert,Dustin	69
Ohka,Tomo	69
Johnson,Josh	69
Meredith,Cla	69
Hernandez,Felix	64
Cabrera,Fernando	63
Jimenez,Ubaldo	58
Hensley,Clay	57
Myers,Brett	56
MacDougal,Mike	56
Penn,Hayden	56
Bonderman,Jeremy	54
Sanchez,Jonathan	54
Sonnanstine,Andrew	51
Mota,Guillermo	48
Jennings,Jason	48
Torres,Salomon	47
Coffey,Todd	46
Stokes,Brian	45
Garcia,Freddy	43
Vanden Hurk,Rick	42
Broxton,Jonathan	41
Frasor,Jason	41
Julio,Jorge	41
Gallardo,Yovani	40
Santana,Ervin	40
Ramirez,Horacio	40
Hamels,Cole	40
Marshall,Jay	40
Colon,Bartolo	39
Saunders,Joe	39
Chamberlain,Joba	39
Burnett,A.J.	39
Crain,Jesse	38
Capuano,Chris	37
Yates,Tyler	36
Bush,David	36
Shields,James	36
Mesa,Jose	35
Kazmir,Scott	35
Towers,Josh	35
Ray,Chris	34
Rodney,Fernando	34
Vargas,Jason	32
Belisle,Matt	32
Olsen,Scott	32
Bedard,Erik	31
Hendrickson,Mark	31
Smith,Joe	31
Matsuzaka,Daisuke	30
Seo,Jae	30
Lidge,Brad	29
Coutlangus,Jon	29
Littleton,Wes	29
Santana,Johan	28
Tejeda,Robinson	28
Baez,Danys	28
Thornton,Matt	28

COLLAPSES and CORRECTIONS

BATTERS	Pos	-
Easley,Damion	4	-78
Guzman,Cristian	6	-68
Bloomquist,Willie	4567	-63
Sanders,Reggie	7	-62
Diaz,Matt	7	-60
Wood,Jason	3	-59
Sosa,Sammy	0	-59
Suzuki,Ichiro	8	-57
Alou,Moises	7	-56
Upton,B.J.	84	-52
Floyd,Cliff	9	-52
Boone,Aaron	3	-51
Renteria,Edgar	6	-49
Norton,Greg	0	-48
Lowell,Mike	5	-48
Phelps,Josh	3	-47
Cabrera,Orlando	6	-46
Vidro,Jose	0	-45
Figgins,Chone	5	-43
Lofton,Kenny	87	-43
Burke,Jamie	2	-42
Aybar,Erick	46	-42
House,J.R.	2	-42
Phillips,Andy	3	-42
Redmond,Mike	2	-41
Linden,Todd	7	-40
Posada,Jorge	2	-38
Castro,Ramon	2	-38
Taveras,Willy	8	-38
Hopper,Norris	87	-38
Kouzmanoff,Kevin	5	-38
Spiezio,Scott	5	-37
Lieberthal,Mike	2	-37
Garciaparra,Nomar	35	-37
Smith,Jason	6	-36
Willits,Reggie	798	-36
Sanchez,Freddy	4	-36
Thome,Jim	0	-35
Kendrick,Howie	4	-35
Ankiel,Rick	98	-35
DeRosa,Mark	459	-34
Mirabelli,Doug	2	-34
Thomas,Frank	0	-34
Infante,Omar	4	-34
Morales,Kendry	3	-34
Lee,Derrek	3	-33
Taguchi,So	87	-33
DaVanon,Jeff	8	-33
Hermida,Jeremy	9	-32
Scutaro,Marco	65	-32
Nixon,Trot	9	-32
Helton,Todd	3	-32
Fukudome,Kosuke	9	-31
Giambi,Jason	0	-31
Miles,Aaron	46	-30
Winn,Randy	987	-30
Kent,Jeff	4	-30
Young,Delmon	98	-30
Brown,Emil	79	-29
Broussard,Ben	39	-29
Hatteberg,Scott	3	-29
Jones,Chipper	5	-29
Ozuna,Pablo	5	-29
Giles,Brian	9	-29
Graffanino,Tony	45	-28
Young,Dmitri	3	-28
Clayton,Royce	6	-28
Francoeur,Jeff	9	-28
Piazza,Mike	0	-27
Johjima,Kenji	2	-27

PITCHERS	-
Owens,Henry	-118
Romero,J.C.	-111
Gonzalez,Mike	-98
Saito,Takashi	-78
Riske,David	-77
Timlin,Mike	-70
Rasner,Darrell	-70
Moylan,Peter	-69
Trachsel,Steve	-68
Brocail,Doug	-65
Putz,J.J.	-64
Herges,Matt	-64
Betancourt,Rafael	-63
Springer,Russ	-58
Weathers,David	-57
Fultz,Aaron	-54
Glavine,Tom	-53
Isringhausen,Jason	-52
Percival,Troy	-51
Hoffman,Trevor	-50
Colome,Jesus	-48
Paronto,Chad	-48
Shouse,Brian	-47
Sosa,Jorge	-47
Janssen,Casey	-47
Donnelly,Brendan	-46
Duckworth,Brandon	-46
Kline,Steve	-45
Wakefield,Tim	-45
Lyon,Brandon	-45
Wood,Kerry	-45
Proctor,Scott	-45
Lowry,Noah	-44
Rogers,Kenny	-44
King,Ray	-43
Jones,Todd	-42
Snyder,Kyle	-42
Washburn,Jarrod	-41
Guerrier,Matt	-41
Otsuka,Akinori	-40
Seay,Bobby	-40
Slaten,Doug	-40
Lannan,John	-40
Alfonseca,Antonio	-39
Beimel,Joe	-39
Bannister,Brian	-39
Hernandez,Orlando	-38
Nathan,Joe	-38
Wilson,Brian	-37
Gardner,Lee	-37
Loaiza,Esteban	-37
Harden,Rich	-36
Walker,Jamie	-36
Bruney,Brian	-35
Batista,Miguel	-35
Hernandez,Livan	-34
Affeldt,Jeremy	-34
Accardo,Jeremy	-34
Williams,Woody	-33
Patton,Troy	-33
Mahay,Ron	-33
Cali,Carmen	-32
Moyer,Jamie	-32
Hampson,Justin	-32
Marte,Damaso	-31
Tallet,Brian	-31
Burton,Jared	-31
Uehara,Koji	-30
Loewen,Adam	-30
Kennedy,Joe	-30

RISK MANAGEMENT

Most DL Days, 2005-2007

NAME	DL
Pavano,Carl	453
Tsao,Chin-hui	452
Escobar,Alex	446
Estes,Shawn	427
Miller,Wade	402
Wood,Kerry	394
Baldelli,Rocco	385
Dotel,Octavio	366
Padilla,Juan	366
Lawrence,Brian	365
Gagne,Eric	352
Prior,Mark	343
Thomson,John	342
McPherson,Dallas	341
Koskie,Corey	338
Backe,Brandon	336
Harden,Rich	335
Ankiel,Rick	332
Martinez,Carlos	330
Brazoban,Yhency	329
Wolf,Randy	320
Van Benschoten,Jol	320
Percival,Troy	320
Walker,Tyler	312
Patterson,John	309
Guzman,Christian	304
Sturtze,Tanyon	301
Clement,Matt	292
Nix,Laynce	286
Wright,Jaret	285
Werth,Jayson	280
Snelling,Chris	274
Ayala,Luis	262
Francisco,Frank	258
Mulder,Mark	257
Miller,Matt	255
Sanchez,Duaner	248
Hudson,Luke	248
Sanders,Reggie	244
Bradley,Milton	239
Wagner,Ryan	234
Acevedo,Jose	232
Colon,Roman	232
Benson,Kris	231
Gonzalez,Mike	230
Liriano,Francisco	217
Martinez,Pedro	216
Sheets,Ben	215
Reitsma,Chris	213
Johnson,Nick	212
Mathieson,Scott	212
Parrish,John	209
Zambrano,Victor	208
Mientkiewicz,Doug	208
Bowie,Micah	207
Politte,Cliff	207
Rhodes,Arthur	204
Crosby,Bobby	204
White,Rondell	199
Valentin,Jose	199
Carpenter,Chris	197
Colon,Bartolo	197
Rupe,Josh	194
Lowe,Mark	191
Hill,Shawn	189
Sweeney,Mike	187

Highest Reliability Scores

1B/DH	POS	Rel
Ortiz,David	0	96
Konerko,Paul	3	85
Teixeira,Mark	3	83
Huff,Aubrey	03	77
Millar,Kevin	30	77
Pujols,Albert	3	74
Youkilis,Kevin	3	73
Gonzalez,Adrian	3	66
Casey,Sean	3	63
Jacobs,Mike	3	60
Vidro,Jose	0	59
Broussard,Ben	39	56
Jackson,Conor	3	55
Wilkerson,Brad	37	52
Cantu,Jorge	3	50
Johnson,Dan	3	47
Garko,Ryan	3	47
Delgado,Carlos	3	45
Howard,Ryan	3	44
Conine,Jeff	3	39
Morneau,Justin	3	39
Berkman,Lance	39	38
Sexson,Richie	3	37
Fielder,Prince	3	34
Hinske,Eric	37	30
LaRoche,Adam	3	30
Cairo,Miguel	35	28
Boone,Aaron	3	26
Overbay,Lyle	3	26
Helton,Todd	3	26
Giambi,Jason	0	23
Lee,Derrek	3	23

Highest Reliability Scores

2B	POS	Rel
Iguchi,Tadahito	4	99
Castillo,Luis	4	90
Grudzielanek,Mark	4	84
Utley,Chase	4	83
Hudson,Orlando	4	81
Belliard,Ronnie	4	81
Hill,Aaron	4	79
Kent,Jeff	4	71
DeRosa,Mark	459	68
Uggla,Dan	4	68
Biggio,Craig	4	60
Lopez,Jose	4	58
Pedroia,Dustin	4	51
Roberts,Brian	4	50
Cano,Robinson	4	49
Giles,Marcus	4	49
Miles,Aaron	46	45
Blum,Geoff	4	43
Ellis,Mark	4	43
Kinsler,Ian	4	41
Graffanino,Tony	45	39
Kennedy,Adam	4	37
Cora,Alex	46	36
Bloomquist,Willie	4567	36
Weeks,Rickie	4	34
Burke,Chris	48	32
Polanco,Placido	4	32
Quintanilla,Omar	4	30
Sanchez,Freddy	4	29
Matsui,Kaz	4	23
Phillips,Brandon	4	23

Highest Reliability Scores

3B	POS	Rel
Feliz,Pedro	5	99
Wright,David	5	94
Iwamura,Akinori	5	90
Ramirez,Aramis	5	89
Beltre,Adrian	5	88
Inge,Brandon	5	87
Cabrera,Miguel	5	83
Glaus,Troy	5	75
Chavez,Eric	5	73
Mora,Melvin	5	70
Figgins,Chone	5	67
Zimmerman,Ryan	5	64
Tracy,Chad	5	57
Wigginton,Ty	54	57
Betemit,Wilson	5	56
Adams,Russ	5	54
Bautista,Jose	59	53
Jones,Chipper	5	52
Rodriguez,Alex	5	52
Counsell,Craig	564	45
Encarnacion,Edwin	5	45
Nunez,Abraham	5	44
Lamb,Mike	53	43
Cintron,Alex	5	40
Castillo,Jose	54	39
Ensberg,Morgan	5	37
Punto,Nick	564	32
Atkins,Garrett	5	32
Dobbs,Greg	5	31
Lowell,Mike	5	27
Blake,Casey	5	22
Rodriguez,Luis	54	21

Highest Reliability Scores

SS	POS	Rel
Cabrera,Orlando	6	92
Rollins,Jimmy	6	88
Young,Michael	6	86
Uribe,Juan	6	83
Betancourt,Yuniesky	6	81
Tejada,Miguel	6	80
Greene,Khalil	6	75
Lugo,Julio	6	73
Furcal,Rafael	6	73
Jeter,Derek	6	73
Wilson,Jack	6	72
Renteria,Edgar	6	66
Loretta,Mark	6435	64
Bartlett,Jason	6	63
Gonzalez,Alex	6	58
Eckstein,David	6	56
Everett,Adam	6	56
Clayton,Royce	6	53
Scutaro,Marco	65	48
Pena,Tony	6	45
Peralta,Jhonny	6	39
Guillen,Carlos	63	38
Barmes,Clint	6	34
Izturis,Cesar	6	33
Lopez,Felipe	64	32
McDonald,John	6	32
Keppinger,Jeff	6	27
Ramirez,Hanley	6	26
Reyes,Jose	6	26
Santiago,Ramon	6	26
Hardy,J.J.	6	25

Highest Reliability Scores

CA	POS	Rel
Martinez,Victor	23	99
Johjima,Kenji	2	77
Pierzynski,A.J.	2	71
Rodriguez,Ivan	2	69
Kendall,Jason	2	68
Molina,Bengie	2	67
Buck,John	2	64
Lo Duca,Paul	2	59
Schneider,Brian	2	58
Estrada,Johnny	2	49
Paulino,Ronny	2	48
Martin,Russell	2	45
Olivo,Miguel	2	44
Hernandez,Ramon	2	41
Ausmus,Brad	2	35
Molina,Jose	2	35

Highest Reliability Scores

OF	POS	Rel
Crawford,Carl	7	99
Burrell,Pat	7	99
Pierre,Juan	8	98
Suzuki,Ichiro	8	94
Guerrero,Vladimir	90	92
Lee,Carlos	7	86
Damon,Johnny	807	83
Ibanez,Raul	7	80
Hunter,Torii	8	79
Gonzalez,Luis	7	78
Nady,Xavier	9	74
DeJesus,David	8	73
Taveras,Willy	8	73
Jenkins,Geoff	7	73
Sizemore,Grady	8	72
Abreu,Bobby	9	72
Green,Shawn	9	71
Kearns,Austin	9	71
Soriano,Alfonso	7	71
Payton,Jay	7	69
Willingham,Josh	7	68
Jones,Jacque	89	68
Holliday,Matt	7	67
Byrnes,Eric	798	67
Mench,Kevin	79	66
Anderson,Garret	70	64
Fukudome,Kosuke	9	62
Crisp,Coco	8	61
Swisher,Nick	893	58
Francoeur,Jeff	9	57
Murton,Matt	97	57
Catalanotto,Frank	7	54
Podsednik,Scott	7	53
Victorino,Shane	9	53
Mackowiak,Rob	79	51
Roberts,Dave	87	51
Cameron,Mike	8	51
Lofton,Kenny	87	50
Stewart,Shannon	7	50
Taguchi,So	87	49
Matthews Jr.,Gary	8	46
Amezaga,Alfredo	8	46
Clark,Brady	7	46
Drew,J.D.	9	46
Nixon,Trot	9	45
Hart,Corey	98	45
Brown,Emil	79	44

RISK MANAGEMENT

Highest Reliability

SP	Rel
Suppan,Jeff	99
Harang,Aaron	97
Oswalt,Roy	97
Lackey,John	96
Lowe,Derek	95
Santana,Johan	92
Robertson,Nate	91
Vazquez,Javier	90
Penny,Brad	90
Washburn,Jarrod	89
Davis,Doug	89
Hernandez,Livan	89
Haren,Dan	88
Byrd,Paul	85
Morris,Matt	85
Hudson,Tim	84
Webb,Brandon	82
Garland,Jon	82
Fogg,Josh	81
Maddux,Greg	80
Arroyo,Bronson	80
Moyer,Jamie	80
Young,Chris	80
Francis,Jeff	79
Contreras,Jose	77
Capuano,Chris	77
Sabathia,C.C.	77
Smoltz,John	77
Marquis,Jason	76
Zito,Barry	75
Millwood,Kevin	75
Batista,Miguel	75
Snell,Ian	74
Pettitte,Andy	73
Peavy,Jake	73
Westbrook,Jake	72
Lilly,Ted	72
Lohse,Kyle	71
Zambrano,Carlos	71
Buehrle,Mark	70
Meche,Gil	69
Silva,Carlos	69
Halladay,Roy	66
Blanton,Joe	66
Kuroda,Hiroki	66
Willis,Dontrelle	64
Weaver,Jeff	63

Highest Reliability

RP	Rel
Rodriguez,Francisco	70
Cordero,Francisco	68
Nathan,Joe	63
Cordero,Chad	62
Dempster,Ryan	59
Valverde,Jose	59
Hendrickson,Mark	58
Tomko,Brett	57
Lidge,Brad	56
Ortiz,Ramon	56
Jenks,Bobby	55
Wagner,Billy	54
Hoffman,Trevor	53
Gregg,Kevin	53
Putz,J.J.	51
Fossum,Casey	50

POWER

PX over 120	PX	Rel
Burrell,Pat	158	99
Ortiz,David	186	96
Wright,David	152	94
Guerrero,Vladimir	128	92
Ramirez,Aramis	141	89
Beltre,Adrian	133	88
Lee,Carlos	128	86
Konerko,Paul	142	85
Cabrera,Miguel	166	83
Utley,Chase	152	83
Teixeira,Mark	169	83
Hunter,Torii	123	79
Greene,Khalil	126	75
Glaus,Troy	145	75
Pujols,Albert	155	74
Nady,Xavier	130	74
Chavez,Eric	133	73
Jenkins,Geoff	139	73
Sizemore,Grady	141	72
Soriano,Alfonso	164	71
Willingham,Josh	132	68
Uggla,Dan	139	68
Holliday,Matt	163	67
Gonzalez,Adrian	136	66
Zimmerman,Ryan	128	64
Buck,John	140	64
Fukudome,Kosuke	121	62
Jacobs,Mike	134	60
Swisher,Nick	144	58
Tracy,Chad	126	57
Wigginton,Ty	132	57
Betemit,Wilson	172	56

COMMAND

CMD over 2.5	CMD	Rel
Harang,Aaron	3.8	97
Oswalt,Roy	3.3	97
Lackey,John	3.0	96
Santana,Johan	4.8	92
Vazquez,Javier	3.9	90
Haren,Dan	3.7	88
Webb,Brandon	3.0	82
Maddux,Greg	3.4	80
Arroyo,Bronson	2.7	80
Francis,Jeff	2.6	79
Sabathia,C.C.	3.9	77
Smoltz,John	3.7	77
Snell,Ian	2.9	74
Peavy,Jake	3.5	73
Rodriguez,Francisco	2.8	70
Cordero,Francisco	3.8	68
Halladay,Roy	2.8	66
Blanton,Joe	2.6	66
Nathan,Joe	3.9	63
Bush,David	3.2	63
Cordero,Chad	2.6	62
Beckett,Josh	3.5	61
Bonderman,Jeremy	3.1	59
Valverde,Jose	2.9	59
Matsuzaka,Daisuke	3.1	58
Lidge,Brad	3.0	56
Jenks,Bobby	3.0	55
Hill,Rich	3.2	54
Wagner,Billy	3.5	54
Hoffman,Trevor	2.6	53
Putz,J.J.	4.6	51

SPEED

SX over 120	SX	Rel
Crawford,Carl	173	99
Pierre,Juan	156	98
Suzuki,Ichiro	136	94
Iwamura,Akinori	121	90
Rollins,Jimmy	167	88
Damon,Johnny	122	83
Furcal,Rafael	138	73
Taveras,Willy	142	73
Sizemore,Grady	128	72
Soriano,Alfonso	122	71
Byrnes,Eric	142	67
Figgins,Chone	158	67
Bartlett,Jason	138	63
Fukudome,Kosuke	121	62
Crisp,Coco	132	61
Podsednik,Scott	126	53
Victorino,Shane	159	53
Roberts,Dave	164	51
Cameron,Mike	125	51
Roberts,Brian	131	50
Lofton,Kenny	142	50
Hart,Corey	127	45
Owens,Jerry	125	40
Logan,Nook	140	34
Weeks,Rickie	153	34
Anderson,Joshua	124	33
Lopez,Felipe	120	32
Cairo,Miguel	131	28
Freel,Ryan	127	28
Granderson,Curtis	148	27
Ramirez,Hanley	147	26
Rios,Alex	124	26

DOMINANCE

DOM over 7.0	DOM	Rel
Harang,Aaron	8.0	97
Lackey,John	7.5	96
Santana,Johan	9.6	92
Vazquez,Javier	8.5	90
Haren,Dan	7.9	88
Webb,Brandon	7.2	82
Young,Chris	8.2	80
Francis,Jeff	7.0	79
Capuano,Chris	7.5	77
Sabathia,C.C.	7.7	77
Smoltz,John	8.1	77
Snell,Ian	8.0	74
Peavy,Jake	9.5	73
Lilly,Ted	7.5	72
Zambrano,Carlos	7.6	71
Rodriguez,Francisco	11.9	70
Cordero,Francisco	11.3	68
Nathan,Joe	9.6	63
Cordero,Chad	7.9	62
Cabrera,Daniel	7.9	61
Beckett,Josh	8.8	61
Bonderman,Jeremy	7.8	59
Dempster,Ryan	7.6	59
Valverde,Jose	10.9	59
Matsuzaka,Daisuke	9.4	58
Lidge,Brad	12.0	56
Jenks,Bobby	8.2	55
Hill,Rich	9.2	54
Cain,Matt	8.0	54
Wagner,Billy	10.1	54
Gregg,Kevin	8.7	53

CONTACT

Ct% over 85%	Ct%	Rel
Martinez,Victor	86	99
Pierre,Juan	94	98
Suzuki,Ichiro	89	94
Guerrero,Vladimir	89	92
Cabrera,Orlando	90	92
Castillo,Luis	91	90
Ramirez,Aramis	88	89
Rollins,Jimmy	88	88
Young,Michael	85	86
Lee,Carlos	89	86
Grudzielanek,Mark	87	84
Damon,Johnny	86	83
Betancourt,Yuniesky	91	81
Belliard,Ronnie	86	81
Tejada,Miguel	89	80
Hill,Aaron	86	79
Gonzalez,Luis	87	78
Johjima,Kenji	92	77
Huff,Aubrey	85	77
Pujols,Albert	90	74
Lugo,Julio	85	73
Furcal,Rafael	87	73
DeJesus,David	86	73
Taveras,Willy	85	73
Wilson,Jack	89	72
Green,Shawn	85	71
Kent,Jeff	86	71
Pierzynski,A.J.	86	71
Payton,Jay	90	69
Kendall,Jason	92	68
Molina,Bengie	90	67
Renteria,Edgar	85	66

OVERALL PITCHING SKILL

BPV over 75	BPV	Rel
Harang,Aaron	98	97
Oswalt,Roy	90	97
Lackey,John	88	96
Santana,Johan	141	92
Vazquez,Javier	103	90
Haren,Dan	97	88
Webb,Brandon	96	82
Sabathia,C.C.	104	77
Smoltz,John	104	77
Snell,Ian	78	74
Peavy,Jake	111	73
Rodriguez,Francisco	117	70
Cordero,Francisco	132	68
Nathan,Joe	132	63
Beckett,Josh	103	61
Bonderman,Jeremy	87	59
Valverde,Jose	110	59
Matsuzaka,Daisuke	95	58
Lidge,Brad	118	56
Jenks,Bobby	99	55
Hill,Rich	93	54
Wagner,Billy	117	54
Gregg,Kevin	84	53
Putz,J.J.	146	51
Bedard,Erik	106	50
Burnett,A.J.	95	49
Rivera,Mariano	150	49
Myers,Brett	86	49
Fuentes,Brian	94	48
Escobar,Kelvim	82	47
Papelbon,Jonathan	145	46

POSITION SCARCITY CHART

30	$30+ players	29	$20-29 players	15	$15-19 players	10	$10-14 players

FIRST BASE

- Pujols, Albert
- Teixeira, Mark
- Howard, Ryan
- Fielder, Prince
- Berkman, Lance
- Lee, Derrek
- Gonzalez, Adrian
- Morneau, Justin
- Pena, Carlos
- Helton, Todd
- Konerko, Paul
- LaRoche, Adam
- Delgado, Carlos
- Garko, Ryan
- Votto, Joey
- Jackson, Conor
- Loney, James
- Youkilis, Kevin
- Jacobs, Mike
- Sexson, Richie
- Kotchman, Casey
- Young, Dmitri
- Wilkerson, Brad
- Overbay, Lyle
- Barton, Daric
- Stairs, Matt
- Johnson, Nick
- Johnson, Dan
- Millar, Kevin
- Gload, Ross
- Casey, Sean
- Mientkiewicz, Doug
- Garciaparra, Nomar
- Aurilia, Rich
- Broussard, Ben
- Clark, Tony
- Hinske, Eric
- Phelps, Josh
- Hatteberg, Scott
- Cantu, Jorge
- Baker, Jeff
- Shealy, Ryan
- Klesko, Ryan
- Ortmeier, Dan
- Thorman, Scott

SECOND BASE

- Utley, Chase
- Phillips, Brandon
- Roberts, Brian
- Cano, Robinson
- Hill, Aaron
- Weeks, Rickie
- Kinsler, Ian
- Matsui, Kaz
- Sanchez, Freddy
- Castillo, Luis
- Pedroia, Dustin
- Uggla, Dan
- Hudson, Orlando
- Johnson, Kelly
- Polanco, Placido
- Cabrera, Asdrubal
- Kendrick, Howie
- Ellis, Mark
- Kent, Jeff
- Lopez, Jose
- Belliard, Ronnie
- DeRosa, Mark
- Richar, Danny
- Iguchi, Tadahito
- Casilla, Alexi
- Durham, Ray
- German, Esteban
- Grudzielanek, Mark
- Burke, Chris
- Antonelli, Matt
- Barfield, Josh
- Frandsen, Kevin
- Kennedy, Adam
- Giles, Marcus
- Aybar, Erick
- Valentin, Jose
- Miles, Aaron
- Fontenot, Mike
- Carroll, Jamey
- Bloomquist, Willie
- Infante, Omar
- Easley, Damion
- Gotay, Ruben
- Quintanilla, Omar
- Cora, Alex

THIRD BASE

- Rodriguez, Alex
- Wright, David
- Cabrera, Miguel
- Braun, Ryan
- Figgins, Chone
- Ramirez, Aramis
- Atkins, Garrett
- Zimmerman, Ryan
- Jones, Chipper
- Beltre, Adrian
- Encarnacion, Edwin
- Lowell, Mike
- Blalock, Hank
- Wigginton, Ty
- Gordon, Alex
- Kouzmanoff, Kevin
- Fields, Josh
- Rolen, Scott
- Glaus, Troy
- Tracy, Chad
- Izturis, Maicer
- LaRoche, Andy
- Longoria, Evan
- Blake, Casey
- Iwamura, Akinori
- Mora, Melvin
- Chavez, Eric
- Crede, Joe
- Bautista, Jose
- Feliz, Pedro
- Inge, Brandon
- Reynolds, Mark
- Ensberg, Morgan
- Betemit, Wilson
- Wood, Brandon
- Moore, Scott
- Marte, Andy
- Lamb, Mike
- Dobbs, Greg
- Spiezio, Scott
- Helms, Wes
- Cintron, Alex
- Punto, Nick
- Abreu, Tony
- Buscher, Brian

SHORTSTOP

- Ramirez, Hanley
- Rollins, Jimmy
- Reyes, Jose
- Guillen, Carlos
- Tulowitzki, Troy
- Furcal, Rafael
- Jeter, Derek
- Young, Michael
- Tejada, Miguel
- Renteria, Edgar
- Cabrera, Orlando
- Theriot, Ryan
- Lugo, Julio
- Lopez, Felipe
- Greene, Khalil
- Bartlett, Jason
- Hardy, J.J.
- Betancourt, Yun
- Peralta, Jhonny
- Drew, Stephen
- Eckstein, David
- Wilson, Jack
- Uribe, Juan
- Keppinger, Jeff
- Harris, Brendan
- Escobar, Yunel
- Pena, Tony
- Loretta, Mark
- Vizquel, Omar
- Gonzalez, Alex
- Crosby, Bobby
- Everett, Adam
- Murphy, Donnie
- Scutaro, Marco
- Ryan, Brendan
- Guzman, Cristian
- Zobrist, Ben
- Cedeno, Ronny
- Jimenez, D'Angelo
- McDonald, John
- Wilson, Josh
- Barmes, Clint
- Izturis, Cesar
- Santiago, Ramon
- Hernandez, Luis

CATCHERS

- Martin, Russell
- Martinez, Victor
- McCann, Brian
- Mauer, Joe
- Posada, Jorge
- Towles, J.R.
- Johjima, Kenji
- Molina, Bengie
- Napoli, Mike
- Hernandez, Ram
- Lo Duca, Paul
- Saltalamacchia, J
- Ruiz, Carlos
- Barrett, Michael
- Soto, Geovany
- Snyder, Chris
- Varitek, Jason
- Pierzynski, A.J.
- Estrada, Johnny
- Bard, Josh
- Rodriguez, Ivan
- Buck, John
- Paulino, Ronny
- Olivo, Miguel
- Torrealba, Yorvit
- Zaun, Gregg
- Navarro, Dioner
- Barajas, Rod
- Ross, Dave
- Montero, Miguel
- Molina, Yadier
- Kendall, Jason
- Schneider, Brian
- Castro, Ramon
- Suzuki, Kurt
- Laird, Gerald
- Valentin, Javier
- Iannetta, Chris
- Shoppach, Kelly
- Thigpen, Curtis
- Lieberthal, Mike
- Redmond, Mike
- House, J.R.
- Mathis, Jeff
- Coste, Chris

OUTFIELDERS

- Holliday, Matt
- Crawford, Carl
- Lee, Carlos
- Soriano, Alfonso
- Pierre, Juan
- Beltran, Carlos
- Guerrero, Vladimir
- Sizemore, Grady
- Suzuki, Ichiro
- Markakis, Nick
- Abreu, Bobby
- Rios, Alex
- Hart, Corey
- Byrnes, Eric
- Victorino, Shane
- Dunn, Adam
- Wells, Vernon
- Dye, Jermaine
- Granderson, Curtis
- Pence, Hunter
- Hunter, Torii
- Bay, Jason
- Ordonez, Magglio
- Young, Chris
- Hawpe, Brad
- Taveras, Willy
- Ramirez, Manny
- Matsui, Hideki
- Upton, B.J.
- Francoeur, Jeff
- Young, Delmon
- Rowand, Aaron
- Damon, Johnny
- Kemp, Matt
- Hamilton, Josh
- Ellsbury, Jacoby
- Hermida, Jeremy
- Burrell, Pat
- Jones, Andruw
- Kearns, Austin
- Guillen, Jose
- Willingham, Josh
- Kubel, Jason
- Pie, Felix
- Patterson, Corey

STARTERS

- Santana, Johan
- Peavy, Jake
- Webb, Brandon
- Bedard, Erik
- Haren, Dan
- Verlander, Justin
- Beckett, Josh
- Kazmir, Scott
- Sabathia, C.C.
- Hernandez, Felix
- Matsuzaka, D
- Vazquez, Javier
- Lackey, John
- Harang, Aaron
- Shields, James
- Gallardo, Yovani
- Hill, Rich
- Oswalt, Roy
- Smoltz, John
- Escobar, Kelvim
- Hamels, Cole
- Burnett, A.J
- Snell, Ian
- Halladay, Roy
- Liriano, Francisco
- McGowan, Dustin
- Martinez, Pedro
- Myers, Brett
- Carmona, Fausto
- Billingsley, Chad
- Lincecum, Tim
- Wainwright, Adam
- Maine, John
- Hudson, Tim
- Francis, Jeff
- Blanton, Joe
- Zambrano, Carlos
- Wang, Chien-Ming
- Bonderman, Jeremy
- Greinke, Zack
- Cain, Matt
- Sheets, Ben
- Lowe, Derek
- Hughes, Philip
- Chamberlain, Joba

RELIEVERS

- Putz, J.J.
- Papelbon, Jonathan
- Nathan, Joe
- Cordero, Francisco
- Rodriguez, Francisco
- Rivera, Mariano
- Jenks, Bobby
- Lidge, Brad
- Valverde, Jose
- Street, Huston
- Wagner, Billy
- Capps, Matt
- Corpas, Manuel
- Saito, Takashi
- Soriano, Rafael
- Cordero, Chad
- Gregg, Kevin
- Soria, Joakim
- Borowski, Joe
- Isringhausen, Jason
- Hoffman, Trevor
- Broxton, Jonathan
- Gagne, Eric
- Betancourt, Rafael
- Wheeler, Dan
- Benoit, Joaquin
- Marmol, Carlos
- Walker, Jamie
- Fuentes, Brian
- Accardo, Jeremy
- Wilson, Brian
- Meredith, Cla
- Ayala, Luis
- Dempster, Ryan
- Rodney, Fernando
- Qualls, Chad
- Reyes, Al
- Weathers, David
- Otsuka, Akinori
- Jones, Todd
- Shields, Scot
- Ryan, B.J.
- Heilman, Aaron
- Bradford, Chad
- Bell, Heath

PORTFOLIO3 PLAN

TIER 1

High Skill, Low Risk

BATTERS	Age	Bats	Pos	Filters: 70 REL	80 Ct%	100 PX	100 SX	R$
*Wright,David	25	R	5	94	81	152	109	$37
*Pujols,Albert	28	R	3	74	90	155	57	$35
*Rollins,Jimmy	29	S	6	88	88	118	167	$33
*Crawford,Carl	26	L	7	99	84	105	173	$32
Utley,Chase	29	L	4	83	82	152	117	$31
*Lee,Carlos	31	R	7	86	89	128	80	$31
Ortiz,David	32	L	0	96	80	186	56	$30
*Pierre,Juan	30	L	8	98	94	42	156	$28
*Guerrero,Vladimir	32	R	90	92	89	128	48	$26
*Ramirez,Aramis	29	R	5	89	88	141	51	$26
*Suzuki,Ichiro	34	L	8	94	89	46	136	$26
*Furcal,Rafael	30	S	6	73	87	79	138	$24
*Hunter,Torii	32	R	8	79	82	123	91	$24
Beltre,Adrian	29	R	5	88	82	133	90	$23
Taveras,Willy	26	R	8	73	85	43	142	$22
*Konerko,Paul	32	R	3	85	82	142	25	$21
Martinez,Victor	29	S	23	99	86	111	27	$21
*Damon,Johnny	34	L	807	83	86	87	122	$20
Hill,Aaron	26	R	4	79	86	110	73	$20
*Cabrera,Orlando	33	R	6	92	90	70	104	$18
*Castillo,Luis	32	S	4	90	91	41	116	$18
*Lugo,Julio	32	R	6	73	85	82	117	$18
*DeJesus,David	28	L	8	73	86	81	113	$17
Hudson,Orlando	30	S	4	81	84	90	116	$17
Youkilis,Kevin	29	R	3	73	80	119	67	$17
*Ibanez,Raul	35	L	7	80	83	109	55	$17
Huff,Aubrey	31	L	03	77	85	104	57	$16
*Kent,Jeff	40	R	4	71	86	113	55	$15
Iguchi,Tadahito	33	R	4	99	81	91	112	$14
Uribe,Juan	29	R	6	83	80	111	46	$11
Millar,Kevin	36	R	30	77	81	106	44	$11

PITCHERS	Age	Thrw	Filters: 70 REL	75 BPV	R$
*Santana,Johan	29	L	92	141	$35
Peavy,Jake	26	R	73	111	$30
*Webb,Brandon	29	R	82	96	$29
*Haren,Dan	27	R	88	97	$28
Sabathia,C.C.	27	L	77	104	$27
*Vazquez,Javier	31	R	90	103	$25
*Lackey,John	29	R	96	88	$25
Rodriguez,Francisco	26	R	70	117	$24
*Harang,Aaron	30	R	97	98	$24
*Oswalt,Roy	30	R	97	90	$23
*Smoltz,John	41	R	77	104	$22
Snell,Ian	26	R	74	78	$21
Maddux,Greg	42	R	80	75	$15

* Asterisked players also appeared on the 2007 list,
  which may indicate even greater stability.

**The following players were on the 2007 list but did
not make it onto the 2008 list:**

Biggio,Craig	Jeter, Derek
Cabrera,Miguel	Kennedy,Adam
Carpenter,Chris	Monroe,Craig
Chavez,Eric	Nathan,Joe
Cordero,Francisco	Overbay,Lyle
Crede,Joe	Podsednik,Scott
Everett,Adam	Teixeira,Mark
Feliz,Pedro	Tejada,Miguel
Figgins,Chone	Wells,Vernon
Freel,Ryan	

TIER 2

High Skill, Mod Risk

BATTERS	Age	Bats	Pos	Filters: 40 REL	80 Ct%	100 PX	100 SX	<$20 R$
Kinsler,Ian	25	R	4	41	84	101	114	$19
Encarnacion,Edwin	25	R	5	45	83	114	81	$19
Garko,Ryan	27	R	3	47	82	127	45	$18
Fukudome,Kosuke	31	L	9	62	80	121	121	$18
Jackson,Conor	26	R	3	55	88	103	53	$17
Crisp,Coco	28	S	8	61	84	79	132	$17
Bartlett,Jason	28	R	6	63	86	71	138	$16
Roberts,Dave	35	L	87	51	85	64	164	$16
Ellis,Mark	30	R	4	43	84	110	87	$16
Ethier,Andre	26	L	97	44	83	117	51	$16
Tracy,Chad	28	L	5	57	82	126	52	$15
Murton,Matt	26	R	97	57	86	112	64	$15
Matthews Jr.,Gary	33	S	8	46	81	109	107	$15
Anderson,Garret	35	L	70	64	85	108	55	$14
Lofton,Kenny	40	L	87	50	90	64	142	$12
Catalanotto,Frank	34	L	7	54	89	100	75	$12
Owens,Jerry	27	L	8	40	85	42	125	$11
Johnson,Dan	28	L	3	47	84	107	34	$11
Jones,Jacque	33	L	89	68	81	102	79	$11
Mench,Kevin	30	R	79	66	90	101	70	$9
Pena,Tony	26	R	6	45	83	61	100	$9
Giles,Marcus	30	R	4	49	81	83	109	$8
Gonzalez,Alex	31	R	6	58	81	110	51	$8
Amezaga,Alfredo	30	S	8	46	87	52	118	$8
Podsednik,Scott	32	L	7	53	83	71	126	$7
Tyner,Jason	31	L	70	42	90	41	104	$7
Cantu,Jorge	26	R	3	50	81	113	46	$6

PITCHERS	Age	Thrw	Filters: 40 REL	50 BPV	<$20 R$
Myers,Brett	27	R	49	86	$19
Hudson,Tim	32	R	84	60	$19
Francis,Jeff	27	L	79	66	$19
Blanton,Joe	27	R	66	63	$19
Zambrano,Carlos	26	R	71	66	$19
Wang,Chien-Ming	28	R	61	50	$18
Bonderman,Jeremy	25	R	59	87	$18
Cain,Matt	23	R	54	73	$18
Cordero,Chad	26	R	62	72	$18
Gregg,Kevin	29	R	53	84	$18
Lowe,Derek	34	R	95	64	$18
Borowski,Joe	37	R	45	70	$17
Meche,Gil	29	R	69	57	$17
Arroyo,Bronson	31	R	80	66	$17
Young,Chris	28	R	80	70	$16
Penny,Brad	29	R	90	53	$16
Pettitte,Andy	35	L	73	57	$16
Lilly,Ted	32	L	72	58	$16
Bush,David	28	R	63	70	$16
Hoffman,Trevor	40	R	53	69	$15
Millwood,Kevin	33	R	75	57	$15
Wheeler,Dan	30	R	41	96	$13
Capuano,Chris	29	L	77	64	$13
Cabrera,Daniel	26	R	61	60	$12
Rodriguez,Wandy	29	L	47	59	$12
Willis,Dontrelle	26	L	64	50	$11
Mussina,Mike	39	R	47	59	$11
Fuentes,Brian	32	L	48	94	$11
Dempster,Ryan	31	R	59	55	$11
Maholm,Paul	25	L	54	52	$10
Lieber,Jon	38	R	43	62	$10
Shields,Scot	32	R	40	89	$10
Hendrickson,Mark	33	L	58	51	$2

PORTFOLIO3 PLAN

TIER 3

R$ | **<$10**

High Skill, High Risk

MIXED LG	Age	Bats	Pos	REL	Ct%	PX	SX
			Filters:	0	80	100	100
Alou,Moises	41	R	7	17	90	116	46
Izturis,Maicer	27	S	54	16	90	74	106
Rivera,Juan	29	R	9	4	88	104	28
Barton,Daric	22	L	3	8	88	103	80
Ruiz,Carlos	29	R	2	23	87	101	78
Pearce,Steven	25	R	9	10	87	117	102
Casilla,Alexi	23	S	4	0	86	49	124
Davis,Rajai	27	R	8	25	86	55	129
Bonds,Barry	43	L	7	0	86	148	34
German,Esteban	30	R	45	10	84	71	125
Gathright,Joey	27	L	7	37	84	38	118
Richar,Danny	24	L	4	0	84	99	108
Duffy,Chris	28	L	8	17	84	65	137
LaRoche,Andy	24	R	5	1	83	112	68
Diaz,Matt	30	R	7	35	83	101	81
Quentin,Carlos	25	R	9	14	82	115	76
Freel,Ryan	32	R	8	28	82	72	127
Overbay,Lyle	31	L	3	26	82	112	56
Bourn,Michael	25	L	7	10	81	58	189
Hairston,Scott	27	R	7	3	81	129	82
Young,Dmitri	34	S	3	17	81	121	40
Thomas,Frank	39	R	0	2	81	123	14
Buck,Travis	24	L	9	0	80	139	107
Stairs,Matt	40	L	37	7	80	145	48
Milledge,Lastings	23	R	9	18	80	111	100

DEEP LG	Age	Bats	Pos	REL	Ct%	PX	SX
Hopper,Norris	29	R	87	20	90	33	107
Ryan,Brendan	26	R	65	4	90	46	109
Redman,Tike	31	L	8	11	90	52	127
Ozuna,Pablo	33	R	5	0	89	44	107
Aybar,Erick	24	S	46	14	89	53	118
Chavez,Endy	30	L	79	8	89	62	114
Cora,Alex	32	L	46	36	89	63	113
Anderson,Joshua	25	L	8	33	87	38	124
Cairo,Miguel	34	R	35	28	87	55	131
Guzman,Cristian	30	S	6	0	87	65	122
Mientkiewicz,Doug	33	L	3	5	86	108	36
Barrett,Michael	31	R	2	24	86	105	46
Carroll,Jamey	34	R	45	8	86	50	103
Schierholtz,Nathan	24	L	9	0	85	100	107
House,J.R.	28	R	2	5	85	104	35
Salazar,Jeff	27	L	9	36	85	81	119
Gwynn,Tony	25	L	8	24	85	38	118
Morgan,Nyjer	27	L	8	4	84	43	135
Zaun,Gregg	37	S	2	28	84	109	38
Wilson,Josh	27	R	64	6	84	72	107
Willits,Reggie	26	S	798	14	84	43	102
Burke,Chris	28	R	48	32	83	83	118
Francisco,Ben	26	R	7	28	83	103	103
Young,Delwyn	25	S	7	23	82	106	70
Barajas,Rod	32	R	2	32	82	113	29
Dukes,Elijah	23	R	8	0	82	102	91
Punto,Nick	30	S	564	32	82	52	114
Marte,Andy	24	R	5	5	82	116	39
Stewart,Ian	23	L	5	0	81	104	79
Gomez,Carlos	22	R	79	0	81	75	139
Bradley,Milton	30	S	7	3	81	122	63
Piazza,Mike	39	R	0	0	81	101	31
Pagan,Angel	26	S	89	2	81	83	114
Upton,Justin	20	R	9	0	81	121	105
Murphy,Donnie	25	R	6	1	81	119	79
Barfield,Josh	25	R	4	17	80	74	115
Ortmeier,Dan	27	S	37	23	80	84	102
Lane,Jason	31	R	8	17	80	105	47

MIXED LG	Age	Thrw	REL	BPV
		Filters:	0	75
Betancourt,Rafael	33	R	20	149
Broxton,Jonathan	23	R	11	137
Meredith,Cla	24	R	2	102
Rodney,Fernando	31	R	0	101
Ryan,B.J.	32	L	2	97
Benoit,Joaquin	30	R	31	96
Howell,J.P.	25	L	12	90
Gagne,Eric	32	R	0	90
Marmol,Carlos	25	R	0	88
Parra,Manny	25	L	0	86
Reyes,Al	38	R	0	86
Qualls,Chad	29	R	37	86
Otsuka,Akinori	36	R	11	85
Bailey,Homer	22	R	0	82
Buchholz,Clay	23	R	0	82
Ayala,Luis	30	R	0	80
Accardo,Jeremy	26	R	39	79
Baker,Scott	26	R	17	77
Clemens,Roger	45	R	37	77

DEEP LG	Age	Thrw	REL	BPV
Bell,Heath	30	R	27	120
Dotel,Octavio	34	R	0	117
Duchscherer,Justin	30	R	0	109
Cruz,Juan	29	R	18	107
Howry,Bob	34	R	37	105
Kuo,Hong-Chih	26	L	0	105
Bray,Bill	24	L	0	101
Hoey,James	25	R	0	95
Wuertz,Mike	29	R	17	95
Marte,Damaso	33	L	19	93
Owens,Henry	29	R	0	92
Frasor,Jason	30	R	28	91
Perez,Rafael	26	L	6	89
Sherrill,George	31	L	9	89
Feliciano,Pedro	31	L	24	88
Sanchez,Jonathan	25	L	0	88
Delcarmen,Manny	26	R	4	87
Heilman,Aaron	29	R	39	87
Turnbow,Derrick	30	R	39	87
Speier,Justin	34	R	0	87
Chulk,Vinnie	29	R	6	86
Miller,Justin	30	R	2	86
Okajima,Hideki	32	L	14	86
Miller,Adam	23	R	0	85
Meloan,Jonathan	23	R	0	84
Lindstrom,Matt	28	R	2	83
Downs,Scott	32	L	29	82
Calero,Kiko	33	R	11	82
Ray,Chris	26	R	13	81
Wilson,C.J.	27	L	24	80
Perez,Chris	22	R	0	78
MacDougal,Mike	31	R	0	77
Flores,Randy	32	L	14	77
Zumaya,Joel	23	R	0	77
Tankersley,Taylor	25	L	0	77
Miller,Andrew	23	L	0	76
Harden,Rich	26	R	0	76
Vizcaino,Luis	33	R	16	76
Wood,Kerry	30	R	0	75
Yates,Tyler	30	R	0	75
Smith,Joe	24	R	0	75

ROTISSERIE AUCTION DRAFT
Top 560 players ranked for 75% depth leagues

NAME	POS	5x5	NAME	POS	5x5	NAME	POS	5x5	NAME	POS	5x5
Rodriguez,Alex	5	$38	Hill,Rich	P	$23	Wang,Chien-Ming	P	$18	Gorzelanny,Tom	P	$16
Wright,David	5	$37	Zimmerman,Ryan	5	$23	Garko,Ryan	3	$18	Penny,Brad	P	$16
Ramirez,Hanley	6	$36	Ordonez,Magglio	9	$23	Soriano,Rafael	P	$18	Nady,Xavier	9	$16
Holliday,Matt	7	$35	Jones,Chipper	5	$23	Willingham,Josh	7	$18	Roberts,Dave	87	$16
Pujols,Albert	3	$35	Beltre,Adrian	5	$23	Bonderman,Jeremy	P	$18	Ellis,Mark	4	$16
Santana,Johan	P	$35	Oswalt,Roy	P	$23	Matsui,Kaz	4	$18	Butler,Billy	0	$16
Cabrera,Miguel	5	$34	Hafner,Travis	0	$22	Wigginton,Ty	54	$18	Ethier,Andre	97	$16
Rollins,Jimmy	6	$33	Smoltz,John	P	$22	Kubel,Jason	70	$18	Betancourt,Yuniesky	6	$16
Braun,Ryan	5	$32	Morneau,Justin	3	$22	Greinke,Zack	P	$18	Pettitte,Andy	P	$16
Reyes,Jose	6	$32	Pena,Carlos	3	$22	Cain,Matt	P	$18	Lilly,Ted	P	$16
Crawford,Carl	7	$32	Young,Chris	8	$22	Sanchez,Freddy	4	$18	Bush,David	P	$16
Utley,Chase	4	$31	Lidge,Brad	P	$22	Cordero,Chad	P	$18	Isringhausen,Jason	P	$15
Teixeira,Mark	3	$31	Hawpe,Brad	9	$22	Cabrera,Orlando	6	$18	Marcum,Shaun	P	$15
Lee,Carlos	7	$31	Escobar,Kelvim	P	$22	Pie,Felix	8	$18	Tracy,Chad	5	$15
Ortiz,David	0	$30	Valverde,Jose	P	$22	McCann,Brian	2	$18	Hoffman,Trevor	P	$15
Peavy,Jake	P	$30	Cano,Robinson	4	$22	Patterson,Corey	8	$18	Broxton,Jonathan	P	$15
Soriano,Alfonso	7	$30	Taveras,Willy	8	$22	Sheets,Ben	P	$18	Teahen,Mark	9	$15
Putz,J.J.	P	$29	Hamels,Cole	P	$22	Gordon,Alex	53	$18	Milledge,Lastings	9	$15
Howard,Ryan	3	$29	Burnett,A.J.	P	$21	Gregg,Kevin	P	$18	Young,Dmitri	3	$15
Webb,Brandon	P	$29	Helton,Todd	3	$21	Castillo,Luis	4	$18	Church,Ryan	78	$15
Bedard,Erik	P	$29	Ramirez,Manny	7	$21	Fukudome,Kosuke	9	$18	Perez,Oliver	P	$15
Fielder,Prince	3	$28	Jeter,Derek	6	$21	Lowe,Derek	P	$18	Kent,Jeff	4	$15
Phillips,Brandon	4	$28	Matsui,Hideki	70	$21	Theriot,Ryan	64	$18	Izturis,Maicer	54	$15
Haren,Dan	P	$28	Street,Huston	P	$21	Lugo,Julio	6	$18	Sheffield,Gary	0	$15
Verlander,Justin	P	$28	Upton,B.J.	84	$21	Pedroia,Dustin	4	$18	Wilkerson,Brad	37	$15
Pierre,Juan	8	$28	Young,Michael	6	$21	Soria,Joakim	P	$18	LaRoche,Andy	5	$15
Beckett,Josh	P	$28	Snell,Ian	P	$21	McLouth,Nate	87	$17	Murton,Matt	97	$15
Kazmir,Scott	P	$28	Tejada,Miguel	6	$21	Votto,Joey	3	$17	Westbrook,Jake	P	$15
Beltran,Carlos	8	$28	Francoeur,Jeff	9	$21	Lopez,Felipe	64	$17	Buehrle,Mark	P	$15
Sabathia,C.C.	P	$27	Halladay,Roy	P	$21	Greene,Khalil	6	$17	Buchholz,Clay	P	$15
Papelbon,Jonathan	P	$27	Konerko,Paul	3	$21	DeJesus,David	8	$17	Peralta,Jhonny	6	$15
Guerrero,Vladimir	90	$26	Wagner,Billy	P	$21	Uggla,Dan	4	$17	Duncan,Chris	7	$15
Berkman,Lance	39	$26	Capps,Matt	P	$21	Hudson,Orlando	4	$17	Matthews Jr.,Gary	8	$15
Hernandez,Felix	P	$26	Young,Delmon	98	$21	Kouzmanoff,Kevin	5	$17	Maddux,Greg	P	$15
Matsuzaka,Daisuke	P	$26	Martinez,Victor	23	$21	Johnson,Kelly	4	$17	Schilling,Curt	P	$15
Figgins,Chone	5	$26	Liriano,Francisco	P	$21	Jackson,Conor	3	$17	Millwood,Kevin	P	$15
Ramirez,Aramis	5	$26	Thome,Jim	0	$20	Loney,James	3	$17	Lopez,Jose	4	$14
Sizemore,Grady	8	$26	McGowan,Dustin	P	$20	Hughes,Philip	P	$17	Thomas,Frank	0	$14
Nathan,Joe	P	$26	Rowand,Aaron	8	$20	Borowski,Joe	P	$17	Bonds,Barry	7	$14
Suzuki,Ichiro	8	$26	Martinez,Pedro	P	$20	Mauer,Joe	2	$17	Davis,Rajai	8	$14
Atkins,Garrett	5	$26	Corpas,Manuel	P	$20	Posada,Jorge	2	$17	Belliard,Ronnie	4	$14
Markakis,Nick	9	$26	Damon,Johnny	807	$20	Cabrera,Melky	8	$17	Diaz,Matt	7	$14
Vazquez,Javier	P	$25	Kemp,Matt	9	$20	Youkilis,Kevin	3	$17	James,Chuck	P	$14
Guillen,Carlos	63	$25	Hamilton,Josh	8	$20	Polanco,Placido	4	$17	Overbay,Lyle	3	$14
Abreu,Bobby	9	$25	Hill,Aaron	4	$20	Chamberlain,Joba	P	$17	Towles,J.R.	2	$14
Lackey,John	P	$25	Ellsbury,Jacoby	7	$20	Fields,Josh	57	$17	Anderson,Garret	70	$14
Rios,Alex	98	$25	LaRoche,Adam	3	$20	Cameron,Mike	8	$17	Longoria,Evan	5	$14
Lee,Derrek	3	$25	Hermida,Jeremy	9	$20	Meche,Gil	P	$17	Santana,Ervin	P	$14
Hart,Corey	98	$25	Weeks,Rickie	4	$20	Ibanez,Raul	7	$17	Drew,Stephen	6	$14
Roberts,Brian	4	$25	Burrell,Pat	7	$19	Rolen,Scott	5	$17	Garza,Matt	P	$14
Cordero,Francisco	P	$25	Kinsler,Ian	4	$19	Cuddyer,Michael	9	$17	DeRosa,Mark	459	$14
Byrnes,Eric	798	$25	Myers,Brett	P	$19	Arroyo,Bronson	P	$17	Johjima,Kenji	2	$14
Victorino,Shane	9	$24	Encarnacion,Edwin	5	$19	Crisp,Coco	8	$17	Hall,Bill	8	$14
Dunn,Adam	7	$24	Carmona,Fausto	P	$19	Cabrera,Asdrubal	4	$17	Gagne,Eric	P	$14
Tulowitzki,Troy	6	$24	Jones,Andruw	8	$19	Drew,J.D.	9	$17	Baker,Scott	P	$14
Wells,Vernon	8	$24	Billingsley,Chad	P	$19	Jacobs,Mike	3	$17	Bailey,Homer	P	$14
Dye,Jermaine	9	$24	Lincecum,Tim	P	$19	Young,Chris	P	$16	Richar,Danny	4	$14
Furcal,Rafael	6	$24	Delgado,Carlos	3	$19	Griffey Jr.,Ken	9	$16	Molina,Bengie	2	$14
Rodriguez,Francisco	P	$24	Saito,Takashi	P	$19	Bartlett,Jason	6	$16	Iguchi,Tadahito	4	$14
Rivera,Mariano	P	$24	Wainwright,Adam	P	$19	Swisher,Nick	893	$16	Blake,Casey	5	$14
Granderson,Curtis	8	$24	Kearns,Austin	9	$19	Sonnanstine,Andrew	P	$16	Freel,Ryan	8	$14
Jenks,Bobby	P	$24	Lowell,Mike	5	$19	Weaver,Jered	P	$16	Napoli,Mike	2	$14
Pence,Hunter	8	$24	Maine,John	P	$19	Scott,Luke	9	$16	Iwamura,Akinori	5	$13
Hunter,Torii	8	$24	Guillen,Jose	9	$19	Huff,Aubrey	03	$16	Betancourt,Rafael	P	$13
Harang,Aaron	P	$24	Hudson,Tim	P	$19	Winn,Randy	987	$16	Wheeler,Dan	P	$13
Shields,James	P	$24	Blalock,Hank	5	$19	Kendrick,Howie	4	$16	Mora,Melvin	5	$13
Bay,Jason	7	$23	Francis,Jeff	P	$19	Sexson,Richie	3	$16	Barton,Daric	3	$13
Gallardo,Yovani	P	$23	Blanton,Joe	P	$19	Kotchman,Casey	3	$16	Gaudin,Chad	P	$13
Martin,Russell	2	$23	Renteria,Edgar	6	$19	Hardy,J.J.	6	$16	Buck,Travis	9	$13
Gonzalez,Adrian	3	$23	Zambrano,Carlos	P	$19	Glaus,Troy	5	$16	Pena,Wily Mo	79	$13

ROTISSERIE AUCTION DRAFT — Top 560 players ranked for 75% depth leagues

NAME	POS	5x5	NAME	POS	5x5	NAME	POS	5x5	NAME	POS	5x5
Pearce,Steven	9	$13	Gathright,Joey	7	$11	Betemit,Wilson	5	$9	Crosby,Bobby	6	$8
Gomes,Jonny	097	$13	Gutierrez,Franklin	9	$11	Miller,Adam	P	$9	Morales,Franklin	P	$8
Duffy,Chris	8	$13	Monroe,Craig	7	$11	Olivo,Miguel	2	$9	Montero,Miguel	2	$8
Capuano,Chris	P	$13	Jones,Jacque	89	$11	Lind,Adam	7	$9	Rogers,Kenny	P	$8
Cruz,Nelson	9	$13	Guthrie,Jeremy	P	$11	Bell,Heath	P	$9	Lamb,Mike	53	$8
Alou,Moises	7	$13	Silva,Carlos	P	$11	Redman,Tike	8	$9	Amezaga,Alfredo	8	$8
Kennedy,Ian	P	$13	Lee,Cliff	P	$11	Wood,Brandon	5	$9	Mitre,Sergio	P	$8
Eckstein,David	6	$13	Ross,Cody	8	$11	Mientkiewicz,Doug	3	$9	Podsednik,Scott	7	$7
Slowey,Kevin	P	$13	Kuroda,Hiroki	P	$11	Escobar,Yunel	654	$9	Peralta,Joel	P	$7
Zito,Barry	P	$13	Maholm,Paul	P	$10	Garciaparra,Nomar	35	$9	Jackson,Edwin	P	$7
Ankiel,Rick	98	$13	Grudzielanek,Mark	4	$10	Howry,Bob	P	$9	Embree,Alan	P	$7
Jenkins,Geoff	7	$13	Litsch,Jesse	P	$10	Olsen,Scott	P	$9	Janssen,Casey	P	$7
Wilson,Jack	6	$13	Volquez,Edinson	P	$10	Sosa,Sammy	0	$9	Neshek,Pat	P	$7
Thames,Marcus	73	$12	Burke,Chris	48	$10	Loewen,Adam	P	$9	Hoey,James	P	$7
Cust,Jack	90	$12	Qualls,Chad	P	$10	Okajima,Hideki	P	$9	Gibbons,Jay	70	$7
Howell,J.P.	P	$12	Francisco,Ben	7	$10	Gonzalez,Luis	7	$9	Dobbs,Greg	5	$7
Chavez,Eric	5	$12	Stewart,Shannon	7	$10	Wakefield,Tim	P	$9	Wise,Matt	P	$7
Lofton,Kenny	87	$12	Barrett,Michael	2	$10	Saunders,Joe	P	$9	Glavine,Tom	P	$7
Hernandez,Ramon	2	$12	Soto,Geovany	2	$10	Aurilia,Rich	35	$9	Hammel,Jason	P	$7
Hairston,Scott	7	$12	Lieber,Jon	P	$10	Broussard,Ben	39	$9	Braden,Dallas	P	$7
Benoit,Joaquin	P	$12	Doumit,Ryan	92	$10	Torrealba,Yorvit	2	$9	Morris,Matt	P	$7
Owings,Micah	P	$12	Reynolds,Mark	5	$10	Lewis,Fred	97	$9	Everett,Adam	6	$7
Correia,Kevin	P	$12	Danks,John	P	$10	Mench,Kevin	79	$9	Wolf,Randy	P	$7
Cabrera,Daniel	P	$12	Green,Shawn	9	$10	Wilson,Preston	9	$9	Tyner,Jason	70	$7
Giles,Brian	9	$12	Reyes,Al	P	$10	Pena,Tony	6	$9	Benson,Kris	P	$7
Brown,Emil	79	$12	Johnson,Randy	P	$10	Clark,Tony	3	$9	Patton,Troy	P	$7
Rodriguez,Wandy	P	$12	Weathers,David	P	$10	Loretta,Mark	6435	$9	Molina,Yadier	2	$7
Crede,Joe	5	$12	Otsuka,Akinori	P	$10	Anderson,Joshua	8	$9	Taguchi,So	87	$7
Rivera,Juan	9	$12	Parra,Manny	P	$10	Upton,Justin	9	$9	Kendall,Jason	2	$7
Bautista,Jose	59	$12	Gomez,Carlos	79	$10	Wilson,C.J.	P	$9	Feliciano,Pedro	P	$7
Catalanotto,Frank	7	$12	Snyder,Chris	2	$10	Frandsen,Kevin	46	$9	Murphy,Donnie	6	$7
Stairs,Matt	37	$12	Varitek,Jason	2	$10	Piazza,Mike	0	$9	Murphy,David	7	$7
Werth,Jayson	97	$12	Washburn,Jarrod	P	$10	Duncan,Shelley	0	$9	Uehara,Koji	P	$7
Robertson,Nate	P	$12	Willits,Reggie	798	$10	Bradley,Milton	7	$9	Schneider,Brian	2	$7
Bannister,Brian	P	$12	Schmidt,Jason	P	$10	Zaun,Gregg	2	$9	Scutaro,Marco	65	$7
Bergmann,Jason	P	$12	Jones,Todd	P	$10	Spilborghs,Ryan	89	$9	Castro,Ramon	2	$7
Willis,Dontrelle	P	$11	Pierzynski,A.J.	2	$10	Lohse,Kyle	P	$9	Nunez,Leo	P	$7
Casilla,Alexi	4	$11	Ensberg,Morgan	5	$10	Gonzalez,Edgar	P	$9	Sanders,Reggie	7	$7
Lo Duca,Paul	2	$11	Harris,Brendan	64	$10	Vizcaino,Luis	P	$9	Marte,Damaso	P	$7
Quentin,Carlos	9	$11	Gload,Ross	3	$10	Dotel,Octavio	P	$8	Marquis,Jason	P	$7
Mussina,Mike	P	$11	Reyes,Anthony	P	$10	Navarro,Dioner	2	$8	Phelps,Josh	3	$7
Davis,Doug	P	$11	Estrada,Johnny	2	$10	Wuertz,Mike	P	$8	Gross,Gabe	9	$7
Marmol,Carlos	P	$11	Casey,Sean	3	$10	Kennedy,Adam	4	$8	Suzuki,Kurt	2	$7
Saltalamacchia,Jarr	23	$11	Kendrick,Kyle	P	$10	Giles,Marcus	4	$8	Botts,Jason	7	$7
Byrd,Paul	P	$11	Jones,Adam	7	$10	Perez,Rafael	P	$8	Aybar,Erick	46	$7
Walker,Jamie	P	$11	Dellucci,David	7	$10	Hinske,Eric	37	$8	Riske,David	P	$7
Durham,Ray	4	$11	Byrd,Marlon	89	$10	Duchscherer,Justin	P	$8	Johnson,Reed	7	$7
German,Esteban	45	$11	Bard,Josh	2	$10	Hill,Shawn	P	$8	Hatteberg,Scott	3	$7
Johnson,Nick	3	$11	Colon,Bartolo	P	$10	Miller,Andrew	P	$8	Spiezio,Scott	5	$6
Bonser,Boof	P	$11	Shields,Scot	P	$10	Linebrink,Scott	P	$8	Carpenter,Chris	P	$6
Feliz,Pedro	5	$11	Suppan,Jeff	P	$10	Pineiro,Joel	P	$8	Carlyle,Buddy	P	$6
Fuentes,Brian	P	$11	Lester,Jon	P	$10	Jones,Brandon	7	$8	Speier,Justin	P	$6
Accardo,Jeremy	P	$11	Rodriguez,Ivan	2	$10	Cruz,Juan	P	$8	Hopper,Norris	87	$6
Contreras,Jose	P	$11	Ryan,B.J.	P	$10	Looper,Braden	P	$8	Logan,Nook	8	$6
Uribe,Juan	6	$11	Gabbard,Kason	P	$10	Frasor,Jason	P	$8	Helms,Wes	5	$6
Inge,Brandon	5	$11	Clemens,Roger	P	$10	Downs,Scott	P	$8	Floyd,Cliff	9	$6
Wilson,Brian	P	$11	Cook,Aaron	P	$9	Vizquel,Omar	6	$8	Cabrera,Fernando	P	$6
Garland,Jon	P	$11	Payton,Jay	7	$9	Hirsh,Jason	P	$8	Cintron,Alex	5	$6
Batista,Miguel	P	$11	Harden,Rich	P	$9	Bray,Bill	P	$8	Cantu,Jorge	3	$6
Ruiz,Carlos	2	$11	Baldelli,Rocco	8	$9	Moore,Scott	5	$8	Delcarmen,Manny	P	$6
Meredith,Cla	P	$11	Heilman,Aaron	P	$9	Weaver,Jeff	P	$8	Sanchez,Jonathan	P	$6
Bourn,Michael	7	$11	Antonelli,Matt	4	$9	Rauch,Jon	P	$8	Petit,Yusmeiro	P	$6
Owens,Jerry	8	$11	Buck,John	2	$9	Barajas,Rod	2	$8	Punto,Nick	564	$6
Vidro,Jose	0	$11	Raburn,Ryan	9	$9	Marte,Andy	5	$8	Sherrill,George	P	$6
Ayala,Luis	P	$11	Padilla,Vicente	P	$9	Ross,Dave	2	$8	Gordon,Tom	P	$6
Keppinger,Jeff	6	$11	Vargas,Claudio	P	$9	McCarthy,Brandon	P	$8	Hernandez,Orland	P	$6
Dempster,Ryan	P	$11	Paulino,Ronny	2	$9	Edmonds,Jim	8	$8	Jurrjens,Jair	P	$6
Rodney,Fernando	P	$11	Giambi,Jason	0	$9	Gonzalez,Alex	6	$8	Abreu,Tony	54	$6
Johnson,Dan	3	$11	Barfield,Josh	4	$9	Pena,Tony	P	$8	Torres,Salomon	P	$6
Millar,Kevin	30	$11	Bradford,Chad	P	$9	Jimenez,Ubaldo	P	$8	Morgan,Nyjer	8	$6

ROTISSERIE SNAKE DRAFT — 15 TEAM MIXED LEAGUE

#	NAME	POS	#	NAME	POS	#	NAME	POS	#	NAME	POS
1	Ramirez,Hanley	6	5	Shields,James	P	9	Johnson,Kelly	4	13	Cain,Matt	P
	Rodriguez,Alex	5		Dunn,Adam	7		Polanco,Placido	4		Sheets,Ben	P
	Wright,David	5		Rivera,Mariano	P		Uggla,Dan	4		Cordero,Chad	P
	Rollins,Jimmy	6		Hunter,Torii	8		Cabrera,Asdrubal	4		Pie,Felix	8
	Reyes,Jose	6		Dye,Jermaine	9		Greene,Khalil	6		Willingham,Josh	7
	Santana,Johan	P		Granderson,Curtis	8		Napoli,Mike	2		Kubel,Jason	70
	Pujols,Albert	3		Harang,Aaron	P		Towles,J.R.	2		Belliard,Ronnie	4
	Holliday,Matt	7		Pence,Hunter	8		Molina,Bengie	2		Lopez,Jose	4
	Utley,Chase	4		Jenks,Bobby	P		Johjima,Kenji	2		Iguchi,Tadahito	4
	Cabrera,Miguel	5		Victorino,Shane	9		Damon,Johnny	807		Drew,Stephen	6
	Braun,Ryan	5		Wells,Vernon	8		LaRoche,Adam	3		Richar,Danny	4
	Crawford,Carl	7		Rodriguez,Francisco	P		Hermida,Jeremy	9		Ruiz,Carlos	2
	Phillips,Brandon	4		Weeks,Rickie	4		Rowand,Aaron	8		Lo Duca,Paul	2
	Teixeira,Mark	3		Hill,Aaron	4		Kemp,Matt	9		Rolen,Scott	5
	Lee,Carlos	7		Posada,Jorge	2		McGowan,Dustin	P		Kouzmanoff,Kevin	5
2	Ortiz,David	0	6	Mauer,Joe	2	10	Ellsbury,Jacoby	7	14	Chamberlain,Joba	P
	Soriano,Alfonso	7		Beltre,Adrian	5		Martinez,Pedro	P		Crisp,Coco	8
	Peavy,Jake	P		Zimmerman,Ryan	5		Thome,Jim	0		McLouth,Nate	87
	Martin,Russell	2		Jones,Chipper	5		Corpas,Manuel	P		Ibanez,Raul	7
	Bedard,Erik	P		Ordonez,Magglio	9		Hamilton,Josh	8		Fields,Josh	57
	Putz,J.J.	P		Hill,Rich	P		Hardy,J.J.	6		Meche,Gil	P
	Webb,Brandon	P		Gallardo,Yovani	P		Betancourt,Yuniesky	6		Jackson,Conor	3
	Howard,Ryan	3		Oswalt,Roy	P		Ellis,Mark	4		Cameron,Mike	8
	Roberts,Brian	4		Bay,Jason	7		Bartlett,Jason	6		Arroyo,Bronson	P
	Verlander,Justin	P		Gonzalez,Adrian	3		Kendrick,Howie	4		Loney,James	3
	Haren,Dan	P		Kinsler,Ian	4		Encarnacion,Edwin	5		Votto,Joey	3
	Pierre,Juan	8		Renteria,Edgar	6		Lowell,Mike	5		Drew,J.D.	9
	Fielder,Prince	3		Lidge,Brad	P		Blalock,Hank	5		Lopez,Felipe	64
	Kazmir,Scott	P		Hawpe,Brad	9		Jones,Andruw	8		Cuddyer,Michael	9
	Beckett,Josh	P		Valverde,Jose	P		Delgado,Carlos	3		Cabrera,Melky	8
3	Beltran,Carlos	8	7	Young,Chris	8	11	Kearns,Austin	9	15	Hughes,Philip	P
	Furcal,Rafael	6		Morneau,Justin	3		Wainwright,Adam	P		Borowski,Joe	P
	Tulowitzki,Troy	6		Smoltz,John	P		Carmona,Fausto	P		Jacobs,Mike	3
	Papelbon,Jonathan	P		Hamels,Cole	P		Myers,Brett	P		DeJesus,David	8
	Sabathia,C.C.	P		Taveras,Willy	8		Lincecum,Tim	P		Youkilis,Kevin	3
	Ramirez,Aramis	5		Hafner,Travis	0		Blanton,Joe	P		Eckstein,David	6
	Figgins,Chone	5		Pena,Carlos	3		Saito,Takashi	P		Wilson,Jack	6
	Atkins,Garrett	5		Escobar,Kelvim	P		Billingsley,Chad	P		Barrett,Michael	2
	Sizemore,Grady	8		Pedroia,Dustin	4		Zambrano,Carlos	P		Soto,Geovany	2
	Matsuzaka,Daisuke	P		Castillo,Luis	4		Francis,Jeff	P		Pierzynski,A.J.	2
	Berkman,Lance	39		Cabrera,Orlando	6		Hudson,Tim	P		Rodriguez,Ivan	2
	Suzuki,Ichiro	8		Matsui,Kaz	4		Burrell,Pat	7		Bard,Josh	2
	Nathan,Joe	P		Sanchez,Freddy	4		Maine,John	P		Varitek,Jason	2
	Hernandez,Felix	P		Lugo,Julio	6		Guillen,Jose	9		Estrada,Johnny	2
	Guerrero,Vladimir	90		Halladay,Roy	P		Kent,Jeff	4		Snyder,Chris	2
4	Markakis,Nick	9	8	Matsui,Hideki	70	12	Peralta,Jhonny	6	16	Glaus,Troy	5
	Cano,Robinson	4		Liriano,Francisco	P		Hernandez,Ramon	2		Sexson,Richie	3
	Rios,Alex	98		Ramirez,Manny	7		Garko,Ryan	3		Weaver,Jered	P
	Cordero,Francisco	P		Martinez,Victor	23		Soriano,Rafael	P		Bush,David	P
	Lee,Derrek	3		Capps,Matt	P		Lowe,Derek	P		Lilly,Ted	P
	Abreu,Bobby	9		Young,Delmon	98		Patterson,Corey	8		Roberts,Dave	87
	Hart,Corey	98		Francoeur,Jeff	9		Wigginton,Ty	54		Ethier,Andre	97
	Guillen,Carlos	63		Street,Huston	P		Fukudome,Kosuke	9		Winn,Randy	987
	Lackey,John	P		Konerko,Paul	3		Gordon,Alex	53		Kotchman,Casey	3
	Vazquez,Javier	P		Burnett,A.J.	P		Gregg,Kevin	P		Young,Chris	P
	Byrnes,Eric	798		Snell,Ian	P		Bonderman,Jeremy	P		Nady,Xavier	9
	Jeter,Derek	6		Wagner,Billy	P		Wang,Chien-Ming	P		Griffey Jr.,Ken	9
	Young,Michael	6		Upton,B.J.	84		Theriot,Ryan	64		Sonnanstine,Andrew	P
	Tejada,Miguel	6		Helton,Todd	3		Soria,Joakim	P		Huff,Aubrey	03
	McCann,Brian	2		Hudson,Orlando	4		Greinke,Zack	P		Scott,Luke	9

ROTISSERIE SNAKE DRAFT — 15 TEAM MIXED LEAGUE

#	NAME	POS
17	Butler, Billy	0
	Swisher, Nick	893
	Penny, Brad	P
	Gorzelanny, Tom	P
	Pettitte, Andy	P
	Paulino, Ronny	2
	Torrealba, Yorvit	2
	Zaun, Gregg	2
	Olivo, Miguel	2
	Buck, John	2
	Tracy, Chad	5
	LaRoche, Andy	5
	Schilling, Curt	P
	Teahen, Mark	9
	Duncan, Chris	7
18	Hoffman, Trevor	P
	Isringhausen, Jason	P
	Maddux, Greg	P
	Milledge, Lastings	9
	Westbrook, Jake	P
	Young, Dmitri	3
	Marcum, Shaun	P
	Buehrle, Mark	P
	Wilkerson, Brad	37
	Murton, Matt	97
	Broxton, Jonathan	P
	Perez, Oliver	P
	Sheffield, Gary	0
	Matthews Jr., Gary	8
	Izturis, Maicer	54
19	Millwood, Kevin	P
	Church, Ryan	78
	Buchholz, Clay	P
	Casilla, Alexi	4
	Keppinger, Jeff	6
	Durham, Ray	4
	Uribe, Juan	6
	Montero, Miguel	2
	Navarro, Dioner	2
	Ross, Dave	2
	Barajas, Rod	2
	Blake, Casey	5
	Longoria, Evan	5
	Freel, Ryan	8
	Thomas, Frank	0
20	Gagne, Eric	P
	Bonds, Barry	7
	DeRosa, Mark	459
	James, Chuck	P
	Anderson, Garret	70
	Baker, Scott	P
	Santana, Ervin	P
	Hall, Bill	8
	Overbay, Lyle	3
	Davis, Rajai	8
	Garza, Matt	P
	Bailey, Homer	P
	Diaz, Matt	7
	Grudzielanek, Mark	4
	Schneider, Brian	2

#	NAME	POS
21	Molina, Yadier	2
	Suzuki, Kurt	2
	Castro, Ramon	2
	Kendall, Jason	2
	Iwamura, Akinori	5
	Mora, Melvin	5
	Duffy, Chris	8
	Gaudin, Chad	P
	Zito, Barry	P
	Cruz, Nelson	9
	Slowey, Kevin	P
	Wheeler, Dan	P
	Barton, Daric	3
	Jenkins, Geoff	7
	Kennedy, Ian	P
22	Ankiel, Rick	98
	Pearce, Steven	9
	Pena, Wily Mo	79
	Gomes, Jonny	097
	Buck, Travis	9
	Capuano, Chris	P
	Alou, Moises	7
	Betancourt, Rafael	P
	Pena, Tony	6
	Barfield, Josh	4
	Antonelli, Matt	4
	Valentin, Javier	2
	Laird, Gerald	2
	Crede, Joe	5
	Chavez, Eric	5
23	Owings, Micah	P
	Howell, J.P.	P
	Cust, Jack	90
	Benoit, Joaquin	P
	Bautista, Jose	59
	Bannister, Brian	P
	Rodriguez, Wandy	P
	Robertson, Nate	P
	Hairston, Scott	7
	Thames, Marcus	73
	Bergmann, Jason	P
	Rivera, Juan	9
	Catalanotto, Frank	7
	Cabrera, Daniel	P
	Stairs, Matt	37
24	Lofton, Kenny	87
	Brown, Emil	79
	Werth, Jayson	97
	Correia, Kevin	P
	Giles, Brian	9
	Vizquel, Omar	6
	Kennedy, Adam	4
	Giles, Marcus	4
	Gonzalez, Alex	6
	Crosby, Bobby	6
	Shoppach, Kelly	2
	Iannetta, Chris	2
	Inge, Brandon	5
	Feliz, Pedro	5
	Batista, Miguel	P

#	NAME	POS
25	Johnson, Nick	3
	Byrd, Paul	P
	Marmol, Carlos	P
	German, Esteban	45
	Guthrie, Jeremy	P
	Jones, Jacque	89
	Mussina, Mike	P
	Contreras, Jose	P
	Kuroda, Hiroki	P
	Silva, Carlos	P
	Walker, Jamie	P
	Willis, Dontrelle	P
	Quentin, Carlos	9
	Saltalamacchia, Jarro	23
	Monroe, Craig	7
26	Davis, Doug	P
	Gathright, Joey	7
	Garland, Jon	P
	Lee, Cliff	P
	Accardo, Jeremy	P
	Gutierrez, Franklin	9
	Wilson, Brian	P
	Meredith, Cla	P
	Ross, Cody	8
	Rodney, Fernando	P
	Ayala, Luis	P
	Fuentes, Brian	P
	Vidro, Jose	0
	Owens, Jerry	8
	Millar, Kevin	30
27	Johnson, Dan	3
	Bonser, Boof	P
	Dempster, Ryan	P
	Bourn, Michael	7
	Murphy, Donnie	6
	Everett, Adam	6
	Redmond, Mike	2
	Lieberthal, Mike	2
	Thigpen, Curtis	2
	Reynolds, Mark	5
	Ensberg, Morgan	5
	Dellucci, David	7
	Jones, Adam	7
	Casey, Sean	3
	Gabbard, Kason	P
28	Lester, Jon	P
	Reyes, Anthony	P
	Colon, Bartolo	P
	Litsch, Jesse	P
	Byrd, Marlon	89
	Gload, Ross	3
	Harris, Brendan	64
	Shields, Scot	P
	Jones, Todd	P
	Parra, Manny	P
	Schmidt, Jason	P
	Green, Shawn	9
	Weathers, David	P
	Washburn, Jarrod	P
	Doumit, Ryan	92

#	NAME	POS
29	Burke, Chris	48
	Willits, Reggie	798
	Lieber, Jon	P
	Clemens, Roger	P
	Maholm, Paul	P
	Danks, John	P
	Volquez, Edinson	P
	Francisco, Ben	7
	Otsuka, Akinori	P
	Gomez, Carlos	79
	Stewart, Shannon	7
	Kendrick, Kyle	P
	Reyes, Al	P
	Qualls, Chad	P
	Suppan, Jeff	P
30	Ryan, B.J.	P
	Johnson, Randy	P
	Valentin, Jose	4
	Mathis, Jeff	2
	Coste, Chris	2
	Miller, Damian	2
	House, J.R.	2
	Molina, Jose	2
	Betemit, Wilson	5
	Wood, Brandon	5
	Heilman, Aaron	P
	Okajima, Hideki	P
	Wilson, Preston	9
	Upton, Justin	9
	Raburn, Ryan	9

SIMULATION LEAGUE DRAFT   TOP 500

NAME	POS	RAR	NAME	POS	RAR	NAME	POS	RAR	NAME	POS	RAR
Rodriguez,Alex	5	52.6	Myers,Brett	P	20.9	Keppinger,Jeff	6	12.8	Millwood,Kevin	P	8.8
Cabrera,Miguel	5	49.6	Halladay,Roy	P	20.8	Chamberlain,Joba	P	12.6	Castro,Ramon	2	8.8
Webb,Brandon	P	44.3	Blalock,Hank	5	20.8	Buchholz,Clay	P	12.3	Wilson,Jack	6	8.8
Wright,David	5	43.6	Hamels,Cole	P	20.7	Richar,Danny	4	12.3	Suzuki,Ichiro	8	8.8
Pujols,Albert	3	42.0	McGowan,Dustin	P	20.5	Buck,Travis	9	12.2	Ibanez,Raul	7	8.6
Howard,Ryan	3	41.9	Cust,Jack	90	20.5	Lidge,Brad	P	12.2	Barton,Daric	3	8.6
Hernandez,Felix	P	41.5	Pedroia,Dustin	4	20.2	Hart,Corey	98	12.2	Alou,Moises	7	8.6
Ramirez,Hanley	6	39.6	Hafner,Travis	0	20.1	Ellis,Mark	4	12.0	Dellucci,David	7	8.5
Utley,Chase	4	38.5	Howell,J.P.	P	20.0	Greene,Khalil	6	11.9	Matthews Jr.,Gary	8	8.4
Ortiz,David	0	36.2	Matsuzaka,Daisuke	P	19.7	Ross,Cody	8	11.9	Buck,John	2	8.4
Teixeira,Mark	3	35.1	Oswalt,Roy	P	19.7	Varitek,Jason	2	11.8	Hughes,Philip	P	8.4
Rollins,Jimmy	6	34.7	Glaus,Troy	5	19.5	Kubel,Jason	70	11.6	Greinke,Zack	P	8.3
Santana,Johan	P	34.3	Markakis,Nick	9	19.4	Maddux,Greg	P	11.5	Francis,Jeff	P	8.2
Braun,Ryan	5	34.3	Meredith,Cla	P	19.4	Griffey Jr.,Ken	9	11.5	Hall,Bill	8	8.2
Holliday,Matt	7	34.3	Ordonez,Magglio	9	19.1	Cordero,Francisco	P	11.4	Wuertz,Mike	P	8.0
Beltran,Carlos	8	33.5	Hermida,Jeremy	9	19.0	Rodriguez,Francisc	P	11.4	Fukudome,Kosuke	9	8.0
Jones,Chipper	5	33.2	Bonderman,Jeremy	P	18.9	Towles,J.R.	2	11.3	Billingsley,Chad	P	8.0
Bedard,Erik	P	32.8	Weeks,Rickie	4	18.9	Drew,Stephen	6	11.1	Valverde,Jose	P	7.9
Ramirez,Manny	7	32.8	Upton,B.J.	84	18.9	Kotchman,Casey	3	11.1	Murton,Matt	97	7.8
Dunn,Adam	7	32.6	Johnson,Kelly	4	18.0	Hardy,J.J.	6	11.1	Zambrano,Carlos	P	7.7
Martin,Russell	2	32.4	Harang,Aaron	P	17.7	Jenks,Bobby	P	11.0	Betancourt,Rafael	P	7.6
Sizemore,Grady	8	31.6	Konerko,Paul	3	17.6	Rowand,Aaron	8	10.8	Clemens,Roger	P	7.6
Liriano,Francisco	P	31.5	Wang,Chien-Ming	P	17.3	Betemit,Wilson	5	10.7	Ensberg,Morgan	5	7.6
Martinez,Victor	23	30.8	Napoli,Mike	2	17.3	Young,Michael	6	10.7	Kearns,Austin	9	7.5
Lowe,Derek	P	30.5	Furcal,Rafael	6	17.2	Downs,Scott	P	10.6	Barajas,Rod	2	7.5
Bonds,Barry	7	30.0	Verlander,Justin	P	17.2	Damon,Johnny	807	10.6	Willingham,Josh	7	7.5
Guillen,Carlos	63	29.7	Lee,Derrek	3	17.0	Soriano,Alfonso	7	10.5	Cuddyer,Michael	9	7.4
Fielder,Prince	3	29.5	Snell,Ian	P	16.8	Mitre,Sergio	P	10.4	Lo Duca,Paul	2	7.4
Posada,Jorge	2	28.8	Lackey,John	P	16.7	Barrett,Michael	2	10.4	Perez,Rafael	P	7.4
Granderson,Curtis	8	28.7	Jeter,Derek	6	16.3	Ethier,Andre	97	10.4	Catalanotto,Frank	7	7.3
Guerrero,Vladimir	90	28.6	Lee,Carlos	7	16.3	Papelbon,Jonathan	P	10.4	Iannetta,Chris	2	7.3
Hawpe,Brad	9	28.2	Hill,Rich	P	16.0	Cabrera,Asdrubal	4	10.4	Lieber,Jon	P	7.2
Tulowitzki,Troy	6	28.1	Rios,Alex	98	16.0	Qualls,Chad	P	10.3	Sexson,Richie	3	7.2
Pena,Carlos	3	27.9	Renteria,Edgar	6	15.9	Phillips,Brandon	4	10.3	Feliciano,Pedro	P	7.2
Burnett,A.J.	P	27.9	Scott,Luke	9	15.9	Cameron,Mike	8	10.3	Thames,Marcus	73	7.1
Peavy,Jake	P	27.3	Lincecum,Tim	P	15.9	Ross,Dave	2	10.3	Gordon,Alex	53	7.1
Berkman,Lance	39	26.9	Kent,Jeff	4	15.8	Pettitte,Andy	P	10.2	Molina,Bengie	2	7.1
Beckett,Josh	P	26.7	Broxton,Jonathan	P	15.5	Bush,David	P	10.2	Cruz,Juan	P	6.9
Carmona,Fausto	P	26.5	Zimmerman,Ryan	5	15.5	Wainwright,Adam	P	10.2	Bruce,Jay	8	6.8
Burrell,Pat	7	26.0	Kinsler,Ian	4	15.3	Tracy,Chad	5	10.2	Bray,Bill	P	6.8
Mauer,Joe	2	25.6	Snyder,Chris	2	15.2	Beltre,Adrian	5	10.2	Moylan,Peter	P	6.8
Haren,Dan	P	25.6	Bay,Jason	7	15.2	Wagner,Billy	P	10.2	Wheeler,Dan	P	6.8
Sabathia,C.C.	P	25.1	Soto,Geovany	2	14.8	Nathan,Joe	P	10.1	Wilson,C.J.	P	6.7
Kazmir,Scott	P	25.0	Westbrook,Jake	P	14.6	Sanchez,Freddy	4	10.0	Benoit,Joaquin	P	6.7
Wells,Vernon	8	24.9	Bard,Josh	2	14.5	LaRoche,Andy	5	10.0	Giles,Brian	9	6.7
Ramirez,Aramis	5	24.7	Rivera,Mariano	P	14.5	Duncan,Chris	7	9.9	Kouzmanoff,Kevin	5	6.6
Helton,Todd	3	24.6	Young,Chris	8	14.2	Chavez,Eric	5	9.9	Sonnanstine,Andre	P	6.6
Hamilton,Josh	8	24.5	Putz,J.J.	P	14.2	Rodney,Fernando	P	9.8	Blanton,Joe	P	6.5
Abreu,Bobby	9	24.5	Hunter,Torii	8	14.1	Stairs,Matt	37	9.7	Cook,Aaron	P	6.5
Swisher,Nick	893	24.3	Miller,Andrew	P	14.1	German,Esteban	45	9.7	Hill,Shawn	P	6.5
Roberts,Brian	4	24.2	Ruiz,Carlos	2	14.1	Maholm,Paul	P	9.5	Bradford,Chad	P	6.5
Smoltz,John	P	24.0	Hudson,Orlando	4	14.0	Uggla,Dan	4	9.4	Johjima,Kenji	2	6.4
Thome,Jim	0	23.9	Fields,Josh	57	13.9	Sheets,Ben	P	9.4	Gomes,Jonny	097	6.4
McCann,Brian	2	23.4	Morneau,Justin	3	13.8	Johnson,Nick	3	9.4	Okajima,Hideki	P	6.4
Hill,Aaron	4	23.2	Lowell,Mike	5	13.7	Longoria,Evan	5	9.4	Overbay,Lyle	3	6.4
Cano,Robinson	4	23.1	Escobar,Kelvim	P	13.6	Corpas,Manuel	P	9.3	Carpenter,Chris	P	6.4
Vazquez,Javier	P	22.9	Polanco,Placido	4	13.6	Street,Huston	P	9.3	Escobar,Yunel	654	6.4
Atkins,Garrett	5	22.8	Bell,Heath	P	13.6	Soria,Joakim	P	9.2	Peralta,Jhonny	6	6.3
Shields,James	P	22.7	Martinez,Pedro	P	13.5	Pie,Felix	8	9.2	Encarnacion,Edwi	5	6.3
Reyes,Jose	6	22.5	Saltalamacchia,Jarr	23	13.4	Saito,Takashi	P	9.1	Shoppach,Kelly	2	6.3
Dye,Jermaine	9	21.8	DeJesus,David	8	13.4	Rolen,Scott	5	9.1	Garza,Matt	P	6.3
Drew,J.D.	9	21.6	Jones,Andruw	8	13.3	Castillo,Luis	4	9.0	Frasor,Jason	P	6.3
Pence,Hunter	8	21.6	Youkilis,Kevin	3	13.2	Hernandez,Ramon	2	8.9	Soriano,Rafael	P	6.3
Hudson,Tim	P	21.6	Wilkerson,Brad	37	13.1	Antonelli,Matt	4	8.9	LaRoche,Adam	3	6.2
Matsui,Hideki	70	21.0	Tejada,Miguel	6	13.1	Wigginton,Ty	54	8.8	DeRosa,Mark	459	6.2
Gallardo,Yovani	P	21.0	Zaun,Gregg	2	13.0	Shields,Scot	P	8.8	Meche,Gil	P	6.1

NAME	POS	RAR	NAME	POS	RAR	NAME	POS	RAR	NAME	POS	RAR
Schneider,Brian	2	6.1	Yates,Tyler	P	3.8	Maybin,Cameron	7	1.9	Valentin,Jose	4	0.6
McLouth,Nate	87	6.0	Pearce,Steven	9	3.7	Pena,Wily Mo	79	1.9	Rauch,Jon	P	0.6
Sanchez,Jonathan	P	6.0	Edmonds,Jim	8	3.7	Jackson,Conor	3	1.9	Buchholz,Taylor	P	0.6
Dotel,Octavio	P	6.0	Schilling,Curt	P	3.7	Estrada,Johnny	2	1.9	Green,Shawn	9	0.6
Heilman,Aaron	P	6.0	Votto,Joey	3	3.7	Doumit,Ryan	92	1.9	Bowen,Rob	2	0.5
Bradley,Milton	7	5.9	Marte,Damaso	P	3.7	Isringhausen,Jason	P	1.9	Rhodes,Arthur	P	0.5
Jimenez,D'Angelo	6	5.9	Miller,Justin	P	3.7	Sherrill,George	P	1.8	Tavarez,Julian	P	0.5
MacDougal,Mike	P	5.7	Guerrier,Matt	P	3.6	Arroyo,Bronson	P	1.8	Owens,Henry	P	0.5
Delcarmen,Manny	P	5.7	Mientkiewicz,Doug	3	3.6	Marmol,Carlos	P	1.8	Gorzelanny,Tom	P	0.5
Iguchi,Tadahito	4	5.6	Litsch,Jesse	P	3.5	Dukes,Elijah	8	1.7	Affeldt,Jeremy	P	0.5
Garko,Ryan	3	5.6	Clement,Matt	P	3.5	Gregg,Kevin	P	1.7	Sanders,Reggie	7	0.4
Capuano,Chris	P	5.6	Turnbow,Derrick	P	3.5	Meloan,Jonathan	P	1.7	Oliver,Darren	P	0.4
Werth,Jayson	97	5.5	Grudzielanek,Mark	4	3.4	Dempster,Ryan	P	1.7	Loe,Kameron	P	0.4
Gonzalez,Alex	6	5.5	Jones,Jacque	89	3.4	Germano,Justin	P	1.7	Geary,Geoff	P	0.3
Figgins,Chone	5	5.4	Howry,Bob	P	3.4	Guzman,Cristian	6	1.6	Ohman,Will	P	0.3
Otsuka,Akinori	P	5.4	Reyes,Dennys	P	3.4	Hatteberg,Scott	3	1.6	Seay,Bobby	P	0.3
Ayala,Luis	P	5.3	Willis,Dontrelle	P	3.3	Brown,Andrew	P	1.6	Franklin,Ryan	P	0.2
Bailey,Homer	P	5.2	Loewen,Adam	P	3.3	Roberts,Dave	87	1.6	Chulk,Vinnie	P	0.2
Loretta,Mark	6435	5.2	Speier,Justin	P	3.3	Rivera,Juan	9	1.5	Suzuki,Kurt	2	0.2
Smith,Joe	P	5.2	Lieberthal,Mike	2	3.3	Clark,Tony	3	1.5	Durham,Ray	4	0.2
Kuo,Hong-Chih	P	5.2	Grabow,John	P	3.2	Molina,Yadier	2	1.5	Miner,Zach	P	0.1
Marcum,Shaun	P	5.2	Penny,Brad	P	3.1	Hawkins,LaTroy	P	1.5	Silva,Carlos	P	0.1
Kendrick,Howie	4	5.2	Shouse,Brian	P	3.0	Towers,Josh	P	1.5	Zumaya,Joel	P	0.1
Fuentes,Brian	P	5.1	Crain,Jesse	P	3.0	Madson,Ryan	P	1.4	Borkowski,Dave	P	0.1
Gagne,Eric	P	5.1	Johnson,Dan	3	3.0	Wagner,Ryan	P	1.4	Schoeneweis,Scott	P	0.0
Rodriguez,Wandy	P	5.1	Johnson,Randy	P	3.0	Cabrera,Fernando	P	1.4	Walker,Jamie	P	0.0
Harden,Rich	P	5.1	Eckstein,David	6	3.0	Danks,John	P	1.3	DaVanon,Jeff	8	-0.0
Belliard,Ronnie	4	5.1	Teahen,Mark	9	3.0	Pavano,Carl	P	1.3	Stewart,Ian	5	-0.0
Church,Ryan	78	5.1	Delgado,Carlos	3	2.9	Cedeno,Ronny	6	1.3	Lyon,Brandon	P	-0.0
Iwamura,Akinori	5	5.1	Perez,Chris	P	2.9	Wood,Kerry	P	1.3	Harris,Brendan	64	-0.0
Crawford,Carl	7	5.0	Saunders,Joe	P	2.9	Belisle,Matt	P	1.3	Riske,David	P	-0.0
Capps,Matt	P	5.0	Thornton,Matt	P	2.8	Lugo,Julio	6	1.3	Contreras,Jose	P	-0.0
Headley,Chase	5	5.0	Peralta,Joel	P	2.8	Brazoban,Yhency	P	1.2	Fossum,Casey	P	-0.1
Duchscherer,Justin	P	5.0	Hinske,Eric	37	2.8	Parra,Manny	P	1.2	Bootcheck,Chris	P	-0.1
Cabrera,Daniel	P	5.0	Gonzalez,Adrian	3	2.8	Mastny,Tom	P	1.2	Gonzalez,Mike	P	-0.1
Lopez,Felipe	64	4.9	Robertson,Nate	P	2.8	Freel,Ryan	8	1.2	Thompson,Brad	P	-0.1
Gabbard,Kason	P	4.8	Navarro,Dioner	2	2.7	Buehrle,Mark	P	1.2	Hannahan,Jack	5	-0.1
Torrealba,Yorvit	2	4.8	Raburn,Ryan	9	2.6	Helms,Wes	5	1.2	Miller,Damian	2	-0.1
Cabrera,Melky	8	4.8	Gordon,Tom	P	2.6	Cordero,Chad	P	1.1	Mota,Guillermo	P	-0.1
Morales,Franklin	P	4.8	Penn,Hayden	P	2.6	Flores,Randy	P	1.1	Parrish,John	P	-0.1
Branyan,Russell	5	4.8	Reyes,Al	P	2.6	Gaudin,Chad	P	1.0	Marte,Andy	5	-0.2
Huff,Aubrey	03	4.7	Embree,Alan	P	2.5	Slaten,Doug	P	1.0	Nolasco,Ricky	P	-0.2
Lofton,Kenny	87	4.7	Logan,Boone	P	2.5	Kemp,Matt	9	1.0	Wise,Matt	P	-0.2
Torres,Salomon	P	4.7	Gobble,Jimmy	P	2.5	Reyes,Anthony	P	1.0	Donnelly,Brendan	P	-0.2
Littleton,Wes	P	4.7	Millar,Kevin	30	2.5	Pena,Tony	P	1.0	Mulder,Mark	P	-0.2
Spilborghs,Ryan	89	4.7	Linebrink,Scott	P	2.5	O'Flaherty,Eric	P	0.9	Wolf,Randy	P	-0.3
Bonser,Boof	P	4.6	Pineiro,Joel	P	2.5	Jenkins,Geoff	7	0.9	Floyd,Gavin	P	-0.3
Vizcaino,Luis	P	4.6	Miller,Adam	P	2.4	Lopez,Javier	P	0.9	Murphy,Donnie	6	-0.3
Colon,Bartolo	P	4.5	Julio,Jorge	P	2.4	Gonzalez,Edgar	P	0.9	Gardner,Lee	P	-0.3
Maine,John	P	4.4	Janssen,Casey	P	2.4	Johnson,Josh	P	0.9	Lilly,Ted	P	-0.3
Accardo,Jeremy	P	4.4	Dinardo,Lenny	P	2.4	Milledge,Lastings	9	0.9	Baez,Danys	P	-0.3
Moore,Scott	5	4.4	Snelling,Chris	8	2.4	Baker,Scott	P	0.8	Graffanino,Tony	45	-0.3
Hoey,James	P	4.3	Cain,Matt	P	2.3	Ray,Chris	P	0.8	Santana,Ervin	P	-0.4
Valentin,Javier	2	4.3	Prior,Mark	P	2.3	Hendrickson,Mark	P	0.8	Nippert,Dustin	P	-0.4
Lindstrom,Matt	P	4.3	Theriot,Ryan	64	2.3	Calero,Kiko	P	0.7	Seanez,Rudy	P	-0.4
Mussina,Mike	P	4.2	Montero,Miguel	2	2.3	Pelfrey,Mike	P	0.7	Treanor,Matt	2	-0.4
Correia,Kevin	P	4.2	Paulino,Ronny	2	2.3	Mahay,Ron	P	0.7	Garcia,Freddy	P	-0.4
Rincon,Juan	P	4.2	Green,Sean	P	2.3	Wood,Brandon	5	0.7	Floyd,Cliff	9	-0.5
Ryan,B.J.	P	4.1	Lamb,Mike	53	2.2	Devine,Joey	P	0.7	Casilla,Santiago	P	-0.5
Upton,Justin	9	4.1	Borowski,Joe	P	2.2	Tankersley,Taylor	P	0.7	Giambi,Jason	0	-0.5
Hochevar,Luke	P	4.0	Crisp,Coco	8	2.2	Miller,Trever	P	0.7	Baldelli,Rocco	8	-0.5
Izturis,Maicer	54	4.0	Wilson,Brian	P	2.2	Neshek,Pat	P	0.6	Britton,Chris	P	-0.6
Reynolds,Mark	5	4.0	House,J.R.	2	2.1	Ellsbury,Jacoby	7	0.6	Hairston,Scott	7	-0.6
Coffey,Todd	P	4.0	Anderson,Garret	70	2.0	Nunez,Leo	P	0.6	Pinto,Renyel	P	-0.6
Gross,Gabe	9	3.8	Phelps,Josh	3	2.0	Jones,Brandon	7	0.6	Igawa,Kei	P	-0.7
Blake,Casey	5	3.8	Farnsworth,Kyle	P	2.0	Braden,Dallas	P	0.6	Young,Dmitri	3	-0.7

VII.
SABERMETRIC
TOOLS

One Glossary
Abbreviations and Beginner Concepts

Avg: Batting average (see also BA)

BA: Batting average (see also Avg)

BABIP: Batting average on balls-in-play (see Hit rate)

Base Performance Indicator (BPI): A statistical formula that measures an isolated aspect of a player's situation-independent raw skill or a gauge that helps capture the effects that random chance has on skill. Although there are many such formulas, there are only a few that we are referring to when the term is used in this book. For batters, the skills BPIs are linear weighted power index (PX), speed score index (SX), walk rate (bb%), contact rate (ct%), batting eye (Eye), ground ball/line drive/fly ball ratios (G/L/F), home run to fly ball rate (hr/f) and expected batting average (xBA). Random chance is measured with hit rate on balls in play (H%). For pitchers, our BPIs are control (bb/9), dominance (k/9), command (k/bb), opposition on base avg (OOB), ground/line/fly ratios (G/L/F) and expected ERA (xERA). Random chance is measured with hit rate (H%), strand rate (S%) and home run to fly ball ratio (hr/f).

Batting Average (BA, or Avg): A grand old nugget that has long outgrown its usefulness. We revere .300 hitting superstars and scoff at .250 hitters, yet the difference between the two is 1 hit every 20 ABs. This 1 hit every five games is not nearly the wide variance that exists in our perceptions of what it means to be a .300 or .250 hitter. BA is a poor evaluator of baseball performance in that it neglects the offensive value of the base on balls and assumes that all hits are created equal.

bb%: Walk rate (hitters)

bb/9: Opposition walks per 9 IP

BF/Gm: Batters faced per game

BIP: Balls-in-play

BPI: Base performance indicator

BPV: Base performance value

Ceiling: The highest professional level at which a player maintains acceptable BPIs. Also, the peak performance level that a player will likely reach, given his BPIs.

Cmd: Command ratio

Ct%: Contact rate

Ctl: Control rate

DIS%: PQS disaster rate

Dom: Dominance rate

DOM%: PQS domination rate

Eye: Batting eye

Fanalytics: The serious, scientific approach to fantasy baseball analysis. A contraction of "fantasy" and "analytics," fanalytic gaming might be considered a mode of play that requires a more strategic and quantitative approach to player analysis and game decisions.

FB%: Fly ball per cent

G/L/F: Ground balls, line drives, and fly balls as percentages of total balls in play (hits *and* outs)

GB%: Ground ball per cent

Gopheritis (also, Acute Gopheritis and Chronic Gopheritis): The dreaded malady in which a pitcher is unable to keep the ball in the ballpark. Pitchers with gopheritis have a fly ball rate of at least 40%. More severe cases have a FB% over 45%.

H%: Hit rate (batters) or Hits allowed per balls in play (pitchers)

hr/9: Opposition home runs per 9 IP

hr/f: Home runs hit (batters), or allowed (pitchers), per fly ball

IP/G: Innings pitched per game appearance

k/9: Dominance rate (opposition strikeouts per 9 IP)

LD%: Line drive per cent

Leading Indicator: A statistical formula that can be used to project likely future performance.

LW: Linear weights

LWPwr: Linear weighted power

Major League Equivalency *(Bill James):* A formula that converts a player's minor or foreign league statistics into a comparable performance in the major leagues. These are not projections, but conversions of current performance. Contains adjustments for the level of play in individual leagues and teams, and the player's age as compared to that level. Works best with Triple-A stats, not quite as well with Double-A stats, and hardly at all with the lower levels. Foreign conversions are still a work in process. James' formula only addressed batting. Our research has devised conversion formulas for pitchers, however, their best use comes when looking at BPI's, not traditional stats.

Mendoza Line: Named for Mario Mendoza, it represents the benchmark for batting futility. Usually refers to a .200 batting average, but can also be used for low levels of other statistical categories. Note that Mendoza's lifetime batting average was actually a much more robust .215.

MLE: Major league equivalency

Noise: Irrelevant or meaningless pieces of information that can distort the results of an analysis. In news, this is opinion or rumor that can invalidate valuable information. In forecasting, these are unimportant elements of statistical data that can artificially inflate or depress a set of numbers.

OB: On base average (batters)

OBA: Opposition batting average (pitchers)

OOB: Opposition on base average (pitchers)

Opposition Strikeouts per Game: See Dominance rate.

Opposition Walks per Game: See Control rate.

OPS: On base plus slugging average

PQS: Pure Quality Starts

Pw: Linear weighted power

PX: Linear weighted power index

R$: Rotisserie value

RAR: Runs above replacement

RC: Runs created

RC/G: Runs created per game

REff%: Relief efficiency per cent

Rotisserie Value (R$): The dollar value placed on a player's performance in a Rotisserie league, and designed to measure the impact that player has on the standings. These values are highly variable depending upon a variety of factors:
- the salary cap limit
- the number of teams in the league
- each team's roster size
- the impact of any protected players
- each team's positional demands at the time of bidding
- the statistical category demands at the time of bidding
- external factors, e.g. media inflation or deflation of value

In other words, **a $30 player is only a $30 player if someone in your draft pays $30 for him.**

There are a variety of methods to calculate value, most involving a delineation of a least valuable performance level (given league size and structure), and then assigning a certain dollar amount for incremental improvement from that base. The method we use is a variation of the Standings Gain Points method described in the book, *How to Value Players for Rotisserie Baseball,* by Art McGee. (2nd edition available now)

People play Rotisserie in many variations. The most popular game is the 5x5 format. Mixed league participation is soaring; here, player pool penetration falls short of the standard 75%.

Since we currently have no idea who is going to play RF for the Mets, or whether Matt Antonelli is going to break camp with San Deigo, all the projected values are slightly inflated. They are roughly based on a 12-team AL and 13-team NL league. We've attempted to take some contingencies into account, but the values will not total to anywhere near $3120, so don't bother adding them up and save your irate e-mails.

A $25 player in this book might actually be worth $21. Or $28. This level of precision is irrelevant in a process that is going to be driven by market forces anyway. *So, don't obsess over it.*

How do other writers publish perfect Rotisserie values over the winter? Do they make arbitrary decisions as to where free agents are going to sign and who is going to land jobs in the spring? I'm not about to make those massive leaps of faith. Bottom line... Some things you can predict, to other things you have to react. As roles become more defined over the winter, our online updates will provide better approximations of playing time, and projected Roto values that add up to $3120.

S%: Strand rate

Save: There are six events that need to occur in order for a pitcher to post a single save...

1. The starting pitcher and middle relievers must pitch well.

2. The offense must score enough runs.

3. It must be a reasonably close game.

4. The manager must choose to put the pitcher in for a save opportunity.

5. The pitcher must pitch well and hold the lead.

6. The manager must let him finish the game.

Of these six events, only one is within the control of the relief pitcher. As such, projecting saves for a reliever has little to do with skill and a lot to do with opportunity. However, pitchers with excellent skills sets may create opportunity for themselves.

SBO: Stolen base opportunity per cent

Situation Independent: Describing a statistical gauge that measures performance apart from the context of team, ballpark, or other outside variables. Home runs, as they are unaffected by the performance of a batter's team, are often considered a situation independent stat (they are, however, affected by park dimensions). Strikeouts and Walks are better examples.

Conversely, RBI's are situation dependent because individual performance varies greatly by the performance of other batters on the team (you can't drive in runs if there is nobody on base). Similarly, pitching wins are as much a measure of the success of a pitcher as they are a measure of the success of the offense and defense performing behind that pitcher, and are therefore a poor measure of pitching performance alone.

Situation independent gauges are important for us to be able to separate a player's contribution to his team and isolate his performance so that we may judge it on its own merits.

Slg: Slugging average

Soft Stats (also, Soft Skills): Batting eyes less than 0.50. Command ratios under 2.0. Strikeout rates below 5.0. Etc.

Soft-tosser: A pitcher with a strikeout rate of 5.5 or less.

Spd: Speed score

Strikeouts per Game: See Opposition strikeouts per game.

Surface Stats: Traditional statistical gauges that the mainstream uses to measure performance. Stats like batting average, wins, and ERA only touch the surface of a player's skill. Component skills analysis digs beneath the surface to reveal true skill.

Sv%: Saves conversion rate

SX: Speed Score Index

Vulture: A pitcher, typically a middle reliever, who accumulates an unusually high number of wins by preying on other pitchers' misfortunes. More accurately, this is a pitcher typically brought into a game after a starting pitcher has put his team behind, and then pitches well enough and long enough to allow his offense to take the lead, thereby "vulturing" a win from the starter.

Walks per Game: See Opposition walks per game.

Wasted talent: A player with a high level skill that is negated by a deficiency in another skill. For instance, basepath speed can be negated by poor on base ability. Pitchers with strong arms can be wasted because home plate is an elusive concept to them.

WHIP: Walks plus Hits divided by Innings Pitched

Wins: There are five events that need to occur in order for a pitcher to post a single win...

1. He must pitch well, allowing few runs.

2. The offense must score enough runs.

3. The defense must successfully field all batted balls.

4. The bullpen must hold the lead.

5. The manager must leave the pitcher in for 5 innings, and not remove him if the team is still behind.

Of these five events, only one is within the control of the pitcher. As such, projecting wins can be an exercise in futility.

xBA: Expected batting average

xERA: Expected ERA

The Other Glossary
Sabermetrics, Fanalytics and Advanced Concepts

Balls-in-play (BIP)

Batting: (AB – K)   *Pitching*: ((IP x 2.82)) + H – K

The total number of batted balls that are hit fair, both hits and outs. An analysis of how these balls are hit – on the ground, in the air, hits, outs, etc. – can provide analytical insight, from player skill levels to the impact of luck on statistical output.

Base Performance Value (BPV): A single value that describes a player's overall raw skill level. This is more useful than traditional statistical gauges to track player performance trends and project future statistical output. The BPV formula combines and weights several BPIs.

Batting BPV: (Batting Eye x 20) + ((Batting Average - .300) / .003) + (Linear Weighted Power Index x 0.43)

This formula combines the individual raw skills of batting eye, the ability to hit safely, and the ability to hit with power. **BENCHMARKS:** The best hitters will have a BPV of 50 or greater. (Note: Batting BPV does not appear in this edition of the *Forecaster* but does in the free projections update.)

Pitching BPV: (Dominance Rate x 6) + (Command Ratio x 21) - (Expected Opp. HR Rate x 30) - ((Opp. Batting Average - .275) x 200)

This formula combines the individual raw skills of power, command, the ability to keep batters from reaching base, and the ability to prevent long hits, all characteristics that are unaffected by most external team factors. In tandem with a pitcher's strand rate, it provides a complete picture of the elements that contribute to a pitcher's ERA, and therefore serves as an accurate tool to project likely changes in ERA. **BENCHMARKS:** A BPV of 50 is the minimum level required for long-term success. The elite of the bullpen aces will have BPV's in excess of 100 and it is rare for these stoppers to enjoy long term success with consistent levels under 75.

Batters faced per game *(Craig Wright)*

((IP x 2.82) + H + BB) / G

A measure of pitcher usage and one of the leading indicators for potential pitcher burnout. (See Usage Warning Flags in the Forecaster's Toolbox.)

Batting average on balls in play *(Voros McCracken)*

Batting BABIP: (H—HR) / (AB – HR - K)

Pitching BABIP: (H—HR) / ((IP x 2.82) + H - K - HR)

Also called Hit rate (H%). The percent of balls hit into the field of play that fall for hits. See Forecaster's Toolbox for a complete discussion. **BENCHMARK:** The league average H% is 30%, which is also the level that individual pitching performances will regress to on a year to year basis. Any +/- variance of 3% or more can affect a pitcher's ERA. Batters tend to regress to their own historical three-year mean level.

Batting eye (Eye)

(Walks / Strikeouts)

A measure of a player's strike zone judgment, the raw ability to distinguish between balls and strikes. **BENCHMARKS:** The best hitters have eye ratios over 1.00 (indicating more walks than strikeouts) and are the most likely to be among a league's .300 hitters. Ratios less than 0.50 represent batters who likely also have lower BA's. (See Forecaster's Toolbox for more.)

Command ratio (Cmd)

(Strikeouts / Walks)

This is a measure of a pitcher's raw ability to get the ball over the plate. There is no more fundamental a skill than this, and so it is used as a leading indicator to project future rises and falls in other gauges, such as ERA. Command is one of the best gauges to use to evaluate minor league performance. **BENCHMARKS:** Baseball's best pitchers will have ratios in excess of 3.0. Pitchers with ratios under 1.0 — indicating that they walk more batters than they strike out — have virtually no potential for long term success. If you make no other changes in your approach to drafting a pitching staff, limiting your focus to only pitchers with a command ratio of 2.0 or better will substantially improve your odds of success. (See the Forecaster's Toolbox for more command ratio research.)

Contact rate (ct%)

((AB - K) / AB)

Measures a batter's ability to get wood on the ball and hit it into the field of play. **BENCHMARKS:** Those batters with the best contact skill will have levels of 90% or better. The hackers of society will have levels of 75% or less.

Control rate (bb/9), or Opposition walks per game

BB Allowed x 9 / IP

Measures how many walks a pitcher allows per game equivalent. **BENCHMARK:** The best pitchers will have bb/9 levels of 3.0 or less.

Dominance rate (k/9), or Opposition Strikeouts per Game

(K Allowed x 9 / IP)

Measures how many strikeouts a pitcher allows per game equivalent. **BENCHMARK:** The best pitchers will have k/9 levels of 5.6 or higher.

ERA variance: The variance between a pitcher's ERA and his xERA, which is a measure of over or underachievement. A positive variance indicates the potential for a pitcher's ERA to rise. A negative variance indicates the potential for ERA improvement. (See Expected ERA) **BENCHMARK:** Discount variances that are under 0.50. Any variance over 1.00 (one run per game) is regarded as a clear indicator of future change.

Expected batting average *(John Burnson)*

xCT% * [xH1% + xH2%]

where

xH1% = GB% * [0.0004 PX + 0.062 ln(SX)]
      + LD% * [0.93 - 0.086 ln(SX)]
      + FB% * 0.12

and

xH2% = FB% * [0.0013 PX - 0.0002 SX - 0.057]
      + GB% * [0.0006 PX]

A hitter's batting average as calculated by multiplying the percentage of balls put in play (contact rate) by the chance that a ball in play falls for a hit. The likelihood that a ball in play falls for a hit is a product of the speed of the ball and distance it is hit (PX), the speed of the batter (SX), and distribution of ground balls, fly balls, and line drives. We further split it out by

non-homerun hit rate (xH1%) and homerun hit rate (xH2%).
BENCHMARKS: In general, xBA should approximate batting average fairly closely. Those hitters who have large variances between the two gauges are candidates for further analysis.

Expected earned run average (Gill and Reeve)

$(.575 x H [per 9 IP]) + (.94 x HR [per 9 IP]) + (.28 x BB [per 9 IP]) - (.01 x K [per 9 IP]) - Normalizing Factor$

"xERA represents the expected ERA of the pitcher based on a normal distribution of his statistics. It is not influenced by situation-dependent factors." xERA erases the inequity between starters' and relievers' ERA's, eliminating the effect that a pitcher's success or failure has on another pitcher's ERA.

Similar to other gauges, the accuracy of this formula changes with the level of competition from one season to the next. The normalizing factor allows us to better approximate a pitcher's actual ERA. This value is usually somewhere around 2.77 and varies by league and year.

BENCHMARKS: xERA should approximate a pitcher's ERA fairly closely. Those pitchers who have large variances between the two gauges are candidates for further analysis.

Projected xERA or projected ERA? Projected xERA is more accurate for looking ahead on a purely skills basis. Projected ERA includes situation-*dependent* events — bullpen support, park factors, etc. — which are reflected better by ERA. The optimal approach is to use *both* gauges as a range of the expectation for the coming year.

Expected earned run average2 (John Burnson)

$(xER * 9)/IP$, where xER is defined as

$xER\% * \{ FB/10 + (1-xS\%) * [(0.3*BIP) + BB] \}$

where

$xER\% = 0.96 - (0.0284 * (GB/FB))$

and

$xS\% = (64.5 + (K/9 * 1.2) - (BB/9 * (BB/9 + 1)) / 20)$
$+ ((0.0012 * (GB\%^2)) - (0.001 * GB\%) - 2.4)$

Note: xERA2 is used in the player boxes for years when G/L/F data is available. Other years use the Gill and Reeve formula.

Expected home run rate (xHR/9): *See Home runs to fly ball rate*

Ground ball, fly ball, line drive percentages (G/F/L): The percentage of all Balls-in-Play that are hit on the ground, in the air and as line drives. For batters, increased fly ball tendency may foretell a rise in power skills; increased line drive tendency may foretell an improvement in batting average. For a pitcher, the ability to keep the ball on the ground can contribute to his statistical output exceeding his demonstrated skill level .

*BIP Type	Total%	Out%
Ground ball	45%	72%
Line drive	20%	28%
Fly ball	35%	85%
TOTAL	*100%*	*69%*

* Data only includes fieldable balls and is net of home runs.

Hit rate (H%): *See Batting average on balls in play*

Home runs to fly ball rate

HR / FB

Also, expected home run rate = $(FB x 0.10) x 9 / IP$

The percent of fly balls that are hit for HRs. BENCHMARK: The league average level is 10%, which is also the level that individual pitching performances will regress to on a year to year basis. Batters tend to regress to their own historical three-year mean level.

Linear weights (Pete Palmer)

$((Singles x .46) + (Doubles x .8) + (Triples x 1.02) + (Home runs x 1.4) + (Walks x .33) + (Stolen Bases x .3) - (Caught Stealing x .6) - ((At bats - Hits) x Normalizing Factor)$

(Also referred to as Batting Runs.) Formula whose premise is that all events in baseball are linear, that is, the output (runs) is directly proportional to the input (offensive events). Each of these offensive events is then weighted according to its relative value in producing runs. Positive events — hits, walks, stolen bases — have positive values. Negative events — outs, caught stealing — have negative values.

The normalizing factor, representing the value of an out, is an offset to the particular level of offense in a given year. As such it changes every season, growing larger in high offense years and smaller in low offense years. The value is usually somewhere around .26 and varies by league.

LW is no longer included in the player forecast boxes, but the LW concept is used with the linear weighted power gauge.

Linear weighted power (LWPwr)

$((Doubles x .8) + (Triples x .8) + (HR x 1.4)) / (At bats- K) x 100$

An excerpt of the linear weights formula that only considers events that are measures of a batter's pure power. BENCHMARKS: Baseball's top sluggers typically top the 17 mark. Weak hitters will have a LWPwr level of under 10.

Linear weighted power index (PX)

$(Batter's LWPwr / League LWPwr) x 100$

LWPwr is presented in this book in its normalized form to get a better read on a batter's accomplishment in each year. For instance, a 30-HR season today is not nearly as much of an accomplishment as 30 HRs hit in a lower offense year like 1995. BENCHMARKS: A level of 100 equals league average power skills. Any player with a value over 100 has above average power skills, and those over 175 are the Slugging Elite.

On base average (OBA)

$(H + BB) / (AB + BB)$

Addressing one of the two deficiencies in BA, OB gives value to those events that get batters on base, but are not hits. (Hit batsmen are often part of this formula.). An OB of .350 can be read as "this batter gets on base 35% of the time." When a run is scored, there is no distinction made as to how that runner reached base. So, two thirds of the time — about how often a batter comes to the plate with the bases empty — a walk really is as good as a hit. BENCHMARKS: We all know what a .300 hitter is, but what represents "good" for OB? That comparable level would likely be .400, with .275 representing the comparable level of futility.

On base plus slugging average (OPS): A simple sum of the two gauges, it is considered as one of the better evaluators of overall performance. OPS combines the two basic elements of offensive production — the ability to get on base (OB) and the ability to advance baserunners (Slg). BENCHMARKS: The game's top batters will have OPS levels over .900. The worst batters will have levels under .600.

Opposition batting average (OBA)

$(Hits Allowed / ((IP x 2.82) + Hits Allowed))$

A close approximation of the batting average achieved by opposing batters against a particular pitcher.

BENCHMARKS: The converse of the benchmark for batters, the best pitchers will have levels under .250; the worst pitchers levels over .300.

Opposition home runs per game (hr/9)

(HR Allowed x 9 / IP)

Measures how many home runs a pitcher allows per game equivalent. **BENCHMARK:** The best pitchers will have hr/9 levels of under 1.0.

Opposition on base average (OOB)

(Hits Allowed + BB) / ((IP x 2.82) + H + BB)

A close approximation of the on base average achieved by opposing batters against a particular pitcher. **BENCHMARK:** The best pitchers will have levels under .300; the worst pitchers levels over .375.

Plus/Minus score: A gauge that measures the probability that a player's future performance will exceed or fall short of the immediate past year's numbers. Positive scores indicate both rebounds and potential breakouts. Negative scores indicate both corrections and potential breakdowns. The further the score is from zero, the higher the likelihood of a performance swing. Two types of variables are tracked for batters and pitchers:

Batting: Multi-year trends in bb%, ct%, PX and SX. Outlying levels for h%, hr/f, xBA and LH/RH variance.

Pitching: Multi-year trends in BPV. Outlying levels for h%, s%, hr/f, xERA and LH/RH variance.

Power/contact rating

(BB + K) / IP

Measures the level by which a pitcher allows balls to be put into play and helps tie a pitcher's success to his team's level of defensive ability. In general, extreme power pitchers can be successful even with poor defensive teams. Power pitchers tend to have greater longevity in the game. Contact pitchers with poor defenses behind them are high risks to have poor W-L records and ERA. **BENCHMARKS:** A level of 1.13 or greater describes the pure throwers. A level of .93 or lower describes the high contact pitcher. Tip... if you have to draft a pitcher from a poor defensive team, going with power over contact will usually net you more wins in the long run.

PQS disaster rate *(Gene McCaffrey):* The percentage of a starting pitcher's outings that rate as a PQS-0 or PQS-1. See the Pitching Logs section for more information on DIS%.

PQS domination rate *(Gene McCaffrey):* The percentage of a starting pitcher's outings that rate as a PQS-4 or PQS-5. See the Pitching Logs section for more information on DOM%.

Pure Quality Starts: PQS is the next step in following pitching lines. The old Quality Start method — minimum 6 IP, maximum 3 earned runs — is simplistic and does not measure any real skill. Bill James' "game score" methodology is better, but is not feasible for quick calculation.

In PQS, we give a starting pitcher credit for exhibiting certain skills in each of his starts. Then by tracking his "PQS Score" over time, we can follow his progress. A starter earns one point for each of the following criteria...

1. The pitcher must have gone a minimum of 6 innings. This measures stamina. If he goes less than 5 innings, he automatically gets a total PQS score of zero, no matter what other stats he produces.

2. He must have allowed no more than an equal number of hits to the number of IP. This measures hit prevention.

3. His number of strikeouts must be no fewer than two less than his innings pitched. This measures dominance.

4. He must have struck out at least twice as many batters as he walked. This measures command.

5. He must have allowed no more than one home run. This measures his ability to keep the ball in the park.

A perfect PQS score would be 5. Any pitcher who averages 3 or more over the course of the season is probably performing admirably. The nice thing about PQS is it allows you to approach each start as more than an all-or-nothing event.

Note the absence of earned runs. No matter how many runs a pitcher allows, if he scores high on the PQS scale, he has hurled a good game in terms of his base skills. The number of runs allowed — a function of not only the pitcher's ability but that of his bullpen and defense — will even out over time.

Reliever efficiency per cent (REff%)

(Wins + Saves + Holds) / (Wins + Losses + SaveOpps + Holds)

This is a measure of how often a reliever contributes positively to the outcome of a game. A record of consistent, positive impact on game outcomes breeds managerial confidence, and that confidence could pave the way to save opportunities. For those pitchers suddenly thrust into a closer's role, this formula helps gauge their potential to succeed based on past successes in similar roles. **BENCHMARK:** Minimum of 80%.

Runs above replacement (RAR): An estimate of the number of runs a player contributes above a "replacement level" player. "Replacement" is defined as the level of performance at which another player can easily be found at little or no cost to a team. What constitutes replacement level is a topic that is hotly debated. There are a variety of formulas and rules of thumb used to determine this level for each position (replacement level for a shortstop will be very different from replacement level for an outfielder). Our estimates appear below.

One of the major values of RAR for fantasy applications is that it can be used to assemble an integrated ranking of batters and pitchers for drafting purposes.

Batters create runs; pitchers save runs. But are batters and pitchers who have comparable RAR levels truly equal in value? Pitchers might be considered to have higher value. Saving an additional run is more important than producing an additional run. A pitcher who throws a shutout is guaranteed to win that game, whereas no matter how many runs a batter produces, his team can still lose given poor pitching support.

To calculate RAR for batters:
Start with a batter's runs created per game (RC/G).
Subtract his position's replacement level RC/G.
Multiply by number of games played: (AB - H + CS) / 25.5.

Replacement levels used in this book, for 2007:

POS	AL	NL
C	4.02	3.79
1B	5.09	5.60
2B	4.13	4.56
3B	4.50	4.78
SS	4.56	3.96
LF	4.72	5.34
CF	4.28	4.56
RF	4.70	5.25
DH	6.02	

To calculate RAR for pitchers:
Start with the replacement level league ERA.
Subtract the pitcher's ERA. (To calculate *projected* RAR, use the pitcher's xERA.)
Multiply by number of games played, calculated as plate appearances (IP x 4.34) divided by 38.

Multiply the resulting RAR level by 1.08 to account for the variance between earned runs and total runs.

RAR can also be used to calculate rough projected team won-loss records. *(Roger Miller)* Total the RAR levels for all the players on a team, divide by 10 and add to 53 wins.

Runs created *(Bill James)*

(H + BB - CS) x (Total bases + (.55 x SB)) / (AB + BB)

A formula that converts all offensive events into a total of runs scored. As calculated for individual teams, the result approximates a club's actual run total with great accuracy.

Runs created per game *(Bill James)*

Runs Created / ((AB - H + CS) / 25.5)

RC expressed on a per-game basis might be considered the hypothetical ERA compiled against a particular batter. Another way to look at it... a batter with a RC/G of 7.00 would be expected to score 7 runs per game if he were cloned nine times and faced an average pitcher in every at bat. However, cloning batters is not a practice we recommend.

BENCHMARKS: Few players surpass the level of a 10.00 RC/G in any given season, but any level over 7.50 can still be considered very good. At the bottom are levels below 3.00.

Runs created per game2 *(Neil Bonner)*

(SS x 37.96) + (ct% x 10.38) + (bb% x 14.81) – 13.04

where SS, or "swing speed" is defined as

((1B x 0.5) + (2B x 0.8) + (3B x 1.1) + (HR x 1.2)) / (AB - K)

This is the version that is currently used in this book.

Saves conversion rate (Sv%)

Saves / Save Opportunities

The percentage of save opportunities that are successfully converted. **BENCHMARK:** We look for a minimum 80% for long-term success.

Slugging average (Slg)

(Singles + (2 x Doubles) + (3 x Triples) + (4 x HR)) / AB

A measure of the total number of bases accumulated (or the minimum number of runners' bases advanced) per at bat. It is a misnomer; it is not a true measure of a batter's slugging ability because it includes singles. Slg also assumes that each type of hit has proportionately increasing value (i.e. a double is twice as valuable as a single, etc.) which is not true. For instance, with the bases loaded, a HR always scores four runs, a triple always scores three, but a double could score two or three and a single could score one, or two, or even three.

BENCHMARKS: The top batters will have levels over .500. The bottom batters will have levels under .300.

Speed score *(Bill James):* A measure of the various elements that comprise a runner's speed skills. Although this formula (a variation of James' original version) may be used as a leading indicator for stolen base output, SB attempts are controlled by managerial strategy which makes Spd somewhat less valuable.

The speed scores in this book are calculated as the mean value of the following four elements...

1. Stolen base efficiency = *(((SB + 3)/(SB + CS + 7)) - .4) x 20*

2. Stolen base freq. = *Square root of ((SB + CS)/(Singles + BB)) / .07*

3. Triples rating = *(3B / (AB - HR - K))* and the result assigned a value based on the following chart:

< 0.001	0
0.001	1
0.0023	2
0.0039	3
0.0058	4
0.008	5
0.0105	6
0.013	7
0.0158	8
0.0189	9
.0223+	10

4. Runs scored as a percentage of times on base = *(((R - HR)/(H + BB - HR)) - .1) / .04*

Speed score index (SX)

(Batter's Spd / League Spd) x 100

Normalized speed scores are presented in this book to get a better read on a runner's accomplishment in context. A level of 100 equals league average speed skill. Values over 100 indicate above average skill, over 200 represent the Fleet of Feet Elite.

Stolen base opportunity per cent (SBO)

(SB + CS) / (BB + Singles)

A rough approximation of how often a base-runner attempts a stolen base. Provides a comparative measure for players on a given team and, as a team measure, the propensity of a manager to give a "green light" to his runners.

Strand rate (S%)

(H + BB - ER) / (H + BB - HR)

Measures the percentage of allowed runners a pitcher strands (earned runs only), which incorporates both individual pitcher skill and bullpen effectiveness. **BENCHMARKS:** The most adept at stranding runners will have S% levels over 75%. Once a pitcher's S% starts dropping down below 65%, he's going to have problems with his ERA. Those pitchers with strand rates over 80% will have artificially low ERAs, which will be prone to relapse. (See the Forecaster's Toolbox for more research.)

Vintage Eck territory: A pitching base performance value (BPV) level of 200 or over. Over the course of his career, Dennis Eckersely posted levels this high four times:

1989	345
1990	347
1991	226
1992	210

Walks plus hits divided by innings pitched (WHIP): Decreed as a base Rotisserie category. **BENCHMARKS:** Usually, a WHIP of under 1.20 is considered top level and over 1.50 is indicative of poor performance. Levels under 1.00 — allowing fewer runners than IP — represent extraordinary performance and are rarely maintained over time.

Walk rate (bb%)

(BB / (AB + BB))

A measure of a batter's plate patience. **BENCHMARKS:** The best batters will have levels over 10%. Those with poor plate patience will have levels of 5% or less.

2008 CHEATER'S BOOKMARK

BATTING STATISTICS — BENCHMARKS

Abbrv	Term	Formula / Descr.	BAD UNDER	'07 LG AVG AL	'07 LG AVG NL	BEST OVER
Avg	Batting Average	h/ab	250	271	266	300
xBA	Expected Batting Average	*See glossary*		270	272	
OB	On Base Average	(h+bb)/(ab+bb)	300	338	334	375
Slg	Slugging Average	total bases/ab	350	423	423	500
OPS	On Base plus Slugging	OB+Slg	650	761	757	875
bb%	Walk Rate	bb/(ab+bb)	5%	9%	9%	10%
ct%	Contact Rate	(ab-k) / ab	75%	81%	81%	85%
Eye	Batting Eye	bb/k	0.50	0.51	0.49	1.00
PX	Power Index	Normalized power skills	80	100	100	120
SX	Speed Index	Normalized speed skills	80	100	100	120
SBO	Stolen Base Opportunity %	(sb+cs)/(singles+bb)		9%	9%	
G/F	Groundball/Flyball Ratio	gb / fb		1.2	1.1	
G	Ground Ball Per Cent	gb / balls in play		44%	42%	
L	Line Drive Per Cent	ld / balls in play		18%	19%	
F	Fly Ball Per Cent	fb / balls in play		38%	39%	
RC/G	Runs Created per Game	*See glossary*	3.00	4.87	5.14	7.50
RAR	Runs Above Replacement	*See glossary*	-0.0			+25.0

PITCHING STATISTICS — BENCHMARKS

Abbrv	Term	Formula / Descr.	BAD OVER	'07 LG AVG AL	'07 LG AVG NL	BEST UNDER
ERA	Earned Run Average	er*9/ip	5.00	4.50	4.43	4.00
xERA	Expected ERA	*See glossary*		4.34	4.37	
WHIP	Baserunners per Inning	(h+bb)/ip	1.50	1.41	1.40	1.25
BF/G	Batters Faced per Game	((ip*2.82)+h+bb)/g	28.0			
PC	Pitch Counts per Start		120	95	93	
OBA	Opposition Batting Avg	Opp. h/ab	290	269	267	250
OOB	Opposition On Base Avg	Opp. (h+bb)/(ab+bb)	350	336	335	300
BABIP	BatAvg on balls in play	(h-hr)/((ip*2.82)+h-k-hr)		309	306	
Ctl	Control Rate	bb*9/ip		3.3	3.3	3.0
hr/9	Homerun Rate	hr*9/ip		1.0	1.0	1.0
hr/f	Homerun per Fly ball	hr/fb		9%	10%	10%
S%	Strand Rate	(h+bb-er)/(h+bb-hr)		70%	71%	
DIS%	PQS Disaster Rate	% GS that are PQS 0/1		24%	26%	20%

Abbrv	Term	Formula / Descr.	BAD UNDER	'06 LG AVG AL	'06 LG AVG NL	BEST OVER
RAR	Runs Above Replacement	*See glossary*	-0.0			+25.0
Dom	Dominance Rate	k*9/ip		6.6	6.7	6.5
Cmd	Command Ratio	k/bb		2.0	2.0	2.2
G/F	Groundball/Flyball Ratio	gb / fb		1.16	1.14	
BPV	Base Performance Value	*See glossary*	50	55	54	75
DOM%	PQS Dominance Rate	% GS that are PQS 4/5		39%	38%	50%
Sv%	Saves Conversion Rate	(saves / save opps)		68%	66%	80%
REff%	Relief Effectiveness Rate	*See glossary*		66%	66%	80%

NOTES

2008 FANTASY BASEBALL
WINNERS RESOURCE GUIDE

http://orders.baseballhq.com/

10 REASONS
why <u>winners</u> rely on
SHANDLER ENTERPRISES, LLC
for fantasy baseball information

1 NO OTHER RESOURCE provides you with more vital intelligence to help you win. Compare the depth of our offerings in these pages with any other information product or service.

2 NO OTHER RESOURCE provides more exclusive information, like cutting-edge component skills analyses, revolutionary strategies like the LIMA Plan, and innovative gaming formats like Quint-Inning. *You won't find these anywhere else on the internet, guaranteed.*

3 NO OTHER RESOURCE has as long and as consistent a track record of success in the top national experts competitions... Our writers have achieved 14 first place, 5 second place and 8 third place finishes since 1997. *No other resource comes remotely close.*

4 NO OTHER RESOURCE has as consistent a track record in projecting impact performances. In 2007, our readers had surprises like Adrian Gonzalez, Khalil Greene, Brad Hawpe, Russ Martin, Dustin Pedroia, Joaquin Benoit, Fausto Carmona, Francisco Cordero, Kevin Gregg, Ted Lilly, Brad Penny, James Shields, Ian Snell and Javier Vazquez on their teams, *and dozens more.*

5 NO OTHER RESOURCE is supported by over 45 top writers and analysts — all paid professionals and proven winners, not weekend hobbyists or corporate staffers.

6 NO OTHER RESOURCE has a wider scope, providing valuable information not only for Rotisserie, but for alternative formats like simulations, salary cap contests, online games, points, head-to-head, dynasty leagues and others.

7 NO OTHER RESOURCE is as highly regarded by its peers in the industry. Baseball HQ is the *only* three-time winner of the Fantasy Sports Trade Association's "Best Fantasy Baseball Online Content" award and Ron Shandler was a key subject in Sam Walker's *Fantasyland.*

8 NO OTHER RESOURCE is as highly regarded *outside* of the fantasy industry. Many Major League general managers are regular customers and several of our writers have been advisors to the St. Louis Cardinals since the 2004 season.

9 NO OTHER RESOURCE has been creating fantasy baseball winners for as long as we have. Our 21 years of stability *guarantees your investment.*

10 Year after year, over 90% of our subscribers report that the products and services of Shandler Enterprises have helped them improve their performance in their fantasy leagues. <u>That's the bottom line</u>.

TO ORDER
MAIL check or money order to: Shandler Enterprises LLC, P.O. Box 20303-A, Roanoke, VA 24018
PHONE 1-800-422-7820
FAX: 540-772-1969
ONLINE secure order form: *http://orders.baseballhq.com/*

Baseball HQ is the one web site where fantasy leaguers go to gain an unbeatable edge. Not just news and stats, HQ provides the fantasy implications, analysis of what the future may hold, and all the tools you need to take your team to victory!

News & Analysis

- Statistical news analysis
- Injury reports
- Ron Shandler's "Fanalytics"
- Ray Murphy's "Speculator"
- Research & Analysis
- Subscriber Forums

Buyers Guides

BATTERS
- Interactive player database
- Daily projections
- Weekly surgers and faders
- Power analysis
- Speed analysis
- Batting Average analysis

PITCHERS
- Interactive player database
- Daily projections
- Weekly surgers and faders
- Starting pitcher logs
- Bullpen indicator charts

TEAMS
- Depth chart center
- Weekly rotation planner
- Ballpark factors

Minor Leagues

- Organization reports
- Full coverage of winter baseball
- Prospect rankings by position
- In-season call-ups analysis
- In-season news and analysis
- Major league equivalent statistics

Gaming Tools

- Custom fantasy draft guides
- Custom cheat sheets
- Custom Rotisserie grids
- Team stat tracker
- Mock drafts
- Strategy columns
- Personal advisory service

Fantasy league winners don't wait until March to prepare for their next title run. Baseball HQ gives you tons of vital intelligence to keep the Hot Stove burning all winter long...

- In-depth statistical and situational analysis of every off-season player move
- Sleepers, gambles and end-game draft picks to tuck away
- 2008 player projections, updated daily from December through September
- 2008 depth charts, bullpen indicators and more
- Strategy columns on keeper decisions, position scarcity and more
- Coverage of Rotisserie, Scoresheet and simulation games, salary cap contests, online gaming, points games, head-to-head and dynasty leagues
- Market research guide, tracking player values across the internet
- Draft guides, cheat sheets and Rotisserie grids
- Comprehensive player database — profile and statistical trend data at a glance.
- Organizational reports on 2008's top prospects
- Scouting reports from the Arizona Fall League, Rule 5 draft, Japanese Leagues and all winter leagues
- Our active subscriber forum community — 24/7/365
- Complete access to our sabermetric archives, pitcher logs, major league equivalents and more — going all the way back to 1998!
- *and much more!*

$99.00	One year subscription
$69.00	6 month subscription
$39.00	3 month subscription

*Please read the **Terms of Service** at http://www.baseballhq.com/terms.html*

Not Ready to Commit?

Get a FREE Weekly Sample of All the Baseball HQ Goodies with…

Fantasy baseball's #1 premium information service brings you the industry's #1 analytical weekly e-mail newsletter — **ABSOLUTELY FREE!**

Baseball HQ Friday is your link to exclusive insights from the experts at Baseball HQ. Every Friday afternoon, you'll receive news analyses and strategies from the top analysts in the game — perennial winners of national experts competitions. It's your direct connection to a fantasy baseball title in 2008!

Every Friday, from January 25 through September 5, you'll receive:

- Comprehensive player analyses
- Cutting edge statistical insight
- Innovative game strategies
- Ron Shandler's Master Notes
- Reviews, discounts and more!

And there's no obligation. It's FREE.

GO TO

http:// www.baseballhq.com/ friday96.shtml

and sign up TODAY!

First Pitch
Forums & Conferences

"The opportunity to interact with experts as well as proven local winners to build strategies and enhance player knowledge is unparalleled... the best roto investment you can make!"
— M.Dodge, Hockessin DE

FIRST PITCH 2008

Get a head start on the 2008 season with a unique opportunity to go one-on-one with some of the top writers and analysts in the fantasy baseball industry. First Pitch Forums bring the experts to some of the top cities in the USA for lively and informative symposium sessions.

This year's theme: "100 Predictions for 2008"
These 3-hour sessions combine player analysis with fantasy drafting, interactive activities and fun! You've never experienced anything so informational and entertaining! We've selected the top issues, topics and strategies that could make or break your fantasy season...

- First-round no-brainers who won't return first round value
- Bullpens that will have new closers by June
- Minor league end-gamers who will have hidden value
- Players who won't be healthy on Opening Day
- Player pool observations that need to shape your draft strategy
- Hitters who will post their first $30 season
- Pitchers you don't want at the price they will probably cost
- and many more predictions!

Ron Shandler and *Baseball Injury Report's* Rick Wilton chair the sessions, bringing a dynamic energy to every event. They are joined by guest experts from Baseball HQ and some of the leading sports media sources.

What you get for your registration...
- Three hours of baseball talk with some of the industry's top analysts
- The chance to have *your* questions answered, 1-on-1 with the experts
- The opportunity to network with fellow fantasy leaguers from your area
- Freebies and discounts from leading industry vendors

Program description, forum sites and directions at
**http://
www.baseballhq.com
/seminars/**

2008 SITES

February 23	**OAKLAND**
February 24	**LOS ANGELES**
March 1	**CLEVELAND**
March 2	**CHICAGO**
March 7	**WASHINGTON DC**
March 8	**NEW YORK**
March 9	**BOSTON**

REGISTRATION RATES
$29 per person in advance
$39 per person at the door

OFFICIAL LOGO MERCHANDISE

TO ORDER THESE PRODUCTS, and MORE:

http://www.cafepress.com/baseballhq

The Industry's Largest Online Library of Rotisserie and Fantasy Tools and Strategies

Other sources give you the news, stats and analysis, but don't tell you **how** to win. RotoHQ.com provides you with a grasp of the economics, an education in the psychology of competition, and a unique perspective on what it takes to win.

RotoHQ.com includes *hundreds* of essays, and *thousands* of tips on league management, draft management, in-season tactical planning, free agent strategies, trading philosophies, and much more. Includes essays, worksheets and checklists.

**2008 Season Subscription $12.95
FREE TOPIC PREVIEW at
www.rotohq.com**

RotoLab
Draft Software

RotoLab is both a draft preparation program and an in-draft management tool. Just make the roster moves and player selections, and the program handles the rest... automatically! All budget calculations, inflation changes, player lists, team stats and standing totals are a single mouse click away. And... **RotoLab comes loaded with industry-leading player projections from BaseballHQ.com!**

- Easy to use interface
- Sort, search and filter data at the click of a mouse
- 5 years of historical and projected stats
- User notes for each player
- Drag-and-drop player moves
- Two-click operation to draft players
- Flexible league setup options
- Customizable valuation process
- User-definable player list
- Roster management from a single screen
- Cheat Sheet and full stat views to draft from

**Download the FREE DEMO at
www.rotolab.com**
HUGE discount for Baseball HQ subscribers!

Deric McKamey's 2008
MINOR LEAGUE BASEBALL ANALYST

Deric McKamey's **Minor League Baseball Analyst** is the first book to fully integrate sabermetrics and scouting. A long-term Bill James disciple and graduate of Major League Baseball's scout school, Deric provides his unique brand of analysis for over 1000 minor leaguers. For baseball analysts and those who play in fantasy leagues with farm systems, the **Analyst** is the perfect complement to the *Baseball Forecaster* and is designed exactly for your needs:

- *Stats and Sabermetrics...* Over three dozen categories for 1000 minor leaguers, including batter skills ratings, pitch repertoires and more
- *Performance Trends...* spanning each player's last five minor league stops, complete with leading indicators
- *Scouting reports...* for all players, including expected major league debuts, potential major league roles and more
- *Major League Equivalents...* Five year scans for every player
- *Mega-Lists...* The Top 100 of 2008, retrospective looks at the Top 100's of 2003-2007, organizational Top 15's, top prospects by position, power and speed prospects, and more
- *Strategy essays...* on drafting and managing your fantasy team's farm system
- *Player Potential Ratings...* Deric's exclusive system that evaluates each player's upside potential and chances of achieving that potential.

Available January 2008

**Minor League
Baseball Analyst**
. . . . $19.95
*plus $5.00 Priority Mail
shipping and handling*

 **BOOKS** from Shandler Enterprises

John Burnson's 2008
GRAPHICAL PLAYER

John Burnson's **Graphical Player 2008** is a new way to view statistics. Instead of columns of numbers, it presents its data in the most natural and immediate way -- visually! The new 5th Edition includes more charts and graphs than ever before — complete profiles of over 750 players, each described in several multi-faceted graphs and charts. It includes:

PITCHERS
- Daily pitching logs
- Rolling rates of strikeouts, walks, and ground balls
- Each pitcher's full career workload
- Career trends in fantasy value for 4x4 and 5x5 leagues
- Each pitcher's hit and strand rates over his career
- A new probabilistic form of Expected ERA

BATTERS
- Daily hitting logs
- Rolling strikeout rates, power index, more
- Games played by position
- Batting average scan, OPS, injuries
- OPS versus RH and LH pitchers and compared to peers at position
- Career trends in power and speed, compared to peers at position

Available NOW!

Graphical Player
. . . . $21.95
*plus $5.00 Priority Mail
shipping and handling*

NEW for 2008... Three-year projections, spray charts, pitch profiles and more!

FANTASY BASEBALL'S *ONLY*
Free-Standing Draft Board

AVAILABLE IN:
10, 12, 14 & 16
TEAM VERSIONS

3 SIZES OF
FREE-STANDING
DRAFT BOARDS

5 SIZES OF
COLOR CODED
LABELS

SHOWN WITH OPTIONAL STAND

These Solid Corrugated Free-Standing Draft Boards
are the same ones used at **NFBC**

> 10, 12, 14, 16 [*OR MORE*] TEAMS AVAILABLE
> 23 ROUNDS OR 30 ROUNDS AVAILABLE

10% Discount to Readers of Baseball Forecaster
Redeem at our special website:

www.fjfantasy.com/disindex.htm

www.FJFantasy.com

TOLL FREE 1-866-200-7493

PHONE 1-814-833-0271
FAX 1-814-835-3610

Order On-line, by phone, by fax, or send check or money order to:
FJ Fantasy Sports, Inc., 5146 Annendale Drive, Erie PA 16506